Fodor's 2015

FLORIDA

WELCOME TO FLORIDA

With its accessible and varied pleasures, Florida is a favorite of many. Drawn to the colonial charm of St. Augustine, Miami's pulsing nightlife, the glitz of Palm Beach, or the quiet expanse of the Everglades, almost all visitors find something to love here. From the powdery white beaches of the Panhandle to the vibrant coral reefs of the Florida Keys, the ocean is always calling—for sailing, fishing, diving, swimming, and other water sports. Stray off the path a few miles, and you might glimpse a bit of the Florida of old, including cigar-makers and mermaids.

TOP REASONS TO GO

★ **Miami:** A vibrant, multicultural metropolis that buzzes both day and night

★ **Beaches:** Surf-pounded on the Atlantic coast, powdery and pure white on the Gulf

★ **Key West:** Quirky, fun, and tacky, it's both family-friendly and decidedly not.

★ **Golf:** Oceanfront and inland, some of the country's finest links are found here.

★ **Theme Parks:** The state has some of the biggest and best, not all of them Disney.

★ **Family Fun:** From shelling in Sanibel to meeting astronauts at Kennedy Space Center

Fodor's FLORIDA 2015

Publisher: Amanda D'Acierno, *Senior Vice President*

Editorial: Arabella Bowen, *Editor in Chief*; Linda Cabasin, *Editorial Director*

Design: Fabrizio La Rocca, *Vice President, Creative Director*; Tina Malaney, *Associate Art Director*; Chie Ushio, *Senior Designer*; Ann McBride, *Production Designer*

Photography: Melanie Marin, *Associate Director of Photography*; Jessica Parkhill and Jennifer Romains, *Researchers*

Maps: Rebecca Baer, *Senior Map Editor*; David Lindroth, Mark Stroud (Moon Street Cartography), *Cartographers*

Production: Linda Schmidt, *Managing Editor*; Evangelos Vasilakis, *Associate Managing Editor*; Angela L. McLean, *Senior Production Manager*

Sales: Jacqueline Lebow, *Sales Director*

Marketing & Publicity: Heather Dalton, *Marketing Director*; Katherine Punia, *Senior Publicist*

Business & Operations: Susan Livingston, *Vice President, Strategic Business Planning*; Sue Daulton, *Vice President, Operations*

Fodors.com: Megan Bell, *Executive Director, Revenue & Business Development*; Yasmin Marinaro, *Senior Director, Marketing & Partnerships*

Copyright © 2015 by Fodor's Travel, a division of Random House LLC

Writers: Kate Bradshaw, Jennifer Greenhill-Taylor, Rona Grindin, Lynne Helm, Jennie Hess, Jill Martin, Steve Master, Gary McKechnie, Paul Rubio, Avery Sumner, Ashley Wright

Editors: Doug Stallings (Lead Editor), Alexis Crisman Kelly
Production Editor: Elyse Rozelle

ISBN 978–0-8041–4271–7

ISSN 0193–9556

All details in this book are based on information supplied to us at press time. Always confirm information when it matters, especially if you're making a detour to visit a specific place. Fodor's expressly disclaims any liability, loss, or risk, personal or otherwise, that is incurred as a consequence of the use of any of the contents of this book.

SPECIAL SALES

This book is available at special discounts for bulk purchases for sales promotions or premiums. For more information, e-mail specialmarkets@randomhouse.com

PRINTED IN THE UNITED STATES OF AMERICA

10 9 8 7 6 5 4 3 2 1

CONTENTS

6 <   **Contents**

ABOUT
THIS GUIDE

Fodor's Recommendations
Everything in this guide is worth doing—
we don't cover what isn't—but exceptional sights, hotels, and restaurants are
recognized with additional accolades.
Fodor's Choice ★ indicates our top recommendations; and **Best Bets** call attention to
notable hotels and restaurants in various
categories. Care to nominate a new place?
Visit Fodors.com/contact-us.

Trip Costs
We list prices wherever possible to help
you budget well. Hotel and restaurant
price categories from **$** to **$$$$** are noted
alongside each recommendation. For
hotels, we include the lowest cost of a
standard double room in high season.
For restaurants, we cite the average price
of a main course at dinner or, if dinner
isn't served, at lunch. For attractions,
we always list adult admission fees; dis-
counts are usually available for children,
students, and senior citizens.

Hotels
Our local writers vet every hotel to recom-
mend the best overnights in each price cat-
egory, from budget to expensive. Unless
otherwise specified, you can expect pri-
vate bath, phone, and TV in your room.
*Hotel reviews have been shortened. For
full information, visit Fodors.com.*

Restaurants
Unless we state otherwise, restaurants are
open for lunch and dinner daily. We men-
tion dress code only when there's a specific
requirement and reservations only when
they're essential or not accepted. *To make
restaurant reservations, visit Fodors.com.*

Credit Cards
The hotels and restaurants in this guide
typically accept credit cards. If not, we'll
say so.

Top Picks
★ Fodor's Choice

Listings
⊠ Address
⊠ Branch address
☎ Telephone
🖷 Fax
⊕ Website
✉ E-mail
🎫 Admission fee
🕘 Open/closed times
Ⓜ Subway
✛ Directions or Map coordinates

Hotels & Restaurants
🏨 Hotel
🛏 Number of rooms
🍽 Meal plans
✗ Restaurant
🍷 Reservations
👔 Dress code
🚫 No credit cards
💲 Price

Other
⇨ See also
☞ Take note
🏌 Golf facilities

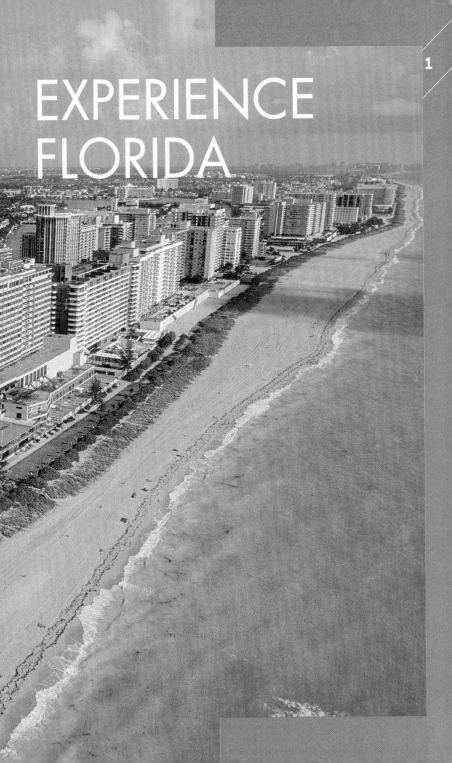

EXPERIENCE
FLORIDA

WHAT'S WHERE

The following numbers refer to chapters.

2 Miami and Miami Beach. Greater Miami is hot—and we're not just talking about the weather. Art-deco buildings and balmy beaches set the scene. Vacations here are as much about lifestyle as locale, so prepare for power shopping, club-hopping, and decadent dining.

3 The Everglades. Covering more than 1.5 million acres, the fabled "River of Grass" is the state's greatest natural treasure. Biscayne National Park (95% of which is underwater) runs a close second. It's the largest marine park in the United States.

4 The Florida Keys. This slender necklace of landfalls, strung together by a 113-mile highway, marks the southern edge of the continental United States. It's nirvana for anglers, divers, literature lovers, and Jimmy Buffett wannabes.

5 Fort Lauderdale with Broward County. The town *Where the Boys Are* has grown up. The beaches that first attracted college kids are now complemented by luxe lodgings and upscale entertainment options.

6 Palm Beach with the Treasure Coast. This area scores points for diversity. Palm Beach and environs are famous for their golden sand and glitzy residents, whereas the Treasure Coast has unspoiled natural delights.

7 The Tampa Bay Area. Tampa's Busch Gardens and Ybor City are only part of the area's appeal. Culture vultures flock to St. Petersburg and Sarasota for concerts and museums, and eco-adventurers veer north to the Nature Coast.

8 The Lower Gulf Coast. Blessed with beaches, this was the last bit of coast to be settled. But as Naples's manicured golf greens and Fort Myers's mansions-cum-museums prove, it is far from uncivilized.

9 Orlando and Environs. Theme parks are what draw most visitors to the area, yet downtown Orlando, Kissimmee, and Winter Park have enough sights, shops, and restaurants to make them destinations in their own right.

10 Walt Disney World. The granddaddy of attractions, Disney is four theme parks in one—Magic Kingdom, Animal Kingdom, Epcot, and Hollywood Studios. Plus, it has a pair of water parks and Downtown Disney (an entertainment zone featuring Cirque du Soleil).

11 Universal Orlando. The movies are brought to life at Universal Studios, while Islands of Adventure delivers gravity-defying rides and special-effects surprises—and the Wizarding World of Harry Potter. Nearby Wet 'n Wild is full of watery adventures.

12 SeaWorld Orlando. Marine mammals perform in SeaWorld's meticulously choreographed shows, and thrill seekers find their adrenaline rush on coasters. Sister park Discovery Cove offers a daylong, swim-with-the-dolphins escape. At Aquatica water park, one slide even dips into a dolphin habitat.

13 Northeast Florida. Though time rewinds in historic St. Augustine, it's on fast-forward in Daytona Beach and the Space Coast, where horse-drawn carriages are replaced by race cars and rocket ships.

14 The Panhandle. Southern gentility and redneck rambunctiousness make the Panhandle a colorful place—but it's the green gulf waters and sugar-white sand that keep devotees coming back.

FLORIDA
TOP ATTRACTIONS

Walt Disney World
(A) Like one of Snow White's dwarfs, Orlando was sleepy until Uncle Walt turned this swampland into the world's most famous tourist attraction. Nowadays Walt Disney World is a 39-square-mile complex and growing, with four separate parks, scores of hotels, and satellite attractions. Thanks to innovative rides and dazzling animatronics, these parks feature prominently in every child's holiday fantasy. Walt Disney World also has grown-up amenities, including championship golf courses, sublime hotels and spas, and fine restaurants. If you have time for only one megapark, choose the original: Walt Disney World's Magic Kingdom. ⇨ *Chapter 10.*

South Beach
(B) You can't miss the distinctive forms, vibrant colors, and extravagant flourishes of SoBe's architectural gems. The world's largest concentration of art deco edifices

is right here. The neighborhood also has enough beautiful people to qualify for the Register of Hippest Places. The glitterati, along with assorted vacationing hedonists, are drawn by übertrendy shops and a surfeit of celeb-studded clubs. Divine eateries are the icing—umm, better make that the ganache—on South Beach's proverbial cake. ⇨ *Chapter 2.*

Key West
(C) These 800-plus islands in the Florida Keys are at once a unique landmass and a mass of contradictions. At the far end of this island chain, Key West is the main attraction. Its laid-back vibe is intoxicating. Eating, drinking, water sports, sunset cruises, kayaking, and more drinking are high on the agenda. Visitors never grow tired of the walking tours through the gingerbread-house-filled streets and channeling the spirit of Ernest Hemingway, who lived and worked here. Today, touring his former digs and toasting his memory at

Sloppy Joe's Bar on Duval Street is almost mandatory. ⇨ *Chapter 4.*

Shopping in Fort Lauderdale and Miami

(D) The Sunshine State is a shopaholic's dream. Visitors travel from overseas with the sole purpose of shopping weekends at Fort Lauderdale's 2-mile, alligator-shape Sawgrass Mills outlet mall. The alfresco addition to the mall, the Shops at Colonnade, caters to well-heeled patrons with a David Yurman jewelry outlet and other shops, including Valentino, Prada, Burberry, Kate Spade New York, and Barneys New York. For more high-end shoppers, Bal Harbour Shops in the swanky Miami suburb is a collection of 100 haute couture shops, boutiques, and department stores. Restaurants and cafés, in tropical garden settings, overflow with style-conscious diners. ⇨ *Chapters 2 and 5.*

Universal Orlando

(E) With rides and attractions more geared toward adults and teens, Universal's two theme parks—Universal Studios and Islands of Adventure—deliver gravity-defying rides and special-effects extravaganzas based on popular television shows and films. The Wizarding World of Harry Potter is the newest "land" at Islands of Adventure, where you'll get to see Hogwarts Castle and drink butter beer! ⇨ *Chapter 11.*

Kennedy Space Center

(F) Though there are enough wide-open expanses to justify the area's moniker, it was NASA that put the "space" in Space Coast—and this is its star attraction. Space memorabilia and aeronautic antiques, ranging from Redstone rockets to the *Apollo XIV* command module, turn an outing here into a trip back in time for anyone who lived through the space race. More down-to-earth types can also visit the Merritt Island National Wildlife Refuge (originally created as a buffer for the space program) and Canaveral National Seashore. ⇨ *Chapter 13.*

Tampa Bay

(G) As a vibrant city with exceptional beaches, Tampa Bay is perfect for indecisive folks who want to enjoy surf and sand without sacrificing urban experiences. Families will love Busch Gardens, a major zoo and theme park. Football and hockey fans will relish the chance to see the Buccaneers and Lightning play. Baseball is big, too: the Rays are based here, and the Yankees descend annually for spring training. ⇨ *Chapter 7.*

The Dalí Museum

(H) St. Petersburg is home to a museum dedicated to the work of Salvador Dalí, showcasing the most comprehensive collection of the surrealist's artwork. This is the kind of first-class museum you'd expect to find in Paris or Madrid, but instead it's here on the Gulf Coast. The state-of-the-art glass building housing the museum is quite a spectacle in and of itself. ⇨ *Chapter 7.*

Sportfishing

(I) Islamorada in the Florida Keys holds steadfast to its claim as Sportfishing Capital of the World. Up in the Panhandle, Destin proves it is the World's Luckiest Fishing Village each October by inviting anglers young and old to compete in the monthlong Destin Fishing Rodeo. However, if you'd prefer to throw fish rather than catch them, head to Pensacola in late April for the Interstate Mullet Toss. (Participants line up to throw dead fish across the Florida–Alabama state line.) ⇨ *Chapter 14.*

Surfing in Cocoa Beach

(J) Cocoa Beach, on the northeast coast, is Surf City for Floridians. Baby boomers may remember it as the place where Major Nelson dreamed of Jeannie. The community is better known today as the hometown of surfing's biggest celeb, Kelly Slater. He has won a record-breaking 10 world championships, and totally tubular types can learn to emulate him at the Ron Jon Surf School. ⇨ *Chapter 13.*

Palm Beach

(**K**) If money could talk, you'd hardly be able to hear above the din in Palm Beach. The upper crust started calling it home—during winter at least—in the early 1900s. And today it remains a ritzy, glitzy enclave for both old money and the nouveau riche (a coterie led by the Donald himself, who owns the landmark Mar-a-Lago Club). Simply put, Palm Beach is the sort of place where shopping is a full-time pursuit and residents don't just wear Polo—they play it. Ooh and aah to your heart's content; then, for more conspicuous consumption, continue south on the aptly named Gold Coast. ⇨ *Chapter 6.*

Broward's Inland Waterways

(**L**) Mariners should set their compass for Fort Lauderdale (aka the Venice of America), where vessels from around the world moor along some two dozen finger isles between the beach and the mainland. Tourists can cruise Broward County's 300 miles of inland waterways by water taxi and tour boat, or bob around the Atlantic in a chartered yacht. If you're in a buying mood, come in late October for the annual Fort Lauderdale International Boat Show. Billed as the world's largest, it has $3 billion worth of boats in every conceivable size, shape, and price range. ⇨ *Chapter 5.*

Little Havana

(**M**) On the streets of Miami's Little Havana, just west of downtown, salsa tunes blare and the smell of spicy chorizo fills the air. (You can get a good whiff of tobacco, too, thanks to the cigar makers who still hand-roll their products here.)

For nearly 50 years, the neighborhood's undisputed heart has been Calle Ocho, the commercial thoroughfare that hosts Carnaval Miami. The roaring 10-day block party each March culminates with the world's longest conga line. Ambience- and amenity-wise, it is as close as you'll get to Cuba without running afoul of the federal government. ⇨ *Chapter 2.*

The Everglades

(N) No trip to southern Florida is complete without seeing the Everglades. At its heart is a river—50 miles wide but merely 6 inches deep—flowing from Lake Okeechobee into Florida Bay. For an up-close look, speed demons can board an airboat that careens through the marshy waters. Purists, alternately, may placidly canoe or kayak within the boundaries of Everglades National Park. Just remember to keep your hands in the boat. The critters that call this unique ecosystem home (alligators, Florida panthers, and cottonmouth snakes for starters) can add real bite to your visit! ⇨ *Chapter 3.*

Sanibel Island

(O) Ready to do something slightly more vigorous than applying SPF 45 and rolling over? Trade beach-bumming for beach-combing in Sanibel, the Shell Capital of the World. Conchs, cockles, clams, coquinas—they're all here (the bounty is due to this barrier island's unusual east–west orientation). Of course, if you'd rather construct sand castles than do the Sanibel Stoop, you need only cross the 3-mile causeway to Fort Myers Beach. It has the finest building material and, every November, professional and amateur aficionados prove it during the American SandSculpting Championship. ⇨ *Chapter 8.*

Ringling Center for the Arts

(P) Sarasota, once winter headquarters for Ringling Bros. and Barnum & Bailey, is proud of its circus heritage. Ringling's former 32-room, 15-bathroom mansion is now the site of the Florida State University's Ringling Center for the Cultural Arts. Within this center, visitors who can't get enough of sawdust and sequins can see an impressive collection of vintage costumes, props, and parade wagons at the stunning Ringling Circus Museum. In addition, the center's John and Mable Ringling Museum of Art showcases 500 years of art, including an impressive collection of tapestries and paintings by Rubens. The adjacent Tibbals Learning Center houses a mind-boggling ¾-inch-scale miniature circus with almost a million pieces. ⇨ *Chapter 8*.

St. Augustine

(Q) History comes to life in St. Augustine . . . and the same can perhaps be said of the undead. Ghosts are plentiful, thanks to all the pirates, plunderers, and other lost souls who formerly lived in this deceptively quiet city. To hear lurid lore about local haunts, sign on for one of the nightly outings organized by Ghost Tours of St. Augustine. These 90-minute lantern-lighted walks recount spirited stories full of goosebump-inducing details. You can also opt for a trolley ride and enter the old jail if you dare, or take a cruise through the harbor shadows in the summer. Top off your tour with an overnight stay at St. Francis Inn (St. Augustine's oldest hostelry) or the Casablanca Inn: both are reputedly haunted. ⇨ *Chapter 13*.

WHEN TO GO

Although Florida is a year-round vacation venue, it divides the calendar into regional tourism seasons. Holidays and school breaks are major factors. However, the clincher is weather, with the best months being designated as peak periods.

High season in southern Florida starts with the run-up to Christmas and continues through Easter. Snowbirds migrate down then to escape frosty weather back home, and festivalgoers flock in because major events are held this time of year to avoid summer's searing heat and high humidity. Winter is also *the* time to visit the Everglades, as temperatures, mosquito activity, and water levels are all lower (making wildlife easier to spot).

Northern Florida, conversely, receives the greatest influx of visitors from Memorial Day to Labor Day. Costs are highest then, but so are temperatures. (In winter, when the mercury dips into the 40s, you'd get a chilly reception on Panhandle beaches.) Specific areas, like Panama City Beach or Daytona Beach, attract throngs—and thongs—during spring break, too. In the latter location, expect revved-up revelers during Speedweeks (late January and February) and Bike Week (early March).

Thanks to its theme parks, Central Florida is a magnet for children, meaning the largest crowds gather, logically enough, whenever class lets out. Lineups at attractions do shrink after they return to school, though this area's hopping all year, with large numbers of international families and kid-free adults coming in the off-season. Spring and fall shoulder seasons are the optimal time to visit, both weather-wise and pricewise.

Climate

Florida is rightly called the Sunshine State—areas like Tampa Bay report 361 days of sunshine a year! But it could also be dubbed the Humid State. From June through September, 90% humidity levels aren't uncommon, nor are accompanying thunderstorms. In fact, more than half of the state's rain falls during these months. Florida's two-sided coastline also makes it a target for tropical storms. Hurricane season officially begins June 1 and ends November 30.

FAQS

I'm not crazy about spending seven nights in hotels. Any affordable alternatives? If you want to pretend you're lucky enough to live here, try a vacation rental. Aside from providing privacy, rentals let you set your own schedule and do your own cooking. The caveat is that you may have to rent in weekly—not nightly—increments. Several companies specialize in the Orlando area, Magical Memories (☎ 866/535–7851 ⊕ *www.magicalmemories.com*) being one reliable bet. But in terms of coverage, geographically and pricewise, HomeAway (☎ 877/228–3145 ⊕ *www.homeaway.com*) wins, listing more than 20,000 Floridian condos, cottages, beach houses, and villas. ⇨ *Apartment and House Rentals under Accommodations in Travel Smart Florida.*

Will I need a car? Public transportation is limited here. So unless you'll be spending your whole vacation on-site at Walt Disney World (where complimentary shuttles are available to resort guests) or in Miami Beach (where dense traffic and limited parking is the norm), having a vehicle is recommended. Renting one on arrival is wise, unless you drive your own. To make car time less tedious, consider occasionally taking the road less traveled. The National Scenic Byways Program website (⊕ *www.byways.org*) spotlights memorable routes within the state, including the Overseas Highway, which has been designated as an "All-American Road" and is one of only 31 roads countrywide to be so honored.

How do I pick between Orlando's parks and Tampa's Busch Gardens? That's a tough call, especially if you haven't yet seen newer attractions like Manta at Sea-World or Jungala at Busch Gardens. The good news is you don't have to

choose, because the Busch Gardens Shuttle Express (☎ 407/423–5566 ⊕ *www.mearstransportation.com*) offers same-day round-trip service between designated locations in Orlando and the Tampa venue for free when you buy a ticket to Busch Gardens, but you may arrive at the park as late as 11:30 am and will return whenever the park closes.

Is Miami OK for families? Absolutely. Despite all the attention paid to G-strings, it retains areas with genuine G-rated appeal. Beyond the beaches, attractions like the interactive Children's Museum and MiaSci (a museum of science) draw kids in droves. Want to go wild? Bypass the nightclubs and head instead to Zoo Miami or the Seaquarium. If you dream of being named "best parent ever," sign your offspring up for a sleepover at the former or a dolphin swim at the latter.

What about hurricanes? The hurricane season begins on June 1 and lasts through November 1 (roughly half the year). However, big storms are much more likely in August and September. Chances are, you'll be just fine if you travel to Florida in June or July, though it's always a good idea to buy travel insurance in case something does happen. In the summer, frequent afternoon thunderstorms are common, especially inland in places like Orlando. On the coast, the weather is almost universally hot and muggy, and rain is common, especially later in the summer.

IF YOU LIKE

Animal Encounters

Florida is home to one supersize mouse and makes an ideal habitat for party animals. Yet there are other types of wildlife here, too. In terms of biodiversity, the state ranks third in the country, with approximately 1,200 different kinds of critters.

■ **Alligators.** Florida has more than 1.3 million resident alligators. You can witness them doing inane tricks at places like **Gatorland** (⇨ *Chapter 9)*, but gator spotting in the wild is far more rewarding. Everglades National Park teems with gators. The best place to get up close and personal with them is **Shark Valley** (⇨ *Chapter 3)*, in the north of the national park.

■ **Birds.** Poised on two major migratory routes, Florida draws about 500 species of birds—and the 2,000-mile **Great Florida Birding Trail** (⇨ *Chapter 8)* helps you track them down. Through detailed guides and highway signs, it identifies sites where you may spy anything from bald eagles to burrowing owls.

■ **Manatees.** They're nicknamed "sea cows" and resemble walruses. But Florida's official marine mammals are most closely related to elephants, which may account for their slow pace and hefty frames. For a chance at swimming with manatees in the wild, take an organized pontoon ride through **Crystal River** (⇨ *Chapter 7)*, near the Upper Gulf Coast.

■ **Sea Turtles.** Ready for a late-night rendezvous with the massive leatherbacks and loggerheads that lumber onto Floridian beaches to lay their eggs between March and October? **Archie Carr National Wildlife Refuge** (⇨ *Chapter 6)*, the Western Hemisphere's largest loggerhead nesting site, organizes free turtle watches in June and July.

Life in the Fast Lane

The Sunshine State has been satisfying visitors' need for speed ever since Henry Ford and his snowbird buddies started using Ormond Beach as a test track. Today roller coasters, stock cars, supersonic jets, and spaceships add momentum to your vacation.

■ **Daytona Beach.** Daytona 500, NASCAR's most prestigious event, pulls in legions of devotees each February. But any time of year you can slip into a driving suit and then into the driver's seat of a Winston Cup–style stock car, courtesy of the Richard Petty Driving Experience at **Daytona International Speedway.** *See* ⇨ *Chapter 13.*

■ **Kennedy Space Center.** Whether you admire Buzz Aldrin or Buzz Lightyear, this spot has the right stuff. See a rocket launch or take your own giant leap with the **Astronaut Training Experience.** The half-day program consists of realistic training exercises culminating in a simulated mission. *See* ⇨ *Chapter 13.*

■ **Pensacola.** The **National Museum of Naval Aviation** displays 150-plus military aircraft and has motion-based simulators that let you "fly" an F/A-18. Better yet, the U.S. Navy Precision Flight Team (familiar to most of us as the Blue Angels) is based here, so you may get to observe them in action at 700 mph. *See* ⇨ *Chapter 14.*

■ **Tampa.** If you think the pursuit of happiness is a high-speed activity, head for **Busch Gardens,** Florida's premier roller-coaster location. SheiKra is one of the world's tallest dive coasters, Kumba features one of the world's largest vertical loops, and Montu (a gut-churning inverted coaster) delivers a g-force of 3.85. *See* ⇨ *Chapter 7.*

Something Old, Something New

You don't have to look far for "New Florida." It's evident in skyscrapers and sprawling suburbs, in malls, multiplexes, and the ubiquitous condo complexes that obscure parts of the coast. Yet it is easy enough to find reminders of the state's rich past.

■ **Apalachicola.** A booming cotton-and-lumber industry turned this Panhandle town into a bustling port in the 19th century. Now it's part of the Forgotten Coast. Hundreds of preserved buildings, ranging from antebellum warehouses to gracious Victorian-style homes, give it a time-warped appeal. *See* ⇨ *Chapter 14.*

■ **Coral Gables.** You can soak up 1920s architecture in Miami Beach. But in nearby Coral Gables you can soak *in* it at the **Venetian Pool,** a vintage municipal lagoon fashioned from a quarry. Back in the day it attracted Johnny Weissmuller, Esther Williams, and other legendary swimmers. *See* ⇨ *Chapter 2.*

■ **Cross Creek.** You can tour the Cracker-style house where Marjorie Kinnan Rawlings wrote *The Yearling* at **Marjorie Kinnan Rawlings Historic State Park** from October through July and visit the surrounding farm and grove year-round. *See* ⇨ *Chapter 13.*

■ **St. Augustine.** Fortify yourself at **Castillo de San Marcos.** Built by the Spanish to defend *La Florida*, this formidable 17th-century structure is America's oldest masonry fort. Even kids whose interest in architecture stops at Cinderella Castle will be impressed by its turrets, moat, and double drawbridge. *See* ⇨ *Chapter 13.*

Hitting the Greens

With more courses than any other state and weather that allows for year-round play, Florida is a dream destination for golfers. Ready to go for it? The tourism board's new, dedicated golf website (⊕ *www.golf.visitflorida.com*) will point you in the right direction.

■ **The Breakers.** Floridians' fascination with golf began in 1897 when the state's first course opened at this Palm Beach resort. (Rockefellers, Vanderbilts, and Astors are all listed in the guest book.) Today, the original 70-par **Ocean Course** offers spectacular Atlantic views and challenging shots on 140 acres. *See* ⇨ *Chapter 6.*

■ **Doral Golf Resort & Spa.** The **Blue Monster** understandably grabs the spotlight here: the par-72 course has been a stop on the PGA tour for more than 45 years. But the Miami resort has four other championship courses (including the new Jim McLean Signature Course) as well as McLean's own golf school. *See* ⇨ *Chapter 2.*

■ **PGA Village.** Owned and operated by the PGA, this Port St. Lucie venue boasts three championship courses designed by Tom Fazio and Pete Dye, plus a 35-acre **Golf Learning and Performance Center** that can turn weekend duffers into scratch players. A free museum of golf memorabilia is also on site. *See* ⇨ *Chapter 6.*

■ **Reunion Resort.** This spot near Orlando just keeps upping its game. Not content with having courses laid out by Tom Watson, Arnold Palmer, and Jack Nicklaus, it recently added the Annika Academy, a golf school named for LPGA phenom Annika Sörenstam and overseen by her coach, Henri Reis. *See* ⇨ *Chapter 9.*

FLORIDA'S
BEST BEACHES

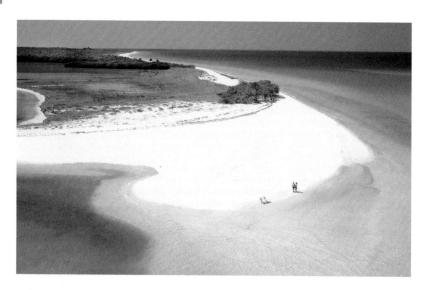

Bahia Honda State Park

Though the Florida Keys aren't renowned for beautiful sandy beaches, this is an exception. The 524-acre park has three superb beaches over 2.5 miles of sandy coastline at the crossroads of the Atlantic and the gulf, idyllic for swimming, snorkeling, kayaking, and fishing. Atlantic-facing Sandspur beach flaunts long stretches of powdery sands. *See ⇨ Chapter 4.*

Bowman's Beach, Sanibel Island

On Sanibel's secluded northwest end, this beach doubles as a shell hunter's paradise and a beach wanderer's great escape. For the former, the likelihood of leaving with a bag full of gorgeous shells is high. For the latter, the chance of serene, inspiring vistas is guaranteed. *See ⇨ Chapter 8.*

Caladesi Island State Park

Accessible only by ferry from Honeymoon Island State Recreation Area, this park offers pure white beaches, beautiful sunsets, and excellent bird-watching. *See ⇨ Chapter 7.*

Clearwater Beach

At what is arguably the state's best beach for families, kids and parents alike love the white stands and shallow, clear, warm waters by day, followed by sunset celebrations nightly, complete with musicians and artists. *See ⇨ Chapter 7.*

Fort de Soto Beach

Another winner of "America's Best Beach," the 1,136-acre park lies at the mouth of Tampa Bay, spread over five islands and housing 7 miles of beach, two fishing piers, and a 4-mile hiking/skating trail. The beaches are super packed on weekends but splendidly quiet on weekdays. *See ⇨ Chapter 7.*

Fort Lauderdale Beach

The former spring-break capital now plays host to a reinvented, more upscale beachfront; however, the downy sands and crystalline waters from the days of *Where the Boys Are* haven't changed. The beach "scene" is

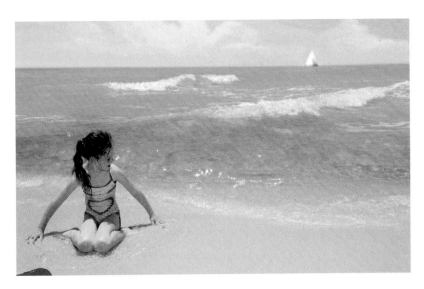

found between Las Olas and Sunrise boulevards. *See ⇨ Chapter 5.*

John Pennekamp Coral Reef State Park

Florida's best bet for diving and snorkeling, this state park adjacent to the Florida Keys National Marine Sanctuary encompasses 78 square miles of ecological treasures, the majority of which are found underwater. Although the beaches here do attract families, the real draw is experiencing the underwater world of the 600 varieties of fish that call this park home. *See ⇨ Chapter 4.*

Panama City Beach

It may be Spring Break Capital of the World come March and April, but the rest of the year this 17-mile expanse of snowy-white sand and sparking emerald-green water attracts families from all across the Southeast to enjoy some awesome fun in the sun. Pier Park offers great shopping and watering holes on the streets opposite the beachfront hotels. *See ⇨ Chapter 14.*

Siesta Key Beach

Crowned "America's Best Beach" in 2012, this one boasts the finest quartz sands in the world. The sand is so fine and powdery it appears like piles of flour and squeaks under your feet when you walk on it. The 40-acre beach park of this island is exceptionally wide and long, providing ample space for families, romantics, and Sunday's Drum Circle celebration. *See ⇨ Chapter 8.*

South Beach

The legend of beautiful people is very much a reality on the sands parallel to deco-drenched Ocean Drive from 5th to 15th Street, and upscale Collins Avenue from 15th to 23rd Street. Expect diesel bodies, plastic surgery, hunky gay guys, pretentious party-goers, and random families coming to see what the fuss is all about. *See ⇨ Chapter 2.*

GREAT ITINERARIES

Florida is a long, lean peninsula anchored to the mainland by a "panhandle," so the distances between destinations may surprise you. Panama City, for example, is closer to New Orleans than to Orlando, and Tallahassee, though only 8 miles from the Georgia border, is a whopping 465 miles from Miami Beach. Key West, similarly, is 494 miles from Jacksonville, yet only 90 miles from Cuba. When plotting your dream trip, study a map to determine how easy it will be to connect the dots—or simply follow one of these tried-and-true itineraries. If you have two or more weeks to drive through the state, you can do them all.

3 to 4 Days: Orlando

Anyone can easily spend a week doing the attractions. (Remember, Walt Disney World alone is roughly the size of San Francisco.) But unless you're a die-hard ride hound, a few days will let you sample them and still enjoy some of Orlando's other amenities. The hard part is deciding where to start. The Magic Kingdom has the greatest concentration of classic sites, and Epcot proves this really is a small world. Film buffs can get reel at Disney's Hollywood Studios or Universal Studios, and thrill seekers can get their hearts pumping at Islands of Adventure. As for wildlife encounters, you can do like Dolittle at Disney's Animal Kingdom or SeaWorld. On top of all that, there's a sufficient number of water parks—including both old favorites such as Wet 'n Wild and newer entries like Aquatica—to make you forget you're inland. In the city itself, art connoisseurs can survey the collection of modern paintings at the Orlando Museum of Art, and flower fans can check out Orlando blooms in the 50-acre Harry P. Leu Gardens. Boaters can take advantage of the area's numerous lakes, and golfers can link up on courses designed by the sport's biggest stars.

2 to 3 Days: Panhandle

Let's be honest: People come to Florida's Panhandle primarily for those white-sand beaches. Some of the best in the country are along this coastline, affectionately known as the Redneck Riviera. But it's possible to work on a tan and still work in some sightseeing. At Gulf Islands National Seashore, for instance, you can soak up the sun, cast a fishing net, take a hike, tour centuries-old forts, and have time left for a trip into historic Pensacola. After beach time around Apalachicola Bay, head north through the canopied roads around Apalachicola National Forest. Then get a true taste of the Old South in moss-draped Tallahassee. Yet another day could be devoted to glorious Grayton Beach, where diving and kayaking can be followed up with a relaxing drive along Route 30A to cute, nostalgia-inducing communities like WaterColor and Seaside. When planning your trip, bear in mind that the Panhandle not only has its own time zone but its own tourism season—summer—and that's prime time for beachgoing.

2 to 3 Days: Space Coast

If you need proof that Florida was the first part of the United States to be settled, look no farther than St. Augustine. It was founded by the Spanish in 1565, and visiting Castillo de San Marcos (its colonial-era fortress) or strolling the streets of the Old City that grew up around it allows you to experience life in the past lane. Taking in the stellar sites at the 150,000-acre Kennedy Space Center has just the opposite effect. Although it may seem centuries removed, the nation's oldest continuously inhabited city is less than two

Panhandle
Pensacola
Gulf Islands
National Seashore
Grayton
Beach
30A
98
WaterColor
and Seaside
Tallahassee
10
10
St. Augustine
75
1
Daytona
Kennedy
Space Center
Canaveral National Seashore
Merritt Island
Gulf of Mexico
Orlando
Caladesi Island
State Park
Walt Disney
World
Tampa
St. Petersburg
95
Sarasota
ATLANTIC
OCEAN
75
Palm Beach
Boca Raton
Fort
Lauderdale
41
Miami
Everglades
City
Biscayne
National Park
Bahia Honda
State Park
John Pennekamp
Coral Reef
State Park
Key West

hours by car from our launch pad to the moon. Between them, you can hear the call of the wild at Merritt Island National Wildlife Refuge, catch a wave like local surfing legend Kelly Slater, or blissfully hit the beach at Canaveral National Seashore. (The 24-mile preserve remains undeveloped, so you lounge in the shelter of dunes, not the shadow of high-rises.) Racier options also await—just reset your GPS for Daytona Beach. Its International Speedway, which has hosted NASCAR's Daytona 500 every February since 1959, is a must-see for stock-car enthusiasts, and there's plenty to do here year-round even if it's not a race day.

2 to 3 Days: Gold Coast and Treasure Coast

The opulent mansions of Palm Beach's Ocean Boulevard give you a glimpse of how the richer half lives. For exclusive boutique shopping, art gallery browsing, and glittery sightseeing, sybarites should wander down "The Avenue" (that's Worth Avenue to non–Palm Beachers). The sporty set will find dozens of places to tee up (hardly surprising given that the PGA is based here), along with tennis courts, polo clubs, even a croquet center. Those who'd like to see more of the Gold Coast can continue traveling south

through Boca Raton to Fort Lauderdale (justifiably known as the Yachting Capital of the World). But to balance the high-brow with the low-key, turn northward for a tour of the Treasure Coast. Notable for its outdoor opportunities and Old Florida ambience, this region was named for the booty spilled by a fleet of Spanish galleons shipwrecked here in 1715, and for centuries treasure kept washing ashore south of Sebastian Inlet. These days you're more likely to discover manatees and golden surfing opportunities. You can also look for the sea turtles that lay their own little treasures in the sands March through October.

2 to 3 Days: Miami Area

Greater Miami lays claim to the country's most celebrated strand—South Beach—and lingering on it tops most tourist itineraries. (The Ocean Drive section, lined with edgy clubs, boutiques, and eateries, is where the see-and-be-seen crowd gathers.) Once you've checked out the candy-color art-deco architecture, park yourself to ogle the parade of stylish people. Or join them in browsing Lincoln Road Mall, and be sure to check out its latest addition, the glittering Frank Gehry–designed New World Symphony. Later, *merengue* over to Calle Ocho, the epicenter of Miami's

Cuban community. Elsewhere in the area, Coconut Grove, Coral Gables, and the Miami Design District (an 18-block area crammed with showrooms and galleries) warrant a visit as well. Because Miami is the sole U.S. city with two national parks and a national preserve in its backyard, it is also a convenient base for eco-excursions. You can take a day trip to the Everglades; get a spectacular view of the reefs from a glass-bottom boat in Biscayne National Park; and then spot some rare wood storks in Big Cypress Swamp, which is best explored via Alligator Alley (Interstate 75).

2 to 3 Days: Florida Keys

Some dream of "sailing away to Key Largo," others of "wasting away again in Margaritaville." In any case, almost everybody equates the Florida Keys with relaxation. And they live up to their reputation, thanks to offbeat attractions and that fabled come-as-you-are, do-as-you-please vibe. Key West, alternately known as the Conch Republic, is a good place to get initiated. The Old Town has a funky, laid-back feel. So take a leisurely walk, pay your respects to Ernest Hemingway, and then (if you haven't imbibed too much at one of the renowned watering holes) rent a moped to tour the rest of the island. Clear waters and abundant marine life make underwater activities another must. After scoping out the parrotfish, you can head back into town and join local Parrotheads in a Jimmy Buffett sing-along. When retracing your route to the mainland, plan a last pit stop at Bahia Honda State Park (it has ranger-led activities plus the Keys' best beach) or John Pennekamp Coral Reef State Park, which offers unparalleled snorkeling and scuba diving.

TIPS

Now that one-way airfares are commonplace, vacationers visiting multiple destinations can fly into and out of different airports. Rent a car in between, picking it up at your point of arrival and leaving it at your point of departure. If you do this itinerary as an entire vacation, your best bet is to fly into and out of Orlando and rent a car from there.

Inquire about scheduled activities when visiting national and state parks or preserves. Many of them run free or low-cost ranger-led programs that run the gamut from walks and talks to campfires and canoe trips.

2 to 3 Days: Tampa Bay Area

Whether you bypassed Orlando's theme parks or simply want to add another one to your list, Busch Gardens is a logical starting point. With hair-raising rides and more than 2,000 animals, it appeals to adrenaline junkies and scaredy cats alike. Later you can catch a sporting event (Tampa has professional baseball, football, and hockey teams) or catch an act in the Spanish-inflected Ybor City entertainment district. If you're more interested in catching some rays, try Caladesi Island State Park to the west of the city or Fort De Soto Park at the mouth of Tampa Bay. After exploring the Riverwalk's new museums, culture vultures can take day trips to the galleries in St. Petersburg and to Sarasota's thriving arts scene. Nature lovers proceed north to Crystal River, where you can snorkel with the manatees that congregate in the warm water November through March.

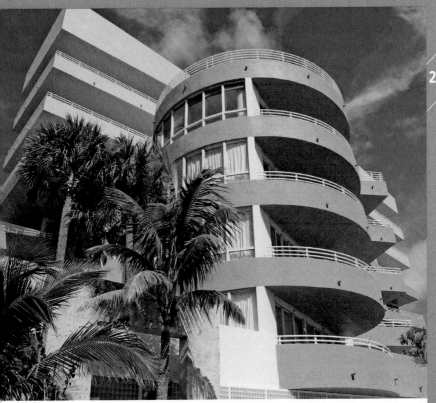

MIAMI AND
MIAMI BEACH

WELCOME TO MIAMI AND MIAMI BEACH

TOP REASONS TO GO

★ **The beach:** Miami Beach has been rated as one of the 10 best in the world. White sand, warm water, and bronzed bodies everywhere provide just the right mix of relaxation and people-watching.

★ **Dining delights:** Miami's eclectic residents have transformed the city into a museum of epicurean wonders, ranging from Cuban and Argentine fare to fusion haute cuisine.

★ **Wee-hour parties:** A 24-hour liquor license means clubs stay open until 5 am, and after-parties go until noon the following day.

★ **Picture-perfect people:** Miami is a watering hole for the vain and beautiful of South America, Europe, and the Northeast. Watch them—or join them—as they strut their stuff and flaunt their tans on the white beds of renowned art-deco hotels.

★ **Art deco district:** Iconic pastels and neon lights accessorize the architecture that first put South Beach on the map in the 1930s.

1 Downtown. Weave through the glass-and-steel labyrinth of new condo construction to catch a game or a new exhibition.

2 Coconut Grove. Catch dinner and a movie, listen to live music, or cruise the bohemian shops.

3 Coral Gables. Dine and shop on family-friendly Miracle Mile, and take a driving tour of the surrounding neighborhoods.

4 Key Biscayne. Explore the pristine parks and stretches of award-winning beaches by boat, kayak, or foot.

5 Wynwood. Eat, shop, and gawk your way through this trendy, creative neighborhood north of downtown.

6 Midtown. Experience yuppie life in this residential enclave chock full of fabulous restaurants and lounges.

7 Design District. Browse the design showrooms and haute boutiques before dining at Miami's trendiest restaurants.

8 Little Haiti. Practice your Creole and sample Haitian food in this interesting ethnic neighborhood.

2

GETTING ORIENTED

Long considered the gateway to Latin America, Miami is as close to Cuba and the Caribbean as you can get within the United States. The 36-square-mile city is at the southern tip of the Florida peninsula, bordered on the east by Biscayne Bay. Over the bay lies a series of barrier islands, the largest being a thin 18-square-mile strip called Miami Beach. To the east of Miami Beach is the Atlantic Ocean. To the south are the Florida Keys.

9 Little Havana. Sip Cuban coffee, roll cigars, and play dominoes in the heart and soul of Cuba's exile community.

10 South Beach. People-watch from sidewalk cafés, admire art deco, and party 'til dawn at the nation's hottest clubs.

11 Mid-Beach. Experience the booming restaurant scene and trendy hotels just beyond South Beach.

12 Fisher and Belle Isle. Be near the pulse of Miami Beach but a man-made island away.

13 North Beach and Aventura. Shop and relax in the quieter northern end of Miami Beach.

CUBAN FOOD

If the tropical vibe has you hankering for Cuban food, you've come to the right place. Miami is the top spot in the country to enjoy authentic Cuban cooking.

The flavors and preparations of Cuban cuisine are influenced by the island nation's natural bounty (yuca, sugarcane, guava), as well as its rich immigrant history, from near (Caribbean countries) and far (Spanish and African traditions). Chefs in Miami tend to stick with the classic versions of beloved dishes, though you'll find some variation from restaurant to restaurant, as recipes have often been passed down through generations of home cooks. For a true Cuban experience, try either the popular **Versailles** (✉ *3555 S.W. 8th St.* ☎ *305/444–0240* ⊕ *www. versaillesrestaurant.com*) or classic **La Carreta** (✉ *3632 S.W. 8th St.* ☎ *305/444–7501*) in Little Havana, appealing to families seeking a home-cooked, Cuban-style meal. For a modern interpretation of Cuban eats, head to Coral Gable's **Havana Harry's** (✉ *4612 S. Le Jeune Rd.* ☎ *305/661–2622*). South Beach eatery **Puerto Sagua Restaurant** (✉ *700 Collins Ave.* ☎ *305/673–1115*) is the beach's favorite Cuban hole-in-the-wall, open daily from 7 am to 2 am.

THE CUBAN SANDWICH

A great *cubano* (Cuban sandwich) requires pillowy Cuban bread layered with ham, garlic-citrus-marinated slow-roasted pork, Swiss cheese, and pickles (plus salami in Tampa, lettuce and tomatoes in Key West), with butter and/or mustard. The sandwich is grilled in a sandwich press until the cheese melts and all the elements are fused together. Try one at **Enriqueta's Sandwich Shop** (✉ 2830 N.E. 2nd Ave. ☎ 305/573–4681 ⊙ Weekdays 6 am–4 pm, Sat. 6 am–2 pm) in Wynwood, or **Exquisito Restaurant** (✉ 1510 S.W. 8th St. ☎ 305/643–0227 ⊙ Daily 7 am–midnight) in Little Havana.

KEY CUBAN DISHES

ARROZ CON POLLO

This chicken-and-rice dish is Cuban comfort food. Found throughout Latin America, the Cuban version is typically seasoned with garlic, paprika, and onions, then colored golden or reddish with saffron or *achiote* (a seed paste), and enlivened with a sizable splash of beer near the end of cooking. Green peas and sliced, roasted red peppers are standard toppings.

BISTEC DE PALOMILLA

This thinly sliced sirloin steak is marinated in lime juice and garlic and fried with onions. The steak is often served with *chimichurri* sauce, an olive oil, garlic, and cilantro sauce that sometimes comes with bread (slather bread with butter and dab on the chimichurri). Also try *ropa vieja*, a slow-cooked, shredded flank steak in a garlic-tomato sauce.

DESSERTS

Treat yourself to a slice of *tres leches* cake. The "three milks" come from the sweetened condensed milk, evaporated milk, and heavy cream that are poured over the cake until it's an utterly irresistible gooey mess. Also, don't miss the *pastelitos*, Cuban fruit-filled turnovers. Traditional flavors include plain guava, guava with cream cheese, and cream cheese with coconut. Yum!

DRINKS

Sip *guarapo* (gwa-RA-poh), a fresh sugarcane juice that isn't really as sweet as you might think, or grab a straw and enjoy a frothy *batido* (bah-TEE-doe), a Cuban-style milk shake made with tropical fruits like mango, *piña* (pineapple), or *mamey* (mah-MAY, a tropical fruit with a melon-cherry taste). For a real twist, try the *batido de trigo*—a wheat shake that will remind you of sugar-glazed breakfast cereal.

FRITAS

If you're in the mood for an inexpensive, casual Cuban meal, have a *frita*—a hamburger with distinctive Cuban flair. It's made with ground beef that's mixed with ground or finely chopped chorizo, spiced with pepper, paprika, and salt, topped with sautéed onions and shoestring potato fries, and then served on a bun slathered with a special tomato-based ketchuplike sauce.

LECHON ASADO

Fresh ham or an entire suckling pig marinated in *mojo criollo* (parsley, garlic, sour orange, and olive oil) is roasted until fork tender and served with white rice, black beans, and *tostones* (fried plantains) or *yuca* (pronounced YU-kah), a starchy tuber with a mild nut taste that's often sliced into fat sticks and deep-fried like fries.

By Paul Rubio

Three quarters of a century after the art deco movement, Miami remains one of the world's trendiest and flashiest hot spots. Luckily for visitors, South Beach is no longer the only place to stand and pose in Miami. North of downtown Miami's megamakeover, the growing Wynwood and Design districts—along with nearby Midtown—are home to Miami's hipster and fashionista scenes, and the South beach "scene" continues to extend both north and west, with the addition of new venues north of 20th Street, south of 5th Street and along the bay on West Avenue. The reopening of the mammoth Fontainebleau and its enclave of nightclubs and restaurants along Mid-Beach paved the way for a mid-beach renaissance, luring in other globally renowned resorts, lounges, and restaurants into the neighborhood, such as the Soho Beach House and Nobu restaurant.

Visit Miami today and it's hard to believe that 100 years ago it was a mosquito-infested swampland, with an Indian trading post on the Miami River. Then hotel builder Henry Flagler brought his railroad to the outpost known as Fort Dallas. Other visionaries—Carl Fisher, Julia Tuttle, William Brickell, and John Sewell, among others—set out to tame the unruly wilderness. Hotels were erected, bridges were built, the port was dredged, and electricity arrived. The narrow strip of mangrove coast was transformed into Miami Beach—and the tourists started to come. They haven't stopped since!

Greater Miami is many destinations in one. At its best it offers an unparalleled multicultural experience: melodic Latin and Caribbean tongues, international cuisines and cultural events, and an unmistakable joie de vivre—all against a beautiful beach backdrop. In Little Havana the air is tantalizing with the perfume of strong Cuban coffee. In Coconut Grove, Caribbean steel drums ring out during the Miami/Bahamas Goombay Festival. Anytime in colorful Miami Beach, restless crowds wait for entry to the hottest new clubs.

Many visitors don't know that Miami and Miami Beach are really separate cities. Miami, on the mainland, is South Florida's commercial hub. Miami Beach, on 17 islands in Biscayne Bay, is sometimes considered America's Riviera, luring refugees from winter with its warm sunshine; sandy beaches; graceful, shady palms; and tireless nightlife. The natives know well that there's more to Greater Miami than the bustle of South Beach and its Art Deco District. In addition to well-known places such as Ocean Drive and Lincoln Road, the less reported spots—like the burgeoning Design District in Miami, the historic buildings of Coral Gables, and the secluded beaches of Key Biscayne—are great insider destinations.

PLANNING

WHEN TO GO

Miami and Miami Beach are year-round destinations. Most visitors come November through April, when the weather is close to perfect; hotels, restaurants, and attractions are busiest; and each weekend holds a festival or event. The "Season" kicks off in December with Art Basel Miami Beach, and hotel rates don't come down until after the college kids have left after spring break in late March.

It's hot and steamy May through September, but nighttime temperatures are usually pleasant. Also, summer is a good time for the budget traveler. Many hotels lower their rates considerably, and many restaurants offer discounts—especially during **Miami Spice** in August and September, when a slew of top restaurants offer special tasting menus at a steep discount. (Check ⊕ *www.iLoveMiamiSpice.com* for details.)

GETTING HERE AND AROUND

Greater Miami resembles Los Angeles in its urban sprawl and traffic. You'll need a car to visit many attractions and points of interest. If possible, avoid driving during the rush hours of 7–9 am and 5–7 pm—the hour just after and right before the peak times also can be slow going. During rainy weather, be especially cautious of flooding in South Beach and Key Biscayne.

AIR TRAVEL

Miami is serviced by Miami International Airport (MIA), 8 miles northwest of downtown, and Fort Lauderdale–Hollywood International Airport (FLL), 26 miles northeast. Many discount carriers, like Spirit Airlines, Southwest Airlines, and JetBlue, fly into FLL, making it a smart bargain if you're renting a car. Otherwise, look for flights to MIA on American Airlines, Delta, and United. MIA recently underwent an extensive face-lift, improving facilities, common spaces, and the overall aesthetic of the airport.

CAR TRAVEL

Interstate 95 is the major expressway connecting South Florida with points north; State Road 836 is the major east–west expressway and connects to Florida's Turnpike, State Road 826, and Interstate 95. Seven causeways link Miami and Miami Beach, with Interstate 195 and Interstate 395 offering the most convenient routes; the Rickenbacker Causeway extends to Key Biscayne from Interstate 95 and U.S. 1. The high-speed lanes on the left-hand side of I–95 require a prepaid toll gadget called a "Sunpass," available in most drug and grocery stores. It is sometimes included with your rental car (and you are billed for the tolls later). Note, the toll on to Key Biscayne is cash only. Also, remember U.S. 1 (aka Biscayne Boulevard)—you'll hear it often in directions. It starts in Key West, hugs South Florida's coastline, and heads north straight through to Maine.

PUBLIC TRANSPORTATION

Some sights are accessible via the public transportation system, run by the **Metro-Dade Transit Agency,** which maintains 740 Metrobuses on 90 routes; the 23-mile Metrorail elevated rapid-transit system; and the Metromover, an elevated light-rail system. Those planning to use public transportation should get an EASY Card or EASY Ticket available at any Metrorail station and most supermarkets. Fares are discounted, and transfer fees are nominal. The bus stops for the **Metrobus** are marked with blue-and-green signs with a bus logo and route information. The fare is $2.25 (exact change only if paying cash). Cash-paying customers must pay for another ride if transferring. Some express routes carry a surcharge of $0.50. Elevated **Metrorail** trains run from downtown Miami north to Hialeah and south along U.S. 1 to Dadeland. The system operates daily 5 am–midnight. The fare is $2.25; $0.60 transfers to Metrobus are available only for EASY Card and EASY Ticket holders. **Metromover** resembles an airport shuttle and runs on two loops around downtown Miami, linking major hotels, office buildings, and shopping areas. The system spans 4 miles, including the 1-mile Omni Loop and the 1-mile Brickell Loop. There is no fee to ride.

Tri-Rail, South Florida's commuter-train system, stops at 18 stations north of MIA along a 71-mile route. There's a Metrorail transfer station two stops north of MIA. Prices range from $2.50 to $6.90 for a one-way ticket.

Contacts Metro-Dade Transit Agency ☎ 305/891–3131, 3-1-1 ⊕ www.miamidade.gov/transit. **Tri-Rail** ☎ 800/874–7245 ⊕ www.tri-rail.com.

TAXI TRAVEL

Except in South Beach, it's difficult to hail a cab on the street; in most cases you'll need to call a cab company or have a hotel doorman hail one for you. Fares run $2.50 for the first ⅙ of a mile and $2.40 every mile thereafter. Flat-rate fares are also available from the airport to a variety of zones (including Miami Beach) for $32. Expect a $2 surcharge on rides leaving from Miami International Airport or the Port of Miami. For those heading from MIA to downtown, the 15-minute, 7-mile trip costs around $22. Many cabs now accept credit cards; inquire before you get in the car.

2

Taxi Companies **Central Cab** ☎ *305/532-5555* ⊕ *www.centralcab.com.*
Tropical Taxi ☎ *305/945-1025* ☞ *Serving Miami Beach only.* **Yellow Cab**
☎ *305/888-8888.*

TRAIN TRAVEL

Amtrak provides service from 500 destinations to the Greater Miami
area. The trains make several stops along the way; north–south service
stops in the major Florida cities of Jacksonville, Orlando, Tampa, West
Palm Beach, and Fort Lauderdale. Note that these stops are often in less
than ideal locations for immediate city access. For extended trips, or if
you want to visit other areas in Florida, you can come via Auto Train
(where you bring your car along) from Lorton, Virginia, just outside
Washington, D.C., to Sanford, Florida, just outside Orlando. From
there it's less than a four-hour drive to Miami. Fares vary, but expect
to pay between around $275 and $350 for a basic sleeper seat and car
passage each way. ■ TIP→ You must be traveling with an automobile to
purchase a ticket on the Auto Train.

VISITOR INFORMATION

For additional information about Miami and Miami Beach, contact the
city's visitor bureaus. You can also pick up a free Miami Beach INcard
at the Miami Beach Visitors Center 10–4seven days a week, entitling
you to discounts and offers at restaurants, shops, galleries, and more.

Contacts **Coconut Grove Chamber of Commerce** ✉ *2820 McFarlane
Rd., Coconut Grove* ☎ *305/444-7270* ⊕ *www.coconutgrovechamber.com.*
Coral Gables Chamber of Commerce ✉ *224 Catalonia Ave., Coral Gables*
☎ *305/446-1657* ⊕ *www.coralgableschamber.org.* **Greater Miami Convention & Visitors Bureau** ✉ *701 Brickell Ave., Ste. 2700, Miami* ☎ *305/539-3000,
800/933-8448 in U.S.* ⊕ *www.miamiandbeaches.com.* **Key Biscayne Chamber
of Commerce and Visitors Center** ✉ *88 W. McIntyre St., Ste. 100, Key Biscayne*
☎ *305/361-5207* ⊕ *www.keybiscaynechamber.org.* **Visit Miami Beach—Visitors
Center** ✉ *1901 Convention Center Dr., Hall C* ☎ *786/276-2763, 305/672-1270
for Miami Beach Tourist Hotline* ⊕ *www.miamibeachguest.com.*

EXPLORING MIAMI AND MIAMI BEACH

If you'd arrived here 50 years ago with a guidebook in hand, chances
are you'd be thumbing through listings looking for alligator wrestlers
and you-pick strawberry fields or citrus groves. Things have changed.
While Disney sidetracked families in Orlando, Miami was developing a
unique culture and attitude that's equal parts beach town/big business,
Latino/Caribbean meets European/American—all of which fuels a great
art and food scene, as well as exuberant nightlife and myriad festivals.

To find your way around Greater Miami, learn how the numbering system works (or better yet, use a GPS). Miami is laid out on a grid with
four quadrants—northeast, northwest, southeast, and southwest—that
meet at Miami Avenue and Flagler Street. Miami Avenue separates east
from west, and Flagler Street separates north from south. Avenues and
courts run north–south; streets, terraces, and ways run east–west. Roads
run diagonally, northwest–southeast. But other districts—Miami Beach,
Coral Gables, and Hialeah—may or may not follow this system, and

along the curve of Biscayne Bay the symmetrical grid shifts diagonally. It's best to buy a detailed map, stick to the major roads, and ask directions early and often. However, make sure you're in a safe neighborhood or public place when you seek guidance; cabdrivers and cops are good resources.

DOWNTOWN

Downtown Miami dazzles from a distance. The skyline is fluid, thanks to the sheer number of sparkling glass high-rises between Biscayne Boulevard and the Miami River. Business is the key to downtown Miami's daytime bustle. However, the influx of massive, modern, and affordable condos has lured a young and trendy demographic to the areas in and around downtown, giving Miami much more of a "city" feel come nightfall. In fact, downtown has become a nighttime hot spot in recent years, inciting a cultural revolution that has fostered burgeoning areas north in Wynwood, Midtown, and the Design District, and south along Brickell Avenue. The pedestrian streets here tend to be very restaurant-centric, complemented by lounges and nightclubs.

The free, 23-mile, elevated commuter system known as the Metromover runs inner and outer loops through downtown and to nearby neighborhoods south and north. Many attractions are conveniently located within a few blocks of a station.

TOP ATTRACTIONS

Adrienne Arsht Center. Culture vultures and other artsy types are drawn to this stunning performing arts center, which includes the 2,400-seat Ziff Ballet Opera House, the 2,200-seat Knight Concet Hall, the Carnival Studio black-box theater, and an outdoor Plaza for the Arts. Throughout the year, you'll find top-notch performances by local and national touring groups, including Broadway hits like *Wicked* and *Jersey Boys,* intimate music concerts, and showstopping ballet. Think of it as a sliver of savoir faire to temper Miami's often over-the-top vibe. The massive development was designed by architect César Pelli, and stands as the largest American performing-arts center constructed since the 1980s. Complimentary one-hour tours of the Arsht Center, highlighting the architecture and its public art, are offered every Saturday and Monday at noon. Restaurateur Barton G. presents his pretheater dining extravaganza at the Arsht Center's restaurant, **Prelude by Barton G.,** with a 2-course, $29 prix-fixe menu (☎ *305/357–7900 ⊕ www.preludebybartong.com*). ✉ *1300 Biscayne Blvd., at N.E. 13th St., Downtown* ☎ *305/949–6722 for box office ⊕ www.arshtcenter.org.*

Freedom Tower. In the 1960s this ornate Spanish-baroque structure was the Cuban Refugee Center, processing more than 500,000 Cubans who entered the United States after fleeing Fidel Castro's regime. Built in 1925 for the *Miami Daily News,* it was inspired by the Giralda, an 800-year-old bell tower in Seville, Spain. Preservationists were pleased to see the tower's exterior restored in 1988. Today, it is owned by Miami Dade College (MDC), functioning as a cultural and educational center; it's also home to the MDC Musueum of Art + Design, which showcases a broad collection of contemporary Latin art as well works in the

Downtown Miami

KEY
Ⓜ Metromover Station
- - - Metromover

genres of minimalism and pop art. ■**TIP**→ **Admission is free to both the tower and museum.** ✉ *600 Biscayne Blvd., at N.E. 6th St., Downtown* ☎ *305/237–7700* ⊕ *www.mdcmoad.org* ⊗ *Wed.–Sun. noon–5.*

HistoryMiami. Discover a treasure trove of colorful stories about the region's history at HistoryMiami, formerly known as the Historical Museum of Southern Florida. Exhibits celebrate the city's multicultural heritage, including an old Miami streetcar and unique items chronicling the migration of Cubans to Miami. ✉ *101 W. Flagler St., between N.W. 1st and 2nd Aves., Downtown* ☎ *305/375–1492* ⊕ *www.historymiami. org* ✉ *$8* ⊗ *Mon.–Sat. 10–5, Sun. noon–5.*

Fodor'sChoice
★

Pérez Art Museum Miami (PAMM). Opened in December 2013, the Pérez Art Museum Miami, known locally as PAMM, shines as the city's first true world-class museum. This über-high-design architectural masterpiece on Biscayne Bay is a sight to behold. Double-story, cylindrical hanging gardens sway from high atop the museum, anchored to stylish wood trusses that help create this gotta-see-it-to-believe-it indoor/outdoor museum. Large sculptures, Asian-inspired gardens, sexy white benches, and steel frames envelop the property. Inside, the 120,000-square-foot space houses multicultural art from the 20th and 21st centuries, some of which were previously on display at the Miami Art Museum (note: downtown's Miami Art Museum no longer exists and the collection has now been incorporated into PAMM). Most of the interior space is devoted to temporary exhibitions, which have included the likes of *Ai Weiwei: According to What?* and *Edouard Duval-Carrié: Imagined Landscapes.* Even if you aren't a "museum type" per se, come check out this magnum opus over lunch at the Verde, the museum's sensational waterfront restaurant and bar. ✉ *1103 Biscayne Blvd., Downtown* ☎ *305/375–3000* ⊕ *www.pamm.org* ✉ *$12* ⊗ *Tues.–Wed. and Fri.–Sun. 10–6, Thurs. 10–9.*

WORTH NOTING

Bayfront Park. This pedestrian-friendly waterfront park sits on a 32-acre site smack in the heart of downtown Miami on Biscayne Bay; there's a small walking trail and three major event spaces: Bicentennial Park, Tina Hills Pavilion, and Klipsch Amphitheater at Bayfront Park. American sculptor Isamu Noguchi helped redesign the park in the late 1980s, gracing the site with several works, including the white *Challenger* Memorial, commemorating the space shuttle that exploded in 1986. If you want to live like a local, join in the free yoga on the bayfront Monday and Wednesday (at 6 pm) or Saturday (at 9 am). At the park's north end, you'll reach the colossal Bayside Marketplace entertainment, dining, and retail complex, which is particularly popular with cruise passengers as well as visitors from South America. ✉ *301 N. Biscayne Blvd., Downtown* ☎ *305/358–7550* ⊕ *www.bayfrontparkmiami.com.*

FAMILY
Jungle Island. Originally located deep in south Miami and known as Parrot Jungle, South Florida's original tourist attraction opened in 1936 and moved closer to Miami Beach in 2003. Located on Watson Island, a small stretch of land off of I–395 between Downtown Miami and South Beach, Jungle Island is far more than a park where cockatoos ride tricycles; this interactive zoological park is home to just about every

unusual and endangered species you would want to see, including a rare albino alligator, a liger (lion and tiger mix), and myriad exotic birds. The most intriguing offerings are the VIP animal tours, including the Lemur Experience ($79.95), in which the highly social primates make themselves at home on your lap or shoulders. Jungle Island offers complimentary shuttle service to most Downtown Miami and South Beach hotels. ⊠ *Watson Island, 1111 Parrot Jungle Trail, off MacArthur Causeway (I–395), Downtown* ☎ *305/400–7000* ⊕ *www.jungleisland. com* 🖃 *$34.95, plus $8 parking* ☉ *Weekdays 10–5, weekends 10–6.*

FAMILY **Miami Children's Museum.** This Arquitectonica-designed museum, both imaginative and geometric in appearance, is directly across the MacArthur Causeway from Jungle Island. Twelve galleries house hundreds of interactive, bilingual exhibits. Children can scan plastic groceries in the supermarket, scramble through a giant sand castle, climb a rock wall, learn about the Everglades, and combine rhythms in the world-music studio. ⊠ *Watson Island, 980 MacArthur Causeway, off I–395, Downtown* ☎ *305/373–5437* ⊕ *www.miamichildrensmuseum.org* 🖃 *$16, parking $1/hr* ☉ *Daily 10–6.*

COCONUT GROVE

A former haven for writers and artists, Coconut Grove has never quite outgrown its image as a small village. You can still feel the Bohemian roots of this artsy neighborhood, but it has grown increasingly mainstream and residential over the past 20 years. Posh estates mingle with rustic cottages, modest frame homes, and stark modern dwellings, often on the same block. If you're into horticulture, you'll be impressed by the Garden of Eden–like foliage that seems to grow everywhere without care. In truth, residents are determined to keep up the Grove's village-in-a-jungle look, so they lavish attention on exotic plantings even as they battle to protect any remaining native vegetation.

The center of the Grove still attracts its fair share of locals and tourists who enjoy perusing the small boutiques, sidewalk cafés, and cute galleries that remind us of the old Grove. Activities here are family-friendly with easy access to bayside parks, museums, and gardens.

TOP ATTRACTIONS

FAMILY **Patricia and Phillip Frost Museum of Science.** In mid-2015 the Patricia and Phillip Frost Museum of Science will relocate to its much larger, hyper-modern new home in downtown's Museum Park. Until then, this small fun museum in Coconut Grove is chock-full of hands-on sound, gravity, and electricity displays for children and adults alike. For animal lovers, its wildlife center houses native Florida snakes, turtles, tortoises, and birds of prey. Check the museum's schedule for traveling exhibits that appear throughout the year. If you're here the first Friday of the month—called Fabulous First Fridays—stick around for the free star show at 7 pm and then gaze at the planets through two powerful Meade telescopes at the Weintraub Observatory. Also enjoy a laser-light rock-and-roll show nightly at 8, 9, 10, or 11 to the tunes of the Doors, Bob Marley, the Beatles, or Pink Floyd to name a few. ⊠ *3280 S. Miami*

Greater Miami

OCEAN

MIAMI BEACH

SOUTH BEACH

Art Deco District

Collins Ave.
Ocean Dr.
A1A

Fisher Island

Virginia Key

Causeway

11

Rickenbacker Causeway

Grove Isle

Miami Children's Museum

Watson Island

Jungle Island

Port Miami

MacArthur Causeway

Venetian Causeway

Julia Tuttle Causeway

JFK Causeway

Biscayne Blvd.

N.E. 2nd Ave.

N. Miami Ave.

1

DESIGN DISTRICT

MIDTOWN

WYNWOOD ARTS DISTRICT

195

441

95

305

41

1

2

7

8

6

9

10

S.W. 13th St.

Brickell Ave.

Coral Way

S.W. 3rd Ave.

S.W. 12th Ave.

27

COCONUT GROVE

S. Dixie Hwy.

N.W. 79th St.

N.W. 62nd St.

N.W. 54th St.

N.W. 36th St.

N.W. 17th Ave.

N.W. 20th St.

Robert Frost Expwy.

Hialeah Dr.

944

9

Miami River

East-West Expressway

N.W. 7th St.

W. Flagler St.

Ponce de León Blvd.

MIAMI

N.W. 27th Ave.

S.W. 8th St.

S.W. 22nd St.

1

S.W. 37th Ave. (Douglas Rd.)

Le Jeune Rd.

Granada Blvd.

Sevilla Ave.

Tamiami Trail

3

4

CocoWalk

Grand Ave.

5

953

972

57th Ave.

976

Bird Rd.

S.W. 8th St.

S.W. 24th St.

826

968

959

836

Dairy Rd.

N.W. 39th St.

N.W. 72nd Ave.

Miami International Airport

27

ATLANTIC

Biscayne Bay

KEY
BISCAYNE

Crandon Park

Crandon
Park

Bill Baggs Cape
Florida State Park

Cape Florida
Lighthouse

0   3 km

0   3 miles

CORAL
GABLES

Coral Gables

Marnada St.

Sunset Dr.

Ponce de León Rd.

Red Rd.

S.W. 72nd St.

Ponce de León Blvd.

Waterway

Cartagena
Plaza

Old Cutler Rd.

Matheson Hammock
Park Beach

SOUTH
MIAMI

Ave., Coconut Grove ☎ *305/646–4200* ⊕ *www.miamisci.org* ✉ *$14.95* ⊗ *Museum daily 10–6; planetarium hrs vary.*

Fodor's Choice
★ **Vizcaya Museum and Gardens.** Of the 10,000 people living in Miami between 1912 and 1916, about 1,000 of them were gainfully employed by Chicago industrialist James Deering to build this European-inspired residence. Once comprising 180 acres, this National Historic Landmark now occupies a 30-acre tract that includes a rockland hammock (native forest) and more than 10 acres of formal gardens with fountains overlooking Biscayne Bay. The house, open to the public, contains 70 rooms, 34 of which are filled with paintings, sculpture, antique furniture, and other fine and decorative arts. The collection spans 2,000 years and represents the Renaissance, baroque, rococo, and neoclassical periods. The 90-minute self-guided Discover Vizcaya Audio Tour is available in multiple languages for an additional $5. Moonlight tours, offered on evenings that are nearest the full moon, provide a magical look at the gardens; call for reservations. ✉ *3251 S. Miami Ave., Coconut Grove* ☎ *305/250–9133* ⊕ *www.vizcayamuseum.org* ✉ *$18* ⊗ *Wed.–Mon. 9:30–4:30.*

WORTH NOTING

Barnacle Historic State Park. A pristine bay-front manse sandwiched between cramped luxury developments, Barnacle is Miami's oldest house still standing on its original foundation. To get here, you'll hike along an old buggy trail through a tropical hardwood hammock and landscaped lawn leading to Biscayne Bay. Built in 1891 by Florida's first snowbird—New Yorker Commodore Ralph Munroe—the large home, built of timber that Munroe salvaged from wrecked ships, has many original furnishings, a broad sloping roof, and deeply recessed verandas that channel sea breezes into the house. If your timing is right, you may catch one of the monthly Moonlight Concerts, and the old-fashioned picnic on July 4 is popular. ✉ *3485 Main Hwy., Coconut Grove* ☎ *305/442–6866* ⊕ *www.floridastateparks.org/thebarnacle* ✉ *$2 park entry, tours $3, concerts $7* ⊗ *Fri.–Mon. 9–5; tours at 10, 11:30, 1, and 2:30. Concerts monthly Sept.–May 6–9 pm; call or check the website for dates.*

CORAL GABLES

You can easily spot Coral Gables from the window of a Miami-bound jetliner—just look for the massive orange tower of the Biltmore Hotel rising from a lush green carpet of trees concealing the city's gracious homes. The canopy is as much a part of this planned city as its distinctive architecture, all attributed to the vision of George E. Merrick nearly 100 years ago.

The story of this city began in 1911, when Merrick inherited 1,600 acres of citrus and avocado groves from his father. Through judicious investment he nearly doubled the tract to 3,000 acres by 1921. Merrick dreamed of building an American Venice here, complete with canals and homes. Working from this vision, he began designing a city based on centuries-old prototypes from Mediterranean countries. Unfortunately for Merrick, the devastating no-name hurricane of 1926, followed by the Great Depression, prevented him from fulfilling many of his plans. He died at 54, an employee of the post office. Today Coral Gables has a population of about 47,000. In its bustling downtown more than 150 multinational companies maintain headquarters or regional offices, and the University of Miami campus in the southern part of the Gables brings a youthful vibrancy to the area. A southern branch of the city extends down the shore of Biscayne Bay through neighborhoods threaded with canals.

TOP ATTRACTIONS

Biltmore Hotel. Bouncing back stunningly from its dark days as an army hospital, this hotel has become the jewel of Coral Gables—a dazzling architectural gem with a colorful past. First opened in 1926, it was a hot spot for the rich and glamorous of the Jazz Age until it was converted to an army–air force regional hospital in 1942. Until 1968, the Veterans Administration continued to operate the hospital after World War II. The Biltmore then lay vacant for nearly 20 years before it underwent extensive renovations and reopened as a luxury hotel in 1987. Its 16-story tower, like the Freedom Tower in downtown Miami, is a replica of Seville's Giralda Tower. The magnificent pool is reportedly the largest hotel pool in the continental United States. Because it functions as a full-service hotel, your ticket in—if you aren't staying here—is to patronize one of the hotel's several restaurants or bars. Sunday champagne brunch is a local legend; try to get a table in the courtyard. ⊠ *1200 Anastasia Ave., near De Soto Blvd., Coral Gables* ☎ *855/311–6903* ⊕ *www.biltmorehotel.com.*

FAMILY

Fodor's Choice

★

Fairchild Tropical Botanic Garden. With 83 acres of lakes, sunken gardens, a 560-foot vine pergola, orchids, bellflowers, coral trees, bougainvillea, rare palms, and flowering trees, Fairchild is the largest tropical botanical garden in the continental United States. The tram tour highlights the best of South Florida's flora; then you can set off exploring on your own. A 2-acre rain-forest exhibit showcases tropical plants from around the world complete with a waterfall and stream. The conservatory, Windows to the Tropics, is home to rare tropical plants, including the Titan Arum (*Amorphophallus titanum*), a fast-growing variety that attracted thousands of visitors when it bloomed in 1998. (It was only the sixth documented bloom in this country in the 20th century.) The Keys Coastal Habitat, created in a marsh and mangrove area in 1995 with assistance from the Tropical Audubon Society, provides food and shelter to resident and migratory birds. Check out the Montgomery Botanical Center, a research facility devoted to palms and cycads. Spicing up Fairchild's calendar are plant sales, afternoon teas, and genuinely special events year-round, such as the International Mango Festival the second weekend in July. The excellent bookstore–gift shop carries books on gardening and horticulture, and the Garden Café serves sandwiches and, seasonally, smoothies made from the garden's own crop of tropical fruits. ⊠ *10901 Old Cutler Rd., Coral Gables* ☎ *305/667–1651* ⊕ *www.fairchildgarden.org* 🎟 *$25* ⊙ *Daily 7:30–4:30.*

FAMILY

Venetian Pool. Sculpted from a rock quarry in 1923 and fed by artesian wells, this 820,000-gallon municipal pool had a major face-lift in 2010. It remains quite popular because of its themed architecture—a fantasy version of a waterfront Italian village—created by Denman Fink. The pool has earned a place on the National Register of Historic Places and showcases a nice collection of vintage photos depicting 1920s beauty pageants and swank soirees held long ago. Paul Whiteman played here, Johnny Weissmuller and Esther Williams swam here, and you should, too (but no kids under 3). A snack bar, lockers, and showers make this must-see user-friendly as well. ⊠ *2701 De Soto Blvd., at Toledo St., Coral Gables* 🕾 *305/460–5306* ⊕ *www.gablesrecreation.com* 🖃 *$11; free parking across De Soto Blvd.* ☉ *Usually Tues.–Sun. 11–4:30, but best to call ahead.*

WORTH NOTING

Miracle Mile. Even with competition from some impressive malls, this half-mile stretch of colorful retail stores continues to thrive because of its intriguing mixture of unique boutiques, bridal shops, art galleries, and charming restaurants. It attracts Latin America's power players, including the overly botoxed women you might see on *The Real Housewives of Miami.* ⊠ *Coral Way, between S.W. 37th and S.W. 42nd Aves.* ⊕ *www.shopcoralgables.com.*

OFF THE BEATEN PATH

Zoo Miami. Don't miss a visit to this top-notch zoo, 14 miles southwest of Coral Gables, in the Miami suburbs. The only subtropical zoo in the continental United States, it has 320-plus acres that are home to more than 2,000 animals, including 40 endangered species, which roam on islands surrounded by moats. Amazon & Beyond encompasses 27 acres of simulated tropical rain forests showcasing 600 animals indigenous to the region, such as giant river otters, harpy eagles, anacondas, and jaguars. The Wings of Asia aviary has about 300 exotic birds representing 70 species flying free within the junglelike enclosure. Florida: Mission Everglades showcases the diverse wildlife of native Florida ecosystems. There's also a petting zoo with a meerkat exhibit and interactive opportunities, such as those at Wacky Barn and Dr. Wilde's World and the Ecology Theater, where kids can touch animals like alligators and opossums. An educational and entertaining wildlife show is given three times daily. ⊠ *12400 S.W. 152nd St. (1 Zoo Blvd.), Richmond Heights* 🕾 *305/251–0400* ⊕ *www.miamimetrozoo.com* 🖃 *$15.95; 45-min tram tour $4.95* ☉ *Daily 9:30–5:30, last admission at 4.*

KEY BISCAYNE

Once upon a time, the two barrier islands that make up the village of Key Biscayne (Key Biscayne itself and Virginia Key) were outposts for fishermen and sailors, pirates and salvagers, soldiers and settlers. The 95-foot Cape Florida Lighthouse stood tall during Seminole Indian battles and hurricanes. Coconut plantations covered two-thirds of Key Biscayne, and there were plans as far back as the 1800s to develop the picturesque island as a resort for the wealthy. Fortunately, the state and county governments set much of the land aside for parks, and both keys are now home to top-ranked beaches and golf, tennis, softball, and picnicking facilities. The long and winding bike paths that run through the islands are favorites for in-line skaters and cyclists. Incorporated in 1991, the village of Key Biscayne is a hospitable community of about 12,500, even though Virginia Key remains undeveloped at the moment. These two playground islands are especially family-friendly.

TOP ATTRACTIONS

FAMILY **Miami Seaquarium.** This classic family attraction stages shows with sea lions, dolphins, and Lolita the killer whale. The Crocodile Flats exhibit has 26 Nile crocodiles. Discovery Bay, an endangered mangrove habitat, is home to sea turtles, alligators, herons, egrets, and ibis. You can also visit a shark pool, a tropical reef aquarium, and West Indian and Florida manatees. A popular interactive attraction is the Stingray Touch Tank, where you can touch and feed cow-nose rays and southern stingrays. Another big draw is the Dolphin Interaction program, including the quite intensive Dolphin Odyssey ($199) experience and the lighter shallow-water Dolphin Encounter ($139). Make reservations for either experience. ⊠ *4400 Rickenbacker Causeway, Virginia Key* ☎ *305/361–5705* ⊕ *www.miamiseaquarium.com* ✍ *$41.95, parking $8 (cash only)* ⊙ *Daily 9:30–6, last admission at 4:30.*

> **SAIL AWAY**
>
> If you can sail in Miami, do. Blue skies, calm seas, and a view of the city skyline make for a pleasurable outing—especially at twilight, when the fabled "moon over Miami" casts a soft glow on the water. Key Biscayne's calm waves and strong breezes are perfect for sailing and windsurfing, and although Dinner Key and the Coconut Grove waterfront remain the center of sailing in Greater Miami, sailboat moorings and rentals sit along other parts of the bay and up the Miami River, too.

WYNWOOD

Fodor's Choice ★ Wynwood actually encompasses three trendy, creative neighborhoods 3 to 4 miles north of downtown and has developed an impressive mix of one-of-a-kind shops and galleries, haute couture boutiques, see-and-be-seen bars, and slick restaurants. One thing is still missing from the landscape: a decent hotel. On a positive note, it's kept the vibe in these neighborhoods more local and less touristy. The downside: you'll need a vehicle to get here, and though in close proximity to one another, you'll also need a vehicle to get between these emerging neighborhoods.

Between I–95 and Miami Avenue from 29th to 22nd streets, the funky and edgy **Wynwood Art District** (⊕ *www.wynwoodmiami.com*) is peppered with galleries, art studios, and private collections accessible to the public. Though the neighborhood hasn't completely shed its dodgy past, artist-painted graffiti walls and reinvented urban, industrial buildings have transformed the area from plain old grimy to super trendy. The Wynwood Walls on Northwest 2nd Avenue between Northeast 25th and 26th streets are a cutting-edge enclave of modern urban murals. However, these avant-garde graffiti displays by renowned artists are just the beginning; in fact, almost every street is colored with funky spray-paint art, making the neighborhood a photographer's dream. Wynwood's retail space is a hodgepodge of cheap garment stores, upscale boutiques, and contemporary galleries (some by appointment only). Your best bet is to visit during Wynwood's monthly gallery walk on the second Saturday evening of each month, when studios and galleries are all open at the same time.

TOP ATTRACTIONS

Margulies Collection at the Warehouse. Make sure a visit to Wynwood includes a stop at the Margulies Collection at the Warehouse. Martin Margulies's collection of vintage and contemporary photography, videos, and installation art in a 45,000-square-foot space makes for eye-popping viewing. Admission proceeds go to the Lotus House, a local homeless shelter for women and children. ⊠ *591 N.W. 27th St., between N.W. 5th and 6th Aves., Wynwood* ☎ *305/576–1051* ⊕ *www. margulieswarehouse.com* 🖾 *$10* ⊗ *Oct.–Apr., Wed.–Sat. 11–4.*

Fodor's Choice ★ **Rubell Family Collection.** Fans of edgy art will appreciate the Rubell Family Collection. Mera and Don Rubell have accumulated work by artists from the 1970s to the present, including Jeff Koons, Cindy Sherman, Damien Hirst, and Keith Haring. Admission always includes a complimentary audio tour; however, true art lovers should opt for a complimentary guided tour of the collection, offered Wednesday through Saturday at 11 am and 3 pm. ⊠ *95 N.W. 29th St., between N. Miami and N.W. 1st Aves., Wynwood* ☎ *305/573–6090* ⊕ *www.rfc.museum* 🖾 *$10* ⊗ *Tues.–Sat. 10–6.*

MIDTOWN

Northeast of Wynwood, Midtown (⊕ *www.midtownmiami.com*) lies between Northeast 29th and 36th streets, from North Miami Avenue to Northeast 2nd Avenue. This sub-city is anchored by a multitower residential complex with prolific retail space, often housing the latest and greatest in dining and shopping trends.

DESIGN DISTRICT

North of Midtown, from about Northeast 38th to Northeast 42nd streets and across the other side of Interstate 195, the Design District (⊕ *www.miamidesigndistrict.net*) is yet another 18 blocks of clothiers, antiques shops, design stores, and bars and eateries. The real draws here are the interior design and furniture galleries as well as über-high-end shopping that's oh-so Rodeo Drive.

LITTLE HAITI

Miami's Little Haiti is the largest Haitian community outside of Haiti itself, and while people of different ethnic backgrounds have begun to move into the neighborhood, people here are still surprised to see tourists. However, owners of shops and restaurants tend to be welcoming. Creole is commonly spoken, although some people—especially younger folks—also speak English. Once a small farming community, Little Haiti is the heart and soul of Haitian society in the U.S. Its northern and southern boundaries are 85th Street and 42nd Street, respectively, with I–95 to the west and Biscayne Boulevard to the east. The best section to visit is along North Miami Avenue from 54th to 59th streets.

LITTLE HAVANA

Fodor's Choice

★

First settled en masse by Cubans in the early 1960s, after Cuba's Communist revolution, Little Havana is a predominantly working-class area and the core of Miami's Hispanic community. Spanish is the principal language, but don't be surprised if the cadence is less Cuban and more Salvadoran or Nicaraguan: the neighborhood is now home to people from all Latin American countries.

If you come to Little Havana expecting the Latino version of New Orleans's French Quarter, you're apt to be disappointed—it's not about the architecture here. Rather, it's a place to soak in the atmosphere. Little Havana is more about great, inexpensive food (not just Cuban; there's Vietnamese, Mexican, and Argentinean here as well), distinctive affordable Cuban-American art, cigars, and great coffee. It's not a prefab tourist destination—this is real life in Spanish-speaking Miami.

Little Havana's semi-official boundaries are 27th Avenue to 4th Avenue on the west, Miami River to the north, and Southwest 13th Street to the south. Much of the neighborhood is residential; however, you'll quickly discover the area's flavor, both literally and figuratively, along Calle Ocho (Southwest 8th Street), between Southwest 11th and 17th avenues, which is lined with cigar factories, cafés selling guava pastries and rose petal flan, *botanicas* brimming with candles, and Cuban clothes and crafts stores. Your "Welcome to Little Havana" photo op shines on 27th Avenue and 8th Street. Giant hand-painted roosters are found scattered throughout the entire neighborhood, an artistic nod to their real-life counterparts that roam the streets here. You'll need to drive into Little Havana, since public transportation here is limited; but once on Calle Ocho, it's best to experience the neighborhood on foot.

TOP ATTRACTIONS

Cuban Memorial Boulevard. Four blocks in the heart of Little Havana are filled with monuments to Cuba's freedom fighters. South of Calle Ocho (8th Street), S.W. 13th Ave. becomes a ceiba tree–lined parkway known as Cuban Memorial Boulevard, divided at the center by a narrow grassy mall with a walking path through the various memorials. Among them is the *Eternal Torch of the Brigade 2506*, blazing with an endless flame and commemorating those who were killed in the failed Bay of Pigs invasion of 1961. Another is a bas-relief map of Cuba depicting each of its *municipios*. There's also a bronze statue in honor of Nestory (Tony) Izquierdo, who participated in the Bay of Pigs invasion and served in Nicaragua's Somozan forces. ⊠ *S.W. 13th Ave., between S.W. 8th and S.W.12th Sts., Little Havana.*

Domino Park. Watch a slice of old Havana come to life in Miami's Little Havana. At Domino Park, officially known as Maximo Gomez Park, guayabera-clad seniors bask in the sun and play dominoes, while onlookers share neighborhood gossip and political opinions. ■ TIP→ There is a little office at the park with a window where you can get information on Little Havana; the office also stores the dominoes for the older gents who play regularly, but it's BYOD ("bring your own dominoes") for everyone else. ⊠ *801 S.W. 15th Ave., Little Havana* ☎ *305/859–2717 for park office.*

NEED A
BREAK?

Las Pinareños Fruteria y Floreria. In the mood for something refreshing or a high-octane jolt? Try Las Pinareños, a *fruteria* (fruit stand) that serves *coco frio* (fresh, cold coconut juice served in a whole coconut), mango juice, and other *jugos* (juices), as well as Cuban coffees and Cuban finger foods. You can order your sweet, hot *cortadito* (coffee with milk) or a *cafecito* (no milk) from the walk-up window and enjoy it at one of the stools in front of the shop or sit at one of the tables inside the fruit and flower market. ⊠ *1334 S.W. 8th St., Little Havana* ☎ *305/285–1135.*

El Titan de Bronze. A peek at the intently focused cigar rollers through the windows doesn't prepare you for the rich, pungent scent that jolts your senses as you step inside the store. Millions of stogies are deftly hand-rolled at this family-owned business every year. Visitors are welcome to watch the rolling action (and of course buy some cigars). ⊠ *1071 S.W. 8th St., Little Havana* ☎ *305/860–1412* ⊕ *www.eltitancigars.com.*

SOUTH BEACH

Fodor's Choice
★

The hub of Miami Beach is South Beach (better known as SoBe), with its energetic Ocean Drive, Collins Avenue, and Washington Avenue. Here life unfolds 24 hours a day. Beautiful people pose in hotel lounges and sidewalk cafés, bronzed cyclists zoom past palm trees, and visitors flock to see the action. On Lincoln Road, café crowds spill onto the sidewalks, weekend markets draw all kinds of visitors and their dogs, and thanks to a few late-night lounges, the scene is just as alive at night. Further north (in Mid-Beach and North Beach), the vibe is decidedly quieter.

TOP ATTRACTIONS

Fodor's Choice
★

Española Way. There's a bohemian feel to this street lined with Mediterranean-revival buildings constructed in 1925. Al Capone's gambling syndicate ran its operations upstairs at what is now the Clay Hotel, a youth hostel. At a nightclub here in the 1930s, future bandleader Desi Arnaz strapped on a conga drum and started beating out a rumba rhythm. Visit this quaint avenue on a weekend afternoon, when merchants and craftspeople set up shop to sell everything from handcrafted bongo drums to fresh flowers. Between Washington and Drexel avenues the road has been narrowed to a single lane and Miami Beach's trademark pink sidewalks have been widened to accommodate sidewalk café's and shops selling imaginative clothing, jewelry, and art. ⊠ *Española Way, between 14th and 15th sts. from Washington to Jefferson Aves., South Beach.*

Holocaust Memorial. A bronze sculpture depicts refugees clinging to a giant bronze arm that reaches out of the ground and 42 feet into the air. Enter the surrounding courtyard to see a memorial wall and hear the music that seems to give voice to the 6 million Jews who died at the hands of the Nazis. It's easy to understand why Kenneth Treister's dramatic memorial is in Miami Beach: the city's community of Holocaust survivors was once the second-largest in the country. ⊠ *1933–1945*

Meridian Ave., at Dade Blvd., South Beach ☎ *305/538–1663* ⊕ *www.
holocaustmmb.org* 🎟 *Free* ⊙ *Daily 9–sunset.*

FAMILY

Fodor'sChoice

★

Lincoln Road Mall. This open-air pedestrian mall flaunts some of Miami's
best people-watching. The eclectic interiors of myriad fabulous restaurants, colorful boutiques, art galleries, lounges, and cafés are often
upstaged by the bustling outdoor scene. It's here among the prolific
alfresco dining enclaves that you can pass the hours easily beholding
the beautiful people. Indeed, outdoor restaurants and café seating take
center stage along this wide pedestrian road adorned with towering date
palms, linear pools, and colorful broken-tile mosaics. Some of the shops
on Lincoln Road are owner-operated boutiques carrying a smart variety
of clothing, furnishings, jewelry, and decorative elements. You'll also
find typical chain stores—H&M, American Eagle Outfitters, Forever
21, and so on. Lincoln Road is fun, lively, and friendly for people—old,
young, gay, and straight—and their dogs.

Two landmarks worth checking out at the eastern end of Lincoln Road
are the massive 1940s keystone building at 420 Lincoln Road, which
has a 1945 Leo Birchanky mural in the lobby, and the 1921 Mission-
style Miami Beach Community Church, at Drexel Avenue. The Lincoln
Theatre (No. 541–545), at Pennsylvania Avenue, is a classical four-story
art deco gem with friezes, which now houses H&M. At Euclid Avenue
there's a monument to Morris Lapidus, the brains behind Lincoln Road
Mall, who in his 90s watched the renaissance of his whimsical South
Beach creation. At Lenox Avenue, a black-and-white art deco movie
house with a Mediterranean barrel-tile roof is now the Colony Theater
(No. 1040), where live theater and experimental films are presented.
✉ *Lincoln Rd., between Washington Ave. and Alton Rd., South Beach*
⊕ *www.lincolnroadmall.com.*

QUICK
BITES

Lincoln Road is a great place to cool down with an icy treat while touring
South Beach. If you visit on a Sunday, stop at one of the many juice
vendors, who'll whip up made-to-order smoothies from mangoes, oranges,
and other fresh local fruits.

Frieze Ice Cream Factory. A true South Beach original, this mom-and-
pop ice cream shop serves what could very well be the best ice cream
in Florida. Delight in mouthwatering homemade ice cream and sorbets
including Indian mango, key lime pie, cashew toffee crunch, and chocolate
decadence. ✉ *1626 Michigan Ave., just south of Lincoln Rd., South Beach*
☎ *305/538-0207* ⊕ *www.thefrieze.com.*

Gelateria 4D. Authentic Italian gelato is scooped up with plenty of authentic Miami attitude at this sleek glass-and-stainless-steel sweet spot. The
gelato is delicious despite the not-so-sweet service and exorbitant price.
✉ *670 Lincoln Rd., between Euclid and Pennsylvania aves., South Beach*
☎ *786/276-9475* ⊕ *www.gelateria4d.com.*

WORTH NOTING

Art Deco Welcome Center. Run by the Miami Design Preservation League, the center provides information about the buildings in the district. An improved gift shop sells 1930s–50s art deco memorabilia, posters, and books on Miami's history. Several tours—covering Lincoln Road, Española Way, North Beach, and the entire Art Deco District, among others—start here. You can choose from a self-guided iPod audio tour or join one of the regular morning walking tours at 10:30 every day. On Thursday a second tour takes place at 6:30 pm. Arrive at the center 15 minutes beforehand and pre-purchase tickets online. All of the options provide detailed histories of the art deco hotels as well as an introduction to the art deco, Mediterranean revival, and Miami Modern (MiMo) styles found within the Miami Beach Architectural Historic District. Don't miss the special boat tours during Art Deco Weekend, in early January. (⇨ *For a map of the Art Deco District and info on some of the sites there, see the "A Stroll Down Deco Lane" in-focus feature.*) ✉ *1001 Ocean Dr., South Beach* ☎ *305/672–2014* ⊕ *www.mdpl.org* 🎫 *Tours $20* ☽ *Daily 9:30–7.*

Bass Museum of Art. Special exhibitions join a diverse collection of European art at this museum whose original building is constructed of keystone and has unique Maya-inspired carvings. An expansion designed by Japanese architect Arata Isozaki houses another wing and an outdoor sculpture garden. Works on permanent display include *The Holy Family,* a painting by Peter Paul Rubens; *The Tournament,* one of several 16th-century Flemish tapestries; and works by Albrecht Dürer and Henri de Toulouse-Lautrec. Docent tours are by appointment but free with entry. ✉ *2100 Collins Ave., South Beach* ☎ *305/673–7530* ⊕ *www.bassmuseum.org* 🎫 *$8* ☽ *Wed.–Sun. noon–5.*

Jewish Museum of Florida—FIU. Listed on the National Register of Historic Places, this former synagogue, built in 1936, contains art deco chandeliers, 80 impressive stained-glass windows, and a permanent exhibit, *MOSAIC: Jewish Life in Florida,* which depicts more than 235 years of the Florida Jewish experience. A partnership with Florida International University, the Jewish Museum also houses a store filled with books, jewelry, and other souvenirs as well as playinh host to traveling exhibits and special events. ✉ *301 Washington Ave., South Beach* ☎ *305/672–5044* ⊕ *www.jmof.fiu.edu* 🎫 *$6* ☽ *Tues.–Sun. 10–5. Museum store closed Sat.*

Wolfsonian–Florida International University. An elegantly renovated 1926 storage facility is now a research center and museum showcasing a 120,000-item collection of modern design and "propaganda arts" amassed by Miami native Mitchell ("Micky") Wolfson Jr., a world traveler and connoisseur. Broad themes of the 19th and 20th centuries—nationalism, political persuasion, industrialization—are addressed in permanent and traveling shows. Included in the museum's eclectic holdings, which represent art deco, art moderne, art nouveau, Arts and Crafts, and other aesthetic movements, are 8,000 matchbooks collected by Egypt's King Farouk. ✉ *1001 Washington Ave., South Beach* ☎ *305/531–1001* ⊕ *www.wolfsonian.org* 🎫 *$7 (free Fri. after 6)* ☽ *Sat.–Tues. and Thurs. noon–6, Fri. noon–9.*

World Erotic Art Museum (WEAM). The sexy collection of more than 4,000 erotic items, all owned by millionaire Naomi Wilzig, unfolds with unique art of varying quality—fertility statues from around the globe and historic Chinese *shunga* books (erotic art offered as gifts to new brides on the wedding night) share the space with some kitschy knickknacks. If this is your thing, an original phallic prop from Stanley Kubrick's *A Clockwork Orange* and an over-the-top Kama Sutra bed is worth the price of admission, but the real standout is "Miss Naomi," who is usually on hand to answer questions and provide behind-the-scenes anecdotes. Kids 17 and under are not admitted. ✉ *1205 Washington Ave., at 12th St., South Beach* ☎ *305/532–9336* ⊕ *www.weam. com* 🖃 *$15* 🕑 *Mon.–Thurs. 11–10, Fri.–Sun. 11–midnight.*

MID-BEACH

Where does South Beach end and Mid-Beach begin? With the massive amount of money being spent on former 1950s pleasure palaces like the Fontainebleau and Eden Roc, it could be that Mid-Beach will soon just be considered part of South Beach. North of 24th Street, Collins Avenue curves its way to 44th Street, where it takes a sharp left turn after running into the Soho House Miami and then the Fontainebleau resort. The area between these two points—24th Street and 96th Street—is Mid-Beach.

FISHER AND BELLE ISLANDS

A private island community near the southern tip of South Beach, Fisher Island is accessible only by the island's ferry service. The island is predominantly residential with a few hotel rooms on offer at the Resort at Fisher Island Club. Belle Island is a small island connected to both the mainland and Miami Beach by road. It is a mile north of South Beach and just west over the Venetian Causeway.

NORTH BEACH AND AVENTURA

Nearing the 100th Street mark on Collins Avenue, Mid-Beach gives way to North Beach. In particular, at 96th Street, the town of Bal Harbour takes over Collins Avenue from Miami Beach. The town runs a mere 10 blocks to the north before the bridge to Sunny Isles. Bal Harbour is famous for its outdoor high-end shops. If you take your shopping seriously, you'll probably want to stay in this area. At 106th Street, the town of Sunny Isles is an appealing, calm, predominantly upscale choice for families looking for a beautiful beach. There's no nightlife to speak of in Sunny Isles, and yet the half-dozen megaluxurious skyscraper hotels that have sprung up here in the past decade have created a niche-resort town from the demolished ashes of much older, affordable hotels. Farther west are the high-rises of Aventura.

BEACHES

CORAL GABLES

FAMILY **Matheson Hammock Park and Beach.** Kids love the gentle waves and warm water of this beach in Coral Gables suburbia, near Fairchild Tropical Botanic Garden. But the beach is only part of the draw: the park includes a boardwalk trail, a playground, and a golf course. Plus the park is a prime spot for kite-boarding. The man-made lagoon, or "atoll pool," is perfect for inexperienced swimmers, and it's one of the best places in mainland Miami for a picnic. ■ TIP→ However, the water can be a bit murky, and with the emphasis on families, it's not the best place for singles. The park also offers a full-service marina. **Amenities:** parking (fee); toilets. **Best for:** swimming. ⊠ *9610 Old Cutler Rd.* ☎ *305/665-5475* ⊕ *www.miamidade.gov/parks/parks/matheson_beach.asp* ⌑ *$5 per vehicle weekdays, $6 weekends* ⊘ *Daily sunrise–sunset.*

KEY BISCAYNE

Fodor's Choice **Bill Baggs Cape Florida State Park.** Thanks to inviting beaches, sunsets, ★ and a tranquil lighthouse, this park at Key Biscayne's southern tip is worth the drive. In fact, the 1-mile stretch of pure beachfront has been named several times in Dr. Beach's revered America's Top 10 Beaches list. It has 18 picnic pavilions available as daily rentals, two cafés that serve light lunches (Lighthouse Café, overlooking the Atlantic Ocean, and the Boater's Grill, on Biscayne Bay), and plenty of space to enjoy the umbrella and chair rentals. A stroll or ride along walking and bicycle paths provides wonderful views of Miami's dramatic skyline. From the southern end of the park you can see a handful of houses rising over the bay on wooden stilts, the remnants of Stiltsville, built in the 1940s and now protected by the Stiltsville Trust. The nonprofit group was established in 2003 to preserve the structures, because they showcase the park's rich history. Bill Baggs has bicycle rentals, a playground, fishing piers, and guided tours of the **Cape Florida Lighthouse,** South Florida's oldest structure. The lighthouse was erected in 1845 to replace an earlier one damaged in an 1836 Seminole attack, in which the keeper's helper was killed. Free tours are offered at the restored cottage and lighthouse at 10 am and 1 pm Thursday to Monday. Be there a half hour beforehand. **Amenities:** food and drink; lifeguards; parking (fee); showers; toilets. **Best for:** solitude; sunsets; walking. ⊠ *1200 S. Crandon Blvd., Key Biscayne* ☎ *305/361–5811* ⊕ *www.floridastateparks.org/capeflorida* ⌑ *$8 per vehicle; $2 per pedestrian* ⊘ *Daily 8–sunset.*

FAMILY **Crandon Park Beach.** This relaxing oasis in northern Key Biscayne offers renowned tennis facilities, a great golf course, a family amusement center, and 2 miles of beach dotted with palm trees. The park is divided by Key Biscayne's main road, with tennis and golf on the bayside, the beaches on the oceanside. Families really enjoy the beaches here—the sand is soft, there are no rip tides, there's a great view of the Atlantic, and parking is both inexpensive and plentiful. However, on weekends, be prepared for a long hike from your car to the beach. There are bathrooms, outdoor showers, plenty of picnic tables, and concession stands. The family-friendly park offers abundant options for those who find it challenging simply to sit and build sand castles. Kite-board rentals and lessons are offered from the north water-sports concessions, as are kayak rentals. Eco-tours and nature trails showcase the myriad ecosystems of Key Biscayne including mangroves, coastal hammock, and sea-grass beds. Bird-watching is great at the southern end of the park. The **Crandon Park Amusement Center** at Crandon Park was once the site of a zoo. There are swans, waterfowl, peacocks, and dozens of huge iguanas running loose. Nearby you'll find a restored carousel (it's open weekends and major holidays 10:30–5, and you get three rides for $2), an old-fashioned outdoor roller rink, a dolphin-shape spray fountain, and a playground. **Amenities:** food and drink; lifeguards; parking (fee); showers; toilets; water sports. **Best for:** swimming; walking. ✉ 6747 Crandon Blvd., Key Biscayne ☎ 305/361–5421 ⊕ www.miamidade. gov/Parks/Parks/crandon_beach.asp ✇ $5 per vehicle weekdays, $6 weekends ⏱ Daily sunrise–sunset.

> ## THE OCEAN DRIVE HUSTLE
>
> As you stroll by the sidewalk restaurants lining Ocean Drive, don't be surprised if you're solicited by a pretty hostess, who'll literally shove a menu in your face to entice you to her café—which is exactly like every other eatery on the strip. Be advised that reputable restaurants refrain from these aggressive tactics. If you're indeed enticed by the fishbowl drinks, use the chance to bargain. A request for free drinks with dinner may very well be accommodated!

SOUTH BEACH

Fodor's Choice ★ **South Beach.** A 10-block stretch of white sandy beach hugging the turquoise waters along Ocean Drive—from 5th to 15th Street—is one of the most popular in America, known for drawing unabashedly modelesque sunbathers and posers. With the influx of new luxe hotels and hotspots from 1st to 5th and 16th to 25th streets, the South Beach stand-and-pose scene is now bigger than ever and stretches yet another dozen-plus blocks. The beaches crowd quickly on the weekends with a blend of European tourists, young hipsters, and sun-drenched locals offering Latin flavor. Separating the sand from the traffic of Ocean Drive is palm-fringed **Lummus Park**, with its volleyball nets and chickee huts (huts made of palmetto thatch over a cypress frame) for shade. The beach at **12th Street** is popular with gays, in a section often marked with rainbow flags. Locals hang out on 3rd Street beach, in an area called **SoFi** (South of Fifth) where they watch fit Brazilians play foot volley, a variation of volleyball that uses everything but the hands. Because much of South Beach leans toward skimpy sunning—women are often in G-strings and casually topless—many families prefer the tamer sections of Mid- and North Beach. Metered parking spots next to the ocean are a rare find. Instead, opt for a public garage a few blocks away and enjoy the people-watching as you walk to find your perfect spot on the sand. **Amenities:** food and drink; lifeguards; parking (fee); showers; toilets.

Best for: partiers; sunrise; swimming; walking. ⌧ *Ocean Dr., from 5th to 15th St., then Collins Ave. to 25th St., South Beach.*

NORTH BEACH AND AVENTURA

Haulover Beach Park. This popular clothing-optional beach is embraced by naturists of all ages, shapes, and sizes; there are even sections primarily frequented by families, singles, and gays. However, Haulover has more claims to fame than its casual attitude toward swimwear—it's also the best beach in the area for bodyboarding and surfing, as it gets what pass for impressive swells in these parts. Plus the sand here is fine-grain white, unusual for the Atlantic coast. Once you park in the North Lot, you'll walk through a short tunnel covered with trees and natural habitat until you emerge on the unpretentious beach, where nudity is rarely met by gawkers. There are volleyball nets, and plenty of beach chair and umbrella rentals to protect your birthday suit from too much exposure—to the sun, that is. The sections of beach requiring swimwear are popular, too, given the park's ample parking and relaxed atmosphere. Lifeguards stand watch. More active types might want to check out the kite rentals, or charter-fishing excursions. **Amenities:** food and drink; lifeguards; parking (fee); showers; toilets. **Best for:** nudists; surfing; swimming; walking. ⌧ *10800 Collins Ave., north of Bal Harbour, North Beach and Aventura* ☎ *305/944–3040* ⊕ *www.hauloverbeach.org* ⌧ *$6 per vehicle if parking in lot* ☉ *Daily 8–sunset.*

FAMILY **Oleta River State Park.** Tucked away in North Miami Beach, this urban park is a ready-made family getaway. Nature lovers will find it easy to embrace the 1,128 acres of subtropical beauty along Biscayne Bay. Swim in the calm bay waters and bicycle, canoe, kayak, and bask among egrets, manatees, bald eagles, and fiddler crabs. Dozens of picnic tables, along with 10 covered pavilions, dot the stunning natural habitat, which was restored with red mangroves to revitalize the ecosystem and draw endangered birds, like the roseate spoonbill. There's a playground for tots, a mangrove island accessible only by boat, 15 miles of mountain-bike trails, a half-mile exercise track, concessions, and outdoor showers. **Amenities:** food and drink; parking (fee); showers; toilets; water sports. **Best for:** solitude; sunrise; sunset; walking. ⌧ *3400 N.E. 163rd St., North Beach and Aventura* ☎ *305/919–1846* ⊕ *www.floridastateparks.org/oletariver* ⌧ *$6 per vehicle; $2 per pedestrian* ☉ *Daily 8–sunset.*

WHERE TO EAT

Miami's restaurant scene has exploded in the past few years, with dozens of great new restaurants springing up left and right. The melting pot of residents and visitors has brought an array of sophisticated, tasty cuisine. Little Havana is still king for Cuban fare, and Miami Beach is swept up in a trend of fusion cuisine, which combines Asian, French, American, and Latin cooking with sumptuous—and pricey—results. Locals spend the most time in Downtown Miami, Wynwood, Midtown, and the Design District, where the city's ongoing foodie and cocktail revolution is most pronounced. Since Miami dining is a part

2

of the trendy nightlife scene, most dinners don't start until 8 or 9 pm, and may go well into the night. To avoid a long wait among the late-night partiers at hot spots, come before 7 or make reservations. Attire is usually casual-chic, but patrons like to dress to impress. Prices tend to stay high in hot spots like Lincoln Road, but if you venture off the beaten path you can find delicious food for reasonable prices. When you get your bill, check whether a gratuity is already included; most restaurants add between 15% and 20% (ostensibly for the convenience of, and protection from, the many Latin American and European tourists who are used to this practice in their homelands), but supplement it depending on your opinion of the service.

Use the coordinate (✛ C2) at the end of each review to locate a property on the Where to Eat in the Miami Area map.

WHAT IT COSTS				
	$	$$	$$$	$$$$
RESTAURANTS	under $15	$16–$20	$21–$30	over $30

Restaurant prices are the average cost of a main course at dinner or, if dinner is not served, at lunch.

DOWNTOWN

$$$$
ECLECTIC
✕ **Azul.** A restaurant known for producing celebrity chefs and delivering dining fantasies of Food Network proportions, Azul is a Miami foodie institution. With its Forbes five-star, award-winning team, Azul offers a haute-cuisine experience on par with a two- or three-Michelin-star restaurant. Chefs fuse disparate ingredients, merging as decadent, gastronomic art. Headliners include Tuna Poke with white soy, scallion, and macadamia nuts and the Basil "Sous-Vide" Salmon with ratatouille and fine herbs. Dine here and you'll undoubtedly experience bold new taste sensations while enjoying one of the finest wine lists in the city and an incomparable skyline view. ⑤ *Average main: $48 ⊠ Mandarin Oriental, Miami, 500 Brickell Key Dr., Downtown* ☎ *305/913–8358* ⊕ *www.mandarinoriental.com/miami* ⌧ *Reservations essential* ✛ *D5.*

$$$$
FRENCH
✕ **db Bistro Moderne Miami.** One of America's most celebrated French chefs, Daniel Boulud brings his renowned cooking to the Miami scene. The menu of Boulud's Miami outpost pays homage to Mediterranean cuisines and the specialties of his homeland. Begin with a cold plate from the fabulous raw bar or the signature house-smoked sturgeon; then feast on *escargots persillade* (wild burgundy snails simmered in parsley, garlic, salted butter with yellow tomatoes and wild mushrooms). For the main course, try the authentic *coq au vin*, which is sure to stir up memories of France through its robust taste and smell. ⑤ *Average main: $31 ⊠ JW Marriott Marquis Miami, 255 Biscayne Blvd. Way, Downtown* ☎ *305/421–8800* ⊕ *www.dbbistro.com/miami* ✛ *D4.*

$$$
STEAKHOUSE
Fodor'sChoice
★
✕ **Edge, Steak & Bar.** It's farm-to-table surf-and-turf at this elegantly understated restaurant in the Four Seasons Hotel Miami, where hefty portions of the finest cuts and freshest seafood headline the menu, prepared by renowned chef Aaron Brooks. The innovative tartares are a

BEST BETS FOR MIAMI DINING

Fodor's writers and editors have selected their favorite restaurants by price, cuisine, and experience in the Best Bets lists below. In the first column, Fodor's Choice designations represent the "best of the best" in every price category. Find specific details about a restaurant in the full reviews, listed alphabetically by neighborhood.

Fodor's Choice ★

Bianca, South Beach, $$$$, p. 67

Bocce Bar, Midtown Miami, $$$, p. 64

De Rodriguez Cuba on Ocean, South Beach, $$$$, p. 68

eating house, Coral Gables, $$$, p. 61

Edge, Steak and Bar, Downtown, $$$, p. 57

Fish Fish, North Beach and Aventura, $$$$, p. 78

Hakkasan, Mid-Beach, $$$$, p. 76

Hy-Vong Vietnamese Cuisine, Little Havana, $$, p. 66

J & G Grill, North Beach and Aventura, $$$$, p. 78

Joe's Stone Crab Restaurant, South Beach, $$$$, p. 69

Juvia, South Beach, $$$$, p. 69

Macchialina Taverna Rustica, South Beach, $$$$, p. 72

Makoto, North Beach and Aventura, $$$$, p. 78

Michael's Genuine Food & Drink, Design District, $$$, p. 65

Oak Tavern, Design District, $$$, p. 65

Pubbelly, South Beach, $$$, p. 73

Rusty Pelican, Key Biscayne, $$$$, p. 63

Sugarcane Raw Bar Grill, Midtown Miami, $$$$, p. 64

SushiSamba Coral Gables, Coral Gables, $$$$, p. 74

Verde at PAMM, Downtown, $, p. 60

Wynwood Kitchen & Bar, Wynwood, $$, p. 64

By Price

$

Verde at PAMM, Downtown, p. 60

$$

Hy-Vong Vietnamese Cuisine, Little Havana, p. 66

$$$

eating house, Coral Gables, p. 61

Oak Tavern, Design District, p. 65

Yardbird, Southern Table & Bar, South Beach, p. 75

$$$$

Hakkasan, Mid-Beach, p. 76

J & G Grill, North Beach and Aventura, p. 78

Juvia, South Beach, p. 69

Sugarcane Raw Bar Grill, Midtown Miami, p. 64

By Cuisine

AMERICAN

Michael's Genuine Food & Drink, Design District, p. 65

ASIAN

Hakkasan, Mid-Beach, p. 76

Makoto, North Beach and Aventura, p. 78

SushiSamba Coral Gables, Coral Gables, p. 74

CUBAN

De Rodriguez Cuba on Ocean, South Beach, p. 68

Versailles, Little Havana, p. 67

ITALIAN

Bianca, South Beach, p. 67

Bocce Bar, Midtown Miami, p. 64

Macchialina Taverna Rustica, South Beach, p. 72

SEAFOOD

Fish Fish, North Beach and Aventura, p. 78

Joe's Stone Crab Restaurant, South Beach, p. 69

STEAKHOUSE

Meat Market, South Beach, p. 72

Prime 112, South Beach, p. 73

surefire way to start the night right—try the corvina with baby cucumber, green apple, and a young celery-leaf, yellow-pepper sauce, or the ahi tuna with pickled shallots, watermelon, and mint. For the main event, Edge offers a variety of small, medium, and large cuts from the infrared grill, the most popular being the black Angus filet mignon. For a more casual experience, enjoy your meal and the restaurant's artisan cocktails under the skies in the alfresco terrace, where you can also enjoy complimentary s'mores around the fire pits. Sunday brunch is also excellent with a well-stocked raw bar (including stone crabs in season) and a make-your-own taco station. ⑤ *Average main: $30* ⊠ *Four Seasons Miami, 1435 Brickell Ave, Downtown* ☎ *305/381–3190* ⊕ *www.edgerestaurantmiami.com* ✛ *D5.*

$$$
BISTRO
✕ **L'Entrecote de Paris.** Simplicity is just one ingredient to the secret sauce that's made this steak-frites restaurant in downtown Miami so popular. The design and cuisine found in this quiet bistro are as close as you'll get to the City of Light in Miami. The *entrecote* (a sliced flank steak) is the only dish offered here, served with baguette, french fries, and salad, and topped with a secret green sauce of 21 ingredients, which requires 36 hours and four cooking processes to produce. The cocktail and dessert menus are far more extensive, the former including fresh profiteroles with Nutella sauce and tarte tatin, the latter including "Excuse my French" cocktails made with French spirits Chandon and Grey Goose—of course. ⑤ *Average main: $26* ⊠ *1053 S.E. 1st Ave., Downtown* ☎ *305/755–9995* ⊕ *www.lentrecotedeparis.com.br* ✛ *D5.*

$$$$
JAPANESE
✕ **NAOE.** By virtue of its petite size (eight patrons max) and strict seating times (twice per night at 6 and 9:30), the Japanese gem, NAOE, will forever remain intimate and original. By virtue of its price ($160 per person), it will forever require deep pockets—but this place is well worth a bit of credit card debt. The all-inclusive menu changes daily, based on the day's best and freshest seafood, but always includes a Bento Box, soup, nigirizushi, and dessert. Every visit ushers in a new exploration of the senses. Chef Kevin Cory prepares the gastronomic adventure a few feet from his patrons, using only the best ingredients and showcasing family treasures, like the renowned products of his centuries' old family *shoyu* (soy sauce) brewery and sake brewery. From start to finish, you'll be transported to Japan through the stellar service, the tastes of bizarre sea creatures and the smoothness of spectacular sakes. ⑤ *Average main: $160* ⊠ *661 Brickell Key Dr., Downtown* ☎ *305/947–6263* ⊕ *www.naoemiami.com* ⚊ *Reservations essential* ⊗ *Closed Sunday* ✛ *D5.*

$$$
ARGENTINE
✕ **Novecento.** This famed Argentine eatery is the Financial District's answer to Ocean Drive: the people are still beautiful, but now they're wearing suits or stilettos. Known for its empanadas (tender chicken or spinach and cheese), simple grilled meats (luscious grilled skirt steak with chimichurri sauce), and the innovative Ensalada Novecento (grilled skirt steak, french fries, and mixed baby greens), it's no wonder Novecento is Brickell Avenue's best weekday power-lunch and happy-hour spot (2-for-1 drinks every day 4–7 pm). It's also a really popular place for late-night dining and people-watching. Come for Sunday brunch and enjoy the signature *parillada,* a small grill with an assortment of steaks, sausages, and sweetbreads. You'll also find several pasta

dishes on the menu, a nod to Argentina's strong Italian influence. ⑤ *Average main: $23* ⊠ *1414 Brickell Ave., Downtown* ☎ *305/403–0900* ⊕ *www.novecento.com* ✛ *D5.*

$$ ╳ **Perricone's Marketplace and Café.** Brickell Avenue south of the Miami
ITALIAN River is a haven for Italian restaurants, and this lunch place for local bigwigs is the biggest and most popular among them. It's housed partially outdoors and partially indoors in an 1880s Vermont barn. Recipes were handed down from generation to generation, and the cooking is simple and good. Buy your wine from the on-premises deli, and enjoy it (for a small corkage fee) with homemade minestrone; a generous antipasto; linguine with a sauté of jumbo shrimp, scallops, and calamari; or gnocchi with four cheeses. The homemade tiramisù and cannoli are top-notch. ⑤ *Average main: $22* ⊠ *Mary Brickell Village, 15 S.E. 10th St., Downtown* ☎ *305/374–9449* ⊕ *www.perricones.com* ✛ *D5.*

$ ╳ **Verde.** As if the new high design Pérez Art Museum Miami (PAMM)
ECLECTIC weren't cool enough, its waterfront restaurant Verde is also making
Fodor's Choice major waves across Biscayne Bay. The slick, contemporary Stephen
★ Starr restaurant offers seating both indoors and out, with design-savvy décor and accessories true to its "green" name that blend seamlessly with the living walls and hanging gardens strewn across the museum's exterior. The exceptionally affordable, one-page menu features eclectic epicurean lunch plates that include a squash blossoms pizza, bigeye tuna tartare, a house chopped salad (with manchego, garbanzo beans, red peppers, cucumber, baby romaine, and smoked tomato vinaigrette), and gourmet cheeseburgers with applewood-smoked bacon and fries. ■TIP→ Museum admission is not required to eat here, but the restaurant is open only during museum hours, meaning lunch only, except on Thursdays, when the museum remains open until 9 pm. ⑤ *Average main: $14* ⊠ *Pérez Art Museum Miami, 1103 Biscayne Blvd., Downtown* ☎ *305/375–3000* ⊕ *www.pamm.org/dining* ☽ *Closed Monday* ✛ *D4.*

COCONUT GROVE

$$$ ╳ **Jaguar Ceviche Spoon Bar & Latam Grill.** A fabulous fusion of Peruvian
PERUVIAN and Mexican flavors, Jaguar is a gastronomic tour of Latin America in a single restaurant. As the name implies, there is a heavy emphasis on ceviches. The best option for experiencing this delicacy is the spoon sampler, which includes six distinct Peruvian and Mexican ceviches served in oversized spoons. Dishes, such the Mexican Tortilla Lasagna (chicken, poblano peppers, corn, tomato sauce, and cream, topped with melted cheese), are colorful, flavorful, and innovative. ⑤ *Average main: $23* ⊠ *3067 Grand Ave., Coconut Grove* ☎ *305/444–0216* ⊕ *www. jaguarhg.com/jaguarspot* ✛ *C5.*

$$$ ╳ **Le Bouchon du Grove.** This petite French bistro with a supercharged
FRENCH atmosphere is a great spot in the heart of the Grove. Waiters tend to lean on chairs while taking orders, and managers and owners freely mix with the clientele, making Le Bouchon one of the last remaining vestige of the Grove's bohemian days. The result is one big happy family, all enjoying traditional French pâtés, gratins, quiches, chicken fricassee, mussels, duck-leg confit, and steak frites. The lively mood inside is

matched by the throngs that parade outside the French doors. Breakfast is served daily. $ *Average main: $24* ✉ *3430 Main Hwy., Coconut Grove* ☎ *305/448–6060* ⊕ *www.lebouchondugrove.com* ✛ *C5*.

$$$
SEAFOOD
FAMILY

✕ **Monty's.** Connected to the Bayshore Landing Marina, Monty's has a Caribbean flair, thanks especially to live calypso and island music on the outdoor terrace. Though it has lost the luster it had back in the '90s, it's still a kid-friendly place where Mom and Dad can kick back early eve and enjoy a beer and the raw bar while the youngsters dance to live music. The extensive menu offers a bit of everything, but the oysters on the half shell and the conch chowder are the best items. $ *Average main: $25* ✉ *Bayshore Landing Marina, 2550 S. Bayshore Dr., at Aviation Ave., Coconut Grove* ☎ *305/856–3992* ✛ *C5*.

$$
AMERICAN
FAMILY

✕ **Peacock Garden Café.** Reinstating the artsy and exciting vibe of Coconut Grove circa once-upon-a-time, this lovely spot offers an indoor-outdoor, tea-time setting for light bites. By day, it's one of Miami's most serene lunch spots. The lushly landscaped courtyard is lined with alfresco seating, drawing some of Miami's most fabulous ladies who lunch. Come evening, the café buzzes with a multigenerational crowd, enjoying the South Florida zephyrs and the delicious flatbreads, salads, homemade soups, and entrées. ■TIP➜ Breakfast is also excellent. $ *Average main: $19* ✉ *2889 McFarlane Rd., Coconut Grove* ☎ *305/774–3332* ⊕ *www.jaguarhg.com/peacockspot* ✛ *C5*.

CORAL GABLES

$$$
ECLECTIC
Fodor'sChoice
★

✕ **eating house.** Check your calorie counter at the door when you enter the hippest eatery in Coral Gables. This microrestaurant sports long wait times, but you'll be talking about your meal here for months to come. The ever-changing small-plates menu teems with extreme culinary innovation and unexpected flavor combinations. Think: first fried cauliflower with lime cream, cotija cheese, and topped with layers of frito dust, followed by chicken "foie-ffles" (fried chicken, foie gras, and waffles smothered with candied bacon, maple syrup, and ranch dressing). Desserts are equally amazing. The famous "dirt cup" indeed resembles a soil-filled flowerpot. However, these roots are made of pretzels, hazelnuts, and *tierra nueva* chocolate ice cream; the "soil" is a mountain of crushed Oreos—and yes, that is a gummy worm, adding a wonderfully campy touch to the dish's creativity. $ *Average main: $23* ✉ *804 Ponce De Leon Blvd., Coral Gables* ☎ *305/448–6524* ⊕ *www.eatinghousemiami.com* ✛ *B5*.

$
CUBAN

✕ **El Palacio de los Jugos.** To the northwest of Coral Gables proper, this joint is one of the easiest and truest ways to see Miami's local Latin life in action. It's also one of the best fruit-shake shacks you'll ever come across (ask for a tropical juice of mamey or guanabana). Besides the rows of fresh tropical fruits and vegetables, and the shakes you can make with any of them, this boisterous indoor-outdoor market has numerous food counters where you can get just about any Cuban food—tamales, rice and beans, a *pan con lechón* (roast pork on Cuban bread for $5), fried pork rinds, or a coconut split before you and served with a straw. Order your food at a counter, and eat it along with local families at rows of outdoor picnic-style tables next to the parking lot.

It's disorganized, chaotic, and not for those cutting calories, but it's delicious and undeniably the real thing. $ *Average main: $6* ⊠ *5721 W. Flagler St., Flagami* ☎ *305/264–8662* ⊕ *www.elpalaciodelosjugos. com/en* ⊟ *No credit cards* ⊹ *B4.*

$$
CUBAN

✕ **Havana Harry's.** When Cuban families want an affordable home-cooked meal with a twist but don't want to cook it themselves or go supercheap at the Cuban fast-food joint, Pollo Tropical, they come to this big, unassuming restaurant. In fact, you're likely to see whole families here representing multiple generations. The fare is traditional Cuban: long thin steaks known as *bistec palomilla* (panfried), roast chicken with citrus marinade, and fried pork chunks; contemporary flourishes—mango sauce and guava-painted pork roast—are kept to a minimum. Most dishes come with white rice, black beans, and a choice of ripe or green plantains. The sweet ripe ones offer a good contrast to the savory dishes. Start with the *$5.25 mariquitas* (plantain chips) with mojo. Finish with the acclaimed flan. $ *Average main: $14* ⊠ *4612 Le Jeune Rd., Coral Gables* ☎ *305/661–2622* ⊕ *www.havanaharrys. net* ⊹ *B5.*

$$$
CARIBBEAN

✕ **Ortanique on the Mile.** Cascading *ortaniques,* a Jamaican hybrid orange, are hand-painted on columns in this warm, welcoming yellow dining room. Food is vibrant in taste and color, as delicious as it is beautiful. Though there is no denying that the strong, full flavors are imbued with island breezes, chef-partner Cindy Hutson's personal "cuisine of the sun" goes beyond Caribbean refinements. The menu centers on fish, since Hutson has a special way with it, and the West Indian Style Bouillabaisse is not to be missed. Ceviches and soups change nightly. The mojitos here—and the cocktails in general—are amazing! Beyond the original Coral Gables location, Ortanique has now spread its island love to the islands themselves, with a location in Grand Cayman and another in Harbour Island, Bahamas. $ *Average main: $32* ⊠ *278 Miracle Mile, Coral Gables* ☎ *305/446–7710* ⊕ *www.ortaniquerestaurants. com* ☺ *No lunch weekends* ⊹ *B5.*

$$$$
FRENCH

✕ **Pascal's on Ponce.** This French gem amid the Coral Gables restaurant district is always full, thanks to chef-proprietor Pascal Oudin's assured and consistent cuisine. Oudin forgoes the glitz and fussiness often associated with French cuisine, and instead opts for a simple, small, refined dining room that won't overwhelm patrons. The equally sensible menu includes a creamy lobster bisque starter. The main course is a tough choice between oven-roasted duck with poached pears and diver sea scallops with beef short rib. Ask your expert waiter to pair dishes with a selection from Pascal's impressive wine list, and, for dessert, order the bittersweet-chocolate soufflé with chocolate ganache. $ *Average main: $34* ⊠ *2611 Ponce de León Blvd., Coral Gables* ☎ *305/444–2024* ⊕ *www.pascalmiami.com* ☺ *Closed Sun. No lunch Sat.* ⊹ *B5.*

$$$$
JAPANESE
FUSION
Fodor's Choice
★

✕ **SushiSamba Coral Gables.** A flavor explosion of East-meets-South, SushiSamba beautifully mingles Japanese, Peruvian, and Brazilian cuisines to create an off-the-grid small-plates experience in the heart of Miracle Mile. The sleek 6,500-square-foot restaurant is at once modernist and welcoming. The colorful menu is divided into small hot plates, Samba Rolls, raw dishes, large plates, and skewers from the robata.

Don't miss the divine *chicharrón de calamar,* a deliciously creative incarnation of fried calamari, topped with tamarind sauce. Indulge in the crispy *taquitos,* stuffed with Maine lobster and hearts of palm. Feast on the specialty sushi roll unique to this location, the spicy Samba Coral Gables, which is loaded with steamed lobster, avocado, jalapeno, rice cracker, sweet chili, and key lime mayo. ■TIP➜ Save room for dessert. The Samba Split—a tower of dulce de leche ice cream, caramelized bananas, coconut flan, coconut mochi, and caramel popcorn—is even better than it sounds! $ *Average main: $34* ⊠ *The Westin Colonnade Hotel, 180 Aragon Ave., Coral Gables* ☎ *305/448–4990* ⊕ *www. sushisamba.com* ✛ *B5.*

KEY BISCAYNE

$$$
MEXICAN

╳ **Cantina Beach.** Leave it to the Ritz-Carlton Key Biscayne to bring a small, sumptuous piece of coastal Mexico to Florida's fabulous beaches. The pool- and oceanside Cantina Beach showcases authentic and divine Mexican cuisine, including fresh guacamole made tableside. The restaurant also boasts the region's only *tequilier,* mixing and matching 110 high-end tequilas. It's no surprise then that Cantina Beach has phenomenal margaritas. And the best part is that you can enjoy them with your feet in the sand, gazing at the ocean. $ *Average main: $21* ⊠ *The Ritz-Carlton Key Biscayne, Miami, 455 Grand Bay Dr., Key Biscayne* ☎ *305/365–4622* ⊕ *www.ritzcarlton.com/keybiscayne* ✛ *D6.*

$$$$
ITALIAN

╳ **Cioppino.** Few visitors think to venture out to the far end of Key Biscayne for dinner, but making the journey to the soothing grounds of this quiet Ritz-Carlton property on the beach is well worth it. Choose your view: the ornate dining room near the exhibition kitchen or the alfresco area with views of landscaped gardens or breeze-brushed beaches. Choosing your dishes may be more difficult, given the many rich, luscious Italian options, including imported cheeses, olive oils, risottos, and fresh fish flown in daily. Items range from the creamy *burrata* mozzarella and authentic pasta dishes to tantalizing risotto with organic spinach and roasted quail, all expertly matched with rare and boutique wines. An after-dinner drink and live music at the old-Havana-style RUMBAR inside the hotel is another treat. $ *Average main: $36* ⊠ *The Ritz-Carlton Key Biscayne, Miami, 455 Grand Bay Dr., Key Biscayne* ☎ *305/365–4156* ⊕ *www.ritzcarlton.com/keybiscayne* ✛ *D6.*

$$$$
MODERN
AMERICAN
Fodor's Choice
★

╳ **Rusty Pelican.** Whether you're visiting Miami for the first or 15th time, a meal at the Rusty Pelican could easily stand out as your most memorable experience. The legendary Key Biscayne restaurant's $7 million reinvention is nothing short of spectacular. Vistas of the bay and Miami skyline are sensational—whether you admire them through the floor-to-ceiling windows or from the expansive outdoor seating area, lined with alluring fire pits. The menu is split between tropically inspired small plates, ideal for sharing, and heartier entrées from land and sea. Standouts include corvina ceviche; baked crab cakes; and the crispy fried, whole local red snapper. $ *Average main: $38* ⊠ *3201 Rickenbacker Causeway, Key Biscayne* ☎ *305/361–3818* ⊕ *www.therustypelican.com* ✛ *D5.*

WYNWOOD

$$ ✕**Joey's.** Veneto-native chef Ivo Mazzon pays homage to fresh ingre-
ITALIAN   dients prepared simply in his small, modern Italian café, which carries
a full line of flatbread pizzas, including the legendary *dolce e piccante*
with figs, Gorgonzola, honey, and hot pepper—it's sweet and spicy
goodness through and through. Joey's also serves the full gamut of Ital-
ian favorites. One of the first nongallery tenants and the first restaurant
in the Wynwood Art District, it's become a favorite in this thriving
neighborhood. The wine list is small but carefully chosen. ⑤ *Average
main: $19* ✉ *2506 N.W. 2nd Ave., Wynwood* ☎ *305/438–0488* ⊕ *www.
joeyswynwood.com* ✛ *D4.*

$$$ ✕**Wynwood Kitchen & Bar.** At the center of Miami's artsy gallery-driven
ECLECTIC   neighborhood, Wynwood Kitchen & Bar offers an experience com-
Fodor'sChoice   pletely different from anything else in the state. While you enjoy Latin-
★   inspired small plates, you can marvel at the powerful, hand-painted
murals characterizing the interiors and exteriors, which also spill out
onto the captivating Wynwood Walls. Designed for sharing, tapas-style
dishes include wood-grilled baby octopus skewers, lemon-pepper calamari, roasted beets, bacon-wrapped dates, and ropa vieja empanadas.
It's best to allot a good chunk of time to thoroughly enjoy the creative
food, the artist-inspired cocktails, and the coolio crowd, and to ven-
erate the sensational works of art all around you. ⑤ *Average main:
$22* ✉ *2550 N.W. 2nd Ave., Wynwood Art District* ☎ *305/722–8959*
⊕ *www.wynwoodkitchenandbar.com* ✛ *C4.*

MIDTOWN

$$$ ✕**Bocce Bar.** A splendid slice of the Italian countryside has landed in
MODERN ITALIAN   Miami's trendy Midtown area, and the impressive 3,200 square-foot
Fodor'sChoice   enclave houses a beautifully appointed rustic Italian restaurant, Miami's
★   first official bocce court, and a throwback-style Italian market. Mosaic-
tiled floors, antique mirrors, and exposed wood beams set the scene
indoors while towering cypress trees, a traditional bocce court, and
alfresco seating aplenty define the front patio. Spectacular design not-
withstanding, it's the food that headlines the overall Bocce Bar experi-
ence. The small plates sharing menu is a gastronomic tour through Italy
with a modern twist. Standouts include the savory salumi and cheese
selections; farm-fresh antipasti dishes like the grilled treviso with shaved
pecorino or creamy polenta with broccoli rabe and poached egg; the
house-made pastas; and the whole branzino over braised fennel. Dishes
are beautifully presented, often accented by edible flowers, and never
fall below a caliber of blow-your-mind deliciousness. ⑤ *Average main:
$29* ✉ *3252 N.E. 1st Ave., Midtown* ☎ *786/245–6211* ⊕ *www.bocce-
bar.com* ✛ *D4.*

$$$$ ✕**Sugarcane Raw Bar Grill.** Midtown's most popular restaurant rages
JAPANESE   seven nights (and days) a week; and it's not hard to see why. The vibrant,
FUSION   supersexy, high-design restaurant perfectly captures Miami's Latin
Fodor'sChoice   vibe while serving eclectic Latin American tapas and modern Japanese
★   delights from three separate kitchens (robata, raw bar, and hot kitchen).
Miami's easy-on-the-eyes crowd often begins the Sugarcane experience

in the alfresco lounge, engaging in a fabulous mix of standing, posing, flirting, and sipping on delicious cocktails. Indoors, the trio of kitchens engineers some 60 small bites that include everything from ceviche to sushi to bacon-wrapped dates and grilled maple-glazed sweet potatoes. Sugarcane has its fair share of out-of-the-ordinary dishes (think BBQ-spice pig's-ear and oxtail paella) but it's the specialty sushi rolls (like the Night Crab Roll, filled with snow crab, shrimp tempura, and caper mustard) and the crudos (like the spicy local catch) that are most popular. ⑤ *Average main: $38* ✉ *3252 N.E. 1st Ave., Midtown* ☎ *786/369–0353* ⊕ *sugarcanerawbargrill.com* ⚑ *Reservations essential* ✥ *D4.*

FULL-MOON DINNERS

The Full Moon Dinner Series at Cioppino is fun, romantic, geeky, and one of Miami's most memorable experiences. Held from October to May on the exact night of the full moon, the dinner is a four-course Italian gastronomic extravaganza. Tabletop telescopes serve as centerpieces. The restaurant's Constellation Concierge visits each table to point out key stars and constellations, and then invites guests to look at the moon through the megatelescope. Meanwhile highly attentive staff members serve the divine creations of Chef de Cuisine Ezio Gamba.

DESIGN DISTRICT

$$$ ✕ **Michael's Genuine Food & Drink.** Michael's is often cited as Miami's top
AMERICAN restaurant, and it's not hard to see why. This indoor-outdoor bistro in
Fodor'sChoice Miami's Design District relies on fresh ingredients and a hip but unpre-
★ tentious vibe to lure diners. Beautifully arranged combinations like crispy, sweet-and-spicy pork belly with kimchi explode with unlikely but satisfying flavor. Owner and chef Michael Schwartz aims for sophisticated American cuisine with an emphasis on local and organic ingredients. He gets it right. Portions are divided into small, medium, and large plates, and the smaller plates are more inventive, so you can order several and explore. Reserve two weeks in advance for weekend tables; also, consider brunch. ⑤ *Average main: $26* ✉ *130 N.E. 40th St., Design District* ☎ *305/573–5550* ⊕ *www.michaelsgenuine.com* ⚑ *Reservations essential* ✥ *D3.*

$$$ ✕ **Oak Tavern.** In the center of Miami's stylish Design District, Oak Tav-
MODERN ern delivers perfect modern American cuisine. The personality-driven
AMERICAN restaurant, covered in reclaimed wood, and named from the giant oak
Fodor'sChoice tree in the alfresco courtyard, is helmed by local celebrity chef David
★ Bracha. Bracha's creative juices flow through his small plates, large plates, and delicacies from the wood oven. Miami A-listers and neighborhood regulars alike return week after week for the *bacalao* croquettes, roasted baby carrots salad, burrata with walnut pesto, artisan pizzas, mushroom-crusted strip steak in truffle butter, and wood-grilled salmon with butternut squash risotto. The crudos and raw oysters are off the charts but not to be outshined by the fire-roasted oysters in chili butter, sizzling out of the wood oven. Excellent mixology is also a highlight of a tavern visit. Spice up your night (or day) with a Frida Kahlo (tequila, crushed tomatoes, fresh rosemary, chilies) or a Green

Mile (gin, cucumber, chili). $ *Average main: $25* ⊠ *35 N.E. 40th St., Design District* ☎ *786/391–1818* ⊕ *www.oaktavernmiami.com* ⊗ *No lunch weekends* ✢ *D3*.

LITTLE HAITI

The east part of Little Haiti is often referred to as the "Upper East Side." Many of the area's newer restaurants are opening here.

$ ✕ **Chez Le Bebe.** Chez Le Bebe offers a short menu of Haitian home cook-
CARIBBEAN ing—it's been going strong for 30 years and has been featured on shows like the Travel Channel's *Bizarre Foods with Andrew Zimmern* and *The Layover with Anthony Bourdain*. If you want to try stewed goat, this is the place to do it! Other dishes include tender and flavorful chicken, fish, oxtail, and fried pork; each plate comes with rice, beans, plantains, and salad, for around $15. $ *Average main: $15* ⊠ *114 N.E. 54th St., Little Haiti* ☎ *305/751–7639* ▭ *No credit cards* ✢ *D3*.

LITTLE HAVANA

$$$$ ✕ **Casa Juancho.** This meeting place for the movers and shakers of the
SPANISH Cuban *exilio* community is also a haven for lovers of fine Spanish regional cuisine. Strolling balladeers serenade amid brown brick, rough-hewn dark timbers, hanging smoked meats, ceramic plates, and oil still lifes: a bit of old España dropped on Calle Ocho. Try the *dorada a la sal* (sea bream baked in a crust of sea salt), *langostinos al vega Sicilia* (jumbo shrimp sautéed with butter and shallots), or one of the many paellas. The house features one of the largest lists of reserve Spanish wines in the United States. In the evening, there's live Latin music in the dining room and in the lounge. $ *Average main: $34* ⊠ *2436 S.W. 8th St., Little Havana* ☎ *305/642–2452* ⊕ *www.casajuancho.com* ✢ *C4*.

$ ✕ **Exquisito Restaurant.** For a true locals' spot and some substantial Cuban
CUBAN eats in the heart of Little Havana, pop into Exquisito Restaurant, a local institution since the 1970s. The unassuming Cuban café serves up delectable, authentic Cuban favorites, including a great cubano and succulent yuca with garlic sauce. There's a quick-serve café on one side; next door is a full-service restaurant. A Cuban coffee is a whopping $0.75. $ *Average main: $14* ⊠ *1510 S.W. 8th St., Little Havana* ☎ *305/643–0227* ⊕ *www.exquisitorestaurant.com* ▭ *No credit cards* ✢ *C5*.

$$ ✕ **Hy-Vong Vietnamese Cuisine.** Florida's best Vietnamese food in the heart
VIETNAMESE of Little Havana? It may sound bizarre, but Hy-Vong will have you
Fodor'sChoice rethinking your drive to Calle Ocho for Cuban cuisine. In fact, people
★ are willing to wait on the sidewalk for hours to sample the delights at this tiny restaurant, like *cha gio* (Vietnamese spring rolls), fish panfried with mango or with *nuoc man* (a garlic-lime fish sauce), not to mention the pork *thit kho* (caramelized braised pork) stewed in coconut milk. Beer-savvy proprietors Kathy Manning and Tung Nguyen serve a half-dozen top brews (Double Grimbergen, Peroni, and Spaten among them) to further inoculate the experience from the ordinary—well, as ordinary as a Vietnamese restaurant on Calle Ocho can be. Arrive early to avoid long waits. $ *Average main: $17* ⊠ *3458 S.W. 8th St., Little*

Havana ☎ *305/446–3674* ⊕ *www.hyvong.com* ⊙ *No lunch; Closed Mon. and Tues.* ✢ *B5.*

$ ✕ **Las Pinareños Fruteria y Floreria.** In the mood for something refreshing
CUBAN or a high-octane jolt? Try Las Pinareños, a *fruteria* (fruit stand) that serves *coco frio* (fresh, cold coconut juice served in a whole coconut), mango juice, and other *jugos* (juices), as well as Cuban coffees and Cuban finger foods. You can order your sweet, hot *cortadito* (coffee with milk) or a *cafecito* (no milk) from the walk-up window and enjoy it at one of the stools in front of the shop or sit at one of the tables inside the fruit and flower market. ⑤ *Average main: $7* ✉ *1334 S.W. 8th St., Little Havana* ☎ *305/285–1135* ✢ *C5.*

$$ ✕ **Versailles.** *¡Bienvenido a Miami!* To the area's Cuban population,
CUBAN Miami without Versailles is like rice without black beans. First-timer Miami visitors looking for that "Cuban food on Calle Ocho" experience, look no further. The storied eatery, where old émigrés opine daily about all things Cuban, is a stop on every political candidate's campaign trail, and it should be a stop for you as well. Order a heaping platter of *lechon asado* (roasted pork loin), ropa vieja, or *picadillo* (spicy ground beef), all served with rice, beans, and fried plantains. Battle the oncoming food coma with a cup of the city's strongest cafecito, which comes in the tiniest of cups but packs a lot of punch. Versailles operates a bakery next door as well—take some pastelitos home. ⑤ *Average main: $15* ✉ *3555 S.W. 8th St., Little Havana* ☎ *305/444–0240* ✢ *C5.*

SOUTH BEACH

$$$$ ✕ **Bianca.** In a hotel where style reigns supreme, this high-profile res-
ITALIAN taurant provides both glamour and solid cuisine. The main attraction
Fodor's Choice of dining here is to see and be seen, but you may leave talking about
★ the food just as much as the outfits, hairdos, and celebrity appearances. This Italian restaurant doles out some pretty amazing fare, including a shaved baby-artichoke salad and truffle tagliatelle—perfection in every bite. The dessert menu may seem a bit back-to-basics, with tiramisù and cheesecake among the favorites, but these sweet classics are done right. For something a bit more casual at the Delano, try sushi from the Philippe Starck countertop sushi bar, Umi, at the front of the hotel. ⑤ *Average main: $50* ✉ *Delano Hotel, 1685 Collins Ave., South Beach* ☎ *305/674–5752* ⊕ *www.delano-hotel.com* ⟐ *Reservations essential* ✢ *H2.*

$$ ✕ **Big Pink.** The décor in this innovative, superpopular diner may remind
AMERICAN you of a roller-skating rink—everything is pink Lucite, stainless steel, and campy (think sports lockers as decorative touches)—and the menu is 3 feet tall, complete with a table of contents. Food is solidly all-American, with dozens of tasty sandwiches, pizzas, turkey or beef burgers, and side dishes, each and every one composed with gourmet flair. Big Pink also makes a great spot for brunch. ⑤ *Average main: $14* ✉ *157 Collins Ave., South Beach* ☎ *305/532–4700* ⊕ *www.mylesrestaurantgroup.com* ✢ *G5.*

$$$$ ✕ **BLT Steak.** This Ocean Drive favorite, renowned for seriously divine
STEAKHOUSE Gruyère cheese popovers and succulent steak and fish dishes, illuminates the vibrant, open lobby of the snazzy Betsy Hotel. It has the

distinction among all of Miami's steakhouses of serving breakfast daily and consistently impressing even the most finicky eaters. You can count on the highest-quality cuts of USDA Prime-certified Black Angus, and American Wagyu beef, in addition to blackboard specials, and sushi and raw-bar selections. Though the name may say steak, the fresh fish is arguably the highlight of the entire menu—the sautéed Dover sole with soy-caper brown butter is legendary. $ *Average main: $42* ⊠ *The Betsy Hotel, 1440 Ocean Dr., South Beach* ☎ *305/673–0044* ⊕ *www. bltrestaurants.com* ⊹ *G2.*

$$$$
CUBAN
Fodor's Choice
★

✕ **De Rodriguez Cuba on Ocean.** If you're seeking a classy, personality-driven joint in which to experience a superlative Miami incarnation of old-world Havana, look no further than this fabulous eatery run by James Beard Award–winning chef Douglas Rodriguez. It captures the essence of circa-1950s Cuba—from the décor to the music to the incredible mojitos. Although you'll find some Cuban classics here, chef Rodriguez truly showcases his creativity and gastronomic prowess across the menu. His sensational ceviches and innovative tapas and appetizers include tuna-watermelon ceviche, Cuban shrimp and sweet-corn grits, smoked marlin tacos, and crispy shrimp *chicharrón*. Larger plates such as the Sugarcane Tuna (thick, fresh, sushi-grade tuna skewered with sugarcanes) served alongside quinoa and Catalan spinach and with squid ink sauce are off-the-charts delicious. Make sure you start your evening here with a Cojito, a coconut mojito made with fresh coconut, coconut rum, lime, and mint. $ *Average main: $36* ⊠ *Hilton Bentley Hotel, 101 Ocean Dr., South Beach* ☎ *305/672–6624* ⊕ *www. drodriguezcuba.com* ⊹ *G5.*

$$$
MODERN ITALIAN

✕ **Dolce Italian.** In the center of the South Beach action, Dolce Italian doles out an irresistible menage à trois: great food, great ambience, and an easy-on-the-eyes crowd. Tucked into the first floors of the renovated Gale South Beach hotel, Miami's "it" crowd clamors for a table to see and be seen feasting on Dolce's spaghetti al pomodoro, Tartufata pizza (with speck, spicy salami, and truffle oil), housemade mozzarella, roasted branzino, and meats from the Tuscan grill. Indeed, Italian-born chef Paolo Dorigato's menu is packed with modern incarnations of Italian classics that would make *nonna* proud. After dinner, stop in the adjacent Regent Cocktail Bar for a classic cocktail in a speakeasy setting or head into the basement to party the night away in the '70s-inspired Rec Room. $ *Average main: $24* ⊠ *1690 Collins Ave., South Beach* ☎ *786/975–2550* ⊕ *www.galehotel.com/dine* ⊹ *G2.*

$$$
AMERICAN

✕ **Florida Cookery.** Originally the brainchild of award-winning Miami chef Kris Wessel (of *Chopped* fame), the Florida Cookery redefined Florida cuisine when it opened. Now that Wessel is gone, it lacks the wow factor it once had but it still delivers taste sensations crafted from just about all things Florida—local fish, stone crabs, and spiny lobster to alligator, Indian River County grapefruit, hearts of palm, and kumquats. Start with the empanadas trio (curry chicken, ropa vieja, and alligator) or the *corvina tiradito*. Splurge on the Miami Paella for your main—a massive skillet of Florida fresh seafood, chorizo, and yellow rice. $ *Average main: $26* ⊠ *The James Royal Palm, 1545 Collins Ave., South Beach* ☎ *786/276–0333* ⊕ *www.florida-cookery.com* ⊹ *H2.*

$$$$
SEAFOOD
Fodor'sChoice
★

✕ **Joe's Stone Crab Restaurant.** In South Beach's decidedly new-money scene, the stately Joe's Stone Crab is an old-school testament to good food and good service. South Beach's most storied restaurant started as a turn-of-the-century eating house when Joseph Weiss discovered succulent stone crabs off the Florida coast. A century later, the restaurant stretches a city block and serves 2,000 dinners a day to local politicians and moneyed patriarchs. Stone crabs, served with legendary mustard sauce, crispy hash browns, and creamed spinach, remain the staple. Though stone-crab season runs from October 15 to May 15, Joe's remains open year-round (albeit with a limited schedule) serving other phenomenal seafood dishes. Finish your meal with tart key lime pie, baked fresh daily. ■TIP→ **Joe's famously refuses reservations, and weekend waits can be three hours long—yes, you read that correctly—so come early or order from Joe's Take Away next door.** $ *Average main: $45 ⊠ 11 Washington Ave., South Beach ☎ 305/673–0365, 305/673–4611 for takeout ⊕ www.joesstonecrab.com ⚑ Reservations not accepted ☉ No lunch Sun. and Mon. and mid-May–mid-Oct. ⊕ G5.*

$$$$
JAPANESE
FUSION
Fodor'sChoice
★

✕ **Juvia.** High atop South Beach's design-driven parking garage, Juvia commingles urban sophistication with South Beach seduction. Towering over the beach's art deco district, the restaurant rises as a bold amalgamation of steel, glass, hanging gardens, and purple accents—a true work of art high in the sky. Three renowned chefs unite to deliver an amazing eating experience that screams Japanese, Peruvian, and French all in the same breath, focusing largely on raw fish and seafood dishes. The see-and-be-seen crowd can't get enough; neither can we! $ *Average main: $42 ⊠ 1111 Lincoln Rd., South Beach ☎ 305/763–8272 ⊕ www. juviamiami.com ⚑ Reservations essential ⊕ F2.*

$$$
ASIAN

✕ **Khong River House.** A James Beard Foundation semifinalist as America's Best New Restaurant 2013, Khong River House brings the exotic flavors of rural Thailand to Miami's storied Lincoln Road. Unlike your typical American Thai restaurant, Khong doles out hefty portions of lesser-known dishes common to the Mekong River and Golden Triangle region, where Myanmar, Thailand, Laos, and Vietnam converge. Ambush your senses with *Kuay Teaw Reau Phama* (Burmese noodle wraps stuffed with chilies, roasted peanuts, palm sugar, and cilantro), *Gang Pah Gai* (northeastern-style jungle stew with chicken, baby corn, and Thai eggplant), or *Ped Pad Cha* (Thai-style crispy duck). The restaurant is also a visual feast for the senses with seductive hardwood walls and furnishings, tastefully placed Buddhist statues, as well as a clandestine, second-floor dining room. $ *Average main: $26 ⊠ 1661 Meridian Ave., South Beach ☎ 305/763–8147 ⊕ www.khongriver.com ⚑ Reservations essential ⊕ G2.*

$$$
MODERN FRENCH

✕ **La Gloutonnerie.** Far removed from South Beach's mass-market deco drive strip, this intimate "vintage kitchen" brings the best of French old-school cuisine to the beach's more refined SoFi (South of Fifth) neighborhood. Executive Chef Christian Testa presents everything you'd desire from a renowned French kitchen from *escargots Bourgogne* to *chateubriand* while adding new-world flavors and fusions to the mix with dishes such as the tuna carpaccio and an assortment of fresh pasta entrees. Within the restaurant, a retro mini-market offers cheese, cold

Where to Eat and Stay in the Miami Area

0 — 2 mi
0 — 2 km

A

Palmetto Expwy. 826
817
N. Miami Beach Blvd.
NORTH MIAMI BEACH
909
N.W. 135th St.
N.E. 135th St. 915
Fish Fish

HIALEAH
932 E. 49th St.
W. 49th St.
N.W. 103rd St.
N.E. 95th St.
NORTH MIAMI
N.W. 95th St.
N.W. 79th St. 441
JFK Causeway
9
N.W. 62nd St.

N.W. 58th St.
27
N.W. 72nd Ave.
Hialeah Dr. 944 N.W. 54th St.
DESIGN DISTRICT
N.W. 40th St. 95
Chez La Bebe
N.W. 39th St.
Airport Expwy.
Oak Tavern
Michael's Genuine
N.W. 36th St.
Bocce Bar/
Julia Tuttle Causeway
N.W. 87th Ave.
Dairy Rd.
Miami River
Sugarcane Raw Bar Grill
Miami International Airport
Wynwood Kitchen & Bar
MIDTOWN
N.W. 20th St. 27
WYNWOOD
Joey's
Doubletree Grand Hotel Biscayne Bay

Dolphin Expwy. 836 395
DOWNTOWN MIAMI
Venetian Causeway
El Palacio de los Jugos
968
db Bistro Moderne
JW Marriott Marquis
Verde
MacArthur Causeway
N.W. 7th St.
Viceroy
Epic Hotel
W. Flagler St.
Casa Juancho
Perricone's Marketplace and Café
Azul
W. Flagler St. 41
Hy-Vong Vietnamese Cuisine
Versailles
NAOE
Tamiami Trail
S.W. 8th St.
41
Mandarin Oriental, Miami
S.W. 8th St. 41
eating house Miami
Exquisito
Conrad Miami
Edge, Steak and Bar
SushiSamba Coral Gables
959
Las Pinareños
L'Entrecote de Paris
24th St. 972
Coral Way
Hotel St. Michel
S.W. 22nd St.
Four Seasons Hotel Miami
Ortanique on the Mile
Novocento
Rusty Pelican
Biltmore Hotel
COCONUT GROVE
826
Pascal's on Ponce
5
40th St. 976
Bird Rd.
CORAL GABLES
953
Le Bouchon de Grove
Monty's
Rickenbacker Causeway
Havana Harry's
Ritz-Carlton, Coconut Grove
S.W. 87th Ave.
Peacock Garden Café
Crandon Park
874
S.W. 57th Ave.
Jaguar Ceviche Spoon Bar & Latam Grill
973 986
S. Dixie Hwy.
S.W. 72nd St.
1
KEY BISCAYNE
N. Kendall Dr.
Red Rd.
Old Cutler Rd.
Cantina Beach
Matheson Hammock Park
Cioppino
Ritz-Carlton, Key Biscayne, Miami
Biscayne Bay

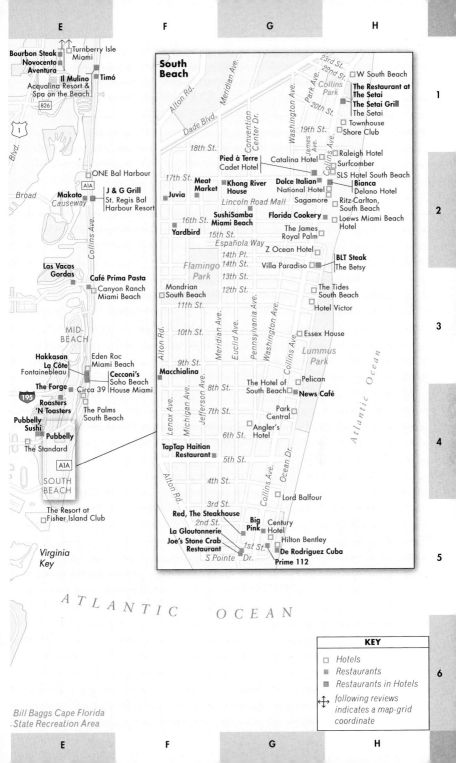

cuts, and imported French products. Add stylish black-and-white décor, stellar service, and a hip crowd, and you have the perfect recipe for keeping history in style. ⑤ *Average main: $28* ⌧ *81 Washington Ave., South Beach* ☎ *305/503–3811* ⊕ *www.lagloutonnerie.com* ✥ *G5.*

$$$$ ✕ **Macchialina Taverna Rustica.** Framed by exposed brick walls, decorated
ITALIAN   with daily specials chalkboards, and packed with gregarious patrons,
Fodor's Choice   this local foodie hangout feels like a cozy, neighborhoody, New Eng-
★   land tavern. And with a gorgeous menu showcasing the prowess of chef Federico Fellini, Macchialina Taverna Rustica nails the concept of modern Italian cuisine. Combining such great ambience and amazing eats, expect one helluva night. Start with some Italian-imported salumi, local burrata, or creamy polenta with sausage ragù and cipollini onions. Then, move on to the house-made pastas, perhaps the beet-filled *mezzaluna,* the *tagliolini al funghi,* or the spaghetti *con vongole,* before feasting on a lavish chicken or fish entrée (local hog snapper, anyone?). Save room for the house *panna cotta,* smothered in candied pistachios and balsamic-reduced strawberries. ⑤ *Average main: $34* ⌧ *820 Alton Rd., South Beach* ☎ *305/534–2124* ⊕ *www.macchialina.com* ✥ *F3.*

$$$$ ✕ **Meat Market.** On Lincoln Road, where most of the restaurants empha-
STEAKHOUSE   size people-watching over good food, this is one spot where you can find the best of both. Indeed, this is a meat market in every sense of the phrase, with great cuts of meat and plenty of sexy people passing by in skimpy clothes and enjoying fruity libations at the bar. Hard-core carnivores go wild over the 14-ounce center-cut prime New York steak as well as the "mixed-grill special," a creative trio of meats and seafood that changes nightly. The tuna tartare is exceptional here, lightly tossed in ginger and soy with mashed avocados and mango mole. Also consider the wood-grilled blackened local snapper cooked to perfection and topped with a light sun-dried-tomato pesto and dollops of black-garlic sauce. The broccolini side makes a nice complement to any meal. ⑤ *Average main: $39* ⌧ *915 Lincoln Rd., South Beach* ☎ *305/532–0088* ⊕ *www.meatmarketmiami.com* ✥ *F2.*

$$ ✕ **News Café.** No trip to Miami is complete without a stop at this Ocean
AMERICAN   Drive landmark, though the food is nothing special. The 24-hour café attracts a crowd with snacks, light meals, drinks, periodicals, and the people-parade on the sidewalk out front. Most prefer sitting outside, where they can feel the salt breeze and gawk at the human scenery. Sea-grape trees shade a patio where you can watch from a quiet distance. Offering a little of this and a little of that—bagels, pâtés, chocolate fondue, sandwiches, and a terrific wine list—this joint has something for everyone. Although service can be indifferent to the point of laissez-faire and the food is mediocre at best, News Café is just one of those places visitors love. ⑤ *Average main: $16* ⌧ *800 Ocean Dr., South Beach* ☎ *305/538–6397* ⊕ *www.newscafe.com* ⌧ *Reservations not accepted* ✥ *G4.*

$$$$ ✕ **Pied à Terre.** This cozy, 36-seat French Contemporary restaurant with
MODERN FRENCH   Mediterranean influence resides in the heart of South Beach, but it's everything the beach is not. Quiet, classic, and elegant, this hidden gastro-sanctuary within the historic Cadet Hotel forgoes glitz and gimmicks for taste and sophistication. The restaurant recalls the ambience

CHEAP EATS ON SOUTH BEACH

Miami Beach is notorious for overpriced eateries, but locals know better. **Pizza Rustica** (⊠ 8th St. and Washington Ave. and 667 Lincoln Rd.) serves up humongous slices overflowing with mozzarella, steak, olives, and barbecue chicken until 4 am. **La Sandwicherie** (⊠ 14th St. between Collins and Washington aves.) is a South Beach classic that's been here since 1988, serving gourmet French sandwiches, a delicious prosciutto salad, and healthful smoothies from a walk-up bar. **Lime Fresh Mexican Grill** (⊠ 1439 Alton Rd., at 14th St.) serves fresh and tangy fish tacos and homemade guacamole.

of a bona fide, intimate Parisian eatery—the kind you'd randomly discover on a side street in the City of Light's 5th or 6th arrondissement—and doles out succulent French contemporary cuisine enhanced by an excellent and reasonably priced wine list. ⑤ *Average main: $42* ⊠ *Cadet Hotel, 1701 James Ave., South Beach* ☎ *305/531–4533* ⊕ *www.cadethotel.com* ⌚ *Reservations essential* ⊘ *Closed Mon. No lunch* ✛ *G2.*

$$$$
STEAKHOUSE
✕ **Prime 112.** This wildly busy steakhouse is particularly renowned for its well-marbled Prime beef, creamed corn, truffle macaroni and cheese, and buzzing scene: while you stand at the bar awaiting your table (everyone has to wait—at least a little bit), you'll clamor for a drink with all facets of Miami's high society, from the city's top real estate developers and philanthropists to striking models and celebrities (Lenny Kravitz, Jay-Z, and Matt Damon are among a big list of celebrity regulars). ⑤ *Average main: $42* ⊠ *112 Ocean Dr., South Beach* ☎ *305/532–8112* ⊕ *www.mylesrestaurantgroup.com* ⌚ *Reservations not accepted* ⊘ *No lunch weekends* ✛ *G5.*

$$$
ECLECTIC
Fodor's Choice
★
✕ **Pubbelly.** Five years after opening, South Beach's favorite neighborhood gastropub still packs the house nightly. The petite eatery, located on a residential street in SoBe's western reaches, attracts the "who's who" of beach socialites, hipsters, and the occasional tourist coming to chow down on inventive Asian-Latin small plates, dumplings, charcuterie, and seasonal large plates by executive chef/owner Jose Mendin. From bay scallops Bourguignon to short-rib tartare to *huitlacoche* (corn truffle) dumplings in squid ink black butter, Pubbelly constantly pushes the envelope on inventive cuisine, and locals simply can't get enough. Expect deservedly long wait times, especially on weekends. But not to worry: after a few rounds of craft beers, sake cocktails, and eclectic wines from the awesome drink menu, your table will be ready in no time! ⑤ *Average main: $28* ⊠ *1418 20th St., South Beach* ☎ *305/532–7555* ⊕ *www.pubbelly.com* ✛ *E4.*

$$$$
JAPANESE
✕ **Pubbelly Sushi.** The team behind South Beach's wildly popular Pubbelly gastropub has teamed up with sushi chef Yuki Ieto to create the Pubbelly Sushi, a 40-seat canteen doling out contemporary, Japanese-inspired sharing plates. Of course you go light with the grade-A sashimi

or meats from the *robata* (Japanese charcoal) grill, but the real fun lies in the flavor-rich Snacks, Pubbelly Rolls, and New England Style Rolls. Start with Rock Shrimp Tempura "Buffalo Style" and graduate to the Bigeye Tuna Roll (spicy tuna over squares of crispy rice) and Navarro (salmon, crab, melted mozzarella, and fried onions). Feast on the Fried Clams New England Roll—five buttermilk-soaked clams smothered with coleslaw on a brioche bun. Wash it all down with the house Vodkasake cocktails. They're all deliciously addicting, but the Basil Berry (basil, strawberries, yuzu, sake) and Spicy Pina (jalapeno, pineapple, sake) go best with a steamy Miami evening. ⑤ *Average main: $38* ⊠ *1424 20th St., South Beach* ☎ *305/531–9282* ⊕ *www.pubbellysushi.com* ✛ *E4*.

$$$$
STEAKHOUSE

✕ **Red, the Steakhouse.** The carnivore glamour den seduces with its red and black dominatrix color scheme and overloads the senses with the divine smells and tastes of the extensive menu. Red boasts an equal number of seafood and traditional carnivorous offerings, each delicately prepared, meticulously presented, and gleefully consumed. Start with the tuna tartare, the mussels *diavolo,* or crisp chili calamari and then continue with fresh lobster or the many variations of Angus Beef Prime. And don't forget about the dozen or so sides, often the most exciting part of any steak house experience. ⑤ *Average main: $50* ⊠ *119 Washington Ave., South Beach* ☎ *305/534–3688* ⊕ *www.redthesteakhouse. com* ⌂ *Reservations essential* ✛ *G5*.

$$$$
ASIAN

✕ **The Restaurant at The Setai.** East meets West in the open-theater kitchen helmed by chef Mathias Gervais, where dishes reflect the divine and disparate flavors of Asia—from Thailand and India to China and Malaysia. Indeed, dining here is a culinary tour of Asia. With its harmonious courtyard reflecting pool and polished-stone interiors, the setting of the Setai is so dramatically beautiful that a less-than-heavenly dining experience would be a blow. Even so, the restaurant exceeds all expectations. Dishes—such as steamed yellowtail snapper with ginger soy, sweet soy, and green onions; perfectly cooked dim sum; and curries— come family-style in native crockery. The leather-bound wine list is 45 pages long. ⑤ *Average main: $50* ⊠ *The Setai Hotel, 2001 Collins Ave., South Beach* ☎ *305/520–6400* ⊕ *www.thesetaihotel.com/dining/ therestaurant* ⌂ *Reservations essential* ✛ *H1*.

$$$$
STEAKHOUSE

✕ **The Setai Grill.** If there's such a thing as an haute steakhouse, the Setai Grill is it. Executive Chef Mathias Gervais reinterprets American classics using the Rolls Royces of the food industry (think Pat LaFrieda beef, Cinco Jotas's Jamón Ibérico, and Marky's caviar) and adding a French, contemporary twist. While the LaFrieda prime cuts and the braised meats exemplify tradition perfected, Gervais goes more avantegarde than his "Butcher's Cuts" with the bites, small plates and medium plates. The Crispy Duck salad, for example, is a sensational taste explosion, as the flavors of duck confit, watercress, fried shallots, lychess, and sweet onion vinaigrette unite. ⑤ *Average main: $77* ⊠ *The Setai Hotel, 101 20th St., South Beach* ☎ *305/520–6800* ⊕ *www.thesetaihotel.com* ⌂ *Reservations essential* ☽ *Closed Mon. and Tues.* ✛ *H1*.

$$$$
JAPANESE
Fodor's Choice
★

✕ **SushiSamba Miami Beach.** Though SushiSamba branched out from NYC to Miami Beach back in 2001, this place is as trendy as ever, with long wait times to prove it. Like its six sister locations, SushiSamba Miami Beach doles out flavor explosions of East-meets-South, fusing

Japanese, Peruvian, and Brazilian cuisines to create an off-the-grid small-plates experience, this time in the heart of pedestrian-friendly Lincoln Road. The results are succulent and superb: skewers of miso-marinated sea bass over roasted corn, crunchy hamachi *taquitos* (yellowtail tartare with spicy aji panca sauce), *mocqueca mista* (Brazilian seafood stew), and South Beach–inspired sushi rolls, including the signature Samba Dromo, filled with lobster, mango, and peanut curry. Always packed with customers, both indoors and out, the blaring beats, great eats, and amazing cocktails are a fabulous rare find of timeless trendiness on South Beach. $ *Average main: $34* ⊠ *600 Lincoln Rd., South Beach* ☎ *305/673–5337* ⊕ *www.sushisamba.com* ✛ *G2.*

$
CARIBBEAN ✕ **Tap Tap Haitian Restaurant.** Tap Tap is anything but SoBe glitz and glam, but this Haitian restaurant will instantly immerse you in Haiti's cuisine and culture. An extensive collection of Haitian folk art is displayed throughout this house turned restaurant so much so that every wall, table, and chair doubles as a piece of colorful art. Menu highlights include *soup joumou* (pumpkin soup), *spagheti kreyol* (pasta, shrimp or herring, and a creole tomato sauce), *kabrit nan sos* (Bolinas goat stew in a mildly spicy tomato-based sauce), and grilled conch (when available). They also have an extensive vegetarian menu, including several vegan dishes. $ *Average main: $14* ⊠ *819 5th St., South Beach* ☎ *305/672–2898* ✛ *F4.*

$$$
SOUTHERN ✕ **Yardbird Southern Table & Bar.** There's a helluva lot of Southern lovin' from the Lowcountry at this lively and funky South Beach spot. Miami's A-list puts calorie-counting aside for decadent nights filled with comfort foods and innovative drinks. The family-style menu is divided between "small plates," "the bird," "plates," and "fixins," but have no doubt the "the bird" takes center stage (or plate) here. You'll rave about Mama's chicken biscuits, the chicken 'n' watermelon 'n' waffles, and Llewellyn's fine fried chicken, which requires a 27-hour marination and slow-cooking process. Oh, and then there are the sides, like house-cut fries with a buttermilk dipping sauce and bacon salt or the super-creamy macaroni and cheese. Don't plan on hitting the beach in a bikini the next day. $ *Average main: $28* ⊠ *1600 Lenox Ave., South Beach* ☎ *305/538–5220* ⊕ *www.runchickenrun.com* ✛ *F2.*

MID-BEACH

$$$
ITALIAN ✕ **Cecconi's.** The wait for a table at this outpost of the iconic Italian restaurant is just as long as its West Hollywood counterpart, and the dining experience just as fabulous. Eating here is a real scene of "who's who" and "who's eating what." Without a doubt, the truffle pizza, which servers shave huge hunks of black or white truffle onto tableside, is the restaurant's most talked about dish. The fish carpaccios are light and succulent while the classically hearty pastas and risottos provide authentic Italian fare. $ *Average main: $28* ⊠ *Soho Beach House, 4385 Collins Ave., Mid-Beach* ☎ *786/507–7900* ⊕ *www.cecconismiamibeach. com* ⌲ *Reservations essential* ✛ *E3.*

$$$$
STEAKHOUSE

✕ **The Forge.** Legendary for its opulence, this restaurant has been wow-ing patrons since 1968. After a renovation, the Forge reemerged in 2010 more decadent than ever—and it hasn't looked back since. It is a steakhouse, but a steakhouse the likes of which you haven't seen before. Antiques, gilt-framed paintings, a chandelier from the Paris Opera House, and Tiffany stained-glass windows from New York's Trinity Church are the fitting background for some of Miami's best cuts. The tried-and-true menu also includes prime rib, bone-in filet, lobster *thermidor,* chocolate soufflé, and sinful side dishes like creamed spinach and roasted-garlic mashed potatoes. For its walk-in humidor alone, the over-the-top Forge is worth visiting. Automated wine machines span the perimeter of the restaurant and allow you to pick your own pour and sample several wines throughout your meal. ⑤ *Average main: $38* ✉ *432 Arthur Godfrey Rd., Mid-Beach* ☎ *305/538–8533* ⊕ *www. theforge.com* ◷ *No lunch* ✛ *E4.*

$$$$
CANTONESE
Fodor's Choice
★

✕ **Hakkasan Miami.** This stateside sibling of the Michelin-star London restaurant brings the haute-Chinese-food movement to South Florida, adding Pan-Asian flair to even quite simple and authentic Cantonese recipes, and producing an entire menu that can be classified as blow-your-mind delicious. Seafood and vegetarian dishes outnumber meat options, with the scallop-and-shrimp dim sum, Szechuan-style braised eggplant, and charcoal-grilled silver cod with champagne and Chinese honey reaching new heights of excellence. ■TIP➔ **It's dinner only here, except on weekends when the restaurant hosts a dim sum lunch.** Superb eats notwithstanding, another reason to experience Hakkasan is that it's arguably the sexiest, best-looking restaurant on Miami Beach. Intri-cately carved, lacquered-black-wood Chinois panels divide seating sec-tions, creating a deceptively cozy dining experience for such a large restaurant. Dress to impress. ⑤ *Average main: $42* ✉ *Fontainebleau Hotel, 4441 Collins Ave., 4th fl., Mid-Beach* ☎ *786/276–1388 after 4 pm, 877/326–7412 before 4 pm* ⊕ *www.hakkasan.com/miami* ⌖ *Reser-vations essential* ◷ *No lunch weekdays* ✛ *E3.*

$$
FRENCH

✕ **La Côte.** With clean white lines, colorful bursts of aqua-blue cushions, and elegant umbrellas, La Côte at the Fontainebleau whisks you away to the coast of southern France. The two-level, predominantly al fresco restaurant snuggled between the beach and the Fontainebleau's pools opens its arms in a generous embrace while flirting with your taste buds, and maybe your man: the female waitstaff wear bikinis and flip-flops. Depending on your tastes, this may or may not foster a relaxed atmo-sphere that complements the simple elegant menu. Try the popular fruits de mer, or order a variety of oysters on the half shell. The vegetable pissaladière is a great vegetarian option for the table. Eating lunch here is an inexpensive way to get a good peek at the Fontainebleau while having a nice meal. ⑤ *Average main: $18* ✉ *Fontainebleau Hotel, 4441 Collins Ave., Mid-Beach* ☎ *305/674–4710* ⊕ *www.fontainebleau.com* ◷ *No dinner Sun.–Wed.* ✛ *E3.*

$$$$
ARGENTINE

✕ **Las Vacas Gordas.** Since 1996 this Argentine steak house has welcomed the who's who of Latin high society, fulfilling their wildest carnivore cravings. Recently expanded and reinvented as a glamorous enclave where the Pampas meets contemporary Miami, Vacas's grill sizzles day and nights to the troves of patrons who patiently wait to feast on mounds of fresh meat from the Argentine lowlands. The reasonably priced house malbecs complement the high-end selections showcased in the floor-to-ceiling, glass-enclosed wine cellar. Those less enthused about massive meat slabs can opt for the *Berecava* (eggplant with tomato sauce and cheese), homemade pastas, grilled peppers, fish and shrimp, or fill up on homemade rolls with spicy chimichurri. ⑤ *Average main: $35* ⊠ *933 Normandy Dr., Mid-Beach* ☎ *305/867–1717* ⊕ *www. lasvacasgordas.com* ⊗ *No lunch weekdays* ✢ *E3.*

$
DELI
FAMILY
╳ **Roasters 'N Toasters.** Formerly the longtime family establishment Arnie and Richie's, Roasters 'N Toasters Miami Beach has preserved an intimate, Jewish deli feel that would make Arnie and Richie proud. The prices are slightly higher than back in the day, but the faithful still come for the onion rolls and smoked whitefish salad, as well as the new "Famous Zaftig Sandwich," a deliciously juicy skirt steak served on twin challah rolls with a side of apple sauce and mini potato pancakes. Service can be brusque, but it sure is quick. ⑤ *Average main: $14* ⊠ *525 Arthur Goddrey Rd., Mid-Beach* ☎ *305/531–7691* ⊕ *www. roastersntoasters.com* ⊗ *Daily 6 am–3:30 pm* ⊗ *No dinner* ✢ *E4.*

NORTH BEACH AND AVENTURA

$$$$
STEAKHOUSE
╳ **Bourbon Steak.** Michael Mina's long-standing South Florida steakhouse has never gone out of style. The restaurant design is seductive, the clientele sophisticated, the service phenomenal, and the food exceptional. Dinner begins with a skillet of fresh potato focaccia and chive butter. Mina then presents a bonus starter—his trio of famous fries (fried in duck fat) with three robust sauces. Appetizers are mainly seafood. The raw bar impresses and classic appetizers like the ahi tuna tartare are delightful and super fresh. Entrees like the Maine lobster pot pie and any of the dozen varieties of butter-poached, wood-grilled steaks (from prime cuts to American wagyu) are cooked to perfection. ⑤ *Average main: $38* ⊠ *Turnberry Isle Miami, 19999 W. Country Club Dr., Aventura* ☎ *786/279–6600* ⊕ *www.michaelmina.net* ⊸ *Reservations essential* ✢ *E1.*

$$
ITALIAN
╳ **Café Prima Pasta.** If Tony Soprano lived in Miami, this is where you'd find him. This famous, bustling Italian eatery is infused with the energy of the Argentine Cea family, whose clan cooks, serves, and operates this place, while somehow finding the time to pose for photos with the hundreds of celebrities who have eaten here over the years (see them in the photos on the walls). It's on a busy street, yet the low light, soothing music, and intimate seating on this restaurant's outdoor veranda can make Café Prima Pasta a romantic spot. Everything is made in-house— from the fragrant rosemary butter to the pasta, which tastes best as crab-stuffed raviolotti or as homemade squid-ink linguine, served with seafood in a lobster sauce. ⑤ *Average main: $20* ⊠ *414 71st St., North Beach and Aventura* ☎ *305/867–0106* ⊕ *www.primapasta.com* ⊗ *No lunch* ✢ *E3.*

$$$$
SEAFOOD
Fodor's Choice
★

✕ **Fish Fish.** This small seafood eatery in North Miami is one of the city's last remaining insider secrets. Tucked away in a small strip mall, the colorful restaurant showcases Florida's superlative fruits of the sea alongside other ocean-to-table favorites from across the United States. The assortment of fresh regional catch on display makes its way straight to the pan for the restaurant's most popular entrée—the family-style "Whole Fish," prepared either crispy or grilled. But beyond this simple yet delicious "Fish Done Right," the small plates, salads, and specialties run a bit more complex. Stellar flavor explosions include a deconstructed grilled Caesar salad, lobster-truffled mac and cheese, and steamed mussels fra diavolo style. The restaurant also incorporates fish and seafood into its house-made pasta and risotto dishes. What's more? The under-the-sea-themed cocktail menu delivers mixology at its finest. Innovative drinks affectionately carry names like the Starfish (pear, ginger, and lime martini) and the Walrus (watermelon and cucumber gin martini). $ *Average main: $34* ✉ *13488 Biscayne Blvd., North Beach and Aventura* ☎ *786/732–3124* ⊕ *www.fishfishmiami.com* ✛ *D2.*

$$$$
ITALIAN

✕ **Il Mulino New York.** For more than two decades, Il Mulino New York has ranked among the top Italian restaurants in Gotham, so it's no surprise that the Miami outpost is similarly venerable. Even before the antipasti arrive, you may find yourself in a phenomenal carb coma from the fresh breads and the bruschetta. Everything that touches your palate is prepared to perfection, from simply prepared fried calamari and gnocchi pomodoro to the more complex scampi oregenata and ever-changing risottos. The restaurant is seductive, quiet, and intimate, and a favorite hangout of A-list celebs seeking a refined spot where crowds won't gawk over their presence. $ *Average main: $52* ✉ *Acqualina Resort, 17875 Collins Ave., Sunny Isles* ☎ *305/466–9191* ⊕ *www. acqualinaresort.com* ⌒ *Reservations essential* ✛ *E1.*

$$$$
MODERN FRENCH
Fodor's Choice
★

✕ **J & G Grill.** Set in the ultraglamorous St. Regis Bal Harbour, celebrity chef Jean-Gorges Vongerichten brings haute French fusion cuisine to the stunning Miami waterfront. The restaurant interiors flaunt a design sophistication that blends seamlessly with its host hotel. From beginning to end, a meal here is a true gastronomic tour de force, where dishes like the lobster bisque with butternut squash espuma and the porcini risotto with truffle brioche nary fall below the level of mind-blowing. While menu items change seasonally, there are always a number of can't-miss J & G signatures such as the Crispy Poached Egg Caviar with vodka crème fraîche. Save room for the decadent desserts from pastry chef Antonio Bachour; his French-inspired delights are pure foodie fantasia. $ *Average main: $46* ✉ *St. Regis Bal Harbour, 9703 Collins Ave., North Beach and Aventura* ☎ *305/993–3300* ⊕ *www.jggrillmiami.com* ✛ *E2.*

$$$$
JAPANESE
Fodor's Choice
★

✕ **Makoto.** Stephen Starr's Japanese headliner is one of the most popular restaurants in the swanky and prestigious Bal Harbor Shops. The ambience, service, and food all impress; and given its location in haute-couture central, the patrons definitely dress to impress. There are two menus, one devoted solely to sushi, sashimi, and maki; the other to Japanese hot dishes like tempuras, meats, and vegetables grilled over Japanese charcoal (robata), rice and noodle dishes, and steaks and fish inspired by the Land of the Rising Sun. $ *Average main: $34* ✉ *Bal Harbour Shops, 9700 Collins Ave., North Beach and Aventura, Bal Harbour* ☎ *305/864–8600* ⊕ *www.makoto-restaurant.com* ✛ *E2.*

$$$

MODERN ARGENTINE

✕ **Novecento Aventura.** Miami can't get enough of this lively Argentine bistro, where empanadas, *picadas* (sharing platters of small bites), sizzling steaks (including a grilled beef tenderloin in a malbec demi-glace), and homemade pastas (a nod to Argentina's Italian heritage) headline the menu. Following Novecento's long-term success in Downtown Miami, NYC, and of course Buenos Aires, the restaurant has recently expanded across Miami and into Mexico and Uruguay, upping its outposts to a lucky 13. Like all Novecentos, the Aventura is a scene of "who's who" in Miami's Latin American society. The dim lighting, seductive ambience, and early-19th-century black-and-white imagery recall a bona fide Buenos Aires bistro, helping patrons forget that they are, in fact, in suburban Aventura. Besides the hearty eats, the wine list is excellent and surprisingly affordable. $ *Average main: $24* ✉ *Town Center Aventura, 18831 N. Biscayne Blvd., North Beach and Aventura* ☎ *305/466–0900* ⊕ *www.novecento.com* ✛ *E1.*

$$$

ITALIAN

✕ **Timó.** In a glorified strip mall 5 miles north of South Beach, Timó (Italian for "thyme") is worth the trip from anywhere in South Florida. It's a kind of locals' secret. The handsome bistro, owned and operated by chef Tim Andriola, has dark-wood walls, Chicago brick, and a stone-encased wood-burning stove. Andriola has an affinity for robust Mediterranean flavors: sweetbreads with bacon, honey, and aged balsamic vinegar; inexpensive, artisanal pizzas; and homemade pastas. Wood-roasted meats and Parmesan dumplings in a truffle broth are not to be missed. Every bite of every dish attests to the care given, and the service is terrific. $ *Average main: $27* ✉ *17624 Collins Ave., Sunny Isles* ☎ *305/936–1008* ⊕ *www.timorestaurant.com* ☽ *No lunch weekends* ✛ *E1.*

WHERE TO STAY

Room rates in Miami tend to swing wildly. In high season, which is January through May, expect to pay at least $200 per night, even at low-budget hotels. With a rebounding local economy and increased tourism, prices skyrocketed in 2013, increasing up to 70% in some cases. Numerous hotels, previously affordable, have moved to our highest price category. In fact, it's common nowadays for rates to begin around $500 at Miami's top hotels. In summer, however, prices can be as much as 50% lower than the dizzying winter rates. You can also find great deals between Easter and Memorial Day, which is actually a delightful time in Miami. Business travelers tend to stay in downtown Miami, and most vacationers stay on Miami Beach, as close as possible to the water. South Beach is no longer the only "in" place to stay. Mid-Beach and downtown have taken the hotel scene by storm in the past few years and become home to some of the region's most avant-garde and luxurious properties to date. If money is no object, stay in one of the glamorous hotels lining Collins Avenue between 15th and 23rd streets. Otherwise, stay on the quiet beaches farther north, or in one of the small boutique hotels on Ocean Drive, Collins, or Washington avenues between 10th and 15th streets. Two important considerations that affect price are balcony and view. If you're willing to have a room without an ocean view, you can sometimes get a much lower price than the standard rate.

Hotel reviews have been shortened. For full information, visit Fodors. com.

Use the coordinate (✛ C2) at the end of each review to locate a property on the Where to Stay in the Miami Area map.

WHAT IT COSTS				
	$	$$	$$$	$$$$
HOTELS	under $200	$201–$300	$301–$400	over $400

Hotel prices are the lowest cost of a standard double room in high season.

DOWNTOWN

Miami's skyline continues to grow by leaps and bounds. With downtown experiencing a renaissance of sorts, the hotel scene here isn't just for business anymore. In fact hotels that once relied solely on their Monday–Thursday traffic are now bustling on weekends, with a larger focus on cocktails around the rooftop pool and less a focus on the business center. These hotels offer proximate access to downtown's burgeoning food and cocktail scene, historic sights, and are a short cab ride away from Miami's beaches.

$$$ **Conrad Miami.** Occupying floors 16 to 26 of a 36-story skyscraper in
HOTEL Miami's Financial District, this chic hotel mixes business with pleasure, offering easy access to the best of Downtown Miami. **Pros:** central downtown location; excellent service. **Cons:** poor views from some rooms; expensive parking. $ *Rooms from: $309* ⊠ *Espirito Santo Plaza, 1395 Brickell Ave., Downtown* ☎ *305/503–6500* ⊕ *www.conradhotels. com* ⤴ *189 rooms, 14 suites* ❑ *No meals* ✛ *D5.*

$ **Doubletree Grand Hotel Biscayne Bay.** Near the Port of Miami at the
HOTEL north end of Downtown, this waterfront hotel offers relatively basic, spacious rooms and convenient access to and from the cruise ships and Downtown, making it a good crash pad for budget-conscious cruise passengers. **Pros:** marina; proximity to port. **Cons:** still need a cab to get around; dark lobby and neighboring arcade of shops; worn rooms. $ *Rooms from: $185* ⊠ *1717 N. Bayshore Dr., Downtown* ☎ *305/372– 0313, 800/222–8733* ⊕ *www.doubletree.com* ⤴ *152 rooms, 56 suites* ❑ *No meals* ✛ *D4.*

$$$ **Epic Hotel.** In the heart of Downtown, Kimpton's pet-friendly, freebie-
HOTEL heavy Epic Hotel has 411 guest rooms, each with a spacious balcony
Fodor's Choice (many of them overlook Biscayne Bay) and fabulous modern ameni-
★ ties—Frette linens, iPod docks, spa-inspired luxury bath products—that match the modern grandeur of the trendy common areas, which include a supersexy rooftop pool. **Pros:** sprawling rooftop pool deck; balcony in every room; complimentary wine hour, coffee, and Wi-Fi. **Cons:**

BEST BETS FOR MIAMI LODGING

Fodor's offers a selective listing of high-quality lodging experiences in every price range, from the city's best budget beds to its most sophisticated luxury hotels. Here, we've compiled our top recommendations by price and experience. The very best properties are designated in the listings with the Fodor's Choice logo. Find specific details about a hotel in the full reviews, listed alphabetically by neighborhood.

Fodor's Choice ★

Acqualina Resort & Spa on the Beach, North Beach and Aventura, $$$$, p. 90

Delano Hotel, South Beach, $$$$, p. 85

Epic Hotel, Downtown, $$$, p. 80

The James Royal Palm, South Beach, $$$, p. 85

The Lord Balfour, South Beach, $, p. 86

Mandarin Oriental, Miami, Downtown, $$$$, p. 82

Ritz-Carlton, South Beach, $$$$, p. 87

SLS Hotel South Beach, South Beach, $$$$, p. 87

St. Regis Bal Harbour Resort, North Beach and Aventura, $$$$, p. 91

Surfcomber Miami, South Beach, $$, p. 88

W South Beach, South Beach, $$$$, p. 88

By Price

$

The Lord Balfour, South Beach, p. 86

$$

Surfcomber Miami, South Beach, p. 88

$$$

Epic Hotel, Downtown, p. 80

The James Royal Palm, South Beach, p. 85

$$$$

Delano Hotel, South Beach, p. 85

Mandarin Oriental, Miami, Downtown, p. 82

St. Regis Bal Harbour Resort, North Beach and Aventura, p. 91

W South Beach, South Beach, p. 88

By Experience

BEST HOTEL BAR

National Hotel, South Beach, p. 86

Viceroy Miami (rooftop bar), Downtown, p. 82

BEST-KEPT SECRET

The Lord Balfour, South Beach, p. 86

Soho Beach House, Mid-Beach, p. 90

BEST LOCATION

The Betsy Hotel, South Beach, p. 84

Surfcomber Miami, South Beach, p. 88

BEST POOL

Biltmore Hotel, Coral Gables, p. 83

Delano Hotel, South Beach, p. 85

Raleigh Hotel, South Beach, p. 87

Viceroy Miami, Downtown, p. 82

BEST SERVICE

Acqualina Resort & Spa on the Beach, North Beach and Aventura, p. 90

The Ritz-Carlton Key Biscayne, Key Biscayne, p. 83

St. Regis Bal Harbour Resort, North Beach and Aventura, p. 91

BEST VIEWS

Epic Hotel, Downtown, p. 80

St. Regis Bal Harbour Resort, North Beach and Aventura, p. 91

W South Beach, South Beach, p. 88

HIPSTER HOTELS

Catalina Hotel & Beach Club, South Beach, p. 84

Shore Club, South Beach, p. 87

Soho Beach House, Mid-Beach, p. 90

2

some rooms have inferior views; congested valet area. ⑤ *Rooms from: $399* ✉ *270 Biscayne Blvd. Way, Downtown* ☎ *305/424–5226* ⊕ *www. epichotel.com* ⟿ *411 rooms* ⦿ *No meals* ✛ *D4.*

$$$$
HOTEL
🏨 **Four Seasons Hotel Miami.** A favorite of business travelers visiting downtown's busy, business-centric Brickell Avenue, this plush sanctuary offers a respite from the nine-to-five mayhem—a soothing water wall greets you, the understated rooms impress you, and the seventh-floor, 2-acre-pool terrace relaxes you. **Pros:** rooms renovated in 2011; sensational service; amazing gym and pool deck. **Cons:** no balconies; caters mostly to business travelers; not near beach. ⑤ *Rooms from: $499* ✉ *1435 Brickell Ave., Downtown* ☎ *305/358–3535* ⊕ *www. fourseasons.com/miami* ⟿ *182 rooms, 39 suites* ⦿ *No meals* ✛ *D5.*

$$$$
HOTEL
🏨 **JW Marriott Marquis Miami.** The marriage of Marriott's JW and Marquis brands has created a truly tech-savvy, contemporary, and stylish business-minded hotel—you may never have seen a Marriott quite like this one. **Pros:** entertainment center; amazing technology; pristine rooms. **Cons:** swimming pool receives limited sunshine; lots of conventioneers on weekdays. ⑤ *Rooms from: $419* ✉ *255 Biscayne Blvd. Way, Downtown* ☎ *305/421–8600* ⊕ *www.jwmarriottmarquismiami. com* ⟿ *257 rooms, 56 suites* ⦿ *No meals* ✛ *D4.*

$$$$
HOTEL
Fodor's Choice
★
🏨 **Mandarin Oriental, Miami.** Clandestinely situated at the tip of prestigious Brickell Key in Biscayne Bay, the Mandarin Oriental feels as exclusive as it does glamorous, with luxurious rooms, exalted restaurants, and the city's top spa, all of which marry the brand's signature Asian style with Miami's bold tropical elegance. **Pros:** impressive lobby; intimate vibe; ultraluxurious. **Cons:** man-made beach; small infinity pool; few beach cabanas. ⑤ *Rooms from: $519* ✉ *500 Brickell Key Dr., Downtown* ☎ *305/913–8288, 866/888–6780* ⊕ *www.mandarinoriental.com* ⟿ *326 rooms, 31 suites* ⦿ *No meals* ✛ *D5.*

$$$$
HOTEL
🏨 **Viceroy Miami.** This hotel cultivates a brash, supersophisticated Miami attitude, likely stemming from its flawless guest rooms decked out with dramatic Kelly Wearstler, Asian-inspired interiors and larger-than-life common areas designed by Philippe Starck. **Pros:** amazing design elements; exceptional pool deck and spa; sleek rooms. **Cons:** poor views from rooms; tiny lobby; some amenities shared with ICON Miami residents. ⑤ *Rooms from: $429* ✉ *485 Brickell Ave., Downtown* ☎ *305/503–4400, 866/781–9923* ⊕ *www.viceroymiami.com* ⟿ *150 rooms, 18 suites* ⦿ *No meals* ✛ *D4.*

COCONUT GROVE

Although this area certainly can't replace the draw of Miami Beach or the business convenience of downtown, about 20 minutes away, it's an exciting bohemian-chic neighborhood with a gorgeous waterfront.

$$
HOTEL
🏨 **The Ritz-Carlton Coconut Grove, Miami.** Overlooking Biscayne Bay, this business-centric Ritz-Carlton hotel in the heart of Coconut Grove received a face-lift in 2012 that gave its lobby and lounge a refreshed, livelier look that complements its sophisticated guest rooms—all with marble baths and private balconies. **Pros:** elevated pool deck; near Coconut Grove and Coral Gables shopping; excellent service. **Cons:**

near residential area; more business- than leisure-oriented. Ⓢ *Rooms from: $299* ✉ *3300 S.W. 27th Ave., Coconut Grove* ☎ *305/644–4680, 800/241–3333* ⊕ *www.ritzcarlton.com* ⬎ *88 rooms, 27 suites* ⦿⊙ *No meals* ✛ *C5.*

CORAL GABLES

Beautiful Coral Gables is set around its beacon, the national landmark Biltmore Hotel. It also has a couple of big business hotels and one smaller boutique property. The University of Miami is nearby.

$$$ **Biltmore Hotel.** Built in 1926, this landmark hotel has had several
HOTEL incarnations over the years—including a stint as a hospital during World War II—but through it all, this grande dame has remained an opulent reminder of yesteryear, with its palatial lobby and grounds, enormous pool (largest in the lower 48), and distinctive 315-foot tower, which rises above the canopy of trees shading Coral Gables. **Pros:** historic property; gorgeous pool; great tennis and golf. **Cons:** in the suburbs; a car is necessary to get around. Ⓢ *Rooms from: $343* ✉ *1200 Anastasia Ave., Coral Gables* ☎ *855/311–6903* ⊕ *www.biltmorehotel. com* ⬎ *241 rooms, 39 suites* ⦿⊙ *No meals* ✛ *B5.*

$ **Hotel St. Michel.** This quiet and charming European bed-and-break-
B&B/INN fast–inspired hotel dates to 1926—original elevator and all—and is right off the Miracle Mile in Coral Gables. **Pros:** coolest elevator in Florida; historical vibe; totally unexpected in South Florida. **Cons:** small rooms; old, individual in-room a/c units; breakfast no longer included at this B&B. Ⓢ *Rooms from: $179* ✉ *162 Alcazar Ave., Coral Gables* ☎ *305/444–1666, 800/848–4683* ⊕ *www.hotelstmichel.com* ⬎ *25 rooms, 3 suites* ⦿⊙ *No meals* ✛ *B5.*

KEY BISCAYNE

There's probably no other place in Miami where slowness is lifted to a fine art. On Key Biscayne there are no pressures, there's no nightlife outside of the Ritz-Carlton's great live Latin music weekends, and the dining choices are essentially limited to the hotel (which has four dining options, including the languorous, Havana-style RUMBAR).

$$$ **The Ritz-Carlton Key Biscayne, Miami.** In this ultra-laid-back Key Bis-
RESORT cayne setting, it's natural to appreciate the Ritz brand of pamper-
FAMILY ing with luxurious rooms, attentive service, four on-property dining options, and ample recreational activities for the whole family. **Pros:** on the beach; quiet; luxurious family retreat. **Cons:** far from South Beach and downtown; beach sometimes seaweed-strewn; rental car almost a necessity. Ⓢ *Rooms from: $499* ✉ *455 Grand Bay Dr., Key Biscayne* ☎ *305/365–4500, 800/241–3333* ⊕ *www.ritzcarlton.com/keybiscayne* ⬎ *365 rooms, 37 suites* ⦿⊙ *No meals* ✛ *D6.*

SOUTH BEACH

If you are looking to experience the postcard image of Miami, look no further than South Beach. Most of the hotels along Ocean Drive, Collins Avenue, and Washington Avenue are housed in history-steeped art deco buildings, each one cooler than the next. From boutique hotels to high-rise structures, all South Beach hotels are in close distance to the beach and never far from the action. Most hotels here cost a pretty penny, and for good reason. They are more of an experience than a place to crash (think designer lobbies, some of the world's best pool scenes, and unparalleled people-watching),

$$$ **Angler's Hotel.** Miami's newest addition to the Kimpton portfolio has
HOTEL an air of serenity and privacy that pervades this discreet little oasis of personality-driven villas (built in 1930 by architect Henry Maloney) and modern tower units, together capturing the feel of a sophisticated private Mediterranean villa community. **Pros:** gardened private retreat; excellent service; daily complimentary wine hour. **Cons:** on busy Washington Avenue; not directly on beach. ⑤ *Rooms from: $339* ⊠ *660 Washington Ave., South Beach* ☎ *305/534–9600* ⊕ *www.anglershotelmiami.com* ⇥ *24 rooms, 20 suites* ◯◯ *No meals* ✛ *G4.*

$$$ **The Betsy Hotel.** An art deco treasure elegantly refurbished and totally
HOTEL retro-chic, The Betsy sits directly on world-famous Ocean Drive and delivers the full-throttle South Beach experience with style, pizzazz and cultural twist—the Betsy offers cultural programs year-round such as poetry readings, live jazz, and art shows. **Pros:** unbeatable location; super-fashionable; great beach club. **Cons:** some small rooms; service can be hit or miss; no pool scene (but there's a rooftop scene). ⑤ *Rooms from: $389* ⊠ *1440 Ocean Dr., South Beach* ☎ *305/531–6100* ⊕ *www. thebetsyhotel.com* ⇥ *41 rooms, 20 suites* ◯◯ *No meals* ✛ *G2.*

$$ **Cadet Hotel.** A former home to World War II air force cadets, this gem
HOTEL has been reimagined as an oasis in South Beach, offering the antithesis of the sometimes maddening jet-set scene with 34 distinctive rooms exuding understated luxury. **Pros:** excellent service; lovely garden and spa pool; originality. **Cons:** tiny swimming pool; limited appeal for the party crowd. ⑤ *Rooms from: $279* ⊠ *1701 James Ave., South Beach* ☎ *305/672–6688, 800/432–2338* ⊕ *www.cadethotel.com* ⇥ *32 rooms, 3 suites* ◯◯ *Breakfast* ✛ *G2.*

$$ **Catalina Hotel & Beach Club.** The Catalina is the budget party spot in
HOTEL the heart of South Beach's hottest block and attracts plenty of twenty-somethings with its free nightly drink hour, airport shuttles, bike rentals, two fun pools, and beach chairs. **Pros:** free drinks; free bikes; free airport shuttle; good people-watching. **Cons:** service not a high priority; loud; rooms not well maintained. ⑤ *Rooms from: $295* ⊠ *1720–1756 Collins Ave., South Beach* ☎ *305/674–1160* ⊕ *www.catalinahotel.com* ⇥ *200 rooms* ◯◯ *No meals* ✛ *G2.*

$ **Century Hotel Miami Beach.** If you're looking for a clean place in the
HOTEL emerging SoFi (South of 5th) area to rest your head for the evening, this very basic and cheap (but tidy) hotel gives you a chance to discover a more residential side of bustling South Beach while staying in a 1939 two-story art deco masterpiece by Henry Hohauser. **Pros:** good location; complimentary breakfast; pet-friendly. **Cons:** no pool; simple rooms; must call to book. ⑤ *Rooms from: $120* ⊠ *140 Ocean Dr., South Beach* ☎ *305/674–8855* ⊕ *www.centurymiamibeach.com* ⇥ *26 rooms* ◯◯ *Breakfast* ✛ *G5.*

$$$$ ⊞ **Delano Hotel.** The hotel that single-handedly made South Beach cool
HOTEL again in the nineties is still making major waves across the beach as
Fodor'sChoice this Philippe Starck powerhouse continues to define the paradigm of
★ South Beach décor and glamour. **Pros:** electrifying design; lounging
among the beautiful and famous. **Cons:** crowded; sceney; entry level
rooms are on small side. ⑤ *Rooms from: $439 ⊠ 1685 Collins Ave.,*
South Beach ☎ *305/672–2000, 800/555–5001* ⊕ *www.delano-hotel.*
com ⮑ *184 rooms, 24 suites* ❄️ *No meals* ✛ *H2.*

$$ ⊞ **Essex House.** This restored art deco gem is a favorite with Europeans
HOTEL desiring good location and a somewhat no-frills practical base—expect
average-size rooms with midcentury-style red furniture and marble tubs.
Pros: a social, heated pool; complimentary beer and wine hour Mon-
day–Friday; in-house sushi restaurant Zen Sai. **Cons:** small pool; not
on the beach. ⑤ *Rooms from: $229 ⊠ 1001 Collins Ave., South Beach*
☎ *305/534–2700* ⊕ *www.essexhotel.com* ⮑ *61 rooms, 15 suites* ❄️ *No*
meals ✛ *G3.*

$$$ ⊞ **Hilton Bentley Miami/South Beach.** One of the area's only kid-friendly
HOTEL boutique hotels, this contemporary, design-driven, and artsy Hilton in
FAMILY the emerging and trendy SoFi (South of 5th) district offers families just
the right mix of South Beach flavor and wholesome fun while still providing couples a romantic base without any party madness. **Pros:** quiet
location; style and grace; family-friendly. **Cons:** small pool; small lobby.
⑤ *Rooms from: $360 ⊠ 101 Ocean Dr., South Beach* ☎ *305/938–4600*
⊕ *www.hilton.com* ⮑ *104 rooms, 5 suites* ❄️ *No meals* ✛ *G5.*

$$$ ⊞ **The Hotel of South Beach.** Fashion designer Todd Oldham preserved the
HOTEL art-deco roots of The Hotel, which inhabits the historic Tiffany build-
ing on Collins Avenue, and has expanded the property with 20 new
deluxe oceanfront rooms and suites along fabulous Ocean Drive. **Pros:**
great service; coolest roof-deck bar in town; good for couples. **Cons:**
pool is tiny; rooms from original building lack good views. ⑤ *Rooms*
from: $329 ⊠ 801 Collins Ave., South Beach ☎ *305/531–2222* ⊕ *www.*
thehotelofsouthbeach.com ⮑ *68 rooms, 5 suites* ❄️ *No meals* ✛ *G4.*

$$ ⊞ **Hotel Victor.** Fresh from a facelift in late 2013, the sleek Hotel Vic-
HOTEL tor, created by the Parisian designer Jacques Garcia, has replaced the
dated jellyfish motif with a newer incarnation of bold modernism.
Pros: views from pool deck; high hip factor; good service. **Cons:** small
rooms; street noise from some rooms; lots of rusty handles. ⑤ *Rooms*
from: $297 ⊠ 1144 Ocean Dr., South Beach ☎ *305/779–8700* ⊕ *www.*
hotelvictorsouthbeach.com ⮑ *91 rooms* ❄️ *No meals* ✛ *G3.*

$$$ ⊞ **The James Royal Palm.** The James Royal Palm is a daily celebration
RESORT of art deco, Art Basel, modernity, and design detail that also dutifully
Fodor'sChoice embodies the mantra of the James brand: "luxury liberated." **Pros:**
★ design blending contemporary style with South Beach identity; impres-
sive spa; multiple pools; unbeatable location; two noteworthy restau-
rants. **Cons:** occasional noise from in-house nightclub; small driveway
for entering. ⑤ *Rooms from: $359 ⊠ 1545 Collins Ave., South Beach*
☎ *786/276–0100* ⊕ *www.jameshotels.com/miami* ⮑ *234 studios, 159*
suites ❄️ *No meals* ✛ *G2.*

$$$ 　🏨 **Loews Miami Beach Hotel.** A two-tower 800-room megahotel with top-
HOTEL 　tier amenities, a massive spa, a great pool, and direct beachfront access,
FAMILY 　the Loews Miami Beach is good for families, businesspeople, groups,
and pet-lovers. **Pros:** top-notch amenities; immense spa; pets welcome.
Cons: insanely large; constantly crowded; pets desperate to go will need
to wait several minutes to make it to the grass. $⑤ Rooms from: 399
$⊠ 1601 Collins Ave., South Beach$ ☎ 305/604–1601, 800/235–6397
⊕ *www.loewshotels.com/miamibeach* ⤳ *733 rooms, 57 suites* ⑩ *No
meals* ✣ *H2.*

$ 　🏨 **The Lord Balfour.** Quickly making a name for itself in South Beach's
HOTEL 　emerging SoFi (South of 5th) neighborhood, the luxurious, boutique,
Fodor's Choice 　and retro-chic Lord Balfour hotel proves that style, sophistication, and
★ 　the full-throttle, present-day Miami Beach experience need not require
the deepest of deep pockets. **Pros:** handcrafted tea-infused cocktails
in the lobby bar; whimsical interior design; excellent service. **Cons:** no
pool yet (under construction); rooms on smaller side; occasional street
noise from some rooms. $⑤ Rooms from: 199 $⊠ 350 Ocean Dr., South
Beach$ ☎ *800/949–4075* ⊕ *www.lordbalfourmiami.com* ⤳ *64 rooms*
⑩ *No meals* ✣ *G4.*

$$$ 　🏨 **Mondrian South Beach.** The Mondrian South Beach infuses life into
HOTEL 　the beach's lesser-known western perimeter and rises as a poster child
of SoBe design glam—head to toe, the hotel is a living and functioning
work of art, an ingenious vision of provocateur Marcel Wanders. **Pros:**
trendy; perfect sunsets; party vibe. **Cons:** busy lobby; doses of South
Beach attitude; no direct beach access. $⑤ Rooms from: 339 $⊠ 1100
West Ave., South Beach$ ☎ *305/514–1500* ⊕ *www.mondrian-miami.
com* ⤳ *233 rooms, 102 suites* ⑩ *No meals* ✣ *F3.*

$$$$ 　🏨 **National Hotel.** The National Hotel has maintained its distinct art
HOTEL 　deco heritage (the chocolate- and ebony-hued pieces in the lobby date
back to the 1930s, and the baby grand piano headlines the throwback
Blues Bar) while also keeping up with SoBe's glossy newcomers with
its renovated cabana wing and art deco tower. **Pros:** stunning pool;
perfect location. **Cons:** street noise on the weekends; rooms don't have
the finesse of neighbors. $⑤ Rooms from: 405 $⊠ 1677 Collins Ave.,
South Beach$ ☎ *305/532–2311, 800/327–8370* ⊕ *www.nationalhotel.
com* ⤳ *143 rooms, 9 suites* ⑩ *No meals* ✣ *H2.*

$$ 　🏨 **Park Central.** This seven-story, oft-photographed 1937 archetypal
HOTEL 　art deco building on Ocean Drive offers a wide range of somewhat
dated, Old Florida–style rooms complete with wicker chairs and black-
and-white photos of old beach scenes. **Pros:** spacious rooftop sundeck;
comfy beds; good location. **Cons:** dated furnishings; small bathrooms;
most rooms have limited views. $⑤ Rooms from: 289 $⊠ 640 Ocean
Dr., South Beach$ ☎ *305/538–1611* ⊕ *www.theparkcentral.com* ⤳ *113
rooms, 12 suites* ⑩ *No meals* ✣ *G4.*

$$$ 　🏨 **Pelican Miami Beach.** Each awesome room of this Ocean Drive bou-
HOTEL 　tique hotel is completely different, fashioned from a mix of antique
and garage-sale furnishings selected by the designer of Diesel's cloth-
ing-display windows. **Pros:** unique, over-the-top design; central Ocean
Drive location. **Cons:** rooms are so tiny that the quirky charm wears
off quickly; not smoke-free. $⑤ Rooms from: 339 $⊠ 826 Ocean Dr.,$

South Beach ☎ 305/673–3373 ⊕ *www.pelicanhotel.com* ⤵ 28 *rooms,* 4 *suites* ○| *No meals* ✛ *G4.*

$$$
HOTEL

Raleigh Hotel. This classy art-deco gem, now part of the sbe hotel group, balances the perfect amount of style, comfort, and South Beach sultriness, highlighted by the beach's sexiest pool, which was created for champion swimmer Esther Williams. **Pros:** amazing historic swimming pool; elegance. **Cons:** lobby is a bit dark; not as social as other South Beach hotels. $ *Rooms from: $315* ✉ *1775 Collins Ave., South Beach* ☎ 305/534–6300 ⊕ *www.raleighhotel.com* ⤵ 95 *rooms, 10 suites* ○| *No meals* ✛ *H2.*

$$$$
HOTEL
FAMILY
Fodor'sChoice
★

The Ritz-Carlton, South Beach. Completely revamped and renovated in 2013, the smoking-hot, art-deco Ritz-Carlton, South Beach is a surprisingly trendy, beachfront bombshell, with a dynamite staff, a snazzy Club Lounge, a "tanning butler," and a long pool deck that leads right out to the beach. **Pros:** luxurious renovated rooms; great service; pool with VIP cabanas; great location. **Cons:** not as small and intimate as other properties. $ *Rooms from: $629* ✉ *1 Lincoln Rd., South Beach* ☎ 786/276–4000, 800/241–3333 ⊕ *www.ritzcarlton.com/southbeach* ⤵ 375 *rooms* ○| *No meals* ✛ *H2.*

$$$$
HOTEL

Sagamore, the Art Hotel. This supersleek, all-white, all-suite hotel in the middle of the action looks and feels like an edgy art gallery, filled with brilliant contemporary works, the perfect complement to the posh, gargantuan, 500-square-foot crash pads. **Pros:** sensational pool; great location; good rate specials. **Cons:** can be quiet on weekdays; patchy Wi-Fi. $ *Rooms from: $429* ✉ *1671 Collins Ave., South Beach* ☎ 305/535–8088 ⊕ *www.sagamorehotel.com* ⤵ 93 *suites* ○| *No meals* ✛ *H2.*

$$$$
RESORT

The Setai. This opulent, all-suite hotel feels like an Asian museum, serene and beautiful, with heavy granite furniture lifted by orange accents, warm candlelight, and the soft bubble of seemingly endless ponds complemented by three oceanfront infinity pools (heated to 75, 85, and 95 degrees) that further spill onto the beach's velvety sands. **Pros:** quiet and classy; beautiful grounds. **Cons:** TVs are far from the beds; high price point. $ *Rooms from: $833* ✉ *101 20th St., South Beach* ☎ 305/520–6000 ⊕ *www.thesetaihotel.com* ⤵ 121 *suites* ○| *No meals* ✛ *H1.*

$$$
HOTEL

Shore Club. In terms of lounging, people-watching, partying, and poolside glitz, the Shore Club still ranks among the ultimate South Beach adult playgrounds; guests generally hang out in the minimalist lobby or by one of the two stylish pools, where a peek behind the cascading white curtains or palm trees can yield a celebrity, a scandal, or a make-out session. **Pros:** hip crowd; good restaurants and bars; nightlife in your backyard. **Cons:** spartan rooms; late-night music. $ *Rooms from: $379* ✉ *1901 Collins Ave., South Beach* ☎ 305/695–3100, 877/640–9500 ⊕ *www.shoreclub.com* ⤵ 309 *rooms, 79 suites* ○| *No meals* ✛ *H1.*

$$$$
RESORT
Fodor'sChoice
★

SLS Hotel South Beach. Smack in the center of South Beach, the SLS Hotel marks designer Philippe Starck's triumphant large-scale return to South Beach; but this time he's teamed up with friends Sam Nazarian, chefs José Andrés and Katsuya Uech, and Lenny Kravitz for the whimsical trip down the rabbit hole, creating the latest and greatest in the evolution of Miami's happening hotel/food/pool/beach scene. **Pros:** great in-house restaurants; masterful design; fun pool scene. **Cons:** sometimes small rooms; no lobby per se; congested valet area. $ *Rooms from: $415* ⊠ *1701 Collins Ave., South Beach* ☎ *305/674–1701* ⊕ *www. slshotels.com/southbeach* ↘ *127 rooms, 13 suites* |○| *No meals* ✛ *H2.*

$$
HOTEL
Fodor's Choice
★

Surfcomber Miami, South Beach. In 2012 the legendary Surfcomber joined the hip Kimpton Hotel group, spawning a fantastic nip-and-tuck that's rejuvenated the rooms and common spaces to reflect vintage luxe and oceanside freshness, and offering a price point that packs the place with a young, sophisticated yet unpretentious crowd. **Pros:** stylish but not pretentious; pet-friendly; on the beach. **Cons:** small bathrooms; front desk often busy. $ *Rooms from: $299* ⊠ *1717 Collins Ave., South Beach* ☎ *305/532–7715* ⊕ *www.surfcomber.com* ↘ *182 rooms, 4 suites* |○| *No meals* ✛ *H2.*

$$$
HOTEL

The Tides South Beach. Formerly the crown jewel of the Viceroy Hotel Group, the Tides South Beach is an exclusive Ocean Drive art deco hotel of just 45 ocean-facing suites adorned with soft pinks and corals, gilded accents, and marine-inspired decor. **Pros:** superior service; great beach location; ocean views from all suites plus the terrace restaurant. **Cons:** tiny elevators; mediocre restaurant. $ *Rooms from: $396* ⊠ *1220 Ocean Dr., South Beach* ☎ *305/604–5070* ⊕ *www.tidessouthbeach.com* ↘ *45 suites* |○| *No meals* ✛ *G3.*

$
HOTEL

Townhouse Hotel. Though sandwiched between the Setai and the Shore Club—two of the coolest hotels on the planet—the Townhouse doesn't try to act all dolled up: it's comfortable being the shabby-chic, lighthearted, relaxed fun hotel on South Beach (and rates include a Parisian-style breakfast). **Pros:** a great budget buy for the style-hungry; direct beach access; hot rooftop lounge. **Cons:** no pool; small rooms not designed for long stays. $ *Rooms from: $195* ⊠ *150 20th St., east of Collins Ave., South Beach* ☎ *305/534–3800* ⊕ *www.townhousehotel. com* ↘ *69 rooms, 2 suites* |○| *Breakfast* ✛ *H1.*

$
B&B/INN

Villa Paradiso. One of South Beach's best deals for budget travelers, Paradiso has huge rooms with kitchens and a charming tropical courtyard with benches for hanging out at all hours. **Pros:** great hangout spot in courtyard; good value; great location. **Cons:** no pool; no restaurant; not trendy. $ *Rooms from: $174* ⊠ *1415 Collins Ave., South Beach* ☎ *305/532–0616* ⊕ *www.villaparadisohotel.com* ↘ *17 studios* |○| *No meals* ✛ *G2.*

$$$$
HOTEL
Fodor's Choice
★

W South Beach. Fun, fresh, and funky, the W South Beach is also the flagship for the brand's evolution towards young sophistication, which means less club music in the lobby, more lighting, and more attention to the multimillion-dollar art collection lining the lobby's expansive walls. **Pros:** pool scene; masterful design; ocean-view balconies in each room. **Cons:** not a classic art deco building; hit-or-miss service. $ *Rooms from: $1379* ⊠ *2201 Collins Ave., South Beach* ☎ *305/938–3000* ⊕ *www. whotels.com/southbeach* ↘ *213 studios, 135 suites* |○| *No meals* ✛ *H1.*

$$$
HOTEL

Z Ocean Hotel South Beach. The lauded firm of Arquitectonica designed the rooms and suites at this glossy and bold hideaway, including 27 rooftop suites endowed with terraces, each complete with Jacuzzi, plush chaise lounges, and a view of the South Beach skyline. **Pros:** incredible balconies; huge rooms; space-maximizing closets. **Cons:** gym is tiny and basic; not much privacy on rooftop suite decks. $⑤ Rooms from: $399 ✉ 1437 Collins Ave., South Beach ☎ 305/672–4554 ⊕ www. zoceanhotelsouthbeach.com ⤴ 79 suites |⦿| No meals ✛ G2.

MID-BEACH

The stretch of Miami Beach called "Mid-Beach" is undergoing a renaissance, as formerly run-down hotels are renovated and new hotels and condos are built.

$$$$
RESORT
Canyon Ranch Miami Beach. Physical and mental well-being top the agenda at this 150-suite beachfront hotel, defined by its 70,000-square-foot wellness spa, including a rock-climbing wall, 54 treatment rooms, and 30 exercise classes daily. **Pros:** directly on the beach; spacious suites (minimum 720 square feet); spa treatments exclusive to hotel guests. **Cons:** far from nightlife; not a very gregarious clientele. $⑤ Rooms from: $480 ✉ 6801 Collins Ave., Mid-Beach ☎ 305/514–7000 ⊕ www. canyonranch.com ⤴ 150 suites |⦿| No meals ✛ E3.

$
HOTEL
Circa 39 Hotel. Located in the heart of Mid-Beach, this stylish yet affordable 100-guest room boutique hotel pays attention to every detail and gets them all right, with amenities that include a swimming pool and sundeck complete with cabanas and umbrella-shaded chaises that invite all-day lounging. **Pros:** affordable; chic; intimate; beach chairs provided; art deco fireplace. **Cons:** not on the beach side of Collins Avenue. $⑤ Rooms from: $187 ✉ 3900 Collins Ave., Mid-Beach ☎ 305/538–4900, 877/824–7223 ⊕ www.circa39.com ⤴ 96 rooms |⦿| No meals ✛ E4.

$$$$
RESORT
Eden Roc Miami Beach. This grand 1950s hotel designed by Morris Lapidus retains its old glamour even after $230 million in renovations and expansions added sparkle to the rooms and grounds, renewing the allure and swagger of a stay at the Eden Roc. **Pros:** modern rooms; great pools; revival of Golden Age glamour. **Cons:** expensive parking; taxi needed to reach South Beach. $⑤ Rooms from: $469 ✉ 4525 Collins Ave., Mid-Beach ☎ 305/531–0000, 800/327–8337 ⊕ www. edenrocmiami.com ⤴ 535 rooms, 92 suites |⦿| No meals ✛ E3.

$$$$
RESORT
FAMILY
Fontainebleau Miami Beach. Vegas meets art deco at this colossal classic, deemed Miami's biggest hotel after its $1 billion reinvention, which spawned more than 1,500 rooms (split among 658 suites in two new all-suite towers and 846 rooms in the two original buildings), 12 renowned restaurants and lounges, LIV nightclub, several sumptuous pools with cabana islands, a state-of-the-art fitness center, and a 40,000-square-foot spa. **Pros:** excellent restaurants; historic design mixed with all-new facilities; fabulous pools. **Cons:** away from the South Beach pedestrian scene; massive size; bizarre mix of guests. $⑤ Rooms from: $489 ✉ 4441 Collins Ave., Mid-Beach ☎ 305/538–2000, 800/548–8886 ⊕ www. fontainebleau.com ⤴ 846 rooms, 658 suites |⦿| No meals ✛ E3.

$$$
HOTEL
The Palms Hotel & Spa. If you're seeking an elegant, relaxed property away from the noise but still near South Beach, the Palms has an exceptional beach, an easy pace, and beautiful gardens with soaring palm trees and inviting hammocks; the rooms look as fabulous as the grounds, which include a 5,000-square-foot Aveda spa and a signature

farm-to-table restaurant, Essensia. **Pros:** tropical garden; relaxed and quiet. **Cons:** standard rooms do not have balconies (but suites do). $ *Rooms from: $359* ⊠ *3025 Collins Ave., Mid-Beach* ☎ *305/534–0505, 800/550–0505* ⊕ *www.thepalmshotel.com* ↝ *220 rooms, 22 suites* ⎮◯⎮ *No meals* ✛ *E4.*

$$$$
HOTEL
⬚ **Soho Beach House.** The Soho Beach House is a throwback to swanky vibes of bygone decades, bedazzled in faded color palates, maritime ambience, and circa-1930s avant-garde furnishings, luring A-listers and wannabes to indulge in the amenity-clad, retro-chic rooms as long as they follow stringent "house rules" (no photos, no mobile phones, no suits, and 1 guest only). **Pros:** trendy; two pools; fabulous restaurant; full spa. **Cons:** members have priority for rooms; lots of pretentious patrons; house rules are a bit much. $ *Rooms from: $495* ⊠ *4385 Collins Ave., Mid-Beach* ☎ *786/507–7900* ⊕ *www.sohobeachhouse. com* ↝ *55 rooms* ⎮◯⎮ *No meals* ✛ *E3.*

FISHER AND BELLE ISLANDS

$$$$
RESORT
⬚ **The Resort at Fisher Island Club.** An exclusive private island, just south of Miami Beach but accessible only by ferry, Fisher Island houses an upscale residential community that includes a small inventory of overnight accommodations, including opulent cottages, villas, and junior suites, which surround the island's original 1920s-era Vanderbilt mansion. **Pros:** great private beaches; never crowded; varied on-island dining choices. **Cons:** ferry ride to get on and off island; limited cell service. $ *Rooms from: $1037* ⊠ *1 Fisher Island Dr., Fisher Island* ☎ *305/535–6000, 800/537–3708* ⊕ *www.fisherislandclub.com* ↝ *50 condo units, 7 villas, 3 cottages* ⎮◯⎮ *No meals* ✛ *E5.*

$$
RESORT
⬚ **The Standard Miami Beach.** An extension of André Balazs's trendy and hip yet budget-conscious hotel chain, the shabby-chic Standard is a mile from South Beach on an island just over the Venetian Causeway and boasts one of South Florida's most renowned spas and hottest pool scenes. **Pros:** free bike and kayak rentals; swank pool scene; great spa; inexpensive. **Cons:** slight trek to South Beach; small rooms with no views. $ *Rooms from: $299* ⊠ *40 Island Ave., Belle Isle* ☎ *305/673–1717* ⊕ *www.standardhotel.com* ↝ *104 rooms, 1 suite* ⎮◯⎮ *No meals* ✛ *E4.*

NORTH BEACH AND AVENTURA

$$$$
RESORT
FAMILY
Fodor's Choice
★
⬚ **Acqualina Resort & Spa on the Beach.** Acqualina raises the bar on Miami beachfront luxury, delivering a fantasy of Mediterranean opulence, with oceanfront lawns and pools that evoke Vizcaya. **Pros:** excellent beach; in-room check-in; luxury amenities; huge spa. **Cons:** no nightlife near hotel; hotel's towering height shades the beach by early afternoon. $ *Rooms from: $625* ⊠ *17875 Collins Ave., Sunny Isles* ☎ *305/918–8000* ⊕ *www.acqualinaresort.com* ↝ *54 rooms, 43 suites* ⎮◯⎮ *No meals* ✛ *E1.*

$$$$
RESORT
⬚ **ONE Bal Harbour.** In one of South Florida's poshest neighborhoods, ONE Bal Harbour exudes contemporary beachfront luxury design with decadent mahogany-floor guest rooms featuring large terraces with

panoramic views of the water and city, over-the-top bathrooms with 10-foot floor-to-ceiling windows, and LCD TVs built into the bathroom mirrors. **Pros:** proximity to Bal Harbour Shops; beachfront; great contemporary-art collection. **Cons:** narrow beach is a bit disappointing; far from nightlife. ⑤ *Rooms from: $759* ✉ *10295 Collins Ave., North Beach and Aventura, Bal Harbour* ☎ *305/455–5400* ⊕ *www. onebalharbourresort.com* ⇆ *124 rooms, 63 suites* ◉ *No meals* ✛ *E2.*

$$$$ 🏨 **St. Regis Bal Harbour Resort.** When this $1 billion–plus resort opened in
RESORT 2012, Miami's North Beach entered a new era of glamour and haute liv-
Fodor'sChoice ing, with A-list big spenders rushing to stay in this 27-story, 243-room,
★ triple-glass-tower masterpiece. **Pros:** beachfront; beyond glamorous; large rooms. **Cons:** limited lounge space around main pool; limited privacy on balconies. ⑤ *Rooms from: $679* ✉ *9703 Collins Ave., North Beach and Aventura, Bal Harbour* ☎ *305/993–3300* ⊕ *www. stregisbalharbour.com* ⇆ *190 rooms, 53 suites* ◉ *No meals* ✛ *E2.*

$$$$ 🏨 **Turnberry Isle Miami.** Golfers and families favor this service-oriented
RESORT 300-acre tropical resort with jumbo-size rooms and world-class ameni-
FAMILY ties, including a majestic lagoon pool (winding waterslide and lazy river included), an acclaimed three-story spa and fitness center, and celeb chef Michael Mina's Bourbon Steak restaurant. **Pros:** great golf, pools, and restaurants; free shuttle to Aventura Mall; situated between Miami and Fort Lauderdale. **Cons:** not on the beach; no nightlife. ⑤ *Rooms from: $459* ✉ *19999 W. Country Club Dr., North Beach and Aventura* ☎ *305/932–6200, 866/612–7739* ⊕ *www.turnberryislemiami.com* ⇆ *408 rooms, 29 suites* ◉ *No meals* ✛ *E1.*

NIGHTLIFE

One of Greater Miami's most popular pursuits is bar hopping. Bars range from intimate enclaves to showy see-and-be-seen lounges to loud, raucous frat parties. There's a New York–style flair to some of the newer lounges, which are increasingly catering to the Manhattan party crowd who escape to South Beach for long weekends. No doubt, Miami's pulse pounds with nonstop nightlife that reflects the area's potent cultural mix. On sultry, humid nights with the huge full moon rising out of the ocean and fragrant night-blooming jasmine intoxicating the senses, who can resist Cuban salsa with some disco and hip-hop thrown in for good measure? When this place throws a party, hips shake, fingers snap, bodies touch. It's no wonder many clubs are still rocking at 5 am. If you're looking for a relatively nonfrenetic evening, your best bet is one of the chic hotel bars on Collins Avenue.

The *Miami Herald* (⊕ *www.miamiherald.com*) is a good source for information on what to do in town. The Weekend section of the newspaper, included in the Friday edition, has an annotated guide to everything from plays and galleries to concerts and nightclubs. The "Ticket" column details the week's entertainment highlights. Or you can pick up the *Miami New Times* (⊕ *www.miaminewtimes.com*), the city's largest free alternative newspaper, published each Thursday. It lists nightclubs, concerts, and special events; reviews plays and movies; and provides in-depth coverage of the local music scene. *MIAMI* (⊕ *www.*

modernluxury.com/miami) and *Ocean Drive* (⊕ *www.oceandrive. com*), Miami's model-strewn, upscale fashion and lifestyle magazines, squeeze club, bar, restaurant, and events listings in with fashion spreads, reviews, and personality profiles. Paparazzi photos of local party people and celebrities give you a taste of Greater Miami nightlife before you even dress up to paint the town.

The Spanish-language *El Nuevo Herald* (⊕ *www.elnuevoherald.com*), published by the *Miami Herald,* has extensive information on Spanish-language arts and entertainment, including dining reviews, concert previews, and nightclub highlights.

DOWNTOWN

BARS AND LOUNGES

Fodor's Choice ★ **Blackbird Ordinary.** This local watering hole has been around since 2011, but it's now trendier than ever. With a vibe that's a bit speakeasy, a bit dive bar, a bit hipster hangout, and a bit Miami sophisticate, it's hands-down one of the coolest places in the city and clearly appeals to a wide range of demographics. Mixology is a huge part of the Blackbird experience—so be prepared for some awesome artisanal cocktails. There's something going on every night of the week, and the stylish outdoor space is great for cocktails under the stars, movie screenings, and live music. ⊠ *729 S.W. 1st Ave., Downtown* ☎ *305/671–3307* ⊕ *www. blackbirdordinary.com.*

Hyde AAA. The Miami outpost of the wildly popular Hyde Lounge is situated within the AmericanAirlines Arena (AAA) for use before/during/after Miami Heat games and arena concerts. The 250-person venue debuted during the Heat's 2012–13 season and quickly became a Miami institution. Located court-level on the south end of the arena, Hyde AAA provides a full-blown, big pimpin' dining, lounge, and nightlife experience that's often better than the event happening in the arena itself. ⊠ *AmericanAirlines Arena, 601 Biscayne Blvd., Downtown* ☎ *855/777–4933* ⊕ *www.hydeaaarena.com.*

Fodor's Choice ★ **Tobacco Road.** Opened in 1912, this classic holds Miami's oldest liquor license: No. 0001. Upstairs, in a space that was occupied by a speakeasy during Prohibition, local and national blues bands perform nightly. There is excellent bar food, a dinner menu, and a selection of single-malt scotches, bourbons, and cigars. This is the hangout of grizzled journalists, bohemians en route to or from nowhere, and club kids seeking a way station before the real parties begin. Live blues, R&B, and jazz bands are on tap, along with food and drink, seven days a week. If you like your food and drink the way you like your blues—gritty, honest, and unassuming—then this vintage joint will quickly earn your respect. ⊠ *626 S. Miami Ave., Downtown* ☎ *305/374–1198* ⊕ *www. tobacco-road.com.*

DANCE CLUBS

Club Space. Want 24-hour partying? Here's the place. Space revolutionized the Miami party scene over a decade ago and still gets accolades as one of the country's best dance clubs. But depending on the month,

Cars whizz by Avalon hotel and other art deco architecture on Ocean Drive, Miami South Beach.

Space wavers between trendy and empty, so make sure you get the up-to-date scoop from your hotel concierge. Created from four downtown warehouses, it has two levels (one blasts house music; the other reverberates with hip-hop), an outdoor patio, a New York–style industrial look, and a 24-hour liquor license. It's open on weekends only, and you'll need to look good to be allowed past the velvet ropes. Note that the crowd can sometimes be sketchy, and take caution walking around the surrounding neighborhood. ⊠ *34 N.E. 11th St., Downtown* ☎ *305/375–0001* ⊕ *www.clubspace.com.*

WYNWOOD

BARS AND LOUNGES

Fodor's Choice ★ **Cafeina Wynwood Lounge.** This awesome Wynwood watering hole takes center stage during the highly social Gallery Night and Artwalk through the Wynwood Art District, the second Saturday of every month, which showcases the cool and hip art galleries between Northwest 20th and Northwest 36 streets west of North Miami Avenue. For those in the know, the evening either begins or ends at Cafeina, a seductive, design-driven lounge with a gorgeous patio and plenty of art on display. Other weekends, this is still a great place to hang out and get a true feel for Miami's cultural revolution. Open only Thursday–Saturday. ⊠ *297 N.W. 23rd St., Wynwood* ☎ *305/438–0792* ⊕ *www.cafeinamiami.com; www.wynwoodartwalk.com.*

SOUTH BEACH

BARS AND LOUNGES

Blues Bar at National Hotel. Dedicate at least one night of your Miami vacation to an art deco pub crawl, patronizing the hotel bars and lounges of South Beach's most iconic buildings, including the National Hotel. Though it's a low-key affair, the nifty wooden Blues Bar here is well worth a stop. The bar is one of many elements original to the 1939 building that give it such a sense of its era that you'd expect to see Ginger Rogers and Fred Astaire hoofing it along the polished terrazzo floor. The adjoining Martini Room has a great collection of cigars, old airline stickers, and vintage Bacardi ads on the walls, but it's only available for private events. ⊠ *National Hotel, 1677 Collins Ave., South Beach* ☎ *305/532–2311* ⊕ *www.nationalhotel.com.*

Fodor's Choice **FDR at the Delano.** The Delano's famous Florida Room was reinvented
★ and reopened in spring 2012 as FDR, an überexclusive subterranean lounge, developed by Las Vegas's Light Group. The world's hottest DJs are on tap for a stylish see-and-be-seen crowd. Seductive lighting illuminates the two-room, 200 person watering hole, decked out in dark and sexy décor. Bottle service is available for high rollers. ⊠ *1685 Collins Ave., South Beach* ☎ *305/672–2000* ⊕ *www.delano-hotel.com.*

Lost Weekend. Slumming celebs and locals often patronize this pool hall–resto–dive bar on quaint Española Way. The hardcore locals are serious about their pastime, so it can be challenging to get a table on weekends. However, everyone can enjoy the pinball machines, the grub, and the full bar, which has 150 kinds of beer (a dozen of which are on tap). Each night, Lost Weekend draws an eclectic crowd, from yuppies to drag queens to celebs on the down-low. So South Beach! ⊠ *218 Española Way, South Beach* ☎ *305/672–1707.*

MOVA. Formerly known as Halo Lounge, this gay bar and lounge off of Lincoln Road is where most LGBT South Beach nights begin (and some end), with ample eye candy to whet the palate for a scintillating night of drinking and partying. The minimalist lounge gives off an undeniably sexy vibe, augmented by the handsome bartenders muddling fresh fruits for the ever-changing avant-garde drink menu. The place gets packed on Friday and Saturday; other nights are hit-or-miss. ⊠ *1625 Michigan Ave., South Beach* ☎ *305/534–8181* ⊕ *www.movalounge.com.*

Mynt Lounge. This is the quintessential celeb-studded, super-VIP, South Beach party where you may or may not be let in, depending on what you wear or who you know. It's the kind of place where back in the day LiLo would act out, Brit-Brit would chill out, and Paris Hilton would zone out, namely because of the club's "no paparazzi" policy. Admittedly, owner Romain Zago says that "Mynt is for the famous and fabulous." Every summer the lounge undergoes renovations to stay at the top of its game, revealing a slightly different look. ⊠ *1921 Collins Ave., South Beach* ☎ *305/532–0727* ⊕ *www.myntlounge.com.*

The Regent Cocktail Club. This classic cocktail bar recalls an intimate gentleman's club (and not the stripper kind) with strong masculine cocktails, dark furnishings, bartenders dressed to the nines, and the sounds

THE VELVET ROPES

How to get past the velvet ropes at the hottest South Beach nightspots? First, if you're staying at a hotel, use the concierge. Decide which clubs you want to check out (consult *Ocean Drive* magazine celebrity pages if you want to be among the glitterati), and the concierge will email, fax, or call in your names to the clubs so you'll be on the guest list when you arrive. This means much easier access and usually no cover charge (which can be upward of $20) if you arrive before midnight. Guest list or no guest list, follow these pointers: Make sure there are more women than men in your group. Dress up: casual chic is the dress code. For men this means no sneakers, no shorts,

no sleeveless vests, and no shirts unbuttoned past the top button. For women, provocative and seductive is fine; overly revealing is not. Black is always right. At the door: don't name-drop—no one takes it seriously. Don't be pushy while trying to get the doorman's attention. Wait until you make eye contact, then be cool and easygoing. If you decide to tip him (which most bouncers don't expect), be discreet and pleasant, not big-bucks obnoxious—a $10 or $20 bill quietly passed will be appreciated, however. With the right dress and the right attitude, you'll be on the dance floor rubbing shoulders with South Beach's finest clubbers in no time.

of jazz legends in the background. The intimate space exudes elegance and timelessness. It's a welcome respite from South Beach's predictable nightlife scene. Cocktails—each with bespoke ice cubes—change daily and are posted on the house blackboard. ⊠ *Gale South Beach, 1690 Collins Ave., South Beach* ☎ *305/673–0199* ⊕ *www.galehotel. com/nightlife.*

Rose Bar at the Delano. Tucked away inside the chic Delano hotel, the Rose Bar is a South Beach mainstay and an essential stop on any South Beach bar crawl. Now managed by Las Vegas's The Light Group, the Rose Bar mixes classic art deco architecture with the best in mixology (and a bit of Vegas bling). The bar pushes the envelope on creative cocktails. ⊠ *Delano Hotel, 1685 Collins Ave., South Beach* ☎ *305/672–2000* ⊕ *www.delano-hotel.com.*

Fodor's Choice ★ **Skybar at the Shore Club.** An entire enclave dedicated to alcohol-induced fun for grown-ups, the Skybar is actually a collection of adjoining lounges at the Shore Club, including a chic outdoor lounge, the indoor Red Room, and the areas in between, which teem with party-hungry visitors. Splendor-in-the-garden is the theme in the outdoor lounge, accessorized with daybeds and glowing Moroccan lanterns. Groove to dance music in the Red Room or have a cocktail (or five) stargazing on the daybeds with your new best friends. ⊠ *Shore Club Hotel, 1901 Collins Ave., South Beach* ☎ *305/695–3100* ⊕ *www.shoreclub.com.*

DANCE CLUBS

Cameo. One of Miami's longest-running dance clubs, Cameo is constantly reinventing itself, but the result always seems to be the same— long lines filled with everyone claiming to be on the guest list, hoochie mamas wearing far too little clothing, and some unsuspecting tourists trying to see what all the fuss is about. The combination makes for some insane partying, especially if the night is headlined by an all-star DJ. You'll find both plentiful dance space and plush VIP lounges. If you can brave the velvet rope, the thuggish crowd, and the nonsense described above, Saturday-night parties are the best. ✉ *1445 Washington Ave., South Beach* ☎ *786/235–5800* ⊕ *www.cameomiami.com.*

Nikki Beach Club. Smack-dab on the beach, the full-service Nikki Beach Club was once upon a time a favorite of SoBe's pretty people and celebrities. Nowadays, it's filled with more suburbanites than the "in" crowd. Nikki's late-night parties are reserved for Sundays only. Other days, the Beach Club is open from 11 to 11 (except Monday and Tuesday when it closes at 6). Visitors can eat at the Nikki Beach Restaurant, and get their food and drink on in the tepees, hammocks, and beach beds (expect rental fees). Sunday brunch at the club's restaurant is pretty spectacular. ✉ *1 Ocean Dr., South Beach* ☎ *305/538–1111* ⊕ *www.nikkibeach.com/miami.*

Fodor's Choice ★   **The Rec Room.** Entering The Rec Room is like stumbling upon an awesome basement party that just happens to be packed with the hottest people ever. This underground space of the Gale Hotel pays homage to everything 1977 (memorabilia included) and features a collection of over 3,000 vinyl records at the disposal of resident DJs. The vibe is totally speakeasy meets modern day. The easy-on-the-eyes crowd lets loose, free of inhibitions, jamming out to old-school hip-hop and eighties and nineties throwbacks. ✉ *Gale South Beach, 1690 Collins Ave., South Beach* ☎ *305/673–0199* ⊕ *www.galehotel.com/nightlife.*

Score. Since the nineties, Score has been the see-and-be-seen HQ of Miami's gay community, with plenty of global hotties coming from near and far to show off their designer threads and six-pack abs. After moving in 2013 to Washington Avenue from its long-time Lincoln Road location, this South Beach powerhouse shows no signs of slowing down. DJs spin five nights a week, but Planeta Macho Latin Tuesday is exceptionally popular, as are the weekend dance-offs—Filthy Gorgeous Fridays and Bigger Saturdays. Dress to impress (and then be ready to go shirtless). ✉ *1437 Washington Ave., South Beach* ☎ *305/535–1111* ⊕ *www.scorebar.net* ⊗ *Closed Mon. and Wed.*

Twist. Twist is a gay institution in South Beach, having been the late-night go-to place for decades, filling to capacity around 2 am after the beach's fly-by-night bars and more established lounges begin to die down (though it's in fact open daily from 1 pm to 5 am). There's never a cover here—not even on holidays or during gay pride events. The dark club has several rooms spread over two levels and patios, pumping out different tunes and attracting completely disparate groups. It's not uncommon to have young college boys partying to Top 40 in one room and strippers showing off their stuff to the straight girls in another area, while an all-out hip-hop throwdown is taking place upstairs. ✉ *1057 Washington Ave., South Beach* ☎ *305/538–9478* ⊕ *www.twistsobe.com.*

LIVE MUSIC

Jazid. If you're looking for an unpretentious alternative to the velvet-rope nightclubs, this unassuming, live-music hot spot is a standout on the SoBe strip. Eight-piece bands play danceable Latin rhythms, as well as reggae, hip-hop, and fusion sounds. Each night caters to a different genre. Get ready for a late night though, as bands are just getting started at 11 pm. Call ahead to reserve a table. ✉ *1342 Washington Ave., South Beach* ☎ *305/673–9372* ⊕ *www.jazid.net.*

MID-BEACH

DANCE CLUBS

Fodor's Choice
★ **LIV Nightclub.** Since its 2009 opening, the Fontainebleau's LIV Nightclub has garnered plenty of global attention. It's not hard to see why—if you can get in, that is (LIV is notorious for lengthy lines, so don't arrive fashionably late). Past the velvet ropes, the dance palladium impresses with its lavish décor, well-dressed international crowd, sensational light-and-sound system, and seductive bilevel club experience. Sometimes the lobby bar, filled with LIV's overflow (and rejects), is just as fun as the club itself. ■ **TIP→ Men beware: Groups of guys entering LIV are often coerced into insanely priced bottle service.** ✉ *Fontainebleau Miami Beach, 4441 Collins Ave., Mid-Beach* ☎ *305/674–4680* ⊕ *www. livnightclub.com.*

SHOPPING

Beyond its fun-in-the-sun offerings, Miami has evolved into a world-class shopping destination. People fly to Miami from all over the world just to shop. The city teems with sophisticated shopping malls—from multistory, indoor climate-controlled temples of consumerism to sun-kissed, open-air retail enclaves—and bustling avenues and streets, lined at once with affordable chain stores, haute couture boutiques, and one-off, "only in Miami"–type shops.

Miami's shopping centers are record breakers. Several chain stores in the massive Aventura Mall bank as the best-selling outposts in the country, while Bal Harbour Shops flaunt the most lucrative square footage of any shopping arena in the country, with its sales reaching up to $2,555 per square foot.

Following the incredible success of the Bal Harbour Shops in the highest of the high-end market (think Chanel, Alexander McQueen, ETRO, and Hermès), the Design District has followed suit. Beyond fabulous designer furniture showrooms, the district's tenants now include Dior Homme, Rolex, and Prada. In addition, an entire LVMH mall is currently under construction to create more upscale retail space.

If you're from a region ripe with the climate-controlled slickness of shopping malls and food-court "meals," you'll love the choices in Miami. Head out into the sunshine and shop the city streets, where you'll find big-name retailers and local boutiques alike. Take a break at a sidewalk café to power up on some Cuban coffee or fresh-squeezed OJ and enjoy the tropical breezes.

Beyond clothiers and big-name retailers, Greater Miami has all manner of merchandise to tempt even the casual browser. For consumers on a mission to find certain items—art-deco antiques or cigars, for instance—the city streets burst with a rewarding collection of specialty shops.

Stroll through Spanish-speaking neighborhoods where shops sell clothing, cigars, and other goods from all over Latin America or even head to Little Haiti for rare vinyl records.

COCONUT GROVE

MALLS

CocoWalk. This three-story indoor-outdoor mall has three floors of nearly 40 shops that stay open almost as late as its popular restaurants. Typically 1990s chain stores like Victoria's Secret and Gap blend with a few specialty shops like Guayabera World; the space mixes the bustle of a mall with the breathability of an open-air market. Touristy kiosks with cigars, beads, incense, herbs, and other small items are scattered around the ground level, and commercial restaurants and nightlife (Cheesecake Factory, Fat Tuesday, and Paragon Grove 13—a multiscreen, state-of-the-art movie theater with a wine bar and lounge) line the upstairs perimeter. Hanging out and people-watching is something of a pastime here for Miami suburbanites. ⊠ *3015 Grand Ave., Coconut Grove* ☎ *305/444–0777* ⊕ *www.cocowalk.net.*

OUTDOOR MARKETS

Coconut Grove Organic Farmers' Market. This pricey, outdoor organic market is a Saturday ritual for Coconut Grove locals. It specializes in a mouthwatering array of local produce as well as such ready-to-eat, raw vegan goodies as cashew butter, homemade salad dressings, and fruit pies. If you are looking for a downright granola crowd and experience, pack your Birkenstocks, because this is it. It's open Saturday from 10 to 7, rain or shine. ⊠ *3300 Grand Ave., Coconut Grove* ☎ *305/238–7747* ⊕ *www.glaserorganicfarms.com.*

ANTIQUES

Worth Galleries. Find an enormous selection of fine European antiques as well as large and eclectic items—railroad crossing signs, statues, English roadsters. This gallery possesses South Florida's largest collection of antique books and antique chandeliers. There's also vintage furniture, modern art, oil paintings, and silverware, all in a cluttered setting that makes shopping an adventure. ⊠ *2520 S.W. 28th La., Coconut Grove* ☎ *305/285–1330* ⊕ *www.worthgalleries.com.*

CORAL GABLES

MALLS

Village of Merrick Park. At this Mediterranean-style, trilevel, shopping-and-dining venue, Neiman Marcus and Nordstrom anchor 115 specialty shops. Designers such as ETRO, Jimmy Choo, Tiffany & Co., Burberry, CH Carolina Herrera, and Gucci fulfill most high-fashion needs, and haute-décor shopping options include Brazilian contemporary-furniture designer Artefacto. International food favorite C'est

Bon and pampering specialist Elemis Day-Spa offer further indulgences. ✉ *358 San Lorenzo Ave., Coral Gables* ☎ *305/529–0200* ⊕ *www.villageofmerrickpark.com.*

SHOPPING DISTRICTS

Miracle Mile. The centerpiece of the downtown Coral Gables shopping district, lined with trees and busy with strolling shoppers, is home to men's and women's boutiques, jewelry and home-furnishings stores, and a host of exclusive couturiers and bridal shops. Running from Douglas Road to LeJeune Road and Aragon Avenue to Andalusia Avenue, more than two dozen first-rate restaurants offer everything from French to Japanese-fusion cuisine, and art galleries and the Actors' Playhouse at the Miracle Theater give the area a cultural flair. ■ TIP➔ If debating Miracle Mile versus Bal Harbour or Lincoln Road or the Design District, check out the others first. ✉ *Miracle Mile (Coral Way), Douglas Rd. to LeJeune Rd., and Aragon Ave. to Andalusia Ave., Coral Gables* ⊕ *www.shopcoralgables.com.*

ANTIQUES

Alhambra Antiques. The collection of high-quality antique French furniture and decorative pieces are acquired on annual jaunts to France. Expect a wide range of classic chandeliers, clocks, chairs, daybeds, tables, and mirrors. While the showroom offers regular hours (Monday–Saturday noon–6), it's usually best to call ahead as many high-end Coral Gables shops prefer to open their stores by appointment only, rather than maintaining an open-door policy during their operating hours. ✉ *2850 Salzedo St., Coral Gables* ☎ *305/446–1688* ⊕ *www.alhambraantiques.com.*

BOOKS

FAMILY

Fodor's Choice ★

Books & Books, Inc. Long live the classic book store! Greater Miami's only independent, English-language bookshop, Books & Books, specializes in contemporary and classical literature as well as in books on the arts, architecture, Florida, and Cuba. The Coral Gables store is the largest of its three South Florida locations. Here, you can sip 'n' read in the courtyard lounge or dine at the old-fashioned in-store café while browsing the photography gallery. Multiple rooms are filled with myriad genres, making for a fabulous afternoon of book shopping—plus there's an entire area dedicated to kids. There are book signings, literary events, poetry, and other readings too. Two smaller locations on Lincoln Road in South Beach and at the Bal Harbour Shops also carry great reads. ✉ *265 Aragon Ave., Coral Gables* ☎ *305/442–4408* ⊕ *www.booksandbooks.com* ⊙ *Sun.–Thurs. 9 am–11 pm, Fri.–Sat. 9 am–midnight.*

CLOTHING

Koko & Palenki. Shoe shopaholics come here for the well-edited selection of trendy footwear by Alexandre Birman, Giuseppe Zanotti, Emilia Castillo, Rachel Zoe, Rebecca Minkoff, and others. Handbags and belts add to the selection. Clothing hails from designers like Catherine Malandrino, Issa, J Brand, and Citizens of Humanity. Koko & Palenki also has a store in Aventura Mall. ✉ *Village of Merrick Park, 342*

San Lorenzo Ave., Ste. 1090, Coral Gables ☎ *305/444–0626* ⊕ *www. kokopalenki.com.*

Silvia Tcherassi. The Colombian designer's signature boutique in the Village of Merrick Park features ready-to-wear, feminine, and frilly dresses and separates accented with chiffon, tuille, and sequins. A neighboring atelier at 4101 Ponce de Leon Boulevard showcases the designer's bridal collection. ⊠ *Village of Merrick Park, 350 San Lorenzo Ave., No. 2140, Coral Gables* ☎ *305/461–0009* ⊕ *www.silviatcherassi.com.*

JEWELRY

Beverlee Kagan. Specializing in vintage and antique jewelry, this jeweler showcases over 30,000 eclectic items, including art deco–era bangles, bracelets, and cuff links. ⊠ *5831 Sunset Dr., Coral Gables* ☎ *305/663– 1937* ⊕ *www.kaganjewelry.com.*

ONLY IN MIAMI

La Casa de las Guayaberas. This clothing shop sells custom-made Ramon Puig guayaberas, the natty four-pocket dress shirts favored by older Cuban men and hipsters alike. Ramon Puig is known as "the King of Guayaberas," and his shirts are top of the line as far as guayaberas go. Hundreds are available off the rack. There are styles for women, too. ⊠ *5840 S.W. 8th St., Coral Gables* ☎ *305/266–9683* ⊕ *www. ramonpuig.com.*

WYNWOOD

SHOPPING NEIGHBORHOODS

Fodor's Choice ★ **Miami Design District.** Miami is synonymous with good design, and this visitor-friendly shopping district—from Northeast 38th to Northeast 42nd Street, between North Miami Avenue and Northeast 2nd Avenue—is an unprecedented melding of public space and the exclusive world of design. There are more than 200 showrooms and galleries, including Baltus, Animadomus, Kartell, Ann Sacks, Poliform USA, and Luminaire Lab. Upscale retail outlets also grace the district. Cartier, En Avance, Louis Vuitton, Prada, Rolex and Scotch & Soda now neighbor the design showrooms. Meanwhile, restaurants like Michael's Genuine Food & Drink also make this trendy neighborhood a hip place to dine. Unlike most showrooms, which are typically the beat of decorators alone, the Miami Design District's showrooms are open to the public and occupy windowed, street-level spaces. Although in some cases you'll need a decorator to secure your purchases, browsers are encouraged to consider for themselves the array of rather exclusive furnishings, decorative objects, antiques, and art. ⊠ *N.E. 2nd Ave. and N.E. 40th St., Miami Design District* ⊕ *www.miamidesigndistrict.net.*

CLOTHING

Fly Boutique. After 13 years on South Beach, Fly Boutique has found its new home in Miami's up and coming MIMO district, north of the Design District. This resale boutique is where Miami hipsters flock for the latest arrival of used clothing. Eighties glam designer pieces fly out at a premium price, but vintage camisoles and Levi's corduroys are still a resale deal. You'll find supercool art, furniture, luggage, and collectibles throughout the boutique. And be sure to look up—the eclectic lanterns are also for sale. ⊠ *7235 Biscayne Blvd., Design District* ☎ *305/604–8508* ⊕ *www.flyboutiquevintage.com.*

ONLY IN MIAMI

ABC Costume Shop. ABC Costume Shop is a major costume source for TV, movie, and theatrical performances. Open to the public, it has over 30,000 costumes in stock—outfits range from Venetian kings and queens to Tarzan and Jane. Hundreds of these costumes and accessories, such as wigs, masks, gloves, tights, and makeup, are available to buy off the rack; others are available to rent. ⊠ *575 N.W. 24th St., Wynwood* ☎ *305/573–5657* ⊕ *www.abccostumeshop.com* ☽ *Closed Sat. in July and Aug.*

FAMILY **Genius Jones.** This is a modern design store for kids and parents. It's the best—and one of the few—places to buy unique children's gifts in Miami. Pick up furniture, strollers, clothing, home accessories, and playthings, including classic wooden toys, vintage-rock T-shirts by Claude and Trunk, and toys designed by Takashi Murakami and Keith Haring. ⊠ *2800 NE 2nd Ave., Wynwood* ☎ *305/571–2000* ⊕ *www.geniusjones.com.*

LITTLE HAITI

MUSIC

Sweat Records. Though Little Haiti's shopping "scene" is mostly botanicas and voodoo supply shops, one of its most popular residents is Sweat Records, a record store with Miami's biggest selection of new LPs; there's also a vegan, organic coffee shop. Sweat sells a wide range of music—rock, pop, punk, electronic, hip-hop, and Latino—as well as turntables and vinyl accessories. ⊠ *5505 N.E. 2nd Ave., Little Haiti* ☎ *786/693–9309* ⊕ *www.sweatrecordsmiami.com.*

LITTLE HAVANA

ONLY IN MIAMI

FAMILY **La Casa de los Trucos (The House of Costumes).** This popular costume store first opened in Cuba in the 1920s; the exiled owners reopened it here in the 1970s. They have cartoon costumes, rockstar costumes, pet costumes, couples costumes, you name it. If you come any time near Halloween, expect to stand in line just to enter the tiny store. Wooden, life-size costume cut-outs in the parking lot make for great photo ops. ⊠ *1343 S.W. 8th St., Little Havana* ☎ *305/858–5029* ⊕ *www.crazyforcostumes.com.*

Lily's Records. The last of a dying breed, Lily's Records sells old-fashioned CDs and records, specializing in hard-to-get beats from across Latin America. The store is divided into sounds from various countries/regions, including (but not limited to) Puerto Rico, Mexico, Argentina, and Dominican Republic. ⊠ *1419 S.W. 8th St., Little Havana* ☎ *305/856–0536* ⊕ *www.lilysrecords.com.*

CIGARS

Sosa Family Cigars. Sosa offers a wide selection of premium and house cigars from around the world. It's one of the only cigar shops in Little Havana where you can sit and play dominoes while smoking stogies. There's a selection of wines for purchase, too. Humidors and other accessories are also available. ⊠ *3475 S.W. 8th St., Little Havana* ☎ *305/446–2606.*

SOUTH BEACH

SHOPPING DISTRICTS

Fodor'sChoice ★ **Collins Avenue.** Give your plastic a workout in South Beach shopping at the many high-profile tenants on this densely packed stretch of Collins between 5th and 10th streets, with stores like Steve Madden, Club Monaco, MAC Cosmetics, Ralph Lauren, Kenneth Cole, and Intermix. Sprinkled among the upscale vendors are hair salons, spas, cafés, and such familiar stores as the Gap and Urban Outfitters. Be sure to head over one street east to Ocean Drive or west to Washington Avenue for a drink or a light bite, or go for more retail therapy on Lincoln Road. ⊠ *Collins Ave. between 5th and 10th Sts., South Beach* ⊕ *www.lincolnroadmall.com/shopping/collins-avenue.*

Lincoln Road Mall. The eight-block-long pedestrian mall is the trendiest place on Miami Beach. Home to more than 150 shops, 20-plus art galleries and nightclubs, about 50 restaurants and cafés, and the renovated Colony Theatre, Lincoln Road, between Alton Road and Washington Avenue, is like the larger, more sophisticated cousin of Ocean Drive. The see-and-be-seen theme is furthered by outdoor seating at every restaurant, where tourists and locals lounge and discuss the people (and pet) parade passing by. An 18-screen movie theater anchors the west end of the street, which is where most of the worthwhile shops are; the far east end is mostly discount and electronics shops. Due to higher rents, you are more likely to see big corporate stores like American Eagles Outfitters, H&M, and Victoria's Secret than original boutiques. However, a few emporiums and stores with unique personalities, like Chroma, Base, and Books & Books, remain. ⊠ *Lincoln Rd. between Alton Rd. and Washington Ave., South Beach* ⊕ *www.lincolnroadmall.com.*

CLOTHING

Base. This is the quintessential South Beach fun-and-funky boutique experience. Stop here for men's eclectic clothing, shoes, jewelry, and accessories that mix Japanese design with Caribbean-inspired materials. Constantly evolving, this shop features an intriguing magazine section, a record section, groovy home accessories, and the latest in men's swimwear and sunglasses. The often-present house-label designer may help select your wardrobe's newest addition. The boutique has small outposts in the Delano Hotel and the Mondrian South Beach, as well as an haute vending machine in the latter. ⊠ *939 Lincoln Rd., South Beach* ☎ *305/531–4982* ⊕ *www.baseworld.com.*

Intermix. This modern New York–based boutique has the variety of a department store. You'll find fancy dresses, stylish shoes, slinky accessories, and trendy looks by sassy and somewhat pricey designers like

Chloé, Stella McCartney, Marc Jacobs, Moschino, and Diane von Furstenberg. There is a branch at the Bal Harbour Shops at 9700 Collins Avenue in North Beach and Aventura. ✉ *634 Collins Ave., South Beach* ☎ *305/531–5950* ⊕ *www.intermixonline.com.*

ONLY IN MIAMI

Fodor'sChoice **Dog Bar.** Just north of Lincoln Road's main drag, this over-the-top pet
★ boutique caters to enthusiastic animal owners with a variety of unique items for the super-pampered pet. From luxurious pet sofas imported from Italy to bling-bling-studded collars to chic poopy-bag holders, Miami's "original pet boutique" carries pretty much every pet accessory imaginable. They also have plenty of gourmet food and treats as well as a wide variety of fancy toys for dogs, large and small. ✉ *1684 Jefferson Ave., South Beach* ☎ *305/532–5654* ⊕ *www.dogbar.com.*

Fodor'sChoice **The Webster Miami.** Occupying an entire circa-1939 art deco building, the
★ Webster is a trilevel, 20,000-square-foot, one-stop shop for fashionistas. This retail sanctuary carries ready-to-wear fashions by more than 100 top designers, plus in-store exclusive shirts, candles, books, and random trendy items you might need for your South Beach experience—a kind of haute Urban Outfitters for grown-ups. Too many choices? Sit down for a café au lait and pastry at the first U.S. outpost of Paris-based patisserie-chocolatier Hugo & Victor, located inside the store. ✉ *1220 Collins Ave., South Beach* ☎ *305/674–7899* ⊕ *www.thewebstermiami.com.*

OUTDOOR MARKETS

Lincoln Road Farmers' Market. With all the familiar trappings of a farmers market (except for farmers—most of the people selling veggies appear to be resellers), this is a weekly South Beach Sunday (9–6:30) ritual. It brings local produce and bakery vendors to Lincoln Road and often features plant workshops, art sales, and children's activities. This is a good place to pick up live orchids, too. ✉ *Lincoln Rd. between Meridian and Washington Aves., South Beach* ☎ *305/531–0038* ⊕ *www. themarketcompany.org.*

VINTAGE CLOTHING

Consign of the Times. Come to this shop for vintage and consignment items by top designers at pre-owned prices, including Chanel suits, Fendi bags, and Celine and Prada treasures. ✉ *1635 Jefferson Ave., South Beach* ☎ *305/535–0811* ⊕ *www.consignofthetimes.com.*

NORTH BEACH AND AVENTURA

MALLS

Fodor'sChoice **Aventura Mall.** This three-story megamall offers the ultimate in South
★ Florida retail therapy. Aventura houses many global top performers such as the most lucrative Abercrombie & Fitch in the United States, a supersize Nordstrom and Bloomingdale's, and 300 other shops like Façonnable, Dior, and Braccialini, which together create the fifth-largest mall in the United States. This is the one-stop, shop-'til-you-drop retail Mecca for locals, out-of-towners, and—frequently—celebrities. ✉ *19501 Biscayne Blvd., North Beach and Aventura* ☎ *305/935–1110* ⊕ *www.aventuramall.com.*

Fodor'sChoice   **Bal Harbour Shops.** Beverly Hills meets the South Florida sun at this
★   swank collection of 100 high-end shops, boutiques, and department
        stores, which include such names as Alexander McQueen, Gucci, Her-
        mès, Salvatore Ferragamo, Tiffany & Co., and Valentino. Many Euro-
        pean designers open their first North American signature store at this
        outdoor, pedestrian-friendly mall, and many American designers open
        their first boutique outside of New York here. Restaurants and cafés, in
        tropical garden settings, overflow with style-conscious diners. People-
        watching on the terrace of the Japenese restaurant Makoto is the best
        in town. The ambience is oh-so Rodeo Drive. ✉ *9700 Collins Ave.,*
        Bal Harbour, North Beach and Aventura ☎ *305/866–0311* ⊕ *www.*
        balharbourshops.com.

JEWELRY

MIA Jewels. This jewelry and accessories boutique is known for its colorful, gem- and bead-laden, gold and silver earrings, necklaces, bracelets,
and brooches by lines such as Cousin Claudine, Amrita, and Alexis
Bittar. This is a shoo-in store for everyone: you'll find things for trend
lovers (gold-studded chunky Lucite bangles), classicists (long, colorful,
wraparound beaded necklaces), and ice lovers (long Swarovski crystal
cabin necklaces) alike. ✉ *Aventura Mall, 19575 Biscayne Blvd., North*
Beach and Aventura ☎ *305/931–2000.*

SPORTS AND THE OUTDOORS

Sun, sand, and crystal-clear water mixed with an almost nonexistent
winter and a cosmopolitan clientele make Miami and Miami Beach
ideal for year-round sunbathing and outdoor activities. Whether the
priority is showing off a toned body, jumping on a Jet Ski, or relaxing
in a tranquil natural environment, there's a beach tailor-made to please.
But tanning and water sports are only part of this sun-drenched picture.
Greater Miami has championship golf courses and tennis courts, miles
of bike trails along placid canals and through subtropical forests, and
skater-friendly concrete paths amidst the urban jungle. For those who
like their sports of the spectator variety, the city offers up a bonanza
of pro teams for every season. There's even a crazy ball-flinging game
called jai alai that's billed as the fastest sport on earth.

In addition to contacting venues directly, get tickets to major events
from **Ticketmaster** (☎ *800/745–3000* ⊕ *www.ticketmaster.com*).

BASEBALL

FAMILY   **Miami Marlins.** Miami's baseball team, formerly known as the Florida
        Marlins, moved into a new home in 2012: Marlins Park—a 37,442-
        seat retractable-roof, air-conditioned baseball stadium on the grounds
        of Miami's famous Orange Bowl. Go see the team that came out of
        nowhere to beat the New York Yankees and win the 2003 World Series.
        Home games are April through early October. ✉ *Marlins Park, 501*
        N.W. 16 Ave., Little Havana ☎ *305/480–1300, 877/627–5467 for tick-*
        ets ⊕ *www.miami.marlins.mlb.com* ⌨ *$10–$395; parking from $20*
        and should be pre-purchased online.

Continued on page 110

A STROLL DOWN

DECO LANE

by Susan MacCallum Whitcomb

"It was an age of miracles, it was an age of art,

it was an age of excess, and it was an age of satire."

—F. Scott Fitzgerald, *Echoes of the Jazz Age*

The 1920s and '30s brought us flappers and gangsters, plunging stock prices and soaring skyscrapers, and plenty of headline-worthy news from the arts scene, from talking pictures and the jazz craze to fashions where pearls piled on and sequins dazzled. These decades between the two world wars also gave us an art style reflective of the changing times: art deco.

Distinguished by geometrical shapes and the use of industrial motifs that fused the decorative arts with modern technology, art deco became the architectural style of choice for train stations and big buildings across the country (think New york's Radio City Music Hall and Empire State Building).

Using a steel-and-concrete box as the foundation, architects dipped into art deco's grab bag of accessories, initially decorating facades with spheres, cylinders, and cubes. They later borrowed increasingly from industrial design, stripping elements used in ocean liners and automobiles to their streamlined essentials.

The style was also used in jewelry, furniture, textiles, and advertising. The fact that it employed inexpensive materials, such as stucco or terrazzo, helped art deco thrive during the Great Depression.

MIAMI BEACH'S ART DECO DISTRICT

With its warm beaches and tropical surroundings, Miami Beach in the early 20th century was establishing itself as America's winter playground. During the roaring '20s luxurious hostelries resembling Venetian palaces, Spanish villages, and French châteaux sprouted up. In the 1930s, middle-class tourists started coming, and more hotels had to be built. Designers like Henry Hohauser chose art deco for its affordable yet distinctive design.

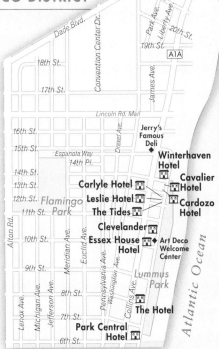

An antidote to the gloom of the Great Depression, the look was cheerful and tidy. And with the whimsical additions of portholes, colorful racing bands, and images of rolling ocean waves painted or etched on the walls, these South Beach properties created an oceanfront fantasy world for travelers.

Many of the candy-colored hotels have survived and been meticulously restored. They are among the more than 800 buildings of historical significance in South Beach's art deco district. Composing much of South Beach, the 1-square-mi district is bounded by Dade Boulevard on the north, the Atlantic Ocean on the east, 6th Street on the south, and Alton Road on the west.

Because the district as a whole was developed so rapidly and designed by like-minded architects—**Henry Hohauser, L. Murray Dixon, Albert Anis,** and their colleagues—it has amazing stylistic unity. Nevertheless, on this single street you can trace the evolution of period form from angular, vertically emphatic early deco to aerodynamically rounded Streamline Moderne. The relatively severe Cavalier and more curvaceous Cardozo are fine examples of the former and latter, respectively.

To explore the district, begin by loading up on literature in the **Art Deco Welcome Center** (✉ *1001 Ocean Dr.* ☎ *305/763–8026* ⊕ *www.mdpl.org*). If you want to view these historic properties on your own, just start walking. A four-block stroll north on Ocean Drive gets you up close to camera-ready classics: the **Clevelander** (1020), the **Tides** (1220), the **Leslie** (1244), the **Carlyle** (1250), the **Cardozo** (1300), the **Cavalier** (1320), and the **Winterhaven** (1400).

ART DECO TOURS

See the bold looks of classic Art Deco architecture along Ocean Drive.

SELF-GUIDED AUDIO TOURS
Expert insight on the architecture and the area's history is yours on the Miami Design Preservation League's (MDPL) 90-minute self-guided walks that use an iPod or iphone and include a companion map. You can pick up the iPod version and companion map at the Art Deco Welcome Center from 9:30 AM to 5 PM daily; the cost is $15.

WALKING TOURS
The tour offers a primer in the three predominate styles found in the Art Deco District: Art Deco, Meditteranean Revival, and Miami Modern (MiMo).

The MDPL's 90-minute "Ocean Drive and Beyond" group walking tour gives you a guided look at area icons, inside and out. (A number of interiors are on the itinerary, so it's a good chance to peek inside spots that might otherwise seem off-limits.) Morning tours depart daily at 10:30 AM from the Art Deco Welcome Center Gift Shop. An additional evening tour departs at 6:30 PM on Thursdays. Buy tickets in advance at ⊕ mdpl.org, or arrive 15–20 minutes early to buy tickets ($20).

BIKE TOURS
Rather ride than walk? Half-day cycling tours of the city's art deco history are organized daily for groups (5 or more) by **South Beach Bike Tours** (☎ 305/673–2002 ⊕ www.southbeachbiketours.com). The $59 cost includes equipment, snacks, and water.

ART DECO WEEKEND

Tours, lectures, film screenings, and dozens of other '30s-themed events are on tap in mid-January, during the annual **Art Deco Weekend** (☎ 305/672-2014, ⊕ www.ArtDecoWeekend.com). Festivities—many of them free—kick off with a Saturday morning parade and culminate in a street fair. More than a quarter of a million people join in the action, which centers on Ocean Drive between 5th and 15th streets.

Celebrate the 1930s during Art Deco Weekend.

ARCHITECTURAL HIGHLIGHTS

Cavalier Hotel

FRIEZE DETAIL, CAVALIER HOTEL

The decorative stucco friezes outside the Cavalier Hotel at 1320 Ocean Drive are significant for more than aesthetic reasons. Roy France used them to add symmetry (adhering to the "Rule of Three") and accentuate the hotel's verticality by drawing the eye upward. The pattern he chose also reflected a fascination with ancient civilizations engendered by the recent rediscovery of King Tut's tomb and the Chichén Itzá temples.

LOBBY FLOOR, PARK CENTRAL HOTEL

Terrazzo—a compound of cement and stone chips that could be poured, then polished—is a hallmark of deco design. Terrazzo floors typically had a geometric pattern, like this one in the Park Central Hotel, a 1937 building by Henry Hohauser at 640 Ocean Drive.

Park Central Hotel

CORNER FACADE, ESSEX HOUSE HOTEL

Essex House Hotel, a 1938 gem that appears permanently anchored at 1001 Collins Avenue, is a stunning example of Maritime deco (also known as Nautical Moderne). Designed by Henry Hohauser to evoke an ocean liner, the hotel is rife with marine elements, from the rows of porthole-style windows and natty racing stripes to the towering smokestack-like sign. With a prow angled proudly into the street corner, it seems ready to steam out to sea.

Essex House Hotel

NEON SPIRE, THE HOTEL

The name spelled vertically in eye-popping neon on the venue's iconic aluminum spire—Tiffany—bears evidence of the hotel's earlier incarnation. When the L. Murray Dixon–designed Tiffany Hotel was erected at 801 Collins Avenue in 1939, neon was still a novelty. Its use, coupled with the spire's rocket-like shape, combined to create a futuristic look influenced by the sci-fi themes then pervasive in popular culture.

The Hotel

ENTRANCE, JERRY'S FAMOUS DELI

Inspired by everything from car fenders to airplane noses, proponents of art deco's Streamline Moderne look began to soften buildings' hitherto boxy edges. But when Henry Hohauser designed Hoffman's Cafeteria in 1940 he took moderne to the max. The landmark at 1450 Collins Avenue (now Jerry's Famous Deli) has a sleek, splendidly curved facade. The restored interior echoes it through semicircular booths and rounded chair backs.

Jerry's Famous Deli

ARCHITECTURAL TERMS

The Rule of Three: Early deco designers often used architectural elements in multiples of three, creating tripartite facades with triple sets of windows, eyebrows, or banding.

Eyebrows: Small shelf-like ledges that protruded over exterior windows were used to simultaneously provide much-needed shade and serve as a counterpoint to a building's strong vertical lines.

Tropical Motifs: In keeping with the setting, premises were plastered, painted, or etched with seaside images. Palm trees, sunbursts, waves, flamingoes, and the like were particularly common.

Banding: Enhancing the illusion that these immobile structures were rapidly speeding objects, colorful horizontal bands (also called "racing stripes") were painted on exteriors or applied with tile.

Stripped Classic: The most austere version of art deco (sometimes dubbed Depression Moderne) was used for buildings commissioned by the Public Works Administration.

(top) Hotel Marlin; (left) Sherbrooke Hotel; (right) U.S. Post Office in Miami Beach.

Miami Beach residential buildings tower over the sand.

BICYCLING

Perfect weather and flat terrain make Miami–Dade County a popular place for cyclists; however, biking here can also be quite dangerous. Be very vigilant when biking on Miami Beach, or better yet, steer clear and bike the beautiful paths of Key Biscayne instead.

Key Cycling. On an island where biking is a way of life, this Key Biscayne bike shop carries a wide range of amazing bikes in its showroom, as well as any kind of bike accessory imaginable. Out-of-towners can rent mountain or hybrid bikes for $15 for two hours, $24 for the day, and $80 for the week. ✉ *Galleria Shopping Center, 328 Crandon Blvd., Ste. 121, Key Biscayne* 🕿 *305/361–0061* ⊕ *www.keycycling.com.*

Miami Beach Bicycle Center. The easiest and most economical place for a bike rental on Miami Beach is this shop near Ocean Drive. Rent a bike for $5 per hour, $18 per day, or $80 for the week. All bike rentals include locks, helmets, and baskets. ✉ *601 5th St., South Beach* 🕿 *305/674–0150* ⊕ *www.bikemiamibeach.com.*

BOATING AND SAILING

Boating, whether on sailboats, powerboats, luxury yachts, WaveRunners, or windsurfers, is a passion in Greater Miami. The Intracoastal Waterway, wide and sheltered Biscayne Bay, and the Atlantic Ocean provide ample opportunities for fun aboard all types of watercraft.

The best windsurfing spots are on the north side of the Rickenbacker Causeway at Virginia Key Beach or to the south at, go figure, Windsurfer Beach. Kite surfing adds another level to the water-sports craze.

OUTFITTERS AND EXPEDITIONS

Playtime Watersports. A regularly scheduled evening sunset cruise through Biscayne Bay on the 50-foot sailing "Great White Catamaran" departs nightly at 6:30 pm from Marbella Marina in downtown; however, Playtime also offers all-inclusive, fully crewed private charters on its catamaran. ⊠ *Marbella Marina, 801 Brickell Ave., Downtown* ☎ *305/216–6967* ⊕ *www.playtimewatersport.com.*

Fodor'sChoice ★ **Sailboards Miami.** Rent paddle boards and kayaks or learn how to windsurf from this permanent, roadside adventure outfitter, directly off Rickenbacker Causeway. These friendly folks say they teach more windsurfers each year than anyone in the United States and promise to teach you to windsurf within two hours—for $79. ⊠ *Mile 6.5 on Rickenbacker Causeway (go right before bridge), Key Biscayne* ☎ *305/892–8992* ⊕ *www.sailboardsmiami.com* ☉ *Fri.–Tues. 10–6.*

GOLF

Greater Miami has more than 30 private and public courses. Costs at most courses are higher on weekends and in season, but you can save by playing on weekdays and after 1 or 3 pm, depending on the course. Call ahead to find out when afternoon-twilight rates go into effect. For information on most courses in Miami and throughout Florida, you can visit ⊕ *www.floridagolferguide.com.*

Biltmore Golf Course. On the grounds of the historic circa 1926 Biltmore hotel, the Biltmore Golf Course provides a golf experience primarily for in-house guests, local residents, and those visiting the Coral Gables area. The 6,800-yard, 18-hole, par-71, championship golf course was designed in 1925 by Scotsman Donald Ross, the "it" golf designer of the Roaring Twenties. Today, the lush, well-maintained course is easily accessible thanks to its advanced online booking system, where you can easily reserve your tee time and decide between pricing, depending on the time of day and year. There's a pro-shop on site, and golf instruction is available through the Biltmore Golf Academy or the more extensive, on-site Total Performance Golf programs. ⊠ *The Biltmore Hotel, 1210 Anastasia Ave., Coral Gables* ☎ *855/311–6903* ⊕ *www.biltmorehotel.com/golf* ⛳ *$113 for 9 holes, $195 for 18 holes* ⅃ *18 holes. 6800 yards. par 71.*

Fodor'sChoice ★ **Crandon Golf at Key Biscayne.** On the serene island of Key Biscayne, overlooking Biscayne Bay, this top-rated, championship municipal golf course is considered one of the state's most challenging par-72 courses. Enveloped by tropical foliage, mangroves, saltwater lakes, and bayside waters, the course also happens to be the only one in North America with a subtropical lagoon. The Devlin/Von Hagge–designed course has a USGA rating of 75.4 and a slope rating of 129 and has received national awards from both *Golfweek* and *Golf Digest*. The course is located on the south side of Crandon Park. Nonresidents should expect to pay $180 (Monday–Thursday) to $225 (Friday–Sunday) for a round during peak hours in peak season (December 15–April) and roughly half that off season. Deeply discounted twilight rates of $40 apply after 3:30 pm. Tee times can be booked online. ⊠ *Crandon Park, 6700*

Crandon Blvd., Key Biscayne ☎ *305/361–9129* ⊕ *www.golfcrandon. com* ☞ *$180 for 18 holes* ⛳ *18 holes. 7400 yards. par 72.*

Fodor's Choice **Trump National Doral Miami.** Just west of Miami proper, Trump National
★ Doral Miami is best known for the par-72 Blue Monster course (renovated in 2013) and the World Golf Championships–Cadillac Championship. The week of festivities planned around this March tournament,
which offers $8.5 million in prize money, brings hordes of pro-golf
aficionados to South Florida. But there's far more to the Trump golf
grounds than the Dick Wilson–designed Blue Monster and the Cadillac Championship. There are four other renowned golf courses—the
Greg Norman–designed Great White Course, the Raymon Floyd–
redesigned Gold Course, the Jim McClean Signature Course, and the
Red Course (under renovation at press time)—and numerous other
tournaments throughout the year. Hence, golf enthusiasts flock here
year-round. ⊠ *4400 N.W. 87th Ave., 36th St. exit off Rte. 826, Doral*
☎ *800/713–6725* ⊕ *www.trumphotelcollection.com/miami* ☞ *$450 for
Blue Monster Course, $250 for Great White Course, $190 for Gold
Course* ⛳ *Blue Monster Course: 18 holes. 7300 yards. par 72. Great
White Course: 18 holes. 7200 yards. par 72. Gold Course: 18 holes.
6600 yards. par 70.*

The Senator Course at Shula's Golf Club. Deep in the suburbs of west Miami,
the Senator Course at Shula's Golf Club boasts the longest championship course in the area (7,055 yards, par 72), a lighted par-3 course,
and a golf school. The championship, classic-style Senator Course was
originally designed in 1962 by Bill Watts, updated by Kipp Schulties
in 1998, and completely refreshed in late 2013, with improvements
that included sparkling new Champion Bermuda greens and new Celebration Bermuda tees. The club hosts dozens of tournaments yearly.
Because of its remote location, greens fees tend to be on the lower side.
They run from $40 to $130, depending on the season and time. You'll
pay in the lower range on weekdays, more on weekends, and $40 after
2 pm. Golf carts are included. For true golf enthusiasts, there's the on-
site Don Shula hotel—a comfortable base to eat, live, and breathe golf.
⊠ *7601 Miami Lakes Dr., 154th St. Exit off Rte. 826, Miami Lakes*
☎ *305/820–8088* ⊕ *www.shulasgolfclub.com* ☞ *$130 for 18 holes*
⛳ *18 holes. 7055 yards. par 70.*

GUIDED TOURS

BOAT TOURS

Duck Tours Miami. Like the campy duck tours that originated in Boston
and are now commonplace in several cities across the U.S., ducked-
themed amphibious WWII vehicles make daily 90-minute tours of
Miami that combine land and sea views. Comedy, quacks, and cheese
are part of the mix. ⊠ *1661 James Ave., South Beach* ☎ *305/673–2217*
⊕ *www.ducktourssouthbeach.com* ☞ *$32.*

Island Queen Cruises. Tours on Island Queen Cruises run the gamut—
sunset cruises, dance cruises, fishing cruises, speedboat rides and their
signature, tours of Millionaire's Row, Miami's waterfront homes of the
rich and famous. *The Island Queen, Island Lady,* and *Miami Lady* are

three double-decker, 140-passenger tour boats docked at Bayside Marketplace that set sail daily for 90-minute narrated tours of the Port of Miami and Millionaires' Row. For the same tour with a lot more speed, take the tour on the high-speed Bayside Blaster. ✉ *401 Biscayne Blvd., Downtown* ☎ *305/379–5119* ⊕ *www.islandqueencruises.com* 💲 *$28.*

WALKING TOURS

Art Deco District Tour. Operated by the Miami Design Preservation League, this is a 90-minute guided walking tour that departs from the league's welcome center at Ocean Drive and 10th Street. It starts at 10:30 am daily, with an extra tour at 6:30 pm Thursday. Alternatively, you can go at your own pace with the league's self-guided iPod audio tour, which also takes roughly an hour and a half. ✉ *1001 Ocean Dr., South Beach* ☎ *305/763–8026* ⊕ *www.mdpl.org* 💲 *$20 guided tour, $15 audio tour.*

Little Havana Cuban Cuisine and Culture Walk. HistoryMiami runs culinary and cultural tours of Little Havana. Enjoy the unique architecture of this ethnic enclave and community history by visiting botanicas, cigar factories, and sipping Cuban coffee. The two-hour tour is offered monthly and leaves from Los Pinareños Fruteria at 10 am. Tours aren't available every month, so check the website ahead of time to book. ✉ *1334 S.W. 8th St., Little Havana* ☎ *305/375–1621* ⊕ *www.historymiami. org* 💲 *$30.*

SCUBA DIVING AND SNORKELING

Diving and snorkeling on the offshore coral wrecks and reefs on a calm day can be very rewarding. Chances are excellent that you'll come face-to-face with a flood of tropical fish. One option is to find Fowey, Triumph, Long, and Emerald reefs in 10- to 15-foot dives that are perfect for snorkelers and beginning divers. On the edge of the continental shelf a little more than 3 miles out, these reefs are just a ¼ mile away from depths greater than 100 feet. Another option is to paddle around the tangled prop roots of the mangrove trees that line the coast, peering at the fish, crabs, and other creatures hiding there. ⇨ *For the best snorkeling in Miami–Dade, head to Biscayne National Park. See the Everglades chapter for more information.*

Artificial Reefs. Perhaps the area's most unusual diving options are its artificial reefs. Since 1981, Miami–Dade County's Department of Environmental Resources Management has sunk tons of limestone boulders and a water tower, army tanks, and almost 200 boats of all descriptions to create a "wreckreational" habitat where divers can swim with yellow tang, barracudas, nurse sharks, snapper, eels, and grouper. The website offers an interactive map of wreck locations. Dive outfitters are familiar with most of these artificial reefs and can take you to the best ones. ✉ *Miami Beach* ⊕ *www.miamidade.gov/environment/reefs-artificial.asp.*

OUTFITTERS

Divers Paradise of Key Biscayne. This complete dive shop and diving-charter service next to the Crandon Park Marina, includes equipment rental and scuba instruction with PADI and NAUI affiliation. Four-hour dive trips are offered Tuesday through Friday at 10:30, weekends at 8:30 and 1:30. The trip is $60. Night dives are offered Saturdays at 5:30. ⊠ *Crandon Park Marina, 4000 Crandon Blvd., Key Biscayne* ☎ *305/361–3483* ⊕ *www.keydivers.com* ⊗ *Closed Mon.*

Fodor's Choice   **South Beach Dive and Surf.** Dedicated to all things ocean, this PADI 5-Star
★   Dive Shop offers multiple diving and snorkeling trips weekly as well as surfboard, paddleboard, and skateboard sales, rentals and lessons. The Discover Scuba course (for noncertified divers) trains newcomers every Monday, Tuesday, Thursday, and Saturday at 8 am which includes two dives in Key Largo's John Pennekamp Marine Sanctuary that same day. Night dives take place each Wednesday at 5, and wreck and reef dives weekends at 7:30 am and noon. The center also runs dives in Key Largo's Spiegel Grove, the second-largest wreck ever to be sunk for the intention of recreational diving, and in the Neptune Memorial Reef, inspired by the city of Atlantis and created in part using the ashes of cremated bodies. The dive shop itself is located in the heart of South Beach, but boats depart from marinas in Miami Beach and Key Largo, in the Florida Keys. ⊠ *850 Washington Ave., South Beach* ☎ *305/531–6110* ⊕ *www.southbeachdivers.com.*

THE EVERGLADES

WELCOME TO
THE EVERGLADES

TOP REASONS
TO GO

★ **Fun fishing:** Cast for some of the world's fight-ingest game fish—600 species of fish in all—in the Everglades' backwaters.

★ **Abundant birdlife:** Check hundreds of birds off your life list, includ-ing—if you're lucky—the rare Everglades snail kite.

★ **Cool kayaking:** Do a half-day trip in Big Cypress National Preserve or reach for the ultimate—the 99-mile Wilderness Trail.

★ **Swamp cuisine:** Hankering for alligator tail and frogs' legs? Or how about swamp cabbage, made from hearts of palm? Better yet, try stone-crab claws fresh from the traps.

★ **Gator-spotting:** This is ground zero for alliga-tor viewing in the United States, and there's a good bet you'll leave having spotted your quota.

Collier-Seminole State Park

Fakahatchee Strand Preserve State Park

Ten Thousand Islands

41

Monroe Station

Everglades City

3 Big Cypress National Preserve

Chokoloskee Island

Loop Road

Everglades National Park

Lostmans R.

Gulf of Mexico

Broad R.

Harney R.

Northwest Cape

Whitewater Bay

Cape Sable

Flamingo

0   20 miles

0   30 km

East Cape

Oyster Keys

Catfish Key

1 **Everglades National Park.** Alligators, Florida panthers, black bears, manatees, dolphins, bald eagles, and roseate spoon-bills call this vast habitat home.

2 **Biscayne National Park.** Mostly under water, this is where the string of coral reefs and islands that form the Florida Keys begins.

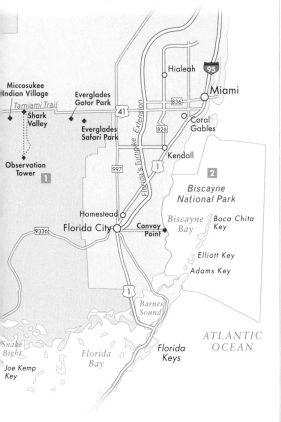

Hialeah

95

Miami

Miccosukee
Indian Village

Everglades
Gator Park

Tamiami Trail

836

◆ Shark
Valley

41

◆ Everglades
Safari Park

Coral
Gables

826

Observation
Tower **1**

997

Kendall

1

2

*Biscayne
National Park*

Homestead

Biscayne
Bay

Boca Chita
Key

9336

Florida City

Convoy
Point

Elliott Key

Adams Key

1

*Barnes
Sound*

ATLANTIC
OCEAN

*Snake
Bight*

*Florida
Bay*

*Florida
Keys*

*Joe Kemp
Key*

GETTING
ORIENTED

3

The southern third of the
Florida peninsula is largely
taken up by protected government land that includes
Everglades National Park,
Big Cypress National
Preserve, and Biscayne
National Park. Miami lies to
the northeast, and Naples
and Marco Island are
northwest. Land access to
Everglades National Park is
primarily by two roads. The
park's main road traverses
the southern Everglades
from the gateway towns of
Homestead and Florida City
to the outpost of Flamingo,
on Florida Bay. To the north,
Tamiami Trail (U.S. 41) cuts
through the Everglades from
the Greater Miami area
on the east coast or from
Naples on the west coast to
the western park entrance in
Everglades City at Route 29.

3 **Big Cypress National
Preserve.** Neighbor to
Everglades National Park, it's
an outdoor-lover's paradise.

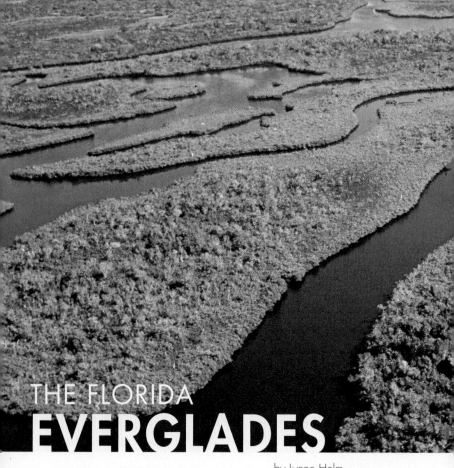

THE FLORIDA
EVERGLADES

by Lynne Helm

Alternately described as elixir of life or swampland muck, the Florida Everglades is one of a kind—a 50-mi-wide "river of grass" that spreads across hundreds of thousands of acres. It moves at varying speeds depending on rainfall and other variables, sloping south from the Kissimmee River and Lake Okeechobee to estuaries of Biscayne Bay, Florida Bay, and the Ten Thousand Islands.

Today, apart from sheltering some 70 species on America's endangered list, the Everglades also embraces more than 7 million residents, 50 million annual tourists, 400,000 acres of sugarcane, and the world's largest concentration of golf courses.

Demands on the land threaten the Everglades' finely balanced ecosystem. Irrigation canals for agriculture and roadways disrupt natural water flow. Drainage for development leaves wildlife scurrying for new territory. Water runoff, laced with fertilizers, promotes unnatural growth of swamp vegetation. What remains is a miracle of sorts, given decades of these destructive forces.

Creation of the Everglades required unique conditions. South Florida's geology, linked with its warm, wet subtropical climate, is the perfect mix for a marshland ecosystem. Layers of porous, permeable limestone create water-bearing rock,

soil, and aquifers, which in turn affects climate, weather, and hydrology.

This rock beneath the Everglades reflects Florida's geologic history—its crust was once part of the African region. Some scientists theorize that continental shifting merged North America with Africa, and then continental rifting later pulled North America away from the African continent but took part of northwest Africa with it—the part that is today's Florida. The Earth's tectonic plates continued to migrate, eventually placing Florida at its current location as a land mass jutting out into the ocean, with the Everglades at its tip.

EXPERIENCING THE ECOSYSTEMS

Eight distinct habitats exist within Everglades National Park, Big Cypress National Preserve, and Biscayne National Park.

ECOSYSTEMS	EASY WAY	MORE ACTIVE WAY
COASTAL PRAIRIE: An arid region of salt-tolerant vegetation lies between the tidal mud flats of Florida Bay and dry land. **Best place to see it: The Coastal Prairie Trail**	Take a guided boat tour of Florida Bay, leaving from Flamingo Marina.	Hike the Coastal Prairie Trail from Eco Pond to Clubhouse Beach.
CYPRESS: Capable of surviving in standing water, cypress trees often form dense clusters called "cypress domes" in natural water-filled depressions. **Best place to see it: Big Cypress National Preserve**	Drive U.S. 41 (also known as Tamiami Trail—pronounced Tammy-Amee), which cuts across Southern Florida, from Naples to Miami.	Hike (or drive) the scenic Loop Road, which begins off Tamiami Trail, running from the Loop Road Education Center to Monroe Station.
FRESH WATER MARL PRAIRIE: Bordering deeper sloughs are large prairies with marl (clay and calcium carbonate) sediments on limestone. Gators like to use their toothy snouts to dig holes in prairie mud. **Best place to see it: Pahayokee Overlook**	Drive there from the Ernest F. Coe Visitor Center.	Take a guided tour, either through the park service or from permitted, licensed guides. You also can set up camp at Long Pine Key.
FRESH WATER SLOUGH AND HARDWOOD HAMMOCK: Shark River Slough and Taylor Slough are the Everglades' two sloughs, or marshy rivers. Due to slight elevation amid sloughs, dense stands of hardwood trees appear as teardrop-shaped islands. **Best place to see it: The Observation Tower**	Take a two-hour guided tram tour from the Shark Valley Visitor Center to the tower and back.	Walk or bike (rentals available) the route to the tower via the tram road and (walkers only) Bobcat Boardwalk trail and Otter Cave Hammock Trail.
MANGROVE: Spread over South Florida's coastal channels and waterways, mangrove thrives where Everglades fresh water mixes with salt water. **Best place to see it: The Wilderness Waterway**	Picnic at the area near Long Pine Key, which is surrounded by mangrove, or take a water tour at Biscayne National Park.	Boat your way along the 99-mi Wilderness Waterway. It's six hours by motorized boat, seven days by canoe.
MARINE AND ESTUARINE: Corals, sponges, mollusks, seagrass, and algae thrive in the Florida Bay, where the fresh waters of the Everglades meet the salty seas. **Best place to see it: Florida Bay**	Take a boat tour from the Flamingo Visitor Center marina.	Canoe or kayak on White Water Bay along the Wilderness Waterway Canoe Trail.
PINELAND: A dominant plant in dry, rugged terrain, the Everglades' diverse pinelands consist of slash pine forest, saw palmettos, and more than 200 tropical plant varieties. **Best place to see it: Long Pine Key trails**	Drive to Long Pine Key, about 6 mi off the main road from Ernest F. Coe Visitor Center.	Hike or bike the 28 mi of Long Pine Key trails.

Lake
Okeechobee

Big Cypress
National
Preserve

EVERGLADES
NATIONAL
PARK

Biscayne
National
Park

Big Cypress
National Preserve

41

997

41

Shark Valley
Visitor Center

Tram Tour

Overlook

Chekika

997

Third Bay
Big Lostmans Bay

Key
McLaughlin

Wilderness Waterway
and Canoe Trail

Shark River Slough

EVERGLADES
NATIONAL PARK

Biscayne
National
Park

Homestead
Florida City

821

Ponce De Leon
Bay

Pa-hay-okee
Overlook

Long Pine
Key

Ernest F Coe
Visitor Center

9336

Royal Palm

Taylor Slough

1

Whitewater
Bay

Mahogany
Hammock

Nine Mile Pond
Canoe Trail

Nine Mile Pond

CAPE SABLE

Bear Lake
Canoe Trail

West Lake

Snake Bight Trail

Christian Point Trail

Flamingo

Flamingo
Visitor Center

Coastal Prairie
Trail

Deer Key

Eagle Key

Nest
Keys

Black Betsy
Keys

Park Key

Shell Key

Russell Key

Key Largo

Corinne Key

Florida Bay

Panhandle
Key

Rabbit Keys

Tavernier
Plantation

Barnes Key

Islamorada

1

TO
KEY WEST

0   8 mi
0   8 km

IN FOCUS THE FLORIDA EVERGLADES

3

**Marine and Estuarine
Water Depths**
☐ 0-3 Feet
☐ 3-6 Feet
☐ over 6 Feet

Land Cover
☐ Coastal Prairie
☐ Cypress
☐ Fresh Water Marl Prairie
☐ Fresh Water Slough
☐ Hardwood Hammock
☐ Mangrove
☐ Pinelands
☐ Urban

👫 Ranger Station
▲ Campground
🛖 Picnic Area
🍴 Restaurant
······· Walking/Hiking Trails
--- Water/Canoe Trails

Habitats within Florida's Everglades
ecosystem support a diverse collection
of plant and animal species encountered
nowhere else. The landscape is dynamic,
and the ecosystems are in constant flux,
subject to changing elements.

FLORA

① Cabbage Palm

It's virtually impossible to visit the Everglades and not see a cabbage palm, Florida's official state tree. The cabbage palm (or sabal palm), graces assorted ecosystems and grows well in swamps. **Best place to see them:** At Loxahatchee National Wildlife Refuge (embracing the northern part of the Everglades, along Alligator Alley), throughout Everglades National Park, and at Big Cypress National Preserve.

② Sawgrass

With spiny, serrated leaf blades resembling saws, sawgrass inspired the term "river of grass" for the Everglades. **Best place to see them:** Both Shark Valley and Pahayokee Overlook provide terrific vantage points for gazing over sawgrass prairie; you also can get an eyeful of sawgrass when crossing Alligator Alley, even when doing so at top speeds.

③ Mahogany

Hardwood hammocks of the Everglades live in areas that rarely flood because of the slight elevation of the sloughs, where they're typically found. **Best place to see them:** Everglades National Park's Mahogany Hammock Trail (which has a boardwalk leading to the nation's largest living mahogany tree).

④ Mangrove

Mangrove forest ecosystems provide both food and protected nursery areas for fish, shellfish, and crustaceans. **Best place to see them:** Along Biscayne National Park shoreline, at Big Cypress National Preserve, and within Everglades National Park, especially around the Caple Sable area.

⑤ Gumbo Limbo

Sometimes called "tourist trees" because of peeling reddish bark (not unlike sunburns). **Best place to see them:** Everglades National Park's Gumbo Limbo Trail and assorted spots throughout the expansive Everglades.

FAUNA

❶ American Alligator

In all likelihood, on your visit to the Everglades you'll see at least a gator or two. These carnivorous creatures can be found throughout the Everglades swampy wetlands.

Best place to see them: Loxahatchee National Wildlife Refuge (also sheltering the endangered Everglades snail kite) and within Everglades National Park at Shark Valley or Anhinga Trail. Sometimes (logically enough) gators hang out along Alligator Alley, basking in early morning or late-afternoon sun along four-lane I–75.

❷ American Crocodile

Crocs gravitate to fresh or brackish water, subsisting on birds, fish, snails, frogs, and small mammals.

Best place to see them: Within Everglades National Park, Big Cypress National Preserve, and protected grounds in or around Billie Swamp Safari.

❸ Eastern Coral Snake

This venomous snake burrows in underbrush, preying on lizards, frogs, and smaller snakes.

Best place to see them: Snakes typically shy away from people, but try Snake Bight or Eco Pond near Flamingo, where birds are also prevalent.

❹ Florida Panther

Struggling for survival amid loss of habitat, these shy, tan-colored cats now number around 100, up from lows of near 30.

Best place to see them: Protected grounds of Billie Swamp Safari sometimes provide sightings during tours. Signage on roadway linking Tamiami Trail and Alligator Alley warns of panther crossings, but sightings are rare.

❺ Green Tree Frog

Typically bright green with white or yellow stripes, these nocturnal creatures thrive in swamps and brackish water.

Best place to see them: Within Everglades National Park, especially in or near water.

● =Extremely Common ● =Very Common ● =Somewhat Common ● =Rare

BIRDS

❶ Anhinga

The lack of oil glands for waterproofing feathers helps this bird to dive as well as chase and spear fish with its pointed beak. The Anhinga is also often called a "water turkey" because of its long tail, or a "snake bird" because of its long neck.

Best place to see them: The Anhinga Trail, which also is known for attracting other wildlife to drink during especially dry winters.

❷ Blue-Winged Teal

Although it's predominantly brown and gray, this bird's powder-blue wing patch becomes visible in flight. Next to the mallard, the blue-winged teal is North America's second most abundant duck, and thrives particularly well in the Everglades.

Best place to see them: Near ponds and marshy areas of Everglades National Park or Big Cypress National Preserve.

❸ Great Blue Heron

This bird has a varied palate and enjoys feasting on everything from frogs, snakes, and mice to shrimp, aquatic insects, and sometimes even other birds! The all-white version, which at one time was considered a separate species, is quite common to the Everglades.

Best place to see them: Loxahatchee National Wildlife Refuge or Shark Valley in Everglades National Park.

❹ Great Egret

Once decimated by plume hunters, these monogamous, long-legged white birds with S-shaped necks feed in wetlands, nest in trees, and hang out in colonies that often include heron or other egret species.

Best place to see them: Throughout Everglades National Park, along Alligator Alley, and sometimes even on the fringes of Greater Fort Lauderdale.

⑤ Greater Flamingo

Flocking together and using long legs and webbed feet to stir shallow waters and mud flats, color comes a couple of years after hatching from ingesting shrimplike crustaceans along with fish, fly larvae, and plankton.

Best place to see them: Try Snake Bight or Eco Pond, near Flamingo Marina.

⑥ Osprey

Making a big comeback from chemical pollutant endangerment, ospreys (sometimes confused with bald eagles) are distinguished by black eyestripes down their faces. Gripping pads on feet with curved claws help them pluck fish from water.

Best place to see them: Look near water, where they're fishing for lunch in the shallow areas. Try the coasts, bays, and ponds of Everglades National Park. They also gravitate to trees You can usually spot them from the Gulf Coast Visitor Center, or you can observe them via boating in the Ten Thousand Islands.

⑦ Roseate Spoonbill

These gregarious pink-and-white birds gravitate toward mangroves, feeding on fish, insects, amphibians, and some plants. They have long, spoon-like bills, and their feathers can have a touch of red and yellow. These birds appear in the Everglades year-round.

Best place to see them: Sandy Key, southwest of Flamingo, is a spoonbill nocturnal roosting spot, but at sunrise these colorful birds head out over Eco Pond to favored day hangouts throughout Everglades National Park.

⑧ Wood Stork

Recognizable by featherless heads and prominent bills, these birds submerge in water to scoop up hapless fish. They are most common in the early spring and often easiest to spot in the morning.

Best place to see them: Amid the Ten Thousand Island areas, Nine Mile Pond, Mrazek Pond, and in the mangroves at Paurotis Pond.

● *=Extremely Common* ● *=Very Common* ● *=Somewhat Common* ● *=Rare*

THE BEST EVERGLADES ACTIVITIES

HIKING

Top experiences: At Big Cypress National Preserve, you can hike along designated trails or push through unmarked acreage. (Conditions vary seasonally, which means you could be tramping through waist-deep waters.) Trailheads for the Florida National Scenic Trail are at Loop Road off U.S. 41 and Alligator Alley at mile marker 63.

What will I see? Dwarf cypress, hardwood hammocks, prairies, birds, and other wildlife.

For a short visit: A 6.5-mi section from Loop Road to U.S. 41 crosses Robert's Lake Strand, providing a satisfying sense of being out in the middle nowhere.

With more time: A 28-mile stretch from U.S. 41 to I–75 (Alligator Alley) reveals assorted habitats, including hardwood hammocks, pinelands, prairie, and cypress.

Want a tour? Big Cypress ranger-led exploration starts from the Oasis Visitor Center, late November through mid-April.

WALKING

Top experiences: Everglades National Park magnets: wheelchair accessible walkways at Anhinga Trail, Gumbo Limbo Trail, Pahayokee Overlook, Mahogany Hammock, and West Lake Trail.

What will I see? Birds and alligators at Anhinga; tropical hardwood hammock at Gumbo Limbo; an overlook of the River of Grass from Pahayokee's tower; a subtropical tree island with massive mahogany growth along Mahogany Hammock; and a forest of mangrove trees on West Lake Trail.

For a short visit: Flamingo's Eco Pond provides for waterside wildlife viewing.

With more time: Shark Valley lets you combine the quarter-mile Bobcat Boardwalk (looping through sawgrass prairie and a bayhead) with the 1-mi-long round-trip Otter Cave, allowing you to steep in subtropical hardwood hammock.

Want a tour? Pahayokee and Flamingo feature informative ranger-led walks.

The Anhinga Trail near the Royal Palm Visitor Center at Everglades National Park

BOATING

Top experiences: Launch a boat from the Gulf Coast Visitors Center or Flamingo Marina. Bring your own watercraft or rent canoes or skiffs at either location.

What will I see? Birds from bald eagles to roseate spoonbills, plus plenty of mangrove and wildlife—and maybe even some baby alligators with yellow stripes.

For a short visit: Canoe adventurers often head for Hells Bay, a 3-mile stretch about 9 mi north of Flamingo. Or put in at the Turner River alongside the Tamiami Trail in the Big Cypress National Preserve and paddle all the way (about eight hours) to Chocoloskee Bay at Everglades City.

With more time: Head out amid the Ten Thousand Islands and lose yourself in territory once exclusively the domain of only the hardiest pioneers and American Indians. If you've got a week or more for paddling, the 99-mile Wilderness Waterway stretches from Flamingo to Everglades City.

Want a tour? Sign on for narrated boat tours at the Gulf Coast or Flamingo visitor center.

BIRD WATCHING

Top experiences: Anhinga Trail, passing over Taylor Slough.

What will I see? Anhinga and heron sightings are a nearly sure thing, especially in early morning or late afternoon. Also, alligators can be seen from the boardwalk.

For a short visit: Even if you're traveling coast to coast at higher speeds via Alligator Alley, chances are you'll spot winged wonders like egrets, osprey, and heron.

With more time: Since bird-watching at Flamingo can be a special treat early in the morning or late in the afternoon, try camping overnight even if you're not one for roughing it. Reservations are recommended. (Flamingo Lodge remains closed after 2005 hurricane damage.)

Want a tour? Ranger-led walks at Pahayokee and from Everglades National Park visitor centers provide solid birding background for novices.

(top left) Tourists cruise the Everglades by airboat; (bottom left) Green Heron; (right) Eastern Meadowlark

THE BEST EVERGLADES ACTIVITIES

BIKING

Top experiences: Shark Valley (where bicycling is allowed on the tram road) is great for taking in the quiet beauty of the Everglades. Near Ernest F. Coe Visitor Center, Long Pine Key's 14-mile nature trail also can be a way to bike happily away from folks on foot.

What will I see? At Shark Valley, wading birds, turtles, and, probably alligators. At Long Pine Key, shady pinewood with subtropical plants and exposed limestone bedrock.

For a short visit: Bike on Shark Valley tram road but turn around to fit time schedule.

With more time: Go the entire 15-mi tram road route, which has no shortcuts. Or try the 22-mile route of Old Ingraham Highway near the Royal Palm Visitor Center, featuring mangrove, sawgrass, and birds (including hawks).

Want a tour? In Big Cypress National Preserve, Bear Island Bike Rides (8 mile round-trip over four to five hours) happen on certain Saturdays.

SNORKELING

Top experiences: Biscayne National Park, where clear waters incorporate the northernmost islands of the Florida Keys.

What will I see? Dense mangrove swamp covering the park shoreline, and, in shallow waters, a living coral reef and tropical fish in assorted colors.

For a short visit: Pick a sunny day to optimize your snorkeling fun, and be sure to use sunscreen.

With more time: Advanced snorkel tours head out from the park on weekends to the bay, finger channels, and around shorelines of the barrier islands. Biscayne National Park also has canoe and kayak rentals, picnic facilities, walking trails, fishing, and camping.

Want a tour? You can swim and snorkel or stay dry and picnic aboard tour boats that depart from Biscayne National Park's visitor center.

(top left) Biking near the Shark Valley Visitor Area. (top right) Snorkeling on the surface in the Atlantic Ocean.

DID YOU KNOW?

You can tell you're looking at a crocodile if you can see its lower teeth protruding when its jaws are shut, whereas an alligator shows no teeth when his mouth is closed. Gators are much darker in color—a grayish black—compared with the lighter tan color of crocodiles. Alligators' snouts are also much broader than their long, thin crocodilian counterparts.

THE STORY OF THE EVERGLADES

Dreams of draining southern Florida took hold in the early 1800s, expanding in the early 1900s to convert large tracts from wetlands to agricultural acreage. By the 1920s, towns like Fort Lauderdale and Miami boomed, and the sugar industry—which came to be known as "Big Sugar"—established its first sugar mills. In 1947 Everglades National Park opened as a refuge for wildlife.

Meanwhile, the sugar industry grew. In its infancy, about 175,000 tons of raw sugar per year was produced from fields totaling about 50,000 acres. But once the U.S. embargo stopped sugar imports from Cuba in 1960 and laws restricting acreage were lifted, Big Sugar took off. Less than five years later, the industry produced 572,000 tons of sugar and occupied nearly a quarter of a million acres.

Fast-forward to 2008, to what was hailed as the biggest conservation deal in U.S. history since the creation of the national parks. A trailblazing restoration strategy hinged on creating a water flow-way between Lake Okeechobee and the Everglades by buying up and flooding 187,000 acres of land. The country's largest producers of cane sugar agreed to sell the necessary 187,000 acres to the state of Florida for $1.75 billion. Environmentalists cheered.

But within months, news broke of a scaled-back land acquisition plan: $1.34 billion to buy 180,000 acres. By spring 2009, the restoration plan had shrunk to $536,000 to buy 73,000 acres. With the purchase still in limbo, critics claim the state might overpay for acreage appraised at pre-recession values and proponents fear dwindling revenues may derail the plan altogether.

The Big Sugar land deal is part of a larger effort to preserve the Everglades. In 2010, two separate lawsuits charged the state, along with the United States Environmental Protection Agency, with stalling Everglades cleanup that was supposed to begin in 2006. "Glacial delay" is how one judge put it. The state must reduce phosphorus levels in water that flows to the Everglades or face fines and sanctions for violating the federal Clean Water Act. The fate of the Everglades remains in the balance.

3

Updated by
Lynne Helm

More than 1.5 million acres of South Florida's 4.3 million acres of subtropical, watery wilderness were given national-park status and protection in 1947 with the creation of Everglades National Park. It's one of the country's largest national parks and is recognized by the world community as a Wetland of International Importance, an International Biosphere Reserve, and a World Heritage Site. Come here if you want to spend the day biking, hiking, or boating in deep, raw wilderness with lots of wildlife.

To the east of Everglades National Park, Biscayne National Park brings forth a pristine, magical, subtropical Florida. It's the nation's largest marine park and the largest national park within the continental United States boasting living coral reefs. A small portion of the park's 172,000 acres consists of mainland coast and outlying islands, but 95% remains under water. Of particular interest are the mangroves and their tangled masses of stiltlike roots that thicken the shorelines. These "walking trees," as some locals call them, have curved prop roots, which arch down from the trunk, and aerial roots that drop from branches. The trees draw fresh water from salt water and create a coastal nursery that sustains myriad types of marine life. You can see Miami's high-rise buildings from many of Biscayne's 44 islands, but the park is virtually undeveloped and large enough for escaping everything that Miami and the Upper Keys have become. To truly escape, don scuba-diving or snorkeling gear and lose yourself in the wonders of the coral reefs.

On the northern edge of Everglades National Park is Big Cypress National Preserve, one of South Florida's least developed watersheds. Established by Congress in 1974 to protect the Everglades, it comprises extensive tracts of prairie, marsh, pinelands, forested swamps, and sloughs. Hunting is allowed, as is off-road-vehicle use. Come here if you like alligators. Stop at the Oasis Visitor Center's boardwalk with alligators lounging underneath, and then drive Loop Road for a backwoods experience. If time permits, kayak the Turner River.

Surrounding the parks and preserve are several communities where you'll find useful outfitters: Everglades City, Florida City, and Homestead.

PLANNING

WHEN TO GO

Winter is the best, and busiest, time to visit the Everglades. Temperatures and mosquito activity are more tolerable, low water levels concentrate the resident wildlife, and migratory birds swell the avian population. In late spring the weather turns hot and rainy, and tours and facilities are less crowded. Migratory birds depart, and you must look harder to see wildlife. Summer brings intense sun and afternoon rainstorms. Water levels rise and mosquitoes descend, making outdoor activity virtually unbearable, unless you swath yourself in netting. Mosquito repellent is a necessity any time of year.

GETTING HERE AND AROUND

Miami International Airport (MIA) is 34 miles from Homestead and 47 miles from the eastern access to Everglades National Park. ⇨ *For MIA airline carrier information, refer to the Miami chapter.* Shuttles run between MIA and Homestead. Southwest Florida International Airport (RSW), in Fort Myers, a little over an hour's drive from Everglades City, is the closest major airport to the Everglades' western entrance. On-demand taxi transportation from the airport to Everglades City is available from MBA Airport Transportation and costs $150 for up to three passengers ($10 each for additional passengers).

Contacts MBA Airport Transportation. MBA is the taxi concessionaire for Southwest Florida International Airport, providing transportation to Everglades City. Call for rates. ☎ *239/225-0428* ⊕ *www.mbaairport.com.*

HOTELS

Accommodations near the parks range from inexpensive to moderate and offer off-season rates in summer, when rampant mosquito populations discourage spending time outdoors, especially at dusk. If you're devoting several days to exploring the east coast Everglades, stay in park campgrounds; 11 miles away in Homestead–Florida City, where there are reasonably priced chain motels and RV parks; in the Florida Keys; or in the Greater Miami–Fort Lauderdale area. Lodgings and campgrounds are also plentiful on the Gulf Coast (in Everglades City, Marco Island, and Naples, the latter of which has the most upscale area accommodations).

Hotel reviews have been shortened. For full information, visit Fodors. com.

RESTAURANTS

Dining in the Everglades area centers on mom-and-pop places serving hearty homestyle food, and small eateries specializing in fresh local fare: alligator, fish, stone crab, frogs' legs, and Florida lobster from the Keys. American Indian restaurants serve local favorites as well as catfish,

Indian fry bread (a flour-and-water flatbread), and pumpkin bread. A growing Hispanic population around Homestead means plenty of authentic, inexpensive Latin cuisine, with an emphasis on Cuban and Mexican dishes. Restaurants in Everglades City, especially those along the river, have fresh seafood including particularly succulent, sustainable stone crab. These places are casual to the point of rustic, and are often closed in late summer or fall. For finer dining, go to Marco Island or Naples.

WHAT IT COSTS				
	$	**$$**	**$$$**	**$$$$**
RESTAURANTS	under $16	$16–$20	$21–$30	over $30
HOTELS	under $201	$201–$300	$301–$400	over $400

Restaurant prices are the average cost of a main course at dinner or, if dinner is not served, at lunch. Hotel prices are the lowest cost of a standard double room in high season.

ABOUT ACTIVITIES

⇨ *While outfitters are listed with the parks and preserve, see our What's Nearby section later in this chapter for information about each town.*

EVERGLADES NATIONAL PARK

45 miles southwest of Miami International Airport.

If you're heading across South Florida on U.S. 41 from Miami to Naples, you'll breeze right through the Everglades. Also known as Tamiami Trail, this mostly two-lane road skirts the edge of Everglades National Park and cuts across the Big Cypress National Preserve. You'll also be near the park if you're en route from Miami to the Florida Keys on U.S. 1, which cuts through Homestead and Florida City—communities east of the main park entrance. Basically, if you're in South Florida, you can't escape at least fringes of the Everglades. With tourist strongholds like Miami, Naples, and the Florida Keys so close, travelers from all over the world typically make day trips to the park.

Everglades National Park has three main entry points: the park headquarters at Ernest F. Coe Visitor Center, southwest of Homestead and Florida City; the Shark Valley area, accessed by Tamiami Trail (U.S. 41); and the Gulf Coast Visitor Center, south of Everglades City to the west and closest to Naples.

Explore on your own or participate in free ranger-led hikes, bicycle or bird-watching tours, and canoe trips. The variety of these excursions is greatest from mid-December through Easter, and some adventures (canoe trips, for instance) typically aren't offered in sweltering summer. Among the more popular are the Anhinga Amble, a 50-minute walk around the Taylor Slough (departs from the Royal Palm Visitor Center), and the Early Bird Special, a 90-minute walk centered on birdlife (departs from Flamingo Visitor Center). Check with the visitor centers for details.

War on Pythons

In 2013, Florida launched its first Python Challenge™ to put the kibosh on Burmese pythons, those deadly snakes literally squeezing the life out of Everglades wonders, from colorful birds to full-grown deer to gators.

The state-sponsored winter competition was a trailblazer, attracting amateurs and professionals alike from 38 states and Canada to help decimate this growing environmental threat. Sadly, only 68 pythons were captured out of the thousands estimated to live in the Everglades.

Even experienced 'Gladesmen with special permits to regularly stalk these predators had trouble finding them—partly because tan, splotchy skin provides natural camouflage for slithering about and causing mayhem within the ecosystem. Unseasonably warm winter weather also left the pythons, which grow up to 26 feet long, without incentive to boldly sun themselves.

In 2012, the U.S. Department of the Interior—hailing a milestone in Everglades protection—announced a nationwide ban on the import of Burmese pythons and other nonnative, large constrictor snakes, including both northern and southern African pythons and the yellow anaconda.

No matter what the future of the state's Python Challenge™, its war against invasive species and the efforts to protect Everglades wildlife continue unabated.

—By Lynne Helm

PARK ESSENTIALS

Admission Fees The fee is $10 per vehicle; and $5 per pedestrian, bicycle, or motorcycle. Payable at gates, the admission is good for seven consecutive days at all park entrances. Annual passes are $25.

Admission Hours The park is open daily, year-round. Both the main entrance near Florida City and Homestead, and the Gulf Coast entrance are open 24 hours. The Shark Valley entrance is open 8:30 am to 6 pm.

COE VISITOR CENTER TO FLAMINGO

About 30 miles from Miami.

The most popular access to Everglades National Park is via the park headquarters entrance southwest of Homestead and Florida City. If you're coming to the Everglades from Miami, take Route 836 West to Route 826/874 South to the Homestead Extension of Florida's Turnpike, U.S. 1, and Krome Avenue (Route 997/old U.S. 27). To reach the Ernest F. Coe Visitor Center from Homestead, go right (west) from U.S. 1 or Krome Avenue onto Route 9336 (Florida's only four-digit route) in Florida City and follow signage to the park entrance.

EXPLORING

To explore this section of the park, follow Route 9336 from the park entrance to Flamingo; you'll find many opportunities to stop along the way, and an assortment of activities to pursue in the Flamingo area.

Ernest F. Coe Visitor Center. Get your park map here, but don't just grab and go; this visitor center's numerous interactive exhibits and films are well worth your time. The 15-minute film *River of Life*, updated frequently, provides a succinct park overview. A movie on hurricanes and a 35-minute wildlife film for children are available upon request. A bank of telephones offers differing viewpoints on the

Great Water Debate, detailing how last century's gung ho draining of swampland for residential and agricultural development also cut off water-supply routes for precious wetlands in the Everglades ecosystem. You'll also find a schedule of daily ranger-led activities, mainly walks and talks; information on the popular Nike missile site tour (harking back to the Cuban missile crisis era); and details about canoe rentals and boat tours at Flamingo. The Everglades Discovery Shop stocks books, kids' stuff, and jewelry including bird-oriented earrings, plus insect repellent, sunscreen, and water. Coe Visitor Center, which has restrooms, is outside park gates, so you can stop in without paying park admission. ⊠ *40001 Rte. 9336, 11 miles southwest of Homestead* ☎ *305/242–7700* ⊙ *Daily 9–5, subject to change.*

Main road to Flamingo. Route 9336 travels 38 miles from the Ernest F. Coe Visitor Center southwest to the Florida Bay at Flamingo. It crosses a section of the park's eight distinct ecosystems: hardwood hammock, freshwater prairie, pinelands, freshwater slough, cypress, coastal prairie, mangrove, and marine-estuarine. Route highlights include a dwarf cypress forest, the transition zone between sawgrass and mangrove forest, and a wealth of wading birds at Mrazek and Coot Bay ponds—where in early morning or late afternoon you can observe them feeding. Be forewarned, however, that flamingo sightings are extremely rare. Boardwalks, looped trails, several short spurs, and observation platforms help you stay dry. You may want to stop along the way to walk several short trails (each takes about 30 minutes): the wheelchair-accessible **Anhinga Trail**, which cuts through sawgrass marsh and allows you to see lots of wildlife (be on the lookout for alligators and the trail's namesake water birds: anhingas); the junglelike—yet, also wheelchair-accessible—**Gumbo-Limbo Trail;** the **Pinelands Trail,** where you can see the park's limestone bedrock; the **Pahayokee Overlook Trail,** ending at an observation tower; and the **Mahogany Hammock Trail** with its dense growth. ■**TIP→** Before heading out on the trails, inquire about insect and weather conditions to plan accordingly, stocking up on bug repellent, sunscreen, and water as necessary. Even on seemingly sunny days, it's smart to bring rain gear.

Royal Palm Visitor Center. Ideal for when there's limited time to experience the Everglades, this small center with a bookstore and vending machines permits access to the **Anhinga Trail boardwalk,** where in winter spotting alligators congregating in watering holes is almost guaranteed.

The neighboring **Gumbo-Limbo Trail** takes you through a hardwood hammock. Combining these short strolls (½ mile or so) allows you to experience two Everglades ecosystems. Rangers conduct daily Anhinga Ambles in season (call ahead for times). A Glades Glimpse program takes place afternoons daily in season, as do starlight walks and bike tours. If you have a mind for history, ask about narrated Nike missile site tours, stemming from the '60s-era Cuban missile crisis. ⊠ *Rte. 9336, 4 miles west of Ernest F. Coe Visitor Center* ☎ *305/242–7700* ☺ *Daily 8–4:15.*

NEED A BREAK? Good spots to pull over for a picnic lunch are **Paurotis Pond**, about 10 miles north of Florida Bay, or **Nine Mile Pond**, less than 30 miles from the main visitor center. Another option is along **Bear Lake**, 2 miles north of the Flamingo Visitor Center.

Flamingo. At the far end of the main road to the Flamingo community along Florida Bay, you'll find a marina with a gift shop, visitor center, and campground, with nearby hiking and nature trails. Despite the name, what you are unlikely to find here are flamingos. To improve your luck for glimpsing these flamboyant pink birds with toothpick legs, check out Snake Bight Trail, starting about five miles from the Flamingo outpost. Before hurricanes Katrina and Wilma washed them away in 2005, a lodge, cabins, and restaurant facilities in Flamingo provided Everglades National Park's only accommodations. Rebuilding of Flamingo Lodge, long projected, has yet to materialize. For now, you can still pitch tents or bring RVs to the campground, where improvements include solar-heated showers and electricity for RV sites. A houseboat rental concession offers a pair of 35-footers each sleeping six and equipped with shower, toilet, bedding, kitchenware, stereo, and depth finder. The houseboats (thankfully air-conditioned) have 60-horsepower outboards and rent for $350 per night, plus a $200 fuel deposit.

Flamingo Marina Store—Everglades National Park Boat Tours 2. Next to the Flamingo Visitor Center, the only general store within Everglades National Park stocks limited groceries, snacks, souvenirs, bait, tackle, firewood, tents, and camping supplies, as well as fuel for boats and vehicles. It's a sister operation to Everglades National Park Boat Tours in Everglades City. ⊠ *Flamingo* ☎ *239/695–3101* ☺ *Daily 7–7.*

Flamingo Visitor Center. Check the schedule here for ranger-led activities, such as naturalist discussions, trail hikes, and evening programs in the 100-seat campground amphitheater, replacing the old gathering spot destroyed by 2005 hurricanes. If you're starving, the center's Buttonwood Cafe serves sandwiches, salads, and pizza. You'll find natural history exhibits and pamphlets on canoe, hiking, and biking trails in the 2nd-floor Florida Bay Flamingo Museum, accessible only by stairway and a steep ramp. ⊠ *1 Flamingo Lodge Hwy., Flamingo* ☎ *239/695–2945, 239/695–3101 for marina* ☺ *Exhibits always open, staffed mid-Nov.–mid-Apr., daily 8–4:30.*

SPORTS AND THE OUTDOORS
BIRD-WATCHING
Some of the park's best birding is in the Flamingo area.

BOATING

The 99-mile inland **Wilderness Trail** between Flamingo and Everglades City is open to motorboats as well as canoes, although, depending on the water level, powerboats may have trouble navigating above Whitewater Bay. Flat-water canoeing and kayaking are best in winter, when temperatures are moderate, rainfall diminishes, and mosquitoes back off—a little, anyway. You don't need a permit for day trips, although there's a seven-day, $5 launch fee for all motorized boats brought into the park. The Flamingo area has well-marked canoe trails, but be sure to tell someone where you're going and when you

GOOD READS

■ *The Everglades: River of Grass.* This circa-1947 classic by pioneering conservationist Marjory Stoneman Douglas (1890–1998) is a must-read.

■ *Everglades Wildguide.* Jean Craighead George gives an informative account of the park's natural history in this official National Park Service handbook.

■ *Everglades: The Park Story.* Wildlife biologist William B. Robertson Jr. presents the park's flora, fauna, and history.

expect to return. Getting lost is easy, and spending the night without proper gear can be unpleasant, if not dangerous.

Flamingo Lodge, Marina, and Everglades National Park Tours. Everglades National Park's official concessionaire operates a marina, runs tours, and rents canoes, kayaks, and skiffs, secured by credit cards. A one-hour, 45-minute backcountry cruise aboard the 50-passenger *Pelican* ($32.50) winds under a heavy canopy of mangroves, revealing abundant wildlife—from alligators, crocodiles, and turtles to herons, hawks, and egrets. Renting a 17-foot, 40-hp skiff from 7 am runs $195 per day (eight hours, if returned by 4 pm), $150 per half day, or $80 for two hours; there is a $100 credit card deposit required. Canoes for up to three paddlers rent for $16 for two hours (minimum), $22 for four hours, $32 for eight hours, and $40 overnight. Family canoes for up to four go for $20 for two hours, $30 for four hours, $40 for eight hours, and $50 for 24 hours. The concessionaire also rents bikes, binoculars, rods, reels, and other equipment by the half or full day. Feeling sticky after a day in the 'Glades? Hot showers are $3. (Flamingo Lodge, a victim of massive hurricane damage in 2005, remains closed pending a fresh start.) ■TIP→ An experimental Eco Tent of canvas and wood, unveiled in winter 2012–13, was immediately booked solid for the season. Built by University of Miami architecture students, Eco Tent sleeps four, has a table and chairs, and wins rave reviews from designers, park officials, and campers. It's a prototype for up to 40 more units, once funding is secured. ⊠ *1 Flamingo Lodge Hwy., on Buttonwood Canal, Flamingo* ☎ *239/695–3101, 239/695–0124 for Eco Tent reservations* ⊕ *www.evergladesnationalparkboattoursflamingo.com.*

GULF COAST ENTRANCE

To reach the park's western gateway, take U.S. 41 west from Miami for 77 miles, turn left (south) onto Route 29, and travel another 3 miles through Everglades City to the Gulf Coast Ranger Station. From Naples

Much skill is required to navigate boats through the shallow, muddy waters of the Everglades.

on the Gulf Coast, take U.S. 41 east for 35 miles, and then turn right onto Route 29.

Gulf Coast Visitor Center. The best place to bone up on Everglades National Park's watery western side is at this center just south of Everglades City (5 miles south of Tamiami Trail) where rangers can give you the park lowdown and address your questions. In winter, backcountry campers purchase permits here and canoeists check in for trips to the Ten Thousand Islands and 99-mile Wilderness Waterway Trail. Nature lovers view interpretive exhibits on local flora and fauna while waiting for naturalist-led boat trips. In season (Christmas through Easter), rangers lead bike tours and canoe trips. A selection of about 30 nature presentations and orientation films are available by request for view on a big screen. Admission is free only to this section, and no direct roads from here link to other parts of the park. ⊠ *815 Oyster Bar La., off Rte. 29, Everglades City* ☎ *239/695–3311* ☼ *Mid-Nov.–mid-Apr., daily 8–4:30; mid-Apr.–mid-Nov., daily 9–4:30.*

SPORTS AND THE OUTDOORS

BOATING AND KAYAKING

Everglades National Park Boat Tours. In conjunction with boat tours at Flamingo, this operation runs 1½-hour trips ($32) through the Ten Thousand Islands National Wildlife Refuge. Adventure-seekers often see dolphins, manatees, bald eagles, and roseate spoonbills. In peak season (November–April), 49-passenger boats run on the hour and half-hour daily. Mangrove wilderness tours ($40) on smaller boats are for up to six passengers. These one-hour, 45-minute trips are the best option to see alligators. The outfitter also rents canoes ($24 per day) and kayaks (from $45 per day). Taxes are additional. ⊠ *Gulf Coast Visitor Center, 815 Oyster Bar La., Everglades City* ☎ *239/695–2591, 866/628–7275* ⊕ *www.evergladesnationalparkboattoursgulfcoast.com/index.php.*

Fodor's Choice ★ **Everglades Rentals & Eco Adventures.** Ivey House Inn houses this established, year-round source for guided Everglades paddling tours and rentals. Canoes cost $35 the first day, $27 daily thereafter. Day-long kayak rentals are from $45. Shuttles deliver you to major launching areas such as Turner River ($25.60 to $32, one-way for up to two people). Highlights include bird and gator sightings, mangrove forests, no-man's-land beaches, and spectacular sunsets. Longer adventures include equipment rental, guide, and meals. ⊠ *Ivey House, 107 Camellia St., Everglades City* ☎ *877/567–0679, 239/695–3299* ⊕ *www. evergladesadventures.com.*

SHARK VALLEY

23½ miles west of Florida's Turnpike, off Tamiami Trail. Approximately 45 mins west of Miami.

You won't see sharks at Shark Valley. The name comes from the Shark River, also called the River of Grass, flowing through the area. Several species of shark swim up this river from the coast (about 45 miles south of Shark Valley) to give birth, though not at this particular spot. Young sharks (called pups), vulnerable to being eaten by adult sharks and other predators, gain strength in waters of the slough before heading out to sea.

EXPLORING

Although Shark Valley is the national park's north entrance, no roads here lead directly to other parts of the park. However, it's still worth stopping to take the two-hour narrated tram tour (reservations recommended; ⇨ *see listing below*). Stop at the halfway point and ascend to the top of the observation tower via a ramp.

Prefer to do the trail on foot? It takes nerve to walk the paved 15-mile loop in Shark Valley, because in the winter months alligators lie alongside the road, basking in the sun—most, however, do move quickly out of the way.

You also can ride a bicycle (the outfitter here rents one-speed, well-used bikes daily 8:30–4 for $8.50 per hour). Behind the bike-rental area a short boardwalk trail meanders through sawgrass, and another passes through a tropical hardwood hammock. An underwater live camera in the canal behind the center (viewed from the gift shop) lets visitors sporadically see the alligators and otters.

Observation Tower. At the Shark Valley trail's end (really, the halfway point of the 15-mile loop), you can pause to navigate this tower, first built in 1984, spiraling 50 feet upward. Once on top, you'll find the River of Grass gloriously spreads out as far as you can see. Observe water birds as well as alligators, and maybe even river otters crossing the road. The tower has a wheelchair-accessible ramp to the top. ⊠ *Shark Valley Loop Rd.*

Shark Valley Visitor Center. This small center has rotating exhibits, an underwater camera, a bookstore (run by the Everglades Association) with hats, postcards, and other souvenirs, plus park rangers ready for your questions. ✉ *36000 S.W. 8th St., Miami* ✛ *23½ miles west of Florida's Turnpike, off Tamiami Trail* ☎ *305/221–8776* ⊘ *Daily 9:15–5:15.*

SPORTS AND THE OUTDOORS

BOATING

Many Everglades-area tours operate only in season, roughly November through April.

Buffalo Tiger's Airboat Tours. A former chief of Florida's Miccosukee tribe founded this Shark Valley area tour operation, although at 94 years and counting, the chief no longer skippers the boat. Savvy guides narrate the trip to an old Indian camp on the north side of Tamiami Trail from the American Indian perspective. Don't worry about airboat noise, since engines are shut down during informative talks. The 45-minute tours run 10–5 Saturday through Thursday at $27.50 per person. Look online for discount coupons. Reservations are not required, and credit cards are now accepted at this once cash-only outpost. ✉ *29708 S.W. 8th St., 5 miles east of Shark Valley, 25 miles west of Florida's Turnpike* ☎ *305/559–5250* ⊕ *www.buffalotigersairboattours.com.*

GUIDED TOURS

Shark Valley Tram Tours. Starting at the Shark Valley visitor center, these popular two-hour, narrated tours ($22) on bio-diesel trams follow a 15-mile loop road—great for viewing gators—into the interior, stopping at a 50-foot observation tower. Bring your own water. Reservations are strongly recommended December through April. ✉ *Shark Valley Visitor Center, Shark Valley Loop Rd.* ☎ *305/221–8455* ⊕ *www. sharkvalleytramtours.com* ⊘ *Tours Dec.–Apr., hrly 9–4; May–Nov., hrly 9–3.*

> ### THE EVERGLADES WITH KIDS
>
> Although kids of all ages can enjoy the park, those six and older will get the most out of the experience. Consider how much you as a supervising adult will enjoy keeping tabs on tiny ones around so much water and so many teeth. Some children are frightened by sheer wilderness.

BIG CYPRESS NATIONAL PRESERVE

Through the early 1960s the world's largest cypress-logging industry prospered in Big Cypress Swamp until nearly all the trees were cut down. With the death of the industry, government entities began buying parcels. Now more than 729,000 acres, or nearly half of the swamp, form this national preserve. "Big" refers not to the new-growth trees but to the swamp, jutting into the north edge of Everglades National Park like a jigsaw-puzzle piece. Size and strategic location make Big Cypress an important link in the region's hydrological system, where rainwater first flows through the preserve, then south into the park, and eventually into Florida Bay. Its variegated pattern of wet prairies, ponds, marshes, sloughs, and strands provides a wildlife sanctuary, and thanks to a policy of balanced land use—"use without abuse"—the watery wilderness is devoted to recreation as well as to research and preservation. Bald cypress trees that may look dead are actually dormant, with green needles springing to life in spring. The preserve allows—in limited areas—hiking, hunting, and off-road vehicle use (airboat, swamp buggy, four-wheel drive) by permit. Compared with Everglades National Park, the preserve is less developed and hosts fewer visitors. That makes it ideal for naturalists, birders, and hikers preferring to see more wildlife than people.

Several scenic drives link from Tamiami Trail, some requiring four-wheel-drive vehicles, especially in wet summer months. A few lead to camping areas and roadside picnic spots. Apart from the Oasis Visitor Center, popular as a springboard for viewing alligators, the newer Big Cypress Swamp Welcome Center features a platform for watching manatees. Both centers, along Tamiami Trail between Miami and Naples, feature a top-notch 25-minute film on Big Cypress.

PARK ESSENTIALS

Admission Fees There's no admission fee to visit the preserve.

Admission Hours The park is open 24 hours daily, year-round. Accessible only by boat, Adams Key is for day use only.

Contacts Big Cypress National Preserve ☎ *239/695–1201* ⊕ *www.nps.gov/bicy.*

EXPLORING

Big Cypress Swamp Welcome Center. As a sister to the Oasis Visitor Center, the newer Big Cypress Swamp Welcome Center on the preserve's western side has lots of information, as well as restrooms, picnic facilities, and a 70-seat auditorium. An outdoor breezeway showcases an interactive Big Cypress watershed exhibit, illustrating Florida water flow. ■ TIP➔ **Love manatees? Here you'll find a platform for viewing these intriguing mammals that are attracted to warm water. (They were possibly once mistaken for mermaids by thirsty or love-starved ancient sailors.)** ✉ *33000 Tamiami Trail E, 5 miles east of SR29, Ochopee* ☎ *239/695–4758* ⊕ *www.nps.gov/bicy/planyourvisit/visitorcenters.htm* ☜ *Free* ⊙ *Daily 9–4:30.*

Clyde Butcher's Big Cypress Gallery. For taking home swamp memories in stark black and white, you can't do better than picking up a postcard, calendar, or more serious piece of artwork by photographer Clyde Butcher at his namesake trailside gallery. Butcher, a big guy with an even bigger beard, is an affable personality renowned for his knowledge of the 'Glades and his ability to capture its magnetism through a large format lens. Even if you can't afford his big stuff, you're warmly invited to gaze. Out back, Butcher and his wife Niki also rent a bungalow ($225 per night, October–April) and a cottage ($275 per night, year-round). ■ TIP→ Ask about Clyde's muck-abouts or Saturday Swamp Walks ($50), September through March. You'll need a hat, long pants, old sneakers, and—because you*will*get wet—a spare set of dry clothing. ⊠ *52388 Tamiami Trail, at mile marker 54.5, Ochopee* ☎ *239/695–2428* ⊕ *www. clydebutchersbigcypressgallery.com* ⊗ *Daily 10–5.*

Oasis Visitor Center. The big attraction at Oasis Visitor Center, on the east side of Big Cypress Preserve, is the observation deck for viewing fish, birds, and other wildlife. A small butterfly garden's native plants seasonally attract winged wonders. Inside, you'll find an exhibit area, bookshop, and a theater showing an informative 25-minute film on Big Cypress Preserve swamplands. Leashed pets allowed, but not on boardwalk deck. ■ TIP→ Get your gator watch on at the center's observation deck where big alligators congregate. ⊠ *52105 Tamiami Trail, Ochopee* ✛ *24 miles east of Everglades City, 50 miles west of Miami, 20 miles west of Shark Valley* ☎ *239/695–1201* ⊕ *www.nps.gov/bicy/ planyourvisit/visitorcenters* ☞ *Free* ⊗ *Daily 9–4:30.*

FAMILY **Ochopee Post Office.** North America's smallest post office is a former irrigation pipe shed on the Tamiami Trail's south side. Blink and you'll risk missing it. To support this picturesque outpost during an era of postal service closures and layoffs, why not buy a postcard of this one-room shack for mailing to whoever would appreciate it? You can mail packages or buy money orders here, too. ⊠ *38000 Tamiami Trail E, 4 miles east of Rte. 29, Ochopee* ☎ *239/695–2099* ⊗ *Weekdays 8–10 and noon–4, Sat. 10–11:30.*

WHERE TO EAT

$ ✕ **Joanie's Blue Crab Cafe.** West of the nation's tiniest post office by a
SEAFOOD quarter mile or so, you'll find this red barn of a place dishing out catfish, frogs' legs, gator, grouper, burgers, salads, and (no surprise here) an abundance of soft-shell crabs, crab cakes, and she-crab soup. Entrées run from $12.95 to market price. Grab an icy beer from the cooler and eat out front or on the back patio—keep an eye out for Gertrude, a neighborhood gator on the loose. Joanie's doors are open from 11 am to 5 pm, so don't be late for supper, and don't be surprised if there's some live entertainment. ⑤ *Average main: $13* ⊠ *39395 Tamiami Trail, Ochopee* ✛ *About 3½ miles east of Rte. 29, less than a mile west of Ochopee post office* ☎ *239/695–2682* ⊕ *www.joaniesbluecrabcafe.com* ⊗ *Closed Mon. (varies seasonally; call to confirm).*

SPORTS AND THE OUTDOORS

There are three types of trails—walking (including part of the extensive Florida National Scenic Trail), canoeing, and bicycling. All three trail types are easily accessed from the Tamiami Trail near the preserve visitor center, and one boardwalk trail departs from the center. Canoe and bike equipment can be rented from outfitters in Everglades City, 24 miles west, and Naples, 40 miles west.

Hikers can tackle the Florida National Scenic Trail, which begins in the preserve and is divided into segments 6.5 to 28 miles each. Two 5-mile trails, Concho Billy and Fire Prairie, can be accessed off Turner River Road, a few miles east. Turner River Road and Birdon Road form a 17-mile gravel loop drive that's excellent for birding. Bear Island has about 32 miles of scenic, flat, looped trails that are ideal for bicycling. Most trails are hard-packed lime rock, but a few miles are gravel. Cyclists share the road with off-road vehicles, most plentiful from mid-November through December.

To see the best variety of wildlife from your car, follow 26-mile Loop Road, south of U.S. 41 and west of Shark Valley, where alligators, raccoons, and soft-shell turtles crawl around beside the gravel road, often swooped upon by swallowtail kites and brown-shouldered hawks. Stop at H. P. Williams Roadside Park, west of the Oasis, and walk along the boardwalk to spy gators, turtles, and garfish in the river waters.

RANGER PROGRAMS

From the Oasis Visitor Center you can get in on the seasonal ranger-led or self-guided activities, such as campfire and wildlife talks, hikes, slough slogs, and canoe excursions. The 8-mile Turner River Canoe Trail begins nearby and crosses through Everglades National Park before ending in Chokoloskee Bay, near Everglades City. Rangers lead four-hour canoe trips and two-hour swamp walks in season; call for days and times. Bring shoes and long pants for the swamp walks and be prepared to wade at least knee-deep in water. Ranger program reservations are accepted up to 14 days in advance.

BISCAYNE NATIONAL PARK

Occupying 172,000 acres along the southern portion of Biscayne Bay, south of Miami and north of the Florida Keys, Biscayne National Park is 95% submerged, its terrain ranging from 4 feet above sea level to 60 feet below. Contained within are four distinct zones: Biscayne Bay, undeveloped upper Florida Keys, coral reefs, and coastal mangrove forest. Mangroves line the mainland shore much as they do elsewhere along South Florida's protected waters. Biscayne Bay serves as a lobster sanctuary and a nursery for fish, sponges, crabs, and other sea life. Manatees and sea turtles frequent its warm, shallow waters. The park hosts legions of boaters and landlubbers gazing in awe over the bay.

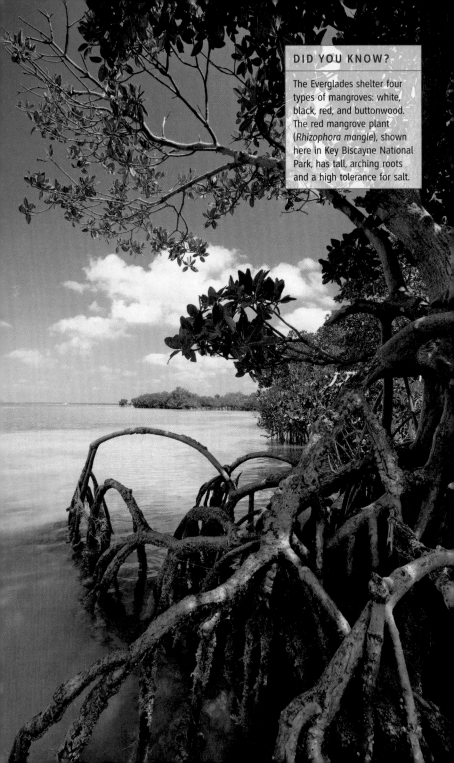

GETTING HERE

To reach Biscayne National Park from Homestead, take Krome Avenue to Route 9336 (Palm Drive) and turn east. Follow Palm Drive about 8 miles until it becomes S.W. 344th Street, and follow signs to park headquarters in Convoy Point. The entry is 9 miles east of Homestead and 9 miles south and east of Exit 6 (Speedway Boulevard/S.W. 137th Avenue) off Florida's Turnpike.

PARK ESSENTIALS

Admission Fees There's no fee to enter Biscayne National Park, and you don't pay a fee to access the islands, but there's a $20 overnight camping fee that includes a $5 dock charge to berth vessels at some island docks. The park concession charges for trips to the coral reefs and islands.

Admission Hours The park is open daily, year-round.

Contacs Biscayne National Park ⊠ *Dante Fascell Visitor Center, 9700 S.W. 328th St., Homestead* ☎ *305/230–7275* ⊕ *www.nps.gov/bisc.*

EXPLORING

Biscayne is a magnet for diving, snorkeling, canoeing, birding, and, to some extent (if you have a private boat), camping. Elliott Key is the best place to hike (⇨ *see The Islands*).

THE CORAL REEF

Biscayne's corals range from soft, flagellant fans, plumes, and whips found chiefly in shallow patch reefs to the hard brain corals, elkhorn, and staghorn forms that can withstand depths and heavier shoreline wave action.

THE ISLANDS

To the east, about 8 miles off the coast, 44 tiny keys stretch 18 nautical miles north to south, and are reached only by boat. No mainland commercial transportation operates to the islands, and only a handful are accessible: Elliott, Boca Chita, Adams, and Sands keys, lying between Elliott and Boca Chita. The rest are wildlife refuges or have rocky shores or waters too shallow for boats. December through April, when the mosquito population is less aggressive, is the best time to explore. Bring repellent, sunscreen, and water.

Adams Key. A stone's throw from the western tip of Elliott Key and 9 miles southeast of Convoy Point, the island is open for day use. It was the onetime site of the Cocolobo Club, a yachting retreat famous for hosting presidents Harding, Hoover, Johnson, and Nixon as well as other luminaries. Hurricane Andrew blew away what remained of club facilities in 1992. Adams Key has picnic areas with grills, restrooms, dockage, and a short trail running along the shore and through a hardwood hammock. Rangers live on-island. Access is by private boat, with no pets or overnight docking allowed. ⊕ *www.nps.gov/bisc/ planyourvisit/adamskey.*

Boca Chita Key. Ten miles northeast of Convoy Point and about 12 miles south of the Cape Florida Lighthouse on Key Biscayne, this key once was owned by the late Mark C. Honeywell, former president of Honeywell Company, and is on the National Register of Historic Places for its 10 historic structures. A ½-mile hiking trail curves around the island's south side. Climb the 65-foot-high ornamental lighthouse (by ranger tour only) for a panoramic view of Miami or check out the cannon from the HMS *Fowey*. There's no fresh water, access is by private boat only, and no pets are allowed. Only portable toilets are on site, with no sinks or showers. A $20 fee for overnight docking (6 pm to 6 am) covers a campsite; pay at the harbor's automated kiosk.

> ## BISCAYNE IN ONE DAY
>
> Most visitors come to snorkel or dive. Divers should plan to spend the morning on the water and the afternoon exploring the visitor center. The opposite is true for snorkelers, as snorkel trips (and one-tank shallow-dive trips) depart in the afternoon. If you want to hike as well, turn to the trails at Elliott Key—just be sure to apply insect repellent (and sunscreen, too, no matter what time of year).

Elliott Key. The largest of the islands, 9 miles east of Convoy Point, Elliott Key has a mile-long loop trail on the bay side at the north end of the campground. Boaters may dock at any of 36 slips (call ahead; Hurricane Sandy forced closure of the boardwalk and harbor in 2012, and at press time docks remained closed). Head out on your own to hike the 6-mile trail along so-called Spite Highway, a 225-foot-wide swath of green that developers mowed down in hopes of linking this key to the mainland. Luckily the federal government stepped in, and now it's a hiking trail through tropical hardwood hammock. Facilities include restrooms, picnic tables, fresh drinking water, cold (occasionally lukewarm) showers, grills, and a campground. Leashed pets are allowed in developed areas only, not on trails. A 30-foot-wide sandy shoreline about a mile north of the harbor on the west (bay) side of the key is the only one in the national park, and boaters like to anchor off here to swim. The beach, fun for families, is for day use only; it has picnic areas and a short trail that cuts through the hammock.

VISITOR CENTER

FAMILY **Dante Fascell Visitor Center.** Go outside on the wide veranda to soak up views across mangroves and Biscayne Bay at this Convoy Point visitor center. Inside the museum, artistic vignettes and on-request videos including the 11-minute *Spectrum of Life* explore the park's four ecosystems, while the Touch Table gives both kids and adults a feel for bones, feathers, and coral. Facilities include the park's canoe and tour concession, restrooms with showers, a ranger information area, gift shop with books, and vending machines. Various ranger programs take place daily during busy fall and winter seasons. On the second Sunday monthly (December through April), the free Family Fun Fest offers hands-on activities. Rangers also give informal tours on Boca Chita key; arrange in advance. A short trail and boardwalk lead to a jetty, and there are picnic tables and grills. This is the only area of the park accessible without a boat. ⌂ *9700 S.W. 328th St., Homestead* ☏ *305/230–7275* ⊕ *www.nps.gov/bisc* 💲 *Free* ☉ *Daily 9–5.*

SPORTS AND THE OUTDOORS

BIRD-WATCHING

More than 170 species of birds have been identified around the park. Expect to see flocks of brown pelicans patrolling the bay—suddenly rising, then plunging beak first to capture prey in their baggy pouches. White ibis probe exposed mudflats for small fish and crustaceans. Although all the keys are excellent for birding, Jones Lagoon (south of Adams Key, between Old Rhodes Key and Totten Key) is outstanding. It's approachable only by nonmotorized craft.

DIVING AND SNORKELING

Diving is great year-around but best in summer, when calmer winds and smaller seas result in clearer waters. Ocean waters, 3 miles east of the keys, showcase the park's main attraction—the northernmost section of Florida's living tropical coral reefs. Some are the size of an office desk, others as large as a football field. Glass-bottom-boat rides, when operating, showcase this underwater wonderland, but you really should snorkel or scuba dive to fully appreciate it.

A diverse population of colorful fish—angelfish, gobies, grunts, parrotfish, pork fish, wrasses, and many more—flits through the reefs. Shipwrecks from the 18th century are evidence of the area's international maritime heritage, and a Maritime Heritage Trail is being developed to link six of the major shipwreck and underwater cultural sites. Thus far, three sites, including a 19th-century wooden sailing vessel, have been plotted with GPS coordinates and marked with mooring buoys. Plastic dive cards are being developed that will contain navigational and background information.

WHAT'S NEARBY

EVERGLADES CITY

35 miles southeast of Naples and 83 miles west of Miami.

Aside from a chain gas station or two, Everglades City is perfect Old Florida. No high-rises (other than an observation tower) mar the landscape at this western gateway to Everglades National Park, just off the Tamiami Trail. It was developed in the late 19th century by Barron Collier, a wealthy advertising entrepreneur, who built it as a company town to house workers for his numerous projects, including construction of the Tamiami Trail. It grew and prospered until the Depression and World War II. Today this ramshackle town draws adventure seekers heading to the park for canoeing, fishing, and bird-watching excursions. Airboat tours, though popular, are banned within the preserve and park because of the environmental damage they cause to the mangroves. The Everglades Seafood Festival, going strong for about 40 years and held the first full weekend of February, draws crowds of more than 50,000 for delights from the sea, music, and craft displays. At quieter times, dining choices are limited to a handful of basic eateries. The town is small, fishing-oriented, and unhurried, making it excellent for boating,

Native plants along the Turner River Canoe Trail hem paddlers in on both sides, and alligators lurk nearby.

bicycling, or just strolling around. You can pedal along the waterfront on a 2-mile strand out to Chokoloskee Island.

Contacts Everglades Area Chamber of Commerce Welcome Center. Pick up brochures and pamphlets for area lodging, restaurants, and attractions, and ask for additional information from friendly staffers. ⊠ *32016 Tamiami Trail E, at Rte. 29* ☎ *239/695–3941* ⊕ *www.evergladeschamber.net.*

EXPLORING

Fakahatchee Strand Preserve State Park. The ½-mile Big Cypress Bend boardwalk through this linear swamp forest provides opportunity to see rare plants, nesting eagles, and Florida's largest stand of native royal palms co-existing—unique to Fakahatchee Strand—with bald cypress under the forest canopy. Fakahatchee Strand, about 20 miles long and 5 miles wide, is also the orchid and bromeliad capital of the continent with 44 native orchids and 14 native bromeliads, many blooming most extravagantly in hotter months. It's particularly famous for its ghost orchids (as featured in Susan Orlean's novel *The Orchid Thief*), visible on guided hikes. In your quest for ghost orchids, keep alert for white-tailed deer, black bears, bobcats, and the Florida panther. For park nature on parade, take the 12-mile-long (one-way) W. J. Janes Memorial Scenic Drive ($3 payable at the honor box; have exact change). Hike its spur trails if you have time. Rangers lead swamp walks and canoe trips November through April. ⊠ *Boardwalk on north side of Tamiami Trail, 7 miles west of Rte. 29; W. J. Janes Memorial Scenic Dr., ¾ mile north of Tamiami Trail on Rte. 29; ranger station at 137 Coastline Dr., Copeland* ☎ *239/695–4593* ⊕ *www.floridastateparks. org/fakahatcheestrand* ⧉ *Free* ☉ *Daily 8 am–sunset.*

Collier-Seminole State Park. The opportunity to try biking, hiking, camping, and canoeing into Everglades territory make this park a prime introduction to this often forbidding land. Of historical interest, a Seminole War blockhouse has been re-created to hold the interpretative center, and one of the "walking dredges"—a towering black machine invented to carve the Tamiami Trail out of the muck—stands silent on grounds amid tropical hardwood forest. Campsites (plans to re-open in 2015) include electricity, water, and picnic tables. Restrooms have hot water showers, and one has a couple of washers and dryers outside. ⊠ *20200 Tamiami Trail E, Naples* 🕾 *239/394–3397* ⊕ *www. floridastateparks.org/collier-seminole* 🖃 *$5 per car, $4 with lone driver, $2 for pedestrians or bikers* ☉ *Daily 8–sunset.*

Florida Panther National Wildlife Refuge. When this refuge opened in 1989, it was off-limits to the public to protect endangered cougar subspecies. In 2005, responding to public demand, the 26,400-acre refuge opened two short loop trails in a region lightly traveled by panthers so visitors could get tastes of wet prairies, tropical hammocks, and pine uplands where panthers roam and wild orchids thrive. The 1.3-mile trail is rugged and often thigh-high under water during summer and fall; it's closed when completely flooded. The shorter 0.3-mile Leslie M. Duncan Memorial Trail is wheelchair-accessible and open year-round. For either, bring drinking water and insect repellent. Although sightings are rare, you may spot deer, black bears, and the occasional panther—or their tracks. Annual events include the Save the Panther Week in March, with an open house, plant walks, and tours. ⊠ *Off Rte. 29, between U.S. 41 and I-75* 🕾 *239/353–8442* ⊕ *www.fws.gov/floridapanther* 🖃 *Free* ☉ *Daily dawn–dusk; trails may be closed July–Nov. because of rain.*

Museum of the Everglades. Through artifacts and photographs you can meet American Indians, pioneers, entrepreneurs, and anglers who played roles in southwest Florida development. Exhibits and a short film chronicle the tremendous feat of building the Tamiami Trail across mosquito-ridden, gator-infested Everglades wetlands. Permanent displays and monthly exhibits rotate works of local artists. The museum is housed in the Laundry Building, completed in 1927 and once used for washing linens from the Rod and Gun Club and Everglades Inn. ⊠ *105 W. Broadway* 🕾 *239/695–0008* 🖃 *Free* ☉ *Tues.–Sat. 9–4.*

WHERE TO EAT

$ ✕ **City Seafood.** Owner Richard Wahrenberger serves up gems from the
SEAFOOD sea delivered fresh from his own boats. Even better, you can chow down on his delectable, sustainable stone crabs—medium, large, jumbo, and colossal based on weight—with clear conscience. After removal of meaty claws, crabs are returned to waters where they grow new ones. Enjoy breakfast, lunch, or dinner inside this rustic haven, or sit outdoors to watch pelicans, gulls, tarpon, manatee, and the occasional gator play off the dock in the Barron River. Relax with a beer or wine by the glass. Appetizers run from deep-fried corn to conch, and sandwiches from hot dogs to pulled pork. Big draws, however, remain stone crabs and baskets of smoked mullet, grouper, shrimp, oysters, blue crab, gator, or frogs' legs. Got a cooler? City Seafood wraps for the road, and also ships. A gift shop sells cutesy crabby-style tanks, boxers, and

tees. $ *Average main: $15* ✉ *702 Begonia St.* ☎ *239/695–4700* ⊕ *www. cityseafood1.com.*

$$ ✕ **Everglades Seafood Depot.** Count on tasty, affordable meals in a scenic
SEAFOOD setting at this storied 1928 Spanish-style stucco structure fronting Lake Placid. Beginning life as the original Everglades train depot, the building later was deeded to the University of Miami for marine research, and appeared in the 1958 film *Winds across the Everglades* (starring Christopher Plummer, Peter Falk, Gypsy Rose Lee, and Burl Ives). Seafood is the star here now including lobster, frogs' legs, crab, and alligator. Steak, seafood, and combo entrées include salad or soup, or an extra-charge option for a salad bar with steamed shrimp. All-you-can-eat specials—fried chicken, a taco bar, or a seafood buffet—are staged on selected nights. Save room for "secret family recipe" coconut guava cake. If you'd like a view, ask for a back porch table or a lakeside window seat. $ *Average main: $20* ✉ *102 Collier Ave.* ☎ *239/695–0075* ⊕ *www.evergladesseafooddepot.com.*

$ ✕ **Havana Cafe.** Cuban specialties are a tasty change from the seafood
CUBAN houses of Everglades City. This cheery eatery with a dozen or so tables inside, has more seating on the porch. Service is order-at-the-counter for breakfast and lunch (7 am–3 pm), with dinner in season on Friday and Saturday nights. Jump-start your day with café con leche and a pressed-egg sandwich, or try a Havana omelet. For lunch, you'll find the ubiquitous Cuban sandwich, burgers, shrimp, grouper, steak, and pork plates with rice and beans and yucca. $ *Average main: $15* ✉ *191 Smallwood Dr., Chocoloskee* ☎ *239/695–2214* ⊕ *www.myhavanacafe.com* ▤ *No credit cards* ⊙ *No dinner Apr.–Oct. or Sun.–Thurs. Nov.–Mar.*

$$ ✕ **Oyster House Restaurant.** One of the town's oldest fish houses, Oyster
SEAFOOD House serves all the local staples—shrimp, gator tail, frogs' legs, oys-
FAMILY ters, stone crab, and grouper—in a lodgelike setting with mounted wild game on walls and rafters. Deep-frying remains an art in these parts, so if you're going to indulge, do it here where you can create your own fried platter for under $25. Try to dine at sunset for golden rays with your watery view. Outside, a 75-foot observation tower affords a terrific overview of the Ten Thousand Islands. $ *Average main: $20* ✉ *901 South Copeland Ave.* ☎ *239/695–2073* ⊕ *www.oysterhouserestaurant. com.*

$$$ ✕ **Rod and Gun Club.** Striking, polished pecky-cypress woodwork in this
SEAFOOD historic building dates from the 1920s, when wealthy hunters, anglers, and yachting parties arrived for the winter season. Presidents Hoover, Roosevelt, Truman, Eisenhower, and Nixon stopped by here, as did Ernest Hemingway, Burt Reynolds, and Mick Jagger. The main dining room holds overflow from the expansive screened porch overlooking the river. Like life in general here, friendly servers move slowly and upkeep is minimal. Fresh seafood dominates, from stone crab in season (October 15–May 15) to a surf-and-turf combo of steak and grouper or a swamp-and-turf duet of frogs' legs and steak (each $26.95), or pasta pairings, from $19.95. For $14.95 you can have your own catch fried, broiled, or blackened, served with salad, veggies, and potato. Pie choices are key lime and chocolate–peanut butter. Separate checks are discouraged at this cash-only venue, and there's a $5 plate-sharing charge.

Yesteryear's main lobby is well worth a look—even if you're eating elsewhere. Arrive by boat or land. Ⓢ *Average main: $25* ⊠ *200 Riverside Dr.* ☎ *239/695–2101* ⊕ *www.evergladesrodandgun.com* ▭ No credit cards ⊘ *Sometimes shuts down in summer; call ahead.*

Ⓢ ✕**Triad Seafood.** Along the Barron River, seafood houses, fishing boats, SEAFOOD and crab traps populate one shoreline; mangroves the other. Selling fresh off the boat, some seafood houses added picnic tables and eventually grew into restaurants. Family-owned Triad Seafood Market & Cafe is one, with a screened dining area, and additional outdoor seating under a breezeway and on a deck (heated in winter) overhanging the river. Here you can savor fresh seafood at its finest, or have it shipped. Nothing fancy (although smoked fish and oyster caesar salad are on the menu), but you'd be hard-pressed to find a better grouper sandwich. An all-you-can-eat fresh stone crab feast with butter or mustard sauce (October 15 to May 15; market prices fluctuate wildly) can thin your wallet, especially for the jumbos. Lunch starts at 11 am with fried shrimp, oyster, crab cake, and soft-shell blue crab baskets, plus reubens, Philly cheesesteaks, burgers, and kids' meals under $5 Ⓢ *Average main: $15* ⊠ *401 School Dr.* ☎ *239/695–0722* ⊕ *www. triadseafoodmarketcafe.com* ⊘ *Closed May 16–Oct. 15.*

WHERE TO STAY

Ⓢ 🏨 **Glades Haven Cozy Cabins.** Bob Miller wanted to build a Holiday Inn HOTEL next to his Oyster House Restaurant on marina-channel shores, but when that didn't fly, he sent for cabin kits and set up mobile-home-size units around a pool on his property as part of "Miller's World." **Pros:** great nearby food options; convenient to ENP boating; free docking; marina. **Cons:** trailer-park-crowded feel with a noisy bar nearby; no phones, no pets. Ⓢ *Rooms from: $95* ⊠ *801 Copeland Ave.* ☎ *239/695– 2746, 888/956–6251* ⊕ *www.gladeshaven.com* ⤳ *24 cabins, 2 3-bedroom houses* ⦿*No meals.*

Ⓢ 🏨 **Ivey House.** A remodeled 1928 boardinghouse originally built for B&B/INN crews working on the Tamiami Trail, Ivey House (originally operated Fodor's Choice by Mr. and Mrs. Ivey) now fits adventurers on assorted budgets. **Pros:** ★ historic; pleasant; affordable. **Cons:** not on water; some small rooms. Ⓢ *Rooms from: $169* ⊠ *107 Camellia St.* ☎ *877/567–0679, 239/695– 3299* ⊕ *www.iveyhouse.com* ⤳*30 rooms, 18 with bath; 1 2-bedroom cottage* ⦿*Breakfast.*

SPORTS AND THE OUTDOORS

AIR TOURS

Wings Ten Thousand Islands Aero Tours. These 20-minute to nearly 2-hour scenic flightseeing tours of the Ten Thousand Islands National Wildlife Refuge, Big Cypress National Preserve, Everglades National Park, and Gulf of Mexico operate November through April. Aboard an Alaskan Bush plane, you can see sawgrass prairies, American Indian shell mounds, alligators, and wading birds. Rates start at $46 and go up to $224 for a two-hour Everglades tour (per person with groups of three or four). Flights can be booked to the Florida Keys, connecting to the Dry Tortugas. ⊠ *Everglades City Airpark, 650 Everglades City Airpark Rd.* ☎ *239/695–3296.*

BOATING AND CANOEING

On the Gulf Coast explore the nooks, crannies, and mangrove islands of Chokoloskee Bay and Ten Thousand Islands National Wildlife Refuge, as well as the many rivers near Everglades City. The Turner River Canoe Trail, a pleasant day trip with almost guaranteed bird and alligator sightings, passes through the mangrove, dwarf cypress, coastal prairie, and freshwater slough ecosystems of Everglades National Park and Big Cypress National Preserve.

SHUTTLES FROM MIAMI

Super Shuttle. This 24-hour service runs air-conditioned vans between MIA and the Homestead–Florida City area; pickup is outside baggage claim and costs around $61 per person depending on your destination. For a return to MIA, reserve 24 hours in advance and know your pickup zip code for a price quote. ☎ 305/871–2000 ⊕ www.supershuttle.com.

Glades Haven Marina. Get out on Ten Thousand Islands waters in a 19-foot Sundance or a 17-foot Flicker fishing boat. Rates start at $200 a day, plus fuel, with half-day and hourly options. The outfitter also rents kayaks and canoes and has a 24-hour boat ramp and dockage for up to 24-ft. vessels. Launch your own boat for $15, a canoe or kayak for $5. ⊠ 801 Copeland Ave. S ☎ 239/695–2628 ⊕ www.gladeshaven.com.

FLORIDA CITY

3 miles southwest of Homestead on U.S. 1.

Florida's Turnpike ends in Florida City, the southernmost town on the peninsula, spilling thousands of vehicles onto U.S. 1 and eventually west to Everglades National Park, east to Biscayne National Park, or south to the Florida Keys. Florida City and Homestead run into each other, but the difference couldn't be more noticeable. As the last outpost before 18 miles of mangroves and water, this stretch of U.S. 1 is lined with fast-food eateries, service stations, hotels, bars, dive shops, and restaurants. Hotel rates increase significantly during NASCAR races at the nearby Homestead-Miami Speedway. Like Homestead, Florida City is rooted in agriculture, with expanses of farmland west of Krome Avenue and a huge farmers' market that ships produce nationwide.

EXPLORING

Tropical Everglades Visitor Center. Run by the nonprofit Tropical Everglades Visitor Association, this pastel pink center with teal signage offers abundant printed material plus tips from volunteer experts on exploring south Dade County, Homestead, Florida City, and the Florida Keys. ⊠ 160 U.S. 1 ☎ 305/245–9180, 800/388–9669 ⊕ www.tropicaleverglades.com.

WHERE TO EAT

$$
ITALIAN

✕ **Capri Restaurant.** This friendly family-owned enterprise has been a magnet for affordable Italian-American classics since 1958. Dine amid red-brick walls at round tables, or at sunny courtyard tables with umbrellas. Options range from the all you care to eat pasta on Tuesdays ($8) to crunchy crust pizza or paninis, or steak, prime rib, and a multitude of seafood-pasta combos. Tuesday is also lobster night. Daily early-birds (4:30–6:30) include soup or salad and potato or spaghetti. Specialty martinis and fruity cocktails supplement an extensive wine list. ⑤ *Average main: $16* ✉ *935 N. Krome Ave.* ☎ *305/247–1542* ⊕ *www.dinecapri.com* ⊘ *No lunch Sun.*

$ ╳ **Farmers' Market Restaurant.** Although this eatery is within the farm-
SEAFOOD ers' market on the edge of town and is big on serving fresh vegetables, seafood figures prominently on the menu. A family of anglers runs the place, so fish and shellfish are only hours from the sea, and there's a fish fry on Friday nights. Catering to farmers, the restaurant opens at 5:30 am, serving pancakes, jumbo eggs, and fluffy omelets with home fries or grits in a pleasant dining room with red and green checked tablecloths. For lunch or dinner, choose among fried shrimp or conch, seafood pasta, country-fried steak, and roast turkey, as well as salads, burgers and sandwiches. ⑤ *Average main: $13* ✉ *300 N. Krome Ave.* ☎ *305/242–0008.*

$$ ╳ **Mutineer Wharf Restaurant.** Families and older couples flock to this
SEAFOOD kitschy roadside outpost with a fish-and-duck pond. Built in 1980 to look like a ship—back when Florida City barely got on maps—etched glass divides bilevel dining rooms, with velvet-upholstered chairs, an aquarium, and nautical antiques. Florida lobster tails, stuffed grouper, shrimp, and snapper top the menu, along with another half-dozen daily seafood specials. Add to that steaks, ribs, and chicken. Yellowfin tuna wraps and grouper sandwiches are filling items for lunch, especially before a trip into Everglades Park. You also can relax for dinner in the restaurant's Wharf Lounge. Friday and Saturday nights feature live entertainment and dancing. ⑤ *Average main: $18* ✉ *11 S.E. 1st Ave. (U.S. 1), at Palm Dr.* ☎ *305/245–3377* ⊕ *www.mutineerrestaurant.com.*

WHERE TO STAY

$ ▦ **Best Western Gateway to the Keys.** For easy access to Everglades and
HOTEL Biscayne national parks as well as the Keys, you'll be well situated at this sprawling, two-story lodging spot two blocks off Florida's Turn-pike. **Pros:** convenient to parks, outlet shopping, and dining; business services; attractive pool area. **Cons:** traffic noise; fills up fast in high season. ⑤ *Rooms from: $135* ✉ *411 S. Krome Ave.* ☎ *305/246–5100, 888/981–5100* ⊕ *www.bestwestern.com/gatewaytothekeys* ⇆ *114 rooms* ⏐◎⏐ *Breakfast.*

$ ▦ **Econo Lodge.** Close to Florida's Turnpike and with access to the
HOTEL Keys, this is a serviceable overnight pullover spot with a complimen-tary breakfast. **Pros:** laundry facility on property; pool; proximity to mall outlet shopping. **Cons:** urban-ugly location; noisy. ⑤ *Rooms from: $89* ✉ *553 N.E. 1st Ave.* ☎ *305/248–9300, 800/553–2666* ⊕ *www.econolodge.com* ⇆ *42 rooms* ⏐◎⏐ *Breakfast.*

$ ▦ **Fairway Inn.** With a waterfall pool, this two-story motel with exterior
HOTEL room entry has some of the area's lowest chain rates, and it's next to the Chamber of Commerce visitor center so you'll have easy access to read-ing and planning material. **Pros:** affordable; convenient to restaurants, parks, and raceway. **Cons:** plain, small rooms; no-pet policy. ⑤ *Rooms from: $89* ✉ *100 S.E. 1st Ave.* ☎ *305/248–4202, 888/340–4734* ⇆ *160 rooms* ⏐◎⏐ *Breakfast.*

$ 🏨 **Quality Inn.** Amid an asphalt complex of hotels, gas stations, and eat-
HOTEL   eries just off U.S. 1, this two-story Quality Inn (previously a Comfort
Inn) with exterior corridors has a friendly front desk staff offering tips
on Everglades or Keys adventures, or action at the nearby track. **Pros:**
close to restaurants and services. **Cons:** no elevator; noisy location.
⑤ *Rooms from: $89* ⊠ *333 S.E. 1st Ave.* ☎ *305/248–4009, 888/352–
2489* ⊕ *www.qualityinn.com* ⟿ *123 rooms* ✺ *Breakfast.*

$ 🏨 **Ramada Inn.** If you're looking for an uptick from other chains, this
HOTEL   pet-friendly property offers more amenities and comfort, such as
32-inch flat-screen TVs, duvet-covered beds, closed closets, and stylish
furnishings. **Pros:** extra room amenities; convenient location. **Cons:**
chain anonymity. ⑤ *Rooms from: $99* ⊠ *124 E. Palm Dr.* ☎ *305/247–
8833* ⊕ *www.hotelfloridacity.com* ⟿ *123 rooms* ✺ *Breakfast.*

SHOPPING

FAMILY   **Robert Is Here.** Want take-home gifts? This remarkable fruit stand sells
more than 100 types of jams, jellies, honeys, and salad dressings along
with its vegetables, juices, fresh-fruit milk shakes (try the key lime),
and some 30 kinds of tropical fruits, including (in season) carambola,
lychee, egg fruit, monstera, sapodilla, dragonfruit, genipa, sugar apple,
and tamarind. Back in 1960, the stand got started when seven-year-old
Robert sat at this spot hawking his father's bumper cucumber crop.
Now Robert (still on the scene daily with his wife and kids), ships
nationwide and donates seconds to needy area families. An assortment
of animals out back—goats to iguanas and emus, along with a splash
pool—creates entertainment value for kids. Picnic tables, benches, and
a waterfall with a koi pond add serenity. On the way to Everglades
National Park, Robert opens at 8 am, operating until at least 7, and
shutting down from Labor Day until November. ⊠ *19200 S.W. 344th
St.* ☎ *305/246–1592.*

HOMESTEAD

30 miles southwest of Miami.

Since recovering from Hurricane Andrew in 1992, Homestead has
redefined itself as a destination for tropical agro- and ecotourism. At
a crossroads between Miami and the Keys as well as Everglades and
Biscayne national parks, the area has the added dimension of shopping centers, residential development, hotel chains, and the Homestead-
Miami Speedway—when car races are scheduled, hotels hike up their
rates and require minimum stays. The historic downtown has become a
preservation-driven Main Street. Krome Avenue, where it cuts through
the city's heart, is lined with restaurants, an arts complex, antiques
shops, and low-budget, sometimes undesirable, accommodations. West
of north–south Krome Avenue, miles of fields grow fresh fruits and
vegetables. Some are harvested commercially, and others beckon with
"U-pick" signs. Stands selling farm-fresh produce and nurseries that
grow and sell orchids and tropical plants abound. In addition to its
agricultural legacy, the town has an eclectic flavor, attributable to its
population mix: descendants of pioneer Crackers, Hispanic growers and

farm workers, professionals escaping the Miami hubbub, and latter-day northern retirees.

EXPLORING

Fruit & Spice Park. Because it officially qualifies for tropical status, this 37-acre park in Homestead's Redland historic agricultural district is the only public botanical garden of its type in the United States. More than 500 varieties of fruit, nuts, and spices typically grow here, and there are 75 varieties of banana alone, plus 160 of mango. Tram tours (included in admission) run three times daily, and you can sample fresh fruit at the gift shop, which also stocks canned and dried fruits plus cookbooks. The Mango Café, open daily, serves mango salsa, smoothies, and shakes along with salads, wraps, sandwiches, and a yummy Mango Passion Cheesecake. Picnic in the garden at provided tables or on your own blankets. Annual park events include January's Redland Heritage Festival and June's Summer Fruit Festival. ⊠ *24801 S.W. 187th Ave.* ☎ *305/247–5727* ⊕ *www.fruitandspicepark.org* ⊠ *$8* ⊙ *Daily 9–5; guided tram tours at 11, 1:30, and 3.*

Schnebly Redland's Winery. Enjoy Homestead's fruity bounty in liquid form at this winery that began producing wines of lychee, mango, guava, and other fruits as a way to avoid waste from family groves each year—bounty not perfect enough for shipping. Over the years, the winery (now with a brewery, too) has expanded with an indoor reception/tasting area serving snacks and a lush plaza area landscaped in coral rock, tropical plants, and waterfalls—topped with an Indian thatched chickee roof. Tours and tastings are offered daily. The Ultimate Tasting ($9.95) includes five wines, and an etched Schnebly glass you can keep. ⊠ *30205 S.W. 217th Ave.* ☎ *305/242–1224, 888/717–9463 (WINE)* ⊕ *www.schneblywinery.com* ⊙ *Weekdays 10–5, Sat. 10–6, Sun. noon–5.*

WHERE TO EAT

$

MEXICAN

✕ **NicaMex.** Among the local Latin population this 68-seat eatery is a low-budget favorite for Nicaraguan and Mexican flavors. It helps if you know Spanish, but the menu is bilingual and some staffers speak English. Although they term it *comidas rapidas* (fast food), the cuisine is not Americanized. Try authentic huevos rancheros or *chilaquiles* (corn tortillas cooked in red-pepper sauce) for breakfast. Specialties include *chicharron en salsa verde* (fried pork skin in hot-green-tomato sauce). Hearty beef soups are top sellers. If you want (or dare), Mexican plates from tacos to tostadas can be made with beef tongue. Choose among domestic or imported beers, and escape south of the border. ⑤ *Average main: $10* ⊠ *32 N.W. 1st St., across from Krome Ave. bandstand* ☎ *305/247–0727.*

WHERE TO STAY

$

HOTEL

🏠 **Hotel Redland.** Of downtown Homestead's smattering of mom-and-pop lodging options, this historic inn is by far the most desirable with its Victorian-style rooms done up in pastels and reproduction antique furniture. **Pros:** historic character; convenient to downtown and near antique shops; well maintained; smoke-free. **Cons:** traffic noise; some

Are baby alligators more to your liking than their daddies? You can pet one at Gator Park.

small rooms. $ *Rooms from: $100* ✉ *5 S. Flagler Ave.* ☎ *305/246–1904, 800/595–1904* ⊕ *www.hotelredland.com* 🛏 *13 rooms* ¶ *No meals.*

SPORTS AND THE OUTDOORS

AUTO RACING

Homestead-Miami Speedway. The speedway buzzes more than 280 days each year with racing, manufacturer testing, car-club events, driving schools, and ride-along programs. The facility has 65,000 grandstand seats, club seating eight stories above racing action, and two tracks—a 2.21-mile continuous road course and a 1.5-mile oval. A packed schedule includes GRAND-AM and NASCAR events. Two tunnels on the grounds are below sea level. ✉ *One Speedway Blvd.* ☎ *866/409–7223* ⊕ *www.homesteadmiamispeedway.com.*

WATER SPORTS

Homestead Bayfront Park. Boaters, anglers, and beachgoers give high ratings to facilities at this recreational area adjacent to Biscayne National Park. The 174-slip marina, accommodating vessels up to 50 feet, has a ramp, dock, bait-and-tackle shop, fuel station, ice, and dry storage. The park also has a snack bar, tidal swimming area, a beach with lifeguards, playground, ramps for people with disabilities, and a picnic pavilion with grills, showers, and restrooms. ✉ *9698 S.W. 328th St.* ☎ *305/230–3033* ⌲ *$6 per passenger vehicle; $12 per vehicle with boat Mon.–Thurs., $15 Fri.–Sun.; $15 per RV or bus* ☉ *Daily sunrise–sunset.*

TAMIAMI TRAIL

U.S. 41, between Naples and Miami

An 80-mile stretch of U.S. 41 (known as the Tamiami Trail) traverses the Everglades, Big Cypress National Preserve, and Fakahatchee Strand Preserve State Park. The road was conceived in 1915 to link Miami to Fort Myers and Tampa. When it finally became a reality in 1928, it cut through the Everglades and altered the natural flow of water as well as the lives of the Miccosukee Indians, who were trying to eke out a living fishing, hunting, farming, and frogging here. The landscape is surprisingly varied, changing from hardwood hammocks to pinelands, then abruptly to tall cypress trees dripping with Spanish moss and back to sawgrass marsh. Slow down to take in the scenery and you'll likely be rewarded with glimpses of alligators sunning themselves along the banks of roadside canals and hundreds of waterbirds, especially in the dry winter season. The man-made landscape includes Native American villages, chickee huts, and airboats parked at roadside enterprises. Between Miami and Naples the road goes by several names, including Tamiami Trail, U.S. 41, 9th Street in Naples, and, at the Miami end, S.W. 8th Street. ■TIP→ Businesses along the trail give their addresses based on either their distance from Krome Avenue, Florida's Turnpike, or Miami on the east coast or Naples on the west coast.

EXPLORING

Everglades Safari Park. A perennial favorite with tour-bus operators, this family-run park has an arena, seating up to 300 for shows with alligator wrestling. Before and after, get a closer look at both alligators and crocodiles on Gator Island, follow a jungle trail, walk through a small wildlife museum, or climb aboard an airboat for a 40-minute ride on the River of Grass (included in admission). There's also a restaurant, gift shop, and an observation platform looking out over the Glades. Smaller, private airboats can be chartered for tours lasting 40 minutes to 2 hours. Check online for coupons. ⊠ *26700 S.W. 8th St., 15 miles west of Florida's Turnpike* ☎ *305/226–6923, 305/223–3804* ⊕ *www.evergladessafaripark.com* ☑ *$23* ⊙ *Daily 9–5, last tour at 3:30.*

FAMILY **Gator Park.** Here you can get face-to-face with and even touch an alligator—albeit a baby one—during the park's Wildlife Show. You also can squirm in a "reptilium" of venomous and nonpoisonous native snakes or learn about American Indians of the Everglades through a reproduction of a Miccosukee village. The park, open rain or shine, also has 35-minute airboat tours as well as a gift shop and restaurant serving fare from burgers to gator tail. ⊠ *24050 Tamiami Trail, 12 miles west of Florida's Turnpike* ☎ *305/559–2255, 800/559–2205* ⊕ *www.gatorpark.com* ☑ *Tours, wildlife show, and airboat ride $22.99* ⊙ *Daily 9–5.*

FAMILY **Miccosukee Indian Village and Gift Shop.** Showcasing the skills and lifestyle of the Miccosukee Tribe of Florida, this cultural center offers craft demonstrations and insight into interaction with alligators. Narrated 30-minute airboat rides take you into the wilderness where natives hid after the Seminole Wars and Indian Removal Act of the mid-1800s. In modern times, many of the Miccosukee have relocated to this village along Tamiami Trail, but most still maintain their hammock farming and hunting camps. The museum shows a film and displays chickee structures and artifacts. Guided tours run throughout the day, and a gift shop stocks dolls, apparel, silver jewelry, beadwork, and other handcrafts. The Miccosukee Everglades Music and Craft Festival falls on a July weekend, and the 10-day Miccosukee Indian Arts Festival is in late December. ⊠ *U.S. 41, just west of Shark Valley entrance, 25 miles west of Florida's Turnpike at MM 70* ☎ *305/552–8365* ⊕ *www. miccosukee.com* ⤬ *Village $8, airboat rides $10* ⊙ *Daily 9–5.*

> ### CROCS OR GATORS?
>
> You can tell you're looking at a crocodile, not an alligator, if you can see its lower teeth protruding when its jaws are shut. Gators are much darker in color—a grayish black—compared with the lighter tan color of crocodiles. Alligator snouts—sort of U-shape—are also much broader than their long, thin A-shape crocodilian counterparts. South Florida is the world's only place where the two coexist. Alligators are primarily found in freshwater habitats, whereas crocodiles (better at expelling salt from water) are typically in coastal estuaries.

WHERE TO EAT

$ ✕ **Coopertown Restaurant.** Make
AMERICAN this a pit stop for local color and cuisine fished straight from the swamp. Started a half century ago as a sandwich stand, this eatery inside an airboat concession storefront has long attracted the famous and the humbly hungry. Besides catfish and shrimp, house specialties are frogs' legs and alligator tail breaded in cornmeal and deep-fried, served with lemon wedges and Tabasco. Sandwich options include burgers, hot dogs, and grilled cheese. $ *Average main: $12* ⊠ *22700 S.W. 8th St., 11 miles west of Florida's Turnpike* ☎ *305/226–6048* ⊕ *www.coopertownairboats.com* ⊙ *No dinner.*

$ ✕ **Miccosukee Restaurant.** For breakfast or lunch (or dinner until 9 pm,
SOUTHWESTERN November–April), this roadside cafeteria a quarter mile from the Miccosukee Indian Village provides the best menu variety along Tamiami Trail in Everglades territory. Atmosphere comes from the view overlooking the River of Grass, servers wearing traditional Miccosukee patchwork vests, and a mural depicting American Indian women cooking while men powwow. Catfish and frogs' legs are breaded and deep-fried. Besides pumpkin and Indian fry bread, you'll also find burgers, salads, and south-of-the-border dishes. The Miccosukee Platter (around $25) offers a sampling of local favorites, including gator bites. $ *Average main: $15* ⊠ *U.S. 41, 18 miles west of Miccosukee Resort & Gaming; 25 miles west of Florida's Turnpike* ☎ *305/894–2374* ⊙ *No dinner May–Oct.*

$ ✕ **Pit Bar-B-Q.** This old-fashioned roadside eatery along Tamiami Trail
BARBECUE near Krome Avenue was launched in 1965 by the late Tommy Little,
FAMILY who wanted to provide easy access to cold drinks and rib-sticking fare for folks heading into or out of the Everglades. This recently spiffed up backwood heritage vision remains a popular, affordable family option. Order at the counter, grab your food, and eat at picnic tables on the screened porch or outdoors. Specialties include barbecued chicken and ribs with a tangy sauce, fries, coleslaw, and a fried biscuit, plus burgers and fish sandwiches. The whopping double-decker beef or

pork sandwich with slaw requires multiple napkins. Latin specialties include deep-fried pork and fried green plantains. Beer is by the bottle or pitcher. Locals flock here with kids on weekends for pony rides. ⑤ *Average main: $12* ✉ *16400 S.W. 8th St., 5 miles west of Florida's Turnpike* ☎ *305/226–2272* ⊕ *www.thepitbarbq.com.*

WHERE TO STAY

$ · ⛨ **Miccosukee Resort & Gaming.** Like an oasis on the horizon of end-
RESORT · less sawgrass, this nine-story resort at the southeastern edge of the Everglades can't help but attract attention, even if you're not on the lookout for 24-hour gaming action. **Pros:** casino; most modern resort in these parts; golf. **Cons:** smoky lobby; hotel guests find parking lot fills with gamblers; feels incompatible with the Everglades. ⑤ *Rooms from: $149* ✉ *500 S.W. 177th Ave., 6 miles west of Florida's Turn-pike* ☎ *305/925–2555, 877/242–6464* ⊕ *www.miccosukee.com* 🛏 *256 rooms, 46 suites* ⎮❍⎮ *No meals.*

SPORTS AND THE OUTDOORS

BOAT TOURS

Many Everglades-area tours operate only in season, roughly November through April.

Coopertown Airboats. In business since 1945, the oldest airboat opera-tor in the Everglades offers 35- to 40-minute tours ($23) that take you 9 miles to hammocks and alligator holes. You also can book private charters of up to two hours. ✉ *22700 S.W. 8th St., 11 miles west of Florida's Turnpike* ☎ *305/226–6048* ⊕ *www.coopertownairboats.com.*

Everglades Alligator Farm. Open daily near the entrance to Everglades National Park, this working farm—home of the 14-foot "Grandpa" gator—runs a 4-mile, 30-minute airboat tour with departures 25 min-utes after the hour. The tour ($23) includes free hourly alligator, snake, and wildlife shows, or see only the gator farm and show ($15.50). Alli-gator feedings are at noon and 3 pm. Look for online coupons. ✉ *40351 S.W. 192nd Ave., Homestead* ☎ *305/247–2628* ⊕ *www.everglades.com.*

Everglades Safari Park. A 30-minute eco-adventure airboat ride costs $23, while longer, smaller, private airboat adventures, like the eco-adventure and sunset tours, cost more. All prices include the alliga-tor show and access to walking trails and exhibits. Look for online discounts. ✉ *26700 S.W. 8th St., 15 miles west of Florida's Turnpike* ☎ *305/226–6923, 305/223–3804* ⊕ *www.evergladessafaripark.com.*

Gator Park Airboat Tours. Open daily rain or shine, Gator Park conducts 45-minute narrated airboat tours ($22.99), including a park tour and wildlife show. Look for significant online discounts. ✉ *24050 S.W. 8th St., 12 miles west of Florida's Turnpike* ☎ *305/559–2255, 800/559–2205* ⊕ *www.gatorpark.com.*

FAMILY · **Wooten's Everglades Airboat Tours.** This classic Florida roadside attraction runs airboat tours (starting at $28 per person) through the Everglades for up to 18 people and swamp-buggy rides ($24 per person) through the Big Cypress Swamp for up to 25 passengers. Each lasts approxi-mately 30 minutes. (Swamp-buggies are giant tractorlike vehicles with huge rubber wheels.) More personalized airboat tours on smaller boats, seating six to eight, last about an hour. An on-site animal sanctuary with a live gator show ($8) shelters the typical Everglades array of alligators, snakes, and other creatures. Ask about packages that include an airboat ride, swamp-buggy adventure, and sanctuary access. Rates change frequently, but check out the website for combo packages. ✉ *32330 Tamiami Trail E, 1½ miles east of Rte. 29, Ochopee* ☎ *239/695–2781, 800/282–2781* ⊕ *www.wootenseverglades.com* ☉ *Daily 8:30–5; last ride departs at 4:30.*

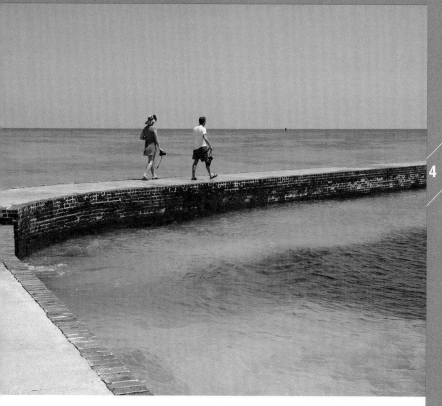

4

THE FLORIDA KEYS

WELCOME TO THE FLORIDA KEYS

TOP REASONS TO GO

★ **John Pennekamp Coral Reef State Park:** A perfect introduction to the Florida Keys, this nature reserve offers snorkeling, diving, camping, and kayaking. An underwater highlight is the massive *Christ of the Deep* statue.

★ **Under the sea:** Whether you scuba dive, snorkel, or ride a glass-bottom boat, don't miss gazing at the coral reef and its colorful denizens.

★ **Sunset at Mallory Square:** Sure, it's touristy, but just once while you're here, you've got to witness the circuslike atmosphere of this nightly celebration.

★ **Duval crawl:** Shop, eat, drink, repeat. Key West's Duval Street and the nearby streets make a good day's worth of window-shopping and people-watching.

★ **Get on the water:** From angling for trophy-size fish to zipping out to the Dry Tortugas, a boat trip is in your future. It's really the whole point of the Keys.

1 The Upper Keys. As the doorstep to the islands' coral reefs and blithe spirit, the Upper Keys introduce all that's sporting and sea-oriented about the Keys. They stretch from Key Largo to the Long Key Channel (MM 105–65).

2 The Middle Keys. Centered on the town of Marathon, the Middle Keys hold most of the chain's historic and natural attractions outside of Key West. They go from Conch (pronounced *konk*) Key through Marathon to the south side of the Seven Mile Bridge, including Pigeon Key (MM 65–40).

3 The Lower Keys. Pressure drops another notch in this laid-back part of the region, where key-deer viewing and fishing reign supreme. The Lower Keys go from Little Duck Key west through Big Coppitt Key (MM 40–9).

THE LOWER KEYS

4 Key West. The ultimate in Florida Keys craziness, this party town isn't for the closed-minded or those seeking a quiet retreat. The Key West area encompasses MM 9–0.

Homestead
TO MIAMI
905A
Card Sound Bridge
1
905
Everglades National Park
9336
Barnes Sound
Whitewater Bay
CAPE SABLE
Flamingo
Key Largo
Mexico
Florida Bay
1
THE UPPER KEYS
Key Largo
Tavernier
John Pennekamp Coral Reef State Park
Windley Key
Plantation Key
Islamorada
Upper Matecumbe Key
Straits of Florida
2
THE MIDDLE KEYS
Layton
Lower Matecumbe Key
Craig Key
Long Key
Marathon Airport
Conch Key
Duck Key
Grassy Key
arathon
Vaca Key
Flat Deer Key
Seven Mile Bridges
ATLANTIC OCEAN

4

GETTING ORIENTED

The Florida Keys are the dribble of islands off the peninsula's southern tip. From Miami International Airport, Key Largo is a 56-mile drive via the Florida Turnpike and U.S. 1. The rest of the keys—Islamorada, Marathon, Bahia Honda Key, and Big Pine Key—fall in succession for the 85 miles between Key Largo and Key West along the Overseas Highway. At their north end, the Florida Keys front Florida Bay, part of Everglades National Park. The Middle and Lower Keys front the Gulf of Mexico; the Atlantic Ocean borders the length of the chain on its eastern shores.

SEAFOOD IN THE FLORIDA KEYS

Fish. It's what's for dinner in the Florida Keys. The Keys' runway between the Gulf of Mexico or Florida Bay and Atlantic warm waters means fish of many fin. Restaurants take full advantage by serving it fresh, whether you caught it or a local fisherman did.

Menus at a number of colorful waterfront shacks such as **Snapper's** (✉ *139 Seaside Ave., Key Largo* ☎ *305/852–5956*) in Key Largo and **Half Shell Raw Bar** (✉ *231 Margaret St., Key West* ☎ *305/294–7496*) range from basic raw, steamed, broiled, grilled, or blackened fish to some Bahamian and New Orleans–style interpretations. Other seafood houses dress up their fish in creative haute cuisine styles, such as **Pierre's** (✉ *MM 81.5 BS, Islamorada* ☎ *305/664–3225* ⊕ *www.pierres-restaurant.com*) hogfish meunière, or yellowtail snapper with pear-ricotta pasta purses with caponata and red pepper coulis at **Café Marquesa** (✉ *600 Fleming St., Key West* ☎ *305/292–1244* ⊕ *www.marquesa.com*). Try a Keys-style breakfast of "grits and grunts"—fried fish and grits—at the **Stuffed Pig** (✉ *3520 Overseas Hwy., Marathon* ☎ *305/743–4059*).

BUILT-IN FISH

You know it's fresh when you see a fish market as soon as you open the door to the restaurant where you're dining. It happens frequently in the Keys. You can even peruse the seafood showcases and pick the fish fillet or lobster tail you want.

Many of the Keys' best restaurants are found in marina complexes, where the commercial fishermen bring their catches straight from the sea. Those in **Stock Island** (one island north of Key West) and at **Keys Fisheries Market & Marina** (✉ *MM 49 BS, end of 35th St., Marathon* ☎ *305/743-4353, 866/743-4353*) take some finding.

CONCH

One of the tastiest legacies of the Keys' Bahamian heritage (and most mispronounced), conch (pronouced *konk*) shows up on nearly every menu in some shape or form. It's so prevalent in local diets that natives refer to themselves as Conchs. Conch fritters are the most popular culinary manifestations, followed by cracked (pounded, breaded, and fried) conch, and conch salad, a ceviche-style refresher. Since the harvesting of queen conch is now illegal, most of the islands' conch comes from the Bahamas.

FLORIDA LOBSTER

Where are the claws? Stop looking for them: Florida spiny lobsters don't have 'em, never did. The sweet tail meat, however, makes up for the loss. Commercial and sport divers harvest these glorious crustaceans from late July through March. Check with local dive shops on restrictions, and then get ready for a fresh feast. Restaurants serve them broiled with drawn butter or in creative dishes such as lobster Benedict, lobster spring rolls, lobster Reuben, and lobster tacos.

GROUPER

Once central to Florida's trademark seafood dish—fried grouper sandwich—its populations have been overfished in recent years, meaning that the state has exerted more control over

bag regulations and occasionally closes grouper fishing on a temporary basis during the winter season. Some restaurants have gone antigrouper to try to bring back the abundance, but most grab it when they can. Black grouper is the most highly prized of the several varieties.

STONE CRAB

In season October 15 through May 15, it gets its name from its rock-hard shell. Fishermen take only one claw, which can regenerate in a sustainable manner. Connoisseurs prefer them chilled with tangy mustard sauce. Some restaurants give you a choice of hot claws and drawn butter, but this means the meat will be cooked twice, because it's usually boiled or steamed as soon as it's taken from its crab trap.

YELLOWTAIL SNAPPER

The preferred species of snappers, it's more plentiful in the Keys than in any other Florida waters. As pretty as it is tasty, it's a favorite of divers and snorkelers. Mild, sweet, and delicate, its meat lends itself to any number of preparations. It's available pretty much year-round, and many restaurants will give you a choice of broiled, baked, fried, or blackened. Chefs top it with everything from key lime beurre blanc to mango chutney. **Ballyhoo's** in Key Largo (⌧ *MM 97.8, in median* ☎ *305/852–0822*) serves it 10 different ways.

Updated by Jill Martin

Your Keys experience begins on your 18-mile drive south on "The Stretch," a portion of U.S. 1 with a specially colored blue median that takes you from Florida City to Key Largo. The real magic begins at mile marker 113, where the Florida Keys Scenic Highway begins. As the only All-American Road in Florida, it is a destination unto itself, one that crosses 42 bridges over water, including the Seven Mile Bridge—with its stunning vistas—and ends in Key West. Look for crocodiles, alligators, and bald eagles along the way.

Key West has a Mardi Gras mood with Fantasy Festival, a Hemingway look-alike contest, and the occasional threat to secede from the Union. It's an island whose eclectic natives, known as "Conchs," mingle well with visitors (of the spring break variety as well as those seeking to escape reality for a while) on this scenic, sometimes raucous 4x2-mile island paradise.

Although life elsewhere in the island chain isn't near as offbeat, it is as diverse. Overflowing bursts of bougainvillea, shimmering waters, and mangrove-lined islands can be admired throughout. The one thing most visitors don't admire much in the Keys are their beaches. They're not many, and they're not what you'd expect. The reason? The coral reef. It breaks up the waves and prevents sand from being dumped on the shores. That's why the beaches are mostly rough sand, as it's crushed coral. Think of it as a trade-off: the Keys have the only living coral reef in the U.S., but that reef prevents miles of shimmering sands from ever arriving.

In season, a river of traffic gushes southwest on this highway. But that doesn't mean you can't enjoy the ride as you cruise along the islands. Gaze over the silvery blue-and-green Atlantic and its living coral reef, with Florida Bay, the Gulf of Mexico, and the backcountry on your right (the Keys extend southwest from the mainland). At a few points the ocean and gulf are as much as 10 miles apart; in most places,

4

however, they're from 1 to 4 miles apart, and on the narrowest landfill islands they're separated only by the road.

While the views can be mesmerizing, to appreciate the Keys you need to get off the highway, especially in more developed regions like Key Largo, Islamorada, and Marathon. Once you do, rent a boat, anchor, and then fish, swim, or marvel at the sun, sea, and sky. Or visit one of the many sandbars, which are popular places to float the day away. Oceanside, dive or snorkel spectacular coral reefs or pursue grouper, blue marlin, mahimahi, and other deepwater game fish. Along Florida Bay's coastline, kayak to secluded islands through mangrove forests, or seek out the bonefish, snapper, snook, and tarpon that lurk in the shallow grass flats and mangrove roots of the backcountry.

PLANNING

WHEN TO GO

High season in the Keys falls between Christmas and Easter. November to mid-December crowds are thinner, the weather is wonderful, and hotels and shops drastically reduce their prices. Summer, which is hot and humid, is becoming a second high season, especially among Floridians, families, and European travelers. If you plan to attend the wild Fantasy Fest in October, book your room at least six months in advance. Accommodations are also scarce during the last consecutive Wednesday and Thursday in July (lobster sport season) and starting the first weekend in August, when the commercial lobster season begins.

Winter is typically 10°F warmer than on the mainland; summer is usually a few degrees cooler. The Keys also get substantially less rain, around 40 inches annually, compared with an average 55–60 inches in Miami and the Everglades. In the summertime, "thunder boomers" (quick-moving thunder storms) pass through most afternoons, although tropical storms can dump rain for two or more days. Winter cold fronts occasionally stall over the Keys, dragging overnight temperatures down to the low 50s.

GETTING HERE AND AROUND

AIR TRAVEL

About 450,000 passengers use the **Key West International Airport (EYW)** each year; its most recent renovation includes a beach where travelers can catch their last blast of rays after clearing security. Because flights are few, many prefer flying into Miami International Airport (MIA) and driving the 110-mile Overseas Highway (aka U.S. 1).

Contact **Key West International Airport** (EYW). ✉ 3491 S. Roosevelt Blvd., Key West ☎ 305/296–5439 ⊕ www.keywestinternationalairport.com.

BOAT AND FERRY TRAVEL

Key West can be reached by high-speed catamaran ferry from Fort Myers and Marco Island through Key West Express.

Boaters can travel to and along the Keys either along the Intracoastal Waterway through Card, Barnes, and Blackwater sounds and into Florida Bay or along the deeper Atlantic Ocean route through Hawk

Channel. The Keys are full of marinas that welcome transient visitors, but there aren't enough slips for all the boats heading to these waters. Make reservations far in advance and ask about channel and dockage depth—many marinas are quite shallow.

Contact **Key West Express** ✉ *100 Grinnell St., Key West* ☎ *888/539–2628* ⊕ *www.seakeywestexpress.com.*

BUS TRAVEL

Those unwilling to tackle the route's 42 bridges and peak-time traffic can take **Greyhound's** Keys Shuttle, which has multiple daily departures from Miami International Airport.

Contacts **Greyhound** ☎ *800/231–2222* ⊕ *www.greyhound.com.* **Keys Shuttle** ✉ *1333 Overseas Hwy., Marathon* ☎ *888/765–9997* ⊕ *www.keysshuttle.com.*

CAR TRAVEL

By car, from Miami International Airport, follow signs to Coral Gables and Key West, which puts you on LeJeune Road, then Route 836 west. Take the Homestead Extension of Florida's Turnpike south (toll road), which ends at Florida City and connects to the Overseas Highway (U.S. 1). Tolls from the airport run approximately $3. Payment is collected via SunPass, a prepaid toll program, or with Toll-By-Plate, a system that photographs each vehicle's license plate and mails a monthly bill for tolls, plus a $2.50 administrative fee, to the vehicle's registered owner.

Vacationers traveling in their own cars can obtain a mini-SunPass sticker via mail before their trip for $4.99 and receive the cost back in toll credits and discounts. The pass also is available at many major Florida retailers and turnpike service plazas. It works on all Florida toll roads and many bridges. For details on purchasing a mini-SunPass, call or visit the website.

For visitors renting cars in Florida, most major rental companies have programs allowing customers to use the Toll-By-Plate system. Tolls, plus varying service fees, are automatically charged to the credit card used to rent the vehicle (along with a hefty service charge in most cases). For details, including pricing options at participating rental-car agencies, check the program website. Under no circumstances should motorists attempt to stop in high-speed electronic tolling lanes. Travelers can contact Florida's Turnpike Enterprise for more information about the all-electronic tolling on Florida's Turnpike.

The alternative from Florida City is Card Sound Road (Route 905A), which has a (cash-only) bridge toll of $1. SunPass isn't accepted. Continue to the only stop sign and turn right on Route 905, which rejoins the Overseas Highway 31 miles south of Florida City. The best Keys road map, published by the Homestead–Florida City Chamber of Commerce, can be obtained for $5.50 from the Tropical Everglades Visitor Center.

Contacts **Florida's Turnpike Enterprise** ☎ *800/749–7453* ⊕ *www. floridasturnpike.com.* **SunPass** ☎ *888/865–5352* ⊕ *www.sunpass.com.*

THE MILE MARKER SYSTEM

Getting lost in the Keys is almost impossible once you understand the unique address system. **Many addresses are simply given as a mile marker (MM) number.** The markers are small, green, rectangular signs along the side of the Overseas Highway (U.S. 1). They begin with MM 126, 1 mile south of Florida City, and end with MM 0, in Key West. **Keys residents use the abbreviation BS for the bayside of Overseas Highway and OS for the oceanside.** From Marathon to Key West, residents may refer to the bayside as the gulfside.

HOTELS

Throughout the Keys, the types of accommodations are remarkably varied, from 1950s-style motels to cozy inns to luxurious resorts. Most are on or near the ocean, so water sports are popular. Key West's lodging portfolio includes historic cottages, restored Conch houses, and large resorts. Some larger properties throughout the Keys charge a mandatory daily resort fee of $15 or more, which can cover equipment rental, fitness-center use, and other services. You can expect another 12.5% (or more) in state and county taxes. Some guesthouses and inns don't welcome children, and many don't permit smoking.

Hotel reviews have been shortened. For full information, visit Fodors.com.

RESTAURANTS

Seafood rules in the Keys, which is full of chef-owned restaurants with not-too-fancy food. Many restaurants serve cuisine that reflects the proximity of the Bahamas and Caribbean (you'll see the term "Floribbean" on many menus). Tropical fruits figure prominently—especially on the beverage side of the menu. Florida spiny lobster should be local and fresh from August to March, and stone crabs from mid-October to mid-May. And don't dare leave the islands without sampling conch, be it in a fritter or in ceviche. Keep an eye out for authentic key lime pie—yellow custard in a graham-cracker crust. If it's green, just say "no." Note: Particularly in Key West and particularly during spring break, the more affordable and casual restaurants can get loud and downright rowdy, with young visitors often more interested in drinking than eating. Live music contributes to the decibel levels. If you're more of the quiet, intimate-dining type, avoid such overly exuberant scenes by eating early or choosing a restaurant where the bar isn't the main focus.

WHAT IT COSTS				
	$	$$	$$$	$$$$
RESTAURANTS	under $16	$16–$20	$21–$30	over $30
HOTELS	under $201	$201–$300	$301–$400	over $400

Restaurant prices are the average cost of a main course at dinner or, if dinner is not served, at lunch. Hotel prices are the lowest cost of a standard double room in high season.

THE UPPER KEYS

Diving and snorkeling are the primary draws in the Upper Keys, thanks to the tropical coral reef that runs a few miles off the seaward coast. Divers of all skill levels benefit from accessible dive sites and an established tourism infrastructure. Fishing is another huge draw, especially around Islamorada, known for its sportfishing in both deep offshore waters and in the backcountry. Offshore islands accessible only by boat are popular destinations for kayakers. In short, if you don't like the water, you might get bored here.

Other nature lovers won't feel shortchanged. Within 1½ miles of the bay coast lie the mangrove trees and sandy shores of Everglades National Park, where naturalists lead tours of one of the world's few saltwater forests. Here you'll see endangered manatees, curious dolphins, and other underwater creatures. Although the number of birds has dwindled since John James Audubon captured their beauty on canvas, the rare Everglades snail kite, bald eagles, ospreys, and a colorful array of egrets and herons delight bird-watchers. At sunset, flocks take to the skies as they gather to find their night's roost, adding a swirl of activity to an otherwise quiet time of day.

The Upper Keys are full of low-key eateries where the owner is also the chef and the food is tasty and never too fussy. The one exception is Islamorada, where you'll find more upscale restaurants. Places to eat may close for a two- to four-week vacation during the slow season between mid-September and late October.

In the Upper Keys the accommodations are as varied as they are plentiful. The majority of lodgings are in small waterfront complexes with furnished one- or two-bedroom units. These places offer dockage and often arrange boating, diving, and fishing excursions. There are also larger resorts with every type of activity imaginable and smaller boutique hotels where the attraction is personalized service.

Depending on which way the wind blows and how close the property is to the highway, there may be some noise from Overseas Highway. If this is an annoyance for you, ask for a room as far from the traffic as possible. Some properties require two- or three-day minimum stays during holiday and high-season weekends. Conversely, discounts may apply for midweek, weekly, and monthly stays.

GETTING HERE AND AROUND

Airporter operates scheduled van and bus pickup service from all Miami International Airport (MIA) baggage areas to wherever you want to go in Key Largo ($50) and Islamorada ($55). Groups of three or more passengers receive discounts. There are three departures daily; reservations are required 48 hours in advance. The SuperShuttle charges about $165 for two passengers for trips from Miami International Airport to the Upper Keys; reservations are required. For a trip to the airport, place your request 24 hours in advance.

Contacts Airporter ☎ 305/852–3413, 800/830–3413. **SuperShuttle** ☎ 305/871–2000 ⊕ www.supershuttle.com.

KEY LARGO

56 miles (90 km) south of Miami International Airport.

The first of the Upper Keys reachable by car, 30-mile-long Key Largo is also the largest island in the chain. Key Largo—named Cayo Largo ("Long Key") by the Spanish—makes a great introduction to the region.

The history of Largo is similar to that of the rest of the Keys, with its succession of native people, pirates, wreckers, and developers. The first settlement on Key Largo was named Planter, back in the days of pineapple, and later, key lime plantations. For a time it was a convenient shipping port, but when the railroad arrived, Planter died on the vine. Today three communities—North Key Largo, Key Largo, and Tavernier—make up the whole of Key Largo.

If you've never tried diving, Key Largo is the perfect place to learn. Dozens of companies will be more than happy to show you the ropes. Nobody comes to Key Largo without visiting John Pennekamp Coral Reef State Park, one of the jewels of the state-park system. Also popular is the adjacent Key Largo National Marine Sanctuary, which encompasses about 190 square miles of coral reefs, seagrass beds, and mangrove estuaries. Both are good for underwater exploration.

Fishing is the other big draw, and world records are broken regularly. There are plenty of charter operations to help you find the big ones and teach you how to hook the elusive (but inedible) bonefish, sometimes known as the ghost fish. On land, restaurants will cook your catch or dish up their own offerings with inimitable style.

Key Largo offers all the conveniences of a major resort town, with most businesses lined up along Overseas Highway (U.S. 1), the four-lane highway that runs down the middle of the island. Cars whiz past at all hours—something to remember when you're booking a room. Most lodgings are on the highway, so you'll want to be as far from the road as possible.

GETTING HERE AND AROUND

Key Largo is 56 miles south of Miami International Airport, with the mile markers going from 105 to 91. The island runs northeast–southwest, with Overseas Highway running down the center. If the highway is your only glimpse of the island, you're likely to feel barraged by its tacky commercial side. Make a point of driving Route 905 in North Key Largo and down side streets to the marinas to get a better feel for it.

VISITOR INFORMATION

Contact **Key Largo Chamber of Commerce**. Stop in for brochures, directions, recommendations, or some colorful Key Largo T-shirts and gifts. ✉ *MM 106 BS, 10600 Overseas Hwy.* ☎ *305/451–4747, 800/822–1088* ⊕ *www.keylargochamber.org.*

EXPLORING

Dagny Johnson Key Largo Hammock Botanical State Park. American crocodiles, mangrove cuckoos, white-crowned pigeons, Schaus swallowtail butterflies, mahogany mistletoe, wild cotton, and 100 other rare critters and plants inhabit these 2,400 acres, sandwiched between Crocodile

Lake National Wildlife Refuge and Pennekamp Coral Reef State Park. The park is also a user-friendly place to explore the largest remaining stand of the vast West Indian tropical hardwood hammock and mangrove wetland that once covered most of the Keys' upland areas. Interpretive signs describe many of the tropical tree species along a wide 1-mile paved road (2-mile round trip) that invites walking and biking. There are also more than 6 miles of nature trails accessible to bikes and wheelchairs. Pets are welcome if on a leash no longer than 6 feet. You'll also find restrooms, information kiosks, and picnic tables. ■TIP➔ Rangers recommend not visiting when it's raining as the trees can drip poisonous sap. ⊠ *Rte. 905 OS, 0.5 mile north of Overseas Hwy., North Key Largo* ☎ *305/451–1202* ⊕ *www.floridastateparks. org/keylargohammock* ☝ *$2.50 (exact change needed)* ☉ *Daily 8–sundown.*

FAMILY **Dolphin Cove.** This educational program begins at the facility's bayside lagoon with a get-acquainted session from a platform. After that, you slip into the water for some frolicking with your new dolphin pals. Options range from a sea lion swim (new at this location), to a shallow-water swim with a dolphin, to a hands-on structured swim with a dolphin. You can also spend the day shadowing a trainer for a hefty $670 fee. ⊠ *MM 101.9 BS, 101900 Overseas Hwy.* ☎ *305/451–4060, 877/365–2683* ⊕ *www.dolphinscove.com* ☝ *$10 admission only; interactive programs from $140* ☉ *Daily 8–5.*

FAMILY **Dolphins Plus.** A sister property to Dolphin Cove, Dolphins Plus offers some of the same programs and the age requirement is lower. The cheapest option, a Natural Swim program, begins with a one-hour briefing; then you enter the water to become totally immersed in the dolphins' world. In this visual orientation, participants snorkel but are not allowed to touch the dolphins. For tactile interaction (kissing, fin tows, etc.), sign up for the Structured Swim program, which is more expensive. ⊠ *MM 99, 31 Corrine Pl.* ☎ *305/451–1993, 866/860–7946* ⊕ *www.dolphinsplus.com* ☝ *Programs from $165* ☉ *Daily 8–5.*

FAMILY **Jacobs Aquatic Center.** Take the plunge at one of three swimming pools: an 8-lane, 25-meter lap pool with two diving boards; a 3- to 4-foot-deep pool accessible to people with mobility challenges; and an interactive children's play pool with a waterslide, pirate ship, waterfall, and sloping zero entry instead of steps. Because so few of the motels in Key Largo have pools, it remains a popular destination for visiting families. ⊠ *Key Largo Community Park, 320 Laguna Ave., at St. Croix Pl.* ☎ *305/453–7946* ⊕ *www.jacobsaquaticcenter.org* ☝ *$12 ($2 discount weekdays)* ☉ *Daily 10–6 (10–7 in summer).*

BEACHES

FAMILY **John Pennekamp Coral Reef State Park.** This state park is on everyone's
Fodor's Choice list for easy access to the best diving and snorkeling in Florida. The
★ underwater treasure encompasses 78 square miles of coral reefs and sea-grass beds. It lies adjacent to the Florida Keys National Marine Sanctuary, which contains 40 of the 52 species of coral in the Atlantic Reef System and nearly 600 varieties of fish, from the colorful parrot fish to the demure cocoa damselfish. Whatever you do, get in the

DID YOU KNOW?

The bronze *Christ of the Deep* (also called *Christ of the Abyss*) statue of Jesus Christ underwater near John Pennekamp Coral Reef State Park is modeled after one in the Mediterranean Sea near where Italian Dario Gonzatti died while scuba diving.

water. Snorkeling and diving trips ($30 and $55, respectively, equipment extra) and glass-bottom-boat rides to the reef ($24) are available, weather permitting. One of the most popular snorkel trips is to see *Christ of the Deep*, the 2-ton underwater statue of Jesus. The park also has nature trails, two man-made beaches, picnic shelters, a snack bar, and a campground. **Amenities:** food and drink; parking (fee); showers; toilets; water sports. **Best for:** snorkeling; swimming. ⌧ *MM 102.5 OS, 102601 Overseas Hwy.* ☎ *305/451–1202 for park, 305/451–6300 for excursions* ⊕ *www.pennekamppark.com, www.floridastateparks.org/ pennekamp* ⌦ *$4.50 for 1 person in vehicle, $8 for 2–8 people, $2 for pedestrians and cyclists or extra people (plus a $0.50 per-person county surcharge)* ⊘ *Daily 8–sunset.*

WHERE TO EAT

$$$
SEAFOOD
Fodor's Choice
★

✕ **Buzzard's Roost Grill and Pub.** The views are nice at this waterfront restaurant but the food is what gets your attention. Burgers, fish tacos, and seafood baskets are lunch faves. Dinner is about seafood and steaks, any way you like them. Try the smoked-fish dip, served with Armenian heart-shaped lavash crackers. Look for the big signs on U.S. 1 that direct you where to turn—it's worth finding. ⑤ *Average main: $21* ⌧ *Garden Cove Marina, 21 Garden Cove Dr., Northernmost Key Largo* ☎ *305/453–3746* ⊕ *www.buzzardsroostkeylargo.com.*

$$$
SEAFOOD

✕ **The Fish House.** Restaurants not on the water have to produce the highest quality food to survive in the Keys. That's how the Fish House has succeeded since the 1980s—so much so that it built the Fish House Encore (a fancier version) next door to accommodate fans. The pan-sautéed catch of the day is a long-standing favorite, as is the "Matecumbe-style" preparation—baked with tomatoes, capers, olive oil, and lemon juice, it will make you moan with pleasure. Prefer shellfish? Choose from shrimp, lobster, and (mid-October to mid-May) stone crab. The smoked fish chunks are the best in the Keys. The only thing bland is their side dishes: simple boiled red potatoes, a hunk of corn on the cob, or black beans and rice. For a sweet ending, the homemade key lime pie is award-winning. ⑤ *Average main: $21* ⌧ *MM 102.4 OS, 102341 Overseas Hwy.* ☎ *305/451–4665* ⊕ *www.fishhouse.com* ⌲ *Reservations not accepted* ⊘ *Closed Sept.* ⌐ *American Express not accepted.*

$
AMERICAN

✕ **Harriette's Restaurant.** If you're looking for comfort food—like melt-in-your-mouth biscuits the size of a salad plate—try this refreshing throwback. The kitchen makes muffins daily in 13 different flavors like mango, coconut, and key lime. Since the early 1980s, owner Harriette Mattson has been here to personally greet guests who come for the to-die-for omelets and old-fashioned hotcakes with sausage or bacon. For something unique, try the conch burger and eggs. At lunch, Harriette shines in the burger department, and her soups—from garlic tomato to chili—are homemade. ⑤ *Average main: $8* ⌧ *MM 95.7 BS, 95710 Overseas Hwy.* ☎ *305/852–8689* ⌲ *Reservations not accepted* ⊘ *No dinner* ⌐ *American Express not accepted.*

$$
SEAFOOD

✕ **JJ's Big Chill.** Owned by former NFL coach, Jimmy Johnson, this waterfront establishment offers three entertaining experiences, and all are big winners. You'll find the best sports bar in the Upper Keys complete with the coach's Super Bowl trophies, a main restaurant with all-glass indoor seating and a waterfront deck, and an enormous outdoor tiki bar with entertainment seven nights a week. There's even a pool and cabana club where (for an entrance fee) you can spend the day sunning. Menu favorites are the Parmesan-crusted snapper and brick-oven roasted chicken wings, but don't miss the tuna nachos—as delicious as they are artfully presented. As the sun sets over the bay, enjoy the views and a slice of white chocolate–macadamia cheesecake. $ *Average main: $16* ✉ *MM 104 BS, 104000 Overseas Hwy.* ☎ *305/453–9066* ⊕ *www. jjsbigchill.com.*

$ ✕ **Key Largo Conch House.** Tucked into the trees along the Overseas High-
AMERICAN way, this Victorian-style home (family-owned since 2004) and its true-to-the-Keys style of cooking is worth seeking out—at least the Food Network and the Travel Channel have thought so in the past. The Old South veranda and patio seating are ideal for winter dining, but indoors the seating is tighter. Raisin pecan French toast and seven varieties of Benedicts, including conch, are reason enough to rise early to get your fresh coffee fix. Lunch and dinner menus cover all bases, from a conch chowder bread bowl and vegetarian wraps to lobster and conch ceviche. Lionfish is proudly served when available, as is local yellowtail snapper. Interesting fact: the restaurant's "loo" was voted "Best of" for local restaurants. $ *Average main: $15* ✉ *MM 100.2, 100211 Overseas Hwy.* ☎ *305/453–4844* ⊕ *www.keylargoconchhouse.com* ⌂ *Reservations essential.*

$ ✕ **Mrs. Mac's Kitchen.** Townies pack the counters and booths at this tiny
SEAFOOD eatery, where license plates are stuck on the walls and made into chandeliers, for everything from blackened prime rib to crab cakes. Every night is themed including Meatloaf Mondays, Italian Wednesdays, and Seafood Sensation (offered Friday and Saturday). There's also a champagne breakfast (at this original location) and an assortment of tasty Angus beef burgers, sandwiches, a famous chili, and key lime freeze (a tangy concoction somewhere between a shake and a float). In season, ask about the hogfish special du jour. A second location, Mrs. Mac's Kitchen 2, is located half a mile south (✉ *MM 99 Center, 99020 Overseas Hwy.*), also in Key Largo. The newer location offers a similar menu, a full bar, and double the seating space. It's also kid-friendly. $ *Average main: $15* ✉ *MM 99.4 BS, 99336 Overseas Hwy.* ☎ *305/451–3722, 305/451–6227* ⊕ *www.mrsmacskitchen.com* ☾ *Closed Sun.*

$$$ ✕ **Sundowners.** The name doesn't lie. If it's a clear night and you can
AMERICAN snag a reservation, this restaurant will treat you to a sherbet-hue sunset over Florida Bay. If you're here in mild weather—anytime other than the dog days of summer or the rare winter cold snap—the best seats are on the patio. The food is excellent: try the key lime seafood, a happy combo of sautéed shrimp, lobster, and lump crabmeat swimming in a tangy sauce spiked with Tabasco served over penne or rice. Wednesday and Saturday are all about prime rib, and Friday draws the crowds with an all-you-can-eat fish fry. Vegetarian and gluten-free options are available. To beat the crowds, stop in for lunch, which offers the same great food, minus the hassle. $ *Average main: $22* ✉ *MM 104 BS, 103900 Overseas Hwy.* ☎ *305/451–4502* ⊕ *sundownerskeylargo.com* ⌂ *Reservations essential.*

WHERE TO STAY

$$
B&B/INN

⬚ **Azul del Mar.** The dock points the way to many beautiful sunsets at this no-smoking, adults-only boutique hotel, which Karol Marsden (an ad exec) and her husband Dominic (a travel photographer) have transformed from a run-down mom-and-pop place into a waterfront gem. **Pros:** great garden; good location; sophisticated design. **Cons:** small beach; high-priced; minimum stays during holidays. $ *Rooms from: $279* ⊠ *MM 104.3 BS, 104300 Overseas Hwy.* ☎ *305/451–0337, 888/253–2985* ⊕ *www.azulkeylargo.com* ⤳ *2 studios, 3 1-bedroom suites, 1 2-bedroom suite* ⎨⎧⎬ *No meals.*

$
RESORT

⬚ **Coconut Bay Resort & Bay Harbor Lodge.** Some 200 feet of waterfront is the main attraction at these side-by-side sister properties that offer a choice between smaller rooms and larger separate cottages. **Pros:** bay front; neatly kept gardens; walking distance to restaurants; complimentary kayak and paddleboat use. **Cons:** a bit dated; small sea-walled sand beach. $ *Rooms from: $175* ⊠ *MM 97.7 BS, 97702 Overseas Hwy.* ☎ *305/852–1625, 800/385–0986* ⊕ *www.coconutbaykeylargo. com* ⤳ *7 rooms, 5 efficiencies, 2 suites, 1 2-bedroom villa, 6 1-bedroom cottages* ⎨⎧⎬ *No meals.*

$$
B&B/INN

⬚ **Coconut Palm Inn.** You'd never find this waterfront haven unless someone told you it was there, as it's tucked into a residential neighborhood beneath towering palms and native gumbo limbos. **Pros:** secluded; quiet; sophisticated feel. **Cons:** Front desk closes early each evening; no access to ice machine when staff leaves; breakfast is ho-hum. $ *Rooms from: $279* ⊠ *MM 92 BS, 198 Harborview Dr., via Jo-Jean Way off Overseas Hwy., Tavernier* ☎ *305/852–3017* ⊕ *www.coconutpalminn.com* ⤳ *13 rooms, 7 suites* ⎨⎧⎬ *Breakfast.*

$$
B&B/INN

⬚ **Dove Creek Lodge.** With its sherbet-hued rooms and plantation-style furnishings, these tropical-style units (19 in all) range in size from simple lodge rooms to luxury two-bedroom suites. **Pros:** luxurious rooms; walk to Snapper's restaurant; complimentary kayaks and Wi-Fi. **Cons:** no beach; some find the music from next door bothersome. $ *Rooms from: $229* ⊠ *MM 94.5 OS, 147 Seaside Ave.* ☎ *305/852–6200, 800/401–0057* ⊕ *www.dovecreeklodge.com* ⤳ *4 room, 10 suites* ⎨⎧⎬ *Breakfast.*

$$
RESORT
Fodor'sChoice
★

⬚ **Hilton Key Largo Resort.** Nestled within a hardwood hammock (localese for uplands habitat where hardwood trees such as live oak grow) near the southern border of Everglades National Park, this sprawling resort had a $12-million renovation in 2012 and offers a full slate of amenities in a woodsy setting. **Pros:** nice nature trail on bay side; pretty pools with waterfalls; awesome trees; bicycles available for rent. **Cons:** some rooms overlook the parking lot; pools near the highway; expensive per-night resort fee. $ *Rooms from: $219* ⊠ *MM 97 BS, 97000 Overseas Hwy.* ☎ *305/852–5553, 888/871–3437* ⊕ *www.keylargoresort.com* ⤳ *190 rooms, 10 suites* ⎨⎧⎬ *No meals.*

$$
RENTAL

⬚ **Island Bay Resort.** When Mike and Carol Shipley took over this off-the-beaten-path resort in 2000, they revamped the 10 bayside cottages, improved the landscaping, and added touches such as hammocks and Adirondack chairs that make you feel like this is your own personal tropical playground. **Pros:** on the water; sunset views. **Cons:** most units are small; no pool; lacks on-site amenities. $ *Rooms from: $209*

☒ *92530 Overseas Hwy.* ☎ *305/852–4087* ⊕ *www.islandbayresort.com* 🛏 *10 units* ⦿ *No meals.*

$$ 🏨 **Kona Kai Resort, Gallery & Botanic Gardens.** Brilliantly colored bougainvillea, coconut palm, and guava trees—and a botanical garden of other rare species—make this 2-acre adult hideaway one of the prettiest places to stay in the Keys. **Pros:** free custom tours of botanical gardens for guests; free use of sports equipment; knowledgeable staff. **Cons:** expensive; some rooms are very close together. $ *Rooms from: $289* ☒ *MM 97.8 BS, 97802 Overseas Hwy.* ☎ *305/852–7200, 800/365–7829* ⊕ *www.konakairesort.com* 🛏 *8 suites, 3 rooms* ⊘ *Closed Sept.* ⦿ *No meals.*

RESORT
Fodor's Choice
★

$ 🏨 **Marriott's Key Largo Bay Beach Resort.** This 17-acre bayside resort has plenty of diversions, from diving to parasailing to a day spa. **Pros:** lots of activities; free covered parking; dive shop on property; free Wi-Fi. **Cons:** rooms facing highway can be noisy; thin walls. $ *Rooms from: $139* ☒ *MM 103.8 BS, 103800 Overseas Hwy.* ☎ *305/453–0000, 866/849–3753* ⊕ *www.marriottkeylargo.com* 🛏 *132 rooms, 20 2-bedroom suites, 1 penthouse suite* ⦿ *No meals.*

RESORT
FAMILY

$ 🏨 **The Pelican.** This 1950s throwback is reminiscent of the days when parents packed the kids into the station wagon and headed to no-frills seaside motels, complete with an old-timer fishing off the dock. **Pros:** free use of kayaks and a canoe; well-maintained dock; reasonable rates. **Cons:** some small rooms; basic accommodations and amenities. $ *Rooms from: $110* ☒ *MM 99.3, 99340 Overseas Hwy.* ☎ *305/451–3576, 877/451–3576* ⊕ *www.hungrypelican.com* 🛏 *13 rooms, 4 efficiencies, 4 suites, 2 trailers* ⦿ *Breakfast.*

HOTEL

NIGHTLIFE

The semiweekly *Keynoter* (Wednesday and Saturday), weekly *Reporter* (Thursday), and Friday through Sunday editions of the *Miami Herald* are the best sources of information on entertainment and nightlife.

Breezers Tiki Bar & Grille. Mingle with locals over cocktails and sunsets at Marriott's Key Largo Bay Beach Resort. ☒ *Marriott Key Largo Bay Beach Resort, 103800 Overseas Hwy.* ☎ *305/453–0000.*

Caribbean Club. Walls plastered with Bogart memorabilia remind customers that the classic 1948 Bogart–Bacall flick *Key Largo* has a connection with this worn watering hole. Although no food is served and the floors are bare concrete, this landmark draws boaters, curious visitors, and local barflies to its humble bar stools and pool tables. But the real magic is around back, where you can grab a seat on the deck and catch a postcard-perfect sunset. Live music draws revelers Thursday through Sunday. ☒ *MM 104 BS, 10404 Overseas Hwy.* ☎ *305/451–4466.*

SHOPPING

For the most part, shopping is sporadic in Key Largo, with a couple of shopping centers and fewer galleries than you find on the other big islands. If you're looking to buy scuba or snorkeling equipment, you'll have plenty of places from which to choose.

Bluewater Potters. Bluewater Potters creates functional and decorative ceramics ranging from signature vases and kitchenware to one-of-a-kind pieces where the owners' creative talent at the wheel blazes. In addition to their main gallery location in Key Largo, find them in the new Morada Way Arts and Culture District in Islamorada at MM 81.5. ✉ *MM 102.9 OS, 102991 Overseas Hwy.* ☎ *305/453–1920* ⊕ *www. bluewaterpotters.com.*

Fodor's Choice ★ **Key Largo Chocolates.** Specializing in key lime truffles made with quality Belgian chocolate, this is the only chocolate factory in the entire Florida Keys. But you'll find much more than just the finest white, milk, and dark chocolate truffles; try their cupcakes, ice cream, and famous "choco-diles." Another fan favorite is the salted turtles, which are worth every calorie. Chocolate classes are also available for kids and adults, and a small gift area showcases local art, jewelry, hot sauces, and other goodies. Look for the bright green and pink building. ✉ *MM 100 BS, 100471 Overseas Hwy.* ☎ *305/453–6613* ⊕ *www.keylargochocolates.com.*

Randy's Florida Keys Gift Co. Since 1989, Randy's has been "the" place for unique gifts. Owner Randy and his wife Lisa aren't only fantastic at stocking the store with a plethora of items, they're well respected in the community for their generosity and dedication. Stop in and say hello then browse the tight aisles and loaded shelves filled with key lime candles, books, wood carvings, jewelry, clothing, T-shirts, and eclectic, tropical decor items. This friendly shop prides itself on carrying wares from local craftsmen and there's something for every budget. ✉ *1102421 Overseas Hwy.* ⊹ *Right on U.S. 1, next to the Sandal Factory Outlet* ☎ *305/453–9229* ⊕ *www.keysmermaid.com.*

SPORTS AND THE OUTDOORS

BOATING

Everglades Eco-Tours. Captain Sterling operates Everglades and Florida Bay ecology tours and more expensive sunset cruises. You can see dolphins, manatees, and birds from the casual comfort of his pontoon boat, equipped with PVC chairs. Bring your own food and drinks. ✉ *Sundowners Restaurant, MM 104 BS, 103900 Overseas Hwy.* ☎ *305/853–5161, 888/224–6044* ⊕ *www.captainsterling.com* ⌧ *From $50.*

M.V. *Key Largo Princess*. Two-hour glass-bottom-boat trips and sunset cruises on a luxury 70-foot motor yacht with a 280-square-foot glass viewing area depart from the Holiday Inn docks three times a day. ✉ *Holiday Inn, MM 100 OS,99701 Overseas Hwy.* ☎ *305/451–4655, 877/648–8129* ⊕ *www.keylargoprincess.com* ⌧ *$30.*

CANOEING AND KAYAKING

Sea kayaking continues to gain popularity in the Keys. You can paddle for a few hours or the whole day, on your own or with a guide. Some outfitters even offer overnight trips. The **Florida Keys Overseas Paddling Trail,** part of a statewide system, runs from Key Largo to Key West. You can paddle the entire distance, 110 miles on the Atlantic side, which takes 9–10 days. The trail also runs the chain's length on the bayside, which is a longer route.

Coral Reef Park Co. At John Pennekamp Coral Reef State Park, this operator has a fleet of canoes and kayaks for gliding around the 2½-mile mangrove trail or along the coast. Powerboat rentals also available. ✉ *MM 102.5 OS, 102601 Overseas Hwy.* ☎ *305/451–6300* ⊕ *www. pennekamppark.com* ⌧ *Rentals from $12 per hr.*

Florida Bay Outfitters. Rent canoes or sea kayaks from this company, which sets up self-guided trips on the Florida Keys Overseas Paddling Trail, helps with trip planning, and matches equipment to your skill level. It also runs myriad guided tours around Key Largo. Take a full-moon paddle or a one- to seven-day canoe or kayak tour to the Everglades, Lignumvitae Key, or Indian Key. ⊠ *MM 104 BS, 104050 Overseas Hwy.* ☎ *305/451–3018* ⊕ *www.kayakfloridakeys.com* 🖅 *From $25.*

FISHING

Private charters and big head boats (so named because they charge "by the head") are great for anglers who don't have their own vessel.

Sailors Choice. Fishing excursions depart twice daily (half-day trips are cash-only), but the company also does private charters. The 65-foot boat leaves from the Holiday Inn docks. Rods, bait, and license are included. ⊠ *Holiday Inn Resort & Marina, MM 100 OS, 99701 Overseas Hwy.* ☎ *305/451–1802, 305/451–0041* ⊕ *www.sailorschoicefishingboat.com* 🖅 *From $40.*

SCUBA DIVING AND SNORKELING

Much of what makes the Upper Keys a singular dive destination is variety. Places like Molasses Reef, which begins 3 feet below the surface and descends to 55 feet, have something for everyone, from novice snorkelers to experienced divers. The *Spiegel Grove*, a 510-foot vessel, lies in 130 feet of water, but its upper regions are only 60 feet below the surface. On rough days, Key Largo Undersea Park's Emerald Lagoon is a popular spot. Expect to pay about $80 for a two-tank, two-site dive trip with tanks and weights, or $35–$40 for a two-site snorkel outing. Get big discounts by booking multiple trips.

Amy Slate's Amoray Dive Resort. This outfit makes diving easy. Stroll down to the full-service dive shop (NAUI, PADI, TDI, and BSAC certified), then onto a 45-foot catamaran. ⊠ *MM 104.2 BS, 104250 Overseas Hwy.* ☎ *305/451–3595, 800/426–6729* ⊕ *www.amoray.com* 🖅 *From $85.*

Conch Republic Divers. Book diving instruction as well as scuba and snorkeling tours of all the wrecks and reefs of the Upper Keys. Two-location dives are the standard, and you'll pay an extra $20 for tank and weights. ⊠ *MM 90.8 BS, 90800 Overseas Hwy.* ☎ *305/852–1655, 800/274–3483* ⊕ *www.conchrepublicdivers.com* 🖅 *From $65.*

Coral Reef Park Co. At John Pennekamp Coral Reef State Park, this company gives 3½-hour scuba and 2½-hour snorkeling tours of the park. In addition to the great location and the dependability it's also suited for water adventurers of all levels. ⊠ *MM 102.5 OS, 102601 Overseas Hwy.* ☎ *305/451–6300* ⊕ *www.pennekamppark.com* 🖅 *From $30.*

Ocean Divers. The PADI five-star facility has been around since 1975 and offers day and night dives, a range of courses, and dive-lodging packages. Two-tank reef dives include tank and weight rental. There are also organized snorkeling trips with equipment. ⊠ *MM 100 OS, 522 Caribbean Dr.* ☎ *305/451–1113, 800/451–1113* ⊕ *www.oceandivers. com* 🖅 *Snorkel trips from $35, diving from $85.*

Fodor'sChoice   **Quiescence Diving Services.** This operator sets itself apart in two ways: it
★   limits groups to six to ensure personal attention and offers both two-
dive day and night dives, as well as twilight dives when sea creatures
are most active. There are also organized snorkeling excursions. ✉ *MM
103.5 BS, 103680 Overseas Hwy.* ☎ *305/451–2440* ⊕ *www.quiescence.
com* 🖃 *Snorkel trips $49, diving from $75.*

ISLAMORADA

Islamorada is between mile markers 90.5 and 70.

Early settlers named this key after their schooner, *Island Home*, but
to make it sound more romantic they translated it into Spanish: *Isla
Morada*. The chamber of commerce prefers to use its literal transla-
tion "Purple Island," which refers either to a purple-shelled snail that
once inhabited these shores or to the brilliantly colored orchids and
bougainvilleas.

Early maps show Islamorada as encompassing only Upper Matecumbe
Key. But the incorporated "Village of Islands" is made up of a string of
islands that the Overseas Highway crosses, including Plantation Key,
Windley Key, Upper Matecumbe Key, Lower Matecumbe Key, Craig
Key, and Fiesta Key. In addition, two state-park islands accessible only
by boat—Indian Key and Lignumvitae Key—belong to the group.

Islamorada (locals pronounce it *eye*-la-mor-*ah*-da) is one of the world's
top sportfishing destinations. For nearly 100 years, seasoned anglers
have fished these clear, warm waters teeming with trophy-worthy fish.
There are numerous options for those in search of the big ones, including chartering a boat with its own crew or heading out on a vessel
rented from one of the plethora of marinas along this 20-mile stretch
of the Overseas Highway.

ESSENTIALS

Visitor Information Islamorada Chamber of Commerce & Visitors Center
✉ *MM 87.1 BS, 87100 Overseas Hwy.* ☎ *305/664–4503, 800/322–5397* ⊕ *www.
islamoradachamber.com.*

EXPLORING

Florida Keys Memorial / Hurricane Monument. On Monday, September 2,
1935, more than 400 people perished when the most intense hurricane
to make landfall in the U.S. swept through this area of the Keys. Two
years later, the Florida Keys Memorial was dedicated in their honor.
Native coral rock, known as keystone, covers the 18-foot obelisk monument that marks the remains of over 300 storm victims. A sculpted
plaque of bending palms and waves graces the front (although many
are bothered that the palms are bending in the wrong direction). In
1995, the memorial was placed on the National Register of Historic
Places. ✉ *MM 81.5, OS, 81000 Overseas Hwy., Upper Matecumbe
Key* 🖃 *Free.*

History of Diving Museum. Adding to the region's reputation for world-
class diving, this museum plunges into the history of man's thirst for
undersea exploration. Among its 13 galleries of interactive and other
interesting displays are a submarine and helmet re-created from the film

Islamorada's warm waters attract large fish and the anglers and charter captains who want to catch them.

20,000 Leagues Under the Sea. Vintage U.S. Navy equipment, diving helmets from around the world, and early scuba gear explore 4,000 years of diving history. For the grand finale, spend $3 for a mouth-piece and sing your favorite tune at the helium bar. There are extended hours (until 7 pm) on the third Wednesday of every month. ⊠ *MM 83 BS, 82990 Overseas Hwy., Upper Matecumbe Key* ☎ *305/664–9737* ⊕ *www.divingmuseum.org* 🖃 *$12* ☉ *Daily 10–5.*

Islamorada Founder's Park. This public park is the gem of Islamorada and boasts a palm-shaded beach, swimming pool, marina, skate park, tennis, and plenty of other facilities. If you want to rent a boat or learn to sail, businesses here can help you. If you're staying in Islamorada, admission is free. Those staying elsewhere pay $8 to enter the park. Either way, you pay an additional $3 to use the Olympic-size pool. A spiffy amphitheater hosts concerts, plays, and shows. The shallow water beach is ideal for swimming and families with little ones. Showers and bathrooms beachside. ⊠ *MM 87 BS, 87000 Overseas Hwy., Plantation Key* ☎ *305/853–1685.*

FAMILY **Robbie's Marina.** Huge, prehistoric-looking denizens of the not-so-deep, silver-sided tarpon congregate around the docks at this marina on Lower Matecumbe Key. Children—and lots of adults—pay $3 for a bucket of sardines to feed them and $1 each for dock admission. Spend some time hanging out at this authentic Keys community, where you can grab a bite to eat indoors or out, shop at a slew of artisans' booths, or charter a boat, kayak, or other water craft. ⊠ *MM 77.5 BS, 77522 Overseas Hwy., Lower Matecumbe Key* ☎ *305/664–9814, 877/664–8498* ⊕ *www.robbies.com* 🖃 *Dock access $1* ☉ *Daily sunrise–sunset.*

FAMILY **Theater of the Sea.** The second-oldest marine-mammal center in the world doesn't attempt to compete with more modern, more expensive parks. Even so, it's among the better attractions north of Key West, especially if you have kids in tow. In addition to marine life exhibits and shows, you can make reservations for up-close-and-personal encounters like a swim with a dolphin or sea lion, or stingray and turtle feedings (which include general admission; reservations required). These are popular, so reserve in advance. Ride a "bottomless" boat to see what's below the waves and take a guided tour of the marine-life exhibits. Nonstop animal shows highlight conservation issues. You can stop for lunch at the grill, shop in the extensive gift shop, or sunbathe and swim at their private beach. This easily could be an all-day attraction. ⊠ *MM 84.5 OS, 84721 Overseas Hwy., Windley Key* ☎ *305/664–2431* ⊕ *www.theaterofthesea. com* 🖃 *$31.95; interaction programs $35–$185* ⊙ *Daily 9:30–5 (last ticket sold at 3:30).*

Upper Matecumbe Key. This was one of the first of the Upper Keys to be permanently settled. Early homesteaders were so successful at grow-ing pineapples in the rocky soil that at one time the island yielded the country's largest annual crop. However, foreign competition and the hurricane of 1935 killed the industry. Today, life centers on fishing and tourism, and the island is filled with everything from bait shops and charter boats to eclectic galleries and fusion restaurants. ⊠ *MM 84–79.*

OFF THE
BEATEN
PATH
Indian Key Historic State Park. Mystery surrounds 10-acre Indian Key, on the ocean side of the Matecumbe islands. Before it became one of the first European settlements outside of Key West, it was inhabited by American Indians for several thousand years. The islet served as a base for 19th-century shipwreck salvagers until an Indian attack wiped out the settlement in 1840. Dr. Henry Perrine, a noted botanist, was killed in the raid. Today his plants grow in the town's ruins. Most people kayak or canoe here from Indian Key Fill or take a boat from Robbie's Marina to tour the nature trails and the town ruins or to snorkel. There are no restrooms or picnic facilities on Indian Key. ☎ *305/664–2540 for park* ⊕ *www.floridastateparks.org/indiankey* 🖃 *Free* ⊙ *Daily 8–5.*

OFF THE
BEATEN
PATH
Lignumvitae Key Botanical State Park. On the National Register of Historic Places, this 280-acre bay-side island is the site of a virgin hardwood forest and the 1919 home of chemical magnate William Matheson. His caretaker's cottage serves as the park's visitor center. Access is by boat—your own, a rented vessel, or a tour operated from Robbie's Marina. The tour leaves at 8:30 am Friday through Sunday and takes in both Lignumvitae and Indian keys (reservations required). Paddling here from Indian Key Fill, at MM 78.5, is a popular pastime. The only way to do the trails is by a guided ranger walk, offered at 10 am and 2 pm Friday to Sunday. Wear long sleeves and pants, and bring mosquito repellent. On the first Saturday in December is the Lig-numvitae Christmas Celebration, when the historic home is decorated 1930s-style. ☎ *305/664–2540 for park, 305/664–8070 for boat tours* ⊕ *www.floridastateparks.org/lignumvitaekey* 🖃 *$1 for ranger tours, $35 for boat tours* ⊙ *Park Thurs.–Mon. 8–5, house tours Fri.–Sun. at 10 and 2.*

Windley Key Fossil Reef Geological State Park. The fossilized-coral reef, dating back about 125,000 years, demonstrates that the Florida Keys were once beneath the ocean. Excavation of Windley Key's limestone bed by the Florida East Coast Railway exposed the petrified reef, full of beautifully fossilized brain coral and sea ferns. Visitors can see the fossils along a 300-foot quarry wall when hiking the park's three trails. There are guided (Friday, Saturday, and Sunday only) and self-guided tours along the trails, which lead to the railway's old quarrying equipment and cutting pits, where you can make rubbings of the quarry walls. The **Alison Fahrer Environmental Education Center** holds historic, biological, and geological displays about the area, including videos. The first Saturday in March is Windley Key Day, when the park sells native plants and hosts environmental exhibits. ⊠ *MM 84.9 BS, Windley Key* ☎ *305/664–2540* ⊕ *www.floridastateparks.org/windleykey* 🖃 *$2.50, plus $2 for guided tours* ⊙ *Education center Fri.–Sun. 9–5 (tours at 10 and 2).*

BEACHES

Anne's Beach Park. On Lower Matecumbe Key this popular village park is named for a local environmental activist. Its "beach" (really a typical Keys-style sand flat with a gentle slope) is best enjoyed at low tide. The nicest feature here is an elevated, wooden half-mile boardwalk that meanders through a natural wetland hammock. Covered picnic areas along the way give you places to linger and enjoy the view. Restrooms are at the north end. Weekends are packed with Miami day-trippers as it's the only public beach until you reach Marathon. **Amenities:** parking (no fee); toilets. **Best for:** partiers; snorkeling; swimming; windsurfing. ⊠ *MM 73.5 OS, Lower Matecumbe Key* ☎ *305/853–1685.*

WHERE TO EAT

$$$ ✕ **Chef Michael's.** Peace. Love. Hogfish. That's the motto of this local
SEAFOOD favorite that's been making big waves since its opening in 2011 with
Fodor'sChoice Chef Michael Ledwith at the helm. Sit outdoors on the covered wood
★ deck and tap your toes to the live music, or dine inside amid dark wood floors and white linens. Seafood is selected fresh daily, then elegantly prepared with a splash of tropical flair. Try hogfish with mango sauce, or the catch "Juliette" with shrimp, scallops, chardonnay butter, and toasted almonds. Carnivores can feast on prime-grade beef, carved in-house—that kind of marbling just melts in your mouth. Chef Michael even grows his own herbs, right out the kitchen door. How about a watermelon mint sangria? Just say yes. Gluten-free and vegetarian dishes are available. 🖹 *Average main: $29* ⊠ *MM 81.7, 81671 Overseas Hwy., Upper Matecumbe Key* ☎ *305/664–0640* ⊕ *www. foodtotalkabout.com* ⊛ *Reservations essential* ⊙ *No lunch Mon.–Sat.*

$$ ✕ **Hungry Tarpon.** As part of the colorful, bustling Old Florida scene
SEAFOOD at Robbie's Marina, you know that the seafood here is fresh and top quality. The extensive menu seems as if it's bigger than the dining space, which consists of a few tables and counter seating indoors, plus tables out back under the mangrove trees, close to where tourists pay to feed the tarpon in the marina. While tarpon are snacking on sardines, diners enjoy quite the impressive smattering of dishes for breakfast, lunch, and dinner. Specialties include biscuits and gravy, grilled ahi tuna nachos, a Matecumbe fish sandwich with provolone and bacon on grilled

sourdough, and a shrimp burrito. $ *Average main: $19* ✉ *MM 77.5 BS, 77522 Overseas Hwy., Lower Matecumbe Key* ☎ *305/664–0535* ⊕ *www.hungrytarpon.com* ⊗ *Reservations not accepted.*

$ ✕ **Islamorada Fish Company.** When a restaurant is owned by Bass Pro

SEAFOOD   Shops, you know the seafood should be as fresh as you can get it. The

FAMILY   fun begins in the parking lot with painted white fish marking the parking spaces. The restaurant is housed in an open-air, oversized tiki hut right on Florida Bay, making this the quintessential Keys experience. There's a small, low-key tiki bar area if you prefer a stool to a table. Menu highlights include cracked conch beaten 'til tender and fried crispy, and Grouper Portofino, which will keep you coming back for more. Each afternoon, the staff feed the fish in the bay. Jump out of your seat and walk over for a close-up view of snapper, large tarpon, and even sharks. $ *Average main: $15* ✉ *MM 81.5 BS, 81532 Overseas Hwy., Windley Key* ☎ *305/664–9271* ⊕ *restaurants.basspro.com/fishcompany/Islamorada* ⊗ *Daily 11–10.*

$ ✕ **Island Grill.** Don't be fooled by appearances; this shack on the water-

SEAFOOD   front takes island breakfast, lunch, and dinner up a notch. The eclectic menu tempts you with such dishes as its famed "original tuna nachos," lobster rolls, and a nice selection of seafood and sandwiches. Southern-style shrimp and andouille sausage with grits join island-style specialties such as grilled ribs with guava barbecue sauce on the list of entrées. There's an air-conditioned dining room and bar as well as open seating under a vaulted porch ceiling. The outdoor bar hosts live entertainment Wednesday to Sunday. Don't be in a hurry; service is usually slow. $ *Average main: $12* ✉ *MM 85.5 OS, 85501 Overseas Hwy., Windley Key* ☎ *305/664–8400* ⊕ *www.keysislandgrill.com* ⊗ *Reservations not accepted.*

$$$ ✕ **Marker 88.** A few yards from Florida Bay, this seafood restaurant

SEAFOOD   has been popular since the late '60s. Large picture windows offer great sunset views, but the bay is lovely no matter what time of day you visit. Outdoor dining is popular, too. Chef Bobby Stoky serves such irresistible entrées as onion-crusted mahimahi, crispy yellowtail snapper, and mangrove-honey-and-chipotle-glazed ribeye. In addition, there are a half-dozen burgers and sandwiches, and you can't miss the restaurant's famous key lime baked Alaska dessert. The extensive wine list is an oenophile's delight. $ *Average main: $28* ✉ *MM 88 BS, 88000 Overseas Hwy., Plantation Key* ☎ *305/852–9315* ⊕ *www.marker88.info* ⊗ *Reservations essential.*

$$$ ✕ **Morada Bay Beach Café.** This bayfront restaurant wins high marks for

ECLECTIC   its surprisingly stellar cuisine, tables planted in the sand, and tiki torches

FAMILY   that bathe the evening in romance. Entrées feature alluring combinations like fresh fish of the day sautéed with Meyer lemon butter and whole fried snapper with coconut rice. Seafood takes center stage, but you can always get roasted organic chicken or prime rib. Tapas and raw bar menus cater to smaller appetites or those who can't decide with offerings like fried calamari, conch fritters, and Wagyu beef sliders. Lunch adds interesting sandwiches to the mix. Sit in a dining room outfitted with surfboards, or outdoors on a beach, where the sunset puts on a mighty show and kids (and your feet) play in the sand. $ *Average* *main: $27* ⊠ *MM 81 BS, 81600 Overseas Hwy., Upper Matecumbe Key* ☎ *305/664–0604* ⊕ *www.moradabay-restaurant.com.*

$$$$ ✕ **Pierre's.** One of the Keys' most elegant restaurants, Pierre's marries
FRENCH colonial style with modern food trends. Full of interesting architec-
Fodor's Choice tural artifacts, the place oozes style, especially the wicker chair–strewn
★ veranda overlooking the bay. Save your best "tropical chic" duds for
dinner here, so you don't stand out from your surroundings. The food,
drawn from French and Floridian influences, is multilayered and beautifully presented. Among the seasonally changing appetizer choices,
you might find smoked hogfish chowder and foie gras sliders with a
butternut squash milk shake. A changing list of entrées might include
hogfish meunière and scallops with pork belly tortellini. The downstairs
bar is a perfect spot for catching sunsets, sipping martinis, and enjoying light eats. $ *Average main: $35* ⊠ *MM 81.5 BS, 81600 Overseas
Hwy., Upper Matecumbe Key* ☎ *305/664–3225* ⊕ *www.moradabay.
com* ⚐ *Reservations essential* ☉ *No lunch.*

WHERE TO STAY

$$ ☗ **Casa Morada.** This relic from the 1950s has been restyled into a suave,
B&B/INN design-forward, all-suites property with outdoor showers and Jacuzzis
Fodor's Choice in some of the suites. **Pros:** cool design; complimentary snacks and
★ bottled water; complimentary use of bikes, kayaks, and snorkel gear.
Cons: trailer park across the street; beach is small and inconsequential.
$ *Rooms from: $299* ⊠ *MM 82 BS, 136 Madeira Rd., Upper Mate-
cumbe Key* ☎ *305/664–0044, 888/881–3030* ⊕ *www.casamorada.com*
⚐ *16 suites* ◯| *Breakfast.*

$$ ☗ **Cheeca Lodge & Spa.** At 27 acres, this may be the largest resort in the
RESORT Keys, and it's also big on included amenities. **Pros:** beautifully land-
Fodor's Choice scaped grounds; new designer rooms; water-sports center on property.
★ **Cons:** expensive rates; expensive resort fee; very busy. $ *Rooms from:
$299* ⊠ *MM 82 OS, Box 527, Upper Matecumbe Key* ☎ *305/664–
4651, 800/327–2888* ⊕ *www.cheeca.com* ⚐ *60 1-bedroom suites, 64
junior suites* ◯| *No meals.*

$ ☗ **Drop Anchor Resort and Marina.** Immaculately maintained, this place has
HOTEL the feel of an old friend's beach house. **Pros:** bright and colorful; attention
to detail; laid-back charm. **Cons:** noise from the highway; beach is better
for fishing than swimming. $ *Rooms from: $149* ⊠ *MM 85 OS, 84959
Overseas Hwy., Windley Key* ☎ *305/664–4863, 888/664–4863* ⊕ *www.
dropanchorresort.com* ⚐ *18 suites* ◯| *No meals.*

$$ ☗ **The Islander, A Guy Harvey Outpost Resort.** Guests here get to choose
RESORT between a self-sufficient townhouse on the bay with room for a boat, or
an oceanfront resort with on-site restaurants and oodles of amenities.
Pros: spacious rooms; nice kitchens; eye-popping views. **Cons:** pricey
for what you get; beach has rough sand. $ *Rooms from: $249* ⊠ *MM
82.1 OS, 82200 Overseas Hwy., Upper Matecumbe Key* ☎ *305/664–
2031, 800/753–6002* ⊕ *www.guyharveyoutpostislamorada.com* ⚐ *114
rooms, 12 suites, 25 townhouses* ◯| *Breakfast.*

$$$ ☗ **The Moorings Village.** This tropical retreat is everything you imag-
HOTEL ine when you think of the Keys—from hammocks swaying between
Fodor's Choice towering trees to sugar-white sand (arguably the Keys' best resort
★ beach) lapped by aqua-green waves. **Pros:** romantic setting; good

dining options with room-charging privileges; beautiful beach. **Cons:** no room service; extra fee for housekeeping; daily resort fee for activities. ⑤ *Rooms from: $375* ✉ *MM 81.6 OS, 123 Beach Rd., Upper Matecumbe Key* ☎ *305/664–4708* ⊕ *www.themooringsvillage.com* ↪ *6 cottages, 12 houses* ⑩ *No meals.*

$$
HOTEL
Fodor'sChoice
★

Ocean House. Islamorada's newest adult boutique hotel is situated right on the Atlantic, yet it's hidden from passersby amidst lush gardens. **Pros:** complimentary use of kayaks, snorkel equipment and bicycles; luxurious facilities and amenities. **Cons:** limited number of units means they're often booked solid; luxury comes at a price. ⑤ *Rooms from: $299* ✉ *MM 82 OS, 82885 Old Hwy., Windley Key* ☎ *866/540–5520* ⊕ *www.oceanhousefloridakeys.com* ↪ *8 suites* ⑩ *Some meals.*

$$
RESORT

Postcard Inn Beach Resort & Marina at Holiday Isle. After an $11-million renovation that encompassed updating everything from the rooms to the public spaces, this iconic property (formerly known as the Holiday Isle Beach Resort) has found new life. **Pros:** large private beach; heated pools; on-site restaurants including Shula's 2. **Cons:** rooms near Tiki bar are noisy; minimum stay required during peak times; bathrooms need updating. ⑤ *Rooms from: $215* ✉ *MM 84 OS, 84001 Overseas Hwy., Plantation Key* ☎ *305/664–2321* ⊕ *www.holidayisle.com/Islamorada-beachclub* ↪ *143 rooms* ⑩ *No meals.*

$
HOTEL
FAMILY

Ragged Edge Resort. Nicely tucked away in a residential area at the ocean's edge, this family-owned hotel draws returning guests who'd rather fish off the dock and grill up dinner than loll around in Egyptian cotton sheets. **Pros:** oceanfront; boat docks and ramp; cheap rates. **Cons:** dated décor; off the beaten path. ⑤ *Rooms from: $110* ✉ *MM 86.5 OS, 243 Treasure Harbor Rd., Plantation Key* ☎ *305/852–5389, 800/436–2023* ⊕ *www.ragged-edge.com* ↪ *6 studios, 1 efficiency, 3 2-bedroom suites* ⑩ *No meals.*

SHOPPING

Art galleries, upscale gift shops, and the mammoth World Wide Sportsman (if you want to look the part of a local fisherman, you must wear a shirt from here) make up the variety and superior style of Islamorada shopping.

Banyan Tree. A sharp-eyed husband-and-wife team successfully combines antiques and contemporary gifts for the home and garden with plants, pots, and trellises in a stylishly sophisticated indoor–outdoor setting. ✉ *MM 81.2 OS, 81197 Overseas Hwy., Upper Matecumbe Key* ☎ *305/664–3433* ⊕ *www.banyantreegarden.com.*

Casa Mar Village. Change is good, and in this case, it's fantastic. What was once a row of worn-down buildings is now a merry blend of gift shops and galleries with the added bonus of a place selling fresh-roasted coffee. By day, these colorful shops glisten at their canalfront location; by nightfall, they're lit up like a lovely Christmastown. The offerings include the Jolly Pelican, Jewels by Vivi, the Little White Gallery, Olive Morada (upscale oils and vinegars), and the Fresh Press Cafe. ✉ *MM 90 OS, 90775 Old Hwy., Upper Matecumbe Key* ☎ *305/522-0330.*

Gallery Morada. This gallery is a go-to destination for one-of-a-kind gifts, beautifully displayed blown glass, original sculptures, paintings, lithographs, and jewelry by 200 artists. Its location, front and center, makes it the gateway to the Morada Way Arts & Cultural District, an area with artist galleries, shops, potters, gardens, and culinary classes. ✉ *MM 81.6 OS, 81611 Old Hwy., Upper Matecumbe Key* ☎ *305/664–3650* ⊕ *www.gallerymorada.com.*

Rain Barrel Artisan Village. This is a natural and unhurried shopping showplace. Set in a tropical garden of shady trees, native shrubs, and orchids, the crafts village has shops selling the work of local and national artists as well as resident artists who sell work from their own studios. Have your photo taken with "Betsy," the giant Florida lobster, roadside. ✉ *MM 86.7 BS, 86700 Overseas Hwy., Plantation Key* ☎ *305/852–3084* ⊕ *www.seefloridaonline.com/rainbarrel/index.html.*

Redbone Gallery. One of the largest sportfishing–art galleries in Florida stocks hand-stitched clothing and giftware, in addition to work by wood and bronze sculptors such as Kendall van Sant; watercolorist C. D. Clarke; and painters Daniel Caldwell, David Hall, Steven Left, and Stacie Krupa. Proceeds benefit cystic fibrosis research. Find them in the Morada Way Arts & Cultural District. ✉ *MM 81.5 OS, 200 Morada Way, Upper Matecumbe Key* ☎ *305/664–2002* ⊕ *www.redbone.org.*

World Wide Sportsman. This two-level retail center sells upscale and everyday fishing equipment, resort clothing, sportfishing art, and other gifts. When you're tired of shopping, relax at the Zane Grey Long Key Lounge, located above the store—but not before you step up and into *Pilar*, a replica of Hemingway's boat. ✉ *MM 81.5 BS, 81576 Overseas Hwy., Upper Matecumbe Key* ☎ *305/664–4615, 800/327–2880.*

SPORTS AND THE OUTDOORS
BOATING
Marinas pop up every mile or so in the Islamorada area, so finding a rental or tour is no problem. Robbie's Marina is a prime example of a salty spot where you can find it all—from fishing charters and kayaking rentals to lunch and tarpon feeding.

Bump & Jump. You can rent both fishing and deck boats here (from 15 to 29 feet) by the day or the week. There's free local delivery for those without trailers. ✉ *MM 81.2 OS, 81197 Overseas Hwy., Upper Matecumbe Key* ☎ *305/664–9404, 877/453–9463* ⊕ *www.keysboatrental.com* 🖃 *Rentals from $145 per day.*

Houseboat Vacations of the Florida Keys. See the islands from the comfort of your own boat (captain's cap optional). The company maintains a fleet of 44- to 55-foot boats that accommodate up to 10 people and come outfitted with everything you need besides food. (You may provision yourself at a nearby grocery store.) There's a three-day minimum; weekly rates are available. Kayaks and paddleboards suitable for bayside use are also available. ✉ *MM 85.9 BS, 85944 Overseas Hwy.* ☎ *305/664–4009* ⊕ *www.baysidetikiboats.com* 🖃 *From $1,150.*

Robbie's Boat Rentals & Charters. This full-service company will even give you a crash course on how not to crash your boat. The rental fleet includes an 18-foot skiff with a 90-horsepower outboard to a 21-foot deck boat with a 130-horsepower engine. Robbie's also rents snorkeling gear (there's good snorkeling nearby) and sells bait, drinks and snacks. Want to hire a guide who knows the local waters and where

Kayak ready to be used on the beach in the Florida Keys

the fish lurk? Robbie's offers offshore-fishing trips, patch-reef trips, and party-boat fishing. Backcountry flats trips are a specialty. ⊠ *MM 77.5 BS, 77522 Overseas Hwy., Lower Matecumbe Key* ☎ *305/664–9814, 877/664–8498* ⊕ *www.robbies.com* ✉ *From $185 per day.*

Treasure Harbor Marine. The Anderson family will provide everything you need for a bareboat sailing vacation at sea. They also give excellent advice on where to find the best anchorages, snorkeling spots, or lobstering sites. Vessels range from a 23.5-foot Hunter to a 41-foot Morgan Out Island. Boats can be rented by the day or week. Marina facilities include water, electric, ice machine, laundry, picnic tables, and restrooms with showers. Transient and longterm dockage available. A store sells snacks, beverages, and sundries. ⊠ *MM 86.5 OS, 200 Treasure Harbor Dr., Plantation Key* ☎ *305/852–2458, 800/352–2628* ⊕ *www.treasureharbor.com* ✉ *From $160 per day.*

FISHING

Here in the self-proclaimed "sportfishing capital of the world," sailfish is the prime catch in the winter and dolphinfish (mahimahi) in the summer. Buchanan Bank just south of Islamorada is a good spot to try for tarpon in the spring. Blackfin tuna and amberjack are generally plentiful in the area, too. ■ TIP➜ **The Hump at Islamorada ranks highest among anglers' favorite fishing spots in Florida because of the incredible offshore marine life.**

Captain Ted Wilson. Go into the backcountry for bonefish, tarpon, redfish, snook, and shark aboard a 17-foot boat that accommodates up to three anglers. Two people can choose half- or full-day trips, two hour sunset bonefishing excursions, or evening fishing excursions. There's an extra

$100 charge for each additional person. ⊠ *MM 79.9 OS, 79851 Overseas Hwy., Upper Matecumbe Key* ☎ *305/942–5224, 305/664–9463* ⊕ *www.captainedwilson.com* ✉ *Bonefishing from $250, half-day trips from $400.*

Florida Keys Fly Fish. Like other top fly-fishing and light-tackle guides, Captain Geoff Colmes helps his clients land trophy fish in the waters around the Keys. ⊠ *105 Palm La., Upper Matecumbe Key* ☎ *305/853–0741* ⊕ *www.floridakeysflyfish.com* ✉ *From $400.*

Florida Keys Outfitters. Long before fly-fishing became popular, Sandy Moret was fishing the Keys for bonefish, tarpon, and redfish. Now he attracts anglers from around the world on a quest for the big catch. His weekend fly-fishing classes include classroom instruction, equipment, and daily lunch. Guided fishing trips can be done for a half day or full day. Packages combining fishing and accommodations at Islander Resort are available. ⊠ *Green Turtle, MM 81.2, 81219 Overseas Hwy., Upper Matecumbe Key* ☎ *305/664–5423* ⊕ *www.floridakeysoutfitters. com* ✉ *Half-day trips from $496.*

Hubba Hubba Charters. Captain Ken Knudsen has fished the Keys waters since the 1970s. A licensed backcountry guide, he's ranked among Florida's top 10 by national fishing magazines. He offers four-hour sunset trips for tarpon and two-hour sunset trips for bonefish, as well as half- and full-day outings. Prices are for one or two anglers, and tackle and bait are included. ⊠ *MM 79.8 OS, Upper Matecumbe Key* ☎ *305/664–9281* ✉ *From $200.*

SCUBA DIVING AND SNORKELING

Florida Keys Dive Center. Dive from John Pennekamp Coral Reef State Park to Alligator Light with this outfitter. The center has two 46-foot Coast Guard–approved dive boats, offers scuba training, and is one of the few Keys dive centers to offer Nitrox and Trimix (mixed gas) diving. ⊠ *MM 90.5 OS, 90451 Overseas Hwy., Plantation Key* ☎ *305/852–4599, 800/433–8946* ⊕ *www.floridakeysdivectr.com* ✉ *Snorkeling from $38, diving from $65.*

Islamorada Dive Center. This one-stop dive shop has a resort, pool, restaurant, lessons, and twice-daily dive and snorkel trips. You can take a day trip with a two-tank dive or a one-tank night trip without equipment. Snorkel trips are also available. ⊠ *MM 84 OS, 84001 Overseas Hwy., Windley Key* ☎ *305/664–3483, 800/327–7070* ⊕ *www. islamoradadivecenter.com* ✉ *Snorkel trips from $45, diving from $80.*

WATER SPORTS

The Kayak Shack. You can rent kayaks for trips to Indian (about 20 minutes one way) and Lignumvitae (about 45 minutes one way) keys, two favorite destinations for paddlers. Kayaks can be rented for a half day—and you'll need plenty of time to explore those mangrove canopies. Pedal kayaks are also available and are a bit more expensive. The company also offers guided three-hour tours, including a snorkel trip to Indian Key. It also rents stand-up paddleboards, including instruction, and canoes. ⊠ *Robbie's Marina, MM 77.5 BS, 77522 Overseas Hwy., Lower Matecumbe Key* ☎ *305/664–4878* ⊕ *www.kayakthefloridakeys. com* ✉ *From $40 for single, $55 for double; guided trips from $45.*

EN
ROUTE

Long Key Viaduct. As you cross Long Key Channel, look beside you at the old viaduct. The second-longest bridge on the former rail line, this 2-mile-long structure has 222 reinforced-concrete arches. The old bridge is popular with cyclists and anglers, who fish off the sides day and night.

THE MIDDLE KEYS

Most of the activity in this part of the Florida Keys centers on the town of Marathon—the region's third-largest metropolitan area. On either end of it, smaller keys hold resorts, wildlife research and rehab facilities, a historic village, and a state park. The Middle Keys make a fitting transition from the Upper Keys to the Lower Keys not only geographically but mentally. Crossing Seven Mile Bridge prepares you for the slow pace and don't-give-a-damn attitude you'll find a little farther down the highway. Fishing is one of the main attractions—in fact, the region's commercial-fishing industry was founded here in the early 1800s. Diving is another popular pastime. There are many natural areas to enjoy in the Middle Keys, where mainland stress becomes an ever more distant memory.

If you get bridge fever—the heebie-jeebies when driving over long stretches of water—you may need a pair of blinders (or a couple of tranquilizers) before tackling the Middle Keys. Stretching from Conch Key to the far side of the Seven Mile Bridge, this zone is home to the region's two longest bridges: Long Key Viaduct and Seven Mile Bridge, both historic landmarks.

DUCK KEY

Duck Key is at mile marker 61.

Duck Key holds one of the region's nicest marina resorts, Hawks Cay, plus a boating-oriented residential community.

EXPLORING

Dolphin Connection. Hawk's Cay Resort's Dolphin Connection offers three programs, including Dockside Dolphins, a 30-minute encounter from the dry training docks; Dolphin Discovery, an in-water program that lasts about 45 minutes and lets you kiss, touch, and feed the dolphins; and Trainer for a Day, a three-hour session with the animal training team. ⊠ *Hawk's Cay Resort, MM 61 OS,61 Hawks Cay Blvd.* ☎ *305/743–7000* ⊕ *www.dolphinconnection.com* ➳ *From $60.*

WHERE TO EAT AND STAY

$$$
LATIN AMERICAN

✕ **Alma.** A refreshing escape from the Middle Keys' same-old menus, Alma serves expertly prepared Florida and Latin-Caribbean dishes in an elegant setting. Nightly changing menus might include a trio of ceviche, ahi tuna with a wonderful garbanzo bean–tomato sauce, gnocchi and exotic mushroom ragout, or pan-seared Wagyu steak. Finish your meal with the silky, smooth, passion fruit crème brûlée, which has just the right amount of tartness to balance the delicate caramelized crust. ⑤ *Average main: $28* ⊠ *Hawks Cay Resort, MM 61 OS, 61*

Hawks Cay Blvd. ☎ *305/743–7000, 888/432–2242* ⊕ *www.hawkscay. com* ☾ *No lunch.*

$$
RESORT
FAMILY
Fodor'sChoice
★

ⓣ **Hawks Cay Resort.** The 60-acre, Caribbean-style retreat with a full-service spa and restaurants has plenty to keep the kids occupied (and adults happy). **Pros:** huge rooms; restful spa; full-service marina and dive shop. **Cons:** no real beach; far from Marathon's attractions. ⑤ *Rooms from: $240* ✉ *MM 61 OS, 61 Hawks Cay Blvd.* ☎ *305/743–7000, 888/432–2242* ⊕ *www.hawkscay.com* ⇌ *161 rooms, 16 suites, 225 2- and 3-bedroom villas* ⑩ *No meals.*

GRASSY KEY

Grassy Key is between mile markers 60 and 57.

Local lore has it that this sleepy little key was named not for its vegetation—mostly native trees and shrubs—but for an early settler by the name of Grassy. The key is inhabited primarily by a few families operating small fishing camps and roadside motels. There's no marked definition between it and Marathon, so it feels sort of like a suburb of its much larger neighbor to the south. Grassy Key's sights tend toward the natural, including a worthwhile dolphin attraction and a small state park.

GETTING HERE AND AROUND

Most visitors arriving by air drive to this destination either from Miami International Airport or Key West International Airport. Rental cars are readily available at both, and in the long run, are the most convenient means of transportation for getting here and touring around the Keys.

EXPLORING

Curry Hammock State Park. Looking for a slice of the Keys that's far removed from tiki bars? On the ocean and bay sides of Overseas Highway are 260 acres of upland hammock, wetlands, and mangroves. On the bay side, there's a trail through thick hardwoods to a rocky shoreline. The ocean side is more developed, with a sandy beach, a clean bathhouse, picnic tables, a playground, grills, and a 28-site campground. Locals consider the paddling trails under canopies of arching mangroves one of the best kayaking spots in the Keys. Manatees frequent the area, and it's a great spot for bird-watching. Herons, egrets, ibis, plovers, and sanderlings are commonly spotted. Raptors are often seen in the park, especially during migration periods. ✉ *MM 57 OS, 56200 Overseas Hwy., Little Crawl Key* ☎ *305/289–2690* ⊕ *www.floridastateparks.org/curryhammock* ⛵ *$4.50 for 1 person, $6 for 2, $0.50 per additional person* ☾ *Daily 8–sunset.*

FAMILY **Dolphin Research Center.** The 1963 movie *Flipper* popularized the notion of humans interacting with dolphins, and Milton Santini, the film's creator, also opened this center, which is home to a colony of dolphins and sea lions. The nonprofit center has educational sessions and programs that allow you to greet the dolphins from dry land or play with them in their watery habitat. You can even paint a T-shirt with a dolphin; you pick the paint, the dolphin "designs" your shirt. The center also offers five-day programs for children and adults with disabilities. ✉ *MM 59*

Continued on page 200

DID YOU KNOW?

The coral making up the Barrier Reef is living and provides an ecosystem for small marine creatures. Bumping against or touching the coral can kill these creatures as well as damage the reef itself.

UNDER THE SEA
SNORKELING AND DIVING
IN THE FLORIDA KEYS by Lynne Helm

Up on the shore they work all day . . .

> While we devotin',
>
> Full time to floatin',
>
> Under the sea . . .

—"Under the Sea,"
from Disney's *Little Mermaid*

All Floridians—even those long-accustomed to balmy breezes and swaying palms—turn ecstatic at the mere thought of tripping off to the Florida Keys. Add the prospect of underwater adventure, and hot diggity, it's unparalleled bliss.

Perennially laid back, the Keys annually attract nearly 800,000 snorkeling and scuba diving aficionados, and why not? There's arguably no better destination to learn these sports that put you up close to the wonders of life under the sea.

THE BARRIER REEF
The continental United States' only living coral barrier reef stretches 5 mi offshore of the Keys and is a teeming backbone of marine life, ranging from brilliant corals to neon-colored fish from blue-striped grunts to green moray eels. This is the prime reason why the Keys are where you descend upon intricate natural coral formations and encrusted shipwrecks, some historic, others sunk by design to create artificial reefs that attract divers

and provide protection for marine life. Most diving sites have mooring buoys (nautical floats away from shore, sometimes marking specific sites); these let you tie up your boat so you don't need to drop anchor, which could damage the reef. Most of these sites also are near individual keys, where dozens of dive operators can cater to your needs.

Reef areas thrive in waters as shallow as 5 feet and as deep as 50 feet. Shallow reefs attract snorkelers, while deeper reefs suit divers of varying experience levels. The Keys' shallow diving offers two benefits: longer time safely spent on the bottom exploring, and more vibrant colors because of sunlight penetration. Most divers log maximum depths of 20 to 30 feet.

(left) Shallow-water coral reef, (top) Nine Foot Stake is a popular site for underwater photography.

WHERE TO SNORKEL AND DIVE

KEY WEST
Mile Marker 0–4

You can soak up a mesmerizing overview of submerged watery wonders at the Florida Keys Eco-Discovery Center, opened in 2007 on Key West's Truman

Nine Foot Stake

Annex waterfront. Both admission and parking are free at the 6,000 square–foot center (🕘 9–4 Tues.–Sat. ☎ 305/809-4750); interactive exhibits here focus on Keys marine life and habitats. Key West's offshore reefs are best accessed via professional charters, but it's easy to snorkel from shore at Key West Marine Park. Marked by a lighthouse, Sand Key Reef attracts snorkelers and scuba divers. Joe's Tug, at 65-foot depths, sets up encounters with Goliath grouper. Ten-Fathom Ledge, with coral caves and dramatic overhangs, shelters lobster. The Cayman Salvor, a buoy tender sunk as an artificial reef in 1985, shelters baitfish. Patch reef Nine Foot Stake, submerged 10 to 25 feet, has soft corals and juvenile marine life. Kedge Ledge features a pair of coral-encrusted anchors from 18th-century sailing vessels. 🔒 Florida Keys main visitor line at ☎ 800/FLA-KEYS (352-5397).

BIG PINE KEY/LOWER KEYS
Mile Marker 4–47

Many devotees feel a Florida dive adventure would not be complete without heading 5 mi from Big Pine Key to Looe Key National Marine Sanctuary, an underwater preserve named for the HMS Looe running aground in 1744. If you time your visit for July, you might hit the one-day free underwater music festival for snorkelers

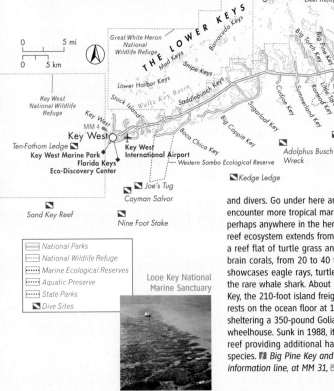

Looe Key National Marine Sanctuary

and divers. Go under here and you'll likely encounter more tropical marine species than perhaps anywhere in the hemisphere. Looe Key's reef ecosystem extends from fossilized corals to a reef flat of turtle grass and large star and brain corals, from 20 to 40 feet. A deeper reef showcases eagle rays, turtles, and sometimes the rare whale shark. About 3 mi west of Looe Key, the 210-foot island freighter Adolphus Busch rests on the ocean floor at 110-foot depths, sheltering a 350-pound Goliath grouper near the wheelhouse. Sunk in 1988, it acts as an artificial reef providing additional habitat for marine species. 🔒 Big Pine Key and Lower Keys Tourist information line, at MM 31, ☎ 800/872-3722.

MARATHON/MIDDLE KEYS

Mile Marker 47–63

The Middle Keys yield a marine wilderness of a spur-and-groove coral and patch reefs. The **Adelaide Baker** historic shipwreck has a pair of stacks in 25 feet of water.

Sombrero Reef

Popular **Sombrero Reef**, with coral canyons and archways, is marked by a 140-foot lighted tower. Six distinct patch reefs known as **Coffin's Patch** have shallow elkhorn forests. **Delta Shoals**, a network of coral canyons fanning seaward from a sandy shoal, attracts divers to its elkhorn, brain, and star coral heads. Marathon's **Thunderbolt**, a 188-foot ship sunk in 1986, sits upright at 115-foot depths, coated with sponge, coral, and hydroid, and attracting angelfish, jacks, and deep-water pelagic creatures. ⬛ *Greater Marathon Chamber and visitors center at MM 53.5,* ☎ *800/262-7284.*

ISLAMORADA Mile Marker 63–90

Islamorada offers shallow coral reefs, mini walls, shipwrecks, and the **Aquarius** (⬛ www.uncw.edu/ aquarius), an underwater habitat for scientific research. Coral heads showcase tropical marine life, from grunt to regal queen angelfish. Green moray eels populate spur-and-groove channels, and nurse sharks linger under overhangs. Submerged attractions include the **Eagle**, a 287-foot ship in 110 feet of water; **Davis Reef**, with gorgonian coral; **Alligator Reef**, where the *USS Alligator* sank while fighting pirates; the sloping **Conch Wall**, with barrel sponges and gorgonian; and **Crocker Wall**, featuring spur-and-groove and block corals. ⬛ *Islamorada Chamber and visitor center at MM 83.2,* ☎ *800/322-5397.*

KEY LARGO Mile Marker 90–112

Key Largo marine conservation got a big leg up with creation of **John Pennekamp Coral Reef State Park** in 1960, the nation's first undersea preserve, followed by 1975's designation of the **Key Largo National Marine Sanctuary**. A popular underwater attraction is the bronze statue of **Christ of the Abyss** between coral formations. Explorers with a "lust for rust" can dive down to 60 to 90 feet and farther to see the murky cemetery for two twin 327-foot U.S. Coast Guard cutters, *Duane* and *Bibb*, used during World War II; *USS Spiegel Grove*, a 510-foot Navy transport ship sunk in 2002 to create an artificial reef; and **Molasses Reef**, showcasing coral heads. ⬛ *Key Largo Chamber at MM 106,* ☎ *800/822-1088.*

SCUBA DIVING

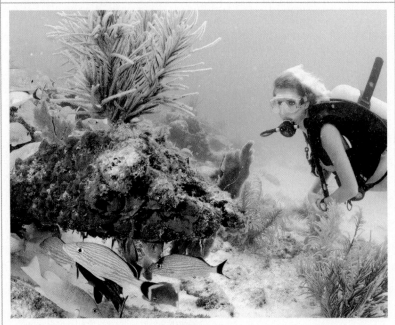

A diver explores the coral reef in the Florida Keys National Marine Sanctuary off Key Largo.

Florida offers wonderful opportunities to spend your vacation in the sun and become a certified diver at the same time. In the Keys, count on setting aside three to five days for entry-level or so-called "Open Water" certification offered by many dive shops. Basic certification (covering depths to about 60 feet) involves classroom work and pool training, followed by one or more open-water dives at the reef. After passing a knowledge test and completing the required water training (often starting in a pool), you become a certified recreational scuba diver, eligible to rent dive gear and book dive trips with most operations worldwide. Learning through video or online computer programs can enable you to complete classroom work at home, so you can more efficiently schedule time in the Keys for completing water skills and getting out to the reef for exploration.

Many would-be divers opt to take the classroom instruction and pool training at home at a local dive shop and then spend only two days in the Keys completing four dives. It's not necessarily cheaper, but it can be far more relaxing to commit to only two days of diving.

Questions you should ask: Not all dive shops are created equal, and it may be worthwhile to spend extra money for a better diving experience. Some of the larger dive shops take out large catamarans that can carry as many as 24 to 40 people. Many people prefer the intimacy of a smaller boat.

Good to know: Divers can become certified through PADI *(www.padi.com)*, NAUI *(www.naui.org)*, or SSI *(www.divessi.com)*. The requirements for all three are similar, and if you do the classroom instruction and pool training with a dive shop associated with one organization, the referral for the open water dives will be honored by most dive shops. Note that you are not allowed to fly for at least 24 hours after a dive, because residual nitrogen in the body can pose health risks upon decompression. While there are no rigid rules on diving after flying, make sure you're well-hydrated before hitting the water.

Cost: The four-day cost can range from $300 to $475, but be sure to ask if equipment, instruction manuals, and log books are extra. Some dive shops have relationships with hotels, so check for dive/stay packages. Referral dives (a collaborative effort among training agencies) run from $285 to $300 and discover scuba runs around $175 to $200.

SNUBA

Beyond snorkeling or the requirements of scuba, you also have the option of "Snuba." The word is a trademarked portmanteau or combo of snorkel and scuba. Marketed as easy-to-learn family fun, Snuba lets you breathe underwater via tubes from an air-supplied vessel above, with no prior diving or snorkel experience required.

NOT CERTIFIED?

Not sure if you want to commit the time and money to become certified? Not a problem. Most dive shops and many resorts will offer a discover scuba day-long course. In the morning, the instructor will teach you the basics of scuba diving: how to clear your mask, how to come to the surface in the unlikely event you lose your air supply, etc. In the afternoon, instructors will take you out for a dive in relatively shallow water—less than 30 feet. Be sure to ask where the dive will take place. Jumping into the water off a shallow beach may not be as fun as actually going out to the coral. If you decide that diving is something you want to pursue, the open dive may count toward your certification.

■ TIP➜ You can often book the discover dives at the last minute. It may not be worth it to go out on a windy day when the currents are stronger. Also the underwater world looks a whole lot brighter on sunny days.

(top) Scuba divers; (bottom) Diver ascending line.

4

IN FOCUS UNDER THE SEA

SNORKELING

Snorkling lets you see the wonders of the sea from a new perspective.

The basics: Sure, you can take a deep breath, hold your nose, squint your eyes, and stick your face in the water in an attempt to view submerged habitats . . . but why not protect your eyes, retain your ability to breathe, and keep your hands free to paddle about when exploring underwater? That's what snorkeling is all about.

Equipment needed: A mask, snorkel (the tube attached to the mask), and fins. In deeper waters (any depth over your head), life jackets are advised.

Steps to success: If you've never snorkeled before, it's natural to feel a bit awkward at first, so don't sweat it. Breathing through a mask and tube, and wearing a pair of fins take getting used to. Like any activity, you build confidence and comfort through practice.

If you're new to snorkeling, begin by submerging your face in shallow water or a swimming pool and breathing calmly through the snorkel while gazing through the mask.

Next you need to learn how to clear water out of your mask and snorkel, an essential skill since splashes can send water into tube openings and masks can leak. Some snorkels have built-in drainage valves, but if a tube clogs, you can force water up and out by exhaling through your mouth. Clearing a mask is similar: lift your head from water while pulling forward on mask to drain. Some masks have built-in purge valves, but those without can be cleared underwater by pressing the top to the forehead and blowing out your nose (charming, isn't it?), allowing air to bubble into the mask, pushing water out the bottom. If it sounds hard, it really isn't. Just try it a few times and you'll soon feel like a pro.

Now your goal is to get friendly with fins—you want them to be snug but not too tight—and learn how to propel yourself with them. Fins won't help you float, but they will give you a leg up, so to speak, on smoothly moving through the water or treading water (even when upright) with less effort.

Flutter stroking is the most efficient underwater kick, and the farther your foot bends forward the more leg power you'll be able to transfer to the water and the farther you'll travel with each stroke. Flutter kicking movements involve alternately separating the legs and then drawing them back together. When your legs separate, the leg surface encounters drag from the water, slowing you down. When your legs are drawn back together, they produce a force pushing you forward. If your kick creates more forward force than it causes drag, you'll move ahead.

Submerge your fins to avoid fatigue rather than having them flailing above the water when you kick, and keep your arms at your side to reduce drag. You are in the water—stretched out, face down, and snorkeling happily away—but that doesn't mean you can't hold your breath and go deeper in the water for a closer look at some fish or whatever catches your attention. Just remember that when you do this, your snorkel will be submerged, too, so you won't be breathing (you'll be holding your breath). You can dive head-first, but going feet-first is easier and less scary for most folks, taking less momentum. Before full immersion, take several long, deep breaths to clear carbon dioxide from your lungs.

If your legs tire, flip onto your back and tread water with inverted fin motions while resting. If your mask fogs, wash condensation from lens and clear water from mask.

TIPS FOR SAFE SNORKELING

- Snorkel with a buddy and stay together.
- Plan your entry and exit points prior to getting in the water.
- Swim into the current on entering and then ride the current back to your exit point.
- Carry your flippers into the water and then put them on, as it's difficult to walk in them.
- Make sure your mask fits properly and is not too loose.
- Pop your head above the water periodically to ensure you aren't drifting too far out, or too close to rocks.
- Think of the water as someone else's home—don't take anything that doesn't belong to you, or leave any trash behind.
- Don't touch any sea creatures; they may sting.
- Wear a T-shirt over your swimsuit to help protect you from being fried by the sun.
- When in doubt, don't go without a snorkeling professional; try a guided tour.

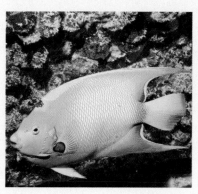

Cayman Salvor

4

IN FOCUS UNDER THE SEA

DID YOU KNOW?

Dolphins in Florida are predominantly of the Atlantic bottlenose variety. These playful and smart creatures love to leap out of the water and synchronize their movements with others. By swimming next to boats, dolphins can conserve energy.

BS, 58901 Overseas Hwy. ☎ 305/289–1121 for info, 305/289–0002 for reservations ⊕ www.dolphins.org ☞ $20 ⊗ Daily 9–4:30.

WHERE TO EAT

$$$ ✕ **Hideaway Café.** The name says it all. Tucked between Grassy Key and
AMERICAN Marathon, it's easy to miss if you're barnstorming through the Middle Keys. When you find it (upstairs at Rainbow Bend Resort), you'll discover a favorite of locals who appreciate a well-planned menu, lovely ocean view, and quiet evening away from the crowds—fancy with white tablecloths, but homey with worn carpeting. For starters, dig into escargots à la Edison (sautéed with vegetables, pepper, cognac, and cream). Then feast on several specialties, such as a rarely found chateaubriand for one, a whole roasted duck, or the seafood medley combining the catch of the day with scallops and shrimp in a savory sauce. ⑤ *Average main: $30* ⊠ *Rainbow Bend Resort, MM 58 OS, 57784 Overseas Hwy.* ☎ *305/289–1554* ⊕ *www.hideawaycafe.com* ⊗ *No lunch.*

MARATHON

Marathon is between mile markers 53 and 47.5.

Marathon is a bustling town, at least compared with other Keys communities. If you get off the main drag, you'll find the few oceanfront hotels, but there are a number of good dining options right on Overseas Highway, so you'll definitely want to stop for a bite even if you're just passing through on the way to Key West.

If you stop a while, you'll find Marathon has the most historic attractions outside of Key West, and the well-worth-visiting Sombrero Beach—though fishing, diving, and boating are the main events here. The town throws tarpon tournaments in April and May, more fishing tournaments in June and September, a seafood festival in March, and lighted boat parades around the winter holidays.

New Englanders founded this former fishing village in the early 1800s. The community on Vaca Key subsequently served as a base for pirates, salvagers (also known as "wreckers"), spongers, and, later, Bahamian farmers who eked out a living growing cotton and other crops. More Bahamians arrived in hopes of finding work building the railroad. According to local lore, Marathon was renamed when a worker commented that it was a marathon task to position the tracks across the 6-mile-long island. During the building of the railroad, Marathon developed a reputation for lawlessness that rivaled that of the Old West. It's said that to keep the rowdy workers from descending on Key West for their off-hours endeavors, residents would send boatloads of liquor up to Marathon. Needless to say, things have quieted down considerably since then. Grassy Key segues into Marathon with little more than a slight increase in traffic and higher concentration of commercial establishments. Marathon's roots are anchored to fishing and boating, so look for marinas to find local color, fishing charters, and good restaurants. At its north end, Key Colony Beach is an old-fashioned island neighborhood worth a visit for its shops and restaurants. Just be warned the police are plentiful and love to catch speeders. Nature lovers shouldn't miss the attractions on Crane Point. Other good places to leave the main road are at Sombrero Beach Road (MM 50), which leads to the beach, and 35th Street (MM 49), which takes you to a funky little marina and restaurant. Overseas Highway hightails through Hog Key and Knight Key before the big leap over Florida Bay and Hawk's Channel via the Seven Mile Bridge.

GETTING HERE AND AROUND

The SuperShuttle charges $102 per passenger for trips from Miami International Airport to the Upper Keys. To go farther into the Keys, you must book an entire 11-person van, which costs about $250 to Marathon. For a trip to or from the airport, place your request 24 hours in advance.

Miami Dade Transit provides daily bus service from MM 50 in Marathon to the Florida City Walmart Supercenter on the mainland. The bus stops at major shopping centers as well as on-demand anywhere along the route during daily round trips on the hour from 6 am to 10 pm. The cost is $2 one-way, exact change required. The Lower Keys Shuttle bus runs from Marathon to Key West ($4 one way), with scheduled stops along the way.

ESSENTIALS

Transportation Contacts Lower Keys Shuttle ☎ 305/809–3910 ⊕ www. kwtransit.com. **Miami Dade Transit** ☎ 305/770–3131 ⊕ www.miamidade.gov/ transit. **SuperShuttle** ☎ 305/871–2000, 800/258–3826 ⊕ www.supershuttle.com.

Visitor Information Greater Marathon Chamber of Commerce and Visitor Center ✉ MM 53.5 BS, 12222 Overseas Hwy. ☎ 305/743–5417, 800/262–7284 ⊕ www.floridakeysmarathon.com.

EXPLORING

FAMILY **Crane Point Museum, Nature Center, and Historic Site.** Tucked away from the highway behind a stand of trees, Crane Point—part of a 63-acre tract that contains the last-known undisturbed thatch-palm hammock—is delightfully undeveloped. This multiuse facility includes the **Museum of Natural History of the Florida Keys,** which has displays about local wildlife, a seashell exhibit, and a marine-life display that makes you feel you're at the bottom of the sea. Kids love the replica 17th-century galleon and pirate dress-up room where they can play, and the re-created **Cracker House** filled with insects, sea-turtle exhibits, and children's activities. On the 1-mile indigenous loop trail, visit the **Laura Quinn Wild Bird Center** and the remnants of a Bahamian village, site of the restored **George Adderly House.** It is the oldest surviving example of Bahamian tabby (a concretelike material created from sand and sea-shells) construction outside of Key West. A boardwalk crosses wetlands, rivers, and mangroves before ending at Adderly Village. From November to Easter, docent-led tours are available; bring good walking shoes and bug repellent during warm weather. ✉ MM 50.5 BS, 5550 Overseas Hwy. ☎ 305/743–9100 ⊕ www.cranepoint.net ⚏ $12.50 ☉ Mon.–Sat. 9–5, Sun. noon–5; call to arrange trail tours.

Pigeon Key. There's much to like about this 5-acre island under the Old Seven Mile Bridge. You might even recognize it from one season finale of the TV show *The Amazing Race*. You can reach it via a ferry that departs from behind the visitors center (look for the old red railroad car on Knight's Key, MM 47 OS). Once there, tour the island on your own or join a guided tour to explore the buildings that formed the early-20th-century work camp for the Overseas Railroad that linked the mainland to Key West in 1912. Later the island became a fish camp, a state park, and then government-administration headquarters. Exhibits in a small museum recall the history of the Keys, the railroad, and railroad baron Henry M. Flagler. The ferry ride with tour lasts two hours; visitors can self-tour and catch the ferry back in a half hour. ⌂ *MM 45 OS, 1 Knights Key Blvd., Pigeon Key* ☎ *305/743–5999* ⊕ *www.pigeonkey.net* 💰 *$12* ⊙ *Daily 9:30–2:30; ferry departures at 10, 12 and 2.*

Seven Mile Bridge. This is one of the most photographed images in the Keys. Actually measuring slightly less than 7 miles, it connects the Middle and Lower Keys and is believed to be the world's longest segmental bridge. It has 39 expansion joints separating its various concrete sections. Each April runners gather in Marathon for the annual Seven Mile Bridge Run. The expanse running parallel to Seven Mile Bridge is what remains of the **Old Seven Mile Bridge,** an engineering and architectural marvel in its day that's now on the National Register of Historic Places. Once proclaimed the Eighth Wonder of the World, it rested on a record 546 concrete piers. No cars are allowed on the old bridge today.

FAMILY **The Turtle Hospital.** More than 100 injured sea turtles check in here every year. The 90-minute guided tours take you into recovery and surgical areas at the world's only state-certified veterinary hospital for sea turtles. In the "hospital bed" tanks, you can see recovering patients and others that are permanent residents due to their injuries. After the tour, you can feed some of the "residents." Call ahead—space is limted and tours are sometimes cancelled due to medical emergencies. The turtle ambulance out front makes for a memorable souvenir photo. ⌂ *MM 48.5 BS, 2396 Overseas Hwy.* ☎ *305/743–2552* ⊕ *www.turtlehospital. org* 💰 *$18* ⊙ *Daily 9–5.*

BEACHES

FAMILY **Sombrero Beach.** No doubt one of the best beaches in the Keys, here you'll find pleasant, shaded picnic areas that overlook a coconut palm–lined grassy stretch and the Atlantic Ocean. Roped-off areas allow swimmers, boaters, and windsurfers to share the narrow cove. Facilities include barbecue grills, a large playground, a pier, a volleyball court, and a paved, lighted bike path off Overseas Highway. Sunday afternoons draw lots of local families toting coolers. The park is accessible for those with disabilities and allows leashed pets. Turn east at the traffic light in Marathon and follow signs to the end. **Amenities:** showers; toilets. **Best for:** families; swimming; windsurfing. ⌂ *MM 50 OS, Sombrero Beach Rd.* ☎ *305/743–0033* 💰 *Free* ⊙ *Daily 8–sunset.*

WHERE TO EAT

$ × **Fish Tales Market and Eatery.** This roadside eatery with its own seafood
SEAFOOD market serves signature dishes such as snapper on grilled rye with coleslaw and melted Muenster cheese and a fried fish burrito. You also can slurp luscious lobster bisque or tomato-based conch chowder. There

are burgers, chicken, and dogs for those who don't do seafood. Plan to dine early; it's only open until 6:30 pm (4 pm on Saturdays). This is a no-frills kind of place with a loyal local following, unfussy ambiance, a couple of outside picnic tables, and friendly service. ⑤ *Average main: $9* ✉ *MM 52.5 OS, 11711 Overseas Hwy.* ☎ *305/743–9196, 888/662–4822* ⊕ *www.floridalobster.com* ⚠ *Reservations not accepted* ☾ *Closed Sun. No dinner Sat.*

$$
ITALIAN
✕ **Key Colony Inn.** The inviting aroma of an Italian kitchen pervades this family-owned favorite with a supper-club atmosphere. As you'd expect, the service is friendly and attentive. For lunch there are fish and steak entrées served with fries, salad, and bread in addition to Italian specialties. At dinner you can't miss with traditional dishes like veal Oscar and New York strip, or such specialties as seafood *Italiano*, a dish of scallops and shrimp sautéed in garlic butter and served with marinara sauce over a bed of linguine. The place is renowned for its Sunday brunch, served from November to April. ⑤ *Average main: $19* ✉ *MM 54 OS, 700 W. Ocean Dr., Key Colony Beach* ☎ *305/743–0100* ⊕ *www.kcinn.com.*

$$
SEAFOOD
FAMILY
✕ **Keys Fisheries Market & Marina.** From the parking lot, you can't miss the enormous tiki bar on stilts, but the walk-up window on the ground floor is the heart of this warehouse-turned restaurant. Order at the window, pick up your food, then dine at one of the waterfront tables outfitted with rolls of paper towels. The menu comprises fresh seafood and a token hamburger and chicken sandwich. A huge lobster reuben ($14.95) served on thick slices of toasted bread is the signature dish. Other delights include the shrimp burger, very rich whiskey-peppercorn snapper, and the Keys Kombo (grilled lobster, shrimp, scallops, and mahimahi for $29). The adults-only upstairs tiki bar offers a sushi and raw bar for eat-in only. Bring quarters for fish food—you can feed the tarpon while you wait for your food. ⑤ *Average main: $16* ✉ *MM 49 BS, 3390 Gulfview Ave., at the end of 35th St. (turn right on 35th St. off Gulfview Ave.)* ☎ *305/743–4353, 866/743–4353* ⊕ *www.keysfisheries. com* ⚠ *Reservations not accepted.*

$$$
SEAFOOD
Fodor's Choice
★
✕ **Lazy Days South.** Tucked into Marathon Marina a half mile north of the Seven Mile Bridge, this restaurant offers views just as spectacular as its highly lauded food. A spin-off of an Islamorada favorite, here you'll find a wide range of daily offerings from fried- or sautéed conch and a coconut-fried fish du jour sandwich to seafood pastas and beef tips over rice. Choose a table on the outdoor deck, or inside underneath paddle fans and surrounded by local art. ⑤ *Average main: $22* ✉ *MM 47.3 OS, 725 11th St.* ☎ *305/289–0839* ⊕ *www.keysdining.com/lazydays.*

$
DINER
✕ **The Stuffed Pig.** With only nine tables and a counter inside, this breakfast-and-lunch place is always hopping. When the weather's right, grab a table out back. The kitchen whips up daily lunch specials like burgers, seafood platters, or pulled pork with hand-cut fries, but a quick glance around the room reveals that the all-day breakfast is the main draw. You can get the usual breakfast plates, but most newcomers opt for oddities like the lobster omelet, alligator tail and eggs, or "grits and grunts" (that's fish, to the rest of us). ⑤ *Average main: $9* ✉ *MM 49*

BS, 3520 Overseas Hwy. ☎305/743–4059 ⊕ www.thestuffedpig.com
⌂ Reservations not accepted ▭ No credit cards ⊗ No dinner.

WHERE TO STAY

$$
RENTAL
🏨 **Glunz Ocean Beach Hotel & Resort.** The Glunz family got it right when they purchased this former timeshare property and put a whole lot of love into renovating it to its full oceanfront potential. **Pros:** oceanfront; convenient amenities; excellent free Wi-Fi. **Cons:** neighbor noise; small elevator; no interior corridors; not cheap. ⑤ *Rooms from: $260* ✉ *MM 53.5 OS, 351 E. Ocean Dr., Key Colony Beach* ☎ *305/289–0525* ⊕ *www. GlunzOceanBeachHotel.com* ⤷ *22 rooms, 16 suites* ⑪ *No meals.*

$$$
RESORT
FAMILY
Fodor's Choice
★
🏨 **Tranquility Bay.** Ralph Lauren could have designed the rooms at this stylish, luxurious resort on a nice beach. **Pros:** secluded setting; gorgeous design; lovely crescent beach. **Cons:** a bit sterile; no real Keys atmosphere; cramped building layout. ⑤ *Rooms from: $399* ✉ *MM 48.5 BS, 2600 Overseas Hwy.* ☎ *305/289–0888, 866/643–5397* ⊕ *www.tranquilitybay.com* ⤷ *16 guestrooms, 45 2-bedroom suites, 41 3-bedroom suites* ⑪ *No meals.*

SPORTS AND THE OUTDOORS

BIKING

Bike Marathon Bike Rentals. "Have bikes, will deliver" could be the motto of this company, which gets beach cruisers to your hotel door, including a helmet and basket. They also rent kayaks. Note that there's no physical location, but services are available Monday through Saturday 9–4 and Sunday 9–2. ☎ *305/743–3204* ⊕ *www.bikemarathonbikerentals. com* 🚲 *$35 per wk.*

Overseas Outfitters. Aluminum cruisers and hybrid bikes are available for rent at this outfitter. It's open weekdays 9–5:30 and Saturday 9–3. All rentals include a helmet and lock. ✉ *MM 48 BS, 1700 Overseas Hwy.* ☎ *305/289–1670* ⊕ *www.overseasoutfitters.com* 🚲 *Rentals from $15 per day.*

BOATING

Sail, motor, or paddle—whatever your choice of modes, boating is what the Keys are all about. Brave the Atlantic waves and reefs or explore the backcountry islands on the calmer gulfside. If you don't have a lot of boating and chart-reading experience, it's a good idea to tap into local knowledge on a charter.

Captain Pip's. This operator rents 20- to 24-foot outboards as well as tackle and snorkeling gear. Fishing charters are also available with a captain and a mate (full-day charters are also available). Ask about multiday deals, or try one of their accommodation packages and walk right from your bayfront room to your boat. ✉ *MM 47.5 BS, 1410 Overseas Hwy.* ☎ *305/743–4403, 800/707–1692* ⊕ *www.captainpips. com* 🚲 *Rentals from $195 per day; half-day charters from $650.*

Fish 'n Fun. Get out on the water on 19- to 26-foot powerboats. Rentals can be for a half or full day. The company also offers free delivery in the Middle Keys. ✉ *Banana Bay Resort & Marina, MM 49.5 OS, 4590 Overseas Hwy.* ☎ *305/743–2275, 800/471–3440* ⊕ *www. fishnfunrentals.com* 🚲 *From $175.*

FISHING

For recreational anglers, the deepwater fishing is superb in the ocean. Marathon West Hump, one good spot, has depths ranging from 500 to more than 1,000 feet. Locals fish from a half dozen bridges, including Long Key Bridge, the Old Seven Mile Bridge, and both ends of Tom's Harbor. Barracuda, bonefish, mahimahi, and tarpon all frequent local waters. Party boats and private charters are available.

Marathon Lady. Morning, afternoon, and night, fish for mahimahi, grouper, and other tasty catch aboard this 73-footer, which departs on half-day excursions from the Vaca Cut Bridge (MM 53), north of Marathon. Join the crew for night fishing ($55) from 6:30 to midnight from Memorial Day to Labor Day; it's especially beautiful on a full-moon night. ✉ *MM 53 OS, at 117th St., 11711 Overseas Hwy.* ☎ *305/743–5580* ⊕ *www.marathonlady.net* ✉ *From $50.*

Sea Dog Charters. Captain Jim Purcell, a deep-sea specialist for ESPN's *The American Outdoorsman,* provides one of the best values in Keys fishing. Next to the Seven Mile Grill, his company offers half- and full-day offshore, reef and wreck, and backcountry fishing trips, as well as fishing and snorkeling trips aboard 30- to 37-foot boats. The per-person for a half-day trip is the same regardless of whether your group fills the boat, and includes bait, light tackle, ice, coolers, and fishing licenses. If you prefer an all-day private charter on a 37-foot boat, he offers those, too, for up to six people. A fuel surcharge may apply. ✉ *MM 47.5 BS, 1248 Overseas Hwy.* ☎ *305/743–8255* ⊕ *www.seadogcharters.net* ✉ *From $60.*

SCUBA DIVING AND SNORKELING

Local dive operations take you to Sombrero Reef and Lighthouse, the most popular down-under destination in these parts. For a shallow dive and some lobster nabbing, Coffins Patch, off Key Colony Beach, is a good choice. A number of wrecks such as *Thunderbolt* serve as artificial reefs. Many operations out of this area will also take you to Looe Key Reef.

Hall's Diving Center & Career Institute. The institute has been training divers for more than 40 years. Along with conventional twice-a-day snorkel and two-tank dive trips to the reefs at Sombrero Lighthouse and wrecks like the *Thunderbolt,* the company has more unusual offerings like rebreather, photography and nitrox courses. ✉ *MM 48.5 BS, 1994 Overseas Hwy.* ☎ *305/743–5929, 800/331–4255* ⊕ *www.hallsdiving.com* ✉ *From $40.*

Spirit Snorkeling. Join regularly scheduled snorkeling excursions to Sombrero Reef and Lighthouse Reef on this company's comfortable catamaran. They also offer sunset cruises, private charters, and new-age yoga cruises. ✉ *MM 47.5 BS, 1410 Overseas Hwy., Slip No. 1* ☎ *305/289–0614* ⊕ *www.spiritsnorkeling.net* ✉ *From $30.*

THE LOWER KEYS

Beginning at Bahia Honda Key, the islands of the Florida Keys become smaller, more clustered, and more numerous—a result of ancient tidal water flowing between the Florida Straits and the gulf. Here you're likely to see more birds and mangroves than other tourists, and more refuges, beaches, and campgrounds than museums, restaurants, and hotels. The islands are made up of two types of limestone, both denser than the highly permeable Key Largo limestone of the Upper Keys. As a result, freshwater forms in pools rather than percolating through the rock, creating watering holes that support alligators, snakes, deer, rabbits, raccoons, and migratory ducks. Many of these animals can be seen in the National Key Deer Refuge on Big Pine Key. Nature was generous with her beauty in the Lower Keys, which have both Looe Key Reef, arguably the Keys' most beautiful tract of coral, and Bahia Honda State Park, considered one of the best beaches in the world for its fine-sand dunes, clear warm waters, and panoramic vista of a historic bridge, hammocks, and azure sky and sea. Big Pine Key is fishing headquarters for a laid-back community that swells with retirees in the winter. South of it, the dribble of islands can flash by in a blink of an eye if you don't take the time to stop at a roadside eatery or check out tours and charters at the little marinas.

GETTING HERE AND AROUND

The Lower Keys in this section include the keys between MM 37 and MM 9. The Seven Mile Bridge drops you into the lap of this homey, quiet part of the Keys.

Heed speed limits in these parts. They may seem incredibly strict given that the traffic is lightest of anywhere in the Keys, but the purpose is to protect the resident key deer population, and officers of the law pay strict attention and will readily issue speeding tickets.

BAHIA HONDA KEY

Bahia Honda Key is between mile markers 38 and 36.

All of Bahia Honda Key is devoted to its eponymous state park, which keeps it in a pristine state. Besides the park's outdoor activities, it offers an up-close look at the original railroad bridge.

EXPLORING

FAMILY

Fodor's Choice

★

Bahia Honda State Park. Most first-time visitors to the region are dismayed by the lack of beaches—but then they discover Bahia Honda Key. The 524-acre park sprawls across both sides of the highway, giving it 2½ miles of fabulous sandy coastline. The snorkeling isn't bad, either; there's underwater life (soft coral, queen conchs, random little fish) just a few hundred feet offshore. Although swimming, kayaking, fishing, and boating are the main reasons to visit, you shouldn't miss biking along the 2½ miles of flat roads or hiking the Silver Palm Trail, with rare West Indian plants and several species found nowhere else in the nation. Along the way you'll be treated to a variety of butterflies. Seasonal ranger-led nature programs take place at or depart from the Sand and Sea Nature Center. There are rental cabins, a campground, snack bar,

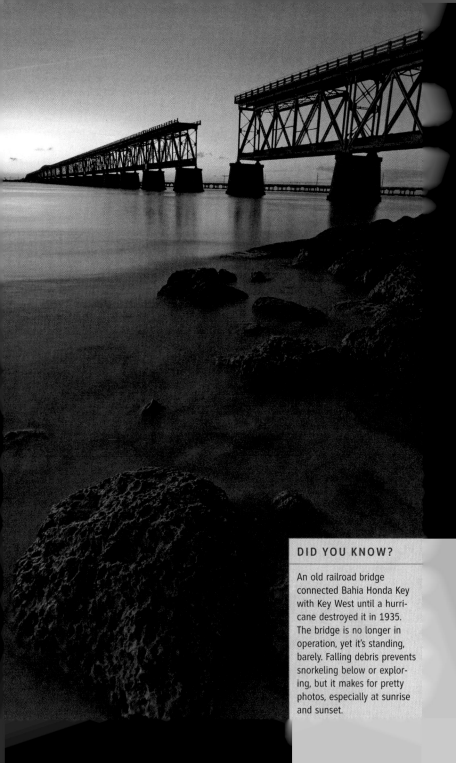

DID YOU KNOW?

An old railroad bridge connected Bahia Honda Key with Key West until a hurricane destroyed it in 1935. The bridge is no longer in operation, yet it's standing, barely. Falling debris prevents snorkeling below or exploring, but it makes for pretty photos, especially at sunrise and sunset.

gift shop, 19-slip marina, nature center, and facilities for renting kayaks and arranging snorkeling tours. Get a panoramic view of the island from what's left of the railroad—the Bahia Honda Bridge. ⊠ *MM 37 OS, 36850 Overseas Hwy.* ☎ *305/872–2353* ⊕ *www.floridastateparks. org/bahiahonda* ➩ *$4.50 for single-occupant vehicle, $9 for vehicle with 2–8 people* ⊙ *Daily 8–sunset.*

BEACHES

Sandspur Beach. Bahia Honda Key State Beach contains three beaches in all—on both the Atlantic Ocean and the Gulf of Mexico. Sandspur Beach, the largest, is regularly declared the best beach in the Florida Keys, and you'll be hard-pressed to argue. The sand is baby-powder soft, and the aqua water is warm, clear, and shallow. With their mild currents, the beaches are great for swimming, even with small fry. **Amenities:** food and drink; showers; toilets; water sports. **Best for:** snorkeling; swimming. ⊠ *MM 37 OS, 36850 Overseas Hwy.* ☎ *305/872–2353* ⊕ *www.floridastateparks.org/bahiahonda* ➩ *$4.50 for single-occupant vehicle, $9 for vehicle with 2–8 people* ⊙ *Daily 8–sunset.*

WHERE TO STAY

$$$ ⬚ **Bahia Honda State Park Cabins.** Elsewhere you'd pay big bucks for
RENTAL the wonderful water views available at these cabins on Florida Bay. **Pros:** great bayfront views; beachfront camping; affordable rates. **Cons:** books up fast; area can be buggy. ⑤ *Rooms from: $183* ⊠ *MM 37 OS, 36850 Overseas Hwy.* ☎ *305/872–2353, 800/326–3521* ⊕ *www. reserveamerica.com* ➩ *6 cabins* ⦿ *No meals.*

SPORTS AND THE OUTDOORS

SCUBA DIVING AND SNORKELING

Bahia Honda Dive Shop. The concessionaire at Bahia Honda State Park manages a 19-slip marina; rents wet suits, snorkel equipment, and corrective masks; and operates twice-a-day offshore-reef snorkel trips. Park visitors looking for other fun can rent kayaks and beach chairs. ⊠ *MM 37 OS, 36850 Overseas Hwy.* ☎ *305/872–3210* ⊕ *www. bahiahondapark.com* ⊙ *Kayak rentals from $10 per hr.; snorkel tours from $30.*

BIG PINE KEY

Big Pine Key runs from mile marker 32 to 30.

Welcome to the Keys' most natural holdout, where wildlife refuges protect rare and endangered animals. Here you've left behind the commercialism of the Upper Keys for an authentic backcountry atmosphere.

How could things get more casual than Key Largo? Find out by exiting Overseas Highway to explore the habitat of the charmingly diminutive Key deer or cast a line from No Name Bridge. Tours explore the expansive waters of National Key Deer Refuge and Great White Heron National Wildlife Refuge, one of the first such refuges in the country. Along with Key West National Wildlife Refuge, it encompasses more than 200,000 acres of water and more than 8,000 acres of land on 49 small islands. Besides its namesake bird, the Great White Heron National Wildlife Refuge provides habitat for uncounted species of birds and three species of sea turtles. It's the only U.S. breeding site for the endangered hawksbill turtle.

ESSENTIALS

Visitor Information Big Pine and the Lower Keys Chamber of Commerce ☎ 305/872–2411, 800/872–3722 ⊕ www.lowerkeyschamber.com.

EXPLORING

National Key Deer Refuge. This 84,824-acre refuge was established in 1957 to protect the dwindling population of the Key deer, one of more than 22 animals and plants federally classified as endangered or threatened, including five that are found nowhere else on earth. The Key deer, which stands about 30 inches at the shoulders and is a subspecies of the Virginia white-tailed deer, once roamed throughout the Lower and Middle Keys, but hunting, destruction of their habitat, and a growing human population caused their numbers to decline to 27 by 1957. The deer have made a comeback, increasing their numbers to approximately 750. The best place to see Key deer in the refuge is at the end of Key Deer Boulevard and on No Name Key, a sparsely populated island just east of Big Pine Key. Mornings and evenings are the best time to spot them. Deer may turn up along the road at any time of day, so drive slowly. They wander into nearby yards to nibble tender grass and bougainvillea blossom, but locals do not appreciate tourists driving into their neighborhoods after them. Feeding them is against the law and puts them in danger.

A quarry left over from railroad days, the **Blue Hole** is the largest body of freshwater in the Keys. From the observation platform and nearby walking trail, you might see the resident alligator, turtles, and other wildlife. There are two well-marked trails, recently revamped: the Jack Watson Nature Trail (0.6 mile), named after an environmentalist and the refuge's first warden; and the Fred Mannillo Nature Trail, one of the most wheelchair-accessible places to see an unspoiled pine-rockland forest and wetlands. The visitor center has exhibits on Keys biology and ecology. The refuge also provides information on the Key West National Wildlife Refuge and the Great White Heron National Wildlife Refuge. Accessible only by water, both are popular with kayak outfitters. ⊠ *Visitor Center–Headquarters, Big Pine Shopping Center, MM 30.5 BS, 28950 Watson Blvd.* ☎ *305/872–2239* ⊕ *www.fws.gov/nationalkeydeer* ᐧ *Free* ⊙ *Daily sunrise–sunset; headquarters weekdays 8–5.*

WHERE TO EAT

$ ✕ **Good Food Conspiracy.** Like good wine, this small natural-foods eat-
VEGETARIAN   ery and market, surrenders its pleasures a little at a time. Step inside to the aroma of brewing coffee, and then pick up the scent of fresh strawberries or carrots blending into a smoothie, the green aroma of wheatgrass juice, followed by the earthy odor of hummus. Order raw or cooked vegetarian and vegan dishes, organic soups and salads, and organic coffees and teas. Bountiful sandwiches include the popular tuna melt or hummus and avocado. Sit at the counter or in the back garden and mingle with the locals as folks have been doing since the early 1980s. Then stock up on healthful snacks like dried fruits, raw nuts, and carob-covered almonds. Gluten-free items, too. ⑤ *Average*

main: *$10* ✉ *MM 30.2 OS, 30150 Overseas Hwy.* ☎ *305/872–3945* ⊕ *www.goodfoodconspiracy.com* ⌂ *Reservations not accepted* ☉ *No dinner Sun.*

$ ✕ **No Name Pub.** This no-frills honky-tonk has been around since 1936,
AMERICAN delighting inveterate locals and intrepid vacationers who come for the excellent pizza, cold beer, and *interesting* companionship. The décor, such as it is, amounts to the autographed dollar bills that cover every inch of the place. The full menu printed on place mats includes a tasty conch chowder, a half-pound fried-grouper sandwich, spaghetti and meatballs, and seafood baskets. The lighting is poor, the furnishings are rough, and the music is oldies. This former brothel and bait shop is just before the No Name Key Bridge in the midst of a residential neighborhood. It's a bit hard to find, but worth the trouble if you want a singular Keys experience. ⑤ *Average main: $15* ✉ *MM 30 BS, 30813 Watson Blvd.* ⌖ *From U.S. 1, turn west on Wilder Rd., left on South St., right on Ave. B, right on Watson Blvd.* ☎ *305/872–9115* ⊕ *www. nonamepub.com* ⌂ *Reservations not accepted.*

WHERE TO STAY

$ ⌂ **Big Pine Key Fishing Lodge.** There's a congenial atmosphere at this lively
HOTEL family-owned lodge-campground-marina—a happy mix of tent camp-ers (who have the fabulous waterfront real estate), RVers (who are pretty permanent), and motel dwellers who like to mingle at the rooftop pool and challenge each other to a game of poker. **Pros:** local fishing crowd; nice pool; great price. **Cons:** RV park is too close to motel; deer will eat your food if you're camping. ⑤ *Rooms from: $114* ✉ *MM 33 OS, 33000 Overseas Hwy.* ☎ *305/872–2351* ⊕ *www.big-pine-key.com/ fishinglodge.php* ⇥ *16 efficiencies* ❍ *No meals.*

$$ ⌂ **Deer Run Bed & Breakfast.** Innkeepers Jen DeMaria and Harry Appel
B&B/INN were way ahead of the green-lodging game when they opened in 2004, and guests love how Key deer wander the grounds of this beachfront B&B on a residential street lined with mangroves. **Pros:** quiet loca-tion; vegan, organic breakfasts; complimentary bikes, kayaks, and state park passes. **Cons:** price is a bit high; hard to find. ⑤ *Rooms from: $255* ✉ *MM 33 OS, 1997 Long Beach Dr.* ☎ *305/872–2015* ⊕ *www. deerrunfloridabb.com* ⇥ *4 rooms* ❍ *Breakfast.*

SPORTS AND THE OUTDOORS
BIKING
A good 10 miles of paved roads run from MM 30.3 BS, along Wilder Road, across the bridge to No Name Key, and along Key Deer Boule-vard into the National Key Deer Refuge. Along the way you might see some Key deer. Stay off the trails that lead into wetlands, where fat tires can do damage to the environment.

Big Pine Bicycle Center. Owner Marty Baird is an avid cyclist and enjoys sharing his knowledge of great places to ride. He's also skilled at select-ing the right bike for the journey, and he knows his repairs, too. His old-fashioned single-speed, fat-tire cruisers rent by the half or full day. Helmets, baskets, and locks are included. ✉ *MM 30.9 BS, 31 County Rd.* ☎ *305/872–0130* ⊕ *www.bigpinebikes.com* 🏷 *From $8.*

BOATING AND FISHING EXCURSIONS

Those looking to fish can cast from No Name Key Bridge or hire a charter to take them into backcountry or deep waters for fishing year-round. If you're looking for a good snorkeling spot, stay close to Looe Key Reef, which is prime scuba and snorkeling territory. One resort caters to divers with dive boats that depart from their own dock. Others can make arrangements for you.

Strike Zone Charters. Glass-bottom-boat excursions venture into the backcountry and Atlantic Ocean. The five-hour Island Excursion emphasizes nature and Keys history; besides close encounters with birds, sea life, and vegetation, there's a fish cookout on an island. Snorkel and fishing equipment, food, and drinks are included. This is one of the few nature outings in the Keys with wheelchair access. Deep-sea charter rates for up to six people can be arranged for a half- or full day. It also offers flats fishing in the Gulf of Mexico. Dive excursions head to the wreck of the 110-foot *Adolphus Busch*, and scuba and snorkel trips to Looe Key Reef, prime scuba and snorkeling territory, aboard glass-bottom boats. ⊠ *MM 29.6 BS, 29675 Overseas Hwy.* ☎ *305/872–9863, 800/654–9560* ⊕ *www.strikezonecharter.com* ⌐ *From $38.*

KAYAKING

There's nothing like the vast expanse of pristine waters and mangrove islands preserved by national refuges from here to Key West. The maze-like terrain can be confusing, so it's wise to hire a guide at least the first time out.

Big Pine Kayak Adventures. There's no excuse to skip a water adventure with this convenient kayak rental service, which delivers them to your lodging or anywhere between Seven Mile Bridge and Stock Island. The company, headed by *The Florida Keys Paddling Guide* author Bill Keogh, will rent you a kayak and then ferry you—called taxi-yakking—to remote islands with clear instructions on how to paddle back on your own. Rentals are by the half day or full day. Three-hour group kayak tours are the cheapest option and explore the mangrove forests of Great White Heron and Key Deer National Wildlife Refuges. More expensive four-hour custom tours transport you to exquisite backcountry areas teeming with wildlife. Kayak fishing charters are also popular. ⊠ *Old Wooden Bridge Fishing Camp* ✛ *From MM 30, turn right at traffic light, continue on Wilder Rd. toward No Name Key; the fishing camp is just before the bridge with a big yellow kayak on the sign out front* ☎ *305/872–7474* ⊕ *www.keyskayaktours.com* ⌐ *From $50.*

LITTLE TORCH KEY

Little Torch Key is between mile markers 29 and 10.

Little Torch Key and its neighbor islands, Ramrod Key and Summerland Key, are good jumping-off points for divers headed for Looe Key Reef. The islands also serve as a refuge for those who want to make forays into Key West but not stay in the thick of things.

The undeveloped backcountry at your door makes Little Torch Key an ideal location for fishing and kayaking. Nearby Ramrod Key, which also caters to divers bound for Looe Key, derives its name from a ship that wrecked on nearby reefs in the early 1800s.

NEED A BREAK?

Baby's Coffee. The aroma of rich roasting coffee beans arrests you at the door of "the Southernmost Coffee Roaster." Buy it by the pound or by the cup along with sandwiches and sweets. ⊠ *MM 15 OS, 3178 Overseas Hwy.* ☎ *305/744–9866, 800/523–2326* ⊕ *www.babyscoffee.com.*

WHERE TO EAT

$$
AMERICAN

✗**Geiger Key Smokehouse Bar & Grill.** There's a strong hint of the Old Keys at this oceanside marina restaurant, which came under new management in 2010 by the same folks who own Hogfish Grill on Stock Island. "On the backside of paradise," as the sign says, its tiki structures overlook quiet mangroves at an RV park marina. Locals usually outnumber tourists. The all-day menu spans an ambitious array of sandwiches, tacos, and seafood. Local fishermen stop here for breakfast before heading out in search of the big one. Don't miss the Sunday BBQ from 4–9. ⑤ *Average main: $16* ⊠ *MM 10, 5 Geiger Key Rd., off Boca Chica Rd., Bay Point, Geiger Key* ☎ *305/296–3553, 305/294–1230* ⊕ *www.geigerkeymarina.com.*

$$
SEAFOOD

✗**Mangrove Mama's Restaurant.** This could be the prototype for a Keys restaurant, given its shanty appearance, lattice trim, and roving sort of indoor-outdoor floor plan. Then there's the seafood, from the ubiquitous fish sandwich (fried, grilled, broiled, or blackened) to lobster reubens, crab cakes, and coconut shrimp. Burgers, steaks, and ribs round out the menu. Hidden in a grove of banana and palm trees, the place opens for lunch, Sunday brunch, and dinner. ⑤ *Average main: $20* ⊠ *MM 20 BS, Sugarloaf Key* ☎ *305/745–3030* ⊕ *www.mangrovemamasrestaurant.com* ⊙ *Closed Sept.*

$$$
SEAFOOD
Fodor'sChoice
★

✗**Square Grouper.** In an unassuming warehouse-looking building right off U.S. 1, chef and owner Lynn Bell is creating seafood magic. Just ask the locals, who wait in line for a table along with visitors in the know. But don't let the exterior fool you: the dining room is surprisingly suave, with butcher paper–lined tables, mandarin-colored walls, and textural components throughout. While the restaurant earns rave reviews, its name still earns snickers. (A "square grouper" is slang for bales of marijuana dropped into the ocean during the drug-running 1970s.) The dishes here not only taste close-your-eyes-and-grin good, their presentation is lovely. For starters, try the flash-fried conch with wasabi drizzle or home-smoked fish dip. Then perhaps order the seafood pasta with key lime butter sauce. It's okay to drool. Upstairs, Chef Lynn has just opened a beatnik-style tapas bar. ⑤ *Average main: $25* ⊠ *MM 22.5 OS, Cudjoe Key* ☎ *305/745–8880* ⊕ *www.squaregrouperbarandgrill.com* ⊙ *Closed Sun., Sept., and several wks in summer.*

WHERE TO STAY

$$$$
RESORT
Fodor'sChoice
★

▥**Little Palm Island Resort & Spa.** *Haute tropicale* best describes this luxury retreat, and "second mortgage" might explain how some can afford the extravagant prices. **Pros:** secluded setting; heavenly spa; easy wildlife viewing. **Cons:** expensive; might be too quiet for some; only accessible by boat or seaplane. ⑤ *Rooms from: $1590* ⊠ *MM 28.5*

OS, 28500 Overseas Hwy. ☎305/872–2524, 800/343–8567 ⊕www.littlepalmisland.com ⇲30 suites ⫿⊙⫿Some meals.

$ ⛵ **Looe Key Reef Resort & Center.** If your Keys vacation is all about div-
HOTEL ing, you'll be well served at this scuba-obsessed operation—the closest place to stay to the stellar reef (and affordable to boot). **Pros:** guests get discounts on dive and snorkel trips; fun bar. **Cons:** small rooms; unheated pool; close to road. ⑤ Rooms from: $89 ⊠ MM 27.5 OS, 27340 Overseas Hwy., Ramrod Key ☎305/872–2215, 877/816–3483 ⊕www.diveflakeys.com ⇲23 rooms, 1 suite ⫿⊙⫿No meals.

$ ⛵ **Parmer's Resort.** Almost every room at this budget-friendly option has
HOTEL a view of South Pine Channel, with the lovely curl of Big Pine Key in the foreground. **Pros:** bright rooms; pretty setting; good value. **Cons:** a bit out of the way; housekeeping costs extra; little shade around the pool. ⑤ Rooms from: $159 ⊠ MM 28.7 BS, 565 Barry Ave. ☎305/872–2157 ⊕www.parmersresort.com ⇲18 rooms, 12 efficiencies, 15 apartments, 1 penthouse, 1 2-bedroom cottage ⫿⊙⫿Breakfast.

SPORTS AND THE OUTDOORS

BOATING AND KAYAKING

Dolphin Marina. Dolphin Marina rents 19- and 22-foot boats with 150 horsepower for up to eight people by the half day and full day. ⊠28530 Overseas Hwy. ☎305/872–2685 ⊕www.dolphinmarina.net ⇲From $200 half-day, from $250 full-day.

Sugarloaf Marina. Rates for one-person kayaks are based on an hourly or daily rental; two-person kayaks are also available. Delivery is free for rentals of three days or more. The folks at the marina can also hook you up with an outfitter for a day of offshore or backcountry fishing. There's also a well-stocked ship store. ⊠ MM 17 BS, 17015 Overseas Hwy., Sugarloaf Key ☎305/745–3135 ⊕www.sugarloafkeymarina.com ⇲From $15 per hr.

SCUBA DIVING AND SNORKELING

In 1744 the HMS *Looe*, a British warship, ran aground and sank on one of the most beautiful coral reefs in the Keys, 5 nautical miles off the coast of Little Torch Key. Today the key owes its name to the ill-fated ship. The 5.3-square-nautical-mile reef, part of the Florida Keys National Marine Sanctuary, has strands of elkhorn coral on its eastern margin, purple sea fans, and abundant sponges and sea urchins. On its seaward side, it drops almost vertically 50 to 90 feet. In its midst, Shipwreck Trail plots the location of nine historic wreck sites in 14 to 120 feet of water. Buoys mark the sites, and underwater signs tell the history of each site and what marine life to expect. Snorkelers and divers will find the sanctuary a quiet place to observe reef life—except in July, when the annual Underwater Music Festival pays homage to Looe Key's beauty and promotes reef awareness with six hours of music broadcast via underwater speakers. Dive shops, charters, and private boats transport about 500 divers and snorkelers to hear the spectacle, which includes classical, jazz, new age, and Caribbean music, as well as a little Jimmy Buffett. There are even underwater Elvis impersonators.

Looe Key Reef Resort & Dive Center. This center, the closest dive shop to Looe Key Reef, offers two affordable trips daily, 7:30 am or 12:15 pm (for divers, snorkelers, or bubble watchers). The maximum depth is 30 feet, so snorkelers and divers go on the same boat. On Wednesday and Sunday, it runs a trip for advanced divers that visits a wreck and a reef in the area. The dive boat, a 45-foot catamaran, is docked at the full-service Looe Key Reef Resort. ⊠ *Looe Key Reef Resort, MM 27.5 OS, 27340 Overseas Hwy., Ramrod Key* ☎ *305/872–2215, 877/816–3483* ⊕ *www.diveflakeys.com* ✉ *From $39.*

EN ROUTE The huge object that looks like a white whale floating over Cudjoe Key (MM 23–21) isn't a figment of your imagination. It's Fat Albert, a radar balloon that monitors local air and water traffic.

KEY WEST

4

Situated 150 miles from Miami, 90 miles from Havana, and an immeasurable distance from sanity, this end-of-the-line community has never been like anywhere else. Even after it was connected to the rest of the country—by the railroad in 1912 and by the highway in 1938—it maintained a strong sense of detachment.

Key West reflects a diverse population: Conchs (natives, many of whom trace their ancestry to the Bahamas), freshwater Conchs (longtime residents who migrated from somewhere else years ago), Hispanics (primarily descendants of Cuban immigrants), recent refugees from the urban sprawl of mainland Florida, military personnel, and an assortment of vagabonds, drifters, and dropouts in search of refuge. The island was once a gay vacation hot spot, and it remains a decidedly gay-friendly destination. Some of the most renowned gay guesthouses, however, no longer cater to an exclusively gay clientele. Key Westers pride themselves on their tolerance of all peoples, all sexual orientations, and even all animals. Most restaurants allow pets, and it's not surprising to see stray cats, dogs, and chickens roaming freely through the dining rooms. The chicken issue is one that government officials periodically try to bring to an end, but the colorful iconic fowl continue to strut and crow, particularly in the vicinity of Old Town's Bahamian Village.

Although the rest of the Keys are known for outdoor activities, Key West has something of a city feel. Few open spaces remain, as promoters continue to churn out restaurants, galleries, shops, and museums to interpret the city's intriguing past. As a tourist destination, Key West has a lot to sell—an average temperature of 79°F, 19th-century architecture, and a laid-back lifestyle. Yet much has been lost to those eager for a buck. Duval Street looks like a miniature Las Vegas lined with garish signs for T-shirt shops and tour-company offices. Cruise ships dwarf the town's skyline and fill the streets with day-trippers gawking at the hippies with dogs in their bike baskets, gay couples walking down the street holding hands, and the oddball lot of locals, some of whom bark louder than the dogs.

KEY WEST'S COLORFUL HISTORY

The United States acquired Key West from Spain in 1821, along with the rest of Florida. The Spanish had named the island Cayo Hueso, or Bone Key, after the Native American skeletons they found on its shores. In 1823 President James Monroe sent Commodore David S. Porter to chase pirates away. For three decades the primary industry in Key West was wrecking—rescuing people and salvaging cargo from ships that foundered on the nearby reefs. According to some reports, when pickings were lean, the wreckers hung out lights to lure ships aground. Their business declined after 1849, when the federal government began building lighthouses.

In 1845 the army began construction on Fort Taylor, which kept Key West on the Union side during the Civil War, even though most of Florida seceded. After the fighting ended, an influx of Cubans unhappy with Spain's rule brought the cigar industry here. Fishing, shrimping, and sponge gathering became important industries, as did pineapple canning. Through much of the 19th century and into the 20th, Key West was

Florida's wealthiest city in per-capita terms. But in 1929 the local economy began to unravel. Cigar making moved to Tampa, Hawaii dominated the pineapple industry, and the sponges succumbed to blight. Then the Depression hit, and within a few years half the population was on relief.

Tourism began to revive Key West, but that came to a halt when a hurricane knocked out the railroad bridge in 1935. To help the tourism industry recover from that crushing blow, the government offered incentives for islanders to turn their charming homes—many of them built by shipwrights—into guesthouses and inns. The wise foresight has left the town with more than 100 such lodgings, a hallmark of Key West vacationing today. In the 1950s the discovery of "pink gold" in the Dry Tortugas boosted the economy of the entire region. Harvesting Key West shrimp required a fleet of up to 500 boats and flooded local restaurants with sweet, luscious shrimp. The town's artistic community found inspiration in the colorful fishing boats.

GETTING HERE AND AROUND
CAR TRAVEL

Between mile markers 4 and 0, Key West is the one place in the Keys where you could conceivably do without a car, especially if you plan on staying around Old Town. If you've driven the 106 miles down the chain, you're probably ready to abandon your car in the hotel parking lot anyway. Trolleys, buses, bikes, scooters, and feet are more suitable alternatives. To explore the beaches, New Town, and Stock Island, you'll probably need a car.

Old Town Key West is the only place in the Keys where parking is a problem. There are public parking lots that charge by the hour or day (some hotels and bed-and-breakfasts provide parking or discounts at municipal lots). If you arrive early, you can sometimes find a spot on side streets off Duval and Whitehead, where you can park for free—just be sure it's not marked for residential parking only. Your best bet is to bike or take the trolley around town if you don't want to walk. You can disembark and reboard the trolley at will.

BUS TRAVEL

Greyhound Lines runs a special Keys shuttle two times a day (depending on the day of the week) from Miami International Airport (departing from Concourse E, lower level) and stops throughout the Keys. Fares run about $45 for Key West (✉ 3535 S. Roosevelt, Key West International Airport). Keys Shuttle runs scheduled service six times a day in 15-passenger vans between Miami Airport and Key West with stops throughout the Keys for $70 to $90 per person.

The City of Key West Department of Transportation has six color-coded bus routes traversing the island from 6:30 am to 11:30 pm. Stops have signs with the international bus symbol. Schedules are available on buses and at hotels, visitor centers, and shops. The fare is $2 one way. The Lower Keys Shuttle bus runs from Marathon to Key West ($4 one way), with scheduled stops along the way.

4

Contacts **City of Key West Department of Transportation** ☎ *305/809–3910 ⊕ www.kwtransit.com.* **Greyhound Lines** ☎ *800/410–5397 for local info, 800/231–2222 ⊕ www.greyhound.com.* **Keys Shuttle** ☎ *305/289–9997, 888/765–9997 ⊕ www.keysshuttle.com.* **SuperShuttle** ☎ *305/871–2000, 800/258–3826 ⊕ www.supershuttle.com.*

BOAT TRAVEL

Key West Express operates air-conditioned ferries between the Key West Terminal (Caroline and Grinnell streets) and Marco Island and Fort Myers Beach. The trip from Fort Myers Beach takes at least four hours each way and costs $86 one-way, $146 round-trip. Ferries depart from Fort Myers Beach at 8:30 am and from Key West at 6 pm. The Marco Island ferry costs $86 one-way and $146 round-trip, and departs at 8:30 am (the return trip leaves Key West at 5 pm). A photo ID is required for each passenger. Advance reservations are recommended. The SuperShuttle charges $102 per passenger for trips from Miami International Airport to the Upper Keys. To go farther into the Keys, you must book an entire 11-person van, which costs about $350 to Key West. You need to place your request for transportation back to the airport 24 hours in advance.

Contact **Key West Express** ✉ *100 Grinnell St.* ☎ *888/539–2628 ⊕ www. seakeywestexpress.com.*

VISITOR INFORMATION

Contact **Greater Key West Chamber of Commerce** ☎ *305/294–2587, 800/527–8539 ⊕ www.keywestchamber.org.*

EXPLORING

OLD TOWN

The heart of Key West, the historic Old Town area runs from White Street to the waterfront. Beginning in 1822, wharves, warehouses, chandleries, ship-repair facilities, and eventually, in 1891, the U.S. Custom House sprang up around the deep harbor to accommodate the navy's large ships and other sailing vessels. Wreckers, merchants, and sea captains built lavish houses near the bustling waterfront. A remarkable number of these fine Victorian and pre-Victorian structures have been restored to their original grandeur and now serve as homes, guesthouses, shops, restaurants, and museums. These, along with the dwellings of famous writers, artists, and politicians who've come to Key West over the past 175 years, are among the area's approximately 3,000 historic structures. Old Town also has the city's finest restaurants and hotels, lively street life, and popular night spots.

TOP ATTRACTIONS

Audubon House and Tropical Gardens. If you've ever seen an engraving by ornithologist John James Audubon, you'll understand why his name is synonymous with birds. See his works in this three-story house, which was built in the 1840s for Captain John Geiger and filled with period furniture. It now commemorates Audubon's 1832 stop in Key West while he was traveling through Florida to study birds. After an introduction by a docent, you can do a self-guided tour of the house and gardens (or just the gardens). An art gallery sells lithographs of the artist's famed portraits. ⊠ *205 Whitehead St.* ☎ *305/294–2116, 877/294–2470* ⊕ *www.audubonhouse.com* ⊠ *$7.50 gardens only; $12 house and gardens* ⊙ *Daily 9:30–5 (last tour at 4:15).*

Fodor's Choice ★ **Ernest Hemingway Home and Museum.** Amusing anecdotes spice up the guided tours of Ernest Hemingway's home, built in 1801 by the town's most successful wrecker. While living here between 1931 and 1942, Hemingway wrote about 70% of his life's work, including classics like *For Whom the Bell Tolls.* Few of his belongings remain aside from some books, and there's little about his actual work, but photographs help you visualize his day-to-day life. The famous six-toed descendants of Hemingway's cats—many named for actors, artists, authors, and even a hurricane—have free rein of the property. Tours begin every 10 minutes and take 30 minutes; then you're free to explore on your own. Be sure to find out why there is a urinal in the garden! ⊠ *907 Whitehead St.* ☎ *305/294–1136* ⊕ *www.hemingwayhome.com* ⊠ *$13* ⊙ *Daily 9–5.*

Fort Zachary Taylor Historic State Park. Construction of the fort began in 1845 but was halted during the Civil War. Even though Florida seceded from the Union, Yankee forces used the fort as a base to block Confederate shipping. More than 1,500 Confederate vessels were detained in Key West's harbor. The fort, finally completed in 1866, was also used in the Spanish-American War. Take a 30-minute guided walking tour of the redbrick fort, a National Historic Landmark, at noon and 2, or self-tour anytime between 8 and 5. In February a celebration called Civil War Heritage Days includes costumed reenactments and demonstrations. From mid-January to mid-April the park serves as an open-air gallery for pieces created for Sculpture Key West. One of its most popular features is its man-made beach, a rest stop for migrating birds in the spring and fall; there are also picnic areas, hiking and biking trails and a kayak launch. ⊠ *Southard St., at the end of the street, through Truman Annex* ☎ *305/292–6713* ⊕ *www.floridastateparks. org/forttaylor* ⊠ *$4 for single-occupant vehicle, $6 for 2–8 people in a vehicle, plus a $0.50 per person county surcharge.* ⊙ *Daily 8–sunset.*

Key West

DREDGERS KEY

ATLANTIC OCEAN

Key West International Airport

Key West Municipal Beach

WISTERIA ISLAND

SUNSET KEY

FLEMING KEY

See inset at left

KEY

▶ ① Sights
① Restaurants & Hotels

Sights

▶
Audubon House and Tropical Gardens **3**
Ernest Hemingway Home and Museum **1**
Fort East Martello Museum & Gardens **11**

Fort Zachary Taylor Historic State Park **8**
Harry S Truman Little White House Museum **4**
Historic Seaport at Key West Bight **7**

Key West Butterfly & Nature Conservatory **9**
Key West Lighthouse Museum and Keeper's Quarters Museum **2**
Key West Museum of Art & History in the Custom House **5**

Key West Tropical Forest & Botanical Garden **12**
Mallory Square and Pier **6**
Southernmost Point **10**

Restaurants

▶
Hogfish Bar & Grill **5**
Salute Ristorante at the Beach **2**

Hotels

▶
Key West Marriott Beachside **4**
Parrot Key Resort **3**
Sunset Key **1**

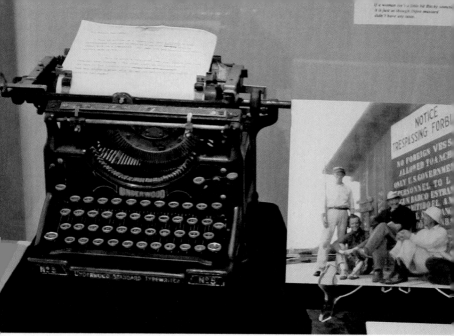
See the typewriter Hemingway used at his home office in Key West. He lived here from 1931 to 1942.

NEED A BREAK? **Key West Library.** Check out the pretty palm garden next to the Key West Library at 700 Fleming Street, just off Duval. This leafy, outdoor reading area, with shaded benches, is the perfect place to escape the frenzy and crowds of downtown Key West. There's free Internet access in the library, too. ⊠ *700 Fleming St.* ☏ *305/292–3595.*

Harry S Truman Little White House Museum. Renovations to this circa-1890 landmark have restored the home and gardens to the Truman era, down to the wallpaper pattern. A free photographic review of visiting dignitaries and presidents—John F. Kennedy, Jimmy Carter, and Bill Clinton are among the chief executives who passed through here—is on display in the back of the gift shop. Engaging 45-minute tours begin every 20 minutes until 4:30. They start with an excellent 10-minute video on the history of the property and Truman's visits. On the grounds of **Truman Annex,** a 103-acre former military parade grounds and barracks, the home served as a winter White House for presidents Truman, Eisenhower, and Kennedy. ■ TIP➔ The house tour does require climbing steps. Visitors can do a free self-guided botanical tour of the grounds with a brochure from the museum store. ⊠ *111 Front St.* ☏ *305/294–9911* ⊕ *www.trumanlittlewhitehouse.com* ⊠ *$16.13* ⊙ *House daily 9–5, grounds daily 7–6.*

Historic Seaport at Key West Bight. What was once a funky—in some places even seedy—part of town is now an 8½-acre historic restoration of 100 businesses, including waterfront restaurants, open-air bars, museums, clothing stores, bait shops, dive shops, docks, a marina, and watersports concessions. It's all linked by the 2-mile waterfront **Harborwalk,**

CLOSE UP

Hemingway Was Here

In a town where Pulitzer Prize–winning writers are almost as common as coconuts, Ernest Hemingway stands out. Bars and restaurants around the island claim that he ate or drank there (except Bagatelle, where a sign in the bar reads, "Hemingway never liked this place").

Hemingway came to Key West in 1928 at the urging of writer John dos Passos and rented a house with wife number two, Pauline Pfeiffer. They spent winters in the Keys and summers in Europe and Wyoming, occasionally taking African safaris. Along the way they had two sons, Patrick and Gregory. In 1931 Pauline's wealthy uncle Gus gave the couple the house at 907 Whitehead Street. Now known as the Ernest Hemingway Home & Museum, it's Key West's number-one tourist attraction. Renovations included the addition of a pool and a tropical garden.

In 1935, when the visitor bureau included the house in a tourist brochure, Hemingway promptly built the brick wall that surrounds it today. He wrote of the visitor bureau's offense in a 1935 essay for *Esquire*, saying, "The house at present is occupied by your correspondent is listed as number eighteen in a compilation of the forty-eight things for a tourist to see in Key West. So there will be no difficulty in a tourist finding it or any other of the sights of the city, a map has been prepared by the local F.E.R.A. authorities to be presented to each arriving visitor. This is all very flattering to the easily bloated ego of your correspondent but very hard on production."

During his time in Key West, Hemingway penned some of his most important works, including *A Farewell to Arms, To Have and Have Not, Green Hills of Africa,* and *Death in the Afternoon.* His rigorous schedule consisted of writing almost every morning in his second-story studio above the pool, and then promptly descending the stairs at midday. By afternoon and evening he was ready for drinking, fishing, swimming, boxing, and hanging around with the boys.

One close friend was Joe Russell, a craggy fisherman and owner of the rugged bar Sloppy Joe's, originally at 428 Greene Street but now at 201 Duval Street. Russell was the only one in town who would cash Hemingway's $1,000 royalty check. Russell and Charles Thompson introduced Hemingway to deep-sea fishing, which became fodder for his writing. Another of Hemingway's loves was boxing. He set up a ring in his yard and paid local fighters to box with him, and he refereed matches at Blue Heaven, then a saloon at 729 Thomas Street.

Hemingway honed his macho image, dressed in cutoffs and old shirts, and took on the name Papa. In turn, he gave his friends new names and used them as characters in his stories. Joe Russell became Freddy, captain of the *Queen Conch* charter boat in *To Have and Have Not.*

Hemingway stayed in Key West for 11 years before leaving Pauline for wife number three. Pauline and the boys stayed on in the house, which sold in 1951 for $80,000, 10 times its original cost.

—Jim and Cynthia Tunstall

4

which runs between Front and Grinnell streets, passing big ships, schooners, sunset cruises, fishing charters, and glass-bottom boats. ⊠ *100 Grinnell St.* ☎ *305/293–8309* ⊕ *www.keywestseaport.com.*

NEED A BREAK?

Coffee Plantation. Get your morning (or afternoon) buzz, and hook up to the Internet in the comfort of a homelike setting in a circa-1890 Conch house. Munch on sandwiches, wraps, and pastries, and sip a hot or cold espresso beverage. ⊠ *713 Caroline St.* ☎ *305/295–9808* ⊕ *www. coffeeplantationkeywest.com.*

FAMILY **Key West Butterfly & Nature Conservatory.** This air-conditioned refuge for butterflies, birds, and the human spirit gladdens the soul with hundreds of colorful wings—more than 45 species of butterflies alone—in a lovely glass-encased bubble. Waterfalls, artistic benches, paved pathways, birds, and lush, flowering vegetation elevate this above most butterfly attractions. The gift shop and gallery are worth a visit on their own. ⊠ *1316 Duval St.* ☎ *305/296–2988, 800/839–4647* ⊕ *www. keywestbutterfly.com* ⊠ *$12* ☉ *Daily 9–5 (gallery and shop until 5:30).*

Key West Lighthouse Museum & Keeper's Quarters Museum. For the best view in town, climb the 88 steps to the top of this 1847 lighthouse. The 92-foot structure has a Fresnel lens, which was installed in the 1860s at a cost of $1 million. The keeper lived in the adjacent 1887 clapboard house, which now exhibits vintage photographs, ship models, nautical charts, and lighthouse artifacts from all along the Key reefs. A kids' room is stocked with books and toys. ⊠ *938 Whitehead St.* ☎ *305/295–6616* ⊕ *www.kwahs.com* ⊠ *$10* ☉ *Daily 9:30–4:30.*

Fodor'sChoice ★ **Key West Museum of Art & History in the Custom House.** When Key West was designated a U.S. port of entry in the early 1820s, a customs house was established. Salvaged cargoes from ships wrecked on the reefs were brought here, setting the stage for Key West to become—for a time—the richest city in Florida. The imposing redbrick-and-terra-cotta Richardsonian Romanesque–style building reopened as a museum and art gallery in 1999. Smaller galleries have long-term and changing exhibits about the history of Key West, including a Hemingway room and a fine collection of folk artist Mario Sanchez's wood paintings. In 2011, to commemorate the 100th anniversary of the railroad's arrival to Key West in 1912, a new permanent Flagler exhibit opened. ⊠ *281 Front St.* ☎ *305/295–6616* ⊕ *www.kwahs.com* ⊠ *$9* ☉ *Daily 9:30–4:30.*

Mallory Square and Pier. For cruise-ship passengers, this is the disembarkation point for an attack on Key West. For practically every visitor, it's the requisite venue for a nightly sunset celebration that includes street performers—human statues, sword swallowers, tightrope walkers, musicians, and more—plus craft vendors, conch fritter fryers, and other regulars who defy classification. (Wanna picture with my pet iguana?) With all the activity, don't forget to watch the main show: a dazzling tropical sunset.

The Southernmost Point. Possibly the most photographed site in Key West (even though the actual geographic southernmost point in the continental United States lies across the bay on a naval base, where you see a satellite dish), this is a must-see. Who wouldn't want his picture taken

Divers examine the intentionally scuttled 327-foot former U.S. Coast Guard cutter *Duane* in 120 feet of water off Key Largo.

next to the big striped buoy that marks the southernmost point in the continental United States? A plaque next to it honors Cubans who lost their lives trying to escape to America and other signs tell Key West history. ⊠ *Whitehead and South sts.*

NEW TOWN

The Overseas Highway splits as it enters Key West, the two forks rejoining to encircle New Town, the area east of White Street to Cow Key Channel. The southern fork runs along the shore as South Roosevelt Boulevard (Route A1A), skirting Key West International Airport. Along the north shore, North Roosevelt Boulevard (U.S. 1) leads to Old Town. Part of New Town was created with dredged fill. The island would have continued growing this way had the Army Corps of Engineers not determined in the early 1970s that it was detrimental to the nearby reef.

Fort East Martello Museum & Gardens. This redbrick Civil War fort never saw a lick of action during the war. Today it serves as a museum, with historical exhibits about the 19th and 20th centuries. Among the latter are relics of the USS *Maine,* cigar factory and shipwrecking exhibits, and the citadel tower you can climb to the top. The museum, operated by the Key West Art and Historical Society, also has a collection of Stanley Papio's "junk art" sculptures inside and out, and a gallery of Cuban folk artist Mario Sanchez's chiseled and painted wooden carvings of historic Key West street scenes. ⊠ *3501 S. Roosevelt Blvd.* ☎ *305/296–3913* ⊕ *www.kwahs.com* ✉ *$9* ⊙ *Daily 9:30–4:30.*

Key West Tropical Forest & Botanical Garden. Established in 1935, this unique habitat is the only frost-free botanical garden in the continental United States. You won't see fancy topiaries and exotic plants, but you'll

THE CONCH REPUBLIC

Beginning in the 1970s, pot smuggling became a source of income for islanders who knew how to dodge detection in the maze of waterways in the Keys. In 1982 the U.S. Border Patrol threw a roadblock across the Overseas Highway just south of Florida City to catch drug runners and undocumented aliens. Traffic backed up for miles as Border Patrol agents searched vehicles and demanded that the occupants prove U.S. citizenship. Officials in Key West, outraged at being treated like foreigners by the federal government, staged a protest and formed their own "nation": the so-called Conch Republic. They hoisted a flag and distributed mock border passes, visas, and Conch currency. The embarrassed Border Patrol dismantled its roadblock, and now an annual festival recalls the city's victory. You can even "apply" for a Conch Republic passport (for entertainment purposes, not travel!). It'll set you back $100, but those who hold one think it's priceless. Begin your journey online at ⊕ *www. conchrepublic.com.*

see a unique ecosystem that naturally occurs in this area and the Caribbean. There are paved walkways that take you past butterfly gardens, mangroves, Cuban palms, lots of birds like herons and ibis, and ponds where you can spy turtles and fish. It's a nice respite from the sidewalks and shops, and offers a natural slice of Keys paradise. ⊠ *5210 College Rd.* ☎ *305/296–1504* ⊕ *www.kwbgs.org* ⊠ *$7* ☉ *Daily 10–4.*

BEACHES

OLD TOWN

Dog Beach. Next to Louie's Backyard, this tiny beach—the only one in Key West where dogs are allowed unleashed—has a shore that's a mix of sand and rocks. **Amenities:** none. **Best for:** walking. ⊠ *Vernon and Waddell sts.* ⊠ *Free* ☉ *Daily sunrise–sunset.*

FAMILY **Fort Zachary Taylor Beach.** The park's beach is the best and safest place to swim in Key West. There's an adjoining picnic area with barbecue grills and shade trees, a snack bar, and rental equipment, including snorkeling gear. A café serves sandwiches and other munchies. **Amenities:** food and drink; showers, toilets; water sports. **Best for:** swimming; snorkeling. ⊠ *Southard St., at the end of the street, through Truman Annex* ☎ *305/292–6713* ⊕ *www.floridastateparks.org/forttaylor* ⊠ *$4 for single-occupant vehicle, $6 for 2–8 people in a vehicle, plus $0.50 per person county surcharge* ☉ *Daily 8–sunset; tours at noon and 2.*

FAMILY **Higgs Beach–Astro City Playground.** This Monroe County park with its groomed pebbly sand is a popular sunbathing spot. A nearby grove of Australian pines provides shade, and the West Martello Tower provides shelter should a storm suddenly sweep in. Kayak and beach-chair rentals are available, as is a volleyball net. The beach also has a marker and cultural exhibit commemorating the gravesite of 295 enslaved Africans who died after being rescued from three South America–bound slave ships in 1860. Across the street, **Astro City Playground** is popular with

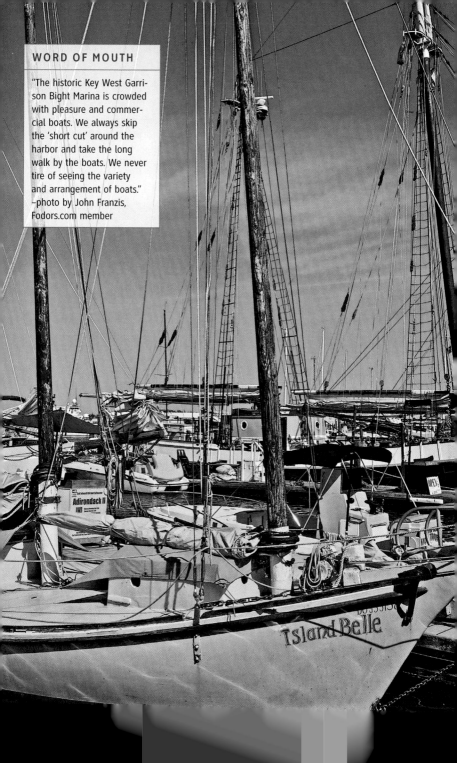

young children. **Amenities:** parking (free); toilets; water sports. **Best for:** swimming; snorkeling. ⊠ *Atlantic Blvd., between White and Reynolds sts.* 🖅 *Free* ☉ *Daily 6 am–11 pm.*

NEW TOWN

C. B. Harvey Memorial Rest Beach. This beach and park were named after Cornelius Bradford Harvey, former Key West mayor and commissioner. Adjacent to Higgs Beach, it has half a dozen picnic areas across the street, dunes, a pier, and a wheelchair and bike path. **Amenities:** none. **Best for:** walking. ⊠ *Atlantic Blvd., east side of White St. Pier* 🖅 *Free* ☉ *Daily 6 am–11 pm.*

Smathers Beach. This wide beach has nearly 1 mile of nice white sand, plus beautiful coconut palms, picnic areas, and volleyball courts, all of which make it popular with the spring-break crowd. Trucks along the road rent rafts, windsurfers, and other beach "toys." **Amenities:** parking (free); toilets; water sports. **Best for:** partiers. ⊠ *S. Roosevelt Blvd.* 🖅 *Free* ☉ *Daily 7 am–11 pm.*

WHERE TO EAT

Bring your appetite, a sense of daring, and a lack of preconceived notions about propriety. A meal in Key West can mean overlooking the crazies along Duval Street, watching roosters and pigeons battle for a scrap of food that may have escaped your fork, relishing the finest in what used to be the dining room of some 19th-century Victorian home, or gazing out at boats jockeying for position in the marina. And that's just the diversity of the setting. Seafood dominates local menus, but the treatment afforded that fish or crustacean can range from Cuban and American to Asian and Continental.

$$ ✕ **Ambrosia.** Ask any savvy local where to get the best sushi on the island
JAPANESE and you'll undoubtedly be pointed to this bright and airy dining room with modern indoor waterfall literally steps from the Atlantic. Grab a seat at the sleek bar, where the back wall glows from purple to blue, or sit at the sushi bar and watch owner and head sushi chef Masa (albeit not the famous chef of the eponymous restaurants in New York and Las Vegas) prepare an impressive array of super fresh sashimi delicacies. Sushi lovers can't go wrong with the Ambrosia special: miso soup served with a sampler of 15 kinds of sashimi, seven pieces of sushi, and sushi rolls. There's an assortment of lightly fried tempura and teriyaki dishes and a killer bento box at lunch. Enjoy it all with a glass of premium sake or a cold glass of Sapporo beer. ⑤ *Average main: $20* ⊠ *Santa Maria Resort, 1401 Simonton St.* ☎ *305/293–0304* ⊕ *www.keywestambrosia. com* ☉ *Closed 2 wks after Labor Day. No lunch weekends.*

$$$ ✕ **Azur Restaurant.** Fuel up on the finest fare at this former gas station,
ECLECTIC now part of the Eden House complex. In a contemporary setting with indoor and outdoor seating, welcoming staff serves breakfast, lunch, and dinner that stand out from the hordes of Key West restaurants by virtue of originality. For instance, key lime–stuffed French toast and yellowtail snapper Benedict make breakfast a pleasant wake-up call. The crab cake BLT, duck Cubano with fontina cheese, and charred marinated octopus command notice on the lunch menu. Four varieties

of homemade gnocchi are a dinner-time specialty, along with tasting plates, "almost entrees" like braised lamb ribs over Moroccan-spiced chickpeas, and main courses that include seafood risotto with chorizo and grilled sea bass. Sunday brunch served. $ *Average main: $26* ✉ *425 Grinnell St.* ☎ *305/292–2987* ⊕ *www.azurkeywest.com* ⚼ *Reservations essential.*

$ ╳ **B.O.'s Fish Wagon.** What started out as a fish house on wheels appears to have broken down on the corner of Caroline and William streets and is today the cornerstone for one of Key West's junkyard-chic dining institutions. Step up to the wood-plank counter window and order the specialty: a grouper sandwich fried or grilled and topped with key lime sauce. Other choices include fish nuts (don't be scared, they're just fried nuggets), hot dogs, cracked conch sandwich, and shrimp or soft-shell-crab sandwich. Talk sass with your host and find a picnic table or take a seat at the plank. Grab some paper towels off one of the rolls hanging around and busy yourself reading graffiti, license plates, and irreverent signs. It's a must-do Key West experience. $ *Average main: $12* ✉ *801 Caroline St.* ☎ *305/294–9272* ⊕ *www.bosfishwagon.com* ▭ *No credit cards.*

SEAFOOD

$$$ ╳ **Blue Heaven.** The outdoor dining area here is often referred to as "the quintessential Keys experience," and it's hard to argue. There's much to like about this historic restaurant where Hemingway refereed boxing matches and customers cheered for cockfights. Although these events are no more, the free-roaming chickens and cats add that "what-a-hoot" factor. Nightly specials include black bean soup, Caribbean BBQ shrimp, bison strip steak with blackberry salad, and jerk chicken. Desserts and breads are baked on the premises. The banana bread and shrimp and grits are hits during breakfast, but the signature meal here is the lobster Benedict with key lime hollandaise. Bring patience as there is always a wait. $ *Average main: $24* ✉ *729 Thomas St.* ☎ *305/296–8666* ⊕ *www.blueheavenkw.com* ⚼ *Reservations not accepted* ⊙ *Closed after Labor Day for 6 wks.*

CARIBBEAN

$ ╳ **The Café.** You don't have to be a vegetarian to love this new-age café decorated with bright artwork and a corrugated tin–fronted counter. Local favorites include homemade soup, veggie sandwiches and burgers (order them with a side of sweet potato fries), grilled portobello mushroom salad, seafood, vegan specialties, stir-fry dinners, and grilled Gorgonzola pizza. There's also a nice selection of draft beer and wines by the glass, plus daily desserts (including vegan selections). $ *Average main: $11* ✉ *509 Southard St.* ☎ *305/296–5515* ⊕ *www.thecafekw.com* ⚼ *Reservations not accepted* ⊙ *Closed Sun.*

VEGETARIAN

$$$ ╳ **Café Marquesa.** Chef Susan Ferry presents seven or more inspired entrées on her changing menu each night; delicious dishes can include yellowtail snapper with pear, ricotta pasta purses with caponata, and Australian rack of lamb crusted with goat cheese and a port-fig sauce. End your meal on a sweet note with key lime napoleon with tropical fruits and berries. There's also a fine selection of wines and custom martinis such as the key limetini and the Irish martini. Adjoining the intimate Marquesa Hotel, the dining room is equally relaxed and elegant.

EUROPEAN
Fodor's Choice
★

$ *Average main: $29* ✉ *600 Fleming St.* ☎ *305/292–1244* ⊕ *www. marquesa.com* ⚅ *Reservations essential* ☾ *No lunch.*

$$$ ✕ **Café Solé.** This little corner of France hides behind a high wall in a
FRENCH residential neighborhood. Inside, French training intertwines with local ingredients, creating delicious takes on classics, including a must-try conch Carpaccio, yellowtail snapper with mango salsa, and some of the best bouillabaisse that you'll find outside of Marseilles. Hog snapper (aka hogfish) is a house specialty here, prepared several ways by Chef John Correa, including with beurre blanc or red pepper–custard sauce. From the land, there is filet mignon with a wild-mushroom demiglaze. Lunch is served from 11 to 2, dinner from 5 to 10. $ *Average main: $27* ✉ *1029 Southard St.* ☎ *305/294–0230* ⊕ *www.cafesole.com* ⚅ *Reservations essential.*

$$$ ✕ **Camille's Restaurant.** Break out the stretchy pants because everything
MODERN on the menu at this affordable hot spot not only sounds scrumptious,
AMERICAN it is. Start your day with a shrimp, lobster, or crab-cake Benedict—the latter was voted best in the Florida Keys. Lunch brings dishes like hand-pulled chicken salad or a mahimahi wrap. Evenings will have you swooning for the famous grilled stone-crab cakes with an addictive Captain Morgan spiced rum–mango sauce. Locals have tried to keep this place a secret for over 20 years, but the word is out. Line up beneath the bright pink awning and happily wait for your seat. Be sure to ask your server about the Barbie dolls—they have a most unique collection, many with a Key West flair. $ *Average main: $21* ✉ *1202 Simonton St., at Catherine St.* ☎ *305/296-4811* ⊕ *www.camilleskeywest.com* ⚅ *Reservations essential.*

$$$ ✕ **Deuce's Off the Hook Grill.** It's a tight fit with only six tables (and six
MODERN counter seats), but if you don't mind sitting close to fellow diners, you
AMERICAN will be rewarded with a made-from-scratch meal almost any time of day. Battered chicken tenders with waffles and huevos rancheros will rev up your morning. Coconut-crusted mahimahi with mango salsa is the signature lunch dish, but the lobster pie (pizza with poached lobster, goat cheese, arugula, and shaved fig) is a close second. Dinners run the gamut with the likes of "The Gobbler" (freshly roasted turkey with bacon smashed potatoes on a sage-stuffed waffle) to grouper in bouillabaisse with fennel. A specials board lists plenty of tempting options too, but be sure to ask the price since seafood risotto might *sound* great, but when the reality hits your bill, your wallet won't be happy. $ *Average main: $21* ✉ *728 Simonton St.* ☎ *305/414–8428* ⚅ *Reservations essential.*

$$ ✕ **El Meson de Pepe.** If you want to get a taste of the island's Cuban
CUBAN heritage, this is the place. Perfect for after watching a Mallory Square sunset, you can dine alfresco or in the dining room on refined versions of Cuban classics. Begin with a megasize mojito while you enjoy the basket of bread and savory sauces. The expansive menu offers *tostones rellenos* (green plantains with different traditional fillings), ceviche, and more. Choose from Cuban specialties such as roasted pork in a cumin mojo sauce and *ropa vieja* (shredded beef stew). At lunch, the local Cuban population and cruise-ship passengers enjoy Cuban sandwiches and smaller versions of dinner's most popular entrées. A Latin band performs outside at the bar during sunset celebration. $ *Average main: $19*

✉ *410 Wall St., Mallory Sq.* ☎ *305/295–2620* ⊕ *www.elmesondepepe.com.*

$ ✕ **El Siboney.** Dining at this family-style restaurant is like going to Mom's
CUBAN for Sunday dinner—if your mother is Cuban. The dining room is noisy, and the food is traditional *cubano*. There are well-seasoned black beans, a memorable paella, traditional ropa vieja, and local seafood served grilled, stuffed, and breaded. Dishes come with plantains and beans and rice or salad and fries. To make a good thing even better, the prices are very reasonable. $ *Average main: $10* ✉ *900 Catherine St.* ☎ *305/296–4184* ⊕ *www.elsiboneyrestaurant.com* ⌲ *Reservations not accepted.*

$$ ✕ **Half Shell Raw Bar.** Smack-dab on the docks, this legendary institution
SEAFOOD gets its name from the oysters, clams, and peel-and-eat shrimp that are
FAMILY a departure point for its seafood-based diet. It's not clever recipes or fine dining (or even air-conditioning) that packs 'em in; it's fried fish, po'boy sandwiches, and seafood combos. For a break from the deep fryer, try the fresh and light conch ceviche "cooked" with lime juice. The potato salad is flavored with dill, and the "PamaRita" is a new twist in Margaritaville. $ *Average main: $16* ✉ *Lands End Village at Historic Seaport, 231 Margaret St.* ☎ *305/294–7496* ⊕ *www.halfshellrawbar.com* ⌲ *Reservations not accepted.*

$ ✕ **Hogfish Bar & Grill.** It's worth a drive to Stock Island, just outside of
SEAFOOD Key West, to sit along one of Florida's last surviving working water-fronts, watch the shrimpers and fishermen unloading their catch, and indulge in the freshness you're witnessing at this down-to-earth spot. Hogfish is of course the specialty. The "Killer Hogfish Sandwich" comes on Cuban Bread (you can also have it as a breakfast Benedict); sprinkle it with one of the house hot sauces. Other favorites include lobster BLT, pulled pork sandwich, hogfish tacos, gator bites, lobster potpie, and barbeque ribs. $ *Average main: $13* ✉ *6810 Front St., Stock Island* ☎ *305/293–4041* ⊕ *www.hogfishbar.com.*

$ ✕ **Lobo's Mixed Grill.** Famous for its selection of wrap sandwiches, Lobo's
AMERICAN has a reputation among locals for its 8-ounce, charcoal-grilled ground
FAMILY chuck burger—thick and juicy and served with lettuce, tomato, and pickle on a toasted bun. Mix it up with toppings like Brie, blue cheese, or portobello mushroom. The menu of 30 wraps includes ribeye, oyster, grouper, Cuban, and chicken Caesar. The menu includes salads and quesadillas, as well as a fried-shrimp-and-oyster combo. Beer and wine are served. This courtyard food stand closes around 5, so eat early. Most of Lobo's business is takeout (it has a half-dozen outdoor picnic tables), and it offers free delivery within Old Town. $ *Average main: $9* ✉ *5 Key Lime Sq., east of intersection of Southard and Duval sts.* ☎ *305/296–5303* ⊕ *www.lobosmixedgrill.com* ⌲ *Reservations not accepted* ☾ *Closed Sun. Apr.–early Dec.*

$$$$ ✕ **Louie's Backyard.** Feast your eyes on a steal-your-breath-away view and
ECLECTIC beautifully presented dishes prepared by executive chef Doug Shook. Once you get over sticker shock on the seasonally changing menu, settle in on the outside deck and enjoy dishes like grilled scallops with portobello relish, grilled king salmon with fried risotto, and mint-rubbed pork chop with salsa verde. A more affordable option upstairs is the Upper Deck, which serves tapas such as flaming ouzo shrimp, roasted

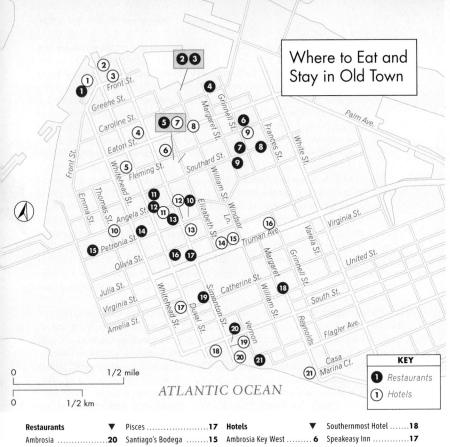

Where to Eat and Stay in Old Town

ATLANTIC OCEAN

olives with onion and feta, and Gruyère and duck confit pizza. If you come for lunch, the menu is less expensive but the view is just as fantastic. For night owls, the tin-roofed Afterdeck Bar serves cocktails on the water until the wee hours. $ *Average main: $36* ⊠ *700 Waddell Ave.* ☎ *305/294–1061* ⊕ *www.louiesbackyard.com* ⌲ *Reservations essential* ☾ *Closed Labor Day to mid-Sept. Upper Deck closed Sun. and Mon. No lunch on Upper Deck.*

$$

ITALIAN

✕ **Mangia Mangia.** This longtime favorite serves large portions of homemade pastas that can be matched with any of their homemade sauces. Tables are arranged in a brick garden hung with twinkling lights and in a cozy, casual dining room in an old house. Everything out of the open kitchen is outstanding, including the *bollito misto di mare* (fresh seafood sautéed with garlic, shallots, white wine, and pasta) or the memorable spaghettini "schmappellini," homemade pasta with asparagus, tomatoes, pine nuts, and Parmesan. The wine list—with more than 350 offerings—includes old and rare vintages, and also has a good by-the-glass selection. $ *Average main: $16* ⊠ *900 Southard St.* ☎ *305/294–2469* ⊕ *www.mangia-mangia.com* ⌲ *Reservations not accepted* ☾ *No lunch.*

$$$

AMERICAN

✕ **Michaels Restaurant.** White tablecloths, subdued lighting, and romantic music give Michaels the feel of an urban eatery. Garden seating reminds you that you are in the Keys. Chef-owner Michael Wilson flies in prime rib, cowboy steaks, and ribeyes from Allen Brothers in Chicago, which has supplied top-ranked steakhouses for more than a century. Also on the menu is a melt-in-your-mouth grouper stuffed with jumbo lump crab, Kobe and tenderloin meat loaf, veal saltimbocca, and a variety of made-to-order fondue dishes (try the pesto pot, spiked with hot pepper and basil). To lighten up, smaller portions of many of the favorites are available until 7:30 Sunday through Thursday. The Hemingway (mojito-style) and the Third Degree (raspberry vodka and white crème de cacao) top the cocktail menu. $ *Average main: $25* ⊠ *532 Margaret St.* ☎ *305/295–1300* ⊕ *www.michaelskeywest.com* ⌲ *Reservations essential* ☾ *No lunch.*

$$$

ECLECTIC

✕ **Nine One Five.** Twinkling lights draped along the lower- and upper-level outdoor porches of a 100-year-old Victorian mansion set an elegant—though unstuffy—stage here. If you like to sample and sip, you'll appreciate the variety of smaller plate selections and wines by the glass. Starters include a cheese platter, crispy duck confit, a tapas platter, and the signature "tuna dome" with fresh crab, lemon-miso dressing, and an ahi tuna–sashimi wrapping. There are also larger plates if you're craving something like seafood soup or steak au poivre frites. Dine outdoors and people-watch along upper Duval, or sit at a table inside while listening to light jazz. $ *Average main: $28* ⊠ *915 Duval St.* ☎ *305/296–0669* ⊕ *www.915duval.com* ⌲ *Reservations essential* ☾ *No lunch.*

$$$$

EUROPEAN

✕ **Pisces.** In a circa-1892 former store and home, chef William Arnel and staff create a contemporary setting with a stylish granite bar, Andy Warhol originals, and glass oil lamps. Favorites include "lobster tango mango," flambéed in cognac and served with saffron butter sauce and sliced mangoes; filet mignon with bordelaise sauce; and yellowtail Atocha with lemon brown butter, shrimp, and scallops. ⑤ *Average main: $35* ✉ *1007 Simonton St.* ☎ *305/294–7100* ⊕ *www. pisceskeywest.com* ⌂ *Reservations essential* ⊘ *No lunch.*

$$
ITALIAN
✕ **Salute Ristorante at the Beach.** Sister restaurant to Blue Heaven, this colorful establishment sits on Higgs Beach, giving it one of the island's best lunch views—and a bit of sand and salt spray on a windy day. The intriguing menu is Italian with a Caribbean flair and will not disappoint. For dinner, popular dishes include linguine with mussels, lasagna, and white bean soup. At lunch the gazpacho refreshes with great flavor and texture, and the calamari marinara, antipasti sandwich, and yellowtail sandwich will having you singing "Amore." ⑤ *Average main: $20* ✉ *1000 Atlantic Blvd., Higgs Beach* ☎ *305/292–1117* ⊕ *www. saluteonthebeach.com* ⌂ *Reservations not accepted.*

$
TAPAS
Fodor's Choice
★
✕ **Santiago's Bodega.** If you've ever wondered where chefs go for a great meal in the lower Keys, this is their secret spot. Picky palates will be satisfied at this funky, dark, and sensuous corner house, which is well off the main drag. Dine on the front porch surrounded by fuchsia bougainvillea or inside amid eclectic paintings and mismatched chandeliers. Waiters recommend choosing three of the small plates per person, then sharing. That number works. Cold tapas include dishes like yellowfin tuna ceviche with large hunks of avocado and mango, and shaved beef carpaccio with smoked sea salt and truffle oil. Favorite hot tapas are filet mignon with creamy Gorgonzola butter and cherry-hoisin-glazed beef shortribs. Dessert? The bread pudding is legendary. Reward yourself for finding this place with a fruit-filled glass of homemade red or white sangria. All bets say you'll eat here over and over again. ⑤ *Average main: $13* ✉ *Bahama Village, 207 Petronia St.* ☎ *305/296–7691* ⊕ *www.santiagosbodega.com* ⌂ *Reservations essential.*

$$$
SEAFOOD
✕ **Seven Fish.** A local hot spot, this intimate, off-the-beaten-track eatery is good for an eclectic mix of dishes like tropical shrimp salsa, wild-mushroom quesadilla, seafood marinara, and old-fashioned meat loaf with real mashed potatoes. For dessert, the sweet potato pie provides an added measure of down-home comfort. Those in the know reserve for dinner early to snag one of the 20 or so tables clustered in the bare-bones dining room. ⑤ *Average main: $26* ✉ *632 Olivia St.* ☎ *305/296–2777* ⊕ *www.7fish.com* ⌂ *Reservations essential* ⊘ *Closed Tues. No lunch.*

$$
SEAFOOD
FAMILY
✕ **Turtle Kraals.** Named for the *kraals*, or corrals, where sea turtles were once kept until they went to the cannery, this place calls to mind the island's history. The lunch-dinner menu offers an assortment of marine cuisine that includes seafood enchiladas, mesquite-grilled fish of the day, and mango crab cakes. The slow-cook wood smoker results in wonderfully tender ribs, brisket, mesquite-grilled oysters with Parmesan and cilantro, and mesquite-grilled chicken sandwich. The open restaurant overlooks the marina at the Historic Seaport. Turtle races entertain during happy hour on Monday and Friday at 6 pm. ⑤ *Average main: $16* ✉ *231 Margaret St.* ☎ *305/294–2640* ⊕ *www.turtlekraals.com.*

WHERE TO STAY

Historic cottages, restored century-old Conch houses, and large resorts are among the offerings in Key West, the majority charging from $100 to $300 a night. In high season, Christmas through Easter, you'll be hard-pressed to find a decent room for less than $200, and most places raise prices considerably during holidays and festivals. Many guest-houses and inns don't welcome children under 16, and most don't permit smoking indoors. Rates often include an expanded continental breakfast and afternoon wine or snack.

$$$
B&B/INN
Ambrosia Key West. If you desire personal attention, a casual atmosphere, and a dollop of style, stay at these twin inns spread out on nearly 2 acres. **Pros:** spacious rooms; poolside breakfast; friendly staff. **Cons:** on-street parking can be tough to come by; a little too spread out. $ *Rooms from: $319* ⊠ *615, 618, 622 Fleming St.* ☎ *305/296–9838, 800/535–9838* ⊕ *www.ambrosiakeywest.com* ⇆ *6 rooms, 3 town houses, 1 cottage, 10 suites* ¡○¡ *Breakfast.*

$
B&B/INN
Angelina Guest House. In the heart of Old Town, this home away from home offers simple, clean, attractively priced accommodations. **Pros:** good value; nice garden; friendly staff. **Cons:** thin walls; basic rooms; shared balcony. $ *Rooms from: $109* ⊠ *302 Angela St.* ☎ *305/294–4480, 888/303–4480* ⊕ *www.angelinaguesthouse.com* ⇆ *13 rooms* ¡○¡ *Breakfast.*

$$
B&B/INN
Azul Key West. The ultramodern—nearly minimalistic—redo of this classic circa-1903 Queen Anne mansion is a break from the sensory overload of Key West's other abundant Victorian guesthouses. **Pros:** lovely building; marble-floored baths; luxurious linens. **Cons:** on a busy street. $ *Rooms from: $249* ⊠ *907 Truman Ave.* ☎ *305/296–5152, 888/253–2985* ⊕ *www.azulhotels.us* ⇆ *10 rooms, 1 suite* ¡○¡ *Breakfast.*

$$$
RESORT
FAMILY
Casa Marina Resort & Beach Club. At any moment, you expect the landed gentry to walk across the oceanfront lawn of this luxurious resort, just as they did when this 13-acre resort was built back in the 1920s. **Pros:** nice beach; historic setting; away from the crowds. **Cons:** long walk to central Old Town; expensive resort fee. $ *Rooms from: $359* ⊠ *1500 Reynolds St.* ☎ *305/296–3535, 866/203–6392* ⊕ *www.casamarinaresort.com* ⇆ *241 rooms, 70 suites* ¡○¡ *No meals.*

$$
B&B/INN
Courtney's Place. If you like kids, cats, and dogs, you'll feel right at home in this collection of accommodations ranging from cigar-maker cottages to shotgun houses. **Pros:** near Duval Street; fairly priced. **Cons:** small parking lot; small pool; minimum-stay requirements. $ *Rooms from: $249* ⊠ *720 Whitmarsh La., off Petronia St.* ☎ *305/294–3480, 800/869–4639* ⊕ *www.courtneysplacekeywest.com* ⇆ *6 rooms, 2 suites, 2 efficiencies, 8 cottages* ¡○¡ *Breakfast.*

$
HOTEL
Crowne Plaza Key West–La Concha. History and franchises can mix, as this 1920s-vintage hotel proves with its handsome faux-palm atrium lobby and sleep-conducive rooms. **Pros:** restaurant and Starbucks in house; close to downtown attractions; free Wi-Fi. **Cons:** high-traffic area; confusing layout; expensive valet-only parking. $ *Rooms from: $199* ⊠ *430 Duval St.* ☎ *305/296–2991* ⊕ *www.laconchakeywest.com* ⇆ *160 rooms, 8 rooms with balconies, 10 suites* ¡○¡ *No meals.*

$ ⬚ **Eden House.** From the vintage metal rockers on the street-side porch
HOTEL   to the old neon hotel sign in the lobby, this 1920s rambling Key West
mainstay hotel is high on character, low on gloss. **Pros:** free parking;
hot tub is actually hot; daily happy hour around the pool; discount at
excellent Azur restaurant. **Cons:** pricey; a bit of a musty smell in some
rooms; no TV in some rooms. ⑤ *Rooms from: $200* ✉ *1015 Fleming St.*
☎ *305/296–6868, 800/533–5397* ⊕ *www.edenhouse.com* ⮑ *36 rooms,*
8 suites ⦿ *No meals.*

$$$ ⬚ **The Gardens Hotel.** Built in 1875, this gloriously shaded, award-win-
HOTEL   ning property was a labor of love from the get-go, and it covers a third
Fodor's Choice   of a city block in Old Town. **Pros:** luxurious bathrooms; secluded gar-
★   den seating; free domestic phone calls and Wi-Fi. **Cons:** hard to get
reservations; expensive; nightly secure-parking fee. ⑤ *Rooms from:*
$385 ✉ *526 Angela St.* ☎ *305/294–2661, 800/526–2664* ⊕ *www.*
gardenshotel.com ⮑ *17 rooms* ⦿ *Breakfast.*

$$ ⬚ **Hyatt Key West Resort and Spa.** With its own man-made beach, the
RESORT   Hyatt Key West is one of few resorts where you can dig your toes in
FAMILY   the sand, then walk a short distance away to the streets of Old Town.
Pros: a little bit away from the bustle of Old Town; plenty of activities.
Cons: beach is small; cramped-feeling property. ⑤ *Rooms from: $290*
✉ *601 Front St.* ☎ *305/809–1234* ⊕ *www.keywest.hyatt.com* ⮑ *118*
rooms ⦿ *No meals.*

$ ⬚ **Key Lime Inn.** This 1854 Grand Bahama–style house on the National
B&B/INN   Register of Historic Places succeeds by offering amiable service, a
great location, and simple rooms with natural-wood furnishings. **Pros:**
free parking; some rooms have private outdoor spaces. **Cons:** standard rooms are pricey; pool faces a busy street; mulch-covered paths.
⑤ *Rooms from: $179* ✉ *725 Truman Ave.* ☎ *305/294–5229, 800/549–*
4430 ⊕ *www.keylimeinn.com* ⮑ *37 rooms* ⦿ *Breakfast.*

$ ⬚ **Key West Bed and Breakfast/The Popular House.** There are accommo-
B&B/INN   dations for every budget, but the owners reason that budget travelers
deserve as pleasant an experience (and lavish a tropical Continental
breakfast) as their well-heeled counterparts. **Pros:** lots of art; tiled outdoor shower; hot tub and sauna area is a welcome hangout. **Cons:** some
rooms are small. ⑤ *Rooms from: $99* ✉ *415 William St.* ☎ *305/296–*
7274, 800/438–6155 ⊕ *www.keywestbandb.com* ⮑ *10 rooms, 6 with*
private bath ⦿ *Breakfast.*

$$$ ⬚ **Key West Marriott Beachside Hotel.** This hotel vies for convention busi-
HOTEL   ness with the biggest ballroom in Key West, but it also appeals to fam-
ilies with its spacious condo units decorated with impeccable taste.
Pros: private beach; poolside cabanas. **Cons:** small beach; long walk
to Old Town; cookie-cutter facade. ⑤ *Rooms from: $340* ✉ *3841 N.*
Roosevelt Blvd., New Town ☎ *305/296–8100, 800/546–0885* ⊕ *www.*
keywestmarriottbeachside.com ⮑ *93 rooms, 93 1-bedroom suites, 10*
2-bedroom suites, 26 3-bedroom suites ⦿ *No meals.*

$$$ ⬚ **Marquesa Hotel.** In a town that prides itself on its laid-back luxury,
HOTEL   this complex of four restored 1884 houses stands out. **Pros:** elegant set-
Fodor's Choice   ting; romantic atmosphere; turndown service. **Cons:** street-facing rooms
★   can be noisy; expensive rates. ⑤ *Rooms from: $345* ✉ *600 Fleming St.*

☎ *305/292–1919, 800/869–4631* ⊕ *www.marquesa.com* ⤴ *27 rooms* �‖ *No meals.*

$$
B&B/INN
⌂ **Merlin Guesthouse.** Key West guesthouses don't usually welcome families, but this laid-back jumble of rooms and suites is an exception. **Pros:** good location near Duval Street; good rates. **Cons:** neighbor noise; street parking. Ⓢ *Rooms from: $279* ⌂ *811 Simonton St.* ☎ *305/296–3336, 800/642–4753* ⊕ *www.merlinguesthouse.com* ⤴ *10 rooms, 6 suites, 4 cottages* �‖ *Breakfast.*

$$
B&B/INN
⌂ **Mermaid & the Alligator.** An enchanting combination of flora and fauna makes this 1904 Victorian house a welcoming retreat. **Pros:** hot plunge pool; massage pavilion; island-getaway feel. **Cons:** minimum stay required (length depends on season); dark public areas; plastic lawn chairs. Ⓢ *Rooms from: $268* ⌂ *729 Truman Ave.* ☎ *305/294–1894, 800/773–1894* ⊕ *www.kwmermaid.com* ⤴ *9 rooms* �‖ *Breakfast.*

$$$$
RESORT
Fodor's Choice
★
⌂ **Ocean Key Resort & Spa.** A pool and lively open-air bar and restaurant sit on Sunset Pier, a popular place to watch the sun sink into the horizon. **Pros:** well-trained staff; lively pool scene; best spa on the island. **Cons:** $20 per night valet parking; too bustling for some; pricey. Ⓢ *Rooms from: $450* ⌂ *Zero Duval St.* ☎ *305/296–7701, 800/328–9815* ⊕ *www. oceankey.com* ⤴ *64 rooms, 36 suites* �‖ *No meals.*

$$$
HOTEL
⌂ **Parrot Key Resort.** This revamped destination resort feels like an old-fashioned beach community with picket fences and rocking-chair porches. **Pros:** four pools; finely appointed units; access to marina and other facilities at three sister properties in Marathon. **Cons:** outside of walking distance to Old Town; no transportation provided; hefty resort fee. Ⓢ *Rooms from: $329* ⌂ *2801 N. Roosevelt Blvd.* ☎ *305/809–2200* ⊕ *www.parrotkeyresort.com* ⤴ *74 rooms, 74 suites, 74 3-bedroom villas* �‖ *No meals.*

$$$$
RESORT
⌂ **Pier House Resort and Caribbean Spa.** The location—on a quiet stretch of beach at the foot of Duval—is ideal as a buffer from and gateway to the action. **Pros:** beautiful beach; good location; nice spa. **Cons:** lots of conventions; poolside rooms are small; not really suitable for children under 16. Ⓢ *Rooms from: $460* ⌂ *1 Duval St.* ☎ *305/296–4600, 800/327–8340* ⊕ *www.pierhouse.com* ⤴ *116 rooms, 26 suites* �‖ *No meals.*

$$
RESORT
⌂ **The Reach Resort.** Embracing Key West's only natural beach, this full-service, luxury resort offers sleek rooms with modern amenities as well as shared access to its sister Casa Marina resort nearby. **Pros:** removed from Duval hubbub; great sunrise views; pullout sofas in most rooms. **Cons:** expensive resort fee; high rates. Ⓢ *Rooms from: $300* ⌂ *1435 Simonton St.* ☎ *305/296–5000, 888/318–4316* ⊕ *www.reachresort.com* ⤴ *72 rooms, 78 suites* �‖ *No meals.*

$$$
RENTAL
Fodor's Choice
★
⌂ **Santa Maria Suites.** It's odd to call this a "hidden gem" when it sits on a prominent corner just one block off Duval, but you'd never know the luxury that awaits behind its concrete facade. **Pros:** amenities galore; front desk concierge services; private parking lot. **Cons:** daily resort fee; beds low to the ground. Ⓢ *Rooms from: $350* ⌂ *1401 Simonton St.* ☎ *866/726–8259, 305/296–5678* ⊕ *www.santamariasuites.com* ⤴ *34 suites* �‖ *No meals.*

Sunset Key cottages are right on the water's edge, far away from the action of Old Town.

$$ **Simonton Court.** A small world all its own, this adult lodging makes
B&B/INN you feel deliciously sequestered from Key West's crasser side, but close
enough to get there on foot. **Pros:** lots of privacy; well-appointed
accommodations; friendly staff. **Cons:** minimum stays required in high
season. $ *Rooms from: $275* ✉ *320 Simonton St.* ☎ *305/294–6386,
800/944–2687* ⊕ *www.simontoncourt.com* ⤴ *17 rooms, 6 suites, 6
cottages* ❚❉❙ *Breakfast.*

$$$ **Southernmost Hotel.** This hotel's location on the quiet end of Duval
HOTEL means you don't have to deal with the hustle and bustle of downtown
unless you want to—it's within a 20-minute walk (but around sunset, this end of town gets its share of car and foot traffic). **Pros:** pool
attracts a lively crowd; access to nearby properties and beach; free
parking and Wi-Fi. **Cons:** can get crowded around the pool and public
areas; expensive nightly resort fee. $ *Rooms from: $359* ✉ *1319 Duval
St.* ☎ *305/296–6577, 800/354–4455* ⊕ *www.southernmostresorts.com*
⤴ *124 rooms* ❚❉❙ *No meals.*

$ **Speakeasy Inn.** During Prohibition, Raul Vasquez made this place
B&B/INN popular by smuggling in rum from Cuba; today its reputation is for
having reasonably priced rooms within walking distance of the beach.
Pros: good location; reasonable rates; kitchenettes. **Cons:** no pool; on
busy Duval. $ *Rooms from: $169* ✉ *1117 Duval St.* ☎ *305/296–2680*
⊕ *www.speakeasyinn.com* ⤴ *4 suites* ❚❉❙ *Breakfast.*

$$$$ **Sunset Key.** This private island retreat with its own sandy beach
RESORT feels completely cut off from the world, yet you're just minutes away
Fodor'sChoice from the action. **Pros:** peace and quiet; roomy verandas; free 24-hour
★ shuttle; free Wi-Fi. **Cons:** luxury doesn't come cheap. $ *Rooms from:*

$695 ⊠245 Front St. ☎305/292–5300, 888/477–7786 ⊕www. westinsunsetkeycottages.com ⇨40 cottages ⎟◯⎟Breakfast.

NIGHTLIFE

Rest up: Much of what happens in Key West does so after dark. Open your mind and have a stroll. Scruffy street performers strum next to dogs in sunglasses. Brawls tumble out the doors of Sloppy Joe's. Drag queens strut across stages in Joan Rivers garb. Tattooed men lick whipped cream off women's body parts. And margaritas flow like a Jimmy Buffett tune.

BARS AND LOUNGES

Capt. Tony's Saloon. When it was the original Sloppy Joe's in the mid-1930s, Hemingway was a regular. Later, a young Jimmy Buffett sang here and made this watering hole famous in his song "Last Mango in Paris." Captain Tony was even voted mayor of Key West. Yes, this place is a beloved landmark. Stop in and take a look at the "hanging tree" that grows through the roof, listen to live music seven nights a week, and play some pool. ⊠428 Greene St. ☎305/294–1838 ⊕www. capttonyssaloon.com.

Durty Harry's. This megasize entertainment complex is home to eight different bars and clubs, both indoor and outdoor. Their motto is, "Eight Famous Bars, One Awesome Night," and they're right. You'll find pizza, dancing, live music, a martini bar, and the infamous Red Garter strip club. ⊠208 Duval St. ☎305/296–5513.

Green Parrot Bar. Pause for a libation in the open air and breathe in the spirit of Key West. Built in 1890 as a grocery store, this property has been many things to many people over the years It's touted as the oldest bar in Key West and the sometimes-rowdy saloon has locals outnumbering out-of-towners, especially on nights when bands play. ⊠601 Whitehead St., at Southard St. ☎305/294–6133 ⊕www.greenparrot.com.

Hog's Breath Saloon. Belly up to the bar for a cold mug of the signature Hog's Breath Lager at this infamous joint, a must-stop on the Key West bar crawl. Live bands play daily 1 pm–2 am (except when the game's on TV). You never know who'll stop by and perhaps even jump on stage for an impromptu concert. ⊠400 Front St. ☎305/296–4222 ⊕www. hogsbreath.com.

Margaritaville Café. A youngish, touristy crowd mixes with aging Parrot Heads. It's owned by former Key West resident and recording star Jimmy Buffett, who has been known to perform here. The drink of choice is, of course, a margarita, made with Jimmy's own brand of Margaritaville tequila. There's live music nightly, as well as lunch and dinner. ⊠500 Duval St. ☎305/292–1435 ⊕www.margaritaville.com.

Pier House. The party here begins with a steel-drum band to celebrate the sunset on the beach (on select Thursdays and Fridays), then moves indoors to the Wine Galley piano bar for live jazz. ⊠1 Duval St. ☎305/296–4600, 800/327–8340 ⊕www.pierhouse.com.

Schooner Wharf Bar. This open-air waterfront bar and grill in the historic seaport district retains its funky Key West charm and hosts live

Sloppy Joe's is one must-stop on most Key West visitors' bar-hop stroll, also known as the Duval Crawl.

entertainment daily. Its margaritas rank among Key West's best, as does the bar itself, voted Best Local's Bar six years in a row. For great views, head up to the second floor and be sure to order up some fresh seafood and fritters and Dark and Stormy cocktails. ✉ *202 William St.* ☎ *305/292–3302* ⊕ *www.schoonerwharf.com.*

Sloppy Joe's. There's history and good times at the successor to a famous 1937 speakeasy named for its founder, Captain Joe Russell. Decorated with Hemingway memorabilia and marine flags, the bar is popular with travelers and is full and noisy all the time. A Sloppy Joe's T-shirt is a de rigueur Key West souvenir, and the gift shop sells them like crazy. Grab a seat (if you can) and be entertained by the bands and by the parade of people in constant motion. ✉ *201 Duval St.* ☎ *305/294–5717* ⊕ *www.sloppyjoes.com.*

The Top. On the seventh floor of the Crowne Plaza Key West La Concha, this is one of the best places in town to view the sunset and enjoy live entertainment on Friday and Saturday nights. ✉ *430 Duval St.* ☎ *305/296–2991* ⊕ *www.laconchakeywest.com.*

Virgilio's Martini Bar. In the best traditions of a 1950s cocktail lounge, this bar serves chilled martinis to the soothing tempo of live jazz and blues. Locals love the late night dancing and $5 Martini Mondays. ✉ *524 Duval St.* ☎ *305/296–8118* ⊕ *www.virgilioskeywest.com.*

SHOPPING

On these streets you'll find colorful local art of widely varying quality, key limes made into everything imaginable, and the raunchiest T-shirts in the civilized world.

MALLS AND SHOPPING CENTERS

Bahama Village. Where to start your shopping adventure? This cluster of spruced-up shops, restaurants, and vendors is responsible for the restoration of the colorful historic district where Bahamians settled in the 19th century. The village lies roughly between Whitehead and Fort streets and Angela and Catherine streets. Hemingway frequented the bars, restaurants, and boxing rings in this part of town. ⊠ *Between Whitehead and Fort sts. and Angela and Catherine sts..*

ARTS AND CRAFTS

Alan S. Maltz Gallery. The owner, declared the state's official wildlife photographer by the Wildlife Foundation of Florida, captures the state's nature and character in stunning portraits. Spend four figures for large-format images on canvas or save on small prints and closeouts. ⊠ *1210 Duval St.* ☏ *305/294–0005* ⊕ *www.alanmaltz.com.*

Art@830. This inviting gallery carries a little bit of everything, from pottery to paintings and jewelry to sculptures. Most outstanding is its selection of glass art, particularly the jellyfish lamps. Take time to admire all that is here. ⊠ *830 Caroline St., Historic Seaport* ☏ *305/295–9595* ⊕ *www.art830.com.*

Gallery on Greene. This is the largest gallery–exhibition space in Key West and it showcases 37 museum-quality artists. They pride themselves on being the leader in the field of representational fine art, painting, sculptures, and reproductions from the Florida Keys and Key West. You can immediately see the love from gallery curator Nancy Frank, who aims to please everyone, from the casual buyer to the established collector. ⊠ *606 Greene St.* ☏ *305/294–1669* ⊕ *www.galleryongreene.com.*

Gingerbread Square Gallery. The oldest private art gallery in Key West represents local and internationally acclaimed artists on an annually changing basis, in mediums ranging from graphics to art glass. ⊠ *1207 Duval St.* ☏ *305/296–8900* ⊕ *www.gingerbreadsquaregallery.com.*

Glass Reunions. Find a collection of wild and impressive fine-art glass here. It's worth a stop in just to see the imaginative and over-the-top glass chandeliers, jewelry, dishes, and platters. ⊠ *825 Duval St.* ☏ *305/294–1720* ⊕ *www.glassreunions.com.*

Key West Pottery. You won't find any painted coconuts here, but you will find a collection of contemporary tropical ceramics. Wife and husband owners Kelly Lever and Adam Russell take real pride in this working studio that, in addition to their own creations, features artists from around the country. This is one of the island's only specialty galleries. ⊠ *929 Truman Ave.* ☏ *305/900–8303* ⊕ *www.keywestpottery.com.*

KW Light Gallery at Island Arts. Historian, photographer, and painter Sharon Wells opened this gallery to showcase her own fine-art photography, painted tiles and canvases. She also offers private tours of Key West. ⊠ *1128 Duval St.* ☏ *305/923–5133* ⊕ *www.keywesttiles.com.*

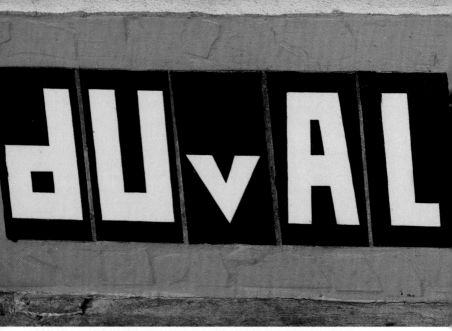

Nightlife, shops, and some interesting street art can all be found on Key West's Duval Street.

Lucky Street Gallery. High-end contemporary paintings are the focus at this gallery with over 30 years of experience and a passionate staff. There are also a few pieces of jewelry by internationally recognized Key West–based artists. Changing exhibits, artist receptions, and special events make this a lively venue. ✉ *1130 Duval St.* ☎ *305/294–3973* ⊕ *www.luckystreetgallery.com.*

Pelican Poop Shoppe. Caribbean art sells in a historic building (with Hemingway connections, of course). For $2 admission or a $10 purchase, you can stroll the tropical courtyard garden. The owners buy directly from the artisans every year, so the prices are very attractive. ✉ *314 Simonton St.* ☎ *305/292–9955.*

BOOKS

Key West Island Bookstore. This home away from home for the large Key West writers' community carries new, used, and rare titles. It specializes in Hemingway, Tennessee Williams, and South Florida mystery writers. ✉ *513 Fleming St.* ☎ *305/294–2904* ⊕ *www.keywestislandbooks.com.*

CLOTHING AND FABRICS

Fairvilla Megastore. Don't leave town without a browse through the legendary shop, where you'll find an astonishing array of fantasy wear, outlandish costumes (check out the pirate section), and other "adult" toys. ✉ *520 Front St.* ☎ *305/292–0448* ⊕ *www.fairvilla.com.*

Kino Sandals. A pair of Kino Sandals was once a public declaration that you'd been to Key West. The attraction? You can watch these inexpensive items being made. The factory has been churning out several styles since 1966. Walk up to the counter, grab a pair, try them on, and lay down some cash. It's that simple. ⊠ *107 Fitzpatrick St.* ☎ *305/294–5044* ⊕ *www.kinosandalfactory.com* ♥ *Closed Sun. in off-season.*

FOOD AND DRINK

Fausto's Food Palace. Since 1926 Fausto's has been the spot to catch up on the week's gossip and to chill out in summer—it has groceries, organic foods, marvelous wines, a sushi chef on duty 8 am–3 pm, and box lunches to go. There are two locations you can shop in Key West (the other is at 1105 White Street), plus a recently opened online store. ⊠ *522 Fleming St.* ☎ *305/296–5663* ⊕ *www.faustos.com.*

Fodor's Choice **Kermit's Key West Lime Shoppe.** You'll see Kermit himself standing on the
★ corner every time a trolley passes, pie in hand. Besides pie, his shop carries a multitude of key lime products from barbecue sauce to jellybeans. His prefrozen pies, dressed with a special long-lasting whipped cream instead of meringue, travels well. This is a must-stop shop while in Key West. The key lime pie is the best on the island; once you try it frozen on a stick, dipped in chocolate, you may consider quitting your job and moving here. Savor every bite on their outdoor patio/garden area. Heaven. ⊠ *200 Elizabeth St., Historic Seaport* ☎ *305/296–0806, 800/376–0806* ⊕ *www.keylimeshop.com.*

GIFTS AND SOUVENIRS

Cayo Hueso y Habana. Part museum, part shopping center, this circa-1879 warehouse includes a hand-rolled cigar shop, one-of-a-kind souvenirs, a Cuban restaurant, and exhibits that tell of the island's Cuban heritage. Outside, a memorial garden pays homage to the island's Cuban ancestors. ⊠ *410 Wall St., Mallory Sq.* ☎ *305/293–7260.*

Cocktails! Key West. Could there possibly be a better location to celebrate the art of the drink than Key West? This celebratory shop carries everything you need for cocktails including beautiful hand-painted stemware, highball, martini, and shot glasses, mugs, accessories, and art that blends perfectly. Most of the designs are made on the island. ⊠ *808 Duval St.* ☎ *305/292–1190* ⊕ *www.cocktailskeywest.com.*

Montage. For that unique (but slightly overpriced) souvenir of your trip to Key West head here, where you'll discover hundreds of handcrafted signs of popular Key West guesthouses, inns, hotels, restaurants, bars, and streets. If you can't find what you're looking for, they'll make it for you. ⊠ *291 Front St.* ☎ *305/395–9101, 877/396–4278* ⊕ *www.montagekeywest.com.*

SPORTS AND THE OUTDOORS

Unlike the rest of the region, Key West isn't known primarily for outdoor pursuits. But everyone should devote at least half a day to relaxing on a boat tour, heading out on a fishing expedition, or pursuing some other adventure at sea. The ultimate excursion is a boat trip to Dry Tortugas National Park for snorkeling and exploring Fort Jefferson. Other excursions cater to nature lovers, scuba divers and snorkelers, anglers, and those who would just like to get out in the water and enjoy the scenery and sunset. For those who prefer their recreation land-based, biking is the way to go.

BIKING

Key West was practically made for bicycles, but don't let that lull you into a false sense of security. Narrow and one-way streets along with car traffic result in several bike accidents a year. Some hotels rent or lend bikes to guests; others will refer you to a nearby shop and reserve a bike for you. Rentals usually start at about $10 a day, but some places also rent by the half day. ■TIP→ **Lock up! Bikes—and porch chairs!—are favorite targets for local thieves.**

A&M Rentals. Rent beach cruisers with large baskets or scooters. Look for the huge American flag on the roof, or call for free airport, ferry, or cruise ship pick-up. ⊠ *523 Truman Ave.* ☎ *305/294–0399* ⊕ *www. amscooterskeywest.com* ⊠ *Bicycles from $15, scooters from $35.*

Eaton Bikes. Tandem, three-wheel, and children's bikes are available in addition to the standard beach cruisers and hybrid bikes. Delivery is free for all Key West rentals. ⊠ *830 Eaton St.* ☎ *305/294–8188* ⊕ *www. eatonbikes.com* ⊠ *From $18 per day.*

Lloyd's Original Tropical Bike Tour. Explore the natural, noncommercial side of Key West at a leisurely pace, stopping on backstreets and in backyards of private homes to sample native fruits and view indigenous plants and trees with a 30-year Key West veteran. The behind-the-scenes tours run two hours and include a bike rental. ⊠ *Truman Ave. and Simonton St.* ☎ *305/304–4700, 305/294–1882* ⊕ *www. lloydstropicalbiketour.com* ⊠ *$39.*

Moped Hospital. This outfit supplies balloon-tire bikes with yellow safety baskets for adults and kids, as well as scooters and even double-seater scooters. ⊠ *601 Truman Ave.* ☎ *305/296–3344, 866/296–1625* ⊕ *www. mopedhospital.com* ⊠ *Bicycles from $12 per day, scooters from $35 per day.*

BOAT TOURS

Dancing Dolphin Spirit Charters. Victoria Impallomeni, a wilderness guide and environmental marine science expert, invites up to six nature lovers—especially children—aboard the *Imp II*, a 25-foot Aquasport, for four-hour and seven-hour ecotours that frequently include encounters with wild dolphins. While island-hopping, you visit underwater gardens, natural shoreline, and mangrove habitats. For her Dolphin Day for Humans tour, Impallomeni pulls you through the water, equipped with mask and snorkel, on a specially designed "dolphin water massage board" that simulates dolphin swimming motions. Sometimes dolphins follow the boat and swim among participants. All equipment is supplied. ⊠ *Murray's Marina, MM 5 OS, 5710 Overseas Hwy.* ☎ *305/304–7562, 888/822–7366* ⊕ *www.captainvictoria.com* ⊠ *From $500.*

White Knuckle Thrill Boat Ride. For something with an adrenaline boost, book with this specially designed jet boat. It holds up to 10 people and does amazing maneuvers like 360s, fishtails, and other water stunts. The cost includes a pickup shuttle from your hotel. ⊠ *Sunset Marina, 555 College Rd.* ☎ *305/797–0459* ⊕ *www.whiteknucklethrillboatride. com* ⊠ *$59.*

BUS AND TROLLEY TOURS

City View Trolley Tours. In 2010, City View Trolley Tours began service, offering a little competition to the Conch Train and Old Town Trolley, which are owned by the same company. Purchase your tickets online or with your smartphone, but you pay double if you pay in person. Tours depart every 30 minutes 9:30–4:30. Passengers can board and disembark at any of nine stops, and can reboard at will. ☎ *305/294–0644* ⊕ *www.cityviewtrolleys.com* ✉ *From $19.*

Conch Tour Train. The Conch Tour Train is a 90-minute narrated tour of Key West, traveling 14 miles through Old Town and around the island. Board at Mallory Square or Angela Street and Duval Street depot every half hour (9–4:30 from Mallory Square). Discount tickets are available online. ☎ *305/294–5161, 888/916–8687* ⊕ *www.conchtourtrain.com* ✉ *$30.45.*

Gay & Lesbian Trolley Tour. Decorated with a rainbow, the Gay and Lesbian Trolley Tour rumbles around the town beginning at 4 pm every Saturday afternoon. The 70-minute tour highlights Key West's gay history. ✉ *513 Truman Ave.* ☎ *305/294–4603* ⊕ *www.gaykeywestfl.com* ✉ *$25.*

Old Town Trolley. Old Town Trolley operates trolley-style buses, departing from the Mallory Square every 30 minutes 9–4:30, for 90-minute narrated tours of Key West. The smaller trolleys go places the larger Conch Tour Train won't fit and you can ride a second consecutive day for free. You may disembark at any of 12 stops and reboard a later trolley. You can save $3 by booking online. It also offers package deals with Old Town attractions. ✉ *201 Front St.* ☎ *305/296–6688, 888/910–8687* ⊕ *www.trolleytours.com* ✉ *$30.*

FISHING

Key West Bait & Tackle. Prepare to catch a big one with the live bait, frozen bait, and fishing equipment provided here. They even offer rod and reel rentals (starting at $15 for 24 hours). Stop by their onsite Live Bait Lounge where you can sip ice-cold beer while telling fish tales. ✉ *241 Margaret St.* ☎ *305/292–1961* ⊕ *www.keywestbaitandtackle.com.*

Key West Pro Guides. This outfitter offers only private charters, and you pay by the half day. Trips include flats and backcountry fishing and reef and offshore fishing. ✉ *G-31 Miriam St.* ☎ *866/259–4205* ⊕ *www.keywestproguides.com* ✉ *From $400.*

GOLF

Key West Golf Club. Key West isn't a major golf destination, but there is one course on Stock Island designed by Rees Jones that will downright surprise you with its water challenges and tropical beauty. It's also the only "Caribbean" golf course in the United States, boasting 200 acres of unique Florida foliage and wildlife. Hole 8 is the famous "Mangrove Hole," which will give you stories to tell. It's a 143-yard par 3 that is played completely over a mass of mangroves with their gnarly roots and branches completely intertwined. Bring extra balls and book your tee time early in season. Nike rental clubs available. ✉ *6450 E. College Rd.* ☎ *305/294–5232* ⊕ *www.keywestgolf.com* ✉ *$52–$97* ⚑ *18 holes. 6500 yards. Par 70.*

KAYAKING

Key West Eco-Tours. Key West is surrounded by marinas, so it's easy to find a water-based activity or tour, whether it's sailing with dolphins or paddling in the mangroves. These sail-kayak-snorkel excursions take you into backcountry flats and mangrove forests without the crowds. The 4½-hour trip includes lunch. Private sunset sails and private charters are also available. ✉ *Historic Seaport, 100 Grinnell St.* ☎ *305/294–7245* ⊕ *www.keywestecotours.com* ✉ *From $115.*

Lazy Dog Kayak Guides. Take a two- or four-hour guided sea kayak–snorkel tour around the mangrove islands just east of Key West. Costs include transportation, bottled water, a snack, and supplies, including snorkeling gear. Paddleboard tours are also available, as are rentals for self-touring. ✉ *5114 Overseas Hwy.* ☎ *305/295–9898* ⊕ *www.lazydog. com* ✉ *From $40.*

SUP Key West. This ancient sport from Hawaii involves a surfboard and a paddle and has quickly become a favorite Florida water sport known as SUP (stand-up paddleboarding). SUP Key West gives lessons and tours of the estuaries. What's more, your tour guides are experts (one's even a PhD) in marine biology and ecology. Call ahead to make arrangements. ✉ *110 Grinnell St.* ☎ *305/240–1426* ⊕ *www.supkeywest.com* ✉ *From $45.*

SCUBA DIVING AND SNORKELING

The Florida Keys National Marine Sanctuary extends along Key West and beyond to the Dry Tortugas. Key West National Wildlife Refuge further protects the pristine waters. Most divers don't make it this far out in the Keys, but if you're looking for a day of diving as a break from the nonstop party in Old Town, expect to pay about $65 and upward for a two-tank dive. Serious divers can book dive trips to the Dry Tortugas.

Captain's Corner. This PADI-certified dive shop has classes in several languages and twice-daily snorkel and dive trips to reefs and wrecks aboard the 60-foot dive boat *Sea Eagle*. Use of weights, belts, masks, and fins is included. ✉ *125 Ann St.* ☎ *305/296–8865* ⊕ *www.captainscorner. com* ✉ *From $40.*

Dive Key West. Operating over 40 years, Dive Key West is a full-service dive center that has charters, instruction, gear rental, sales, and repair. You can take either snorkel excursions and regular scuba trips. ✉ *3128 N. Roosevelt Blvd.* ☎ *305/296–3823* ⊕ *www.divekeywest.com* ✉ *Snorkeling from $59, scuba from $75.*

Snuba of Key West. Safely dive the coral reefs without getting a scuba certification. Ride out to the reef on a catamaran, then follow your guide underwater for a one-hour tour of the coral reefs. You wear a regulator with a breathing hose that is attached to a floating air tank on the surface. No prior diving or snorkeling experience is necessary, but you must know how to swim. The price includes beverages. ✉ *Garrison Bight Marina, Palm Ave. between Eaton St. and N. Roosevelt Blvd.* ☎ *305/292–4616* ⊕ *www.snubakeywest.com* ✉ *From $99.*

WALKING TOURS

West Martello Tower. Among the arches and ruins of this redbrick Civil War–era fort, the Key West Garden Club maintains lovely gardens of native and tropical plants, fountains, and sculptures. It also holds art, orchid, and flower shows February through April and leads private garden tours one weekend in March. ⊠ *Atlantic Blvd. and White St.* ☎ *305/294–3210* ⊕ *www.keywestgardenclub.com* ✉ *Donations welcome* ⊙ *Daily 9:30–5.*

DRY TORTUGAS NATIONAL PARK

70 miles southwest of Key West.

History buffs might remember long-deactivated Fort Jefferson as the prison that held Dr. Samuel Mudd for his role in the Lincoln assassination. But today's "guests" are much more captivated by this sanctuary's thousands of birds and marine life.

GETTING HERE AND AROUND

At this writing, the ferryboat *Yankee Freedom II* departs from a marina in Old Town and does day trips to Garden Key. Key West Seaplane Adventures has half- and full-day trips to the Dry Tortugas, where you can explore Fort Jefferson, built in 1846, and snorkel on the beautiful protected reef. Departing from the Key West airport, the flights include soft drinks and snorkeling equipment for $280 (half day) and $495 (full day), plus there's a $5 (cash only) park fee. If you want to explore the park's other keys, look into renting a boat or hiring a private charter. ⇨ *For more information on the two ferries and the seaplane, see Exploring.*

ESSENTIALS

Visitor Information Dry Tortugas National Park ☎ *305/242–7700* ⊕ *www. nps.gov/drto.*

EXPLORING

Dry Tortugas National Park. This park, 70 miles off the shores of Key West, consists of seven small islands. Tour the fort, then lay out your blanket on the sunny beach for a picnic before you head out to snorkel on the protected reef. Many people like to camp here ($3 per person per night, eight sites plus group site and overflow area; first come, first served), but note that there's no freshwater supply and you must carry off whatever you bring onto the island.

The typical visitor from Key West, however, makes it no farther than the waters of Garden Key. Home to 19th-century Fort Jefferson, it is the destination for seaplane and fast ferry tours out of Key West. With 2½ to 6½ hours to spend on the island, visitors have time to tour the mammoth fort-cum-prison and then cool off with mask and snorkel along the fort's moat wall.

History buffs might remember long-deactivated Fort Jefferson, the largest brick building in the western hemisphere, as the prison that held Dr. Samuel Mudd, who unwittingly set John Wilkes Booth's leg after the assassination of Abraham Lincoln. Three other men were also held there for complicity in the assassination. Original construction on the fort began in 1846 and continued for 30 years, but was never completed because the invention of the rifled cannon made it obsolete. That's when it became a Civil War prison and later a wildlife refuge. In 1935 President Franklin Roosevelt declared it a national monument for its historic and natural value.

The brick fort acts as a gigantic, almost 16-acre reef. Around its moat walls, coral grows and schools of snapper, grouper, and wrasses hang out. To reach the offshore coral heads requires about 15 minutes of swimming over sea-grass beds. The reef formations blaze with the color and majesty of brain coral, swaying sea fans, and flitting tropical fish. It takes a bit of energy to swim the distance, but the water depth pretty much measures under 7 feet all the way, allowing for sandy spots to stop and rest. (Standing in sea-grass meadows and on coral is detrimental to marine life.)

Serious snorkelers and divers head out farther offshore to epic formations, including Palmata Patch, one of the few surviving concentrations of elkhorn coral in the Keys. Day-trippers congregate on the sandy beach to relax in the sun and enjoy picnics. Overnight tent campers have use of restroom facilities and achieve a total getaway from noise, lights, and civilization in general. Remember that no matter how you get here, the park's $5 admission fee must be paid in cash.

Birders in the know bring binoculars to watch some 100,000 nesting sooty terns at their only U.S. nesting site, Bush Key, adjacent to Garden Key. Noddy terns also nest in the spring. During winter migrations, birds fill the airspace so thickly they literally fall from the sky to make their pit stops, birders say. Nearly 300 species have been spotted in the park's seven islands, including frigatebirds, boobies, cormorants, and broad-winged hawks. Bush Key is closed to foot traffic during nesting season, January through September. ⊕ *www.nps.gov/drto* ✉ *$5.*

Yankee Freedom III. The fast, sleek, 110-foot catamaran *Yankee Freedom III* travels to the Dry Tortugas in 2¼ hours. The time passes quickly on the roomy vessel equipped with four restrooms, three warm freshwater showers, and two bars. Stretch out on two decks that are both air-conditioned, with cushioned seating. There is also an open sundeck with sunny and shaded seating. Continental breakfast and lunch are included. On arrival, a naturalist leads a 45-minute guided tour, which is followed by lunch and a free afternoon for swimming, snorkeling (gear included), and exploring. The vessel is ADA-certified for visitors using wheelchairs. ■**TIP→ The Dry Tortugas lies in the Central time zone.** ⊠ *Lands End Marina, 240 Margaret St., Key West* ☎ *305/294–7009, 800/634–0939* ⊕ *www.yankeefreedom.com* ✉ *$170, parking $5* ☉ *Trips daily at 8 am (check in 7:15 am).*

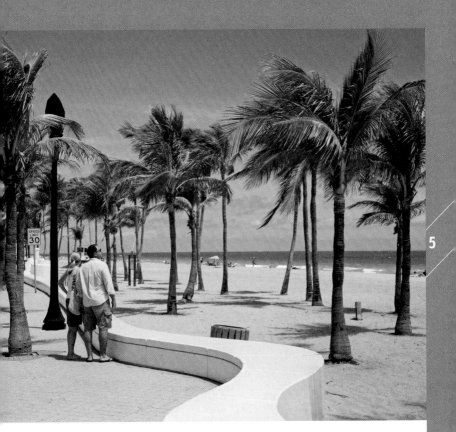

FORT LAUDERDALE

With Broward County

WELCOME TO FORT LAUDERDALE

TOP REASONS TO GO

★ **Blue waves:** Sparkling Lauderdale beaches spanning Broward County's entire coast were Florida's first to capture Blue Wave Beach status from the Clean Beaches Council.

★ **Inland waterways:** More than 300 miles of inland waterways, including downtown Fort Lauderdale's historic New River, create what's known as the Venice of America.

★ **Everglades access:** Just minutes from luxury hotels and golf courses, the rugged Everglades tantalize with alligators, colorful birds, and other wildlife.

★ **Vegas-style gaming:** Since slots and blackjack tables hit Hollywood's glittering Seminole Hard Rock Hotel & Casino in 2008, smaller competitors have followed this lucrative trend on every square inch of Indian Territory.

★ **Cruise gateway:** Port Everglades—home port for *Allure* and *Oasis of the Seas,* the world's largest cruise vessels—hosts ships from major cruise lines.

1 **Fort Lauderdale.** Anchored by the fast-flowing New River and its attractive Riverwalk, Fort Lauderdale embraces high-rise condos along with single-family homes, museums, parks, and attractions. Las Olas Boulevard, lined with boutiques, sidewalk cafés, and restaurants, links downtown with 20 miles of sparkling beaches.

2 **North on Scenic A1A.** Stretching north on Route A1A, old-school seaside charm abounds, from high-rise Galt Ocean Mile to quiet, low-rise resort communities farther north.

3 **Hollywood.** From its beachside Broadwalk to historic Young Circle (the latter transformed into an Arts Park) to South Broward's main destination provides grit, glitter, and diversity in attractions.

441
91
811
Deerfield
Beach
A1A
Coconut
Creek
1
Hillsboro
Beach
Sample Rd.
Powerline Rd.
811
834
Hillsboro
Lighthouse
7 **Butterfly** ◆
World
Margate
Dixie Hwy.
Federal Hwy.
Coconut Cr.
Pkwy.
North
Lauderdale
Atlantic Blvd.
Pompano
Beach
95
1
Sawgrass Expwy.
Cypress Creek Rd.
Commercial Blvd.
Lauderdale-
by-the-Sea
2
Oakland Park Blvd.
N. Andrews Ave.
A1A
Lauderdale
Lakes
441
Sunrise Blvd.
Seminole Dr.
S.W. 31st Ave.
**Fort
Lauderdale**
Broward Blvd.
1 Las Olas
Blvd.
Davie Blvd.
Melrose
Park
84
S.E. 17th St.
Causeway
7
595
◆ Port Everglades
**Fort Lauderdale-Hollywood
International Airport**
Griffin Rd.
1
Dania Beach
Blvd.
Stirling Rd.
Dania
Beach
A1A
Sheridan St.
822
95
Dixie Hwy.
Hollywood Blvd.
Hollywood
Pembroke Rd.
3
Hallandale Blvd.
Hallandale

ATLANTIC OCEAN

0   3 mi
0   3 km

GETTING ORIENTED

Along the southeast's Gold Coast, Fort Lauderdale and Broward County anchor a delightfully chic middle ground between the posh and elite Palm Beaches and the international hubbub of Miami. From downtown Fort Lauderdale, it's about a four-hour drive to either Orlando or Key West, but there's plenty to keep you in Broward. All told, Broward boasts 31 communities from Deerfield Beach to Hallandale Beach along the coast, and from Coral Springs to Southwest Ranches closer to the Everglades. Big—in fact, huge—shopping options await in the western suburbs, home of Sawgrass Mills, the upscale Colonnade Outlets at Sawgrass, and IKEA Sunrise.

5

By Paul Rubio

Collegians of the 1960s returning to Fort Lauderdale would be hard-pressed to recognize the onetime "Sun and Suds Spring Break Capital of the Universe." Back then, Fort Lauderdale's beachfront was lined with T-shirt shops, and downtown consisted of a lone office tower and dilapidated buildings waiting to be razed. Not anymore!

The beach and downtown have since exploded with upscale shops, restaurants, and luxury resort hotels equipped with enough high-octane amenities to light up skies all the way to western Broward's Alligator Alley. At risk of losing small-town 45-rpm magic in iPod times—when hotel parking fees alone eclipse room rates of old—Greater Fort Lauderdale somehow seems to meld disparate eras into nouveau nirvana, seasoned with a lot of Gold Coast sand.

The city was named for Major William Lauderdale, who built a fort at the river's mouth in 1838 during the Seminole Indian wars. It wasn't until 1911 that the city was incorporated, with only 175 residents, but it grew quickly during the Florida boom of the 1920s. Today's population hovers around 165,000, and suburbs keep growing—1.75 million live in Broward County's 31 municipalities and unincorporated areas.

As elsewhere, many speculators busily flipping property here got caught when the sun-drenched real-estate bubble burst, leaving Broward's foreclosure rate to skyrocket. But the worst is far behind us. By the time the city began celebrating its centennial in 2011, it had resumed the renaissance that began before the economic crisis. The 20-mile shoreline—with wide ribbons of golden sand for beachcombing and sunbathing—remains the anchor draw for Fort Lauderdale and Broward County, but amazing beaches are now complemented by show-stopping hotels, an exploding foodie scene, and burgeoning cultural scene. In a little more than 100 years, Fort Lauderdale has grown into Fort Fabulous.

PLANNING

WHEN TO GO

Peak season runs Thanksgiving through April, when concert, art, and entertainment seasons go full-throttle. Expect heat and humidity and some rain in summer. Hurricane winds come most notably in August and September. Golfing tee-time waits are longer on weekends year-round. Regardless of season, remember that Fort Lauderdale sunshine can burn even in cloudy weather.

GETTING HERE AND AROUND

AIR TRAVEL

Serving more than 23 million travelers a year, **Fort Lauderdale–Hollywood International Airport** is 3 miles south of downtown Fort Lauderdale, just off U.S. 1 between Fort Lauderdale and Hollywood, and near Port Everglades and Fort Lauderdale Beach. Other options include **Miami International Airport**, about 32 miles to the southwest, and the far less chaotic **Palm Beach International Airport**, about 50 miles to the north. All three airports link to **Tri-Rail**, a commuter train operating seven days through Palm Beach, Broward, and Miami-Dade counties.

Airport Information **Fort Lauderdale–Hollywood International Airport** (FLL). ⊠ Ft. Lauderdale 🕿 866/435–9355 ⊕ www.broward.org/airport. **Miami International Airport** (MIA). ⊠ Miami 🕿 305/876–7000 ⊕ www.miami-airport. com. **Palm Beach International Airport** (PBI). ⊠ Palm Beach 🕿 561/471–7420 ⊕ www.pbia.org. **Tri-Rail** 🕿 800/874–7245 ⊕ www.tri-rail.com.

BUS TRAVEL

Broward County Transit operates bus route No. 1 between the airport and its main terminal at Broward Boulevard and Northwest 1st Avenue, near downtown Fort Lauderdale. Service from the airport is every 20 minutes and begins at 5:22 am on weekdays, 5:37 am Saturday, and 8:41 am Sunday; the last bus leaves the airport at 11:38 pm Monday–Saturday and 9:41 pm Sunday. The fare is $1.75 (coins only). ⚠ **The Northwest 1st Avenue stop is in a crime-prone part of town. Exercise special caution there, day or night. Better yet, take a taxi to and from the airport.** Broward County Transit (BCT) also covers the county on 303 fixed routes. The fare is $1.75 (cash only). Service starts around 5 am and continues to 11:30 pm, except on Sunday.

Bus Contact **Broward County Transit** 🕿 954/357–8400 ⊕ www.broward.org/BCT.

CAR TRAVEL

Renting a car to get around Broward County is highly recommended. Taxis are scarce and costly. Public transportation is rarely used.

By car, access to Broward County from north or south is via Florida's Turnpike, Interstate 95, U.S. 1, or U.S. 441. Interstate 75 (Alligator Alley, requiring a toll despite being part of the nation's interstate-highway system) connects Broward with Florida's west coast and runs parallel to State Road 84 within the county. East–west Interstate 595 runs from westernmost Broward County and links Interstate 75 with Interstate 95 and U.S. 1, providing handy access to the airport and seaport.

Route A1A, designated a Florida Scenic Highway by the state's Department of Transportation, parallels the beach.

TRAIN TRAVEL

Amtrak provides daily service to Fort Lauderdale and stops at Deerfield Beach and Hollywood.

HOTELS

Back-to-back openings of luxury beachfront hotels have created Fort Lauderdale's upscale "hotel row"—with the Atlantic Resort & Spa, the Hilton Beach Resort, the Ritz-Carlton, the W, and the Westin all less than a decade old. More upscale places to hang your hat are on the horizon, whereas smaller family-run lodging spots are disappearing. You can also find chain hotels along the Intracoastal Waterway. If you want to be *on* the beach, be sure to ask specifically when booking your room, since many hotels advertise "waterfront" accommodations that are along inland waterways or overlooking the beach from across Route A1A.

Hotel reviews have been shortened. For full information, visit Fodors. com.

RESTAURANTS

References to "Fort Liquordale" from spring-break days of old have given way to au courant allusions for the decidedly cuisine-oriented "Fork Lauderdale." Greater Fort Lauderdale offers some of the finest, most varied dining of any U.S. city its size, spawned in part by the advent of new luxury hotels and upgrades all around. From among more than 4,000 wining-and-dining establishments in Broward, choose from basic Americana or cuisines of Asia, Europe, or Central and South America, and enjoy more than just food in an atmosphere with subtropical twists.

WHAT IT COSTS				
	$	$$	$$$	$$$$
RESTAURANTS	under $16	$16–$20	$21–$30	over $30
HOTELS	under $201	$201–$300	$301–$400	over $400

Restaurant prices are the average cost of a main course at dinner or, if dinner is not served, at lunch. Hotel prices are the lowest cost of a standard double room in high season.

FORT LAUDERDALE

Like many southeast Florida neighbors, Fort Lauderdale has long been revitalizing. In a state where gaudy tourist zones often stand aloof from workaday downtowns, Fort Lauderdale exhibits consistency at both ends of the 2-mile Las Olas corridor. The sparkling look results from upgrades both downtown and on the beachfront. Matching the downtown's innovative arts district, cafés, and boutiques is an equally inventive beach area, with hotels, cafés, and shops facing an undeveloped shoreline, and new resort-style hotels replacing faded icons of yesteryear. Despite wariness of pretentious overdevelopment, city leaders have allowed a striking number of glittering high-rises. Nostalgic locals and frequent visitors fret over the diminishing vision of sailboats bobbing in waters near downtown; however, Fort Lauderdale remains the yachting capital of the world, and the water toys don't seem to be going anywhere. Sharp demographic changes are also altering the faces of Greater Fort Lauderdale communities, increasingly cosmopolitan with more minorities, including Hispanics and people of Caribbean descent, as well as gays and lesbians. In Fort Lauderdale, especially, a younger populace is growing, whereas longtime residents are heading north, to a point where one former city commissioner likens the change to that of historic New River—moving with the tide and sometimes appearing at a standstill: "The river of our population is at still point, old and new in equipoise, one pushing against the other."

GETTING HERE AND AROUND

The Fort Lauderdale metro area is laid out in a grid system, and only myriad canals and waterways interrupt the mostly straight-line path of streets and roads. Nomenclature is important here. Streets, roads, courts, and drives run east–west. Avenues, terraces, and ways run north–south. Boulevards can (and do) run any which way. For visitors, boutique-lined Las Olas Boulevard is one of the most important east–west thoroughfares from the beach to downtown, whereas Route A1A—referred to as Atlantic Boulevard, Ocean Boulevard, and Fort Lauderdale Beach along some stretches—runs along the north–south oceanfront. These names can confuse visitors, since there are separate streets called Atlantic and Ocean in Hollywood and Pompano Beach. Boulevards, composed of either pavement or water, give Fort Lauderdale its distinct "Venice of America" character.

The city's transportation system, though less congested than elsewhere in South Florida, suffers from traffic overload. I–595 connects the city and suburbs and provides a direct route to the Fort Lauderdale–Hollywood International Airport and Port Everglades, but lanes slow to a crawl during rush hours. The Intracoastal Waterway, paralleling Route A1A, is the nautical equivalent of an interstate highway. It runs north–south between downtown Fort Lauderdale and the beach and provides easy boating access to neighboring beach communities.

Catch an orange-bottomed, yellow-topped Sun Trolley, running every 15 minutes, for as little as $0.50 each way. Sun Trolley's *Convention Connection* runs round-trip from Cordova Road's Harbor Shops near Port Everglades (where you can park free) to past the Convention Center, over the 17th Street Causeway, and north along Route A1A to Beach Place. Sun Trolley's Las Olas Beaches route passes from downtown through Las Olas and then north on A1A. Wave at trolley drivers—yes, they'll stop—for pickups anywhere along the route.

Meters in Yellow Cab taxis run at rates of $4.50 for the first mile and $2.40 for each additional mile; waiting time is $0.40 per minute. There's a $10-fare minimum to or from seaport or airport, and an additional $2 service charge when you are collected from the airport. All Yellow Cab vehicles accept major credit cards.

Transportation Contacts Sun Trolley ☎ *954/761–3543* ⊕ *www.suntrolley. com.* **Yellow Cab** ☎ *954/777–7777* ⊕ *www.yellowcabbroward.com.*

TOURS

Honeycombed with some 300 miles of navigable waterways, Fort Lauderdale is the home port for about 44,000 privately owned vessels, but you don't need to be a boat owner to ply the waters. For a scenic way to really see this canal-laced city, take a relaxing boat tour or simply hop on a Water Taxi, part of Fort Lauderdale's water-transportation system. See why the city is called the "Venice of America."

Carrie B Harbor Tours. Board a 300-passenger day cruiser for a 90-minute tour on the New River and Intracoastal Waterway. Cruises depart at 11, 1, and 3 daily November through May and Thursday–Monday between June and October. The cost is $22.95. ■ TIP→ **Book ahead online.** ✉ *440 N. New River Dr. E, off Las Olas Blvd.* ☎ *954/642–1601* ⊕ *www.carriebcruises.com.*

FAMILY **Fort Lauderdale Duck Tours.** Quack, quack! The famous 45-passenger amphibious Hydra-Terra tours, which first gained popularity in Boston, have arrived in Fort Lauderdale. Ninety-minute tours include lots of land/water family fun, cruising and driving through Venice of America neighborhoods, historic areas, and the Intracoastal Waterway. Several tours depart daily and cost just under $34. Schedule varies and ducks sometimes don't run in low season, so check ahead of time. △ **The website shares its booking engine with the Duck Tours South Beach, so be sure to book for the correct location!** ✉ *17 S. Fort Lauderdale Beach Blvd., at Beach Pl.* ☎ *954/761–4002* ⊕ *www.fortlauderdaleducktours.com.*

Jungle Queen Riverboat. The kitsch *Jungle Queen* riverboat seats more than 550 and cruises up the New River through the heart of Fort Lauderdale, as it has for more than 75 years. It's old-school and totally touristy but that's half the fun! The sightseeing cruises at 9:30 and 1:30 cost $19.95, and the 6 pm all-you-can-eat BBQ dinner cruise costs $42.95. ✉ *Bahia Mar Beach Resort, 801 Seabreeze Blvd.* ☎ *954/462–5596* ⊕ *www.junglequeen.com.*

FAMILY
Fodor's Choice
★
Water Taxi. A great way to experience the multimillion-dollar homes, hotels, and seafood restaurants along Fort Lauderdale's waterways is via the public Water Taxi, which runs every 30 minutes beginning at 10 am and ending at midnight. There are 14 regularly scheduled pickup stations in Fort Lauderdale, including Las Olas Riverfront, the Shops of Las Olas, Bahia Mar, and Gallery ONE near the Galleria Mall. An unlimited day pass serves as both a tour and a means of transportation between Fort Lauderdale's hotels and hot spots, though Water Taxi is most useful when viewed as a tour. It's possible to cruise all afternoon while taking in the waterfront sights. Captains and helpers indulge guests in fun factoids about Fort Lauderdale, white lies about the city's history, and bizarre tales about the celebrity homes along the Intracoastal. A day pass is $22. Water Taxi also connects Fort Lauderdale to Hollywood, where there are seven scheduled stops. ☎ *954/467–6677* ⊕ *www.watertaxi.com.*

5

VISITOR INFORMATION

Greater Fort Lauderdale Convention and Visitors Bureau ☎ *954/765–4466* ⊕ *www.sunny.org.*

EXPLORING

DOWNTOWN AND LAS OLAS

The jewel of downtown along New River is the small Arts and Entertainment District, with Broadway shows, ballet, and theater at the riverfront Broward Center for the Performing Arts. Clustered within a five-minute walk are the Museum of Discovery & Science, the expanding Fort Lauderdale Historical Museum, and the Museum of Art—home to stellar touring exhibits. Restaurants, sidewalk cafés, bars, and dance clubs flourish along Las Olas and its downtown extension. Tying these areas together is the Riverwalk, extending 2 miles along the New River's north and south banks. Tropical gardens with benches and interpretive displays fringe the walk on the north, boat landings on the south.

TOP ATTRACTIONS

Fort Lauderdale History Center. Surveying city history from the Seminole era to more recent times, the Fort Lauderdale Historical Society's museum has expanded into several adjacent buildings, including the historic King-Cromartie House (typical early 20th-century-style Fort Lauderdale home), the 1905 New River Inn (Broward's oldest remaining hotel building), and the Hoch Heritage Center, a public research facility archiving original manuscripts, maps, and more than 250,000 photos. Daily docent-led tours run on the hour from 1–3 pm. ⊠ *231 S.W. 2nd Ave., Downtown and Las Olas* ☎ *954/463–4431* ⊕ *www. oldfortlauderdale.org* 💰 *$10* ☉ *Tues.–Sun. noon–4.*

Fodor's Choice ★ **Las Olas Boulevard.** What Lincoln Road is to South Beach, Las Olas Boulevard is to Fort Lauderdale. The terrestrial heart and soul of Broward County, Las Olas is the premier street for restaurants, art galleries, shopping, and people-watching. From west to east the landscape of Las Olas transforms from modern downtown high-rises to original boutiques and ethnic eateries. Beautiful mansions and traditional Floridian homes line the Intracoastal and define Fort Lauderdale. The streets of Las Olas connect to the pedestrian friendly Riverwalk, which continues to the edge of the New River on Avenue of the Arts. ⊠ *E. Las Olas Blvd., Downtown and Las Olas* ⊕ *www.lasolasboulevard.com.*

Museum of Art Fort Lauderdale. Currently in an Edward Larrabee Barnes–designed building that's considered an architectural masterpiece, activists started this museum in a nearby storefront more than 50 years ago. MOAFL, part of Nova Southeastern University, hosts world-class touring exhibits and has an impressive permanent collection of 6,000 works of 20th-century European and American art, including pieces by Picasso, Calder, Dalí, Mapplethorpe, Warhol, and Stella, as well as works by celebrated Ashcan School artist William Glackens. ■ TIP→ The lobby-level store and café combo, Museum Cafe, is a cool local hangout. ⊠ *1 E. Las Olas Blvd., Downtown and Las Olas*

☎ 954/525–5500 ⊕ *www.moafl.org* ✉ *$10* ⊙ *Tues.–Wed. and Fri.–Sat.*
11–5, Thurs.11–7, Sun. noon–5 ⊙ *Closed Mon.*

FAMILY
Fodor'sChoice
★

Museum of Discovery & Science/AutoNation IMAX Theater. With more than
200 interactive exhibits, the aim here is to entertain children—*and*
adults—with the wonders of science and the wonders of Florida. In
2012, the museum doubled in size, meaning twice the fun! Exhibits
include the Ecodiscovery Center with an Everglades Airboat Adventure
ride, resident otters, and an interactive Florida storm center. Florida
Ecoscapes has a living coral reef, plus sharks, rays, and eels. Runways to
Rockets offers stimulating trips to Mars and the moon while nine different cockpit simulators let you try out your pilot skills. The AutoNation
IMAX theater, part of the complex, shows films (some in 3-D) on an
80-foot by 60-foot screen with 15,000 watts of digital surround sound
broadcast from 42 speakers. ✉ *401 S.W. 2nd St., Downtown and Las
Olas* ☎ *954/467–6637 for museum, 954/463–4629 for IMAX* ⊕ *www.
mods.org* ✉ *Museum $14 ($19 with one IMAX show)* ⊙ *Mon.–Sat.
10–5, Sun. noon–6.*

Riverwalk. Lovely views prevail on this paved promenade on the New
River's north bank. On the first Sunday of every month a free jazz festival attracts visitors. From west to east, the Riverwalk begins at the
residential New River Sound, passes through the Arts and Science District, then the historic center of Fort Lauderdale, and wraps around the
New River until it meets with Las Olas Boulevard's shopping district.

Stranahan House. The city's oldest residence, on the National Register
of Historic Places, and increasingly dwarfed by high-rise development,
was once home to businessman Frank Stranahan, who arrived in 1892.
With his wife, Ivy, the city's first schoolteacher, he befriended and traded
with Seminole Indians, and taught them "new ways." In 1901 he built
a store that would later become his home after serving as a post office,
a general store, and a restaurant. Frank and Ivy's former residence is
now a museum, with many period furnishings, and tours. The historic home remains Fort Lauderdale's principal link to its brief history.
Note that self-guided tours are not allowed. ✉ *335 S.E. 6th Ave., at
Las Olas Blvd., Downtown and Las Olas* ☎ *954/524–4736* ⊕ *www.
stranahanhouse.org* ✉ *$12* ⊙ *Tours Oct.–Aug., daily at 1, 2, and 3 pm.*

QUICK
BITES

Kilwins Ft. Lauderdale. The sweet smell of waffle cones lures pedestrians to an old-fashioned confectionery in the heart of Las Olas Boulevard
that also sells hand-paddled fudge and scoops of homemade ice cream.
✉ *809 E. Las Olas Blvd., Downtown and Las Olas* ☎ *954/523–8338* ⊕ *www.
kilwins.com/ftlauderdale.*

ALONG THE BEACH

Fodor'sChoice
★

Bonnet House Museum & Gardens. A 35-acre oasis in the heart of the beach
area, this subtropical estate on the National Register of Historic Places
stands as a tribute to the history of Old South Florida. This charming
home, built in the 1920s, was the winter residence of the late Frederic
and Evelyn Bartlett, artists whose personal touches and small surprises
are evident throughout. If you're interested in architecture, artwork,
or the natural environment, this place is worth a visit. After admiring

THE GHOSTS OF STRANAHAN HOUSE

These days the historic Stranahan House is as famous for its nighttime ghost tours as it is for its daytime history tour. Originally built as a trading post in 1901 and later expanded into a town hall, a post office, a bank, and the personal residence of Frank Stranahan and his wife, Ivy Cromartie, the historic Stranahan House was more than plagued by a number of tragic events and violent deaths, including Frank's suicide. After financial turmoil, Stranahan tied himself to a concrete sewer grate and jumped into New River, leaving his widow to carry on. Sunday night at 7:30, house staff reveal the multiple tragic tales from the Stranahan crypt during the River House Ghost Tour ($25) and help visitors communicate with "the other side." Using special tools and snapping photos to search for orbs, guests are encouraged to field energy from the supposed five ghosts in the house. Given the high success rate of reaching out to the paranormal, the Stranahan House has become a favorite campground for global ghost hunters and television shows. Advance reservations are required.

the fabulous gardens, be on the lookout for playful monkeys swinging from trees. Interesting fact: The Bonnet House was the final stop in the 2005 season of CBS's Amazing Race hit television show. ⊠ *900 N. Birch Rd., Along the beach* ☎ *954/563–5393* ⊕ *www.bonnethouse.org* ✉ *$20 for house tours, $10 for gardens only* ☉ *Tues.–Sun. 9–4; tours hourly from 9:30–3:30.*

NEED A BREAK?

Casablanca Café. For respite from the sun, duck in for a nice glass of chardonnay or a light bite. ⊠ *3049 Alhambra St., Along the beach* ☎ *954/764–3500.*

Steak 954. Recover from a long day in the sun with a much-deserved, refreshing cocktail. ⊠ *401 N. Fort Lauderdale Beach Blvd., Along the beach* ☎ *954/414–8333.*

WESTERN SUBURBS AND BEYOND

West of Fort Lauderdale is ever-growing suburbia, with most of Broward's golf courses, shopping, casinos, and chain restaurants. As you head farther west, the terrain takes on more characteristics of the Everglades, and you'll occasionally see alligators sunning on canal banks. Eventually, you reach the Everglades themselves after hitting the airboat outfitters on the park's periphery. Tourists flock to these airboats, but the best way of seeing the Everglades is to visit the Everglades National Park itself.

FAMILY **Ah-Tah-Thi-Ki Museum.** A couple of miles from Billie Swamp Safari is Ah-Tah-Thi-Ki Museum, whose name means "a place to learn, a place to remember." This museum documents the traditions and culture of the Seminole Tribe of Florida through artifacts, exhibits, and reenactments of rituals and ceremonies. The 60-acre site includes a living-history Seminole village, nature trails, and a wheelchair-accessible boardwalk through a cypress swamp. ■TIP→ Guided tours are available daily,

but call for exact times. Self-guided audio tours are available anytime. There are also children's programs. ✉ *34725 W. Boundary Rd., Clewiston* ☎ *877/902–1113* ⊕ *www.ahtahthiki.com* ✉ *$9* ⊘ *Daily 9–5.*

FAMILY **Billie Swamp Safari.** At the Billie Swamp Safari, experience the majesty of the Everglades firsthand. Daily tours of wildlife-filled wetlands and hammocks yield sightings of deer, water buffalo, raccoons, wild hogs, hawks, eagles, and alligators. Animal and reptile shows entertain audiences. Ecotours are conducted aboard motorized swamp buggies, and airboat rides are available, too. The on-site Swamp Water Café serves gator nuggets, frogs' legs, catfish, and Indian fry bread with honey. ✉ *Big Cypress Seminole Indian Reservation, 30000 Gator Tail Trail, Clewiston* ☎ *863/983–6101, 800/949–6101* ⊕ *www.swampsafari.com* ✉ *Swamp Safari Day Package $49.95 (includes ecotour, shows, exhibits, and airboat ride)* ⊘ *Daily 9–6.*

FAMILY **Butterfly World.** As many as 80 butterfly species from South and Central
Fodor'sChoice America, the Philippines, Malaysia, Taiwan, and other Asian nations
★ are typically found within the serene 3-acre site inside Tradewinds Park in the northwest reaches of Broward County. A screened aviary called North American Butterflies is reserved for native species. The Tropical Rain Forest Aviary is a 30-foot-high construction, with observation decks, waterfalls, ponds, and tunnels filled with thousands of colorful butterflies. There are lots of birds, too, and kids love going in the lorikeet aviary, where the colorful birds land on every limb! ✉ *Tradewinds Park, 3600 W. Sample Rd., Coconut Creek* ☎ *954/977–4400* ⊕ *www. butterflyworld.com* ✉ *$24.95* ⊘ *Mon.–Sat. 9–5, Sun. 11–5.*

FAMILY **Everglades Holiday Park.** This 30-acre park provides a decent glimpse of the Everglades and Florida's wild west circa 1950. Take an hour-long airboat tour, look at an 18th-century-style American Indian village, or catch the alligator wrestling. The airboats tend to be supersized and the experience very commercialized. Most episodes of Animal Planet's *Gator Boys* are filmed here. ✉ *21940 Griffin Rd., Western Suburbs and Beyond* ☎ *954/434–8111* ⊕ *www.evergladesholidaypark.com* ✉ *Park free, airboat tour $26.50* ⊘ *Daily 9–5.*

FAMILY **Flamingo Gardens.** Gators, crocodiles, river otters, and birds of prey lie in wait at Flamingo Gardens, with a walk-through aviary, plant house, and Everglades museum in the pioneer Wray Home. A half-hour guided tram ride winds through a citrus grove and wetlands area, and the gift shop helps you ship oranges, grapefruit and tangerines home. ✉ *3750 S. Flamingo Rd., Davie* ☎ *954/473–2955* ⊕ *www.flamingogardens.org* ✉ *$18, tram ride $4* ⊘ *Daily 9:30–5.*

FAMILY **Sawgrass Recreation Park.** A half-hour airboat ride through the Everglades allows you to view a good variety of plants and wildlife, from ospreys and alligators to turtles, snakes, and fish. Besides the ride, your entrance fee covers admission to an Everglades nature exhibit; a native Seminole village; and exhibits on alligators, other reptiles, and birds of prey. Supercool airboat nights tours are offered on Wednesday and Saturday at 8:30 to experience the nocturnal world of the 'glades. Reservations required for night tours. ✉ *1006 N. U.S. 27, Weston*

☎ 888/424–7262 ⊕ *www.evergladestours.com* ✉ *$19.50, night tours $40* ☾ *Airboat rides daily 9–5.*

BEACHES

Fodor's Choice
★

Fort Lauderdale Beach. The same downy sands that once welcomed America's youth-gone-wild (aka wild spring breakers) now frame a multimile shoreline of beachside sophistication. Alone among Florida's major beachfront communities, Fort Lauderdale's principal beach remains gloriously open and uncluttered. Walkways line both sides of the beach roadway, and traffic has been trimmed to two gently curving northbound lanes. Fort Lauderdale Beach unofficially begins between the Sheraton Fort Lauderdale and Hilton's Bahia Mar Resort, starting with the quiet **South Beach Park**, where picnic tables and palm trees rule. Going north, the younger, barely legal crowd gravitates toward the section of sand at the mouth of Las Olas Boulevard. The beach is actually most crowded between Las Olas and Sunrise Boulevards, directly in front of the major hotels and condominiums, namely in front of **Beach Place**, home to the Marriott time-share building and touristy places like Hooters and Fat Tuesday (and a beach-themed CVS Pharmacy). Gay men and women get their fix of vitamin D along **Sebastian Beach**, on Sebastian Street, just north of The Ritz-Carlton, Fort Lauderdale.

Families with children enjoy hanging out between Seville Street and Vistamar Street, between the Westin Fort Lauderdale Beach and the Atlantic Resort and Spa. **Amenities:** food and drink; lifeguards; parking (fee). **Best for:** sunrise; swimming; walking. ⊠ *Rte. A1A from Holiday Dr. to Sunrise Blvd., Along the beach.*

Harbor Beach. The posh neighborhood of Harbor Beach boasts Fort Lauderdale's most opulent homes along the Intracoastal Waterway. Due east of this community, and just south of Fort Lauderdale's South Beach Park, a stunning swath of beach has adopted the name of its neighborhood—Harbor Beach. This section offers some of the few private beaches in Fort Lauderdale, most of which belong to big hotel names like the Marriott Harbor Beach and the Lago Mar. (Only hotel guests can access these beaches.) Such status permits the hotels to offer full-service amenities and eating and drinking outlets on their bespoke slices of sugarloafed heaven. **Amenities:** water sports. **Best for:** solitude; swimming; walking. ⊠ *S. Ocean La. and southern tip of Holiday Dr., Along the beach.*

Hugh Taylor Birch State Recreation Area. North of Fort Lauderdale's bustling beachfront, past Sunrise Boulevard, the quieter sands of Fort Lauderdale beach run parallel to Hugh Taylor Birch State Recreation Area, a nicely preserved patch of primeval Florida. The 180-acre tropical park sports lush mangrove areas along the Intracoastal waterway, and lovely nature trails. Visit the Birch House Museum, enjoy a picnic, play volleyball, or paddle a rented canoe. Since parking is limited on Route A1A, park here and take a walkway underpass to the beach (which can be accessed daily 9–5). **Amenities:** toilets. **Best for:** solitude; walking. ⊠ *3109 E. Sunrise Blvd., Along the beach* ☎ *954/564–4521* ⊕ *www. floridastateparks.org/HughTaylorBirch* ⊠ *$6 per vehicle, $2 per pedestrian* ☼ *Daily 8–sunset.*

WHERE TO EAT

DOWNTOWN AND LAS OLAS

$$
MODERN
AMERICAN
Fodor'sChoice
★

✕ **American Social.** A charming slice of Americana in the heart of Las Olas Boulevard, American Social flaunts a sexy nerd vibe, packing the house nightly with Fort Lauderdale's hottest twenty- and thirtysomethings. The intimate restaurant and bar are adorned with framed *Life* magazine covers and library books, fostering an ambience that is oh-so Boston. The drinks here rock, and the modern American cuisine is equally awesome. Choose from 16 beers on tap or some tantalizing mixology (e.g. the Strawberry Honey Smash—vodka, strawberries, simple syrup, honey liqueur, and fresh lemon juice). Feast on the seafood mac-and-cheese skillet, shrimp pesto flatbread, and the full gamut of gourmet burgers with sides of Parmesan and truffle fries or sweet-potato fries. ▪**TIP**➜ **Arrive early on weekends as the restaurant quickly reaches capacity.** Ⓢ *Average main: $20* ⊠ *721 E. Las Olas Blvd., Downtown and Las Olas* ☎ *954/764–7005* ⊕ *www.americansocialbar.com.*

$$$
MODERN
AMERICAN
FAMILY
Fodor'sChoice
★

×**Big City Tavern.** A Las Olas landmark, Big City Tavern is the boulevard's most consistent spot for good food, good spirits, and good times. The diverse menu commingles Asian entrées like pad thai, Italian options like homemade meatballs and cheese ravioli in a toasted garlic marinara, and American dishes like the grilled skirt-steak Cobb salad. Don't forget to ask about the crispy flatbread of the day, and make sure to save room for the homemade desserts. The pistachio brown-butter bundt cake with honey-roasted spiced peaches and pistachio gelato, the caramelized banana sundae in a Mason jar, and the devil's-food-cake ice-cream sandwich are all heaven on earth. ■TIP→ Big City is open late into the night for drinks, desserts, and even offers a special late-night menu. Ⓢ *Average main: $24* ✉ *609 E. Las Olas Blvd., Downtown and Las Olas* ☎ *954/727–0307* ⊕ *www.bigtimerestaurants.com.*

$
AMERICAN

×**The Floridian.** This classic diner is plastered with photos of Monroe, Nixon, and local notables past and present in a succession of brightly painted rooms with funky chandeliers. The kitchen dishes up typical grease-pit breakfast favorites (no matter the hour), with oversized omelets that come with biscuits, toast, or English muffins, plus a choice of grits or tomatoes. The restaurant also has good hangover eats, but don't expect anything exceptional (besides the location and the rock-bottom prices). It's open 24 hours—even during hurricanes, as long as the power holds out. Ⓢ *Average main: $13* ✉ *1410 E. Las Olas Blvd., Downtown and Las Olas* ☎ *954/463–4041* ▭ *No credit cards.*

$
CAFÉ
Fodor'sChoice
★

×**Gran Forno Cafe.** The gamble of importing an entire Italian bakery direct from Brescia, Italy definitely paid off. Most days, the sandwiches, fresh baked breads, and pastries sell out even before lunchtime. All products are made fresh daily (except Monday), beginning at 4 am, by a team of bakers who can be seen hard at work through the café's glass windows. Customers line up at the door early in the morning to get their piping-hot artisanal breads, later returning for the scrumptious paninis and decadent desserts. A second branch, five blocks east on Las Olas at No. 704, called Gran Forno Pronto, offers full service and a more extensive menu seven days a week, but it's only open until 7 pm. Ⓢ *Average main: $12* ✉ *1235 E. Las Olas Blvd., Downtown and Las Olas* ☎ *954/467–2244* ⊕ *www.granforno.com* ☾ *Closed Mon.*

$$$
STEAKHOUSE

×**Grille 401.** Enveloped in panes of wine bottles, floor-to-ceiling glass windows, and masculine wood panels, seductive Grille 401 is part avant-garde steakhouse, part pan-Asian eatery, part chic lounge—all together 100% fabulous. With a diverse menu that includes Osaka-style pressed sushi, classic filet mignon, crispy crab fritters, wood-grilled lobster, as well as a "light and healthy" menu for the lithe and calorie-conscious, there's something special for just about everyone. For the not-so-calorie-conscious, the homemade desserts, including a white-chocolate brioche bread pudding and, arguably, the world's best carrot cake are must tries. By day, Grille 401 caters to a power-lunch crowd escaping the ordinary in the Las Olas financial district; by night, Grille 401 is all about sophisticated dining and excellent cocktails. Ⓢ *Average main: $28* ✉ *401 E. Las Olas Blvd., Downtown and Las Olas* ☎ *954/767–0222* ⊕ *www.grille401.com.*

$$$$
SEAFOOD
Fodor'sChoice
★
✕ **Lobster Bar Sea Grille.** A spectacular, high-design restaurant at the crossroads of Las Olas's financial and shopping districts, Lobster Bar Sea Grille brings a much-needed infusion of sophisticated dining to the Fort Lauderdale scene. The intricately tiled archways and high ceilings of the restaurant recall New York's Grand Central station while the nautical-inspired décor is meant to evoke an ambience of fine dining on a yacht. Mission accomplished. The seafood and fish selections here are sublime, specializing in simply prepared, fresh whole fish and flash-fried lobster tails. There's also a range of custom-aged prime steaks with the full gamut of sides from Parmesan-baked asparagus to cauliflower gratin. $ *Average main: $46* ✉ *450 E. Las Olas Blvd., Downtown and Las Olas* ☎ *954/772–2675* ⊕ *www.buckheadrestaurants.com/lobster-bar-sea-grille* ⚱ *Reservations essential.*

$$$
MODERN
MEXICAN
Fodor'sChoice
★
✕ **Rocco's Tacos & Tequila Bar.** The busiest spot on the Las Olas strip, Rocco's is more of a scene than just a restaurant. With pitchers of margaritas a-flowin', the middle-age crowd is boisterous and fun, recounting (and reliving) the days of spring-break debauchery from their preprofessional years. In fact, Rocco's drink menu is even larger than its sizeable food menu. Guacamole is made tableside, and Mexican dishes such as chimichangas and enchiladas have been reinvented (and made far less spicy) for the American palate. Expect a wild night and lots of fun! $ *Average main: $23* ✉ *1313 E. Las Olas Blvd., Downtown and Las Olas* ☎ *954/524–9550* ⊕ *www.roccostacos.com.*

$$$
CAJUN
Fodor'sChoice
★
✕ **Royal Pig Pub.** Fort Lauderdale's coolest gastro-pub revels in doling out hefty portions of cajun comfort cuisine and potent, creative libations. As the name implies, this is indeed the place to be a pig and unapologetically pig out on the beer and butter-soaked New Orleans–style BBQ shrimp; grilled fish-of-the-day atop cheese grits and mussel étouffée; sweet-potato fries with honey-cider drizzle; and grilled free-range turkey burgers loaded with exotic condiments. Plenty of folks come here just for the awesome drinks. In fact, it's one of Fort Lauderdale's busiest watering holes. The pub's arched ceilings are lined with flat-screen TVs, and the bar occupies nearly half the restaurant. Rub elbows with Fort Lauderdale's yuppies and hotties over dragon fruit cosmos and spiked, cucumber and mint berry lemonades. $ *Average main: $22* ✉ *350 E. Las Olas Blvd., Downtown and Las Olas* ☎ *954/617–7447* ⊕ *www.royalpigpub.com.*

$$$$
SEAFOOD
✕ **Wild Sea Oyster Bar & Grille.** In the heart of tony Las Olas Boulevard, this oyster bar and grille keeps things simple with a small menu focused on a beautiful raw bar and ever-changing preparations of diverse catches from Florida, Hawaiian, and New England waters. With everything filleted and/or shucked in house, the just-caught freshness is evident in each bite. Make sure to try the ahi tuna *poke* (Hawaiian raw fish salad) as well as the fruity West Florida grouper with mango, heirloom tomatoes, and blackberry drizzle. $ *Average main: $39* ✉ *Riverside Hotel, 620 E. Las Olas Blvd, Downtown and Las Olas* ☎ *954/467–0671* ⊕ *www.wildsealasolas.com* ⊘ *Closed Sun. and Mon. No lunch.*

$$$
AMERICAN
✕ **YOLO.** The now-overused term YOLO stands for "You Only Live Once," but you will definitely want to eat here more than once. For Fort Lauderdale's bourgeoisie, this is the place to see and be seen and

to show off your hottest wheels in the driveway. For others, it's an upscale restaurant with affordable prices and a great ambience. The restaurant serves the full gamut of new American favorites like tuna sashimi, fried calamari, garden burgers, and short ribs with a sophisticated spin. For example, the Szechuan calamari is flash-fried, and then covered in garlic-chili sauce, chopped peanuts, and sesame seeds; the garden burger is made from bulgur wheat, cremini mushrooms, and cashews and served with thin-cut fries. $ *Average main: $24* ⊠ *333 E. Las Olas Blvd., Downtown and Las Olas* 🕾 *954/523–1000* ⊕ *www. yolorestaurant.com.*

ALONG THE BEACH

$$
×**Casablanca Cafe.** Located along Route A1A in the heart of Fort Lau-
ECLECTIC derdale's hotel row, Casablanca Cafe offers alfresco and indoor dining with a fabulous ocean view. The historic two-story Moroccan-style villa was built in the 1920s by local architect Francis Abreu. The menu at this piano bar and restaurant showcases a global potpourri of American, Mediterranean, and Asian flavors; however, the recommended "house favorites" focus on eclectic preparations of Florida fish. The food isn't particularly delicious, but the location and ambience are excellent. Prepare for long waits to eat in the outdoor section; it's wildly popular morning, noon, and night with tourists and locals alike. $ *Average main: $18* ⊠ *3049 Alhambra St., Along the beach* 🕾 *954/764–3500* ⊕ *www.casablancacafeonline.com.*

$$$
×**Dos Caminos.** An institution in New York City's Mexican dining scene,
MEXICAN Dos Caminos opened its first Florida outpost at the Sheraton Fort Lauderdale Beach Hotel. Rounds of traditional and nontraditional margaritas (like the pineapple–brown sugar margarita) begin the journey south of the border. Chips are served with a trio of authentic salsas, usually followed by fantastic guacamole, made to order. The house specialties, tacos, quesadillas, and enchiladas are a commingling of traditional Mexican and neo-Mexican gastronomy, reinvented with an American flair. $ *Average main: $21* ⊠ *Sheraton Fort Lauderdale Beach Hotel, 1140 Seabreeze Blvd., Along the beach* 🕾 *954/727–7090* ⊕ *www.doscaminos.com.*

$$
×**Oasis Cafe.** On a spit of land near Route A1A, this outdoor-only
AMERICAN spot has swing-glide tables covered by green-striped awnings affording plenty of shade. The swinging tables are enticing, but the food you'll get is just okay (except the key lime pie). Drinks are great though! Friendly staffers serve up libations and casual fare from burgers and wraps to salads and steak. Be aware that a gratuity is tacked on no matter what your party size. A free valet assists with cramped parking. $ *Average main: $18* ⊠ *600 Seabreeze Blvd., Along the beach* 🕾 *954/463–3130* ⊕ *www.oasiscafefortlauderdalebeach.com.*

$$$$
×**Ocean 2000.** This waterfront restaurant and lounge at the Pelican
SEAFOOD Grand Beach Resort is a favorite of locals in the know, renowned for its
Fodor's Choice stunning Atlantic ocean views and excellent fish and seafood (prepared
★ with a Latin flair). Expect succulent and savory dishes that include local fish ceviche, swordfish "sashimi style," and Florida yellowtail snapper *á la plancha* (skillet-grilled). If indulging in the wildly popular Sunday brunch or a casual seaside lunch, make sure to request seating

on the oceanfront patio, arguably the best seats in any house in Fort Lauderdale. Come nightfall, the slick dining room comes to life, illuminated by futuristic chandeliers, ubiquitous candles, and the moonlight over the ocean through oversized windows. ⑤ *Average main: $34* ✉ *Pelican Grand Beach Resort, 2000 N. Ocean Blvd., Along the beach* ☎ *954/556–7667* ⊕ *www.pelicanbeach.com/ocean2000.*

$$$ ✕ **S3.** S3 stands for the fabulous trio of sun, surf, and sand, paying
SEAFOOD homage to its prime beachfront location. Located on the ground floor of the Hilton Fort Lauderdale Beach Resort, S3 flaunts a fun, fresh, sophisticated, beachside swagger. On any given night, you'll have an even mix of locals and tourists loving life, taking Twit-pics of their S3 cocktail sampler—a tray of adorable miniature versions of the signature libations. The menu features a variety of Japanese-inspired raw dishes, sushi rolls, and small plates, all meant for sharing and delivered as soon as they're ready. A few must-tries: the spicy Kamikaze roll, the crunchy mac 'n' cheese with smoked gouda and crispy prosciutto, and the shrimp toast from the wood-fired oven. ⑤ *Average main: $29* ✉ *Hilton Fort Lauderdale Beach Resort, 505 N. Fort Lauderdale Beach Blvd., Along the beach* ⊕ *www.s3restaurant.com.*

$$$$ ✕ **SAIA Sushi.** The superlative locale for getting your sushi fix in Fort
SUSHI Lauderdale, SAIA offers innovative rolls and perfectly executed clas-
Fodor'sChoice sics as well as a great selection of hot Thai and Japanese dishes. SAIA's
★ master chef, Subin Chenkosorn, hails from the renowned Blue Sea at the Delano in Miami and has brought his amazing skill set to the Fort Lauderdale shoreline. The stylish restaurant doubles as a gregarious lounge come late evening, perfect for enjoying another round of saketinis, soju-based cocktails, and other specialty drinks like the divine SAIA-rita and Ruby Foo, after a fabulous dinner. ⑤ *Average main: $35* ✉ *Sonesta Fort Lauderdale, 999 N. Fort Lauderdale Beach Blvd., Along the beach* ☎ *954/302–5252* ⊕ *saiasushi.com.*

$$$$ ✕ **Shula's on the Beach.** For anyone who gets positively misty-eyed at the
STEAKHOUSE mere mention of Don Shula's Miami Dolphins 17–0 Perfect Season of 1972, the good news is that this beachfront spot also turns out culinary winners just as handily. Despite dozens of new, trendy steakhouses in Miami and Fort Lauderdale, Shula's on the Beach remains staunch competition. Carnivores rejoice over the aged premium Black Angus beef grilled over a super-hot fire for quick charring. The seafood is excellent, too, and served in generous portions. The jumbo sea scallops and jumbo lump crab cakes are indeed "jumbo" and überdelicious. For a more casual affair, check out the lively bar area adorned with sports memorabilia and large-screen TVs. ⑤ *Average main: $52* ✉ *The Westin Beach Resort & Spa, Fort Lauderdale, 321 N. Fort Lauderdale Beach Blvd., Along the beach* ☎ *954/355–4000* ⊕ *www.donshula.com/ shulas-on-the-beach-ft-lauderdale.*

$$$$ ✕ **Steak 954.** It's not just the steaks that impress at Stephen Starr's super-
STEAKHOUSE star restaurant. The lobster and crab-coconut ceviche and the red snap-
Fodor'sChoice per tiradito are divine; the butter-poached Maine lobster is perfection;
★ the raw bar showcases only the best and freshest seafood on the market; and the ice cream sandwiches are pure foodie fantasia. Located on the 1st floor of the swanky W Fort Lauderdale, Steak 954 offers spectacular

Sand can sometimes be forgiving if you fall, and bicyclists also appreciate the ocean views.

views of the ocean for those choosing outdoor seating; inside, there's a sexy, sophisticated ambience for those choosing to dine in the main dining room, with bright tropical colors balanced with dark woods and an enormous jellyfish tank spanning the width of the restaurant. Sunday brunch is very popular, so arrive early for the best views. ⑤ *Average main: $55* ✉ *W Fort Lauderdale, 401 N. Fort Lauderdale Beach Blvd., Along the beach* ☎ *954/414–8333* ⊕ *www.steak954.com.*

$$$$ ✕ **3030 Ocean.** 3030 Ocean has been the talk of the town for decades.
SEAFOOD Previously under the direction of celebrity chef Dean Max, Fort Lau-
Fodor's Choice derdale's most legendary fish and seafood restaurant is now helmed by
★ another top chef—Paula DaSilva of 1500 Degrees fame (who, interest-
ingly enough, got her start at 3030 more than a decade ago). Constantly
evolving with new flavors and fusions, 3030 Ocean gives plenty of
great reasons to return time and time again. The ahi tuna poke—a tuna
tartare tossed with macadamia nuts, chili sauce, and cucumber—is so
fresh, it melts in your mouth. The pan-seared branzino over gnocchi
and sautéed Maine scallops over curried corn purée are nothing short
of experiential. The martini menu is also heaven sent, advancing mixology with basil-and-passion-fruit martinis, Bellini martinis, and açai-
and-sage martinis. ⑤ *Average main: $32* ✉ *Marriott's Harbor Beach Resort & Spa, 3030 Holiday Dr., Along the beach* ☎ *954/765–3030* ⊕ *www.3030ocean.com.*

INTRACOASTAL AND INLAND

$$ ✕ **Anthony's Coal Fired Pizza.** Before this legendary "pizza well done"
PIZZA spread to nearly 50 outposts across five states, Anthony's original coal-
FAMILY fired oven was heating up Fort Lauderdale in a big way. The petite first

location of the wildly popular pizza joint still packs the house nightly serving a simple menu of coal-fired pizza, chicken wings, and salad. Vegetarians and nonvegetarians alike love the cheeseless Eggplant Marino pizza and the Roasted Cauliflower pizza, with olive oil and whole garlic cloves, bread crumbs, and Romano and mozzarella cheeses. $ *Average main: $16* ✉ *2203 South Federal Hwy., Intracoastal and Inland* ☎ *954/462-5555* ⊕ *www.anthonyscoalfiredpizza.com.*

$$$$
SOUTHWESTERN

✕**Canyon Southwest Cafe.** Southwestern fusion fare helps you escape the ordinary at this small, magical enclave, managed hands-on by executive chef Chris Wilber. Order, for example, bison medallions with scotch bonnets, a tequila-jalapeño smoked salmon tostada, coriander-crusted tuna, or blue-corn fried oysters. Chipotle, wasabi, mango, and red chilies accent fresh seafood and wild game. Cocktail lovers should start off with a signature prickly-pear margarita or choose from a well-rounded wine list or beer selection. ■TIP➔ On every night but Saturday ladies get the special price of $6 margaritas and ½ off small plates. $ *Average main: $32* ✉ *1818 E. Sunrise Blvd., Intracoastal and Inland* ☎ *954/765-1950* ⊕ *www.canyonfl.com* ☾ *No lunch.*

$$$$
STEAKHOUSE

✕**The Capital Grille, Fort Lauderdale.** The Capital Grille is a rare example of a restaurant chain that has managed to uphold the superlative food quality and stellar service on which it was founded, regardless of expansion. Indeed, the Fort Lauderdale outpost of this American darling never fails to impress, every dish cooked being to perfection and meticulously presented. The dining room feels warm and welcoming, buzzing with the constant chatter of patrons raving about the food and ordering another round of "Stoli dolis" (Stoli vodka marinating in a tub of fresh-cut pineapples for two weeks and then served as a smooth martini). Though the steaks and sides are the main draw, the calamari appetizer, shrimp cocktail, sushi-grade tuna steak, and salmon should not be overlooked; they are all phenomenal. $ *Average main: $34* ✉ *Galleria Fort Lauderdale, 2430 E. Sunrise Blvd., Intracoastal and Inland* ☎ *954/446-2000* ⊕ *www.thecapitalgrille.com.*

$$$$
ITALIAN

✕**Casa D'Angelo Ristorante.** Casa D'Angelo is packed year-round and for good reason. Owner-chef Angelo Elia has created a gem of a Tuscan-style white-tablecloth restaurant in Fort Lauderdale and the city can't get enough, so expect long waits. Casa D'Angelo's oak oven turns out marvelous seafood and beef dishes. The pappardelle with porcini mushrooms takes pasta to pleasant heights. Another favorite is antipasto "Angelo," an assortment of seasonal grilled vegetables and mozzarella. Ask about the oven-roasted fish of the day at market price. The restaurant's raging popularity has lead to a handful of other outposts by Chef Angelo in the South Florida area. $ *Average main: $38* ✉ *1201 N. Federal Hwy., #5A, Intracoastal and Inland* ☎ *954/564-1234* ⊕ *www. casa-d-angelo.com* ☾ *No lunch.*

$$$
ASIAN
Fodor's Choice
★

✕**Coco Asian Bistro & Bar.** The best of Thai and Japanese cuisine unite under one roof at Coco Asian Bistro & Bar, a locally famous gastronomic gem in a jazzy Fort Lauderdale strip mall. Chef Mike Ponluang's expansive menu spans authentic Asian to pan-Asian flavors better-suited to the American palate to downright avant-garde interpretations of Asian cuisine. You'll never go wrong with the traditional pad thai or the

5

variety of classic curries, but there are also dishes like the Emerald Scallops, a decadent marriage of diver scallops, asparagus, and portobello mushrooms in a green curry, as well as the off-the-menu lobster pad thai served in the shell. The oversize sushi rolls are beautifully crafted, often mingling at least five flavors, fostering utter sushitopia. Try, for example, Mike's Roll, a taste explosion of tuna, spinach, avocado, tempura flakes, and kampyo rolled in sweet, black sticky rice and served with sweet chili sauce for dipping. The artisan cocktails are also excellent; don't leave without having a lycheetini or two! $ *Average main: $27* ⊠ *1841 Cordova Rd., Intracoastal and Inland* ☏ *954/525–3541* ⊕ *www.cocoasianbistro.com* ⊗ *No lunch weekends.*

$$$
MODERN
AMERICAN

✕ **d.b.a./café.** Expect the unexpected at this small, eclectic, and artsy eatery that serves food with both modern American and modern French accents. With a dozen or so tables in a dimly lit space lined with exposed brick and adorned with family photos, this neighborhood restaurant exudes a true one-of-a-kind flair and serves up some pretty amazing food, too. Entrées are served in either half or full portions, catering either to those who like hearty mains or to those who want to have a variety of small plates. Enjoy simple sensations like pan-seared sea scallops with porcini-mushroom butter and fresh ricotta gnocchi with gorgonzola sauce, or dive into personality-driven dishes like the flavorful onion-crusted Florida grouper with saffron-vanilla beurre blanc, mushroom risotto, and spinach. A full roster of nightly specials and the desserts of the evening are posted on the restaurant's blackboard menu. $ *Average main: $24* ⊠ *2364 N. Federal Hwy., Intracoastal and Inland* ☏ *954/565–3392* ⊕ *www.dbacafeandwinebar.com* ⌲ *Reservations essential* ⊗ *Closed Mon. No lunch.*

$$
PIZZA

✕ **Giorgio's 17th Street.** The delicious brick-oven pizza lures customers to this tiny restaurant, but it's really the salads and sandwiches that provide the wow factor. The blackened-chicken Caesar salad and the monstrous grilled-chicken sandwiches (with grilled peppers and fresh mozzarella on freshly baked bread) are both memorable. Nevertheless, the homemade seafood salad is still Giorgio's best seller, a healthy mix of tender squid, shrimp, and scallops in a light vinaigrette. All meals are served with piping hot rolls and homemade hummus. $ *Average main: $18* ⊠ *1499 S.E. 17th St., Intracoastal and Inland* ☏ *954/767–8300* ⊕ *www.letseat.at/giorgios* ⊗ *No lunch Sun.*

$$$$
MODERN
AMERICAN
Fodor's Choice
★

✕ **Market 17.** Using only the best ingredients from regional farmers and local fishermen, Market 17 leads the organic farm-to-table revolution in South Florida. The menu at this chic restaurant shifts seasonally, lending to an ever-changing kaleidoscope of mouthwatering creations. The Florida wahoo crudo in citrus marinade and the pan-basted Florida yelloweye snapper with leek puree are two local favorites. The desserts, too, are outstanding and include homemade ice creams in flavors like bananas Foster, chocolate cake batter, and ginger and honey. For something awesome and different with a small group, Market 17 offers "dining in the dark," where dinner is served in a blacked-out room, forcing you to rely on your senses of touch, taste, and smell to figure out what you're eating and drinking. $ *Average main: $36* ⊠ *1850 S.E.*

17th St., Ste. 109, Intracoastal and Inland ☎ *954/835–5507* ⊕ *www. market17.net* ⚓ *Reservations essential* ⊘ *No lunch.*

$ ✕ **Pelican Landing.** In this age of globalization and instant information,
SEAFOOD   it's nearly impossible to remain the city's "best-kept secret," but some-
Fodor's Choice   how Pelican Landing has managed to do exactly that. Located on a
★   second-story terrace in the Pier Sixty-Six Marina, the serene outdoor
restaurant serves mouthwatering beach-shack-style eats surrounded by
picturesque panoramas of boats, sea, and sunset. The fish is caught
daily, served blackened or grilled, presented with sides, on a salad, or
in a burrito. The ceviches and conch fritters are some of the best in
South Florida. And matched with frozen drinks and pitchers of mojitos, you'll quickly reach a state of "paradise found!" ⑤ *Average main:
$14* ⊠ *Hyatt Regency Pier Sixty Six, 2301 S.E. 17th St. Causeway, at
end of main dock, Intracoastal and Inland* ☎ *954/525–6666* ⊕ *www.
pier66.hyatt.com.*

$$$$ ✕ **Ruth's Chris Steak House.** Service at the Fort Lauderdale outpost of the
STEAKHOUSE   steakhouse juggernaut is outstanding, and waitstaff are eager to guide
you through the protein-rich menu. Steaks are served on a sizzling
500-degree plate to keep them piping hot and are dripping with melted
butter. Appetizers include the "crabtini," a generous portion of lump
crabmeat, lightly dressed in a chilled martini glass, and the sensational
lobster bisque. ■ TIP→ **Save room for a decadent dessert: the caramelized banana cream pie and chocolate sin cake are off-the-charts delicious.** ⑤ *Average main: $38* ⊠ *2525 N. Federal Hwy., Intracoastal and
Inland* ☎ *954/565–2338* ⊕ *www.ruthschris.com.*

$ ✕ **Southport Raw Bar.** You can't go wrong at this unpretentious spot
SEAFOOD   where the motto, on bumper stickers for miles around, proclaims, "eat
fish, live longer, eat oysters, love longer, eat clams, last longer." Raw or
steamed clams, raw oysters, and peel-and-eat shrimp are market price.
Sides range from Bimini bread to key lime pie, with conch fritters, beer-
battered onion rings, and corn on the cob in between. Order wine by
the bottle or glass, and beer by the pitcher, bottle, or can. Eat outside
overlooking the Intracoastal, or inside at booths, tables, or in the front
or back bars. Limited parking is free, and a grocery-store parking lot
is across the street. ⑤ *Average main: $14* ⊠ *1536 Cordova Rd., Intra-
coastal and Inland* ☎ *954/525–2526* ⊕ *www.southportrawbar.com.*

$$ ✕ **Sublime.** Pamela Anderson, Alec Baldwin, Alicia Silverstone and their
VEGETARIAN   celebrity pals are not the only vegetarians that love this vegan power-
Fodor's Choice   house. The vegan sushi, the portobello stack, and innovative pizzas and
★   pastas surprisingly can satisfy even carnivore cravings. All dishes are
organic and void of any animal by-products, showing the world how
vegan eating does not compromise flavor or taste. Even items like the
key lime cheesecake, and chicken scaloppini use alternative ingredients
and headline an evening of health-conscious eating. ⑤ *Average main:
$17* ⊠ *1431 N. Federal Hwy., Intracoastal and Inland* ☎ *954/539–9000*
⊕ *www.sublimerestaurant.com* ⊘ *Closed Mon.*

$$$ ✕ **Thasos Greek Taverna.** A small, heavenly slice of the Greek Isles has
GREEK   floated ashore between Fort Lauderdale's beach and the Intracoastal
Waterway. Upon entering Thasos Greek Taverna, you'll immediately
think Greek chic, with the white-washed walls, blue trim, streaming

images of Greece on the walls, and the easy-on-the-eyes crowd. Plan on eating family-style. Start with a variety of *pikilia* (Greek spreads), which include spicy whipped feta, divine *tzatziki* (a garlicky yogurt-cucumber dip), and melt-in-your-mouth *taramosalata* (whitefish caviar). Then move onto the *mezedes* (hot shared plates) that include shrimp *saganaki* (fried with tomatoes, olives, and feta), stuffed grape leaves, and the oh-so-tender fire-grilled octopus. Finally, expand your waistline with a main course, including specialties like the traditional *moussaka* (soufflé of ground lamb and eggplant). ⑤ *Average main: $28* ✉ *3330 E. Oakland Park Blvd., between N. Ocean Blvd and N.E. 33rd Ave., Intracoastal and Inland* ☎ *954/200–6006* ⊕ *www.thasostaverna.com* ⚑ *Reservations essential.*

$
MEXICAN
Fodor's Choice
★

✕ **Zona Fresca.** A local favorite on the cheap, Zona Fresca serves healthful, Mexican fast food with the best chips, salsas, burritos, and quesadillas in town. Everything is made fresh on the premises, including the authentic salsas, presented in a grand salsa bar. Zona is busy seven days a week for both lunch and dinner and offers both indoor and outdoor seating. It's likely to be your best (and cheapest) lunch in Fort Lauderdale. ⑤ *Average main: $8* ✉ *1635 N. Federal Hwy., Intracoastal and Inland* ☎ *954/566–1777* ⊕ *www.zonafresca.com.*

WESTERN SUBURBS

$$
PIZZA
FAMILY

✕ **D' Angelo: Pizza, Wine Bar, and Tapas.** Expanding the D'Angelo restaurant empire, Florida's famous restaurateur and Tuscan chef Angelo Elia has opened an outpost of his casual pizza, tapas, and wine bar in the western suburbs of Fort Lauderdale. D'Angelo serves affordable small plates, salads, ceviches, and pizzas (based with either red or white sauce) and has quickly become a neighborhood favorite. Both kids and adults love the rotating selections of homemade gelatos. Don't miss the zucchini flowers stuffed with mozzerella, the spinach gnocchi with four cheeses and pine nuts, and the Sorrentina pizza with eggplant, mozzarella, fresh tomato, and basil oil. This is superb Italian comfort food! ⑤ *Average main: $20* ✉ *Country Isle Shopping Center, 1370 Weston Rd., Weston* ☎ *954/306–0037* ⊕ *www.dangelopizza.com.*

$
SOUTHERN

✕ **Georgia Pig.** When heading out to the area's western reaches, this postage-stamp-size outpost can add down-home zing to your day—if you can find it, that is (signage has been known to disappear), and if you don't mind the somewhat gritty atmosphere. Breakfast, which includes sausage gravy and biscuits, is served 6–11 am, but the big attraction is barbecue beef, pork, or chicken, on platters or in sandwiches for lunch through dinner until about 8 pm. Alternatives include a spicy Brunswick stew and fried jumbo shrimp. There's apple, peach, cherry, and pecan pie, and a small-fry menu. Order takeout or eat at the counter, at wooden tables, or at a half dozen or so booths. ⑤ *Average main: $12* ✉ *1285 S. State Rd. 7 (U.S. 441) just south of Davie Blvd., Western Suburbs and Beyond* ☎ *954/587–4420* ▬ *No credit cards* ⊙ *Closed Sun. No dinner Sat.*

$$$$
STEAKHOUSE

✕ **Ireland's Steakhouse.** Don't let the name fool you. Ireland's Steakhouse is not particularly Irish nor is it just a steakhouse. In fact, this restaurant is most popular for its sustainable seafood menu. Promoting a holistic philosophy of green eating, the restaurant meticulously chooses its ingredients and the purveyors that supply them, while staying true to the international "Seafood Watch" guide. The restaurant is a warm and woodsy enclave in the back corner of the Bonaventure Resort & Spa. In keeping with trends of other steakhouses, hearty mains (like the cherry balsamic yellowfin tuna and the 20-oz. bone-in ribeye) are paired with loads of decadent sides made for sharing (like lobster mac 'n' cheese and lobster fries). ⑤ *Average main: $36* ✉ *Bonaventure Resort & Spa, 250 Racquet Club Rd., Weston* ☎ *800/327–8090* ⊕ *www.bonaventureresortandspa.com* ⊘ *Closed Sun. and Mon. No lunch.*

$$
SOUTHERN
✕ **Swank Southern Kitchen.** This hip, personality-driven eatery is the type of joint you'd expect to find in a big city, not in the suburbs. The farmhouse-chic restaurant is all about Southern hospitality, high-cal comfort food, and some darn good cocktails. First-timers are bound to start the night with "Swamp Water," a mason jar filled with a greenish concoction of 100% blue agave tequila, blue curaçao, orange juice, and gummy worms. The eating frenzy often begins with fried green tomatoes and crab hush puppies before moving on to the chicken and waffles or the beer-can chicken (smothered in beer gravy). After a few mason jars, head to the old-fashioned, dress-up photo booth to shoot some incriminating, for-your-eyes-only, photos. ⑤ *Average main: $20* ✉ *4198 S. University Dr., Western Suburbs and Beyond* ☎ *954/727–5497* ⊕ *www.swanksouthern.com* ⊘ *No lunch.*

WILTON MANORS AND OAKLAND PARK

$$$
AMERICAN
✕ **Lips.** The 1990s trend of drag dining is still alive and well in Fort Lauderdale. The hit restaurant and show bar Lips is a favorite for large groups celebrating birthdays, bachelorette parties, and other milestones. Expect some show-stopping entertainment while you eat, peppered with quite a few embarrassing moments as the queens love to drag guests up on stage. ■**TIP➔ Locals tend to visit Lips on Sunday for Sunday Gospel Brunch, the only "church" service with unlimited sparkling wine.** Besides the meal, there's a show charge that ranges from $5 to $10. ⑤ *Average main: $25* ✉ *1421 E. Oakland Park Blvd., Oakland Park* ☎ *954/567–0987* ⊕ *www.floridalips.com* ⊘ *Closed Mon.*

$$$$
SOUTH PACIFIC
FAMILY
✕ **Mai-Kai.** Touristy to some yet exciting to others, the South Pacific meets South Florida at this torch-lit landmark. It's undeniably gimmicky, but droves arrive for the popular Polynesian dance review and fire shows, Peking duck, and umbrella-garnished exotic tropical drinks. The Pacific allure is maintained with freshly planted palms, thatch, and bamboo, and a wood-planked bridge rebuilt to make arriving cars sound like rumbling thunder. An expanded wine list embraces boutique vintages from around the world. Valet parking is available. ⑤ *Average main: $39* ✉ *3599 N. Federal Hwy., Wilton Manors and Oakland Park* ☎ *954/563–3272* ⊕ *www.maikai.com.*

$$$$
SEAFOOD
✕ **Sunfish Grill.** The former Pompano Beach institution migrated south in 2009 and hasn't looked back since. Quickly establishing itself in the Oakland Park area (albeit in a quiet strip mall), Sunfish Grill doles out beautifully presented contemporary American cuisine, namely well-executed, outside-the-box seafood and fish dishes. The spaghetti Bolognese is made with ground tuna instead of beef; the Sunfish Caesar with Maytag Blue Cheese instead of Parmesan; the "not the usual" key lime

pie with coconut sorbet instead of whipped cream. The results of this ingenuity are fantastic. $ *Average main: $36* ⊠ *2775 E. Oakland Park Blvd., Wilton Manors and Oakland Park* ☎ *954/561–2004* ⊕ *www. sunfishgrill.com.*

WHERE TO STAY

DOWNTOWN AND LAS OLAS

$$ ⏥ **Pineapple Point.** Tucked a few blocks behind Las Olas Boulevard in the
B&B/INN residential neighborhood of Victoria Park, clothing-optional Pineapple Point is a magnificent maze of posh tropical cottages and dense foliage catering to the gay community and is nationally renowned for its stellar service. **Pros:** superior service; tropical setting. **Cons:** difficult to find at first; need a vehicle for beach jaunts. $ *Rooms from: $289* ⊠ *315 N.E. 16th Terr., Downtown and Las Olas* ☎ *954/527–0094* ⊕ *www. pineapplepoint.com* ⤳ *25 rooms* ⦿⎮ *Breakfast.*

$$ ⏥ **Riverside Hotel.** On Las Olas Boulevard, just steps from boutiques,
HOTEL restaurants, and art galleries, Fort Lauderdale's oldest hotel (circa 1936) evokes a time bygone with historical photos gracing hallways, and guest rooms outfitted with antique oak furnishings, ornamental palm trees, and a bold tropical color palate with a Tommy Bahamas throwback flair. **Pros:** historic appeal; in the thick of Las Olas action; nice views. **Cons:** questionable room décor; dated lobby; small bathrooms. $ *Rooms from: $239* ⊠ *620 E. Las Olas Blvd., Downtown and Las Olas* ☎ *954/467–0671, 800/325–3280* ⊕ *www.riversidehotel.com* ⤳ *208 rooms, 6 suites* ⦿⎮ *No meals.*

ALONG THE BEACH

$$$ ⏥ **The Atlantic Resort & Spa.** The hotel that catalyzed Fort Lauderdale's
HOTEL luxe revolution circa 2000 continues to be a beautiful and well-run gem, and the skyscraping, oceanfront beauty seems well positioned to stay at the top of her contemporary game for years to come. **Pros:** sophisticated lodging option; en-suite kitchenettes; hotel received full renovation in 2011. **Cons:** no complimentary water bottles in room; expensive parking. $ *Rooms from: $323* ⊠ *601 N. Fort Lauderdale Beach Blvd., Along the beach* ☎ *954/567–8020, 877/567–8020* ⊕ *www. atlantichotelfl.com* ⤳ *61 rooms, 58 suites, 4 penthouses* ⦿⎮ *No meals.*

$ ⏥ **Bahia Mar Fort Lauderdale Beach Hotel, A DoubleTree by Hilton.** This nicely
HOTEL situated Fort Lauderdale beachfront classic received a long-overdue nip/tuck in 2011–12 that included cheery, refreshed guestrooms and rebranding as a DoubleTree hotel. **Pros:** crosswalk from hotel to beach; on-site yacht center; easy to navigate Fort Laud with on-site water-taxi stop. **Cons:** dated exteriors; small bathrooms; popcorn ceilings. $ *Rooms from: $189* ⊠ *801 Seabreeze Blvd., Along the beach* ☎ *954/764–2233* ⊕ *www.bahiamarhotel.com* ⤳ *296 rooms* ⦿⎮ *No meals.*

$$ ⏥ **Hilton Fort Lauderdale Beach Resort.** This 26-story oceanfront sparkler
RESORT features 374 tastefully appointed guest rooms and a fabulous 6th-floor
FAMILY pool deck, colorfully and whimsically decorated. **Pros:** excellent gym;
Fodor's Choice most rooms have balconies; great location. **Cons:** charge for Wi-Fi; no
★   outdoor bar; expensive valet parking. $ *Rooms from: $279* ⊠ *505 N.*

Fort Lauderdale Beach Blvd., Along the beach ☎ *954/760–7177* ⊕ *www. fortlauderdalebeachresort.hilton.com* ⇆ *374 rooms* ⊚ *No meals.*

$$$$
RESORT
FAMILY
🏨 **Lago Mar Resort and Club.** The sprawling, kid-friendly Lago Mar, owned by the Banks family since the early 1950s, retains its sparkle and a refreshed old Florida feel thanks to frequent renovations; brilliantly colored bougainvillea edges the swimming lagoon, and you have direct access to a large private beach in an exclusive neighborhood. **Pros:** secluded setting; plenty of activities; on the very private Harbor beach. **Cons:** not easy to find; far from restaurants and beach action. ⑤ *Rooms from: $425* ✉ *1700 S. Ocean La., Along the beach* ☎ *954/523–6511, 800/524–6627* ⊕ *www.lagomar.com* ⇆ *52 rooms, 160 suites* ⊚ *No meals.*

$$$
RESORT
FAMILY
Fodor's Choice
★
🏨 **Marriott Harbor Beach Resort.** Bill Marriott's personal choice for his annual four-week family vacation, the Marriott Harbor Beach Resort sits on a quarter-mile swath of private beach and bursts with the luxe beachfront personality of an upscale Caribbean resort. **Pros:** excellent gym; all rooms have balconies; great eating outlets; no resort fees. **Cons:** Wi-Fi isn't free; expensive parking; interiors are new but feel a little cookie-cutter. ⑤ *Rooms from: $379* ✉ *3030 Holiday Dr., Along the beach* ☎ *954/525–4000* ⊕ *www.marriottharborbeach.com* ⇆ *650 roooms, 31 suites* ⊚ *No meals.*

$$
RESORT
FAMILY
🏨 **Pelican Grand Beach Resort.** Smack on Fort Lauderdale beach, this yellow spired, Key West–style, Noble House property fuses a heritage of Old Florida seaside charm with understated luxury; there's renovated rooms upstairs, an amazing beachfront, an old-fashioned emporium, and Fort Lauderdale's only lazy river. **Pros:** free popcorn in the Postcard Lounge; directly on the beach; Ocean 2000 restaurant. **Cons:** high tide can swallow most of beach area; small fitness center. ⑤ *Rooms from: $272* ✉ *2000 N. Atlantic Blvd., Along the beach* ☎ *954/568–9431, 800/525–6232* ⊕ *www.pelicanbeach.com* ⇆ *156 rooms* ⊚ *No meals.*

$$$
B&B/INN
🏨 **The Pillars Hotel.** Once a "small secret" kept by locals in the know, this elegant boutique gem, sandwiched between Fort Lauderdale beach and the Intracoastal Waterway, rarely falls below capacity since it invariably lands on reader's choice lists. **Pros:** attentive staff; lovely décor; idyllic pool area. **Cons:** small rooms; not for families with young kids given proximity to dock and water with no lifeguard on duty. ⑤ *Rooms from: $309* ✉ *111 N. Birch Rd., Along the beach* ☎ *954/467–9639* ⊕ *www. pillarshotel.com* ⇆ *13 rooms, 5 suites* ⊚ *No meals.*

$$$$
HOTEL
Fodor's Choice
★
🏨 **The Ritz-Carlton, Fort Lauderdale.** Inspired by the design of an opulent luxury liner, 24 dramatically tiered, glass-walled stories rise from the sea, forming a sumptuous Ritz-Carlton hotel with guest rooms that reinvent a golden era of luxury travel, a lavish tropical sundeck and infinity-edge pool peering over the ocean, and a Club Lounge that spans an entire floor. **Pros:** prime beach location; modern seaside elegance deviates dramatically from traditional Ritz-Carlton décor; sensational Club Lounge. **Cons:** no complimentary Wi-Fi; expensive valet parking. ⑤ *Rooms from: $429* ✉ *1 N. Fort Lauderdale Beach Blvd., Along the beach* ☎ *954/465–2300* ⊕ *www.ritzcarlton.com/FortLauderdale* ⇆ *138 rooms, 54 suites* ⊚ *No meals.*

$$ ⬚ **Sheraton Fort Lauderdale Beach Hotel.** As part of its global rebranding,
HOTEL   Sheraton has reinvented (and renamed) its Fort Lauderdale landmark—
once the Sheraton Yankee Clipper Hotel—with updated interiors and
public spaces throughout its four towers of rooms and suites. **Pros:** Fri-
day night retro mermaid show in swimming pool; proximity to beach;
excellent gym. **Cons:** small rooms; low ceilings in lobby; faded exte-
riors. *⑤ Rooms from: $229 ✉ 1140 Seabreeze Blvd., Along the beach
☎ 954/524–5551 ⊕ www.sheratonftlauderdalebeach.com ⇌ 486 rooms
❖ No meals.*

$$ ⬚ **The Westin Beach Resort & Spa, Fort Lauderdale.** Smack-dab in the center
RESORT   of Fort Lauderdale Beach and connected directly to the beach through a
FAMILY   private overpass, the hotel once known as the Sheraton Yankee Trader
has been transformed into a modern convention-centric Westin. **Pros:**
direct beach access; heavenly beds and spa. **Cons:** lengthy walks to
get to some rooms; fee for Wi-Fi; a lot of conventioneers. *⑤ Rooms
from: $289 ✉ 321 N. Fort Lauderdale Beach Blvd., Along the beach
☎ 954/467–1111 ⊕ www.westin.com/fortlauderdalebeach ⇌ 433
rooms ❖ No meals.*

$$$ ⬚ **W Fort Lauderdale.** Fort Lauderdale's trendiest hotel—equipped with
HOTEL   a rooftop see-through swimming pool, a wide range of spectacular
Fodor's Choice   contemporary rooms and suites, and an easy-on-the-eyes youthful
★   crowd—boasts a vibe highly reminiscent of South Beach. **Pros:** trendy
and flashy; tony scene; amazing pool; great spa. **Cons:** party atmo-
sphere not for everyone; impersonal service. *⑤ Rooms from: $355
✉ 435 N. Fort Lauderdale Beach Blvd., Along the beach ☎ 954/462–
1633 ⊕ www.wfortlauderdalehotel.com ⇌ 346 rooms, 171 condo-
miniums ❖ No meals.*

$ ⬚ **Worthington Guest House.** Located five minutes from gay Sebastian
B&B/INN   Beach, this hotel is one of Fort Lauderdale Beach's 27 clothing-optional
guesthouses for gay men. **Pros:** fresh-squeezed orange juice in the morn-
ing; nice pool area; ability to also hang out at sister properties Alcazar
and Villa Venice. **Cons:** not on the beach; windows open towards fence
or other buildings. *⑤ Rooms from: $165 ✉ 543 N. Birch Rd., Along
the beach ☎ 954/563–6819 ⊕ www.theworthington.com ⇌ 14 rooms
❖ Breakfast.*

INTRACOASTAL AND INLAND

$$ ⬚ **Gallery ONE by DoubleTree.** A condo hotel favored by vacationers
HOTEL   preferring longer stays, the residential-style Gallery ONE rises over the
Intracoastal, within short walking distance of both Fort Lauderdale
Beach and the city's popular Galleria Mall. **Pros:** walking distance to
both beach and supermarket; easy water taxi access; good for longer
stays. **Cons:** pool area needs refurbishment; kitchens don't have stoves;
no bathtubs. *⑤ Rooms from: $209 ✉ 2670 E. Sunrise Blvd., Intra-
coastal and Inland ☎ 954/565–3800 ⊕ www.doubletree.com ⇌ 231
rooms ❖ No meals.*

$ ⬚ **Hilton Fort Lauderdale Marina.** After a $72 million renovation in 2011,
RESORT   the mammoth, 589-room, 20-boat-slip Hilton Fort Lauderdale Marina
FAMILY   infused luxury and modernity into its charming Key West style. **Pros:**
Fodor's Choice   sexy fire pit; outdoor bar popular with locals; easy water taxi access.
★   **Cons:** no bathtubs in tower rooms; small fitness center. *⑤ Rooms from:*

Lago Mar Resort and Club in Fort Lauderdale has its own private beach on the Atlantic Ocean.

$189 ✉ *1881 S.E. 17th St., Intracoastal and Inland* ☎ *954/463–4000* ⊕ *www.fortlauderdalemarinahotel.com* ⌂ *589 rooms* �‖*No meals.*

$$
RESORT
🏨 **Hyatt Regency Pier Sixty-Six Resort & Spa.** Don't let the 1970s exterior of the iconic 17-story tower fool you; this lovely 22-acre resort teems with contemporary interior-design sophistication and remains one of Florida's few hotels where a rental car isn't necessary. **Pros:** great views; plenty of activities; free shuttle to beach; easy Water Taxi access. **Cons:** tower rooms are far less stylish than lanai rooms; totally retro rotating rooftop is used exclusively for private events. ⑤ *Rooms from: $219* ✉ *2301 S.E. 17th St. Causeway, Intracoastal and Inland* ☎ *954/525– 6666* ⊕ *www.pier66.hyatt.com* ⌂ *384 rooms* �‖*No meals.*

$$
HOTEL
FAMILY
🏨 **Il Lugano Luxury Suite Hotel.** This all-suite condo hotel on Fort Lauderdale's northern Intracoastal waterway offers all the comforts of home (washer, dryer, kitchenette, fridge, sleeper sofa, huge terraces) with all the glamour of a hyper-modern trendsetting hotel. **Pros:** 800-square-foot rooms; easy water taxi access; good for longer stays. **Cons:** limited sunlight in pool area; need wheels to reach main beach and downtown area. ⑤ *Rooms from: $289* ✉ *3333 N.E. 32nd Ave., Intracoastal and Inland* ☎ *954/564–4400* ⊕ *www.illugano.com* ⌂ *28 suites* �‖*No meals.*

WESTERN SUBURBS

$
HOTEL
FAMILY
🏨 **Bonaventure Resort & Spa.** This massive suburban enclave—formerly a Hyatt Regency–flagged resort—targets conventioneers and business executives as well as international vacationers who value golf, the Everglades, and shopping over beach proximity. Factor in the allure of the huge and soothing aLaya Spa and the "Choose Your Journey" package

that includes a spa treatment with the room, and you'll see why. **Pros:** lush landscaping; pampering spa; great in-house restaurant, Ireland's Steakhouse. **Cons:** difficult to find; in the suburbs; poor views from some rooms. ⑤ *Rooms from: $169* ⊠ *250 Racquet Club Rd., Westin* ☎ *954/389–3300* ⊕ *www.bonaventureresortandspa.com* ⌁ *501 rooms* ⍗ *No meals.*

NIGHTLIFE AND PERFORMING ARTS

For the most complete weekly listing of events, check "Showtime!," the *South Florida Sun-Sentinel*'s tabloid-size entertainment section and events calendar published on Friday. "Weekend," in the Friday Broward edition of the *Herald,* also lists area happenings. The weekly *City Link* and *New Times Broward* are free alternative newspapers, detailing plenty of entertainment and nightlife options. For the latest happenings in GLBT nightlife, visit **Mark's List** (⊕ *www.jumponmarkslist.com*), the online authority of all things GLBT in South Florida or pick up one of the weekly gay rags, *MARK* or *Hot Spots.*

NIGHTLIFE

DOWNTOWN AND LAS OLAS

The majority of Fort Lauderdale nightlife takes place near downtown, beginning on Himmarshee Street (2nd Street) and continuing on to the Riverfront, and then to Las Olas Boulevard. The downtown Riverfront tends to draw a younger demographic somewhere between underage teens and late twenties. On Himmarshee Street, a dozen rowdy bars and clubs, ranging from the seedy to the sophisticated, entice a wide range of partygoers. Toward East Las Olas Boulevard, near the financial towers and boutique shops, bars cater to the yuppie crowd.

Maguire's Hill 16. With the requisite lineup of libations and pub-style food, this classic Irish pub is good for no-frills fun, fried eats, and daily live music. It's famous locally as the oldest award-winning Traditional Irish Pub and Restaurant in Fort Lauderdale. Live music is on tap every Wednesday, Friday, and Saturday night. ⊠ *535 N. Andrews Ave., Downtown and Las Olas* ☎ *954/764–4453* ⊕ *www.maguireshill16.com.*

O Lounge. This lounge and two adjacent establishments, **Yolo** and **Vibe,** on Las Olas and under the same ownership, cater to Fort Lauderdale's sexy yuppies, business men, desperate housewives, and hungry cougars letting loose during happy hour and on the weekends. Crowds alternate between Yolo's outdoor fire pit, O Lounge's chilled atmosphere and lounge music, and Vibe's more intense beats. Expect flashy cars in the driveway and a bit of plastic surgery. ⊠ *333 E. Las Olas Blvd., Downtown and Las Olas* ☎ *954/523–1000* ⊕ *www.yolorestaurant.com.*

Off the Hookah. After a not-very-visible $21 million renovation in 2012, the downtown space formerly home to Voodoo Lounge returned as Off the Hookah. Totally revamped from top to bottom and filled with VIP areas, Hookah attempts to reinstate the late-night electro and pop parties that made downtown Fort Lauderdale famous circa 2006. The club also regularly hosts local and national talent. The long-running Sunday gay-straight mixer, Life's a Drag, continues on from its Voodoo days. It's a fun-filled night of drag performances and incriminating debauchery.

✉ *111 S.W. 2nd Ave., Downtown and Las Olas* ☎ *954/761–8686* ⊕ *www.offthehookah.com.*

ROK: BRG. Downtown Fort Lauderdale warmly welcomed this personality-driven burger bar and gastro-pub in early 2011, giving the grown-ups something to enjoy in teenage-infested downtown. The long and narrow venue, adorned with exposed-brick walls and flat-screen TVs is great for watching sports and for mingling on weekends. Locals come here for the great cocktails and beer selection. ✉ *208 S.W. 2nd St., Downtown and Las Olas* ☎ *954/525–7656* ⊕ *www.rokbrgr.com.*

Fodor'sChoice ★ **Tap 42 Bar and Kitchen.** With 42 rotating draft beers from around the U.S., 50-plus bourbons, a few dozen original cocktails (including beer cocktails), and 66 bottled craft beers, awesome drinks and good times headline a typical evening at classy cool Tap 42. Although the indoor/outdoor gastro-pub is a bit off the beaten path, it's well worth the detour. The 42 drafts protrude from a stylish wall constructed of pennies, surfacing more like a work of art than a beer-filling station. The venue attracts large crowds of young professionals for nights of heavy drinking and highly caloric new-age bar eats. ✉ *1411 S. Andrews Ave., Downtown and Las Olas* ☎ *954/463–4900* ⊕ *www.tap42.com.*

Fodor'sChoice ★ **Tarpon Bend.** This casual two-story restaurant transforms into a jovial resto-bar in the early evening, ideal for enjoying a few beers, mojitos, and some great bar food. It's consistently busy, day, night, and late night with young professionals, couples, and large groups of friends. It's one place that has survived all the ups and downs of downtown Fort Lauderdale. ✉ *200 S.W. 2nd St., Downtown and Las Olas* ☎ *954/523–3233* ⊕ *www.tarponbend.com.*

ALONG THE BEACH

Given its roots as a beachside party town, it's hard to believe that Fort Lauderdale Beach offers very few options in terms of nightlife. A few dive bars are at opposite ends of the main strip, near Sunrise Boulevard and Route A1A, as well as Las Olas Boulevard and A1A. On the main thoroughfare between Las Olas and Sunrise, a few high-end bars at the beach's show-stopping hotels have become popular, namely those at the W Fort Lauderdale.

Elbo Room. You can't go wrong wallowing in the past, lifting a drink, and exercising your elbow at the Elbo, a noisy, suds-drenched hot spot since 1938. It seems like nothing has changed here since Fort Lauderdale's spring-break heyday, and the clientele still includes far too many scantily clad girls that will do anything for booze. At least the bathrooms were redone in 2011. The watering hole phased out food (except for light nibbles) ages ago, but kept a hokey sense of humor: upstairs a sign proclaims, "We don't serve women here. You have to bring your own." ✉ *241 S. Fort Lauderdale Blvd., Along the beach* ☎ *954/463–4615* ⊕ *www.elboroom.com.*

Living Room at the W. The large living-room-like space next to the lobby of the W Fort Lauderdale transforms into a major house-party-style event, mainly on weekends. There are plenty of plush couches, but it's usually standing-room-only early for this South Beach–style throw-down, with great DJs, awesome libations, and an easy-on-the-eyes crowd. A breezy and beautiful outdoor area is idyllic for the overflow, as is the downstairs lounge, Whiskey Blue (which is only open Thursday–Saturday). ⊠ *W Fort Lauderdale, 401 N. Fort Lauderdale Beach Blvd., Along the beach* ☎ *954/414–8300* ⊕ *www.wfortlauderdalehotel. com/living-room.*

Parrot Lounge. An old-school Fort Lauderdale hangout, this dive bar/ sports bar is particularly popular with Philadelphia Eagles fans, those longing to recall *Where the Boys Are,* and folks reminiscing about Fort Lauderdale's big-hair, sprayed-tan, Sun-In-bright 1980s heyday. This place is stuck in the past, but it's got great libations, wings, fingers, poppers, and skins. 'Nuff said. ⊠ *911 Sunrise La., Along the beach* ☎ *954/563–1493* ⊕ *www.parrotlounge.com.*

INTRACOASTAL AND INLAND

Bars and pubs along Fort Lauderdale's Intracoastal cater to the city's large, transient boating community. Heading inland along Sunrise Boulevard, the bars around Galleria Mall target thirty- and fortysomething singles.

Blue Martini Fort Lauderdale. A hot spot for thirtysomething-plus adults gone wild, Blue Martini's menu is filled with tons of innovative martini creations (42 to be exact) and lots of cougars on the prowl, searching for a first, second, or even third husband. And the guys aren't complaining! The drinks are great and the scene is fun for everyone, even those who aren't single and looking to mingle. ⊠ *Galleria Fort Lauderdale, 2432 E. Sunrise Blvd., Intracoastal and Inland* ☎ *954/653–2583* ⊕ *www. bluemartinilounge.com.*

Kim's Alley Bar. Around since 1948, Kim's Alley Bar is the ultimate no-frills South Florida dive bar, a neighborhood spot in a strip mall near the Intracoastal. It has two smoke-filled bar areas, a jukebox, and pool tables that provide endless entertainment (if the patrons aren't providing enough diversion). ⊠ *The Gateway, 1920 E. Sunrise Blvd., Intracoastal and Inland* ☎ *954/763–2143.*

WILTON MANORS AND OAKLAND PARK

Fort Lauderdale's gay nightlife is most prevalent in Wilton Manors, affectionately termed Fort Lauderdale's "gayborhood." Wilton Drive, known as "the Drive," has dozens of bars, clubs, and lounges that cater to all types of GLBT subcultures.

Georgie's Alibi. A Fort Lauderdale GBLT institution, Georgie's Alibi is an anchor for the Wilton Manors gay community. The gargantuan pub fills to capacity for $3, 32-ounce Long Island Iced Tea Thursdays (from 9 pm 'til close). Any night of the week, Alibi stands out as a kind of gay Cheers of Fort Lauderdale—a neighborhood bar with darts, pool, libations, and some eye candy, offering a no-frills, laid-back attitude. ⊠ *2266 Wilton Dr., Wilton Manors and Oakland Park* ☎ *954/565–2526* ⊕ *www.alibiwiltonmanors.com.*

The Manor. Inspired by The Abbey in West Hollywood, The Manor sought to offer a one-stop gay party shop in the heart of the Wilton Manors gayborhood. It didn't quite work out that way, but the multifaceted two-story enclave is still open Friday for the campy pop night Bubble Gum Fridays and the circuit-party style Epic Saturdays.

✉ *2345 Wilton Dr., Wilton Manors and Oakland Park* ☎ *954/626–0082* ⊕ *www.themanorcomplex.com.*

Fodor's Choice ★ **Rosie's Bar and Grill.** Rosie's is consistently lively, pumping out tons of pop tunes and volumes of joyous laughter to surrounding streets. The former Hamburger Mary's has become an institution in South Florida as the go-to gay-friendly place for cheap drinks, decent bar food, and great times. Most of the fun at Rosie's is meeting new friends and engaging in conversation with the person seated next to you. Drink specials change daily. Sunday brunch with alternating DJs is wildly popular. ✉ *2449 Wilton Dr., Wilton Manors and Oakland Park* ☎ *954/563–0123* ⊕ *www.facebook.com/RosiesBarAndGrill.*

Sidelines. One of the most popular and consistently busy joints on "The Drive" is this spacious sports and video bar that taps into the butch side of gay culture. The bar is often locally awarded the "Best Gay Bar in South Florida," and its all-welcoming vibe draws crowds both young and old, men and women. Expect large crowds during major football and basketball games. ✉ *2031-A Wilton Dr., Wilton Manors* ☎ *954/563–8001* ⊕ *www.sidelinessports.com.*

WESTERN SUBURBS AND BEYOND

Florida's cowboy country, Davie, offers country-western fun out in the 'burbs. In addition, South Florida's Native American tribes have long offered gambling on Indian Territory near Broward's western suburbs. With new laws, Broward's casinos offer Vegas-style slot machines and even blackjack. Hollywood's Seminole Hard Rock Hotel & Casino offers the most elegant of Broward's casino experiences. ⇨ *See Nightlife in Hollywood.*

SHOPPING

MALLS

Galleria Fort Lauderdale. Fort Lauderdale's most upscale mall is just west of the Intracoastal Waterway. The split-level emporium entices with Neiman Marcus, Dillard's, Macy's, an Apple Store plus 150 specialty shops for anything from cookware to exquisite jewelry. Chow down at Capital Grille, Truluck's, P. F. Chang's, or Seasons 52, or head for the food court, which will defy expectations with its international food-market feel. The mall itself is open Monday through Saturday 10–9, Sunday noon–6. The standalone restaurants and bars, like Capital Grille and Blue Martini Fort Lauderdale, are open later. ✉ *2414 E. Sunrise Blvd., Intracoastal and Inland* ☎ *954/564–1036* ⊕ *www.galleriamall-fl.com.*

FAMILY Fodor's Choice ★ **Sawgrass Mills.** This alligator-shaped megamall draws 26 million shoppers a year to its collection of 400 outlet stores and name-brand discounters. The mall claims to be the second-largest attraction in Florida—second only to Disney World. Though that claim is probably an exaggeration, you should prepare for insane crowds even during off-peak hours and seasons. ✉ *12801 W. Sunrise Blvd., at Flamingo Rd., Sunrise* ⊕ *www.sawgrassmills.com.*

Swap Shop. For those who grew up in Fort Lauderdale, the Swap Shop's cheesy commercials of yesteryear will forever remain. "Where's the bargains?" "At the Swap Shop!" The South's largest flea market, with 2,000 vendors, is open daily. Thankfully, they've done away with the awful circus after years of protests by animal-rights activists. While exploring this indoor–outdoor entertainment-and-shopping complex, hop on the carousel, try some fresh sugarcane juice, or stick around for movies at the 14-screen Swap Shop drive-in. ⊠ *3291 W. Sunrise Blvd., Western Suburbs and Beyond* ☎ *954/791–7927* ⊕ *www.floridaswapshop.com.*

SHOPPING DISTRICTS

The Gallery at Beach Place. Just north of Las Olas Boulevard on Route A1A, this shopping gallery is attached to the mammoth Marriott Beach Place timeshare. Spaces are occupied by touristy shops that sell everything from sarongs to alligator heads, chain restaurants like Hooter's, bars serving frozen drinks, and a supersize CVS pharmacy, which sells everything you need for the beach. ■TIP➔ **Beach Place has covered parking, and usually has plenty of spaces, but you can pinch pennies by using a nearby municipal lot that's metered.** ⊠ *17 S. Fort Lauderdale Beach Blvd., Along the beach* ⊕ *www.galleryatbeachplace.com.*

Fodor'sChoice   **Las Olas Boulevard.** Las Olas Boulevard is the heart and soul of Fort Lau-
★   derdale. Not only are fifty of the city's best boutiques, thirty top restaurants, and a dozen art galleries found along this beautifully landscaped street, but Las Olas links Fort Lauderdale's growing downtown with its superlative beaches. Though you'll find a Cheesecake Factory on the boulevard, the thoroughfare tends to shun chains and welcomes one-of-a-kind clothing boutiques, chocolatiers, and ethnic eateries. Window shopping allowed. ⊠ *East Las Olas Blvd., Downtown and Las Olas* ⊕ *www.lasolasboulevard.com.*

FOOD

Chef Jean-Pierre Cooking School. Catering to locals, seasonal snowbirds, and folks winging in for even shorter stays, Jean-Pierre Brehier (former owner of the Left Bank Restaurant on Las Olas) teaches the basics, from boiling water onward. The enthusiastic Gallic transplant has appeared on NBC's *Today* among other shows. Choose from demonstration classes, hands-on classes, and a full series of cooking classes. Book ahead as classes often fill up. For souvenir hunters, this fun cooking facility also sells nifty pots, pastas, oils, and other great items. ⊠ *1436 N. Federal Hwy., Intracoastal and Inland* ☎ *954/563–2700* ⊕ *www.chefjp.com* ✉ *From $65 per demonstration class, $125 hands-on class; "Cooking 101" and "Cooking 102" series $350 each* ☉ *Store Mon.–Sat. 10–7, class schedules vary.*

SPORTS AND THE OUTDOORS

BIKING

Among the most popular routes are Route A1A and Bayview Drive, especially in early morning before traffic builds, and a 7-mile bike path that parallels State Road 84 and New River and leads to Markham Park, which has mountain-bike trails. ■TIP➔ **Alligator alert: Do not dangle your legs from seawalls.**

Broward B–cycle. The big-city trend of "pay and ride" bicycles has now reached Broward County. With 40 station locations over 20 scenic miles, from as far south as Hallandale to as far north as Pompano Beach and Coconut Creek, bikes can be rented for as little as 30 minutes or as long as a week, and can be picked up and dropped off at any and all stations in Broward County. Most stations are found downtown and along the beach. This is an excellent green and health-conscious way to explore Fort Lauderdale. Please note, however, that helmets are not provided at the kiosks. ⊕ *www.broward.bcycle.com.*

FISHING

Bahia Mar Marina. If you're interested in a saltwater charter, check out the offerings at the marina of the Bahia Mar Fort Lauderdale Beach Hotel, A DoubleTree by Hilton. Sportfishing and drift-fishing bookings can be arranged. Snorkeling and diving outfitter Sea Experience also leaves from here, as does the famous *Jungle Queen* steamboat. In addition, the water taxi makes regular stops here. ⊠ *Bahia Mar Fort Lauderdale Beach Hotel, A DoubleTree by Hilton, 801 Seabreeze Blvd., Along the beach* ☎ *954/627–6309.*

RODEOS

Davie Pro Rodeo. It may sound strange, but South Florida has a rather large cowboy scene, concentrated in the western suburb of Davie. And for over four decades, the Bergeron Rodeo Grounds has surfaced as Davie's biggest tourist attraction. Throughout the year, the Rodeo hosts national tours and festivals as well as the annual Southeaster Circuit Finals. Check the website for the exact dates of these rodeos. ⊠ *Davie Pro Rodeo Arena, 4271 Davie Rd., Davie* ☎ *954/680–8005* ⊕ *www. davieprorodeo.com.*

SCUBA DIVING AND SNORKELING

Lauderdale Diver. A PADI 5-Star Certification Agency, this dive center facilitates daily trips on a variety of dive boats up and down Broward's shoreline (they don't have their own boat but work with a handful of preferred outfitters). A variety of snorkeling, reef diving, and wreck diving trips are offered daily as well as scuba diving lessons. ⊠ *1334 S.E. 17th St., Intracoastal and Inland* ☎ *954/467–2822* ⊕ *www. lauderdalediver.com.*

FAMILY **Sea Experience.** The *Sea Experience I* leaves daily at 10:15 am and 2:15 pm for two-hour glass-bottom-boat and snorkeling combination trips that explore Fort Lauderdale's offshore reefs. The tour costs $28 ($7 more to snorkel, equipment provided). They also offer beginner and more advanced scuba diving experiences. ⊠ *Bahia Mar Fort Lauderdale Beach Hotel, A DoubleTree by Hilton, 801 Seabreeze Blvd., Along the beach* ☎ *954/770–3483* ⊕ *www.seaxp.com.*

SEGWAY TOURS

FAMILY
Fodor'sChoice
★
M.Cruz Rentals. M.Cruz Rentals offers Segway tours of Fort Lauderdale Beach four times per day and bicycle rentals by the hour. The rental facility is at the beach entrance of Hugh Taylor Birch State Park, just north of hotel row. The Segway Tours leave from here as well. Staff are exceptionally friendly and accommodating. ⊠ *Hugh Taylor Birch*

State Park, 3109 E. Sunrise Blvd., Along the beach ☎ *954/235–5082* ⊕ *www.mcruzrentals.com.*

TENNIS

Jimmy Evert Tennis Center. With 22 courts (18 lighted clay courts, 3 hard courts, and a low-compression sand "beach" court), this is the crown jewel of Fort Lauderdale's public tennis facilities. Legendary champ Chris Evert learned her two-handed backhand here under the watchful eye of her now-retired father, Jimmy, the center's tennis pro for 37 years. ⊠ *Holiday Park, 701 N.E. 12th Ave., Intracoastal and Inland* ☎ *954/828–5378* ⊕ *www.fortlauderdale.gov/tennis/jetc.htm* 🖃 *$18 day pass (for Broward nonresidents)* ⊗ *Weekdays 7:45 am–9 pm, weekends 7:45 am–6 pm.*

NORTH ON SCENIC A1A

North of Fort Lauderdale's Birch Recreation Area, Route A1A edges away from the beach through a stretch known as Galt Ocean Mile, and a succession of oceanside communities line up against the sea. Traffic can line up, too, as it passes through a changing pattern of beach-blocking high-rises and modest family vacation towns and back again. As far as tourism goes, these communities tend to cater to a different demographic than Fort Lauderdale. Europeans and cost-conscious families head to Lauderdale-by-the-Sea, Pompano, and Deerfield for fewer frills and longer stays.

Towns are shown on the Broward County map.

LAUDERDALE-BY-THE-SEA

Lauderdale-by-the-Sea is 5 miles north of Fort Lauderdale.

Just north of Fort Lauderdale's northern boundary, this low-rise family resort town traditionally digs in its heels at the mere mention of high-rises. The result is choice shoreline access that's rapidly disappearing in nearby communities. Without a doubt, Lauderdale-by-the-Sea takes delight in embracing its small beach-town feel and welcoming guests to a different world of years gone by.

GETTING HERE AND AROUND

Lauderdale-by-the-Sea is just north of Fort Lauderdale. If you're driving from Interstate 95, exit east onto Commercial Boulevard and head over the Intracoastal Waterway. From U.S. 1 (aka Federal Highway), turn east on Commercial Boulevard. If coming from A1A, just continue north from Fort Lauderdale Beach.

ESSENTIALS

Visitor Information Lauderdale-by-the-Sea Chamber of Commerce ☎ *954/776–1000* ⊕ *www.lbts.com.*

BEACHES

FAMILY **Lauderdale-by-the-Sea Beach.** Especially popular with divers and snorkelers, this laid-back stretch of sand provides great access to lovely coral reefs. When you're not underwater, look up and you'll likely see

a pelican flying by. Gentle trade winds make this an utterly relaxing retreat from the hubbub of Fort Lauderdale's busier beaches. That said, the southern part of the beach at Commercial Boulevard and A1A is often busy due to a concentrated number of restaurants at the intersection, including the wildly popular Aruba Beach Café. Going north from Commercial Boulevard the beach is lined with no-frills hotels and small inns for families and vacationers visiting Fort Lauderdale for longer periods of time, mainly Europeans. Look for metered parking around Commercial Boulevard and A1A. **Amenities:** food and drink; lifeguards; parking (fee). **Best for:** solitude; snorkeling; swimming. ⊠ *Commercial Blvd. at Rte. A1A.*

WHERE TO EAT

$$ ✕ **Aruba Beach Café.** This casual beachfront eatery is always crowded
CAFÉ   and always fun. One of Lauderdale-by-the-Sea's most famous restau-
FAMILY   rants, Aruba Beach serves a wide range of American and Caribbean cuisine, including Caribbean conch chowder and conch fritters. There are also fresh tropical salads, sandwiches, and seafood. The café is famous for its divine fresh-baked Bimini bread with Aruba glaze (think challah with donut glaze). A band performs day and night, so head for the back corner with excellent views of the beach if you want conversation while you eat and drink. Sunday breakfast buffet starts at 9 am. ⑤ *Average main: $20* ⊠ *1 Commercial Blvd.* ☎ *954/776–0001* ⊕ *www. arubabeachcafe.com.*

$$$ ✕ **Blue Moon Fish Company.** Most tables have stellar views of the Intra-
SEAFOOD   coastal Waterway, but Blue Moon East's true magic comes from the kitchen, where the chefs create moon-and-stars-worthy seafood dishes. It's also the best deal in town with a two-for-one word-of-mouth lunch special Monday through Saturday. Start with whole roasted garlic and bread and continue on to the mussels, the baby spinach and pecan-crusted goat-cheese-fritter salad (with caramelized onions and blackened shrimp), or pan-seared fresh-shucked oysters. For Sunday's champagne brunch book early, even in the off-season. They now also offer Saturday brunch, too, but it's an à la carte menu not like Sunday's grand buffet. ⑤ *Average main: $40* ⊠ *4405 W. Tradewinds Ave.* ☎ *954/267–9888* ⊕ *www.bluemoonfishco.com.*

$ ✕ **LaSpada's Original Hoagies.** The crew at this seaside hole-in-the-wall
AMERICAN   puts on quite a show of ingredient-tossing flair while assembling takeout hoagies, subs, and deli sandwiches. Locals rave that they are the best around. LaSpada's popularity has resulted in higher prices and the addition of four other South Florida locations, taking away from the joint's former one-of-a-kind appeal. Fill up on the foot-long "Monster" (ham, cheese, roast beef, and turkey piled high), "Hot Meatballs Marinara," or an assortment of salads. ⑤ *Average main: $12* ⊠ *4346 Seagrape Dr.* ☎ *954/776–7893* ⊕ *www.laspadashoagies.com.*

WHERE TO STAY

$ 🏨 **Blue Seas Courtyard.** Husband-and-wife team Cristie and Marc Furth
B&B/INN   run this quaint Mexican-themed motel across the street from Lauderdale-by-the-Sea's family-friendly beaches. **Pros:** south-of-the-border vibe; friendly owners; vintage stoves from 1971; memory-foam mattress toppers. **Cons:** rooms lack ocean views; old bathtubs in some rooms.

$ *Rooms from: $163* ⊠ *4525 El Mar Dr.* ☎ *954/772–3336* ⊕ *www. blueseascourtyard.com* ⟿ *12 rooms* ⦿⨾ *Breakfast.*

$$ ⛭ **High Noon Beach Resort.** Family-run since 1961, this hotel sits on
HOTEL 300 feet of beautiful beach, with plenty of cozy spots and an old-school homey ambience that keeps repeat visitors coming back for more. **Pros:** smack on the beach; friendly vibe; great staff. **Cons:** early booking required; not on "happening" part of beach. $ *Rooms from: $201* ⊠ *4424 El Mar Dr.* ☎ *954/776–1121, 800/382–1265* ⊕ *www. highnoonresort.com* ⟿ *40 rooms* ⦿⨾ *Breakfast.*

$ ⛭ **Sea Lord Hotel & Suites.** This attractive oceanside hotel received major
HOTEL upgrades in 2010, including a new pool deck, restaurant, lobby, sundeck, entranceway, small fitness center, and room enhancements. **Pros:** terrific beach location; void of the moldy smell in nearby older hotels. **Cons:** shaky elevators; limited parking. $ *Rooms from: $170* ⊠ *4140 El Mar Dr.* ☎ *954/776–1505, 800/344–4451* ⊕ *www.sealordhotel.com* ⟿ *47 rooms* ⦿⨾ *Breakfast.*

$$ ⛭ **Tropic Seas Resort Motel.** This two-story property has an unbeatable
HOTEL location—directly on the beach, flanking 150 feet of pristine sands and
FAMILY sparkling blues—and is a favorite of annual European vacationers looking for longer stays. **Pros:** family-owned friendliness; great lawn furniture. **Cons:** must reserve far ahead; dated bathrooms. $ *Rooms from: $205* ⊠ *4616 El Mar Dr.* ☎ *954/772–2555, 800/952–9581* ⊕ *www. tropicseasresort.com* ⟿ *16 rooms* ⦿⨾ *Breakfast.*

SPORTS AND THE OUTDOORS

Anglin's Fishing Pier. This longtime favorite for 24-hour fishing has a fresh, renovated appearance after shaking off repeated storm damage that closed the pier at intervals during the past decade. ⊠ *2 Commercial Blvd.* ☎ *954/491–9403* ⊕ *www.boatlessfishing.com/anglins.htm.*

HOLLYWOOD

Hollywood has had several face-lifts to shed its old-school image, but there's still something delightfully retro about the city. Young Circle, once down-at-heel, is now Broward's first Arts Park. On Hollywood's western outskirts, the flamboyant Seminole Hard Rock Hotel & Casino has enlivened this previously downtrodden section of the State Road 7/U.S. 441 corridor, drawing local weekenders, architecture buffs, partiers, and gamblers. But Hollywood's redevelopment efforts don't end there: new shops, restaurants, and art galleries open at a persistent clip, and the city has continually spiffed up its boardwalk—a wide pedestrian walkway along the beach—where local joggers are as commonplace as sun-seeking snowbirds from the north. On the coast of Hallandale, the beach is backed by older, towering condominiums. Inland, Hallandale has been trying to get some business from neighboring Aventura and Sunny Isles in Dade County with the development of the high-end Village at Gulfstream Park, a luxury retail arcade anchored by a reinvented casino and race track.

GETTING HERE AND AROUND

From Interstate 95, exit east on Sheridan Street or Hollywood Boulevard for Hollywood or Hallandale Beach Boulevard for either Hollywood or Hallandale.

ESSENTIALS

Visitor Information Hollywood Community Redevelopment Agency
☎ 954/924–2980 ⊕ www.visithollywoodfl.org.

EXPLORING

FAMILY **Arts Park at Young Circle.** This 10-acre urban park has completely transformed the run-down traffic circle linking downtown Hollywood with its beaches into a beautiful, lively public space. There's no shortage of things to do here: a huge playground beckons for the little ones, a state-of-the-art amphitheater hosts regular concerts, and educational workshop spaces host regular events, like Friday glassblowing workshops and jewelry-making classes. ⊠ *1 Young Circle, Hollywood Blvd. and U.S. 1* ☎ *954/921–3500* ⊕ *www.visithollywoodfl.org/artspark.aspx.*

Downtown Hollywood Art & Design District. From 21st Avenue to Young Circle on Hollywood Boulevard and Harrison Street, the streets are peppered with boutiques, bistros, sidewalk cafés, and galleries featuring original artwork (eclectic paintings, sculpture, photography, and mixed media).

IGFA Fishing Hall of Fame and Museum. This creation of the International Game Fishing Association is a shrine to the sport. It has an extensive museum and research library where seven galleries feature fantasy fishing and other interactive displays. At the Catch Gallery, you can cast off virtually to reel in a marlin, sailfish, trout, tarpon, or bass. (If you suddenly get an urge to gear up for your own adventures, a Bass Pro Shops Outdoor World is next door.) ⊠ *300 Gulf Stream Way* ☎ *954/922–4212* ⊕ *www.igfa.org* ⊡ *$10* ⊗ *Mon.–Sat. 10–6, Sun. noon–6.*

FAMILY **West Lake Park.** Rent a canoe, kayak, or take the 40-minute boat tour at this park bordering the Intracoastal Waterway. At 1,500 acres, it is one of Florida's largest urban nature facilities. Extensive boardwalks traverse mangrove forests that shelter endangered and threatened species. A 65-foot observation tower showcases the entire park. At the free **Anne Kolb Nature Center,** named after Broward's late environmental advocate, there's a 3,500-gallon aquarium. The center's exhibit hall has 27 interactive displays. ⊠ *1200 Sheridan St.* ☎ *954/357–5161* ⊕ *www.broward.org/parks/WestLakePark* ⊡ *Weekends $1.50, weekdays free* ⊗ *Park daily 9–6:30, Nature Center daily 9–5.*

BEACHES

FAMILY **Hollywood Beach and Broadwalk.** The name might be Hollywood, but
Fodor's Choice there's nothing hip or chic about **Hollywood North Beach Park**, which
★ sits at the north end of Hollywood (Route A1A and Sheridan Street), before the pedestrian Broadwalk begins. And that's a good thing. It's just a laid-back, old-fashioned place to enjoy the sun, sand, and sea. The film *Marley & Me*, starring Jennifer Aniston and Owen Wilson and

filmed in Greater Fort Lauderdale, spurred a comeback for dog beaches in South Florida, and ever since then, the year-round **Dog Beach of Hollywood** in North Beach Park has allowed dogs to enjoy fun in the sun from 3 to 7 pm Friday–Sunday (4 to 8 pm during Daylight Savings Time). Farther south on Hollywood beach, the 2.5-mile **Broadwalk** is a delightful throwback to the '50s, with mom-and-pop stores, ice cream parlors, elderly couples going for long strolls, and families building sand castles on the beach. Thanks to millions in investment, this popular stretch of beach has spiffy features like a pristine pedestrian walkway, a concrete bike path, a crushed-shell jogging path, an 18-inch decorative wall separating the Broadwalk from the sand, and places to shower off after a dip. Expect to hear French spoken throughout Hollywood, since its beaches have long been a favorite getaway for Quebecois. **Amenities:** food and drink; lifeguards; parking (fee); toilets. **Best for:** sunrise; swimming; walking. ⊠ *Rte. A1A from Dania Beach Blvd. to Halladale Beach Blvd.* 🚗 *Parking in public lots is $1.75 per hr.*

John U. Lloyd Beach State Recreation Area. The once pine-dotted natural area was restored to its natural state, thanks to government-driven efforts to pull out all but indigenous plants. Now native sea grape, gumbo-limbo, and other native plants offer shaded ambience. Nature trails and a marina are large draws as is canoeing on Whiskey Creek. The beaches are also excellent, but beware of mosquitos in summer! **Amenities:** parking (fee); toilets. **Best for:** solitude; sunrise. ⊠ *6503 N. Ocean Dr.* ☎ *954/923–2833* ⊕ *www.floridastateparks.org/lloydbeach* 🚗 *$6 per vehicle for 2–8 passengers, $4 for lone driver* ⊙ *Daily 8–sunset.*

WHERE TO EAT

$$$
ITALIAN
Fodor'sChoice
★

✕ **Café Martorano.** Located within Seminole Hard Rock's adjoining entertainment and restaurant zone, this Italian-American institution pays homage to anything and everything that has to do with the "Godfather" and impresses with humongous family-style portions. Dishes run the full Italian-American gamut, from the classic parmigianas to the lobster and snapper francese. The homemade mozzarella and fried calamari are excellent choices for starters. It's easy to gorge here since each dish is so succulent and savory. The ever-present *Godfather* motif is taken to the extreme—dinner is interrupted hourly with clips from the movie played on the surrounding flat screens. There's an undeniable nightclub vibe to the joint, especially later into the night. $ *Average main: $27* ⊠ *5751 Seminole Way* ☎ *954/584–4450* ⊕ *www.cafemartorano.com* ⊙ *No lunch.*

$$$$
STEAKHOUSE
Fodor'sChoice
★

✕ **Hollywood Prime.** Hollywood's superlative choice for fine dining, the intimate 15-table Hollywood Prime is a classic American steakhouse done right. A living slice of golden-age glamour, the restaurant's ambience recalls a bygone era of dress-up dining in South Florida, where decked-out patrons are rightfully treated as VIPs. Perfected steakhouse classics headline the menu: jumbo shrimp cocktail, lobster bisque, onion soup gratinée, Caesar salad, 21-day dry-aged prime steaks including a 28-ounce prime porterhouse and an 18-ounce prime ribeye as well as a 3½-pound Maine lobster (yes, you read correctly!). All this is complemented by a wine list with more than 600 fine wines. It doesn't get much better than this. Oh wait, it does! The key lime pie is a divine intervention of creamy tart pie, buttery crust, fresh whipped cream, and white chocolate. ⑤ *Average main: $67* ⊠ *The Westin Diplomat Resort & Spa, 3555 S. Ocean Dr.* ☎ *954/602–8347* ⊕ *www.hollywoodprime. com* ⌲ *Reservations essential* ⊘ *No lunch.*

$ × **Jaxson's Ice Cream Parlour & Restaurant.** This 1950s landmark whips
AMERICAN up malts, shakes, and jumbo sundaes from ice creams prepared daily
FAMILY on premises, plus sandwiches and salads, amid an antique-license-plate
Fodor'sChoice décor. Owner Monroe Udell's trademarked Kitchen Sink—a small sink
★ full of ice cream, topped by sparklers—for parties of four or more goes for $12.75 per person (no sharing). Those wanting a sample before committing to a flavor, think again. The oh-so-popular Jaxson's doesn't give samples! ⑤ *Average main: $13* ⊠ *128 S. Federal Hwy.* ☎ *954/923–4445* ⊕ *www.jaxsonsicecream.com.*

$$ × **LeTub.** Once a Sunoco gas station, this quirky waterside saloon has an
AMERICAN enduring affection for claw-foot bathtubs. Hand-painted porcelain is everywhere—under ficus, sea grape, and palm trees. If a potty doesn't appeal, there's a secluded swing facing the water north of the main dining area. Despite molasses-slow service and an abundance of flies at sundown, this eatery is favored by locals, and management seemed genuinely appalled when hordes of trend-seeking city slickers started jamming bar stools and tables after Oprah declared its thick, juicy Angus burgers the best around. A 13-oz. Sirloin burger and large fries will run you around $16. ⚠ **There's no children's menu and no children allowed after 8 pm.** ⑤ *Average main: $16* ⊠ *1100 N. Ocean Dr.* ☎ *954/921–9425* ⊕ *www.theletub.com.*

$$$ × **Taverna Opa.** It's a Greek throwdown every night at this Hollywood
GREEK institution, chock-full of loud music, belly dancers, napkin throwing, and most importantly, delectable Greek food. Expect a lively night of great eats (including amazing hot and cold meze, wood-fire grilled meats, and seafood), tabletop dancing, and awkward moments (especially when suburban dads with two left feet decide to get in on the act). ■TIP➜ **Best experienced with a large group and plenty of alcohol.** ⑤ *Average main: $23* ⊠ *410 N. Ocean Dr.* ☎ *954/929–4010* ⊕ *www. www.tavernaopa.com/hollywood.*

WHERE TO STAY

$ ⛺ **Manta Ray Inn.** Canadians Donna and Dwayne Boucher run this
RENTAL immaculate, affordable circa 1940s, two-story complex of apartment units that sits right on the beach. **Pros:** on the beach; low-key atmosphere. **Cons:** no restaurant; no pool (but access to one next door is included). ⑤ *Rooms from: $199* ⊠ *1715 S. Surf Rd.* ☎ *954/921–9666, 800/255–0595* ⊕ *www.mantarayinn.com* ⌲ *12 units* ⃒⊙⃒ *No meals.*

$$ ⛺ **Seminole Hard Rock Hotel & Casino.** On the industrial flatlands of west-
HOTEL ern Hollywood, the Seminole Hard Rock Hotel & Casino serves as a magnet for pulsating Vegas-style entertainment and folks looking for 24 hours of casino, clubbing, and hedonism. **Pros:** nonstop entertainment; plenty of activities; rooms renovated in 2012. **Cons:** in an unsavory

neighborhood; no tourist sights in close proximity; endless entertainment can be exhausting. $ *Rooms from: $259* ⊠ *1 Seminole Way* ☎ *866/502–7529, 800/937–0010* ⊕ *www.seminolehardrockhollywood. com* ⤳ *395 rooms, 86 suites* ⦿| *No meals.*

$$$$
RESORT
FAMILY
Fodor's Choice
★
The Westin Diplomat Resort & Spa. This colossal 39-story, contemporary, triple-tower property effectively brings style, sophistication, and pizzazz to Hollywood Beach with its massive, 60-foot-high atrium, casual-chic guest rooms, a 120-foot bridged infinity pool (extending from lobby to oceanfront), one of South Florida's largest and most high-design spas, and a handful of excellent restaurants. **Pros:** heavenly beds for adults and kids; excellent gym; eye-popping architecture. **Cons:** large complex; numerous conventioneers. $ *Rooms from: $415* ⊠ *3555 S. Ocean Dr.* ☎ *954/602–6000, 888/627–9057* ⊕ *www.diplomatresort.com* ⤳ *902 rooms, 96 suites* ⦿| *No meals.*

NIGHTLIFE

Fodor's Choice
★
Seminole Hard Rock Casino. The glitzy, Vegas-style Seminole Hard Rock Casino is the superlative gaming and entertainment complex in Florida. Though located in a somewhat downtrodden area of inland Hollywood, once inside the Hard Rock enclave, you'll be mesmerized by the excitement radiating from the 145,000-square-foot casino, the 5,500-seat arena (Hard Rock Live), a dozen restaurants, and near dozen bars and nightclubs. The casino has blackjack, baccarat, three-card poker, more than 2,500 gaming machines, and just under 100 tables. It's open 24/7 and is connected to a hotel tower and entertainment complex, including great nightlife options such as an Improv Comedy Club, an outpost of the famous European club Pangaea, a classic piano bar, and two other multilevel nightclubs. While weekends are guaranteed party-hard mayhem, not all clubs are open on weekdays so check Hard Rock's detailed, user-friendly website for schedules. ■**TIP→ The Seminole Hard Rock is not to be confused with its neighbor, the smoky and seedy Seminole Casino of Hollywood.** ⊠ *1 Seminole Way* ☎ *866/502–7529* ⊕ *www. seminolehardrockhollywood.com.*

SPORTS AND THE OUTDOORS

FISHING

Sea Legs III. *Sea Legs III* goes out three times daily, fishing for wahoo, yellowtail, grouper, and kingfish. Two 4½-hour drift-fishing trips run during the day (one at 8 am, the other at 1:30 pm), and bottom-fishing trips run nightly from 7 to midnight. Day trips cost $38, night trips $40, both including rod rental. ⊠ *5398 N. Ocean Dr.* ☎ *954/923–2109* ⊕ *www.deepseafishingsealegs.com.*

PALM BEACH AND THE TREASURE COAST

WELCOME TO PALM BEACH

TOP REASONS TO GO

★ **Exquisite resorts:** Two grandes dames, the Breakers and the Boca Raton Resort & Club, perpetually draw the rich, the famous, and anyone else who can afford the luxury. The Eau Palm Beach and Four Seasons sparkle with service fit for royalty.

★ **Beautiful beaches:** From Jupiter, where dogs run free, to Stuart's tubular waves, to the broad stretches of sand in Delray Beach and Boca Raton, swimmers, surfers, sunbathers—and sea turtles looking for a place to hatch their eggs—all find happiness.

★ **Top-notch golf:** The Champion Course and re-envisioned Fazio Course at PGA National Resort & Spa are world-renowned; pros sharpen up at PGA Village.

★ **Horse around:** Wellington, with its popular polo season, is often called the winter equestrian capital of the world.

★ **Excellent fishing:** The Atlantic Ocean, teeming with kingfish, sailfish, and wahoo, is a treasure chest for anglers.

1 Greater Palm Beach. With Gatsby-era architecture, stone-and-stucco estates, and extravagant dining, Palm Beach is a must-see for travelers to the area. Plan to spend time on Worth Avenue, also known as the Mink Mile, a collection of more than 200 chic shops, and Whitehall, the palatial retreat for Palm Beach's founder, Henry Flagler. West Palm Beach and its environs—Lake Worth, Palm Beach Gardens, and Singer Island—are bustling with their own identities. Culture fans have plenty to cheer about with the Kravis Center and Norton Museum of Art; sports enthusiasts will have a ball golfing or boating; and kids love Lion Country Safari.

2 Delray Beach. Its lively downtown, with galleries, independent boutiques, and trendy restaurants right by the water, is perfect for strolling. To the west is the unique Morikami Museum and Japanese Gardens.

3 Boca Raton. An abundance of modern shopping plazas mix with historic buildings from the 1920s, masterpieces by renowned architect Addison Mizner. Parks line much of the oceanfront.

4 Treasure Coast. Northern Palm Beach County and beyond remains blissfully low-key, with fishing towns, spring-training stadiums, and ecotourism attractions until you hit the cosmopolitan—yet understated—Vero Beach.

GETTING ORIENTED

This diverse region extends 120 miles from laid-back Sebastian to tony Boca Raton. The area's glitzy epicenter, Palm Beach, attracts socialites, the well-heeled, and interested onlookers. The northernmost cities are only about 100 miles from Orlando, making that area an ideal choice for families wanting some beach time to go with their visit to Mickey Mouse. Delightfully funky Delray Beach is only an hour north of Miami. The Intracoastal Waterway runs parallel to the ocean and transforms from a canal to a tidal lagoon separating islands from the mainland, starting with Palm Beach and moving northward to Singer Island (Palm Beach Shores and Riviera Beach), Jupiter Island, Hutchinson Island (Stuart, Jensen Beach, and Fort Pierce), and Orchid Island (Vero Beach and Sebastian).

6

By Paul Rubio A golden stretch of the Atlantic shore, the Palm Beach area resists categorization, and for good reason: the territory stretching south to Boca Raton, appropriately coined the Gold Coast, defines old-world glamour and new-age sophistication.

To the north you'll uncover the comparatively undeveloped Treasure Coast—liberally sprinkled with seaside gems and wide-open spaces along the road awaiting your discovery. Speaking of discovery, its moniker came from the 1715 sinking of a Spanish fleet that dumped gold, jewels, and silver in the waters; today the *Urca de Lima*, one of the original 11 ships and now an undersea "museum," can be explored by scuba divers.

Altogether, there's a delightful disparity between Palm Beach, pulsing with old-money wealth, and under-the-radar Hutchinson Island. Seductive as the gorgeous beaches, eclectic dining, and leisurely pursuits can be, you should also take advantage of flourishing commitments to historic preservation and the arts, as town after town yields intriguing museums, galleries, theaters, and gardens.

Palm Beach, proud of its status as America's first luxe resort destination and still glimmering with its trademark Mediterranean-revival mansions, manicured hedges, and highbrow shops, can rule supreme as the focal point for your sojourn any time of year. From there, head off in one of two directions: south toward Delray Beach and Boca Raton along an especially scenic estate-dotted route known as A1A, or back north to the beautiful barrier islands of the Treasure Coast. For rustic inland activities such as bass fishing and biking on the dike around Lake Okeechobee, head west.

PLANNING

WHEN TO GO

The weather is optimal from November through May, but the trade-off is that roadways and hotels are more crowded and prices higher. If the scene is what you're after, try the early weeks of December when the "season" isn't yet in full swing. However, be warned that after Easter, the crowd relocates to the Hamptons, and Palm Beach feels like another universe. For some, that's a blessing—and a great time to take advantage of lower summer lodging rates (the Breakers runs promos at a fourth its regular cost). Hurricanes can show up from June to November, but there's always plenty of notice. More important, you'll need to bring your tolerance for heat, humidity, and afternoon downpours.

GETTING HERE AND AROUND

AIR TRAVEL

If you're flying into the area, the most convenient airport is Palm Beach International Airport in West Palm, but it's possible (and sometimes cheaper) to fly to Fort Lauderdale or Orlando. Try to rent a car if you plan on exploring. Interstate 95 runs north–south, linking West Palm Beach with Fort Lauderdale and Miami to the south and with Daytona, Jacksonville, and the rest of the Atlantic Coast to the north. Florida's Turnpike runs from Miami north through West Palm Beach before angling northwest to reach Orlando. U.S. 1 threads north–south along the coast, connecting most coastal communities, whereas the more scenic Route A1A, also called Ocean Boulevard or Ocean Drive, depending on where you are, ventures out onto the barrier islands. I–95 runs parallel to U.S. 1, but a few miles inland.

From the airport, call Southeastern Florida Transportation Group, a local hotline for cabs, airport shuttles, and private sedans.

Airport Palm Beach International Airport (*PBI*). ⊠ *1000 Turnage Blvd., West Palm Beach* ☎ *561/471–7420* ⊕ *www.pbia.org.*

Airport Transfers Southeastern Florida Transportation Group ☎ *561/777–7777* ⊕ *www.yellowcabflorida.com.*

BUS TRAVEL

The county's bus service, Palm Tran, runs two routes (nos. 44 and 40) that offer daily service connecting the airport, the Tri-Rail stop near it, and locations in central West Palm Beach. A network of 34 routes joins towns all across the area; it's $5 for a day pass. The free Downtown Trolley connects the West Palm Beach Amtrak station and the Tri-Rail stop in West Palm on its Green Line. Its Yellow Line makes continuous loops down Clematis Street, the city's main stretch of restaurants and watering holes interspersed with stores, and through CityPlace, a shopping-dining-theater district. Hop on and off at any of the seven stops. The trolley's Yellow Line runs Sunday to Wednesday 11–9 and Thursday to Saturday 11–11. The trolley's Green Line, which stretches farther east, west, and south, runs weekdays 7–6, Saturday 9–6, and Sunday 11–6.

Contacts **Downtown Trolley** ☎ 561/833–8873 ⊕ www.westpalmbeachdda. com/transportation. **Palm Tran** ☎ 561/841–4287 ⊕ www.pbcgov.com/palmtran.

TRAIN TRAVEL

Amtrak stops daily in West Palm Beach. The West Palm Beach station is at the same location as the Tri-Rail stop, so the same free shuttle, the Downtown Trolley (⊕ *www. westpalmbeachdda.com/transportation*), is available (via the trolley's Green Line).

Tri-Rail Commuter Service is a rail system with 18 stops altogether between West Palm Beach and Miami; tickets can be purchased at each stop, and a one-way trip from the first to the last point is $6.90 weekdays, $5 weekends. Three stations—West Palm Beach, Lake Worth, and Boca—have free shuttles to their downtowns, and taxis are on call at others.

Contacts **Amtrak** ☎ 800/872–7245 ⊕ www.amtrak.com. **Tri-Rail** ☎ 800/874–7245 ⊕ www.tri-rail.com.

HOTELS •

Palm Beach has a number of smaller hotels in addition to the famous Breakers. Lower-priced hotels and bed-and-breakfasts can be found in West Palm Beach and Lake Worth. Heading south, the oceanside town of Manalapan has the Eau Palm Beach Resort & Spa. The Seagate Hotel & Spa sparkles in Delray Beach, and the posh Boca Beach Club lines the superlative swathe of shoreline in Boca Raton. In the opposite direction there's the PGA National Resort & Spa, and across from it by the water is the Marriott on Singer Island, a well-kept secret for spacious, sleek suites. Even farther north, Vero Beach has a collection of luxury boutique hotels, as well as more modest options along the Treasure Coast. To the west, towns close to Lake Okeechobee offer country-inn accommodations.

Hotel reviews have been shortened. For full information, visit Fodors. com.

RESTAURANTS

Numerous elegant establishments offer upscale American, Continental, and international cuisine, but the area also is chock-full of casual waterfront spots serving affordable burgers and fresh seafood feasts. Grouper, fried or blackened, is especially popular here, along with the ubiquitous shrimp. Happy hours and early-bird menus, Florida hallmarks, typically entice the budget-minded with several dinner entrées at reduced prices offered during certain hours, usually before 5 or 6.

WHAT IT COSTS				
	$	$$	$$$	$$$$
RESTAURANTS	under $16	$16–$20	$21–$30	over $30
HOTELS	under $201	$201–$300	$301–$400	over $400

Restaurant prices are the average cost of a main course at dinner or, if dinner is not served, at lunch. Hotel prices are the lowest cost of a standard double room in high season.

VISITOR INFORMATION

Contacts **Palm Beach County Convention and Visitors Bureau** ✉ *1555 Palm Beach Lakes Blvd., Ste. 800, West Palm Beach* ☎ *561/233–3000* ⊕ *www. palmbeachfl.com.*

PALM BEACH

70 miles north of Miami, off I–95.

Long reigning as the place where the crème de la crème go to shake off winter's chill, Palm Beach, which is actually on a barrier island, continues to be a seasonal hotbed of platinum-grade consumption. The town celebrated its 100th birthday in 2011, and there's no competing with its historic social supremacy. It's been the winter address for heirs of the iconic Rockefeller, Vanderbilt, Colgate, Post, Kellogg, and Kennedy families. Even newer power brokers, with names like Kravis, Peltz, and Trump, are made to understand that strict laws govern everything from building to landscaping, and not so much as a pool awning gets added without a town council nod. Only three bridges allow entry, and huge tour buses are a no-no.

To learn "who's who" in Palm Beach, it helps to pick up a copy of the *Palm Beach Daily News*—locals call it the Shiny Sheet because its high-quality paper avoids smudging society hands or Pratesi linens—for, as it's said, to be mentioned in the Shiny Sheet is to be Palm Beach.

All this fabled ambience started with Henry Morrison Flagler, Florida's premier developer, and cofounder, along with John D. Rockefeller, of Standard Oil. No sooner did Flagler bring the railroad to Florida in the 1890s than he erected the famed Royal Poinciana and Breakers hotels. Rail access sent real-estate prices soaring, and ever since, princely sums have been forked over for personal stationery engraved with 33480, the zip code of Palm Beach (which didn't actually get its status as an independent municipality until 1911). Setting the tone in this town of unparalleled Florida opulence is the ornate architectural work of Addison Mizner, who began designing homes and public buildings here in the 1920s and whose Moorish-Gothic Mediterranean-revival style has influenced virtually all landmarks.

But the greater Palm Beach area is much larger and encompasses several communities on the mainland and to the north and south. To provide Palm Beach with servants and other workers, Flagler created an off-island community across the Intracoastal Waterway (also referred to as Lake Worth in these parts). West Palm Beach, now cosmopolitan and noteworthy in its own right, evolved into an economically vibrant business hub and a sprawling playground with some of the best nightlife and cultural attractions around, including the glittering Kravis Center for the Performing Arts, the region's principal entertainment venue. The mammoth Palm Beach County Judicial Center and Courthouse and the State Administrative Building underscore the breadth of the city's governmental and corporate activity.

The burgeoning equestrian development of Wellington, with its horse shows and polo matches, lies a little more than 10 miles west of downtown, and is the site of much of the county's growth.

Spreading southward from the Palm Beach/West Palm Beach nucleus set between the two bridges that flow from Royal Poinciana Way and Royal Palm Way into Flagler Drive on the mainland are small cities like Lake Worth, with its charming artsy center, Lantana, and Manalapan (home to the fabulous Eau resort, formerly the Ritz-Carlton Palm Beach). All three have turf that's technically on the same island as Palm Beach, and at its bottom edge across the inlet is Boynton Beach, a 20-minute drive from Worth Avenue.

Most visitors don't realize that West Palm Beach itself doesn't have any beaches, so locals and guests hop over to Palm Beach or any of the communities just mentioned—or they head 15 minutes north to the residential Singer Island towns of Palm Beach Shores and Riviera Beach, known for their marinas and laid-back vibe. Another option is Peanut Island, which sits in the Intracoastal between Palm Beach and Singer Island, and to Juno Beach. Suburban Palm Beach Gardens, a paradise for golfers and shoppers (malls abound), is inland from Singer Island and 15 minutes northwest of downtown West Palm Beach. Because of its upscale slant, it has a ton of restaurants and bars (both independents and chains).

GETTING HERE AND AROUND
Palm Beach is 70 miles north of Miami. To access Palm Beach off I–95, exit east at Southern Boulevard, Belvedere Road, or Okeechobee Boulevard. To drive from Palm Beach to Lake Worth, Lantana, Manalapan, and Boynton Beach, head south on Ocean Boulevard/Route A1A; Lake Worth is roughly 6 miles south, and Boynton is another 6. Similarly, to reach them from West Palm Beach, take U.S. 1 or I–95. To travel between Palm Beach and Singer Island, you must cross over to West Palm before returning to the beach. Once there, go north on U.S. 1 and then cut over on Blue Heron Boulevard/Route 708. If coming straight from the airport or somewhere farther west, take I–95 up to the same exit and proceed east. The main drag in Palm Beach Gardens is PGA Boulevard/Route 786, which is 4 miles north on U.S. 1 and I–95; A1A merges with it as it exits the top part of Singer Island. Continue on A1A to reach Juno Beach.

TOURS
FAMILY **DivaDuck Amphibious Tours.** Running 75 minutes, these duck tours go in and out of the water on USCG-inspected amphibious vessels around West Palm Beach and Palm Beach. The tours depart two or three times most days for $25 per person; there are big discounts for kids. ⊠ *City-Place, 600 S. Rosemary Ave., corner of Hibiscus St. and Rosemary Ave., West Palm Beach* ☎ *877/844–4188* ⊕ *www.divaduck.com.*

Island Living Tours. Book a private mansion-viewing excursion around Palm Beach, and hear the storied past of the island's upper crust. Owner Leslie Diver also hosts an Antique Row Tour and a Worth Avenue Shopping Tour. All vehicle tours are 3 hours and from $60 per person to $150 per person, depending on the vehicle used. Leslie also

Draped in European elegance, the Breakers in Palm Beach sits on 140 acres along the oceanfront.

runs 90-minute bicycle tours through Palm Beach ($35, not including bike rental). One bicycle tour explores the Estate Section and historic Worth Avenue; another explores the island's lesser-known North End. Call in advance for location and to reserve. ☎ 561/868-7944 ⊕ *www. islandlivingpb.com.*

EXPLORING

PALM BEACH
Most streets around major attractions and commercial zones have free parking as well as metered spaces. If you can stake out a place between a Rolls Royce and a Bentley, do so, but beware of the "Parking by Permit Only" signs, as a $25 ticket might take the shine off your spot. Better yet, if you plan to spend an entire afternoon strolling Worth Avenue, valet-park at the garage next to Saks Fifth Avenue that's a block in from Ocean Boulevard (if you've reached South County Road you've gone too far); some stores will validate your parking ticket.

TOP ATTRACTIONS
Bethesda-by-the-Sea. Donald Trump and his wife, Melania were married here in 2005, but this gothic-style Episcopal church had a claim to fame upon its creation in 1926: it was built by the first Protestant congregation in southeast Florida. Church lecture tours, covering Bethesda's history, architecture, and more, are offered at 12:15 on the second and fourth Sunday each month from September to May (excluding December) and at 11:15 on the fourth Sunday each month from June to August. Adjacent is the formal, ornamental Cluett Memorial

Garden. ✉ *141 S. County Rd.* ☎ *561/655–4554* ⊕ *www.bbts.org*
⌦ *Free* ⊙ *Church and gardens daily 9–5.*

Fodor's Choice **The Breakers.** Built by Henry Flagler in 1896 and rebuilt by his descen-
★ dants after a 1925 fire, this magnificent Italian Renaissance–style resort
helped launch Florida tourism with its Gilded Age opulence, attracting influential wealthy Northerners to the state. The hotel, still owned
by Flagler's heirs, is a must-see even if you aren't staying here. Walk
through the 200-foot-long lobby, which has soaring arched ceilings
painted by 72 Italian artisans and hung with crystal chandeliers, and
the ornate Florentine Dining Room, decorated with 15th-century Flemish tapestries. ▪TIP➔ **Book a pampering spa treatment or dine on top
of the Seafood Bar's whimsical aquarium counter, where leggy green
starfish prance below your plate, and the $20 parking is free.** ✉ *1 S.
County Rd.* ☎ *561/655–6611* ⊕ *www.thebreakers.com.*

Fodor's Choice **Henry Morrison Flagler Museum.** The worldly sophistication of Florida's
★ Gilded Age lives on at Whitehall, the plush 55-room "marble palace"
Henry Flagler commissioned in 1901 for his third wife, Mary Lily
Kenan. Architects John Carrère and Thomas Hastings were instructed
to create the finest home imaginable—and they outdid themselves.
Whitehall rivals the grandeur of European palaces and has an entrance
hall with a baroque ceiling similar to Louis XIV's Versailles. Here you'll
see original furnishings; a hidden staircase Flagler used to sneak from
his bedroom to the billiards room; an art collection; a 1,200-pipe organ;
and Florida East Coast Railway exhibits, along with Flagler's personal
railcar, No. 91, showcased in an 8,000-square-foot beaux-arts-style
pavilion behind the mansion. Docent-led tours and audio tours are
included with admission. The museum's Café des Beaux-Arts, open
from Thanksgiving through mid-April, offers a Gilded Age–style early
afternoon tea for $40 (11:30–2:30); the price includes museum admis-
sion. ✉ *1 Whitehall Way* ☎ *561/655–2833* ⊕ *www.flaglermuseum.us*
⌦ *$18* ⊙ *Tues.–Sat. 10–5, Sun. noon–5.*

WORTH NOTING

El Solano. No Palm Beach mansion better represents the town's luminous
legacy than the Spanish-style home built by Addison Mizner as his own
residence in 1925. Mizner later sold El Solano to Harold Vanderbilt,
and the property was long a favorite among socialites for parties and
photo shoots. Vanderbilt held many a gala fund-raiser here. Beatle John
Lennon and his wife, Yoko Ono, bought it less than a year before Lennon's death. It's still privately owned and not open to the public, but
it's well worth a drive-by on any self-guided Palm Beach mansion tour.
✉ *720 S. Ocean Blvd.*

Mar-a-Lago. Breakfast-food heiress Marjorie Merriweather Post com-
missioned a Hollywood set designer to create Ocean Boulevard's famed
Mar-a-Lago, a 114-room, 110,000-square-foot Mediterranean-revival
palace. Its 75-foot Italianate tower is visible from many areas of Palm
Beach and from across the Intracoastal Waterway in West Palm Beach.
Owner Donald Trump has turned it into a private membership club.
So you'll have to enjoy the view from the car window unless you have

Palm Beach and
West Palm Beach

CLOSE UP

The Mansions of Palm Beach

Whether you aspire to be a Kennedy, Donald Trump, or Rod Stewart—all onetime or current Palm Beach residents—no trip to the island is complete without gawking at the megamansions lining its perfectly manicured streets.

No one is more associated with how the island took shape than Addison Mizner, architect extraordinaire and society darling of the 1920s. But what people may not know is that a "fab four" was really the force behind the residential streets as they appear today: Mizner, of course, plus Maurice Fatio, Marion Sims Wyeth, and John Volk.

The four architects dabbled in different genres, some more so than others, but the unmissable style is Mediterranean revival, a Palm Beach hallmark mix of stucco walls, Spanish red-tile roofs, Italianate towers, Moorish-Gothic carvings, and the uniquely Floridian use of coquina, a grayish porous limestone made of coral rock with fossil-like imprints of shells. As for Mizner himself, he had quite the repertoire of signature elements, including using differently sized and shaped windows on one facade, blue tile work inside and out, and tiered roof lines (instead of one straight-sloping panel across, having several sections overlap like scales on a fish).

The majority of preserved estates are clustered in three sections: along Worth Avenue; the few blocks of South County Road after crossing Worth and the streets shooting off it; and the 5-mile stretch of South Ocean Boulevard from Barton Avenue to near Phipps Ocean Park, where the condos begin cropping up.

If 10 miles of riding on a bike while cars zip around you isn't intimidating, the two-wheeled trip may be the best way to fully take in the beauty of the mansions and surrounding scenery. Many hotels have bicycles for guest use. Another option is the dependable Palm Beach Bicycle Trail Shop (☎ 561/659–4583 ⊕ www.palmbeach-bicycle.com). Otherwise, driving is a good alternative. Just be mindful that Ocean Boulevard is a one-lane road and the only route on the island to cities like Lake Worth and Manalapan, so you can't go too slowly, especially at peak travel times.

If gossip is more your speed, in-the-know concierges rely on Leslie Diver's "Island Living Tours" (☎ 561/868–7944 ⊕ www.islandlivingpb.com); she's one of the town's leading experts on architecture *and* dish, both past and present.

Top 10 Self-Guided Stops: (1) Casa de Leoni, 450 Worth Avenue (Addison Mizner); (2) Villa des Cygnes, 456 Worth Avenue (Addison Mizner and Marion Sims Wyeth); (3) 17 Golfview Road (Marion Sims Wyeth); (4) 220 and 252 El Bravo Way (John Volk); (5) 126 South Ocean Boulevard (Marion Sims Wyeth); (6) El Solano, 720 South Ocean Boulevard (Addison Mizner); (7) Casa Nana, 780 South Ocean Boulevard (Addison Mizner); (8) 920 and 930 South Ocean Boulevard (Maurice Fatio); (9) Mar-a-Lago, 1100 South Ocean Boulevard (Joseph Urban); (10) Il Palmetto, 1500 South Ocean Boulevard (Maurice Fatio).

—Dorothea Hunter Sönne

The Armory Art Center in West Palm Beach helps students of all ages create works of art in various mediums.

a membership. ✉ *1100 S. Ocean Blvd.* ☎ *561/832–2600* ⊕ *www.maralagoclub.com.*

WEST PALM BEACH

Long considered Palm Beach's less privileged stepsister, West Palm Beach has come into its own over the past 35 years, and just in this millennium the $30 million Centennial Square waterfront complex at the eastern end of Clematis Street, with piers, a pavilion, and an amphitheater, has transformed West Palm into an attractive, easy-to-walk downtown area—not to mention there's the Downtown Trolley that connects the shopping-and-entertainment mecca CityPlace with restaurant-and-lounge-lined Clematis Street. West Palm is especially well regarded for its arts scene, with unique museums and performance venues.

The city's outskirts, vast flat stretches with fast-food outlets and car dealerships, may not inspire, but are worth driving through to reach attractions scattered around the southern and western reaches. Several sites are especially rewarding for children and other animal and nature lovers.

TOP ATTRACTIONS

Ann Norton Sculpture Gardens. This landmarked complex is a testament to the creative genius of the late American sculptor Ann Weaver Norton (1905–1982), who was the second wife of the Norton Museum founder, industrialist Ralph H. Norton. A set of art galleries in the studio and main house where she lived is surrounded by two acres of gardens with 300 species of rare palm trees, eight brick megaliths, a monumental figure in Norwegian granite, and plantings designed to attract native birds. ⊠ *253 Barcelona Rd.* ☎ *561/832–5328* ⊕ *www.ansg.org* 🖃 *$10* ⊗ *Wed.–Sun. 10–4.* ⊗ *Closed Aug.*

FAMILY **Lion Country Safari.** Drive your own vehicle along four miles of paved roads through a cageless zoo with free-roaming animals (chances are you'll have a giraffe nudging at your window) and then let loose in a 55-acre fun-land with camel rides, bird feedings, and a pontoon-boat cruise past islands with monkeys. A CD included with admission narrates the winding trek past white rhinos, zebras, and ostriches grouped into exhibits like Gir Forest that's modeled after a sanctuary in India and has native twisted-horned blackbuck antelope and water buffalo. (For obvious reasons, lions are fenced off, and no convertibles or pets are allowed.) Aside from dozens more up-close critter encounters after debarking, including a petting zoo, kids can go paddleboating, do a round of mini-golf, climb aboard carnival rides, or have a splash in a 4,000-square-foot aquatic playground (some extra fees apply). ⊠ *2003 Lion Country Safari Rd., at Southern Blvd.* W ☎ *561/793–1084* ⊕ *www. lioncountrysafari.com* 🖃 *$29.95, $6 parking* ⊗ *Mid-Dec.–Aug., daily 9:30–5:30 (last entry at 4:30); Sept.–Dec., daily 10–5 (last entry at 4).*

Mounts Botanical Garden. The oldest public green space in the county is, unbelievably, across the road from the West Palm Beach airport; but the planes are the last thing you notice while walking around and relaxing amid the nearly 14 acres of exotic trees, rain-forest flora, and butterfly and water gardens. The gift shop contains a selection of rare gardening books on tropical climes. ⊠ *531 N. Military Trail* ☎ *561/233–1757* ⊕ *www.mounts.org* 🖃 *$5 (suggested donation)* ⊗ *Mon.–Sat. 8:30–4, Sun. noon–4.*

National Croquet Center. The world's largest croquet complex, the 10-acre center is also the headquarters for the U.S. Croquet Association. Vast expanses of orderly lawns are the stage for fierce competitions. There's also a clubhouse with a pro shop and the Croquet Grille, with verandas for dining and viewing (armchair enthusiasts can enjoy the games for no charge). You don't have to be a member to try your hand out on the lawns, and on Saturday morning at 10 am, there's a free group lesson with an introduction to the game and open play; call in advance to reserve a spot. ⊠ *700 Florida Mango Rd., at Summit Blvd.* ☎ *561/478–2300* ⊕ *www.croquetnational.com* 🖃 *Center free; full day of croquet $25* ⊗ *Tues.–Sun. 9–5.*

Fodor's Choice **Norton Museum of Art.** Constructed in 1941 by steel magnate Ralph H.
★ Norton and his wife, Elizabeth, it has grown to become one of the most impressive museums in South Florida with an extensive collection of 19th- and 20th-century American and European paintings—including works by Picasso, Monet, Matisse, Pollock, Cassatt, and O'Keeffe— plus Chinese art, earlier European art, and photography. There is a sublime outdoor sculpture garden, a glass ceiling by Dale Chihuly, a gift shop, and a schedule of lectures, programs, and concerts for adults and children. Galleries showcase traveling exhibits, too. ■TIP➔ **One of the city's best-kept secrets is the gourmet restaurant Fratelli Lyon in the West Courtyard of the Museum. Lunch is served Tuesday–Sunday; an a la carte dinner menu is available on Thursday evenings.** ⊠ *1451 S.*

Olive Ave. ☎ *561/832–5196* ⊕ *www.norton.org* ✉ *$12* ☾ *Tues.–Wed. and Fri.–Sat. 10–5, Thurs. 10–9, Sun. 11–5.*

WORTH NOTING

Richard and Pat Johnson Palm Beach County History Museum. A beautifully restored 1916 courthouse downtown opened its doors in 2008 as the permanent home of the Historical Society of Palm Beach County's collection of artifacts and records dating back before the town's start—a highlight is furniture and decorative objects from Mizner Industries (a real treat since many of his mansions are not open to the public). ✉ *300 N. Dixie Hwy.* ☎ *561/832–4164* ⊕ *www.historicalsocietypbc. org* ✉ *Free* ☾ *Tues.–Sat. 10–5.*

FAMILY **South Florida Science Museum.** Aside from permanent exhibits with outta-this-world finds like moon and Mars rocks and a 232-pound meteorite, there are fresh- and saltwater aquariums, daily planetarium shows, and even 9 holes of mini-golf. On the second Saturday of each month, the planetarium offers three separate laser shows (at 6:30, 7:30, and 8:30) incorporating music from the likes of Dave Matthews, Pink Floyd, and Michael Jackson. ✉ *4801 Dreher Trail N* ☎ *561/832–1988* ⊕ *www. sfsciencecenter.org* ✉ *$15, laser show $10* ☾ *Weekdays 10–5, weekends 10–6.*

LAKE WORTH

For years, tourists looked here mainly for inexpensive lodging and easy access to Palm Beach, since a bridge leads from the mainland to a barrier island with Lake Worth's beach. Now Lake Worth has several blocks of restaurants, nightclubs, shops, and art galleries, making this somewhat a worthy destination on its own.

Museum of Polo and Hall of Fame. Start here in Lake Worth for an introduction to polo. See memorabilia, art, and a film on the history of the sport. Then, treat yourself to a Sunday match; polo season runs January through April. ✉ *9011 Lake Worth Rd.* ☎ *561/969–3210* ⊕ *www. polomuseum.com* ✉ *Free (donations accepted)* ☾ *Jan.–Apr., weekdays 10–4, Sat. 10–2; May–Dec., weekdays 10–4.*

LANTANA

Lantana—just a bit farther south from Palm Beach than Lake Worth—has inexpensive lodging and a bridge connecting the town to its own beach on a barrier island. Tucked between Lantana and Boynton Beach is **Manalapan,** a tiny but posh residential community.

BOYNTON BEACH

In 1884, when fewer than 50 settlers lived in the area, Nathan Boynton, a Civil War veteran from Michigan, paid $25 for 500 acres with a mile-long stretch of beachfront thrown in. How things have changed, with today's population at about 118,000 and property values still on an upswing. Far enough from Palm Beach to remain low-key, Boynton Beach has two parts, the mainland and the barrier island—the town of Ocean Ridge—connected by two bridges.

FAMILY **Arthur R. Marshall Loxahatchee National Wildlife Refuge.** The most robust part of the northern Everglades, this 221-square-mile refuge is one of two huge water-retention areas accounting for much of the "River of

The posh Palm Beach area has its share of luxury villas on the water; many are Mediterranean in style.

Grass" outside the national park near Miami. Start at the visitor center, which has fantastic interactive exhibits and videos like *Night Sounds of the Everglades* and an airboat simulator. From there, you can take a marsh trail to a 20-foot-high observation tower, or stroll a ½-mile boardwalk lined with educational signage through a dense cypress swamp. There are also guided nature walks (including some specifically for bird-watching), and there's great bass fishing (bring your own poles and bait) and a 5½-mile canoe trail loop (a rental kiosk is by the fishing pier). ⊠ *10216 Lee Rd., off U.S. 441, between rtes. 804 and 806* ☎ *561/734–8303* ⊕ *www.loxahatcheefriends.com* 🖾 *$5 per vehicle; $1 per pedestrian* ☉ *Daily sunrise–sunset, visitor center daily 9–4.*

SINGER ISLAND

Across the inlet from the northern end of Palm Beach is Singer Island, which is actually a peninsula that's big enough to pass for a barrier island, rimmed with mom-and-pop motels and high-rises. Palm Beach Shores occupies its southern tip (where tiny Peanut Island is a stone's throw away); farther north are Riviera Beach and North Palm Beach, which also straddle the inlet and continue on the mainland.

Palm Beach Maritime Museum. Though the main building of the Palm Beach Maritime Museum is found in Currie Park in West Palm Beach, its main treasure—the restored "Kennedy Bunker," a bomb shelter built for President John F. Kennedy, and a historic Coast Guard station—is located on Peanut Island. You can take a guided tour of the bunker through the museum's Peanut Island outpost. The museum also has a nice little gift shop, an outdoor deck on the water, and a lawn where you can play games including horseshoes. To get there, catch a water taxi from Riviera Beach Municipal Marina (⊕ www.peanutislandwatertaxi. com), but call ahead as the boats won't run in choppy waters. ⊠ *Peanut Island, Riviera Beach* ☏ *561/848–2960* ⊕ *www.pbmm.org* ⊠ *$14 (not including water transportation)* ⊙ *Thurs.–Sun. 11–4.*

PALM BEACH GARDENS

About 15 minutes northwest of Palm Beach is this relaxed, upscale residential community known for its high-profile golf complex, the **PGA National Resort & Spa.** Although not on the beach, the town is less than a 15-minute drive from the ocean.

JUNO BEACH

This small town east of Palm Beach Gardens has 2 miles of shoreline that becomes home to thousands of sea turtle hatchlings each year, making it one of the world's densest nesting sites. A 990-foot-long pier lures fishermen and beachgoers seeking a spectacular sunrise.

Fodor'sChoice
★
Loggerhead Park Marine Life Center of Juno Beach. Located in a certified green building in Loggerhead Park—and established by Eleanor N. Fletcher, the "turtle lady of Juno Beach"—the center focuses on the conservation of sea turtles with three core competencies of education, research, and rehabilitation. The education center houses displays of coastal natural history, detailing Florida's marine ecosystems and the life and plight of the various species of sea turtles found on Florida's shores. You can visit recovering turtles in their tanks out back; volunteers are happy to tell you the turtles' heroic tales of survival. The center has regularly scheduled activities, such as Kid's Story Time and Junior Vet Lab, and most are free of charge. During nesting season, the center hosts night walks to experience turtle nesting in action. Given that the adjacent beach is part of the second biggest nesting ground for loggerhead turtles in the world, your chances of seeing this natural phenomenon is pretty high (over 13,000 loggerheads nested here in 2012). ⊠ *14200 U.S. 1* ☏ *561/627–8280* ⊕ *www.marinelife.org* ⊠ *Free* ⊙ *Mon.–Sat. 10–5, Sun. noon–4.*

OFF THE
BEATEN
PATH
Forty miles west of West Palm Beach, amid the farms and cattle pastures rimming the western edges of Palm Beach and Martin counties, is **Lake Okeechobee,** the second-largest freshwater lake completely within the United States. It's girdled by 120 miles of road yet remains shielded from sight for almost its entire circumference. Lake Okeechobee—the Seminole's Big Water and the gateway of the great Everglades watershed—measures 730 square miles, at its longest roughly 33 miles north–south and 30 miles east–west, with an average natural depth of only 10 feet (flood control brings the figure up to 12 feet and deeper). Six major lock systems and 32 separate water-control structures manage the water. Encircling the lake is a 34-foot-high grassy levee that locals call "the wall," and the Lake Okeechobee Scenic Trail, a segment of the Florida National Scenic Trail that's an easy, flat ride for bikers. Anglers have a field day here as well, with great bass and perch catches. ■TIP➔ There's no shade, so wear a hat, sunscreen, and bug repellent. Be sure to bring lots of bottled water, too, because restaurants and stores are few and far between.

BEACHES

PALM BEACH

Phipps Ocean Park. About 2 miles south of "Billionaire's Row" on Ocean Boulevard sits this public oceanside park, with two metered parking lots separated by a fire station. The north side is better for beachgoers and currently houses the sole entry point to the beach itself (the other three entry points are closed for repairs). At the southern entrance, there is a six-court tennis facility. The beach is narrow and has natural rock formations dotting the shoreline, making it ideal for snorkelers. There are picnic tables and grills on site, as well as the Little Red Schoolhouse, an 1886 landmark that hosts educational workshops for local kids. If a long walk floats your boat, venture north to see the megamansions, but don't go too far inland, because private property starts just a few feet from the surf. There's a 2-hour time limit for free parking. **Amenities:** parking (no fee); showers; toilets; lifeguards. **Best for:** walking; solitude. ⊠ *2201 S. Ocean Blvd.* 🕾 *561/838–5400, 561/227–6450 for tennis reservations* 🎫 *Free* ⊙ *Daily 8–8.*

Town of Palm Beach Municipal Beach. You know you're here if you see Palm Beach's younger generation frolicking on the sands and non-xenophobic locals setting up chairs as the sun reflects off their gleaming white veneers. The Worth Avenue clock tower is within sight, but the gateways to the sand are actually on Chilean Avenue, Brazilian Avenue, and Gulfstream Road. It's definitely the most central and longest lifeguarded strip open to everyone and a popular choice for hotel guests from the Colony and Chesterfield. Lifeguards are present from Brazilian Avenue down to Chilean Avenue. It's also BYOC (Bring Your Own Chair). You'll find no water-sport or food vendors here; however, casual eateries are a quick walk away. Metered spots line A1A. **Amenities:** lifeguards; showers. **Best for:** swimming; sunsets. ⊠ *S. Ocean Blvd. from Brazilian Ave. to Gulfstream Rd.* 🕾 *561/838–5483 for beach patrol* ⊙ *Daily 8–8.*

LAKE WORTH

FAMILY **Lake Worth Beach.** This public beach bustles with beachgoers of all ages thanks to the prolific family offerings. The waterfront retail promenade—the old fashioned non-gambling Lake Worth "casino"—has a Mulligan's Beach House Bar & Grill, a T-shirt store, a pizzeria, and a Kilwin's ice cream shop. The beach also has a municipal Olympic-size public swimming pool, a playground, a fishing pier—not to mention the pier's wildly popular daytime eatery, Benny's on the Beach. Omphoy and Four Seasons guests are steps away from the action. **Amenities:** food and drink; lifeguards; parking (no fee); showers; toilets; water sports. **Best for:** sunsets; swimming. ⊠ *10 S. Ocean Blvd., at Rte. A1A and Lake Ave.* ⊕ *www.lakeworth.org/visitors/casino-building-and-beach-complex* 🎫 *$1 to enter pier, $3 to enter and fish; $2 per hr for parking.*

LANTANA

Town of Lantana Public Beach. Ideal for quiet ambles, this sandy stretch is also noteworthy for a casual restaurant, the no-frills breezy Dune Deck Café, which is perched above the waterline and offers great views for an oceanfront breakfast or lunch. The beach's huge parking lot is directly adjacent to the Eau Palm Beach, and diagonally across the street is a sizeable strip mall with all sorts of conveniences, including more eateries. Note: the beach is very narrow and large rocks loom in the water. However, these are some of the clearest waters along the Florida coastline, and they make an idyllic background for long walks and great photos. Bring plenty of quarters for the old school parking meters. **Amenities:** food and drink; lifeguards; parking (fee); showers; toilets. **Best for:** walking. ⊠ *100 E. Ocean Ave.* 🖅 *$1.50 per hr for parking.*

SINGER ISLAND

FAMILY

Fodor's Choice

★

John D. MacArthur Beach State Park. If getting far from rowdy crowds is your goal, this spot on the north end of Singer Island is a good choice. Encompassing 2 miles of beach and a lush subtropical coastal habitat, inside you'll find a great place for kayaking, snorkeling at natural reefs, bird-watching, fishing, and hiking. You might even get to see a few manatees! A 4,000-square-foot nature center has aquariums and displays on local flora and fauna, and there's a long roster of monthly activities, such as surfing clinics, art lessons, and live bluegrass music. Guided sea turtle walks are available at night in season, and daily nature walks depart at 10 am. Check the website for times and costs of activities. **Amenities:** water sports; parking (fee); showers; toilets. **Best for:** swimming; walking; solitude; surfing. ⊠ *10900 Jack Nicklaus Dr., North Palm Beach* 🕿 *561/624–6952* ⊕ *www.macarthurbeach.org* 🖅 *Parking $5, bicyclists and pedestrians $2* ⊙ *Park daily 8–sunset; nature center and gift shop daily 9–5.*

Peanut Island Park. Partiers, families, and overnight campers all have a place to go on the 79 acres here. The island, in a wide section of the Intracoastal between Palm Beach Island and Singer Island with an open channel to the sea, is accessible only by private boat or water taxi, two of which set sail regularly from the Riviera Beach Municipal Marina (www.peanutislandwatertaxi.com) and the Sailfish Marina (www.sailfishmarina.com/water_taxi). Fun-loving seafarers looking for an afternoon of Jimmy Buffett and brewskis pull up to the day docks or the huge sandbar on the north—float around in an inner tube, and it's spring-break déjà vu. Walk along the 20-foot-wide paved path encircling the island, and you'll hit a 170-foot fishing pier, a campground, the lifeguarded section to the south that is particularly popular with families because of its artificial reef, and last but not least, the Palm Beach Maritime Museum's "Kennedy Bunker" (a bomb shelter prepared for President John F. Kennedy that was restored and opened to the public in 1999). There are picnic tables and grills, but no concessions. ■ TIP➔ **A new ordinance means alcohol possession and consumption is restricted to permit areas.** **Amenities:** lifeguards (summer only); showers; toilets. **Best for:** partiers; walking; swimming; sunrise. ⊠ *6500 Peanut Island Rd., Riviera Beach* 🕿 *561/845–4445* ⊕ *www.pbcgov.com/parks/peanutisland* 🖅 *Beach free, water taxi $10.*

JUNO BEACH

FAMILY

Juno Beach Ocean Park. An angler's dream, this beach has a 990-foot pier that's open daily, like the beach, from sunrise to sunset. From November through February, pier gates open at 6 am and don't close until 10 pm on weeknights and midnight on weekends, making it an awesome place to catch a full sunrise and sunset (that is, if you don't mind paying the small admission fee). A concession stand on the pier sells fish food as well as such human favorites as burgers, sandwiches, and ice cream. Families adore this shoreline because of the amenities and vibrant atmosphere. There are plenty of kids building castles but also plenty of teens having socials and hanging out along the beach. **Amenities:** lifeguards; food and drink; parking (no fee); showers; toilets. **Best for:** sunrise; sunset; swimming. ⊠ *14775 U.S. 1* ☎ *561/799–0185 for pier* ⊕ *www.pbcgov.com/parks/locations/junobeach.htm* ☒ *$4 to fish, $1 to enter pier* ⊙ *Daily sunrise–sunset.*

WHERE TO EAT

PALM BEACH

$$$$ ✕ **bûccan.** Lanterns cast a soft glow as young bluebloods rocking D&G
ECLECTIC   jeans slip into tightly packed copper-topped tables alongside groups of
Fodor'sChoice   silver-haired oil scions. It's island casual in its trendiest, most boisterous
★   yet still refined incarnation, with a menu to match. Chef-owner Clay Conley's small plates to share (wood-fired wild mushroom pizza with black truffle vinaigrette) with unfussy presentations (house-made squid-ink orecchiette stewed with sausage, conch, and chilies in a mini–Le Creuset cocotte) and inventive, sophisticated flavor combinations and textures (hamachi sashimi with yuzu and crisped lotus root) make this the place to see and be seen—and the best-tasting meal at a price more expected of the mainland. ⑤ *Average main: $32* ⊠ *350 S. County Rd., Palm Beach* ☎ *561/833–3450* ⊕ *www.buccanpalmbeach.com* ⌒ *Reservations essential* ⊙ *No lunch.*

$$$$ ✕ **Café Boulud.** Palm Beach socialites just can't get enough of this prized
FRENCH   restaurant by celebrated chef Daniel Boulud. This posh French-Amer-
Fodor'sChoice   ican venue in the Brazilian Court hotel is casual yet elegant, with a
★   palette of honey, gold, and citron. Plenty of natural light spills through arched glass doors opening to a lush courtyard that's just the place to be on a warm evening. Lunch and dinner entrées on the restaurant's signature four-section menu include classic French, seasonal, vegetarian, and a rotating roster of international dishes. The lounge, with its illuminated amber glass bar, is the perfect perch to take in the jet-set crowd that comes for a hint of the south of France in South Florida. ⑤ *Average main: $38* ⊠ *The Brazilian Court Hotel & Beach Club, 301 Australian Ave., Palm Beach* ☎ *561/655–6060* ⊕ *www.cafeboulud.com* ⌒ *Reservations essential.*

$$$$ ✕ **Chez Jean-Pierre.** With walls adorned with avant-garde Dalí- and
FRENCH   Picasso-like art, this bistro is where the Palm Beach old guard likes to let down its hair, all the while partaking of sumptuous French cuisine and an impressive wine selection. Forget calorie or cholesterol concerns, and indulge in scrambled eggs with caviar or homemade foie gras, along with desserts like frozen hazelnut soufflé or profiteroles au chocolat. Jackets are not required, although many men wear them. The main entrance is through a courtyard in the back. ⑤ *Average main: $39* ⊠ *132 N. County Rd., Palm Beach* ☎ *561/833–1171* ⊕ *www.chezjean-pierre.com* ⌒ *Reservations essential* ⊙ *Closed Sun. No lunch.*

$$$
ASIAN
╳**Echo.** Palm Beach's window on Asia has a sleek sushi bar and floor-to-ceiling glass doors separating the interior from the popular terrace dining area. Chinese, Japanese, Thai, and Vietnamese selections are neatly categorized: Wind (small plates starting your journey), Water (seafood mains), Fire (open-flame wok creations), Earth (meat dishes), and Flavor (desserts, sweets). Pick from dim sum to sashimi, pad thai to Szechuan beef, steamed sea bass to shrimp lo mein. On weekdays, come for the early shift (5–6:30 pm) for half-price sushi and cocktails in the restaurant's Dragonfly Lounge. $ *Average main: $30* ⊠ *230-A Sunrise Ave., Palm Beach* ☎ *561/802–4222* ⊕ *www.echopalmbeach. com* ☉ *Closed Mon. No lunch.*

$$
PIZZA
╳**Pizza Al Fresco.** The secret-garden setting is the secret to the success of this European-style pizzeria, where you can dine under a canopy of century-old banyans in an intimate courtyard. Specialties are 12-inch hand-tossed brick-oven pizzas with such interesting toppings as prosciutto, arugula, and caviar. There's even a carbonara breakfast pizza (part of a small morning menu) and a Nutella dessert pizza. Piping-hot calzones, salads, and baked pastas round out the choices. Next to the patio, look for the grave markers of Addison Mizner's beloved pet monkey, Johnnie Brown, and Rose Sachs's dog, Laddie (she and husband Morton bought Mizner's villa and lived there 47 years). Delivery is available. This bistro is dog-friendly. $ *Average main: $19* ⊠ *14 Via Mizner, at Worth Ave., Palm Beach* ☎ *561/832–0032* ⊕ *www.pizzaalfresco.com.*

$$$$
ITALIAN
╳**Renato's.** Here, at one of the most romantic restaurants in Palm Beach, guests can dine in the beautiful courtyard under the stars and twinkling lights on the bougainvillea or in the intimate, low-lighted dining room flickering with candles and enhanced with fresh flowers and quiet classical music. Be sure to try the split-pea soup with small cubes of ham (a meal in itself) and the sautéed swordfish with white wine, lemon butter, and capers when it's offered. All are served on pretty, flowered porcelain plates atop crisp white-linen tablecloths. Although pricey, dinner here is worth every penny. Jackets are encouraged. $ *Average main: $37* ⊠ *87 Via Mizner, Palm Beach* ☎ *561/655–9752* ⊕ *www.renatospalmbeach. com* ⌂ *Reservations essential* ☉ *No lunch Sun.*

$$$
AMERICAN
FAMILY
╳**Testa's Palm Beach.** Attracting a loyal clientele since 1921, this restaurant is still owned by the Testa family. Lunches range from burgers to crab salad, and dinner specialties include snapper Florentine and jumbo lump-crab cakes. You can dine inside in an intimate pine-paneled room with cozy bar, out back in a gazebo-style room for large groups, or outside at tables that are pet-friendly. Don't miss the signature strawberry pie made with fresh Florida berries. $ *Average main: $27* ⊠ *221 Royal Poinciana Way, Palm Beach* ☎ *561/832–0992* ⊕ *www.testasrestaurants.com.*

WEST PALM BEACH

$
AMERICAN
╳**Belle and Maxwell's.** Palm Beach's ladies who lunch gladly leave the island for an afternoon at Belle and Maxwell's. Hidden among the antique stores, every day looks like a storybook tea party at this quaint teahouse. Expect colorful luncheonette dresses and great soups, salads, and sandwiches at surprisingly affordable prices. People also frequent Belle and Maxwell's solely for its coffee and homemade desserts (including a $12 sweet sampler platter that gives you four different treats to

taste). $ *Average main: $12* ✉ *3700 S. Dixie Hwy., West Palm Beach* ☎ *561/832–4449* ⊕ *www.belleandmaxwells.net* ✓ *Closed Sun.*

$
AMERICAN

✕ **Howley's.** Since 1950 this diner's eat-in counter and "cooked in sight, it must be right" motto have made it a congenial setting for meeting old friends and making new ones. Nowadays, Howley's prides itself on its kitsch factor and old-school eats like turkey potpie and a traditional Thanksgiving feast, as well as its retro-redux dishes like potato-and-brisket burrito. Forgo the counter for the retro tables or sit out on the covered patio. The café attracts a loyal clientele into the wee hours (it's open weekdays until 2 am and weekends until 5 am and has a full bar). $ *Average main: $13* ✉ *4700 S. Dixie Hwy., West Palm Beach* ☎ *561/833–5691* ⊕ *www.sub-culture.org/howleys.*

$$$
ITALIAN
FAMILY

✕ **Il Bellagio.** In the heart of CityPlace, this European-style eatery offers Italian specialties and a wide variety of fine wines. The menu includes classics like chicken parmigiana, risotto, and fettuccine alfredo. Pizzas from the wood-burning oven are especially good. Service is friendly and efficient, but the overall noise level tends to be high. Sit at the outdoor tables next to the main plaza's dancing fountains if you can. $ *Average main: $23* ✉ *CityPlace, 600 S. Rosemary Ave., West Palm Beach* ☎ *561/659–6160* ⊕ *www.ilbellagiocityplace.com.*

$
MIDDLE EASTERN
Fodor'sChoice
★

✕ **Middle East Bakery.** This hole-in-the-wall Middle Eastern bakery, deli, and market is packed at lunchtime with regulars who are on a first-name basis with the gang behind the counter. From the nondescript parking lot the place doesn't look like much, but inside, delicious hot and cold Mediterranean treats await. Choose from traditional gyro sandwiches and lamb salads with sides of grape leaves, tabbouleh, and couscous. There's a big take-out business, as seating is limited, and it closes shop at 6 pm (4:30 pm on Saturdays). $ *Average main: $10* ✉ *327 5th St., West Palm Beach* ☎ *561/659–7322* ✓ *Closed Sun.*

$$$
FRENCH

✕ **Pistache French Bistro.** Although "the island" is no doubt a bastion of French cuisine, this cozy bistro across Lake Worth on the Clematis Street waterfront entices a lively crowd looking for a good meal with pretention checked at the door. The outdoor terrace can't be beat, and the fabulous modern French menu (revamped in early 2014), including roasted sliced duck with truffled polenta rather than the ubiquitous *à l'orange,* are a delight. Save room for dessert: the house-made pudding Breton, a fluffy, raisin-accented brioche bread pudding paired with Crème Anglaise, could be straight out of a Parisian café. $ *Average main: $27* ✉ *101 N. Clematis St., West Palm Beach* ☎ *561/833–5090* ⊕ *www.pistachewpb.com.*

$$$
MODERN
AMERICAN

✕ **Rhythm Cafe.** West Palm Beach's Rhythm Cafe is a true one-of-a-kind and anything but Palm Beach formal (think décor like a feathered pink flamingo perched on terrazzo floors). Fun, funky, cheesy, campy, and cool all at once, the former 1950's drugstore-cum-restaurant on West Palm Beach's Antique Row features an ever-changing creative menu of house-made items with Italian, Greek, American, and Creole influences. Favorites include "tapas-tizers" like the lemon-doused *saganaki* (flaming cheese) and the goat cheese pie; and main courses like the graham-cracker-crusted chicken in key lime sauce and fresh fish of the day prepared six totally different ways. The dessert menu features a variety of homemade ice creams. $ *Average main: $24* ⊠ *3800 S. Dixie Hwy., West Palm Beach* ☎ *561/833–3406* ⊕ *www.rhythmcafe.cc* ⊙ No lunch.

LAKE WORTH

$ ✕ **Benny's on the Beach.** Perched on the Lake Worth Pier, Benny's has a walk-up bar, a take-out window, and a full-service, no-frills restaurant serving diner-style food that's cheap and filling. Eat-in diners come here for long afternoons of beer and cocktails, enjoying prolific alfresco seating and a spectacular view of the sun glistening on the water and the waves crashing directly below. ■ TIP➔ **Though officially open for just breakfast and lunch, on weekends Benny's usually serves until sunset.** $ *Average main: $12* ⊠ *Lake Worth Beach, 10 S. Ocean Blvd., Lake Worth* ☎ *561/582–9001* ⊕ *www.bennysonthebeach.com* ⊙ No dinner.

AMERICAN

$$ ✕ **Bizaare Ave Café.** Decorated with a mix of artwork and antiques, this cozy bistro housed in a circa-1926 building and inspired by TV's *Friends*, fits right into downtown Lake Worth's groovy, eclectic scene. Artwork and furnishings can be purchased. Daily specials are available on both the lunch and dinner menus, where crêpes, pizzas, pastas, and salads are the staples. A more formal dining space is now open on the second floor. $ *Average main: $18* ⊠ *921 Lake Ave., Lake Worth* ☎ *561/588–4488* ⊕ *www.bizaareavecafe.com*.

ECLECTIC

LANTANA

$$ ✕ **Old Key Lime House.** An informal seafood spot covered by a chickee-hut roof built by Seminole Indians, it's perched on the Intracoastal Waterway and is open and airy, with observation decks that wrap around the back. In 1889, the Lyman family, some of the earliest settlers in Lantana, built this as their house, and it has grown over the years into the popular island-style eatery it is today. Kids love feeding the fish below. Of course, order the namesake key lime pie—the house specialty has been featured in *Bon Appétit*. $ *Average main: $20* ⊠ *300 E. Ocean Ave., Lantana* ☎ *561/582–1889* ⊕ *www.oldkeylimehouse.com*.

SEAFOOD
FAMILY

PALM BEACH GARDENS

$$$$ ✕ **Café Chardonnay.** At the end of a strip mall, Café Chardonnay is surprisingly elegant and has some of the most refined food in the suburban town of Palm Beach Gardens. Soft lighting, warm woods, white table-cloths, and cozy banquettes set the scene for a quiet lunch or romantic dinner. The place consistently receives praise for its innovative, continually changing menu and outstanding wine list. Starters can include wild-mushroom strudel and pancetta-wrapped diver scallops. Entrées might be grilled filet mignon or a pan-roasted veal chop with Parmesan risotto and brandy morel sauce. $ *Average main: $34* ⊠ *The Gardens Square Shoppes, 4533 PGA Blvd., Palm Beach Gardens* ☎ *561/627–2662* ⊕ *www.cafechardonnay.com* ⊙ No lunch weekends.

AMERICAN

$$$$ ✕ **Ironwood Steak & Seafood.** Located in the PGA National Resort & Spa, this eatery draws guests, locals, and tourists alike eager for a taste of its fired-up Vulcan steaks (Vulcan to meat-eaters is like Titelist to golfers—the best equipment around). The she-crab soup with sherry is a favorite from the sea, as are the raw bar items, like the jumbo shrimp cocktail and tuna tartare. Bright red banquettes, slate-tile walls, private rooms, and an impressive glass-walled wine cellar create a relaxed,

STEAKHOUSE

contemporary setting that spills out onto the equally chic adjoining lobby bar, which becomes quite the scene on weekend nights when a DJ spins. $ *Average main: $38* ⊠ *PGA National Resort & Spa, 400 Ave. of the Champions, Palm Beach Gardens* ☎ *561/627–4852* ⊕ *www. pgaresort.com/restaurants/ironwood-grille.*

$$$

SEAFOOD

✕ **Spoto's Oyster Bar.** If you love oysters and other raw bar nibbles, head here, where black-and-white photographs of oyster fisherman adorn the walls. The polished tables give the eatery a clubby look. Spoto's serves up a delightful bowl of New England clam chowder and a truly impressive variety of oysters and clams. The Caesar salad with crispy croutons and anchovies never disappoints. Sit outside on the patio to take advantage of the area's perfect weather. $ *Average main: $26* ⊠ *PGA Commons, 4560 PGA Blvd., Palm Beach Gardens* ☎ *561/776–9448* ⊕ *www.spotosoysterbar.com.*

WHERE TO STAY

PALM BEACH

$$$$

HOTEL

Fodor'sChoice

★

🏨 **The Brazilian Court Hotel.** This posh boutique hotel, stomping ground of Florida's well-heeled, is full of historic touches and creature comforts—from its yellow facade with dramatic white-draped entry, to modern draws like the renowned spa and Daniel Boulud restaurant. **Pros:** Stylish and hip local crowd; charming courtyard; free beach shuttle; award-winning restaurant; plush spa. **Cons:** small fitness center; nondescript pool; 10-minute ride to ocean and suggested 24-hour advance reservation for shuttle. $ *Rooms from: $409* ⊠ *301 Australian Ave., Palm Beach* ☎ *561/655–7740* ⊕ *www.thebraziliancourt.com* ⌧ *80 rooms* ⎮◯⎮ *No meals.*

$$$$

RESORT

FAMILY

Fodor'sChoice

★

🏨 **The Breakers Palm Beach.** More than an opulent hotel, the Breakers is a legendary 140-acre self-contained jewel of a resort built in an Italian Renaissance style and loaded with amenities, from a 20,000-square-foot luxury spa and grandiose beach club to 10 tennis courts and two 18-hole golf courses—not to mention Henry Flagler's heirs still run the place and invest $20 million a year to keep it at the cutting edge. **Pros:** impeccable attention to detail; fantastic service; beautiful room views; extensive activities for families. **Cons:** big price tag; short drive to reach off-property attractions. $ *Rooms from: $579* ⊠ *1 S. County Rd., Palm Beach* ☎ *561/655–6611, 888/273–2537* ⊕ *www.thebreakers. com* ⌧ *608 rooms* ⎮◯⎮ *No meals.*

$$$

HOTEL

🏨 **The Chesterfield Palm Beach.** A distinctly upper-crust northern European feel pervades the peach stucco walls and elegant rooms here; the hotel sits just north of the western end of Worth Avenue, and high tea, a cigar parlor, and daily turndown service recall a bygone, more refined era. **Pros:** gracious, attentive staff; Leopard Lounge entertainment; free valet parking. **Cons:** long walk to beach; only one elevator; to some, can come off as a bit stuffy. $ *Rooms from: $389* ⊠ *363 Cocoanut Row, Palm Beach* ☎ *561/659–5800, 800/243–7871* ⊕ *www.chesterfieldpb. com* ⌧ *41 rooms, 11 suites* ⎮◯⎮ *No meals.*

$$$$

HOTEL

🏨 **The Colony.** This legendary British colonial-style hotel has sunny rooms, suites, and villas with traditional furnishings and a slight Caribbean flair in a particularly convenient location, just one block from

Worth Avenue and one block from a pretty beach on the Atlantic Ocean. **Pros:** unbeatable location; famous polo bar; pillow-top mattresses; full English breakfast included. **Cons:** lobby is small; elevators are tight. ⑤ *Rooms from: $440* ✉ *155 Hammon Ave., Palm Beach* ☎ *561/655–5430, 800/521–5525* ⊕ *www.thecolonypalmbeach.com* ↘ *83 rooms, 7 villas* ⦿ *Breakfast.*

$$$$
RESORT
FAMILY
Fodor's Choice
★

Four Seasons Resort Palm Beach. Couples and families seeking relaxed seaside elegance in a ritzy yet understated setting will love this manicured 6-acre oceanfront escape at the south end of Palm Beach, with serene, bright, airy rooms in a cream-colored palette and spacious marble-lined baths. **Pros:** accommodating service; all rooms have balconies; outstanding complimentary kids' program. **Cons:** 10-minute drive to downtown Palm Beach (but can walk to Lake Worth); pricey. ⑤ *Rooms from: $499* ✉ *2800 S. Ocean Blvd., Palm Beach* ☎ *561/582–2800, 800/432–2335* ⊕ *www.fourseasons.com/palmbeach* ↘ *210 rooms* ⦿ *No meals.*

$$$$
RESORT

The Omphoy Ocean Resort. From the monumental entrance and the lobby's exotic ebony pillars to a lounge with Balinese art and a pool table to the bronze-infused porcelain tile floors, this Zen-like boutique hotel has a sexy, sophisticated look and a loyal following with young, hip travelers. **Pros:** most rooms have beautiful views of the private beach; ultracontemporary vibe; luxury setting. **Cons:** a hike from shopping and nightlife; the infinity pool is across the driveway. ⑤ *Rooms from: $425* ✉ *2842 S. Ocean Blvd., Palm Beach* ☎ *561/540–6440, 888/344–4321* ⊕ *www.omphoy.com* ↘ *144 rooms* ⦿ *No meals.*

WEST PALM BEACH

$$
B&B/INN

Casa Grandview West Palm Beach. In West Palm's charming Grandview Heights historic district—and just minutes away from both downtown and the beach—this warm and personalized B&B offers a wonderful respite from South Florida's big-hotel norm. **Pros:** daily dry cleaning of all linens; complimentary soft drinks, coffee, and snacks (and lots of them) in lobby; simple keyless entry (number code lock system). **Cons:** cottages and suites have seven-day minimum; free breakfast in B&B rooms only; art deco suites don't have air-conditioning; in a residential area. ⑤ *Rooms from: $225* ✉ *1410 Georgia Ave., West Palm Beach* ☎ *561/655–8932* ⊕ *www.casagrandview.com* ↘ *17 rooms* ⦿ *Multiple meal plans.*

$$
B&B/INN

Grandview Gardens Bed & Breakfast. Defining the Florida B&B experience, this 1925 Mediterranean Revival home overlooks a serene courtyard pool and oozes loads of charm and personality, while the fabulous owners provide heavy doses of bespoke service. **Pros:** multilingual owners; outside private entrances to rooms; innkeepers offer historic city tours. **Cons:** not close to the beach; in a residential area; rental car needed. ⑤ *Rooms from: $219* ✉ *1608 Lake Ave., West Palm Beach* ☎ *561/833–9023* ⊕ *www.grandview-gardens.com* ↘ *5 rooms, 2 cottages* ⦿ *Breakfast.*

$
HOTEL

Hotel Biba. In the El Cid historic district, this 1940s-era motel has gotten a fun stylish revamp from designer Barbara Hulanicki: each room has a vibrant mélange of colors, along with handcrafted mirrors, mosaic bathroom floors, and custom mahogany furnishings. **Pros:** cool, punchy design and luxe fixtures; popular wine bar; free continental breakfast with Cuban pastries. **Cons:** water pressure is weak; bathrooms are tiny; noisy when the bar is open late; not all rooms have central A/C. ⑤ *Rooms from: $129* ✉ *320 Belvedere Rd., West Palm Beach* ☎ *561/832–0094* ⊕ *www.hotelbiba.com* ↝ *43 rooms* ⦿ *Breakfast.*

LAKE WORTH

$

B&B/INN

⚏ **Sabal Palm House.** Built in 1936, this romantic, two-story B&B is a short walk from Lake Worth's downtown shops, eateries, and the Intracoastal Waterway, and each room is decorated with antiques and inspired by a different artist, including Renoir, Dalí, Norman Rockwell, and Chagall. **Pros:** on quiet street; hands-on owners; chairs and totes with towels provided for use at nearby beach. **Cons:** no pool; peak times require a two-night minimum stay; no parking lot. ⑤ *Rooms from: $159* ✉ *109 N. Golfview Rd., Lake Worth* ☎ *561/582–1090, 888/722–2572* ⊕ *www.sabalpalmhouse.com* ↝ *5 rooms, 2 suites* ⦿ *Breakfast.*

SOUTH PALM BEACH AND MANALAPAN

$$$$

RESORT

FAMILY

Fodor's Choice

★

⚏ **Eau Palm Beach.** In the coastal town of Manalapan (just south of Palm Beach), this sublime, glamorous destination resort (formerly the Ritz-Carlton) showcases a newer, younger face of luxury, including a 3,000-square-foot oceanfront terrace, two sleek pools, a huge fitness center, a deluxe spa, and richly upholstered furnishings with contemporary, beachy patterns. **Pros:** magnificent aesthetic details throughout; indulgent pampering services; excellent on-site dining; kids love the cool cyber-lounge just for them. **Cons:** golf course is off property; 15-minute drive to Palm Beach. ⑤ *Rooms from: $459* ✉ *100 S. Ocean Blvd., Manalapan* ☎ *561/533–6000, 800/241–3333* ⊕ *www.eaupalmbeach.com* ↝ *310 rooms* ⦿ *No meals.*

SINGER ISLAND

$$$

RESORT

FAMILY

⚏ **Palm Beach Marriott Singer Island Beach Resort & Spa.** Families with a yen for the cosmopolitan but requiring the square footage and comforts of home revel in these spacious marble-tiled, granite-topped, Kitchen Aid–outfitted condos; couples wanting a private beach without the same level of sticker shock or bustle found 10 minutes to the south also appreciate the infinity pool and quiet sundeck. **Pros:** wide beach; genuinely warm service; plenty of kids' activities; sleek spa. **Cons:** no upscale dining or shopping nearby; unspectacular room views for an oceanside hotel. ⑤ *Rooms from: $399* ✉ *3800 N. Ocean Dr., Singer Island, Riviera Beach* ☎ *561/340–1700, 877/239–5610* ⊕ *www.marriott.com* ↝ *202 suites* ⦿ *No meals.*

$

HOTEL

⚏ **Sailfish Marina Resort.** A marina with deepwater slips—and prime location at the mouth to the Atlantic Ocean on the Intracoastal Waterway across from Peanut Island—lures boaters and anglers here to these rather basic rooms, studios, and efficiencies. **Pros:** inexpensive rates; great waterfront restaurant; has a water taxi; pretty grounds. **Cons:** no real lobby; not directly on beach; area attracts a party crowd and can be noisy; dated décor. ⑤ *Rooms from: $90* ✉ *98 Lake Dr., Palm Beach Shores* ☎ *561/844–1724* ⊕ *www.sailfishmarina.com* ↝ *30 units* ⦿ *No meals.*

PALM BEACH GARDENS

$$ ⚐ **PGA National Resort & Spa.** A soup-to-nuts renovation completed in
RESORT 2012 elevated this golfer's paradise (five championship courses and the
Fodor's Choice site of the yearly Honda Classic pro-tour tournament) from its *Cad-*
★ *dyshack*-style beginnings to a sleek modern playground with a gorgeous
zero-entry lagoon pool, seven different places to eat, and a full-service
spa with unique mineral-salt therapy pools. **Pros:** dream golf facilities;
affordable rates for top-notch amenities; close to shopping malls. **Cons:**
no beach shuttle; difficult to get around if you don't have a car; long
drive to Palm Beach proper. ⑤ *Rooms from: $279* ⊠ *400 Ave. of the
Champions, Palm Beach Gardens* ☎ *561/627–2000, 800/633–9150*
⊕ *www.pgaresort.com* ⇱ *280 rooms, 59 suites* ⊙ *No meals.*

NIGHTLIFE AND PERFORMING ARTS

PALM BEACH

NIGHTLIFE

Palm Beach is teeming with restaurants that turn into late-night hot
spots, plus hotel lobby bars perfect for tête-à-têtes.

Fodor's Choice **bûccan.** A hip Hamptons-esque scene with society darlings crowds the
★ lounge, throwing back killer cocktails like the Basil Rathbone (gin,
orange juice, mint, basil, strawberry) and Buccan T (vodka, black tea,
cranberry, citrus, basil, and agave nectar). ⊠ *350 S. County Rd., Palm
Beach* ☎ *561/833–3450* ⊕ *www.buccanpalmbeach.com.*

Cucina Dell' Arte. Though this spot is popular for lunch and dinner, it's
even more popular later in the night. The younger, trendier set comes
late to dance and mingle and have a great time. ⊠ *257 Royal Poinci-
ana Way, Palm Beach* ☎ *561/655–0770* ⊕ *www.cucinadellarte.com/
palmbeach.*

The Leopard Lounge. In the Chesterfield hotel, this enclave feels like an
exclusive club. The trademark ceiling and spotted floors of the reno-
vated lounge are a nod to this hotel's historic roots, but the rest of the
décor is new age Palm Beach glam. Though it starts each evening as a
restaurant, as the night progresses the Leopard is transformed into an
old-fashioned club with live music for Palm Beach's old guard. ⊠ *The
Chesterfield Palm Beach, 363 Cocoanut Row, Palm Beach* ☎ *561/659–
5800* ⊕ *www.chesterfieldpb.com.*

WEST PALM BEACH

NIGHTLIFE

West Palm is known for its exuberant nightlife—Clematis Street and
CityPlace are the prime party destinations. In fact, downtown rocks
every Thursday from 6 pm on with Clematis by Night (⊕ *www.wpb.
org/clematis-by-night*), a celebration of music, dance, art, and food at
Centennial Square.

Blue Martini. The CityPlace outpost of this South Florida hot spot for
thirty, forty, and fiftysomething adults gone wild has a menu filled with
tons of innovative martini creations (42 to be exact), and lots of cou-
gars on the prowl, searching for a first, second, or even third hus-
band. And the guys aren't complaining! The drinks are great and the

scene is fun for everyone, even those who aren't single and looking to mingle. Expect DJs some nights, live music others. ⊠ *CityPlace, 550 S. Rosemary Ave. #244, West Palm Beach* ☎ *561/835–8601* ⊕ *www. bluemartinilounge.com.*

ER Bradley's Saloon. People of all ages congregate to hang out and socialize at this kitschy open-air restaurant and bar to gaze at the Intracoastal Waterway; the mechanical bull is a hit on Saturday. Live music's on tap five to seven nights a week. ⊠ *104 Clematis St., West Palm Beach* ☎ *561/833–3520* ⊕ *www.erbradleys.com.*

Fodor'sChoice ★ **Rocco's Tacos and Tequila Bar.** In the last few years, Rocco's has taken root in numerous South Florida downtowns and become synonymous with wild nights of chips 'n' guac, margaritas, and intoxicating fun. This is more of a scene than just a restaurant. With pitchers of margaritas a-flowin', the middle-age crowd is boisterous and fun, recounting (and reliving) the days of spring break debauchery from their pre-professional years. Get your party started here with more than 220 choices of tequila. There's another branch at 5250 Town Center Circle in Boca Raton. ⊠ *224 Clematis St., West Palm Beach* ☎ *561/650–1001* ⊕ *www. roccostacos.com.*

PERFORMING ARTS

Palm Beach Dramaworks (pbd). Housed in an intimate venue with only 218 seats in downtown West Palm Beach, their modus operandi is "theater to think about" with plays by Pulitzer Prize winners on rotation. ⊠ *201 Clematis St., West Palm Beach* ☎ *561/514–4042* ⊕ *www. palmbeachdramaworks.org.*

Fodor'sChoice ★ **Raymond F. Kravis Center for the Performing Arts.** This is the crown jewel amid a treasury of local arts attractions, and its marquee star is the 2,195-seat Dreyfoos Hall, a glass, copper, and marble showcase just steps from the restaurants and shops of CityPlace. The center also boasts the 289-seat Rinker Playhouse, 170-seat Persson Hall, and the Gosman Amphitheatre, which holds 1,400 total in seats and on the lawn. A packed year-round schedule features a blockbuster lineup of Broadway's biggest touring productions, concerts, dance, dramas, and musicals; Miami City Ballet and the Palm Beach Pops perform here. ⊠ *701 Okeechobee Blvd., West Palm Beach* ☎ *561/832–7469 for box office* ⊕ *www.kravis.org.*

SHOPPING

As is the case throughout Florida, many of the smaller boutiques in Palm Beach close in the summer, and most stores are closed on Sunday. Consignment stores in Palm Beach are definitely worth a look; you'll often find high-end designer clothing in impeccable condition.

PALM BEACH

SHOPPING AREAS

Royal Poinciana Way. Cute shops like resort-wear favorite Joy of Palm Beach (⊕ *www.joyofpalmbeach.com*) dot the north side of Royal Poinciana Way between Bradley Place and North County Road. Wind through the courtyards past upscale consignment stores to Sunset Avenue, then stroll down Sunrise Avenue: this is the place for specialty items like out-of-town newspapers, health foods, and rare books. ⊠ *Worth Ave., between Bradley Pl. and N. County Rd., Palm Beach.*

Fodor's Choice
★

Worth Avenue. One of the world's premier showcases for high-quality shopping runs half a mile from east to west across Palm Beach, from the beach to Lake Worth. The street has more than 200 shops (more than 40 of them sell jewelry), and many upscale chain stores (Gucci, Hermès, Pucci, Saks Fifth Avenue, Neiman Marcus, Louis Vuitton, Chanel, Cartier, Tiffany & Co., and Tourneau) are represented—their merchandise appealing to the discerning tastes of the Palm Beach clientele. Don't miss walking around the *vias*, little courtyards lined with smaller boutiques; historic tours are available each month during "season" from the Worth Avenue Association. ■TIP→ For those looking to go a little lighter on the pocket book, just north of Worth Avenue, the six blocks of South Country Road have interesting and somewhat less expensive stores. ⊠ *Worth Ave., between Cocoanut Row and S. Ocean Blvd., Palm Beach* ⊕ *www.worth-avenue.com.*

RECOMMENDED STORES

Betteridge at Greenleaf & Crosby. Jewelry is very important in Palm Beach, and for more than 119 years the diverse selection here has included investment pieces. Window shopping is allowed. ⊠ *236 Worth Ave., Palm Beach* ☏ *561/655–5850* ⊕ *www.betteridge.com.*

Calypso St. Barth. For those boutiques that are represented in the wealthiest cities across the country, having an outpost here on Via Encantada on Worth Avenue is almost obligatory. For its Palm Beach store (one of four Florida outposts—the others are in Bal Harbour, Naples, and Coral Gables), Calypso has curated a lively collection of resort wear like beautifully embroidered tunics and patterned bikinis as well as shoes, fragrances, and accessories for the pampered lady. ⊠ *247-B Worth Ave., Palm Beach* ☏ *561/832–5006* ⊕ *www.calypsostbarth.com.*

The Church Mouse. Many high-end resale boutique owners grab their merchandise at this thrift store run by the Episcopal Church of Bethesda-by-the-Sea, in business since 1970. The mouse accepts cheese from October to June, Monday–Saturday 10–4. You can feel good about your purchases here: proceeds go to regional nonprofits. ⊠ *378 S. County Rd., Palm Beach* ☏ *561/659–2154* ⊕ *www.bbts.org/churchmouse.*

Déjà Vu. There are so many gently used, top-quality pieces from Chanel here that this could be a resale house for the brand. There's no digging through piles here; clothes are in impeccable condition and are well organized. Sadly, Maxie Barley, owner of the store and Palm Beach legend, passed away in October 2013. ⊠ *Via Testa, 219 Royal Poinciana Way, Palm Beach* ☏ *561/833–6624.*

FAMILY   **Spring Flowers.** Specializing in European labels, beautiful children's clothing starts with newborn gown sets by Petit Bateau and grows into fashions by Léon and Fleurisse. ⊠ *320 Worth Ave., Palm Beach* ☏ *561/832–0131* ⊕ *www.springflowerschildren.com.*

WEST PALM BEACH

Fodor's Choice ★ **Antique Row.** West Palm's U.S. 1, "South Dixie Highway," is the destination for those who are interested in interesting home décor. From thrift shops to the most exclusive stores, it is all here within 40 stores—museum-quality furniture, lighting, art, junk, fabric, frames, tile, and rugs. So if you're looking for an art deco, French provincial, or Mizner pièce de résistance, big or small, schedule a few hours for an Antique Row stroll. You'll find bargains during the off-season (May to November). Antique Row runs north–south from Belvedere Road to Forest Hill Boulevard, although most stores are bunched between Belvedere Road and Southern Boulevard. ⊠ *U.S. 1, between Belvedere Rd. and Forest Hill Blvd., West Palm Beach* ⊕ *www.westpalmbeachantiques.com.*

CityPlace. The 72-acre, four-block-by-four-block commercial and residential complex centered on Rosemary Avenue attracts people of all ages to with restaurants like Italian-inspired Il Bellagio, bars like Blue Martini, a 20-screen Muvico and IMAX, the Harriet Himmel Theater, and a 36,000-gallon water fountain and light show. The dining, shopping, and entertainment are all family-friendly; at night a lively crowd likes to hit the outdoor bars. Among CityPlace's stores are such popular national retailers as Macy's, H&M, Pottery Barn, Banana Republic, and Restoration Hardware. There are also shops unique to Florida: Behind the punchy, brightly colored clothing in the front window of **C. Orrico** (☎ *561/832–9203*) are family fashions and accessories by Lily Pulitzer. ⊠ *700 S. Rosemary Ave., West Palm Beach* ☎ *561/366–1000* ⊕ *www.cityplace.com.*

FAMILY **Clematis Street.** If lunching is just as important as window-shopping, the renewed downtown West Palm around Clematis Street that runs west to east from South Rosemary Avenue to Flagler Drive is the spot for you. Centennial Park by the waterfront has an attractive design—and fountains where kids can cool off—which adds to the pleasure of browsing and resting at one of the many outdoor cafés. Hip national retailers such as Design Within Reach (⊕ *www.dwr.com*) mix with local boutiques, and both blend in with restaurants and bars. ⊠ *Clematis St., between S. Rosemary Ave. and Flagler Dr., West Palm Beach* ⊕ *www. westpalmbeach.com/clematis.*

PALM BEACH GARDENS

Downtown at The Gardens. This open-air pavilion down the street from The Gardens Mall has boutiques, chain stores, day spas, a 16-screen movie theater, and a lively restaurant and nighttime bar scene that includes the Dirty Martini and Cabo Flats, which both feature live music. ⊠ *11701 Lake Victoria Gardens Ave., Palm Beach Gardens* ☎ *561/340–1600* ⊕ *www.downtownatthegardens.com.*

Fodor's Choice ★ **The Gardens Mall.** One of the most refined big shopping malls in America, the 160-store Gardens Mall in northern Palm Beach County has stores like Burberry, Chanel, Gucci, Louis Vuitton, and David Yurman. There are also plenty of reasonably priced national retailers like H&M and Abercrombie & Fitch. This beautiful mall has prolific seating pavilions, making it a great place to spend a humid summer afternoon.

✉ *3101 PGA Blvd., Palm Beach Gardens* ☎ *561/775–7750* ⊕ *www. thegardensmall.com.*

SPORTS AND THE OUTDOORS

You can have a baseball bonanza while on vacation in the greater Palm Beach area by venturing up to the Treasure Coast's spring-training facilities, winter home to several major league teams and minor leagues the rest of the year. Northern towns like Palm Beach Gardens are only minutes away.

PALM BEACH

Palm Beach Island has two good golf courses—the Breakers and the Palm Beach Par 3 Golf Course, but only the latter is open to the public. Not to worry, there are more on the mainland, as well as myriad other outdoor sports opportunities.

BIKING

Bicycling is a great way to get a closer look at Palm Beach. Only 14 miles long, half a mile wide, flat as the top of a billiard table, and just as green, it's a perfect biking place.

Fodor's Choice
★ **Palm Beach Bicycle Trail Shop.** Open daily year-round, the shop rents bikes by the hour or day, and it's about a block from the north Lake Trail entrance. The shop has maps to help you navigate your way around the island, or you can download the main map from the shop's website. They are experts on the nearby, palm-fringed 4-mile Lake Trail. ✉ *223 Sunrise Ave., Palm Beach* ☎ *561/659–4583* ⊕ *www. palmbeachbicycle.com.*

GOLF

Fodor's Choice
★ **Palm Beach Par 3 Golf Course.** This course has been named the best par-3 golf course in the United States by *Golf Digest* magazine. The 18-hole course—originally designed by Dick Wilson and Joe Lee in 1961—was redesigned in 2009 by Hall of Famer Raymond Floyd. The par-3 course includes six holes directly on the Atlantic Ocean, with some holes over 200 yards. The grounds are exquisitely landscaped, as one would expect in Palm Beach. There's also a lavish clubhouse that houses Al Fresco, an Italian-inspired restaurant. Greens fees are $46; cart is an extra $25, but walking is encouraged. ✉ *2345 S. Ocean Blvd., Palm Beach* ☎ *561/547–0598* ⊕ *www.golfontheocean.com* ✏ *$46 for 18 holes.* 🏌 *18 holes. 2458 yards. par 58.*

WEST PALM BEACH
POLO

Fodor's Choice
★ **International Polo Club Palm Beach.** Attend matches and rub elbows with celebrities who make the pilgrimage out to Palm Beach polo country (the western suburb of Wellington) during the January-through-April season. The competition is not just among polo players. High society dresses in their best polo couture week after week, each outfit more fabulous than the next. An annual highlight at the polo club is the U.S. Open Polo Championship at the end of season. ◼TIP→ One of the best ways to experience the polo scene is by enjoying a gourmet brunch on the veranda of the International Polo Club Pavilion; it'll cost

Worth Avenue is the place in Palm Beach for high-end shopping, from international boutiques to independent jewelers.

you from $100–$120 per person depending on the month, but it's well worth it. ⊠ *3667 120th Ave. S, Wellington* ☎ *561/204–5687* ⊕ *www. internationalpoloclub.com.*

LAKE WORTH
GOLF
Palm Beach National Golf and Country Club. Despite the name, this classic 18-hole course resides in Lake Worth, not in Palm Beach. It is, however, in Palm Beach County and prides itself on being "the most fun and friendly golf course" in Palm Beach County. The championship layout was designed by Joe Lee in the 1970s and is famous for its 3rd and 18th holes. The 3rd: a par-3 island hole with a sand bunker. The 18th: a short par 4 of 358 yards sandwiched between a wildlife preserve and water. Due to the challenging nature of the course, it's more popular with seasoned golfers. The Steve Haggerty Golf Academy is also based here. ⊠ *7500 St. Andrews Rd., Lake Worth* ☎ *561/965–0044* ⊕ *www. palmbeachnational.com* ✉ *$89 for 18 holes* ⚐ *18 holes. 6734 yards. par 72.*

SINGER ISLAND
FISHING
Sailfish Marina. Book a full or half day of deep-sea fishing for up to six people with the seasoned captains and large fleet of 28- to 65-foot boats. ⊠ *Sailfish Marina Resort, 98 Lake Dr., Palm Beach Shores* ☎ *561/844–1724* ⊕ *www.sailfishmarina.com.*

PALM BEACH GARDENS

GOLF

Fodor'sChoice **PGA National Resort & Spa.** If you're the kind of traveler who takes along
★ a set of clubs, you'll achieve nirvana on the greens of PGA National
Resort & Spa. The five championship courses are open only to hotel
guests and club members, which means you'll have to stay to play. The
Champion Course, redesigned by Jack Nicklaus and famous for its Bear
Trap holes, is the site of the yearly Honda Classic pro tournament. The
four other challenging courses are also legends in the golfing world: the
Palmer, named for its architect, the legendary Arnold Palmer; the Fazio
(formerly the "Haig," the resort's first course re-opened in November
2012 after a major renovation) and the Squire, both from Tom and
George Fazio; and the Karl Litten–designed Estates, the sole course
not on the property (it is located five miles west of the PGA resort).
Lessons are available at the David Leadbetter Golf Academy. ⊠ *PGA
National Resort & Spa, 1000 Ave. of the Champions, Palm Beach
Gardens* ☏ *561/627–1800* ⊕ *www.pgaresort.com/golf/pga-national-
golf* ⌧ *$347 for 18 holes for Champion Course, Fazio Course, and
Squire Course. $258 for 18 holes for Palmer Course and Estates Course.
🏌. Champion Course: 18 holes. 7048 yards. par 72. Palmer Course: 18
holes. 7079 yards. par 72. Fazio Course: 18 holes. 6806 yards. par 72.
Squire Course: 18 holes. 6465 yards. par 72. Estates Course: 18 holes.
6694 yards. par 72.*

DELRAY BEACH

15 miles south of West Palm Beach.

A onetime artists' retreat with a small settlement of Japanese farmers,
Delray has grown into a sophisticated beach town. Delray's current
popularity is caused in large part by the fact that it has the feel of an
organic city rather than a planned development or subdivision—and
it's completely walkable. Atlantic Avenue, the once-dilapidated main
drag, has evolved into a more-than-a-mile-long stretch of palm-dotted
sidewalks, lined with stores, art galleries, and dining establishments.
Running east–west and ending at the beach, it's a happening place for a
stroll, day or night. Another active pedestrian area, the Pineapple Grove
Arts District, begins at Atlantic and stretches northward on Northeast
2nd Avenue about half a mile, and yet another active pedestrian way
begins at the eastern edge of Atlantic Avenue and runs along the big,
broad swimming beach that extends north to George Bush Boulevard
and south to Casuarina Road.

GETTING HERE AND AROUND

To reach Delray Beach from Boynton Beach, drive 2 miles south on
I–95, U.S. 1, or Route A1A.

ESSENTIALS

VISITOR INFORMATION

Contacts **Palm Beach County Convention and Visitors Bureau** ⊠ *1555
Palm Beach Lakes Blvd., Ste. 800, West Palm Beach* ☏ *561/233–3000* ⊕ *www.
palmbeachfl.com.*

CLOSE UP

The Morikami: Essence of Japan in Florida

A magical 200-acre garden where the Far East meets the South lies just beyond Palm Beach's allure of sun, sea, and glittering resorts. It's called the Morikami Museum and Japanese Gardens and is a testament to one man's perseverance. One of the largest Japanese gardens outside of Japan, it's also a soothing destination for reflection, with a pine forest, trails, and lakes.

In 1904, Jo Sakai, a New York University graduate, returned to his homeland of Miyazu, Japan, to recruit hands for farming what is now northern Boca Raton. With help from Henry Flagler's East Coast Railroad subsidiary, they colonized as Yamato, an ancient name for Japan. When crops fell short, everyone left except for George Sukeji Morikami, who carried on cultivating local crops, eventually donating his land to memorialize the Yamato Colony in the mid-1970s to Palm Beach County. His dream took on a new dimension with the 1977 opening of the Morikami complex, a living monument bridging cultural understanding between Morikami's two homelands.

The original Yamato-kan building chronicles the Yamato Colony, and a 32,000-square-foot main museum that opened in 1993 has rotating exhibits with 7,000 art objects and artifacts from the permanent collection, including 200 examples of textiles and a 500-piece collection of tea-ceremony items. No visit is complete without exploring the expansive Japanese gardens that have strolling paths, a tropical bonsai collection, and lakes teeming with koi. Enjoy a demonstration of *sado,* the Japanese tea ceremony, in the Seishin-an teahouse (check website for schedule), learn about Japanese history in the 5,000-book library, or register in advance for classes like calligraphy, bonsai, art, and intro to sushi making. The gift shop has some great finds for the whole family, and the Cornell Café has excellent pan-Asian fare and a relaxing terrace that overlooks the gardens.

6

EXPLORING

Colony Hotel. The chief landmark along Atlantic Avenue since 1926 is this sunny Mediterranean revival–style building, which is a member of the National Trust's Historic Hotels of America. Walk through the lobby to the parking lot where original garages still stand—relics of the days when hotel guests would arrive via chauffeured cars and stay there the whole season. ⊠ *525 E. Atlantic Ave.* ☎ *561/276–4123* ⊕ *www. thecolonyhotel.com.*

FAMILY **Delray Beach Center for the Arts at Old School Square.** Instrumental in the revitalization of Delray Beach circa 1995, this cluster of galleries and event spaces were established in restored school buildings dating from 1913 and 1925. The **Cornell Museum of Art & American Culture** offers ever-changing exhibits on fine arts, crafts, and pop culture, plus a hands-on children's gallery. From November to April, the 323-seat **Crest Theatre** showcases national-touring Broadway musicals, cabaret concerts, dance performances, and lectures. ⊠ *51 N. Swinton Ave.*

Morikami Museum and Japanese Gardens gives a taste of the Orient through its exhibits and tea ceremonies.

☎ 561/243–7922 ⊕ www.oldschool.org ✉ $10 for museum ⊙ Museum Tues.–Sat. 10:30–4:30, Sun. 1–4:30.

FAMILY
Fodor's Choice
★

Morikami Museum and Japanese Gardens. The boonies west of Delray Beach seems an odd place to encounter one of the region's most important cultural centers, but this is exactly where you can find a 200-acre cultural and recreational facility heralding the Yamato Colony of Japanese farmers that settled here in the early 20th century. A permanent exhibit details their history, and all together the museum's collection has more than 7,000 artifacts and works of art on rotating display. Traditional tea ceremonies are conducted monthly from October to June, along with educational classes on topics like calligraphy and sushi-making (these require advance registration and come with a fee). The six main gardens are inspired by famous historic periods in Japanese garden design and have South Florida accents (think tropical bonsai), and the on-site Cornell Café serves light Asian fare at affordable prices and was recognized by the Food Network as being one of the country's best museum eateries. ✉ 4000 Morikami Park Rd. ☎ 561/495–0233 ⊕ www.morikami.org ✉ $14 ⊙ Tues.–Sun. 10–5.

BEACHES

Fodor's Choice
★

Delray Municipal Beach. If you're looking for a place to see and be seen, head for this wide expanse of sand, the heart of which is where Atlantic Avenue meets A1A, close to restaurants, bars, and quick-serve eateries. Singles, families, and water-sports enthusiasts alike love it here. Lounge chairs and umbrellas can be rented every day, and lifeguards man stations half a mile out in each direction. The most popular section of beach is south of Atlantic Avenue on A1A, where the street parking is found. There are also two metered lots with restrooms across from A1A at Sandoway Park and Anchor Park (bring quarters if parking here!). On the beach by Anchor Park, north of Casuarina Road, are six volleyball nets and a kiosk that offers Hobie Wave rentals, surfing lessons, and snorkeling excursions to the 1903 SS *Inchulva* shipwreck half a mile offshore. The beach itself is open 24 hours, if you're at a nearby hotel and fancy a moonlight stroll. **Amenities:** water sports; food and drink; lifeguards; parking (fee); toilets; showers. **Best for:** windsurfing; partiers; swimming. ⊠ *Rte. A1A and E. Atlantic Ave.* ◳ *$1.50 per 1 hr parking* ☉ *Daily 24 hrs.*

WHERE TO EAT

$$
BRITISH
✕ **Blue Anchor.** Yes, this pub was actually shipped from England, where it had stood for 150 years in London's historic Chancery Lane. There it was a watering hole for famed Englishmen, including Winston Churchill. The Delray Beach incarnation has stuck to authentic British pub fare. Chow down on a ploughman's lunch (a chunk of Stilton cheese, a piece of bread, English pork pie, and pickled onions), fish-and-chips, and bangers and mash (sausages with mashed potatoes). This is a pub's pub—nothing fancy, very hearty. Don't be surprised to find a soccer game on TV. English beers and ales are available on tap and by the bottle. It's also a late-night place and has live music on weekends. $ *Average main: $18* ⊠ *804 E. Atlantic Ave.* ☎ *561/272–7272* ⊕ *www.theblueanchor.com.*

$$$
SEAFOOD
Fodor's Choice
★
✕ **City Oyster & Sushi Bar.** This trendy restaurant mingles the personalities and flavors of a New England oyster bar, a modern sushi eatery, an eclectic seafood grill, and an award-winning dessert bakery to create a can't-miss foodie haven in the heart of Delray's bustling Atlantic Avenue. With fruits of the sea delivered fresh daily and a winning culinary team, dishes like the New England clam chowder, New Orleans–style shrimp and crab gumbo, tuna crudo, and lobster fried rice are simply sublime. What's more? The restaurant's colossal bakery adds an unexpected element of carb bliss with a full roster of house-made breads and desserts, including the decadent, seasonal pies (ranging from chocolate–peanut butter to mixed berries) and the insanely divine pecan pie in a glass, smothered in salted caramel, pecan brittle, butter-pecan ice cream, and topped with whipped cream. Pastas are also made in-house. The wine list and craft beer menus are off the charts. $ *Average main: $23* ⊠ *213 E. Atlantic Ave.* ☎ *561/272–0220* ⊕ *www.cityoysterdelray.com.*

$$$
ITALIAN
✕ **D'Angelo Trattoria.** One of South Florida's most renowned Italian chefs, Angelo Elia, continues to expand his empire with this lively trattoria off Atlantic Avenue in Delray Beach. In a refurbished and reinvented beach house, the restaurant delivers hefty portions of original Italian favorites—such as gnocchi *quattro formaggi* (four cheeses) and seafood risotto—as well as Italian-American delights, like jumbo-shrimp parmigiana over spicy linguini. The wood oven also commands a lot of attention for its excellent pizzas, from the more traditional margherita to the more avant-garde, like the Integrale made with whole-wheat flour and topped with mozzarella, brie, zucchini, and smoked salmon. Come

hungry and prepare yourself for a major food hangover that's worth every bite. $ *Average main: $28* ⊠ *9 S.E. 7th Ave.* ☎ *561/330–1237* ⊕ *www.dangelotrattoria.com* ⊘ *No lunch.*

$$$ × **Max's Harvest.** A few blocks off Atlantic Avenue in the artsy Pine-
MODERN   apple Grove neighborhood, a tree-shaded, fenced-in courtyard wel-
AMERICAN   comes foodies eager to dig into its "farm-to-fork" offerings. The menu
Fodor's Choice   encourages people to experiment with "to share," "start small," and
★   "think big" plates. An ideal sampling: organic deviled eggs with chives and truffle sea salt; tequila-cured salmon; ricotta gnocchi, boiled then sautéed with porcini mushrooms and truffle tremor (goat cheese with truffles); and a pork chop over mustard spaetzle. Sunday brunch is wildly popular and includes an unlimited interactive Bloody Mary bar and champagne cocktails. $ *Average main: $27* ⊠ *169 N.E. 2nd Ave.* ☎ *561/381–9970* ⊕ *www.maxsharvest.com* ⊘ *No lunch Mon.–Sat.*

$$$ × **The Office.** Scenesters line the massive indoor-outdoor bar from noon
AMERICAN   'til the wee hours at this cooler-than-thou retro library restaurant, but
Fodor's Choice   it's worth your time to stop here for the best burger in town. There's a
★   whole selection, but the Prime CEO steals the show: Maytag bleu cheese and Gruyere with tomato-onion confit, arugula, and bacon. It's so juicy, you'll quickly forget the mess you're making. Other upscale renditions of comforting classics like nachos (a delicate puff of whipped crab per chip served with jicama slaw), fried green tomatoes (panko-and-corn-meal crusted with crisped bits of Serrano ham), and "naughty" alcoholic shakes are worth every indulgent calorie. $ *Average main: $24* ⊠ *201 E. Atlantic Ave.* ☎ *561/276–3600* ⊕ *www.theofficedelray.com.*

$$$$ × **32 East.** Although restaurants come and go every year on Atlantic
AMERICAN   Avenue, 32 East remains one of the best—if not the best—in Delray
Fodor's Choice   Beach. An ever-changing daily menu defines modern American cuisine.
★   Depending on what is fresh and plentiful, you might indulge in oak-fired organic dates and pears wrapped in bacon or perfectly prepared cumin-chili spiced cobia over black bean–tomato salad. Medium-tone wood accents and dim lighting make this brasserie seem cozy. There's a packed bar in front, an open kitchen in back, and patio seating on the sidewalk. ■TIP→ If you splurge on one dinner in Delray, make it 32 East. $ *Average main: $36* ⊠ *32 E. Atlantic Ave.* ☎ *561/276–7868* ⊕ *www.32east.com* ⚏ *Reservations essential* ⊘ *No lunch.*

WHERE TO STAY

$ ⊡ **Colony Hotel & Cabaña Club.** Not to be confused with the luxurious
HOTEL   Colony in Palm Beach, this charming hotel in the heart of downtown Delray dates back to 1926; and although it's landlocked, it does have a cabana club 2 miles away for hotel guests only. **Pros:** pet-friendly; full breakfast buffet included with rooms; free use of cabanas, umbrellas, and hammocks. **Cons:** no pool at main hotel building; must walk to public beach for water sport rentals. $ *Rooms from: $195* ⊠ *525 E. Atlantic Ave.* ☎ *561/276–4123, 800/552–2363* ⊕ *www.thecolonyhotel. com* ⚏ *48 rooms, 22 suites* ⍟*Breakfast.*

$$ ⊡ **Delray Beach Marriott.** By far the largest hotel in Delray Beach, the Mar-
HOTEL   riott has two towers on a stellar plot of land at the east end of Atlantic
FAMILY   Avenue—it's the only hotel that directly overlooks the water, yet it is still

within walking distance of restaurants, shopping, and nightlife. **Pros:** fantastic ocean views; pampering spa; two pools. **Cons:** chain-hotel feel; charge for parking; must rent beach chairs. [$] *Rooms from: $279* ✉ *10 N. Ocean Blvd.* ☎ *561/274–3200* ⊕ *www.delraybeachmarriott. com* ➵ *181 rooms, 88 suites* ○| *No meals.*

$$$
RESORT
FAMILY
Fodor'sChoice
★

🛏 **The Seagate Hotel & Spa.** Those who crave 21st-century luxury in its full glory (ultraswank tilework and fixtures, marble vanities, seamless shower doors) will love this LEED-certified hotel that offers a subtle Zen coastal motif throughout. **Pros:** two swimming pools; fabulous beach club; exceptionally knowledgeable concierge team. **Cons:** main building not directly on beach; daily resort fee; separate charge for parking. [$] *Rooms from: $369* ✉ *1000 E. Atlantic Ave.* ☎ *561/665–4800, 877/577–3242* ⊕ *www.theseagatehotel.com* ➵ *154 rooms* ○| *No meals.*

$
B&B/INN
Fodor'sChoice
★

🛏 **Sundy House.** Just about everything in this bungalow-style B&B is executed to perfection—especially its tropical, verdant grounds, which are actually a nonprofit botanical garden (something anyone can check out during free weekday tours) with a natural, freshwater swimming pool where your feet glide along limestone rocks and mingle with fish. **Pros:** charming eclectic décor; each room is unique; renowned restaurant with popular indoor-outdoor bar and free breakfast; in quiet area off Atlantic Avenue. **Cons:** need to walk through garden to reach rooms (i.e., no covered walkways); beach shuttle requires roughly half-hour advance notice; no private beach facilities. [$] *Rooms from: $199* ✉ *106 Swinton Ave.* ☎ *561/272–5678, 877/434–9601* ⊕ *www.sundyhouse. com* ➵ *11 rooms* ○| *Breakfast.*

NIGHTLIFE

Boston's on the Beach. You'll find beer flowing and the ocean breeze blowing at this beach bar and eatery, a local watering hole since 1983. The walls are laden with paraphernalia from the Boston Bruins, New England Patriots, and Boston Red Sox, including a shrine to Ted Williams. Boston's can get loud and rowdy (or lively, depending on your taste) later at night. Groove to reggae on Monday, live blues music on Tuesday, and other live music from rock to country on Friday, Saturday, and Sunday. ✉ *40 S. Ocean Blvd.* ☎ *561/278–3364* ⊕ *www. bostonsonthebeach.com.*

Dada. Bands play in the living room of a historic house. It's a place where those who don't drink will also feel comfortable, and excellent gourmet nibbles are a huge bonus (a full dinner menu is available, too). ✉ *52 N. Swinton Ave.* ☎ *561/330–3232* ⊕ *www.sub-culture.org/dada.*

Jellies Bar at the Atlantic Grille. Within the Seagate Hotel, the fun and fabulous bar at the Atlantic Grille is known locally as Jellies Bar. The over-30 set consistently floats over to this stunning bar to shimmy to live music Tuesday to Saturday; the namesake jellyfish tank never fails to entertain as well. ✉ *The Seagate Hotel & Spa, 1000 E. Atlantic Ave.* ☎ *561/665–4900* ⊕ *www.theatlanticgrille.com.*

SHOPPING

Atlantic Avenue and Pineapple Grove, both charming neighborhoods for shoppers, have maintained Delray Beach's small-town integrity. Atlantic Avenue is the main drag, with art galleries, boutiques, restaurants, and bars lining it from just west of Swinton Avenue all the way east to the ocean. The up-and-coming Pineapple Grove Arts District is centered on the half-mile strip of Northeast 2nd Avenue that goes north from Atlantic.

Furst. This studio-shop gives you the chance to watch designer Flavie Furst or her pupils at work—and then purchase their fine, hand-crafted gold, gold-filled, and silver jewelry. ⊠ *123 N.E. 2nd Ave.* ☎ *561/272–6422* ⊕ *www.flaviefurst.com* ☺ *Closed Sun.*

Snappy Turtle. Jack Rogers sandals and Trina Turk dresses mingle with other fun resort fashions for the home and family at this family-run store. ⊠ *1100 E. Atlantic Ave.* ☎ *888/762–7798* ⊕ *www.snappy-turtle.com.*

SPORTS AND THE OUTDOORS

BIKING

There's a bicycle path in Barwick Park, but the most popular place to ride is up and down the special oceanfront bike lane along Route A1A. The city also has an illustrated and annotated map on key downtown sights available through the Palm Beach Convention and Visitors Bureau.

Richwagen's Bike & Sport. Rent bikes by the hour, day, or week (they come with locks, baskets, and helmets); Richwagen's also has copies of city maps on hand. A 7-Speed Cruiser rents for $55 per week. ⊠ *298 N.E. 6th Ave.* ☎ *561/276–4234* ⊕ *www.delraybeachbicycles.com.*

TENNIS

Delray Beach Tennis Center. Each year this complex hosts simultaneous professional tournaments where current stars like Andy Roddick and Juan Martin del Potro along with legends like Ivan Lendl and Michael Chang duke it out (⊕ *www.yellowtennisball.com*), as well as Chris Evert's Pro-Celebrity Tennis Classic charity event (⊕ *www.chrisevert. org*). The rest of the time, you can practice or learn on 14 clay courts and 7 hard courts; private lessons and clinics are available, and it's open from 7:30 am to 9 pm weekdays and until 6 pm weekends. Since most hotels in the area do not have courts, tennis players visiting Delray Beach often come here to play. ⊠ *201 W. Atlantic Ave.* ☎ *561/243–7360* ⊕ *www.delraytennis.com.*

BOCA RATON

6 miles south of Delray Beach.

Less than an hour south of Palm Beach and anchoring the county's south end, upscale Boca Raton has much in common with its fabled cousin. Both reflect the unmistakable architectural influence of Addison Mizner, their principal developer in the mid-1920s. The meaning of the name Boca Raton (pronounced boca rah-*tone*) often arouses curiosity, with many folks mistakenly assuming it means "rat's mouth." Historians say the probable origin is Boca Ratones, an ancient Spanish geographical term for an inlet filled with jagged rocks or coral. Miami's Biscayne Bay had such an inlet, and in 1823 a mapmaker copying Miami terrain confused the more northern inlet, thus mistakenly labeling this area Boca Ratones. No matter what, you'll know you've arrived in the heart of downtown when you spot the historic town hall's gold dome on the main street, Federal Highway. Much of the Boca landscape was heavily planned, and many of the bigger sights are clustered in the area around town hall and Lake Boca, a wide stretch of the Intracoastal Waterway between Palmetto Park Road and Camino Real (two main east–west streets at the southern end of town).

GETTING HERE AND AROUND
To get to Boca Raton from Delray Beach, drive south 6 miles on Interstate 95, Federal Highway (U.S. 1), or Route A1A.

ESSENTIALS
VISITOR INFORMATION
Contacts Palm Beach County Convention and Visitors Bureau ✉ *1555 Palm Beach Lakes Blvd., Ste. 800, West Palm Beach* ☎ *561/233–3000* ⊕ *www. palmbeachfl.com.*

6

EXPLORING

FAMILY **Boca Raton Museum of Art.** Changing-exhibition galleries on the first floor showcase internationally known artists—both past and present—at this museum in a spectacular building that's part of the Mizner Park shopping center; the permanent collection upstairs includes works by Picasso, Degas, Matisse, Klee, Modigliani, and Warhol, as well as notable African and pre-Columbian art. Daily tours are included with admission. In addition to the treasure hunts and sketchbooks you can pick up from the front desk, there's a roster of special programs that cater to kids, including studio workshops and gallery walks. Another fun feature is the cell phone audio guide—certain pieces of art have a corresponding number you dial to hear a detailed narration. ✉ *501 Plaza Real, Mizner Park* ☎ *561/392–2500* ⊕ *www.bocamuseum.org* 🔖 *$14* ⊘ *Tues., Thurs., and Fri. 10–5, Wed. 10–9, weekends noon–5.*

FAMILY **Gumbo Limbo Nature Center.** A big draw for kids, this stellar spot has four huge saltwater tanks brimming with sea life, from coral to stingrays to spiny lobsters, plus a sea turtle rehabilitation center. Nocturnal walks in spring and early summer, when staffers lead a quest to find nesting female turtles coming ashore to lay eggs, are popular; so are the hatching releases in August and September. Call to purchase tickets in advance as there are very limited spaces. Gumbo Limbo is one of only a handful of centers that offer the chance to observe the babies departing into the ocean. There is also a nature trail and butterfly garden, a ¼-mile boardwalk, and a 40-foot observation tower, where you're likely to see brown pelicans and osprey. ✉ *1801 N. Ocean Blvd.* ☎ *561/544–8605*

⊕ *www.gumbolimbo.org* ✉ *Free ($5 suggested donation), turtle walks $15* ⊗ *Mon.–Sat. 9–4, Sun. noon–4.*

Old Floresta. This residential area was developed by Addison Mizner starting in 1925 and is beautifully landscaped with palms and cycads. Its houses are mainly Mediterranean in style, many with balconies supported by exposed wood columns. Explore by driving northward on Paloma Avenue (Northwest 8th Avenue) from Palmetto Park Road, then weave in and out of the side streets. ✉ *Paloma Ave. north of W. Palmetto Park Rd.*

BEACHES

Boca's three city beaches (South Beach, Red Reef Park, and Spanish River Park, south to north, respectively) are beautiful and hugely popular; but unless you're a resident or enter via bicycle, parking can be very expensive. Save your receipt if you care to go in and out, or park hop—most guards at the front gate will honor a same-day ticket from another location if you ask nicely. Another option is the county-run South Inlet Park that's walking distance from the Boca Raton Bridge Hotel at the southern end of Lake Boca; it has a metered lot for a fraction of the cost, but not quite the same charm as the others.

FAMILY **Red Reef Park.** The ocean with its namesake reef that you can wade up to is just one draw: a fishing zone on the Intracoastal Waterway across the street, a 9-hole golf course next door, and the Gumbo Limbo Environmental Education Center at the northern end of the park can easily make a day at the beach into so much more. But if pure old-fashioned fun-in-the-sun is your focus, to that end there are tons of picnic tables and grills, and two separate playgrounds. Pack snorkels and explore the reef at high tide when fish are most abundant. Swimmers, be warned: once lifeguards leave at 5, anglers flock to the shores and stay well past dark. **Amenities:** lifeguards; parking (fee); showers; toilets. **Best for:** snorkeling; swimming; walking. ✉ *1400 N. Rte. A1A* ☎ *561/393–7974, 561/393–7989 for beach conditions* ⊕ *www.ci.boca-raton.fl.us/rec/parks/redreef.shtm* ✉ *$16 parking (weekdays), $18 parking (weekends)* ⊗ *Daily 8 am–10 pm.*

South Beach Park. Perched high up on a dune, a large open-air pavilion at the east end of Palmetto Park Road offers a panoramic view of what's in store below on the sand that stretches up the coast. Serious beachgoers need to pull into the main lot ¼ mile north on the east side of A1A, but if a short-but-sweet visit is what you're after, the 15 or so one-hour spots with meters in the circle driveway will do (and not cost you the normal $15 parking fee). During the day, pretty young things blanket the shore, and windsurfers practice tricks in the waves. Quiet quarters are farther north. **Amenities:** lifeguards; parking (fee); showers; toilets. **Best for:** sunsets; windsurfing; walking; swimming. ✉ *400 N. Rte A1A* ⊕ *www.ci.boca-raton.fl.us/rec/parks/southbeach.shtm* ✉ *$15 parking (weekdays), $17 parking (weekends)* ⊗ *Daily 8–sunset.*

Spanish River Park. At 76 acres and including extensive nature trails, this is by far one of the largest ocean parks in the southern half of Palm Beach County and a great pick for people who want more space and fewer crowds. Big groups, including family reunions, favor it because of the number of covered picnic areas for rent, but anyone can snag a free table (there are plenty!) under the thick canopy of banyan trees. Even though the vast majority of the park is separated from the surf, you never actually have to cross A1A to reach the beach, because tunnels run under it at several locations. **Amenities:** lifeguards; parking (fee); showers; toilets. **Best for:** swimming; walking; solitude. ⊠ *3001 N. Rte. A1A* ☏ *561/393-7815* ⊕ *www.ci.boca-raton.fl.us/rec/parks/ spanishriver.shtm* 🎟 *$16 parking (weekdays), $18 parking (weekends)* ☉ *Daily 8–sunset.*

WHERE TO EAT

$$$$
TUSCAN
Fodor's Choice
★

✕ **Casa D'Angelo Ristorante.** The lines are deservedly long at Chef Angelo Elia's upscale Tuscan restaurant in tony Boca Raton. The third outpost of his renowned Casa D'Angelo chain impresses with an outstanding selection of antipasti, carpaccios, pastas, and specialties from the wood-burning oven. From staples like the antipasto *angelo* (grilled vegetables and buffalo mozzarella) and linguine with white-water clams and garlic, to the ever-changing gnocchi, risotto, veal scaloppine, and fish specials of the day, Angelo's dishes deliver pure perfection in every bite. The wine list is also exceptional with hundreds of Italian and American wines to choose from. ⑤ *Average main: $38* ⊠ *171 E. Palmetto Park Rd.* ☏ *561/996–1234* ⊕ *www.casa-d-angelo.com* ⊛ *Reservations essential* ☉ *No lunch.*

$$$
AMERICAN

✕ **Racks Downtown Eatery & Tavern.** Whimsical indoor–outdoor décor and comfort food with a twist help define this popular eatery in tony Mizner Park. Instead of dinner rolls, pretzel bread and mustard get things started. Share plates like bacon-wrapped shrimp and sea bass lettuce cups to promote convivial social dining. Move on to creative wood-fired pizzas and burgers; there's also a sushi menu. Happy hour at the bar is 4–7 and offers half-price drinks and appetizers. ⑤ *Average main: $23* ⊠ *402 Plaza Real, Mizner Park* ☏ *561/395–1662* ⊕ *www. racksboca.com.*

$$$$
SEAFOOD
Fodor's Choice
★

✕ **Truluck's.** This popular Florida and Texas seafood chain is so serious about its fruits of the sea that it supports its own fleet of 16 fishing boats. Stone crabs are the signature dish, and you can have all you can eat on Monday night from October to May. Other recommended dishes include salmon topped with blue crab and shrimp, hot-and-crunchy trout, crab cakes, and blackened Florida grouper. Portions are huge, so you might want to make a meal of appetizers. And don't miss the warm carrot cake—it's heaven on a plate! The place comes alive each night with its popular piano bar. ⑤ *Average main: $35* ⊠ *351 Plaza Real, Mizner Park* ☏ *561/391–0755* ⊕ *www.trulucks.com.*

$$$
CHINESE

✕ **Uncle Tai's.** The draw at this upscale eatery is some of the best Hunan cuisine on Florida's east coast. Specialties include sliced duck with snow peas and water chestnuts in a tangy plum sauce, and orange beef delight—flank steak stir-fried until crispy and then sautéed with pepper sauce, garlic, and orange peel. They'll go easy on the heat on request. The service is quietly efficient. The early-bird crowd will appreciate the very filling Sunset Dinner specials (5–6:15 pm), which come with a

6

starter, a dessert, and a main dish. ⑤ *Average main: $21* ✉ *5250 Town Center Circle* ☎ *561/368–8806* ⊕ *www.uncletais.com.*

WHERE TO STAY

$$$
RESORT
FAMILY
Fodor's Choice
★

Boca Beach Club. Dotted with turquoise lounge chairs, ruffled umbrellas, and white-sand beaches, this newly reconceived and rebranded hotel is now part of the Waldorf-Astoria collection and looks as if it was carefully replicated from a retro-chic postcard. **Pros:** great location on the beach; kids' activity center. **Cons:** pricey; shuttle ride away from the main building. ⑤ *Rooms from: $399* ✉ *900 S. Ocean Blvd.* ☎ *888/564–1312* ⊕ *www.bocabeachclub.com* ⇄ *212 rooms* ⍥ *No meals.*

$$
RESORT
FAMILY
Fodor's Choice
★

Boca Raton Resort & Club. Addison Mizner built this Mediterranean-style hotel in 1926, and additions over time have created a sprawling, sparkling resort, one of the most luxurious in all of South Florida and part of the Waldorf-Astoria collection. **Pros:** super-exclusive—grounds are closed to the public; décor strikes the right balance between historic roots and modern comforts; plenty of activities. **Cons:** daily resort charge; conventions often crowd common areas. ⑤ *Rooms from: $249* ✉ *501 E. Camino Real* ☎ *561/447–3000, 888/543–1277* ⊕ *www.bocaresort.com* ⇄ *635 rooms* ⍥ *No meals.*

NIGHTLIFE

Fodor's Choice
★

Rustic Cellar. Warm and intimate, this dark cozy nook is modeled after a Napa Valley tasting room and is perhaps the best wine bar in Palm Beach County. More than 300 hand-selected vintages, most from top domestic and foreign vintners, are served—and nearly all are available by the glass. There's also an impressive collection of craft beers. ✉ *Royal Palm Place, 409 S.E. Mizner Blvd.* ☎ *561/392–5237* ⊕ *www.rusticcellar.com.*

SHOPPING

Mizner Park. This distinctive 30-acre shopping center off Federal Highway, one block north of Palmetto Park Road, intersperses apartments and town houses among its gardenlike commercial areas. Some three dozen national and local retailers line the central axis that's peppered with fountains and green space, restaurants, galleries, a movie theater, the Boca Raton Museum of Art, and an amphitheater that hosts major concerts as well as community events. ✉ *327 Plaza Real* ☎ *561/362–0606* ⊕ *www.miznerpark.com.*

Royal Palm Place. The retail enclave of Royal Palm is filled with independent boutiques selling fine jewelry and apparel. By day, stroll the walkable streets and have your pick of sidewalk cafés for lunch alongside Boca's ladies who lunch. Royal Palm Place assumes a different personality come nightfall, as its numerous restaurants and lounges attract throngs of patrons for great dining and fabulous libations. ✉ *101 Plaza Real S* ☎ *561/392–8920* ⊕ *www.royalpalmplace.com.*

Town Center at Boca Raton. Over on the west side of Boca, this indoor megamall has over 220 stores, with anchor stores including Saks and

Neiman Marcus and just about every major high-end designer, including Bulgari and Anne Fontaine. But not every shop here requires deep pockets. The Town Center at Boca Raton is also firmly rooted with a variety of more affordable national brands like Gap and Guess. ⊠ *6000 Glades Rd.* ☎ *561/368–6000* ⊕ *www.simon.com/mall/ town-center-at-boca-raton.*

SPORTS AND THE OUTDOORS

GOLF

Red Reef Park Executive Golf Course. This executive golf course offers 9 holes with varying views of the Intracoastal and the Atlantic Ocean. The Joe Palloka and Charles Ankrom designed course dates back to 1957. It was refreshed in 2001 through a multimillion-dollar renovation. The scenic holes are between 54 and 227 yards each—great for a quick round. The greens fees range from $16.25 to walk in the off-season to $25.75 with a cart in season. Park in the lot across the street from the main beach entrance, and put the greens-fees receipt on the dash; that covers parking. ⊠ *1221 N. Ocean Blvd.* ☎ *561/391–5014* ⊕ *www. bocacitygolf.com* ✉ *$25.75 for 9 holes* ⚡ *9 holes. 1357 yards. par 32.*

SCUBA AND SNORKELING

Force-E. This company rents, sells, and repairs scuba and snorkeling equipment—and organizes about 80 dive trips a week throughout the region. The PADI-affiliated five-star center has instruction for all levels and offers private charters, too. They have two other outposts besides this Boca Raton location—one north in Riviera Beach and one south in Pompano Beach. ⊠ *2181 N. Federal Hwy.* ☎ *561/368–0555, 866/307– 3483* ⊕ *www.force-e.com.*

TREASURE COAST

In contrast to the glitzy, überplanned Gold Coast that includes Greater Palm Beach and Boca Raton, the more bucolic Treasure Coast stretches from northernmost Palm Beach County into Martin, St. Lucie, and Indian River counties. Along the east are barrier islands all the way to Sebastian and beyond, starting with Jupiter Island, then Hutchinson Island, and finally Orchid Island—and reefs, too. Those reefs are responsible for the region's nickname: they've caused ships carrying riches dating back as far as 1715 to fall asunder and cast their treasures ashore. The Intracoastal Waterway here is called the Indian River starting at the St. Lucie Inlet in Stuart and morphs into a broad tidal lagoon with tiny uninhabited islands and wildlife galore. Inland, there's cattle ranching and tracts of pine and palmetto scrub, along with sugar and citrus production.

Despite a growing number of malls and beachfront condominiums, much of the Treasure Coast remains untouched, something not lost on ecotourists, game fishers, and people who want a break from the oversaturated digital age. Consequently, there are fewer lodging options in this region of Florida, but if 30 minutes in the car sounds like a breeze, culture vultures can live in the lap of luxury in Vero Beach and detour south to Fort Pierce's galleries and botanical gardens. Likewise, families will revel in every amenity imaginable at the Hutchinson Island Marriott and be able to swing northwest to hit up the Mets spring-training stadium in Port St. Lucie or down to Jupiter for the Cardinals and the Marlins.

JUPITER AND VICINITY

12 miles north of West Palm Beach.

Jupiter is one of the few towns in the region not fronted by an island, and it's still quite close to the fantastic hotels, shopping, and dining of the Palm Beach area. The beaches here are on the mainland, and Route A1A runs for almost 4 miles along the beachfront dunes and beautiful homes.

Northeast across the Jupiter Inlet from Jupiter is the southern tip of Jupiter Island, which stretches about 15 miles to the St. Lucie Inlet. Here expansive and expensive estates often retreat from the road behind screens of vegetation, and the population dwindles the farther north you go. At the very north end, sea turtles come to nest. To the west, on the mainland, is the little community of Hobe Sound.

GETTING HERE AND AROUND

If you're coming from the airport in West Palm Beach, take I–95 to Route 706. Otherwise, Federal Highway (U.S. 1) and Route A1A are usually more convenient.

Contacts Palm Beach County Convention and Visitors Bureau ⊠ *1555 Palm Beach Lakes Blvd., Ste. 800, West Palm Beach* ☎ *561/233–3000* ⊕ *www. palmbeachfl.com.*

EXPLORING

Fodor's Choice ★ **Blowing Rocks Preserve.** Managed by the Nature Conservancy, this protected area on Jupiter Island is headlined by an almost otherworldly-looking limestone shelf that fringes South Florida's most turquoise waters. Also protected within its 73 acres are plants native to beach-front dunes, coastal strand (the landward side of the dunes), mangrove swamps, and tropical hardwood forests. There are two short walking trails on the Intracoastal side of the preserve, as well as an education center and a butterfly garden. The best time to come and seeing the "blowing rocks" is when a storm is brewing: If high tides and strong offshore winds coincide, the sea blows spectacularly through the holes in the eroded outcropping. During a calm summer day, you can swim in crystal clear waters on the mile-long beach and climb around the rock formations at low tide. Park in one of the two lots because police ticket cars on the road. ⊠ *574 S. Beach Rd., CR 707, Hobe Sound* ☎ *561/744–6668* ⊕ *www.nature.org/blowingrocks* ⊠ *$2* ☉ *Daily 9–4:30.*

FAMILY
Fodor's Choice ★ **Hobe Sound Nature Center.** Though located in the Hobe Sound National Wildlife Refuge, this nature center is an independent organization. The exhibit hall houses live baby alligators, crocodiles, a scary-looking tarantula, and more—and is a child's delight. ■ TIP→ Among the center's more popular events are the annual nighttime sea turtle walks, held between May and June; reservations are accepted as early as April

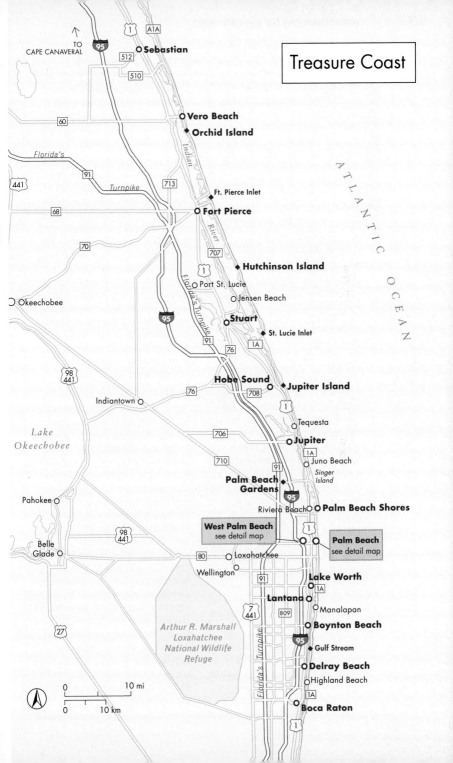

Treasure Coast

TO CAPE CANAVERAL

95
1
A1A

512
510

O **Sebastian**

60

Florida's
91
Turnpike

713

O **Vero Beach**
◆ **Orchid Island**

Indian

441

68

◆ Ft. Pierce Inlet

O **Fort Pierce**

70

River

707

1

◆ **Hutchinson Island**

Florida's Turnpike

O Port St. Lucie

O Okeechobee

O Jensen Beach

95

O **Stuart**

91
76
1A

◆ St. Lucie Inlet

98
441

76

Hobe Sound O
708

◆ **Jupiter Island**

Indiantown O

1

Lake
Okeechobee

706

O Tequesta

O **Jupiter**
1A

710

91

O Juno Beach
Singer
Island

Pahokee O

**Palm Beach
Gardens** ◆

95

98
441

Riviera Beach O

O **Palm Beach Shores**

Belle
Glade O

West Palm Beach
see detail map

1

Palm Beach
see detail map

80
O Loxahatchee

Wellington O

91

Lake Worth
1A

Lantana O

7
441

809

O Manalapan

ATLANTIC OCEAN

27

Arthur R. Marshall
Loxahatchee
National Wildlife
Refuge

Florida's Turnpike

O **Boynton Beach**

95

◆ Gulf Stream

O **Delray Beach**

O Highland Beach

1A

0   10 mi
0   10 km

O **Boca Raton**

1

CLOSE UP

Florida's Sea Turtles: The Nesting Season

From May to October, turtles nest all along the Florida coast. Female loggerhead, Kemp's ridley, and other species living in the Atlantic Ocean or Gulf of Mexico swim as much as 2,000 miles to the Florida shore. By night they drag their 100- to 400-pound bodies onto the beach to the dune line. Then each digs a hole with her flippers, drops in 100 or so eggs, covers them up, and returns to sea.

The babies hatch about 60 days later. Once they burst out of the sand, the hatchlings must get to sea rapidly or risk becoming dehydrated from the sun or being caught by crabs, birds, or other predators.

Instinctively, baby turtles head toward bright light, probably because for millions of years starlight or moonlight reflected on the waves was the brightest light around, serving to guide hatchlings to water. But now light from beach development can lead the babies in the wrong direction, toward the street rather than the water. To help, many coastal towns enforce light restrictions during nesting months. Florida homeowners are asked to dim their lights on behalf of baby sea turtles.

At night, volunteers walk the beaches, searching for signs of turtle nests. Upon finding telltale scratches in the sand, they cordon off the sites, so beachgoers will leave the spots undisturbed. Volunteers also keep watch over nests when babies are about to hatch, and assist if the hatchlings get disoriented.

It's a hazardous world for baby turtles. They can die after eating tar balls or plastic debris, or they can be gobbled by sharks or circling birds. Only about one in a thousand survives to adulthood. After reaching the water, the babies make their way to warm currents. East Coast hatchlings drift into the Gulf Stream, spending years floating around the Atlantic.

Males never return to land, but when females attain maturity, in 15–20 years, they return to shore to lay eggs. Remarkably, even after migrating hundreds and even thousands of miles out at sea, most return to the very beach where they were born to deposit their eggs. Each time they nest, they come back to the same stretch of beach. In fact, the more they nest, the more accurate they get, until eventually they return time and again to within a few feet of where they last laid their eggs. These incredible navigation skills remain for the most part a mystery despite intense scientific study.

Several local organizations offer nightly turtle walks during nesting season. Most are in June and July, starting around 8 pm and sometimes lasting until midnight. Expect a $10 to $15 fee. Call in advance to confirm times and to reserve a spot—places usually take reservations as early as April. If you're in southern Palm Beach County, contact Boca Raton's **Gumbo Limbo Nature Center** (☎ 561/338-1473 ⊕ www.gumbolimbo.org). The **John D. MacArthur Beach State Park** (☎ 561/624-6952 ⊕ www.macarthurbeach.org) is convenient for Palm Beach–area visitors at the northern end of Singer Island. **Hobe Sound Nature Center** (☎ 772/546-2067 ⊕ www.hobesoundnaturecenter.com) is farther up. Treasure Coasters in or near Vero Beach can go to **Sebastian Inlet State Park** (☎ 321/984-4852 ⊕ www.floridastateparks.org/sebastianinlet).

Away from developed shorelines, Blowing Rocks Preserve on Jupiter Island lets you wander the dunes.

1. Just off the center's entrance is a mile-long nature trail loop that snakes through three different kinds of habitats: coastal hammock, estuary beach, and sand pine scrub, which is one of Florida's most unusual and endangered plant communities and what composes much of the refuge's nearly 250 acres. ⊠ 13640 S.E. U.S. 1, Hobe Sound 🕾 772/546–2067 ⊕ www.hobesoundnaturecenter.com ✉ Free (donation requested) ☉ Mon.–Sat. 9–3.

FAMILY
Fodor'sChoice
★

Jonathan Dickinson State Park. This serene state park provides a glimpse of pre-development "real" Florida. A beautiful showcase of Florida inland habitat, the park teems with endangered gopher tortoises and manatees. From Hobe Mountain, an ancient dune topped with a tower, you are treated to a panoramic view of this park's more than 11,000 acres of varied terrain and the Intracoastal Waterway. The Loxahatchee River, which cuts through the park, is home to plenty of charismatic manatees in winter and alligators year-round; two-hour boat tours of the river depart daily (⇨ see Jonathan Dickinson State Park River Tours). Kayak rentals are available, as is horseback riding (it was reintroduced after a 30-year absence). Among the amenities are a dozen newly redone cabins for rent, tent sites, bicycle and hiking trails, two established campgrounds and some primitive campgrounds, and a snack bar. Don't skip the Elsa Kimbell Environmental Education and Research Center, which has interactive displays, exhibits, and a short film on the natural history of the area. The park is also a fantastic birding location, with about 150 species to spot. ⊠ 16450 S.E. U.S. 1, Hobe Sound 🕾 772/546–2771 ⊕ www.floridastateparks.org/jonathandickinson ✉ Vehicles $6, *bicyclists and pedestrians $2 ⊙ Daily 8–sunset, Elsa Kimbell Environmental Education and Research Center daily 9–5.*

Fodor'sChoice ★ **Jupiter Inlet Lighthouse & Museum.** Designed by Civil War hero Lieutenant George Gordon Meade, this brick lighthouse has been under the Coast Guard's purview since 1860. Tours of the 108-foot-tall landmark are held approximately every half-hour and are included with admission. (Children must be at least 4 feet tall to go to the top.) The museum tells about efforts to restore this graceful spire to the way it looked from 1860 to 1918; its galleries and outdoor structures, including a pioneer home, also showcase local history dating back five thousand years. ⊠ *Lighthouse Park, 500 Capt. Armour's Way* ☎ *561/747–8380* ⊕ *www.jupiterlighthouse.org* ⊠ *$9 ⊙ Jan.–Apr., daily 10–5; May–Dec., Tues.–Sun. 10–5. Last tour at 4.*

BEACHES

Carlin Park. About ½ mile south of the Jupiter Beach Resort and Indiantown Road, the quiet beach here is just one draw; otherwise, the manicured park, which straddles A1A, is chock-full of activities and amenities. Two bocce ball courts, six lighted tennis courts, a baseball diamond, a wood-chip-lined running path, and an amphitheater that hosts free concerts and Shakespeare productions are just some of the highlights. Locals also swear by the Lazy Loggerhead Café that's right off the seaside parking lot for a great casual breakfast and lunch. **Amenities:** lifeguards; food and drink; parking (no fee); showers; toilets. **Best for:** swimming; walking. ⊠ *400 S. Rte. A1A* ⊕ *www.pbcgov.com/parks/locations/carlin.htm.*

Hobe Sound National Wildlife Refuge. Nature lovers seeking to get as far as possible from the madding crowds will feel at peace at this refuge managed by the U.S. Fish & Wildlife service. It's a haven for people who want some quiet while they walk around and photograph the gorgeous coastal sand dunes, where turtle nests and shells often wash ashore. The beach has been severely eroded by high tides and strong winds (surprisingly, surfing is allowed and many do partake). You can't actually venture within most of the 735 protected acres, so if hiking piques your interest, head to the refuge's main entrance a few miles away on Hobe Sound (⊠ *13640 S.E. U.S. 1 in Hobe Sound*) for a mile-long trek close to the nature center, or to nearby Jonathan Dickinson State Park (⊠ *16450 S.E. U.S. 1 in Hobe Sound*). **Amenities:** parking (fee); toilets. **Best for:** solitude; surfing; walking. ⊠ *198 N. Beach Rd., at end of N. Beach Rd., Jupiter Island* ☎ *772/546–6141* ⊕ *www.fws.gov/hobesound* ⊠ *$5.*

Fodor'sChoice ★ **Jupiter Beach.** Famous throughout all of Florida for a unique pooch-loving stance, the town of Jupiter's beach welcomes Yorkies, Labs, pugs—you name it—along its 2½-mile oceanfront. Dogs can frolic unleashed or join you for a dip. Free parking spots line A1A in front of the sandy stretch, and there are multiple access points and continuously refilled dog-bag boxes (29 to be exact). The dog beach starts on Marcinski Road (Beach Marker #25) and continues north until Beach Marker #5. Before going, read through the guidelines posted on the Friends of Jupiter Beach website; the biggest things to note are be sure to clean up after your dog and to steer clear of lifeguarded areas to the north and south. **Amenities:** showers; toilets. **Best for:** walking. ⊠ *2188 Marcinski Rd., across the street from the parking lot* ☎ *561/748–8140* ⊕ *www.friendsofjupiterbeach.com.*

WHERE TO EAT

$$
SEAFOOD

✗ **Guanabanas.** Expect a wait for dinner, which is not necessarily a bad thing at this island paradise of a waterfront restaurant and bar. Take the wait time to explore the bridges and trails of the open-air tropical oasis and nibble on some conch fritters at the large tiki bar until your table is ready. Try the lemon-butter hogfish for dinner and stick around for the live music (a full concert calendar is on the website). Breakfast, offered only on weekends, is good, too. That said, it's more about the view than the food here. ⑤ *Average main: $18* ⊠ *960 N. Rte. A1A* ☎ *561/747–8878* ⊕ *www.guanabanas.com* ⌂ *Reservations not accepted.*

$$
SEAFOOD

✗ **Little Moir's Food Shack.** This local favorite is not much to look at and a bit tricky to find, but well worth the search. The fried-food standards you might expect at such a casual place that uses plastic utensils are not found on the menu; instead there are fried tuna rolls with basil, and panko-crusted fried oysters with spicy fruit salad. A variety of beers are fun to pair with the creatively prepared seafood dishes that include wahoo, mahimahi, and snapper. ⑤ *Average main: $17* ⊠ *103 S. U.S. 1* ☎ *561/741–3626* ⊕ *www.littlemoirs.com/food-shack* ⌂ *Reservations not accepted* ☉ *Closed Sun.*

$$$$
SEAFOOD

✗ **Sinclair's Ocean Grill.** Remodeled in late 2012 to give it a slick, contemporary look, this upscale restaurant at the Jupiter Beach Resort & Spa is a favorite of locals in the know. The menu has a daily selection of fresh fish, such as Atlantic black grouper over lemon crab salad, sesame-seared tuna, and mahimahi with fruit salsa. There are also thick, juicy cuts of meat, including New York strip steak and beef tenderloin, as well as mouth-watering chicken and lamb dishes. The new Sinclair's Lounge is idyllic for a pre-dinner aperitif. For something more casual, dine outside on the terrace to hear the waves lapping and take in the beachscape. ⑤ *Average main: $31* ⊠ *Jupiter Beach Resort, 5 N. Rte. A1A* ☎ *561/746–2511* ⊕ *www.jupiterbeachresort.com.*

$$
AMERICAN

✗ **Taste Casual Dining.** Located in the center of historic Hobe Sound, this cozy dining spot with a pleasant, screened-in patio offers piano dinner music on Fridays. Locals like to hang out at the old, English-style wine bar; however, the food itself is the biggest draw here. Try a lobster roll and the signature Gorgonzola salad for lunch, and any fish dish for dinner. On weekend nights, order the excellent, slow-cooked prime rib, another specialty. ⑤ *Average main: $18* ⊠ *11750 S.E. Dixie Hwy., Hobe Sound* ☎ *772/546–1129* ⊕ *www.tastehobesound.com* ☉ *Closed Sun. May–Oct.*

WHERE TO STAY

$$$
RESORT
FAMILY
Fodor'sChoice
★

▣ **Jupiter Beach Resort & Spa.** Families love this nine-story hotel filled with rich Caribbean-style rooms containing mahogany sleigh beds and armoires. All rooms have balconies, and many have stunning views of the ocean and local landmarks like the Jupiter Lighthouse and Juno Pier. **Pros:** fantastic beachside pool area with hammocks and a fire pit; marble showers; great restaurant. **Cons:** $25 nightly resort fee; no covered parking; bathtubs only in suites. ⑤ *Rooms from: $360* ⊠ *5 N. Rte. A1A* ☎ *561/746–2511, 800/228–8810* ⊕ *www.jupiterbeachresort. com* ⇆ *134 rooms, 34 suites* ⦿ *No meals.*

SPORTS AND THE OUTDOORS

BASEBALL

Roger Dean Stadium. It's a spring training doubleheader! Both the St. Louis Cardinals and the Miami Marlins call this 6,600-seat facility home base from February to April. The rest of the year two minor league teams (Jupiter Hammerheads and Palm Beach Cardinals) share its turf. In the Abacoa area of Jupiter, the grounds are surrounded by a mix of restaurants and sports bars for pre- and postgame action. ⊠ *4751 Main St.* ☎ *561/775–1818* ⊕ *www.rogerdeanstadium.com.*

BOATING AND CANOEING

Fodor'sChoice
★
Canoe Outfitters of Florida. See animals from otters to eagles along 8 miles of the Loxahatchee River in Riverbend County Park daily except Tuesday and Wednesday. Canoe and kayak rentals are $26.50 for four hours. Bike rentals are available, too. ⊠ *Riverbend County Park, 9060 W. Indiantown Rd.* ☎ *561/746–7053* ⊕ *www.canoeoutfittersofflorida. com* ⊗ *Closed Tues. and Wed.*

FAMILY
Fodor'sChoice
★
Jonathan Dickinson State Park River Tours. Boat tours of the Loxahatchee River and guided horseback rides, along with canoe, kayak, bicycle, and boat rentals are offered daily. The popular Wilderness Guided Boat Tour leaves four times daily at 9, 11, 1, and 3 pm and costs $18.87 (for best wildlife photos take the 11 or 1 tour). The pontoon cruises up the Loxahatchee in search of manatees, herons, osprey, alligators, and more. The skipper details the region's natural and cultural history; and from Thursday to Monday the boat also stops at the Trapper Nelson Interpretive Site for a tour of the home of a local legend, the so-called "Wildman" of the Loxahatchee. ⊠ *Jonathan Dickinson State Park, 16450 S.E. U.S. 1, Hobe Sound* ☎ *561/746–1466* ⊕ *www. floridaparktours.com.*

GOLF

Abacoa Golf Club. Built in 1999, the tag line for this Joe Lee–designed 18-hole course in Jupiter is "public golf at its finest." Most of the courses in this golfing community are private, but the range at Abacoa is on par with them and membership (nor deep pockets) *isn't* required. One of the course's more interesting features includes the several elevation changes throughout, which is a rarity in flat Florida. The course caters to golfers at all skill levels. The greens fees range from $30 to $99 (including cart), depending on time of year, time of day, and weekday versus weekend. ⊠ *105 Barbados Dr.* ☎ *561/622–0036* ⊕ *www.abacoagolfclub.com* ⦾ *$89 for 18 holes* ⅄ *18 holes. 7200 yards. par 72.*

Golf Club of Jupiter. Locally owned and operated since 1981, this Lamar Smith–designed golf club features a public, championship golf course—the "Jupiter" course—with 18 holes of varying difficulty. It has a course rating of 69.9 and a slope rating of 117 on Bermuda grass. There's a full-time golf pro on staff and an on-site bar and restaurant. ⊠ *1800 S.*

Central Blvd. ☎*561/747–6262* ⊕*www.golfclubofjupiter.com* ▱*$70 for 18 holes.* ⚐*. 18 holes. 6275 yards. par 70.*

STUART AND JENSEN BEACH

10 miles north of Hobe Sound.

The compact town of Stuart lies on a peninsula that juts out into the St. Lucie River off the Indian River and has a remarkable amount of shoreline for its size. It scores huge points for its charming historic district and is the self-described "Sailfish Capital of the World." On the southern end, you'll find Port Salerno and its waterfront area, the Manatee Pocket, which are a skip away from the St. Lucie Inlet.

Immediately north of Stuart is down-to-earth Jensen Beach. Both Stuart and Jensen Beach straddle the Indian River and occupy Hutchinson Island, the barrier island that continues into the town of Fort Pierce. Between late April and August, hundreds, even thousands, of turtles come here to nest along the Atlantic beaches. Residents have taken pains to curb the runaway development that has created commercial crowding to the north and south, although some high-rises have popped up along the shore.

6

GETTING HERE AND AROUND

To get to Stuart and Jensen Beach from Jupiter and Hobe Sound, drive north on Federal Highway (U.S. 1). Route A1A crosses through downtown Stuart and is the sole main road throughout Hutchinson Island. Route 707 runs parallel on the mainland directly across the tidal lagoon.

ESSENTIALS

Visitor Information Martin County Convention & Visitors Bureau ☎ *772/288–5451, 877/585–0085* ⊕ *www.discovermartin.com.*

EXPLORING

Strict architectural and zoning standards guide civic-renewal projects in the heart of Stuart. Antiques stores, restaurants, and more than 50 specialty shops are rooted within the two-block area of Flagler Avenue and Osceola Street north of where A1A cuts across the peninsula (visit ⊕ *www.stuartmainstreet.org* for more information). A self-guided walking-tour pamphlet is available at assorted locations to clue you in on this once-small fishing village's early days.

Elliott Museum. Opened in March 2013, the museum's glittering, green-certified 48,000-square-foot facility is double its previous size and houses a permanent collection along with traveling exhibits pertaining to art, history, and technology. The original museum was founded in 1961 in honor of Sterling Elliott, an inventor of an early automated-addressing machine, the egg crate, and a four-wheel bicycle, and it celebrates history, art, and technology, much of it viewed through the lens of the automobile's effect on American society. There's an impressive array of antique cars, plus paintings, historic artifacts, and nostalgic goods like vintage baseball cards and toys. ⊠ *825 N.E. Ocean Blvd., Jensen Beach* ☎*772/225–1961* ⊕*www.elliottmuseumfl.org* ▱*$12* ☉ *Daily. 10–5.*

FAMILY **Florida Oceanographic Coastal Center.** This hydroland is the place to go for an interactive marine experience and to live the center's mission "to inspire environmental stewardship of Florida's coastal ecosystems through education and research." Petting and feeding stingrays can be done at various times; in the morning, a sea turtle program introduces you to three full-time residents. Make sure to catch the "feeding frenzy" when keepers toss food into the 750,000-gallon lagoon tank and sharks, tarpon, and snook swarm the surface. Join a 1-mile guided walk through the coastal hardwood hammock and mangrove swamp habitats, or explore the trails on your own—you may see a dolphin or manatee swim by. ⊠ *890 N.E. Ocean Blvd.* ☎ *772/225–0505* ⊕ *www. floridaocean.org* ⊠ *$12* ⊘ *Mon.–Sat. 10–5, Sun. noon–4. Nature trails close at 4.*

Gilbert's House of Refuge Museum. Built in 1875 on Hutchinson Island, this is the only remaining example of ten such structures that were erected by the U.S. Life-Saving Service (a predecessor of the Coast Guard) to aid stranded sailors. The displays here include antique life-saving equipment, maps, artifacts from nearby wrecks, and boatbuilding tools. The museum is affiliated with the nearby Elliott Museum. ⊠ *301 S.E. MacArthur Blvd., Jensen Beach* ☎ *772/225–1875* ⊕ *www. houseofrefugefl.org* ⊠ *$8* ⊘ *Mon.–Sat. 10–4, Sun. 1–4.*

BEACHES

FAMILY **Stuart Beach.** When the waves robustly roll in, the surfers are rolling in, too. Beginning surfers are especially keen on Stuart Beach because of its ever-vigilant lifeguards, and pros to the sport like the challenges that the choppy waters here bring. Families enjoy the snack bar known for its chicken fingers, the basketball courts, the large canopy-covered playground, and the three walkways interspersed throughout the area for easy ocean access. **Amenities:** lifeguards; food and drink; parking (no fee); showers; toilets. **Best for:** surfing; swimming. ⊠ *889 N.E. Ocean Blvd.* ⊘ *Daily 24 hrs.*

WHERE TO EAT

$$$ ✕ **Conchy Joe's.** Like a hermit crab sliding into a new shell, Conchy
SEAFOOD   Joe's moved up from West Palm Beach in 1983 to its current home, a 1920s rustic stilt house on the Indian River. It's full of antique fish mounts, gator hides, and snakeskins and is a popular tourist spot—but the waterfront location, casual vibe, and delicious seafood lures locals, too. Grouper marsala (the house specialty), coconut shrimp, and fried Bahamian cracked conch are menu fixtures, and live reggae gets people out of their shells Thursday through Sunday. Ⓢ *Average main: $27* ⊠ *3945 N.E. Indian River Dr., Jensen Beach* ☎ *772/334–1130* ⊕ *www. conchyjoes.com.*

$$$ ✕ **Courtine's.** A husband-and-wife team oversees this quiet and hospi-
FRENCH   table restaurant under the Roosevelt Bridge. French and American influences are clear in the Swiss chef's dishes, from rack of lamb with Dijon mustard to grilled filet mignon stuffed with Roquefort and fresh spinach. The formal dining room has subtle, elegant touches, such as votive candlelight and white tablecloths. A more casual menu is available at

the bar. $ *Average main: $25* ✉ *514 N. Dixie Hwy.* ☎ *772/692–3662* ⊕ *www.courtines.com* ⊗ *Closed Sun. and Mon. No lunch.*

$$$$
ECLECTIC

✕ **11 Maple Street.** This cozy spot is as good as it gets on the Treasure Coast. Soft music and a friendly staff set the mood in the antiques-filled dining room, which holds only 21 tables. An extensive list of small plates can be ordered as starters or mains and include tasty treats like black-rice-and-calamari fritters with Thai sauce and Wagyu hanger steak with onion rings and salsa verde. The limited but superb selection of entrées include wood-grilled elk with roasted faro and Wagyu ribeye with port wine. All desserts are made from scratch and are also seductive, including white-chocolate custard with blackberry sauce. $ *Average main: $42* ✉ *3224 N.E. Maple Ave., Jensen Beach* ☎ *772/334–7714* ⊕ *www.elevenmaple.com* ⟵ *Reservations essential* ⊗ *Closed Sun. and Mon. No lunch.*

WHERE TO STAY

$
RESORT
FAMILY

⌂ **Hutchinson Island Marriott Beach Resort & Marina.** With a 77-slip marina, a full water sports program, a golf course, tons of tennis courts, and children's activities, this self-contained resort is excellent for families, most of whom prefer to stay in the tower directly on the ocean. **Pros:** attentive, warm staff; rooms are comfortable and casually chic; all rooms have balconies. **Cons:** only one sit-down indoor restaurant; common areas are a bit dated; no spa; extra charge for parking. $ *Rooms from: $189* ✉ *555 N.E. Ocean Blvd., Hutchinson Island* ☎ *772/225–3700, 800/775–5936* ⊕ *www.marriott.com* ⤳ *204 rooms, 70 suites* ⦿ *No meals.*

$
RESORT

⌂ **Pirate's Cove Resort & Marina.** This cozy enclave on the banks of the Manatee Pocket with ocean access at the southern end of Stuart is the perfect place to set forth on a day at sea or wind down after one—it's relaxing and casual, and has amenities like a swimming pool courtyard, restaurant, and fitness center. **Pros:** spacious tropical-themed rooms; great for boaters, with a 50-slip full-service marina; each room has a balcony overlooking the water; free Wi-Fi and parking. **Cons:** lounge gets noisy at night; décor and furnishings are pretty but not luxurious; pool is on the small side. $ *Rooms from: $150* ✉ *4307 S.E. Bayview St., Port Salerno* ☎ *772/287–2500* ⊕ *www.piratescoveresort.com* ⤳ *50 rooms* ⦿ *No meals.*

SHOPPING

More than 60 restaurants and shops with antiques, art, and fashion have opened downtown along Osceola Street.

B&A Flea Market. A short drive from downtown and operating for more than two decades, the oldest and largest flea market on the Treasure Coast has a street-bazaar feel, with shoppers happily scouting the 500 vendors for the practical and unusual. If you have an open mind and love to shop garage sales, you'll do just fine here. ✉ *2885 S.E. U.S. 1* ☎ *772/288–4915* ⊕ *www.bafleamarket.com* ⬚ *Free* ⊗ *Weekends 8–3.*

SPORTS AND THE OUTDOORS

FISHING

Sailfish Marina of Stuart. Nab a deep-sea charter here, the closest public marina to the St. Lucie Inlet. ⊠ *3565 S.E. St. Lucie Blvd.* ☎ *772/283–1122* ⊕ *www.sailfishmarinastuart.com.*

FORT PIERCE AND PORT ST. LUCIE

11 miles north of Jensen Beach.

About an hour north of Palm Beach, Fort Pierce has a distinctive rural feel—but it has a surprising number of worthwhile attractions for a town of its size, including those easily seen while following Route 707 on the mainland (A1A on Hutchinson Island). A big draw is an inlet that offers fabulous fishing and excellent surfing. Nearby Port St. Lucie is largely landlocked southwest of Fort Pierce and is almost equidistant from there and Jensen Beach. It's not a big tourist area except for two sports facilities near I–95: the St. Lucie Mets' training grounds, Tradition Field, and the PGA Village. If you want a hotel directly on the sand or crave more than simple, motel-like accommodations, stay elsewhere and drive up for the day.

GETTING HERE AND AROUND

You can reach Fort Pierce from Jensen Beach by driving 11 miles north on Federal Highway (U.S. 1), Route 707, or Route A1A. To get to Port St. Lucie, continue north on U.S. 1 and take Prima Vista Boulevard west. From Fort Pierce, Route 709 goes diagonally southwest to Port St. Lucie, and I–95 is another choice.

ESSENTIALS

Visitor Information St. Lucie County Tourist Development Council ⊠ *2300 Virginia Ave.* ☎ *800/344-8443* ⊕ *www.visitstluciefla.com.*

EXPLORING

Heathcote Botanical Gardens. Stroll through this 3½-acre green space, which includes a palm walk, a Japanese garden, and a collection of 100 bonsai trees. There is also a gift shop with whimsical and botanical knickknacks. Guided tours are available by appointment for an extra fee. ⊠ *210 Savannah Rd.* ☎ *772/464–0323* ⊕ *www. heathcotebotanicalgardens.org* ☝ *$6* ⏱ *Nov.–Apr., Tues.–Sat. 9–5; May–Oct., Tues.–Sat. 9–5, Sun. 1–5.*

National Navy UDT-SEAL Museum. Commemorating the more than 3,000 troops who trained on these shores during World War II when this elite military unit got its start, there are weapons, vehicles, and equipment on view. Exhibits honor all frogmen and underwater demolition teams and depict their history. The museum houses the lifeboat from which SEALs saved the *Maersk Alabama* captain from Somali pirates in 2009. ⊠ *3300 N. Rte. A1A* ☎ *772/595–5845* ⊕ *www.navysealmuseum.com* ☝ *$8* ⏱ *Tues.–Sat. 10–4, Sun. noon–4.*

FAMILY   **Savannas Recreation Area.** Once a reservoir, the 550 acres have been returned to their natural wetlands state. Today the wilderness area has trails and a boat ramp, and the recreation area is open year-round. Canoe and kayak rentals are available Thursday through Monday.

✉ *1400 E. Midway Rd.* ☎ *772/464–7855* ⊕ *www.stlucieco.gov/parks/ savannas.htm* 🎫 *Free* ☉ *Daily 6 am–7:30 pm.*

BEACHES

Fort Pierce Inlet State Park. Across the inlet at the northern side of Hutchinson Island, a fishing oasis lures beachgoers who can't wait to reel in snook, flounder, and bluefish, among others. The park is also known as a prime wave-riding locale, thanks to a reef that lies just outside the jetty. Summer is the busiest season by a long shot, but don't be fooled: it's a laid-back place to sun and surf. There are covered picnic tables but no concessions; however, from where anglers perch, a bunch of casual restaurants can be spotted on the other side of the inlet that are a quick drive away. Note that the area of Jack Island Preserve has been closed indefinitely. **Amenities:** lifeguards (summer only); parking (fee); showers; toilets. **Best for:** surfing; walking; solitude. ✉ *905 Shorewinds Dr.* ☎ *772/468–3985* ⊕ *www.floridastateparks.org/fortpierceinlet* 🎫 *Vehicle $6, bicyclists and pedestrians $2* ☉ *Daily 8–sunset.*

WHERE TO STAY

$
HOTEL

Dockside Inn. This hotel is the best of the lodgings lining the scenic Fort Pierce Inlet on Seaway Drive (and that's not saying much). It's a practical base for fishing enthusiasts with nice touches like two pools and a waterfront restaurant. **Pros:** good value; overnight boat docking available; reasonable rates at marina; parking included. **Cons:** basic décor; some steps to climb; grounds are nothing too fancy but have great views. ⑤ *Rooms from: $109* ✉ *1160 Seaway Dr.* ☎ *772/468–3555, 800/286– 1745* ⊕ *www.docksideinn.com* 🍽 *36 rooms* ⊙*No meals.*

SPORTS AND THE OUTDOORS

BASEBALL

Tradition Field. Out west by I–95, this Port St. Lucie baseball stadium, formerly known as Digital Domain Park as well as Thomas J. White Stadium, is where the New York Mets train; it's also the home of the St. Lucie Mets minor league team. ✉ *525 N.W. Peacock Blvd., Port St. Lucie* ☎ *772/871–2115* ⊕ *www.stluciemets.com.*

GOLF

PGA Village. Owned and operated by the PGA of America, the national association of teaching pros, PGA Village is the winter home to many northern instructors, along with permanent staff. The facility is a little off the beaten path and the clubhouse is basic, but serious golfers will appreciate the three championship courses by Pete Dye and Tom Fazio and the chance to sharpen their skills at the 35-acre PGA Center for Golf Learning and Performance, which has nine practice bunkers mimicking sands and slopes from around the globe. Between the Fazio-designed Wanamaker Course, the Ryder Course, and the Dye-designed Dye Course, there is a total of 54 holes of championship golf at PGA Village. Beginners can start out on the lesser-known (and easier) PGA Short Course and the Country Club Course. ✉ *1916 Perfect Dr., Port St. Lucie* ☎ *772/467–1300, 800/800–4653* ⊕ *www.pgavillage.com* 🎫 *$119 for 18 holes* ⚑*Wanamaker Course: 18 holes. 7123 yards. par 72. Ryder Course: 18 holes. 7037 yards. par 72. Dye Course: 18 holes. 7279 yards. par 72.*

6

SCUBA DIVING

The region's premier dive site is actually on the National Register of Historic Places. The *Urca de Lima* was part of the storied treasure fleet bound for Spain that was destroyed by a hurricane in 1715. It's now part of an underwater archaeological preserve about 200 yards from shore, just north of the National Navy UDT-SEAL Museum and under 10 to 15 feet of water. The remains contain a flat-bottom, round-bellied ship and cannons that can be visited on an organized dive trip.

Dive Odyssea. This full-service dive shop offers kayak rentals, tank rentals, and scuba lessons. Guided dive excursions (two-tank dive trips starting at $65) can be arranged to nearby reefs or the Urca de Lima Underwater Archaeological Preserve, a shipwreck from 1715 that's listed on the National Register of Historic Places. This shipwreck was part of the storied treasure fleet bound for Spain that was destroyed by a hurricane in 1715. It's about 200 yards from shore and under 10 to 15 feet of water; the remains contain a flat-bottom, round-bellied ship and cannons. ⊠ *Fort Pierce Inlet, 621 N. 2nd St.* ☎ *772/460–1771* ⊕ *www.diveodyssea.com.*

VERO BEACH AND SEBASTIAN

12 miles north of Fort Pierce.

Tranquil and picturesque, these Indian River County towns have a strong commitment to the environment and culture, particularly to the upscale yet low-key Vero Beach, which is home to eclectic galleries and even trendy restaurants. Sebastian, a coastal fishing village that feels as remote as possible between Jacksonville and Miami Beach, has plenty of outdoor activities—including those at the Sebastian Inlet State Park, one of Florida's biggest and best recreation areas (and a paradise for surfers). It's actually within the boundaries of the federal government's massive protected Archie Carr National Wildlife Refuge, which encompasses several smaller parks within its boundaries. Downtown Vero is centered on the historic district on 14th Avenue, but much of the fun takes place across the Indian River (aka the Intracoastal Waterway) around Orchid Island's beaches.

GETTING HERE AND AROUND

To get here, you have two basic options: Route A1A along the coast (not to be confused with Ocean Drive, an offshoot on Orchid Island), or either U.S. 1 or Route 605 (also called Old Dixie Highway) on the mainland. As you approach Vero on the latter, you pass through an ungussied-up landscape of small farms and residential areas. On the beach route, part of the drive bisects an unusually undeveloped section of the Florida coast. If flying in, consider Orlando International Airport, which is larger (more flights and lower prices) and a smidge closer than Palm Beach International Airport.

ESSENTIALS

Visitor Information Indian River County Chamber of Commerce ⊠ *1216 21st St.* ☎ *772/567–3491* ⊕ *www.indianriverchamber.com.* **Sebastian River Area Chamber of Commerce** ⊠ *700 Main St., Sebastian* ☎ *772/589–5969* ⊕ *www.sebastianchamber.com.*

EXPLORING

Environmental Learning Center. Off of Wabasso Beach Road, the 64 acres here are almost completely surrounded by water. In addition to a 600-foot boardwalk through the mangrove shoreline and a 1-mile canoe trail, there are aquariums filled with Indian River creatures. Boat and kayak trips to see the historic Pelican Island rookery are also on offer. Call or check the center's website for times. ✉ *255 Live Oak Dr.* ☎ *772/589–5050* ⊕ *www.discoverelc.org* 🎫 *$5* ⊗ *Tues.–Fri. 10–4, Sat. 9–noon (until 4 in winter), Sun. 1–4.*

Fodor'sChoice
★

McKee Botanical Garden. On the National Register of Historic Places, the 18-acre plot is a tropical jungle garden—one of the most lush and serene around. This is *the* place to see spectacular water lilies, and the property's original 1932 Hall of Giants, a rustic wooden structure that has stained-glass and bronze bells, contains the world's largest single-plank mahogany table at 35 feet long. There's a Seminole bamboo pavilion, a gift shop, and café, which serves especially tasty snacks and sandwiches. ✉ *350 U.S. 1* ☎ *772/794–0601* ⊕ *www.mckeegarden.org* 🎫 *$12* ⊗ *Tues.–Sat. 10–5, Sun. noon–5.*

McLarty Treasure Museum. On a National Historic Landmark site on the southern boundary of Sebastian Inlet State Park, this museum underscores the credo, "Wherever gold glitters or silver beckons, man will move mountains." It has displays of coins, weapons, and tools salvaged from the fleet of Spanish treasure ships that sank here in the 1715 storm, leaving some 1,500 survivors struggling to shore between Sebastian and Fort Pierce. The museum sits on the site of the survivors' camp. The museum's last video showing of *The Queen's Jewels and the 1715 Fleet* begins at 3:15. ✉ *Sebastian Inlet State Park, 13180 Rte. A1A, Sebastian* ☎ *772/589–2147* ⊕ *www.floridastateparks.org/sebastianinlet/activities. cfm* 🎫 *$2* ⊗ *Daily 10–4.*

Mel Fisher's Treasure Museum. You'll really come upon hidden loot when you enter this place operated by the family of late treasure hunter Mel Fisher. See some of what he recovered in 1985 from the Spanish *Atocha* that sank in 1622 and dumped 100,000 gold coins, Colombian emeralds, and 1,000 silver bars into Florida's high seas—and what his team still salvages each year off the Treasure Coast. The museum certainly piques one's curiosity about what is still buried, and the website is all about the quest for more booty. ✉ *1322 U.S. 1, Sebastian* ☎ *772/589–9875* ⊕ *www.melfisher.com* 🎫 *$6.50* ⊗ *Mon.–Sat. 10–5, Sun. noon–5* ⊗ *Closed Sept.*

Pelican Island National Wildlife Refuge. Founded in 1903 by President Theodore Roosevelt as the country's first national wildlife refuge, the park encompasses the historic Pelican Island rookery itself—a small island in the Indian River Lagoon and important nesting place for 16 species of birds such as endangered wood storks and, of course, brown pelicans—and the land surrounding it overlooking Sebastian. The rookery is a closed wilderness area, so there's no roaming alongside animal kingdom friends; however, there is an 18-foot observation tower across from it with direct views and more than 6 miles of nature trails in the refuge. Another way to explore is via guided kayak tours from

6

the Florida Outdoor Center (⇨ *See listing below*). ⊠ *Rte. A1A, 1 mile north of Treasure Shores Park* ✛ *Take A1A and turn on Historic Jungle Trail* ☎ *772/581–5557* ⊕ *www.fws.gov/pelicanisland* ▣ *Free* ☉ *Daily 7:30–sunset.*

BEACHES

Most of the hotels in the Vero Beach area are clustered around South Beach Park or line Ocean Drive around Beachland Boulevard just north of Humiston Park. Both parks have lifeguards daily. South Beach, at the end of East Causeway Boulevard, is one of the widest, quietest shores on the island, and has plenty of hammock shade before the dunes to picnic in, plus volleyball nets on the beach. Humiston Park is smackdab in the main commercial zone with restaurants galore, including the lauded Citrus Grillhouse at its southern tip.

Humiston Park. Just south of the Driftwood Resort on Ocean Drive sits Humiston Park, one of the best beaches in town. Parking is free and plentiful, as there's a large lot on Easter Lily Lane and there are spots all over the surrounding business district. The shore is somewhat narrow and there isn't much shade, but the vibrant scene and other amenities make it a great choice for people who crave lots of activity. With lifeguards on call daily, there's a children's playground, plus a ton of hotels, restaurants, bars, and shops within walking distance. **Amenities:** food and drink; lifeguards; showers; toilets, free parking. **Best for:** swimming; partiers; sunsets; walking. ⊠ *3000 Ocean Dr., at Easter Lily La.* ☎ *772/231–5790.*

FAMILY   **Sebastian Inlet State Park.** The 578-acre park, which spans from the tip
Fodor's Choice   of Orchid Island across the passage to the barrier island just north,
★   is one of the Florida park system's biggest draws, especially because of the inlet's highly productive fishing waters. Views from either side of the tall bridge are spectacular, and a unique hallmark is that the gates never close—an amazing feature for die-hard anglers who know snook bite better at night. The park has two entrances, the entrance in Vero Beach and the main entrance in Melbourne (⊠ *9700 Rte. A1A*). Within its grounds, you'll discover a wonderful two-story restaurant that overlooks the ocean, a fish and surfing shop (by the way, this place has some of the best waves in the state, but there are also calmer zones for relaxing swims), two museums, guided sea turtle walks in season, 51 campsites with water and electricity, and a marina with powerboat, kayak, and canoe rentals. **Amenities:** food and drink; parking (fee); showers; toilets; water sports. **Best for:** surfing; sunrise; sunset; walking. ⊠ *14251 N. Rte. A1A* ☎ *321/984–4852* ⊕ *www.floridastateparks.org/sebastianinlet* ▣ *$8 vehicles with up to 8 people, $4 single drivers, $2 bicyclists and pedestrians* ☉ *Daily 24 hrs (gates never close).*

FAMILY   **Wabasso Beach Park.** A favorite for local surfboarding teens and the families at the nearby Disney's Vero Beach Resort, the park is nestled in a residential area at the end of Wabasso Road, about 8 miles up from the action on Ocean Drive and 8 miles below the Sebastian Inlet. Aside from regular amenities like picnic tables, restrooms, and a dedicated parking lot (which really is the "park" here—there's not much green space—and it's quite small, so arrive early), the Disney crowd walks there for its

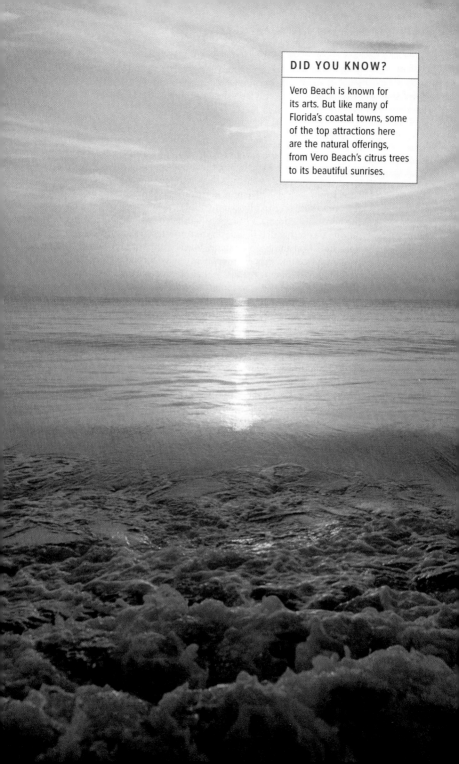

lifeguards (the strip directly in front of the hotel is unguarded) and the local crowd appreciates its conveniences, like a pizzeria and a store that sells sundries, snacks, and beach supplies. **Amenities:** food and drink; lifeguards; parking (no fee); showers; toilets. **Best for:** swimming; surfing. ⊠ *1820 Wabasso Rd.* ⊙ *Daily 7–sunset.*

WHERE TO EAT

$$$

MODERN

AMERICAN

Fodor'sChoice

★

✕**Citrus Grillhouse.** There are rooms with a view, and then there's this view: uninterrupted sea from a wraparound veranda at the southern end of Humiston Park. Even better, the food here is a straightforward, delicious celebration of fresh and fabulous. One such dish—the fire-roasted baby squid with grilled lemon, garlic, toasted crouton—is an exercise in restraint that you can't help but gobble up. Speaking of gobble-gobble, the herb-roasted breast of turkey sandwich with arugula, tomato, red onion, and red-wine vinaigrette on a toasted sesame roll is the idyllic light lunch on the beach. Sunset lovers (and bargain hunters) rejoice over the 3-course prix-fixe menu Monday through Thursday from 5 to 6:30 pm. ⓢ *Average main: $24* ⊠ *Humiston Park, 1050 Easter Lily La.* ☎ *772/234–4114* ⊕ *www.citrusgrillhouse.com* ⊙ *No lunch Sun.*

$$

DINER

FAMILY

✕**The Lemon Tree.** If Italy had old-school luncheonettes, this is what they'd look like: a storefront of yellow walls, dark-green booths, white linoleum tables, and cascading sconces of faux ivy leaves and hand-painted Tuscan serving pieces for artwork. It's self-described by the husband-and-wife owners (who are always at the front) as an "upscale diner," and locals swear by it for breakfast, lunch, and dinner (breakfast only on Sunday), so expect a short wait in season at peak hours. There's always a treat on the house—like a glass of sorbet to finish lunch—and don't miss the shrimp scampi: the sauce is so good, you'll want to dip every bit of the fresh focaccia in it. ⓢ *Average main: $20* ⊠ *3125 Ocean Dr.* ⊕ *www.lemontreevero.com* ⊙ *No lunch or dinner Sun. No dinner June–Sept.*

$$$

ECLECTIC

Fodor'sChoice

★

✕**The Tides.** A charming cottage restaurant west of Ocean Drive prepares some of the best food around—not just in Vero Beach, but all of South Florida. The chefs, classically trained, present a trip around the globe through food, but the setting, although effortlessly elegant (think pale blue coral-printed fabrics and a brick fireplace), is down-to-earth. Putting the crab in crab cake, an appetizer's two jumbo patties have scarcely anything but sweet, fresh flesh; the Southern-inspired corn-and-pepper sauce surrounding them is heavenly. For dinner, the inside-out chicken saltimbocca (rolled up, stuffed, and sliced) hits a high note, and the English pudding dessert is perfectly sticky and sweet. To boot, there's a notable wine list. ⓢ *Average main: $27* ⊠ *3103 Cardinal Dr.* ☎ *772/234–3966* ⊕ *www.tidesofvero.com* ⌂ *Reservations essential* ⊙ *No lunch.*

WHERE TO STAY

$

HOTEL

🔲 **Capt Hiram's Resort.** Popular with boaters, this Key West–style inn on Sebastian's Riverfront has a lobby embellished with a classic surfboard collection and no-frills guestrooms, all of which have private balconies (and most, oak furnishings). **Pros:** great location for fishing; good price; plenty of amenities. **Cons:** eastern rooms can be noisy; simple décor. $ *Rooms from: $125* ✉ *1580 U.S. 1, Sebastian* ☎ *772/388–8588* ⊕ *www.hirams.com* ⇆ *67 rooms* ⏹️ *No meals.*

$$
RESORT
Fodor'sChoice
★

🏨 **Costa d'Este Beach Resort.** This stylish, contemporary boutique hotel in the heart of Vero's bustling Ocean Drive area has a gorgeous infinity pool overlooking the ocean and a distinctly Miami Beach vibe—just like its famous owners, singer Gloria Estefan and producer Emilio Estefan, who bought the property in 2004. **Pros:** all rooms have balconies or secluded patios; huge Italian marble showers; complimentary signature mojitos on arrival. **Cons:** spa is on small side; rooms have only black-out shades; daily resort fee. $ *Rooms from: $239* ✉ *3244 Ocean Dr.* ☎ *772/562–9919* ⊕ *www.costadeste.com* ⇆ *94 rooms* ⏹️ *No meals.*

$
RESORT
FAMILY

🏨 **The Driftwood Resort.** On the National Register of Historic Places, the two original buildings of this 1935 inn were built entirely from ocean-washed timbers; over time more buildings were added, and all are now decorated with such artifacts as ship's bells, Spanish tiles, and a cannon from a 16th-century Spanish galleon, which create a quirky, utterly charming landscape. **Pros:** central location and right on the beach; free Wi-Fi; laundry facilities; weekly treasure hunt is a blast. **Cons:** older property; rooms can be musty; no-frills furnishings. $ *Rooms from: $150* ✉ *3150 Ocean Dr.* ☎ *772/231–0550* ⊕ *www.verobeachdriftwood. com* ⇆ *100 rooms* ⏹️ *No meals.*

$$
RESORT
FAMILY
Fodor'sChoice
★

🏨 **Vero Beach Hotel & Spa.** With a sophisticated, relaxed British West Indies feel, this luxurious five-story beachfront hotel at the north end of Ocean Drive is an inviting getaway and, arguably, the best on the Treasure Coast. **Pros:** beautiful pool; daily complimentary wine hour with hors d'oeuvres. **Cons:** separate charge for valet parking; some rooms overlook parking lot. $ *Rooms from: $279* ✉ *3500 Ocean Dr.* ☎ *772/231–5666* ⊕ *www.verobeachhotelandspa.com* ⇆ *102 rooms* ⏹️ *No meals.*

SHOPPING

The place to go when in Vero Beach is **Ocean Drive.** Crossing over to Orchid Island from the mainland, the Merrill P. Barber Bridge turns into Beachland Boulevard; its intersection with Ocean Drive is the heart of a commercial zone with a lively mix of upscale clothing stores, specialty shops, restaurants, and art galleries.

Just under 3 miles north of that roughly eight-block stretch on A1A is a charming outdoor plaza, the **Village Shops.** It's a delight to stroll between the brightly painted cottages that have more unique, high-end offerings.

Back on the mainland, take 21st Street westward and you'll come across a small, modern shopping plaza with some independent shops and national chains. Keep going west on 21st Street, and then park around 14th Avenue to explore a collection of art galleries and eateries in the historic downtown.

SHOPPING CENTERS AND MALLS

Vero Beach Outlets. Need some retail therapy? Just west of I–95 off Route 60 is a discount shopping destination with 50 high-end brand-name stores, including Ann Taylor, Polo Ralph Lauren, Restoration Hardware, White House/Black Market, and Jones New York. ✉ *1824 94th*

6

Dr. ✛ On Rte. 60, west of I–95 at Exit 147 ☎ 772/770–6097 ⊕ www.
verobeachoutlets.com.

SPORTS AND THE OUTDOORS

BOATING AND FISHING

Most of the region's fishing outfitters are based at the Capt. Hiram's
Resort marina in Sebastian.

Big Easy Fishing Charters. For over forty years, Big Easy has offered Sebastian off-shore fishing, including guided backwater and deep-sea excursions. ⊠ *Capt Hiram's Resort, 1606 N. Indian River Dr., Sebastian*
☎ *772/538–1072* ⊕ *www.bigeasyfishingcharter.com.*

Sebastian Watercraft Rentals. Based at Capt Hiram's Resort, this rental
company has a fleet that ranges from 16-passenger pontoons to jet
skis, and the company also organizes fishing charters on the Indian
River. ⊠ *Capt Hiram's Resort, 1606 N. Indian River Dr., Sebastian*
☎ *772/589–5560* ⊕ *www.floridawatercraftrentals.com.*

Skipper Sportfishing Charters. Based at the marina at Capt Hiram's Resort,
Captain Eric Olsen offers full- and half-day ocean and river fishing
trips at $500 and $300, respectively. ⊠ *Capt Hiram's Resort, 1606 N.*
Indian River Dr., Sebastian ☎ *772/589–8505* ⊕ *www.skipperfish.com.*

GOLF

Sandridge Golf Club. The Sandridge Golf Club features two public 18-hole
courses designed by Ron Garl: the Dunes course, with six holes located
on a sand ridge; and the Lakes course, named for—you guessed it—the
ubiquitous lakes around the course. The Dunes course, opened in 1987,
follows a history-steeped pathway once used during mining operations.
The Lakes course, opened in 1992, is renowned for the very challenging, par-4 14th hole with an island green. There's a pro-shop on site
offering lessons and clinics. ⊠ *5300 73rd St.* ☎ *772/770–5000* ⊕ *www.*
sandridgegc.com ▱ *$50 for 18 holes.* ⚲ *Dunes course: 18 holes. 6817*
yards. par 72. Lakes course: 18 holes. 6181 yards. par 72.

GUIDED TOURS

Florida Outdoor Center. Guided tours explore the area's natural wonders
like the Pelican Island National Wildlife Refuge and begin at only $35
per person. Tours include: Adventure Walk, a Bird Biking Safari, or
Wildlife Watching Paddling Excursion. The company is mobile and,
therefore, flexible. ☎ *772/202–0220* ⊕ *www.floridaoutdoorcenter.com.*

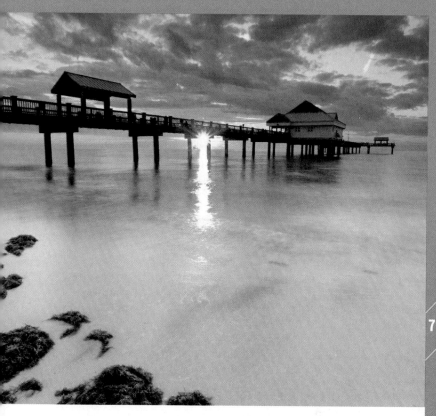

THE TAMPA
BAY AREA

WELCOME TO
THE TAMPA BAY AREA

TOP REASONS
TO GO

★ **Art gone wild:** Whether you take the guided tour or chart your own course, experience the one-of-a-kind collection at the Salvador Dalí Museum, which has relocated to a gorgeous waterfront building in downtown St. Petersburg.

★ **Cuban roots:** You'll find great food and vibrant nightlife in historic Ybor City, just east of downtown Tampa.

★ **Beachcomber bonanza:** Caladesi Island State Park has some of the best shelling on the Gulf Coast, and its five-star sunsets are a great way to end the day.

★ **Culture fix:** If you love the arts, there's no finer offering in the Bay Area than at the Florida State University Ringling Center for the Cultural Arts in Sarasota.

1 Tampa. Situated on a large bay of the same name, Tampa is a growing waterfront metropolis that's packed with state-of-the-art zoos, plenty of museums, and inviting shopping districts. Among the main draws is Busch Gardens, which doubles as a theme park and a zoo.

2 St. Petersburg. Although downtown St. Petersburg can be rowdy, there are also pockets of culture. The mellow but pricey Pinellas County beach towns include St. Pete Beach and Treasure Island.

3 Clearwater and Vicinity. Quiet during the winter, the beach areas north of St. Petersburg buzz all spring and summer. In addition to Clearwater, the area includes Dunedin and Tarpon Springs.

4 Sarasota and Vicinity. Sarasota County's barrier islands lure travelers to a battery of white-sand beaches, but Sarasota's cultural treasures are the true draw for many of its visitors.

GETTING ORIENTED

On the east side of the bay, Tampa is a sprawling cosmopolitan city offering attractions like Busch Gardens and Ybor City. To the west, St. Petersburg and Clearwater boast lovely barrier island beaches. Moving to the south, Sarasota's arts scene is among the finest in Florida.

7

Updated
by Kate
Bradshaw

If you seek a destination that's no one-trick pony, the Tampa Bay region is a spot you can't miss. Encompassing an area from Tarpon Springs to Tampa proper and all the way south to Sarasota, it's one of those unsung places as dynamic as it is appealing—and word has definitely started to spread about its charms. With its long list of attractions—from pristine beaches to world-class museums—it's easy to see why.

First and foremost, Tampa Bay's beaches are some of the best in the country. Whether you want coarse or fine sand, and whether you seek a mellow day of shelling or a raucous romp on a crowded stretch of waterfront, this place has it all. Of course, you can choose from a range of water activities, including charter fishing, parasailing, sunset cruises, kayaking, and more.

The region has its share of boutique districts spotted with shops and sidewalk cafés. Tampa's Hyde Park Village and downtown St. Petersburg's Beach Drive are among the top picks if you're looking to check out some upscale shops and dine alfresco while getting the most of the area's pleasant climate. Vibrant nightlife tops off Tampa Bay's list of assets. Ybor City attracts the club set, and barrier islands like St. Pete Beach offer loads of live music and barefoot dancing into the wee hours.

Tampa Bay has lots of family-friendly attractions, too. You can check out Busch Gardens, Adventure Island, and the Clearwater Marine Aquarium, to name a few. And art fanatics will find an astonishing array of attractions, including Sarasota's Ringling Museum of Art, St. Petersburg's enrapturing Salvador Dalí and Dale Chihuly collections (both permanent and housed in exquisite new digs), and Tampa's Museum of Art. Come prepared to explore and see for yourself what a compelling, unforgettable place the Tampa Bay area really is.

PLANNING

WHEN TO GO

Winter and spring are high season, and the amount of activity during this time is double that of the off-season. Beaches do stay pretty packed throughout the sweltering summer, which is known for massive, almost-daily afternoon thunderstorms. Summer daytime temperatures hover around or above 90°F. Luckily the mercury drops to the mid-70s at night, and the beaches have a consistent onshore breeze that starts just before sundown, which enabled civilization to survive here before air-conditioning arrived.

GETTING HERE AND AROUND

AIR TRAVEL

Tampa International Airport, the area's largest and busiest airport, with 19 million passengers per year, is served by most major carriers and offers ground transportation to surrounding cities. Many of the large U.S. carriers also fly into and out of Sarasota–Bradenton International Airport. St. Petersburg–Clearwater International Airport, 9 miles west of downtown St. Petersburg, is much smaller than Tampa International and has limited service.

Airport Transfers: SuperShuttle is one of the easiest ways to get to and from the airport if you forgo a rental car. All you need to do is call or visit the SuperShuttle website to book travel—they'll pick you up and drop you off wherever you're staying at any hour. Basic service costs around $28.

Blue One Transportation provides service to and from Tampa International Airport for areas including Hillsborough (Tampa, Plant City), Pinellas (St. Petersburg, St. Pete Beach, Clearwater), and Polk (Lakeland) counties. Rates vary by pickup location, destination, and fuel costs.

Airport Sarasota–Bradenton International Airport ✉ *Sarasota* ☎ *941/359–2777* ⊕ *www.srq-airport.com.* **St. Petersburg–Clearwater International Airport** ✉ *Clearwater* ☎ *727/453–7800* ⊕ *www.fly2pie.com.* **Tampa International Airport** ✉ *Tampa* ☎ *813/870–8700* ⊕ *www.tampaairport.com.*

Airport Transfers Blue One Transportation ☎ *813/282–7351* ⊕ *www.blueonetransportation.com.* **SuperShuttle** ☎ *800/258–3826* ⊕ *www.supershuttle.com.*

BOAT TRAVEL

Dolphin Landings Charter Boat Center has daily four-hour cruises to unspoiled Egmont Key at the mouth of Tampa Bay. Hubbard's Marina also operates a ferry to Egmont Key on most days. Climb aboard the glass-bottom boats of St. Nicholas Boat Line to take a sightseeing cruise of Tarpon Springs' historic sponge docks and see a diver at work.

On Captain Memo's Pirate Cruise, crew members dressed as pirates take you on sightseeing and sunset cruises in a replica of a 19th-century sailing ship. Starlite Cruises operates two very different ships for lunch, sightseeing, and dinner cruises: the *Starlite Majesty,* a sleek, yacht-style vessel; and *Starlite Princess,* an old-fashioned paddle wheeler that sails out of St. Pete Beach.

Tour Operators Captain Memo's Pirate Cruise ⊠ *Clearwater Beach Marina, 25 Causeway Blvd., at the end of Rte. 60, Clearwater Beach* ☎ *727/446–2587* ⊕ *www.captainmemo.com.* **Dolphin Landings Charter Boat Center** ⊠ *4737 Gulf Blvd., St. Pete Beach* ☎ *727/360–7411* ⊕ *www.dolphinlandings.com.* **St. Nicholas Boat Line** ⊠ *693 Dodecanese Blvd., Tarpon Springs* ☎ *727/942–6425.* ***Starlite Cruises*** ⊠ *Clearwater Beach Marina, 25 Causeway Blvd., at the end of Rte. 60, Clearwater Beach* ☎ *727/462–2628* ⊕ *www.starlitecruises.com.*

BUS AND TROLLEY TRAVEL

Hillsborough Area Regional Transit and TECO Line Street Cars replicate Tampa's first electric streetcars, transporting cruise-ship passengers to Ybor City and downtown Tampa. Pinellas Suncoast Transit Authority offers bus service throughout Pinellas County, from the county's inland parts out to the beaches. PSTA also runs the Suncoast Beach Trolley, which takes passengers up and down the beaches—from Pass-A-Grille all the way up to Clearwater Beach and downtown Clearwater—for $2 each way.

Manatee County Area Transit (MCAT) has buses throughout Bradenton and the nearby towns of Palmetto and Ellenton, as well as connections to Sarasota attractions. Service is inexpensive, but it's really no substitute for a car.

St. Petersburg Trolley will get you to key destinations throughout downtown St. Pete, and even offers free service between the Chamber of Commerce Visitor's Bureau and certain destinations.

Contacts Hillsborough Area Regional Transit ☎ *813/254–4278* ⊕ *www. gohart.org.* **Pinellas Suncoast Transit Authority** ☎ *727/540–1900* ⊕ *www. psta.net.* **St. Petersburg Trolley** ☎ *727/821–5166* ⊕ *www.stpetetrolley.com.* **TECO Line Street Cars** ☎ *813/254–4278* ⊕ *www.tecolinestreetcar.org.*

CAR TRAVEL

Interstates 75 and 275 span the Bay Area from north to south. Coming from Orlando, you're likely to drive west into Tampa on Interstate 4. Along with Interstate 75, U.S. 41 (the Tamiami Trail) stretches the length of the region and links the business districts of many communities; avoid this route during rush hours (7–9 am and 4–6 pm).

HOTELS

Many convention hotels in the Tampa Bay area double as family-friendly resorts—taking advantage of nearby beaches, marinas, spas, tennis courts, and golf links. However, unlike Orlando and some other parts of Florida, the area has been bustling for more than a century, and its accommodations often reflect a sense of its history.

You'll find a turn-of-the-20th-century beachfront resort where Zelda and F. Scott Fitzgerald stayed, a massive all-wood building from the 1920s, plenty of art deco, and Spanish-style villas. But one thing they all have in common is a certain Gulf Coast charm.

Hotel reviews have been shortened. For full information, visit Fodors. com.

RESTAURANTS

Fresh gulf seafood is plentiful—raw bars serving oysters, clams, and mussels are everywhere. Tampa's many Cuban and Spanish restaurants serve paella with seafood and chicken, *boliche criollo* (sausage-stuffed eye-round roast) with black beans and rice, *ropa vieja* (shredded flank steak in tomato sauce), and other treats. Tarpon Springs adds classic Greek specialties. In Sarasota the emphasis is on ritzier dining, though many restaurants offer extra-cheap early-bird menus.

WHAT IT COSTS				
	$	$$	$$$	$$$$
RESTAURANTS	under $16	$16–$20	$21–$30	over $30
HOTELS	under $201	$201–$300	$301–$400	over $400

Restaurant prices are the average cost of a main course at dinner or, if dinner is not served, at lunch. Hotel prices are the lowest cost of a standard double room in high season.

VISITOR INFORMATION

Contacts Bradenton Area Convention and Visitors Bureau. This organization has all you need to know about everything Bradenton, Anna Maria Island, Palmetto, and Ellenton have to offer. ☎ 941/729-9177 ⊕ www.bradentongulfislands.com. **Manatee County Area Transit** ⊕ www.mymanatee.org. **Sarasota Convention and Visitors Bureau.** This organization has the skinny on South Tampa Bay. ✉ 701 N. Tamiami Trail, Sarasota ☎ 941/957-1877 ⊕ www.sarasotafl.org. **Tampa Bay & Company** ✉ 401 E. Jackson St., Ste. 2100, Tampa ☎ 800/448-2672, 813/223-1111 ⊕ www.visittampabay.com. **Tampa Bay Beaches Chamber of Commerce.** The staff here will give you the lowdown on the Pinellas County beaches. ✉ 6990 Gulf Blvd., St. Pete Beach ☎ 727/360-6957 ⊕ www.tampabaybeaches.com.

TAMPA

84 miles southwest of Orlando via I–4.

Tampa, the west coast's business-and-commercial hub, has a sprinkling of high-rises and heavy traffic. A concentration of restaurants, nightlife, stores, and cultural events is amid the bustle. The city has really come into its own in recent years. The downtown Tampa waterfront features stunning views and excellent museums. Animal lovers flock here for attractions like Lowry Park Zoo, Busch Gardens, Big Cat Rescue, and Giraffe Ranch. Revelers will enjoy the strip of bars and clubs that constitutes Ybor City, a historic area with a heavy Cuban influence. The city also abounds with art museums, shops, and a wide array of restaurants. Downtown and Ybor City are both excellent spots to look for live music. Not too far out of town are some great golf courses and nature trails. Tampa is also a short drive from a long stretch of gorgeous Gulf Coast beaches.

GETTING AROUND

Downtown Tampa's Riverwalk, on Ashley Drive at the Hillsborough River, connects waterside entities such as the Florida Aquarium, the Channelside shopping-and-entertainment complex, and Marriott Waterside. The landscaped park is 6 acres and extends along the Garrison cruise-ship channel and along the Hillsborough River downtown. The walkway is being expanded as waterside development continues.

Although downtown Tampa, the Channelside District, and Ybor City are easy to navigate without a car, you'll want to rent one if you plan on hitting the beaches or heading to Busch Gardens, Hyde Park, International Plaza, or any of the zoos.

VISITOR INFORMATION

Contacts Tampa Bay & Company ✉ *401 E. Jackson St., Ste. 2100* ☎ *800/448–2672, 813/223–1111* ⊕ *www.visittampabay.com.* **Tampa Bay Beaches Chamber of Commerce.** The staff here will give you the lowdown on the Pinellas County beaches. ✉ *6990 Gulf Blvd., St. Pete Beach* ☎ *727/360–6957* ⊕ *www.tampabaybeaches.com.* **Ybor City Chamber Visitor Bureau** ✉ *1800 E. 9th Ave.* ☎ *813/248–3712* ⊕ *www.ybor.org.*

EXPLORING

TOP ATTRACTIONS

Fodor's Choice ★ **Big Cat Rescue.** Suburban Citrus Park in North Tampa is probably the last place you'd expect to be able to get face-to-face with an 800-pound tiger. Yet at the end of a shaded road just yards off the Veterans' Expressway, you can do just that. This rescue center is home base for a nonprofit organization that serves as a sanctuary for tigers, ocelots, bobcats, cougars, and members of any other large cat species you can imagine. Each and every one of these marvelous creatures has a unique story. Some arrived here after narrowly avoiding becoming an expensive coat. Others were kept as pets until the owners realized how pricey 15 pounds of meat per day (what it takes to feed some of these creatures) can be. They're all kept in large enclosures. A volunteer guide will lead you around the property and tell you every cat's story. You'll also get an earful of little-known facts about these big cats, from the true origin of the white tiger to why some cats have white spots on the backs of their ears. Tours (no unescorted visits are allowed) are every day but Thursday, but kids under 10 are only allowed on a special kids' tour at 9 am on Saturday and Sunday. Night tours, feeding tours, and appointment-only private tours are also available. ✉ *12802 Easy St., Citrus Park* ☎ *813/920–4130* ⊕ *bigcatrescue.org* ⤳ *$29* ⊙ *Mon.–Wed. and Fri. at 3; weekends at 10 and 1; kids' tour weekends at 9. Other special tours available by reservation only, at varying costs.*

FAMILY

Fodor's Choice ★ **Busch Gardens.** The Jungala exhibit at Busch Gardens brings Bengal tigers to center stage and puts them at eye level—allowing you to view them from underground caves and underwater windows. The big cats are just one of the reasons the theme park attracts some 4.5 million visitors each year. This is a world-class zoo, with more than 2,000 animals, and a live-entertainment venue that provides a full day (or more) of fun for the whole family. If you want to beat the crowds, start in the back of the park and work your way around clockwise.

The 335-acre adventure park's habitats offer views of some of the world's most endangered and exotic animals. For the best animal sightings, go to their habitats early, when it's cooler. You can experience up-close animal encounters on the Serengeti Plain, a 65-acre free-roaming habitat, home to reticulated giraffes, Grevy's zebras, white rhinos, bongos, impalas, and more. Myombe Reserve allows you to view lowland gorillas and chimpanzees in a lush, tropical-rain-forest environment. Down Under–themed Walkabout Way offers those ages five and up an opportunity to hand-feed kangaroos and wallabies (a cup of vittles is $5).

Interested in watching a tiger get a dental checkup? Then head over to the Animal Care & Nutrition Center, where you can observe veterinary care for many of the park's animals.

The park's newest thrill ride is Falcon's Fury, a 335-foot drop that is reportedly the tallest freestanding drop ride on the continent. It's the centerpiece of a the park's newest "land," Pantopia, a colorful collection of rides, cafés, and retail space that replaces its Timbuktu section.

Many consider the seven roller coasters to be the biggest lure. On the wings of an African hawk, SheiKra—North America's first dive coaster—takes riders on a three-minute journey 200 feet up, then (gulp!) plunges 90 degrees straight down at 70 mph. The park's coaster lineup also includes steel giants Kumba, Scorpion, and Montu; a double, wooden roller coaster called Gwazi; and Sand Serpent, a five-story family coaster full of hairpin turns and breathtaking dips. When it's running, the Cheetah Hunt is an absolutely exhilarating 4,429-foot-high launch coaster. With three different launch points, this coaster takes you through the Serengeti and into a rocky gorge with a top speed of 60 mph.

The off-road safari Rhino Rally brings you face-to-face with zebras, elephants, and white rhinos. Catering to the shorter set, the Sesame Street Safari of Fun is a 5-acre kids' playground with Sesame-themed rides, shows, and water adventures. The Air Grover Rollercoaster takes kids (and parents) on minidives and twisty turns over the Sahara, while Jungle Flyers gets them swinging and screeching. If you're looking to cool off, your best bets are Congo River Rapids, Tanganyika Tidal Wave, Stanleyville Falls (a flume ride), or Bert & Ernie's Water Hole—complete with bubblers, geysers, water jets, and dumping buckets. Character lunches are available (but you might want to wait until after your rides). ⊠ *10165 N. Malcolm McKinley Dr., Central Tampa* ☎ *813/987–5000, 888/800–5447* ⊕ *www.buschgardens.com* ⊠ *$92, parking $15* ☉ *Daily 9:30–6.*

FAMILY **Florida Aquarium.** Although eels, sharks, and stingrays are the headliners, the Florida Aquarium is much more than a giant fishbowl. This architectural landmark features an 83-foot-high, multitier, glass dome; 250,000 square feet of air-conditioned exhibit space; and more than 20,000 aquatic plants and animals representing species native to Florida and the rest of the world—from black-tip sharks to leafy sea dragons.

Floor-to-ceiling interactive displays, behind-the-scenes tours, and in-water adventures allow kids to really get hands-on—and even get their feet wet. Adventurous types (certified divers age 15 and up) can dive with mild-mannered sharks and sea turtles, participate in shark-feeding programs (age 12 and up), or shallow-water swim with reef fish such as eels and grouper (age 6 and up).

However, you don't have to get wet to have an interactive experience: the Ocean Commotion exhibit offers virtual dolphins and whales and multimedia displays and presentations. The Coral Reef Gallery is a 500,000-gallon tank with viewing windows, an awesome 43-foot-wide panoramic opening, and a walk-through tunnel that gives the illusion of venturing into underwater depths. There you see a thicket of elkhorn coral teeming with tropical fish, and a dark cave reveals sea life you would normally see only on night dives. The new Journey to Madagascar exhibit features ring-tailed lemurs, hissing cockroaches, and an Indian Ocean coral reef to showcase the nation's vast diversity of creatures and ecosystems.

If you have an an extra 90 minutes, try the Wild Dolphin Adventure Cruise, which takes up to 130 passengers onto Tampa Bay in a 72-foot catamaran for an up-close look at bottlenose dolphins and other wildlife. The outdoor Explore a Shore exhibit, which gives younger kids a chance to release some energy, is an aquatic playground with a water-slide, water-jet sprays, and a climbable replica pirate ship. Last but not least, two black-footed South African penguins make daily appearances in the Coral Reef Gallery. For an extra cost, you can get an up-close look at the daily lives of these penguins during the half-hour-long Penguins: Backstage Pass demonstration. ⊠ *701 Channelside Dr., Downtown* ☎ *813/273–4000* ⊕ *www.flaquarium.org* ✉ *Aquarium $21.95; Aquarium/Adventure Cruise combo $37.95; Penguins: Backstage Pass combo $48.95; Behind the Scenes Combo $29.95; Dive with the Sharks $175; Swim with the Fishes $75; parking $6* ⊙ *Daily 9:30–5.*

OFF THE BEATEN PATH **Giraffe Ranch.** Rural Dade City is known mostly for its strawberries, but word is quickly spreading about something else that makes people flock here: giraffes. These graceful creatures are the headliners at this nearly 50-acre ranch. You can view them as part of a safari-style vehicle tour or from the back of a camel; on either tour, you can hand-feed them cabbage leaves. You'll also see tons of zebras, a pair of pygmy hippos, a couple of rhinos, ostriches, and many other animal species roaming the grounds. Near the ranch's welcome center and gift shop is a corral of enclosures where you can watch guinea pigs chomp on sweet-potato chunks, hold a baby goat, and, for a little extra cash, feed grapes to lemurs or bathe a rhino. The ranch's proprietors have encyclopedic knowledge of the animal kingdom, and the overall experience is meant to impart a sense of connection to the animal world—and the environment—on those who visit. Tours take about two hours, and reservations are required. Credit cards are not accepted. ⊠ *38650 Mickler Rd., Dade City* ☎ *813/482–3400* ⊕ *www.girafferanch.com* ✉ *$69 for tour in safari van, $150 for tour by camelback* ⊙ *Tours daily at 11 and 2, by reservation only.*

FAMILY **Glazer Children's Museum.** It's all about play here, and with 53,000-square-feet, more than a dozen themed areas, and 175 "interactives," there's plenty of opportunity for it. Areas designed to nurture imagination and strengthen confidence allow children and families to experience everything from flying an airplane to shopping for groceries. Kids can also create art, control the weather, navigate a mini–shipping channel, and "drive" a miniature (stationary) fire truck through Tampa. A Water's Journey Tree lets kids climb the tree to the second floor and mimics the water cycle. ⊠ *110 W. Gasparilla Plaza, Downtown* ☎ *813/443–3861* ⊕ *wwww.glazermuseum.org* ✉ *$15 adult* ⊙ *Weekdays 10–5, Sat. 10–6, Sun. 1–6.*

FAMILY **Lowry Park Zoo.** Natural-habitat exhibits include Safari Africa, where a herd of African elephants (including two calves) is free to roam, make the 56-acre Lowry Park Zoo one of the best midsize zoos in the country. Asia gardens features two clouded snow leopards, and residents of the nearby Ituri Forest include a cheetah and lovably plump pygmy hippos. As you stroll through, keep an eye out for okapis, a rare forest giraffe from Central Africa. The stars at Primate World range from cat-size lemurs to a family of heavyweight Bornean orangutans that love to ham for the camera.

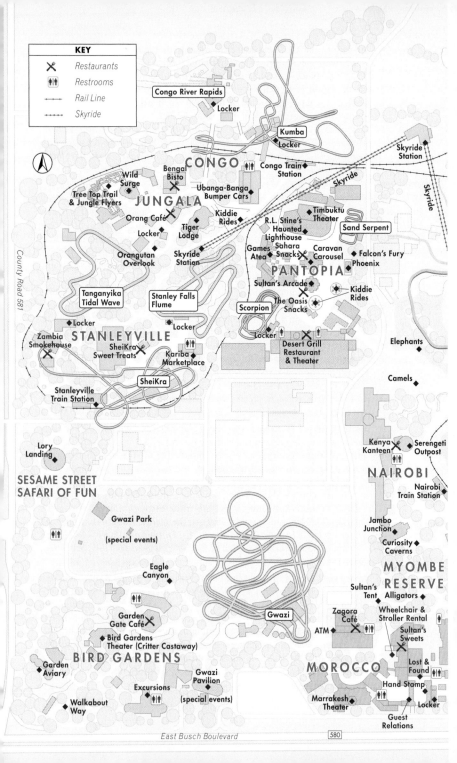

KEY

✕ Restaurants
🚻 Restrooms
+—+—+ Rail Line
••••••• Skyride

County Road 581

Congo River Rapids
Locker
Kumba
Locker
Skyride Station

CONGO
Congo Train Station
Skyride
Skyride

Wild Surge
Bengal Bistro
Ubanga-Banga Bumper Cars
Tree Top Trail & Jungle Flyers
JUNGALA
Orang Café
Kiddie Rides
Timbuktu Theater
Sand Serpent
Locker
Tiger Lodge
R.L. Stine's Haunted Lighthouse
Orangutan Overlook
Skyride Station
Games Atea
Sahara Snacks
Caravan Carousel
Falcon's Fury
Phoenix
PANTOPIA
Sultan's Arcade
Kiddie Rides
Tanganyika Tidal Wave
Stanley Falls Flume
Scorpion
The Oasis Snacks
Locker
Locker
Desert Grill Restaurant & Theater
Elephants

Zambia Smokehouse
STANLEYVILLE
SheiKra Sweet Treats
Kariba Marketplace
Camels

Stanleyville Train Station
SheiKra

Kenya Kanteen
Serengeti Outpost
NAIROBI
Nairobi Train Station

Lory Landing
SESAME STREET SAFARI OF FUN

Jambo Junction
Curiosity Caverns
MYOMBE RESERVE

Gwazi Park
(special events)

Eagle Canyon

Sultan's Tent
Alligators
Zagora Café
Wheelchair & Stroller Rental
Gwazi
ATM
Sultan's Sweets

Garden Gate Café
Bird Gardens Theater (Critter Castaway)
BIRD GARDENS

Lost & Found
Hand Stamp

Garden Aviary
Gwazi Pavilion
(special events)
MOROCCO

Excursions
Marrakesh Theater
Locker

Walkabout Way
Guest Relations

East Busch Boulevard   580

Busch Gardens Tampa Bay

Rhino Rally

SERENGETI PLAIN

McKinley Drive

Skyride

EDGE OF AFRICA

Cheetah Hunt

Skyride Station

CHEETAH HUNT

Crown Colony House

Crown Colony Pizza

Tut's Tomb

Montu

Sand Dig Games Area

Locker

EGYPT

Cheetah Run

Moroccan Palace Theater

Iceploration

Nairobi Gate

ATM

PARK ENTRANCE & EXIT

PARKING

East Busch Boulevard   580

BUSCH GARDENS
NAME

Name	Min. Height	Type of Entertainment	Duration	Suits	Crowds	Strategy
Egypt						
Edge of Africa	n/a	Walk thru	Up to you	All	OK	Go after lunch
Montu	54"	Thrill ride	3 mins	14 and up	Yes!	Go here first
Skyride	n/a	Ride	5 mins	All	Yes	Can get busy
Tut's Tomb	n/a	Walk thru	10 mins	All	OK	Go after Montu
Morocco						
Gwazi	48"	Thrill ride	2½ mins	10 and up	Yes!	Expect to wait
Iceploration	n/a	Show	30 mins	All	Yes	Arrive 15 mins early
Myombe Reserve	n/a	Walk thru	Up to you	All	OK	Before noon photo op
Bird Gardens						
Backyard Wildlife Habitat	n/a	Walk thru	Up to you	All	Yes	Good anytime
Critter Castaway	n/a	Show	25 mins	All	Yes	Do after Gwazi
Garden Aviary	n/a	Walk thru	Up to you	All	OK	Go after lunch
Lory Landing	n/a	Walk thru	Up to you	All	OK	Bring money to feed
Sesame Street Safari of Fun						
Air Grover	n/a	Junior thrill ride	2 mins	Under 6	Yes!	Expect a wait
Bert and Ernie's Watering Hole	n/a	Play area	Up to you	All	OK	Bring a bathing suit
Big Bird's 123-Smile With Me	n/a	Walk thru	Up to you	All	Yes	Photo/autograph op
Big Bird's Whirly Birdy	n/a	Ride	3 mins	Under 6	OK	Excellent for toddlers
Cookie Monster's Canopy Crawl	n/a	Play area	Up to you	Under 6	OK	Good for energetic children
The Count's Zambezi Rally	n/a	Ride	Up to you	Under 6	Yes	Go early in the day
Elmo's Safari Go-Round	n/a	Ride	3 mins	Under 6	Yes	Good anytime
Elmo's Treehouse Trek	n/a	Play area	Up to you	Under 6	OK	May be hard to keep track of toddlers
Oscar's Swamp Stomp	n/a	Play area	Up to you	All	OK	Bring a towel
Rosita's Djembe Fly-Away	n/a	Junior thrill ride	2 mins	Under 6	Yes	Older toddlers may enjoy this more
Slimey's Sawara Sand	n/a	Play area	Up to you	All	OK	Chance for parents to relax
Telly's Jungle Jam	n/a	Play area	Up to you	All	OK	Slow- paced area
Zoe-Petra & the Hippos of the Nile	n/a	Junior thrill ride	3 mins	Under 6	Yes	Good cool-off spot

Stanleyville

	Height	Type	Duration	Age		Notes
Sheikra	54"	Thrill ride	2½ mins	14 and up	Yes!	Use the lockers
Stanley Falls Flume	46"	Thrill ride	3 mins	10 and up	Yes	Lengthy lines
Tanganyika Tidal Wave	48"	Thrill ride	2 mins	10 and up	Yes	Bring a change of clothes or poncho

Jungala

Jungle Flyers	48"	Junior thrill ride	3 mins	6 to 13	Yes	Skip for other rides
Jungala Stiltwalkers	n/a	Show	15 mins	All	OK	Very entertaining
Orangutan Overlook	n/a	Walk thru	Up to you	All	Yes	Morning photo op
Tree Top Trails	n/a	Walk thru	Up to you	All	Yes	Gets crowded
Tiger Lodge	n/a	Walk thru	Up to you	All	Yes	Close-up views
Wild Surge	38"	Thrill ride	2 mins	5 and up	Yes!	

Congo

Congo River Rapids	42"	Thrill ride	6 mins	10 and up	Yes!	Bring extra clothes or poncho
Kumba	54"	Thrill ride	3 mins	14 and up	Yes!	Go early or before closing
Ubanga-Banga Bumper Cars	42"	Ride	2 mins	8 and up	Yes	Long wait times

Pantopia

Animal Care Center	n/a	Educational Exhibit	n/a	5 and up	No	Slow-paced ride
Carousel Caravan	n/a	Ride	3 mins	All	OK	Expect lines
Cheetah Hunt	48"	Thrill ride	3½ mins	12 and up	Yes!	Arrive 15 mins before show
Dance to the Music	n/a	Seasonal show	20 mins	All	Yes	Very long wait time
Falcon's Fury	48"	Thrill ride	2 mins	12 and up	Yes	Arrive 15 mins early
Pirate 4-D Movie	n/a	Show	15 mins	All	OK	Go after Scorpion
Phoenix	48"	Thrill ride	2 mins	12 and up	Yes	Very popular
Sand Serpent	46"	Junior thrill ride	2 mins	All	Yes	Go during Dance to the Music show
Scorpion	42"	Thrill ride	2 mins	14 and up	Yes	Good break from the sun
Sesame Street Presents Lights, Camera, Action!	n/a	Show	20 mins	All	OK	

Nairobi

Curiosity Caverns	n/a	Walk thru	Up to you	All	No	Good to get out of the sun
Edge of Africa	n/a	Walk thru	Up to you	All	OK	Great break from the crowds
Elephant Habitat	n/a	Walk thru	Up to you	All	OK	Go during Meet the Keeper
Rhino Habitat	n/a	Walk thru	Up to you	All	Yes	Earlier the better
Rhino Rally	39"	Vehicle ride	10 mins	10 and up	Yes	This ride is bumpy—hold on to your valuables
Serengeti Express	n/a	Vehicle ride	12–35 mins	All	No	Great way to relax and see the park

DID YOU KNOW?

One of six roller coasters at Busch Gardens, the steel, 60-foot-tall Scorpion twists and turns at speeds near 50 mph and then throws you into a 360-degree vertical loop. During the two-minute ride you'll experience a 3.5 g-force.

For hands-on experiences, Lowry has more options than most large parks, including chances to feed a giraffe, hold a colorful lorikeet, or touch a slippery stingray. Majestic red-tailed hawks and other raptors put on a show at the Birds of Prey Center, and a flock of majestic macaws soars through the zoo in a one-of-a-kind free-flight experience each day at 10 and 2. You can come face-to-face with Florida manatees at the Manatee Aquatic Center, the only nonprofit manatee hospital on the planet.

Dwindling native species like Florida panthers, black bears, and red wolves may be tough to find in the wild, but you can easily find them at the Florida Wildlife Center. Kookaburras, koala, emus, and wallabies populate the Wallaroo Station children's zoo. There are also water-play areas, rides (all of which are included with zoo admission), shows, and restaurants. ✉ *1101 W. Sligh Ave., Central Tampa* ☏ *813/935–8552* ⊕ *www.lowryparkzoo.com* ☑ *$24.95* ◷ *Daily 9:30–5.*

Fodor's Choice ★ **Ybor City.** Tampa's lively Latin quarter is one of only a few National Historic Landmark districts in Florida. Bordered by I–4 to the north, 22nd Street to the east, Adamo Drive to the south, and Nebraska Avenue to the West, it has antique-brick streets and wrought-iron balconies. Cubans brought their cigar-making industry to Ybor (pronounced *ee-bore*) City in 1886, and the smell of cigars—hand-rolled by Cuban immigrants—still wafts through the heart of this east Tampa area, along with the strong aroma of roasting coffee. These days the neighborhood is one of Tampa's hot spots, if at times a rowdy one, as empty cigar factories and historic social clubs have been transformed into trendy boutiques, art galleries, restaurants, and nightclubs. ✉ *Ybor City.*

WORTH NOTING

FAMILY **Adventure Island.** From spring until fall, rides named Everglides, Gulf Scream, and Key West Rapids promise heat relief at Busch Gardens' water park. Tampa's most popular "wet" park features waterslides and artificial wave pools, along with tranquil "beaches" in a 30-acre package. One of the attraction's headliners, Riptide, challenges you to race three other riders on a sliding mat through twisting tubes and hairpin turns. Planners of this park also took the younger kids into account, with offerings such as Fabian's Funport, which has a scaled-down pool and interactive water gym. Along with a volleyball complex and a rambling river, there are cafés, snack bars, picnic and sunbathing areas, changing rooms, and private cabanas. ✉ *10001 N. McKinley Dr., less than 1 mile north of Busch Gardens, Central Tampa* ☏ *813/987–5660, 888/800–5447* ⊕ *www.adventureisland.com* ☑ *$47; parking $12* ◷ *Mid-Mar.–Aug., daily 10–5; Sept.–Oct., weekends 10–5.*

Centennial Park. You can step back into the past at Centennial Park, which re-creates a period streetscape and hosts a farmer's market called the "Fresh Market" every Saturday, among a host of other events like festivals and pottery classes. ✉ *1800 E. 8th Ave., Ybor City.*

Tampa Museum of Art. Housed in an exquisitely designed new building, the Tampa Museum of Art is emblematic of the city's efforts to revitalize the downtown riverfront. The facility overlooks Curtis Hixon Park, the towering minarets of the University of Tampa, and the Hillsborough

River. The museum's 66,000 square feet of gallery space displays an impressive permanent collection of 20th- and 21st-century sculpture as well as Greek and Roman antiquities. Five additional galleries host traveling exhibits ranging from the classics to some of the most prominent artists working today. Also notable is Sono, the museum's cafe, which is operated by Mise en Place, one of Tampa's top restaurants. ⊠ *120 W. Gasparilla Plaza, Downtown* ☎ *813/274–8130* ⊕ *www.tampamuseum. org* 🖼 *$10* ⊙ *Mon.–Thurs. 11–7, Fri. 11–8, weekends 11–5.*

Ybor City Museum State Park. This park provides a look at the history of the cigar industry. Admission includes a tour of La Casita, one of the shotgun houses occupied by cigar workers and their families in the late 1890s, held every half-hour between 10 and 3. ⊠ *1818 E. 9th Ave., between Nuccio Pkwy. and 22nd St. from 7th to 9th Ave., Ybor City* ☎ *813/247–6323* ⊕ *www.ybormuseum.org* 🖼 *$4* ⊙ *Daily 9–5.*

WHERE TO EAT

$$$$
STEAKHOUSE
Fodor's Choice
★

✕ **Bern's Steak House.** With the air of an exclusive club, this is one of Florida's finest steakhouses. Rich mahogany paneling and ornate chandeliers define the legendary Bern's, where the chef ages his own beef, grows much of his own produce, and roasts his own coffee. There's also a Cave Du Fromage, housing a discriminating selection of artisanal cheeses from around the world. Cuts of topmost beef are sold by weight and thickness. There's a 60-ounce strip steak that's big enough to feed your pride (of lions), but for most appetites the veal loin chop or 8-ounce chateaubriand is more than enough. The wine list includes approximately 7,000 selections (with 1,000 dessert wines). After dinner, tour the kitchen and wine cellar before having dessert upstairs in a cozy booth. The dessert room is a hit. For a real jolt, try the Turkish coffee with an order of Mississippi mud pie. Casual business attire is recommended. Those looking for the Bern's touch but aren't up for donning a jacket and tie should opt for Side Bern's, the steakhouse's more low-key sister property a few blocks up the road. ⑤ *Average main: $32* ⊠ *1208 S. Howard Ave., Hyde Park* ☎ *813/251–2421* ⊕ *www.bernssteakhouse. com* ⌲ *Reservations essential* 🏛 *Jacket and tie.*

$$$
ASIAN FUSION

✕ **BT.** Local restaurateur B. T. Nguyen has earned quite a following since opening her first eatery more than two decades ago. Her modern take on conscientiously sourced local ingredients fits well within its upscale South Tampa surroundings, and the high-style Vietnamese cuisine features fresh herbs grown on site and a drink list that includes organic sake martinis—some flavored with herbs from that same garden. With a motto like "eat local, think global," the menu is inevitably sophisticated yet simple, with creative offerings like Shaken beef, a go-to dish for regulars, consisting of cubed filet mignon flavored with cognac and shallots. Vegetarians and vegans can rest easy here, with options such as Food Karma (braised tofu, edamame, eggplant, and ginger in coconut broth over black rice). Casual dress is acceptable, but patrons tend to dress up. ⑤ *Average main: $28* ⊠ *2507 S. MacDill Ave., Suite B, Hyde Park* ☎ *813/258–1916* ⊕ *www.restaurantbt.com.*

$$ ✕ **Café Dufrain.** Dogs can tag along if you dine on the front patio at pet-
ECLECTIC   friendly Café Dufrain, an eatery right on the Hollsborough River across
from the Tampa Bay Times Forum. Creative menu items, which vary by
season, include fried chicken and waffles (a Southern classic) and cevi-
che with sweet potato and toasted macadamia nuts. The bar menu has
a nice selection of craft beers. In mild weather, opt for the waterfront
view of downtown Tampa. ⑤ *Average main: $20* ⊠ *707 Harbour Post
Dr., Downtown* ☎ *813/275–9701* ⊕ *www.cafedufrain.com.*

$ ✕ **Cappy's Pizza.** Chicago may be the first place you think of when you
PIZZA   hear the words "deep dish pizza," which is why the high-quality pies
this local chain offers may surprise (and please) you. The menu at this
family-friendly spot is pretty simple: choose either a Chicago- or New
York–style crust, and select your toppings. The "Cappy" features a
blend of pepperoni, ham, onions, green pepper, sausage, and mush-
rooms. You can also go with a calzone. There's no hostess here, so put
your name on the (usually long) list you see when you first walk in.
If it's not too packed, try to get garden seating. The feel inside is very
nostalgic; vintage signs and an old toy train set adorn the walls. You'll
find a lengthy list of craft brews, and the kids might enjoy an IBC root
beer. This location is cash-only, but there is an ATM on site. ⑤ *Average
main: $12* ⊠ *4910 N. Florida Ave., Seminole Heights* ☎ *813/238–1516*
⊕ *cappyspizzaonline.com* ⌂ *Reservations not accepted* ▭ *No credit
cards* ⊘ *No lunch.*

$$ ✕ **Columbia.** Make a date for some of the best Latin cuisine in Tampa.
SPANISH   A fixture since 1905, this magnificent structure with an old-world air
Fodor's Choice   and spacious dining rooms takes up an entire city block and seems to
★   feed the entire city—locals as well as visitors—throughout the week, but
especially on weekends. The paella, bursting with seafood, chicken, and
pork, is arguably the best in Florida, and the 1905 salad—with ham,
olives, cheese, and garlic—is legendary. The menu has Cuban classics
such as *boliche criollo* (tender eye of round stuffed with chorizo), *ropa
vieja* (shredded beef with onions, peppers, and tomatoes), and *arroz
con pollo* (chicken with yellow rice). Don't miss the flamenco dancing
show every night but Sunday. This place is also known for its sangria. If
you can, walk around the building and check out the elaborate, antique
décor along every inch of the interior. ⑤ *Average main: $19* ⊠ *2117 E.
7th Ave., Ybor City* ☎ *813/248–4961* ⊕ *www.columbiarestaurant.com.*

$ ✕ **Kojak's House of Ribs.** Few barbecue joints can boast the staying power
SOUTHERN   of this family-owned and -operated pit stop. Located along a shaded
stretch in South Tampa, it debuted in 1978 and has since earned a following of sticky-fingered regulars who have turned it into one of the
most popular barbecue stops in central Florida. It's located in a 1927
house complete with veranda, pillars supporting the overhanging roof,
and brick steps. Day and night, three indoor dining rooms and an
outdoor dining porch have a steady stream of hungry patrons digging
into tender pork spareribs that are dry-rubbed and tanned overnight
before visiting the smoker for a couple of hours. Then they're bathed
in the sauce of your choice. Kojak's also has a nice selection of sandwiches, including chopped barbecue chicken and country-style sausage.
This is definitely not the kind of place you'd want to bring a vegan.

7

$ *Average main: $14* ✉ *2808 Gandy Blvd., South Tampa* ☎ *813/837–3774* ⊕ *www.kojaksbbq.net* ⊘ *Closed Mon.*

$ ✕ **Mel's Hot Dogs.** This is a must after a long day of riding roller coasters
HOT DOG and scoping out zebras at Busch Gardens. Visitors as well as passersby usually are greeted by a red wiener-mobile parked on the north side of the highway near Busch Gardens. Venture inside to find walls dotted with photos from fans and a hot-diggity menu that's heaven for tube-steak fans. You can order a traditional dog, but try something with a little more pizzazz, such as a bacon-cheddar reuben-style bowwow on a poppy-seed bun, or the Mighty Mel, a quarter-pounder decked out with relish, mustard, and pickles. Herbivores, fear not: there's a vegan option on the menu, and it's mighty tasty. To avoid lunch crowds, arrive before 11:30 or after 1:30. $ *Average main: $8* ✉ *4136 E. Busch Blvd., Central Tampa* ☎ *813/985–8000* ⊕ *www.melshotdogs.com* ▭ *No credit cards* ⊘ *Closed Sun.*

$$$ ✕ **Mise en Place.** Known to locals as "Mise" (pronounced *meez*), this
MODERN upscale, modern downtown space is a popular lunch spot for Tam-
AMERICAN pa's political and social elite. At night, it transforms into an elegant, understated dining destination with a menu that offers adventurous yet meticulously crafted modern American cuisine. The menu changes every week, save for staples like the chicken-liver pâté and the rack of lamb. Another thing that doesn't change is the intricacy of every item listed—whether it's tandoori-crusted tofu or pumpkin-spiced rubbed scallops. The long list of boutique wines and specialty cocktails further demonstrate the intelligence and imagination that go into the crafting of the menu. This place is on the western edge of downtown, just across the street from University of Tampa's shining minarets. Parking and entry are behind the building. $ *Average main: $29* ✉ *442 W. Kennedy Blvd., Ste. 110, Downtown* ☎ *813/254–5373* ⊕ *www.miseonline.com* ⊘ *Closed Sun. and Mon.*

$ ✕ **Taco Bus.** It's a Mexican joint with a simple name in a less-than-mag-
MEXICAN nificent location, but that matters not to anyone who's ever eaten to this legendary late-night establishment. Its popularity has turned what was little more than a food truck into a small local chain. You have a long list of meat, seafood, and vegetarian/vegan options, which employ-ees will stuff into the casing of your choice and hand to you through the window of a stationary bus. Don't let the low-key nature of this establishment fool you—the menu features classier items like ceviche, butternut-squash tostadas, and chicken mole among the quesadillas and carne asada. There is also a downtown Tampa location (✉ *505 Franklin St.*) as well as one in St. Petersburg's Grand Central District (✉ *2324 Central Ave.*). $ *Average main: $9* ✉ *913 E. Hillsborough Ave., Central Tampa* ☎ *813/232–5889.*

OFF THE BEATEN PATH
✕ **Pearl in the Grove.** For those who need a break from the urban sprawl, or are just in search of a decent early dinner after a Giraffe Ranch excur-sion, this farm-to-table eatery will hit the spot. Situated in an old one-story farmhouse in the middle of a kumquat grove, this spot serves as a low-key escape for the most cultured of Tampa Bay residents (though casual dress is fine here). Popular dishes include, as one might expect, fried green tomatoes, shrimp creole, honey-chili-glazed quail, and rabbit

confit, but keep in mind that the menu is ever-changing with the seasons. The beer menu features local brews, and the wine list is extensive. Brunch (11–2) is offered Sunday. $ *Average main: $20* ⊠ *31916 St. Joe Rd., Dade City* ☎ *352/588–0008* ⊕ *pearlinthegrove.com* ⛃ *Reservations essential* ⊘ *Closed Mon. and Tues. No dinner Sun.; no lunch.*

WHERE TO STAY

$
B&B/INN
Don Vicente de Ybor Historic Inn. Built as a home in 1895 by town founder Don Vicente de Ybor, this inn shows that the working-class cigar city had an elegant side, too. **Pros:** elegant rooms; rich in history; walking distance to nightlife. **Cons:** rowdy neighborhood on weekend nights. $ *Rooms from: $150* ⊠ *1915 Republica de Cuba, Ybor City* ☎ *813/241–4545, 866/206–4545* ⊕ *www.donvicenteinn.com* ⤴ *14 rooms, 2 suites* ⦿ *Breakfast.*

$$
HOTEL
Fodor'sChoice
★
Epicurean. Brought to you in part by the people at Bern's Steak House (which happens to be across the street), this vibrant, cuisine-centric installment of Marriott's Autograph Collection is an absolute must for foodies, but it doesn't make nonfoodies feel left out. **Pros:** excellent service; great location; tons of amenities. **Cons:** can get pricey; exclusive vibe. $ *Rooms from: $240* ⊠ *1207 S. Howard Ave., SoHo* ☎ *813/999–8701, 855/829–2536* ⊕ *epicureanhotel.com* ⤴ *142 rooms, 5 suites* ⦿ *No meals.*

$
HOTEL
Floridan Palace Hotel. This newly restored 1926 hotel at the northern end of downtown Tampa offers a well-manicured glimpse into a bygone era amid a bustling modern urban core. **Pros:** great downtown location; historic hotel. **Cons:** far from beaches. $ *Rooms from: $189* ⊠ *905 Florida Ave., Downtown* ☎ *813/225–1700* ⊕ *www.floridanpalace.com* ⤴ *195 rooms, 18 suites* ⦿ *No meals.*

$
RESORT
Grand Hyatt Tampa Bay. Situated on the western edge of Tampa, near the airport and overlooking the Courtney Campbell Causeway, the Grand Hyatt has a lot to offer—both in its guest rooms and on the property. **Pros:** extensive amenities; amazing views; world-class dining. **Cons:** far from beach; getting here can be tough due to traffic and awkward road layout. $ *Rooms from: $169* ⊠ *2900 Bayport Dr., West Tampa* ☎ *813/874–1234* ⊕ *www.grandtampabay.hyatt.com* ⤴ *442 rooms* ⦿ *No meals.*

$
HOTEL
Hilton Garden Inn Tampa Ybor Historic District. Although its modern architecture makes it seem out of place in this historic district, this chain hotel's location across from Centro Ybor is a plus. **Pros:** located in top cultural and nightlife district; reasonable rates. **Cons:** neighborhood can be rowdy on weekends; chain-hotel feel. $ *Rooms from: $179* ⊠ *1700 E. 9th Ave., Ybor City* ☎ *813/769–9267* ⊕ *www.hiltongardeninn.com* ⤴ *81 rooms, 14 suites* ⦿ *No meals.*

$$
RESORT
Saddlebrook Resort Tampa. If you can't get enough golf and tennis, here's your fix. **Pros:** away from urban sprawl; great choice for the fitness minded. **Cons:** a bit isolated. $ *Rooms from: $249* ⊠ *5700 Saddlebrook Way, Wesley Chapel* ☎ *813/973–1111, 800/729–8383* ⊕ *www.saddlebrookresort.com* ⤴ *540 rooms, 407 suites* ⦿ *No meals.*

$
HOTEL
Tampa Marriott Waterside Hotel & Marina. Across from the Tampa Convention Center, this downtown hotel was built for conventioneers

Where to Eat and Stay in Tampa

Restaurants ▼

Hotels ▼

KEY

1 *Restaurants*

1 *Hotels*

but is also convenient to tourist spots such as the Florida Aquarium and the Ybor City and Hyde Park shopping and nightlife districts. **Pros:** great downtown location; near sights, dining, nightlife. **Cons:** gridlock during rush hour; streets tough to maneuver; area sketchy after dark. ⑤ *Rooms from: $190* ✉ *700 S. Florida Ave., Downtown* ☎ *888/268–1616, 813/221-4900* ⊕ *www.marriott.com* ↘ *683 rooms, 36 suites* ⦵ *No meals.*

$ ⚏ **Westin Tampa Harbour Island.** Few folks think of the islands when
HOTEL visiting Tampa, but this 12-story hotel on a 177-acre man-made islet is a short drive from downtown Tampa and even closer to the cruise terminal. **Pros:** close to downtown; nice views; on the TECO streetcar line. **Cons:** a bit far from the action; chain-hotel feel. ⑤ *Rooms from: $169* ✉ *725 S. Harbour Island Blvd., Harbour Island* ☎ *813/229–5000* ⊕ *www.westintampaharbourisland.com* ↘ *299 rooms, 19 suites* ⦵ *No meals.*

NIGHTLIFE

When it comes to entertainment, there's never a dull moment in Tampa. Colorful Ybor City, a heavily Cuban-influenced area minutes from downtown, is a case in point. It has by far the biggest concentration of nightclubs (too many to list here), all situated along 7th and 8th avenues. Ybor comes alive at night and on weekends, when a diverse array of bars and clubs open their doors to throngs of partygoers. Whether it's bumping house music or some live rock and roll you seek, you'll find it here. Downtown Tampa is also becoming a formidable nightlife destination. When it comes to the arts—visual, musical, performing, or otherwise—Tampa is one of the South's leading spots.

BARS

Blue Martini Lounge. This spot in International Plaza has live entertainment nightly, except Sunday, and a menu of killer martinis. ✉ *2223 N. West Shore Blvd., West Tampa* ☎ *813/873–2583* ⊕ *www. bluemartinilounge.com.*

Centro Cantina. There are lots of draws here: a balcony overlooking the crowds on Seventh Avenue, live music Thursday through Sunday nights, a large selection of margaritas, and more than 30 brands of tequila. Food is served until 2 am. ✉ *1600 E. 8th Ave., Ybor City* ☎ *813/241–8588* ⊕ *www.centrocantina.com.*

Cigar City Brewing Tasting Room. Offering the fruits of the adjacent Cigar City brewery, the large tasting room here puts Tampa on the map for craft beer enthusiasts. On tap, it offers mainstay brews like Jai Alai IPA and Maduro Brown Ale as well as an interesting rotation of seasonal beers. It's a cozy spot with friendly staff and generally good music. But beware: happy hour can be packed. Brewery tours are available on the hour Wednesday through Saturday between 11 am and 2 pm for a nominal fee. ✉ *3924 W. Spruce St., Ste. A, Central Tampa* ☎ *813/348–6363* ⊙ *Sun.–Thurs. 11–11, Fri.–Sat. 11 am–1 am.*

Fly Bar. A happy hour mecca for hip young professionals, Fly Bar and Restaurant offers an intriguing selection of creative cocktails. Consider the Huck Cinn, made from huckleberry vodka, cinnamon syrup, and fresh lemon. East of Eden is a cocktail consisting of bison grass vodka, Calvados, and chai syrup. The list goes on. If you're hungry, you'll find a food menu to match. There's live music on weekends and occasionally during the week. A huge draw is the rooftop deck, which offers views of surrounding downtown Tampa. ⊠ *1202 N. Franklin St., Downtown* ☏ *813/275–5000* ⊕ *www.flybarandrestaurant.com.*

Gaspar's Grotto. Spanish pirate Jose Gaspar was known for swashbuckling up and down Florida's west coast in the late 18th and early 19th century. His legend has inspired a massive, raucous street festival each winter. This Ybor City drinkery has adopted his name, and rightly so. Decked out in tons of pirate memorabilia, it's the cornerstone to any night spent barhopping on the Ybor strip. The sangria is a good choice, but the aged rums may be a better fit here. You'll also find a food menu that goes well beyond standard bar fare. ⊠ *1805 E. 7th Ave., Ybor City* ☏ *813/248–5900* ⊕ *www.gasparsgrotto.com.*

Hub. Considered something of a dive—but a lovable one—by a loyal and young local following that ranges from esteemed jurists to nose-ring-wearing night owls, the Hub is known for strong drinks and a jukebox that goes well beyond the usual. ⊠ *719 N. Franklin St., Downtown* ☏ *813/229–1553* ⊕ *www.thehubbartampa.com.*

CASINO

Seminole Hard Rock Hotel & Casino. In addition to playing one of the hundreds of Vegas-style slot machines, gamers can get their kicks at the casino's poker tables and video-gaming machines. The lounge serves drinks 24 hours a day. Hard Rock Cafe, of course, has live music, dinner, and nightlife. There is a heavy smell of cigarette smoke here, as with most casinos. ⊠ *5223 N. Orient Rd., off I–4 at N. Orient Rd. exit, East Tampa* ☏ *866/502–7529* ⊕ *www.seminolehardrock.com* ☉ *Daily 24 hrs.*

MUSIC CLUB

Skippers Smokehouse. A junkyard-style restaurant and oyster bar, Skippers has live reggae on Wednesday, Uncle John's Band (a long-running Grateful Dead cover act) on Thursday, and great smoked fish every night. Check their calendar for exceptional musical lineups on the weekends. ⊠ *910 Skipper Rd., Northeast Tampa* ☏ *813/971–0666* ⊕ *www. skipperssmokehouse.com.*

SHOPPING

MALLS

Centro Ybor. Ybor City's destination within a destination is this dining-and-entertainment palace. It has shops, trendy bars and restaurants, and a 20-screen movie theater. ⊠ *1600 E. 8th Ave., Ybor City* ⊕ *www. centroybor.com.*

Channelside Bay Plaza. Right next to Tampa's cruise-ship terminal, this mall offers a vast array of shopping and dining options, as well as live music in a large courtyard. Look out for Qachbals Chocolatier, Tinatapa's (for a mojito), and Splitsville, a bowling alley and restaurant chain targeting a younger crowd. ⊠ *615 Channelside Dr., Downtown* ⊕ *www.channelsidebayplaza.com.*

International Plaza. If you want to grab something at Neiman Marcus or Nordstrom, this is the place. You'll also find Juicy Couture, Burberry, Michael Kors, Louis Vuitton, and many other upscale shops. Stick around after hours, when watering holes in the mall's courtyard become a high-end club scene. ⊠ *2223 N. West Shore Blvd., Airport Area* ⊕ *www.shopinternationalplaza.com.*

Old Hyde Park Village. It's a typical upscale shopping district in a quiet, shaded neighborhood near the water. Williams-Sonoma and Anthropologie are mixed in with bistros and sidewalk cafés. ⊠ *1602 W. Swann Ave., Hyde Park* ⊕ *www.hydeparkvillage.net.*

SPORTS AND THE OUTDOORS

FOOTBALL

Tampa Bay Buccaneers. Seeing the National Football League play isn't easy without connections, though catching a Bucs home game is a little easier than most. Tickets can be found for some games at the box office, though it's a safer bet when you buy them online in advance. ⊠ *Raymond James Stadium, 4201 N. Dale Mabry Hwy., Central Tampa* ☎ *813/879–2827* ⊕ *www.buccaneers.com.*

GOLF

Bloomingdale Golfers Club. In addition to an 18-hole, par-72 course, this club has a two-tiered driving range, a 1-acre putting green, and a restaurant. Greens fees are $30–$80. ⊠ *4113 Great Golfers Pl., Valrico* ☎ *813/685–4105* ⊕ *www.bloomingdalegolf.com.*

The Claw at USF. Named for its many doglegged fairways, the 18-hole, par-71 course is on a preserve with moss-draped oaks and towering pines. Greens fees are $20–$45. ⊠ *13801 N. 46th St., North Tampa* ☎ *813/632–6893* ⊕ *www.theclawatusfgolf.com.*

Saddlebrook Golf Club. There's a lot on offer at this resort, which is half an hour northeast of Tampa: 36 holes and 70- and 71-par courses, a driving range, a golf shop, on-site pros, and a resort spa. The greens fees range from $50 to $105, depending on the season. ⊠ *Saddlebrook Resort, 5700 Saddlebrook Way, Wesley Chapel* ☎ *813/973–1111* ⊕ *www.saddlebrook.com.*

Tournament Players Club of Tampa Bay. This public 18-hole 71-par course 15 miles north of Tampa was designed by Bobby Weed and Chi Chi Rodriguez; greens fees run $79–$159. ⊠ *5300 W. Lutz Lake Fern Rd., Lutz* ☎ *813/949–0090* ⊕ *www.tpctampabay.com.*

WALKING

Bayshore Boulevard Trail. Considered the world's longest continuous sidewalk, this 4.5-mile trail is a good spot for just standing still and taking it all in, with its spectacular views of downtown Tampa and the Hillsborough Bay area. Of course, you can also walk, talk, jog, bike, and in-line skate with locals. The trail is open from dawn to dusk daily. ⊠ *Bayshore Blvd.* ☎ *813/274–8615.*

ST. PETERSBURG

21 miles west of Tampa.

Nicknamed the Sunshine City, St. Pete is much more than a mass of land between the airport and the beaches. In recent years it's seen a fierce arts and cultural revival, which you can plainly see as you stroll through the city's lively downtown area. The new Salvador Dalí Museum building is a testament to the great pride residents of the 'Burg take in their waterfront city. But the city has other arts-oriented attractions, including the Dale Chihuly Collection, the Fine Arts Museum, and the burgeoning young artist hub known as the 600 Block, where eateries and bars attract crowds in the evening. Beach Drive offers some upscale options, whereas Central Avenue appeals more to night owls. The Grand Central District offers some unique vintage and antiques shopping. Gulfport is a stylishly low-key suburb southwest of St. Petersburg. The long strip of barrier islands lining St. Pete's west coast offer miles of gorgeous white beaches as well as dining, nightlife, and phenomenal sunsets. Beach towns here include St. Pete Beach, Treasure Island, Madeira Beach, and Redington Shores. No trip to this area is complete without a visit to the remote, pristine beaches of Fort De Soto.

GETTING HERE AND AROUND

Interstate 275 heads west from Tampa across Tampa Bay to St. Petersburg, swings south, and crosses the bay again on its way to Terra Ceia, near Bradenton. U.S. 19 is St. Petersburg's major north–south artery; traffic can be heavy, and there are many lights, so try to avoid it. Alternatives include 66th and 4th streets. One key thing to remember about St. Pete is that the roads form an easy-to-navigate grid: streets run north to south; avenues run east to west. Central Avenue connects downtown to the beaches.

Around St. Petersburg, Pinellas Suncoast Transit Authority serves Pinellas County. Look for buses that cover the beaches and downtown exclusively.

Contacts Pinellas Suncoast Transit Authority ☎ 727/540–1800 ⊕ www.psta.net.

TOURS

All About Fun Tours. What sets this tour apart from others is you are not going by bus or boat; your self-guided chariot is a motorized Segway. Each tour starts with an easy 15- to 20-minute training session. Tours are 60 or 90 minutes and are offered up to three times daily. It's a carefree way to see downtown St. Petersburg, the park system, and the waterfront while learning about local history. Reservations are required. ⊠ *335 N.E. 2nd Ave.* ☎ 727/896–3640 ⊕ *www.gyroglides. com* 🖃 *Tours $35–$50* ⊗ *Tues.–Sat. at 10:30 and 2, Sun. at 12:30 and 2:30, Mon. call for availability.*

Dolphin Landings Tours. This operation runs a four-hour shelling trip, a two-hour dolphin-sighting excursion powered mostly by sail, back-bay or party-boat fishing, and other outings to Egmont Key and Shell Key. It's not easy to spot from the road: the boats are docked behind a

St. Petersburg
and Vicinity

Gulf of Mexico

■ Crabby Bill's
■ Salt Rock Grill
REDINGTON
BEACH
Redington
Beach
699

Doubletree
Beach Resort
Tampa Bay

MADEIRA
BEACH

TREASURE
ISLAND

Treasure
Island Beach

■ Sloppy Joe's
on the Beach

SUNSET
BEACH

Sunset Beach

699

■ Ted Peters
Famous
Smoked Fish

■ Steam & Chili
Upham Beach

UPHAM
BEACH

TradeWinds Island
Grand Resort
St. Petersburg Municipal Beach
Dolphin Beach Resort
Loews Don CeSar Hotel
Pass-a-Grille Beach

Postcard Inn

BELLE
VISTA

682

Hurricane
Seafood Restaurant
Island's End
Resort

Peg's
Cantina

Seminole Blvd

Vonn Rd.

66th St. N.

82nd Ave. N.

Park Blvd.

694

62nd Ave. N.

54th Ave. N.

693

38th Ave. N.

22nd Ave. N.

9th Ave. N.
5th Ave. N.

1st Ave. N.
1st Ave. S.

22nd Ave. S.

Gulf Blvd.

56th St.

58th Ave. N.

19

49th St. N.

34th St. N.

28th St. N.

19

9th St. N.

Gandy Blvd.

PINELLAS
PARK

275

92

4th St. N.

Weedon Island
State Preserve

92

See Downtown
St Petersburg Map

ST
PETERSBURG

31st St. S.

9th St. S.

4th St. S.

Boyd Hill
Nature Park

54th Ave. S.

COQUINA
KEY

Pinellas Point

Pinellas
Point

Tampa Bay

♦ Egmont Key
♦ Fort De Soto Park
♦ North Beach
♦ Shell Key

275

KEY
□ Hotels
■ Restaurants

0   2 mi
0   2 km

strip mall. ⊠ 4737 Gulf Blvd., St. Pete Beach ☎ 727/360–7411 ⊕ www.
dolphinlandings.com.

VISITOR INFORMATION

Contacts St. Petersburg Area Chamber of Commerce ☎ 727/821–4069
⊕ www.stpete.com. **St. Petersburg/Clearwater Area Convention and Visitors
Bureau** ☎ 727/464–7200, 877/352–3224 ⊕ www.visitstpeteclearwater.com.

EXPLORING

TOP ATTRACTIONS

Fodor's Choice
★

Chihuly Collection. For the uninitiated, those passing this collection's
polished exterior may think it's a gallery like any other. Yet what's
contained inside is an experience akin to *Alice in Wonderland*. This,
the first permanent collection of world-renowned glass sculptor Dale
Chihuly's work, has such impossibly vibrant, larger-than-life pieces as
"Float Boat" and "Ruby Red Icicle." You can tour the museum independently or with one of its volunteer docents (no added cost; tours are
given hourly on the half hour during the week). Each display is perfectly
lit, which adds to the drama of Chihuly's designs. After passing under
a hallway with a semi-transparent ceiling through which a brilliant
array of smaller glass pieces shine, you'll wind up at the breathtaking

finale, "Mille Fiore" ("Thousand Flowers"), a spectacular, whimsical glass montage mimicking a wildflower patch, critters and all. Check out the gift shop at the end if you'd like to take some of the magic home with you. A combination ticket gets you a glimpse into Morean Arts Center's off-site glass-blowing studio, where you can watch resident artisans create a unique glass piece before your eyes. ⊠ *400 Beach Dr., Downtown* ☎ *727/822–7872* ⊕ *www.moreanartscenter.com.* 🏷 *$15* ⊙ *Mon.–Sat. 10–5, Sun. 12–5.*

Fodor's Choice **The Dalí Museum.** Inside and out, the waterfront Dalí Museum, which
★ opened on 1/11/11 (Dali is said to have been into numerology), is almost as remarkable as the Spanish surrealist's work. The state-of-the-art building has a surreal geodesic-like glass structure called the Dalí Enigma, as well as an outdoor labyrinth and a DNA-inspired spiral staircase leading up to the collection. All this, before you've even seen the collection, which is one of the most comprehensive of its kind—courtesy of Ohio magnate A. Reynolds Morse, a friend of Dalí's.

Here, you can scope out his early impressionistic works and see how the painter evolved into the visionary he's now seen to be. The mind-expanding paintings in this downtown headliner include *Eggs on a Plate Without a Plate, The Hallucinogenic Toreador,* and more than 90 other oils. You'll also discover more than 2,000 additional works including watercolors, drawings, sculptures, photographs, and objets d'art. The museum also hosts temporary collections from the likes of Andy Warhol. Free hour-long tours are led by well-informed docents. ⊠ *1 Dali Blvd.* ☎ *727/823–3767* ⊕ *www.thedali.org* 🏷 *$21* ⊙ *Mon.–Wed. and Fri.–Sat. 10–5:30, Thurs. 10–8, Sun. noon–5:30.*

FAMILY **Sunken Gardens.** A cool oasis amid St. Pete's urban clutter, this lush 4-acre plot was created from a lake that was drained in 1903. Explore the cascading waterfalls and koi ponds, and walk through the butterfly house and exotic gardens where more than 50,000 tropical plants and flowers from across the globe thrive amid groves of some of the area's most spectacular palm trees. The on-site restaurant and hands-on kids' museum make this place a family favorite. ⊠ *1825 4th St. N* ☎ *727/551–3102* ⊕ *www.sunkengardens.org* 🏷 *$8* ⊙ *Mon.–Sat. 10–4:30, Sun. noon–4:30.*

WORTH NOTING

Florida Holocaust Museum. The downtown Florida Holocaust Museum is one of the largest of its kind in the United States. It has the permanent History, Heritage, and Hope exhibit, an original boxcar, and an extensive collection of photographs, art, and artifacts. One compelling display includes portraits and biographies of Holocaust survivors. The museum, which also has a series of rotating exhibits, was conceived as a learning center for children, so many of the exhibits avoid overly graphic content; signs are posted outside galleries if the subject matter might be too intense for kids. ⊠ *55 5th St. S* ☎ *727/820–0100* ⊕ *www.flholocaustmuseum.org* 🏷 *$16* ⊙ *Daily 10–5.*

FAMILY **Fort De Soto Park.** Spread over five small islands, 1,136-acre Fort De Soto Park lies at the mouth of Tampa Bay. It has 7 miles of waterfront (much of it beach), two fishing piers, a 4-mile hiking and skating trail, picnic-and-camping grounds, and a historic fort that kids of any age can explore. The fort for which it's named was built on the southern end of Mullet Key to protect sea lanes in the gulf during the Spanish-American War. Roam the fort or wander the beaches of any of the islands within the park. Kayaks and beach cruisers are available for rental. While most of Tampa Bay's beaches don't allow dogs, Fort De Soto has a somewhat lengthy dog beach for those who can't bear to hit the sand without their best buddy. ⊠ *3500 Pinellas Bayway St., Tierra Verde* ☎ *727/582–2267* ⊕ *www.pinellascounty.org/park/05_ft_desoto.htm* 🎫 *$5* ⊙ *Beaches daily sunrise–sunset, fishing and boat ramp 24 hrs.*

FAMILY **Great Explorations.** "Don't touch" are words never spoken here. The museum is hands-on through and through, with a Robot Lab, Climb Wall, Lie Detector, Fire House, Vet's Office, and other interactive play areas. Smart exhibits like the Tennis Ball Launcher, which uses compressed air to propel a ball through a series of tubes, and Sound Waves, where Styrofoam pellets in a clear tube show differences in sound frequencies, employ low-tech to teach high-tech principles. ⊠ *1925 4th St. N* ☎ *727/821–8992* ⊕ *www.greatexplorations.org* 🎫 *$10* ⊙ *Mon.–Sat. 10–4:30, Sun. noon–4:30.*

Museum of Fine Arts. One of the city's cornerstones, this museum is a gorgeous Mediterranean-revival structure that houses outstanding collections of Asian, African, Native American, European, and American art. Major works here by American artists range from Hassam to O'Keeffe to Bellows and Morisot, but the museum is known for its collection of French artists, including Cézanne, Monet, Rodin, Gauguin, and Renoir. There are also photography exhibits that draw from a permanent collection of more than 14,000 works. The recent Hazel Hough Wing more than doubled the museum's exhibit space. A café offers visitors a lunch respite and a beautiful view of the bay. Docents give narrated gallery tours. ⊠ *255 Beach Dr. NE* ☎ *727/896–2667* ⊕ *www.fine-arts.org* 🖃 *$17* ☉ *Mon.–Wed. and Fri.–Sat. 10–5, Sun. 12–5, Thurs. 10–8.*

BEACHES

Egmont Beach. An undeveloped island teeming with birds, shells, and native plants is a short ferry ride away. You'll find serene lengths of beach, abandoned former military buildings, and a lighthouse. You can grab a ferry here from Fort De Soto for as little as $15. **Amenities:** none. **Best for:** solitude; walking. ⊠ *Accessible by boat only, Tierra Verde* ☎ *727/867–6569.*

Madeira Beach. Known to locals as "Mad Beach," this lively barrier island town occupies the southern tip of Shell Key. The beachfront consists of a long stretch of soft, shell-strewn sand, and it's often crowded with families as well as clusters of twentysomething beachgoers. You can get to the beach via numerous public access points, but your best bet is to park at the municipal beach parking lot and head to the sand from there. It's easily accessible from Treasure Island, northern St. Petersburg, and Clearwater Beach. **Amenities:** food and drink; parking (fee); showers; toilets. **Best for:** partiers; swimming; walking. ⊠ *14400 Gulf Blvd., Madeira Beach.*

North Beach, Fort De Soto. Pretty much anywhere you go in this county park can make you feel like you're hundreds of miles from civilization, but the beach on the northern tip of this island chain has perhaps the most remote feel. Sure, it gets pretty packed with weekend revelers and family reunions, but you can easily find your own space on this award-winning beach. It starts out wide at the entrance, and narrows as you go north, so it's perfect for those who enjoy a good stroll. There are some striking panoramic views of the park's undeveloped wetlands. Be warned that once you get past a certain point, the beach becomes clothing optional. **Amenities:** food and drink; parking (fee); showers; toilets. **Best for:** solitude; sunset; swimming; walking. ⊠ *3500 Pinellas Bayway, head right at the flag, Tierra Verde.*

FAMILY

Fodor's Choice

★

Pass-a-Grille Beach. At the southern tip of St. Pete Beach (past the Don Cesar), this is the epitome of Old Florida. One of the most popular beaches in the area, it skirts the west end of charming, historic Pass-a-Grille, a neighborhood that draws tourists and locals alike with its stylish yet low-key mom-and-pop motels and restaurants. On weekends, check out the Art Mart, an open-air market off the boulevard between 9th and 10th avenues that showcases the work of local artisans.

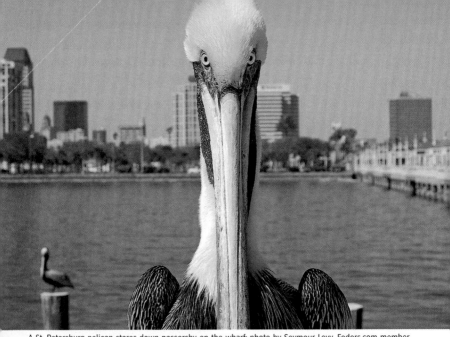

A St. Petersburg pelican stares down passersby on the wharf; photo by Seymour Levy, Fodors.com member.

Amenities: food and drink; parking (fee); showers; toilets. **Best for:** sunset; windsurfing. ⊠ *1000 Pass-a-Grille Way, St. Pete Beach.*

Redington Beach. Sand Key, the landmass that is home to Madeira Beach at the south end and Belleaire Beach in the north, is spotted with public beach access points. This particular spot has a bigger parking area than the others, though it's not free. It's also within walking distance of the Redington Pier, one of the most popular areas for fishing. **Amenities:** food and drink; parking (fee); toilets. **Best for:** solitude; swimming; walking. ⊠ *160th Ave. at Gulf Blvd., Redington Beach.*

Shell Key. If you want to find the most pristine beach possible without heading to some remote outpost, this is your best bet. The shuttle to this seemingly remote paradise runs out of Pass-A-Grille. You can catch it most days at 10, noon, and 2. If you do, expect some amazing snorkeling, shelling, and bird-watching. You can also kayak or canoe here from a launch near Fort DeSoto. Overnight camping is allowed here in the part of the island not designated as a bird sanctuary. Watch for rip currents when swimming, as they can be pretty strong. **Amenities:** none. **Best for:** solitude; swimming; walking. ⊠ *801 Pass-A-Grille Way, Pass-A-Grille, St. Pete Beach* ☎ *727/360–1348.*

St. Petersburg Municipal Beach. Though the beach is technically in the city of Treasure Island, the city of St. Pete Beach owns and maintains this stretch. Due in part to a concession stand and playground, it's excellent for families. The beach here is very, very wide, near hotels, and great for beach volleyball. **Amenities:** food and drink; parking (fee); showers; toilets. **Best for:** solitude; partiers; sunset; swimming. ⊠ *11260 Gulf Blvd., Treasure Island.*

FAMILY **Sunset Beach.** Technically part of Treasure Island, this 2-mile-long outcrop is one of Tampa Bay's best-kept secrets. The northern end has a mixed crowd—from bikers to spring breakers—the middle portion is good for families (there's a pavilion and playground at around 78th and West Gulf Boulevard), and the southern tip attracts the LGBT crowd. Surfers hit up Sunset Beach on the rare occasion that the gulf has some swells to offer. Once you turn onto West Gulf, you can find parking on the side streets, but make sure you park legally—it's all too easy to unwittingly get a barrage of parking tickets here. There are several pay lots starting to your right just south of 82nd Ave. **Amenities:** parking (fee); toilets. **Best for:** solitude; partiers; sunset. ⊠ *W. Gulf Blvd., Treasure Island.*

Treasure Island. Large, wide swaths of sand sans crowd abound, but you can also find some good crowds, especially on weekends. The Sunday-evening drum circle, which happens around sunset just southwest of the Bilmar, makes for some interesting people-watching, as do the many festivals occurring here each month. It's also the only beach that allows alcohol, as long as it's not contained in glass. Plus, getting here is super easy—just head west on St. Petersburg's Central Avenue, which dead-ends smack-dab in the middle of T.I. (that's what the locals call it), where the iconic Thunderbird Beach Resort sign towers over the boulevard. Hang a left at the light. There's a Publix right across the street if you're up for an impromptu picnic or don't want to pay beach-bar prices for a beer. **Amenities:** food and drink; parking (fee); showers; toilets. **Best for:** solitude; partiers; sunsets. ⊠ *10400 Gulf Blvd., Treasure Island.*

Upham Beach. One of the most notable things about this popular beach is the series of large objects that look like yellow school buses buried in the sand. These are actually designed to stabilize the shoreline (this beach is known for rapid erosion). The structures, called T-groins, may not please the eye, but that doesn't keep locals from flocking here. Upham is a wide beach with tons of natural landscaping, and it's near Postcard Inn and the TradeWinds. **Amenities:** food and drink; showers; toilets. **Best for:** partiers; sunset; swimming; walking. ⊠ *900 Gulf Way, St. Pete Beach.*

WHERE TO EAT

$$ ✕ **Bella Brava New World Trattoria.** This trendy eatery is one of the more
ITALIAN sought-after places on equally trendy Beach Drive. It offers a fresh, imaginative approach to Italian fare; a classic dish like ravioli Genovese is stuffed with fresh goat cheese and toasted pine nuts. Pork belly rigatoni and the trattoria burger, which is loaded with Gorgonzola and garlic aioli, are some of the more decadent menu items, while a spate of colorful salads and flatbreads make up the lighter side of things. Specials often feature fresh, local seafood. There's almost always a lengthy wait for a table, even on a weeknight, so reservations are really a must. However, sitting at the bar, which has an equally creative beer, wine, and cocktail menu, is also an option. $ *Average main: $18* ⊠ *204 Beach Dr.*

NE, Downtown ☎ *727/895–5515* ⊕ *www.bellabrava.com* ⤳ *Reservations essential.*

$$$ ✕ **Birch & Vine.** Seasonal, locally sourced ingredients work equally well
MODERN in both the surf and the turf columns at Birch & Vine, which has turned
AMERICAN The Birchwood hotel lobby and patio into an evening dining destination for hunger diners in downtown St. Petersburg. Take particular note of the orange miso scallops, and the sous vide filet mignon, contemporary preparations that complement the reimagined 1920s property. Umbrella-covered patio tables face Beach Drive and North Straub Park to provide the best people watching. The lively weekend scene can create conversational challenges at the interior tables and banquettes; for a quiet dinner, reserve on Monday or Tuesday, or arrange to rent one of the private dining rooms for up to 12 guests. Ⓢ *Average main: $28* ⊠ *The Birchwood, 340 Beach Dr. NE, Downtown* ☎ *727/896–1080* ⊕ *www.thebirchwood.com/birch-vine.html.*

$$ ✕ **Crabby Bill's.** Nothin' fancy about the crab-man's place—just some
SEAFOOD of the area's tastiest seafood served family-style (picture long picnic-style tables). Crustaceans are the house specialty, meaning your choice of blue or soft-shell, and, from October to May, delicious—though costly—stone crabs, among others. There's also a good selection of other treats, including scallops and oysters. Seafood aficionados will want to stick with items for which this place is best known, as the menu can be hit-or-miss. The views alone are a great reason to check it out. This restaurant sits on the beach front, something that turns the rooftop deck into prime real estate at sunset. Diners usually dress in the official uniform of the gulf coast beaches: shorts, T-shirts, and flip-flops. Ⓢ *Average main: $18* ⊠ *5100 Gulf Blvd., St. Pete Beach* ☎ *727/360–8858* ⊕ *www.crabbybills.com.*

$ ✕ **Hurricane Seafood Restaurant.** Sunsets and gulf views are the bait that
SEAFOOD hooks regulars as well as travelers who find their way to this somewhat
Fodor'sChoice hidden pit stop in historic Pass-A-Grille. Dating to 1977, it's mainly her-
★ alded as a watering hole where you can hoist a cold one while munching on one of the area's better grouper sandwiches. (Speaking of this sweet white fish, it's the real deal here, which—be warned—isn't always a guarantee in some restaurants.) There's also a range of seafood and steak entrées, and the crab cakes are legendary. The aforementioned sunsets are best seen from the rooftop deck. Ⓢ *Average main: $15* ⊠ *809 Gulf Way, St. Pete Beach* ☎ *727/360–9558* ⊕ *www.thehurricane.com.*

$$$ ✕ **Marchand's Bar & Grill.** Opened in 1925, this wonderful restaurant in
ECLECTIC the posh Renaissance Vinoy Resort has frescoed ceilings and a spectacular view of Tampa Bay. Upscale and special-occasion diners are drawn to Marchand's by an imaginative menu, which changes often and has recently embraced a farm-to-table approach. You'll always see salmon and Cornish game hen on the menu. More recent additions include gluten-free and veggie options, such as a squash and corn taco. For early birds, the 1925 menu (named for the year the hotel originally opened) offers a four-course meal for just—as you may have guessed—$19.25. Sushi is available Thursday through Saturday. The wine list is extensive, including a number of by-the-glass selections. Ⓢ *Average main:*

$28 ⊠ *Renaissance Vinoy Resort, 501 5th Ave. NE* ☎ *727/824–8072* ⊕ *www.marchandsbarandgrill.com.*

$$
ECLECTIC
✕ **Nitally's ThaiMex Fusion.** For those who take pride in their ability to handle the heat, this casual yet acclaimed fusion eatery is a must. It's run by a married couple, one of whom is from Thailand and the other from, as you may have guessed, Mexico. The resulting menu consists of many a match made in heaven by melding the spice and nuances of either cuisine into a spate of tasty options—think panang-mole curry or chorizo pad thai. (Some of these are even suitable for spice-phobes.) The bravest of souls can try the "inferno soup," which is less of a dish than a double dare, featuring a giant bowl of Thai chicken soup flavored with ghost peppers (finish it in a half hour and you win a cash prize). Regardless of what you order, go for a shade less spicy than you normally would: their idea of medium is what most restaurants consider hot. Portions are massive; if you order a burrito, you may actually receive two. Finally, keep in mind that this place can get packed at dinnertime, especially on weekends, so call ahead. $ *Average main: $18* ⊠ *2462 Central Ave.* ☎ *727/321–8424* ⊕ *www.nitallys.com* ☽ *Closed Sun.*

$
MODERN
MEXICAN
✕ **Peg's Cantina.** A favorite watering hole for Tampa Bay's craft beer enthusiasts, Peg's also offers a variety of specialty pizzas and healthy Mexican options. Housed in an old bungalow along Gulfport's famed Beach Boulevard, it features excellent outdoor seating, and, in perfect Gulfport form, hospitable service for the canine set. Cyclists enjoy cruising here from the Pinellas Trail. Tap beers include house-brand brews as well as options from regional and national breweries. $ *Average main: $15* ⊠ *3038 Beach Blvd. S, Gulfport* ☎ *727/328–2720* ⊕ *www. pegscantina.com* ☽ *Closed Mon. No lunch Tues.–Thurs.*

$$$
STEAKHOUSE
✕ **Rococo.** Yet another happening spot inspired by the St. Pete of yesteryear, this newly minted steakhouse sits in what was once a historic YWCA building. Possibly the only independent steakhouse in St. Petersburg, it gets its name from the late-baroque art movement and displays the work of local artists on its walls. Steak is obviously the main draw—corn-fed, aged, though the menu goes well beyond the normal steakhouse bounds. On a given night, you can find elk, swordfish, or any number of less typical denizens of the land and sea, for those who are not enamored of beef. The chef is also attentive to special diets here, including the needs of gluten-free, vegetarian, and vegan diners. Craft cocktails have a local flair, and the beer and wine selection is expansive. It's really one of the best options in town for a romantic night out in St. Pete. $ *Average main: $30* ☎ *655 2nd Ave. S* ☎ *727/822–0999* ⊕ *www. rococosteak.com* ⊜ *Reservations essential* ☽ *No lunch.*

$$$
SEAFOOD
✕ **Salt Rock Grill.** This hot spot is where tourists and locals converge to enjoy a fun and lively waterfront atmosphere. The rock-solid (if slightly less than imaginative) menu is the best reason to come. Don't believe the Caribbean lobster is a "monster"—at 1¼ pounds it's on the small side, but it's twice-cooked—including a finish on the grill—and quite tasty. Those more into the turf side of things might be interested in the "Chicken Rock'n Bleu," which adds fresh spinach and champagne-mushroom sauce into a classic chicken dish. In fair weather, dine on the dock; otherwise ask for a table with a view of the water.

⑤ *Average main: $25* ✉ *19325 Gulf Blvd., Indian Shores* ☎ *727/593–7625* ⊕ *www.saltrockgrill.com.*

$ ✕ **Steam & Chill.** This eatery is a bit of a rare gem on St. Pete Beach,
CAFÉ offering creative breakfast options that tend to be a bit healthier and more worldly than their greasy-spoon counterparts (think vegan hash and berry-and-Brie crêpes). It's also pretty much the only neighborhood spot where you'll find proper espresso drinks, not to mention formidable brunch and tapas menus. At night, the dining room transforms into a tapas bar with live music and flowing sangria. ⑤ *Average main: $12* ✉ *7400 Gulf Blvd., St. Pete Beach* ☎ *727/360–8080* ⊕ *www.steamandchill.com.*

$ ✕ **Ted Peters Famous Smoked Fish.** Picture this: flip-flop-wearing anglers
SEAFOOD and beach-towel-clad bathers lolling on picnic benches, sipping a beer,
Fodor'sChoice and devouring oak-smoked salmon, mullet, mahimahi, and mackerel.
★ Dinner comes to the table with heaped helpings of potato salad and coleslaw. If you're industrious enough to have hooked your own fish, the crew will smoke it for about $1.50 per pound. If not, there's always what many consider to be the best burger in the region. The popular smoked fish spread and Manhattan clam chowder are available to go. There's also indoor seating at Ted's, which has been a south-side fixture for more than six decades. Closing time is 7:30 pm, so dinner is only for early diners. ⑤ *Average main: $13* ✉ *1350 Pasadena Ave. S, South Pasadena* ☎ *727/381–7931* ⊕ *www.tedpetersfish.com* ⌲ *Reservations not accepted* ▬ *No credit cards* ⊙ *Closed Tues.*

WHERE TO STAY

$$ ⌂ **The Birchwood.** Few things are as emblematic of Beach Drive's renais-
B&B/INN sance than this boutique hotel, which, like many of downtown St. Pete's best attractions, seamlessly blends old and new. **Pros:** highly sought-after location; exquisite furnishings; close to downtown attractions. **Cons:** service seems more B&B than hotel and is often MIA; not the best choice for families with kids; 20 minutes from the beach. ⑤ *Rooms from: $220* ✉ *340 Beach Dr. NE, Downtown* ☎ *727/896–1080* ⊕ *3thebirchwood.com* ⌁ *18 rooms.*

$ ⌂ **Dolphin Beach Resort.** If you don't want to stay at a chain but can't
RESORT afford a huge resort, this beachfront spot is probably a good choice. **Pros:** good bargain; on the beach. **Cons:** décor seems a little dated. ⑤ *Rooms from: $159* ✉ *4900 Gulf Blvd., St. Pete Beach* ☎ *727/360–7011* ⊕ *www.dolphinbeach.com* ⌁ *173 rooms* ⎟⊙⎟ *No meals.*

$ ⌂ **Doubletree Beach Resort Tampa Bay.** This hotel from the Hilton family
RESORT offers the chain's well-known luxury without diminishing the mellow charm of the surrounding area. **Pros:** lauded facility; quiet, beachfront location. **Cons:** few attractions nearby. ⑤ *Rooms from: $179* ✉ *17120 Gulf Blvd., N. Redington Beach* ☎ *727/391–4000* ⊕ *www.doubletreeresort.com* ⌁ *126 rooms* ⎟⊙⎟ *No meals.*

$$ ⌂ **Island's End Resort.** We love this converted 1950s-vintage motel
HOTEL because it has some of the area's best sunrise and sunset views and, like the rest of historic Pass-A-Grille, is totally friendly and totally Old Florida. **Pros:** good value; nice views; near restaurants and shops. **Cons:** access via a traffic-clogged road; parking can be tricky. ⑤ *Rooms from:*

$229 ⊠ *1 Pass-A-Grille Way, St. Pete Beach* ☎ *727/360–5023* ⊕ *www. islandsend.com* ↩ *6 cottages* ¶⊙¶ *Breakfast.*

$$
RESORT
Fodor's Choice
★

⛉ **Loews Don CeSar Hotel.** Today the "Pink Palace," as it's called thanks to its paint job, is a storied resort and gulf-coast architectural landmark, with exterior and public areas oozing turn-of-the-20th-century elegance. **Pros:** romantic destination; great beach; tasty dining options. **Cons:** small rooms; can be quite pricey. ⑤ *Rooms from: $269* ⊠ *3400 Gulf Blvd., St. Pete Beach* ☎ *727/367–6952, 800/282–1116* ⊕ *www. doncesar.com* ↩ *277 rooms, 40 suites, 70 condos* ¶⊙¶ *No meals.*

$
HOTEL
Fodor's Choice
★

⛉ **Postcard Inn.** Take a Waikiki surf shack from back in Duke's day, shake it up with a little Miami chic (circa 1955), and give it a clean modern twist—that's this ultrahip beachfront hotel to a T. **Pros:** lively, fresh feel; on the beach; walking distance to restaurants and nightlife; friendly staff. **Cons:** can be crowded; not for squares. ⑤ *Rooms from: $169* ⊠ *6300 Gulf Blvd., St. Pete Beach* ☎ *727/367–2611, 800/237– 8918* ⊕ *www.postcardinn.com* ↩ *196 rooms* ¶⊙¶ *Breakfast.*

$$
RESORT
FAMILY

⛉ **TradeWinds Island Grand Resort.** The only resort on the beach offering up its own fireworks display, the island-chic TradeWinds is very popular with foreign travelers and the go-to place for beach weddings; it's also one of the few pet-friendly resorts in the area, with a play area and a room-service menu for dogs and cats. **Pros:** great beachfront location; close to restaurants. **Cons:** large, sprawling complex; lots of conventions; pesky resort fee. ⑤ *Rooms from: $219* ⊠ *5500 Gulf Blvd., St. Pete Beach* ☎ *727/363–2212* ⊕ *www.tradewindsresort.com* ↩ *584 rooms, 103 suites* ¶⊙¶ *No meals.*

$$
RESORT
Fodor's Choice
★

⛉ **Vinoy Renaissance Resort & Golf Club.** Built in 1925, (making it roughly the same vintage as the Don CeSar), the Vinoy is a luxury resort in St. Petersburg's gorgeous Old Northeast.Thoughtful renovations keep its yesteryear glamour and spot on the National Register of Historic Places. **Pros:** charming property; friendly service; close to downtown museums. **Cons:** pricey; small rooms. ⑤ *Rooms from: $269* ⊠ *501 5th Ave. NE* ☎ *727/894–1000* ⊕ *www.vinoyrenaissanceresort.com* ↩ *346 rooms, 15 suites* ¶⊙¶ *No meals.*

NIGHTLIFE

LIVE MUSIC VENUES

Ruby's Elixir. If you want to scope out some vintage jazz, blues, or swing, this is the place to do it. It has much better ventilation than most other bars downtown, and you can bring your beverages to one of the outdoor tables—if you can snag one. It's also a great place to find a unique cocktail. ⊠ *15 3rd St. N, Downtown* ☎ *727/898–7829* ⊕ *www.rubyselixir.com.*

BARS AND PUBS

Ale and the Witch. Situated in the courtyard of an office building just off trendy Beach Drive, this establishment is a live-music hub—mostly jam bands—as well as the cornerstone of St. Petersburg's exploding craft-beer scene. Fans of IPAs, saisons, stouts, you name it, will find their beer of choice somewhere amid the lengthy list of brews on tap. There's some seating inside, but all the action happens outside in the courtyard, where there are plenty of tables and a makeshift band shell. Patrons are welcome to grab food from one of the complex's several restaurants to go along with their brews. Although it's a late-night draw, kids and dogs are welcome. ✉ *111 2nd Ave. NE, Downtown* ☎ *727/821–2533* ⊕ *www.thealeandthewitch.com.*

Daiquiri Shak. If frozen DayGlo concoctions spinning around in washing mashine–like mechanisms are your thing, this place should certainly be on your list. If not, this is still a good go-to weekend watering hole on Madeira Beach (technically, it's across the street from the beach). In addition to cocktails like the Grape Ape and the Voodoo Loveshake, there's a respectable selection of beer on tap and a full bar. Entertainment ranges from a weekly pub quiz to full-on funk and rock bands on weekends. The menu includes loads of seafood, of course (oysters are a winner), and the late-night menu is served until 1:30 am. ✉ *14995 Gulf Blvd., Madeira Beach* ☎ *727/393–2706* ⊕ *www.daiquirishak.com.*

Green Bench Brewing Company. The name of this bar is a nod to the green benches that once lined Central Avenue, which retirees occupied in a bygone era. St. Pete has shaken its rap as a sleepy retirement town, and this brewery embodies the Sunshine City's recent revival as a craft-beer town. Barkeeps here serve up brews made on site as well as a few guest batches. The interior has a lodgelike feel (as much as a bar can in Florida), but the real ambience lies outside, where Adirondack chairs and badminton sets are scattered across the lawn. It's also conveniently located a couple of blocks from Tropicana Field, so the place can get packed before and after the Rays play. ✉ *1133 Baum Ave., Downtown* ☎ *727/800–9836* ⊕ *www.greenbenchbrewing.com.*

Jimmy B's. The default beach bar for tourists and locals alike overlooks the vast dunes leading down to the beach. There's live music virtually every night. ✉ *6200 Gulf Blvd., behind the Beachcomber Resort, St. Pete Beach* ☎ *727/367–1902.*

The Mandarin Hide. Perhaps the epitome of downtown St. Pete's bold transformation into a stylish nightlife destination, this place exudes a classy yet jubilant speakeasy vibe. A claw-foot bathtub is one of the first things you see when you walk in the door. Just as vintage as the décor is the drinks menu, which features numerous classic cocktails (made the old-fashioned way), tasty concoctions you'll find nowhere else, and craft beers. You'll find either live music or a DJ most nights. On Sunday they open early to serve up a mean bloody mary. It's closed on Monday and Tuesday. ✉ *231 Central Ave., Downtown* ☎ *727/231–4007* ⊕ *www. mandarinhide.com.*

World of Beer. The name says it all. This local chain is less than a decade old, but it's caught on beyond Tampa Bay. There are now locations throughout the state, including outlets in Tampa and West Palm Beach, but this one fits right in with the downtown St. Pete vibe and locals' endless thirst for craft brew. A new and improved version of the neighborhood pub, WOB offers bottle and draft beers from as far away as New Zealand and as nearby as St. Pete or Tampa. There's live music on weekends. ✉ *100 4th St. S, Downtown* ☎ *727/823–2337* ⊕ *www. wobusa.com.*

SHOPPING

There's no need for a trip to the mall here. Few places in the Tampa Bay area offer so many eclectic shopping options as the St. Petersburg area. Downtown St. Petersburg's Beach Drive is sprinkled with tons of smart yet pricey boutiques. The Grand Central district has plenty of antiques and vintage clothing shops. Beach shopping hubs John's Pass Village and 8th Avenue offer souvenir shopping that goes well beyond the norm. Each of these is also packed with a range of enticing eateries, many with outdoor seating and live entertainment.

Epitomizing St. Petersburg's cultural rebirth, the block-long stretch of Central Avenue between 6th and 7th streets has loads of art galleries and indie shops, as well as dive bars frequented by tattooed hipsters. The central point is Crislip Arcade, where you'll find a vintage clothing shop (Ramblin' Rose), local art galleries (eve-N-odd and Olio, to name a couple), and a unique jewelry shop (Kathryn Cole). Local businesses line the street, including one that specializes in Moroccan imports (Treasures of Morocco), one that hawks a colorful array of vintage clothing and campy memorabilia (Star Booty), and a smoky bar specializing in craft beer and punk rock (Fubar). Local 662 and the State Theater are two music venues on this block that attract national indie music acts.

Art Village. It's hard to believe that the low-key yet vibrant artist enclave of Gulfport was once a blighted fishing village. Now, it's a colorful waterfront community that's very welcoming to the LGBT community. It's pretty much in between St. Pete Beach and St. Petersburg proper, and Beach Boulevard's Art Village sports a high volume of locally owned boutiques, galleries and eclectic eateries. Highlights include Hula Hula, a shop dealing in vintage tropical attire and décor, and Domain, where you can find items—Floridiana or otherwise—you'll find nowhere else, given that much of it was forged at the hands of local artisans. An Art Walk occurs every first Friday and third Saturday of the month, and there's a farmer's market every Tuesday. Keep an eye out for cool local events, as there are many here. ⊠ *Beach Blvd. at Shore Dr., Gulfport.*

Florida Craftsmen Galleries. Downtown St. Pete's bursting art revival is epitomized at Florida Craftsmen Galleries, a nonprofit that gives 125 local crafts people a chance to exhibit glassware, jewelry, furniture, and more. (Think: a vivid coral reef seascape made entirely out of yarn. Stuff like that.) While you're here, take a stroll along Central Avenue's 600-block for a real glimpse into downtown St. Pete's fresh, burgeoning art scene. The gallery is open Monday through Saturday, from 10 to 5:30. ⊠ *501 Central Ave.* ☎ *727/821–7391* ⊕ *www.floridacraftsmen.net.*

Haslam's. One of the state's most notable bookstores, this family-owned emporium has been doing business in St. Petersburg's Grand Central District since the 1930s. Rumored to be haunted by the ghost of *On the Road* author Jack Kerouac (indeed the renowned Beat Generation author used to frequent Haslam's before he died in St. Pete in 1969), the store carries some 300,000 volumes, from cutting-edge best-sellers to ancient tomes. If you value a good book or simply like to browse, you could easily spend an afternoon here. ⊠ *2025 Central Ave.* ☎ *727/822–8616* ⊕ *www.haslams.com.*

7

John's Pass Village and Boardwalk. This collection of shops and restaurants is in an old-style fishing village, where you can watch pelicans cavorting and dive-bombing for food or check out some mellow island music. This is also one of your bests bet for finding a place to rent a Jet Ski or catch a parasailing boat. There's even a live gator attraction here, where patrons can pay to feed the enormous Florida icons large slabs of meat. ⊠ *12901 Gulf Blvd., Madeira Beach* ⊕ *www.johnspass.com.*

Pass-A-Grille 8th Avenue. Pass-A-Grille, the extremely laid-back portion of St. Pete Beach, is well known for its serene beaches, historic buildings, and small-town vibe. What many visitors—and locals—don't know is that eight blocks north of the island's southern tip lies a strip of upscale local shops and art galleries. Favorites include Evander Preston's (who also brews a beer sold locally), Paradiso (resortwear, etc.), and Mountcastle International Trading Company (featuring hand-crafted items from across the globe). An interesting variety of restaurants and bars, including a sweets shop, an all-vegan eatery, and Shadrack's, a quintessential beach dive, also line the street. ⊠ *8th Ave., St. Pete Beach.*

SPORTS AND THE OUTDOORS

BASEBALL

Tampa Bay Rays. Major League Baseball's Tampa Bay Rays completed an improbable worst-to-first turnaround when they topped the American League Eastern Division in 2008, and again in 2010. Then there was that dramatic end-of-season comeback in 2011. Tickets are available at the box office for most games, but you may have to rely on the classifieds sections of the *Tampa Tribune* and *Tampa Bay Times* for popular games. Get here early; parking is often at a premium (pre-gaming at Ferg's is always a safe bet). ⊠ *Tropicana Field, 1 Tropicana Dr., off I–175* ☎ *727/825–3137* ⊕ *www.tampabay.rays.mlb.com.*

CLEARWATER AND VICINITY

Clearwater is 12 miles north of St. Petersburg via U.S. 19.

In Clearwater itself, residential areas are a buffer between the commercial zone that centers on U.S. 19 and the beach, which is moderately quiet during winter but buzzing with life during spring break and in summer. There's a quaint downtown area on the mainland, just east of the beach. You'll find a nightly sunset celebration on the beach and tons of options for dining and entertainment. Among this area's celebrity residents is Winter, the young dolphin who was fitted with a prosthetic tail and depicted in the 2011 film *Dolphin Tale*. She's helping to put this place and its renowned beaches on the map.

If you're up for a day trip, you have two good options if you head north on U.S. 19. One is Dunedin, a Scottish settlement that's packed with cute shops, restaurants, and craft beer bars. You'll find some gorgeous beaches to the west.

Continued on page 402

SPRING TRAINING, FLORIDA-STYLE

by Jim Tunstall and Connie Sharpe

Sunshine, railroads, and land bargains were Florida's first tourist magnets, but baseball had a hand in things, too. The Chicago Cubs led the charge when they opened spring training in Tampa in 1913 — the same year the Cleveland Indians set up camp in Pensacola.

Over the next couple of decades, World War I and the Great Depression interrupted normal lives, but the Sunshine State became a great fit for the national pastime. Soon, big-league teams were flocking south to work off the winter rust.

At one point, the Florida "Grapefruit League" held a monopoly on spring training, but in 1947 Arizona's "Cactus League" started cutting into the action.

Today, roughly half of Major League Baseball's 30 teams arrive in Florida in February for six weeks of calisthenics, tryouts, and practice games. The clubs range from the Detroit Tigers, who have been in the same city (Lakeland) longer than any other team (since 1934), to the Tampa Bay Rays, who moved to a new spring home (Port Charlotte) in 2009.

The Los Angeles Dodgers play the Washington Nationals in Viera during a spring training game.

HERE COME THE FANS

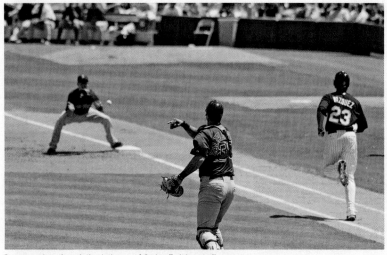

Fan appreciate the relative intimacy of Spring Training stadiums.

Florida's spring training teams play 25 or 30 home and away games, to the delight of 1.68 million annual ticker buyers. Diehards land as soon as the first troops—pitchers and catchers—come to practice around the third week of February. Inter-squad games start in the fourth week, while the real training schedule begins by the end of February or first of March and lasts until the end of the month or early April. These games don't count in the regular season, but they give managers and fans a good idea of which players will be on the opening-day rosters, and who will be   traded, sent to the teams' minor leagues, or told it's time to find a regular day job.

Spring training games provide a great excuse for local baseball fans to cut out of work early, while visitors from the North can leave ice, snow, and sleet behind. And who doesn't want a few chili dogs,

brats, burgers, and brews on a March day? Spring training's draw is more than just a change of venue with an early sample of concession-stand staples. There is also the ample choice of game sites. Teams are scattered around most of the major tourist areas of central and southern Florida, so those coming to watch the games can try a different destination each spring—or even make a road trip to several. Baseball fans also like that it's a melting pot—teams from more than a dozen cities are represented here.

Finally, you can't beat the price—tickets are usually cheaper than during the regular season—nor the access you have to baseball celebrities. In fact, the relaxed atmosphere of spring training makes most players more willing to sign your ball, glove, or whatever. You can get autographs during pregame workouts (practice sessions), which are free, as well as after the game.

4 TIPS

■ **Have a game plan.** Don't just show up. Most teams only have about 15 home games, and those involving popular teams often sell out weeks in advance. Consider buying tickets ahead of time, and if needed, make hotel room reservations at the same time.

■ **Beat the crowds.** The best chance to do this is to go to a weekday game. You'll still encounter lots of fans, but weekday games generally aren't as well attended as weekenders. Also, each team only has a few night games.

■ **Pack a picnic.** Some stadiums let you bring coolers through the turnstiles. Many game attendees also gather for a tailgate party, grilling burgers and sipping a lemonade or beer while jawing with fellow fans (have a chair in tow).

■ West coast games get a lot of sun. Seats in the shade are premium.

(above) Hammond Stadium in Ft. Myers is where the Minnesota Twins practice.
(right) St. Louis Cardinals Chris Duncan is tagged out at Roger Dean Stadium in Jupiter.

Atlanta Braves	**2**	New York Yankees	**4**
Baltimore Orioles	**7**	Philadelphia Phillies	**1**
Boston Red Sox	**14**	Pittsburgh Pirates	**10**
Detroit Tigers	**9**	St. Louis Cardinals/ Florida Marlins	**12**
Houston Astros	**11**	Tampa Bay Rays	**3**
Minnesota Twins	**8**	Toronto Blue Jays	**5**
New York Mets	**6**	Washington Nationals	**13**

PLAY BALL!

Spring training schedules are determined around Thanksgiving. Ticket prices change each year. For all of these teams, you also can order spring training tickets through Ticketmaster (☎ 866/448–7849 ⊕ www.ticketmaster.com) or through the respective team's box office or team Web site. For more information about any of the teams, visit ⊕ www.florida-grapefruitleague.com.

SPRING TRAINING GUIDE
Order a free Guide to *Florida Spring Training* from the **Florida Sports Foundation** (✉ 2930 Kerry Forest Parkway, Tallahassee, FL ☎ 850/488–8347 ⊕ www.flasports.com). Published in February each year, it's packed with information about teams, sites, tickets, and more.

New York Mets catcher Ramon Castro.

ATLANTA BRAVES
Home Field: Champion Stadium, Walt Disney World Wide World of Sports, 700 S. Victory Way, Lake Buena Vista. **Tickets:** $10–$49 ☎ 407/939–4263 ⊕ www.braves.mlb.com

BALTIMORE ORIOLES
Home Field: Ed Smith Stadium, 2700 12th St., Sarasota. **Tickets:** $8–$32
☎ 941/954–4101 ⊕ www.orioles.mlb.com

BOSTON RED SOX
Home Field: JetBlue Park, 11500 Fenway South Dr., Fort Myers. **Tickets:** $10–$46
☎ 239/334–4700, 888/733–7696 ⊕ www.redsox.mlb.com

DETROIT TIGERS
Home Field: Joker Marchant Stadium, 2301 Lakeland Hills Blvd., Lakeland. **Tickets:** $10–$32
☎ 863/686–8075 ⊕ www.tigers.mlb.com

HOUSTON ASTROS
Home Field: Osceola County Stadium, 631 Heritage Parkway, Kissimmee. **Tickets:** $15–$27
☎ 321/697–3200 ⊕ www.astros.mlb.com

MIAMI MARLINS
Home Field: Roger Dean Stadium (shared with St. Louis Cardinals), 4751 Main St., Jupiter. **Tickets:** $15–$28
☎ 561/775–1818 ⊕ www.marlins.mlb.com

MINNESOTA TWINS
Home Field: Lee County Sports Complex, 14100 Six Mile
Cypress Parkway, Fort Myers. **Tickets:** $13–$29
☏ 800/338–9467 ⊕ www.twins.mlb.com

NEW YORK METS
Home Field: Mets Field, 525 NW Peacock Blvd., Port St. Lucie.
Tickets: $8–$25
☏ 772/871–2115 ⊕ www.mets.mlb.com

NEW YORK YANKEES
Home Field: George M. Steinbrenner Field, 1 Steinbrenner Dr.,
Tampa. **Tickets:** $17–$33
☏ 813/879–2244 ⊕ www.yankees.mlb.com

PHILADELPHIA PHILLIES
Home Field: Bright House Networks Field, 601 N. Old
Coachman Rd., Clearwater. **Tickets:** $14–$39
☏ 727/467–4457 ⊕ www.phillies.mlb.com

PITTSBURGH PIRATES
Home Field: McKechnie Field, 1611 9th St. W,
Bradenton. **Tickets:** $12–$22
☏ 941/747–3031 ⊕ www.pirates.mlb.com

ST. LOUIS CARDINALS
Home Field: Roger Dean Stadium (shared with Miami Marlins),
4751 Main St., Jupiter. **Tickets:** $15–$28
☏ 561/630–1828 ⊕ www.cardinals.mlb.com

TAMPA BAY RAYS
Home Field: Charlotte County Sports Park, 2300 El Jobean Rd.,
Port Charlotte. **Tickets:** $10–$27
☏ 888/326–7297 ⊕ www.rays.mlb.com

TORONTO BLUE JAYS
Home Field: Florida Auto Exchange Park, 373 Douglas Ave.,
Dunedin. **Tickets:** $15–$30
☏ 727/733–0429 ⊕ www.bluejays.mlb.com

WASHINGTON NATIONALS
Home Field: Space Coast Stadium, 5800 Stadium Parkway,
Viera. **Tickets:** $12–$26
☏ 321/633–4487 ⊕ www.nationals.mlb.com

Farther north is charming Tarpon Springs, which has a highly Greek-influenced downtown. Here, you'll find historic sponge docks, a Greek restaurant or two, and some great beaches for watching the sunset.

GETTING HERE AND AROUND

Clearwater is due west from Tampa International Airport via State Road 60, and it's about 45 minutes north of St. Petersburg. If you want to fly directly to Clearwater instead of Tampa, though, St. Pete/Clearwater International Airport is another option. From St. Pete you can get here via U.S. 19, which is notorious for its congestion, Alternate U.S. 19, or County Road 1. If you're up for a scenic yet slower drive, Gulf Boulevard takes you all the way to Clearwater from St. Pete Beach—as does a beach trolley that runs along that route.

VISITOR INFORMATION

Contacts **Clearwater Regional Chamber of Commerce** ☎ 727/461–0011 ⊕ www.clearwaterflorida.org. **Greater Dunedin Chamber of Commerce** ☎ 727/733–3197 ⊕ www.dunedin-fl.com. **Tarpon Springs Chamber of Commerce** ☎ 727/937–6109 ⊕ www.tarponspringschamber.com.

EXPLORING

Clearwater Marine Aquarium. This aquarium gives you the opportunity to participate in the work of saving and caring for endangered marine species. Many of the sea turtles, dolphins, and other animals living at the aquarium were brought here to be rehabilitated from an injury or saved from danger. The dolphin exhibit has an open-air arena giving the dolphins plenty of room to jump during their shows. This aquarium is also home to Winter, a dolphin fitted with a prosthetic tail that was the subject of the 2011 film *Dolphin Tale*. The aquarium conducts tours of the bays and islands around Clearwater, including a daily cruise on a pontoon boat (you might just see a wild dolphin or two), and kayak tours of Clearwater Harbor and St. Joseph Sound. ✉ 249 *Windward Passage* ☎ 727/441–1790 ⊕ *www.seewinter.com* 🎫 *$20* ☉ *Daily 9–6.*

Konger Tarpon Springs Aquarium. Although it's not on par with larger facilities in Tampa and Clearwater, this is certainly an entertaining attraction. There are some good exhibits, including a 120,000-gallon shark tank complete with a coral reef. (Divers feed the sharks several times daily.) Also look for tropical fish exhibits and a tank where you can touch baby sharks and stingrays. ✉ *850 Dodecanese Blvd., off U.S. 19, Tarpon Springs* ☎ 727/938–5378 ⊕ *www.tarponspringsaquarium. com* 🎫 *$7.75* ☉ *Mon.–Sat. 10–5, Sun. noon–5.*

FAMILY **Pier 60.** This spot is the terminus of State Road 60 (hence the name), which runs under various names between Vero Beach on the east coast and Clearwater Beach on the west coast. Around 3:30 pm each day, weather permitting, the area surrounding the pier starts to liven up. Local artists and craftspeople populate their folding tables with beaded jewelry, handmade skin-care products, and beach landscape paintings. Jugglers, musicians, breakdancers, and fire breathers put on some lively shows for those in attendance. And the grand finale is the sun setting over the Gulf of Mexico. On weekends when the weather is mild, there

Clearwater's Bait House lures in those heading to the pier to fish. —photo by watland, Fodors.com member.

are also free, family-friendly movie screenings. ✉ *10 Pier 60 Dr., Clearwater Beach* ☎ *727/449–1036* ⊕ *www.sunsetsatpier60.com.*

The Sponge Factory. This shop, museum, and cultural center reveals more than you ever imagined about how a lowly sea creature created the industry that built this village. See a film about these much-sought-after creatures from the phylum *porifera* and how they helped the town prosper in the early 1900s. You'll come away converted to (and loaded up with) natural sponges. ✉ *15 Dodecanese Blvd., off Alt. U.S. 19, Tarpon Springs* ☎ *727/938–5366* ⊕ *www.spongedocks.net* 🖼 *Free* ☉ *Daily 9–6.*

BEACHES

Caladesi Island State Park. Quiet, secluded, and still wild, this 3½-mile-long barrier island is one of the best shelling beaches on the Gulf Coast, second only to Sanibel. The park also has plenty of sights for birders—from common sandpipers to majestic blue herons to rare black skimmers—and miles of trails through scrub oaks, saw palmettos, and cacti (with tenants such as armadillos, rabbits, and raccoons). The landscape also features mangroves and dunes, and the gradual slope of the sea bottom makes this a good spot for novice swimmers and kids. You have to get to Caladesi Island by private boat (there's a 108-slip marina) or through its sister park, Honeymoon Island State Recreation Area, where you take the hourly ferry ride ($14 per person) across to Caladesi. **Amenities:** food and drink; showers; toilets. **Best for:** solitude; swimming. ✉ *Dunedin Causeway, Dunedin* ☎ *727/469–5918* ⊕ *www. floridastateparks.org/caladesiisland* 🖼 *$8 per boat; $2 per kayaker* ☉ *Daily 8–sunset.*

Fodor'sChoice ★ **Clearwater Beach.** On a narrow island between Clearwater Harbor and the gulf is a stretch of sand with a widespread reputation for beach volleyball. It's also the site of a nightly sunset celebration, complete with musicians and artisans. It's one of the area's nicest and busiest beaches, especially on weekends and during spring break, but it's also one of the costliest in terms of parking fees, which can reach $2 per hour. **Amenities:** food and drink; parking (fee); showers; toilets. **Best for:** partiers; sunset; walking. ⊠ *Western end of Rte. 60, 2 miles west of downtown Clearwater.*

Honeymoon Island State Park. If you're seeking an almost completely undeveloped beach that's still easily accessible by car, this is one of your best bets. Northwest of Clearwater, this large state park offers some of the best shell hunting you'll find, as well as thousands of feet of serene beachfront. If you head north along the park road, you find extensive hiking trails, along which you'll see an astonishing array of birds. **Amenities:** food and drink; showers; toilets. **Best for:** solitude; swimming; walking. ⊠ *1 Causeway Blvd., Dunedin* ⊕ *www.floridastateparks.org/honeymoonisland* ⌂ *$8 single-occupant vehicle* ☉ *Daily 8 am–sunset.*

Indian Rocks Beach. This beach community is a mellow alternative to the oft-crowded shorelines of Clearwater and St. Pete Beach along the gulf coast. This is a town in which the road narrows to two lanes and is lined with upscale residential condos instead of busy hotels. There are quite a few beach access points, though your best bet is a landscaped facility offering ample parking, nearby food and drink, and an occasional event. **Amenities:** food and drink; parking (fee); showers; toilets. **Best for:** solitude; swimming; walking. ⊠ *Indian Rocks Beach Nature Preserve, 1700 Gulf Blvd., Indian Rocks Beach* ⊕ *www.indian-rocks-beach.com.*

Sand Key Park. This is a mellow counterpart to often-crowded Clearwater Beach to the north. It has a lovely beach, plenty of green space, a playground, and a picnic area in an otherwise congested area. **Amenities:** food and drink; lifeguards; showers; toilets. **Best for:** solitude; sunset; swimming. ⊠ *1060 Gulf Blvd.* ☎ *727/588–4852.*

Sunset Beach. As the name suggests, this beach park is known as one of the best places in North Pinellas County to watch the sunset. It's a small beach but a great place to barbecue. April through November there's a weekly concert. **Amenities:** toilets. **Best for:** sunset; swimming. ⊠ *1800 Gulf Rd., Tarpon Springs.*

WHERE TO EAT

$$$
AMERICAN ✕**Bob Heilman's Beachcomber.** The Heilman family has fed hungry diners since 1920. Although it's very popular with tourists, you'll also rub shoulders with devoted locals. Despite the frequent crowds, the service is fast and friendly. The sautéed chicken is an American classic—arriving with mashed spuds, gravy, veggie du jour, and fresh baked bread. Or try some Gulf shrimp prepared in nearly any way you can imagine, including lightly breaded and fried, tossed with pasta primavera and sautéed vegetables, or served Rockefeller-style. ⑤ *Average main: $25* ⊠ *447 Mandalay Ave., Clearwater Beach* ☎ *727/442–4144* ⊕ *www.bobheilmans.com.*

$$$
EUROPEAN

✕**Bon Appétit.** Known for its creative fare, this waterfront restaurant has a menu that changes frequently, offering such entrées as broiled rack of lamb in herbed walnut crust, and red snapper on a bed of lobster hash. The creative grouper options, i.e. grouper gyros, get well-deserved plaudits from many patrons. Bon Appétit has staying power, having served at the same location for more than three decades. It's a great place to catch a sunset over the Gulf of Mexico. There's live music every night, and a pianist plays Wednesday through Sunday evenings and at Sunday brunch. ⑤ *Average main: $25* ✉ *148 Marina Plaza, Dunedin* ☎ *727/733–2151* ⊕ *www.bonappetitrestaurant.com.*

$
MEXICAN

✕**Casa Tina.** At this colorful Dunedin institution, vegetarians can veg out on roasted *chiles rellenos* (cheese-stuffed peppers), enchiladas with vegetables, and a cactus salad that won't prick your tongue but will tickle your taste buds with the tantalizing flavors of tender pieces of cactus, cilantro, tomatoes, onions, lime, and *queso fresco* (a mild white cheese). The stuffed sapote squash also makes the grade. Tamales, tacos, and tortillas are prepared in dozens of ways. The place is often crowded, and service can be slow as a result, but there's a reason everyone's eating here. ⑤ *Average main: $15* ✉ *365 Main St., Dunedin* ☎ *727/734–9226.*

$
SEAFOOD

✕**Frenchy's Rockaway Grill.** Quebec native Mike "Frenchy" Preston runs four eateries in the area, including the fabulous Rockaway Grill. Visitors and locals alike keep coming back for the grouper sandwiches that are moist and not battered into submission. (It's also real grouper, something that's not a given these days.) Frenchy also gets a big thumbs-up for the she-crab soup, and, on the march-to-a-different-drummer front, the grouper eggrolls. In mild weather, eat on the deck, though the screaming yellow awning can be nearly as blinding as the sun. ⑤ *Average main: $15* ✉ *7 Rockaway St.* ☎ *727/446–4844* ⊕ *www. frenchysonline.com.*

$$
SEAFOOD

✕**Palm Pavilion Beachside Grill & Bar.** Long heralded as one of the best spots for watching sunsets, this place also gets high marks for its fresh seafood offerings. The grouper sandwich in particular gets rave reviews. Healthier fare includes an array of wraps. The restaurant is casual but not too casual. It's got a bit of a Tommy Bahama feel to it, so you may want to ditch the beach attire if you plan to dine here. Be advised that it gets pretty packed around sunset, when a live band plays island music and the margaritas flow. ⑤ *Average main: $15* ✉ *10 Bay Esplande, Clearwater Beach* ☎ *727/446–2642* ⊕ *www.palmpavilion.com.*

WHERE TO STAY

$$
HOTEL

⌂**Hilton Clearwater Beach.** This marquee property has a look that is clean and modern without losing the Clearwater Beach vibe, and staying here may be a little less pricey than you might expect. **Pros:** on the beach; about as modern as you can get. **Cons:** chain hotel feel; lots of conventions; resort fee. ⑤ *Rooms from: $219* ✉ *400 Mandalay Ave., Clearwater Beach* ☎ *727/461–3222* ⊕ *www.hiltonclearwaterbeach.com* ⇨ *416 rooms, 12 suites* ⊠◎ *No meals.*

$$$$
RESORT

⌂**Hyatt Regency Clearwater Beach.** One of the more recent additions to the Clearwater Beach skyline, this upscale resort towers above almost everything else in the immediate area, both in terms of height and

luxury. **Pros:** gorgeous facility; plenty of amenities; near the action. **Cons:** beach is across busy street; some floors are residential; expensive. ⑤ *Rooms from: $450* ✉ *301 S. Gulfview Blvd.* ☎ *727/373–1234* ⊕ *www.clearwaterbeach.hyatt.com* ⤴ *250 suites* ⦿| *No meals.*

$ 🏨 **Innisbrook Resort & Golf Club.** A massive pool complex with a 15-foot
RESORT waterfall, two winding waterslides, and a sandy waterfront are part of the allure of this sprawling resort, but it may be the 72 holes of golf, including the challenging Copperhead course, that are the real draw. **Pros:** great for serious golfers; varied dining options. **Cons:** far from attractions. ⑤ *Rooms from: $179* ✉ *36750 U.S. 19 N, Palm Harbor* ☎ *727/942–2000, 888/794–8627* ⊕ *www.innisbrookgolfresort.com* ⤴ *50 rooms, 550 suites* ⦿| *No meals.*

$$ 🏨 **Safety Harbor Resort & Spa.** Those who enjoy old-school pampering
RESORT love this hotel's exceptional 50,000-square-foot spa, which has the latest in therapies and treatments. **Pros:** charm to spare; good choice for pampering. **Cons:** far from beach; not ideal for families with children. ⑤ *Rooms from: $269* ✉ *105 N. Bayshore Dr., Safety Harbor* ☎ *727/726–1161, 877/784–6835* ⊕ *www.safetyharborspa.com* ⤴ *175 rooms, 16 suites* ⦿| *No meals.*

$$ 🏨 **Sandpearl Resort.** Two things set this expansive, luxurious Clearwater
RESORT Beach resort apart from other upscale accommodations in the vicinity: it's not part of a major chain, and the property has deep local ties. **Pros:** on the beach; tons of amenities and dining options. **Cons:** resort fee; lots of conventions. ⑤ *Rooms from: $279* ✉ *500 Mandalay Ave.* ☎ *727/441–2425* ⊕ *www.sandpearl.com* ⤴ *203 rooms, 50 suites* ⦿| *No meals.*

$$ 🏨 **Sheraton Sand Key Resort.** Expect something special when you stay
RESORT here, including a modern property and one of the few uncluttered beaches in the area. **Pros:** private beach; great views; no resort fee, and parking is also free. **Cons:** near crowded Clearwater Beach; views come with a high price tag. ⑤ *Rooms from: $230* ✉ *1160 Gulf Blvd., Clearwater Beach* ☎ *727/595–1611* ⊕ *www.sheratonsandkey.com* ⤴ *375 rooms, 15 suites* ⦿| *No meals.*

NIGHTLIFE

Dunedin Brewery. Tampa Bay is seen by many as a flourishing craft-beer hub. If it weren't for Dunedin Brewery, that might not be the case. It was the first of its kind in the area and continues to offer delicious brews to throngs of patrons. It doesn't hurt that it offers live music many nights of the week, either. ✉ *937 Douglas Ave., Dunedin* ☎ *727/736–0606* ⊕ *www.dunedinbrewery.com.*

SPORTS AND THE OUTDOORS

BIKING

Pinellas Trail. This 42-mile paved route spans Pinellas County, from near the southernmost point all the way north to Tarpon Springs. Along a former railway line, the trail runs adjacent to major thoroughfares, no more than 10 feet from the roadway, so you can access it from almost any point. The trail, also popular with in-line skaters, has spawned trailside businesses such as repair shops and health-food cafés. There are also many lovely rural areas to bike through and plenty of places to rent bikes. Be wary of traffic in downtown Clearwater and on the congested areas of the Pinellas Trail, which still needs more bridges for crossing over busy streets, and avoid the trail at night. To start riding from the route's south end, park at Trailhead Park (37th Street South at 8th Avenue South) in St. Petersburg. To ride south from the north end, park your car in downtown Tarpon Springs (East Tarpon Avenue at North Stafford Avenue). ☎ 727/549–6099 ⊕ www.pinellascounty. org/trailgd.

GOLF

Dunedin Golf Club. Dunedin is Tampa Bay's little Scotland, the birthplace of golf, so it's only natural that one of the area's better courses is here. Designed by influential golf-course architect Donald Ross, this semi-private, recently restored facility also has a driving range, a pro shop, and clubhouse. The course itself offers numerous challenging holes with names like "It Isn't Easy," "Calamity Jane," and "Devil's Kick," with the twists and turns to match. Water hazards aren't too overwhelming here, except on the 14th hole, known as "Round the Lake." ⊠ *1050 Palm Blvd., Dunedin* ☎ *727/733–7836* ⊕ *www.dunedingolfclub.com* ☞ *$50 for 18 holes* ⅄ *18 holes. 6625 yards. par 72.*

Innisbrook. Considered one of the top 100 golf destinations in Florida, this resort is home to Larry Packard–designed Copperhead Course, which hosts the the annual PGA Tour Valspar Championship. Open to resort guests as well as the public, the four courses here take full advantage of the fact that they're on the coast, with plenty of ponds and sand traps adding to the scenery as well as the challenge. Fairways here on the Copperhead Course consist of rolling hills lined with trees, which are prime for spotting blue herons, squirrels, and even an alligator or two. The Island Course offers narrow fairways, some of which are lined by Lake Innisbrook, others by tall stands of pine and cypress trees. The North Course features tight fairways, numerous bunkers and eleven water hazards, while the South Course has more of a links course–like layout. The Fox Squirrel Course is a quick 9-hole course available to guests only. ⊠ *36750 U.S. 19 N, Palm Harbor* ☎ *888/794–8627, 727/942–2000* ⊕ *innisbrookgolfresort.com* ☞ *Copperhead Course: $280. Island Course: $240. North and South Courses: $190.* ⅄ *Copperhead Course: 18 holes. 7430 yards. par 72. Island Course: 18 holes. 7310 yards. par 70. North Course: 18 holes,6325 yards, par 70. South Course: 18 holes. 6620 yards. par 71. Fox Squirrel Course: 9 holes. 1236 yards. par 36 (resort guests only, closed during high season).*

Saddlebrook. The courses of this golf-centric resort 30 minutes northeast of Tampa are open to the public, and offer a remoteness that's hard to find in such a densely populated metro area. The star here is the Palmer Course, which, as one might expect, is named for Arnold Palmer, who designed it. It's characterized by a hilly terrain uncharacteristic of Florida as well as island-dotted ponds and plenty of troublesome bunkers. The Saddlebrook Course is more scenic than it is challenging (but is very much both), with long fairways lined with rows of pine trees. There's a pro on site Tuesday, Thursday, and Saturday to help you perfect your game, not to mention a full-fledged golf academy. ⊠ *5700 Saddlebrook Way, Wesley Chapel* ☎ *813/907-4401* ⊕ *www.saddlebrook.com* ⬚ *$96 for 9 holes, $145 for 18 holes* ⅃. *Palmer Course: 18 holes. 6641 yards. par 71. Saddlebrook Course: 18 holes. 6564 yards. par 70.*

SURFING

FlowRider at Surf Style. Surf Style, in the towering Hyatt, is a chain store that sells beach essentials like sarongs, sunblock, and souvenirs. But what sets this particularly enormous store apart is the FlowRider, an indoor pool that generates artificial waves suitable for surfing. For $20 per half hour, you and the kids can surf or learn to surf, something you can't usually do out in the gulf. An instructor is on hand to show you the ropes. ⊠ *Hyatt Regency Clearwater Beach, 311 S. Gulfview Blvd.* ☎ *727/446–6566* ⊕ *www.surf-style.com.*

CITRUS COUNTY

The coastal and western inland areas of Citrus County north of Tampa and St. Petersburg are sometimes called the Nature Coast, and aptly so. Flora and fauna have been well preserved in this area, and West Indian manatees are showstoppers. These gentle vegetarian marine mammals, distantly related to elephants, remain an endangered species, though their numbers have grown to 3,500 or more today. Many manatees have massive scars on their backs from run-ins with boat propellers. Extensive nature preserves and parks have been created to protect them and other wildlife indigenous to the area, and these are among the best spots to view manatees in the wild. Although they're far from mythical beauties, it's believed that manatees inspired ancient mariners' tales of mermaids. This is one of the only spots in the world where you can legally swim with—and even touch—these gentle creatures.

GETTING HERE AND AROUND

U.S. 19 and the Suncoast Parkway, a toll road, are the prime north–south routes through this rural region, and traffic flows freely once you've left the congestion of St. Petersburg, Clearwater, and Port Richey. In most cases, the Suncoast Parkway is a far quicker drive than U.S. 19, though you'll have to pay several dollars in tolls. If you're planning a day trip from the Bay Area, pack a picnic lunch before leaving, since most of the sights are outdoors.

WEEKI WACHEE

Weeki Wachee Springs. At Weeki Wachee Springs, the spring flows at the remarkable rate of 170 million gallons a day with a constant temperature of 74°F. The spring has long been famous for its live "mermaids," clearly not the work of Mother Nature, as they wear bright costumes and put on an Esther Williams–like underwater choreography show that's been virtually unchanged since the park opened in 1947. The park is considered a classic piece of Florida history and culture, also features snorkel tours and canoe trips on the river, and a wilderness boat ride gives an up-close look at raccoons, otters, egrets, and other semitropical Florida wetlands wildlife. In summer, Buccaneer Bay water park opens for swimming, beaching, and riding its thrilling slides and flumes.

✉ *6131 Commercial Way, at U.S. 19 and Rte. 50* ☏ *352/592–5656*
⊕ *www.weekiwachee.com* ▤ *$13* ⊙ *Daily 9–5:30.*

HOMOSASSA SPRINGS
65 miles north of St. Petersburg on U.S. 19.

A little more than an hour north of Clearwater, you'll come upon this
small and friendly hub for water lovers. Along with a phenomenal
manatee-centric state park, you'll find more than a handful of charming
restaurants, some featuring live music in the evening. This and Crystal River provide you with the once-in-a-lifetime chance to swim with
manatees, something best done in winter. Summer's scallop season is
also a massive draw.

EXPLORING

FAMILY **Ellie Schiller Homosassa Springs Wildlife State Park.** Here you can see many
manatees and several species of fish through a floating glass observatory known as the Fish Bowl—except in this case the fish are outside
the bowl and you are inside it. The park's wildlife walk trails lead you
to excellent manatee, alligator, and other animal programs. Among
the species are bobcats, a western cougar, white-tailed deer, a black
bear, pelicans, herons, snowy egrets, river otters, whooping cranes,
and even a hippopotamus named Lu, a keepsake from the park's days
as an exotic-animal attraction. Boat cruises on Pepper Creek lead you
to the Homosassa wildlife park (which takes its name from a Creek
Indian word meaning "place where wild peppers grow"). ✉ *4150 S.
Suncoast Blvd., U.S. 19* ☏ *352/628–5343* ⊕ *www.floridastateparks.
org/homosassasprings* ▤ *$13* ⊙ *Daily 9–5:30; last boat departs at 3:15.*

Yulee Sugar Mill Ruins Historic State Park. This state park has the remains
of a circa-1851 sugar mill and other remnants of a 5,100-acre sugar
plantation owned by Florida's first U.S. senator, David Levy Yulee. It
makes for pleasant picnicking and dog-walking, although it is somewhat lacking visually. ✉ *Rte. 490 (Yulee Dr.), 3 miles off U.S. 19/98*
☏ *352/795–3817* ⊕ *www.floridastateparks.org/yuleesugarmill* ▤ *Free*
⊙ *Daily 8 am–sunset.*

WHERE TO EAT

$ ✗ **Dan's Clam Stand.** Four reasons to go: the fried grouper sandwich, the
SEAFOOD clam "chowda," anything else seafood, and the beef burgers. The origi-
nal location is about 2 miles east of Homosassa Springs State Wildlife
Park. It's very popular among locals—just check out the packed parking
lot at lunch and dinner. New England–style seafood is a house specialty,
including whole-belly clams and lobster, but the grouper and mahimahi
are fresh from local waters. Best of all, Dan's won't bust your budget.
There's another branch in Crystal River. $ *Average main: $10* ✉ *7364
Grover Cleveland Blvd.* ☏ *352/628–9588* ▭ *No credit cards* ⊙ *Closed
Sun.* $ *Average main: $10* ✉ *2315 N. Sunshine Path, off Rte. 44, Crystal River* ☏ *352/795–9081*

$ ✗ **Museum Cafe.** A short trip west of Homosassa Springs State Wildlife
CUBAN Refuge, this tiny eatery housed in the Olde Mill House Printing Museum
is known for its Cuban sandwiches. It's only open for lunch, but it's well
worth making room for a visit here in your itinerary. You can sit at a
table within the museum itself or one of the tables in the very casual

main dining room. Another option is to get your lunch to go and picnic at nearby Yulee Sugar Mill Ruins State Park. $ *Average main: $10* ✉ *10466 W. Yulee Dr.* ☎ *352/628–1081* ⊘ *No dinner.*

$ ✕**Neon Leon's Zydeco Steakhouse.** If you couldn't already tell, the Nature
SEAFOOD   Coast is about as Southern as you can get. This place is a case in point. This roadhouse-style eatery is co-owned by family members of former Lynyrd Skynyrd bassist Leon Wilkeson. Legend has it that Wilkeson had long dreamed of opening a restaurant serving Southern and Cajun food like fried okra and gator tail, with music to match. You'll hear nightly live zydeco here, and the menu offers Dixieland staples like jambalaya (a favorite here), frog legs, and catfish. It may have a roadhouse feel and plenty of musical memorabilia, but it's also smoke-free and pretty family-friendly. A word of caution: the music can get loud. $ *Average main: $15* ✉ *10350 Yulee Dr.* ☎ *352/621–3663* ⊕ *www. neonleonszydecosteakhouse.com* ⊘ *Closed Mon.*

CRYSTAL RIVER
6 miles north of Homosassa Springs on U.S. 19.

Situated along the peaceful Nature Coast, this area is *the* low-key getaway spot in one of the most pristine and beautiful areas in the state. It's also one of the only places on the planet where you can legally swim with manatees. The river's fed by a spring that's a constant 72°F, which is why manatees enjoy spending their winters here. Boating and snorkeling are popular, as is scalloping in the summer. This is a true paradise for nature lovers, and absolutely worth making room for in your vacation itinerary.

EXPLORING
Crystal River National Wildlife Refuge. This is a U.S. Fish and Wildlife Service sanctuary for the endangered manatee. Kings Bay, around which manatees congregate in winter (generally from November to March), feeds crystal-clear water into the river at 72°F year-round. This is one of the sure-bet places to see manatees in winter since hundreds congregate near this 90-acre refuge. The small visitor center has displays about the manatee and other refuge inhabitants. If you want to get an even closer look at these gentle giants, several dive companies provide opportunities for you to swim among them—if you don't mind shelling out some extra cash, donning a wetsuit, and adhering to some strict interaction guidelines. In warmer months, when most manatees scatter, the main spring is fun for a swim or scuba diving. ✉ *1502 S.E. Kings Bay Dr.* ☎ *352/563–2088* ⊕ *www.fws.gov/crystalriver* 🎫 *Free* ⊘ *Daily 7:30–4.*

BEACH
Fort Island Gulf Beach. This is one of the most remote beaches you will find north of Fort De Soto, the isolated beach south of St. Petersburg. One of the best parts of coming here is the drive. The beach sits as the terminus of Fort Island Trail, the same road where you'll find the Plantation Inn & Golf Resort. A 9-mile drive through the wetlands gets you here, offering sweeping views along the way (though the Crystal River nuclear plant looms to the north). The beach itself is raw and subdued, though there are picnic shelters, barbecues and a fishing pier. Don't expect many frills, but if you need to relax after a long day of playing

in the water, this is your place. **Amenities:** showers; toilets. **Best for:** solitude, sunset. ✉ *16000 W. Fort Island Trail.*

MANATEE DIVES

American Pro Diving Center. This is one of several local operators in the area conducting manatee tours of Crystal River National Wildlife Refuge or Homosassa River, something you can't legally do pretty much anywhere else in the country. Tours start at around $30. ✉ *821 S.E. U.S. 19* ☎ *352/563–0041* ⊕ *www.americanprodiving.com.*

Crystal Lodge Dive Center. This dive center is one of the more popular operators offering dives, swims, and snorkel trips to see manatees, with rates starting as low as $25. ✉ *525 N.W. 7th Ave.* ☎ *352/795–6798* ⊕ *www.manatee-central.com.*

Plantation Dive Shop. An obvious choice if you're staying at the Plantation on Crystal River, this dive tour company stands on its own as a manatee tour operator. The guides bring you out to various spots along the river to interact with manatees, and tend to be longtime residents who know their subject well. If the weather is warm, that means no manatees, so opt for a sunset cruise instead. ✉ *Plantation on Crystal River, 9301 Fort Island Trail* ☎ *352/795–5797* ⊕ *www.crystalriverdivers.com* 🖄 *$30 plus equipment.*

SARASOTA AND VICINITY

Widely thought of as one of the best places in Florida to live, Sarasota County anchors the southern end of Tampa Bay. A string of barrier islands borders it with 35 miles of gulf and bay beaches. Sarasota County has something for everyone, from the athletic to the artistic. Thirteen public beaches, two state parks, 22 municipal parks, plus more than 60 public and private golf courses will help keep the active in motion. Spring training was an original destination attraction that now shares the stage with international rowing, swimming, and sailing events. Add to that a plentiful cultural scene dating to the era of circus magnate John Ringling, who chose this area for the winter home of his circus and his family.

BRADENTON

49 miles south of Tampa.

In 1539 Hernando de Soto landed near this Manatee River city, which has some 20 miles of beaches. Bradenton is well situated for access to fishing, both fresh- and saltwater, and it also has its share of golf courses and historic sites dating to the mid-1800s. Orange groves and cattle ranches mix with farmlands between Bradenton's beaches and Interstate 75.

GETTING HERE AND AROUND

You can get to Bradenton via Interstate 75, Interstate 275, and U.S. 41/301. West Manatee Avenue gets you out to the beaches. Manatee County Area Transit (MCAT) has buses throughout Bradenton and the nearby towns of Palmetto and Ellenton, as well as connections to Sarasota attractions. Fares for local bus service range from $1.25 to $3 (for an all-day pass); exact change is required. A $30 monthly "M-Card" is available for unlimited rides on all MCAT routes. However, if you want to get around efficiently—and want access to more places—you're best off renting a car.

Contacts Manatee County Area Transit ⊕ *www.mymanatee.org.*

VISITOR INFORMATION

Contacts Bradenton Area Convention and Visitors Bureau. This organization has all you need to know about everything Bradenton, Anna Maria Island, Palmetto, and Ellenton have to offer. ☎ *941/729–9177* ⊕ *www. bradentongulfislands.com.*

EXPLORING

Fodor's Choice
★

De Soto National Memorial. One of the first Spanish explorers to land in North America, Hernando de Soto came ashore with his men and 200 horses near what is now Bradenton in 1539; this federal park commemorates De Soto's expedition and the Native Americans he and his crew encountered. During the height of tourist season, from mid-December to late April, park staff and volunteers dress in period costumes at Camp Uzita, demonstrate the use of 16th-century weapons, and show how European explorers prepared and preserved food for their overland journeys. The season ends with a reenactment of the explorer's landing. The site also offers a film and short nature trail through the mangroves. ⊠ *8300 De Soto Memorial Hwy.* ☎ *941/792–0458* ⊕ *www. nps.gov/deso* ⊠ *Free (donations accepted)* ☉ *Visitor center daily 9–5, grounds daily dawn–dusk.*

OFF THE
BEATEN
PATH

Gamble Plantation Historic State Park. Built in the 1840s, this antebellum mansion five miles northeast of Bradenton was home to Major Robert Gamble and is the headquarters of an extensive sugar plantation. It is the only surviving plantation house in South Florida. The Confederate secretary of state took refuge here when the Confederacy fell to Union forces. Picnic tables are available. Guided tours of the house are available six times a day. ⊠ *3708 Patten Ave., Ellenton* ☎ *941/723–4536* ⊕ *www.floridastateparks.org/gambleplantation* ⊠ *Free, tours $6* ☉ *Sun.–Sat. 8–sunset, tours Thurs.–Mon. 8–5:40.*

Pine Avenue. Anna Maria Island's newly restored "Main Street" features numerous pricey mom-and-pop boutiques, including upscale yet beach-appropriate clothiers, beach-inspired home décor stores, and antique furniture shops. You can also find shops offering items such as quality vintage clothing and infused olive oil. The Anna Maria City Pier, which overlooks the southern end of Tampa Bay, sits at the end of the street. ⊠ *Pine Ave., Anna Maria* ☎ *941/592–6642* ⊕ *www.pineavenueinfo. com.*

OFF THE
BEATEN
PATH

Solomon's Castle. For a visit to the wild and weird side, particularly fun for children, head to this castle about 45 minutes east of Bradenton through orange groves and cattle farms. Artist and Renaissance man Howard Solomon began building the 12,000-square-foot always-in-progress work out of thousands of aluminum offset printing plates. Inside, you'll find tons of intrigues—everything from a knight assembled with Volkswagen parts to a chair fashioned out of 86 beer cans to an elephant made from seven oil drums. A restaurant serves sit-down lunches in a full-scale model of a Spanish galleon. It is also open Friday and Saturday nights in season. ⊠ *4585 Solomon Rd., Ona* ☎ *863/494–6077* ⊕ *www.solomonscastle.org* ⌂ *$10* ⊙ *Tues.–Sun 11–4. Closed July–Sept.*

FAMILY **South Florida Museum and Parker Manatee Aquarium.** Snooty, the oldest manatee in captivity, is the headliner here. Programs about the endangered marine mammals run four times daily. View changing exhibits such as digital images of water and other natural resources in the East Gallery; glass cases and roll-out drawers on the second floor allow you to look at exhibits normally out of public view. At the Bishop Planetarium (with a domed theater screen), programs presented range from black holes to Jimi Hendrix, Pink Floyd, and other rockers. ⊠ *201 10th St. W* ☎ *941/746–4131* ⊕ *www.southfloridamuseum.org* ⌂ *$18* ⊙ *Mon.–Sat. 10–5, Sun. noon–5. Closed Mon. May, Jun., and Aug.–Dec.*

BEACHES

Anna Maria Island, Bradenton's 7-mile barrier island to the west, has a number of worthwhile beaches, as does Longboat Key. Manatee Avenue connects the mainland to the island via the Palma Sola Causeway, adjacent to which is a long, sandy beach fronting Palma Sola Bay. There are boat ramps, a dock, and picnic tables.

Anna Maria Bayfront Park. This narrow yet secluded beach fronts Tampa Bay at Passage Key Inlet and the Gulf of Mexico. It's also situated between two fishing piers. Don't forget to bring the picnic gear to this unforgettably scenic stretch of shoreline. **Amenities:** lifeguards; showers; toilets. **Best for:** solitude; sunset. ⊠ *310 North Bay Blvd., adjacent to a municipal pier, Anna Maria Island.*

Coquina Beach. Singles and families flock to Coquina Beach, a wider swath of sand is at the southern end of Anna Maria Island. Beach walkers love this stretch since it's Anna Maria's longest beach, and it also attracts crowds of young revelers. **Amenities:** food and drink; lifeguards; showers; toilets. **Best for:** solitude; swimming; walking. ⊠ *1800 Gulf Dr. S, Anna Maria Island.*

Cortez Beach. Towering Australian pines greet you at the entrance of this popular beach park, a favorite among locals and visitors alike. **Amenities:** lifeguards; showers; toilets. **Best for:** solitude; swimming; walking. ⊠ *Gulf Blvd. between 5th and 13th aves., Bradenton Beach.*

Greer Island Beach. Just across the inlet on the northern tip of Longboat Key, Greer Island Beach is accessible by boat or by car via North Shore Boulevard. You'll also hear this place referred to as Beer Can Island. The secluded peninsula has a wide beach and excellent shelling, but no facilities. **Amenities:** none. **Best for:** solitude; walking. ⊠ *7500 Gulf of Mexico Dr., Longboat Key.*

Manatee Beach Park. In the middle of Anna Maria Island, Manatee County Beach is popular with beachgoers of all ages. Paid parking is in the gravel lot next to the beach. **Amenities:** food and drink; parking

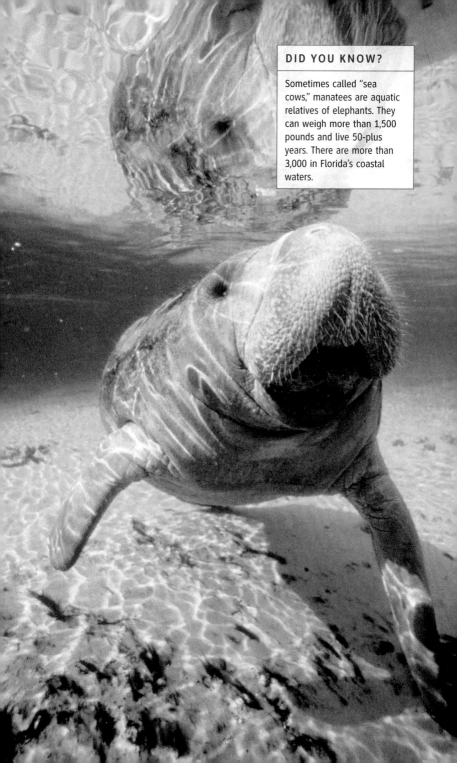

(fee); showers; toilets. **Best for:** solitude; swimming; walking. ⊠ *4000 S.R. 64, at Gulf Dr., Holmes Beach.*

WHERE TO EAT

$$$$ ✕**Euphemia Haye.** A lush tropical setting on the barrier island of Long-
STEAKHOUSE boat Key, this is one of the most romantic restaurants around. The
Fodor's Choice staff is friendly and gracious, the food delightful, and the atmosphere
★ contagious. Its popular dessert display is a sweet ending to the pricey
menu items that feature signature dishes such as crisp roast duckling
with bread stuffing, and flambéed prime peppered steak. The upstairs
Haye Loft, once the home of the original owner's grandson, has been
converted into a more casual bistro and lounge. ⑤ *Average main: $40*
⊠ *5540 Gulf of Mexico Dr., Longboat Key* ☎ *941/383–3633* ⊕ *www.
euphemiahaye.com* ⌂ *Reservations essential* ⊘ *No lunch.*

$ ✕**Gulf Drive Café & Tiki.** Especially popular for breakfast (served all
AMERICAN day), this unassuming landmark squats on the beach and serves cheap
sit-down eats: mostly sandwiches, but also a sampling of entrées after
4 pm. ⑤ *Average main: $14* ⊠ *900 N. Gulf Dr. N, Bradenton Beach*
☎ *941/778–1919.*

$$$ ✕**Sandbar Seafood & Spirits.** If the grouper is not fresh, it is not on the
AMERICAN menu at this beachfront restaurant. Ordered blackened, it can hold its
own against the Island Salad made with mangoes, Gorgonzola, pas-
sion fruit, and pralines. The popular fish also goes over well here in
taco form. Other fresh seafood options include a spicy Szechuan tilapia
sandwich, and crab cakes and crab-crusted sea scallops, a blend of the
Chesapeake and the Gulf. The outside deck sits on the beach—the view
is spectacular and a great place to watch the sunset. ⑤ *Average main:*
$22 ⊠ *100 Spring Ave., Anna Maria Island* ☎ *941/778–0444* ⊕ *www.
groupersandwich.com.*

WHERE TO STAY

$$ 🏨**BridgeWalk.** This circa-1947 Caribbean colonial-style property is
RENTAL across from the beach and a community within itself. **Pros:** great
location; variety of lodging and dining experiences. **Cons:** can be
pricey. ⑤ *Rooms from: $210* ⊠ *100 Bridge St., Bradenton Beach*
☎ *941/779–2545, 866/779–2545* ⊕ *www.silverresorts.com* ⊃ *28
apartments* ⦿ *No meals.*

$$$ 🏨**Longboat Key Club & Resort.** This spectacularly landscaped property
RESORT is one of the best places to play golf in the state, and among the top
tennis resorts in the country. **Pros:** upscale vibe; lovely grounds; most
rooms have private balconies. **Cons:** service can feel snooty. ⑤ *Rooms*
from: $379 ⊠ *220 Sands Point Rd., Longboat Key* ☎ *941/383–8821,*
888/237–5545 ⊕ *www.longboatkeyclub.com* ⊃ *218 rooms and suites*
⦿ *No meals.*

$ 🏨**Silver Surf Gulf Beach Resort.** A sister to BridgeWalk, the Silver Surf
RESORT has the air of a well-maintained 1960s motel with a modern twist,
thanks to recent renovations to all of the studios and full apartments.
Pros: location; freshly renovated rooms and exterior; good value. **Cons:**
while nice, the rooms are still pretty basic (this is not luxury). ⑤ *Rooms*
from: $160 ⊠ *1301 Gulf Dr. N, Anna Maria Island* ☎ *941/778–6626,*
800/441–7873 ⊕ *www.silverresorts.com* ⊃ *50 rooms* ⦿ *No meals.*

Ringling Mansion Sarasota

SARASOTA

30 miles south of Tampa and St. Petersburg.

Sarasota is a year-round destination and home to some of Florida's most affluent residents. Circus magnate John Ringling and his wife, Mable, started the city on the road to becoming one of the state's hotbeds for the arts. Today sporting and cultural events can be enjoyed anytime of the year, and there's a higher concentration of upscale shops, restaurants, and hotels here than in other parts of the Tampa Bay area. Across the water from Sarasota lie the barrier islands of Siesta Key and Lido Key, with myriad beaches, shops, hotels, condominiums, and houses.

GETTING HERE AND AROUND

Sarasota is accessible from Interstate 75, Interstate 275, and U.S. 41. The town's public transit company is Sarasota County Area Transit (SCAT). Fares for local bus service range from $0.75 to $3 (for an all-day pass); exact change is required. A $60 monthly "R-Card" is available for unlimited rides on all SCAT and Manatee County Area Transit (MCAT) routes. If you want to make it to the farther reaches of the area, though, renting a car is probably your best bet.

Contacts Sarasota County Area Transit (SCAT) ☎ *941/861–1234* ⊕ *www.scgov.net/scat.*

VISITOR INFORMATION

Contacts Sarasota Convention and Visitors Bureau. This organization has the skinny on South Tampa Bay. ✉ *701 N. Tamiami Trail* ☎ *941/957–1877* ⊕ *www.sarasotafl.org.*

EXPLORING
TOP ATTRACTIONS

FAMILY **John and Mable Ringling Museum of Art.** Administered by Florida State
Fodor'sChoice University, the museum encompasses the entire Ringling estate, far more
★ than just the art museum; there's also the Tibbals Learning Center and
Circus Museums as well as Ca' d'Zan Mansion, the original Ringling home, and its expansive gardens. The entire compound covers 20
waterfront acres and also has the Historic Asolo Theater, restaurants,
and a research library.

The **Art Museum** was a dream long in the making for John Ringling (of
Ringling Brothers fame). Finally finished in 1931 after setbacks including a land bust and the death of his wife Mable, this enormous museum
was originally built to house Ringling's mindblowingly expansive art
collection. You'll find works ranging from Indian doorways elaborately
carved with Jain deities to opalescent baroque paintings from the likes
of Rubens. There seems to be an endless number of rooms, themselves
decorated in an appropriately gorgeous manner, housing these masterpieces. A wing that features traveling exhibits serves as a temporary home to many thought-provoking pieces throughout the year. The
museum's exit opens out into an enormous courtyard, over which a
towering statue of David replica presides, flanked by royal palms.

Circus magnate John Ringling's grand home, **Ca' d'Zan,** which was
built along Sarasota Bay, was patterned after the Doge's Palace in Venice. This exquisite mansion of 32 rooms, 15 bathrooms, and a 61-foot
Belvedere Tower was completed in 1925, and today is the crowning
jewel at the site of the Ringling Estate. Its 8,000-square-foot terrace
overlooks the dock where Ringling's wife, Mable, moored her gondola.
Mansion tours occur on the hour, and last half an hour. If you don't
want a guided tour, show up on the half-hour for a self-guided your.

Allot some extra time to wander around in the Mable Ringling's **Rose
Garden,** a lush labyrinth surrounded by towering banyans and full of
rare roses and haunting statues.

Don't let the name **Tibbals Learning Center** fool you. This Ringling
estate attraction offers a colorful glimpse into a most wondrous element of of a bygone era: the traveling circus. The center focuses on the
history of the American circus and the collection of Howard Tibbals,
master model builder, who spent 40 years building the world's largest
miniature circus. Perhaps the center's main attraction, this impressive
to-scale replica of the circa 1920s and '30s Ringling Bros. and Barnum & Bailey Circus is an astonishingly accurate portrayal of a circus
coming through town—the number of pancakes the circus cooks are
flipping, the exact likenesses and costumes of the performers, the cor-
rect names of the animals marked on the miniature mess buckets—you
name it. Tibbals's passion to re-create every exact detail continues in
his on-site workshop, where kids can ask him questions and watch him
carving animals and intricate wagons.

If you're looking for clown noses, ringmaster hats, and circus-themed
T-shirts, don't leave before checking out the **Ringling Museum of Art
Store.**

Sarasota County

Anna Maria
1 ANNA MARIA ISLAND

LITTLE BIRD KEY

Memphis

2

Palmetto

4

Ellenton

75

Holmes Beach

PERICO ISLAND

Manatee River

64   Manatee Ave

Bradenton

3

5

Anna Marie Island

Tamiami Rd.

Samoset

Bradenton Beach   Cortez

684   Cortez Rd.

Oneco Rd.

Oneco

70

Longboat Key

789

41

Sarasota-Bradenton Airport

Tallevast

Manatee County
Sarasota County

University Rd.

6   DeSoto   Rd.

Lockwood Ridge Rd.

LONGBOAT KEY

N Tamiami Trail

7

Gulf of Mexico Drive

Sarasota Bay

Gulf

of

Mexico

8   Fruitville Rd.

9   Sarasota

BIRD KEY

Tuttle Rd.

Bee Ridge

LIDO KEY

S. Tamiami Trail

Bee Ridge   Rd.

South Lido Park

Proctor Rd.

PALM ISLAND
Siesta Beach

Beneva Rd.

Clark   Rd.

0   3 mi
0   3 km

SIESTA KEY
TO TURTLE BEACH

De Soto National
Memorial **2**

Gamble Plantation
Historic State Park **4**

John and Mabel Ringling
Museum of Art **6**

Marie Selby
Botanical Gardens **8**

Mote Aquarium **9**

Pine Avenue **1**

Sarasota Jungle
Gardens **7**

Solomon's Castle **5**

South Florida Museum
& Parker Manatee
Aquarium **3**

The **Historic Asolo Theater** is also on the estate grounds and is home to the Asolo Repertory Company. ⊠ *5401 Bay Shore Rd., ½ mile west of Sarasota-Bradenton Airport* ☎ *941/359–5700* ⊕ *www.ringling.org* ▨ *$25 (art museum free Mon.)* ☉ *Grounds daily 9:30–6; museums and mansion daily 10–5 (until 8 Thurs.).*

Marie Selby Botanical Gardens. Orchids make up nearly a third of the 20,000 species of flowers and plants here. You can stroll through the Tropical Display House, home of orchids and colorful bromeliads gathered from rain forests, and wander the garden pathway past plantings of bamboo, ancient banyans, and mangrove forests along Little Sarasota Bay. Although spring sees the best blooms, the greenhouses make this an attraction for all seasons. The added bonus is a spectacular view of downtown. There are rotating exhibits of botanical art and photography in a 1934 restored Southern Colonial mansion. Enjoy lunch at the Local Coffee + Tea, a café in the historic Selby House. ⊠ *811 S. Palm Ave.* ☎ *941/366–5731* ⊕ *www.selby.org* ▨ *$19* ☉ *Daily 10–5.*

WORTH NOTING

FAMILY **Mote Aquarium.** A renowned research facility, the Mote is also a popular tourist attraction that draws families and others interested in its international array of ocean creatures. A 135,000-gallon shark tank lets you view various types of sharks from above and below the surface. Other tanks show off eels, rays, and other marine creatures native to the area. There's also a touch tank where you can get friendly with horseshoe crabs, conchs, and other creatures. Fossil Creek offers aspiring marine paleontologists a chance to sift through a bucket of sand for ancient shark teeth and fossilized stingray tails. The expanded Seahorse Conservation Lab offers a glimpse into the unusual creatures' lives and how the aquarium is working to help them survive and thrive. Hugh and Buffett are the resident manatees and, though not as venerable as Snooty at the Parker Manatee Aquarium, they have lived here since 1996 as part of a research program. There's also a permanent sea-turtle exhibit. For an extra fee, Sarasota Bay Explorers *(⇨ see the separate listing under Boat Tours in Sports and the Outdoors)* offers boat tours from the museum's dock (reservations required), guided kayak tours through the mangroves, private tours and a "Nature Safari." ⊠ *1600 Ken Thompson Pkwy., City Island* ☎ *941/388–4441* ⊕ *www.mote.org* ▨ *Aquarium $19.75* ☉ *Aquarium daily 10–5, boat tours daily at varying times.*

FAMILY **Sarasota Jungle Gardens.** One of Old Florida's charming, family-owned and -operated attractions, Sarasota Jungle Gardens fills 10 acres with native and exotic animals as well as tropical plants. The lush gardens date to 1939, and still have the small-world feel of yesterday's Florida. You'll find red-tailed hawks and great horned owls in the birds of prey show, American alligators and a variety of snakes in the reptile encounter, and bugs of many varieties in a show called Critters and Things. You can talk to trainers and get to know such plants as the rare Australian nut tree and the Peruvian apple cactus in the gardens. Also on site are flocks of flamingos that guests can hand-feed, plus reptiles and a butterfly garden. ⊠ *3701 Bay Shore Rd.* ☎ *941/355–5305* ⊕ *www. sarasotajunglegardens.com* ▨ *$15* ☉ *Daily 10–5.*

BEACHES

FodorśChoice **Siesta Beach.** With 40 acres of nature trails, this park is popular; you'll
★ find tons of amenities. This beach has fine, powdery quartz sand that
squeaks under your feet, very much like the sand along the state's northwestern coast. Don't forget to bring a volleyball—or a tennis racket.
Amenities: food and drink; lifeguards; toilets. **Best for:** partiers; sunset;
swimming; walking. ⊠ *948 Beach Rd., Siesta Key.*

South Lido Park. At the southern tip of the island, South Lido Park has
one of the best beaches in the region, but there are no lifeguards. The
100-acre park interacts with four significant bodies of water: the Gulf
of Mexico, Big Pass, Sarasota Bay, and Brushy Bayou. The sugar-sand
beach has plenty of early morning sand dollars and is a popular place to
fish. Picnic as the sun sets through the Australian pines into the water.
Facilities include nature trails, canoe and kayak trails, restrooms, and
picnic grounds. This park was purchased by John Ringling in 1920
as part of his ambitious plan to develop island properties. His plan
collapsed with the great Florida Land bust of 1926. Because of swift
rip currents, swimming here is not recommended. **Amenities:** showers;
toilets. **Best for:** solitude; walking. ⊠ *2201 Ben Franklin Dr., Lido Key.*

Turtle Beach. A 14-acre beach-park that's popular with families, Turtle
has 2,600 linear feet of beach frontage and is more secluded than most
gulf beaches. Though narrower than most of the region's beaches, it's
also much less crowded, so it doesn't feel so narrow. It's known for
abundant sea turtles. It has covered picnic shelters, grills, and a volleyball court. Locals like the 40-site campground that is also open to
visitors with advance reservations. Fittingly enough, this beach is near
the übermellow Turtle Beach Resort. **Amenities:** toilets. **Best for:** solitude; sunset; swimming; walking. ⊠ *8918 Midnight Pass Rd., Siesta
Key* ☎ *941/349–3839.*

WHERE TO EAT

$$$ ✕ **Bijou Café.** Once a 50-seat 1920 gas-station-turned-restaurant, the
CAFÉ Bijou is now a 140-seat restaurant with the type of enchanting décor
FodorśChoice you might expect in a quaint, modern European café—think French
★ windows and doors, sparkling glassware, bouquets of freshly picked
flowers, and the soft glow of candlelight. Lunches begin with an inspired
soup, salads, or sandwiches such as the pesto chicken-salad croissant.
Dinners emphasize fresh local produce and sustainable seafood. Opera
season—typically February and March—is the only time Sunday din-
ner is served. ⑤ *Average main: $30* ⊠ *1287 1st St.* ☎ *941/366–8111*
⊕ *www.bijoucafe.net* ☉ *Closed Sun. Apr.–Jan. No lunch weekends.*

$$ ✕ **Café Baci.** Specializing in Tuscan and Roman cuisine, Café Baci appeals
ITALIAN to loyal locals and savvy travelers alike. Its menu highlights original
family recipes; specialties range from fresh, succulent seafood dishes and
homemade pastas to traditional veal recipes such as *piccata de vitella*
simmered with white wine, lemon, and capers or grilled salmon served
on spinach pesto risotto. From the moment you walk through the door,
you'll enjoy the peaceful, elegant, Italian-inspired atmosphere. ⑤ *Average main: $20* ⊠ *4001 S. Tamiami Trail* ☎ *941/921–4848* ⊕ *www.
cafebacisarasota.com* ☉ *No lunch weekends*

$$$$ ✕ **Café L'Europe.** Located in St. Armand's Circle, this sidewalk and
CAFÉ   indoor café has a spectacular menu featuring tableside specialties such
as chateaubriand for two. Other popular entrées range from potato-
crusted grouper and brandied duckling to rack of lamb. There's also
a nice choice of wines by the glass. Veranda tables are a great place to
watch shoppers and strollers. ⑤ *Average main: $33* ⊠ *431 St. Armand's
Circle, Lido Key* ☎ *941/388–4415* ⊕ *www.cafeleurope.net.*

$$$ ✕ **Michael's on East.** Not only do the lounge and piano bar, with their
AMERICAN   extensive wine list and vintage cocktails, lure the after-theater set, but
inspired cuisine and superior service also entice. Inside its Midtown
Plaza shopping center location, you'll find décor similar to that of New
York's better bistros of the 1930s and '40s, but there is plenty of veranda
seating for enjoying Sarasota's balmy weather. The fare ranges from
bow-tie pasta with grilled chicken and sun-dried tomatoes to porcini-
rubbed rack of lamb to roasted swordfish with red potatoes. The pecan-
graham-crusted key lime tart served under a cloud of baked meringue
is only one of the creative combinations for concluding your cuisine
adventure. ⑤ *Average main: $26* ⊠ *1212 East Ave. S* ☎ *941/366–0007*
⊕ *www.michaelsoneast.com* ♥ *Closed Sun. No lunch Sat.*

$ ✕ **The Old Salty Dog.** A menu of steamer and raw-bar options has been
AMERICAN   added to the much-enjoyed old favorites, including quarter-pound
hot dogs, fish-and-chips, wings, and burgers. With views of New Pass
between Longboat and Lido Keys, this is a popular stop for locals and
visitors en route from Mote Aquarium and the adjoining bayfront park.
Open-air dining area is comfortable even in summer, thanks to a pleas-
ant breeze. Its bar is shaped from the hull of an old boat. There's another
branch on Siesta Key (⊠ *5023 Ocean Blvd.* ☎ *941/349–0158*). ⑤ *Aver-
age main: $15* ⊠ *1601 Ken Thompson Pkwy., City Island* ☎ *941/388–
4311* ⊕ *www.theoldsaltydog.com* ⚘ *Reservations not accepted.*

$$$$ ✕ **Ophelia's on the Bay.** Florida the way it should be: you can watch as
AMERICAN   dolphins swim past while blue herons lounge on the dock. Enjoy the
flowering gardens while dining alfresco on the outdoor patio on its dock
at Market #48 or in one of two casually elegant dining rooms. An ever-
evolving menu highlights the Florida surroundings with selections such
as Gulf of Mexico hog snapper with cracked pepper and orange honey,
and Chilean salmon with blueberry lavender sauce. The tuna (bigeye,
yellowfin, and more) is flown in from Hawaii thanks to owner Jane
Ferro, who is also the grandniece of the restaurant's namesake. ⑤ *Aver-
age main: $32* ⊠ *9105 Midnight Pass Rd., Siesta Key* ☎ *941/349–2212*
⊕ *www.opheliasonthebay.net* ♥ *No lunch.*

$$ ✕ **Owen's Fish Camp.** Nestled in a banyan-shaded corner of the hip Burns
SOUTHERN   Court district of downtown Sarasota, this spot dishes out quintessen-
tially Southern fare (though the menu is not geographically limited) that
is particularly heavy on the seafood options—everything from an oyster
po' boy with bacon to grilled giant prawns with chili, a popular appetizer. The restaurant is a converted cottage built in 1923, and the setting
gives an additional layer of charm to a casual eatery that's already won
the hearts of tourists and locals alike. Takeaway "jars" offered include
shrimp and avocado cocktail, fried pickles, and boiled peanuts. Note:
There can often be a wait, so get here early because you can't reserve a

table. $ *Average main: $16 ⊠ 526 Burns Ct. ☎ 941/951–6936 ⊕ www. owensfishcamp.com ⌂ Reservations not accepted ⊘ No lunch.*

$ ✕ **Yoder's.** Lines for meals stretch well beyond the hostess's podium here.
AMERICAN Pie—key lime, egg custard, banana cream, peanut butter, strawberry rhubarb, and others—is the main event at this family restaurant in the heart of Sarasota's Amish community. Daily specials typically include zesty goulash, chicken and dumplings, and pulled smoked pork. For breakfast, choose from French toast stuffed with cream cheese or perhaps a hearty stack of pancakes. Sandwiches include Manhattans (roast beef, turkey, or meat loaf on homemade bread with mashed potatoes and gravy). The entire village is always crowded, but there's plenty of waitstaff who keep tables clean and cleared, so the flow is steady. The décor retains its Old Florida efficiency appearance. $ *Average main: $10 ⊠ 3434 Bahia Vista ☎ 941/955–7771 ⊕ www.yodersrestaurant. com ⌂ Reservations not accepted ⊘ Closed Sun.*

WHERE TO STAY

$$ ⊞ **The Cypress, a Bed & Breakfast Inn.** The only bed-and-breakfast in
B&B/INN downtown Sarasota, the inn has a delightful assortment of themed rooms. **Pros:** friendly staff; convenient to downtown; a five-minute drive (or a pleasant walk) from the beaches at Lido Key. **Cons:** no in-room phones. $ *Rooms from: $279 ⊠ 621 Gulfstream Ave. S ☎ 941/955–4683 ⊕ www.cypressbb.com ↘ 2 rooms, 3 suites ⦿ Multiple meal plans.*

$ ⊞ **Gulf Beach Resort.** Lido Key's first motel, this beachfront condo com-
RENTAL plex has been designated a historic property. **Pros:** near shopping; well maintained; lots of beach; free Wi-Fi. **Cons:** basic rooms; motel feel. $ *Rooms from: $140 ⊠ 930 Ben Franklin Dr., Lido Key ☎ 941/388–2127, 800/232–2489 ⊕ www.gulfbeachsarasota.com ↘ 8 rooms, 41 suites ⦿ No meals.*

$$ ⊞ **Hyatt Regency Sarasota.** Popular among business travelers, the Hyatt
HOTEL Regency is contemporary in design and sits in the heart of the city across from the Van Wezel Performing Arts Hall. **Pros:** great location; stellar views. **Cons:** chain-hotel feel. $ *Rooms from: $250 ⊠ 1000 Blvd. of the Arts ☎ 941/953–1234, 800/233–1234 ⊕ www.sarasota.hyatt.com ↘ 294 rooms, 12 suites ⦿ Multiple meal plans.*

$$ ⊞ **Lido Beach Resort.** Superb gulf views can be found at this stylish beach-
RENTAL front resort. **Pros:** beachfront location; many rooms have kitchens. **Cons:** bland, somewhat dated furnishings. $ *Rooms from: $210 ⊠ 700 Ben Franklin Dr., Lido Key ☎ 941/388–2161, 800/441–2113 ⊕ www. lidobeachresort.com ↘ 158 rooms, 64 suites ⦿ No meals.*

$$$$ ⊞ **Ritz-Carlton, Sarasota.** With a style that developers like to say is cir-
HOTEL cus magnate John Ringling's realized dream, The Ritz is appointed with fine artwork and fresh-cut flowers. **Pros:** Ritz-style glitz; lots of amenities; attentive staff. **Cons:** long distance to golf course; not on the beach. $ *Rooms from: $450 ⊠ 1111 Ritz-Carlton Dr. ☎ 941/309–2000, 800/241–3333 ⊕ www.ritzcarlton.com/sarasota ↘ 266 rooms, 30 suites ⦿ No meals.*

7

$$
HOTEL
Fodor's Choice
★

Ⓩ **Turtle Beach Resort.** Reminiscent of a quieter time, many of the cottages at this friendly, affordable, family- and pet-friendly resort date to the 1940s, a romantic plus for yesteryear lovers. **Pros:** nice location; romantic setting; self-serve laundry and Wi-Fi included. **Cons:** far from the area's cultural attractions. ⑤ *Rooms from: $299* ⊠ *9049 Midnight Pass Rd., Siesta Key* ☎ *941/349–4554* ⊕ *www.turtlebeachresort.com* ↻ *7 rooms, 3 suites, 10 cottages* ⑩ *No meals.*

NIGHTLIFE AND PERFORMING ARTS

NIGHTLIFE

Blase Cafe and Lounge. Siesta Key Village doesn't shut down after the dinner crowd vacates its eateries. To the contrary, there are quite a few places to grab a beverage or two. Blase is a good pick if you're in a martini mood. While the cafe has some pretty sophisticated fare, you can be dressed casual if you want to belly up to the circular bar. ⊠ *5263 Ocean Blvd., Siesta Key* ☎ *941/349–9822* ⊕ *www.theblasecafe.com.*

Burns Court Cinemas. There aren't many places in the Tampa Bay area where you can catch indie and foreign films. Since it first opened on the edge of downtown Sarasota in 1993, this has been one of the few. It's less than a block from Burns Square's many stylish yet low-key dining offerings, and, unlike your average corporate movie theater, admission doesn't cost an arm and a leg. ⊠ *506 Burns Ct.* ☎ *941/955–3456* ⊕ *www.filmsociety.org.*

5 O'clock Club. If you find yourself in Southside Village after dinner and are looking for a watering hole that offers live music, look no further. This spot has been one of Sarasota's key music venues for years. Musical offerings differ by night, but you can expect to hear blues, jazz, or rock covers on a given night. If you're looking for a more upscale club, look elsewhere; this is a no-frills kind of place. ⊠ *1930 Hillview St.* ☎ *941/366–5555* ⊕ *www.5oclockclub.net.*

Gator Club. A famous nightclub located in a beautifully restored, brick historic cornerstone building downtown, the Gator Club has live music and dancing 365 days a year. ⊠ *1490 Main St.* ☎ *941/366–5969* ⊕ *www.thegatorclub.com.*

Straight Up Night Club @ 15 South. St. Armand's Circle is a pretty bustling place in the daytime, but the action continues into the wee hours—if you know where to find it. This bar, which is upstairs from an upscale restaurant of the same name, has an excellent martini list and plenty of live music, especially salsa. ⊠ *15 S. Blvd. of the Presidents, Lido Key* ☎ *941/388–1555* ⊕ *www.15southristorante.com.*

PERFORMING ARTS

Asolo Repertory Theatre. One of the best theaters in Sarasota stages productions from November to June in varying venues, which include the Historic Asolo Theater in the Ringling Estate. ⊠ *5555 Tamiami Trail* ☎ *941/351–8000* ⊕ *www.asolorep.org.*

The Players Theatre. A long-established community theater, having launched such actors as Montgomery Clift and Paul Reubens, this troupe performs comedies, special events, live concerts, and musicals.

✉ *838 N. Tamiami Trail, U.S. 41 and 9th St.* ☎ *941/365–2494* ⊕ *www. theplayers.org.*

Sarasota Opera. Performing in a historic 1,122-seat downtown theatre, the Sarasota Opera features internationally known artists singing the principal roles, supported by a professional chorus of young apprentices. ✉ *The Edwards Theater, 61 N. Pineapple Ave.* ☎ *941/328–1300* ⊕ *www.sarasotaopera.org.*

SHOPPING

St. Armand's Circle has a cluster of oh-so-exclusive shops and laid-back restaurants. It's just east of Lido Beach.

SHOPPING AREAS

Siesta Key Village. Not too far from Siesta Key's wildly popular beaches is a cluster of shops, restaurants, and watering holes you won't want to miss. This is a great place to shop and grab a bite after the beach—or earlier if it's not a beach day. Park in the municipal lot at the end of Avenida Madera, then stroll down Ocean Boulevard, where you'll find clusters of upscale shops and a range of restaurants and bars. ✉ *Ocean Blvd. between Beach Rd. and Av. Madera, Siesta Key* ⊕ *www. siestakeyvillage.org.*

Southside Village. This is one of Sarasota's newer spots, with tons of sidewalk cafés, hip boutiques, jewelry stores, and an excellent gourmet market. This place hasn't gotten as much attention as St. Armand's Circle, but it's also got a much shorter history. It's popular among locals and is now starting to get on the radar for visitors. ✉ *Osprey Ave. at Hillview St.* ☎ *941/366–0771.*

St. Armand's Circle. No visit to Sarasota is complete without a visit to this busy yet laid-back shopping and dining hub. One can literally refer to it as a hub because it's arranged around a large traffic circle in the middle of Lido Key. You'll find a sprinkling of upscale retail chains, including White House Black Market, but the area's small, imaginative boutiques are the real draw. Among them is Foxy Lady, which sells trendy women's clothing. The Met is also a good option for women's fashion. St. Armand's Circle also offers plenty of dining/dessert (especially ice cream) options, nightlife, and just plain people-watching. Some days you can even spot a busker or two performing on one of the area's many street corners. ✉ *300 Madison Dr.* ☎ *941/388–1554* ⊕ *www. starmandscircleassoc.com.*

SPORTS AND THE OUTDOORS

BOAT TOURS

Sarasota Bay Explorers. Many visitors to the Mote Aquarium take the 105-minute boat trip onto Sarasota Bay. Conducted by Sarasota Bay Explorers, all boat trips are done in conjunction with the aquarium and leave from the aquarium's dock. The crew brings marine life on board, explains what it is, and throws it back to swim away. You are almost guaranteed to see bottlenose dolphins. Reservations are recommended. You can also charter the *Miss Explorer*, a 24-foot Sea Ray Sundeck, or take a guided kayak or nature tour. ✉ *Mote Aquarium, 1600 Ken Thompson Pkwy.* ☎ *941/388–4200* ⊕ *www.sarasotabayexplorers.com*

7

🚤 *Boat tour $27, kayak tour $55, nature tour $45, charters $295–$445* ☉ *Tours daily at 11, 1:30, and 4 (reservations required).*

FISHING

Flying Fish Fleet. Several boats can be chartered for deep-sea fishing, and there are daily group trips on a "party" fishing boat. ✉ *2 Marina Plaza, off U.S. 41, on the bay front at Marina Jack* ☎ *941/366–3373* ⊕ *www.flyingfishfleet.com.*

GOLF

Bobby Jones Golf Course. This public 45-hole course is over a century old and caters to a range of golfers. The setting is lush and green, with plenty of live oak trees and water. The grounds here are so pleasant that many choose to walk their chosen course, of which there are three. The American Course is best for less experienced golfers or those who want to practice their short shot, and features a range of lakes and varied terrain. The British Course is slightly more challenging, offering longer fairways dotted with water hazards and sand bunkers. The Gillespie Executive Course is recommended for beginners or those lacking the time needed for a full 18 holes. A large ravine divides much of the course from several of its greens approaches. ✉ *1000 Circus Blvd.* ☎ *941/365–2200* ⊕ *www.bobbyjonesgolfclub.com* 💲 *$25 for 9 holes, $35 for 18 holes* 🏌 *American Course: 18 holes. 6031 yards. par 71. British Course: 18 holes. 6710 yards. par 72. Gillespie Executive Course: 9 holes. 1716 yards. par 30.*

KAYAKING

Sarasota Bay Explorers, which operates from the Mote Aquarium, also offers guided kayaking trips *(see ⇨ Boat Tours).*

Siesta Sports Rentals. Up for rent here are kayaks, bikes, beach chairs, scooters, and beach wheelchairs and strollers. Guided kayaking trips are also available. ✉ *6551 Midnight Pass Rd., Siesta Key* ☎ *941/346–1797* ⊕ *www.siestasportsrentals.com.*

THE LOWER GULF COAST

With Fort Myers, Naples, and
the Coastal Islands

WELCOME TO
THE LOWER GULF COAST

TOP REASONS
TO GO

★ **Heavenly beaches:**
Whether you go to the
beach to sun, swim,
gather shells, or watch
the sunset, the region's
Gulf of Mexico beaches
rank among the best.

★ **Edison & Ford Winter
Estates:** A rare complex
of two famous inventors'
winter homes comes
complete with botanical-
research gardens, Edison's
lab, and a museum.

★ **Island hopping:** Rent
a boat or jump aboard a
charter for lunch, picnicking, beaching, or shelling
on a subtropical island
adrift from the mainland.

★ **Naples shopping:**
Flex your buying power
in downtown Naples's
charming shopping dis-
tricts or in lush outdoor
centers around town.

★ **Watch for wildlife:** On
the edge of Everglades
National Park, the region
protects vast tracts of
fragile land and water
where you can see alliga-
tors, manatees, dolphins,
roseate spoonbills, and
hundreds of other birds.

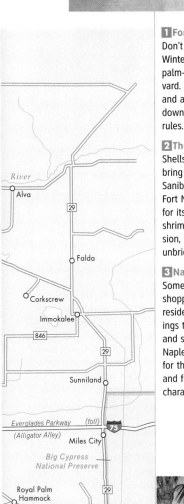

1 **Fort Myers and Vicinity.**
Don't miss the Edison & Ford
Winter Estates along royal
palm–lined McGregor Boulevard. For museums, theater,
and art, the up-and-coming
downtown River District
rules.

2 **The Coastal Islands.**
Shells and wildlife refuges
bring nature lovers to
Sanibel and Captiva islands.
Fort Myers Beach is known
for its lively clubs and
shrimp fleet. For true seclusion, head to the area's
unbridged island beaches.

3 **Naples and Vicinity.**
Some of the region's best
shopping and dining take up
residence in historic buildings trimmed with blossoms
and street sculptures in Old
Naples. Hit Marco Island
for the boating lifestyle
and funky fishing-village
character.

GETTING ORIENTED

The Lower Gulf Coast of
Florida, as its name sug-
gests, occupies a stretch of
coastline along southernmost
west Florida, bordered
by the Gulf of Mexico. It
lies south of Tampa and
Sarasota, directly on the
other side of the state from
West Palm Beach and Fort
Lauderdale. In between the
two coasts stretch heart-
land agricultural areas and
Everglades wilderness. The
region encompasses the
major resort towns of Fort
Myers, Fort Myers Beach,
Sanibel Island, Naples, and
Marco Island, along with a
medley of suburban com-
munities and smaller islands.

8

Updated by
Jill Martin and
Avery Sumner

With its subtropical climate and beckoning family-friendly beaches known for their powdery sand, calm surf, and nary a freighter in sight, the Lower Gulf Coast, also referred to as the state's southwestern region, is a favorite vacation spot of Florida residents as well as visitors. Vacationers tend to spend most of their time outdoors—swimming, sunning, shelling, fishing, boating, and playing tennis or golf.

The region has several distinct travel destinations. Small and historic downtown Fort Myers rises inland along the Caloosahatchee River, and the rest of the town sprawls in all directions. It got its nickname, the City of Palms, from the hundreds of towering royal palms that inventor Thomas Edison planted between 1900 and 1917 along McGregor Boulevard, a historic residential street and site of his winter estate. Edison's idea caught on, and more than 2,000 royal palms now line 14-mile-long McGregor Boulevard. Museums and educational attractions are the draw here. Across the river, Cape Coral has evolved from a mostly residential community to a resort destination for water sports enthusiasts.

Off the coast west of Fort Myers are more than 100 coastal islands in all shapes and sizes. Connected to the mainland by a 3-mile causeway, Sanibel is known for its superb shelling, fine fishing, beachfront resorts, and wildlife refuge. Here and on Captiva, to which it is connected by a short bridge, multimillion-dollar homes line both waterfronts. Just southwest of Fort Myers is Estero Island, home of busy Fort Myers Beach, and farther south, Lovers Key State Park and Bonita Beach.

Farther down the coast lies Naples, once a small fishing village and now a thriving and sophisticated enclave. It's like a smaller, more understated version of Palm Beach, with fine restaurants, chichi shopping areas, luxury resorts, and—locals will tell you—more golf holes per capita than anywhere else in the world. A half hour south basks Marco Island, best known for its beaches and fishing. See a maze of pristine miniature mangrove islands when you take a boat tour from the island's marinas into Ten Thousand Islands National Wildlife Refuge. Although high-rises line much of Marco's waterfront, the tiny fishing village of Goodland, an outpost of Old Florida, tries valiantly to stave off new development.

PLANNING

WHEN TO GO

In winter this is one of the warmest areas of the United States. Occasionally temperatures drop in December or January, but rarely below freezing. From February through April you may find it next to impossible to find a hotel room.

Numbers drop the rest of the year, but visitors within driving range, European tourists, and convention clientele still keep things busy. Temperatures and humidity spike, but discounted room rates make summer attractive. Summer is also rainy season, but most storms occur in the afternoon and last for a flash. Hurricane season runs from June through November.

GETTING HERE AND AROUND

AIR TRAVEL

The area's primary airport is in Fort Myers, where many airlines offer flights; private pilots land at both RSW and Page Field, also in Fort Myers. Gulf Coast Airways to Key West and a couple of private charter services also land at Naples Municipal Airport, and North Captiva Island has a private airstrip.

Contacts Naples Municipal Airport ✉ *160 Aviation Dr. N, Naples* ☎ *239/643–0733* ⊕ *www.flynaples.com.* **Southwest Florida International Airport** (*RSW*). ✉ *11000 Terminal Access Rd., Fort Myers* ☎ *239/590–4800* ⊕ *www.flylcpa.com.*

Airport Transfer Contacts Aaron Airport Transportation ☎ *239/768–1898* ⊕ *www.aarontaxi.com.* **Sanibel Taxi** ☎ *239/472–4160, 888/527–7806* ⊕ *www. sanibeltaxi.com.*

CAR TRAVEL

If you're driving, U.S. 41 (the Tamiami Trail) runs the length of the region. Sanibel Island is accessible from the mainland via the Sanibel Causeway (toll $6 round-trip). Captiva Island lies across a small pass from Sanibel's north end, accessible by bridge.

Be aware that the destination's popularity, especially during winter, means traffic congestion at peak times of day. Avoid driving when the locals are getting to and from work and visitors to and from the beach.

HOTELS

Lodging in Fort Myers, the islands, and Naples can be pricey, but there are affordable options even during the busy winter season. If these destinations are too rich for your pocket, consider visiting in the off-season, when rates drop drastically, or look to Fort Myers Beach and Cape Coral for better rates. Beachfront properties tend to be more expensive; to spend less, look for properties away from the water. In high season—Christmastime and Presidents' Day through Easter—always reserve ahead for the top properties. Fall is the slowest season: rates are low and availability is high, but this is also hurricane season (June–November).

8

Hotel reviews have been shortened. For full information, visit Fodors. com.

RESTAURANTS

In this part of Florida, fresh seafood reigns supreme. Succulent native stone-crab claws, a particularly tasty treat, in season from mid-October through mid-May, are usually served hot with drawn butter or chilled with tangy mustard sauce. Supplies are typically steady, since claws regenerate in time for the next season. Other seafood specialties include fried grouper sandwiches and Sanibel pink shrimp. In Naples's highly hailed restaurants and sidewalk cafés, mingle with locals, winter visitors, and other travelers, and catch up on the latest culinary trends.

WHAT IT COSTS				
	$	$$	$$$	$$$$
Restaurants	under $16	$16–$20	$21–$30	over $30
Hotels	under $201	$201–$300	$301–$400	over $400

Restaurant prices are the average cost of a main course at dinner or, if dinner is not served, at lunch. Hotel prices are the lowest cost of a standard double room in high season.

TOURS

Captiva Cruises. Shelling, dolphin, luncheon, beach, sunset, and history cruises run to and around the out islands of Cabbage Key, Useppa Island, Cayo Costa, and Gasparilla Island. Night sky cruises and excursions also go to the Edison and Ford Winter Estates. Excursions cost $27 to $70 each. ⊠ *McCarthy's Marina, 11401 Andy Rosse La., Captiva* ☎ *239/472–5300* ⊕ *www.captivacruises.com.*

Manatee Sightseeing Adventure. You are guaranteed to see manatees or you don't pay. Tourd depart at Port of the Islands. Discount tickets are available online. ⊠ *525 Newport Dr., Naples* ☎ *239/642–8818* ⊕ *www. see-manatees.com.*

Tarpon Bay Explorers. One of the best ways to see the J. N. "Ding" Darling National Wildlife Refuge is by taking one of these guided or self-guided nature tours. There are many options to choose depending on your activity level and desire—including a sea life cruise, open-air tram tours, and nature cruises, to name a few. Rentals of kayaks, canoes, stand-up paddleboards, bikes, and pontoon boats are right on site. Charter boats are also available. ⊠ *900 Tarpon Bay Rd., Sanibel* ☎ *239/472–8900* ⊕ *www.tarponbayexplorers.com.*

FORT MYERS AND VICINITY

In parts of Fort Myers, old Southern mansions and their modern-day counterparts peek out from behind stately palms and blossomy foliage. Views over the broad Caloosahatchee River, which borders the city's small but businesslike cluster of office buildings downtown, soften the look of the area. These days it's showing the effects of age and urban sprawl, but planners work at reviving what has been termed the River

District at the heart of downtown. North of Fort Myers are small fishing communities and new retirement towns, including Boca Grande on Gasparilla Island; Englewood Beach on Manasota Key; and Port Charlotte, north of the Peace River.

FORT MYERS

80 miles southeast of Sarasota, 125 miles west of Palm Beach.

The city core lies inland along the banks of the Caloosahatchee River, a half hour from the nearest beach. The town is best known as the winter home of inventors Thomas A. Edison and Henry Ford.

GETTING HERE AND AROUND

The closest airport to Fort Myers is Southwest Florida International Airport (RSW), about 15 miles southeast of town. A taxi for up to three passengers costs about $20–$40. Extra people are charged $10 each. LeeTran bus service serves most of the Fort Myers area.

If you're driving here from Florida's East Coast, consider Alligator Alley, a toll section of Interstate 75 that runs from Fort Lauderdale to Naples. I–75 then runs north–south the length of the region. U.S. 41 (the Tamiami Trail, also called South Cleveland Avenue in Fort Myers) runs parallel to the interstate to the west and goes through downtown Naples and Fort Myers. McGregor Boulevard (Route 867) and Summerlin Road (Route 869), Fort Myers's main north–south city streets, head toward Sanibel and Captiva islands. San Carlos Boulevard (Route 865) runs southwest from Summerlin Road to Fort Myers Beach, and Pine Island–Bayshore Road (Route 78) leads from North Fort Myers through northern Cape Coral onto Pine Island.

Key West Express operates a ferry from Fort Myers Beach (year-round) to Key West.

Bus Contacts LeeTran ☎ 239/275–8726, 239/533–8726 ⊕ www.rideleetran. com.

Ferry Contacts Key West Express ⊠ 1200 Main St., Fort Myers Beach ☎ 239/394–9700, 888/539–2628 ⊕ www.keywestexpress.us.

VISITOR INFORMATION

Contacts Lee County Visitor & Convention Bureau ⊠ 2201 2nd St., Ste. 600 ☎ 239/338–3500, 800/237–6444 ⊕ www.fortmyers-sanibel.com.

EXPLORING

TOP ATTRACTIONS

Fodor'sChoice **Edison & Ford Winter Estates.** Fort Myers's premier attraction pays homage
★ to two of America's most ingenious inventors: Thomas A. Edison, who gave the world the stock ticker, the incandescent lamp, and the phonograph, among other inventions; and his friend and neighbor, automaker Henry Ford. Donated to the city by Edison's widow, his once 12-acre estate has been expanded into a remarkable 25 acres, with three homes, two caretaker cottages, a laboratory, botanical gardens, and a museum. The laboratory contains the same gadgets and gizmos as when Edison last stepped foot into it. Visitors can see many of his inventions, along with historic photographs and memorabilia, in the museum. Edison

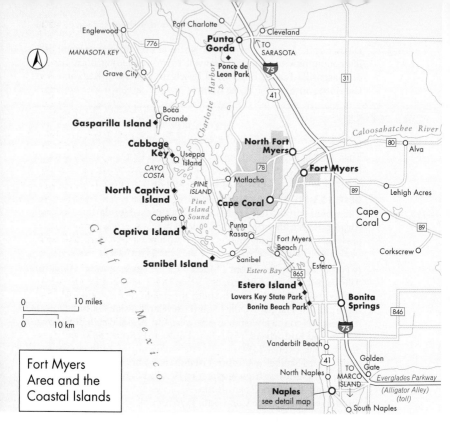

Naples
see detail map

Fort Myers
Area and the
Coastal Islands

traveled south from New Jersey and devoted much of his time here to inventing things (there are 1,093 patents to his name), experimenting with rubber for friend and frequent visitor Harvey Firestone, and planting hundreds of plant species collected around the world. Next door to Edison's two identical homes is Ford's "Mangoes," the more modest seasonal home of Edison's fellow inventor. The property's oldest building, the Edison Caretaker's House, dates to 1860. Tours are guided or audio self-guided. One admission covers homes of both men; museum and laboratory-only tickets and botanical-garden tour tickets are also available. ⊠ *2350 McGregor Blvd.* ☎ *239/334–7419* ⊕ *www. edisonfordwinterestates.org* ✑ *Complete Estate Tour $20 (other tours available)* ☉ *Daily 9–5:30, tours hrly 10–4.*

FAMILY
Fodor's Choice
★

Imaginarium Science Center. Kids can't wait to get their hands on the wonderful interactive exhibits at this lively museum–aquarium combo that explores technology, physics, weather, and other science topics. Check out the stingrays and other marine life in the aquariums, touch tanks, and the living-reef tank; feed the fish, turtles, and swans in the outdoor lagoon; visit a tarantula, python, hissing cockroach, juvenile alligator, and other live critters in the Animal Lab; dig for dinosaur bones; score in the Sporty Science sports simulator; watch a 3-D movie in the theater; take part in a hands-on Animal Encounter demonstration;

and touch a cloud, then prepare to get blown away in the Hurricane Experience. Other highlights include the Tiny Town early childhood area, Backyard Nature, Discovery Lab exploration station, Idea Lab engineering design center, as well as Build-Your-Own-Coaster and Science of Motion. ⊠ *2000 Cranford Ave.* ☎ *239/321–7420* ⊕ *www. imaginariumfortmyers.com* ⌚ *$12* ⊙ *Tues.–Sat. 10–5, Sun. noon–5.*

FAMILY **Manatee Park.** Here you may glimpse Florida's most famous, yet often hard to spot, marine mammal. When gulf waters drop to 68°F or below—usually from November to March—the sea cows congregate in these waters, which are warmed by the outflow of a towering nearby power plant. Pause at any of the three observation decks (the first nearest the outflow and last at the lagoon usually yield the most sightings, as does the Fishing Pier) and watch for bubbles. Hydrophones on the last deck allow you to eavesdrop on their songs. Periodically, one of these gentle giants—mature adults weigh an average of 1000 pounds—will surface. Calusa Blueway Outfitters *(⇨ see Kayaking in Sports and the Outdoors)* run the visitor center/gift shop and offer kayak and canoe rentals, as well as clinics and tours to paddle the canals and get a closer look. ⊠ *10901 Palm Beach Blvd., 1¼ mile east of I–75 Exit 141* ☎ *239/690–5030* ⊕ *www.leeparks.org* ⌚ *Park free. Parking Apr.–Nov., $1 per hr, $5 daily; Dec.–Mar., $2 per hr, $5 daily* ⊙ *Park daily 8–sunset. Visitor center: Nov.–Mar., daily 9–4, Apr.–Oct., weekends 9–1.*

WORTH NOTING

FAMILY **Calusa Nature Center & Planetarium.** Get a look at Florida's native animals and habitats. Boardwalks and trails lead through subtropical wetlands, a birds-of-prey aviary, and a screened-in butterfly house. There are snake, alligator, butterfly, and other live-animal demonstrations several times daily. Museum exhibits include an Exotic Species room and the Insectarium. The domed, state-of-the-art, 90-seat planetarium hosts astronomy shows daily and special laser shows. ⊠ *3450 Ortiz Ave.* ☎ *239/275–3435* ⊕ *www.calusanature.org* ⌚ *$10* ⊙ *Mon.–Sat. 10–5, Sun. 11–5.*

Sidney & Berne Davis Art Center. The River District has become a haven for independent galleries, and in 2003 Florida Arts, Inc., a non-profit organization, stepped in to turn an abandoned post office from 1933 into a space for edgy, up-and-coming visual artists, musical acts, films, and theater. Even if your taste runs more to Broadway and Monet than M-Pact and Marcus Jansen, a visit is worthwhile for the neoclassical revival facade: eight towering coral-rock Ionic columns give way to swaths of intricately detailed window screens. The friendly staff is happy to answer questions about the building's history. Renovations are still in progress with the upper floors slated to open in late 2013. ■ TIP➔ **Plan a trip around the first or third Friday every month for Art Walk or Music Walk; the center stays open late for the throngs of pass-**ersby. ⊠ *2301 1st St.* ☎ *239/333–1933* ⊕ *www.sbdac.com* ⌚ *$5 suggested donation* ⊙ *Weekdays 9–5, performances most weekend nights.*

Southwest Florida Museum of History. A restored railroad depot serves as a showcase for the area's history dating to 800 BC. Displays include prehistoric animals and Calusa artifacts, a reconstructed *chickee* hut,

8

View 200 phonographs, an invention Thomas Edison patented in 1878, at his Fort Myers winter estate.

a dugout canoe, clothing and photos from Seminole settlements, historical vignettes, changing exhibits, and a replicated Florida Cracker house. A favorite attraction is the *Esperanza*, a private, restored 1929 Pullman rail car. ✉ *2031 Jackson St.* ☎ *239/321–7430* ⊕ *www.swflmuseumofhistory.com* 🖃 *$9.50* ☉ *Tues.–Sat. 10–5.*

WHERE TO EAT

$$$ ✕ **Bistro 41.** Shoppers and businesspeople meet here for some of the
AMERICAN town's most dependable and inventive cuisine. Amid brightly painted, textured walls and a display kitchen, the menus roam from "41 Prime Dip" sandwich and the popular bistro salad with portobellos and a pesto drizzle to a delicious pork pot roast. To experience the kitchen at its imaginative best, check the night's specials, which often include daringly done seafood (crabmeat-crusted triple-tail fish with caramelized plantains and passion-fruit beurre blanc, for instance). Small appetite? Half portions and small plates are on offer. When weather permits, ask for a table on the patio. ⑤ *Average main: $23* ✉ *13499 S. Cleveland Ave.* ☎ *239/466–4141* ⊕ *www.bistro41.com* ⌂ *Reservations essential.*

$ ✕ **Chile Ranchero.** Latinos and gringos alike converge on this authentic
MEXICAN little corner of Mexicana in a strip mall along busy Tamiami Trail. The décor is humble, but you can't beat the prices or the portions. The warm and inviting staff speaks Spanish and so does the menu, with English subtitles. The intensely flavorful dishes appeal to American and Latin palates, with a range from fajitas and steak ranchero to seafood soup and excellent nachos con ceviche. ⑤ *Average main: $12* ✉ *11751 S. Cleveland Ave. #18* ☎ *239/275–0505.*

$$$
ITALIAN

✕ **Cibo.** Its flavor-bursting Italian food and its propensity for fresh, quality ingredients keep Cibo at the head of the class for local Italian restaurants. In contrast to the sophisticated black-and-white setting, the menu comes in colors from the classic Cesare salad with shaved Grana Padano and spaghetti and meatballs to salmon piccata and veal porterhouse with porcini risotto. The lasagna Napoletana is typical of the standards set here—a generous square of pasta layered with fluffy ricotta, meat ragù, mozzarella, and the totally fresh-tasting, garlicky pomodoro sauce. ⑤ *Average main: $24* ✉ *12901 McGregor Blvd.* ☎ *239/454–3700* ⊕ *www.cibofortmyers.com* ⚓ *Reservations essential* ⊘ *No lunch.*

$$$
VIETNAMESE

✕ **Saigon Paris Bistro.** Irish omelets, Belgian waffles, crêpes, steak au poivre, Vietnamese sea bass, Waldorf chicken salad: this eatery's extensive menu clearly travels farther abroad than its name implies. And it does so with utmost taste and flavor, as its faithful local clientele will attest. The best deals are the lunchtime Vietnamese entrées and chicken egg-drop soup. The restaurant is known for its gigantic bowls of *pho* (traditional soup), which can be ordered any time of day (some people have them for breakfast). It also offers three-course Vietnamese or Parisian dinners for $30. Leave room for crêpes à la Grand Marnier, prepared tableside. The interior is pleasant, if a bit old-fashioned, but provides a soothing surprise in this busy part of town with its fireplace, floral motif, and classic columns. ⑤ *Average main: $21* ✉ *12995 S. Cleveland. Ave. #118* ☎ *239/936–2233* ⊕ *www.saigonparisbistro.com* ⊘ *Closed Mon. June–Sept.*

$
SEAFOOD
FAMILY

✕ **Shrimp Shack.** Seafood lovers, families, and retired snowbirds flock to this venue with its vivacious staff, bustle, and colorful, cartoonish wall murals. There's a wait for lunch in winter season and a brisk take-out business with drive-through. Southern-style deep frying prevails—whole-belly clams, grouper, shrimp, onion rings, hush puppies, and fried pork loins—though you can get certain selections broiled or blackened, and there's some New England flavor with seafood rolls at lunch. Create your own combo by selecting two or three fried, broiled, or blackened choices. Kids love this place for the buzzing atmosphere and parents love the inexpensive kids meals. For more savings, print out the restaurant's "Kids Eat Free" coupon from the website. This is your place if you like your seafood simple. ⑤ *Average main: $13* ✉ *13361 Metro Pkwy.* ☎ *239/561–6817* ⊕ *www.shrimpshackusa.com.*

$$$$
SOUTHERN

✕ **The Veranda.** Restaurants come and go quickly as downtown reinvents itself, but this one has endured since 1978. A favorite of business and government bigwigs at lunch (the fried green tomato salad is signature), it serves imaginative Continental fare with a trace of a Southern accent for dinner. Notable are tournedos with smoky sour-mash-whiskey sauce, rack of lamb with rosemary-merlot sauce, herb-crusted honey-grilled salmon, and a grilled seafood sampler with saffron fettuccine, all served with homemade honey-drizzled bread and corn muffins with pepper jelly. The restaurant is a combination of two turn-of-the-20th-century homes, with a two-sided central brick fireplace, and sconces and antique oil paintings on its pale-yellow walls. Ask for an outdoor courtyard table when weather permits. ⑤ *Average main: $34* ✉ *2122*

8

2nd St. ☎ *239/332–2065* ⊕ *www.verandarestaurant.com* ⊘ *Closed Sun. No lunch Sat.*

WHERE TO STAY

$ **Crowne Plaza Hotel Fort Myers at the Bell Tower Shops.** Baseball fans often
HOTEL make this hotel home base since spring training and other sports parks are just a few miles away, while singles love the sports bar downstairs and being a stroll from the Bell Tower Shops, and families appreciate the minirefrigerators and microwaves in the rooms. **Pros:** free airport shuttle; complimentary transportation within a 3-mile radius; laundry facilities. **Cons:** showing signs of age; rooms a bit tight; meeting traffic crowds the lobby. ⑤ *Rooms from: $180* ⊠ *13051 Bell Tower Dr.* ☎ *239/482–2900* ⊕ *www.cpfortmyers.com* ⇥ *225 rooms* ⦿ *No meals.*

$ **Hilton Garden Inn Fort Myers.** This compact, prettily landscaped low-
HOTEL rise is near Fort Myers's cultural and commercial areas, and a business clientele favors it for its convenience. **Pros:** near performing-arts center; enjoyable restaurant; large rooms. **Cons:** chain feel; small pool; at busy intersection. ⑤ *Rooms from: $199* ⊠ *12600 University Dr.* ☎ *239/790–3500* ⊕ *www.fortmyers.stayhgi.com* ⇥ *126 rooms* ⦿ *Breakfast.*

$ **Hotel Indigo, Ft. Myers Downtown River District.** The only modern bou-
HOTEL tique hotel downtown, it attracts a cosmopolitan set that wants to be in the center of the River District's art, dining, and shopping scene—and just minutes from other attractions. **Pros:** sleek design; walking distance to restaurants and nightlife; tower built in 2009 and lobby part of historic arcade; rooftop bar. **Cons:** must drive to beach; no suites have full kitchens. ⑤ *Rooms from: $169* ⊠ *1520 Broadway* ☎ *239/337–3446* ⊕ *www.hotelindigo.com* ⇥ *60 rooms, 7 suites* ⦿ *No meals.*

$$$ **Sanibel Harbour Marriott Resort & Spa.** Vacationing families and busi-
RESORT nesspeople who want luxury pick this sprawling resort complex that
FAMILY towers over the island-studded San Carlos Bay at the last mainland
Fodor's Choice exit before the Sanibel Causeway. **Pros:** top-notch accommodations;
★ full amenities; updated spa. **Cons:** daily-parking fee as well as resort fee added to rate; unspectacular beach. ⑤ *Rooms from: $369* ⊠ *17260 Harbour Pointe Dr.* ☎ *239/466–4000, 800/767–7777* ⊕ *www.sanibel-resort.com* ⇥ *283 rooms, 64 suites* ⦿ *No meals.*

NIGHTLIFE AND PERFORMING ARTS

PERFORMING ARTS

Broadway Palm Dinner Theatre. Buffet dinners come along with some of Broadway's best comedies and musicals. There's also a 98-seat black-box theater that hosts smaller-scale productions. ⊠ *1380 Colonial Blvd.* ☎ *239/278–4422* ⊕ *www.broadwaypalm.com.*

Florida Rep. In the restored circa-1915 Arcade Theatre downtown, this top professional company stages Tony- and Pulitzer-winning plays and musicals. There's also an adjacent, more intimate space for edgier works and a Lunchbox Theatre Series for children. ⊠ *2267 1st St.* ☎ *239/332–4488* ⊕ *www.floridarep.org.*

NIGHTLIFE

Bratta's Seafood, Steaks & Pasta. Steaks grilled to order, truly dazzling seafood creations, and 15 different pasta dishes make for an enticing menu. For dessert, their signature chocolate piano filled with silky mousse is worth every calorie. Full bar available, and there is entertainment most nights. ✉ *12984 S. Cleveland Ave.* ☎ *239/433–4449* ⊕ *www.brattasristorante.com* ☉ *No lunch weekends.*

Crü. Trendsters in the mood for a drink and excellent global tapas crowd the lounge area of this cutting-edge restaurant. The lounge serves food until midnight on weekends. ✉ *13499 S. Cleveland Ave., Ste. 241* ☎ *239/466–3663* ⊕ *www.eatcru.com.*

Groove Street Grille & Discotheque. Dance to those fabulous songs of the 1970s and hot hits from today. Happy hour, ladies' night, and good food add to the fun atmosphere. Comedy shows play regularly in the Laugh-In Comedy Cafe, which is in the same building. ✉ *College Plaza, 8595 College Pkwy. #300* ☎ *239/437–2743* ⊕ *www.groovestreet.com* ☉ *Thurs. 9 pm–2 am, Fri. 5 pm–2 am, Sat. 8 pm–2 am.*

The Happy Buddha. A giant gold statue of his Zen-ness out front greets fans—a fun mix of frat boys, retirees, and young professionals—who crowd the casual, smoky bar and groove to hits from live bands and DJs. This is a local favorite. ✉ *12701 McGregor Blvd.* ☎ *239/482–8565.*

Laugh-In Comedy Cafe. South of downtown comedians perform Friday and Saturday. ✉ *College Plaza, 8595 College Pkwy. #300* ☎ *239/479–5233* ⊕ *www.laughincomedycafe.com.*

Stevie Tomato's Sports Page. Five miles up on I–75 from the buzzing Gulf Coast Town Center bars, this is a low-key spot to catch a late game and feast on good munchies; earlier in the evening it's very family-friendly. ✉ *9510 Market Place Rd.* ☎ *239/939–7211* ⊕ *www.stevietomatossportspage.com.*

SHOPPING

Bell Tower Shops. This open-air shopping center has about 40 stylish boutiques and specialty shops, a Saks 5th Avenue, some of Fort Myers's best restaurants and bars, as well as 20 movie screens. ✉ *S. Cleveland Ave. at Daniels Pkwy.* ☎ *239/489–1221* ⊕ *www.thebelltowershops.com.*

Edison Mall. The largest air-conditioned indoor mall in Fort Myers houses several major department stores and some 160 specialty shops. ✉ *4125 Cleveland Ave.* ☎ *239/939–1933* ⊕ *www.edison-mall-fl.com.*

Fleamasters Fleamarket. Just east of downtown, more than 900 vendors sell new and used goods Friday through Sunday 9–5. Its music hall hosts live entertainment. ✉ *4135 Dr. Martin Luther King Jr. Blvd., 1.7 miles west of I–75 Exit 138* ☎ *239/334–7001* ⊕ *www.fleamall.com.*

Gulf Coast Town Center. This a megamall of stores and chain restaurants includes a 130,000-square-foot Bass Pro Shops, Ron Jon Surf Shop, Best Buy, Costco, Golf Galaxy, and movie theaters. ✉ *9903 Gulf Coast Main St.* ☎ *239/267–0783* ⊕ *www.gulfcoasttowncenter.com.*

Sanibel Tanger Factory Outlets. Its boardwalks are lined with outlets for Nike, Van Heusen, Maidenform, Coach, Coldwater Creek, Bath & Body Works, and Samsonite, among others. ✉ *20350 Summerlin Rd.* ☎ *888/471–3939* ⊕ *www.tangeroutlet.com/fortmyers.*

SPORTS AND THE OUTDOORS
BASEBALL

The region is a popular outpost for spring training teams, with two in Fort Myers.

Boston Red Sox. The Sox settled into new digs in 2012 at JetBlue Park at Fenway South, a new $77 million, 10,823-capacity stadium and 106-acre training facility. The field itself is an exact duplicate of their famous home turf, with a Green Monster wall and manual scoreboard. ⊠ *JetBlue Park, 11581 Daniels Pkwy.* ☎ *239/334–4700, 888/733–7696* ⊕ *boston.redsox.mlb.com.*

Minnesota Twins. The team plays exhibition games in town during March and early April. From April through September, the Miracle (⊕ *www. miraclebaseball.com*), a Twins single-A affiliate, plays home games at Hammond Stadium. ⊠ *Lee County Sports Complex, 14100 6 Mile Cypress Pkwy.* ☎ *800/338–9467* ⊕ *minnesota.twins.mlb.com.*

BIKING

One of the longest bike paths in Fort Myers is along Summerlin Road. It passes commercial areas and gets close to Sanibel through dwindling wide-open spaces. Linear Park, which runs parallel to Six Mile Cypress Parkway, offers more natural, less congested views. Trailhead Park is linked to the new John Yarbrough Linear Park to create a 30-mile pathway, the longest in Lee County.

Bike Route. Since 1974, this is the place to come for a good selection of rentals. ⊠ *8595 College Pkwy., Ste. 200* ☎ *239/481–3376* ⊕ *www. thebikeroute.com.*

BOATING AND SAILING

Southwest Florida Yachts. Charter a sailboat or powerboat, or take lessons. With 30 years in the business, they can help you explore Southwest Florida like a native. ⊠ *3444 Marinatown La. NW, North Fort Myers* ☎ *239/656–1339, 800/262–7939* ⊕ *www.swfyachts.com.*

GOLF

Eastwood Golf Course. Golfers love how this Robert von Hagge and Bruce Devlin–designed course is in an area where there is little development, meaning no homes around the course, just plenty of water, trees, and wildlife (aka gators). The driving range and course are affordable, too, especially if you don't mind playing at unfavorable times (midday in summer, for example). Test your skills on the short par 4 on No. 7, where your second shot is over water. The 10th hole will have you shooting over water, too. ⊠ *4600 Bruce Herd La.* ☎ *239/321–7487* ⊕ *www.cityftmyers.com/eastwood* ⌑ *$50, club rentals $15* ⚲ *18 holes. 6772 yards. par 72.*

Fort Myers Country Club. Walk in the footsteps of Thomas Edison and Henry Ford when you play this course known as "The Fort" to its huge fan base. Located less than a mile from the winter estates of these famous inventors, this course is one of the oldest on Florida's west coast. In fact, it was designed in 1916 by Donald Ross and opened in 1917. Number 10 is a par 3 where you can hit anything from a 7-iron to a hybrid as the hole stretches out 203 yards. The Coors Light Open is held here each February. Next door is a lively restaurant and bar, The

Edison. ⊠ *3591 McGregor Blvd.* ☎ *239/321–7488* ⊕ *www.cityftmyers. com/countryclub* 🎫 *$40–$60* ⛳ *18 holes. 6400 yards. par 72.*

Shell Point Golf Club. Newbies to heavy hitters enjoy the layout of this Gordon Lewis–designed course with its challenging fairways and share of water hazards—eight tees on every hole. The front nine play like a symphony, but the back nine can be rough and slow with the wind and their somewhat compacted layouts. If you're looking for a 19th hole where you can toast your one-under-par score, you won't find it here as no alcohol is served. One nice feature at "The Shell" is that they offer Laser Link for accurate yardage to the pin. ⊠ *17401 On Par Blvd.* ☎ *239/433–9790* ⊕ *www.shellpointgolf.com* 🎫 *$95* ⛳ *18 holes. 6880 yards. par 71.*

KAYAKING

Calusa Blueway Outfitters. Paddling enthusiasts can rent kayaks to explore the Manatee Park environs daily from Thanksgiving to Easter and on weekends in the summer; clinics and guided tours are also available, but go in winter if spotting sea cows is your aim. ⊠ *Manatee Park, 10901 Palm Beach Blvd., 1¼ mile east of I–75 Exit 141* ☎ *239/481–4600* ⊕ *www.calusablueway outfitters.com.*

CAPE CORAL, PINE ISLAND, AND NORTH FORT MYERS

13 miles from downtown Fort Myers.

Cape Coral is determinedly trying to move from its pigeonhole as a residential community by attracting tourism with its downtown reconfiguration, the Resort at MarinaVillage, and destination restaurants at the Cape Harbour residential marina development.

GETTING HERE AND AROUND

Four bridges cross from Fort Myers to Cape Coral and North Fort Myers. Pine Island–Bayshore Road (Route 78) leads from North Fort Myers through northern Cape Coral onto off-the-beaten path Pine Island, known for its art galleries, fishing, and exotic fruit farms.

EXPLORING

Calusa Heritage Trail. Affiliated with the University of Florida's natural history museum in Gainesville, this 0.7-mile interpretive walkway explores the site of an ancient Amerindian village—more than 1,500 years old—with excellent signage, two intact shell mounds you can climb, the remains of a complex canal system, and ongoing archaeological research. Guided tours are given 3 times a week from January to April. Check the website for special tours and lecture events. ⊠ *Randell Research Center, 13810 Waterfront Dr., Bokeelia, Pine Island, Pineland* ☎ *239/283–2157* ⊕ *www.flmnh.ufl.edu/rrc* 🎫 *$7 (suggested donation)* ☉ *Daily 10–4. Restrooms and gift shop closed Sun.*

FAMILY **Shell Factory & Nature Park.** This entertainment complex, once just a quirky shopping destination and a survivor from Florida's roadside-attraction era, now contains eateries, museum displays, an arcade, bumper boats, miniature golf, and a mining sluice where kids can pan for shells, fossils, and gemstones. Strolling the grounds is free, but some activities carry individual fees, and a separate admission is required to

PUNTA GORDA DAY TRIP

A half hour (23 miles) north of Fort Myers, the small, old town of Punta Gorda merits a day trip for its restaurants and historic sites. If you're driving to Boca Grande via U.S. 41, it also makes a nice stop along the way. On the mouth of the Peace River, where it empties into Charlotte Harbor, a new riverfront park, water views, and murals enliven the compact downtown historic district. Away from the downtown area, a classic-car museum, wildlife rehabilitation center, and waterfront shopping complex built into an old fish-packing plant fills out a day of sightseeing. Fishing and nature-watching tours also depart from the Fishermen's Village complex.

enter the Nature Park, which has the feel of a small zoo. There you can find llamas and a zebra to ogle; a petting farm with sheep, pigs, and goats; a walk-through aviary; an EcoLab with reptiles and small animals; and a gator slough. The Shell Factory also hosts annual events such as the Gumbo Fest in January. ⊠ *2787 N. Tamiami Trail, North Fort Myers* ☎ *239/995–2141* ⊕ *www.shellfactory.com* ☞ *Shell Factory free, attractions starting at $2 each; Nature Park $12* ⊗ *Shell Factory daily 9–7, Nature Park daily 10–5.*

FAMILY

Fodor'sChoice
★

Sun Splash Family Waterpark. Head here to cool off when summer swelters. Nearly two dozen wet and dry attractions include ten thrill waterslides; the Sand Dollar Walk, where you step from one floating "sand dollar" to another; pint-sized Pro Racer flumes; a professional sand volleyball court; a family pool and Tot Spot; and a river-tube ride. Rates go down after 2 pm, plus the park offers Family Fun Night specials. ⊠ *400 Santa Barbara Blvd.* ☎ *239/574–0558* ⊕ *www.sunsplashwaterpark.com* ☞ *$17.95* ⊗ *Mar.–Sept., weekends and some weekdays 10–5; call or visit the website for hrs.*

OFF THE
BEATEN
PATH

Babcock Wilderness Adventures. To see what Florida looked like centuries ago, visit Babcock's Crescent B Ranch, northeast of Fort Myers. During the 90-minute swamp-buggy-style excursion you ride in a converted school bus through several ecosystems, including the unusual and fascinating Telegraph Cypress Swamp. Along the way an informative and typically amusing guide describes the area's social and natural history while you keep an eye peeled for alligators, wild pigs, all sorts of birds, Florida panthers, and other denizens of the wild. The tour also takes in the ranch's resident cattle and cougar in captivity. Reservations are needed for tours. An on-site restaurant servers "Cracker" chow in season. ⊠ *8000 Rte. 31, Punta Gorda* ☎ *800/500–5583* ⊕ *www.babcockwilderness.com* ☞ *Eco-tour $24; cost for other specialty tours varies* ⚠ *Reservations essential* ⊗ *Oct.–May, tours daily; June–Sept., tours Tues.–Sat. All tours by reservation only; some specialty tours are offered only monthly or seasonally.*

WHERE TO EAT

$ ✕ **Bert's Bar & Grill.** Looking to hang out with the locals of Pine Island?
AMERICAN   Here you'll find cheap eats, live entertainment, a pool table, and a
water view to boot. Speaking of boots, you're likely to see some of the
clientele wearing white rubber fishing boots, known here as Pine Island
Reeboks. Order fried oysters, a burger, pizza, or a grouper Reuben melt
from the no-nonsense menu, and enjoy live music most days. ⑤ *Average
main: $9* ✉ *4271 Pine Island Rd., Matlacha* ☎ *239/282–3232* ⊕ *www.
bertsbar.com* ⚓ *Reservations not accepted.*

$ ✕ **Rumrunners.** Cape Coral's best casual cuisine is surprisingly afford-
AMERICAN   able, considering the luxury condo development that rises around it and
the size of the yachts that pull up to the docks. Caribbean in spirit, with
lots of indoor and outdoor views of a mangrove-fringed waterway, it
serves bistro specialties such as conch fritters, seafood potpie, bronzed
salmon, and a warm chocolate bread pudding that is addictive. Bar
staff is affable and welcoming. ⑤ *Average main: $13* ✉ *Cape Harbour
Marina, 5848 Cape Harbour Dr., off Chiquita Blvd.* ☎ *239/542–0200*
⊕ *www.rumrunnersrestaurant.com.*

$ ✕ **Siam Hut.** Lunch and dinner menus at this Cape Coral fixture let you
THAI   design your own stir-fry, noodle, or fried-rice dish. Dinner specialties
include fried crispy frogs' legs with garlic and black pepper, a sizzling
shrimp platter, fried whole tilapia with curry sauce, salads, and pad thai.
Get your food fiery-hot or extra-mild. Two traditional Thai tables allow
you to sit on floor pillows (conveniently with backs), or you can opt for
a more conventional table or booth. ⑤ *Average main: $12* ✉ *4521 Del
Prado Blvd.* ☎ *239/945–4247* ⊕ *www.siamhutcapecoral.com* ⊗ *Closed
Sun. No lunch Sat.*

WHERE TO STAY

$ 🏨 **Casa Loma Motel.** Stay at this pretty little motel, 15 minutes from
HOTEL   Fort Myers at the end of the Croton Canal, to be close to Cape Coral's
attractions and escape the sticker shock of beachfront lodgings. **Pros:**
kitchen facilities in rooms; free Wi-Fi; large sundeck with canal access.
Cons: must drive to beach; on a busy street; décor a bit dated; no restaurant. ⑤ *Rooms from: $119* ✉ *3608 Del Prado Blvd.* ☎ *239/549–6000,
877/227–2566* ⊕ *www.casalomamotel.com* ⊸ *48 efficiencies, 1 suite*
🍴 *No meals.*

$$ 🏨 **The Westin Cape Coral Resort at MarinaVillage.** Cape Coral's only luxury
RESORT   resort, this modern 19-story tower sits alongside a marina fringed with
mangroves and caters to families and water sports enthusiasts. **Pros:**
full-service marina; designer appointments; three pools; great kayak-
ing. **Cons:** 45-minute ferry to beach; high-rise. ⑤ *Rooms from: $299*
✉ *5951 Silver King Blvd.* ☎ *239/541–5000, 888/372–9256* ⊕ *www.
marinavillageresort.com* ⊸ *83 studios, 83 1-bedroom condos, 82
2-bedroom condos, 16 3-bedroom condos* 🍴 *No meals.*

THE COASTAL ISLANDS

A maze of islands in various stages of habitation fronts Fort Myers
mainland, separated by the Intracoastal Waterway. Some are accessible
via a causeway; to reach others, you need a boat. If you cut through

bay waters, you have a good chance of being escorted by bottlenose dolphins. Mostly birds and other wild creatures inhabit some islands, which are given over to state parks. Traveler-pampering hotels on Sanibel, Captiva, and Fort Myers Beach give way to rustic cottages, old inns, and cabins on quiet Cabbage Key and Pine Island, which have no beaches because they lie between the barrier islands and mainland. Others are devoted to resorts. When exploring barrier island beaches, keep one eye on the sand: collecting seashells is a major pursuit in these parts.

GASPARILLA ISLAND (BOCA GRANDE)

43 miles northwest of Fort Myers.

Before roads to the Lower Gulf Coast were even talked about, wealthy Northerners came by train to spend the winter at the Gasparilla Inn. The inn was completed in 1913 in Boca Grande on Gasparilla Island, named, legend has it, for a Spanish pirate who set up headquarters in these waters. Although condominiums and modern mansions occupy the rest of Gasparilla, much of the town of Boca Grande evokes another era. The mood is set by the Old Florida homes and tree-framed roadways. The island's calm is disrupted in the spring when anglers descend with a vengeance on Boca Grande Pass, considered among the best tarpon-fishing spots in the world.

GETTING HERE AND AROUND

Boca Grande is more than an hour's drive northwest of Fort Myers. Day-trippers can catch a charter boat or rent a boat, dock at a marina, and rent a bike or golf cart for a day of exploring and lunching. North of it stretches a long island, home to Don Pedro Island State Park and Palm Island Resort, both accessible only by boat. Also nearby is the off-the-beaten-path but car-accessible island of Manasota Key and its fishing resort community of Englewood Beach.

EXPLORING

Gasparilla Island State Park and Port Boca Grande Lighthouse Museum. The island's beaches are its greatest prize and lie within the state park at the south end. The long, narrow beach ends at Boca Grande Pass, famous for its deep waters and tarpon fishing. The pretty, two-story, circa-1890 lighthouse once marked the pass for mariners. In recent years it has been restored as a museum that explores the island's fishing and railroad heritage. The lighthouse is closed in August. ⊠ *880 Belcher Rd., Boca Grande* ☎ *941/964–0060* ⊕ *www.floridastateparks.org/gasparillaisland* 🖼 *$3 per vehicle; $2 suggested donation to lighthouse (exact change only)* ☉ *Park daily 8–sunset. Lighthouse Nov.–April, Mon.–Sat. 10–4, Sun. noon–4; May–July, Sept., and Oct., Wed.–Sat. 10–4, Sun. noon–4.*

WHERE TO EAT

$$$
AMERICAN

✕ **The Loose Caboose.** Revered by many—including Katharine Hepburn in her time—for its homemade ice cream, this is also a good spot for solid, affordable fare, from burgers and a Thanksgiving wrap (turkey and cranberry sauce) to chicken potpie and crispy duck with orange-teriyaki sauce. Housed in the town's historic depot, it offers indoor and patio seating in an all-American setting. ⑤ *Average main: $24* ⊠ *433 W.*

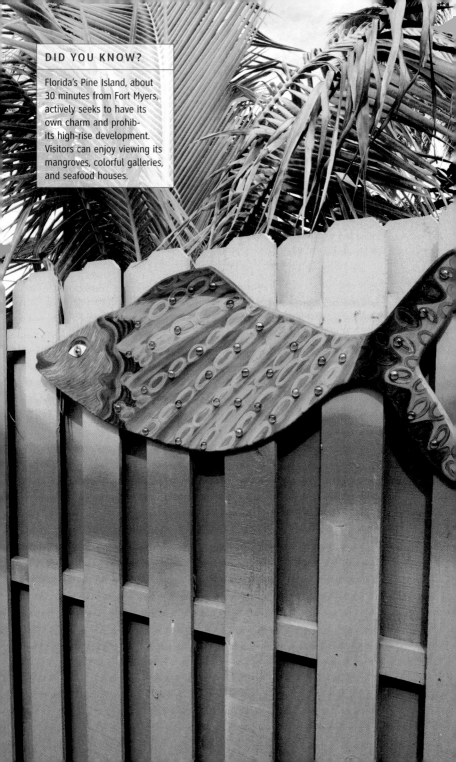

4th St., Boca Grande ☎ *941/964–0440* ⊕ *www.loosecaboose.biz* ⊘ *No dinner Wed. or Apr.–Dec.*

WHERE TO STAY

$$$ 🏨 **Gasparilla Inn & Club.** Once the playground of social-register mem-
HOTEL   bers such as the Vanderbilts and DuPonts, the gracious pale-yellow
wooden hotel was built by shipping industrialists in the early 1900s.
Pros: historic property; nicely renovated. **Cons:** expensive rates; the
quirks of a very old building. ⑤ *Rooms from: $395* ✉ *500 Palm Ave.,
Boca Grande* ☎ *941/964–2201, 800/996–1913* ⊕ *www.gasparillainn.
com* ⤳ *137 rooms, 18 cottages* ⑩ *Multiple meal plans.*

CABBAGE KEY

5 miles south of Boca Grande.

Cabbage Key is the ultimate island-hopping escape in these parts. Some
say Jimmy Buffett was inspired to write "Cheeseburger in Paradise"
after a visit to its popular restaurant.

GETTING HERE AND AROUND

You'll need to take a boat—from Bokeelia or Pineland, on Pine Island,
or from Captiva Island—to get to this island, which sits at mile marker
60 on the Intracoastal Waterway. Local operators offer day trips and
luncheon cruises.

WHERE TO STAY

$ 🏨 **Cabbage Key Inn.** Atop an ancient Calusa Indian shell mound and
HOTEL   accessible only by boat, the friendly, somewhat quirky inn built by nov-
elist and playwright Mary Roberts Rinehart in 1938 welcomes guests
seeking quiet and isolation. **Pros:** plenty of solitude; Old Florida charac-
ter. **Cons:** two-night minimum stay; accessible only by boat or seaplane;
limited amenities, some rooms have no TV; in season the restaurant is
busy. ⑤ *Rooms from: $175* ☎ *239/283–2278* ⊕ *www.cabbagekey.com*
⤳ *6 rooms, 8 cottages* ⑩ *No meals.*

SANIBEL AND CAPTIVA ISLANDS

23 miles southwest of downtown Fort Myers.

Sanibel Island is famous as one of the world's best shelling grounds,
a function of the unusual east–west orientation of the island's south
end. Just as the tide is going out and after storms, the pickings can be
superb, and shell seekers performing the telltale "Sanibel stoop" patrol
every beach carrying bags of conchs, whelks, cockles, and other bivalves
and gastropods. (Remember, it's unlawful to pick up live shells.) Away
from the beach, flowery vegetation decorates small shopping com-
plexes, pleasant resorts and condo complexes, mom-and-pop motels,
and casual restaurants. But much of the two-lane road down the spine
of the island is bordered by nature reserves that have made Sanibel as
well known among bird-watchers as it is among seashell collectors.

Captiva Island, connected to the northern end of Sanibel by a bridge,
is quirky and engaging. At the end of a twisty road lined with million-
dollar mansions lies a delightful village of shops, eateries, and beaches.

GETTING HERE AND AROUND

Sanibel Island is approximately 23 miles southwest of downtown Fort Myers, and Captiva lies north of 12-mile-long Sanibel. If you're flying into Southwest Florida International Airport, an on-demand taxi for up to three passengers to Sanibel or Captiva costs about $60–$68; additional passengers are charged $10 each. Sanibel Island is accessible from the mainland via the Sanibel Causeway (toll $6 round-trip). Captiva Island lies across a small pass from Sanibel's north end, accessible by bridge.

ESSENTIALS

Visitor Information Sanibel and Captiva Islands Chamber of Commerce ⊠ *1159 Causeway Rd., Sanibel* ☎ *239/472–1080* ⊕ *www.sanibel-captiva.org.*

EXPLORING

FAMILY
Fodor's Choice
★
Bailey-Matthews Shell Museum. More than 25 vignettes and exhibits explore shells in the environment, art, and history, including a life-size display of native Calusa and how they used shells for tools and vessels and new exhibits on cowrie shells and the biggest shells in the world. Visit the shell-identifier wheel, which categorizes specimens from local waters in sizes ranging from tiny to huge. Handle shell specimens and play games in the colorful kids' lab. Watch a movie all about shells: how they form and where to find them. A six-foot globe at the center of the museum rotunda highlights shells from around the world. The gift shop is filled with unique items that reflect an upscale nautical theme. ⊠ *3075 Sanibel–Captiva Rd., Sanibel* ☎ *239/395–2233, 888/679–6450* ⊕ *www.shellmuseum.org* ☏ *$9* ☉ *Daily 10–5.*

Clinic for the Rehabilitation of Wildlife (C.R.O.W.). In existence for more than 40 years, the clinic currently cares for more than 4,000 wildlife patients each year. The center offers a look inside the world of wildlife medicine through exhibits, videos, interactive displays, touch screens, and critter cams that feed live footage from four different animal spaces. It's an excellent facility, but the displays may be too graphic for young visitors. ⊠ *3883 Sanibel–Captiva Rd., Sanibel* ☎ *239/472–3644* ⊕ *www.crowclinic.org* ☏ *$5* ☉ *Tues.–Sat. 10–4.*

FAMILY
Fodor's Choice
★
J. N. "Ding" Darling National Wildlife Refuge. More than half of Sanibel is occupied by the subtly beautiful 6,300 acres of wetlands and mangrove forests named after a conservation-minded Pulitzer Prize–winning political cartoonist. The masses of roseate spoonbills and ibis and the winter flock of white pelicans here make for a good show even if you're not a die-hard bird-watcher. Birders have counted some 230 species, including herons, ospreys, and the timid mangrove cuckoo. Raccoons, otters, alligators, and a lone American crocodile also may be spotted. The 4-mile Wildlife Drive is the main way to explore the preserve; drive, walk, or bicycle along it, or ride a specially designed open-air tram with an on-board naturalist. New QR codes signs link to interactive You Tube videos. There are also a couple of short walking trails, including one to a Calusa shell mound. Or explore from the water via canoe or kayak (guided tours are available). The best time for bird-watching is in the early morning and about an hour before or after low tide; the observation tower along the road offers prime viewing. Interactive

Continued on page 452

SHELL-BENT ON SANIBEL ISLAND
by Chelle Koster Walton

Sanibel Island beachgoers are an unusual breed: they pray for storms; they muck around tidal pools rather than play in the waves; and instead of lifting their faces to the sun, they have their heads in the sand—almost literally—as they engage in the so-called "Sanibel Stoop."

Odd? Not when you consider that this is Florida's prime shelling location, thanks to the island's east-west bend (rather than the usual north-south orientation of most beaches along the coastline). The lay of the land means a treasure trove of shells—more than 400 species—wash up from the Caribbean.

These gifts from the sea draw collectors of all levels. Come winter, when the cold and storms kill the shellfish and push them ashore, a parade of stoopers forms on Sanibel's shores.

The reasons people shell are as varied as the shellers themselves. The hardcore compete and sell, whereas others collect simply for the fun of discovery, for displaying, for use in gardens, or for crafts. The typical Sanibel tourist who comes seeking shells is usually looking for souvenirs and gifts to take home.

WHERE TO SHELL

Shelling is good anywhere along Sanibel's gulf-front. Remote **Bowman's Beach** (*off Sanibel-Captiva Road at Bowman's Beach Rd.*) offers the least competition. Other public accesses include **Lighthouse Beach** (Periwinkle Way), **Tarpon Bay Beach** (Tarpon Bay Rd.), and **Turner Beach** (Sanibel-Captiva Rd.). If you want to ditch your car (and crowds), walk or bike using **resident access beaches** (along the Gulf drives). If you want to search with others and get a little guidance, you can join shelling cruises from Sanibel and Captiva islands to the un-bridged island of Cayo Costa. For information contact, **Captiva Cruises** (☎ 239/472-5300, 🌐 www.captivacruises.com) or **Adventures in Paradise** (☎ 239/472-8443, 🌐 www.adventureinparadiseinc.com).

Captiva
Island

○Captiva

Turner
Beach

Bowman's
Beach

SANIBEL ISLAND

Lighthouse
Beach

○
Sanibel

Tarpon Bay
Beach

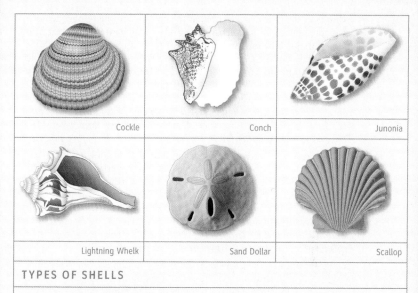

| Cockle | Conch | Junonia |

| Lightning Whelk | Sand Dollar | Scallop |

TYPES OF SHELLS

Cockles: The common Sanibel bivalve (hinged two-shelled mollusk), the heart cockle (named for its Valentine shape) is larger and more bowl-like than the scallop, which makes it a popular, colorful find for soap dishes, ashtrays, and catch-alls.

Conchs: Of the large family of conchs, fighting conchs are most commonly found on Sanibel. Contrary to its macho name, the fighting conch is one of the few vegetarian gastropods. While alive, the shell flames brilliant orange; it fades under tropical sunshine.

Junonias: These olive-shaped, spotted gastropods (single-shell mollusks) are Sanibel's signature, though somewhat rare, finds. People who hit upon one get their picture in the local paper. Resorts have been accused of planting them on their beaches for publicity.

Lightning Whelks: The lightning variety of whelk is "left-handed"—opening on the opposite side from most gastropods. Early islanders used them for tools. The animals lay their miniature shell eggs in papery egg-case chains on the beach.

Sand Dollars: Classified as an echinoderm not a mollusk, the thin sand dollar is brown and fuzzy while alive, studded with tiny tubes for breathing and moving. Unoccupied shells bleach to a beautiful white textured pattern, ideal for hanging on Christmas trees.

Scallops: No surprise that these pretty little bivalves have "scalloped" edges. They invented the word. Plentiful on Sanibel beaches, they come in a variety of colors and sizes.

SHELLING LIKE A PRO

Veteran shell-seekers go out before the sun rises so they can be the first on the beach after a storm or night of high tides. (Storms and cold fronts bring in the best catches.)

Most shellers use a bag to collect their finds. But once you're ready to pack shells for transit, wash them thoroughly to remove sand and debris. Then wrap fragile species such as sand dollars and sea urchins in tissue paper or cotton, then newspaper. Last, place your shells in a cardboard or plastic box. To display them, restore the shell's luster by brushing it with baby oil.

Sanibel shops sell books and supplies for identifying your finds and turning them into craft projects.

exhibits in the free visitor center, at the entrance to the refuge, demonstrate the refuge's various ecosystems and explain its status as a rest stop along a major bird-migration route. A new hands-on manatee exhibit was recently unveiled, too. Wildlife Drive is closed to vehicular traffic on Friday, but you can still kayak and do tours from the Tarpon Bay Recreation Area. ✉ 1 Wildlife Dr., off Sanibel–Captiva Rd. at MM 2, Sanibel ☎ 239/472–1100 for refuge, 239/472–8900 for kayaking and tours ⊕ www.fws.gov/dingdarling 🖃 $5 per car, $1 for pedestrians and bicyclists, tram $13 ۞ Education Center: Jan.–Apr., daily 9–5; May–Dec., daily 9–4. Wildlife Drive Sat.–Thurs. 7:30–½ hr before sunset.

FAMILY **Sanibel–Captiva Conservation Foundation.** For a good look at night herons and other inhabitants of Sanibel's interior wetlands, follow the 4½ miles of walking trails and climb the observation tower. See island research projects, Nature Center exhibits including live turtles, snakes and a touch tank, and visit a butterfly house. Guided walks are available seasonally on and off property. Kids under 17 are free. ✉ 3333 Sanibel–Captiva Rd., Sanibel ☎ 239/472–2329 ⊕ www.sccf.org 🖃 $5 ۞ Oct.–May, weekdays 8:30–4; June–Sept., weekdays 8:30–3.

Sanibel Historical Museum & Village. Charming buildings from the island's past include a general store, a one-room schoolhouse, 1927 post office, a tea room, 1925 winter-vacation cottage, a 1898 fishing cottage, and the 1913 Rutland House Museum, containing old documents and photographs, artifacts, and period furnishings. All buildings are authentic and have been moved from their original locations to the museum grounds. ✉ 950 Dunlop Rd., Sanibel ☎ 239/472–4648 ⊕ www.sanibelmuseum. org 🖃 $10 ۞ Nov.–Apr., Wed.–Sat. 10–4; May–mid-Aug., Wed.–Sat. 10–1; closed mid-Aug.–Oct.

BEACHES

Red tide, an occasional natural beach occurrence that kills fish, also has negative effects on the human respiratory system. It causes scratchy throats, runny eyes and noses, and coughing. Although the effects aren't long-term, it's a good idea to avoid the beach when red tide is in the vicinity (look for posted signs).

SANIBEL

FAMILY **Bowman's Beach.** This long, wide beach on Sanibel's northwest end is the island's most secluded strand, but it also has the most amenities. Park facilities include a playground, a fitness trail, picnic tables, and a canoe launch. It is famed for its shell collecting and spectacular sunsets at the north end—try to spot the green flash, said to occur just as the sun sinks below the horizon. For utmost seclusion, walk north from the two main access points where bridges cross an estuary to reach the beach. It's a long walk from the parking lot over the estuary to the beach, so pack accordingly and plan on a long stay. Tall Australian pines provide shade behind the white sands. Typically gentle waves are conducive to swimming and wading with kids. **Amenities:** parking (fee); showers; toilets. **Best for:** sunsets; swimming; walking. ✉ Bowman Beach Rd., at Blind Pass, Sanibel ☎ 239/472–3700 🖃 Parking $2 per hr.

FAMILY **Gulfside Park Preserve.** The beach is quiet, safe from strong currents, and good for solitude, bird-watching, and shell-finding. There are restrooms, and long stretches to stroll. The white sand is slightly coarse and borders a park with shade, picnic tables, and a loop nature trail. Low-rise resorts and homes lie to the east and west of the parking lot accesses. **Amenities:** parking (fee); toilets. **Best for:** swimming; walking. ⊠ *Algiers La., off Casa Ybel Rd., Sanibel* ☎ *239/472–3700* 🅿 *Parking $2 per hr.*

Lighthouse Beach. At Sanibel's eastern tip, the beach is guarded by the frequently photographed Sanibel Lighthouse, built in 1884, before the island was settled. The lighthouse is not currently open to the public, but there's talk of refurbishing the tower so visitors can climb to the top. The park rounds the island's east end for waterfront on both the gulf and bay, where a fishing pier draws avid anglers. Shaded nature trails connect the two shores. The park is listed on the Great Florida Birding Trail because of its fall and spring migration fall-outs. A pair of ospreys frequently perch on the lighthouse railing; look and listen for these local residents while you're there. **Amenities:** parking (fee); toilets. **Best for:** sunrise; walking; windsurfing; fishing. ⊠ *East end of Periwinkle Way, Sanibel* ☎ *239/472–3700* 🅿 *Parking $2 per hr.*

Tarpon Bay Beach. This centrally located beach is safer for swimming than beaches at the passes, where waters move swiftly. It is, however, one of the more populated beaches, lined with low-rise condos and resorts set back behind vegetation. Casa Ybel Resort lies east of the public access; other smaller resorts can be found along the stretch to the west. The parking lot is a five-minute walk from the beach, so drop off your gang and gear before you park (the lot is open daily from 7 to 7). At the beach, you can walk for miles in either direction on soft white sand studded with shells. **Amenities:** parking (fee); toilets. **Best for:** swimming; walking. ⊠ *Off Sanibel–Capriva Rd., Tarpon Bay Rd. at Gulf Dr., Sanibel* ✛ *Drive to the end of West Gulf Dr. and east to Casa Ybel Rd.* ☎ *239/472–3700* 🅿 *Parking $2 per hr.*

CAPTIVA

FAMILY **Alison Hagerup Beach Park.** This park, once called Captiva Beach, is acclaimed as one of the nation's most romantic beaches for its fabulous sunsets—the best view on Sanibel and Captiva. Shells stud the white, wide sands. The parking lot is small, so arrive early, and bring an umbrella if you need shade. The beach can get crowded, especially in the busy winter/spring season. Facilities are limited to portable restrooms and a volleyball net, but stores and restaurants are nearby. South Seas Island Resort lines the north end of the beach. **Amenities:** parking (fee); toilets. **Best for:** sunsets; swimming; walking. ⊠ *Captiva Dr., at the north end, Captiva* 🅿 *Parking $2 per hr, $10 for 8 hrs.*

Turner Beach. Looking for some romance? This is a prime sunset-watching spot on the southern point of Captiva. Strong currents through Blind Pass make swimming tricky but shelling amazing, and parking is limited. Surfers head here when winds whip up the waves. The beach is narrower than in other parts of the island. No buildings sit on the beach, but 'Tween Waters Resort is across the road to the north of the public access, and Castaways Beach & Bay Cottages is beachfront across the bridge on the Sanibel side of Blind Pass. Restaurants are nearby.

Amenities: parking (fee); toilets. **Best for:** sunsets; surfing; walking. ⊠ *Captiva Dr. at Blind Pass, Captiva* 🚗 *Parking $2 per hr.*

WHERE TO EAT

SANIBEL

$ ✕ **Lazy Flamingo.** At two Sanibel locations, plus two more in neighbor-
AMERICAN   ing Fort Myers and Pine Island Sound, this is a friendly neighborhood
FAMILY   hangout enjoyed by locals and visitors alike. All of these restaurants have a funky nautical look à la Key West and a popular following for their Dead Parrot Wings (buffalo wings coated with tongue-scorching hot sauce), mesquite-grilled grouper sandwiches, burgers, and steamer pots. The Flamingo garlic bread is always a hit, and the grouper caesar salad is cheesy and award-winning. Kids' meals are served on a Frisbee that makes not only a great souvenir but also a cool new beach toy. The second Sanibel location is at 1036 Periwinkle Way (☎ 239/472–6939). ⑤ *Average main: $12* ⊠ *6520C Pine Ave., Sanibel* ☎ *239/472–5353* ⊕ *www.lazyflamingo.com* ⟡ *Reservations not accepted.*

$$ ✕ **Over Easy Café.** Locals head to this chicken-theme eatery mainly for
AMERICAN   breakfast and lunch, although it also serves dinner in season. Kick-start the day with the egg reuben, veggie Benedict, pancakes, or omelets such as crab and asparagus or "meat-lovers." Breakfast is available until 3 pm. The lunch and dinner menu includes a vast variety of salads, sandwiches, wraps, and seafood. Indoor dining is cheerful; outdoors, and pet-friendly. While waiting for a table, you can shop for gifts next door. ⑤ *Average main: $16* ⊠ *630-1 Tarpon Bay Rd., Sanibel* ☎ *239/472–2625* ⊕ *www.overeasycafesanibel.com* ⟡ *Reservations not accepted* ☾ *No dinner.*

$$$ ✕ **Sweet Melissa's Cafe.** You've seen them before: those people who take
MODERN   photos of their food. You'll become one of them when you eat here.
AMERICAN   Choose from full portions or small plates, but the latter are recom-
Fodor'sChoice   mended so that you can savor more outstanding dishes in one sitting.
★   For starters, the cured Japanese yellowtail is delicately placed atop avocado puree with jalapeños, cilantro, and ponzu. Even if you don't like duck, you'll love it here. Fish stew, grilled smoked beef tenderloin, fresh mahimahi: they all are good choices for people who don't mind sharing. Chef Melissa also makes her own sorbet. Dine indoors, on the patio, at the bar, or at the chef's bar overlooking the exhibition kitchen. Live guitar music adds to the experience. ⑤ *Average main: $25* ⊠ *1625 Periwinkle Way, Sanibel* ☎ *239/472–1956* ⊕ *www.sweetmelissascafe. com* ⟡ *Reservations essential* ☾ *No lunch weekends.*

$$$$ ✕ **Thistle Lodge Restaurant.** Now this is romance: the Lodge was built as a
CONTEMPORARY   wedding gift from a husband to his wife and is now a gift to those lucky
Fodor'sChoice   enough to dine here. Lush green grounds are right outside the window,
★   then just beyond is the Gulf of Mexico and Sanibel's seashell-laden shores. But it's more than the views that will lull you into a dreamy mood. The food is fresh, elegant, and flavorful. Entrées include everything from mojito-glazed black grouper to brûléed Gorgonzola filet. Frequent patrons back in the day included Thomas Edison and Henry Ford. ⑤ *Average main: $35* ⊠ *Casa Ybel Resort, 2255 West Gulf Dr., Sanibel* ☎ *239/472–9200* ⊕ *www.thistlelodge.com.*

Where to Eat
and Stay on
Sanibel and Captiva

KEY

☐ Hotels
◾ Restaurants
◼ Restaurants in Hotels

Gulf of Mexico

*CAPTIVA
ISLAND*

Alison Hagerup
Beach

**The Mucky
Duck**

South Seas
Island Resort

◼ **Bubble Room**
◼ **Green Flash**

'Tween Waters Inn
Captiva House

Captiva Dr.

BUCK KEY

Turner
Beach

Lazy Flamingo

Blind Pass
Beach

*Pine Island
Sound*

Bowman's
Beach

*PINE
ISLAND*

Stringfellow Rd.

8

*SANIBEL
ISLAND*

Sanibel-Captiva Rd.

*J. N. Darling
National Wildlife
Refuge*

*St. James
City*

West Wind Inn ☐

W Gulf Dr.

Island Inn ☐
Waterside Inn ☐

*Tarpon
Bay*

**Over Easy
Café** ◼

**Timbers
Restaurant &
Fish Market** ◼

Tarpon Bay
Rd.

Periwinkle Wy.

Sanibel Q. R.

*San Carlos
Bay*

Tarpon Bay
Beach

**Thistle Lodge
Restaurant**
Casa Ybel Resort

Casa Ybel Rd.

**Sweet Melissa's
Cafe** ◼

Traders ◼
Store & Café

Middle Gulf Dr.

Gulfside
City Park

Sundial
Beach Resort
and Spa

Sanibel Siesta
on the Beach

**Lazy
Flamingo** ◼

E Gulf Dr.

Sanibel Causeway

Seaside Inn

Lighthouse
Beach

0 ___ 1 mi
0 ___ 1 km

$$$ ✕**Timbers Restaurant & Fish Market.** One of Sanibel's longest-running
SEAFOOD restaurants successfully satisfies visitors and residents with consistent
quality and a full net of nightly catches and specials. The fish market
inside the door is a sure sign of freshness, and most of the dishes show-
case seafood simply and flavorfully. The oysters Romanoff with caviar,
shallots, and sour cream are a nice twist on oyster "sliders." Corn
flakes grant the crunchy grouper and shrimp rights to their names.
Choose to have your fresh catch blackened, fried, or broiled, or go for
a sirloin or beef filet. House salad or soup du jour comes with each
entrée, or you can upgrade to the crab bisque, which just might be
the best on the island. For lighter fare and a sports bar vibe, Sanibel
Grill shares the same space. ⑤ *Average main: $21* ⊠ *703 Tarpon Bay
Rd., Sanibel* ☎ *239/472–3128* ⊕ *www.prawnbroker.com* ⌲ *Reserva-
tions not accepted.*

$$$ ✕**Traders Store & Café.** In the midst of a warehouse-size store, this bis-
AMERICAN tro, accented with artifacts from exotic places, is a favorite of locals.
Fodor'sChoice The marvelous sesame-seared tuna lunch salad with Asian slaw and
★ wasabi vinaigrette exemplifies the creative fare. For dinner, try the
barbecued baby back ribs, macadamia-crusted grouper, or any of
the day's finely crafted specials. A local band entertains two nights a
week. The bar serves light nibbles and happy-hour twofers. ⑤ *Average
main: $26* ⊠ *1551 Periwinkle Way, Sanibel* ☎ *239/472–7242* ⊕ *www.
traderssanibel.com* ⌲ *Reservations not accepted.*

CAPTIVA

$$$ ✕**Bubble Room.** This lively, kitschy visitors' favorite is fun for families
AMERICAN and nostalgic types with fat wallets. Servers wear scout uniforms and
FAMILY funny headgear. Electric trains circle overhead, glossies of Hollywood
stars past and present line the walls, and glass tabletops showcase old-
time toys. There's so much going on that you might not notice your
food is not quite as happening, and somehow that's okay. After grazing
your basket of cheesy bubble bread and sweet, yeasty sticky buns, go for
slow-cooked prime rib or shrimp sautéed in spicy tequila garlic butter.
The homemade triple-layer cakes, delivered in hefty wedges, are noto-
rious, and the gooey orange crunch cake is a signature favorite. Kids
are welcome and will love to gawk at the Christmas Room before or
after they gobble up the hand-breaded chicken fingers. Be prepared to
wait for a table in season. ⑤ *Average main: $25* ⊠ *15001 Captiva Dr.,
Captiva* ☎ *239/472–5558* ⊕ *www.bubbleroomrestaurant.com* ⌲ *Reser-
vations not accepted.*

$$$$ ✕**Captiva House.** This wonderfully romantic restaurant is casual, com-
SEAFOOD fortable, and considered by many to be the best fine-dining restaurant
Fodor'sChoice on Captiva Island. Executive Chef Jason Miller adds a fresh, Florida
★ flair to seafood dishes like the island snapper wrap (moist snapper
wrapped in crispy phyllo then drizzled with an aged balsamic glaze).
Tempting appetizers, creative salads, juicy steaks, and tantalizing des-
serts round out the menu. The restaurant has its own baker on site
for sweet and savory breads and cakes. No need to dress up; island
casual is welcome. Make time to enjoy the fantastic sunsets just across
the street at the beach. ⑤ *Average main: $32* ⊠ *'Tween Waters Inn,*

15951 Captiva Dr., Captiva ☏*239/472–5161* ⊕ *www.tween-waters. com/dining.php* ⌫ *Reservations essential.*

$$$ ✕ **Green Flash.** Good food and sweeping views of quiet waters and a
SEAFOOD mangrove island keep boaters and others coming back to this casual indoor-outdoor restaurant. Seafood dominates, but there's a bit of everything on the menu, from barbecued shrimp and bacon to grilled swordfish to pork tenderloin wrapped in prosciutto and puff pastry. For lunch, try the Green Flash sandwich (smoked turkey and prosciutto or vegetables, both with cheese on grilled focaccia). Grouper tacos are filling and dripping with freshness. On cool, sunny days, grab a table out back dockside. $ *Average main: $23* ⊠ *15183 Captiva Dr., Captiva* ☏ *239/472–3337* ⊕ *www.greenflashcaptiva.com.*

$$$ ✕ **The Mucky Duck.** A longtime fixture on Captiva's beach, it parodies
SEAFOOD British pubs with its name and sense of humor. Since 1975, it has consistently drawn crowds that occupy themselves with walking the beach and watching sunset while waiting for their name to be called for a table indoors or out. A little Brit, a lot Florida, the revamped menu has kept some favored specialties such as barbecued shrimp wrapped in bacon appetizer, crab cakes, fish and chips, and frozen key lime pie. $ *Average main: $24* ⊠ *11546 Andy Rosse La., Captiva* ☏ *239/472–3434* ⊕ *www. muckyduck.com* ⌫ *Reservations not accepted.*

WHERE TO STAY

SANIBEL

$$$$ ⌂ **Casa Ybel Resort.** Palm trees, quiet ponds, and gazebos set the mood at
RESORT this resort on 23 acres of gulf-facing grounds. **Pros:** on the beach; good
FAMILY restaurants; lots of recreational opportunities. **Cons:** spa treatments in-
Fodor'sChoice room only; minimum stay requirement in some units. $ *Rooms from:*
★ *$559* ⊠ *2255 W. Gulf Dr., Sanibel* ☏ *239/472–3145, 800/276–4753* ⊕ *www.casaybelresort.com* ⇱ *40 1-bedroom units, 74 2-bedroom units* ⦿ *No meals.*

$$$ ⌂ **Island Inn.** Choose from your own cottage on the beach, or take
RESORT your pick from six different styles of modernized hotel rooms at the most established inn on Sanibel. **Pros:** right on the beach; free breakfast; laundry facilities. **Cons:** minimum stays in season; furniture and bathrooms are dated in some units. $ *Rooms from: $360* ⊠ *3111 West Gulf Dr., Sanibel* ☏ *239/472–1561* ⊕ *www.islandinn.com* ⇱ *49 rooms, 6 cottages* ⦿ *Breakfast.*

$$$ ⌂ **Sanibel Siesta on the Beach.** You might want to move right in and never
RENTAL leave once you discover these luxurious two-bedroom/two-bath con-
FAMILY dos right on the sand. **Pros:** on the beach; swimming pool; free Wi-Fi.
Fodor'sChoice **Cons:** minimum stays; office closes early. $ *Rooms from: $325* ⊠ *1246*
★ *Fulgur St., Sanibel* ☏ *239/472–4117* ⊕ *www.sanibelsiesta.com* ⇱ *67 2-bedroom condos* ⦿ *No meals.*

$$ ⌂ **Seaside Inn.** Tucked among the tropical greenery, this beachfront
HOTEL inn is a pleasant alternative to the area's larger resorts. **Pros:** intimate feel; lots of character; beautiful beachfront. **Cons:** no onsite restaurant; cramped parking lot. $ *Rooms from: $289* ⊠ *541 E. Gulf Dr., Sanibel* ☏ *239/472–1400, 866/565–5092* ⊕ *www.seasideinn.com* ⇱ *32 rooms, 6 cottages, 4 suites* ⦿ *Breakfast.*

8

$$
RESORT
FAMILY

☒ **Sundial Beach Resort and Spa.** Renovated in 2013 to the tune of $5 million, Sanibel's largest resort encompasses 400 privately owned studio, one-, two-, and three-bedroom low-rise condo units, about half of which are in its rental program. **Pros:** great beach; plenty of amenities; no charge for beach chairs. **Cons:** conference crowds; packed pool area, $30 per night resort fee. $ *Rooms from: $279* ☒ *1451 Middle Gulf Dr., Sanibel* ☎ *239/472–4151, 866/565–5093* ⊕ *www.sundialresort. com* ⇥ *184 1-, 2-, and 3-bedroom units (varies according to rental program participants)* ⊚ *No meals.*

$$
HOTEL

☒ **Waterside Inn.** Palm trees, sea-grape trees, pastel cottages, and a tiki on the Gulf set the scene at this quiet beachside vacation spot. **Pros:** beachfront location; intimate feel; small pets allowed in most cottages. **Cons:** office closes at night; cottage interiors are a bit worn; parking for only one car per unit. $ *Rooms from: $278* ☒ *3033 W. Gulf Dr., Sanibel* ☎ *239/472–1345, 800/741–6166* ⊕ *www.watersideinn.net* ⇥ *4 rooms, 10 efficiencies, 13 cottages* ⊚ *No meals.*

$$$
HOTEL

☒ **West Wind Inn.** Families and couples flock to this resort not only for its quiet, upscale West Gulf Drive location, but also for its affordability. **Pros:** on the beach; quiet side of the island; laundry facilities on site. **Cons:** Wi-Fi can be sporadic; pool towels are small and wafer-thin. $ *Rooms from: $313* ☒ *3345 West Gulf Dr., Sanibel* ☎ *239/472–1541* ⊕ *www.westwindinn.com* ⇥ *103 rooms.* ⊚ *No meals.*

CAPTIVA

$$$
RESORT
FAMILY
Fodor's Choice
★

☒ **South Seas Island Resort.** This full-service 330-acre resort feels as lush as its name suggests, and with 18 swimming pools (one with two tubular slides), private restaurants and shops, a full-service spa, a nature center stocked with live animals, a family interactive center, and a 9-hole golf course, it won't disappoint. **Pros:** full range of amenities; exclusive feel; car-free transportation. **Cons:** high rates in season; a bit isolated; spread out. $ *Rooms from: $339* ☒ *5400 Plantation Rd., Captiva* ☎ *239/472–5111, 888/222–7848* ⊕ *www.southseas.com* ⇥ *106 rooms, 365 suites* ⊚ *No meals.*

$$
B&B/INN

☒ **'Tween Waters Inn.** Besides its great beach-to-bay location, this inn has historic value and in 2011 was listed in the National Register of Historic Places. **Pros:** great views; lots of water-sports options; free Wi-Fi. **Cons:** beach is across the road. $ *Rooms from: $250* ☒ *Captiva Dr., Captiva* ☎ *239/472–5161, 800/223–5865* ⊕ *www.tween-waters.com* ⇥ *48 rooms, 24 studios, 41 1-bedroom suites, 4 2-bedroom suites, 2 3-bedroom suites, 19 cottages* ⊚ *Breakfast.*

SHOPPING

Sanibel is known for its art galleries, shell shops, and one-of-a-kind boutiques; the several small open-air shopping complexes are inviting, with their tropical flowers and shady ficus trees.

SANIBEL

Periwinkle Place. The largest complex of outdoor Sanibel shopping has about 25 shops in a parklike setting. ☒ *2075 Periwinkle Way, Sanibel* ☎ *734/769–2289* ⊕ *www.periwinkleplace.com.*

Seashells.com. Among the island's cache of shell shops, this one is favored by serious collectors and crafters because of its reasonable prices and the knowledgeable family that runs it. For shell gifts, the family operates another little shop right behind the warehouse-sized one. It's super easy to find, right on the main drag. ✉ *905 Fitzhugh St., Sanibel* 🕾 *239/472–1603* ⊕ *www.seashells.com.*

She Sells Sea Shells. At She Sells Sea Shells, everything imaginable is made from shells, from mirrors to lamps to Christmas ornaments. The owner wrote the book on shell art, and you can buy it here. You can also purchase local shells, like the prized junonia and pick up a T-shirt at a fair price. ✉ *1157 Periwinkle Way, Sanibel* 🕾 *239/472–6991* ⊕ *www. sanibelshellcrafts.com.*

CAPTIVA

Fodor's Choice ★ **Jungle Drums.** Expect the unexpected in wildlife art, where fish, sea turtles, and other wildlife are depicted with utmost creativity and touches of whimsy. If you're looking for souvenirs above and beyond the usual, or unique jewelry, paintings, sculptures, and pottery—this is the place. ✉ *11532 Andy Rosse La., Captiva* 🕾 *239/395–2266* ⊕ *www. jungledrumsgallery.com.*

SPORTS AND THE OUTDOORS

BIKING

Everyone bikes around flat-as-a-pancake Sanibel and Captiva—on bikeways that edge the main highway in places, on the road through the wildlife refuge, and along side streets. Free maps are available at bicycle liveries.

Billy's Bikes. Rent by the hour or the day from this Sanibel outfitter, which also rents motorized scooters and leads Segway tours. ✉ *1470 Periwinkle Way, Sanibel* 🕾 *239/472–5248* ⊕ *www.billysrentals.com.*

Yolo Watersports. Bikes (and watersport recreation rentals) of all kinds are available at this Captiva operator. Gear is also for sale. ✉ *11534 Andy Rosse La., Captiva* 🕾 *239/472–1296* ⊕ *www.yolowatersports.com.*

CANOEING AND KAYAKING

Tarpon Bay Explorers. One of the best ways to scout out the wildlife refuge is by paddle. Rent a canoe or kayak from the refuge's official concessionaire and explore at your leisure. The kayak water trail is easy to follow, simply paddle your way along 17 markers and see a bevy of birds and other wildlife. Guided tours by kayak or pontoon boat are also offered and worthwhile for visitors unfamiliar with the ecosystem. Their on-site touch tank gives a hands-on learning experience with local aquatic life. ✉ *900 Tarpon Bay Rd., Sanibel* 🕾 *239/472–8900* ⊕ *www.tarponbayexplorers.com.*

FISHING

Local anglers head out to catch mackerel, pompano, grouper, snook, snapper, tarpon, and shark.

'Tween Waters Marina. On Captiva, this is the place to look for guides. You can also rent kayaks, canoes, stand-up paddleboards, and other recreational watercrafts. ✉ *'Tween Waters Inn, 15951 Captiva Dr., Captiva* 🕾 *239/472–5161* ⊕ *www.tween-waters.com/marina.php.*

8

GOLF

Dunes Golf & Tennis Club. When your back nine are sanctioned as a wildlife preserve by the Audubon Cooperative Society—even if you play poorly—you're rewarded with lusher than lush fairways and more wildlife than you can shake a stick at. Bring your camera if you golf here, as it's not every day that bald eagles watch you play. Water hazards at every hole will have you losing more balls than usual, so bring plenty. Hole no. 10 is the toughest, which explains why most wish it were a par 5 instead of a par 4. Go for a long, straight tee shot and watch out for the water (and the gators). ✉ *949 Sandcastle Rd., Sanibel* ☎ *239/472–2535* ⊕ *www.dunesgolfsanibel.com* 🖱 *$110* ⛳ *18 holes. 5583 yards. par 70.*

FORT MYERS BEACH (ESTERO ISLAND)

18 miles southwest of Fort Myers.

Crammed with motels, hotels, and restaurants, Estero Island is one of Fort Myers's more frenetic gulf playgrounds. Dolphins frequently frolic in Estero Bay, part of the Intracoastal Waterway, and marinas provide a starting point for boating adventures, including sunset cruises, sightseeing cruises, and deep-sea fishing. At the southern tip, a bridge leads to Lovers Key State Park.

GETTING HERE AND AROUND

San Carlos Boulevard in Fort Myers leads to Fort Myers Beach's high bridge, Times Square, and Estero Boulevard, the island's main drag. Estero Island is 18 miles southwest of Fort Myers.

BEACHES

Lovers Key State Park. Once a little-known secret, this out-of-the-way park encompassing 1,616 acres on four barrier islands and several uninhabited islets is popular among beachgoers and birders. Bike, hike, walk, or paddle the park's trails (rentals available); go shelling on its 2½ miles of white-sand beach; take a boat tour; or have a beach picnic under the trees. Trams run regularly from 9 to 4:30 to deliver you and your gear to South Beach. The ride is short but often dusty. North Beach is a five-minute walk from the concession area and parking lot. Watch for osprey, bald eagles, herons, ibis, pelicans, and roseate spoonbills, or sign up for a free excursion to learn fishing and nature photography. On the park's bay side, across the road from the beach entrance, playgrounds and a picnic area cater to families, plus there are boat ramps, kayak rentals, and a bait shop. **Amenities:** food and drink; parking (fee); showers; toilets; water sports. **Best for:** swimming; walking. ✉ *8700 Estero Blvd.* ☎ *239/463–4588* ⊕ *www.floridastateparks. org/loverskey* 🖱 *$4–$8 per vehicle, $2 for pedestrians and bicyclists* ☉ *Daily 8–sunset.*

FAMILY **Lynn Hall Memorial Park.** At the 17-acre park in the commercial northern part of Estero Island, the wide, sandy shore slopes gradually into the usually tranquil and warm gulf waters, providing safe swimming for children. And since houses, restaurants, condominiums, and hotels (including the Best Western Beach Resort and Pink Shell Resort north of the parking lot) line most of the beach, you're never far from civilization.

There are picnic pavilions and barbecue grills, as well as playground equipment and a free fishing pier. The park is part of a pedestrian mall with a number of beach shops and restaurants steps away. The parking lot fills early on sunny days. **Amenities:** food and drink; parking (fee); showers; toilets; water sports. **Best for:** partiers; sunsets; walking. ⊠ *Estero Blvd. at San Carlos Blvd., to Bowditch Point Park* ☎ *239/463–1116* ⊕ *www.leeparks.org* ᴤ *Parking $2 per hr* ☉ *Daily 7 am–11 pm.*

WHERE TO EAT

$$ ✕ **Doc Ford's Rum Bar & Grille.** For dependably well-prepared food with a water view, Doc Ford's is the top choice in Fort Myers Beach. A spinoff of a Sanibel Island original, its name and theme come from a murder-mystery series by local celebrity author Randy Wayne White. The Yucatan shrimp—steamed in the shell with spicy key lime butter—has earned acclaim. Other choice picks include the beach bread, pulled pork sandwich, banana leaf–wrapped snapper, shrimp and grits with tomatillo sauce, and penne with rock shrimp. Live bands play weekend and Wednesday nights. ⑤ *Average main: $20* ⊠ *708 Fisherman's Wharf* ☎ *239/765–9660* ⊕ *www.docfordsfortmyersbeach.com* ᴤ *Reservations not accepted.*

MODERN AMERICAN

$$ ✕ **Matanzas Inn.** Watch boats coming and going whether you sit inside or out at this rustic Old Florida–style restaurant right on the docks alongside the Intracoastal Waterway. When the weather cooperates, enjoy the view from the shaded outdoor tables. Inside, a rustic shack gives way to a more formal dining area in the back; there's a bar upstairs with sweeping views, pizza, and live music nightly. You can't miss with shrimp from the local fleets—delicately cornmeal-breaded, stuffed, or dipped in rum and coconut. Landlubbers can choose from ribs and steak. This is true Fort Myers Beach style, meaning service can be a bit gruff—and slow. ⑤ *Average main: $18* ⊠ *416 Crescent St.* ☎ *239/463–3838* ⊕ *www. matanzas.com* ᴤ *Reservations not accepted.*

SEAFOOD

$$ ✕ **Parrot Key Caribbean Grill.** For something more contemporary than Fort Myers Beach's traditional shrimp and seafood houses, head to San Carlos Island on the east side of the high bridge where the shrimp boats dock. Parrot Key sits marinaside near the shrimp docks and exudes merriment with its Floribbean cuisine and island music. The all-day menu takes tropical cues with dishes such as habanero-pepper wings; corned beef, turkey, or grouper reuben; filet topped with blue cheese; and day's catch with your choice of sauce. There's live entertainment most nights. ⑤ *Average main: $20* ⊠ *2500 Main St.* ☎ *239/463–3257* ⊕ *www.myparrotkey.com* ᴤ *Reservations not accepted.*

SEAFOOD

$ ✕ **The Plaka.** A casual longtimer and a favorite for a quick breakfast, lunch breaks, and sunset dinners, Plaka—Greek for "fun"—has typical Greek fare such as moussaka, pastitsio, gyros, and roast lamb, as well as burgers, sandwiches, fried seafood, and strip steak. It lies along a row of casual sidewalk restaurants in a pedestrian mall near the beach. There's indoor dining, but grab a seat on the porch or under an umbrella on the patio for the best people-watching and sunset view. ⑤ *Average main: $13* ⊠ *1001 Estero Blvd.* ☎ *239/463–4707* ᴤ *Reservations not accepted.*

GREEK

8

WHERE TO STAY

$$ ⛉ **DiamondHead.** This 12-story resort sits on the beach, and many of the
RESORT   suites, especially those on higher floors, have stunning views. **Pros:** on
FAMILY   the beach; nice views; kitchen facilities. **Cons:** heavy foot and car traf-
fic; tiny fitness center; not the best value on the beach. ⑤ *Rooms from:*
$289 ✉ 2000 Estero Blvd. ☎ 239/765–7654, 888/765–5002 ⊕ www.
diamondheadfl.com ⇄ 121 suites ⦿⦿| *No meals.*

$$ ⛉ **Harbour House.** This condo-hotel adds a degree of beach luxury with
RENTAL   brightly painted and sea-motif studios and one- and two-bedroom
condos, all privately owned. **Pros:** close to lots of restaurants; roomy
units; all have private balconies or lanais; free covered parking. **Cons:**
a walk to the beach; not great views from most rooms. ⑤ *Rooms from:*
$220 ✉ 450 Old San Carlos Blvd. ☎ 239/463–0700, 866/998–9250
⊕ *www.harbourhouseattheinn.com ⇄ 6 studios, 15 1-bedroom condos,*
13 2-bedroom condos ⦿⦿| *No meals.*

$$ ⛉ **Lovers Key Resort.** Views can be stupendous from upper floors in this
RENTAL   14-story tower just north of Lovers Key State Park. **Pros:** excellent
views; off the beaten path; spacious accommodations. **Cons:** not a true
beach; far from shopping and restaurants; limited amenities. ⑤ *Rooms*
from: $270 ✉ 8771 Estero Blvd. ☎ 239/765–1040, 877/798–4879
⊕ *www.loverskey.com ⇄ 100 condominiums* ⦿⦿| *No meals.*

$ ⛉ **Outrigger Beach Resort.** On a wide gulf beach, this casual resort has
RESORT   rooms and efficiencies with configurations to suit different guests'
FAMILY   needs. **Pros:** beautiful beach; water-sports rentals; family-friendly vibe.
Cons: can be noisy; crowded pool area; old-school feel. ⑤ *Rooms from:*
$199 ✉ 6200 Estero Blvd. ☎ 239/463–3131, 800/657–5659 ⊕ www.
outriggerfmb.com ⇄ 76 rooms, 68 efficiencies ⦿⦿| *No meals.*

SPORTS AND THE OUTDOORS

BIKING

Fort Myers Beach has no designated trails, so most cyclists ride along
the road.

Fun Rentals. Bike rentals are available from anywhere between two
hours and a week. ✉ *1901 Estero Blvd. ☎ 239/463–8844 ⊕ www.*
funrentals.org.

Lover's Key Adventures and Events. This company rents one-speed bikes,
kayaks, canoes and concessions in Lovers Key State Park. Fees for adult
bikes are $20 for a half day, $25 for a full day. ✉ *8700 Estero Blvd.*
☎ *239/765–7788 ⊕ www.loverskeyadventures.com.*

CANOEING

Lover's Key Adventures and Events. Lovers Key State Park offers kayak
and canoe rentals and guided kayaking tours of its bird-filled estu-
ary. Guided tours cost $55 (call for dates and times). Rentals begin
at $38 for a half day. ✉ *8700 Estero Blvd. ☎ 239/765–7788 ⊕ www.*
loverskeyadventures.com.

FISHING

Getaway Deep Sea Fishing. Arrange anything from half-day party-boat
charters to full-day excursions, fishing equipment included. Rates start
at $60 for a half-day trip. ✉ *18400 San Carlos Blvd. ☎ 800/641–3088,*
239/466–3600 ⊕ www.getawaymarina.com.

FAMILY **SoulMate Charters.** Local "REEL Talk" radio host Captain Rob Modys takes care of everything from the fishing license to the rods and bait on the half-, three-quarter-, and full-day fishing charters he offers around the scenic back bays and tiny islands near Fort Myers Beach. He's a local guide who knows every "honey hole" and will no doubt find fish for you to catch. As a father himself, he's great with kids and has the patience to teach budding anglers. He is based out of Fish Tale Marina. ✉ *7225 Estero Blvd.* ☎ *239/851–1242* ⊕ *www.soulmatecharters.com.*

GOLF

Fort Myers Beach Golf Club. This semi-private executive course designed by Gordon Lewis is open to the public year-round and boasts a half mile of fairways on the bay. Although the greens are not in the best of shape, it's a fun, short course for all levels and ideal for practicing your short game. The course itself and its practice range sit in the midst of a condo community, and you'll find more than snow birds here in the winter. So if you're remotely into wildlife, you should enjoy your round even more. ✉ *4200 Bay Beach La., off Estero Blvd.* ☎ *239/463–2064* ⊕ *www.fmbgolfclub.com* ✉ *$54.95* ⌁ *18 holes. 3091 yards. par 60.*

NAPLES AND VICINITY

As you head south from Fort Myers on U.S. 41, you soon come to Estero and Bonita Springs, followed by the Naples and Marco Island areas, which are sandwiched between Big Cypress Swamp and the Gulf of Mexico. East of Naples the land is largely undeveloped and mostly wetlands, all the way to Fort Lauderdale. Naples itself is a major vacation destination that has sprouted pricey high-rise condominiums and golfing developments, plus a spate of restaurants and shops to match. A similar but not as thorough evolution has occurred on Marco Island, the largest of the Ten Thousand Islands.

ESTERO/BONITA SPRINGS

10 miles south of Fort Myers via U.S. 41.

Towns below Fort Myers have started to flow seamlessly into one another since the opening of Florida Gulf Coast University in San Carlos Park and as a result of the growth of Estero and Bonita Springs, which were agricultural communities until the 1990s. In recent years the area has become a shopping mecca of mega–outdoor malls mixing big-box stores, smaller chains, and restaurants. Bonita Beach, the closest beach to Interstate 75, has evolved from a fishing community into a strip of upscale homes and beach clubs built to provide access for residents of inland golf developments.

GETTING HERE AND AROUND

U.S. 41 (Tamiami Trail) runs right through the heart of these two adjacent communities. You can also reach them by exits 123 and 116 off Interstate 75.

EXPLORING

FAMILY **Everglades Wonder Gardens.** Opened in 1936 by two retired moonshiners from Detroit, the Everglades Wonder Gardens was one of the first roadside attractions in the state and remained little changed until 2013, when the family decided to close its doors—and thus a rich chapter of Florida tourism history—forever. In stepped Florida landscape photographer John Brady, who negotiated a lease with the founding family and transformed the old-style cramped zoological gardens (that once featured Florida panthers, black bears, crocodiles, alligators, and tame Florida deer) into a botanical garden by conserving the flora and fauna following contemporary standards. Now in focus are diverse gardens that include old-growth trees like kapok, banyan, candle nut, egg fruit, plumeria, jaboticaba, mahogany, cashew, avocado and mango, as well as integrated animal exhibits with tortoises, turtles, smaller alligators, flamingos, and a butterfly garden. The original buildings have been preserved and made into a modern gallery that showcases Brady's photography. ⊠ *27180 Old U.S. 41* ☏ *239/992–2591* ⊕ *www. evergladeswondergardens.net* ⊡ *$12* ⊙ *Daily 9–5.*

Koreshan State Historic Site. Tour one of Florida's quirkier chapters from the past. Named for a religious cult that was active at the turn of the 20th century, Koreshan preserves a dozen structures where the group practiced arts, worshipped a male-female divinity, and created its own branch of science called cosmogony, which claimed the universe existed within a giant hollow sphere. The cult floundered when leader Cyrus Reed Teed died in 1908, and in 1961 the four remaining members deeded the property to the state. Rangers and volunteers lead tours and demonstrations, and the grounds are lovely for picnicking and camping. Canoeists paddle the Estero River, fringed by a forest of exotic vegetation the Koreshans planted. ⊠ *3800 Corkscrew Rd., at U.S. 41, Estero* ☏ *239/992–0311* ⊕ *www.floridastateparks.org/koreshan* ⊡ *$5 per vehicle with up to 8 passengers; $4 for single motorist; $2 per bicyclist, pedestrian, or extra passenger* ⊙ *Daily 8–sunset.*

BEACHES

Barefoot Beach Preserve. This one isn't exactly easy to find since it's accessible only by a quiet neighborhood road around the corner from buzzing Bonita Beach Park, but it's well worth the effort if you appreciate natural coastal habitats with fun interpretive programs. Shells here are bountiful, as are gopher tortoises that may park in shade of your car. Stop by the nature center to join a ranger-led walk through the trails and gardens, or take up a paddle and go kayaking. There's no towel-jockeying here along the wide-open space (the preserve as a whole is 342 acres), and refreshments and beach rentals provide ample comfort while you unwind in the pristine sands. **Amenities:** parking (fee); food and drink; showers; toilets; water sports. **Best for:** solitude; walking. ⊠ *5901 Bonita Beach Rd., at Barefoot Beach Rd.* ☏ *239/591–8596* ⊕ *www.collierparks.com* ⊡ *Parking $8.*

Bonita Beach Park. The joint is always jumping on this rowdy stretch of coast, the easiest by far to reach from the inland areas south of Fort Myers. Local favorite hangout Doc's Beach House, open from breakfast until the wee hours of the night, keeps bellies full and libations flowing.

Other food and sports vendors camp out here, too, making it nearly impossible to resist an ice cream or a ride on a Jet Ski. Shaded pavilions between the parking lot and dunes are a great way to cool off from the sweltering heat—just don't sit too close to the picnickers barbecuing. **Amenities:** showers; toilets; parking (fee); food and drink; water sports. **Best for:** partiers; windsurfing. ⊠ *27954 Hickory Blvd., at Bonita Beach Rd.* ☎ *239/949–4615* ⊕ *www.leeparks.org* 🚗 *Parking $2 per hr.*

WHERE TO EAT

$$$ ✕ **Angelina's Ristorante.** Here it's all about the experience—one of the
ITALIAN most indulgent, pampered meals you'll ever eat. Formally trained wait-
Fodor's Choice staff attend to your every need in this temple of traditional Italian
★ cuisine. A dramatic wine tower hovers over the main room; the plush private booths surrounding it are the best tables (call early to snag one). The taste circus begins with an amuse bouche. Pick between antipasti, crispy flatbreads, and wholesome soups before moving on to homemade pastas and grilled meats. Absolutely try the butternut squash ravioli, an inventive version with citrus-tomato butter and truffled almonds. The evening ends with a complimentary nightcap. There is also a great prix-fixe menu. ■TIP→ **This is an upscale restaurant. Don't show up in flip-flops, jeans, or shorts; the staff may be too polite to turn you away, but you will be uncomfortable.** ⑤ *Average main: $25* ⊠ *24041 U.S. 41* ☎ *239/390–3187* ⊕ *www.angelinasofbonitasprings.com* ⌓ *Reservations essential* ⊗ *No lunch.*

$$$ ✕ **Blue Water Bistro.** For the convenience of shoppers at Coconut Point,
SEAFOOD several excellent restaurants cluster in the midst of the shopping center. Most are hooked to a chain. This one, although part of a Naples–Bonita Springs dining dynasty, has a personality all its own with a suave indoor–outdoor bar scene and seafood that's anything but timid. Its specialty is grilled fish from around the globe that you can mix and match with a choice of sauces and sides. For instance, try swordfish with a sweet-and-sour mango sauce and coconut sticky rice. Other specialties include a classic burger, Thai lobster, and excellent shrimp scampi taglioni. ⑤ *Average main: $22* ⊠ *Coconut Point, 23151 Village Shops Way* ☎ *239/949–2583* ⊕ *www.bluewaterbistro.net* ⊗ *No lunch.*

$ ✕ **Doc's Beach House.** Right next door to the public access point for Bare-
AMERICAN foot Beach, Doc's has fed hungry beachgoers for decades. Come bare-
FAMILY foot and grab a quick libation or meal downstairs, outside on the beach, or in the courtyard. When the thermometer reaches "searing," take refuge on the air-conditioned second floor, with its great view of beach action. Basic fare on the breakfast and all-day menu includes a popular Angus burger, Chicago-style pizza, and seafood plates. The conch chowder is some of the best in these parts, with just the right amount of fire. ⑤ *Average main: $10* ⊠ *27908 Hickory Blvd.* ☎ *239/992–6444* ⊕ *www.docsbeachhouse.com* ⌓ *Reservations not accepted* ▭ *No credit cards.*

$ ✕ **Old 41 Restaurant.** Locals vote this "best breakfast" and "best Philly
AMERICAN cheesesteak," and mostly locals populate its cheery dining room with its Philadelphia allegiance. For breakfast, don't miss the incredible Texas French toast with homemade caramel and pecans, Carbon's malted Belgian waffles, or eggs and homemade hash with Boar's Head meat. Besides cheesesteak, lunch specialties include Boar's Head hoagies,

8

burgers, in-house-roasted beef or turkey sandwiches, and other comfort food—all served until 3 pm. ■TIP→ Though you can't make a reservation here, you can call ahead to get your name on the waiting list. ⑤ *Average main: $7* ✉ *25091 Bernwood Dr.* ☎ *239/948–4123* ⊕ *www. old41.com* ⚓ *Reservations not accepted* ⊙ *No dinner.*

WHERE TO STAY

$$
RESORT
FAMILY
Fodor'sChoice
★

Hyatt Regency Coconut Point Resort & Spa. This secluded luxury resort, with its marble-and-mahogany lobby and championship golf course, makes a lovely sanctuary for families who want a refined atmosphere, plus fun features like a 140-foot waterslide, a rock climbing wall, and a s'mores fire pit. **Pros:** pampering spa; great ceviche bar; rooms upgraded in 2012. **Cons:** need water shuttle to reach the beach; expensive restaurants. ⑤ *Rooms from: $259* ✉ *5001 Coconut Rd.* ☎ *239/444–1234, 800/554–9288* ⊕ *www.coconutpoint.hyatt.com* ⇗ *454 rooms and suites* ▯◯▯ *No meals.*

$$
HOTEL

Trianon Bonita Bay. Convenient to Bonita Springs's best shopping and dining, this branch of a refined downtown Naples favorite has a peaceful, sophisticated feel and a poolside-lakeside alfresco bar and grill. **Pros:** spacious rooms; intimate atmosphere; complimentary breakfast. **Cons:** sometimes less-than-friendly staff; far from beach; slightly stuffy. ⑤ *Rooms from: $210* ✉ *3401 Bay Commons Dr.* ☎ *239/948–4400, 800/859–3939* ⊕ *www.trianon.com* ⇗ *100 rooms* ▯◯▯ *Breakfast.*

SHOPPING

FAMILY
Coconut Point. A 500-acre planned community is host to one of the area's largest shopping complexes with upscale and big-box stores and restaurants. There's a boardwalk for a breather between impulse purchases, and a castle-theme kids' play area. ✉ *23106 Fashion Dr.* ☎ *239/992–9966* ⊕ *www.shopcoconutpoint.com.*

Miromar Outlets. The complex includes Adidas, Coach, Michael Kors, Nike, Nautica, and more than 140 other stores and eateries, plus a free Playland for kids. ✉ *10801 Corkscrew Rd., Exit 123 off I–75, near Germain Arena* ☎ *239/948–3766* ⊕ *www.miromaroutlets.com.*

SPORTS AND THE OUTDOORS
BIRDING
The last leg of the Great Florida Birding Trail has more than 20 stops in the Lower Gulf Coast. Go to ⊕ *www.floridabirdingtrail.com* for a complete list.

CANOEING
The meandering Estero River is pleasant for canoeing as it passes through Koreshan State Historic Site to the bay.

Estero River Outfitters. The company rents canoes, kayaks, and equipment. ✉ *20991 Tamiami Trail S, Estero* ☎ *239/992–4050* ⊕ *www. esteroriveroutfitters.com.*

NAPLES

21 miles south of Bonita Springs, on U.S. 41.

Poised between the Gulf of Mexico and the Everglades, Naples belies its wild setting and Indian past with the trappings of wealth—neo-Mediterranean-style mansions, neatly manicured golfing developments, revitalized downtown streets lined with galleries and one-of-a-kind shops, and a reputation for lively and eclectic dining. Visitors come for its luxury hotels—including two Ritz-Carltons—its fabulous white-sand beaches, fishing, shopping, theater and arts, and a lofty reputation for golf. Yet with all the highfalutin living, Naples still appeals to families, especially with its water park and the Golisano Children's Museum of Naples that opened in 2012.

Old Naples, the historic downtown section, has two main commercial areas, 5th Avenue South and 3rd Street South, and there's also a small cluster of restaurants right by City Dock on Naples Bay. Farther north on U.S. 41 (the Tamiami Trail, or 9th Street here), hotels, shopping centers, and developments have fast been filling in the area around and south of Vanderbilt Beach, including the dining and shopping meccas Waterside Shops, and the Village on Venetian Bay.

GETTING HERE AND AROUND

A taxi for up to three passengers is about $60–$90 from Southwest Florida International Airport (RSW) in Fort Myers to Naples; each additional person is charged $10. You don't need to reserve in advance; simply go to the ground-transportation booth. If you prefer to book a car or limo pickup in advance, three major companies are Aaron Airport Transportation, Naples Taxi & Limo Services, and Naples Airport Shuttle. In Naples and Marco Island, Collier Area Transit runs regular routes.

Downtown Naples is 15 miles south of Bonita Springs, on U.S. 41. If you're driving here from Florida's east coast, consider Alligator Alley, a toll section of Interstate 75 that's a straight shot from Fort Lauderdale to Naples. In Naples, east–west county highways exiting off Interstate 75 include, from north to south, Immokalee Road (Route 846), Pine Ridge Road (Route 896), and Collier Boulevard (Route 951), which actually goes north–south and takes you also to Marco Island.

Contacts Aaron Airport Transportation ☎ *239/768–1898* ⊕ *www.aarontaxi. com.* **Collier Area Transit (CAT)** ☎ *239/252–7777* ⊕ *www.colliergov. net.* **Naples Airport Shuttle** ☎ *239/430–4747, 888/569–2227* ⊕ *www. naplesairportshuttle.com.* **Naples Taxi & Limo Services** ☎ *239/435-0000, 800/472–1371* ⊕ *www.naplestaxiflorida.com.*

TOURS

If you want someone to be your guide as you go about town, Naples Trolley Tours offers eight narrated tours daily, covering more than 100 points of interest in town. The tour ($27) lasts about two hours, but you can get off and on at no extra cost.

Contacts Naples Trolley Tours ✉ *1010 6th Ave. S* ☎ *239/262–7300, 800/592–0848* ⊕ *www.naplestrolleytours.com* ⊘ *Daily 8:30–5:30.*

VISITOR INFORMATION

Contacts Naples, Marco Island, Everglades Convention and Visitors Bureau ☎ *800/688–3600, 239/225–1013* ⊕ *www.paradisecoast.com.*

EXPLORING

TOP ATTRACTIONS

FAMILY **Collier County Museum.** To get a feel for local history, stroll the nicely presented indoor vignettes and traveling exhibits and outdoor parklike displays at this museum. A Seminole chickee village, native plant garden, swamp buggy, reconstructed 19th-century fort, steam logging locomotive, and more capture important Naples-area developments from prehistoric times to the World War II era. ⊠ *3331 Tamiami Trail E* ☎ *239/252–8476* ⊕ *www.colliermuseums.com* ☜ *Free* ⊙ *Weekdays 9–5.*

FAMILY **Conservancy of Southwest Florida Nature Center.** On 21 acres bordering a tidal lagoon teeming with wildlife, the conservancy finished a massive makeover of its facilities in 2013. Kids of all ages now enjoy the new Dalton Discovery Center, with interactive exhibits on six Florida ecosystems, a sea turtle tank, and other live wildlife exhibits with roughly 150 animals, including a saltwater touch tank. The opening of the wildlife hospital tripled the space of the old one, complete with a new viewing area where you can see staff working on any number of animals. Guided walks through an endangered gopher tortoise preserve and electric boat tours (for ages two and older) on the mangrove-bordered Gordon River depart several times daily. Kayaks are available for rent. ■TIP→ **The electric boat tours are free, and you don't have to pay the admission fee for the center to ride.** ⊠ *1495 Smith Preserve Way* ☎ *239/262–0304* ⊕ *www.conservancy.org* ☜ *$12.95* ⊙ *Mon.–Sat. 9:30–4:30.*

Fodor's Choice **Corkscrew Swamp Sanctuary.** To get a feel for what this part of Florida
★ was like before civil engineers began draining the swamps, drive 17 miles east of North Naples to these 14,000 acres of pine flatwood and cypress, grass-and-sedge "wet prairie," saw-grass marshland, and lakes and sloughs filled with water lettuce. Managed by the National Audubon Society, the sanctuary protects North America's largest remaining stand of ancient bald cypress, 600-year-old trees as tall as 130 feet, as well as endangered birds, such as wood storks, which often nest here. This is a favorite destination for serious birders and is the gateway to the Great Florida Birding and Wildlife Trail. If you spend a couple of hours to take the 2¼-mile self-guided tour along the boardwalk, you'll spot ferns, orchids, and air plants, as well as wading birds and possibly alligators and river otters. A nature center educates you about this precious, unusual habitat with a dramatic re-creation of the preserve and its creatures in the Swamp Theater. ⊠ *375 Sanctuary Rd. W, 17 miles east of I–75 on Rte. 846* ☎ *239/348–9151* ⊕ *www.corkscrew.audubon. org* ☜ *$12* ⊙ *Daily 7–5:30.*

FAMILY **Golisano Children's Museum of Naples.** This bright, cheery 30,000-square-foot ode to playful learning burst onto Naples's cultural scene in 2012 after a decade of much-anticipated planning, and its 12 state-of-the-art permanent galleries do not disappoint. Kids of many ages and abilities (exhibits were designed to be accessible for children with special needs, too) will love the gigantic Banyan Tree, a focal point at 45 feet

Sights ▼

Clam Pass
Beach Park **3**

Collier County
Museum **8**

Conservancy
of Southwest
Florida Nature
Center **5**

Corkscrew Swamp
Sanctuary **13**

Delnor–Wiggins
Pass State Park ..**1**

Golisano Children's
Museum of Naples
(C'mon) **12**

Lowdermilk
Park **6**

Naples Botanical
Garden **10**

Naples Zoo **4**

Palm Cottage **7**

Patty & Jay Baker
Naples Museum
of Art **2**

Rookery Bay
Environmental
Learning Center .**9**

Sun-N-Fun
Lagoon **11**

Restaurants ▼

Baleen **3**

Barbatella **20**

The Bay House ...**4**

Bha! Bha! Persian
Bistro **13**

Chops City Grill **18**

Fernández
The Bull **5**

The Local **7**

Old Naples Pub **21**

Osteria Tulia ... **16**

Sea Salt **19**

USS *Nemo* **10**

Hotels ▼

Bellasera Hotel **14**

Edgewater Beach
Hotel **11**

Inn on Fifth **15**

LaPlaya Beach &
Golf Resort **2**

Naples Bay
Resort **22**

The Naples
Beach Hotel &
Golf Club **12**

Park Shore
Resort **9**

Ritz-Carlton
Golf Resort **6**

Ritz-Carlton,
Naples **1**

Trianon
Old Naples **17**

Waldorf Astoria
Naples **8**

KEY

1 *Sights*

(1) *Restaurants
and Hotels*

tall and a climbing obstacle of sorts; the Farm & Market, a cooperative playground where roles are assigned (a harvester or cashier, for example) to subtly enforce team building and math skills; and the Green Construction zone, where hard hats and ecofriendly building materials will inspire future architects. ■TIP→ It's in the same park as Sun-n-Fun Lagoon, and it's possible to do both in one day. ✉ *North Collier Regional Park, 15080 Livingston Rd.* ☎ *239/514–0084* ⊕ *www.cmon. org* ⌖ *$10* ⊗ *Tues.–Sat. 10–5, Sun. 11–4.*

Naples Botanical Garden. An expansion and renovation of the botanical gardens that finished in 2010 elevated this attraction to one of Naples's most culturally and botanically exciting. Its "gardens with latitude" flourish with plants and architectural and decorative elements from Florida and other subtropical locales including Asia, Brazil, and the Caribbean. Highlights of the 170 acres include a Children's Garden with a butterfly house, treehouse, waterfall, cave, Florida Cracker house, and hidden garden; an infinity water lily pool; an aromatic Enabling Garden with a how-to theme; and a dramatic waterfall feature. At this writing, a new visitor center, café, and restaurant were set to open sometime in fall 2014. ✉ *4820 Bayshore Dr.* ☎ *239/643–7275* ⊕ *www.naplesgarden. org* ⌖ *$12.95* ⊗ *Fri.–Wed. 9–5, Thurs. 8–5.*

FAMILY   **Naples Zoo at Caribbean Gardens.** The lush 44-acre zoo got its start as a botanical garden in 1919 and has since drawn visitors curious to see lions, tigers, bears, leopards, gazelles—and a wildly popular giraffe herd added in 2011. For an extra fee you can feed the gentle, eyelash-batting giants or, in the winter season only, ride aboard dromedary camels. Other exhibits include the cult-favorite honey badgers (only four U.S. zoos have them), whose innocuous-sounding name belies their ferocious ways; a "Snakes Live" interactive area; a pair of endangered Madagascar fossas; a giant ant eater in the South American exhibit added in 2014; and the "Primate Expedition Cruise" that sails past islands populated with monkeys and lemurs. Youngsters can amuse themselves in three play zones, and there are daily meet-the-keeper times, alligator feedings, and live animal shows. ■TIP→ Purchase tickets online for a $3 discount per ticket. ✉ *1590 Goodlette-Frank Rd.* ☎ *239/262–5409* ⊕ *www.napleszoo.org* ⌖ *$19.95, giraffe feeding and camel rides $5 each* ⊗ *Daily 9–5 (gates close at 4).*

Fodor'sChoice   **Patty & Jay Baker Naples Museum of Art.** This cool, contemporary museum
★   in the Naples Philharmonic Center for the Arts displays provocative, innovative pieces, including renowned miniatures, antique walking sticks, modern American and Mexican masters, and traveling exhibits. Dazzling installations by glass artist Dale Chihuly include a fiery cascade of a chandelier and an illuminated ceiling layered with many-hued glass bubbles, glass corkscrews, and other shapes that suggest the sea; alone, this warrants a visit. In 2010, the multimillion-dollar donation of a massive 12-piece Louise Nevelson sculpture installation greatly boosted the museum's importance. ✉ *5833 Pelican Bay Blvd.* ☎ *239/597–1900, 800/597–1900* ⊕ *www.thephil.org* ⌖ *$10* ⊗ *Tues. 10–8, Wed.–Sat. 10–4, Sun. noon–4.*

FAMILY **Rookery Bay Environmental Learning Center.** In the midst of 110,000-acre Rookery Bay National Marine Estuary, the center dramatically interprets the Everglades environment and local history with interactive models, aquariums, an art gallery, a film, tours, and "coastal connections" programs (45 minutes, at 11 and 2 daily). It's on the edge of the estuary, about five minutes east of Marco's north bridge on Collier Boulevard. In 2009 the center debuted a 440-foot pedestrian bridge that spans the reserve's creek from the center's second floor, and connects with a half-mile nature trail for guided or self-guided walks. Kayak and boat tours are also available through advance registration. Exhibits include an interactive research boat, a display on the importance of the Gulf of Mexico to coastal communities, and another on global climate change. ■TIP➜ Kids go free on Fridays in June and July. Also, visit the website for a printable coupon for admission. ⊠ *300 Tower Rd.* ☎ *239/530–5940* ⊕ *www.rookerybay.org* ≊ *$5* ⊗ *May–Oct., weekdays 9–4; Nov.–Apr., Mon-Sat. 9–4.*

WORTH NOTING

Palm Cottage. Houses in 19th-century South Florida were often built of a concrete-like material made of sand and seashells called tabby mortar. For a fine example of such construction, stop by Palm Cottage, built in 1895 and one of the Lower Gulf Coast's few surviving tabby homes. The historically accurate interior contains simple furnishings typical of the period. Next door to the cottage, Norris Gardens was designed to reflect turn-of-the-last-century garden trends. ⊠ *137 12th Ave. S* ☎ *239/261–8164, 800/979–3370 for historic district reservations* ⊕ *www.napleshistoricalsociety.org* ≊ *$10* ⊗ *Tues.–Sat. 1–4.*

FAMILY **Sun-N-Fun Lagoon.** This is a splashy water park across from the children's museum along the eastern edge of town. Interactive water features throughout such as dumping buckets and spray guns will delight younger kids, and there's a Tadpole Pool geared to those age six and under. The whole family will go for the diving pool, lazy river, and slides. The park is generally closed from October to President's Day weekend (except during some local school breaks). ⊠ *North Collier Regional Park, 15000 Livingston Rd.* ☎ *239/252–4021* ⊕ *www.napleswaterpark.com* ≊ *$12* ⊗ *Memorial Day–late Aug., daily 10–5; fall and spring, weekends 10–5 (check website for hrs).*

BEACHES

FAMILY **City of Naples Beach.** There's something here for everyone just west of the Third Street South shopping area, but what gets the most attention by far is the historic pier that extends deep into the gulf and has the best free dolphin-viewing seats around. Sunsets are a nightly ritual, and dodging anglers' poles is par for the course. For a charming landscape away from the commotion, head south on Gulf Shore Boulevard and take your pick of the public access points. They may not have the amenities of the pier—or amenities, period—but the solitude can't be beat. **Amenities:** food and drink; parking (fee); showers; toilets. **Best for:** sunsets; swimming. ⊠ *12th Ave. S at Gulf Shore Blvd.* ☎ *239/213–3062* ≊ *Parking $0.25 per 10 mins* ⊗ *Daily 7–sunset.*

8

Clam Pass Beach Park. A quiet day at the beach gets an adventurous start when you board a tram and careen down a ¾-mile boardwalk through shaded mangroves and a network of canals. At the end is a pretty, secluded patch of sand that still has notable activities because of the family-vacation-magnet Waldorf Astoria Naples just a few steps from the public parking lot. The surf is calm, perfect for swimming, and aside from the usual lying out, shelling, and sand-castle building, you can spring for a kayak and meander around the marsh for a different kind of water experience. **Amenities:** food and drink; parking (fee); showers; toilets; water sports. **Best for:** solitude; swimming. ⊠ *465 Seagate Dr.* ☎ *239/252–4000* ⊕ *www.collierparks.com* 🖃 *Parking $8* ⊘ *Daily 8–sunset.*

Fodor's Choice ★ **Delnor-Wiggins Pass State Park.** This wide, virtually untouched expanse— about 166 acres—of open beach makes visitors feel transported from the bustling high-rises and resorts just a few blocks south. A full roster of eco-inclined features, like a designated fishing zone, hard-bottom reef (one of the only ones in the region and close enough to swim up to), boat dock, and observation tower, hook anglers, nature lovers, and water sports enthusiasts drawn to the peaceful, laid-back vibe. A new concession stand was added in 2013, making food, drinks and beach gear easily accessible to those less inclined to self-catering. **Amenities:** food and drink; parking (fee); showers; toilets; water sports. **Best for:** snorkeling; solitude; walking. ⊠ *11135 Gulf Shore Dr. N* ☎ *239/597–6196* ⊕ *www.floridastateparks.org/delnorwiggins* 🖃 *$6 per vehicle with up to 8 people, $4 for single drivers, $2 for pedestrians and bicyclists* ⊘ *Daily 8–sunset.*

FAMILY **Lowdermilk Park.** Do you prefer your beach loud and active with a big dose of good old-fashioned fun? Kids running around in the surf, volleyballers hitting the sand, and tykes getting up close and personal with the park's most colorful residents, the red-throated Muscovy ducks, are all part of the Lowdermilk experience. Shallow waters and little-to-no wave action beg for a dip from even the most hesitant swimmer, and thatched umbrellas dotting the shoreline complete the happy tiki vibe and are yours for the taking—assuming you can snag one (they are strictly first come, first served). **Amenities:** food and drink; parking (fee); showers; toilets. **Best for:** swimming; walking. ⊠ *1301 Gulf Shore Blvd. N* ☎ *239/213–3029* 🖃 *Parking 25¢ per 10 min.* ⊘ *Daily 8–sunset.*

Vanderbilt Beach. If a day at the shore just doesn't seem quite complete without a piña colada and serious people-watching, this place is for you. The white powdery sand often looks like a kaleidoscope, with multihued towels and umbrellas dotting the landscape in front of the nearly 3 miles of tony north Naples condos and luxe resorts, including the Ritz-Carlton and LaPlaya. If you walk far enough—which many people do—you come across eye candy of a different kind: the architecturally stunning megamansions of Bay Colony perched up on the dunes. The beach really comes alive at sunset with onlookers. **Amenities:** food and drink; parking (fee); showers; toilets; water sports. **Best for:** partiers; sunsets; walking. ■TIP→ **Stroll up to Gumbo Limbo at the Ritz for the best Floribbean, yet surprisingly not wallet-busting, lunches and panoramic views from a shaded deck.** ⊠ *100 Vanderbilt*

Beach Rd. ☎ *239/252–4000* ⊕ *www.collierparks.com* 🅿 *Parking $8* ☉ *Daily 8–sunset.*

WHERE TO EAT

$$$$
SEAFOOD

✕**Baleen.** The mood cast in this well-appointed dining room and the romantic gulf-view patio that spills onto the sand feels like the perfect Florida restaurant experience. There's only one small problem: lighting is so low at dinner that you can't read the menu, even with its built-in flashlight. Too bad, because that means you also miss the effect of the beautifully presented dishes: Asian pear–and-arugula salad, black grouper with tamarind glaze, grilled scallops paired with polenta and serrano chilies, Grand Marnier crème brûlée, and the like. (Thankfully, there's a great prix-fixe option.) At breakfast, the house-made corned beef hash is divine. For lunch, the lobster Cobb salad is a popular choice. ⑤ *Average main: $37* ✉ *La Playa Beach & Golf Resort, 9891 Gulf Shore Dr.* ☎ *239/598–5707, 800/237–6883* ⊕ *www.laplayaresort. com* ⌂ *Reservations essential.*

$$
ITALIAN

✕**Barbatella.** This trattoria with an edge was the most buzzed-about opening in 2012; it's still just as popular. The restaurant has three dining spaces to suit any whim: the wine bar, with sleek eclectic décor, has a communal table, green ceiling medallions, crystal chandeliers wrapped in birdcages, and a wine dispenser that allows guests to sip their way through 32 bottles (Italian, of course) by the 1-, 3-, or 6-ounce glass. The brick room, with 150-year-old recycled floors, is more casual and open to the kitchen; and the central patio is shaded and relaxed. The menu, straight-up Italian and expertly done, stars refined versions of classics, including bruschetta, fried calamari, lasagna, and wood-fired pizza. Don't miss the house's sweetest treat: a gelateria that's open to passersby on Third Street South is a partnership with artisan-chocolate king Norman Love. ⑤ *Average main: $20* ✉ *1290 3rd St. S* ☎ *239/263–1955* ⊕ *www.barbatellanaples.com.*

$$$$
SEAFOOD

✕**The Bay House.** Nestled in a hidden expanse of twisted mangrove trees and flowing canals is one of the area's best restaurants for casual fine dining—and beautifully natural scenery. Restored wooden rowboats and modern chandeliers hang from the ceiling of the main dining room, which is packed almost every night in season. The food is a serious celebration of the sea with Southern accents, like locally caught fish with shrimp hash and green tomato jam. Adjacent Tierney's Tavern & Claw Bar shares the same kitchen but focuses on chilled shellfish and other Southern delights with nightly live music and a more casual vibe. ■TIP➔ Saturday lunches are surprisingly quiet and a perfect time to snag one of the coveted tables closest to the windows. ⑤ *Average main: $32* ✉ *799 Walkerbilt Rd.* ☎ *239/591–3837* ⊕ *www.bayhousenaples. com* ⌂ *Reservations essential* ☉ *No lunch May–Nov.*

$$$
MIDDLE EASTERN

✕**Bha! Bha! Persian Bistro.** Long considered one of Naples's best ethnic restaurants, loyal fans of Bha! Bha! have flocked to a tiny north Naples strip mall year in and year out to indulge in the restaurant's chic Persian atmosphere and cuisine. On the eve of its 15th birthday came a well-deserved present: a brand-new location on bustling Fifth Avenue South. But the move didn't spoil the cooking or the following. All of the old favorites still garner loyal reviews, including plum lamb with

8

DID YOU KNOW?

Beaches are for so much more than sunning and sand-castle building. Many are used for fishing, weddings, and horseback riding. And come July 4, some, like the city of Naples Beach (shown here), draw people at night for viewing fireworks over the water.

tomato-pomegranate sauce, mango-garlic shrimp (which was featured in *Bon Appétit*), and spicy beef in saffron sauce with cucumber yogurt—all made completely from scratch on premises. $ *Average main: $25* ⊠ *865 Fifth Ave. S* ☎ *239/594–5557* ⊕ *www.bhabhapersianbistro.com* ⌂ *Reservations essential.*

$$$$
ECLECTIC

✕ **Chops City Grill.** Count on high-quality cuisine that fuses, as its name suggests, chopstick cuisine and steakhouse mainstays. Sophisticated yet resort-wear casual, it draws everyone from young businesspeople to local retirees. Sushi and Pacific Rim inspirations such as shrimp spring rolls rub elbows with beef carpaccio and watermelon salad with goat cheese and pecans. Grilled seafood and fine cuts of meat like dry-aged ribeyes and strip steaks come with side options such as "wild" sherry-laced mushrooms and four-cheese mac. For dessert, sip a frothy Chocolate Kiss martini. Dine alfresco or inside with a view of the kitchen. There's a second location at Brooks Grand Plaza, U.S. 41 at Coconut Road, in Bonita Springs (☎ *239/992–4677*). $ *Average main: $32* ⊠ *837 5th Ave. S* ☎ *239/262–4677* ⊕ *www.chopscitygrill. com* ⌂ *Reservations essential* ⊘ *No lunch.*

$$
CUBAN

✕ **Fernández The Bull.** Intrepid palates venture several miles inland to get a taste of authentic, home-cooked Cuban specialties at this simple store-front café. Stick to the basics, and don't miss the lemony *lechon asado* (slow-roasted pork that's grilled and basted with garlic) or *ropa vieja* (shreds of flank steak simmered in tomato sauce with heaps of peppers and onions). In chichi Naples, the prices are good, and the portions are better: one entrée is enough for dinner and lunch the next day, as all are served with salads, big slabs of toasted garlic bread, and two sides. The bar is wine-and-beer only; the mojitos are faux-jitos but still pretty tasty. $ *Average main: $17* ⊠ *1201 Piper Blvd. #10* ☎ *239/254–9855* ⊕ *www.fernandezthebull.com.*

$$
CONTEMPORARY
Fodor's Choice
★

✕ **The Local.** You'll find an epicurean take on healthy eating at this farm-and-sea-to-table bistro that, as the name declares, looks almost exclusively to local suppliers to stock its kitchen. Though in a strip mall a few blocks inland, the setting is hip and polished with an interior that evokes both the beach and the farm, no doubt a reflection of the young and stylish owners' passion for nourishment. Foodies, the health-conscious, hipsters, and retirees mix equally at The Local, where ingredient origins are proudly traced: microgreens come from Herban Gardens in Fort Myers, dairy and cheese from Winter Park, and organic produce from any number of Florida growers. Choose from healthy options like a superfood salad to more savory indulgences like pork shoulder in natural jus with mango mustard. $ *Average main: $18* ⊠ *5323 Airport Pulling Rd. N* ☎ *239/596–3276* ⊕ *www.thelocalnaples.com.*

$
AMERICAN

✕ **Old Naples Pub.** Local blue- and white-collar workers gather with shoppers for affordable sandwiches and seafood in the vaulted, vine-twisted courtyard of this traditional pub, which has been tucked away from shopping traffic at 3rd Street Plaza since the late 1980s. It strikes one as an everybody-knows-your-name kind of place, with jars of pickles on the tables and friendly bartenders. Taste any of 25 kinds of beer and order fried "ungrouper" sandwiches (made with "mild flaky white filet" as grouper becomes rarer), burgers, crispy chicken salad,

8

and nachos, as well as such not-so-traditional pub grub as grilled fresh catch-of-the-day and fried gator tail. There's musical entertainment Wednesday and Sunday year-round. ⑤ *Average main: $15* ✉ *255 13th Ave. S* ☎ *239/649–8200* ⊕ *www.naplespubs.com* ⚄ *Reservations not accepted.*

$$$
ITALIAN
Fodor's Choice
★

✕**Osteria Tulia.** An ancestral air pervades at this intimate yet lively restaurant on 5th Avenue, where the Sicilian-born chef (and part owner) drives an authentic celebration of the Italian table. Opened in 2013, the concept is a refreshing departure from long, ornate menus and focuses on simple, finely produced house-made Italian cuisine in a rustic, refined setting. Everything wooden was crafted from a dilapidated barn in north Florida, and the 1940s-era bricks came from a reclaimed Chicago firehouse. The signature fennel sausage is homemade from a family recipe, and the kitchen cures its own pancetta, makes its own mozzarella and ricotta cheeses, and makes and extrudes all pastas on-site. Peasant recipes for things like rabbit and wild boar shine on the menu next to more traditional mains like heritage pork and free-range chicken. ⑤ *Average main: $25* ✉ *466 5th Ave. S.* ☎ *239/213–2073* ⊕ *www.tulianaples.com.*

$$$$
MEDITERRANEAN
Fodor's Choice
★

✕**Sea Salt.** Naples's hottest upscale restaurant draws a crowd of connoisseurs to its modern coral-rock dining room that spills out onto the sidewalk. Venetian-born Chef Fabrizio Aielli puts a New World spin on traditional Italian with his nightly changing menu often incorporating local and organic ingredients. Everyone gets a sea-salt sampler. The best way to start is to dabble in charcuterie and European cheese. The finest quality meats and seafood go into dishes including Wagyu beef and Kurobuta pork, grilled local black grouper, and dry-packed scallops with lemon-caper oil. At lunch, choose between creative sandwiches and salads. ⑤ *Average main: $35* ✉ *1186 3rd St. S* ☎ *239/434–7258* ⊕ *www.seasaltnaples.com* ⚄ *Reservations essential.*

$$$
SEAFOOD
Fodor's Choice
★

✕**USS Nemo.** Don't be fooled by the tacky glowing sign from the highway: most Neapolitans swear this is *the* place for seafood in town, which is why you should still make a reservation even in the heat of summer. The food is in the vein of fine dining but served in a whimsical setting with portholes, antique bronze diving gear, and colorful sculptures of fish. Speaking of fish, almost all are locally caught and reach new depths of deliciousness with eclectic, often Asian-inspired preparations. The house signature miso-broiled sea bass with citrus-ginger butter strikes the right balance between sweet and savory; the ginger-steamed halibut with soy-lime dressing and the herb-grilled tuna with warm goat cheese and lobster risotto are also winners. ⑤ *Average main: $24* ✉ *3745 Tamiami Trail N* ☎ *239/261–6366* ⊕ *www.ussnemorestaurant. com* ⚄ *Reservations essential* ⊘ *No lunch weekends.*

WHERE TO STAY

$$$
HOTEL

▦**Bellasera Hotel.** This downtown hotel is just far enough "off Fifth" to be away from the dining-and-shopping foot traffic but close enough for convenience, and it feels like a lovely Italian villa with its red tile roofs and burnt-ochre stucco. **Pros:** spacious accommodations with full home amenities (kitchens, living areas, porches and balconies); on-site restaurant and near downtown restaurants; free bikes for guests; first-come, first-served private cabanas at pool. **Cons:** must take shuttle to beach; on a busy highway (though surprisingly quiet). $ *Rooms from: $309* ⊠ *221 9th St. S* ☎ *239/649–7333, 888/612–1115* ⊕ *www. bellaseranaples.com* ⟿ *10 studios, 30 1-bedroom suites, 48 2-bedroom suites, 12 3-bedroom suites* ⦿ *No meals.*

$$$ **Edgewater Beach Hotel.** At this all-suite, beachfront property at the
HOTEL north end of scenic Gulf Shore Boulevard, the rooms are large and refreshing, exuding a relaxed, contemporary vibe. **Pros:** beautiful beach; quiet; exquisite views. **Cons:** far from shopping; surrounded closely by high-rises; no tubs in some rooms. $ *Rooms from: $389* ⊠ *1901 Gulf Shore Blvd. N* ☎ *239/403–2000, 888/564–1308* ⊕ *www. edgewaternaples.com* ⟿ *97 1-bedroom suites, 28 2-bedroom suites* ⦿ *No meals.*

$$$ **Inn on Fifth.** You can't top this luxe hotel if you want to plant your-
HOTEL self in the heart of Naples nightlife and shopping, and its $15 million expansion across the street in 2012 added 32 new club-level suites with their own private lobby and roof deck. **Pros:** central location; metro vibe; spa has free sauna for guests. **Cons:** pool is eye-level with power lines; beach is a long stroll or shuttle ride away. $ *Rooms from: $385* ⊠ *699 5th Ave. S* ☎ *239/403–8777, 888/403–8778* ⊕ *www.innonfifth. com* ⟿ *117 rooms, 2 suites* ⦿ *No meals.*

$$$$ **LaPlaya Beach & Golf Resort.** LaPlaya bespeaks posh and panache down
RESORT to the smallest detail—note the Balinese-style spa, marble bathrooms,
Fodor's Choice and a stuffed sea turtle toy to cuddle during your stay. **Pros:** right on the
★ beach; high-end amenities; beautiful rooms (renovated in 2012). **Cons:** golf course is off property; no locker rooms in spa. $ *Rooms from: $619* ⊠ *9891 Gulf Shore Dr.* ☎ *239/597–3123, 800/237–6883* ⊕ *www. laplayaresort.com* ⟿ *180 rooms, 9 suites* ⦿ *No meals.*

$$$ **Naples Bay Resort.** This place, a boater's dream, has the class, polish,
RESORT and services associated with a property its size and scope (20 prime
FAMILY canal-front acres) but has the feel of a boutique hotel. **Pros:** on-site marina; free shuttle to beach; walking distance to downtown; $5 water taxi to other bayside hot spots. **Cons:** tennis courts and most pools a trek from main building; no beach; some highway noise. $ *Rooms from: $369* ⊠ *1500 5th Ave. S* ☎ *239/530–1199, 866/605–1199* ⊕ *www.naplesbayresort.com* ⟿ *20 rooms, 29 1-bedroom suites, 36 2-bedroom suites, 108 cottages (minimum 6-night stay in cottages)* ⦿ *No meals.*

$$$$ **The Naples Beach Hotel & Golf Club.** Family-owned and -managed since
RESORT 1946, this art-deco resort is a piece of Naples history—and its stretch
FAMILY of powdery sand has lots of action at all times. **Pros:** terrific beach scene; golf course and driving range on property; complimentary kids' program. **Cons:** expensive nightly rates; have to cross street to reach spa and breakfast dining; though interiors are freshly renovated, signature old-school exterior may not appeal to sleek tastes. $ *Rooms from: $459* ⊠ *851 Gulf Shore Blvd. N* ☎ *239/261–2222, 800/237–7600* ⊕ *www.naplesbeachhotel.com* ⟿ *267 rooms, 42 suites, 10 efficiencies* ⦿ *No meals.*

8

$ **Park Shore Resort.** Well situated near the beaches and shopping off
RENTAL   Gulf Shore Boulevard, this hidden retreat is practical and comfortable,
Fodor'sChoice   offering spacious suites (all with kitchens and screened balconies), a
★   tropical pool and grounds (with upscale gas grills), and a casual calm.
Pros: unbeatable price in Naples; tropical pool and shaded grounds;
quiet. **Cons:** no restaurant; long walk to beach; no shuttle service.
⑤ *Rooms from: $179* ✉ *600 Neoplitan Way* ☎ *800/548–2077* ⊕ *www.
parkshorefl.com* ⤵ *156 rooms* ❍⦿❍ *No meals.*

$$$$ **Ritz-Carlton Golf Resort, Naples.** Ardent golfers with a yen for lux-
RESORT   ury will find their dream vacation at Naples's most elegant golf resort
Fodor'sChoice   where Ritz style prevails and service exceeds your wildest expectations.
★   **Pros:** best golf academy in area; two championship courses at the front
door; plush setting; access to Ritz spa and beach via shuttle; service par
excellence. **Cons:** 10-minute drive to beaches; expensive rates; farther
inland than most properties. ⑤ *Rooms from: $649* ✉ *2600 Tiburón Dr.*
☎ *239/593–2000* ⊕ *www.ritzcarlton.com* ⤵ *295 rooms* ❍⦿❍ *No meals.*

$$$$ **Ritz-Carlton, Naples.** This is a regal Ritz-Carlton, with marble statues
RESORT   and antique furnishings blended with artistic modernity in the rooms,
FAMILY   which were renovated in 2013, and restaurants that now breathe airy
Fodor'sChoice   light-blue and natural tones. **Pros:** flawless service; fun tiki bar and
★   water-sports options; near north Naples shopping and restaurants; private, ultraindulgent spa (guests and members only). **Cons:** high price
tag; hike to downtown; valet parking only; extra charge for beach
umbrellas annoying at this nice a place. ⑤ *Rooms from: $999* ✉ *280
Vanderbilt Beach Rd.* ☎ *239/598–3300* ⊕ *www.ritzcarlton.com* ⤵ *450
rooms* ❍⦿❍ *No meals.*

$$ **Trianon Old Naples.** Refined ladies and gents will feel at home in this
HOTEL   classy boutique hotel that's right smack in the central historic district,
yet enrobed in an aura of privacy two quiet residential blocks south
of Fifth Avenue's bustle. **Pros:** can't-beat location for urbanites; large
rooms; continental breakfast included. **Cons:** limited facilities; must
drive to beach. ⑤ *Rooms from: $289* ✉ *955 7th Ave. S* ☎ *239/435–
9600, 877/482–5228* ⊕ *www.trianon.com* ⤵ *55 rooms, 3 suites*
❍⦿❍ *Breakfast.*

$$ **Waldorf Astoria Naples.** Beach access, a golf club, and top-shelf luxury
RESORT   are all yours at this ultramodern high-rise formerly known as the Naples
FAMILY   Grande; it has a big following with families because of its immense
Fodor'sChoice   free-form pool with a 100-foot waterslide. **Pros:** indulgent spa; great
★   tennis, golf, and kayaking; attentive service; selection of eateries; three
swimming pools. **Cons:** not directly on the beach; golf facility is 6
miles away with no shuttle. ⑤ *Rooms from: $299* ✉ *475 Seagate Dr.*
☎ *239/597–3232, 888/722–1267* ⊕ *www.waldorfastorianaples.com*
⤵ *395 rooms, 79 suites* ❍⦿❍ *No meals.*

NIGHTLIFE AND PERFORMING ARTS
PERFORMING ARTS
Naples is the cultural capital of this stretch of coast.

Naples Players. Musicals and dramas are performed year-round; winter
shows often sell out well in advance. ✉ *Sugden Community Theatre,
701 5th Ave. S* ☎ *239/263–7990* ⊕ *www.naplesplayers.org.*

Philharmonic Center for the Arts. This 1,473-seat performance center hosts plays, concerts, and exhibits year-round, the bulk from September to May. It's home to the 85-piece Naples Philharmonic Orchestra, which presents both classical and pop concerts. The Miami City Ballet performs here during its winter season. ⊠ *5833 Pelican Bay Blvd.* ☎ *239/597–1900, 800/597–1900* ⊕ *www.thephil.org.*

NIGHTLIFE

The heart of Old Naples, 5th Avenue South, already known for its scene of lively bars and sidewalk cafés, has undergone a renaissance of sorts. In 2012 alone at least three new spots debuted.

Avenue Wine Café. Young, casual oenophiles camp out here; there's also an impressive craft-beer list (that includes brews from the new Naples Beach Brewery) as well as cigars. ⊠ *483 5th Ave. S* ☎ *239/403–9463.*

Burn by Rocky Patel. At this part cigar bar, part dance club, you can expect pretty young things grooving to a house DJ. ⊠ *9110 Strada Pl.* ☎ *239/653–9013* ⊕ *www.burnbyrockypatel.com.*

Naples Beach Brewery. With the opening of Naples Beach Brewery in 2013, the Naples scene isn't only about fine wine anymore. This microbrewery's concoctions can be found in almost 50 local bars and restaurants including some of Naples's finest dining establishments. Eight brews range from the straw-color Weizen to the Naples Beach Stout. Look for a plam tree logo on bottles and taps signifying the local craft beers, or head directly to the brewery on Friday and Saturday afternoons for guided tours and tastings. But don't expect to be wowed by a big gleaming factory, as this brewery is small and authentic, located in an industrial neighborhood sandwiched between hardware manufacturers–the real deal. ⊠ *4110 Enterprise Ave, Ste. 217* ☎ *239/304–8795* ⊕ *www.naplesbeachbrewery.com* ⌑ *$15* ☉ *Fri. 4 pm–8 pm, Sat. 3 pm–7 pm.*

Osetra. A hint of SoBe on the Gulf Coast serves champagne and caviar in a sleek setting on 5th Avenue South. ⊠ *469 Fifth Ave. S* ☎ *239/776–7938* ⊕ *www.osetranaples.com.*

The Pub. Long lists of brews, flat-screens, and fun British décor attract a lively crowd to this popular outpost of a small, family-run chain. ⊠ *9118 Strada Pl.* ☎ *239/594–2748* ⊕ *www.experiencethepub.com.*

Vergina. The mature crowd hits the dance floor to Gloria Gaynor and the Bee Gees. ⊠ *700 Fifth Ave. S* ☎ *239/659–7008* ⊕ *www.verginarestaurant.com.*

SHOPPING
SHOPPING AREAS

Tin City. Near 5th Avenue South, a collection of tin-roof former boat docks along Naples Bay has more than 30 boutiques, eateries, and souvenir shops, with everything from jewelry and T-shirts to Jet Ski rentals and seafood. ⊠ *1200 5th Ave. S* ⊕ *www.tin-city.com.*

Village on Venetian Bay. Stroll along the classy boutiques, nearly 30 in all, that line the water's edge, and grab a bite at one of the excellent restaurants, all with fantastic views. ⊠ *4200 Gulf Shore Blvd. N* ⊕ *www.venetianvillage.com.*

8

Waterside Shops. Only in South Florida can you find more than four dozen upscale stores plus eateries wrapped around a series of waterfalls, waterways, and shaded open-air promenades. Saks 5th Avenue and Nordstrom are the main anchors; Burberry, Cartier, Ralph Lauren, and St. John are in the mix. ⊠ *5415 Tamiami Trail N* ☎ *239/598–1605* ⊕ *www.watersideshops.com.*

SPECIALTY SHOPS

Gattle's. This downtown shop stocks pricey-but-pretty linens. ⊠ *1250 3rd St. S* ☎ *239/262–4791, 800/344–4552* ⊕ *www.gattles.com.*

It's New to You. The most upscale clothes sometimes go to this consignment shop. ⊠ *933 Creech Rd.* ☎ *239/263–8400.*

Marissa Collections. *The* destination in Naples for ultra-high-end designer women's wear. ⊠ *1167 3rd St. S* ☎ *239/263–4333* ⊕ *www. marissacollections.com.*

Options. Naples's ladies who lunch often donate their year-old Armani castoffs and fine collectibles to this terrific thrift shop whose proceeds benefit the Shelter for Abused Women & Children. ⊠ *968 2nd Ave. N* ☎ *239/434–7115* ⊕ *www.optionsnaples.org.*

Regatta. Among 5th Avenue South's selection with a decidedly local flair, this shop sells personal and home accessories with a sense of humor and style. ⊠ *760 5th Ave. S* ☎ *239/262–3929.*

SPORTS AND THE OUTDOORS

BIKING

Naples Cyclery. For daily rentals, rates range from $6 to $32 for two hours and selections include two- and four-passenger surreys, tandems, and more; weekly rentals are also available. ■ **TIP→ If you need a little boost, have breakfast, lunch, or an espresso at the store's Fit & Fuel Café, where there's a serious fitting room if you're in the market for a custom-fit bike.** ⊠ *Pavilion Shopping Center, 813 Vanderbilt Beach Rd.* ☎ *239/566–0600* ⊕ *www.naplescyclery.com.*

BOATING AND FISHING

Mangrove Outfitters. Take a guided boat and learn to cast and tie flies. ⊠ *4111 Tamiami Trail E* ☎ *239/793–3370, 888/319–9848* ⊕ *www. mangroveoutfitters.com.*

Naples Watersports at Port-O-Call Marina. A nineteen-foot center-console boat and several 22-foot deck boats start at $130 for two hours. ⊠ *550 Port-O-Call Way* ☎ *239/774–0479* ⊕ *www.naples-boatrentals.com.*

FAMILY　**Pure Naples.** Half-day deep-sea and backwater fishing trips depart twice daily. Sightseeing cruises and thrilling jet tours are also available, along with jet ski and boat rentals and private charters. ⊠ *Tin City, 1200 5th Ave. S* ☎ *239/263–4949* ⊕ *www.purenaples.com.*

GOLF

Lely Resort Golf and Country Club. Flamingo Island (designed by Robert Trent Jones) and The Mustang (designed by Lee Trevino) are the two championship courses open to the public at Lely Resort. Flamingo Island features white-sand bunkers, hourglass fairways, and large greens, along with its signature 3200-yard hole no. 5 with a water-rimmed rolling fairway, bunkers, and two bridges providing the only access to the mainland. The Mustang features 12 lakes and rolling fairways. There's also a John Jacobs' golf school on premises. ✉ *8004 Grand Lely Blvd.* ☎ *239/793–2600* ⊕ *www.lelyresortgolfandcountryclub.com* 🖃 *$169* 🏌 *Flamingo Island: 18 holes. 7171 yards. par 72. The Mustang: 18 holes. 7217 yards. par 72.*

The Naples Beach Hotel & Golf Club. This historic club has weekly clinics, a driving range, a putting green, and is replete with nostalgia as the region's oldest course, built in 1929. It was last redesigned in 1998 by golf architect Ron Garl, and refurbished in 2011. ■**TIP→ It has been voted "Top 50 Women Friendly Golf Courses in the U.S." by the magazine** *Golf for Women.* ✉ *851 Gulf Shore Blvd. N* ☎ *239/435–2475* ⊕ *www. naplesbeachhotel.com* 🖃 *$55 for 9 holes, $125 for 18 holes* 🏌 *18 holes. 6488 yards. par 72.*

Tiburón Golf Club. There are two 18-hole Greg Norman–designed courses, the Gold and the Black—an especially difficult course carved right out of a cypress preserve. Challenging and environmentally pristine, the links include narrow fairways, stacked sod wall bunkers, coquina sand, and no roughs. There's also a Rick Smith Golf Academy. ■**TIP→ You cannot book months in advance unless you're staying at one of the Ritz-Carlton hotels. Nonguests can book 10 days out.** ✉ *Ritz-Carlton Golf Resort, 2620 Tiburón Dr.* ☎ *239/593–2201* ⊕ *www.tiburongcnaples. com* 🖃 *$195* 🏌 *Tiburón Gold: 18 holes. 7271 yards. par 74.9. Tiburón Black: 18 holes. 6949 yards. par 75.01.*

MARCO ISLAND

20 miles south of Naples via Rte. 951.

High-rises dominate part of the shores of Marco Island, which is connected to the mainland by two bridges. Yet because of its distance from downtown Naples, it retains an isolated feeling much appreciated by those who love this corner of the world. Some natural areas have been preserved, and the down-home fishing village of Goodland, a 20-minute drive from historic Old Marco, resists change. Fishing, boating, sunning, swimming, and tennis are the primary activities here.

GETTING HERE AND AROUND

From Naples, Collier Boulevard (Route 951) takes you to Marco Island. If you're not renting a car, taxi rides cost about $100 from the regional airport in Fort Myers, and Collier Area Transit (CAT) runs regular buses through the area. Key West Express operates a ferry from Marco Island (from Christmas through Easter) and Fort Myers Beach (year-round) to Key West. The cost for the round trip (less than four hours each way) is $147 from either Fort Myers Beach or Marco Island.

Contacts Collier Area Transit (CAT) ☎ *239/252–7777* ⊕ *www.colliergov. net.* **Key West Express** ✉ *951 Bald Eagle Dr.* ☎ *239/394–9700, 888/539–2628* ⊕ *www.keywestexpress.us.*

8

VISITOR INFORMATION

Contacts Marco Island Area Chamber of Commerce ⊠ *1102 N. Collier Blvd.* ☎ *239/394–7549, 888/330–1422* ⊕ *www.marcoislandchamber.org.* **Naples, Marco Island, Everglades Convention and Visitors Bureau** ☎ *800/688–3600, 239/225–1013* ⊕ *www.paradisecoast.com.*

EXPLORING

Marco Island Historical Museum. Marco Island was once part of the ancient Calusa kingdom. The Marco Cat, a statue found in 1896 excavations, has become symbolic of the island's prehistoric significance. The original is part of the Smithsonian Institution's collection, but a replica of the Marco Cat is among displays illuminating the ancient past at this museum, which opened in January 2011. Three rooms examine the island's history with dioramas, artifacts, and signage: the Calusa Room, Pioneer Room, and Modern Marco Room. A fourth hosts traveling exhibits focusing on the settlement history of the island. Outside, the yard was built to look like a Calusa village atop a shell mound with a water feature and chickee structure. ⊠ *180 S. Heathwood Dr.* ☎ *239/642–1440* ⊕ *www.colliermuseums. com* ☜ *Free* ⊘ *Tues.–Sat. 9–4.*

BEACHES

FAMILY **Tigertail Beach.** On the northwest side of the island is 2,500 feet of both developed and undeveloped areas. Once gulf front, in recent years a sand spit known as Sand Dollar Island has formed, which means the stretch especially at the north end has become mud flats—great for birding. There's plenty of powdery sand further south and across the lagoon that draws a broad base of fans flocking there for its playgrounds, butterfly garden, volleyball nets, and kayak and umbrella rentals. Beach wheelchairs are also available for free use. ∎TIP➔ **The Conservancy of Southwest Florida conducts free educational beach walks at Tigertail Beach every weekday from 8:30am to 9:30am from January to mid-April. Amenities:** food and drink; parking (fee); showers; toilets; water sports. **Best for:** sunset; swimming; walking. ⊠ *490 Hernando Dr.* ☎ *239/252–4000* ⊕ *www.collierparks.com* ☜ *Parking $8* ⊘ *Daily 8–sunset.*

WHERE TO EAT

$$ ✕ **Arturo's.** This place is huge, with expansive Romanesque dining

ITALIAN rooms and more seating on the patio. Still, it fills up year-round with a

Fodor'sChoice strong well-dressed following that appreciates a fun attitude and seri-

★ ous Italian cuisine done comprehensively and traditionally. Start with the plump mussels marinara, then choose from a lengthy list of classic Italian entrées, including homemade pasta. The stuffed pork chop, a nightly special, is a winner, as is the New York–style cheesecake. ⑤ *Average main: $20* ⊠ *844 Bald Eagle Dr.* ☎ *239/642–0550* ⊕ *www. arturosmarcoisland.com* ⌣ *Reservations essential* ⊘ *No lunch.*

$ ✕ **Crazy Flamingo.** Burgers, conch fritters, and chicken wings draw

AMERICAN mostly locals to this neighborhood bar, where there's counter service only and seating indoors and outdoors on the sidewalk. Try the peel-and-eat shrimp, sushi, mussels marinara, chicken bistro salad, or fried grouper basket. ⑤ *Average main: $11* ⊠ *Marco Island Town Center, 1035 N. Collier Blvd.* ☎ *239/642–9600* ⊕ *www.thecrazyflamingo.com.*

$$$ ✕**Old Marco Lodge Crab House.** Built in 1869, this waterfront restau-
SEAFOOD   rant is Goodland's oldest landmark. Boaters often cruise in and tie up
dockside to sit on the veranda and dine on local seafood and pasta
entrées. The crab-cake sandwich is a popular lunch option. For dinner,
start with a wholesome bowl of vegetable crab soup and then a trip to
the salad bar (included in the price of entrées). The menu has all man-
ner of seafood dishes, including a teriyaki shrimp wrap, a basket of
fried oysters, and a soft-shell crab sandwich. There are also steak and
chicken dishes for landlubbers. Save room for the authentic key lime pie.
⑤ *Average main: $25* ⊠ *401 Papaya St., Goodland* ☎ *239/642–7227*
⊕ *www.oldmarcolodge.com* ▭ *No credit cards* ⊙ *Closed Aug. and Sept.*

$$$ ✕**Sale e Pepe.** Marco's best dining view comes also with some of its
ITALIAN   finest cuisine. The name means "salt and pepper," an indication that
this palatial restaurant with terrace seating overlooking the beach
adheres to the basics of Southern Italian cuisine. Pastas, sausages,
and ice cream are made right here in the kitchen. Simple, artfully presented dishes—butternut squash ravioli, Cornish hen with grilled oyster mushrooms, yellow-pepper-and-shrimp soup, baked salmon with
lobster sauce, chianti-braised short ribs, and tomato-crusted Atlantic
salmon—explode with home-cooked, long-simmered flavors. With the
exception of a handful of pizzas, lunch is more traditional, less Italian.
⑤ *Average main: $25* ⊠ *Marco Beach Ocean Resort, 480 S. Collier
Blvd.* ☎ *239/393–1400* ⊕ *www.sale-e-pepe.com.*

$$$ ✕**Snook Inn.** On the water with live entertainment in the tiki bar and
SEAFOOD   a loaded salad bar: no wonder this place has been a casual favorite
for locals and visitors for decades. Signature items include the spicy
conch chowder, beer-battered grouper sandwich, Caribbean BBQ baby
back ribs, and grouper in a bag with mushroom crab sauce. ⑤ *Aver-
age main: $21* ⊠ *1215 Bald Eagle Dr., Old Marco* ☎ *239/394–3313*
⊕ *www.snookinn.com* ⬧ *Reservations not accepted.*

$$$ ✕**Verdi's American Bistro.** There's a Zen feel to this intimate bistro built
ECLECTIC   on creative American-Italian-Asian fusion cuisine. You might start with
steamed littleneck clams in garlic butter or duck potstickers, then move
on to entrées such as grilled swordfish with pumpkin seeds, miso-glazed
shrimp, pasta pomodoro, or the New Zealand rack of lamb. Cuban
coffee crème brûlée and deep-dish apple strudel are among the tempting desserts. ⑤ *Average main: $28* ⊠ *Sand Dollar Plaza, 241 N. Col-
lier Blvd.* ☎ *239/394–5533* ⊕ *www.verdisbistro.com* ⊙ *Closed Sept.
No lunch.*

WHERE TO STAY

$ ⊡ **The Boat House Motel.** For a great location at a good price, check
HOTEL   into this modest but appealing two-story motel at the north end of
the island on a canal close to the Gulf. **Pros:** away from busy beach
traffic; affordable; boating docks and access. **Cons:** no beach; hard
to find; tight parking area. ⑤ *Rooms from: $177* ⊠ *1180 Edington
Pl.* ☎ *239/642–2400, 800/528–6345* ⊕ *www.theboathousemotel.com*
⤴ *20 rooms* ⦿❘ *No meals.*

$$$ ⊡ **Hilton Marco Island Beach Resort and Spa.** This 11-story hotel is smaller
RESORT   and more conservative than the Marriott—but it seems less busy and
crowded—and rooms, redesigned starting in 2012 with a contemporary

8

beachy style, are spacious and have private balconies with full or partial ocean views. **Pros:** gorgeous, wide beach; complete business services; exclusive feel. **Cons:** a little stuffy; charges for Wi-Fi and self-parking; business focus. $ *Rooms from: $379* ✉ *560 S. Collier Blvd.* ☎ *239/394–5000, 800/445–8667* ⊕ *www.hiltonmarcoisland.com* ⌐⇗ *271 rooms, 22 suites, 4 penthouses* ⦿⊙ *No meals.*

$$$
RESORT
Fodor's Choice
★

🖼 **Marco Beach Ocean Resort.** One of the island's first condo hotels, this 12-story class act has luxurious one- and two-bedroom suites decorated in elegant neutral tones with the finest fixtures; all rooms face the water and look down onto the crescent-shaped rooftop pool (on the fifth floor). **Pros:** gourmet dining; intimate; on beach; sophisticated crowd. **Cons:** steep prices; squeezed between high-rises; near a busy resort. $ *Rooms from: $399* ✉ *480 S. Collier Blvd.* ☎ *239/393–1400, 800/715–8517* ⊕ *www.marcoresort.com* ⌐⇗ *83 1-bedroom and 15 2-bedroom suites* ⦿⊙ *No meals.*

$$$$
RESORT
FAMILY

🖼 **Marco Island Marriott Beach Resort.** A circular drive and manicured grounds with rock waterfalls front this hilltop, beachfront resort made up of twin 11-story towers and villa-like suites, two large pools, and the widest stretch of sand on the island. **Pros:** top-notch amenities; great spa and restaurants; appeals to children and adults; two private golf courses. **Cons:** huge size; lots of convention business; paid parking across the street in an uncovered lot. $ *Rooms from: $499* ✉ *400 S. Collier Blvd.* ☎ *239/394–2511, 800/438–4373* ⊕ *www.marcoislandmarriott.com* ⌐⇗ *664 rooms, 62 suites* ⦿⊙ *No meals.*

$$
RENTAL

🖼 **Olde Marco Island Inn & Suites.** This Victorian with tin roofs and royal-blue shutters and awnings used to be the only place to stay on the island when lodging back then was in the circa-1883 historic building that now holds the restaurant; today guests check into newer hotel sections with comfortable condo suites. **Pros:** quiet part of the island; full kitchen in every room; free Wi-Fi; laundry facilities; free covered parking. **Cons:** must drive to beach; annexed to a shopping center; office closes at night. $ *Rooms from: $279* ✉ *100 Palm St.* ☎ *239/394–3131, 877/475–3466* ⊕ *www.oldemarcoinn.com* ⌐⇗ *51 suites, 2 penthouses* ⦿⊙ *No meals.*

SPORTS AND THE OUTDOORS

FISHING

Sunshine Tours. Try a deep-sea ($120 per person for half-day) or back-country ($65 per person for three hours) fishing charter with this outfitter. ✉ *Rose Marina, 951 Bald Eagle Dr.* ☎ *239/642–5415* ⊕ *www.sunshinetoursmarcoisland.com.*

ORLANDO AND ENVIRONS

WELCOME TO ORLANDO AND ENVIRONS

TOP REASONS TO GO

★ **Magic and Fantasy:** Unleash your inner child, in the glow of Cinderella Castle, at WDW's Magic Kingdom. Fireworks transform the night skies—and you—at this park and at Epcot. And, over at Universal Orlando we have just two words: Harry Potter.

★ **Around:** Visit Epcot's 11 countries, complete with perfect replicas of foreign monuments, unique crafts, and traditional cuisine.

★ **Amazing Animals:** Safari through Africa in Disney's Animal Kingdom, get splashed by Shamu at SeaWorld, kiss a dolphin at Discovery Cove, and watch gators wrestle at Gatorland.

★ **Shopping Opps:** Hit the national chains at Orlando's upscale malls, or browse Winter Park's unique Park Avenue boutiques. Don't forget the mouse ears: Main Street U.S.A. and Downtown Disney are filled with the best classic souvenirs and some quirkier items as well.

1 Orlando and Environs. Once you've exhausted the theme parks, or have been exhausted by them, turn your attention to a wealth of offerings, including museums, parks, and gardens, in Winter Park, Kissimmee, and elsewhere. Thanks to Disney World, Orlando is the gateway for many visitors to central Florida. Edging Orlando to the south is Kissimmee, with home-grown attractions like Gatorland. Looking for more laid-back local flavor? You'll find it just 20 miles northeast of Orlando in the charming Winter Park suburb.

Orlando

CENTRAL FLORIDA

TO MAITLAND
AND ALTAMONT SPRINGS

WINTER PARK

SEMINOLE COUNTY
ORANGE COUNTY

University of
Central Florida

Colonial Dr.

EXIT 83A
EXIT 83
EXIT 82B
EXIT 82A

ORLANDO

Orlando
Executive
Airport

EXIT 80

Hafner Av.

Beachline Expwy. (Toll)

Central Florida Greenway (Toll)

Florida's Turnpike (Toll)

Pkwy

Orlando
International
Airport

0   4 mi
0   4 km

ORANGE COUNTY
OSCEOLA COUNTY

KISSIMMEE

East Lake
Tohopekaliga

GETTING ORIENTED

Central Florida runs from Tampa/St. Petersburg in the west through Orlando to the coastal attractions of Daytona Beach and Cape Canaveral on the east coast. Orlando is more or less equidistant, about 90 minutes by car to the Gulf of Mexico. Walt Disney World is not, contrary to advertising, in Orlando, but lies about 25 miles southwest of the city.

9

2 Walt Disney World. Walt Disney's original decree that his parks be ever-changing, along with some healthy competition from Universal Studios and SeaWorld, has kept the Disney Imagineers dreaming up new entertainment and installing higher-tech thrills and attractions.

3 Universal Orlando. While Disney creates a fantasy world for those who love fairy tales, Universal Orlando is geared to older kids, adults, and anyone who enjoys pop culture. Movie and TV fans love this place. Two other parks—Islands of Adventure (IOA) and Wet 'n Wild—add to the fun.

4 SeaWorld and Discovery Cove. Less glitzy than Walt Disney World or Universal, SeaWorld and Discovery Cove are worth a visit for a low-key, relaxing, ocean-theme experience. If you want to get more keyed up, pay a call on SeaWorld's Aquatica water park.

Updated by
Rona Grindin,
Jennifer Green-
hill-Taylor, and
Jennie Hess

Most Orlando locals look at the theme parks as they would an unruly neighbor: it's big and loud, but it keeps a nice lawn. Central Florida's many theme parks can become over-powering for even the most enthusiastic visitor, and that's when an excursion into the "other" Orlando—the one the locals know and love—is in order.

There are ample opportunities for day trips. If the outdoors is your thing, you can swim or canoe at Wekiwa Springs State Park or one of the area's many other sparkling springs, where the water remains a refreshing 72°F no matter how hot the day. Alternatively, you can hike, horseback ride, canoe, and camp in the Ocala National Forest.

If museums are your thing, charming Winter Park has the Charles Hosmer Morse Museum of American Art with its huge collection of Tiffany glass, and the Cornell Fine Arts Museum on the oak-tree-covered Rollins College campus. While in Winter Park, you can indulge in some high-end shopping and dining on Park Avenue or take a leisurely boat tour of the lakefront homes.

Got kids to educate and entertain? Check out WonderWorks or the Orlando Science Center, where you can view live gators and turtles. Even more live gators (some as long as 14 feet) can be viewed or fed (or even eaten) at Gatorland, just south of Orlando.

Do the kids prefer rockets and astronauts? Don't miss a day trip to Kennedy Space Center, where you can tour a rocket forest, sit in a space capsule, or see a space shuttle up close.

Kissimmee is a 19th-century cattle town south of Orlando that proudly hangs on to its roots with a twice-yearly rodeo where real cowboys ride bulls and rope cattle. The town sits on Lake Tohopekaliga, a favorite spot for airboat rides or fishing trips.

PLANNING

Updated by
Jennie Hess

Orlando is a diverse town. The Downtown area, though small, is dynamic, thanks to an ever-changing skyline of high-rises, sports venues, museums, restaurants, nightspots, a history museum, and several annual cultural events—including film festivals and a world-renowned theater fest. Downtown also has a central green, Lake Eola Park, which offers a respite from otherwise frantic touring.

Neighborhoods such as Thornton Park (great for dining) and College Park (an outpost of great dining and live theater) are fun to wander. Not too far to the north, you can come in contact with natural Florida—its manatees, gators, and crystal clear waters in spring-fed lakes.

Closer to the theme-park action, International Drive, the hub of resort and conference hotels, offers big restaurants and even bigger outlet-mall bargains. Sand Lake Road, between the two, is Orlando's Restaurant Row, with plenty of exciting dining prospects.

GETTING HERE AND AROUND

Orlando is spread out. During rush hour, car traffic crawls along the often-crowded Interstate 4, which runs to both coasts. If you're heading east, you can also take Route 528 (aka the Beachline), a toll road that heads directly for Cape Canaveral and points along the Space Coast; no such option leads west.

If you avoid rush-hour traffic, traveling to points of interest shouldn't take too much time out of your vacation. Winter Park is no more than 20 minutes from Downtown; International Drive and the theme parks are about 30 minutes away in heavier traffic. Orlando International Airport is only 9 miles south of Downtown, but it will take about 30 minutes via a circuitous network of highways (Interstate 4 west to Florida's Turnpike south to Route 528 east).

ESSENTIALS

Visitor Information Orlando Visitors Bureau ☎ *407/363–5872, 800/972–3304* ⊕ *www.visitorlando.com.*

9

EXPLORING

CENTRAL ORLANDO

Fodor'sChoice
★

Harry P. Leu Gardens. A few miles outside of downtown—on the former lakefront estate of a citrus entrepreneur—is this 50-acre garden. Among the highlights are a collection of historical blooms (many varieties of which were established before 1900), ancient oaks, a 50-foot floral clock, and one of the largest camellia collections in eastern North America (in bloom November–March). Mary Jane's Rose Garden, named after Leu's wife, is filled with more than 1,000 bushes; it's the largest formal rose garden south of Atlanta. The simple 19th-century Leu House Museum, once the Leu family home, preserves the furnishings and appointments of a well-to-do, turn-of-the-20th-century Florida family. ⊠ *1920 N. Forest Ave., Lake Ivanhoe* ☎ *407/246–2620* ⊕ *www.*

Central Orlando

0   1/2 mi

0   1/2 km

TO WINTER PARK

Orlando Shakespeare Theater ◆

Rock & Roll Heaven ◆
Washburn Imports ◆

Wally's ◆

Bull and Bush Pub ◆

Orlando Executive Airport

TO ORLANDO INT'L AIRPORT via Route 436 (Semoran Blvd.)

Bob Carr Performing Arts Centre ◆

Firestone Live ◆

The Social/Sky 60 ◆

Tangueray's ◆
Amway Center
Chillers ◆

Monkey Bar ◆

Mad Cow Theatre ◆
Bösendorfer Lounge ◆

Dr. Phillips Performing Arts Center ◆

Parliament House Resort ◆

Florida Mall ◆
Mall at Millenia ◆
Orlando Harley-Davidson ◆

Streets & Roads
Mercy Dr.
John Young Pkwy.
Old Winter Garden Rd.
Colonial Dr.
Princeton St.
Edgewater Dr.
Lakeview St.
Orange Blossom Terr.
Tampa Av.
Orange Av.
Marks St.
Virginia Dr.
Mills Av.
Corrine Dr.
General Rees Av.
Winter Park Rd.
Bennet Rd.
Maguire Blvd.
Primrose Dr.
Bumby Av.
Hampton Av.
Ferncreek Av.
Washington St.
South St.
Central Blvd.
Livingston St.
Robinson St.
Summerlin Av.
Broadway Av.
Magnolia Av.
Garland Av.
Hughey Av.
Parramore Av.
Washington St.
Church St.
South St.

Lakes
Lake Sue
Lake Rowena
Lake Ivanhoe
Lake Concord
Spring Lake
Rock Lake
Lake Lorna Doone
Lake Sylvan
Lake Underhill

leugardens.org ✉ *$10, free 1st Mon. of month* ⊗ *Garden daily 9–5; guided house tours daily on hr and ½ hr 10–3:30.*

FAMILY **Lake Eola Park.** This beautifully landscaped 43-acre park is the verdant heart of downtown Orlando, its mile-long walking path a gathering place for families, health enthusiasts out for a run, and culture mavens exploring area offerings. The well-lighted playground is alive with children, and ducks, swans, and native Florida birds call the lake home. A farmers' market takes up residence on Sunday afternoon.

The lakeside Walt Disney Amphitheater is a dramatic site for concerts, ethnic festivals, and spectacular Fourth of July fireworks. Don't resist the park's biggest draw: a ride in a swan-shape pedal boat. Up to five adults can fit comfortably into each. (Children under 16 must be accompanied by an adult.)

The Relax Grill, by the swan-boat launch, is a great place for a snack. There are also several good restaurants in the upscale Thornton Park neighborhood along the park's eastern border. The ever-expanding skyline rings the lake with modern high-rises, making the peace of the park even more welcome. After a lightning strike in 2009, the landmark fountain was revamped and features an LED light and music show on summer evenings at 9:30. ✉ *195 N. Rosalind Ave., Downtown Orlando* ☎ *407/246–4485 park, 407/246–4485 swan boats* ✉ *Swan boat rental $15 per ½ hr* ⊗ *Park daily 6 am–midnight; swan boats Sun.–Tues. 10–7, Wed.–Sat. 10–10.*

Mennello Museum of American Folk Art. One of the few museums in the United States devoted to folk art has intimate galleries, some with lovely lakefront views. Look for the nation's most extensive permanent collection of Earl Cunningham paintings as well as works by many other self-taught artists. There's a wonderful video about Cunningham and his "curio shop" in St. Augustine. Temporary exhibitions have included the works of Wyeth, Cassatt, and Michael Eastman. At the museum shop you can purchase folk-art books, toys, and unusual gifts. The Mennello is the site of the annual Orlando Folk Festival, held the second weekend of February. ✉ *900 E. Princeton St., Lake Ivanhoe* ☎ *407/246–4278* ⊕ *www.mennellomuseum.org* ✉ *$5* ⊗ *Tues.–Sat. 10:30–4:30, Sun. noon–4:30.*

FAMILY **Orange County Regional History Center.** Exhibits here take you on a journey back in time to discover how Florida's Paleo-Indians hunted and fished the land, what the Sunshine State was like when the Spaniards first arrived, and how life in Florida was different when citrus was king. Visit a cabin from the late 1800s, complete with Spanish moss–stuffed mattresses and mosquito netting over the beds. Seminole Indian displays include interactive activities, and the Tourism Before Disney exhibit previews Florida's destiny as a future vacation mecca. Traveling exhibits bring modern technology and art to the Museum. ✉ *65 E. Central Blvd., Downtown Orlando* ☎ *407/836–8500, 800/965–2030* ⊕ *www.thehistorycenter.org* ✉ *$15* ⊗ *Mon.–Sat. 10–5, Sun. noon–5.*

FAMILY
Fodor'sChoice
★
Orlando Science Center. With all the high-tech glitz and imagined worlds of the theme parks, is it worth visiting Orlando's reality-based science center? If you're a kid crazy about science, the answer is an

The 300-seat Dr. Phillips CineDome, a movie theater with an eight-story screen at the Orlando Science Center, offers large-format iWERKS films.

overwhelming "yes." With exhibits about the human body, mechanics, computers, math, nature, the solar system, and optics, the science center has something for every child's inner geek.

The four-story internal atrium is home to live gators and turtles and is a great spot for simply gazing at what Old Florida once looked like. The 300-seat Dr. Phillips CineDome, a movie theater with a giant eight-story screen, offers large-format iWERKS films and planetarium programs. The Crosby Observatory and Florida's largest publicly accessible refractor telescope are here, as are several smaller telescopes; some weekends you can safely view spots and flares on the sun's surface.

Adults like the science center, too, thanks to events like the annual Science of Wine and Cosmic Golf Challenge; evenings of stargazing in the Crosby Observatory, live music, art, and film; and Otronicon, the annual interactive technology expo. ⊠ *777 E. Princeton St., Lake Ivanhoe* ☎ *407/514–2000* ⊕ *www.osc.org* ✉ *$19 (all-inclusive); parking $5* ⊙ *Daily 10–5; closed Wed.*

INTERNATIONAL DRIVE

FAMILY **Fun Spot America.** Four go-kart tracks offer a variety of driving experiences. Though drivers must be at least 10 years old and meet height requirements, parents can drive younger children in two-seater cars on several of the tracks, including the Conquest Track. Nineteen rides range from the dizzying Paratrooper to an old-fashioned Revolver Ferris Wheel to the twirling toddler Teacups. Fun Spot recently expanded from five to 15 acres and now features Central Florida's only wooden roller coaster as well as the Freedom Flyer steel suspension family coaster, a kiddie coaster, and what's billed as the world's second-tallest (250 feet) SkyCoaster—part skydive, part hang-glide. The tallest, at 300 feet, is located at sister park Fun Spot USA, in Kissimmee. There's also an arcade. From Exit 75A, turn left onto International Drive, then left on Fun Spot Way. ⌧ *5700 Fun Spot Way, I-Drive area* ☎ *407/363–3867* ⊕ *www.funspotattractions.com* ⬛ *$39.95 for all rides (online discounts available) or pay per ride; admission for nonriders free; arcade extra; parking free* ☉ *Apr.–Oct., daily 10 am–midnight; Nov.–Mar., weekdays noon–11, weekends 10 am–midnight.*

Ripley's Believe It or Not! Odditorium. A 10-foot-square section of the Berlin Wall. A pain and torture chamber. Two African fertility statues that women swear have helped them conceive. These and almost 200 other oddities (shrunken heads included) speak for themselves in this museum-cum-attraction in the heart of tourist territory on International Drive. The building itself is designed to appear as if it's sliding into one of Florida's notorious sinkholes. Give yourself an hour or two to soak up the weirdness, but remember: this is a looking, not touching, experience; it might drive antsy youngsters—and their parents—crazy. ■ TIP➡ Buy tickets online ahead of time, and you can get discounts. ⌧ *8201 International Dr., I-Drive area* ☎ *407/351–5803* ⊕ *www. ripleysorlando.com* ⬛ *$19.99; parking free* ☉ *Daily 9 am–midnight; last admission at 11.*

FAMILY **WonderWorks.** The building seems to be sinking into the ground. Not only that, but it seems to be sinking into the ground at a precarious angle and upside down. Many people stop to take pictures in front of the topsy-turvy facade, complete with upended palm trees and broken skyward-facing sidewalks. Inside, the upside-down theme continues only as far as the lobby. After that, it's a playground of 100 interactive experiences—some incorporating virtual reality, others educational (similar to those at a science museum), and still others pure entertainment. You can experience an earthquake or a hurricane, land a space shuttle using simulator controls, make giant bubbles in the Bubble Lab, play laser tag in the enormous laser-tag arena and arcade, design and ride your own roller coaster, lie on a bed of real nails, and play baseball with a virtual Major League batter. ⌧ *9067 International Dr., I-Drive area* ☎ *407/351–8800* ⊕ *www.wonderworksonline.com/ orlando* ⬛ *$24.99; laser tag and Outta Control Magic Comedy Dinner Show extra (online discounts available); parking $3–$9* ☉ *Daily 9 am–midnight.*

KISSIMMEE

18 miles south of Orlando, 10 miles southeast of Walt Disney World (WDW).

Although Kissimmee is primarily known as the gateway to Disney (technically, the vast Disney property of theme parks and resorts lies in both Osceola and Orange counties), its non-WDW attractions just might tickle your fancy. They range from throwbacks to old-time Florida to dinner shows for you and 2,000 of your closest friends. Orlando used

International Drive

EXIT 78

Conroy Rd.

Mall at Millenia

423

EXIT 77

Orlando Premium Outlets
International Drive

Lake Marsha

UNIVERSAL STUDIOS ORLANDO

EXIT 75

Outdoor World

Artegon Orlando

OAK RIDGE

Dr. Phillips Blvd.

Wallace Rd.

iFLY Orlando

EXIT 74B

Congo River 6

Wet 'n Wild

TANGELO PARK

Apopka Vineland Rd.

Spring Lake

EXIT 74A

482

Sand Lake Rd.

Florida's Turnpike (Ronald Reagan Turnpike)

John Young Pkwy.

482

Lake Tibet

435

Little Sand Lake

7

423

Big Sand Lake

4

Pirate's Cove Adventure Golf

Cafe Tu Tu Tango

ICEBAR

Hawaiian Rumble

Adventure Golf

Lake Sheen

8

B.B. King's Blues Club

Pointe Orlando

528

EXIT 72

528

International Drive

Beachline Expwy.

Big Sand Lake

Turkey Lake Rd.

EXIT 71

SEAWORLD ORLANDO

WILLIAMSBURG

Central Florida Pkwy.

WHISPER LAKES

VINELAND

Apopka Vineland Rd.

Palm Pkwy.

435

John Young Pkwy.

535

Orlando Premium Outlets
Vineland Avenue

International Drive

Shingle Creek

423

Buena Vista Dr.

WALT DISNEY WORD

EXIT 68

417

535

Lake Bryan

EXIT 67

4

International Drive

536

417

Central Florida Greenway

0   1 mi

0   1 km

to be prime cattle country, and the best sampling of what life was like is here during the Silver Springs Rodeo in February and June.

With at least 100,000 acres of freshwater lakes, the Kissimmee area brings anglers and boaters to national fishing tournaments and speedboat races. A 50-mile-long series of lakes, the Kissimmee Waterway, connects Lake Tohopekaliga—a Native American name that means "Sleeping Tiger"—with huge Lake Okeechobee in South Florida, and from there, to both the Atlantic Ocean and the Gulf of Mexico.

FAMILY **Gatorland.** This campy attraction near the Orlando–Kissimmee border on U.S. 441 has endured since 1949 without much change, despite competition from the major parks. Over the years, the theme park and registered conservancy has gone through some changes while retaining its gator-rasslin' spirit. Kids get a kick out of this unmanufactured, old-timey thrill ride.

The Gator Gulley Splash Park is complete with giant "egrets" spilling water from their beaks, dueling water guns mounted atop giant gators, and other water-park splash areas. There's also a small petting zoo and an aviary. A free train ride is a high point, taking you through an alligator breeding marsh and a natural swamp setting where you can spot gators, birds, and turtles. A three-story observation tower overlooks the breeding marsh, swamped with gator grunts, especially come sundown during mating season.

For a glimpse of 37 giant, rare, and deadly crocodiles, check out the Jungle Crocs of the World exhibit. To see eager gators leaping out of the water to catch their food, come on cool days for the Gator Jumparoo Show (summer heat just puts them to sleep). The most thrilling is the first one in the morning, when the gators are hungriest. There's also a Gator Wrestlin' Show, and although there's no doubt who's going to win the match, it's still fun to see the handlers take on those tough guys with the beady eyes. In the educational Upclose Encounters show, the show's host handles a variety of snakes. Recent park additions include Panther Springs, featuring brother-and-sister endangered panthers, and the Screamin' Gator Zip Line (additional cost). This is a real Florida experience, and you leave knowing the difference between a gator and a croc. ⊠ *14501 S. Orange Blossom Trail, between Orlando and Kissimmee* ☎ *407/855–5496, 800/393–5297* ⊕ *www.gatorland.com* ✉ *$26.99 (discount coupons online)* ⊙ *Daily 10–5.*

LEGOLAND

50 miles southwest of Orlando.

The quiet town of Winter Haven is home to numerous lakes and a waterskiing school. From 1936 until 2009, it was also home to the Sunshine State's first theme park, Cypress Gardens. Today the spot holds the world's largest LEGOLAND, set on 150 acres and built using nearly 56 million LEGOS. In addition to its 1:20-scale miniature reproductions of U.S. cities, the park features more than 50 rides, shows, and attractions throughout 10 different zones, as well as the marvelous botanical gardens from the original park. Just opened mid-2013, the World of Chima

Kissimmee's Lake Tohopekaliga (affectionately known as Lake Toho) is famous with fishers the world over. It's also great for wildlife spotting—an especially exhilarating experience when done from an airboat.

presented by Cartoon Network invites guests into a fantastical world of animal tribal habitats anchored by an interactive water ride, the Quest for CHI. In Chima's new Speedorz Arena, participants compete to win a supply of the mystical CHI energy source. A 4-D movie and Chima-character meet and greets round out the experience.

The Danish toy company's philosophy is to help children "play well." And play they do, as LEGOLAND attractions are very hands-on. Kids can hoist themselves to the top of a tower, power a fire truck, or navigate a LEGO robot. Sights include huge LEGO dragons, wizards, knights, pirates, castles, roller coasters, racetracks, villages, and cities.

The cityscapes in Miniland USA fascinate children and adults, who delight in discovering what's possible when you have enough bricks. Miniland opens with Kennedy Space Center, where a 6-foot shuttle waits on the launch pad. Miami Beach features bikini-clad bathers and art deco hotels; St. Augustine and its ancient fort play into LEGO's pirate theme; Key West's Mallory Square is accurate right down to the trained cats leaping through rings of fire. The rest of the United States is not ignored: New York City, Las Vegas, San Francisco, and Washington D.C. appear in intricate detail. Visitors spend hours looking for amusing details hidden in each city, like New York's purse-snatcher.

Among other highlights are LEGO Kingdoms, whose castle towers over a jousting area and a roller coaster where knights, damsels, dragons, and ogres are found; Land of Adventure, where you can explore hidden tombs and hunt for treasure; and the Imagination Zone, showcasing LEGO Mindstorms robots, where a giant head of Albert Einstein invites kids to explore and invent. Things get wild in LEGO Technic, the most active of the park's zones, where Test Track, Aquazone Wave Racers, and Technicycle let the family expend some energy. And Pirates' Cove provides a chance to sit in the shade and watch a full-sized pirate battle, with actors wearing LEGO suits defending the huge ship from attacking pirates on water skis.

LEGOLAND Water Park features a wave pool; Build-a-Raft, where families construct a LEGO vessel and float down a lazy river; a 375-foot pair of intertwined waterslides that plunge riders into a pool; and a DUPLO toddler water play area. Not to be forgotten, Cypress Gardens, at the heart of the park, preserves one of Florida's treasures. Families can wander the lush, tropical foliage and gasp at one of the world's largest banyan trees.

The trip to Winter Haven is worth it. The rides, interactive games, gardens, water park, and other attractions will amuse and engage. Round-trip transportation from Orlando Premium Outlets, on Vineland Avenue, leaves at 9 and costs $5. ⊠ *1 Legoland Way, Winter Haven* ☎ *877/350–5346* ⊕ *www.legoland.com* 🖃 *$84; parking $14* ⊙ *Hrs vary seasonally.*

BOK TOWER GARDENS

57 miles southwest of Orlando, 42 miles southwest of WDW.

Fodor's Choice
★
You'll see citrus groves as you ride south along U.S. 27 to the small town of Lake Wales and the Bok Tower Gardens. This appealing sanctuary of plants, flowers, trees, and wildlife has been something of a local secret for years. Shady paths meander through pine forests with silvery moats, mockingbirds and swans, blooming thickets, and hidden sundials. The majestic, 200-foot Bok Tower is constructed of coquina—from seashells—and pink, white, and gray marble. The tower houses a carillon with 60 bronze bells that ring out each day at 1 and 3 pm during 30-minute recitals that might include early-American folk songs, Appalachian tunes, Irish ballads, or Latin hymns. The bells are also featured in recordings every half hour after 10 am, and sometimes even moonlight recitals.

The landscape was designed in 1928 by Frederick Law Olmsted, Jr., son of the planner of New York's Central Park. The grounds include the 20-room, Mediterranean-style Pinewood Estate, built in 1930 and open for self-guided touring. January through April, guides lead you on a 60-minute tour of the gardens (included in the admission price); tours of the inside of the tower are a benefit of membership ($100 and up).

Take Interstate 4 to Exit 55 and head south on U.S. 27 for about 23 miles. Proceed past Eagle Ridge Mall, then turn left after two traffic lights onto Mountain Lake Cut Off Road, and follow the signs. ⊠ *1151 Tower Blvd., Lake Wales* ☎ *863/676–1408* ⊕ *www.boktower. org* 🖃 *$12–$18* ⊙ *Daily 8–6.*

Wildlife-rich Wekiwa Springs State Park is a great place to camp, hike, picnic, canoe, fish, swim, or snorkel.

WEKIWA SPRINGS STATE PARK

13 miles northwest of Orlando, 28 miles north of WDW.

FAMILY
Fodor's Choice
★

"Wekiva" is a Creek Indian word meaning "flowing water"; *wekiwa* means "spring of water." The river, springs, and surrounding 6,400-acre Wekiwa Springs State Park are well suited to camping, hiking, picnicking, swimming, canoeing, and fishing. The area is also full of Florida wildlife: otters, raccoons, alligators, bobcats, deer, turtles, and birds.

Canoe trips can range from a simple hour-long paddle around the lagoon to observe a colony of water turtles to a full-day excursion through the less congested parts of the river, which haven't changed much since the area was inhabited by the Timacuan Indians. You can rent canoes ($17.98 for two hours and $3.20 per hour after that) in the town of Apopka, near the park's southern entrance.

The park has 60 campsites: some are "canoe sites" that you can reach only via the river, and others are "trail sites," meaning you must hike a good bit of the park's 13½-mile trail to reach them. Most, however, are for the less hardy—you can drive right up to them. Sites go for $24 a night with electric and water hookups.

To get here, take Interstate 4 Exit 94 (Longwood) and turn left on Route 434. Go 1¼ mile to Wekiwa Springs Road; turn right and go 4½ miles to the entrance, on the right. ✉ *1800 Wekiva Circle* ☎ *407/884–2008, 800/326–3521 for campsites, 407/884–4311 for canoe rentals* ⊕ *www. floridastateparks.org/wekiwasprings/default.cfm* ✍ *$2 per pedestrian or bicycle; $6 per vehicle* ⊙ *Daily 8–dusk.*

WINTER PARK

6 miles northeast of Orlando, 20 miles northeast of WDW.

This peaceful, upscale community may be just outside the hustle and bustle of Orlando, but it feels like a different country. The town's name reflects its early role as a warm-weather haven for those escaping the frigid blasts of Northeast winters. From the late 1880s until the early 1930s, wealthy industrialists and their families would travel to Florida by rail on vacation, and many stayed, establishing grand homes and cultural institutions. The lovely, 8-square-mile village retains its charm with brick-paved streets, historic buildings, and well-maintained lakes and parkland. Even the town's bucolic 9-hole golf course is on the National Register of Historic Places.

On Park Avenue you can spend a few hours sightseeing, shopping, or both. The street is lined with small boutiques and fine restaurants and bookended by world-class museums: the Charles Hosmer Morse Museum of American Art, with the world's largest collection of artwork by Louis Comfort Tiffany, and the Cornell Fine Arts Museum, on the campus of Rollins College (the oldest college in Florida).

TOURS

Scenic Boat Tour. Head east from Park Avenue and, at the end of Morse Boulevard, you'll find the launching point for this tour, a Winter Park tradition since 1938. The one-hour cruise takes in 12 miles of waterways, including three lakes and narrow, oak- and cypress-shaded canals built in the 1800s as a transportation system for the logging industry. A well-schooled skipper shares stories about the moguls who built their mansions along the shore and points out wildlife and remnants of natural Florida still surrounding the expensive houses. Cash or check only is accepted. ⊠ *312 E. Morse Blvd.* ☎ *407/644–4056* ⊕ *www.scenicboattours.com* 🎫 *$12* ⊘ *Daily 10–4.*

EXPLORING

Fodor'sChoice **Charles Hosmer Morse Museum of American Art.** The world's most com-
★ prehensive collection of work by Louis Comfort Tiffany—including immense stained-glass windows, lamps, watercolors, and desk sets—is in this museum, which also contains American decorative art and paintings from the mid-19th to the early 20th centuries.

Among the draws is the 1,082-square-foot Tiffany Chapel, originally built for the 1893 World's Fair in Chicago. It took craftsmen 2½ years to painstakingly reassemble the chapel here. Many of the works were rescued from Tiffany's Long Island estate, Laurelton Hall, after a 1957 fire destroyed much of the property. The 12,000-square-foot Laurelton Hall wing, opened in 2011, allows for much more of the estate's collection to be displayed at one time. Exhibits in the wing include architectural and decorative elements from Laurelton's dining room, living room, and Fountain Court reception hall. There's also a re-creation of the striking Daffodil Terrace, so named for the glass daffodils that serve as the capitals for the terrace's marble columns. ⊠ *445 N. Park Ave.* ☎ *407/645–5311* ⊕ *www.morsemuseum.org* 🎫 *$5, free Nov.–Apr., Fri. 4–8* ⊘ *Tues.–Sat. 9:30–4, Sun. 1–4; Nov.–Apr., Fri. until 8.*

9

WHERE TO EAT

Updated by
Rona Gindin

You'll find burger-and-fries combos everywhere in Orlando, yet the ambitious chefs behind Orlando's theme-park and independent restaurants provide loads of better options—much better. Locally sourced foods, creative preparations, and clever international influences are all the rage here. Theme-park complexes have some of the best restaurants in town, although you may opt for a rental car to seek out the local treasures.

The signs of Orlando's dining progress is most evident in the last place one would look: Disney's fast-food outlets. Every eatery on Disney property offers a tempting vegetarian option, and kiddie meals come with healthful sides and drinks unless you specifically request otherwise. Chefs at Disney's table-service restaurants consult face-to-face with guests about food allergies.

Around town, locals flock to the Ravenous Pig, the Rusty Spoon, the Smiling Bison, and other gastropubs where the menu changes regularly; Luma on Park, a suave home of thoughtfully created cutting-edge meals; and any number of dining establishments competing to serve the very finest steak. Orlando's culinary blossoming began in 1995, when Disney's signature California Grill debuted, featuring farm-to-table cuisine and wonderful wines by the glass. Soon after, celebrity chefs started opening up shop. And in 2013, Disney completely revamped California Grill so it's a trendsetter once again.

Orlando's destination restaurants can be found in the theme parks, as well as in the outlying towns. Sand Lake Road is now known as Restaurant Row for its eclectic collection of worthwhile tables. Here you'll find fashionable outlets for sushi and seafood, Italian and chops, Hawaiian fusion and upscale Southwestern. Heading into the residential areas, the neighborhoods of Winter Park (actually its own city), Thornton Park, and College Park are prime locales for chow. Scattered throughout Central Florida, low-key ethnic restaurants specialize in the fare of Turkey, India, Peru, Thailand, Vietnam—you name it. Prices in these family-owned finds are usually delightfully low.

Use the coordinate (✛ 1:B2) at the end of each review to locate a site on the Where to Eat and Stay in the Orlando Area map.

MEAL PLANS

Disney Magic Your Way Plus Dining Plan allows you one table-service or buffet meal, one counter-service meal, and one snack per day of your trip at more than 100 theme-park and resort restaurants, provided you stay in a Disney hotel. You'll also receive a refillable drink mug for use at your hotel's fast-fooderies. For more money, you can upgrade the plan to include more; to save, you can downgrade to a counter-service-only plan. Used wisely, a Disney dining plan is a steal, but be careful to buy only the number of meals you'll want to eat. Moderate eaters can end up turning away appetizers and desserts to which they're entitled. Plan ahead, and use "extra" meals to your advantage by swapping two table-service meals for a Disney dinner show, say, or an evening at a high-end restaurant like California Grill.

Universal Meal Deal offers one sit-down and one quick-service meal at participating walk-up eateries inside Universal Studios and Islands of Adventure, plus a snack and soft drink. Daily prices are $46 and $18 (both parks) and must be purchased with a resort stay. A quick-service-only arrangement, with one meal a day, is $20 and $13. All-you-can-drink soft drinks are $12 daily for all.

WHAT IT COSTS				
	$	**$$**	**$$$**	**$$$$**
AT DINNER	under $15	$15–$21	$22–$30	over $30

Prices are per person for a median main course, at dinner, excluding tip and tax of 6.5%.

RESERVATIONS

Reservations are strongly recommended throughout the theme parks. Indeed, make reservations for Disney restaurants and character meals at both Universal and Disney at least 90 (and up to 180) days out. And be sure to ask about the cancellation policy—at a handful of Disney restaurants, for instance, you may be charged penalties if you don't give 24 to 48 hours' notice.

For restaurant reservations within Walt Disney World, call ☎ 407/939–3463 (*WDW–DINE*) or book online at ⊕ *www.disneyworld.com/dining*. You can also get plenty of information on the website, including the meal periods served, price range, and specialties of all Disney eateries. Menus for all restaurants are posted online and tend to be up to date. For Universal Orlando reservations, call ☎ 407/224–9255 (theme parks and CityWalk) or ☎ 407/503–3463 (hotels). Learn about the complex's 50-plus restaurants at ⊕ *www.universalorlando.com/dining*.

In our reviews, reservations are mentioned only when they're essential or not accepted. Unless otherwise noted, the restaurants listed are open daily for lunch and dinner.

9

WALT DISNEY WORLD AREA

MAGIC KINGDOM

$$$
BRASSERIE
Fodor'sChoice
★

✕ **Be Our Guest.** Traverse a bridge flanked by gargoyles and gas lamps to reach the Beast's castle, home of this massive new restaurant with a *Beauty and the Beast* theme, French flair, and the Magic Kingdom's first and only wine and beer served at dinner. The 500-seat restaurant has three rooms: a gilded ballroom, whose ceiling sports cherubs with the faces of Imagineers' children; the tattered West Wing, with a slashed painting that changes from prince to beast during faux storms; and the Rose Gallery. Décor comprises French provincial furniture, suits of armor, and heavy drapes. Food, scratch-prepared on site, includes pan-seared salmon, grilled steak, and maybe a pork rack with red wine au jus. The signature kids' soft drink comes in a light-up castle cup, and desserts, while sweet, are made without refined sugar. Be sure to accept a dollop of "the gray stuff—it's delicious." Lunch is a no-reservations fast-casual affair with the likes of quinoa salad and a braised pork stew

Map 1: Where to Explore, Eat, and Stay in the Orlando Area

PINE HILLS

Silver Star Rd.

W Colonial Dr.

Florida's Turnpike

W Colonial Dr.

Beulah

Gotha

Lake Hiawassa

Lake Down

Turkey Lake

Windermere

Summer Beach

Lake Butler

Conroy Rd.

Hard Rock Hotel

Doubletree by Hilton at the Entrance to Universal Orlando

Mama Della's Ristorante ■

Loews Portofino Bay Hotel □

Isleworth

Finnegan's Bar & Grille ■

Mel's Drive-In

EXIT 78

Lake Speer

UNIVERSAL STUDIOS FLORIDA

Three Broomsticks ■

Mythos ■

EXIT 75

Lake Hancock

Loews Royal Pacific Resort at Universal Orlando

Emeril's Tchoup Chop

Universal's Cabana Bay Beach Resort

Lake Reams

Lake Tibet

International Dr. (I-Dr.)

EXIT 74

PIRATE'S COVE ADVENTURE

Lake Mabel

Lake Sheen

Big Sand Lake

Seasons 52 ■

Vines Grille & Wine Bar

Café Tu Tu Tango

HAWAII

POINTE ORLANDO ◆

Hyatt Regency Orlando □

Taverna Opa ■

WONDERWORKS

EXIT 72

Bay Lake

WALT DISNEY WORLD

Epcot Center Dr.

World Dr.

EXIT 71

ORLANDO PREMIUM OUTLETS VINEYARD AVE. ◆

Central Florida

International Dr.

GRAND CYPRESS GOLF RESORT ◆

EXIT 68

Lake Bryan

Buena Vista Dr.

EXIT 67

See Map 2

Osceola Pkwy.

LAKE BUENA VISTA FACTORY STORES □

Stingle

EXIT 64

Lake Cecile

Poinciana Blvd.

Meliá Orlando Suite Hotel at Celebration □

Celebration

192 FLEA

Irlo Bronson

◆ **BOK TOWER GARDENS**
◆ **CHAMPIONSGATE GOLF CLUB**
◆ **LEGOLAND FLORIDA**

0   5 mi

0   5 km

E **F** **G** **H**

WEKIWA SPRINGS ↑ TO ↑
STATE PARK DAYTONA
TO
LEESBURG

WINTER
PARK
The Ravenous
Pig

■ Luma on Park
■ 4Rivers Smokehouse
◆ CHARLES HOSMER MORSE MUSEUM OF AMERICAN ART

17
92

ORLANDO SCIENCE CENTER ◆   ◆ MENNELLO MUSEUM OF AMERICAN FOLK ART

423   441

◆ HARRY P. LEU GARDENS
■ Hawkers
E Colonial Dr. 50

1

ORLANDO

TO
CHRISTMAS →

The Rusty Spoon ■
ORANGE COUNTY
REGIONAL HISTORY CENTER

◆ LAKE EOLA PARK
□ Grand Bohemian
Anderson St.

408

EXIT 82

552

Kaley St.

2

Michigan St.

Conway Rd.

Semoran Blvd.

EXIT 80

527

Holden Ave.   Gatlin Ave.

15

◆ MALL AT MILLENIA
◆ FUN SPOT AMERICA
◆ RIPLEY'S BELIEVE IT OR NOT! ODDITORIUM

Hoffner Ave.

○ Edgewood

ORLANDO PREMIUM OUTLETS
DRIVE   Oak Ridge Rd.
Pine
Castle

Lake
Conway

436

3

Judge Rd.

■ Canfisco Grille
■ Emeril's Orlando
■ NASCAR Sports Grille

○ Sky Lake
Sand Lake Rd.

Orange Ave.

528

Toll

VE
GOLF

428

EXPWY.

○ Taft

IAN RUMBLE ADVENTURE GOLF

528   91

achline

□ Ritz-Carlton Orlando
Grande Lakes

Primo
JW Marriott
Orlando
Grande Lakes

527

4

ORLANDO
INTERNATIONAL
AIRPORT

Pkwy.
■ **Norman's**

River   Pkwy.

92

Orange Blossom Trail

Florida's Turnpike

○ Flamingo

Mud
Lake

423

Central   Florida   Greenway

417

5

◆ GATORLAND

441

436

John Young Pkwy.

US 441

Blvd.

N

Dart

KISSIMMEE

A MARKET OUTLET

Mem. Hwy. W. Vine St. E. Vine St. 441

W.   N. Main   St.

East Lake
Tohopekaliga

6

KEY
□ Hotels
■ Restaurants
✥ following reviews indicates a map-grid coordinate

E **F** **G** **H**

BEST BETS FOR ORLANDO AND THE PARKS DINING

Orlando is not all fast food. Quality restaurants operate within the parks, Downtown Disney, and several Orlando neighborhoods. Here are our top recommendations, organized by price, cuisine, and experience. The restaurants we consider the very best are indicated in the listings with the Fodor's Choice logo.

Fodor's Choice ★

Be Our Guest, $$$, p. 501

Boma—Flavors of Africa, $$$$, p. 509

California Grill, $$$$, p. 509

Emeril's Orlando, $$$$, p. 514

Flying Fish, $$$$, p. 512

4 Rivers Smokehouse, $, p. 518

Hawkers, $$, p. 518

Jiko, $$$$, p. 512

Luma on Park, $$$, p. 519

Monsieur Paul, $$$$, p. 506

Norman's, $$$$, p. 516

Primo, $$$$, p. 517

The Ravenous Pig, $$$, p. 519

The Rusty Spoon, $$$, p. 518

Todd English's bluezoo, $$$$, p. 512

Victoria & Albert's, $$$$, p. 513

By Price

$

Confisco Grille, p. 514

4 Rivers Smokehouse, p. 518

Mel's Drive-In, p. 513

$$

50's Prime Time Café, p. 507

Hawkers, p. 518

Mama Melrose's Ristorante Italiano, p. 507

Mythos, p. 514

$$$

Be Our Guest, p. 501

Luma on Park, p. 519

The Ravenous Pig, p. 519

The Rusty Spoon, p. 518

$$$$

Boma—Flavors of Africa, p. 509

California Grill, p. 509

Emeril's Orlando, p. 514

Emeril's Tchoup Chop, p. 515

Flying Fish, p. 512

Jiko, p. 512

Monsieur Paul, p. 506

Norman's, p. 516

Primo, p. 517

Todd English's bluezoo, p. 512

Victoria & Albert's, p. 513

By Cuisine

AMERICAN

California Grill, $$$$, p. 509

Cinderella's Royal Table, $$$$, p. 505

50's Prime Time Café, $$, p. 507

Luma on Park, $$$, p. 519

The Ravenous Pig, $$$, p. 519

The Rusty Spoon, $$$, p. 518

Victoria & Albert's, $$$$, p. 513

Wolfgang Puck Grande Cafe, $$$, p. 508

ITALIAN

La Luce by Donna Scala, $$$, p. 517

Mama Della's Ristorante, $$$, p. 515

Primo, $$$$, p. 517

SEAFOOD

Flying Fish, $$$$, p. 512

Todd English's bluezoo, $$$$, p. 512

By Experience

BEST BUFFET

Boma—Flavors of Africa, $$$$, p. 509

Chef Mickey's, $$$$, p. 509

BEST DISNEY RESTAURANT

Be Our Guest, $$$, p. 501

Boma—Flavors of Africa, $$$$, p. 509

California Grill, $$$$, p. 509

Jiko, $$$$, p. 512

Monsieur Paul, $$$$, p. 506

Victoria & Albert's, $$$$, p. 513

BEST OFF-SITE RESTAURANT

Luma on Park, $$$, p. 519

Norman's, $$$$, p. 516

Primo, $$$$, p. 517

The Ravenous Pig, $$$, p. 519

with mashed potatoes, ordered on a touch screen and delivered to the table. $ *Average main: $25* ⊠ *Fantasyland* ☎ *407/939–3463* ⊕ *www. disneyworld.disney.go.com/dining* ⟁ *Reservations essential* ✛ *2:B1.*

$$$$ ✕ **Cinderella's Royal Table.** Cinderella and other Disney princesses appear
AMERICAN at this eatery in the castle's old mead hall; you should book reservations up to 180 days in advance to be sure to see them. The Fairytale Breakfast offers all-you-can-eat options such as lobster-crab crêpes, and caramel apple–stuffed French toast. The Fairytale Lunch and Dinner, prix-fixe table-service meals, include entrées like gnocchi with roasted vegetables or roasted bone-in pork with sweet potato hash. When you arrive at the Cinderella Castle, a photographer snaps a shot of your group in the lobby. A package of photographs will be delivered to your table during your meal. $ *Average main: $59* ⊠ *Cinderella Castle* ☎ *407/939–3463* ⊕ *www.disneyworld.disney.go.com/dining* ⟁ *Reservations essential* ✛ *2:B1.*

$$$$ ✕ **Liberty Tree Tavern.** This "tavern" is dry, but it's a prime spot on the
AMERICAN parade route, so you can catch a good meal while you wait. Order Colonial-period comfort food for lunch like hearty pot roast cooked with a cabernet-mushroom sauce, or turkey and dressing with mashed potatoes. Dinner is the family-style Patriot's Platter, with turkey, carved beef, sliced pork, and sides. The restaurant is decorated in lovely Williamsburg colors with Early American–style antiques and lots of brightly polished brass. Each of the six dining rooms commemorates a historical U.S. figure, like Betsy Ross or Benjamin Franklin. $ *Average main: $32* ⊠ *Liberty Square* ☎ *407/939–3463* ⊕ *www.disneyworld.disney. go.com/dining* ✛ *2:B1.*

EPCOT

$$$$ ✕ **Akershus Royal Banquet Hall.** This restaurant has character buffets at all
SCANDINAVIAN three meals, with an array of Disney princesses, including Ariel, Belle, Jasmine, Snow White, Mulan, Mary Poppins, and even an occasional cameo appearance by Cinderella. The breakfast menu is American, but lunch and dinner find an ever-changing assortment of Norwegian specialties. Appetizers are offered buffet style, and usually include herring, goat-milk cheese, peppered mackerel, and *gravlax* (cured salmon served with mustard sauce) or *fiskepudding* (a seafood mousse with herb dressing). For your main course, chosen à la carte, you might try traditional ground pork and beef *kjottkake* (dumplings) or roasted rack of lamb. Aquavit, wine, and specialty drinks are offered. All meals are fixed-price. $ *Average main: $52* ⊠ *Norway Pavilion* ☎ *407/939–3463* ⊕ *www.disneyworld.disney.go.com/dining* ⟁ *Reservations essential* ✛ *2:E4.*

$$$$ ✕ **Biergarten.** Oktoberfest runs 365 days a year here. The cheerful, some-
GERMAN times raucous, crowds are what you would expect in a place with an oompah band. The menu and level of frivolity are the same at lunch and dinner. Mountains of sauerbraten, bratwurst, chicken or pork schnitzel, German sausage, spaetzle, apple strudel, Bavarian cheesecake, and Black Forest cake await you at the all-you-can-eat buffet. Patrons pound pitchers of all kinds of beer and wine on the long communal tables— even when the yodelers, singers, and dancers aren't egging them on. Prices change seasonally. $ *Average main: $40* ⊠ *Germany Pavilion*

9

☎ 407/939–3463 ⊕ *www.disneyworld.disney.go.com/dining* ⌕ *Reservations essential* ✛ 2:E4.

$$$ ✕ **Les Chefs de France.** What some consider the best restaurant at Disney was created by three of France's most famous chefs: Paul Bocuse, Gaston Lenôtre, and Roger Vergé. Classic escargots, a good starter, are prepared in a casserole with garlic butter; you might follow up with roasted breast and leg of duck confit, or grilled beef tenderloin with black pepper sauce. Make sure you finish with profiteroles drizzled with chocolate sauce. The three-course prix-fixe menu is a great value when it's available. An Audio-Animatronics Remy, from the movie *Ratatouille,* makes the rounds atop a roving chef's cart. $ *Average main: $30* ✉ *France Pavilion* ☎ 407/939–3463 ⊕ *www.disneyworld. disney.go.com/dining* ✛ 2:D4.

FRENCH

$$$$ ✕ **Monsieur Paul.** A mere staircase away from Epcot's busy World Showcase, Monsieur Paul is a subdued and sophisticated fine-dinery. It's owned by Chef Jerome Bocuse and named for his world-famous father, the Culinary Institute of America's Chef of the Century, Paul Bocuse. The restaurant is expensive and sophisticated—in odd juxtaposition to the rumpled clothing and sneakers of most diners—and a delightful diversion from the theme park's bustle. The menu is overtly French while incorporating the best of America. For example, the signature fish dish, which has "scales" of potato, braised fennel, and rosemary sauce, is made with Florida red snapper instead of the original's red mullet. Escargot is presented in large raviolis and a parsley cream. The seared scallops and roasted duck breast are especially interesting entrées. Although the service isn't as polished as the menu, it is heartening to hear the waitstaff converse in French. $ *Average main: $41* ✉ *France Pavilion* ☎ 407/939–3463 ⊕ *www.disneyworld.disney.go.com/dining* ☽ *No lunch* ✛ 2:D4.

FRENCH

Fodor's Choice
★

$$$ ✕ **Rose & Crown.** If you're an Anglophile and you love a beer so thick you could stand a spoon up in your mug, this is the place to soak up both the suds and British street culture. "Wenches" serve up traditional English fare—fish-and-chips, cottage or shepherd's pie (ground beef or lamb with onions, carrots, and peas, topped with mashed potatoes and cheddar cheese), and, at times, the ever-popular bangers and mash (sausage over mashed potatoes). Scotch egg makes a good appetizer. Vegetarians can always find one item adapted for them, such as vegetable pie 'n' mash. For dessert, try the sticky toffee pudding. The terrace has a splendid view of IllumiNations. $ *Average main: $23* ✉ *United Kingdom Pavilion* ☎ 407/939–3463 ⊕ *www.disneyworld. disney.go.com/dining* ✛ 2:D4.

BRITISH

$$$ ✕ **Via Napoli.** When the Patina Restaurant Group decided to open a second Italian eatery in Epcot (the first was Tutto Italia Ristorante), they opted to specialize in authentic Neapolitan wood-fired pizza, importing the mozzarella from Italy and using only San Marzano tomatoes. The result is crusty, thin pies topped with your choice of pepperoni; portobello and crimini mushrooms; or eggplant, artichokes, cotto ham, and mushrooms. The eggplant parmigiana is an outstanding alternative. $ *Average main: $24* ✉ *Italy Pavilion* ☎ 407/939–3463 ⊕ *www. disneyworld.disney.go.com/dining* ✛ 2:E4.

PIZZA

DISNEY'S HOLLYWOOD STUDIOS

$$ ✕ **50's Prime Time Café.** Who says you can't go home again? If you grew
AMERICAN
FAMILY
up in middle America in the 1950s, just step inside. While *I Love Lucy* and *The Donna Reed Show* clips play on a television screen, you can feast on meat loaf, pot roast, or fried chicken, all served on a Formica tabletop. At $16, the meat loaf is one of the best inexpensive, filling dinners in any local theme park. Enjoy it with a malted-milk shake or root-beer float (or a bottle of wine). The place offers some fancier dishes, like the olive oil–poached salmon, which is a good choice for lighter eaters. If you're not feeling totally wholesome, go for Dad's Electric Lemonade (rum, vodka, blue curaçao, sweet-and-sour mix, and Sprite), which is worth every bit of the $10.75 price tag. Just like Mother, the menu admonishes, "Keep your elbows off the table." $ *Average main: $18* ⊠ *Echo Lake* ☎ *407/939–3463* ⊕ *www.disneyworld. disney.go.com/dining* ✛ *2:D5.*

$$$$ ✕ **Hollywood Brown Derby.** At this reproduction of the famous 1940s
AMERICAN
Hollywood restaurant, the walls are lined with movie-star caricatures, just as in Tinseltown. The specialty is the Cobb salad, which by legend was invented by Brown Derby founder Robert Cobb; the salad consists of finely chopped lettuce enlivened by loads of tomato, bacon, turkey, blue cheese, chopped egg, and avocado, all tossed tableside. Other menu choices include grilled salmon with black beluga–lentil stew and lemon-thyme sabayon, and filet of beef with white truffle oil forest mushroom mashed potatoes. Dining with an Imagineer is a special option; you will have lunch or dinner with one of Disney's creative engineers while enjoying a set-price four-course meal including soup, salad, entrée, and dessert. If you request the Fantasmic! dinner package, make a reservation for no later than two hours before the start of the show. $ *Average main: $30* ⊠ *Hollywood Blvd.* ☎ *407/939–3463* ⊕ *www.disneyworld. disney.go.com/dining* ✛ *2:D5.*

$$ ✕ **Mama Melrose's Ristorante Italiano.** To replace the energy you've no
ITALIAN
doubt depleted by miles of theme-park walking, you can load up on carbs at this casual Italian restaurant that looks like an old warehouse. Good main courses include spaghetti with meatballs, and wood-grilled chicken in a four-cheese sauce with pasta and vegetables. Wood-fired flatbreads are available as an entrée choice here (a great bargain at $13 and up) with toppings ranging from grilled chicken with ricotta and onion to wild mushroom. The sangria is popular. Ask for the Fantasmic! dinner package if you want priority seating for the show. $ *Average main: $22* ⊠ *Streets of America* ☎ *407/939–3463* ⊕ *www.disneyworld. disney.go.com/dining* ✛ *2:D5.*

$$ ✕ **Sci-Fi Dine-In Theater Restaurant.** If you don't mind zombies leering at
AMERICAN
you while you eat, then head to this enclosed faux drive-in, where you can sit in a fake candy-color '50s convertible and watch trailers from classics like *Attack of the 50 Foot Woman* and *Teenagers from Outer Space.* The menu includes choices like steak and garlic-mashed potatoes, an Angus or veggie burger, shrimp with pasta, and a huge reuben sandwich with fries or cucumber salad. End with a hot-fudge sundae. $ *Average main: $22* ⊠ *Commissary La.* ☎ *407/939–3463* ⊕ *www. disneyworld.disney.go.com/dining* ✛ *2:D5.*

9

DISNEY'S ANIMAL KINGDOM

$ ✕ **Flame Tree Barbecue.** This counter-service eatery is one of the rela-
FAST FOOD tively undiscovered gems of Disney's culinary offerings. There's nothing
fancy here, but you can dig into ribs and pulled-pork sandwiches. For
something with a lower calorie count, try the smoked turkey sandwich
served with cranberry mayo or a great barbecued chicken served with
baked beans and cole slaw. The outdoor tables, set beneath intricately
carved wood pavilions, make great spots for a picnic, and they're not
usually crowded. $ *Average main: $12* ✉ *Discovery Island* ⊕ *www.
disneyworld.disney.go.com/dining* 🚫 *Reservations not accepted* ✛ *2:B5.*

$$$ ✕ **Yak & Yeti.** The location of this pan-Asian cuisine, sit-down eatery—
ASIAN the only full-service restaurant inside Disney's Animal Kingdom—cer-
tainly makes sense. It's just at the entrance to the Asia section, in a
two-story, 250-seat building that is pleasantly faux-Asian, with cracked
plaster walls, wood carvings, and tile mosaic tabletops. Standout entrées
include seared miso salmon, roasted duck with orange-wasabi glaze,
and tempura shrimp with jasmine rice and chili-plum sauce. Also tasty,
if not authentically Asian, are the baby back ribs with a hoisin barbecue
sauce and sweet chili slaw. $ *Average main: $22* ✉ *Asia* ☎ *407/939–
3463* ⊕ *www.disneyworld.disney.go.com/dining* ✛ *2:B5.*

DOWNTOWN DISNEY

$$$ ✕ **Raglan Road Irish Pub.** An authentic Irish pub in Downtown Disney
IRISH seems oxymoronic, particularly when that pub seats 600 people. But if
Irish grub's your thing, Raglan's is the place to go. The shepherd's pie
served here is of higher quality than the usual version, prepared with
beef and lamb and jazzed up with house spices. And you don't have
to settle for plain fish-and-chips (though you can for $19); there's also
baked salmon with smoked salmon and maple glaze; shiitake risotto;
and lamb shanks braised with rosemary jus. Massive and ornate bars,
imported from Ireland and more than a century old, help anchor the
pub. The entertainment alone makes this place worth the visit. The
house bands play nightly, and a troupe of Irish dancers performs every
evening and during Sunday brunch. Another band plays outside for
guests dining alfresco. $ *Average main: $22* ✉ *1640 E. Buena Vista
Dr., Downtown Disney* ☎ *407/938–0300* ⊕ *www.raglanroadirishpub.
com* ✛ *2:F4.*

$$$ ✕ **Wolfgang Puck Grand Cafe.** There are lots of choices here, from wood-
AMERICAN oven pizza at the informal Puck Express to fine-dining meals in the
upstairs formal dining room. There's also a sushi bar and an informal
café; the café is quite literally a happy medium, and may be the best bet
for families hoping for a bit of elegance without the pressure of a for-
mal dinner. At Express try the butternut squash soup or the Margherita
pizza. At the café, midprice entrées like rosemary chicken Alfredo and
crispy pork loin with shaved fennel, oranges, and radishes are winners,
and you can always have a personal pizza, such as barbecued chicken
with smoked mozzarella. The dining room offers creative entrées liked
seared chicken with truffled polenta. $ *Average main: $21* ✉ *1482
E. Buena Vista Dr., West Side, Downtown Disney* ☎ *407/938–9653*
⊕ *www.wolfgangpuckcafeorlando.com* ✛ *2:F4.*

WDW RESORTS

$$$$
AFRICAN
Fodor'sChoice
★

✕ **Boma—Flavors of Africa.** Boma takes Western-style ingredients and prepares them with an African twist—then invites guests to walk through an African marketplace–style dining room to help themselves at the extraordinary buffet. The dozen or so serving stations have entrées such as roasted pork, Durban-style chicken, spice-crusted beef, and fish served with tamarind and other robust sauces; intriguing salads; and some of the best hummus this side of the Atlantic. Don't pass up the soups, as the coconut-curry seafood stew is excellent. The zebra dome dessert is chocolate mousse covered with white chocolate and striped with dark chocolate. All meals are prix fixe, and prices change seasonally. The South African wine list is outstanding. $ *Average main:* $44 ⊠ *Animal Kingdom Lodge, 2901 Osceola Pkwy., Animal Kingdom Resort Area* ☎ *407/939–3463* ⊕ *www.disneyworld.disney.go.com/ dining* ⚄ *Reservations essential* ⊗ *No lunch* ✛ *2:A5.*

$$$$
AMERICAN
Fodor'sChoice
★

✕ **California Grill.** The view from the surrounding Disney parks from this 15th-floor restaurant—the World's signature dining establishment since 1995—is as stunning as the food, especially after dark, when you can watch the nightly Magic Kingdom fireworks. The entire space and menu underwent major transformations in 2013, from new midcentury modern furnishings and chandeliers to kitchen equipment such as a cast-iron flat grill designed specifically for cooking fish. Expect locally sourced foods where possible, made-from-scratch items such as the sausage-in-a-duck sampler appetizer, and many items cooked in the wood-fired oven. Sushi remains a highlight, alongside creative, globally inspired entrées. Specialties include a short-rib fillet cooked at a low temperature for 24 hours sous-vide-style and served with red-wine butter, and scallops with homemade gnocchi, smoked pork, and Parmesan foam. A 10- to 14-course *omakase* (tasting menu) is available. $ *Average main:* $41 ⊠ *Contemporary Resort, 4600 N. World Dr., Magic Kingdom Resort Area* ☎ *407/939–3463* ⊕ *www.disneyworld.disney. go.com/dining* ⚄ *Reservations essential* ⊗ *No lunch* ✛ *2:C1.*

$$$$
AMERICAN

✕ **Chef Mickey's.** This is the holy shrine for character meals, with Mickey, Minnie, or Goofy around for breakfast and dinner. Folks come here for entertainment and comfort food, not a quiet spot to read the *Orlando Sentinel.* The breakfast buffet includes "pixie-dusted" challah French toast, mountains of pancakes, and even a breakfast pizza. The dinner buffet doesn't disappoint with Thai-curry-chipotle barbecue chicken, roasted ham, and spice-rubbed beef sirloin. Finish off your meal at the all-you-can-eat dessert bar of sundaes. $ *Average main:* $44 ⊠ *Contemporary Resort, 4600 N. World Dr., Magic Kingdom Resort Area* ☎ *407/939–3463* ⊕ *www.disneyworld.disney.go.com/dining* ⊗ *No lunch* ✛ *2:C1.*

$$
AMERICAN

✕ **ESPN Club.** Not only can you watch sports on a big-screen TV here (the restaurant has about 100 monitors), but you can also periodically see ESPN programs being taped in the club itself and be part of the audience of sports-radio talk shows. Food ranges from a variety of half-pound burgers, made with Angus chuck (and one topped with lobster salad), to an excellent Reuben with plenty of corned beef, sauerkraut, and cheese. If you want an appetizer, try the Pub Nachos for Two,

9

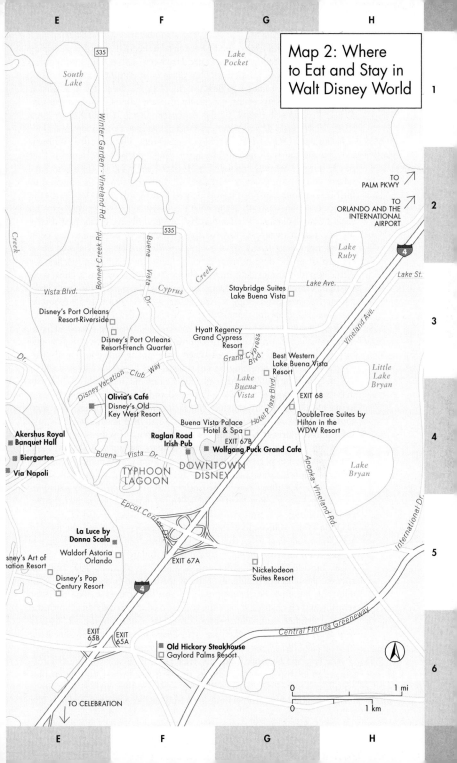

Map 2: Where to Eat and Stay in Walt Disney World

crispy corn tortilla chips piled high with barbecued pulled pork, spicy chili, shredded cheddar cheese, cheddar cheese sauce, sour cream, pico de gallo, and sliced jalapeños. This place is open quite late by Disney standards—until 1 am daily. Beware, the place can be pretty loud during any broadcast sports event, especially football games. $ *Average main: $16* ⊠ *BoardWalk Inn, 2101 Epcot Resorts Blvd., Epcot Resort Area* ☎ *407/939–3463* ⊕ *www.disneyworld.disney.go.com/dining* ✢ *2:D5.*

$$$$
SEAFOOD
Fodor's Choice
★

✕ **Flying Fish.** One of Disney's best restaurants, Flying Fish is whimsically decorated with murals along the upper portion of the walls that pay tribute to Atlantic seaboard spots of the early 1900s. This is a place where you put on your "resort casual" duds to "dine," as opposed to putting on your flip-flops and shorts to "chow down." The chefs take the food so seriously that the entire culinary team takes day trips to local farms to learn their foodstuffs' origins. Flying Fish's best dishes include potato-wrapped red snapper, which is so popular it has been on the menu for several years, and oak-grilled salmon. Groups of up to six can sit at the counter that directly faces the exhibition kitchen for a five-course wine tasting menu. The restaurant now hosts Dine with an Imagineer meals. $ *Average main: $36* ⊠ *BoardWalk Inn, 2101 Epcot Resorts Blvd., Epcot Resort Area* ☎ *407/939–2359* ⊕ *www. disneyworld.disney.go.com/dining* ⊘ *No lunch* ✢ *2:D5.*

$$$$
AFRICAN
Fodor's Choice
★

✕ **Jiko.** The name of this restaurant means "the cooking place" in Swahili, and it is certainly that. The dining area surrounds two big, wood-burning ovens and a grill area where you can watch cooks in North African–style caps working on your meal. The menu here is more African-inspired than purely African, but it does include authentic flavors in entrées like peri-peri chicken flatbread and Zanzibar fish stew. Menu items often change, but entrées might include maize-crusted fish with tomato-butter sauce or spicy Botswana-style beef short ribs with cassava-potato puree. The restaurant offers dozens of wines by the glass, including a large selection of South African vintages. Ask about the wine-and-dine experiences, the Wanyama vehicle safari-dinner combo (only for hotel guests), and the Wednesday wine tastings. $ *Average main: $36* ⊠ *Animal Kingdom Lodge, 2901 Osceola Pkwy., Animal Kingdom Resort Area* ☎ *407/939–3463* ⊕ *www.disneyworld.disney. go.com/dining* ⊜ *Reservations essential* ⊘ *No lunch* ✢ *2:A5.*

$$
AMERICAN

✕ **Olivia's Café.** This is like a meal at Grandma's—provided she lives in Key West and likes to gussy up her grub with trendy twists. The menu ranges from a shrimp pasta with sun-dried tomato to grilled pork chops with chipotle barbecue sauce and a side of smoked-cheddar mac 'n' cheese. Desserts are indulgent, such as the banana-bread-pudding sundae with bananas Foster topping and vanilla ice cream. The outdoor seating, which overlooks a waterway, is a nice place to dine any time the midsummer heat is not bearing down. $ *Average main: $21* ⊠ *Old Key West Resort, 1510 N. Cove Rd., Downtown Disney Resort Area* ☎ *407/939–3463* ⊕ *www.disneyworld.disney.go.com/dining* ✢ *2:E4.*

$$$$
SEAFOOD
Fodor's Choice
★

✕ **Todd English's bluezoo.** Celebrity chef Todd English oversees this cutting-edge seafood eatery, a sleek, modern restaurant that resembles an underwater dining hall, with blue walls and carpeting, aluminum fish suspended from the ceiling, and bubble-like lighting fixtures. The menu is creative and pricey, with entrées like the two-pound Maine "Cantonese lobster," fried and tossed in a sticky soy glaze, and the daily "dancing fish," cooked on an upright rotisserie with an apple-soy marinade. If you don't care for fish, you can opt for seasonal chicken or steak preparations. The children's menu is especially good. $ *Average main: $44* ⊠ *Walt Disney World Dolphin, 1500 Epcot Resorts Blvd., Epcot Resort Area* ☎ *407/934–1111* ⊕ *www.thebluezoo.com* ⊗ *No lunch* ✛ *2:C4.*

$$$$
MODERN
AMERICAN
Fodor'sChoice
★

✕ **Victoria & Albert's.** At this ultraposh, award-winning Disney restaurant, a well-polished service team will anticipate your every need during a gourmet extravaganza. This is one of the plushest fine-dining experiences in Florida, with an ambiance so sophisticated that children under 10 aren't on the guest list. The seven-course, prix-fixe menu changes daily, and you'd do well to supplement the $135 tab with a $65 wine pairing. Appetizer choices may include roast duck with mango vinaigrette, octopus with black-garlic aioli, and masago-crusted shrimp with coconut-curry sauce. Entrées may feature braised oxtail and cherry ravioli or Australian Kobe-style beef with smoked garlic-potato puree. For most of the year, there are two seatings, at 5:45 and 9. In July and August, however, there's generally just one seating at 6:30 pm. For a more luxe experience, reserve a table in the intimate Queen Victoria Room or at the Chef's Table, which has more courses (10 to 12) and a bigger bill ($210, wine pairing $105). $ *Average main: $173* ⊠ *Grand Floridian, 4401 Floridian Way, Magic Kingdom Resort Area* ☎ *407/939–3862* ⊕ *www.victoria-alberts.com* ⌲ *Reservations essential* 🏛 *Jacket required* ⊗ *No lunch* ✛ *2:B1.*

UNIVERSAL ORLANDO AREA

UNIVERSAL STUDIOS

$$
IRISH

✕ **Finnegan's Bar & Grill.** In an Irish pub that would look just right in downtown New York during the Ellis Island era, Finnegan's offers classic Irish comfort food like shepherd's pie, corned beef and cabbage, bangers and mash (sausage and mashed potatoes), and fish-and-chips, plus Guinness on tap. If shepherd's pie isn't your thing, opt instead for a steak, burger, entrée salad, or sandwich. Irish folk music, sometimes live, completes the theme. $ *Average main: $16* ⊠ *New York* ☎ *407/363-8757* ⊕ *www.universalorlando.com* ✛ *1:D3.*

$
AMERICAN

✕ **Mel's Drive-In.** At the corner of Hollywood and Vine is a flashy '50s eatery with a pink-and-white 1956 Ford Crown Victoria parked out in front. For burgers and fries, this is one of the best choices in the park, and it comes complete with a roving doo-wop group during peak seasons. You're on vacation, so go ahead and have that extra-thick shake or the decadent chili-cheese fries. Mel's is also a great place to meet up, in case you decide to go your separate ways in the park. $ *Average main: $9* ⊠ *Hollywood* ☎ *407/363–8766* ⊕ *www.universalorlando.com* ⌲ *Reservations not accepted* ✛ *1:D3.*

9

ISLANDS OF ADVENTURE

$ ✕ **Confisco Grille.** You could walk right past this full-service restaurant
AMERICAN without noticing it, but if you want a good meal and sit-down service, don't pass by too quickly. This is one of the better eateries inside
the theme parks. The menu changes often, but typical entrées include
pad thai, grilled or blackened fresh fish of the day with mashed potatoes and sautéed spinach in a lemon-butter-cilantro sauce, and penne
puttanesca—the vodka-cream tomato sauce is enhanced with sausage, kalamata olives, fried pepperoncini, and roasted garlic. Wash it
all down with refreshing sangria, available by glass, pitcher, and half
pitcher. ⓈⒶ *Average main: $13* ✉ *Port of Entry* ☎ *407/224–4404* ⊕ *www.*
universalorlando.com ☾ *No dinner.* ✛ *1:E3*

$$ ✕ **Mythos.** The name may be Greek, but the dishes are eclectic. The sea-
ECLECTIC sonally changing menu usually includes such mainstays as pad Thai and
pan-seared salmon with pineapple sauce. The building itself—which
looks like a giant rock formation from the outside and a huge cave
(albeit one with plush upholstered seating) from the inside—is enough
to grab your attention, but so do sandwiches like crab-cake sliders and
roast beef paninis with caramelized yellow onions, roasted red peppers,
and pepperoncini. Mythos also has a waterfront view of the big lagoon
in the center of the theme park. When it's slow in the park, the restau-
rant is open only for lunch. Ⓢ *Average main: $15* ✉ *The Lost Continent*
☎ *407/224–4533* ⊕ *www.universalorlando.com* ✛ *1:D3.*

$ ✕ **Three Broomsticks.** Now Harry Potter fans can taste pumpkin juice
BRITISH (with hints of honey and vanilla) and butterbeer (sort of like bubbly
butterscotch cream soda; some say it tastes like shortbread cookies).
They're on the menu along with British foodstuffs at this Hogsmeade
restaurant modeled after the fantasy books. Rickety staircases and
gaslit chandeliers set the tone for the counter-service restaurant, where
families gobble down ample portions of shepherd's pie, fish-and-chips,
chargrilled ribs, and smoked chicken. In the adjacent Hog's Head pub,
a faux hog's head sneers now and then. Ⓢ *Average main: $12* ✉ *Wizard-*
ing World of Harry Potter ☎ *407/224–4233* ⊕ *www.universalorlando.*
com ⓐ *Reservations not accepted* ✛ *1:D3.*

CITYWALK

$$$$ ✕ **Emeril's Orlando.** The popular eatery is a culinary shrine to Emeril
CAJUN Lagasse, the famous TV chef who occasionally makes an appearance.
Fodor's Choice And although the modern interior of the restaurant with its 30-foot
★ ceilings, blond woods, second-story wine loft, and lots of galvanized
steel looks nothing like the French Quarter, the hardwood floors and
linen tablecloths create an environment befitting the stellar nature of
the cuisine. Entrées, which change frequently, may include andouille-
crusted pan-roasted redfish with creole meunière sauce, pork chop with
green mole sauce and tamarind glaze, and barbecue-glazed salmon with
homemade andouille. Reservations are usually essential, but there's a
chance of getting a walk-in seating if you show up for lunch (11:30 am)
or early for dinner (5:30 pm). Ⓢ *Average main: $39* ✉ *6000 Universal*
Blvd. ☎ *407/224–2424* ⊕ *www.emerils.com* ⓐ *Reservations essential*
✛ *1:E3.*

$$
AMERICAN
✕ **NASCAR Sports Grille.** Filled with race-car simulator games as well as arcade and racing memorabilia, this eatery might not look like the place to grab a sublime meal, but that's not the case. This theme restaurant has a reputation as a good place for grub. Selections worth trying include the Southern-style pot roast and the slow-roasted baby back rib platter; the Talladega cheeseburger with a side of fries is a cut above the standard theme-park burger. ⑤ *Average main: $19* ⊠ *6000 Universal Blvd.* ☎ *407/224–7223* ⊕ *www.nascarsportsgrilleorlando.com* ✛ *1:E3.*

UNIVERSAL HOTELS

$$$$
SOUTH PACIFIC
✕ **Emeril's Tchoup Chop.** The bold interior décor—with lots of bamboo, bright glazed tile, an exposition kitchen, and a long zero-edge pool with porcelain lily pads running the length of the dining room—is just as ambitious as the food at Emeril Lagasse's Pacific-influenced restaurant. Following the theme of the Royal Pacific Resort, Lagasse melds his signature bold flavors with Asian- and Polynesian-fusion tastes. A *robata* (charcoal) grill that heats to 1,000°F churns out appetizers and side dishes; try the Thai-spiced lamb satay. Entrées change regularly, but representative dishes include Hawaiian-style snapper with ginger, cilantro, and sesame soy sauce; and a grilled pork chop with Korean barbecue sauce and mango salsa. Sushi varieties are offered. For dessert, get the Hawaiian-style *malasadas* doughnuts. They're served with three sauces in plastic bottles; you insert the tip into the donuts and squirt in the fillings yourself. ⑤ *Average main: $32* ⊠ *Loews Royal Pacific Resort, 6300 Hollywood Way* ☎ *407/503–2467* ⊕ *www.emerils.com* ⌚ *Reservations essential* ✛ *1:D3.*

$$$
ITALIAN
✕ **Mama Della's Ristorante.** This playfully themed Italian restaurant happens to have excellent food. The premise is that you're eating at a home-turned-restaurant owned by an Italian woman. That woman, Mama Della, is played by an actress, whose warmth enhances the experience (as does the serenade by an accordionist, guitar player, and vocalist). The menu features Italian classics like chicken parmigiana and lasagna as well as more ambitious dishes like salmon with fennel soffritto and braised lamb with eggplant caponata. Outdoor seating on the patio provides a view of the hotel's nightly *Musica Della Notte* (*Music of the Night*) opera show. ⑤ *Average main: $29* ⊠ *Loews Portofino Bay Hotel, 5601 Universal Blvd.* ☎ *407/503–3463* ⊕ *www.loewshotels.com* ⊗ *No lunch* ✛ *1:D3.*

ORLANDO METRO AREA

KISSIMMEE

$$$$
STEAKHOUSE
✕ **Old Hickory Steakhouse.** This upscale steakhouse is designed to look like rustic cabins in the Everglades. Beyond the playful facade is a polished restaurant with a classic steakhouse menu—bone-in ribeye, porterhouse, and filet mignon, supplemented by rack of lamb, veal chop, and Atlantic salmon, all priced for the hotel's conventiongoers. The chef gets creative with appetizers like a warm pear-and-goat-cheese tart, but most are standards such as onion soup, shrimp cocktail, and tomato-onion salad. Artisanal cheese plates are on the menu, and desserts are interesting, such as fudge-dipped derby pie. ⑤ *Average main:*

$50 ⊠ Gaylord Palms Resort, 6000 W. Osceola Pkwy., I–4 Exit 65 🕾 407/586–1600 ⊕ www.gaylordpalms.com ✺ No lunch ✛ 2:F6.

INTERNATIONAL DRIVE

$$$ ✕ **Café Tu Tu Tango.** The food here is served tapas-style—everything is

ECLECTIC   appetizer-size but plentiful, and relatively inexpensive. If you want a compendium of cuisines at one go, try the black-bean soup with cilantro sour cream, guava barbecue-glazed pork ribs, hazelnut-lemongrash fish, and spiced alligator bites. The wine list includes more than 35 wines from several countries, with all but a handful by the bottle and the glass, and 50+ craft beers. The restaurant is designed to resemble an artist's loft; artists paint at easels while diners take a culinary trip around the world. Belly dancers, flamenco dancers, Bolivian dancers, and African drummers are among the entertainers who perform in the evening. Thanks to a patio, diners can also share their small plates alfresco. ⑤ *Average main: $23* ⊠ *8625 International Dr., I-Drive area* 🕾 *407/248–2222* ⊕ *www.cafetututango.com* ⌲ *Reservations not accepted* ✛ *1:D4.*

$$$ ✕ **Taverna Opa.** This high-energy Greek restaurant bills itself as offering

GREEK   "fun with a capital F." Here the ouzo flows like a mountain stream, the Greek music almost reaches the level of a rock concert, and the roaming belly dancers actively encourage diners to take part in the mass Zorba dancing, which often happens on the tops of dining tables. The only thing missing is the Greek restaurant tradition of throwing dinner plates, made up in part by the throwing of torn-up paper napkins, which sometimes reaches near-blizzard level. The food, by the way, is also excellent. Standouts include traditional staples like spanakopita, *saganaki* (the traditional flaming cheese appetizer), *avgolemono* (lemony chicken-rice soup), and perhaps the most famous Greek entrée, moussaka. Family-style meals for groups of four and up are available at $33 and $44 per person. The best dessert is the baklava. ⑤ *Average main: $27* ⊠ *Pointe Orlando, 9101 International Dr., I-Drive area* 🕾 *407/351-8660* ⊕ *www.opaorlando.com* ✛ *1:D4.*

SOUTH ORLANDO

$$$$ ✕ **Norman's.** Celebrity-chef Norman Van Aken brings impressive creden-

ECLECTIC   tials to the restaurant that bears his name, as you might expect from the

Fodor's Choice   headline eatery in the Ritz-Carlton Orlando Grande Lakes. Van Aken's

★   culinary roots go back to the Florida Keys, where he's credited with creating "Floribbean" cuisine, a blend that is part Key West and part Caribbean—although he now weaves in flavors from all continents. The Orlando operation is a formal, sleek restaurant with marble floors, starched tablecloths, servers in ties and vests, eight certified sommeliers, and a creative, if expensive, menu. In addition to exceptional ceviches and a signature appetizer called Down Island French toast made with Curacao-marinated foie gras, favorites include a Mongolian-marinated veal chop, pan-cooked Florida snapper with citrus butter, and pork Havana with "21st-century mole sauce." A six-course tasting menu is $95, more with beverage pairings. Covered terrace seating is also available. ⑤ *Average main: $46* ⊠ *Ritz-Carlton Orlando Grande Lakes,*

4000 Central Florida Pkwy. ☎ *407/393–4333* ⊕ *www.normans.com* ⊙ *No lunch* ✤ *1:E4.*

$$$$
ITALIAN
Fodor'sChoice
★

✕ Primo. James Beard Award–winner Melissa Kelly cloned her Italian-organic Maine restaurant in an upscale Orlando hotel and brought her farm-to-table sensibilities with her. Here the daily dinner menu pays tribute to Sicily's lighter foods, made with produce grown in the hotel garden. Homemade pasta is served with veal meatballs or braised rabbit; if the butternut-squash ravioli with butter-poached Maine lobster is available, order it. Dry-aged prime New York strip steak is enhanced with crispy potato and horseradish raviolini. Fish plays prominently, such as a refreshing Florida snapper fillet with Italian couscous and heirloom tomato sauce. Desserts are just as special, with the likes of warm Belgian chocolate *budino* (pudding) cake or hot zeppole tossed in cinnamon and sugar. ⑤ *Average main: $38* ✉ *JW Marriott Orlando Grande Lakes, 4040 Central Florida Pkwy.* ☎ *407/393–4444* ⊕ *www.primorestaurant.com* ⊙ *No lunch* ✤ *1:E4.*

LAKE BUENA VISTA

$$$
ITALIAN

✕ La Luce by Donna Scala. Having made a name for herself at California's Bistro Don Giovanni, Donna Scala brought the same Italian cuisine with a Napa Valley farm-fresh flair to this upscale Hilton at the edge of Disney World. The walls are decorated with chalk art, which changes twice a year. Equal effort goes into the menu, where pastas are made fresh. Try the ricotta gnocchi with wild mushrooms and artichokes, the ribeye with fennel, or a simple seared salmon fillet with tomato chive butter sauce. ⑤ *Average main: $30* ✉ *Hilton Orlando Bonnett Creek, 14100 Bonnet Creek Resort La., Bonnet Creek* ☎ *407/597–3600* ⊕ *www.laluceorlando.com* ⊙ *No lunch* ✤ *2:F5.*

SAND LAKE ROAD

$$
AMERICAN

✕ Seasons 52. Parts of the menu change every week at this innovative restaurant that serves different foods at different times of year, depending on what's in season. Meals here tend to be healthful (butter is banned) yet hearty and very flavorful. The beef and black-bean chili starter is to die for. For an entrée, you might have wood-roasted pork tenderloin with polenta, portobello mushrooms, caramelized cipollini, and roasted onion jus, or caramelized grilled sea scallops with sun-dried tomato–mushroom pearl pasta. An impressive wine list with dozens of selections by the glass complements the menu. For dessert, have mini-indulgence classics like pecan pie, rocky road, carrot cake, and key lime pie served in petite portions. Although the cuisine is haute, the prices are modest—not bad for a snazzy, urbane bistro and wine bar. It has live music nightly to boot. Another Seasons is located in Altamonte Springs. ⑤ *Average main: $20* ✉ *Plaza Venezia, 7700 Sand Lake Rd., Exit 75A off I-4, Sand Lake Rd. Area* ☎ *407/354–5212* ⊕ *www.seasons52.com* ✤ *1:D3.*

9

$$$$
STEAKHOUSE

✕ Vines Grille & Wine Bar. Live jazz and blues music fills the night at the bar section of this dramatically designed restaurant, but the food and drink in the snazzy main dining room are headliners in their own right. The kitchen bills itself as a steakhouse, but it really is far more than that. Entrées range from a porterhouse (alas, no longer dry-aged) to pan-seared Chilean sea bass with lobster risotto and basil *beurre blanc,* from a one-pound Wagyu burger with truffle fries to pork osso bucco with brown butter Boursin grits. Be sure to start with the grilled octopus, which is simply prepared with red onions, capers, and roasted fennel. The wine list here is extensive, and the cocktails are serious business, too. The crowd tends to dress up, but jackets and ties are not required. ⑤ *Average main: $48* ⊠ *The Fountains, 7533 W. Sand Lake Rd., Sand Lake Rd. Area* ☎ *407/351–1227* ⊕ *www.vinesgrille. com* ⊗ *No lunch* ✦ *1:D3.*

CENTRAL ORLANDO

$$ ✕**Hawkers.** Hipsters, families, and business groups dine side by side at this popular restaurant, a laid-back spot that specializes in serving Asian street food. Travel the continent with $3 to $7.50 appetizer-size portions of scratch-made specialties from Malaysia, Singapore, Thailand, and Vietnam. Musts for adventurous diners include *roti canai,* a flaky bread with a chicken-curry dip; curry *laksa,* a noodle soup with exotic flavors; and stir-fried udon noodles. More timid eaters adore the marinated beef skewers with Malaysian satay sauce, peanuty chilled sesame noodles, duck tacos, and any of the Americanized (but flavorful) lettuce wraps. ⑤ *Average main: $15* ⊠ *1103 Mills Ave., Mills 50 District* ☎ *407/237–0606* ⊕ *www.facebook.com/hawkersstreetfare* ✦ *1:F1.*

ASIAN
Fodor's Choice
★

$$$ ✕**The Rusty Spoon.** Lovingly raised animals and locally grown produce are the menu foundation at this Downtown gastropub, an ideal spot for a business lunch or a pre–basketball game, -theater, or -concert dinner. The wood-and-brick dining room is a comfortable backdrop to hearty American meals with a Southern bent. Creatively stuffed eggs and buttermilk-soaked Vidalia onion rings are top starters. The salads—with ultrafresh greens—are always sensational. All pastas are made from scratch, whether a butternut squash lasagna or a winter pappardelle with wilted escarole, parsnips, toasted walnuts, and fried sage. The Dirty South seafood stew is a Dixie take on bouillabaisse. End with a very grown-up take on s'mores. One Sunday a month, there's brunch. ⑤ *Average main: $22* ⊠ *55 W. Church St., Downtown Orlando* ☎ *407/401–8811* ⊕ *www.therustyspoon.com* ⊗ *No lunch weekends* ✦ *1:F1.*

SOUTHERN
Fodor's Choice
★

WINTER PARK

$ ✕**4 Rivers Smokehouse.** Obsessed with Texas-style barbecue brisket, John Rivers decided to turn his passion into a business upon retiring from the corporate world. The result is the überpopular 4 Rivers, which turns out barbecue standards like pulled pork and cornbread, plus more unusual items like the addicting bacon-wrapped smoked jalapeño peppers, the Six Shooter with cheese grits, and a sausage-filled pastry called *kolache.* Old-time soft drinks such as Frostie Root Beer and Cheerwine are for sale, along with desserts like the kiddie favorite Chocolate Awesomeness, an indulgent layering of chocolate cake, chocolate pudding, Heath Bar, whipped cream, and chocolate and caramel sauces. Some units have a Sweet Shop that sells whole oversized cakes. Additional 4 Rivers are

BARBECUE
Fodor's Choice
★

scattered throughout Central Florida. $ *Average main: $14* ✉ *1600 W. Fairbanks Ave.* ☎ *407/474–8377* ⊕ *www.4rsmokehouse.com* ⟋ *Reservations not accepted* ⊙ *Closed Sun.* ✛ *1:F1.*

$$$ ✕ **Luma on Park.** Indisputably one of the Orlando area's best restaurants,
MODERN Luma on Park is a popular spot for progressive American cuisine served
AMERICAN in a fashionable setting. Every ingredient is carefully sourced from local
Fodor's Choice producers when possible, and scratch preparation—from pastas to sau-
★ sages to pickled rhubarb—is the mantra among its dedicated clique of chefs. The menu changes daily. You might discover chestnut agnolotti with Maine lobster or a cauliflower-onion tart as starters, followed by tilefish with tangerine-fennel broth or a duck breast with kale, toasted pine nuts, parsnip purée, and pickled white asparagus. The wine cellar is a high point, holding 7,000 bottles—80 varieties, all available by the half glass, glass, and bottle. The restaurant offers a three-course, prix-fixe dinner Sunday through Tuesday for $35 per person, $45 with wine pairings. $ *Average main: $26* ✉ *290 S. Park Ave., Park Ave.* ☎ *407/599–4111* ⊕ *www.lumaonpark.com* ⟋ *Reservations essential* ⊙ *No lunch Mon.–Thurs.* ✛ *1:F1.*

$$$ ✕ **The Ravenous Pig.** A trendy, vibrant gastropub in one of Orlando's most
MODERN affluent enclaves, the Pig is arguably Orlando's most popular foodie des-
AMERICAN tination. Run by husband-and-wife chefs James and Julie Petrakis, the
Fodor's Choice restaurant dispenses delicacies such as pork porterhouse with German
★ potato salad and apple-cider gastrique, and five-spice Florida cobia with bacon–brussels sprout hash, poached apple, and apple whiskey broth. The menu changes daily and always includes less expensive pub fare like lobster tacos and homemade pretzels with a taleggio-porter fondue. All charcuterie is made in house, from spiced orange salami to game-bird terrine. The signature dessert is the Pig Tails, essentially a basket full of piping hot, pig tail–shaped doughnuts with a chocolate-espresso dipping sauce. $ *Average main: $25* ✉ *1234 N. Orange Ave., Orange Ave.* ☎ *407/628–2333* ⊕ *www.theravenouspig.com* ⟋ *Reservations essential* ⊙ *Closed Sun. and Mon.* ✛ *1:F1.*

9

WHERE TO STAY

Updated by Jennifer Greenhill-Taylor
With tens of thousands of lodging choices available in the Orlando area, from tents to deluxe villas, there is no lack of variety in price or amenities. Narrowing down the possibilities can be part of the fun.

More than 50 million visitors come to the Orlando area each year, making it the most popular tourism destination on the planet. More upscale hotels are opening as visitors demand more luxurious surroundings, such as luxe linens, tasteful and refined décor, organic toiletries, or ergonomic chairs and work desks. But no matter what your budget or desires, lodging comes in such a wide range of prices, themes, color schemes, brands, meal plans, and guest-room amenities, you will have no problem finding something that fits.

Resorts on and off Disney property combine function with fantasy, as befits visitor expectations. Characters in costume perform for the kids, pools are pirates' caves with waterfalls, and some, like the Gaylord Palms, go so far as to re-create Florida landmarks under a gargantuan glass roof, giving visitors the illusion of having visited more of the state than they expected.

The area around the expanded Orange County Convention Center is going more upscale as the center draws more and more savvy conventioneers who bring their families along to visit the theme parks. Central Florida has weathered the tough economic times of the past few years so well, in fact, that prices are on the rise, and a wide range of new hotels are popping up.

Many hotels have joined the trend toward green lodging, bringing recycling, water conservation, and other environmentally conscious practices to the table. Best of all, the sheer number and variety of hotel rooms means you can still find relative bargains throughout the Orlando area, even on Disney property, by researching your trip well, calling the lodgings directly, negotiating packages and prices, and shopping wisely.

RESERVATIONS

When booking by phone, expect a robot first, then a real person.

WDW Central Reservations Office. You can book many accommodations—Disney-owned hotels and some non-Disney-owned hotels—through the WDW Central Reservations Office. The website allows you to compare prices at the various on-site resorts. ☎ *407/934–7639* ⊕ *www. disneyworld.com.*

WDW Special Request Reservations. People with disabilities can call WDW Special Request Reservations, or check the website for specific needs. ☎ *407/824–4321, 407/TTY: 827–5141* ⊕ *www.disneyworld.com.*

Walt Disney Travel Co. Packages can be arranged through the Walt Disney Travel Co. Guests can find planning tools on the website that allow them to customize vacation itineraries to suit interests as well as special needs based on age, height restrictions and medical needs. ☎ *407/939–5277* ⊕ *www.disneyworld.com.*

WHAT IT COSTS			
$	**$$**	**$$$**	**$$$$**
FOR TWO PEOPLE	under $175	$175–$249	$250–$350	over $350

ABOUT OUR REVIEWS

Prices: Prices in the hotel reviews are the lowest cost of a standard double room in high season, excluding taxes, service charges, and meal plans (except at all-inclusives). Prices for rentals are the lowest per-night cost for a one-bedroom unit in high season. Note that taxes in Central Florida can be as high as 12.5%.

Maps: *Throughout the chapter, you'll see mapping symbols and coordinates (✤ 3:F2) after property names or reviews. Maps are within the chapter. The first number after the ✤ symbol indicates the map number. After that is the property's coordinate on the map grid.*

Hotel reviews have been shortened. For full information, visit Fodors. com.

WALT DISNEY WORLD

Disney-operated hotels are fantasies unto themselves. Each is designed according to a theme (quaint New England, the relaxed culture of the Polynesian Islands, an African safari village, and so on), and each offers the same perks: free transportation from the airport and to the parks, the option to charge all of your purchases to your room, special guest-only park-visiting times, and much more. If you stay on site, you'll have better access to the parks and be more immersed in the Disney experience.

MAGIC KINGDOM RESORT AREA

$$$$
RESORT
▦ **Disney's Contemporary Resort.** You're paying for location at this sleek, modern, luxury resort next to the Magic Kingdom, as the monorail runs right through the lobby, making park hopping a breeze, and offering quick respite for families seeking relief from the midday heat. **Pros:** monorail access; Chef Mickey's, the epicenter of character-meal world; health and wellness suites. **Cons:** a mix of conventioneers and vacationers means it can be too frenzied for the former and too staid for the latter. ⑤ *Rooms from: $487* ✉ *4600 N. World Dr., Magic Kingdom Resort Area* ☎ *407/824–1000* ⤳ *1,013 rooms, 25 suites* ⦿*No meals* ✛ *2:C1.*

$$$$
RESORT
Fodor'sChoice
★
▦ **Disney's Grand Floridian Resort & Spa.** On the shores of the Seven Seas Lagoon, so close to the Magic Kingdom that you can see the colors change on the Cinderella Castle, this red-roofed Victorian emulates the style of the great railroad resorts of the past with beautifully appointed rooms, rambling verandas, delicate, white-painted woodwork, and brick chimneys. **Pros:** old-Florida ambience; on the monorail route; Victoria & Albert's offers an evening-long experience in dining; if you're a couple with no kids, this is definitely the most romantic on-property hotel; right next to Disney's Wedding Pavilion. **Cons:** pricey; convention clientele and vacationing singles may be more comfortable than families with young children. ⑤ *Rooms from: $655* ✉ *4401 Floridian Way, Magic Kingdom Resort Area* ☎ *407/824–3000* ⊕ *www.disneyworld. disney.go.com/resorts* ⤳ *867 rooms, 90 suites* ⦿*No meals* ✛ *2:B1.*

$$$$
RESORT
▦ **Disney's Polynesian Resort.** You may not think you're in Fiji, but families with kids can have fun pretending in this South Pacific-themed resort directly across the lagoon from the Magic Kingdom, especially after hearing the drumming and chanting that occasionally fill the three-story atrium of the Great Ceremonial House—aka the lobby—or, in the case of the adults in the party, downing a few of the tropical drinks available at the bar. **Pros:** on the monorail; great atmosphere; free Wi-Fi. **Cons:** pricey; not good for those bothered by lots of loud children. ⑤ *Rooms from: $584* ✉ *1600 Seven Seas Dr., Magic Kingdom Resort Area* ☎ *407/824–2000* ⊕ *www.disneyworld.disney.go.com/resorts* ⤳ *847 rooms, 5 suites* ⦿*No meals* ✛ *2:B2.*

$$$$
RESORT
▦ **Disney's Wilderness Lodge.** The architects outdid themselves in designing this seven-story hotel modeled after majestic turn-of-the-20th-century lodges in the American Northwest, with a cavernous lobby, supported by towering tree trunks, an 82-foot-high, fireplace made of rocks from the Grand Canyon, two 55-foot-tall hand-carved totem poles that pay homage to the region's Native American culture, all

9

BEST BETS FOR ORLANDO AND THE PARKS LODGING

With thousands of hotels to choose from, ask yourself first what your family truly wants to do in Orlando during your visit. This invariably leads to an on-property versus off-property debate, and more questions. To assist you, here are our top recommendations by price (any property listed here has at least some rooms in the noted range) and experience. The very best properties—those that provide a particularly remarkable experience in their price range—are designated in the listings with the Fodor's Choice logo.

Fodor's Choice ★

Best Western Lake Buena Vista Resort, $, p. 527

Disney's All-Star Sports Resort, $, p. 525

Disney's Animal Kingdom Lodge, $$$$, p. 525

Disney's Coronado Springs Resort, $$$, p. 525

Disney's Grand Floridian Resort & Spa, $$$$, p. 521

Hyatt Regency Grand Cypress Resort, $$, p. 530

Loews Portofino Bay Hotel at Universal Orlando, $$$$, p. 528

Loews Royal Pacific Resort at Universal Orlando, $$$, p. 528

Meliá Orlando Suite Hotel at Celebration, $$, p. 529

Nickelodeon Suites Resort, $, p. 530

Ritz-Carlton Orlando, Grande Lakes, $$$$, p. 530

Universal's Cabana Bay Beach Resort, $, ` p. 529

Waldorf Astoria Orlando, $$$, p. 530

By Price

$

Disney's All-Star Sports Resort, p. 525

Disney's Art of Animation Resort, p. 525

Nickelodeon Suites Resort, p. 530

$$

Hyatt Regency Grand Cypress Resort, p. 530

Meliá Orlando Suite Hotel at Celebration, p. 529

$$$

Disney's Coronado Springs Resort, p. 525

Loews Royal Pacific Resort at Universal Orlando, p. 528

$$$$

Disney's Animal Kingdom Lodge, p. 525

Disney's Grand Floridian Resort & Spa, p. 521

Loews Portofino Bay Hotel at Universal Orlando, p. 528

Ritz-Carlton Orlando, Grande Lakes, p. 530

Waldorf Astoria Orlando, p. 530

By Experience

BEST BUDGET

Disney's Art of Animation Resort, $, p. 525

Staybridge Suites Lake Buena Vista, $, p. 530

BEST POOLS

Hyatt Regency Grand Cypress Resort, $$, p. 530

JW Marriott Orlando Grande Lakes, $$$$, p. 529

Loews Portofino Bay Hotel at Universal Orlando, $$$$, p. 528

Ritz-Carlton Orlando, Grande Lakes, $$$$, p. 530

MOST KID-FRIENDLY

Disney's All-Star Sports Resort, $, p. 525

Disney's Contemporary Resort, $$$$, p. 521

Nickelodeon Suites Resort, $, p. 530

WHERE SHOULD WE STAY?

	VIBE	PROS	CONS
Disney	Thousands of rooms at every price; convenient to Disney parks; free transportation all over WDW complex.	Perks like early park entry and Magical Express, which lets you circumvent airport bag checks.	Without a rental car, you likely won't leave Disney. On-site buses, although free, can take a big bite of time out of your entertainment day; convenience comes at a price.
Universal	On-site hotels offer luxury, convenience, and value. There are less expensive options just outside the gates.	Central to Disney, Universal, SeaWorld, malls, and I–4; free water taxis to parks from on-site hotels.	Most on-site hotels are pricey; expect heavy rush-hour traffic during drives to and from other parks.
I-Drive	A hotel, convention center, and activities bonanza. A trolley runs from one end to the other.	Outlet malls provide bargains; world-class restaurants; the Orlando Eye lifts visitors up for a bird's-eye view; many hotels offer free park shuttles.	Transportation can be pricey, in cash and in time, as traffic is often heavy. Crime is up, especially after dark, although area hotels and businesses have increased security.
Kissimmee	It offers mom-and-pop motels and upscale choices, restaurants, and places to buy saltwater taffy.	It's just outside Disney, very close to Magic Kingdom. Lots of Old Florida charm and low prices.	Some of the older motels here are a little seedy. Petty crime in which tourists are victims is rare—but not unheard-of.
Lake Buena Vista	Many hotel and restaurant chains here. Adjacent to WDW, which is where almost every guest in your hotel is headed.	Really close to WDW; plenty of dining and shopping options; easy access to I–4.	Heavy peak-hour traffic. As in all neighborhoods near Disney, a gallon of gas will cost 10%–15% more than elsewhere.
Central Orlando	Parts of town have the modern high-rises you'd expect. Other areas have oak tree–lined brick streets winding among small, cypress-ringed lakes.	Locally owned restaurants, trendy hotels, vibrant nightlife, and some quaint B&Bs. City buses serve the parks. There's good access to I–4.	You'll need to rent a car. And you will be part of the traffic headed to WDW. Expect the 25-mile drive to take at least 45 minutes.
Orlando International Airport	Mostly business and flight-crew hotels and car-rental outlets.	Great if you have an early flight or just want to shop in a mall. There's even a Hyatt on site.	Watching planes, buses, taxis, and cars arrive and depart is all the entertainment you'll get.

lighted by enormous tepee-shaped chandeliers. **Pros:** impressive architecture; boarding point for romantic cruises or free water taxi to Magic Kingdom; elegant dining options; children's activity center, free Wi-Fi. **Cons:** no direct bus to Magic Kingdom, no monorail. [$] *Rooms from: $431 ⊠ 901 Timberline Dr., Magic Kingdom Resort Area ☎ 407/824–3200 ⊕ www.disneyworld.disney.go.com/resorts ⇨ 727 rooms, 31 suites ¶◎ No meals ✦ 2:C2.*

DISNEY AND UNIVERSAL RESORT PERKS

DISNEY PERKS

Extra Magic Hours. You get special early and late-night admission to certain Disney parks on specified days. Call ahead for details so you can plan your early- and late-visit strategies.

Free Parking. Parking is free for Disney hotel guests at Disney hotel and theme-park lots.

Magical Express. If you're staying at a select Disney hotel, this free airport service means you don't need to rent a car or think about finding a shuttle or taxi or worry about baggage handling.

At your hometown airport, you check your bags in and won't see them again till you get to your Disney hotel. At Orlando International Airport you're met by a Disney rep, who leads you to a coach that takes you to your hotel. Your luggage is delivered separately and usually arrives in your room an hour or two after you do. If your flight arrives before 5 am or after 10 pm, you will have to pick up your luggage and deliver it to the coach.

On departure, the process works in reverse (though only on some participating airlines, so check in advance). You get your boarding pass and check your bags at the hotel. At the airport you go directly to your gate, skipping check-in. You won't see your bags until you're in your hometown airport. Participating airlines include American, Delta, JetBlue, Southwest, and United.

Charging Privileges. You can charge most meals and purchases throughout Disney to your hotel room.

Package Delivery. Anything you purchase at Disney—at a park, a hotel, or in Downtown Disney—can be delivered to the gift shop of your Disney hotel for free.

Priority Reservations. Disney hotel guests get priority reservations at Disney restaurants and choice tee times at Disney golf courses up to 30 days in advance.

Guaranteed Entry. Disney theme parks sometimes reach capacity, but on-site guests can enter even when others would be turned away.

UNIVERSAL PERKS

Head-of-the-Line Access. Your hotel key (except for guests of Cabana Bay) lets you go directly to the head of the line for most Universal Orlando attractions. Unlike Disney's Fastpass program, you don't need to use this at a specific time; it's always good. Hotel guests also get early admission to the often-crowded Harry Potter attraction.

Priority Seating. Many of Universal's restaurants offer priority seating to those staying at on-site hotels.

Charging Privileges. You can charge most meals and purchases throughout Universal to your hotel room.

Delivery Services. If you buy something in the theme parks, you can have it sent directly to your room, so you don't have to carry it around.

Free Loaners. Some on-site hotels have a "Did You Forget?" closet that offers everything from kids' strollers to dog leashes to computer accessories. There's no fee for using this service.

EPCOT RESORT AREA

$
RESORT

Disney's Art of Animation Resort. This brightly colored three-story value resort is a kid's version of paradise: each of its four wings features images from *Finding Nemo, Cars, The Lion King,* or *The Little Mermaid,* and in-room linens and carpeting match the wing's theme. **Pros:** direct transportation to airport; free parking; images that kids adore; free Wi-Fi. **Cons:** can be crowded; standard rooms fill up fast. $ *Rooms from: $165 ⊠ 1850 Animation Way, Epcot Resort Area ☎ 407/938–7000 ⊕ www.disneyworld.disney.go.com/resorts ↝ 1,984 rooms, 1,120 suites* ❦ *No meals* ✛ *2:E5.*

$$$$
RESORT

Disney's Yacht Club and Beach Club Resorts. These big Crescent Lake inns next door to Epcot seem straight out of a Cape Cod summer, with their nautical décor, waterfront locale, airy light-filled rooms, rocking-chair porches, and family-friendly water-based activities. **Pros:** location, location, location—it's easy to walk or hop a ferry to Epcot, the BoardWalk, or Hollywood Studios; free Wi-Fi. **Cons:** distances within the hotel—like from your room to the front desk—can seem vast; high noise factor. $ *Rooms from: $517 ⊠ 1700 Epcot Resorts Blvd., Epcot Resort Area ☎ 407/934–8000 for Beach Club, 407/934–7000 for Yacht Club ⊕ www.disneyworld.disney.go.com/resorts ↝ 1,213 rooms, 112 suites* ❦ *No meals* ✛ *2:D4.*

ANIMAL KINGDOM RESORT AREA

$
RESORT
FAMILY
Fodor's Choice
★

Disney's All-Star Sports Resort. Stay here if you want the quintessential Disney-with-your-kids experience, or if you're a couple to whom all that pitter-pattering of little feet is a reasonable tradeoff for a good deal on a room. **Pros:** unbeatable price for a Disney property; free Wi-Fi. **Cons:** no kids' clubs or programs, possibly because this is on the bottom tier of Disney hotels in terms of room rates; distances between rooms and on-site amenities can seem vast; furthest resort from Magic Kingdom means you'll spend time on the bus. $ *Rooms from: $145 ⊠ 1701 W. Buena Vista Dr., Animal Kingdom Resort Area ☎ 407/939–5000 ⊕ www.disneyworld.disney.go.com/resorts ↝ 1,920 rooms* ❦ *No meals* ✛ *2:C6.*

$$$$
RESORT
FAMILY
Fodor's Choice
★

Disney's Animal Kingdom Lodge. Giraffes, zebras, and other wildlife roam three 11-acre savannas separated by the encircling arms of this grand hotel, designed to resemble a *kraal,* or animal enclosure in Africa. **Pros:** extraordinary wildlife and cultural experiences; excellent on-site restaurants (Jiko, Boma, and Sanaa); breakfast buffet in Boma is a bargain. **Cons:** shuttle to parks other than Animal Kingdom can take more than an hour; guided savanna tours available only to guests on the concierge level, where the least expensive room is $100 a night higher than the least expensive rooms in other parts of the hotel. $ *Rooms from: $524 ⊠ 2901 Osceola Pkwy., Animal Kingdom Resort Area ☎ 407/938–3000 ⊕ www.disneyworld.disney.go.com/resorts ↝ 972 rooms, 499 suites and villas* ❦ *No meals* ✛ *2:A5.*

$$$
RESORT
Fodor's Choice
★

Disney's Coronado Springs Resort. Popular with conventiongoers who love the huge meeting spaces, and with families who appreciate its casual Southwestern architecture; lively, Mexican-style food court; and elaborate swimming pool, colorful Coronado Springs Resort also offers a moderate price. **Pros:** great pool with a play-area arcade for

9

kids and a bar for adults; lots of outdoor activities, free Wi-Fi. **Cons:** some accommodations are a long trek from the restaurants; standard rooms are on the small side; as in many Disney lakefront properties, the lake is for looking at and boating on, not for swimming in. ⑤ *Rooms from: $261* ✉ *1000 W. Buena Vista Dr., Animal Kingdom Resort Area* ☎ *407/939–1000* ⊕ *www.disneyworld.disney.go.com/resorts* ↗ *1,917 rooms* ⦿ *No meals* ✛ *2:C5.*

DOWNTOWN DISNEY RESORT AREA

$$
HOTEL

🖭 **Disney's Port Orleans Resort–French Quarter.** Ornate Big Easy–style row houses with wrought iron–clad balconies cluster around magnolia-shaded squares in this relatively quiet resort, which appeals to couples more than families. **Pros:** authentic (or as authentic as Disney can make it) fun, New Orleans–style; moderate price; lots of water recreation options, including boat rentals; free Wi-Fi. **Cons:** even though there are fewer kids here, public areas can still be quite noisy; shuttle service is slow; food court is the only on-site dining option. ⑤ *Rooms from: $227* ✉ *1251 Riverside Dr., Downtown Disney Resort Area* ☎ *407/934–5000* ⊕ *www.disneyworld.disney.go.com/resorts* ↗ *1,008 rooms* ⦿ *No meals* ✛ *2:F3.*

OTHER ON-SITE DISNEY HOTELS

Although not operated by the Disney organization, the Swan and the Dolphin, just outside Epcot; Shades of Green, near the Magic Kingdom; and the hotels along Hotel Plaza Boulevard near Downtown Disney call themselves "official" Walt Disney World hotels. Whereas the Swan, Dolphin, and Shades of Green have the special privileges of on-site Disney hotels, such as free transportation to and from the parks and early park entry, the Downtown Disney resorts may use Disney transportation, but don't have all the same perks.

EPCOT RESORT AREA
Take I–4 Exit 64B or 65.

$$$
RESORT

🖭 **Walt Disney World Dolphin.** A pair of 56-foot-tall sea creatures book-end this 25-story glass pyramid, a luxe resort designed, like the adjoining Swan, by world-renowned architect Michael Graves. **Pros:** access to all facilities at the Swan; easy walk or boat ride to BoardWalk and Epcot; excellent on-site restaurants. **Cons:** daily self-parking fee; a daily resort fee covers Wi-Fi and Internet access, use of health club, and local phone calls; room-charge privileges stop at the front door and don't extend to the Disney parks. ⑤ *Rooms from: $325* ✉ *1500 Epcot Resorts Blvd., Epcot Resort Area* ☎ *407/934–4000, 800/227–1500* ⊕ *www. swandolphin.com* ↗ *1,509 rooms, 112 suites* ⦿ *No meals* ✛ *2:D4.*

$$$
RESORT

🖭 **Walt Disney World Swan.** With Epcot and Hollywood Studios close by, guests here can hit the parks in the morning, return for a swim or nap on a hot afternoon, and go back to the parks refreshed and ready to play until the fireworks. **Pros:** charge privileges and access to all facilities at the Dolphin (but not inside Disney World); easy walk to Board-Walk; free boats to BoardWalk and Epcot; good on-site restaurants. **Cons:** long bus ride to Magic Kingdom; daily resort fee. ⑤ *Rooms from: $274* ✉ *1200 Epcot Resorts Blvd., Epcot Resort Area* ☎ *407/934–3000,*

800/325–3535 ⊕*www.swandolphin.com* ⇨*756 rooms, 55 suites* ❘○❘*No meals* ⊹*2:D4.*

DOWNTOWN DISNEY RESORT AREA
Take I–4 Exit 68.

$

RESORT

Fodor'sChoice

★

🏨 **Best Western Lake Buena Vista Resort.** Only a few minutes' walk from Downtown Disney, this towering resort with its airy lobby offers luxury linens, flat-screen TVs, and, in many rooms, a bird's-eye view of the nightly Disney World fireworks. **Pros:** A quick walk takes you to Downtown Disney; a $12 resort fee covers Wi-Fi, parking and other amenities, making it one of the best bargains on Hotel Row. **Cons:** inconvenient to Universal and Downtown Orlando; transportation to the parks can eat up time. Ⓢ*Rooms from: $129* ⊠*2000 Hotel Plaza Blvd., Downtown Disney Resort Area* ☎*407/828–2424, 800/348–3765* ⊕*www. lakebuenavistaresorthotel.com* ⇨*325 rooms* ❘○❘*No meals* ⊹*2:G3.*

$$

RESORT

🏨 **Buena Vista Palace Hotel & Spa.** This large and amenity-filled hotel, just yards from Downtown Disney, caters to business and leisure guests and gets kudos as much for its on-site charms as for its location. **Pros:** easy walk to Downtown Disney; good restaurants and bars on site; kids' activities; pool is heated; spa is large and luxurious. **Cons:** inconvenient to Universal and Downtown Orlando; daily resort fee for Wi-Fi and fitness center. Ⓢ*Rooms from: $189* ⊠*1900 E. Buena Vista Dr., Downtown Disney Resort Area* ☎*407/827–2727* ⊕*www.buenavistapalace. com* ⇨*1,014 rooms* ❘○❘*No meals* ⊹*2:G4.*

$$

HOTEL

🏨 **DoubleTree Suites by Hilton in the WDW Resort.** Price and location make this all-suites, Hilton-owned hotel a good choice for families and business travelers, as there are amenities for both, and it's a quick, free bus ride to any of the Disney parks. **Pros:** family and business traveler amenities; restaurants on site; adult pool and splash pad for kids, adults; free shuttle to Disney attractions; quick access to I–4. **Cons:** of the properties on Hotel Plaza Blvd., this is the furthest away from Downtown Disney; inconvenient to Universal and Downtown Orlando; daily fees for parking, Wi-Fi. Ⓢ*Rooms from: $199* ⊠*2305 Hotel Plaza Blvd., Downtown Disney Resort Area* ☎*407/934–1000, 800/222–8733* ⊕*www. doubletreeguestsuites.com* ⇨*229 units* ❘○❘*No meals* ⊹*2:G4.*

UNIVERSAL ORLANDO AREA

Universal Orlando's on-site hotels were built in a little luxury enclave that has everything you need, so you never have to leave Universal property. In minutes, you can walk from any hotel to CityWalk, Universal's dining and entertainment district, or take a ferry that cruises the adjacent artificial river.

The newest Universal lodging, Cabana Bay Beach Resort, with 900 family suites and 900 standard rooms, is so close to Islands of Adventure, you may see the spires of Hogwarts Castle from your room. This more affordable, motor court–style resort is designed to evoke 20th-century driving vacations with a hip, retro look.

A burgeoning hotel district across Kirkman Road and down to Sand Lake Road offers convenient accommodations and some even less

9

expensive rates. Although these off-property hotels don't have the perks of the on-site places, you'll probably be smiling when you see your hotel bill.

$

HOTEL

⬚ **DoubleTree by Hilton at the Entrance to Universal Orlando.** The name is a mouthful, but it's an accurate description for this hotel, which caters to business-trippers and pleasure seekers alike, thanks to a location close to the Universal Orlando entrance and not far from the Convention Center. **Pros:** three on-site restaurants; within walking distance of Universal, shops, and restaurants; free shuttle to Universal; on I-Drive trolley route; free Wi-Fi. **Cons:** fee for parking; on a fast-lane tourist strip; need a car to reach Disney and Downtown Orlando. Ⓢ *Rooms from: $139 ✉ 5780 Major Blvd., Universal Orlando Area, Orlando* ☎ *407/351–1000, 800/327–2110 ⊕ www.doubltreeorlando.com ☞ 742 rooms, 19 suites* ⦿| *No meals* ✛ *1:D3.*

$$$$

HOTEL

⬚ **Hard Rock Hotel.** Music rules in this California Mission–style building, where guests can pretend they are rock stars as their hotel key card lets them skip the lines at Universal and grants early park admission. **Pros:** shuttle, water taxi, or short walk to Universal Parks and CityWalk; preferential treatment at Universal rides; charge privileges extend to the other on-property Universal hotels. **Cons:** rooms and meals are pricey; resort fee for parking, gym, and in-room Wi-Fi; loud rock music in public areas, even the pool, but that's why you're here, right? Ⓢ *Rooms from: $354 ✉ 5800 Universal Blvd., Universal Orlando Area, Orlando* ☎ *407/503–7625, 800/232–7827 ⊕ www.hardrockhotelorlando.com* ☞ *621 rooms, 29 suites* ⦿| *No meals* ✛ *1:D3.*

$$$$

HOTEL

Fodor's Choice

★

⬚ **Loews Portofino Bay Hotel at Universal Orlando.** The charm and romance of Portofino, Italy—destination of Europe's rich and famous—are conjured up at this lovely luxury resort, where part of the fun is exploring the waterfront "village" from end to end and not knowing what you'll find around a corner or down some steps. **Pros:** Italian villa atmosphere; large spa; restaurants on site; short walk or ferry ride to CityWalk, Universal Studios, and Islands of Adventure; guests skip lines at Universal rides; kids' activities; shuttles to SeaWorld. **Cons:** rooms and meals are pricey; daily fee for in-room high-speed Internet or Wi-Fi as well as for parking. Ⓢ *Rooms from: $378 ✉ 5601 Universal Blvd., Universal Orlando Area, Orlando* ☎ *407/503–1000, 800/232–7827* ⊕ *www.loewshotels.com/Portofino-Bay-Hotel ☞ 750 rooms, 49 suites* ⦿| *Breakfast* ✛ *1:D3.*

$$$

RESORT

Fodor's Choice

★

⬚ **Loews Royal Pacific Resort at Universal Orlando.** The entrance—a broad, covered footbridge high above a tropical stream—sets the tone for the Pacific Rim theme of this hotel, which lies amid 53 acres of lush shrubs, soaring bamboo, orchids, and palms. **Pros:** preferential treatment at Universal rides; early admission to Islands of Adventure (Wizarding World of Harry Potter); serene, Zen garden vibe. **Cons:** rooms can feel cramped; steep fees for in-room Internet access, fitness center, and parking. Ⓢ *Rooms from: $309 ✉ 6300 Hollywood Way, Universal Orlando Area, Orlando* ☎ *407/503–3000, 800/232–7827* ⊕ *www. universalorlando.com ☞ 1,000 rooms, 113 suites* ⦿| *No meals* ✛ *1:D3.*

$ ⊞ **Universal's Cabana Bay Beach Resort.** Arriving at Universal's latest on-
RESORT site hotel, Cabana Bay Beach Resort, is a bit like going back in time to
FAMILY a 1950s Florida beach town with a modern, ironic twist. **Pros:** early
Fodor'sChoice and easy access to Universal parks; food court on property; two swim-
★ ming pools with sand beaches. **Cons:** access to Disney or Downtown
Orlando requires a journey via busy Interstate 4. ⑤ *Rooms from: $174*
✉ *6550 Adventure Way, Universal Orlando Area, Orlando* ☎ *407/503–
4000* ⊕ *www.loewshotels.com/Cabana-Bay* ⇝ *1,800 rooms, 900 suites*
❑ *No meals* ✛ *1:D3.*

ORLANDO METRO AREA

KISSIMMEE, CELEBRATION, AND POINTS SOUTH

$$$ ⊞ **Gaylord Palms Resort and Convention Center.** Built in the style of a grand
RESORT turn-of-the-20th-century Florida resort, this huge building is meant to
inspire awe: inside its enormous atrium, covered by a 4-acre glass roof,
are re-creations of Florida destination icons such as the Everglades,
Key West, and old St. Augustine. **Pros:** you could have a great vacation
without ever leaving the grounds; free shuttle to Disney. **Cons:** daily
resort and parking fee; rooms can be pricey; not much within walking
distance (although the hotel is so big that you can take quite a hike
inside the building); shuttles to Universal and SeaWorld are available
for a fee. ⑤ *Rooms from: $279* ✉ *6000 W. Osceola Pkwy., I–4 Exit
65, Kissimmee* ☎ *407/586–0000* ⊕ *www.gaylordpalms.com* ⇝ *1,406
rooms, 86 suites* ❑ *No meals* ✛ *2:F6.*

$$ ⊞ **Meliá Orlando Suite Hotel at Celebration.** Much like a European bou-
HOTEL tique hotel in style and service, the Meliá Orlando is very human in
Fodor'sChoice scale and crisply minimalist in décor, and is only minutes from Disney.
★ **Pros:** shuttle to Celebration, Disney parks, Universal, and SeaWorld;
golf privileges at Celebration Golf; spa privileges at Celebration Day
Spa. **Cons:** busy U.S. 192 is close by; daily resort fee; need a car to go
anywhere besides Celebration and the parks. ⑤ *Rooms from: $199*
✉ *225 Celebration Pl., Celebration* ☎ *866/404–6662, 407/964–7000*
⊕ *www.solmelia.com* ⇝ *240 suites* ❑ *Breakfast* ✛ *1:B6.*

INTERNATIONAL DRIVE

$$ ⊞ **Hyatt Regency Orlando.** This deluxe, high-rise conference hotel, for-
RESORT merly the Peabody, offers anything a full-service resort customer could
want, with richly appointed rooms, two pools with cabanas, a full-
service spa and fitness center the size of your local Y, two large restau-
rants, and a 360-seat glass-walled lounge overlooking the pool. **Pros:**
good spa; close to shops and more restaurants. **Cons:** check-in can take
a while if a convention is arriving; long walk from end to end; daily
resort fee. ⑤ *Rooms from: $199* ✉ *9801 International Dr., I-Drive area*
☎ *407/284-1234* ⊕ *www.orlandoregency.hyatt.com* ⇝ *1,641 rooms,
193 suites, 5 penthouse suites* ❑ *No meals.* ✛ *1:D4.*

SOUTH ORLANDO

$$$$ ⊞ **JW Marriott Orlando Grande Lakes.** With more than 70,000 square feet
RESORT of meeting space, this lush resort caters to a convention clientele, but
leisure-seekers and families are certainly not ignored: a European-style

9

spa, a Greg Norman–designed golf course, and a lazy river–style pool complex offer plenty of family fun. **Pros:** pool is great for kids and adults; shares amenities with the Ritz, including huge spa; golf course; free shuttle to SeaWorld and Universal. **Cons:** daily resort fees for parking and in-room Wi-Fi; the resort is huge and spread out; need a car to reach Disney or shopping. $ *Rooms from: $409* ⊠ *4040 Central Florida Pkwy.* ☎ *407/206–2300, 800/576–5750* ⊕ *www.grandelakes. com* ↗ *1,000 rooms, 64 suites* ⫶○⫶ *Multiple meal plans* ✦ *1:E4.*

$$$$ ⫶⫶ **Ritz-Carlton Orlando, Grande Lakes.** Orlando's only Ritz-Carlton is a
RESORT   particularly extravagant link in the luxury chain, with exemplary ser-
Fodor's Choice   vice that extends from the porte-cochere entrance to the 18-hole golf
★   course, restaurants, children's programs, and 40-room spa. **Pros:** truly luxurious; impeccable service; great spa; golf course; award-winning restaurants; transportation to theme parks. **Cons:** pricey; remote from theme parks, attractions; lots of convention and meeting traffic; resort fee. $ *Rooms from: $499* ⊠ *4012 Central Florida Pkwy.* ☎ *407/206– 2400, 800/576–5760* ⊕ *www.ritzcarlton.com* ↗ *582 rooms, 63 suites* ⫶○⫶ *Multiple meal plans* ✦ *1:E4.*

LAKE BUENA VISTA

$$ ⫶⫶ **Hyatt Regency Grand Cypress Resort.** Sitting amid 1,500 palm-filled
RESORT   acres just outside Disney's back gate, this huge luxury resort hotel has
Fodor's Choice   a private lake with watercraft, three golf courses, and miles of trails for
★   strolling, bicycling, jogging, and horseback riding. **Pros:** huge pool; lots of recreation options, for kids and adults, including nearby equestrian center; free Wi-Fi. **Cons:** need a car or taxi to get to Downtown Orlando or Universal; steep resort fee. $ *Rooms from: $239* ⊠ *1 Grand Cypress Blvd., Lake Buena Vista area* ☎ *407/239–1234, 800/233–1234* ⊕ *www. hyattgrandcypress.com* ↗ *815 rooms* ⫶○⫶ *No meals* ✦ *2:G3.*

$ ⫶⫶ **Nickelodeon Suites Resort.** This 24-acre Nickelodeon-themed resort is
RESORT   so kid-friendly that you can barely take a step without bumping into
FAMILY   images of SpongeBob, Dora the Explorer, Jimmy Neutron, or other Nick
Fodor's Choice   characters. **Pros:** extremely kid-friendly; Disney, Universal, and SeaWorld
★   shuttles included in resort fee; discounts (up to 50% off standard rates) for active-duty military; mini-golf course. **Cons:** daily resort fee of $30; not within walking distance of Disney or Downtown Disney; way too frenetic for folks without kids. $ *Rooms from: $149* ⊠ *14500 Continental Gateway, Lake Buena Vista area* ☎ *407/387–5437, 866/462–6425* ⊕ *www.nickhotel.com* ↗ *777 suites* ⫶○⫶ *No meals* ✦ *2:G5.*

$ ⫶⫶ **Staybridge Suites Lake Buena Vista.** Just minutes from a Disney entrance,
HOTEL   this sparkling all-suites (one- and two-bedroom, two-bath) accommodation offers its own brand of luxury, perfect for a big family on a small budget. **Pros:** free scheduled shuttle service to Disney; free hot breakfast; free Wi-Fi and parking. **Cons:** no restaurant, no shuttles to other parks. $ *Rooms from: $144* ⊠ *8751 Suiteside Dr., Lake Buena Vista area, Orlando* ☎ *407/238–0777* ⊕ *www.staybridge.com* ↗ *150 suites* ⫶○⫶ *Multiple meal plans.* ✦ *2:G3.*

$$$ ⫶⫶ **Waldorf Astoria Orlando.** While it doesn't duplicate the famed Wal-
RESORT   dorf Astoria Hotel in New York, this Waldorf echoes the original with
Fodor's Choice   imagination and flair, from the iconic clock in the center of the circu-
★   lar lobby to tiny, black-and-white accent tiles on guest room floors.

Pros: lavish and luxurious hotel with spa and golf, next to Disney; free transportation to Disney parks. **Cons:** pricey, but you knew that; if you can bear to leave your cabana, you'll need a car to see anything else in the area; steep daily resort fee. ⑤ *Rooms from: $339* ✉ *14200 Bonnet Creek Resort La., Bonnet Creek, Orlando* ☎ *407/597–5500* ⊕ *www.waldorfastoriaorlando.com* ⇆ *328 rooms, 169 suites* ⊙ *Breakfast* ✛ *2:F5.*

NIGHTLIFE

Updated by
Jennie Hess

Outside of Downtown Disney and Universal's CityWalk, the focal point of adult Orlando nightlife is Downtown. If you stand on the corner of Orange Avenue and Church Street long enough, you can watch all types of gussied-up revelers walk by. The bars and music clubs here hop even after the 2 am last call.

CENTRAL ORLANDO

BARS

Sky Sixty. You have to head up to the roof using the side staircase of The Social nightclub to reach this breezy hot spot. The great view of busy Orange Avenue is accompanied by dance-friendly DJ beats and cool mojitos. Score a cozy cabana seat for prime people-watching. Sunday Funday features mimosa and other drink discounts. ✉ *60 N. Orange Ave., Downtown Orlando* ☎ *407/246–1599* ⊕ *www.skysixty. com* ⊙ *Thurs.–Sat. 10 pm–2 am, Sun. 5–11.*

Wally's. One of Orlando's oldest bars (circa 1954), this longtime local favorite is a hangout for a cross section of cultures and ages. Some would say it's a dive, but that doesn't matter to the students, bikers, lawyers, and barflies who land here to drink surrounded by the go-go-dancer wallpaper and '60s-era interior. Just grab a stool at the bar to take in the scene and down a cold one. ✉ *1001 N. Mills Ave., Downtown Orlando* ☎ *407/896–6975* ⊕ *www.wallysonmills.com* ⊙ *Mon.– Sat. 7:30 am–2 am.*

MUSIC CLUBS

Firestone Live. Based in an old automotive repair shop, this multilevel, high-energy club draws international music acts. Something's always going on to make the crowd hop: DJ mixes, big band, jazz, hip-hop, rock. Often the dance floor is more like semicontrolled chaos than a place to just listen, so be prepared. Hours and prices vary by event; check the website. ✉ *578 N. Orange Ave., Downtown Orlando* ☎ *407/872–0066* ⊕ *www.firestonelive.net.*

Fodor's Choice
★

The Social. Beloved by locals, The Social is a great place to see touring and area musicians. Up to seven nights a week you can sip trademark martinis while listening to anything from indie rock to rockabilly to undiluted jazz. Several now-national acts got their start here, including Matchbox Twenty, Seven Mary Three, and other groups that don't have numbers in their names. Hours vary. ✉ *54 N. Orange Ave., Downtown*

9

Orlando ☎ *407/246–1419* ⊕ *www.thesocial.org* ✉ *$5–$30, depending on entertainment.*

INTERNATIONAL DRIVE AREA

MUSIC CLUBS

B.B. King's Blues Club. The blues great was doing quite well as a musician before becoming a successful entrepreneur, with blues clubs in Memphis, Nashville, Las Vegas, and West Palm Beach as well as Orlando. Like the others, this club has music at its heart. There's a dance floor and stage for live performances by the B.B. King All-Star Band or visiting musicians seven nights a week. You can't really experience Delta blues without Delta dining, so the club doubles as a restaurant with fried dill pickles, catfish bites, po'boys, ribs, and other comfort foods. Oh, yeah, and there's a full bar. ⊠ *Pointe Orlando, 9101 International Dr., I-Drive area* ☎ *407/370–4550* ⊕ *www.bbkingclubs.com/?page=orlhome* ⊗ *Fri. and Sat. noon–2 am, Sun.–Thurs. noon–midnight.*

NIGHTCLUBS

ICEBAR. Thanks to the miracle of refrigeration, this is Orlando's coolest bar—literally and figuratively. Fifty tons of pure ice is kept at a constant 27°F and has been cut and sculpted by world-class carvers into a cozy (or as cozy as ice can be) sanctuary of tables, sofas, chairs, and a bar. The staff loans you a thermal cape and gloves (upgrade to a fur coat for $10), and when you enter the frozen hall your drink is served in a glass made of crystal-clear ice. There's no cover charge if you just want to hang out in the Fire Lounge or outdoor Polar Patio, but you will pay $19.95 to spend as much time as you can handle in the subfreezing ICEBAR. There's no beer or wine inside; it's simply too cold. ⊠ *Pointe Orlando, 8967 International Dr., I-Drive area* ☎ *407/426–7555* ⊕ *www.icebarorlando.com* ⊗ *Fri. and Sat. 7 pm–2 am, Sun.–Wed. 7–midnight, Thurs. 7–1.*

SPORTS AND THE OUTDOORS

Updated by
Jennie Hess

There are many ways to enjoy the outdoors here, but a few activities stand out. You can keep your feet planted firmly on the ground and play golf (or miniature golf), or you can take to the "skies."

BALLOONING

Fodor's Choice
★

Bob's Balloons. Bob's offers one-hour rides over protected marshland and even flies over the Disney area if wind and weather conditions are right. You meet at Champions Gate, near Disney World, at dawn, where Bob and his assistant take you by van to the launch site. It takes about 15 minutes to get the balloon in the air, and then you're off on an adventure that definitely surpasses Peter Pan's Flight in the Magic Kingdom.

You'll see farm and forest land for miles, along with horses, deer, wild boar, cattle, and birds flying *below* you. Bob may take you as high as 1,000 feet, and you may be able to see such landmarks as the Animal Kingdom's Expedition Everest mountain and Epcot's Spaceship Earth

sphere. Several other balloons are likely to go up near you—there's a tight-knit community of balloonists in the Orlando area—so you'll view these colorful sky ornaments from an unparalleled sightline. There are seats in the basket, but you'll probably be too thrilled to sit down. Check the website for specials and call Bob to reserve. ☎ 407/466–6380, 877/824–4606 ⊕ *www.bobsballoons.com* ✉ *$175 per person.*

GOLF

If golf is your passion, you already know that Arnold Palmer and Gary Player—in fact, almost half of the PGA tour—make Orlando their off-road home. It's not by accident that the Golf Channel originates from here. The Bay Hill Invitational and several LPGA tourneys (the headquarters is in Daytona) come to Orlando every year. And with more than 80 public and private courses, there's ample opportunity for you to play on world-class courses such as Grand Cypress or Champions Gate.

MINIATURE GOLF

FAMILY **Hawaiian Rumble Adventure Golf.** Who can resist golfing around an erupting volcano? Hawaiian Rumble combines a tropical setting with waterfalls, tunnels, tiki gods, and flame-belching mountains. There's also a location in the Lake Buena Vista area. ✉ *8969 International Dr., I-Drive area* ☎ 407/351–7733 ⊕ *www.hawaiianrumbleorlando.com* ✉ *$9.95–$11.95* ☉ *Sun.–Thurs. 9 am–11:00 pm, Fri. and Sat. 9 am–11:30 pm.*

Fodor's Choice
★

FAMILY **Pirate's Cove Adventure Golf.** Two 18-hole courses wind around artificial mountains, through caves, and into lush foliage. The beginner's course is called Captain Kidd's Adventure; the more advanced course is Blackbeard's Challenge. There's another Pirate's Cove on International Drive. ✉ *12545 State Rd. 535, Lake Buena Vista* ☎ 407/827–1242 ⊕ *www.piratescove.net* ✉ *$10.45–$14.95* ☉ *Daily 9 am–11 pm.*

SKYDIVING

Fodor's Choice
★

iFLY Orlando. OK, you technically aren't skydiving, but you come pretty close in a 12-foot-high, 1,000-horsepower wind tunnel that lets you experience everything skydivers do, but closer to the ground. The experience starts with instruction, after which you suit up and hit the wind tunnel, where you soar like a bird under your instructor's watchful eye. It's all so realistic that skydiving clubs come to hone their skills. The attraction is safe for anyone under 250 pounds and older than 3. You can purchase a video of your "jump" for $24.95. ✉ *6805 Visitors Circle, I-Drive area* ☎ 407/903–1150 ⊕ *www.skyventureorlando.com* ✉ *$59.95 and up, depending on package* ☉ *Daily 10–10:30.*

SHOPPING

Updated by
Jennie Hess

Visitors from as far away as Britain and Brazil often arrive in Orlando with empty suitcases for their purchases. Although shopping has all but disappeared from Downtown, the metro area is filled with options. There really is something for everyone—from high-end fashion to outlet-mall chic, from the world's largest flea market to a boutique-filled town, from an antique treasure to a hand-hewn Florida find.

The College Park area, once an antiques-hunter's dream, still has some treasures to be found along North Orange Avenue and Edgewater Drive, including the largest vinyl-record shop in Florida.

The simultaneously glitzy and kitschy International Drive has almost 500 designer outlet stores and odd, off-brand electronics shops. The factory outlets on the north end of the Drive once consisted of shops with merchandise piled on tables; today the shops here are equal to their higher-priced first-run cousins. The strip also has plenty of restaurants and, for those in your group who don't feel like shopping, movie theaters.

CENTRAL ORLANDO

MALLS

Fodor's Choice
★ **Mall at Millenia.** "Deluxe" is the word for this mall, a high-end collection of designer shops, including Gucci, Burberry, Chanel, Jimmy Choo, Hugo Boss, Cartier, Tiffany, and Ferragamo. You'll also find Neiman Marcus, Bloomingdale's, and an Apple store, but the biggest attraction may be the adjacent IKEA. A few minutes northeast of Universal, the mall is easy to reach via Interstate 4 Exit 78. ⊠ *4200 Conroy Rd., South Orlando* ☎ *407/363-3555* ⊕ *www.mallatmillenia.com* ☉ *Mon.–Sat. 10–9, Sun. 11–7.*

INTERNATIONAL DRIVE AREA

MALLS

Pointe Orlando. What was once an enclosed shopping center is now a dining, shopping, and entertainment hot spot—one that's within walking distance of five top hotels and the Orange County Convention Center. In addition to WonderWorks and the enormous Regal IMAX theater, the complex has specialty shops such as Armani Exchange, Tommy Bahama, Chico's, Tommy Hilfiger, Hollister, Charming Charlie, and Victoria's Secret. Restaurants have become a reason to visit, with the very high-end Capital Grille, the Oceanaire Seafood Room, Cuba Libre Restaurant and Rum Bar, The Pub, Marlow's Tavern, the popular Funky Monkey Wine Company, B.B. King's Blues Club, and Taverna Opa. Blue Martini and Minus5 Ice Bar provide after-hours adult beverages. Parking ($3 for 15 minutes–two hours, $6 daily) can be validated by the movie theater and many of the restaurants. ⊠ *9101 International Dr., I-Drive area* ☎ *407/248-2838* ⊕ *www.pointeorlando.com* ☉ *Oct.–May, Mon.–Sat. noon–10, Sun. noon–8; June–Sept. Fri.–Sat. noon–9, Sun.–Thurs. noon–8.*

FACTORY OUTLETS

Orlando Premium Outlets International Drive. This is a prime destination for international shoppers who can find shoes, clothing, cosmetics, electronics, and household goods at a fraction of their home-country prices. The massive complex at the north tip of International Drive includes Saks Fifth Avenue OFF 5TH, Coach, Kate Spade New York, Victoria's

9

536 < **Orlando and Environs**

Secret Outlet, and a Disney outlet. Searching for bargains works up an appetite, and there are plenty of places to eat here, either in the well-lit food court or in one of several sit-down and highly regarded restaurants. ✉ *4951 International Dr., I-Drive area* ☎ *407/352–9600* ⊕ *www. premiumoutlets.com* ⊗ *Mon.–Sat. 10 am–11 pm, Sun. 10–9.*

Orlando Premium Outlets Vineland Avenue. This outlet capitalizes on its proximity to Disney (it's at the confluence of Interstate 4, State Road 535, and International Drive). It's easier to see from the highway than to enter, and parking is tedious and scarce, but smart shoppers have lunch on International Drive and take the I-Ride Trolley right to the front entrance (it runs every 15 minutes). The center's design makes this almost an open-air market, so walking can be pleasant on a nice day. You'll find Prada, Gap, Nike, Adidas, Tory Burch, Polo Ralph Lauren, Giorgio Armani, Burberry, Tommy Hilfiger, Reebok, and about 100 other stores. ✉ *8200 Vineland Ave., I-Drive area* ☎ *407/238–7787* ⊕ *www.premiumoutlets.com* ⊗ *Mon.–Sat. 10 am–11 pm, Sun. 10–9.*

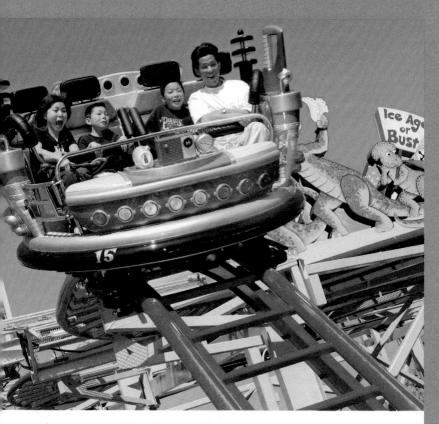

WALT DISNEY
WORLD

WELCOME TO WALT DISNEY WORLD

TOP REASONS TO GO

★ **Nostalgia:** Face it— Mickey and Company are old friends. And you probably have childhood pictures of yourself in front of Cinderella Castle. Even if you don't, nobody does yesteryear better: head to Main Street, U.S.A, or Hollywood Boulevard and see.

★ **Memories in the Making:** Who doesn't want to snap photos of Sis on the Dumbo ride or of Junior after his Splash Mountain experience? The urge to pass that Disney nostalgia on to the next generation is strong.

★ **The Thrills:** For some this means roller coasting to an Aerosmith soundtrack or simulating space flight; for others it's about cascading down a waterslide or going on safari.

★ **The Chills:** If the Pirates of the Caribbean cave doesn't give you goose bumps, try the Haunted Mansion or Twilight Zone Tower of Terror.

★ **The Spectacle:** The list is long—fireworks, laser-light displays, arcade games, parades . . .

1 Magic Kingdom. Disney's emblematic park is home to Space Mountain, Pirates of the Caribbean, and an expanded Fantasyl-and full of new experiences.

2 Epcot. Future World's focus is science, technology, and hands-on experiences. In the World Showcase, you can tour 11 countries without getting jet-lagged.

3 Disney's Hollywood Studios. Attractions at this re-creation of old-time Hollywood include Rock 'n' Roller Coaster Starring Aerosmith and Twilight Zone Tower of Terror.

4 Disney's Animal Kingdom. Amid a 403-acre wildlife preserve are an Asian-themed water ride, an African safari ride, a runaway-train coaster, and shows.

5 Blizzard Beach. Water thrills range from steep flume rides to tubing expeditions in the midst of a park that you'd swear is a slowly melting ski resort. There's plenty for little ones, too.

GETTING ORIENTED

Walt Disney World straddles Orange and Osceola counties to the west of Interstate 4. Four exits will get you to the parks and resort areas: 64B, 65, 67, and 68. To reach hotels along I-Drive, use Exit 72, 74A, or 75A.

6 Typhoon Lagoon. Sandy beaches, oceanlike waves, and a themed water coaster invite castaways to enjoy a day of fun and relaxation. Take the kids on Bay Slides and don snorkels to explore Shark Reef.

7 Disney's Other Worlds. Downtown Disney is the place to go for shopping, dining, and great entertainment from morning through late night. Disney's Board-Walk is a nostalgia trip, with bicycles built for two, surreys with a fringe on top, pizza, bars, and a dance hall.

10

Updated by
Jennie Hess

Mickey Mouse. Tinker Bell. Cinderella. What would child-hood be like without the magic of Disney? When kids and adults want to go to *the* theme park, they're heading to Disney. Here you're walking amid people from around the world and meeting characters like Snow White and Donald Duck while rides whirl nonstop and the irrepressible "it's a small world" tune and lyrics run through your head. You can't help but believe dreams really do come true here.

The **Magic Kingdom** is the heart and soul of the Walt Disney World empire. It was the first Disney outpost in Florida when it opened in 1971, and it's the park that launched Disney's presence in France, Japan, and Hong Kong. For a landmark that wields such worldwide influence, the 142-acre Magic Kingdom may seem small—indeed, Epcot is more than double the size of the Magic Kingdom, and Animal Kingdom is almost triple the size when including the park's expansive animal habitats. But looks can be deceiving. Packed into six different "lands" are nearly 50 major crowd-pleasers, and that's not counting all the ancillary attractions: shops, eateries, live entertainment, character meet-and-greet spots, fireworks shows, and parades.

Nowhere but at **Epcot** can you explore and experience the native food, entertainment, culture, and arts and crafts of countries in Europe, Asia, North Africa, and the Americas. What's more, employees at the World Showcase pavilions actually hail from the countries the pavilions represent.

Epcot, or "Experimental Prototype Community of Tomorrow," was the original inspiration for Walt Disney World. Walt envisioned a future in which nations coexisted in peace and harmony, reaping the miraculous harvest of technological achievement. The Epcot of today is both more and less than his original dream. Less, because the World Showcase presents views of its countries that are, as an Epcot guide once put it, "as Americans perceive them"—highly idealized. But this is a minor quibble in the face of the major achievement: Epcot is that rare paradox—a successful educational theme park that excels at entertainment, too.

Disney's Hollywood Studios were designed to be a trip back to Tinseltown's golden age, when Hedda Hopper, not tabloids, spread celebrity gossip and when the girl off the bus from Ohio could be the next Judy Garland.

The result is a theme park that blends movie-production capabilities and high-tech wonders with breathtaking rides and nostalgia. The park's old-time Hollywood atmosphere begins with a rosy-hued view of the moviemaking business presented in a dreamy stage set from the 1930s and '40s, amid sleek art-moderne buildings in pastel colors, funky diners, kitschy decorations, and sculptured gardens populated by roving actors playing, well, roving actors. There are also casting directors, gossip columnists, and other colorful characters.

Thanks to a rich library of film scores, the park is permeated with music, all familiar, all evoking the magic of the movies, and all constantly streaming from the camouflaged loudspeakers at a volume just right for humming along. The park icon, a 122-foot-high Sorcerer Mickey Hat that serves as a gift shop and Disney pin-trading station, towers over Hollywood Boulevard.

Disney's Animal Kingdom explores the stories of all animals—real, imaginary, and extinct. Enter through the Oasis, where you hear exotic background music and find yourself surrounded by gentle waterfalls and gardens alive with exotic birds, reptiles, and mammals.

At 403 acres and several times the size of the Magic Kingdom, Animal Kingdom is the largest in area of all Disney theme parks. Animal habitats take up much of that acreage. Creatures here thrive in careful re-creations of landscapes from Asia and Africa. Throughout the park, you'll also learn about conservation in a low-key way.

Amid all the nature are thrill rides, a 3-D show (housed in the "root system" of the iconic Tree of Life), two first-rate musicals, and character meet and greets. Cast members are as likely to hail from Kenya or South Africa as they are from Kentucky or South Carolina. It's all part of the charm. New park areas based on the movie *Avatar* are expected to open in 2017, a fitting addition, since the film's theme of living in harmony with nature reflects the park's eco-philosophy.

10

Typhoon Lagoon and **Blizzard Beach** are two of the world's best water parks. What sets them apart? It's the same thing that differentiates all Disney parks—their detailed themes. Whether you're cast away on a balmy island at Typhoon Lagoon or washed up on a ski-resort-turned-seaside-playground at Blizzard Beach, the landscaping and clever architecture will add to the fun of flume and raft rides, wave pools, and splash areas. Another plus: the vegetation has matured enough to create shade. The Disney water parks give you that lost-in-paradise feeling on top of all those high-speed, wedgie-inducing waterslides. They're so popular that crowds often reach overflow capacity in summer. If you're going to Disney for five days or more between April and October, add the Water Park Fun & More option to your Magic Your Way ticket.

PLANNING

ADMISSION

At the gate, the per-person, per-day price is $90 for adults (ages 10 and older) and $84 for children (ages 3–9). You can buy tickets at the Ticket and Transportation Center (TTC) in the Magic Kingdom, from booths at other park entrances, in all on-site resorts if you're a guest, at the Disney store in the airport, and at various other sites around Orlando. You can also buy them in advance online—the best way to save time and money.

If you opt for a multiday ticket, you'll be issued a nontransferable pass that uses your fingerprint for ID. Slide your pass through the reader, just like people with single-day tickets, and also slip your finger into the V-shaped reader. A new option, the MyMagic+ wristband, serves as park ticket, attraction FastPass+, and even hotel room key.

OPERATING HOURS

Walt Disney World operates 365 days a year. Opening and closing times vary by park and by season, with the longest hours during prime summer months and year-end holidays. The parking lots open at least an hour before the parks do.

In general, openings hover around 9 am, though certain attractions might not start up till 10 or 11. Closings range between 5 and 8 pm in the off-season and between 8 and 10, 11, or even midnight in high season. Downtown Disney and BoardWalk shops stay open as late as 11 pm.

EXTRA MAGIC HOURS

The Extra Magic Hours program gives Disney resort guests free early and late-night admission to certain parks on specified days—check ahead (⊕ www.disneyworld.disney.go.com/calendars) for information about each park's "magic hours" days to plan your early- and late-visit strategies.

PARKING AND IN-PARK TRANSPORT

Parking at Disney parks is free to resort guests; all others pay $17 for cars and $18 for RVs and campers. Parking is free for everyone at Typhoon Lagoon, Blizzard Beach, Downtown Disney, and the Board-Walk. Trams take you between the theme-park lots (*note your parking location!*) and turnstiles. Disney's buses, boats, and monorails whisk you from resort to park and park to park. If you're staying on Disney property, you can use this system exclusively. Either take a Disney bus or drive to Typhoon Lagoon and Blizzard Beach. Once inside the water parks, you can walk, swim, slide, or chill out. Allow up to an hour for travel between parks and hotels on Disney transportation.

FASTPASS+

FastPass+ helps you avoid lines, and it's included in regular park admission. Using the new My Disney Experience app or FastPass+ kiosks in each park, you can select up to three attractions at one time; each appointment will give you a one-hour window within which you can experience each attraction. The FastPass+ appointments are loaded directly to your plastic theme-park ticket or your new MagicBand. It's best to make appointments only for the most popular attractions and to stick with the standby queue for attractions that aren't in such demand. Strategy is everything.

Guests can get FastPass+ reservations for some designated character greetings, parades, and shows. These "experience" FastPass+ reservations count just the same as those for the rides. You get three to start with (in a single park) and can add as many more as you have time for (and these can be in a different park if you have the Park Hopper option). Best FastPass+ practices are explained by the program. It will direct you to the attractions where FastPass+ is most helpful. If these attractions don't meet your family's specific needs—your kids are too young to ride coasters, for example—the program will also help you customize your FastPass+ selections.

DISNEY STRATEGIES

Keep in mind these essential strategies, tried and tested by generations of Disney fans.

■ **Buy tickets before leaving home.** It saves money and gives you time to look into all the ticket options. It also offers an opportunity for you to consider vacation packages and meal plans and to register with the My Disney Experience program and mobile app for vacation planning.

■ **Make dining reservations before leaving home.** If you don't, you might find yourself eating fast food (again) or leaving Disney for dinner. On-site restaurants, especially those featuring character appearances, book up months ahead.

■ **Arrive at least 30 minutes before the parks open.** We know, it's your vacation and you want to sleep in. But you probably want to make the most of your time and money, too. Plan to be up by 7:30 am each day to get the most out of your park visits. After transit time, it'll take you 15–20 minutes to park, get to the gates, and pick up your park guide maps and *Times Guide.*

■ **See top attractions in the morning.** And we mean *first thing.* Decide in advance on your can't-miss attractions, find their locations, and hotfoot it to them before 10 am.

■ **Use FastPass+.** The system is free, easy, more streamlined than ever with the new FastPass+ online prebooking system, and it's your ticket to the top attractions with little or no waiting in line. Even if you wait to book once you're in the park, you can now schedule up to three Fast-Pass+ reservations at one time; paper tickets and FastPass+ are obsolete. Instead, your attraction appointments are loaded onto your MagicBand or plastic ticket, whichever you choose to use.

■ **Use Baby Swap.** Disney has a theme-park "rider switch" policy that works like this: one parent waits with the baby or toddler while the other parent rides the attraction. When the ride ends, they switch places with minimal wait.

■ **Build in rest time.** Start early and then leave the parks around 3 or 4 pm, thus avoiding the hottest and often most crowded period. After a couple of hours' rest at your hotel, head back for a nighttime spectacle or to ride a big-ticket ride (lines often are shorter around closing time).

10

■ **Create an itinerary, but leave room for spontaneity.** Don't try to plot your trip hour by hour. If you're staying at a Disney resort, find out which parks have Extra Magic Hours on which days.

■ **Eat at off hours.** To avoid the mealtime rush hours, have a quick, light breakfast at 7 or 8 am, lunch at 11, and dinner at 5 or 6.

OTHER DISNEY SERVICES

If you can shell out $315–$380 an hour (with a six-hour minimum), you can take a customized **VIP Tour** with guides who help you park hop and get good seats at parades and shows. These tours don't help you skip lines, but they make navigating easy. Groups can have up to 10 people; book up to three months ahead.

WDW Tours. Reserve with WDW Tours up to 180 days in advance for behind-the-scenes tours. Participant age requirements vary, so be sure to check before you book. ☎ 407/939–8687.

DISNEY CONTACTS

Cruise Line: ☎ 800/370–0097 ⊕ www.disneycruise.com

Dining Reservations: ☎ 407/939–3463

Extra Magic Hours: ⊕ www.disneyworld.disney.go.com/calendars

Fairy-Tale Weddings: ☎ 321/939–4610 ⊕ www.disneyweddings.disney.go.com

Golf Reservations: ☎ 407/939–4653

Guest Info: ☎ 407/824–4321

VIP Tours: ☎ 407/560–4033

WDW Travel Company: ☎ 407/828–8101

Web: ⊕ www.disneyworld.disney.go.com

THE MAGIC KINGDOM

Whether you arrive at the Magic Kingdom via monorail, boat, or bus, it's hard to escape that surge of excitement or suppress that smile upon sighting the towers of Cinderella Castle or the spires of Space Mountain. So what if it's a cliché by now? There's magic beyond the turnstiles, and you aren't going to miss one memorable moment.

Most visitors have some idea of what they'd like to see and do during their day in the Magic Kingdom. Popular attractions like Space Mountain and Splash Mountain are on the lists of any thrill seeker, and the recently expanded Fantasyland is Destination One for parents of small children. Visitors who steer away from wilder rides are first in line at the Jungle Cruise or Pirates of the Caribbean in Adventureland.

It's great to have a strategy for seeing the park's attractions, grabbing a bite to eat, or scouring the shops for souvenir gold. But don't forget that Disney Imagineers—the creative pros behind every themed land and attraction—are famous for their attention to detail. Your experience will be richer if you take time to notice the extra touches—from the architecture to the music to the costumes. The same genius is evident even in the landscape, from the tropical setting of Adventureland to the red-stone slopes of Frontierland's Big Thunder Mountain Railroad.

Wherever you go, watch for hidden Mickeys—silhouettes and abstract images of Mickey Mouse—tucked by Imagineers into every corner of the Kingdom. For instance, at the Haunted Mansion, look for him in the place settings in the banquet scene.

Much of the Magic Kingdom's pixie dust is spread by the people who work here, the costumed cast members who do their part to create fond memories for each guest who crosses their path. Maybe the grim ghoul who greets you solemnly at the Haunted Mansion will cause you to break down and giggle. Or the sunny shop assistant will help your daughter find the perfect sparkly shoes to match her princess dress. You get the feeling that everyone's in on the fun; in fact, you wonder if they ever go home!

PLANNING

GETTING ORIENTED
The park is laid out on a north–south axis, with Cinderella Castle at the center and the various lands surrounding it in a broad circle.

As you pass underneath the railroad tracks, symbolically leaving behind the world of reality and entering a world of fantasy, you'll immediately notice the adorable buildings lining Town Square and Main Street, U.S.A, which runs due north and ends at the Hub (also called Central Plaza), in front of Cinderella Castle. If you're lost or have questions, cast members are available at almost every turn to help you.

PARK AMENITIES
Guest Relations: To the left in Town Square as you face Main Street, **City Hall** houses Guest Relations (aka Guest Services), the Magic Kingdom's principal information center (☎ 407/824–4521). Here you can search for misplaced belongings or companions, ask questions of staffers, and pick up a guide map and a *Times Guide* with schedules of events and character-greeting information. ■ TIP➔ If you're trying for a last-minute lunch or dinner reservation, you may be able to book it at City Hall.

Lockers: Lockers ($7 or $9 plus $5 deposit) are in an arcade under the Main Street railroad station. If you're park hopping, use your locker receipt to get a free locker at the next park.

Lost People and Things: Instruct your kids to talk to anyone with a Disney name tag if they lose you. **City Hall** also has a lost and found and a computerized message center, where you can leave notes for your companions in the Magic Kingdom and other parks.

VISITING TIPS
■ Try to come toward the end of the week, because most families hit the Magic Kingdom early in a visit.

■ Ride a star attraction during a parade; lines ease considerably. (But be careful not to get stuck on the wrong side of the parade route when it starts, or you may never get across.)

TOP ATTRACTIONS

FOR AGES 7 AND UP

Big Thunder Mountain Railroad. An Old West–theme, classic coaster that's not too scary; it's just a really good, bumpy, swervy thrill.

Buzz Lightyear's Space Ranger Spin. A shoot-'em-up ride where space-ranger wannabes compete for the highest score.

Haunted Mansion. With its razzle-dazzle special effects, this classic is always a frightful hoot.

Pirates of the Caribbean. Don't miss this family cruise through pirate territory, especially if you're a fan of the movies.

Seven Dwarfs Mine Train. It's the newest coaster on the block, with train cars that swing to and fro during the rollicking, musical ride through a mine full of glittery gems.

Space Mountain. The Magic Kingdom's scariest ride zips you along the tracks in near-total darkness except for the stars.

FOR AGES 6 AND UNDER

Dumbo the Flying Elephant. The elephant ears get them every time, and the renovated ride offers double the number of pachyderm vehicles.

Enchanted Tales with Belle. Young girls and boys, and some parents, too, clamor to play characters from "Beauty and the Beast" in this well-done interactive story adventure.

The Magic Carpets of Aladdin. On this must-do for preschoolers, you can make your carpet go up and down to avoid occasional water spurts as mischievous camels spit at you.

The Many Adventures of Winnie the Pooh. Hang on to your honey pot as you get whisked along on a windy-day adventure with Pooh, Tigger, Eeyore, and friends.

Under the Sea: Journey of the Little Mermaid. Wander past waterfalls and tide pools into the cave beneath Prince Eric's Castle for some interactive fun and a clamshell ride through Ariel's story.

■ At City Hall, near the park's Town Square entrance, pick up a map and a *Times Guide,* which lists showtimes, character-greeting times, and hours for attractions and restaurants.

■ Book character meals early. Main Street, U.S.A's The Crystal Palace, A Buffet with Character has breakfast, lunch, and dinner with Winnie the Pooh, Tigger, and friends. All three meals at the Fairy Tale Dining experience in Cinderella Castle are extremely popular—so much so that you should reserve your spot six months out. The same advice goes for booking the full-service dinner at the new Be Our Guest Restaurant in the Beast's Castle in Fantasyland.

EXPLORING THE MAGIC KINGDOM

MAIN STREET, U.S.A.

With its pastel Victorian-style buildings, antique automobiles ahoohga-oohga-ing, sparkling sidewalks, and an atmosphere of what one writer has called "almost hysterical joy," Main Street is more than a mere

Adventure Number 1: Being shipwrecked with the Swiss Family Robinson and exploring their treehouse.

conduit to the other enchantments of the Magic Kingdom. It's where the spell is first cast.

You emerge from beneath the Walt Disney World Railroad Station into a realization of one of the most tenacious American dreams. The perfect street in the perfect small town in a perfect moment of time is burnished to jewel-like quality, thanks to a four-fifths-scale reduction, nightly cleanings with high-pressure hoses, and constant repainting. And it's a very sunny world, thanks to an outpouring of welcoming entertainment: live bands, barbershop quartets, and background music from Disney films and American musicals played over loudspeakers. Horse-drawn trolleys and omnibuses with their horns tooting chug along the street. Vendors in Victorian costumes sell balloons and popcorn. And Cinderella's famous castle floats whimsically in the distance where Main Street disappears.

Although attractions with a capital A are minimal on Main Street, there are plenty of inducements—namely, shops and eateries—to while away your time and part you from your money. The largest of these, the Emporium, is often the last stop for souvenir hunters at day's end. At the Main Street Bakery, you can find your favorite Starbucks latte and a sandwich or baked treats like cupcakes and brownies. If you can't resist an interactive challenge while making your way through the park, head first to the Firehouse, next to City Hall, to join the legendary wizard Merlin in the Sorcerers of the Magic Kingdom role-playing game. For no extra charge, you can take ownership of special cards with "magic spells" that help you search for symbols and bring down Disney villains like Yzma and Kronk from the Disney film *The Emperor's New*

Fort Sam
Clemens

Haunted
Mansion

it's a
small world

Pinocchio
Village Haus

Rivers of America

Rivers of America

Peter Pan's
Flight

Mickey's
PhilharMagic

Big Thunder
Mountain
Railroad

Columbia
Harbour
House

FRONTIERLAND

LIBERTY
SQUARE

Liberty Square
Riverboat

WDW Railroad
Station
Frontierland
Depot

Tom Sawyer
Island

Hall of
Presidents

Parade Route

Splash
Mountain

Liberty Tree
Tavern

Pecos Bill
Tall Tale
Inn Café

Country Bear
Jamboree

Frontierland
Shooting
Gallery

Diamond
Horseshoe

Golden Oak
Outpost

Agrabah
Bazaar

Aloha
Isle

ATM

Tip Board

Sunshine Tree
Terrace

The Magic
Carpets
of Aladdin

Swiss Family
Treehouse

Crystal
Palace

Tortuga
Tavern

Enchanted
Tiki Room

ADVENTURELAND

First Aid/
Baby Care Center

The Pirates
League

Pirates of
the Caribbean

Jungle
Cruise

Emporium

WDW Railroad

City Hall
Guest Relations

ATM

Package Pickup

Newsstand

Monorail
Station

The Magic
Kingdom

0   100 yards

0   100 m

MAGIC KINGDOM

NAME	Height req.	Type of Entertainment	Duration	Crowds	Audience	Tips
Adventureland						
Enchanted Tiki Room	n/a	Show	12 mins.	Light	All Ages	Visit when you need a refresher in a/c.
Jungle Cruise	n/a	Cruise	10 mins.	Heavy	All Ages	Use FastPass+ or come during the parade.
The Magic Carpets of Aladdin	n/a	Thrill Ride for Kids	3 mins.	Heavy	All Ages	Visit while waiting for a FastPass+ appointment.
Pirates of the Caribbean	n/a	Cruise	10 mins.	Moderate	All Ages	A good destination in the heat of the afternoon.
Swiss Family Treehouse	n/a	Walk-through	Up to you	Moderate	All Ages	Visit while waiting for a FastPass+.
Fantasyland						
The Barnstormer	35"	Thrill Ride for Kids	1 min.	Heavy	All but Young Kids	Ride early after hopping train to Fantasyland.
★ Dumbo the Flying Elephant	n/a	Thrill Ride for Kids	2 mins.	Heavy	Young Kids	New circus tent queue offers air-conditioned play area.
★ Enchanted Tales with Belle	n/a	Show	15 mins.	Heavy	All Ages	Go while waiting for Mermaid FastPass+ appointment.
it's a small world	n/a	Cruise	11 mins.	Moderate	All Ages	Tots may beg for a repeat ride; it's worth it.
Mad Tea Party	n/a	Thrill Ride for Kids	2 mins.	Moderate	Young Kids	Skip it if wait is 30 mins.
★ The Many Adventures of Winnie the Pooh	n/a	Thrill Ride for Kids	3½ mins.	Heavy	All Ages	Use FastPass+. Come early, late in the afternoon, or after dark.
Mickey's PhilharMagic	n/a	3-D Film	12 mins.	Heavy	All but Young Kids	Use FastPass+ or arrive early or during a parade.
Peter Pan's Flight	n/a	Thrill Ride for Kids	2½ mins.	Heavy	All Ages	Try evening or early morning. Use FastPass+ first.
Prince Charming Regal Carrousel	n/a	Thrill Ride for Kids	2 mins.	Moderate to Heavy	Families	Come while waiting for Peter Pan's Flight FastPass+, during after-noon parade, or after dark.
★ Seven Dwarves Mine Train	At least 38"	Thrill Ride	2½ mins.	Heavy	All but Young Kids	This ride just opened use a FastPass+.
Under the Sea: Journey of the Little Mermaid	n/a	Ride-Through	7 mins.	Absolutely!	All Ages	You can get a FastPass+, but you'll miss the interactive queue.

Frontierland

	Name	Height	Type	Duration	Crowds	Ages	Comments
★	Big Thunder Mountain Railroad	At least 40"	Thrill Ride	4 mins.	Absolutely!	All but Young Kids	Use FastPass+. Most exciting at night when you can't anticipate the curves.
	Country Bear Jamboree	n/a	Show	17 mins.	Heavy	All Ages	Visit before 11 am. Stand to the far left lining up for the front rows.
★	Splash Mountain	At least 40"	Thrill Ride with Water	11 mins.	Yes!	All but Young Kids	Use FastPass+. Get in line early, or ride during meal or parade time. You may get wet.

Liberty Square

	Name	Height	Type	Duration	Crowds	Ages	Comments
	Hall of Presidents	n/a	Show/Film	22mins.	Moderate	All but Young Kids	Visit anytime.
★	Haunted Mansion	n/a	Thrill Ride	8 mins.	Moderate	All Ages	Nighttime adds extra fear factor.
	Liberty Square Riverboat	n/a	Cruise	15 mins.	Moderate	All Ages	Good for a break from the crowds.

Main Street U.S.A.

	Name	Height	Type	Duration	Crowds	Ages	Comments
	Walt Disney World Railroad	n/a	Railroad	21 mins.	Moderate to Heavy	All Ages	Board with young children for an early start in Frontierland or Fantasyland or hop on midafternoon.

Tomorrowland

	Name	Height	Type	Duration	Crowds	Ages	Comments
	Astro-Orbiter	n/a	Thrill Ride for Kids	2 mins.	Moderate to Heavy	All Ages	Skip unless there's a short line.
★	Buzz Lightyear's Space Ranger Spin	n/a	Interactive Ride	5 mins.	Heavy	All Ages	Come in the early morning and use FastPass+. Kids will want more than one ride.
	Monster's Inc. Laugh Floor	n/a	Film with special effects	15 mins.	Moderate to Heavy	All Ages	Come when you're waiting for your Buzz Lightyear or Space Mountain FastPass+.
★	Space Mountain	At least 44"	Thrill Ride	2½ mins.	You Bet!	All but Young Kids	Use FastPass+, or come at the beginning or the end of day or during a parade.
	Stitch's Great Escape	At least 40"	Simulator Exp.	15 mins.	Moderate to Heavy	All but Young Kids	Visit early after Space Mountain.
	Tomorrowland Speedway	54" to drive	Thrill Ride for Kids	5 mins.	Moderate	All but Young Kids	Come in the evening or during a parade; skip on a first-time visit; 32" height requirement to ride shotgun.
	Tomorrowland PeopleMover	n/a	Railroad	10 mins.	Light	All Ages	Come with young kids if you need a restful ride.
	Walt Disney's Carousel of Progress	n/a	Show	20 mins.	Light to Moderate	All Ages	Skip on a first-time visit unless you're heavily into nostalgia.

★ **Fodor's** Choice

Groove. Don't worry—you'll have time between fireball battles and cyclone spells to ride Space Mountain.

The Harmony Barber Shop lets you step back in time for a haircut ($15 for children 12 and under, $19 for anyone older). Babies or tots get free Mickey Ears, a souvenir lock of hair, and a certificate if it's their first haircut ever, but you pay $19 for the experience. Tweens like to get colored hair gel or "pixie dust" applications (about $8 a pop). At the Town Square Theater (formerly Exposition Hall), presented by Kodak, Mickey Mouse meets you for photos and autographs. And, for the first time in Disney history, you can pick up a FastPass+ appointment for such meet and greets. While you're here, stock up on batteries and memory cards or disposable cameras.

ADVENTURELAND

From the scrubbed brick, manicured lawns, and meticulously pruned trees of the Central Plaza, an artfully dilapidated wooden bridge leads to the jungles of Adventureland. Here, South African cape honeysuckle droops, Brazilian bougainvillea drapes, Mexican flame vines cling, spider plants clone, and three varieties of palm trees sway. The bright, all-American sing-along tunes that fill the air along Main Street and Central Plaza are replaced by the recorded repetitions of trumpeting elephants, pounding drums, and squawking parrots. The architecture is a mishmash of the best of Thailand, the Middle East, the Caribbean, Africa, and Polynesia, arranged in an inspired disorder that recalls comic-book fantasies of far-off places.

Once contained within the Pirates of the Caribbean attraction, Captain Jack Sparrow and the crew of the Black Pearl are brazenly recruiting new hearties at the Pirates League, adjacent to the ride entrance. You can get pirate and mermaid makeovers (for lots of doubloons) here. On a nearby stage furnished with pirate booty, the captain instructs scurvy dog recruits on brandishing a sword at Captain Jack Sparrow's Pirate Tutorial (several shows a day). And that's not all! The new "A Pirate's Adventure: Treasures of the Seven Seas" sends park guests on an interactive quest with a pirate map and talisman to complete "raids" through Adventureland as they fight off pirate enemies along the way. Shiver me timbers—it's a pirate's life for ye!

FRONTIERLAND

Frontierland evokes the American frontier and is planted with mesquite, twisted Peruvian pepper trees, slash pines, and cacti. The period seems to be the latter half of the 19th century, and the West is being won by Disney cast members dressed in checked shirts, leather vests, cowboy hats, and brightly colored neckerchiefs. Banjo and fiddle music twangs from tree to tree, and snackers walk around munching turkey drumsticks so large that you could best an outlaw single-handedly with one. (Beware of hovering seagulls that migrate to the parks during cooler months—they've been known to snatch snacks.)

The screams that drown out the string music aren't the result of a cowboy surprising an Indian. They come from two of the Magic Kingdom's more thrilling rides: Splash Mountain, an elaborate flume ride, and Big Thunder Mountain Railroad, a roller coaster. The Walt Disney World

Coasting down Splash Mountain in Frontierland will put some zip in your doo-dah and some water on your clothes.

Railroad tunnels past a colorful scene in Splash Mountain and drops you off between it and Thunder Mountain.

LIBERTY SQUARE

The rough-and-tumble Western frontier gently folds into Colonial America as Liberty Square picks up where Frontierland leaves off. The weathered siding gives way to solid brick and neat clapboard. The mesquite and cactus are replaced by stately oaks and masses of azaleas. The theme is Colonial history, which Northerners will be happy to learn is portrayed here as solid Yankee. The buildings, topped with weather vanes and exuding prosperity, are pure New England.

A replica of the Liberty Bell, crack and all, seems an appropriate prop to separate Liberty Square from Frontierland. There's even a Liberty Tree, a more than 150-year-old live oak, transported here from elsewhere on Disney property. Just as the Sons of Liberty hung lanterns on trees as a signal of solidarity after the Boston Tea Party, the Liberty Tree's branches are decorated with 13 lanterns representing the 13 original colonies. Around the square are tree-shaded tables for an alfresco lunch and plenty of carts and fast-food eateries to supply the goods.

FANTASYLAND

Walt Disney called this "a timeless land of enchantment," and Fantasyland does conjure pixie dust. Perhaps that's because the fanciful gingerbread houses, gleaming gold turrets, and, of course, the rides are based on Disney-animated movies.

Many of these rides, which could ostensibly be classified as rides for children, are packed with enough delightful detail to engage the adults who accompany them. Fantasyland has always been the most heavily trafficked area in the park, and its rides and shows are almost always crowded.

The good news is that Fantasyland has undergone the largest expansion in the park's history to add several new attractions and experiences. Dumbo the Flying Elephant now is double the size, flying above circus-themed grounds that also include the Great Goofini coaster, starring Goofy as stuntman. There's also a Walt Disney World Railroad station in Fantasyland. And a circus-themed Casey Jr. Splash 'N' Soak Station provides water-play respite for kids. Ariel of *The Little Mermaid* invites you to her own state-of-the-art attraction, Under the Sea: Journey of the Little Mermaid. Disney princesses welcome you for a photo op in the glittering Princess Fairytale Hall. You can be part of the show when you join Belle, Lumiere, and Madame Wardrobe of *Beauty and the Beast* at the Enchanted Tales with Belle attraction for a story performance. Meanwhile, Beast may be brooding in his castle, where the Be Our Guest dining room beckons to lunch and dinner guests. And the musical Seven Dwarfs Mine Train family coaster just opened in 2014 to complete the expansion.

You can enter Fantasyland on foot from Liberty Square, Tomorrowland, or via the Walt Disney World Railroad, but the classic introduction is through Cinderella Castle. As you exit the castle's archway, look left to discover a charming and often overlooked touch: Cinderella Fountain, a lovely brass casting of the castle's namesake, who's dressed in her peasant togs and surrounded by her beloved mice and bird friends.

From the southern end of Liberty Square, head toward the park hub and stop at the Disney PhotoPass picture spot for one of the park's best, unobstructed ground-level views of Cinderella Castle. It's a great spot for that family photo.

TOMORROWLAND

The "future that never was" spins boldly into view as you enter Tomorrowland, where Disney Imagineers paint the landscape with whirling spaceships, flashy neon lights, and gleaming robots. This is the future as envisioned by sci-fi writers and moviemakers in the 1920s and '30s, when space flight, laser beams, and home computers were fiction, not fact. Retro Jetsonesque styling lends the area lasting chic.

Gamers who want a break from the crowds can find their favorite video challenges in the arcade attached to Space Mountain. SEGA race car, NASCAR, and Fast and Furious Super Bikes games draw tweens and teens; Lil' Hoops give young kids a manageable basketball challenge. Though Tomorrowland Transit Authority (TTA) PeopleMover isn't a big-ticket ride, it's a great way to check out the landscape from above as it zooms in and out of Space Mountain and curves around the entire land.

TOP MAGIC KINGDOM SPECTACLES

Fodor'sChoice
★
Disney Festival of Fantasy Parade. Who'd want to miss a parade that delivers in 12 entertainment-packed minutes a lineup of Disney characters and royalty, a Steampunk-inspired, fire-breathing dragon, elaborate towering floats, and handsome pairs of dancers twirling to some of Disney's best tunes? This newest daily 3 pm parade celebrates Walt's legacy with vignettes featuring the glamour, drama, and fun of classic films like *Sleeping Beauty* and *Peter Pan* while also catering to fans of contemporary box-office hits like *Brave* and *Frozen*. The colorful pageant of nine floats out-performs its predecessors with übercreative costuming, inventive float technology, a cast of nearly 100 gung-ho performers, and a new musical score that invites singing along with familiar medleys. From the 50-foot-long topiary garden float of Disney royal couples led by dancers in swan-neck-collared ballgowns with iridescent feathers to the 32-foot-tall Airship float finale with Mickey and Minnie, the parade energizes spectators as it rolls past. A Lost Boy from *Peter Pan* may grab your hand and kiss it. A stilt-walker might lean into your camera for a snapshot. You'll hear viewers gasp or shout when the towering 53-foot-long, green-eyed Maleficent Dragon, created with help from Tony-award-winning designer Michael Curry, rears its head and spews flames. **For people with disabilities:** There are viewing areas for guests in wheelchairs along the route; ask any cast member for guidance. A sign-language schedule is available at Guest Relations. ■TIP➔ The parade runs from Frontierland to Town Square. Check your guidemap for the complete route. Disney now distributes a limited number of FastPass+ reservations, but book as far ahead as possible. Otherwise, find shade beneath a Frontierland porch at least an hour before showtime. If you've seen the parade, this is a good time to head for popular rides while crowds gather along the route. ⊠ *Magic Kingdom* ☞ *Duration: 12 mins. Crowds: Heavy. Audience: All Ages.*

Fodor'sChoice
★
Main Street Electrical Parade. The Main Street parade, with 23 illuminated floats, 80 performers, and a half-million lights in all, first debuted at Disneyland in California in 1972. It lights up Magic Kingdom nights with plenty of power and its distinctive synthesizer-infused "Baroque Hoedown" musical theme. The lead float features Tinker Bell showering guests with 25,000 pixie-dusted points of light, and a finale float with a patriotic tribute that includes a majestic bald eagle shining with golden lights. Check *Times Guide*; the parade sometimes runs twice in one night and occasionally not at all. ■TIP➔ Take your place on the curb at least 40 minutes before the parade begins. ⊠ *Magic Kingdom* ☞ *Duration: 20 mins. Crowds: Heavy. Audience: All Ages.*

10

Fodor'sChoice
★
Wishes. When the lights dim on Main Street and orchestral music fills the air, you know this fireworks extravaganza is about to begin. In Wishes, Jiminy Cricket's voice comes to life and tries to convince you that your wishes really can come true. He gets plenty of support from the Disney stars of classic films such as *Pinocchio, Fantasia, Cinderella,* and *The Little Mermaid*. Portions of famous film songs play over loudspeakers, and you hear the voices of film characters like Peter Pan and Aladdin as more than 680 individual fireworks paint the night sky. Oh, and

don't worry that Tinker Bell may have been sealed in her jar for the night—she comes back to fly above the crowd in grand pixie-dust style. Check the *Times Guide* for performance time, which varies seasonally. ■TIP→ Best views are in the Castle forecourt or on surrounding bridges; or find a place near the front of the park for a quick post-show exit. ⊠ *Magic Kingdom* ☞ *Duration: 12 mins. Crowds: Heavy. Audience: All Ages.*

EPCOT

Walt Disney said that Epcot would "take its cue from the new ideas and new technologies that are now emerging from the creative centers of American industry." He wrote that Epcot—never completed, always improving—"will never cease to be a living blueprint of the future, a showcase to the world for the ingenuity of American free enterprise."

But the permanent settlement that Disney envisioned wasn't to be. Epcot opened in 1982—16 years after his death—as a showcase, ostensibly, for the concepts that would be incorporated into the real-life Epcots of the future. (Disney's vision *has* taken an altered shape in the self-contained city of Celebration, an urban-planner's dream opened in 1996 on Disney property near Kissimmee.)

Epcot, the theme park, has two key areas: Future World, where most pavilions are collaborations between Walt Disney Imagineering and U.S. corporations and are designed to demonstrate technological advances through innovative shows and attractions; and the World Showcase, where shops, restaurants, attractions, and live entertainment create microcosms of 11 countries from four continents.

For years, Epcot was considered the more staid park, a place geared toward adults. But after its 10th anniversary, Epcot began to evolve into a livelier, more child-friendly park, with interactive fun at Innoventions and such "wow" attractions as Future World's Test Track, Mission: SPACE, and Soarin'.

There's something for everyone here. The World Showcase appeals to younger children with the Kidcot Fun Stop craft stations and the Norway pavilion's Princess Storybook Dining. Soarin', in The Land Pavilion, is a family favorite. And The Seas with Nemo & Friends—with one of the world's largest saltwater aquariums and a Nemo-theme ride—is a must-see for all. The hottest new ticket? The greatly improved Test Track presented by Chevrolet, where you can design your own custom concept car, then put it through its high-speed paces.

Wear comfortable shoes—there's *a lot* of territory to cover here. Arrive early, and try to stay all day, squeezing in extras like high-tech games at Innoventions and a relaxing meal. If you enter through International Gateway before 11 am, cast members will direct you to Future World, which usually opens two hours before World Showcase.

PLANNING

GETTING ORIENTED

Epcot is composed of two areas: Future World and the World Showcase. The inner core of Future World's pavilions has the Spaceship Earth geosphere and a plaza anchored by the computer-animated Fountain of Nations. Also at the core is Innoventions, popular for its hands-on, high-tech exhibits, and immersion entertainment.

TOP ATTRACTIONS

The American Adventure

IllumiNations

Mission: SPACE

Soarin'

Test Track

Six pavilions compose Future World's outer ring. Each of the three east pavilions has a ride and the occasional postride showcase; a visit rarely takes more than 30 minutes. The blockbuster exhibits on the west side contain rides and interactive displays; each exhibit can take up to 90 minutes for the complete experience.

World Showcase pavilions are on the promenade that circles the World Showcase Lagoon. Each houses shops, restaurants, and friendly international staffers; some have films or displays. Mexico and Norway offer tame rides. Live entertainment is scheduled at every pavilion except Norway.

Disney's monorail and buses drop you off at the main entrance in front of Future World. But if you're staying at one of the Epcot resorts (the BoardWalk, Yacht Club, Beach Club, Dolphin, or Swan), you can use the International Gateway entrance between World Showcase's France and U.K. pavilions.

PARK AMENITIES

Guest Relations: To the right of the ticket windows at the park entrance and to the left of Spaceship Earth inside the park, this is the place to pick up schedules and maps. You also can get maps at the park's International Gateway entrance and most shops. Guest Relations will also assist with dining reservations, ticket upgrades, and services for guests with disabilities.

Epcot Lost and Found: Located in the Guest Relations lobby east of Spaceship Earth. ⊠ *Future World, Epcot* ☎ *407/560–7500.*

Lockers: Lockers ($7 and $9, with $5 refundable deposit) are at the International Gateway and to the west of Spaceship Earth. Coin-operated lockers also are at the bus information center by the bus parking lot.

Lost People and Things: Instruct children to speak to someone with a Disney name tag if you become separated. Guest Relations has a computerized message center for contacting companions in any of the parks.

Stroller Rentals: You can rent strollers on the east side of the Entrance Plaza and at the International Gateway. Singles are $15 daily, $13 for multiday rental; doubles cost $31 daily, $27 for multiple days. Even preschoolers will be glad for a stroller in this large park.

10

Epcot

PARKING

Monorail

Entrance
Plaza

Monorail

Festival
Center

Mission:
SPACE

Tip
Board

Test
Track

UNIVERSE
OF ENERGY

Ellen's Energy
Adventure

Stroller &
Wheelchair
Rental

Guest
Relations

Innoventions
East

Odyssey
Center

Spaceship
Earth

Electric
Umbrella

Guest
Relations

Lockers

Earth
Station

Tip Board

FUTURE WORLD

Fountain of
Nations

Turtle Talk
with Crush

Coral Reef
Restaurant

Innoventions
West

Tip
Board

THE SEAS WITH
NEMO & FRIENDS

Tip
Board

Journey Into Imagination
with Figment

Captain EO

THE LAND

Circle of
Life

Sunshine Seasons

IMAGINATION!

Garden
Grill

Le Cellier
Steakhouse

Living with
the Land

Soarin'

O Canada!

CANADA

Avenue of the Stars

World Showcase
Events Pavilion

KEY

- Monorail
- X Restaurants
- Restrooms

Epcot Resorts Blvd.

Avenue of the Stars

MEXICO

NORWAY

CHINA

Maelstrom

✕ Lotus Blossom
Café

Reflections
of China

Kringla Bakeri
Og Kafe

Gran Fiesta Tour
Starring The
Three Caballeros

✕ San Angel Inn
✕ La Cava del Tequila

✕ Nine Dragons

Africa
Coolpost

✕ Princess Storybook Dining
at Royal Akershus
Banquet Hall

✕ Saluting
Africa Outpost

First Aid &
Baby Care

✕ La Hacienda de
San Angel and
La Cantina Restaurant

GERMANY

Biergarten

✕ Sommerfest

WORLD
SHOWCASE
PLAZA

Via Napoli
Ristorante e Pizzeria ✕

ITALY

Tutto Italia ✕

World Showcase
Lagoon

Tutto Gusto
Wine Cellar

WORLD SHOWCASE

Fife & Drum ✕

ATM

America Gardens
Theatre ◆

✕ Liberty Inn

AMERICAN
ADVENTURE

Katsura
Grill

Rose & Crown
✕ Pub & Dining Room

Teppan Edo
& Tokyo Dining ✕

✕ Yorkshire County
Fish Shop

JAPAN

UNITED
KINGDOM

INTERNATIONAL
GATEWAY

✕ Tangierine Cafe

Stroller &
Wheelchair
Rental ◆

FRANCE

MOROCCO

✕ Les Chefs de France

✕ Restaurant
Marrakesh

✕ Monsieur Paul

✕ Les Halles Boulangerie
& Pâtisserie

Impressions
de France ◆

0   400 yards

0   400 m

EPCOT

NAME	Height Req.	Type of Entertainment	Duration	Crowds	Audience	Tips
Future World						
Captain EO (Imagination!)	n/a	3-D Film	17 mins.	Moderate to Heavy	All but Young Kids	Come in the early morning or just before closing. Take off the 3-D glasses if little kids get scared.
Journey into Imagination with Figment (Imagination!)	n/a	Ride-Through	8 mins.	Light	Young Kids	Ride after Captain EO. Warn toddlers about darkness at the end of the ride.
Ellen's Energy Adventure (Universe of Energy)	n/a	Ride-Through	45 mins.	Moderate	All but very Young Kids	Best seats are to the far left and front of the theater.
Innoventions	n/a	Walk-Through	Up to you	Moderate to Heavy	All Ages	Come anytime.
The Circle of Life (The Land)	n/a	Film	20 mins.	Moderate to Heavy	All Ages	Come early or for your toddler's afternoon nap.
Living with the Land (The Land)	n/a	Cruise	14 mins.	Moderate	Small Kids	The line moves quickly, so come anytime.
Soarin' (The Land) ★	At least 40"	Simulator Ride	5 mins.	Heavy	All but very Young Kids	Use FastPass+, or come early, or just before closing.
The Seas with Nemo & Friends	n/a	Ride- and Walk-Through	Up to you	Moderate to Heavy	All Ages	Get Nemo fans here early in the morning.
Turtle Talk with Crush	n/a	Animated Show	20 mins.	Moderate to Heavy	Young Kids and Families	Line up after "clamobile" ride.

				You Bet!		
★ Mission: SPACE	At least 44"	Thrill Ride	4 mins.		All but Young Kids	Come before 10 am or use FastPass+. Don't ride on a full stomach.
Spaceship Earth	n/a	Ride-Through	15 mins.	Moderate to Heavy	All Ages	Ride while waiting for Mission: SPACE or Soarin' FastPass+ appointment or just before closing.
★ Test Track	At least 40"	Thrill Ride	5 mins.	Heavy	All but Young Kids	Come early or use FastPass+. The ride can't function on wet tracks, so don't come after a downpour.
World Showcase						
★ The American Adventure Show	n/a	Show/Film	20 mins.	Heavy	All Ages	Arrive 10 mins. before the Voices of Liberty or the Spirit of America Fife & Drum Corps are slated to perform.
America Gardens Theatre	n/a	Live Show	Varies	Varies	Varies	Arrive more than an hour or so ahead of time for holiday and celebrity performances.
Gran Fiesta Tour Starring the Three Caballeros	n/a	Cruise	9 mins.	Light to Moderate	All Ages	Especially good if you have young children.
Impressions de France	n/a	Film	20 mins.	Moderate	All Ages	Come anytime.
Maelstrom	n/a	Thrill Ride for Kids with Water	10 mins.	Moderate to Heavy	All Ages	Use FastPass+ for after lunch or dinner.
O Canada!	n/a	Film	14 mins.	Moderate to Heavy	All Ages	Stop in any time. Be prepared to stand for the film. No strollers permitted.
Reflections of China	n/a	Film	14 mins.	Moderate	All Ages	Come anytime. Be prepared to stand during the film. No strollers permitted.

★ Fodor'sChoice

VISITING TIPS

■ Epcot is so vast and varied that you really need two days to explore. With just one day, you'll have to be highly selective.

■ Go early in the week, when others are at Magic Kingdom.

■ If you like a good festival, visit during the International Flower & Garden Festival (early to mid-March through May) or the International Food & Wine Festival (late September through mid-November).

■ Once through the turnstiles at either the main Future World entrance or the back World Showcase entrance, make a beeline for the popular Mission: SPACE and Test Track (for fast-paced thrills) or The Seas with Nemo & Friends and Soarin' (for family fun). Or make a FastPass+ reservation.

EXPLORING EPCOT

FUTURE WORLD

Future World's inner core is composed of the iconic Spaceship Earth geosphere and, beyond it, a plaza anchored by the awe-inspiring computer-animated Fountain of Nations, which shoots water 150 feet skyward. Don't miss interactive fun at Innoventions.

Six pavilions compose Future World's outer ring. On the east side, they are the Universe of Energy, Mission: SPACE, and Test Track. Each pavilion presents a single, self-contained ride and an occasional postride showcase; a visit rarely takes more than 30 minutes, but it depends on how long you spend in the postride area. On the west side are The Seas with Nemo & Friends, The Land, and Imagination! These blockbuster exhibits contain both rides and interactive displays; you could spend at least 1½ hours at each of these pavilions, but there aren't enough hours in the day, so prioritize.

■TIP→ Before setting out, look into the Disney PhotoPass at the Camera Center in the Entrance Plaza. It tracks photos of your group shot by Disney photographers, which you can view and purchase later at the center or online.

WORLD SHOWCASE

Nowhere but at Epcot can you explore a little corner of nearly a dozen countries in one day. As you stroll the 1 ½ miles around the 40-acre World Showcase Lagoon, you circumnavigate the globe-according-to-Disney by experiencing native food, entertainment, culture, and arts and crafts at pavilions representing countries in Europe, Asia, North Africa, and the Americas. Pavilion employees are from the countries they represent—Disney hires them as part of its international college program.

Instead of rides, you have solid film attractions at the Canada, China, and France pavilions; several art exhibitions; and the chance to try your foreign language skills with the staff. Each pavilion also has a designated Kidcot Fun Stop, open daily from 11 or noon until about 8 or 9, where youngsters can try a cultural crafts project. Live entertainment is an integral part of the experience, and you'll enjoy watching the incredibly talented Jeweled Dragon Acrobats in China, singing along with terrific British rock band impersonators in the United Kingdom

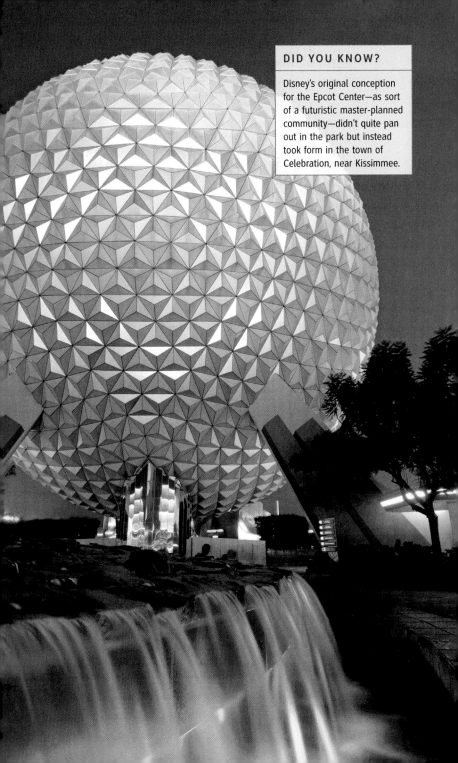

and the Off Kilter band in Canada, or laughing along with some improv fun in the Italy courtyard.

Dining is another favorite pastime at Epcot, and the World Showcase offers tempting tastes of the authentic cuisines of the countries here.

TOP EPCOT SPECTACLE

Fodor's Choice
★
IllumiNations: Reflections of Earth. This marvelous nighttime spectacular takes place over the World Showcase Lagoon every night before closing. Be sure to stick around for the lasers, lights, flames, fireworks, fountains, and music that fill the air over the water. The show's Earth Globe—a gigantic, spherical, video-display system rotating on a 350-ton floating island—is three stories tall with 180,000 light-emitting diodes. It houses six computer processors and 258 strobe lights and projects images celebrating the diversity and unified spirit of humankind. The globe opens like a lotus flower in the grand finale, revealing a huge torch that rises 40 feet into the air as additional flames spread light across the lagoon. Nearly 2,800 fireworks shells paint colorful displays across the night sky.

Although there's generally good viewing from all around the lagoon, some of the best spots are in front of the Italy pavilion, on the bridge between France and the United Kingdom, on the promenade in front of Canada, at the World Showcase Plaza, and at La Hacienda de San Angel and La Cantina de San Angel in Mexico. **For people with disabilities:** During the show, certain areas along the lagoon's edge at Showcase Plaza, Canada, and Germany are reserved for guests using wheelchairs. ■TIP➜ For best views (and if you have young children), find your place 45 minutes in advance and send someone in your group for ice cream or other treats. ✉ *World Showcase, Epcot* ☞ *Duration: 13 mins. Crowds: Heavy. Audience: All Ages.*

NIGHTLIFE

BARS

Cava del Tequila. Set inside the Mexico pavilion, this intimate bar serves tasty tapas, tequila flights, and some of the best margaritas anywhere, including the Cava Organic Skinny Lime Margarita. ✉ *World Showcase, Mexico, Epcot.*

Rose & Crown Pub. Great piano sets by the Hat Lady and, on busy nights, four-to-six-deep at the bar guarantees good times at this United Kingdom watering hole. The fish-and-chips are first rate, and the Trio of United Kingdom Cheeses includes aged Irish cheddar and Stilton. Grab a beer or a cordial and let the fun begin! ✉ *World Showcase, United Kingdom, Epcot.*

Tutto Gusto. This cool, cozy wine cellar adjoining Tutto Italia is the ideal place to kick back at a table or on a sofa and sip a bubbly prosecco or a glass of Italian wine while noshing on antipasto or tapas-sized pastas. For quicker service, head straight for the bar. ✉ *World Showcase Italy pavilion, Epcot.*

The Temple of Quetzalcoatl (ket-zel-co-WAH-tal) at Teotihuacán (tay-o-tee-wah-CON), just outside Mexico City, is the model for the pyramid at the Mexico pavilion.

DISNEY'S HOLLYWOOD STUDIOS

The first thing you notice when you pass through the Hollywood Studios turnstiles is the laid-back California attitude. Palm-lined Hollywood Boulevard oozes glamour—but in a casual way that makes you feel as if you belong, even without your slinky Michael Kors jersey and Jimmy Choos.

When the park opened in May 1989 its name was Disney-MGM Studios. Disney changed the name in 2008 to broaden its appeal. Unlike the first movie theme park—Universal Studios in California—Hollywood Studios combined Disney detail with MGM's motion-picture legacy and Walt Disney's own animated classics. Imagineers built the park with real film and television production in mind, and during its first decade, the Studios welcomed films like *Ernest Saves Christmas* and TV shows like *Wheel of Fortune* to its soundstages.

The Animation Studios, too, were busy. Stories such as *Aladdin* and *Lilo & Stitch* came to life on the easels and computers of Disney's Florida animators. Though production has mostly halted at the park, you can enjoy plenty of attractions that showcase how filmmakers practice their craft. Want to see how special effects are created? Visit the Studio Backlot Tour. If you're wowed by action-film stunts, you can learn the tricks of the trade at the Indiana Jones Epic Stunt Spectacular! or the Lights, Motors, Action! Extreme Stunt Show. No trip to the Studios would be complete without a tour of the Magic of Disney Animation, where you can sit down and draw a character like Mickey or Donald.

TOP ATTRACTIONS

AGES 8 AND UP

The American Idol Experience. If you don't get chosen to test your pipes, you can vote for your favorite Idol wannabe.

Indiana Jones Epic Stunt Spectacular! The show's cast reenacts *Raiders of the Lost Ark* scenes with panache.

The Magic of Disney Animation. It's always fun to immerse yourself in Disney's world of animation.

Rock 'n' Roller Coaster Starring Aerosmith. Blast off to rockin' tunes on a high-speed, hard-core coaster.

Star Tours—The Adventures Continue. Prepare for a high-speed chase on this updated simulator thrill ride through multiple scenarios in the *Star Wars* galaxy.

Toy Story Midway Mania! 3-D glasses? Check. Spring-action shooter? Check. Ride and shoot your way through the midway with Buzz, Woody, and others.

Twilight Zone Tower of Terror. The TV classic theming of this free-fall "elevator" screamer is meticulous.

AGES 7 AND UNDER

Beauty and the Beast—Live on Stage. Memorable music, talented performers, dancing kitchen objects, and a fairy-tale ending make this a must-see show.

Disney Junior—Live on Stage! The preschool crowd can't get enough of the characters here from Disney Channel shows like *Jake and the Never Land Pirates, Mickey Mouse Clubhouse, Doc McStuffins,* and *Sofia the First.*

Honey, I Shrunk the Kids Movie Set Adventure. Youngsters love to romp among the giant blades of grass and bugs.

Muppet*Vision 3-D. Children (and most adults) shriek with laughter during this 3-D movie.

In a savvy effort to grab a big piece of the pop-culture pie, in late 2008 Disney opened its own *American Idol* attraction, where performers earn audience votes to compete in an end-of-day contest for a spot in the TV show's regional audition process. (This attraction is scheduled to close in January 2015.) Imagineers continue to "bring it," with big-hit attractions such as Toy Story Midway Mania! and new twists on old favorites like the 3-D Star Wars–themed simulator ride, Star Tours—The Adventures Continue.

PLANNING

GETTING ORIENTED

The park is divided into sightseeing clusters. **Hollywood Boulevard** is the main artery to the heart of the park, and is where you find the glistening replica of Graumann's Chinese Theater.

Encircling it are **Sunset Boulevard,** the **Animation Courtyard, Mickey Avenue, Pixar Place, Commissary Lane,** the **Streets of America area,** and **Echo Lake.**

The entire park is 135 acres, and has just 20 major attractions (compared with Magic Kingdom's 40-plus). It's small enough to cover in a day and even repeat a favorite ride or two.

If you're staying at one of the Epcot resorts (BoardWalk, Yacht or Beach Club, Swan, or Dolphin), getting to the Entrance Plaza on a motor launch is part of the fun. Disney resort buses also drop you at the entrance.

If you're staying off-property and driving, your parking ticket will remain valid for parking at another Disney park later in the day—provided, of course, you have the stamina.

PARK AMENITIES

Disney's Hollywood Studios Lost and Found: Report lost or found articles at Guest Relations. ✉ *Hollywood Blvd., Disney's Hollywood Studios* ☎ *407/560–4666.*

Guest Relations: You'll find it just inside the turnstiles on the left side of the Entrance Plaza. The **Studios Tip Board**, with updated information on events and attraction wait times, is at the corner of Hollywood and Sunset boulevards.

Lockers: You can rent lockers at the Crossroads of the World kiosk in the center of the Entrance Plaza. The cost is $7 or $9 with a $5 refundable key deposit. The lockers themselves are at Oscar's Super Service.

Lost People and Things: Instruct your kids to go to a Disney staffer with a name tag if they can't find you. If you lose them, ask any cast member for assistance; logbooks of lost children's names are kept at Guest Relations, which also has a computerized message center where you can leave notes for companions.

Stroller Rentals: Oscar's Super Service rents strollers. Single strollers are $15 daily, $13 for more than one day; doubles are $31 daily, $27 multiday.

VISITING TIPS

■ Visit early in the week, when most people are at Magic Kingdom and Animal Kingdom.

10

■ Check the Tip Board periodically for attractions with short wait times to visit between FastPass+ appointments.

■ Be at the Fantasmic! amphitheater at least an hour before showtime if you didn't book the dinner package.

■ Need a burst of energy? On-the-run hunger pangs? Grab a slice at **Pizza Planet** at Streets of America. Alternatively, **Hollywood Scoops ice cream** on Sunset is the place to be on a hot day.

EXPLORING DISNEY'S HOLLYWOOD STUDIOS

HOLLYWOOD BOULEVARD

With its palm trees, pastel buildings, and flashy neon, Hollywood Boulevard paints a rosy picture of 1930s Tinseltown. There's a sense of having walked right onto a movie set of old, with art-deco storefronts and roving starlets and nefarious agents—actually costumed actors known as the Citizens of Hollywood. Throughout the park, characters

Catastrophe Canyon
on Studio Backlot Tour

Earffel
Tower

Soundstages

Stage Lane

Lights, Motors, Action!
Extreme Stunt Show

Toy Story
Midway Mania!

The Legend of
Captain Jack
Sparrow

Walt Disney:
One Man's
Dream

Studio
Backlot
Tour

PIXAR PLACE

MICKEY AVENUE

Studio
Catering Co.

Hey Howdy
Hey Take Away

Great Movie
Ride

STREETS OF
AMERICA

Sorceror
Mickey's Hat

Honey, I Shrunk the Kids
Movie Set Adventure

San Francisco Ave.

ABC
Commissary

Sci-Fi Dine-In
Theater Restaurant

COMMISSARY LANE

ATM

New York St.

Min & Bill's
Dockside Diner

Echo Lake

Muppet*Vision
3-D

ATM

ECHO LAKE

Mama Melrose's
Ristorante
Italiano

Pizza Planet
Arcade

50's Prime
Time Café

Jedi Training
Academy

Star
Tours

Tatooine Alley

Indiana Jones Epic
Stunt Spectacular!

Backlot
Express

Prospect Ave.

KEY

✗ Restaurants

🚹🚺 Restrooms

•••• Parade Route

S. Studio Dr.
(from World Dr.)

0		50 yards
0		50 m

Disney's Hollywood Studios

Cypress Dr.

Theatre of the Stars Dr.

Highland Ave.

The Magic of
Disney Animation

Voyage of the
Little Mermaid
ANIMATION
COURTYARD

Rock 'n' Roller
Coaster Starring
Aerosmith

Cypress Dr.

Disney Junior—
Live on Stage!

Rosie's
All-American
Cafe

Hollywood Brown
Derby

Catalina
Eddie's

Toluca Legs
Turkey Co.

Starring Rolls
Cafe

Tip
Board

Hollywood
Junction
Restaurant
Reservations

SUNSET BOULEVARD

Fairfax
Fare

Twilight Zone
Tower of Terror

HOLLYWOOD
BOULEVARD

Beauty and the Beast—
Live on Stage

Lockers,
strollers

Hollywood
& Vine

ATM

First Aid

Prospect Ave.

Baby Care
Center

Main
Entrance

Perimeter Rd.

Guest
Relations

Fantasmic!

Walt Disney World
Water Transportation

Disney Resort
Bus Facility

Parking

walkway to Epcot Resorts

N. Studio Dr.
(to/from Buena Vista Blvd.)

DISNEY'S HOLLYWOOD STUDIOS

NAME	Height Req.	Type of Entertainment	Duration	Crowds	Audience	Tips
Animation Courtyard						
Disney Junior—Live on Stage!	n/a	Show	24 mins.	Moderate to Heavy	Young Kids	Come first thing in the morning, when your child is most alert and lines are shorter.
The Magic of Disney Animation	n/a	Tour	15+ mins.	Moderate	All Ages	Come in the morning or late afternoon. Toddlers may get bored.
Voyage of the Little Mermaid	n/a	Show	15 mins.	Heavy	All Ages	Come first thing in the morning. Otherwise, wait until after 5.
Echo Lake						
The American Idol Experience	n/a	Show	25 mins./ 45 mins.	Yes!	All but Young Kids	Check *Times Guide*, for showtimes. Arrive at least 30 minutes early for seats inside the theater.
Indiana Jones Epic Stunt Spectacular!	n/a	Show	30 mins.	Moderate to Heavy	All but Young Kids	Come at night, when the idol's eyes glow. Sit up front to feel the heat of a truck on fire.
★ Star Tours 3-D—The Adventure Continues	At least 40"	Simulator Exp.	6 mins.	Heavy	All but Young Kids	Get a FastPass+. Sit in rear for wildest ride.
Hollywood Boulevard						
Great Movie Ride	n/a	Ride/Tour	22 mins.	Moderate	All but Young Kids	Come while waiting for FastPass+ appointment. Lines out the door mean 25-min. wait–or longer.
Mickey Avenue						
Walt Disney: One Man's Dream	n/a	Walk-Through/ Film	15+ mins.	Light to Moderate	All but Young Kids	See this attraction while waiting for a FastPass+ appointment.

Name	Height	Type	Duration	Crowds	Audience	Notes
The Legend of Captain Jack Sparrow	n/a	Show/Film	12 mins.	Moderate	All but Young Kids	Standing room only; children may be restless.
Pixar Place						
Toy Story Midway Mania!	n/a	Interactive Ride	7 mins.	Heavy	All Ages	Come early; use FastPass+.
Streets of America						
Honey, I Shrunk the Kids Movie Set Adventure	n/a	Playground	Up to you	Moderate	Young Kids	Come after you've done several shows and your kids need to cut loose. Keep an eye on toddlers who can quickly get lost in the caves and slides.
Lights, Motors, Action! Extreme Stunt Show	n/a	Show	38 mins.	Heavy	All but Young Kids	For the best seats, line up for the show while others are lining up for the parade.
Muppet*Vision 3-D	n/a	3-D Film	25 mins.	Moderate	All Ages	Arrive 10 mins. early. And don't worry—there are no bad seats.
Studio Backlot Tour	n/a	Tour	35 mins.	Moderate	All but very Young Kids	People sitting on the left can get wet. Come early; it closes at dusk.
Sunset Boulevard						
Beauty and the Beast—Live on Stage!	n/a	Show	30 mins.	Moderate to Heavy	All Ages	Come 30 mins. before showtime for good seats. Performance times vary, so check ahead.
★ Rock 'n' Roller Coaster Starring Aerosmith	At least 48"	Thrill Ride	1 min., 22 secs.	Huge	All but Young Kids	Ride early, then use FastPass+ for another go later.
★ Twilight Zone Tower of Terror	At least 40"	Thrill Ride	10 mins.	You Bet!	All but Young Kids	Use FastPass+. Come early or late evening.

★ Fodor'sChoice

from Disney movies new and old—from *Mickey Mouse* to *Toy Story* friends—pose for photos and sign autographs.

SUNSET BOULEVARD

This avenue honors Hollywood with facades derived from the Cathay Circle, the Beverly Wilshire Theatre, and other City of Angels landmarks. Three of the park's most popular attractions are found here: the live Beauty and the Beast show, The Twilight Zone Tower of Terror, and the Aerosmith-powered Rock 'n' Roller Coaster.

ANIMATION COURTYARD

As you exit Sunset Boulevard, veer right through the high-arched gateway to the Animation Courtyard. Straight ahead are *Disney Junior— Live on Stage!,* the Magic of Disney Animation, and *Voyage of the Little Mermaid.*

PIXAR PLACE

Pixar Place has a fresh look tied to one of the park's biggest attractions, Toy Story Midway Mania! Where TV- and film-production soundstages once stood, warm brick facades welcome you to the land of Woody and Buzz. Open-air kiosks invite you to browse for themed toys and souvenirs. The brick building featuring Toy Story Friends is the place to mix and mingle with characters from the blockbuster movie *Toy Story.* Check schedules on your *Times Guide.*

STREETS OF AMERICA

It's fun to tour the New York and San Francisco sets here on foot so that you can check out the windows of shops and apartments, the taxicabs, and other details. If you're lucky (or smart enough to check the *Times Guide* show schedule), you'll join the street party for a performance by Mulch, Sweat & Shears—Live in Concert, as they play a 30-minute set of rock classics or rockin' seasonal tunes during holidays. The band also performs later in the day by the Sorcerer Hat on Hollywood Boulevard.

ECHO LAKE

In the center of an idealized slice of Southern California is a cool, blue lake—an oasis fringed with trees, benches, and things like pink-and-aqua, chrome-trimmed restaurants with sassy waitresses and black-and-white TVs at the tables; the shipshape Min & Bill's Dockside Diner; and Gertie, an emotive dinosaur that dispenses ice cream (seasonally) as well as Disney souvenirs and the occasional puff of smoke. (Look for Gertie's giant footprints in the sidewalk.) The hot ticket here is the American Idol Experience, where you can act out your own *American Idol* ambitions. You'll also find two of the park's longest-running attractions, the Indiana Jones Epic Stunt Spectacular! and Star Tours—The Adventures Continue, where a 3-D attraction transformation jazzes up the galaxy.

ANIMAL KINGDOM

If you're thinking, "Oh, it's just another zoo, let's skip it," think again. Walt Disney World's fourth theme park, opened in 1998, takes its inspiration from humankind's enduring love for animals and pulls out all the stops. Your day will be packed with unusual animal encounters, enchanting entertainment, and themed rides that'll leave you breathless.

A large chunk of the park is devoted to animal habitats, especially the forest and savanna of Africa's Kilimanjaro Safaris. Towering acacia trees and tall grasses sweep across the land where antelopes, giraffes, and wildebeests roam. A lion kopje, warthog burrows, a zebra habitat, and an elephant watering hole provide ample space for inhabitants.

About 94 acres contain foliage like hibiscus and mulberry, perfect for antelope and many other species. The largest groups of Nile hippos and African elephants in North America live along the winding waterway that leads to the savanna. The generously landscaped Pangani Forest Exploration Trail provides roaming grounds for troops of gorillas and authentic habitats for meerkats, birds, fish, and other creatures.

TOP ATTRACTIONS
Africa
Festival of the Lion King
Kilimanjaro Safaris
Asia
Expedition Everest
DinoLand U.S.A.
DINOSAUR.
Finding Nemo: The Musical
Discovery Island
Tree of Life: It's Tough to Be a Bug!
Tour
Wild Africa Trek

Beyond the park's Africa territory, similar large spaces are set aside for the homes of Asian animals like tigers and giant fruit bats, as well as for creatures such as Galápagos tortoises and a giant anteater.

Disney Imagineers didn't forget to include their trademark thrills, from the Kali River Rapids ride in Asia to the fast-paced DINOSAUR journey in DinoLand U.S.A. Expedition Everest, the park's biggest thrill attraction, is a "runaway" train ride on a faux rugged mountain complete with icy ledges, dark caves, and a yeti legend. Next up: Imagineers are designing a new land in the former Camp Minnie-Mickey location based on the blockbuster film *Avatar* and expected sequels.

The only downside to the Animal Kingdom layout is that walking paths and spaces can get very crowded and hot in the warmest months. Your best bet is to arrive very early and see the animals first before the heat makes them (and you) woozy.

Just before the park opens, Minnie Mouse, Pluto, and Goofy arrive at the iconic Tree of Life in a safari vehicle to welcome the first guests into the heart of the park. Let the adventure begin!

PLANNING

GETTING ORIENTED

Animal Kingdom's hub is the Tree of Life, in the middle of Discovery Island. The park's lands, each with a distinct personality, radiate from Discovery Island. To the southwest, home of the former Camp Minnie-Mickey, Disney Imagineers are creating the new land of Pandora based on the *Avatar* film and upcoming sequels. The new area is expected to open in 2017. North of the hub is Africa, where Kilimanjaro Safaris travel across extensive savanna. In the northeast corner is Rafiki's Planet Watch with conservation activities.

Asia, with thrills like Expedition Everest and Kali River Rapids, is east of the hub, and DinoLand U.S.A. brings *T. rex* and other prehistoric creatures to life in the park's southeast corner.

If you're staying on site, you can take a Disney bus to the Entrance Plaza. If you drive, the $15 parking fee allows you to park at other Disney lots throughout the day.

Although this is technically Disney's largest theme park, most of the land is reserved for the animals. Pedestrian areas are actually quite compact, with relatively narrow passageways. The only way to get around is on foot or in a wheelchair or electronic convenience vehicle (ECV).

PARK AMENITIES

Animal Kingdom Lost and Found: To retrieve lost articles on the same day, visit or call Lost and Found, which is at Guest Relations. ⊠ *Oasis, Animal Kingdom* ☎ *407/938–2785.*

Guest Relations: This office will help with tickets at a window to the left just before you pass through the turnstile. Once you've entered, Guest Relations staffers in the Oasis can provide park maps, schedules, and answers to questions. They can also assist with dining reservations, ticket upgrades, and services for guests with disabilities.

Lockers: Lockers are in Guest Relations in the Oasis. Rental fees are $7 to $9 (depending on size) for a day plus a $5 key deposit.

Lost People and Things: Instruct your kids to speak to someone with a Disney name tag if you become separated. Lost children are taken to the baby-care center, where they can watch Disney movies, or to Guest Relations, whichever is closer. If you do lose your child, contact any cast member immediately and Disney security personnel will be notified.

Stroller Rentals: Garden Gate Gifts in the Oasis rents strollers. Singles are $15 daily, $13 for more than one day; doubles run $31 daily, $27 multiday.

VISITING TIPS

■ Try to visit during the week. Pedestrian areas are compact, and the park can feel uncomfortably packed on weekends.

■ Plan on a full day here. That way, while exploring Africa's Pangani Forest Exploration Trail, say, you can spend 10 minutes (rather than just two) watching vigilant meerkats stand sentry or tracking a mama gorilla as she cares for her youngster.

■ Arrive a half hour before the park opens as much to see the wild animals at their friskiest (morning is a good time to do the safari ride) as to get a jump on the crowds.

■ For updates on line lengths, check the Tip Board, just after crossing the bridge into Discovery Island.

On Asia's Expedition Everest, you'll chug, twist, turn, and plunge up, through, and down Mt. Everest on nearly a mile of track. Oh, yeah, and beware of the yeti!

■ Good places to rendezvous include the outdoor seating area of Tusker House restaurant in Africa, in front of DinoLand U.S.A.'s Boneyard, or on one of the benches outside Expedition Everest in Asia.

EXPLORING ANIMAL KINGDOM

THE OASIS

This entrance makes you feel as if you've been plunked down in the middle of a rain forest. Cool mist, the aroma of flowers, playful animals, and colorful birds enliven a miniature landscape of streams and grottoes, waterfalls, and glades fringed with banana leaves and jacaranda. On mornings when mists shroud the landscape, it's the scene setter for the rest of your day. It's also where you can take care of essentials before entering. Here you'll find guide maps, stroller and wheelchair rentals, Guest Relations, and an ATM.

DISCOVERY ISLAND

The park hub and site of the Tree of Life, this island is encircled by Discovery River, which isn't an actual attraction but makes for attractive views from the bridge to Harambe and another between Asia and DinoLand U.S.A. The island's whimsical architecture, with wood carvings from Bali, lends charm and a touch of fantasy. The Discovery Island Trails that lead to the Tree of Life provide habitats for African crested porcupines, lemurs, Galápagos tortoises, and other creatures you won't want to miss.

You'll discover some great shops and good counter-service eateries here, and the island is also the site of the daily Mickey's Jammin' Jungle

Affection
Section

Conservation Station

RAFIKI'S PLANET WATCH

Habitat Habit!

Wildlife Express Train

SAFARI AREA

Wildlife Express Train

Pangani Forest Exploration Trail

Mombasa Marketplace

AFRICA

Kilimanjaro Safaris

Harambe Fruit Market

Kusafiri Coffee Shop & Bakery

Tusker House Restaurant

Festival of the Lion King

KEY	
✕	*Restaurants*
🚻	*Restrooms*
••••	*Parade Route*

0   200 yards

0   200 m

Disney's Animal Kingdom

ASIA

Kali River Rapids

Expedition Everest

Anandapur Ice Cream Truck

Maharajah Jungle Trek

Lockers

Yak & Yeti Restaurant

Flights of Wonder

Finding Nemo— The Musical

Discovery River

Upcountry

Bradley Falls

Mr Kamal's

Beastly Kiosk

Mickey's Jammin' Jungle Parade

Flame Tree Barbecue

Trilo-Bites

Primeval Whirl

Fossil Fun Games

Boneyard

TriceraTop Spin

ATM

DINOLAND U.S.A.

It's Tough to Be a Bug!

Tree of Life

DISCOVERY ISLAND

Disney Outfitters

Isle of Java

Restaurantosaurus

DinoSue

DINOSAUR

Tamu Tamu Refreshments

Discovery Island Trails

Tips and Showtimes

Mickey's Jammin' Jungle Parade

Island Mercantile

Dawa Bar

First Aid/ Baby Care Center

Pizzafari

Garden Gate Gifts

Strollers & Wheelchairs

ATM

OASIS

Lockers

Guest Relations

Entrance

COMING SOON: AVATAR

Guest Relations

Rainforest Café

ANIMAL KINGDOM

NAME	Height Req.	Type of Entertainment	Duration	Crowds	Audience	Tips
Africa						
★ Festival of the Lion King	n/a	Show	30 mins.	Moderate	All Ages	Arrive 30–40 mins. before showtime. Sit in one of the front rows to increase your kid's chance of being chosen to participate in a show number.
★ Kilimanjaro Safaris	n/a	Riding Tour	22 mins.	Moderate to Heavy	All Ages	Do this first thing in the morning or use FastPass+. If you arrive at the park late morning, save it for day's end, when it's not so hot.
Pangani Forest Exploration Trail	n/a	Zoo/Aviary	Up to you	Light to Moderate	All Ages	Come while waiting for your safari FastPass+; try to avoid coming at the hottest time of day, when the gorillas like to nap.
Asia						
★ Expedition Everest	At least 44"	Thrill Ride	2½ mins.	Huge	All but Young Kids	Arrive early or use FastPass+. This is the park's biggest thrill ride.
Flights of Wonder	n/a	Show	25 mins.	Light	All Ages	Arrive 15 mins. before showtime, and find a shaded seat beneath one of the awnings—the sun can be brutal.
Kali River Rapids	At least 38"	Thrill Ride	7 mins.	Heavy	All but Young Kids	Use your FastPass+ or come during the parade. You'll get wet.
Maharajah Jungle Trek	n/a	Zoo/Aviary	Up to you	Light to Moderate	All Ages	Come anytime.
DinoLand U.S.A.						
Boneyard	n/a	Playground	Up to you	Moderate to Heavy	Young Kids	Play here while waiting for DINOSAUR FastPass+, or come late in the day.

	Height	Type	Duration	Crowds	Age	Tips
DINOSAUR	At least 40"	Thrill Ride	4 mins.	Heavy	All but Young Kids	Come first thing in the morning or at the end of the day, or use FastPass+.
★ Finding Nemo—The Musical	n/a	Show	40 mins.	Heavy	All Ages	Arrive 40 mins. before showtime. Take young kids here while older kids wait for Expedition Everest.
Fossil Fun Games	n/a	Arcade/Fair	Up to you	Light	All Ages	Bring a stash of ones to buy play tickets.
Primeval Whirl	At least 48"	Thrill Ride	2½ mins.	Heavy	All but Young Kids	Kids may want to ride twice. Take your first spin early, then use FastPass+ if the wait is more than 20 mins.
TriceraTop Spin	n/a	Thrill Ride for Young Kids	2 mins.	Heavy	Young Kids	Ride early while everyone else heads for the safari or while waiting for your FastPass+ appointment for DINOSAUR.

Discovery Island

	Height	Type	Duration	Crowds	Age	Tips
★ Tree of Life—It's Tough to Be a Bug!	n/a	3-D film	20 mins.	Moderate to Heavy	All but Young Kids	Do this after Kilimanjaro Safaris or Expedition Everest. Small children may be frightened.

Rafiki's Planet Watch

	Height	Type	Duration	Crowds	Age	Tips
Affection Section	n/a	Petting Yard	Up to you	Light	All Ages	Pet exotic goats and other rare domesticated animals.
Conservation Station	n/a	Walk-Through	Up to you	Light to Moderate	All Ages	Wait for the critter encounter and learn how to protect endangered species.
Habitat Habit!	n/a	Trail Walk	Up to you	Light	All Ages	Watch cotton-top tamarins along this discovery trail.
Wildlife Express Train	n/a	Train Ride	5 mins.	Moderate	All Ages	Head straight to Affection Section with little kids to come face-to-face with domesticated critters.

Parade. Visitor services that aren't in the Oasis are here, on the border with Harambe, including the baby-care center and the first-aid center.

DINOLAND U.S.A.

Just as it sounds, this is the place to come in contact with re-created pre-historic creatures, including the fear-inspiring carnotaurus and the gentle iguanodon. The landscaping includes live plants that have evolved over the last 65 million years. In collaboration with Chicago's Field Museum, Disney displays a complete, full-scale skeleton cast of Dino-Sue—also known as "Sue"—the 65-million-year-old *Tyrannosaurus rex* discovered near the Black Hills of South Dakota.

After admiring Sue, you can go on the thrilling DINOSAUR ride, play in the Boneyard, or take in the Finding Nemo: The Musical show at the Theater in the Wild. Kids will want to try the TriceraTop Spin and the Primeval Whirl family coaster, which has spinning "time machines." There's no need to dig for souvenirs at Chester and Hester's Dinosaur Treasures gift shop—all you need is your wallet.

ASIA

Meant to resemble an Asian village, this land is full of remarkable rain-forest scenery and ruins. Groupings of trees grow from a crumbling tiger shrine, and massive towers—representing Thailand and Nepal—are the habitat for gibbons, whose hooting fills the air.

AFRICA

This largest of the lands is an area of forests and grasslands, predominantly an enclave for wildlife from the continent. Harambe, on the northern bank of Discovery River, is Africa's starting point. Inspired by several East African coastal villages, this Disney town has so much detail that it's mind-boggling to try to soak it all up. Signs on the apparently peeling stucco walls of the buildings are faded, as if bleached by the sun, and everything has a hot, dusty look. For souvenirs with both Disney and African themes, browse through the Mombasa Marketplace and Ziwani Traders.

RAFIKI'S PLANET WATCH

While in the Harambe, Africa, section, board the 250-passenger rustic Wildlife Express steam train for a ride to a unique center of eco-awareness named for the wise baboon from *The Lion King*. Small children especially enjoy the chance to explore these three animal-friendly areas.

TYPHOON LAGOON AND BLIZZARD BEACH

The beauty of Disney's water parks is that you can make either experience fit your mood. Like crowds? Head for the lounge chairs along the Surf Pool at Typhoon Lagoon or Melt-Away Bay at Blizzard Beach. Prefer peace? Walk past lush foliage along each park's circular path until you spot a secluded lean-to or tree-shaded patch of sand.

TYPHOON LAGOON

According to Disney legend, Typhoon Lagoon was created when the lush Placid Palms Resort was struck by a cataclysmic storm. It left a different world in its wake: surfboard-sundered trees, once-upright palms imitated the Leaning Tower of Pisa, and part of the original lagoon was cut off, trapping thousands of tropical fish—and a few sharks. Nothing, however, topped the fate of *Miss Tilly*, a shrimp boat from "Safen Sound, Florida," which was hurled high in the air and became impaled on Mt. Mayday, a magical volcano that periodically tries to dislodge *Miss Tilly* with huge geysers.

TOP ATTRACTIONS

Typhoon Lagoon

Crush 'n' Gusher

Storm Slides

Typhoon Lagoon Surf Pool

Blizzard Beach

Slush Gusher

Summit Plummet

Tike's Peak

Ordinary folks, the legend continues, would have been crushed by such devastation. But the resourceful residents of Placid Palms were made of hardier stuff—and from the wreckage they created 56-acre Typhoon Lagoon, the self-proclaimed "world's ultimate water park."

GETTING ORIENTED

The layout is so simple. The wave and swimming lagoon is at the park's center. Note that the waves are born in the Mt. Mayday side and break on the beaches closest to the entrance. Any attraction requiring a gravitational plunge starts around the summit of Mt. Mayday. Shark Reef and Ketchakiddee Creek flank the head of the lagoon, to Mt. Mayday's right and left, respectively, as you enter. The Crush 'n' Gusher water coaster is due right of Singapore Sal's.

You can take WDW bus transportation or drive to Typhoon Lagoon. There's no parking charge. Once inside, your options are to walk, swim, or slide.

WDW Information: Call WDW Information or check ⊕ *www.disney-world.com*'s park calendars for days of operation. ⊠ *Blizzard Beach* ☎ *407/824–4321.*

WHAT TO EXPECT

You can speed down waterslides with names like Crush 'n' Gusher and Humunga Kowabunga or bump through rapids and falls at Mt. Mayday. You can also bob along in 5-foot waves in a surf pool the size of two football fields or, for a mellow break, float in inner tubes along the 2,100-foot Castaway Creek. Go snorkeling in Shark Reef, rubberneck as fellow human cannonballs are ejected from the Storm Slides, or hunker down in a hammock or lounge chair and read a book. Ketchakiddee Creek, for young children, replicates adult rides on a smaller scale. It's Disney's version of a day at the beach—complete with friendly Disney lifeguards. Most people agree that kids under 7 and older adults prefer Typhoon Lagoon. Bigger kids and teens like Blizzard Beach.

10

During the off-season between October and April, Typhoon Lagoon closes for several weeks for routine maintenance and refurbishment.

PARK AMENITIES

Dressing Rooms and Lockers: There are thatched-roof dressing rooms and lockers to the right on your way into the park. It costs $8 a day to rent a small locker and $10 for a large one; there's also a $5 deposit. There are restrooms in every nook and cranny. Most have showers and are much less crowded than the dressing rooms. If you forgot your towel, rent ($2) or buy one at Singapore Sal's.

Guest Services: The staff at Typhoon Lagoon's Guest Services window outside the entrance turnstiles, to your left, can answer many questions. ■TIP➔ A chalkboard inside gives water temperature and surfing information.

Lost People and Things: Ask about your misplaced people and things at the Guest Services window near the entrance turnstiles. Lost children are taken to an area by the Tip Board near the front of the park, where Disney cast members entertain them with games.

Private Patios: The park has a dozen premium, roped-off Beachcomber Shacks (patios, really) that groups of as many as six can rent. They generally offer shade and sun as well as plush loungers and other chairs, a table with an umbrella, and an ice chest with two bottles of water per guest (up to six). Each guest also gets two beach towels and a refillable soft-drink mug. The whole group gets a locker to share and an attendant to take and deliver food orders (cost of meals not included). The patios cost $345 during peak season (usually March through late August), $240 in September, and $160 the rest of the year. Reserve (☎407/939–8687) well in advance or arrive very early to book one at High 'N Dry. In summer, any patio that isn't prebooked sells out within a half hour of the park opening.

VISITING TIPS

■ In summer, come first thing in the morning (early birds can ride several times before the lines get long), late in the afternoon when park hours run later, or when the weather clears after a thundershower (rainstorms drive away crowds). Afternoons are also good in cooler weather, as the water is a bit warmer. To make a whole day of it, avoid weekends, when locals and visitors pack in.

■ Women and girls should wear one-piece swimsuits unless they want to find their tops somewhere around their ears at the bottom of the waterslide.

■ Invest in sunscreen and water shoes. Plan to slather sunscreen on several times throughout the day. An inexpensive pair of water shoes will save tootsies from hot sand and walkways and from restroom floors.

■ Arrive 30 minutes before opening so you can park, buy tickets, rent towels, and snag inner tubes before the crowds descend and, trust us, it gets very crowded.

BLIZZARD BEACH

With its oxymoronic name, Blizzard Beach promises the seemingly impossible—a seaside playground with an alpine theme. As with its older cousin, Typhoon Lagoon, Disney Imagineers have created a legend to explain the park's origin.

The story goes that after a freak winter storm dropped snow over the western side of Walt Disney World, entrepreneurs created Florida's first downhill ski resort. Sauna-like temperatures soon returned. But as the 66-acre resort's operators were ready to close up shop, they spotted a playful alligator sliding down the 120-foot-tall "liquid ice" slopes. The realization that the melting snow had created the world's tallest, fastest, and most exhilarating water-filled ski and toboggan runs gave birth to the ski resort–water park.

From its imposing ski-jump tower to its 1,200-foot series of rushing waterfalls, Blizzard Beach delivers cool fun even in the hot summertime. Where else can you wear your swimsuit on the slopes?

GETTING ORIENTED

The park layout makes it fairly simple to navigate. Once you enter and rent a locker, you'll cross a small bridge over Cross Country Creek before choosing a spot to park your towels and cooler. To the left is the Melt-Away Bay wave pool. Dead ahead you can see Mt. Gushmore, a chairlift to the top, and the park's many slopes and slides.

If thrills are your game, come early and line up for Summit Plummet, Slush Gusher, and Downhill Double Dipper before wait times go from light to moderate (or heavy). Anytime is a good time for a dip in Melt-Away Bay or a tube trip around Cross Country Creek. Parents with young children should claim their spot early at Tike's Peak, to the park's right even before you cross the bridge.

You can take WDW bus transportation or drive to Blizzard Beach. There's no charge for parking. Once inside, your options are to walk, swim, or slide.

WHAT TO EXPECT

Disney Imagineers have gone all out here to create the paradox of a ski resort in the midst of a tropical lagoon. Lots of verbal puns and sight gags play with the snow-in-Florida motif. The centerpiece is Mt. Gushmore, with its 120-foot-high Summit Plummet. Attractions have names like Teamboat Springs, a white-water raft ride. Themed speed slides include Toboggan Racers, Slush Gusher, and Snow Stormers. Between Mt. Gushmore's base and its summit, swim-skiers can also ride a chairlift converted from ski-resort to beach-resort use—with multihued umbrellas and snow skis on their undersides. Older kids and devoted waterslide enthusiasts generally prefer Blizzard Beach to other water parks.

PARK AMENITIES

Dressing Rooms and Lockers: Dressing rooms, showers, and restrooms are in the village area, just inside the main entrance. There are other restrooms in Lottawatta Lodge, at the Ski Patrol Training Camp, and just past the Melt-Away Bay beach area. Lockers are near the entrance, next

From the wreckage—like that shown here—in the wake of a storm, Placid Palms Resort residents created 56-acre Typhoon Lagoon. Or so the story goes…

to Snowless Joe's Rentals, and near Tike's Peak (the children's area and the most convenient if you have little swim-skiers in tow). It costs $8 to rent a small locker and $10 for a large one, and there's a $5 deposit. Note that there are only small lockers at Tike's Peak. The towels for rent ($2) at Snowless Joe's are tiny. If you forgot yours, you're better off buying a proper one at the Beach Haus.

Guest Services: Disney staffers at Blizzard Beach's Guest Services window, to the left of the ticket booth as you enter the park, can answer most of your questions. Get free life vests or rent towels and lockers at **Snowless Joe's**. Inner tubes, rafts, and slide mats are provided at the rides. Buy beach gear or rent towels or lockers at **Beach Haus. Shade Shack** is the place for a new pair of sunglasses.

Lost People and Things: Instruct youngsters to let a lifeguard know if they get lost. The lost-children station is beneath a large beach umbrella near the front of the park. And don't worry about the kids—a Disney cast member will keep them busy with activities.

Private Patios: The park has 14 Polar Patios to rent to groups of as many as six people. For $345 a day in peak season (usually March through late August), $240 in September, and $160 off-peak, you get plush loungers, chairs, a table with umbrella, refillable beverage mugs, an ice chest with two water bottles per person, a group locker, and an attendant who will take your orders for and deliver lunch and snacks (food costs extra). It's best to book a patio far ahead of time (☎ 407/939–8687). If you arrive early enough, there might be an open patio; check at the Shade Shack.

DISNEY'S OTHER WORLDS

Budget a few hours to explore Disney's "other" places. Several are no-admission-required charmers; one is a high-tech, high-cover-charge gaming wonderland.

DOWNTOWN DISNEY

EXPLORING

East of Epcot and close to Interstate 4 along a large lake, this shopping, dining, and entertainment complex currently has three areas: the Marketplace, West Side, and the connecting district, Pleasure Island. Major changes are in store by 2016 after a massive makeover featuring new shops, restaurants, and promenades is complete and the area is renamed Disney Springs. A huge parking garage will open in early 2015. You can rent lockers, strollers, or wheelchairs, and there are two Guest Relations centers.

DisneyQuest. In a five-story virtual-reality mini-theme park in Downtown Disney's West Side, DisneyQuest lets you pay a hefty cover to participate in high-tech virtual adventures and play video games. To be fair, you can play all day, and there are cutting-edge games and interactive adventures that make the admission worthwhile. It's also a great place for teens and older tweens (children under 10 must be accompanied by an adult). Newest game with play consoles on every floor: Fix-It Felix, Jr. from the popular Disney movie *Wreck-It Ralph*.

In **Explore Zone,** fly through the streets of Agrabah with the help of a virtual-reality helmet on Aladdin's Magic Carpet Ride. Take a Virtual Jungle Cruise down the roiling rapids of a prehistoric world, and paddle (yes, *really* paddle) to adventure amid volcanoes, dinosaurs, and other cretaceous threats. At Pirates of the Caribbean: Battle for Buccaneer Gold, you and the gang must brave the high seas and sink pirate ships to acquire treasure.

In the **Score Zone,** battle super villains while flying, headset firmly intact, through a 3-D comic world in Ride the Comix. Escape evil aliens and rescue colonists during Invasion! An ExtraTERRORestrial Alien Encounter. Or hip-check your friends in a life-size Mighty Ducks Pinball Slam game.

10

In the **Create Zone** learn the secrets of Disney animation at the Animation Academy. Create your own twisted masterpiece at Sid's Create-A-Toy, based on the popular animated film *Toy Story*. Or, at Living Easels, make a *living* painting on a giant electronic screen. Thrills await at Cyberspace Mountain, where you can design your own roller coaster on a computer screen, then climb aboard a 360-degree pitch-and-roll simulator for the ride of your dreams. At Radio Disney SongMaker, produce your own hit.

Classic free-play machines like Pac Man reside in the **Replay Zone.** You can also sit with a partner in an asteroid cannon–equipped bumper car and blast others to make their cars do a 360-degree spin in Buzz Lightyear's AstroBlaster.

All attractions are wheelchair accessible, but most require transfer from wheelchair to the attraction itself. You can, however, wheel right onto Pirates of the Caribbean: Battle for Buccaneer Gold, Aladdin's Magic Carpet Ride, and Mighty Ducks Pinball Slam. Rent wheelchairs at the DisneyQuest Emporium or at Downtown Disney Marketplace Guest Relations ($12 per day for hand operated, plus $100 refundable credit-card deposit); electric chairs are $50 plus deposit at the Marketplace location only. Guide dogs are permitted in all areas but aren't allowed to ride several attractions. Strollers are *not* permitted.

Four attractions have height requirements: Cyberspace Mountain (51 inches), Buzz Lightyear's AstroBlaster (51 inches), Mighty Ducks Pinball Slam (48 inches), and Pirates of the Caribbean (35 inches). Little ones 2–7 can enjoy a Kids' Area on the fourth floor, where they can play smaller versions of video and other games like air hockey, basketball, and bowling.

Lost and Found is at the Guest Relations window, film can be purchased at the Emporium, and cash is available at ATMs inside the House of Blues merchandise shop not far from the DisneyQuest entrance. ⊠ *West Side, Downtown Disney* ☎ *407/828–4600* ☒ *$45* ☽ *Sun.–Thurs. 11:30–10, Fri. and Sat. 11:30–11.*

Marketplace. In the Marketplace, the easternmost Downtown Disney area, you can meander along winding sidewalks and explore hidden alcoves. Children love to splash in fountains that spring from the pavement and ride the miniature train and old-time carousel ($2). Toy stores entice with creation-stations and too many treasures to comprehend. There are plenty of spots to grab a bite or sip a cappuccino along the lakefront. The Marketplace is open from 9:30 am to 11 pm weekdays and until 11:30 Friday and Saturday. ⊠ *Downtown Disney.*

Pleasure Island. When it was a hopping nightlife destination, this area offered a mix of bars, comedy clubs, and dance spots. But the nightclubs are long closed, and the Island has become more of a family-oriented dining and entertainment district. Raglan Road Irish Pub & Restaurant offers great food by Raglan Road's Irish celebrity chef Kevin Dundon, indoor and patio dining, live Irish music, and traditional dance performances every night. Paradiso 37 also welcomes diners indoors and alfresco. This area is part of the Downtown Disney renovation to be renamed Disney Springs by 2016, if not before. ⊠ *Downtown Disney.*

West Side. The main attractions in the hip West Side are the House of Blues music hall, Cirque du Soleil, Splitsville Luxury Lanes, and DisneyQuest virtual indoor theme park and arcade. You can also take a ride in the Characters in Flight helium balloon tethered here ($18), shop in boutiques, or dine in such restaurants as the Wolfgang Puck Café and Planet Hollywood. Shops open at 9:30 or 10:30 am, and closing time is between 11 pm and 2 am. The Splitsville entertainment center offers plenty of fresh fun with 30 bowling lanes on two floors, weekend DJs, and upscale eats like filet sliders and sushi at indoor and outdoor tables. Starbucks plans to move in as part of the mega-makeover that will transform the area to Disney Springs. ⊠ *Downtown Disney.*

NIGHTLIFE

Bongos Cuban Café. Latin rhythms provide the beat at this restaurant and bar with a pre-Castro theme owned by pop singer Gloria Estefan. Four bars are especially busy on weekends, when a Latin band kicks it up a notch with *muy caliente* music. Samba, tango, salsa, and merengue rhythms roll throughout the week. ⊠ *West Side, Downtown Disney* ☎ *407/828–0999* ⊗ *Sun.–Thurs. 11–10:30, Fri. and Sat. 11 am–2 am.*

House of Blues. The restaurant serves up live blues performances and rib-sticking Mississippi Delta cooking all week long. The attached concert hall has showcased such artists as Aretha Franklin, David Byrne, Steve Miller, Willie Nelson, and Journey. Many swear by the "World Famous Gospel Brunch" each Sunday. ⊠ *West Side, Downtown Disney* ☎ *407/934–2583* 💲 *Covers vary* ⊗ *Restaurant Sun.–Thurs. 11:30–11, Fri. and Sat. 11:30–1 am. Concert times vary.*

EPCOT RESORT AREA

In the good ol' days, Americans escaped their city routines for breezy seaside boardwalks. Disney's BoardWalk is within walking distance of Epcot, across Crescent Lake from Disney's Yacht and Beach Club Resorts, and fronting a hotel of the same name. You may be drawn to its good restaurants, bars, shops, surreys, and performers. After sunset, the mood is festive. ■TIP→ If you're here when Epcot is ready to close, you can watch the park fireworks from the bridge that connects BoardWalk to the Yacht and Beach Club Resorts.

NIGHTLIFE

Atlantic Dance Hall. This high-energy Top 40 dance club has a huge screen showing videos requested by the crowd. The parquet dance floor is set off by furnishings of deep blue, maroon, and gold, and the ceiling glows with gold stars and twinkling lights. Signature cocktails are in demand, and you can sip cognac or choose from a selection of popular beers to inspire your dance floor moves. ⊠ *BoardWalk, Epcot Resort Area* ☎ *407/939–2444* 💲 *No cover* ⊗ *Tues.–Sat. 9 pm–1:45 am.*

Big River Grille & Brewing Works. Disney World's only brewpub has intimate tables where brew masters tend to their potions. You can order an $8 sampler with five-to-seven 3-ounce pours of whatever's on tap that day, usually including Red Rocket, Southern Flyer Light Lager, Gadzooks Pilsner, and Steamboat Pale Ale. Upscale pub grub and sandwiches pair well. There's also a sidewalk café. ⊠ *BoardWalk, Epcot Resort Area* ☎ *407/560–0253* 💲 *No cover* ⊗ *Daily 11–11.*

ESPN Club. The sports motif here is carried into every nook and cranny— the main dining area looks like a sports arena, with a basketball-court hardwood floor and a giant scoreboard that projects the day's big game. While you watch, munch on wings, nachos, and linebacker-sized burgers. There are more than 100 TVs throughout (even in the restrooms). The place is packed for big games; call ahead to see if special seating rules are in effect. ⊠ *BoardWalk, Epcot Resort Area* ☎ *407/939–1177* 💲 *No cover* ⊗ *Daily 11:30 am–1 am.*

10

Jellyrolls. In this rockin', boisterous piano bar, comedians act as emcees and play dueling grand pianos nonstop. The steady stream of conventions at Disney makes this the place to catch CEOs doing the conga to Barry Manilow's "Copacabana"—if that's your idea of a good time. ⊠ *BoardWalk, Epcot Resort Area* ☎ *407/560–8770* ✉ *$12 cover* ⊙ *Daily 7 pm–1:45 am.*

UNIVERSAL ORLANDO

With Wet 'n Wild

11

Visit Fodors.com for advice, updates, and bookings

WELCOME TO UNIVERSAL ORLANDO

TOP REASONS TO GO

★ **The Variety:** Universal Orlando is much more than just a single Hollywood-theme amusement park. It's also the fantasy-driven Islands of Adventure (IOA) theme park; the clubs and restaurants of the CityWalk entertainment complex; and the upscale, on-site Hard Rock Hotel, Portofino Bay, and Royal Pacific resorts. Nearby Wet 'n Wild water park is also affiliated with Universal.

★ **Theme-Park Powerhouse:** Neither SeaWorld nor any of Disney's four theme parks can match the collective energy at Universal Studios and Islands of Adventure. Wild rides, clever shows, constantly updated attractions, and an edgy attitude all push the envelope here.

★ **Party Central:** Throughout the year, Universal hosts festive park-wide events such as Mardi Gras, Halloween Horror Nights, Grinchmas, the Summer Concert Series, and the Rock the Universe Christian-music celebration.

1 Universal Studios Florida. The centerpiece of Universal Orlando is a creative and quirky tribute to Hollywood past, present, and future. Overall, the collection of wild rides, quiet retreats, live shows, street characters, and clever movies (both 3-D and 4-D) are as entertaining as the motion pictures

CENTRAL FLORIDA

Orlando

Tropical Lake

EXIT 77

Millenia Lake

Shingle Creek

Kirkman Rd.

ajor Blvd.

Millenia Blvd.

Florida's Turnpike (Ronald Reagan Turnpike)

W. Oak Ridge Rd.

EXITS
75A (WESTBOUND)

D)
ND)

Id

435

Vanguard St.

Carrier Dr.

Municipal Dr.

Mandarin Dr.

Pomelo Dr.

Sand Lake Rd.

GETTING ORIENTED

Universal Orlando is tucked into a corner created by the intersection of Interstate 4 and Kirkman Road (Highway 435), midway between Downtown Orlando and the Walt Disney World Resort. Here you'll be about 15 minutes from each and just 10 minutes from SeaWorld.

they celebrate (and they're always adding something new).

2 Islands of Adventure. Certainly the most significant addition to any Orlando theme park came when IOA introduced an entire land dedicated to Harry Potter, which, in turn, sparked a substantial surge

in attendance. Also at IOA are Spider-Man, the Hulk, velociraptors, the Cat in the Hat, and dozens of other characters that give guests every reason to head to the islands.

3 CityWalk. Even when the parks are closed (especially when the parks are closed), locals and visitors come to

this sprawling entertainment and retail complex to watch movies; dine at theme restaurants; shop for everything from cigars to surf wear; and stay up late at nightclubs celebrating the French Quarter, Jamaica, and the coolest clubs of NYC.

By Gary
McKechnie

Universal Orlando's personality is revealed the moment you arrive on property. Mood music, cartoonish architecture, abundant eye candy, subtle and overt sound effects, whirling and whizzing rides plus a throng of fellow travelers will follow you to nearly every corner of the park. For peace and quiet, seek out a sanctuary at one of the resort hotels.

At a breathless pace, there's a chance you could visit both Universal parks in a single day, but to do that you'll have to invest in an Express Pass. Without it, you'll spend a good portion of that day waiting in line at the premium attractions. So allow two days, perhaps three; a day for each park and a "pick-up" day to return to your favorites at a leisurely pace. Which attractions are the main attractions? At IOA, it's definitely The Wizarding World of Harry Potter (especially the high-volume/low-capacity Ollivanders wand shop), and at Universal Studios you'll find long lines at The Mummy and The Simpsons.

Universal Studios appeals primarily to those who like loud, fast, high-energy attractions—generally teens and adults. Covering 444 acres, it's a rambling montage of sets, shops, and soundstages housing themed attractions, reproductions of New York and San Francisco, and some genuine moviemaking paraphernalia.

When Islands of Adventure (IOA) first opened in 1999, it took attractions to a new level. Most—from Marvel Super Hero Island and Toon Lagoon to Seuss Landing and the Lost Continent—are impressive; some even out-Disney Disney. In 2010, IOA received well-deserved worldwide attention when it opened the 20-acre Wizarding World of Harry Potter. And it's destined to receive even more coverage with the arrival of two new Potter-related areas—one atop the old Amity area at Universal Studios, and another tacked onto the Wizarding World by the Lost Continent.

PLANNING

GETTING HERE AND AROUND

East on Interstate 4 (from WDW and Tampa), exit at Universal Boulevard (75A); take a left into Universal Orlando, and follow the signs. Heading west on Interstate 4 (from Downtown or Daytona), exit at Universal Boulevard (74B), turn right, and follow Hollywood Way.

Both Universal Studios and IOA require a lot of walking—a whole lot of walking. Start off by using the parking area's moving walkways as much as possible. Arrive early at either park, and you may be able to complete a single lap that will get you to the main attractions.

OPERATING HOURS

Universal Studios and IOA are open 365 days a year, from 9 am to 7 pm, with hours as late as 10 pm in summer and at holidays. Wet 'n Wild is also open 365 days a year, weather permitting, but with widely varying hours. Usually it's open from 9 to 6—sometimes earlier, often much later, with summer hours from 9:30 am until 9 pm. Call for exact hours during holiday periods.

PARKING

Universal's two garages total 3.4 million square feet, so *note your parking space*. The cost is $16 for cars and motorcycles ($5 after 6 pm and free after 10), $22 for RVs and preferred parking. Although moving walkways get you partway, you could walk up to a half mile to reach the gates. Valet parking ($15 for up to two hours, $30 for more than two hours) is much closer.

ADMISSION

The at-the-gate, per-person, per-day rate for either Universal Studios Florida or IOA is $92 (ages 10 and up) and $86 for children (ages 3–9). Far less expensive are multiday passes.

EXPRESS PASSES

The Express Pass ranges in price from about $20 off-season to $80 in peak season. Why so much? This pass gets you to the front of most lines and saves a tremendous amount of time. If crowds are thin and lines are moving fast, skip this pass. Also, if you're a guest at a Universal hotel, this perk is free; your room key card serves as the pass. Last tip: if you don't mind riding alone, ask the host about the single-rider option—it'll whisk you through the line much more quickly.

UNIVERSAL DINING PLAN

If you prefer to pay in advance, Quick Service meals include, for adults, one meal, two snacks, and a nonalcoholic beverage ($19). The kids' version covers a kids meal, one snack, and a nonalcoholic beverage ($13). Universal Studios locations include Mel's Drive-In, Louie's Italian, Beverly Hills Boulangerie, and the Classic Monsters Café. At Islands of Adventure, your choices are the Comic Strip Café, Croissant Moon, the Burger Digs, and Café 4.

UNIVERSAL STRATEGIES

Arrive early. Come as early as 8 am if the parks open at 9. Seriously. Better to share them with hundreds of people than with thousands.

Visit on a weekday. Crowds are lighter, especially fall through spring, when kids are in school.

Don't forget anything in your car. Universal's parking areas are at least a half mile from park entrances, and a round-trip hike will eat up valuable time. Consider valet parking—if you can swing it. It costs $30 for longer than two hours before 6 pm (almost twice as much as regular parking), but it puts you much closer to Universal's park entrances and just steps from CityWalk.

Know the restrictions. A few things aren't allowed in the parks: alcohol and glass containers; hard-sided coolers; soft-sided coolers larger than 8½ inches wide by 6 inches high by 6 inches deep; and coolers, suitcases, and other bags with wheels. But if your flight's leaving later, you can check your luggage at the parks (unless you just leave them in your car).

Look into the Express Pass. Jumping to the front of the line with this pass really is worth the extra cost on busy days—unless you stay at a resort hotel, in which case front-of-line access is one of the perks (*a very valuable perk*).

Ride solo. At Universal some rides have a Single Rider line that moves much faster than regular lines.

Get expert advice. The folks at Guest Services (aka Guest Relations) have great insight. The reps can even create a custom itinerary free of charge.

Check out Child Swap. At certain Universal attractions, one parent can enter the attraction, take a spin, and then return to take care of the baby while the other parent rides without having to wait in line again.

FOR PEOPLE WITH DISABILITIES

The *Studio Guide for Guests with Disabilities* (aka *Rider's Guide*) details attractions with special entrances and viewing areas, interpreters, Braille scripts, and assistance devices. In general, if you can transfer from your wheelchair unassisted or with the help of a friend, you can ride many attractions. Some rides have carts that accommodate manual wheelchairs, though not motorized wheelchairs or electronic convenience vehicles (ECVs).

CONTACTS

Universal ☎ *407/363–8000* ⊕ *www.universalorlando.com*

Universal Dining & Tickets ☎ *407/224–7840*

Universal (Loews Resorts) Room Reservations ☎ *877/819–7884*

Universal Vacation Packages ☎ *800/407–4275*

Wet 'n Wild ☎ *407/351–1800 or 800/992–9453* ⊕ *www.wetnwild.com*

UNIVERSAL STUDIOS

Inspired by the California original and opened in Orlando in 1990 (when the city assumed it would become "Hollywood East"), Universal Studios celebrates the movies. The park is a jumble of areas and attractions. But the same is true of back-lot sets at a film studio. Suspend any disbelief you might have, and just enjoy the motion-picture magic.

At Production Central large soundstages house attractions based on TV programs and films like *Shrek, Despicable Me,* and *Twister.* Because it's right near the entrance it may be the park's most crowded area.

Here you see first-hand that not every film or program based in New York is actually shot in New York. Cleverly constructed sets mean that nearly every studio can own its own Big Apple. Universal is no exception. As you explore Production Central, a collection of sparkling public buildings, well-worn neighborhoods, and back alleys are the next-best thing to Manhattan itself.

As you enter the area known as San Francisco, you're roughly one-third of the way through the park. The crowds spread out, and the pace seems to slow. You can stop to see a show starring Beetlejuice or dine at the waterfront Lombard's Seafood Grille.

There's not much shaking between San Francisco and World Expo and its two large attractions—MEN IN BLACK: Alien Attack and the Simpsons Ride. The scarcity of rides here is, however, offset by the colorful spectacle surrounding the Simpson's hometown of Springfield and the abundant attractions at Woody Woodpecker's KidZone. It matches the energy of toddlers and the under-10 crowd with diversions that include a junior-size roller coaster, a mini–water park, and a chance to meet E.T. and Barney the dinosaur. In Hollywood, quiet parks and flashy Rodeo Drive really do make you think you've stepped into vintage Tinseltown.

All in all, Universal Studios fulfills its promise: to put you in the movies.

PLANNING

GETTING ORIENTED

On a map, the park appears neatly divided into six areas positioned around a huge lagoon. There's Production Central, which covers the entire left side of the Plaza of the Stars; New York, with street performances at 70 Delancey; San Francisco; futuristic World Expo; Woody Woodpecker's KidZone; and Hollywood.

What's tricky is that—because it's designed like a series of movie sets—there's no straightforward way to tackle the park. You'll probably make some detours and do some backtracking. To save time and shoe leather, ask theme-park hosts for itinerary suggestions and time-saving tips. Here are a few of our own suggestions.

TOURING TIPS

We highly recommend you purchase your tickets online because it gives you plenty of time to consider your many options and includes a discount. Entering Universal Studios can be overwhelming as you and thousands of others flood through the turnstiles at once. Pick up a map in the entryway to CityWalk or by the park turnstiles and spend a few minutes reviewing it. Map out a route, find show schedules, and select restaurants. If a host is nearby, ask for insider advice on what to see first.

The "right" way. Upon entering, avoid the temptation to go left toward the towering soundstages, looping the park clockwise. Instead, head right—bypassing shops, restaurants, and some crowds to primary attractions like the Simpsons Ride and MEN IN BLACK: Alien Attack.

Universal Studios

TO ISLANDS OF ADVENTURE (100 yards) ←

TO CITYWALK (100 yards) ↓

Beetlejuice's Graveyard Revue

First-Aid

START

Canal St.

Revenge of the Mummy

42nd St.

Louie's Italian Restaurant

NEW YORK

Twister... Ride It Out

STOP

5th Ave.

Parade Route

Finnegan's Bar & Grill

South St.

Park Ave.

Delancey St.

57th St.

8th Ave.

The Lagoon

Monster's Cafe

Transformers: The Ride 3D

South St.

Sunset Blvd.

PRODUCTION CENTRAL

Amblin Ave.

Mel's Drive-In

Vine St.

Blue Man Group

Despicable Me: Minion Mayhem

Shrek 4-D

Parade Route

Parade Route

Hollywood Blvd.

END

Hollywood Rip Ride Rockit

Lucy: A Tribute

Universal Orlando's Horror Make-Up Show

Nickelodeon Way

HOLLYWOOD

Beverly Hills Boulangerie

Lockers

Strollers and Wheelchairs

Plaza of the Stars

Lockers

Smart Lockers

Terminator 2: 3-D

ATM

First-Aid

Backlot Dr.

Guest Services

Main Entrance

UNIVERSAL STUDIOS

NAME	Height Req.	Type of Entertainment	Duration	Crowds	Audience	Tips
Hollywood						
Lucy: A Tribute	n/a	Walk-Through	15 mins.	Light	Adults	Save this for a hot afternoon or for on your way out.
Terminator 2 3-D	n/a	3-D Film/ Simulator Exp.	21 mins.	Heavy	All but Young Kids	Come first thing in the morning or use Express Pass.
★ Universal Orlando's Horror Make-Up Show	n/a	Show	25 mins.	Moderate	All but Young Kids	Come in the afternoon or evening. Young children may be frightened; older children eat up the blood-and-guts comedy.
Production Central						
★ Hollywood Rip Ride Rockit!	At least 51"	Thrill Ride	2 mins.	You Bet!	All but Young Kids	Come early, late, or use a Express Pass. Be patient.
Shrek 4-D	n/a	3-D Film	12 mins.	Heavy	All Ages	Come early or late, or use Express Pass.
New York						
Revenge of the Mummy	At least 48"	Thrill Ride	3 mins.	Heavy	All but Young Kids	Use Express Pass, or come first thing in the morning.
Twister . . . Ride It Out	n/a	Show/ Simulator Exp.	3 mins.	Heavy	All but Young Kids	Come first thing in morning or at closing. This "ride" involves standing and watching the action unfold.
San Francisco/Amity						
Beetlejuice's Graveyard Revue	n/a	Show	25 mins.	Light to Moderate	All but Young Kids	You can use Express Pass here, but there's really no need as there's little chance of a wait.

Disaster!	n/a	Thrill Ride	20 mins.	Heavy	All but Young Kids	Come early, before closing, or use Universal Express Pass. This is loud.
TRANSFORMERS	40"	3-D Thrill Ride	5 mins.	Heavy	All but Young Kids	No Express Pass. Come early.
Woody Woodpecker's KidZone						
A Day in the Park with Barney	n/a	Show	20 mins.	Light	Young Kids	Arrive 10–15 mins. early on crowded days for a good seat—up close and in the center. Can use Express Pass.
Animal Actors on Location!	n/a	Show	20 mins.	Moderate to Heavy	All Ages	Stadium seating, but come early for a good seat. Express Pass accepted.
Curious George Goes to Town	n/a	Playground with Water	Up to you	Moderate	Young Kids	Come in late afternoon or early evening. Bring a towel.
E.T. Adventure	At least 34"	Thrill Ride for Kids	5 mins.	Moderate to Heavy	All Ages	Come early morning or use Express Pass.
Fievel's Playland	n/a	Playground with Water	Up to you	Light to Moderate	Young Kids	Generally light crowds, but there are waits for the waterslide. On hot days come late.
Woody Woodpecker's Nuthouse Coaster	At least 36"	Thrill Ride for Kids	1½ mins.	Moderate to Heavy	Young Kids	Come at park closing, when most little ones have gone home. Try Express Pass.
World Expo						
MEN IN BLACK: Alien Attack	At least 42"	Thrill Ride	4½ mins.	Heavy	All but Young Kids	Solo riders can take a faster line, so split up. This ride spins. Use Express Pass.
★ The Simpsons Ride	40"	Thrill Ride/Simulator Exp.	6 mins.	Heavy	All but Young Kids	Use Express Pass.

★ Fodor's Choice

TOP ATTRACTIONS

AGES 7 AND UP

Hollywood Rip Ride Rockit. On this superwild coaster, you select the soundtrack.

MEN IN BLACK: Alien Attack. The "world's first ride-through video game" gives you a chance to compete for points by plugging away at an endless swarm of aliens.

Revenge of the Mummy. It's a jarring, rocketing indoor coaster that takes you past scary mummies and billowing balls of fire (really).

Shrek 4-D. The 3-D film with sensory effects picks up where the original film left off—and adds some creepy extras in the process.

The Simpsons Ride. It puts you in the heart of Springfield on a wild-and-crazy virtual-reality experience.

Transformers: The Ride—3D. Universal Studios' version of IOA's fantastic Spider-Man experience, but this one features a rough-and-tumble encounter with the mechanical stars of the film franchise.

Twister . . . Ride It Out. Okay, it's just a special-effects show—but what special effects! You experience a tornado without having to head to the root cellar.

Universal Orlando's Horror Make-Up Show. This sometimes gross, often raunchy, but always entertaining demonstration merges the best of stand-up comedy with creepy effects.

AGES 6 AND UNDER

Animal Actors on Location! It's a perfect family show starring a menagerie of animals whose unusually high IQs are surpassed only by their cuteness and cuddle-ability.

Curious George Goes to Town. The celebrated simian visits the Man with the Yellow Hat in a small-scale water park.

A Day in the Park with Barney. Small children love the big purple dinosaur and the chance to sing along.

Photo ops. Universal Studios posts signs that indicate photo spots and show how best to frame your shot.

Rendezvous. Good meeting spots include Lucy: A Tribute, near the entrance; Mel's Drive-In, midway through the park on the right; and Beetlejuice's Graveyard Revue midway through the park on the left.

PARK AMENITIES

Guest Services: Get strategy advice *before* visiting by calling Guest Services at ☎ 407/224–4233.

Lockers: Daily rates for lockers near the park entrance are $8 for a small unit and $10 for a larger one. There are free lockers near the entrances of some high-speed attractions (such as MEN IN BLACK: Alien Attack and Revenge of the Mummy), where you can stash your stuff before your ride; they're available to you for up to 90 minutes total.

Lost People and Things: If you plan to split up, be sure everyone knows where and when to reconnect. Staffers take lost children to Guest Services near the main entrance. This is also where you might find lost personal items.

Stroller Rentals: Just inside the main entrance, there are strollers for $15 (single) and $25 (double) a day. You can also rent small kiddie cars ($18) or large ones ($28) by the day.

Wheelchair Rentals: You can rent manual wheelchairs ($12 per day) at the parking garages and inside the main entrance. Because there are limited quantities of electronic convenience vehicles (ECVs, available in the park for $50), reserve one in advance. A photo ID and a $50 deposit on a credit card are required for wheelchairs.

EXPLORING UNIVERSAL STUDIOS

PRODUCTION CENTRAL
Expect plenty of loud, flashy, rollicking rides that appeal to tweens, teens, and adults. Clear the turnstiles and go straight. You can use Express Pass at all attractions.

NEW YORK
Universal has gone all out to re-create New York's skyscrapers, commercial districts, ethnic neighborhoods, and back alleys—right down to the cracked concrete. Hidden within these structures are restaurants, arcades, gift shops, and key attractions. And, although they're from Chicago, the Blues Brothers drive from the Second City to New York City in their Bluesmobile for free performances at 70 Delancey. Here you can use Express Pass at Revenge of the Mummy and Twister.

SAN FRANCISCO
This area celebrates the West Coast with the wharves and warehouses of San Francisco's Embarcadero and Fisherman's Wharf districts. *Use your Express Pass at both attractions.*

WORLD EXPO
At the far end of the park is a futuristic set of buildings containing a few of Universal Studios' most popular attractions, MEN IN BLACK: Alien Attack, the Simpsons Ride, and the new Kang & Kodos' Twirl 'n' Hurl, which offer fast admission with Express Pass.

WOODY WOODPECKER'S KIDZONE
With its colorful compilation of rides, shows, and play areas, this entire section caters to preschoolers. It's a pint-size Promised Land, where kids can try out a roller coaster and get sprayed, splashed, and soaked in a water-park area. It's also a great place for parents, since it gives them a needed break after nearly circling the park. All shows and attractions except Curious George and Fievel accept Universal Express Pass.

HOLLYWOOD
The quintessential tribute to the golden age of the silver screen, this area to the right of the park entrance celebrates icons like the Brown Derby, Schwab's Pharmacy, and art-deco Hollywood. There are only a few attractions here, and all except Lucy accept Universal Express Pass.

DIAGON ALLEY OPENS

Impressed by the success of the Wizarding World of Harry Potter's Hogsmeade Village at Islands of Adventure, Universal Studios saw an opportunity. Razing the midway and tired JAWS attraction in the Amity Section, it's created an entire land called Diagon Alley.

Having opened in July 2014, like its IOA counterpart, this area features a variety of shops and experiences centered around a single major attraction, Harry Potter and the Escape from Gringotts. The goblin-managed bank is the focal point of this land, and when you enter its hallowed halls, the ride itself is similar to the sensory overload you feel at attractions like Harry's Forbidden Journey and the Amazing Adventures of Spider-Man, as you spin, twist, and twirl through a blend of fast-moving virtual effects (and encounter Harry, Ron, and Hermione along the way).

Throughout the district are shops familiar to anyone who knows of Harry's adventures. There is Universal Studios' version of Ollivanders wand shop as well as Weasleys' Wizard Wheezes (magical jokes and novelty items), the Magical Menagerie (all creatures furry, feathered, or scaly), Madam Malkin's Robes for All Occasions (wizard wear), as well as Wiseacre's Wizarding Equipment and Quality Quidditch Supplies. For practitioners of the Dark Arts, venture down Knockturn Alley and step inside Borgin and Burkes.

J. K. Rowling's vivid descriptions helped paint a picture for designers and they've created spot-on re-creations from the pages of the Potter series. You'll see this at the Leaky Cauldron, the land's signature restaurant, and at Florean Fortescue's Ice-Cream Parlour. And when you're ready to head to Hogwarts, make sure you have a park-to-park pass before stepping aboard the new *Hogwarts Express*—now departing to Islands of Adventure from Platform 9¾, at an impressive re-creation of Kings Cross Station.

ISLANDS OF ADVENTURE

More so than just about any other theme park, Islands of Adventure has gone all out to create settings and attractions that transport you from reality into the surreal. What's more, no one island here has much in common with any other, so in a way, a visit here is almost like a visit to half a dozen different parks.

IOA's unique nature is first revealed when you arrive at the Port of Entry and are greeted by a kaleidoscope of sights and a cacophony of sounds. It's all designed to put you in the frame of mind for adventure.

When you reach the central lagoon, your clockwise journey commences with Marvel Super Hero Island and its tightly packed concentration of roller coasters and thrill rides. Of special note is the amazingly high-tech and dazzling Amazing Adventures of Spider-Man. In just minutes you'll have experienced a day's worth of sensations—and you've only just begun.

Stepping into Toon Lagoon is like stepping into the pages of a comic book, just as entering the upcoming island, Jurassic Park, is like entering a research center where reconstituted dinosaur DNA is being used to create a new breed of *brontosaurus*.

You move from the world of science into the world of magic when you segue into the Wizarding World of Harry Potter. For the first time anywhere, you—and not just a few fortunate actors—can wander through the magnificently fictional, yet now very realistic, realm of the young wizard and his Hogwarts classmates and tutors. Beyond belief.

But that's not the end of it. In the Lost Continent the mood is that of a Renaissance fair, where crafters work inside colorful tents. It's as pronounced an atmosphere as that of the final island, Seuss Landing, which presents the incredible, topsy-turvy world of Dr. Seuss. It's a riot of colors and shapes and fantastic wildlife that pay tribute to the good doctor's vivid imagination.

TOP ATTRACTIONS

Ages 7 and Up

Amazing Adventures of Spider-Man

Dudley Do-Right's Ripsaw Falls

Harry Potter and the Forbidden Journey

Incredible Hulk Coaster

Ages 6 and Under

The Cat in the Hat

Flight of the Hippogriff

Popeye & Bluto's Bilge-Rat Barges

PLANNING

GETTING ORIENTED

Getting your bearings at IOA is far easier than at its sister park, Universal Studios. Brochures in a multitude of languages are in a rack a few steps beyond the turnstiles. The brochures include a foldout map that will acquaint you with the park's simple layout (it's a circle). And, ahead by the lagoon, boards are posted with up-to-the-minute ride and show information—including the length of lines at the major attractions.

You pass through the turnstiles and into the Port of Entry plaza, a bazaar that brings together bits and pieces of architecture, landscaping, music, and wares from many lands—Dutch windmills, Indonesian pedicabs, African masks, restrooms marked "Loo's Landing," and Egyptian figurines that adorn a massive archway inscribed with the notice "The Adventure Begins." From here, themed islands—arranged around a large lagoon—are connected by walkways that make navigation easy. When you've done the full circuit, you'll recall the fantastic range of sights, sounds, and experiences and realize there can be truth in advertising. This park really *is* an adventure.

TOURING TIPS

Hosts. Just about any employee is a host, whether they're at a kiosk or attraction or turnstile. Ask them about their favorite experiences—and for suggestions for saving time.

Photo Ops. Islands of Adventure posts signs that indicate picture spots and show how best to frame your shot.

In the Jurassic Park Discovery Center, your kids might just learn something about dinosaurs that they didn't already know.

Retreat. Explore little-used sidewalks and quiet alcoves to counter IOA's manic energy.

Split the difference. If the park's open late, split the day in half. See part of it in the morning, head off-site to a restaurant for lunch (your parking ticket is good all day) then head to your hotel for a swim or a nap (or both). Return in the cooler, less crowded evening.

PARK AMENITIES

Guest Services. Guest Services is right near the turnstiles, both before and after you enter Islands of Adventure (IOA). ☎ *407/224–6350* ⊕ *www. universalorlando.com.*

Lockers: There are $8-a-day lockers across from Guest Services at the entrance; for $10 a day you can rent a family-size model. You have unlimited access to both types throughout the day—although it's a hike back to retrieve things. Scattered strategically throughout the park—notably at the Incredible Hulk Coaster, Jurassic Park River Adventure, and Forbidden Journey—are so-called Smart Lockers. These are free for the first 45 to 75 minutes, $2 per hour afterward, and max out at $14 per day. Stash backpacks and cameras here while you're being drenched on a watery ride or going through the spin cycle on a twisty one.

Lost People and Things: If you've misplaced something, head to Guest Services in the Port of Entry. This is also where park staffers take lost children.

Stroller Rentals: You can rent strollers ($15 per day for singles, $25 for doubles) at the Port of Entry to your left after the turnstiles. You can also rent kiddie cars—small ones for $18, and large ones for $28.

Eighth Voyage
of Sindbad

Mystic
Fountain

Poseidon's
Fury

LOST
CONTINENT

Dragon
Challenge

Hogsmeade
Station

Fire Eater's
Grill

Triwizard
Spirit Rally

Hagrid's
Hut

Three
Broomsticks

Mythos

THE WIZARDING
WORLD OF
HARRY POTTER:
HOGSMEADE

Flight of the
Hippogriff

Harry Potter
and the
Forbidden Journey

Islands
of Adventure
Lagoon

Jurassic Park
Discovery Center

The Burger
Digs

Me Ship,
The Olive

Guest
Services

TOON
LAGOON

Jurassic Park
River Adventure

JURASSIC
PARK

Popeye & Bluto's
Bilge-Rat Barges

Pteranodon
Flyers

Blondie's

Camp
Jurassic

Comic Strip
Cafe

Thunder Falls
Terrace

Dudley Do-Right's
Ripsaw Falls

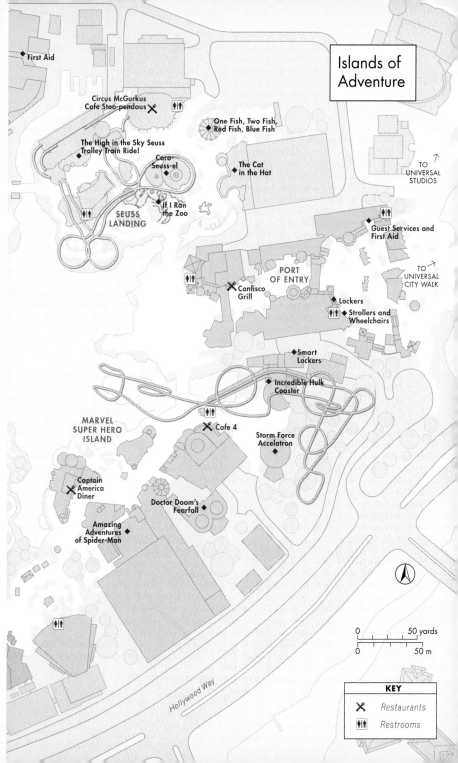

Islands of Adventure

First Aid

Circus McGurkus
Cafe Stoo-pendous ✕ 🚻

One Fish, Two Fish,
Red Fish, Blue Fish ◆

The High in the Sky Seuss
Trolley Train Ride! ◆

Caro-
Seuss-el ◆

The Cat
in the Hat ◆

TO
UNIVERSAL
STUDIOS →

🚻

SEUSS
LANDING

If I Ran
the Zoo ◆

Guest Services and
First Aid ◆

🚻 ✕ Confisco
Grill

PORT
OF ENTRY

TO
UNIVERSAL
CITY WALK →

Lockers ◆

🚻 ◆ Strollers and
Wheelchairs

Smart ◆
Lockers

Incredible Hulk ◆
Coaster

🚻 ✕ Cafe 4

MARVEL
SUPER HERO
ISLAND

Storm Force ◆
Accelatron

Captain ✕
America
Diner

Doctor Doom's ◆
Fearfall

Amazing ◆
Adventures
of Spider-Man

🚻

| 0 | | | | | 50 yards |
| 0 | | | | | 50 m |

Hollywood Way

KEY	
✕	Restaurants
🚻	Restrooms

ISLANDS OF ADVENTURE

NAME	Height Req.	Type of Entertainment	Duration	Crowds	Audience	Tips
Jurassic Park						
Camp Jurassic	n/a	Playground	Up to you	Light to Moderate	All Ages	Come anytime.
Jurassic Park Discovery Center	n/a	Walk-Through	Up to you	Light	Young Kids to Teens	Come anytime.
Jurassic Park River Adventure	At least 42"	Thrill Ride with Water	6 mins.	Heavy	All but Young Kids	Use Express Pass. Come early or late.
Pteranodon Flyers	36" to 56"	Thrill Ride for Kids	2 mins.	Heavy	All Ages	Skip this on your first visit. 36" to 48" can ride but must do so with an adult.
Lost Continent						
Eighth Voyage of Sindbad	n/a	Show	25 mins.	Heavy	All but Young Kids	Stadium seating for everyone, but arrive at least 15 mins. early. Don't sit too far up front. Use Express Pass.
Poseidon's Fury	n/a	Walk-through Simulator Exp.	20 mins.	Heavy	All but Young Kids	Come at the end of the day. Stay to the left for best spot. Get in first row each time. Express Pass accepted.
Marvel Super Hero Island						
★ The Amazing Adventures of Spider-Man	At least 40"	Simulator Exp.	4½ mins.	Absolutely	All but Young Kids	Use Express Pass, or come early or late in day. Don't miss the bad guys in the wanted posters. Try it twice if you can.
Doctor Doom's Fearfall	At least 52"	Thrill Ride	1 min.	Light to Moderate	All but Young Kids	Use Express Pass, or come later in the day. Regardless, come with an empty stomach.
Incredible Hulk Coaster	At least 54"	Thrill Ride	2¼ mins.	Yes!	All but Young Kids	Come here first. Effects are best in the morning. The front row is best.
Storm Force Accelatron	n/a	Thrill Ride	2 mins.	Light	All but Young Kids	Come whenever—except right after eating.
Seuss Landing						

Caro-Seuss-el	n/a	Thrill Ride for Kids	2 mins.	Moderate	All Ages	Use Express Pass, or end your day here.
The Cat in the Hat	n/a	Thrill Ride for Kids	4½ mins.	Heavy	All Ages	Use Express Pass here, or come early or at the end of the day.
High in the Sky Seuss Trolley Train Ride!	At least 34"	Railroad	3 mins.	Heavy	All Ages	Kids love trains, so plan to get in line! 34" to 48" can ride but must do so with an adult. Express Pass accepted.
If I Ran the Zoo	n/a	Playground with Water	Up to you	Heavy	Young Kids	Come toward the end of your visit.
One Fish, Two Fish, Red Fish, Blue Fish	n/a	Thrill Ride for Kids	2+ mins.	Heavy	Young Kids	Use Express Pass, or come early or late in day. Skip it on your first visit.
Toon Lagoon						
Dudley Do-Right's Ripsaw Falls	At least 44"	Thrill Ride with Water	5½ mins.	Heavy	All but Young Kids	Ride the flume in late afternoon to cool down, or at day's end. There's no seat where you can stay dry. Express Pass accepted.
Me Ship, The Olive	n/a	Playground	Up to you	Heavy	Young Kids	Come in the morning or at dinnertime.
Popeye and Bluto's Bilge-Rat Barges	At least 42 "	Thrill Ride with Water	5 mins.	Heavy	All but Young Kids	Come early in the morning or before closing. You will get wet. Express Pass accepted.
The Wizarding World of Harry Potter						
Dragon Challenge	At least 54"	Thrill Ride	3 mins.	Heavy	All but Young Kids	Use Express Pass. Avoid if you're prone to motion sickness.
Flight of the Hippogriff	At least 36"	Thrill Ride for Kids	1 min.	Moderate	Young Kids	Keep an eye on the line, and come when there's an opening. Express Pass accepted.
★ Harry Potter and the Forbidden Journey	At least 48"	Walk-Through/ Ride-Through/ Thrill Ride	50 mins.	Yes!	All but Young Kids	Come early and use Express Pass. Steer clear if you have a queasy stomach.

EXPLORING ISLANDS OF ADVENTURE

MARVEL SUPER HERO ISLAND

The facades on Stanley Boulevard (named for Marvel's famed editor and co-creator Stan Lee) put you smack in the middle of an alternatively pleasant and apocalyptic comic-book world—complete with heroes, villains, and cartoony colors and flourishes. Although the spiky, horrific towers of Doctor Doom's Fearfall and the vivid green of the Hulk's coaster are focal points, the Amazing Adventures of Spider-Man is the must-see attraction. At various times Doctor Doom, Spider-Man, and the Incredible Hulk are available for photos, and sidewalk artists are on hand to paint your face like your favorite hero (or villain). All rides here accept Universal Express Pass.

TOON LAGOON

The main street, Comic Strip Lane, makes use of cartoon characters that are recognizable to anyone—anyone born before 1940, that is. Pert little Betty Boop, gangly Olive Oyl, muscle-bound Popeye, Krazy Kat, Mark Trail, Flash Gordon, Pogo, and Alley Oop are all here, as are the relatively more contemporary Dudley Do-Right, Rocky, Bullwinkle, Beetle Bailey, Cathy, and Hagar the Horrible. With its colorful backdrops, chirpy music, hidden alcoves, squirting fountains, and highly animated scenery, Toon Town is a natural for younger kids (even if they don't know who these characters are). All attractions here accept Universal Express Pass except Me Ship, The Olive.

JURASSIC PARK

Pass through the towering gates of Jurassic Park and the music becomes slightly ominous, the vegetation tropical and junglelike. All of this, plus the high-tension wires and warning signs, does a great job of re-creating the Jurassic Park of Steven Spielberg's blockbuster movie (and its insipid sequels). The half-fun, half-frightening Jurassic Park River Adventure (the only attraction here that uses Universal Express Pass) is the standout, bringing to life key segments of the movie's climax.

THE WIZARDING WORLD OF HARRY POTTER: HOGSMEADE

In mid-2010, Islands of Adventure fulfilled the fantasy of Harry Potter devotees when it unveiled the biggest theme-park addition since the arrival of Disney's Animal Kingdom in 1998. At the highly publicized premiere, even the actors from the Potter film franchise were amazed. Having performed their roles largely before a green screen, they had never seen anything like this. Neither have you. It's fantastic and unbelievable. The movie-magic-perfect re-creations of mythical locales such as Hogwarts, Hogsmeade Village, and Diagon Alley are all here, while playing supporting roles are a handful of candy shops, souvenir stores, and restaurants expertly and exquisitely themed to make you believe you've actually boarded the *Hogwarts Express* and arrived in the incredible fantasy world of J. K. Rowling. Wands, candy, novelties, and more are unique to this magical land. Expect to be impressed—and to wait in line. Even if you owned a wand and were a real wizard, the only attractions in this land that accept the Universal Express Pass are Flight of the Hippogriff and Dragon Challenge. In fact, the land is so popular that in peak season it sometimes reaches capacity, and you have to wait for others to leave before you can enter.

LOST CONTINENT

Just beyond a wooden bridge, huge mythical birds guard the entrance to a land where trees are hung with weathered metal lanterns, and booming thunder mixes with chimes and vaguely Celtic melodies. Farther along the path, the scene looks similar to a Renaissance fair. Seers and fortune-tellers practice their trade in tents, and, in a huge theater, Sindbad leaps and bounces all over Arabia. This stunt show and Poseidon let you bypass lines using Universal Express Pass.

SEUSS LANDING

This 10-acre tribute to Dr. Seuss puts you in the midst of his classic children's books. This means spending quality time with the Cat, Things 1 and 2, Horton, the Lorax, and the Grinch. From topiary sculptures to lurching lampposts to curvy fences (there was never a straight line in any of the books) to buildings that glow in lavenders, pinks, peaches, and oranges, everything seems surreal. It's a wonderful place to wrap up a day. Even the Cat would approve. All rides here except If I Ran the Zoo accept Express Pass.

CITYWALK

With an attitude that's distinctly non-Disney, Universal has created nightlife for adults who want to party. The epicenter here is CityWalk, a 30-acre entertainment and retail complex at the hub of promenades that lead to both Universal parks.

When it comes to retail, much of the merchandise includes things you can find elsewhere—and most likely for less. But when you're swept up in the energy of CityWalk and dazzled by the degree of window-shopping (not to mention the fact that you're on vacation and you're more inclined to spend), chances are you'll want to drop into stores selling everything from surf wear and cigars to tattoos and timepieces.

In addition to stores, the open and airy gathering place includes an over-the-top discotheque, a theater for the fabulous and extremely popular Blue Man Group, and a huge hall where karaoke's king. There's a New Orleans bar, a Jamaican reggae lounge, a casual Key West hangout and, as of 2012, Hollywood Drive-In Golf, a pair of fun-filled 1950s sci-fi-movie-theme miniature golf courses. On weeknights you find families and conventioneers; weekends a decidedly younger crowd parties until the wee hours.

Clubs have individual cover charges, but it's far more economical to pay for the whole kit and much of the caboodle. Choose a Party Pass (a one-price-all-clubs admission) for $11.99, or upgrade to a Party Pass-and-a-Movie for $15.98 (tax included); a Party Pass-and-a-Meal for $21; a Movie-and-a-Meal for $21.95; or a Meal and a Mini-Golf Deal for $23.95

At AMC Universal Cineplex, with its 20 screens (including IMAX), there's certain to be something you like—including nightly midnight

movies. Meals (tax and gratuity included) are served at Jimmy Buffett's Margaritaville, the Hard Rock Cafe, NASCAR Sports Grille, and others. And as if these deals weren't sweet enough, after 6 the $15 parking fee drops to $5. Nevertheless, it's a long haul from the garage to CityWalk—if you prefer, simply call a cab. They run at all hours. ☎ *407/354–3374, 407/363–8000 for Universal main line* ⊕ *www.citywalkorlando.com.*

NIGHTLIFE

With the wide range of nightlife you'll find at Universal, you may get the feeling that you're vacationing not in Orlando, but in New York City. CityWalk's stores open by midmorning, and its restaurants come to life between lunchtime and late afternoon. Eateries that double as nightclubs (such as Pat O'Brien's, Bob Marley's, and the Red Coconut Club) start charging a cover before dusk and apply age restrictions (usually 21) around 9. For details on a particular establishment, check with Guest Services.

BARS AND CLUBS

Bob Marley—A Tribute to Freedom. Modeled after the King of Reggae's home in Kingston, Jamaica (even down to the A/C window units), in a way this nightclub is also part museum, with more than 100 photographs and paintings showing pivotal moments in Marley's life. Though the place does serve meals, most patrons are at the cozy bar or by the patio, where they can be jammin' to a (loud) live band that plays nightly. For a nice souvenir, pose by the wonderful Marley statue outside the club. Legendary Thursdays feature drink specials for everyone, and Sunday is ladies' night from 9 pm until closing. ■TIP➔ Often on Monday and Tuesday, CityWalk's pace is slow enough where some clubs will offer free admission. Ask before you pay. ⊠ *CityWalk* ☎ *407/224–2692* ⊕ *www.universalorlando.com* ⊡ *$7 after 9 pm* ⊙ *Daily 4 pm–2 am.*

CityWalk's Rising Star. Here you and other hopeful (and hopeless) singers can really let loose. Instead of singing to recorded music, you're accompanied by a band complete with backup singers—in front of a live audience. Backup singers are on hand every night, while the live band plugs in Tuesday through Saturday, and a full bar is always on tap. ⊠ *6000 Universal Blvd. #717, CityWalk* ☎ *407/224–2961* ⊕ *www.universalorlando.com* ⊡ *$7, no charge to sing* ⊙ *Nightly 8 pm–2 am.*

the groove. In this cavernous hall images flicker rapidly on several screens, and the lights, music, and mayhem appeal to a mostly under-30 crowd. Prepare for lots of fog, swirling lights, and sweaty bodies. The '70s-style Green Room is filled with beanbag chairs and everything you threw out when Duran Duran hit the charts. The Blue Room is sci-fi Jetson-y, and the Red Room is hot and romantic in a bordello sort of way. The music is equally diverse: Top 40, hip-hop, R&B, techno and the occasional live band. ⊠ *6000 Universal Blvd., CityWalk* ☎ *407/224–2692* ⊕ *www.universalorlando.com* ⊡ *$7* ⊙ *Daily 9 pm–2 am.*

Jimmy Buffett's Margaritaville. Buffett tunes fill the air at the restaurant here and at the Volcano, Land Shark, and 12 Volt bars. Inside there's a miniature Pan Am Clipper suspended from the ceiling, music videos

The Cat and his Hat, McGurkus and the Circus, and fish both red and blue are among the attractions geared to the under-7 set at Seuss Landing.

projected onto sails, limbo and hula-hoop contests, a huge margarita blender that erupts "when the volcano blows," and live music nightly—everything that Parrotheads need to roost. Across the promenade, another full-size seaplane (emblazoned with "Jimmy Buffett, Captain") is the setting for the Lone Palm Airport, a pleasing and surprisingly popular outdoor waterfront bar. ⊠ *6000 Universal Studios Plaza #704, CityWalk* ☎ *407/224–2692* ⊕ *www.margaritavilleorlando.com* ✉ *$7 after 10 pm* ☉ *Daily 11:30 am–2 am.*

Pat O'Brien's. An exact reproduction of the legendary New Orleans original, this comes complete with flaming fountain and dueling pianists who are playing for highly entertained regulars and visitors—even on weekday afternoons. Outside, the cozy and welcoming Patio Bar has a wealth of tables and chairs, allowing you to do nothing but enjoy the outdoors and your potent, rum-based Hurricanes in Orlando's version of the Big Easy. ⊠ *6000 Universal Blvd., CityWalk* ☎ *407/224–2692* ⊕ *www.patobriens.com* ✉ *$7 after 9 pm* ☉ *Patio Bar daily 4 pm–2 am; piano bar daily 5 pm–2 am (21 and up after 9).*

Red Coconut Club. Paying tribute to kitsch design of the 1950s, the interior here is part Vegas lounge, part Cuban club, and part Polynesian tiki bar. It's "where tropical meets trendy." There are three full bars on two levels, signature martinis, an extensive wine list, and VIP bottle service. Hang out in the lounge, on the balcony, or at the bar. On a budget? Take advantage of the daily happy hours and gourmet appetizer menu. A DJ (Sunday–Wednesday) or live music (Thursday–Saturday) pushes the energy with tunes ranging from Sinatra to rock. Thursday is ladies' night. ⊠ *6000 Universal Blvd., CityWalk* ☎ *407/224–2425*

⊕ *www.universalorlando.com* ⌦ *$7 after 9 pm* ☉ *Sun.–Wed. 8 pm–2 am, Thurs.–Sat. 6 pm–2 am.*

SHOWS

Blue Man Group. At their own venue, the Sharp-Aquos Theatre, the ever-innovative Blue Men continue to pound out new music, sketches, and audience interaction that is nothing like you've ever seen. Attempting to understand the apps on a GiPad (a gigantic iPad), they may appear clueless and perplexed about cutting-edge technology (which for them can be as basic as a can of paint), but they're always excited when they can drum out rhythms on lengths of PVC pipes and throw a rave-party finale for all in attendance. The show is a surreal comic masterpiece, so if you have the time and a little extra in your vacation budget, this is a must. Three levels of admission (Poncho, Tier 1, and Tier 2) hint at how messy things can get when the Blue Men cut loose. ⊠ *CityWalk, Orlando, Florida, USA* ☎ *407/258–3626* ⊕ *www.universalorlando.com* ⌦ *Adults $69 in advance, $84 at box office* ☉ *Daily showtimes vary; call for schedule.*

SHOPPING

This 30-acre entertainment and retail complex is at the hub of prom-enades that lead to Universal Studios and Islands of Adventure. Shops here sell fine jewelry, cool beachwear, fashionable clothing, and stylish accessories. The best stores are near the entrance/exit of the complex.

Cigarz. For years, this perfectly themed cigar sanctuary has lured cigar aficionados with an impressive range of cigars preserved in a well-stocked humidor, as well as a good selection of pipes, lighters, and accessories. A cozy bar has become a popular gathering spot for in-the-know locals and soon-to-be friends. FYI: Smoking's permitted. ⊠ *600 Universal Blvd., Suite 740, CityWalk* ☎ *407/370–2999* ⊕ *cigarzcity-walk.com.*

Fresh Produce. Featuring fashions that look right at home in sunny Florida, this boutique showcases comfortable and colorful swimwear, blouses, Capri slacks, dresses, footwear, beach gear, and accessories designed for coastal comfort. ⊠ *CityWalk.*

P!Q. Although it's a small shop, there's enough room to hold hundreds of fun and mind-bending toys and books and games for kids (and adults) to teach them about math and physics and sometimes just plain fun stuff—like beer steins. Always interesting. ⊠ *6000 Universal Blvd., Suite 745J, CityWalk* ⊕ *www.p!qproducts.com.*

Quiet Flight. Granted the closest beach is about 60 miles east, you can still get outfitted like a surfer at this shop, which sports an inventory featur-ing brand names such as Billabong, Quicksilver, Hurley, and Oakley. In addition to shorts and shirts, Quiet Flight also sells sandals, watches, sunglasses (Ray-Ban, Prada, and D&G among the featured names), and . . . surfboards! ⊠ *CityWalk.*

Brain Wash is one of Wet 'n Wild's most thrilling slides.

WET 'N WILD

When you were a kid, chances are all you needed for unlimited summer fun was a simple inflatable pool and a garden hose or sprinkler. Well, about the same time that you were growing up, so were water parks. They started with a few simple slides and are now the aquatic equivalents of megamalls.

It all began in 1977 with Wet 'n Wild, created by George Millay, who was also one of the founders of SeaWorld. Although it's now far from alone, Wet 'n Wild remains extremely popular, thanks to its quality, service, and ability to create more heart-stopping waterslides, rides, and tubing adventures than its competitors. Indeed, new rides seem to be added like clockwork, old ones improved, and settings developed for the comfort of guests. There's a complete water playground for kids, numerous high-energy slides for adults, a lazy-river ride, and some quiet, sandy beaches on which you can stretch out and get a tan.

Speaking of high energy, this is a park that requires a lot of it. A day here is often a marathon of climbing steps, sliding, swimming, and splashing, though you may not notice just how much your stamina is being drained as you scamper from slide to slide. Plan to take breaks: laze in a beach chair and eat high-protein meals and snacks to maintain your strength. You can bring in a cooler for a picnic or eat at a restaurant in one of several food courts.

If you're not a strong swimmer, don't worry. There are plenty of low-key attractions, and all of the ride entrances are marked with warnings to let you know which ones are safe for you. Plus, during peak season,

11

there are as many as 200 lifeguards on duty daily. Also note that all the pools (if not the rides) are ADA-compliant and are heated in cooler weather. This, combined with Orlando's temperate climate, means that Wet 'n Wild is one of the few water parks in the country to stay open year-round.

Surf's up!

PLANNING

GETTING ORIENTED

If you arrive early, when crowds are light to moderate, you should have plenty of time to do each ride once, and possibly twice or more. From the Surf Lagoon straight ahead, head counterclockwise to the most thrilling experiences (Bomb Bay, Der Stuka, The Storm) first. By the time you've circled the park and are worn out, your kids should still have plenty of energy to deplete at Blastaway Beach.

PARK AMENITIES

Guest Services: Get maps and other information at Guest Services (aka Guest Relations), to the left as you enter.

Lockers: There are dressing rooms with lockers in three different sizes (personal $6/$3 deposit, standard $9/$3 deposit, family $11/$3 deposit) as well as showers and restrooms to the left of the entrance gates. Additional restrooms are on the island inside the lazy river and near the First-Aid Stand and the Surge.

Lost People and Things: The Lost and Found is at Guest Services, to the left just after you enter the park. This is also where lifeguards and other staffers take lost children.

Wheelchair Rentals: Near the entrance, you can rent modified wheelchairs (they have large tires that can handle the sand) for $5 per day with a $25 refundable deposit. Note that although many of the paths are flat and accessible, none of the rides accommodates people using wheelchairs.

ESSENTIALS

Admission: Basic admission is about $55 for adults (ages 10 and up) and $50 for children (but look for discount coupons in flyers and magazines displayed in stores and restaurants throughout the I-Drive area). Full price covers admission for any or all of the next 14 consecutive days, even when you buy in advance online (and by doing so, you'll save an additional $10 per ticket). Other money-saving options include the FlexTicket, which bundles Wet 'n Wild with parks and attractions at Universal Orlando, SeaWorld, and Busch Gardens.

Parking: Costing $12 for cars, vans, and motorcycles and $16 for RVs and cars with trailers, parking is in a large lot along Universal Boulevard.

Wet 'n Wild. For general information, call Wet 'n Wild or visit online. ✉ *Wet 'n Wild* ☎ *407/351–3200 for recorded info, 407/351–1800 for park operations* ⊕ *www.wetnwildorlando.com.*

TOURING TIPS

■ Want to save a bundle? Admission drops to half price during the afternoon; exactly when depends on closing time, but can be as late as 5 pm in the summer. Call ahead for the magic hour. Even better, if you pay for a full-price ticket, you can return for free for 14 consecutive days. It's a great deal for families in town for an extended stay. You can see the big three (Disney, Universal, SeaWorld) during the day and return here in the evening.

■ When you arrive, it's a good idea to pick up a map, scan the park layout, and stake out a spot on the beach before heading on or in. To claim a prime beach spot, arrive 30 minutes before the park opens, or visit on a cloudy day. If it looks like rain all day, though, head elsewhere.

■ Men should wear a true bathing suit, and women should opt for a one-piece rather than a bikini. Cutoff shorts and garments with rivets, metal buttons, buckles, or zippers aren't allowed.

■ Wading slippers are a good idea—hot sidewalks and sandpaper-like pool bottoms can do a number on your feet—but put them in a locker or carry them when taking a plunge, since they can catch on slides.

■ Items too large to carry should be stashed in a locker. Some picnic tables have lockable containers (secured to the umbrella stand) that are just large enough to hold smaller items such as keys, glasses, and cell phones.

■ For extra privacy, a quiet oasis in the middle of the lazy river features cabanas with a fan, chaise lounges, and a fridge stocked with a dozen bottles of water. It's a nice base for stowing your things, but the privilege costs an extra $150. Don't want to get up? Servers will bring food to you.

■ Be patient with the lines here. Just when you think you've arrived, you discover there's another level or two to go.

■ To bypass lines at the popular rides, get an Express Pass (available seasonally), accepted at most rides. Prices change based on park attendance and time of day, so call Park Operations at ☎ *407/351–1800* for details. A limited number of passes are sold each day—all the more reason to get here early.

■ Okay. So you remembered your swimsuit and towel. But what about sunscreen? You can buy it and other necessities or souvenirs at the **Breakers Beach Shop,** near the park entrance. And if you did forget a towel, renting one here costs $4 with a $3 deposit. Rent a three-pack, though, and you save $2.

SEAWORLD

With Discovery Cove and Aquatica

WELCOME TO SEAWORLD, DISCOVERY COVE, AND AQUATICA

TOP REASONS TO GO

★ **Animal Magnetism:** If you love animals—slick, shiny, feathery, or furry— SeaWorld, Discovery Cove, and Aquatica are where you want to be. No robotic wildlife here; just well-cared-for and talented dolphins, whales, seals, otters, penguins, cats, dogs . . .

★ **A Slower Pace:** The shows and natural settings of SeaWorld and Discovery Cove let you enjoy a theme-park vacation without racing from one attraction to the next. Living in the moment is the lesson here.

★ **Getting Smarter:** No one leaves these parks without learning a little something about nature through shows, backstage tours, instructional signage, and well-versed educators and naturalists who are always ready to answer questions.

★ **Memories in the Making:** Chances are SeaWorld and Discovery Cove will afford you the chance to pet a penguin, feed a dolphin, or watch a 5-ton whale leap out of the water. You can't forget things like that.

1 SeaWorld. With the exception of a handful of thrill rides, the original park (which opened in 1973 to reroute visitors heading to the then recently opened Walt Disney World) maintains a slow and easy pace. Here it's all about clever shows, shaded sidewalks, and plenty of opportunities to enjoy the natural grace and intriguing personalities of marine life and other animals.

12

GETTING ORIENTED

SeaWorld is just off the intersection of Interstate 4 and the Beachline Expressway, equidistant from Universal Orlando and the Walt Disney World Resort, which are only about five minutes away. SeaWorld is also a mere 10 minutes from Downtown Orlando and 15 minutes from the airport. Discovery Cove is its own oasis across the street from SeaWorld. Aquatica, a little ways down the road from both, is the first of the three that you'll see after exiting the expressway.

TO WET 'N WILD &
UNIVERSAL STUDIOS

EXIT 2

528

EXIT 1

EXIT 3A
AND
EXIT 3B

3 AQUATICA

1 SEAWORLD

Universal Blvd.

Gateway Ave.

Orangewood Blvd.

International Dr.

423

0   1/4 mi

0   1/4 km

2 Discovery Cove.
SeaWorld spun off this park to give you the chance to enjoy a lot more time (and to spend a little more cash) with the animals. A trip to this aquatic oasis feels like a trip to the islands; a daylong, all-inclusive experience that includes breakfast and lunch, drinks, a private beach, snorkeling equipment, and—for approximately an extra $100—the chance to swim with dolphins. Paradise.

3 Aquatica. SeaWorld's water park offers the chance to slip and slide at adrenaline-rush speeds, relax in the current of two wave pools, laze on a wide beach, and take the wee ones to pint-size play areas of their very own. All in all, there's something for everyone, showcased in a tropical, tiki-theme setting.

By Gary
McKechnie

Just as Walt Disney World and Universal Orlando are much more than just a single park, the same is true of SeaWorld. The original park—which includes the Shamu shows as well as presentations featuring dolphins and seals—has expanded to include Discovery Cove (an immersive tropical retreat), and Aquatica (a water park loaded with aquatic excitement). So, as you plan your vacation, consider that SeaWorld can easily fill a single day or, if you're really eager to take to the waters, perhaps a day or two more.

There's a whole lot more to SeaWorld and Discovery Cove than being splashed by Shamu. You can see manatees face-to-snout, learn to love a shark, swim with dolphins, and be spat at by a walrus. These two parks celebrate all the mammals, birds, fish, and reptiles that live in and near the ocean.

Then there's Aquatica, a wild water park that takes its cues from Sea-World and Discovery Cove in design and mood—marine-life motifs are everywhere. It also gives competitor water parks a run for their money with thrilling slides, broad beaches, calming rivers, and an area for small kids.

The park also takes some tips from the tropics. Right after you clear the parking lot, you see a tropical pastiche of buildings. Yup. That's definitely an island vibe you're detecting. Upon entering Aquatica, you feel as if you've left Central Florida for the Caribbean or Polynesia, even.

You might be drawn to the series of superfast waterslides (some of which conclude by sending you into serene streams), or you might feel the pull of the white-sand beaches beside the twin wave pools, where you can laze in the sun, venturing out every so often to try a ride or climb into an inner tube and float down a river. Whether you're spending the day at SeaWorld, Discovery Cove, or Aquatica, just go with it. Get into a groove, relax, and enjoy yourself at some of the most pleasant theme parks in Orlando.

PLANNING

GETTING HERE AND AROUND

Heading west on Interstate 4 (toward Disney) take Exit 72; heading east, take Exit 71. After that you'll be going east on the Beachline Expressway (aka Route 528), and the first right-hand exit leads you to International Drive. Turn left, and you'll soon see the entrance to Aquatica on your left. Sea Harbor Drive—leading to SeaWorld's entrance—will be on your right. To reach Discovery Cove, follow International Drive past Aquatica ½ mile to the Central Florida Parkway and turn right. The park's entrance will be on your left.

OPERATING HOURS

SeaWorld opens daily at 9 am and usually closes at 7 pm, with extended hours during the summer and holidays. Hours at Discovery Cove also vary seasonally, although it's generally open daily from 8 to 5:30, with check-in beginning 30 minutes earlier—which is not a bad idea considering Discovery Cove serves a complimentary breakfast until 10 am. Aquatica is open at 9 am, with closing times varying between 5 and 9 pm, depending on the season. Allow a full day to see each attraction.

ADMISSION

SeaWorld, Discovery Cove, Aquatica, and Busch Gardens Tampa Bay fall under the SeaWorld Parks & Entertainment umbrella, and you can save by buying combo tickets. Regular one-day tickets to **SeaWorld** cost $92 (adults) and $87 (children ages 3–9), excluding tax, but if you order in advance over the phone or online, you'll save $10 per ticket—which just may be the best money-saving option you'll find. Combo-park admission prices, which include 14 days at each park, are as follows:

SeaWorld/Aquatica *$129 adults/$124 children*

SeaWorld/Busch Gardens Tampa *$129/$121*

SeaWorld/Aquatica/Busch Gardens Tampa *$159/$154*

Flex Ticket (14 days at SeaWorld/Aquatica/Busch Gardens Tampa) *$345/$325*

Aquatica at-the-gate admission is $56 (adults) and $51 (children 3–9), but if you order online you'll save around $10 per ticket. Add a Banana Beach all-you-can-eat option, and the online price is $55 adults, $50 children.

Reserve **Discovery Cove** visits well in advance—attendance is limited to about 1,000 a day. Tickets (with a dolphin swim) start at about $229 (off-season, in January and February) but are generally around $289. Forgo the dolphin swim and save approximately $100. This park has what's called dynamic pricing (meaning prices change by season, and also at other times without notice). Admission is less expensive the earlier you book (so call well in advance) and includes access to all beach and snorkeling areas and the free-flight aviary; meals and snacks; use of a mask, snorkel, swim vest, towel, locker, and sunscreen; parking; and a pass for 14 days of unlimited admission to SeaWorld Orlando and Aquatica. Upgrade to an "ultimate" pass (about $20), which includes admission (and free transportation) to Busch Gardens Tampa.

All-Day Dining Deal. Available at select SeaWorld restaurants (Voyager's Smokehouse, Seaport Pizza, Terrace Garden Buffet, The Spice Mill, Seafire Inn, and Mango Joe's), adults will pay from $32.99 and kids from $17.99 to chow down on an entrée, side dish, drink, and dessert for each meal Skip it if you plan on having just one meal in the park.

Quick Queue Passes. SeaWorld's Quick Queue passes (✉ $19–$35 per person, depending on the season) get you to the front of the line at major attractions and shows for one admission each. The higher-price unlimited pass is good for unlimited admissions. Neither Discovery Cove nor Aquatica has such a pass.

SEAWORLD STRATEGIES

Avoid weekend and school-holiday visits. These are the busiest times, so plan around them if you can.

Wear sneakers or water shoes—no heels or slip-on sandals. It may not seem like it, but there'll be a whole lot of walking as you roam from one end of the park to the other, stand in line, and walk through attractions.

Pack dry clothes. You can get wet just by being toward the front at the Shamu show or riding Journey to Atlantis. Alternatively, carry a rain poncho.

Budget for food for the animals. Participating in animal feedings is a major part of the SeaWorld experience, although it comes at a price: a small carton of fish costs $5.

Pick up a map-and-show schedule inside the entrance. SeaWorld has its show schedule down to a science. If you start by catching the show closest to the entrance, shortly after that one's over, guests are moving farther into the park to grab a seat at the next performance so you'll end up moving with the crowd. Instead, start off at a show further inside the park so you are ahead of the crowds. So spend a few minutes planning so you can casually stroll from show to show and have time for learning, testing out thrill rides, *and* enjoying a leisurely meal.

Be open to learning. SeaWorld's trainers and educators are always at the ready to share information about the park's wildlife.

DISCOVERY COVE STRATEGIES

Make reservations well in advance. Prized June dates, for instance, can sell out in March. If there aren't openings when you call, though, don't despair. Call back often to inquire about cancellations.

Think about your eyewear. Park masks don't accommodate glasses, but there are a limited number of near- and far-sighted prescription masks (first-come, first-served) available. Just step into a booth and you'll be able to try on a few different pairs with different magnifications. If you don't mind risking lost contacts, just wear those beneath a non-prescription mask.

Don't bring your own wet suit or fins. Every guest must wear a Discovery Cove–issued wet suit or vest—not a bad idea, as the water can be cold.

Leave belongings in your locker. The plastic passes you're given are all you need to pick up your meals, soft drinks, and—if you're over 21—alcoholic drinks.

DID YOU KNOW?

Performers ski atop the backs of two dolphins, divers leap from towers, and an acrobat does an aerial ballet during the Blue Horizons show. It's a show that blends everything SeaWorld does best above and below the water.

Be flexible when it comes to weather. If the weather on your reserved day looks like it'll be an all-day downpour, attempts will be made to reschedule your visit while you're in town. If that's not possible, you'll have to settle for a refund.

Have a dolphin relay a message. The Special Occasion Package enlists the help of a bottlenose dolphin to deliver love notes, wedding proposals, birthday or anniversary greetings, and the like.

AQUATICA STRATEGIES

■ **Buy tickets in advance.** Tickets bought ahead of time online or at another SeaWorld park allow early entry (and discounts) to Aquatica, which, in turn, increases your chances of hitting all the big-deal flume and tube rides—possibly more than once.

■ **Be open to animal encounters.** The Commerson's dolphins of Dolphin Plunge have scheduled feeding times, and you can see macaws perched on tree limbs and small mammals on display in Conservation Cabanas—usually attended to by knowledgeable educators.

■ **Pack beach supplies.** You'll save a few bucks by having your own towels, lotion, water shoes, and snacks.

■ **Take care of yourself.** Fight fatigue by eating a good breakfast, drinking plenty of water, and nibbling on high-energy snacks. Avoid sunburn by reapplying sunscreen often—even the waterproof stuff washes off.

■ **Save your soles.** Water shoes protect your feet from hot sand and sidewalks and the rough surfaces in some pools.

CONTACTS

Aquatica ☏ *888/800–5447* ⊕ *www.aquaticabyseaworld.com*

Busch Gardens Tampa ☏ *888/800–5447* ⊕ *www.buschgardens.com/bgt*

Discovery Cove ☏ *877/557–7404* ⊕ *www.discoverycove.com*

SeaWorld ☏ *888/800–5447* ⊕ *www.seaworld.com*

Parking. Parking is $15 for a car or motorcycle, $20 for an RV or camper. For $25 you can pull into one of the six Preferred Parking rows closest to the front gate and for $30 a valet will take the wheel. At Aquatica, cars and motorcycles are charged $12, RVs $16—although if you already have your parking slip from that day at SeaWorld, it's free. Parking is free at Discovery Cove.

SEAWORLD

Just as you wouldn't expect to arrive at Disney and see nothing but Mickey Mouse, don't expect to arrive at SeaWorld and see only Shamu. Only a few steps into the park you'll find baby dolphins and their mothers, a pool filled with stingrays, colorful flamingos, rescued sea turtles, rescued pelicans, and even rescued manatees. SeaWorld's objective is to educate as well as entertain.

You'll see how lumbering manatees live and what they look like up close; watch otters and seals perform slapstick routines based on their natural behaviors; learn about the lives of giant tortoises and sea turtles;

12

and be absolutely amazed at the scope of marine life celebrated throughout the park.

Then there are the attractions, each and every one designed not only to showcase the marine world but also to demonstrate ways in which humans can protect the earth's waters and wildlife. And, because there are more exhibits and shows than rides, the difference between SeaWorld and other theme parks is that you can go at your own pace, without that hurry-up-and-wait feeling. It's also worth noting that because shows, attractions, and exhibits are based primarily on nature and animals, designers have created a natural layout as well, with winding lanes and plenty of places to relax by the waterfront or beside bouquets of flowers. There's never a nagging urge to race through anything; indeed, the entire park encourages you to slow down and move at a casual pace.

PLANNING

GETTING ORIENTED

SeaWorld's performance venues, attractions, and activities surround a 17-acre lagoon, and the artful landscaping, curving paths, and concealing greenery sometimes lead to wrong turns. But armed with a map that lists showtimes, it's easy to plan an approach that lets you move fluidly from one show and attraction to the next and still have time for rest stops and meal breaks.

TOURING TIPS

Before investing in front-of-the-line Quick Queue passes (✉ $19–$35), remember that there are only a handful of big-deal rides, and space is seldom a problem at shows.

If you bring your own food, remove all straws and lids before you arrive—they can harm fish and birds.

Arrive at least 30 minutes early for the Shamu show, which generally fills to capacity. Prepare to get wet in the "splash zone" down front.

In Discovery Cove make the aviary one of your first stops, since the 250-plus birds within will be more active in the morning. Check-in starts at around 7:30 am.

PARK AMENITIES

Guest Services: Ticket booths have become the new Guest Services (aka Guest Relations) center. If you ordered your tickets online, have questions about dining or attractions, or just need tickets to begin with, you can find it here.

Information and Reservation Center: Right inside the entrance you can pick up the park map (which also has info on showtimes, services, and amenities); make dinner reservations; and buy tickets for Discovery Cove, Aquatica, and park tours.

Lockers: One-time-use, coin-op lockers ($1) are near flip-over coasters like Kraken and Manta, Journey to Atlantis, and Shamu's Happy Harbor as well as inside SeaWorld's main entrance. Also near the entrance, next to Shamu's Emporium, are day lockers ($8 small, $10 large per day). At Discovery Cove free lockers await you near the cabanas.

SeaWorld Orlando

← TO AQUATICA

Kraken

Pacific Point Preserve

Shark Encounter

Shark's Underwater Grill

Clyde and Seamore Take Pirate Island (Sea Lion & Otter Theater)

Spice Mill Café

Lockers

Antarctica: Empire of the Penguins

ATM

Pearl Dive

Lockers

Journey to Atlantis

Voyager Smokehouse

Antarctic Market

Seaport Pizza

Guest Services, Information

Seaport Theater/ Pets Ahoy

THE WATERFRONT

Reservations and Show Schedules

Blue Horizons (Dolphin Theater)

Manta

Turtle Trek

Lockers

Seafire Inn

Dolphin Nursery

Pelican Preserve

Dolphin Cove

ATM

ATM

Lockers

KEY WEST

Cypress Bakery

Stingray Lagoon

Captain Pete's Island Eats

Key West at SeaWorld

First Aid

Information and Reservations

SeaWorld Rescue

Parking

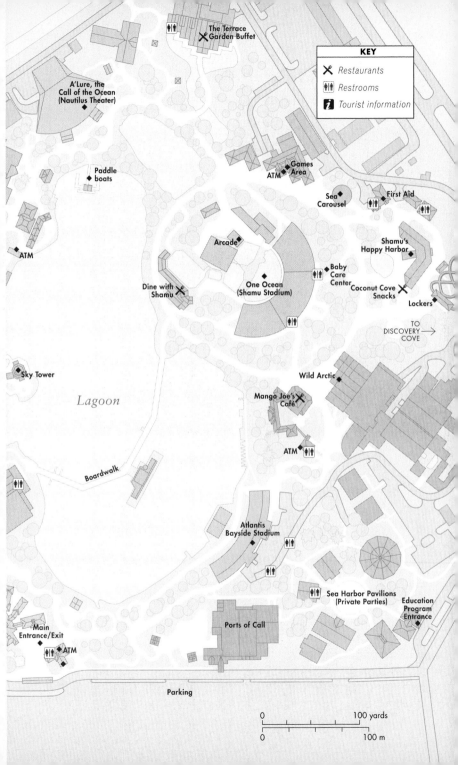

KEY

✕ *Restaurants*
🚻 *Restrooms*
ℹ️ *Tourist information*

The Terrace Garden Buffet

A'Lure, the Call of the Ocean (Nautilus Theater)

Paddle boats

ATM

Games Area

Sea Carousel

First Aid

ATM

Arcade

Shamu's Happy Harbor

Dine with Shamu

One Ocean (Shamu Stadium)

Baby Care Center

Coconut Cove Snacks

Lockers

TO DISCOVERY COVE →

Sky Tower

Lagoon

Wild Arctic

Mango Joe's Café

ATM

Boardwalk

Atlantis Bayside Stadium

Sea Harbor Pavilions (Private Parties)

Education Program Entrance

Main Entrance/Exit

ATM

Ports of Call

Parking

0   100 yards

0   100 m

SEAWORLD ORLANDO AND DISCOVERY COVE

SeaWorld

NAME	Height Req.	Type of Entertainment	Duration	Crowds	Audience	
Antarctica: Empire of the Penguins	48"	Tour/Thrill Ride	5 mins.	Heavy	All Ages	Come early.
A'Lure, the Call of the Ocean	n/a	Show	20 mins.	Heavy	All Ages	Plenty of seats, but arrive 15 mins. early for a wide selection.
Blue Horizons	n/a	Show	20 mins.	Heavy	All Ages	Arrive 20 mins. before showtime.
Dolphin Nursery	n/a	Aquarium	Up to you	Light	All Ages	Come during a Shamu show so the kids can be up front.
Journey to Atlantis	At least 42"	Thrill Ride with Water	6 mins.	Heavy	All but Young Kids	You can make a beeline here first thing or come about an hour before closing. But the best time for this is at night.
Key West at SeaWorld	n/a	Walk-Through/ Aquarium	Up to you	Light to Moderate	All Ages	If too crowded, wander until crowds disperse.
★ Kraken	At least 54"	Thrill Ride	6 mins.	Heavy	All but Young Kids	Get to the park when it opens and head straight to Kraken; otherwise, hit it near closing time or during a Blue Horizons show.
Manatees Rescue	n/a	Aquarium	Up to you	Light to Moderate	All Ages	Come during a Shamu show but *not* right after a dolphin show.
★ Manta	At least 54"	Thrill Ride with Water	6 mins.	You Bet!	All but Young Kids	Come first thing or late in the day, or purchase a Quick Queue pass for front-of-ride access.
Pacific Point Preserve	n/a	Aquarium	Up to you	Light	All Ages	Come anytime.
Pets Ahoy	n/a	Show	15–20 mins.	Moderate to Heavy	All Ages	Gauge the crowds, and come here early if necessary.
★ Sea Lion & Otter Stadium	n/a	Show	40 mins.	Heavy	All Ages	Sit toward the center for the best view, and don't miss the pre-show mime. Plenty of seats.

					Young Kids	
Shamu's Happy Harbor	n/a	Playground with Water	Up to you	Heavy	All Ages	Don't come first thing in morning, or you'll never drag your child away. Bring a towel to dry them off.
★ Shamu Stadium (One Ocean)	n/a	Show	25 mins.	Moderate to Heavy	All Ages	Show itself lasts 25 minutes, but there's a 30-minute pre-show; plan accordingly.
Shark Encounter	n/a	Aquarium	Up to you	Light to Moderate	All Ages	Come during the sea lion show.
Sky Tower	48"	Tour/Thrill Ride	6 mins.	Light	All Ages	Come whenever there's no line. Note the extra $4 charge, though.
Stingray Lagoon	n/a	Aquarium	Up to you	Moderate to Heavy	All Ages	Walk by if it's crowded, but return before dusk.
Turtle Point	n/a	Zoo	Up to you	Light	All Ages	Come anytime.
Wild Arctic	At least 42"	Simulator Exp./Aquarium	5+ mins.	Moderate to Heavy	All Ages	Come during a Shamu show. You can skip the ride if you just want to see the mammals.
Discovery Cove						
Beaches	n/a	Beach Area	Up to you	Light	All Ages	Arrive early and head to the far side for a private spot.
★ Dolphin Lagoon	n/a	Pool	45–60 mins.	n/a	All but Young Kids	Be mindful of your appointment time.
Explorer's Aviary	n/a	Aviary	Up to you	Light to Moderate	All Ages	Come early, when the birds are most active.
Tropical Reef	n/a	Aquarium/Pool Area	Up to you	Light to Moderate	All Ages	Monitor crowds and come when they're lightest. Popular with teens.
Wind-Away River	n/a	Aquarium	Up to you	Light to Moderate	All Ages	When it gets hot, slip into the water. Popular with teens.

★ **Fodor's** Choice

Lost People and Things: SeaWorld's Main Information Center operates as the park's Lost and Found. Lost children are brought here, and it's the place to report lost children. A park-wide paging system also helps reunite parents with kids. At Discovery Cove lost kids and items eventually find their way to the check-in lobby.

ANIMAL ENCOUNTERS AND TOURS

SeaWorld has several programs that put you closer to the animals. Up-Close and Behind-the-Scenes tours last 60 to 90 minutes and cost about $10 to $50. The six-hour VIP Tour starts at around $100 for adults and $80 for children.

You can book tours up to three months in advance. For a list, check the SeaWorld website (⊕ *www.seaworld.com*) or call the park (☎ *407/351–3600*).

Behind the Scenes Tour. On this 90-minute program, you'll have a chance to see how SeaWorld's animal experts care for rescued manatees and sea turtles. Where else can you touch a shark, step inside a hidden polar bear den, and play with a penguin? From $29 adults, $9 children. ⊕ *www.seaworldparks.com*.

DISCOVERY COVE

If you were pleasantly surprised by the pace at SeaWorld, believe it or not, it's even slower at Discovery Cove. Here your mission is to spend an entire day doing nothing but savoring a 32-acre tropical oasis. It's a task made easier by an all-inclusive admission that covers all meals, towels, a wet suit, masks, sunscreen, and the option of springing for the highlight of the day: a unique swimming experience with a bottlenose dolphin.

Even without a dolphin encounter, you can have a great time splashing around coral reefs, swimming into a spacious aviary, floating down a quiet river, and lazing on a sandy beach beneath lovely palms. In 2012, Freshwater Oasis, a tropical rain-forest environment of sparkling clear springs, opened offering face-to-face encounters with playful otters and curious marmoset monkeys. Thanks to a special diving helmet, SeaVenture lets you walk underwater through a reef filled with tropical fish and rays, which you can literally reach out and touch.

PLANNING

GETTING ORIENTED

Thanks to Discovery Cove's daily cap on crowds, it may seem as if you have the park to yourself. Navigating the grounds is simple; signs point to swimming areas, cabanas, or the free-flight aviary—aflutter with

At Discovery Cove's Explorer's Aviary, you can attract exotic birds with fruit or feed. You might even get one (or two) to hop onto your shoulder. Get the camera ready.

exotic birds and accessible via walkway or (even better) by swimming to it beneath a waterfall.

TOURING TIP

In Discovery Cove make the aviary one of your first stops, since the 250-plus birds within will be more active in the morning. Remember that check-in starts at 7:30 am, and the waterways open around 9.

PARK AMENITIES

Guest Services: You can get information on meals, cabanas, lockers, dolphin swims, merchandise, souvenir photos, and other aspects of the park at the **Discovery Cove Check-In Lobby** when you arrive, or at Guest Services (**aka Guest Relations**) just after you enter.

Lost People and Things: Lost kids and items are usually turned over to Discovery Cove attendants, who bring them to the attendants at the Check-In Lobby.

ANIMAL ENCOUNTERS

Trainer for a Day. This opportunity (from $428, but often $500-plus) rivals SeaWorld's Marine Mammal Keeper Experience. General admission includes meals, wet suits, and diving gear; this tour adds a gift bag, waterproof camera, trainer T-shirt, 30-minute dolphin swim, a private photo session with two dolphins, feeding fish in the Grand Reef, a meet-and-greet with tropical birds and small animals, and an almost exclusive (only eight guests in the entire lagoon) interaction that includes a "double-foot push" (two dolphins propel you across the lagoon by the soles of your feet). Ready for more? Shadow a trainer all day: head to the dolphin back area for a private tour and talk to trainers about

how they teach and care for these amazing animals. Like other Discovery Cove admissions, this includes unlimited access to SeaWorld and Aquatica for 14 days. Call ahead to arrange a tour. ☎ *407/351–3600, 877/557–7404* ⊕ *www.discoverycove.com.*

AQUATICA

Just across International Drive from SeaWorld, Aquatica is the 60-acre water park that does a wonderful job angling water-park lovers away from Disney's Typhoon Lagoon and Blizzard Beach and Universal's Wet 'n Wild. And, sure, Aquatica has all the slides you'd expect, but it also has plenty of whimsical SeaWorld touches.

Aquatica takes cues from SeaWorld and Discovery Cove in design and mood. The park also takes its cues from the tropics. Right after you clear the parking lot, you see a tropical pastiche of buildings that may convince you your ship just sailed into the Caribbean. So go with it. Get into a groove, relax, and enjoy yourself. In addition to super-slippery waterslides, there are quiet coves, phenomenally creative kids' play areas, lazy streams, and an atmosphere that is guaranteed to relieve your pre-vacation stress.

Ideally you'll have arrived with some snacks and drinks to combat the fatigue you'll feel after scaling to the tops of all those watery thrill rides. If not, fear not—there are plenty of places to find food and drink.

You should also be toting beach towels, sunscreen, and water shoes. Again, if not, fear not—there are a number of shops and kiosks where you can buy (or rent) all of this stuff and more.

Many of the rides have height restrictions, so if you're traveling with kids, have their heights checked at the Information Center, which you'll see right when you enter the park. Each child will be issued a colored wristband that alerts attendants to which rides are appropriate for him or her (or just look for the height requirement signposted at the entrance to each attraction—and check our reviews). If anyone in your group isn't comfortable in the water, this is also a good place to inquire about the swimming lessons that are offered.

After stashing excess supplies in a locker and generally settling in, it's time to explore. Unless it's peak season, several hours should be enough to visit each ride and attraction once or twice, and will also allow for some downtime, lazing on the beach, or enjoying a leisurely meal.

PLANNING

GETTING ORIENTED

Initially, you might find it hard to get your bearings amid the towering slides, Caribbean palms, winding sidewalks, and the seemingly random layout of restaurants, rides, slides, and facilities. And there are no paper maps, only posted diagrams throughout the park. But in reality, the park is fairly easy to navigate—its layout forms a simple circle. The services (restaurants, changing rooms, shops) form a core around which the attractions are situated.

At the entrance, turn right and you'll be at the premier attraction, Dolphin Plunge, but after that you may want to do an about-face and head straight to the shores of the beach at Cutback Cove. This way, you can set up a base and then work your way to other attractions around the circle while remaining conveniently close to meals at Waterstone Grill and the Banana Beach Cookout.

TOURING TIPS

Be aware of the sun. Avoid sunburn by reapplying sunscreen (they suggest SPF 30) often—even waterproof sunblock washes off. For even more sun protection, rent a standard cabana (about $60) or go all out and splurge on the "ultimate cabana" for eight, which includes an all-day locker, bottled water, towels, and discount coupons for merchandise.

Be aware of your feet. Wear sandals or water shoes (or even socks) to protect your feet from hot sand, sidewalks, and rough pool surfaces. At the major thrill rides, a "sneaker keeper" offers a place to stash your footwear while you experience the ride.

Buy tickets in advance. Prepurchased tickets get you early entrance, and this head start will enable you to hit the major flume and tube rides more than once.

Commune with nature. You can catch Commerson's dolphins at feeding times; spot macaws on tree limbs; or see small mammals in the Conservation Cabanas, where docents answer questions. A variety of animals are on display around the park.

PARK AMENITIES

Information: The Main Information Center is at the park entrance, just past the ticket kiosks. Also at the entrance are an ATM, telephones, and restrooms. This is where you check out the posted park map and plan your approach. On the walkways outside the information center and leading into the park, attendants are stationed to help you get your bearings and point out where to find strollers and wheelchairs, help you with lost-and-found inquiries, and describe combination-ticket packages.

Lockers: There are three areas with unlimited-access lockers to rent for a day. One is near the splashdown area at Walhalla Wave and HooRoo Run; two others are at the center and far end of the park, where there are also nursing facilities. You pay $15 for a small locker (enough for one backpack) and $30 for a large one (for about two backpacks); there's also a $5 deposit, which is refunded when you leave. The central locker area also rents towels for $4 ($1 of which is refunded upon return).

Lost People and Things: Lost items and people are taken to a small tent called the Concierge Cabana, which is right by the entrance to the beach area.

NORTHEAST
FLORIDA

WELCOME TO NORTHEAST FLORIDA

TOP REASONS TO GO

★ **Get out and play:** Beautiful beaches and a wealth of state and national parks mean swimming, sunbathing, kayaking, fishing, hiking, bird-watching, and camping opportunities are all nearby.

★ **Golfer's paradise:** "Above par" describes the golf scene, from award-winning courses to THE PLAYERS Championship to the World Golf Hall of Fame.

★ **Start your engines:** Few things get racing fans as revved up as tours of Daytona International Speedway, home of the Daytona 500, Coke Zero 400, and Rolex 24 at Daytona.

★ **Be in the now:** Whether you want a yoga retreat or the ultimate in sybaritic pampering, the oceanfront spas at Amelia Island and Ponte Vedra Beach make this region the place to be.

★ **The rest is history:** The nation's oldest city, St. Augustine, is a must-see for anyone interested in history.

1 Jacksonville. With a metro-area population of 1.3 million, Jacksonville has the social and cultural appeal of a big city (think pro sports teams, fine dining, museums, nightlife, and shopping) but the down-to-earth charm of a small town. At Amelia Island/Fernandina Beach, just to the north, you'll find a historic downtown, beautiful beaches, and two superlative resorts: the Omni Amelia Island Plantation Resort and the Ritz-Carlton.

2 St. Augustine. You don't have to be a history buff to enjoy America's oldest city, founded in 1565. Foodies, golfers, art lovers, and beach bums generally find plenty to do here, too.

3 Daytona Beach and Inland Towns. The Daytona 500, Bike Week, and spring break put it on the map, but places like New Smyrna Beach, the Ocala National Forest, and Ocala are popular with vacationing families, too. Gainesville is home to the University of Florida and its Gators.

4 The Space Coast. This area includes Canaveral National Seashore; the Kennedy Space Center; Cocoa, offering quiet appeal; and Cocoa Beach, the ultimate surf and bodyboard destination.

GETTING ORIENTED

13

Northeast Florida has historic port cities like Amelia Island/Fernandina Beach and St. Augustine and inland towns like Micanopy and Gainesville, as well as the urban hub of Jacksonville. About two hours south of Jacksonville, on Interstate 95, Titusville is the entry point for the Kennedy Space Center. It marks the northern perimeter of the Space Coast, which includes Cocoa and Melbourne. If you take U.S. 1, it lengthens the trip, but the scenery makes up for the inconvenience. Route A1A/Atlantic Avenue is the main road on all the barrier islands. In many places on A1A, you can see the area's beautiful beaches from your car window.

Kingsland
St. Marys
Fernandina Beach
Callahan • Amelia Island
Fort George
Jacksonville
Atlantic Beach
Neptune Beach
Jacksonville Beach
Ponte Vedra Beach
South Ponte VedraBeach
Vilano Beach
Green Cove prings
St. Augustine 2
ANASTASIA ISLAND
ostwick
Crescent Beach
Palatka
Summer Haven
Crescent Lake
Palm Coast
Flager Beach
Bunnell
Ormond Beach
Lake George
Astor
Daytona Beach 3
South Daytona
Port Orange
Ocala National Forest
De Land
New Smyrna Beach
Eustis
Sanford
ATLANTIC OCEAN
Oviedo
Apopka
Winter Park
Titusville
Orlando
John F. Kennedy Space Center
CAPE CANAVERAL
Kissimmee
Cocoa
Cape Canaveral
Cocoa Beach 4
Satellite Beach
Holopaw
Indialantic
Melbourne
Floridana Beach
Kenansville
Sebastian

0   20 mi
0   20 km

Updated by
Steve Master

For many travelers, Florida is about fantasy, thanks in no small part to Central Florida's make-believe kingdoms. But the northeastern part of the state—you could call it "authentic Florida"—has its own allure, with unspoiled beaches and rivers, historic small towns, and urban arts and culture.

Northeastern Florida's beaches have wide, shell-strewn expanses of soft sand and breakers just the right height for kids to jump. Thanks to the temperate climate and waters warmed by the Gulf Stream, these beaches are a year-round playground—when it's too cold to swim, you can still enjoy surf-fishing or just strolling the shoreline looking for shells and sharks' teeth.

Sun and surf aren't the only reasons to explore northeastern Florida, though. There's historic St. Augustine and its horse-drawn carriages, Daytona and its classic spring-break flavor, and the Space Coast and its sense of discovery. Along the way is an array of little towns—from Fernandina and its shrimp fleets to Micanopy and its antiques stores—that invite quiet exploration.

There's city life in the northeast, too. In the last decade or so, Jacksonville has revitalized its institutions and infrastructure. And with the revitalization has come an arts renaissance—from virtuoso productions in the theaters of the Times-Union Center for the Performing Arts to world-class exhibits in the Museum of Contemporary Art.

So, even if the ultimate reason for your Florida sojourn is Mickey and his friends, there's no reason to miss the northeast. Indeed, you'll find some authentic benefits—among them, a dearth of crowds and lines and an abundance of southern hospitality, plus good value for the money.

PLANNING

WHEN TO GO
It's not 90°F and sunny here every day. In winter the weather is fair, averaging in the low 50s in Jacksonville and low 60s in Cocoa Beach, but the temperature sometimes dips below freezing for a day or two.

Summer temperatures hover around 90°F, but the humidity makes it seem hotter, and late-afternoon thunderstorms are frequent. April and May are good months to visit, because the ocean is beginning to warm up and the beaches aren't yet packed. Fall is usually pleasant, too.

GETTING HERE AND AROUND

AIR TRAVEL

Jacksonville International Airport (JAX) is the region's air hub. A welcome center with information on local attractions, including St. Augustine and Amelia Island, is on the ground floor at the foot of the escalator near baggage claim. It's open daily 9 am–10 pm.

Daytona Beach International (DAB) and Gainesville Regional (GNV) are smaller operations with fewer flights; that said, they may be more convenient in certain travel situations.

Although Orlando isn't part of the area, visitors to northeastern Florida often choose to arrive at Orlando International Airport (MCO), because cheaper flights are usually available. Driving east from Orlando on toll-road 528 (aka the Beachline Expressway) brings you to Cocoa Beach in about an hour. To reach Daytona from Orlando, take Interstate 4 or the Beachline Expressway to Interstate 95 and drive north for an hour or so.

CAR TRAVEL

East–west traffic travels the northern part of the state on Interstate 10, a cross-country highway stretching from Jacksonville, Florida, to Santa Monica, California. Farther south, Interstate 4 connects Florida's west and east coasts. Signs on Interstate 4 designate it an east–west route, but actually the road rambles northeast from Tampa to Orlando, then heads north–northeast to Daytona. Two interstates head north–south on Florida's peninsula: Interstate 95 on the east coast and Interstate 75 on the west.

If you want to drive as close to the Atlantic as possible, choose Route A1A, but accept the fact that it will add considerably to your drive time. It runs along the barrier islands, changing its name several times along the way.

The Buccaneer Trail, which overlaps part of Route A1A, goes from St. Augustine north to Mayport, through marshlands and beaches, and then finally into Fort Clinch State Park. The extremely scenic Route 13, also known as the William Bartram Trail, runs from Jacksonville to East Palatka along the east side of St. Johns River through tiny hamlets. U.S. 17 travels the west side of the river, passing through Green Cove Springs and Palatka. Route 40 runs east–west through the Ocala National Forest, giving a nonstop view of stately pines and bold wildlife.

HOTELS

For the busy seasons—during summer in and around Jacksonville and during summer and holiday weekends all over Florida—reserve well ahead for top properties. Jacksonville's beach hotels fill up quickly for PGA's THE PLAYERS Championship in mid-May. Daytona Beach presents similar problems during the Daytona 500 (late February), Bike Week (late February–early March), spring break (March), and the Coke Zero 400 (early July).

St. Augustine stays busy all year. In fall rates are low and availability is high, but it's also hurricane season. Although the area hasn't been hit directly since 1964, it's possible for threatening storms to disrupt plans.

Hotel reviews have been shortened. For full information, visit Fodors.com.

RESTAURANTS

The ocean, St. Johns River, and numerous lakes and smaller rivers teem with fish, and so, naturally, seafood dominates local menus. Northeast Florida also has fine-dining restaurants, and its ethnic eateries include some excellent Middle Eastern places. And then there are the barbecue joints—more of them than you can shake a hickory chip at.

WHAT IT COSTS				
	$	$$	$$$	$$$$
RESTAURANTS	under $16	$16–$20	$21–$30	over $30
HOTELS	under $201	$201–$300	$301–$400	over $400

Restaurant prices are the average cost of a main course at dinner or, if dinner is not served, at lunch. Hotel prices are the lowest cost of a standard double room in high season.

TOURS

TourTime, Inc. This company offers custom group and individual motor-coach tours of Jacksonville, Amelia Island, Jekyll Island, and St. Augustine, as well as river cruises and trips to Silver Springs, Kennedy Space Center, Orlando, Okefenokee Swamp, and Savannah. Advance reservations are required. ☎ 904/282–8500 ⊕ *www.tourtimeinc.com.*

JACKSONVILLE

399 miles north of Miami, on I-95.

Jacksonville is an underrated vacation spot. It offers appealing downtown riverside areas, handsome residential neighborhoods, a thriving arts scene, and, for football fans, the NFL's Jaguars and the NCAA Gator Bowl.

Although the city has become the largest in area of the continental United States (841 square miles), its Old South flavor remains, especially in the Riverside/Avondale historic district. Here moss-draped oak trees frame prairie-style bungalows and Tudor Revival mansions, and palm trees, Spanish bayonet, and azaleas populate the landscape.

GETTING HERE AND AROUND

The main airport for the region is Jacksonville International Airport. Free shuttles run from the terminal to all parking lots (except the garage) around the clock, and transportation service into the city is available from numerous companies in vehicles that range from taxis to vans to elegant limousines. Check beforehand on prices, which vary widely, and on which credit cards are accepted. The average cost per person from airport to downtown is $35 to $45; it's $45 to $55 for trips to the beaches. The larger companies usually operate 24/7, but the smaller (and often less expensive ones) may be by appointment only.

Connecting the north and south banks of the St. Johns River, the Jacksonville Water Taxi runs between several locations, including Crowne Plaza Jacksonville Riverfront and Jacksonville Landing. The one-way trip takes about five minutes. During football season the water taxi also makes trips to EverBank Field on game days and for special events. The water taxi runs Sunday through Thursday, 11 to 9, and Friday and Saturday from 11 to 11 (except during rain or other bad weather), with special hours on game days and for special events. One-way fare is $3; special-event fare is $5.

Jacksonville Transportation Authority buses and shuttles serve the city and its beaches. The city also operates a small monorail system that links the convention center and a few downtown areas to several other stations across the river on the Southbank and San Marco. It is free and runs weekdays from 6 am to 9 pm and Saturday and Sunday during special events only.

Airport Jacksonville International Airport (*JAX*). ☏ *904/741–4902* ⊕ *www. flyjax.com.*

Airport Transfers Carey Jacksonville ☏ *904/221–5466.*

Taxis Gator City Taxi ☏ *904/355–8294.* **Jacksonville Transportation Authority** (*JTA*). ☏ *904/630–3100* ⊕ *www.jtafla.com.* **Jacksonville Water Taxi** ☏ *904/834–4011* ⊕ *www.jaxwatertaxi.com.* **Yellow Cab–Jacksonville** ☏ *904/999–9999.*

VISITOR INFORMATION

Contact Visit Jacksonville ☏ *904/798–9111, 800/733–2668* ⊕ *www. visitjacksonville.com.*

EXPLORING

Jacksonville was settled along both sides of the twisting St. Johns River, and a number of attractions are on or near its banks. Both sides of the river, which is spanned by myriad bridges, have downtown areas and waterfront complexes of shops, restaurants, parks, and museums.

You can reach some attractions by water taxi or Skyway Express monorail system—scenic alternatives to driving back and forth across the bridges. That said, a car is generally necessary.

In addition to the visitor information center at the airport, there's one at the Jacksonville Landing marketplace and another in Jacksonville Beach at the Beaches Historical Museum (✉ *425 Beach Blvd.*) that is open Tuesday through Saturday 10–4:30 and Sunday noon–4.

TOP ATTRACTIONS

Cummer Museum of Art & Gardens. The Wark Collection of early 18th-century Meissen porcelain is just one reason to visit this former riverfront estate, which includes 13 permanent galleries with more than 5,500 items spanning more than 8,000 years, and 3 acres of riverfront gardens reflecting northeast Florida's blooming seasons and indigenous

Rainbox lorikeet might pop by and say hello while you're touring the Jacksonville Zoo.

varieties. Art Connections allows kids to experience art through hands-on, interactive exhibits. The Thomas H. Jacobsen Gallery of American Art focuses on works by American artists, including Max Weber, N. C. Wyeth, and Paul Manship. A new sculptor garden and outdoor plaza opened in 2013. ✉ *829 Riverside Ave., Riverside* ☎ *904/356-6857* ⊕ *www.cummer.org* ✎ *$10 (free Tues. 4–9)* ⊙ *Tues. 10–9, Wed.–Fri. 10–4, Sat. 10–5, Sun. noon–4.*

Jacksonville Landing. During the week, this riverfront market caters to locals and tourists alike, with specialty shops, full-service restaurants—including a sushi bar, Italian bistro, and a steak house—and an internationally flavored food court. The Landing hosts more than 250 weekend events each year, ranging from the good clean fun of the Lighted Boat Parade and Christmas Tree Lighting to the just plain obnoxious Florida/Georgia game after-party, as well as live music (usually of the local cover-band variety) in the courtyard. ✉ *2 W. Independent Dr., Downtown* ☎ *904/353-1188* ⊕ *www.jacksonvillelanding. com* ✎ *Free* ⊙ *Mon.–Thurs. 10–8, Fri.–Sat. 10–9, Sun. noon–5:30; restaurant hrs vary.*

FAMILY
Fodor's Choice
★

Jacksonville Zoo and Gardens. What's new at the zoo? Plenty. Not only has it seen the births of a rare Amur leopard and a greater kudu calf, but it now offers Tuxedo Coast, a controlled environment for a group of Magellanic penguins, and Land of the Tiger, a 2.5-acre attraction featuring Sumatran and Malayan tigers. Among the other highlights are rare waterfowl and the African Reptile Building, which showcases some of the world's most venomous snakes. Wild Florida is a 2½-acre area with black bears, bald eagles, white-tailed deer, and other animals native to Florida. The African Loop has elephants, white rhinos, and two highly endangered leopards, among other species of African birds and mammals. The Range of the Jaguar, winner of the Association of Zoos and Aquariums Exhibit of the Year, includes 4 acres of exotic big cats as well as 20 other species of animals. Play Park contains a Splash Ground, forest play area, two mazes, and discovery building; Stingray Bay has a 17,000-gallon pool where visitors can pet and feed the mysterious creatures; and Butterfly Hollow is a flower-filled "fairy world" open seasonally. Parking is free. ✉ *370 Zoo Pkwy., off Heckscher Dr. E* ☎ *904/757–4463* ⊕ *www.jaxzoo.org* 🎟 *$15.95* ☉ *Daily 9–5.*

Fodor's Choice
★
Museum of Contemporary Art Jacksonville. In this loftlike downtown building, the former headquarters of the Western Union Telegraph Company, a permanent collection of 20th-century art shares space with traveling exhibitions. The museum encompasses five galleries and ArtExplorium, a highly interactive educational exhibit for kids, as well as a funky gift shop and Café Nola, open for lunch on weekdays and for dinner on Thursday. MOCA Jacksonville also hosts film series and workshops throughout the year, and packs a big art-wallop into a relatively small 14,000 square feet. A once-a-month Art Walk is free to all. ✉ *Hemming Plaza, 333 N. Laura St.* ☎ *904/366–6911* ⊕ *www.mocajacksonville.org* 🎟 *$8* ☉ *Tues., Wed., Fri., and Sat. 11–5, Thurs. 11–9, Sun. noon–5; Art Walk 1st Wed. of month 5–9.*

WORTH NOTING

Anheuser-Busch Jacksonville Brewery Tour. Guided tours give a behind-the-scenes look at how barley, malt, rice, hops, and water form the King of Beers. Or you can hightail it through the self-guided tour and head straight to the free beer tastings (if you're 21 years or older, that is). ✉ *111 Busch Dr.* ☎ *904/696–8373* ⊕ *www.budweisertours.com* 🎟 *Free* ☉ *Mon.–Sat. 10–4; guided tours, call for availability.*

Karpeles Manuscript Library Museum. File this one under "hidden treasure," given that even many residents have never visited Karpeles. That's too bad, because this 1921 neoclassical building on the outskirts of downtown has displayed some priceless documents: the original draft of the Bill of Rights, the Emancipation Proclamation signed by Abraham Lincoln, handwritten manuscripts of Edgar Allan Poe and Charles Dickens, and musical scores by Beethoven and Mozart. Manuscript exhibits change every four months or so and coincide with bi-monthly art exhibits. Also on the premises is an antique-book library, with volumes dating from the late 1800s. ✉ *101 W. 1st St.* ☎ *904/356–2992* ⊕ *www.karpeles.com* 🎟 *Free* ☉ *Tues.–Fri. 10–3, Sat. 10–4.*

FAMILY
Museum of Science & History. Also known locally as MOSH, this museum is home to the Bryan-Gooding Planetarium. As a next-generation planetarium, it can project 3-D laser shows that accompany the ever-popular weekend Cosmic Concerts. For those taking in the planetarium shows, the resolution is significantly sharper than that of the biggest 1080p hi-def TV currently on the market. Whether you're a kid taking in Sesame Street's *One World, One Sky,* or an adult star-gazing in the *Skies over Jacksonville* tour of the night sky, the experience is awesome. MOSH also has a wide variety of interactive exhibits and programs

Jacksonville

that include JEA Science Theater, where you can participate in live science experiments; JEA PowerPlay: Understanding our Energy Choices, where you can energize the future city of MOSHtopia as you learn about alternative energy resources and the science of energy; the Florida Naturalist's Center, where you can interact with northeast Florida wildlife; and the Currents of Time, where you'll navigate 12,000 years of Northeast Florida history, from the region's earliest Native American settlers to modern day events. Nationally acclaimed traveling exhibits are featured along with signature exhibits on regional history. ⊠ *1025 Museum Circle* ☎ *904/396–6674* ⊕ *www.themosh.org* ⊠ *Museum $10, museum and planetarium $15, Cosmic Concerts $5; Fri. $5 all admissions* ⊗ *Mon.–Thurs. 10–5, Fri. 10–8, Sat. 10–6, Sun. noon–5.*

WHERE TO EAT

$$$ ✕ **bb's.** Sleek yet cozy, this hip bistro is as popular with corporate types
AMERICAN   looking to close a deal as it is with young lovebirds seemingly on the verge of popping the question (though shouting the question might be more appropriate, considering how loud the dining room can get on weekends). The concrete floors and a stainless-steel wine bar provide an interesting backdrop for comfort-food-inspired entrées and daily specials that might include char-grilled beef tenderloin, pan-seared diver

scallops with housemade parsnip pierogies, or linguini with Catalan-style black-angus meatballs. On the lighter side, grilled pizzas, sandwiches, and salads, especially the warm goat-cheese salad, are favorites. Although a wait is common, you can pass the time sizing up the display of diet-destroying desserts. Ⓢ *Average main: $21* ✉ *1019 Hendricks Ave., San Marco* ☎ *904/306–0100* ⊕ *www.bbsrestaurant.com* ◷ *Closed Sun.*

THE BIGGEST CITY?

It's nearly impossible to visit Jacksonville without hearing locals brag that their city is the largest in the United States. In fact, the River City's 841 square miles pale in comparison to the actual title holder: 4,710-square-mile Sitka, Alaska. More accurately, Jacksonville is the largest city in the continental United States.

13

$$$ ✕ **Biscottis.** The local artwork on
AMERICAN the redbrick walls is a mild distraction from the jovial yuppies, soccer moms, and metrosexuals—all of whom are among the crowd jockeying for tables in this midsize restaurant. Elbows almost touch, but no one seems to mind. The constantly rotating dinner menu offers the unexpected: wild mushroom ravioli with a broth of corn, leek, and dried apricot; or curry-grilled swordfish with cucumber-fig bordelaise sauce. Be sure to sample from Biscottis's decadent desserts (courtesy of "b the bakery"). Brunch, a local favorite, is served until 3 on weekends. Ⓢ *Average main: $21* ✉ *3556 St. Johns Ave.* ☎ *904/387–2060* ⊕ *www. biscottis.net* ◿ *Reservations not accepted.*

$$$ ✕ **Bistro Aix.** When a Jacksonville restaurant can make Angelenos feel
ECLECTIC like they haven't left home, that's saying a lot. With its slick leather booths, 1940s brickwork, olive drapes, and intricate marbled globes, Bistro Aix (pronounced "X") is just that place. Regulars can't get enough of the creamy onion soup or escargot appetizers, prosciutto and goat cheese salad, or entrées like oak-grilled fish Aixoise, steak frites, or mushroom and fontina wood-fired pizza. Most items (salads included) come in full or lighter-appetite portions, and you'll definitely want to save room for dessert. Aix's in-house pastry team ensures no sweet tooth leaves unsatisfied, with offerings such as profiteroles (mini cream puffs filled with vanilla ice cream and topped with chocolate and caramel sauce) and warm chocolate banana walnut bread pudding. Call for preferred seating. Ⓢ *Average main: $25* ✉ *1440 San Marco Blvd., San Marco* ☎ *904/398–1949* ⊕ *www.bistrox.com* ◿ *Reservations essential* ◷ *No lunch weekends.*

$$ ✕ **Clark's Fish Camp.** It's out of the way, but every mile will be forgot-
SEAFOOD ten once you step inside this former bait shop overlooking Julington Creek. Clark's has more than 160 appetizers and entrées, including the usual—shrimp, catfish, and oysters—and the unusual—ostrich, rattlesnake, and kangaroo. In keeping with the more bizarre entrées is the décor, best described as early American taxidermy: hundreds of stuffed critters gaze upon you in the main dining room, and preserved lions, gazelles, baboons, even a rhino, keep a watchful eye in the bar. One person's kitschy may be another's creepy. Be careful not to park illegally—tickets are expensive. Ⓢ *Average main: $20* ✉ *12903 Hood*

Landing Rd., Mandarin ☎ *904/268–3474* ⊕ *www.clarksfishcamp.com* ⊗ *No lunch weekdays.*

$ ✕**European Street Café.** Wicker baskets and lofty shelves brimming with
AMERICAN   European confections and groceries like Toblerone and Nutella fill practically every inch of space not occupied by café tables. The menu is similarly overloaded, with nearly 100 deli sandwiches and salads. Notable are raspberry-almond chicken salad and the Blue Max, with pastrami, corned beef, Swiss cheese, sauerkraut, hot mustard, and blue-cheese dressing. This quirky spot is favored by area professionals looking for a quick lunch, as well as the under-forty set doing 23-ounce curls with one of the restaurant's 20-plus beers on tap (plus more than 100 in bottles). The San Marco and Beach Boulevard locations offer live music several nights a week. $ *Average main: $9* ⊠ *2753 Park St.* ☎ *904/384–9999* ⊕ *www.europeanstreet.com* ⌂ *Reservations not accepted* ⊠ *1704 San Marco Blvd., San Marco* ☎ *904/398–9500* ⊠ *5500 Beach Blvd., Southside* ☎ *904/398–1717.*

$$$ ✕**Matthew's.** No one can accuse chef Matthew Medure of resting on
ECLECTIC   his laurels. Widely praised for culinary creativity and dazzling pre-
Fodor'sChoice   sentation at his signature San Marco restaurant, Medure has transi-
★   tioned from French-influenced to Italian-inspired cuisine, complete with a pasta course and a create-your-own cheese and charcuterie spread "for the table." While the regulars (and there are many) are sure to miss their favorites, new menu items such as house-made rigatoni with mussels, local shrimp, shiitake mushrooms, and peas; air-dried duck breast with duck confit, stuffed squash bottoms and roasted apricots; and veal-and-shortrib meatballs (an appetizer) are more than worthy substitutes. Complement your meal with one of 450 wines (topping out at more than $1,000 per bottle). And for those worried that Medure has done away with his famous warm soufflé, relax. Some things are sacred. $ *Average main: $25* ⊠ *2107 Hendricks Ave., San Marco* ☎ *904/396–9922* ⊕ *www.matthewsrestaurant.com* ⌂ *Reservations essential* ⊗ *Closed Sun. No lunch.*

WHERE TO STAY

$ ▦ **Hotel Indigo.** Despite the name, don't expect this Southside hotel to be
HOTEL   moody and blue: it's bright, bold, and visually different from any other Jacksonville property. **Pros:** reasonable rates; free Wi-Fi throughout; 24-hour business center; loaner PC. **Cons:** wood floors can be noisy; convenient to business parks but not downtown and its sights; lots of traffic at rush hour. $ *Rooms from: $94* ⊠ *9840 Tapestry Park Circle, Southside* ☎ *904/996–7199, 877/270–1392* ⊕ *www.hotelindigo.com* ⤳ *96 rooms, 4 suites* ⦿*No meals.*

$ ▦ **Hyatt Regency Jacksonville Riverfront.** It doesn't get much more con-
HOTEL   venient than this 19-story, downtown, waterfront hotel within walking distance of Jacksonville Landing, EverBank Field, Florida Theatre, Times-Union Center, corporate office towers, and the county courthouse. **Pros:** riverfront location; rooftop pool and hot tub; free Wi-Fi in public areas; 24-hour gym and business center. **Cons:** not all rooms are riverfront; slow valet service; no minibars; fee for in-room Wi-Fi. $ *Rooms*

from: $159 ✉ *225 E. Coastline Dr., Downtown* ☎ *904/588–1234* ⊕ *www.jacksonville.hyatt.com* ⤷ *963 rooms, 21 suites* ¶◯¶ *No meals.*

$ 🏨 **Omni Jacksonville Hotel.** Jacksonville's most luxurious and glamorous
HOTEL hotel last underwent a major update in 2011—right down to new flat-
FAMILY screen HD TVs in its chic, spacious guest rooms—with more work in
2012. **Pros:** four-diamond on-site restaurant; downtown location; large
rooms; rooftop pool; great kids' offerings. **Cons:** congested valet area;
restaurant pricey; can be chaotic when there's a show at the Times-
Union Center across the street. $ *Rooms from: $179* ✉ *245 Water St.*
☎ *904/355–6664, 800/843–6664* ⊕ *www.omnijacksonville.com* ⤷ *354*
rooms, 4 two-bedroom suites ¶◯¶ *No meals.*

$ 🏨 **Riverdale Inn.** In the early 1900s, Jacksonville's wealthiest residents
B&B/INN built mansions along Riverside Avenue—dubbed the Row—and the
three-story Riverdale Inn is only one of two such homes remaining.
Pros: close to area restaurants and shops; private baths. **Cons:** small
rooms; limited parking; strict cancellation policy. $ *Rooms from:*
$150 ✉ *1521 Riverside Ave., Riverside* ☎ *904/354–5080* ⊕ *www.*
riverdaleinn.com ⤷ *10 rooms, 3 suites* ¶◯¶ *Breakfast.*

$ 🏨 **St. Johns House.** You can enjoy the grace and elegance of the past and
B&B/INN all the modern amenities at this surprisingly inexpensive B&B. **Pros:**
historic home; beautiful Riverside location near parks, restaurants,
and river; elegant antique furnishings. **Cons:** only open six months a
year. $ *Rooms from: $99* ✉ *1718 Osceola St., Riverside* ☎ *904/384–*
3724 ⊕ *www.stjohnshouse.com* ⤷ *3 rooms* ☾ *Closed Mar. June–Oct.*
¶◯¶ *Breakfast.*

NIGHTLIFE

Brewster's Megaplex. Live music abounds at this entertainment complex featuring four night clubs—Edge Concert Hall, Lava Lounge, The
Pit, and Roc Bar. ✉ *845 University Blvd. N* ☎ *904/223–9850* ⊕ *www.*
brewstersmegaplex.com.

Club TSI Discotheque. Billing itself as the city's premier underground
venue, TSI hosts local and national indie performers like Break Science, Derek Van Scoten, Archnemesis, and Elliot Lipp. ✉ *333 E. Bay*
St., Downtown ⊕ *www.clubtsi.com.*

Comedy Zone. The area's premier comedy club is inside the Ramada
Inn Mandarin. ✉ *3130 Hartley Rd.* ☎ *904/292–4242* ⊕ *www.*
comedyzone.com.

The Grotto. Vinophiles, rejoice! Here you can enjoy more than 70 wines
by the glass. ✉ *2012 San Marco Blvd., San Marco* ☎ *904/398–0726*
⊕ *www.grottowine.com.*

Harmonious Monks. This place claims to have "the world's most talented waitstaff." They certainly might be the most energetic, performing
throughout the night and encouraging customers to dance on the bar.
✉ *10550 Old St. Augustine Rd., Mandarin* ☎ *904/880–3040* ⊕ *www.*
harmoniousmonks.net.

Jack Rabbits. It's the place to catch the latest and greatest indie bands and
budding rock stars. ✉ *1528 Hendricks Ave.* ☎ *904/398–7496.*

DID YOU KNOW?

The Jacksonville Jazz Festival takes place in a five-block area centered on Laura Street in the heart of downtown. Festival highlights include performances by renowned jazz musicians, and jazz piano and youth jazz talent competitions.

Latitude 30. This place could be called a pleasure complex, offering "luxury bowling," a video-game arcade, billiards, casual restaurants, sports bars, and "cinegrille" movie-screening rooms, all at one 50,000-square-foot facility. ✉ *10370 Phillips Hwy., Southside* ☎ *904/365–5555* ⊕ *www.latthirty.com* 🏷 *Admission free; bowling $4–$5 game; others vary* ◷ *Sun.–Wed. 11 am–midnight, Thurs.–Sat. 11 am–2 am.*

Mark's. This self-proclaimed "neighborhood lounge with a dash of dance club style" attracts beautiful people to a fairly classy bar with a small dance floor and a popular happy hour. ✉ *315 E. Bay St., Downtown* ☎ *904/355–5099* ⊕ *www.marksjax.com.*

Metro. It's more than just a gay bar: it's like eight gay bars rolled into one, including a piano bar, dance club, lounge, and drag-show cabaret. ✉ *859 Willow Branch Ave., Riverside* ☎ *904/388–8719* ⊕ *www. metrojax.com.*

13

SHOPPING

SHOPPING AREAS

Five Points. This small but funky shopping district less than a mile southwest of downtown has new and vintage-clothing boutiques, shoe stores, and antiques shops. It also has a handful of eateries and bars, not to mention some of the city's most colorful characters. ✉ *Intersection of Park, Margaret, and Lomax sts., Riverside* ⊕ *www.5pointsjax.com.*

MALLS

San Marco Square. Dozens of interesting apparel, home, and jewelry stores and restaurants are in 1920s Mediterranean revival–style buildings. ✉ *San Marco and Atlantic blvds., San Marco* ⊕ *www. mysanmarco.com.*

The Shoppes of Avondale. The highlights here include upscale clothing and accessories boutiques, art galleries, home-furnishings shops, a chocolatier, and trendy restaurants. ✉ *St. Johns Ave. between Talbot Ave. and Dancy St., Avondale* ⊕ *www.shoppesofavondale.com.*

St. Johns Town Center. Some of the shops at this huge outdoor "lifestyle center" aren't found anywhere else in northeast Florida, including Anthropologie, Apple, Lucky Brand Jeans, and Sephora, as well as the Cheesecake Factory, P. F. Chang's China Bistro, and Maggiano's Little Italy. ✉ *4663 River City Dr., Southside* ☎ *904/998–7156* ⊕ *www. stjohnstowncenter.com.*

MARKETS

Riverside Arts Market. The unique location—under the Fuller-Warren Bridge, a block from the Cummer Museum of Art & Gardens—might be as much of a draw as the merchandise. Regardless, since its first Saturday in 2009, RAM has attracted larger and larger crowds of singles, couples, families, and their dogs. They all come to shop for locally created art and crafts, sample food from vendors that include some excellent area restaurants, and check out street performers or the live music shows on the riverfront stage.

Quality is high in every aspect—artists and vendors all go through a fairly rigorous application/audition process—and what there is to see or hear or eat varies from week to week. Sometimes there's also a farmers' market, with licensed farmers and growers selling everything from just-laid eggs and local honey to salad greens that were still in the earth the day before. Inside the Children's Activity Center tent, several organizations offer free educational arts activities to kids.

Because it's sheltered by the bridge, RAM goes on rain or shine. Free parking is available at EverBank and other adjacent businesses, and a "bike valet" service encourages people to travel on two wheels. ✉ 715 Riverside Ave., Riverside 🕿 904/349–2449 ⊕ www.riversideartsmarket. com ✉ Free ⊘ Mar.–Dec., Sat. 10–4.

SPORTS AND THE OUTDOORS

BASEBALL

FAMILY **Jacksonville Suns.** The AA minor-league affiliate of the Miami Marlins plays at the $34-million Baseball Grounds of Jacksonville. The Suns were Southern League champions in 2009 and 2010. ✉ Baseball Grounds of Jacksonville, 301 A. Philip Randolph Blvd., Downtown 🕿 904/358–2846 ⊕ www.jaxsuns.com.

BOAT TOURS

River Cruises. Relaxing lunch and dinner-dancing cruises and private sightseeing charters are offered aboard this operation's Annabelle Lee and Lady St. Johns paddleboats; schedules and prices vary. ✉ 1501 Riverplace Blvd., Southbank 🕿 904/306–2200 ⊕ www.jaxrivercruises.com.

JACKSONVILLE AREA

JACKSONVILLE BEACHES

Atlantic Beach is 20 miles east of Jacksonville, on U.S. 90 (Beach Blvd.).

Perhaps because the Intracoastal Waterway isn't all that wide where it separates the mainland from the beaches, people here aren't likely to think of themselves as "islanders." But they are, indeed, living on a barrier island, functioning with its own rhythms and led by its own elected officials. And, although there's only one island, there are four beaches with beach communities, each with its own mayor and city officials, tax base, and local legislation. They are, from north to south, Atlantic Beach, Neptune Beach, Jacksonville Beach, and Ponte Vedra Beach. Technically, Ponte Vedra, which is home to the PGA Tour, is just across the border between Duval County and St. Johns County, but the four communities are all considered "Jacksonville's beaches."

Oceanfront properties here can be worth millions, but a few blocks from the beach, things become more affordable. That means kids grow up and go to school together, and then stick around to live in and govern the towns together. Instead of pouring money into attractions designed to rake in tourism dollars, locals are likely to concentrate on stodgy subjects like good schools and parks. Because of this, some visitors might find area beaches to be a little calmer and quieter than they expected.

But there's a real sense of community—and a laid-back pace. You might want to embrace it all. In fact, many vacationers like the easy pace so much that they decide to make the area their permanent home.

EXPLORING

FAMILY **Adventure Landing and Shipwreck Island Water Park.** With go-karts, two miniature-golf courses, laser tag, batting cages, kiddie rides, and an arcade, Adventure Landing is more like an old-time boardwalk than a high-tech amusement park. But when the closest theme park is more than two hours away, you make do. The largest family-entertainment center in northeast Florida also encompasses Shipwreck Island Water Park, which features a lazy river for tubing, a 500,000-gallon wave pool, and four extreme slides—the Rage, HydroHalfpipe, Eye of the Storm, and Undertow. ⊠ *1944 Beach Blvd., Jacksonville Beach* ☎ *904/246–4386* ⊕ *www.adventurelanding.com* 🖃 *Adventure Landing free (fees for rides and games), Shipwreck Island $27.99* ⊘ *Adventure Landing: Sun.–Thurs. 10–10, Fri. and Sat. 10–midnight. Shipwreck Island: late Mar.–late Sept., hrs vary.*

Beaches Historical Museum. This museum has exhibits about the history of the beaches communities, the St. Johns River, the fishing and shrimping industry, and the area's settlers. Its gift shop is a good place to find Florida souvenirs of every variety, from tasteful to pure kitsch. Admission

Beaches make great places to drop a line and see if the fish are biting.

here includes a guided tour of the adjacent Pablo Historical Park with its 1911 steam locomotive, railroad foreman's house, and the Mayport Depot. ✉ *381 Beach Blvd., Jacksonville Beach* ☏ *904/241-5657* ⊕ *www.beachesmuseum.org* ✉ *$5* ⊗ *Tues.–Sat. 10–4.*

J. Johnson Gallery. Built by photographer and art collector Jennifer Johnson, this stunning Mediterranean building just a block from the ocean in Jacksonville Beach hosts contemporary art exhibits you'd expect to find only in the nation's largest and most sophisticated cities. Exhibits like "Multiplicity" and "Contemporary Complexities" include work by emerging artists as well as established names. The gallery also presents experimental and project work. ✉ *177 4th Ave. N, Jacksonville Beach* ☏ *904/435-3200* ⊕ *www.jjohnsongallery.com* ✉ *Free* ⊗ *Tues.– Fri. 10–5, Sat. 1–5.*

BEACHES

Atlantic Beach. If you're looking for sun-soaked relaxation, head for Atlantic Beach, where you can sink your feet into its white, sugary sands or catch some waves in the warm surf. You can even rejuvenate with some prime pampering at the One Ocean resort's spa. Hotel guests and those wandering in from the beach can both use this luxurious oceanfront hotel's beach rental services, which offer umbrellas, lounge chairs, body boards, kayaks, and surfboards for a fee. Beachgoers with canine companions are welcome at Atlantic Beach during the day and evening as long as the dog is leashed. Atlantic Beach and next-door Neptune Beach share the trendy Town Center, which has lots of tempting dining and shopping within a block of the beach. **Amenities:** food and drink; lifeguards (seasonal); showers; water sports. **Best for:** sunrise;

surfing; swimming; walking. ☒ *Beach Ave. between 18th and 20th sts., Dewees Ave. between 1st and 16th sts., Ahern St. and Atlantic Blvd., Atlantic Beach.*

Jacksonville Beach. Enjoy the waves at one of Jacksonville's busier beaches, which stretches along the coast for 4.1 miles. A boardwalk and a bevy of beachfront restaurants and shops are also draws, so expect moderate crowds during spring and summer school breaks. The municipal Seawalk Pavilion hosts outdoor movies, concerts, and festivals, and the 2-acre Oceanfront Park (1st Street South, between 5th Avenue South and 6th Avenue South) has a small playground, volleyball court, and picnic areas. Anglers can fish without a license from the wheelchair-accessible 1,320-foot fishing pier ($4, $1 spectator; daily 6 am–10 pm), which also has free fish-cleaning stations, a bait-and-tackle shop, and free parking. The historic Casa Marina Hotel, which opened its doors here in 1925, has a popular Sunday brunch. **Amenities:** food and drink; lifeguards (seasonal); parking (no fee); showers; toilets. **Best for:** partiers; sunrise; surfing; swimming. ☒ *1st St. between Seagate and S. 16th aves., Jacksonville Beach* ☎ *904/241–1515 for fishing pier* ☺ *Daily 8–5.*

Neptune Beach. Nestled between Atlantic and Jacksonville beaches, this is a great destination for those wishing to combine a day at the beach with other activities. The beach, with its light-beige sand, is a great family spot, as it tends to be less crowded than Jacksonville Beach. And because Neptune and Atlantic beaches share Atlantic Avenue's Town Center, with its assortment of restaurants, galleries, stores, and boutiques, beachgoers can escape the sun when they're ready for great food, shopping, and live entertainment. Slider's Bar and Grill is a local favorite, or stop in Pete's Bar for a beer so you can say you were there. **Amenities:** food and drink; lifeguards (seasonal); showers. **Best for:** sunrise; swimming; walking. ☒ *Strand St. between Atlantic Blvd. and Gaillardia Pl., Oak St. and Rose Pl., North St. and 20th Ave., Neptune Beach.*

Ponte Vedra Beach. Although this upscale coastal community 18 miles southeast of downtown Jacksonville is primarily known for its golf courses and swanky homes, it also has beautiful beaches that attract wealthy residents, as well as a number of resorts: the Ponte Vedra Inn & Club, The Lodge & Club, and the Sawgrass Marriott. Public beach access for nonresort guests is minimal in most areas because of heavily restricted parking. However, thanks to its free public parking, Mickler's Landing, south of most residences, is the most popular beach access point. It's also famous for producing sharks' teeth. **Amenities:** lifeguards (seasonal); parking (no fee); showers; toilets. **Best for:** solitude; sunrise; walking. ☒ *East of intersection of A1A S and Ponte Vedra Blvd., Ponte Vedra Beach.*

WHERE TO EAT

ATLANTIC BEACH

$ ✗ **Al's Pizza.** The beach locations of this popular restaurant defy all expectations of a neighborhood pizza joint. Bright colors and geometric patterns accent the dining room, which manages to look retro (soda-fountain chairs) and modern (steel columns) at the same time. The

ITALIAN

menu is fairly predictable; there's pizza by the slice and by the pie, plus standbys like lasagna and ravioli. The clientele, too, is typical beachgoer, with lots of young surfer dudes and dudettes and sunburned families, as well as a fair representation of older Atlantic Beach couples, who come for the food more than the scene. Service is quick, but finding parking at peak hours can be a problem. Check behind the restaurant as well as out front. There's also a branch in Ponte Vedra Beach. $ *Average main: $10* ⊠ *303 Atlantic Blvd.* ☎ *904/249–0002* ⊕ *www.alspizza.com* ⌂ *Reservations not accepted.*

$$$

SEAFOOD

✕ **The Fish Company Restaurant and Oyster Bar.** If you want fresh fish, this is the place. Owners Bill and Ann Pinner have lots of street cred: among other area culinary achievements, they helped establish the Ragtime Tavern as an institution. Options include perfectly blended crab cakes, oh-so-lightly fried Mayport shrimp (never a heavy batter that might cover up the flavor), seafood salads, and delicious sides. And there are offerings for meat lovers in the family, too. There's also a raw bar, outdoor seating, and a full bar with happy-hour prices 2–7 Monday through Saturday and all day on Sunday. $ *Average main: $22* ⊠ *725-12 Atlantic Blvd.* ☎ *904/246–0123* ⊕ *www.thefishcojax.com* ⌂ *Reservations not accepted.*

$$$

ECLECTIC

Fodor's Choice

★

✕ **Ocean 60.** Despite being a block from the Atlantic Ocean, this lively restaurant–wine bar–martini room has gone largely undiscovered by visitors, who might think fine dining and flip-flops don't mix. Those who do stumble upon it, however, are pleasantly surprised to find that a casual aura befits Ocean 60's eclectic seasonal menu, with signature items like salmon gratin (seared salmon topped with a parmesan and tomato gratin served over butternut squash risotto), rosemary grilled New York strip, and wild mushroom crepes. Things are anything but laid-back on Thursday, Friday, and Saturday nights, however, thanks to live music and potent cocktails. $ *Average main: $22* ⊠ *60 Ocean Blvd.* ☎ *904/247–0060* ⊕ *www.ocean60.com* ⊘ *Closed Sun.*

$$

CAJUN

✕ **Ragtime Tavern & Seafood Grill.** A New Orleans theme prevails at this loud place that attracts a lively crowd ranging in age from 21 to midlife-crisis. Grouper oscar (seared and topped with crabmeat, asparagus, and béarnaise sauce) and Ragtime shrimp (deep-fried fresh shrimp rolled in coconut) are specialties (as are microbrews made on the premises), or try a po'boy sandwich or fish sizzled on the grill. Brunch is served Sunday only. $ *Average main: $18* ⊠ *207 Atlantic Blvd.* ☎ *904/241–7877* ⊕ *www.ragtimetavern.com.*

JACKSONVILLE BEACH

$

AMERICAN

FAMILY

✕ **Ellen's Kitchen.** Once upon a time, Ellen's Kitchen was a breakfast-and-lunch place inside Silver's Drug Store at First and Atlantic, a landmark from time immemorial. Silver's is no more, and Ellen's long ago relocated to a shopping strip, but it's still an institution, and probably will be for generations. It's also a great place to bring the kids, thanks to the kid-friendly menu, very reasonable prices, and relaxed atmosphere. Sure, you can get your eggs over-easy and your bacon crisp, but if you want to be mistaken for a local, ask for a Hippie or a Surfer, two poached-egg-on-English-muffin creations that are far better than anybody's eggs Benedict. If it's hollandaise sauce you're craving, though, the crab cake Benedict is brunch perfection. Breakfast is served until the doors close at 2 pm, but the lunch menu is also fairly extensive. Don't expect too much chat from your server at "rush hour" on weekend mornings—everyone's usually working at warp speed. Regardless, though, the staffers do their best to please, no matter how crowded. Ⓢ*Average main: $9* ⊠ *1824 3rd St. S* ☎ *904/246–1572* ⌂ *Reservations not accepted* ☉ *No dinner.*

$ ✕ **European Street Café.** This colorful, quirky, family-owned eatery has a

AMERICAN menu with an ambitious list of sandwiches, salads, and soups; an overflowing gourmet-food section; a mind-boggling beer list; and cookies big enough to knock someone unconscious. Thirsty locals belly up to the impressive, hand-carved bar for monthly beer tastings and daily happy hour (2–7 pm). More mature crowds prefer to sip their zinfandel in the bustling dining room. Ⓢ *Average main: $9* ⊠ *992 Beach Blvd.* ☎ *904/249–3001* ⊕ *www.europeanstreet.com* ⌂ *Reservations not accepted.*

$ ✕ **Mojo Kitchen BBQ Pit & Blues Bar.** True barbecue aficionados know

BARBECUE that the country's really divided into four territories: North Carolina, Memphis, Kansas City, and Texas, each renowned for its own barbecue style. Owner Todd Lineberry did some serious research into each region before deciding his restaurants would honor all four traditions—along with some original flavor. In addition to great barbecue, you'll find Deep South sides like cheese grits and fried green tomatoes as well as some truly delicious sweet tea and banana pudding. The beach location brings both young and old, blue collar and no-collar (plus pukashells), all ready to chow down on generous portions, with a backdrop of bright, bold-color walls and edgy portraits of blues royalty. Mojo's appreciation for the blues doesn't end with the interior design. There's good recorded blues at all times, and on occasion, some great live blues as well. Ⓢ *Average main: $14* ⊠ *1500 Beach Blvd.* ☎ *904/247–6636* ⊕ *www.mojobbq.com* ⌂ *Reservations not accepted.*

PONTE VEDRA BEACH

$$$ ✕ **Aqua Grill.** Come hungry. That might be the best advice for visitors to

ECLECTIC this highly acclaimed restaurant. The menu covers all the bases—steaks, pasta, fork-tender pork shank—but eclectic preparation of fresh seafood is what Aqua Grill does best. The constantly rotating menu might include crispy red snapper Bangkok or pan-seared local triggerfish with pork belly confit and fried leeks. Portions are huge, so share an appetizer. The most popular is the fried green tomatoes with bacon, goat cheese, Thai-chili remoulade and Cajun shrimp salad. The restaurant is a popular spot for locals celebrating special occasions, but it's more casual than formal and has a charming lakeside patio dining area surrounded by waterfalls. Kids—and adults—love observing the colorful saltwater aquarium in the dining room. There's a lively bar scene, with sports showing on seven HD TVs. The full menu is available at the bar, but there's bar food, too, such as the chef's El Presidente wings. Ⓢ *Average main: $25* ⊠ *950 Sawgrass Village* ☎ *904/285–3017* ⊕ *www. aquagrill.net.*

WHERE TO STAY
ATLANTIC BEACH

$$
RESORT
FAMILY

One Ocean. Atlantic Beach's only high-rise oceanfront hotel captures the serenity of the ocean through a color palette of sea-foam green, sand, and sky blue, and reflective materials like glass and marble. **Pros:** exceptional service; walking distance to restaurants and shops; all rooms have floor-to-ceiling ocean views; 24-hour room service. **Cons:** tiny bathrooms; no self-parking on property; resort fee. $ *Rooms from: $209* ⊠ *1 Ocean Blvd.* ☎ *904/249–7402* ⊕ *www.oneoceanresort.com* ⤳ *190 rooms, 3 suites* ⦿ *No meals.*

NEPTUNE BEACH

$
HOTEL

Sea Horse Oceanfront Inn. This bright-pink-and-aqua 1950s-era throwback caters to budget-minded guests seeking an ultracasual, laid-back vibe. **Pros:** beach access with private walk-over; popular bar on site; walking distance to restaurants and shops; free breakfast baskets available at front desk. **Cons:** no frills; no room service. $ *Rooms from: $129* ⊠ *120 Atlantic Blvd.* ☎ *904/246–2175, 800/881–2330* ⊕ *www.jacksonvilleoceanfronthotel.com* ⤳ *37 rooms, 1 suite.* ⦿ *Breakfast.*

PONTE VEDRA BEACH

$$$
RESORT
FAMILY
Fodor's Choice
★

The Lodge & Club. This Mediterranean-revival oceanfront resort— with its white-stucco exterior and Spanish roof tiles—is luxury lodging at its best. **Pros:** high-end accommodations; excellent service; private beach. **Cons:** most recreation facilities are a few blocks away at Ponte Vedra Inn & Club; gratuity charge automatically added to bill nightly. $ *Rooms from: $319* ⊠ *607 Ponte Vedra Blvd.* ☎ *904/273–9500, 800/243–4304* ⊕ *www.pontevedra.com* ⤳ *42 rooms, 24 suites* ⦿ *No meals.*

$$$
RESORT
FAMILY
Fodor's Choice
★

Ponte Vedra Inn & Club. Considered northeast Florida's premier resort for decades, this 1928 landmark continues to wow guests with its stellar service and large guest rooms housed in white-brick, Spanish-style buildings lining the beach. **Pros:** accommodating, friendly staff; private beach; adults-only pool. **Cons:** charge for umbrellas and chaises on the beach; crowded pool at some times of year. $ *Rooms from: $322* ⊠ *200 Ponte Vedra Blvd.* ☎ *904/285–1111, 800/234–7842* ⊕ *www.pontevedra.com* ⤳ *217 rooms, 33 suites* ⦿ *No meals.*

$$
RESORT
FAMILY
Fodor's Choice
★

Sawgrass Marriott Golf Resort & Spa. Here you can laze about in the highly regarded spa or by one of four swimming pools, get active out on a golf course, or fish in a freshwater lake or pond. **Pros:** championship golf courses; beautiful surroundings; readily available shuttle; efficient staff. **Cons:** beach not within walking distance; no free parking; fee for in-room Wi-Fi. $ *Rooms from: $219* ⊠ *1000 PGA Tour Blvd.* ☎ *904/285–7777, 800/457–4653* ⊕ *www.sawgrassmarriott.com* ⤳ *489 rooms, 21 suites* ⦿ *No meals.*

NIGHTLIFE
JACKSONVILLE BEACH

Free Bird Live. This medium-size (it holds 700) concert venue owned by Judy Van Zant-Jenness (widow of Lynyrd Skynyrd's Ronnie Van Zant) draws some complaints about its standing-room-only tickets and slow bar service. But it also gets raves for the chance to see great blues, rock, funk, rockabilly, and jam bands in an intimate setting.

✉ *200 1st St. N* ☎ *904/246–2473* ⊕ *www.freebirdlive.com* ✉ *Admission varies by show.*

Lynch's Irish Pub. Hoist a pint o' Guinness and enjoy live local music. ✉ *514 N. 1st St.* ☎ *904/249–5181* ⊕ *www.lynchsirishpub.com.*

Penthouse Lounge. If you'd rather gawk at sports stars in person than on the tube, head to this oceanfront spot, where local NFL and PGA stars have been known to congregate. ✉ *Casa Marina Hotel, 691 N. 1st St.* ☎ *904/270–0025* ⊕ *www.casamarinahotel.com.*

13

Sneakers Sports Grille. With nearly 80 TVs and an impressive menu (by sports-bar standards anyway), this is the go-to sports bar at the beach. ✉ *111 Beach Blvd.* ☎ *904/482–1000* ⊕ *www.sneakerssportsgrille.com.*

NEPTUNE BEACH

Pete's Bar. The oldest bar in the Jacksonville area is also notable for the cheapest drinks, cheapest pool tables, and most colorful clientele. Authors like John Grisham and James W. Hall have written about this hole-in-the-wall, probably because it's across from The BookMark, a great independent bookstore where writers love to give readings. ✉ *117 1st St.* ☎ *904/249–9158.*

SHOPPING

The BookMark. It may be small in size, but this bookshop is big in prestige. Thanks to its knowledgeable owners, many famous authors love this place and always include it on their publicity tours. Once you've bought books here a time or two, the staff will be able to recommend ones you'll like with amazing accuracy. ✉ *220 1st St., Neptune Beach* ☎ *904/241–9026* ⊕ *www.bookmarkbeach.com* ☉ *Mon.–Wed. 10–7, Thurs.–Sat. 10–8, Sun. 11–5.*

SPORTS AND THE OUTDOORS

BIKING

Champion Cycling. You can rent beach cruisers by the hour or the day. ✉ *1303 N. 3rd St., Jacksonville Beach* ☎ *904/241–0900* ⊕ *www.championcycling.net.*

Ponte Vedra Bicycles. This outfitter includes free bike maps with your rental. ✉ *250 Solana Rd., Ponte Vedra Beach* ☎ *904/273–0199.*

GOLF

Every May millions of golf fans watch golf's most elite competitors vie for the prestige of winning THE PLAYERS Championship. The event—considered by many to be the sport's "unofficial fifth major"—takes place each year at the Tournament Players Club (TPC) Sawgrass in Ponte Vedra Beach, 20 miles southeast of Jacksonville. Designed and built for major tournament golf, TPC has an elevated seating area that gives more than 40,000 fans a great view of the action. And while you're in the area, be sure to visit the World Golf Hall of Fame a few miles down the road in St. Augustine.

Tournament Players Club Sawgrass. There are two courses here: the Stadium Course (with its world-renowned Island Green), which hosts THE PLAYERS Championship each year, and the Pete Dye–designed Valley Course. In conjunction with the Sawgrass Marriott, TPC offers packages like the Tour Player Experience, which not only provides access to the TPC's player area, but also gives you a caddie who wears your name on the back of his golf shirt just like he does when caddying for the pros. How cool is that? The Dye's Valley Course, though not as lauded as the Stadium Course, has hosted its share of major golf events, such as the Senior Players Championship and the NFL Golf Classic. Though challenging, it has wider fairways and more expansive greens than the Stadium Course, which was designed to test the world's best players. If you want to play a round of golf and aren't staying at the Marriott, check out the Resort Day Passes. ⌧ *110 Championship Way, Ponte Vedra Beach* ☎ *904/273–3235, 800/457–4653* ⊕ *www.tpc.com/ sawgrass* ⌦ *Stadium Course $400 for 18 holes; Dye's Valley Course $195 for 18 holes* ⯅ *Stadium Course: 18 holes. 7215 yards. par 72. Dye's Valley Course: 18 holes. 6864 yards. par 72.*

MAYPORT

20 miles northeast of downtown Jacksonville, on Rte. A1A/105.

Dating back more than 300 years, this is one of the oldest fishing communities in the United States. It has several excellent and very casual seafood restaurants and a commercial shrimp-boat fleet. It's also home to one of the largest naval facilities in the country, Naval Station Mayport.

GETTING HERE AND AROUND

St. Johns River Ferry. The arrival of the *Jean Ribault* ferry in 1948 made everyday life here more convenient—and fun. The 153-vessel continues to delight passengers young and old as they embark on the 10-minute cruise across the river between Mayport and Fort George Island. The cost is $5 per motorcycle, $6 per car. Pedestrians enjoy the ride for just $1 each way. Call for departure times. ☎ *904/241–9969* ⊕ *www. stjohnsriverferry.com.*

EXPLORING

Fodor's Choice
★

Kathryn Abbey Hanna Park. This 450-acre oceanfront park just north of Atlantic Beach is beloved by surfers, swimmers, campers, hikers, and especially bikers, who regularly hit the many off-road bike trails from novice right up to those named Grunt and Misery. You can rent canoes, kayaks, or paddleboats to go out on the 60-acre freshwater lake. Younger kids delight in the lakefront playground and a water park with fountains and squirting hoses. There are restrooms, picnic areas, and grills throughout, and from Memorial Day to Labor Day lifeguards supervise all water activities. ⌧ *500 Wonderwood Dr.* ☎ *904/249–4700* ⌦ *$3 per vehicle* ⊙ *Apr.–Oct., daily 8–8; Nov.–Mar., daily 8–6.*

FORT GEORGE ISLAND

25 miles northeast of Jacksonville, on Rte. A1A/105.

One of the oldest inhabited areas of Florida, Fort George Island is lush with foliage, natural vegetation, and wildlife. A 4-mile nature and bike trail meanders across the island, revealing shell mounds dating as far back as 5,000 years.

EXPLORING

Kingsley Plantation. Built in 1792 by Zephaniah Kingsley, an eccentric slave trader, this is the oldest remaining cotton plantation in the state. The ruins of 23 tabby (a concretelike mixture of sand and crushed shells) slave houses, a barn, and the modest Kingsley home are open to the public via self-guided tours and reachable by bridge. ⊠ *Rte. A1A–Heckscher Dr.* ☎ *904/251–3537* ⊕ *www.nps.gov/timu* ☒ *Free* ☼ *Daily 9–5. Plantation house weekends only; call ahead for reservations.*

Talbot Island State Parks. These parks, including Big and Little Talbot islands, have 17 miles of gorgeous beaches, sand dunes, and golden marshes that hum with birds and native waterfowl. Come to picnic, fish, swim, snorkel, or camp. Little Talbot Island, one of the few undeveloped barrier islands in Florida, has river otters, marsh rabbits, raccoons, alligators, and gopher tortoises. Canoe and kayak rentals are available, and the north area is considered the best surfing spot in northeast Florida. A 4-mile nature trail winds across Little Talbot, and there are several smaller trails on Big Talbot. ⊠ *12157 Heckscher Dr.* ☎ *904/251–2320* ⊕ *www.floridastateparks.org/littletalbotisland* ☒ *$5 per vehicle, up to 8 people; $4 single occupants, motorcyclists; $2 pedestrians, bicyclists* ☼ *Daily 8–sunset.*

AMELIA ISLAND AND FERNANDINA BEACH

35 miles northeast of Jacksonville.

At the northeasternmost reach of Florida, Amelia Island has beautiful beaches with enormous sand dunes along its eastern flank, a state park with a Civil War fort, sophisticated restaurants, interesting shops, and accommodations that range from bed-and-breakfasts to luxury resorts. The town of Fernandina Beach is on the island's northern end; a century ago casinos and brothels thrived here, but those are gone. Today there's little reminder of the town's wild days, though one event comes close: the Isle of Eight Flags Shrimp Festival, held during the first weekend of May.

TOURS

Amelia River Cruises and Charters. Narrated tours glide near the area's marshes, rivers, and wilderness beaches. ⊠ *1 N. Front St.* ☎ *904/261–9972, 877/264–9972* ⊕ *www.ameliarivercruises.com.*

VISITOR INFORMATION

Contact Amelia Island Convention and Visitors Bureau ☎ *904/277–0717* ⊕ *www.ameliaisland.com.*

EXPLORING

Amelia Island Historic District. This district in Fernandina Beach has more than 50 blocks of buildings listed on the National Register of Historic Places; 450 ornate structures built before 1927 offer some of the nation's finest examples of Queen Anne, Victorian, and Italianate homes. Many date from the haven's mid-19th-century glory days. Pick up a self-guided-tour map at the Chamber of Commerce, in the old train depot—once a stopping point on the first cross-state railroad—and take your time exploring the quaint shops, restaurants, and boutiques that populate the district, especially along Centre Street.

FAMILY
Fodor'sChoice
★

Fort Clinch State Park. One of the country's best-preserved and most complete 19th-century brick forts, Fort Clinch was built to discourage further British intrusion after the War of 1812 and was occupied in 1863 by the Confederacy; a year later it was retaken by the North. During the Spanish-American War it was reactivated for a brief time, but no battles were ever fought on its grounds (which explains why it's so well preserved). Wander through restored buildings, including furnished barracks, a kitchen, and a repair shop. Living-history reenactments of Civil War garrison life are scheduled throughout the year. The 1,086-acre park surrounding the fort has full-facility camping, nature trails, carriage rides, a swimming beach, and surf and pier fishing. Nature buffs enjoy the variety of flora and fauna, especially since Fort Clinch is the only state park in northeast Florida designated by the Florida Fish and Wildlife Conservation Commission as a viewing destination for the eastern brown pelican, green sea turtle, and loggerhead sea turtle. ⊠ *2601 Atlantic Ave.* ☎ *904/277-7274* ⊕ *www.floridastateparks.org/fortclinch* ⌲ *$6 per vehicle, up to 8 people; $4 single-occupancy vehicles, motorcycles; $2 pedestrians, bicyclists* ⊙ *Daily 8–sunset; fort 9-5.*

BEACHES

There are a number of places on Amelia Island where driving on the beach is allowed in designated areas, including Seaside Park, Peters Point, Burney Park, and Amelia Island State Park. If you have a four-wheel-drive vehicle (and a lot of beach equipment to haul), you may want to try this. Be warned, though: it's easier to get stuck than you might think, and towing is expensive. You also need to watch the tides carefully if you don't want your car floating out to sea. And unless you're a county resident or disabled, you must buy a permit, which is available at the Nassau County Historic Courthouse (⊠ *416 Centre St., Fernandina Beach* ☎ *904/491–6430*), Hall's Beach Store (⊠ *2012 S. Fletcher Ave., Fernandina Beach* ☎ *904/310–6124*), and several other locations. All city beaches have free admission.

Huguenot Memorial Park. Though it's officially a Jacksonville city park, this popular spot on the northern side of the St. Johns River is usually grouped with Amelia's beaches. Among a handful of places where driving on the beach is permitted, it's unusual in that no special permit is required. Families with lots of beach equipment like the option of parking close to the water, but it takes vigilance to avoid soft sand and incoming tides. The ocean side offers good surfing, body boarding, and surf fishing. On the western side is a shallow, sheltered lagoon that's a favorite with windsurfers, paddleboarders, and parents of small children. The park is also an important stop for migrating birds, so at certain times of the year, some areas are closed to vehicles. **Amenities:** lifeguards (seasonal); parking (no fee); showers; toilets. **Best for:** surfing; swimming; windsurfing. ⊠ *10980 Heckscher Dr.* ☎ *904/251–3335* ⌲ *$1 per person 8–10 am, $3 per car after 10* ⊙ *Apr.–Oct., daily 8–8; Nov.–Mar., daily 8–6.*

WORD OF MOUTH

"On this particular day, the beach was strewn with starfish. They were everywhere. And they were still alive. I took a quick picture and then proceeded to run up and down the beach trying to save every one of them. I hope that I succeeded." —photo by funin-thetub, Fodors.com member

Main Beach. Of all Fernandina Beach access points (there are 40), this is likely to be the most crowded—but also the most fun for kids and teens. Not only are there sand volleyball courts, a beachfront playground, picnic tables, and barbecue grills at the park itself, but there's old-school fun to be had at the adjacent skate park and vintage miniature-golf course, whose concession stand sells cold drinks, ice cream, and snow cones. A casual restaurant and bar are right on the beach. **Amenities:** food and drink; lifeguards (seasonal); parking (no fee); showers; toilets. **Best for:** swimming. ⊠ *Atlantic Ave. and S. Fletcher Ave.*

A BANNER BEACH

Fernandina Beach is also known as the "Isle of Eight Flags," a moniker derived from the fact that it's the only American site to have been under eight different flags (French, Spanish, British, Patriots, Green Cross of Florida, Mexican Revolutionary, National Flag of the Confederacy, and United States). Every May the Isle of Eight Flags Shrimp Festival celebrates another of Fernandina's claims to fame: birthplace of the modern shrimping industry.

Peters Point Beach. At the south end of the island, this beach allows you free access to the same gorgeous sands used by vacationers at the Ritz-Carlton. It has a large parking area, a picnic area, barbecue grills, and three lifeguard towers. **Amenities:** lifeguards (seasonal); parking (no fee); showers; toilets. **Best for:** sunrise; surfing; swimming; walking. ⊠ *1974 S. Fletcher Ave.*

Seaside Park Beach. Like Main Beach to the north and Peters Point to the south, Seaside Park allows limited beach driving if you have a permit, but beware—vehicles here frequently get stuck and have to be towed. There are several picnic tables and dune walkovers to the beach. It's a great place to fish or to ride bikes at low tide. Bikes and other beach equipment can be rented at Hall's Beach Store (⊠ *2021 S. Fletcher Ave.*). Also nearby, Sliders Seaside Grill is a venerable oceanfront restaurant where you can enjoy food and drinks inside or at the tiki bar overlooking the beach, often with live music. **Amenities:** food and drink; lifeguards (seasonal); parking (no fee); showers; toilets. **Best for:** surfing; swimming; walking. ⊠ *Sadler Rd. and S. Fletcher Ave.*

Talbot Islands State Parks Beaches. A few miles south of Fernandina Beach, the Talbot Islands State Parks system consists of seven parks, three of which have beach settings. All of the oceanfront parks have picnic areas and a small admission charge but free parking. **Little Talbot** is popular for swimming and beachcombing. Sand dollars are often found at the far north end. **Big Talbot,** with its Boneyard Beach of wind-twisted trees, is not recommended for swimming but is a photographer's paradise. **Amelia Island State Park** is best known for letting you horseback ride on the beach as well as for the adjacent George Crady fishing pier. Kayak and canoe tours can be booked through the parks system's vendor, Kayak Amelia. **Amenities:** lifeguards (seasonal); parking (no fee); showers; toilets. **Best for:** solitude; sunrise; swimming; walking. ⊠ *Rte. A1A, south of Fernandina Beach* ⊕ *www.floridastateparks.org* ✉ *Little*

Talbot $5 per vehicle; Big Talbot $3 per vehicle for The Bluffs picnic area; Amelia Island $2 per person.

WHERE TO EAT

$$
ECLECTIC

✕**Kelley's Courtyard Café.** Few places embody the charm of the historic district like this casual courtyard restaurant, where locals and tourists alike gather as much for the garden setting as the eclectic cuisine. There's an indoor seating area, too, but most prefer the umbrella- and palm-shaded courtyard tables surrounding a soothing brick fountain. The rotating dinner menu might include sweet potato soup, seafood enchiladas, or blue cheese–crusted filet mignon. Lunch offers a tasty respite from shopping, with refreshing salads, wraps, and signature sandwiches such as a BLT with spinach and goat cheese. Wines by the glass (mostly $6) are reasonable for a tourist town. And if there's such a thing as a destination dessert, Granny Mutt's blueberry squares with vanilla ice cream would certainly qualify. $ *Average main: $19* ✉ *19 S. 3rd St.* ☎ *904/432–8213* ⊕ *www.kelleyscourtyardcafe.com* ⊗ *Closed Sun.*

$$$
ECLECTIC

✕**PLAE.** Short for People Laughing and Eating, PLAE has an extensive wine list and an upscale but eclectic menu with French, Asian and Mediterranean influences. Adventurous diners love to order the Chef's Plate, not knowing exactly what delights the chef has prepared for the evening until they appear at the table. PLAE's atmosphere varies greatly depending on your seating choice. Indoors has a sleek, contemporary ambience with intimate, high-backed booths. Dining on the outdoor patio provides a view over the beautiful natural surroundings of the adjacent golf course. Although PLAE's location at the Spa & Shops at Omni Amelia Island Plantation makes it a favorite with Plantation visitors, it's an independently owned restaurant (the only one on property) and equally popular with locals. $ *Average main: $29* ✉ *Omni Amelia Island Plantation, 80 Amelia Village Circle* ☎ *904/277–2132* ⌨ *Reservations essential* ⊗ *Closed Sun.*

$$$$
ECLECTIC
Fodor's Choice
★

✕**Salt.** The Ritz-Carlton restaurant's inventive cuisine highlights seasonal ingredients that might include Florida snapper with Calypso beans and clams, or Darling Downs Wagyu ribeye cooked on a wood-burning grill. The wine list has more than 300 bottles (24 by the glass), service is nothing short of impeccable, and there's a view of the Atlantic from every table. For a unique dining experience, reserve A Seat in the Kitchen, a private dining room within the kitchen, where you can watch the chefs at work and enjoy a personalized five-course meal. To learn the secrets of Salt's cuisine, consider taking one of the two-day Salt cooking school sessions. They've proven so popular, the Ritz-Carlton has expanded the schedule to several a year. Long pants and collared shirts are recommended (for dining, we mean; cooking students get their own Ritz-Carlton aprons). $ *Average main: $46* ✉ *The Ritz-Carlton, Amelia Island, 4750 Amelia Island Pkwy.* ☎ *904/277–1000* ⊕ *www.ritzcarlton. com* ⌨ *Reservations essential* ⊗ *Closed Mon. No lunch.*

$$
SEAFOOD
FAMILY

✕**Sliders Seaside Grill.** After the condo-building boom of the last decade or so, not many oceanfront restaurants remain, but thankfully this is one of them. Indeed there aren't many places where you can enjoy an ocean view like this—a surf break offshore makes it a good place to watch surfers do their thing—and even fewer with a moderately priced menu that allows for an affordable family outing. These are some of the reasons Sliders has evolved into a local favorite, but another is its award-winning Florida seafood dishes, including shrimp and grits, and Apalachicola oysters in season. Sliders also has three bars and live music every night, including the region's favorite reggae band, Pili Pili, on Wednesday. $ *Average main: $18* ⊠ *1998 S. Fletcher Ave.* ☎ *904/277–6652* ⊕ *www.slidersseaside.com.*

$$$$
SEAFOOD
✕ **Verandah Restaurant.** Although it's at the Amelia Island Plantation, this family-friendly restaurant is open to nonresort guests, many of whom drive in from Jacksonville. The dining room has a casual vibe, with plush, roomy booths and tables overlooking the tennis facility, but the menu is all business. Start with the crab cake—nearly 100% blue crab—or deviled eggs topped with pecanwood-smoked bacon. Fresh seafood entrées are a highlight, including the Florida fish muddle (fresh catch with Mayport shrimp and clams) and line-caught pink snapper with Cohen Farm's pecans and local strawberries. And if you luck out and find she-crab soup on the menu (it's seasonal and not always available), order yourself the biggest bowl or bucket they have. $ *Average main: $33* ⊠ *Omni Amelia Island Plantation, 39 Beach Lagoon, Amelia Island* ☎ *904/261–6161* ⊕ *www.omnihotels.com* ⌔ *Reservations essential* ⊗ *Closed Tues. No lunch.*

WHERE TO STAY

$
HOTEL
FAMILY
🛏 **Amelia Hotel at the Beach.** Across the street from the beach, this mid-size inn is not only convenient but an economical and family-friendly alternative to the area's luxury resorts and romantic and kid-unfriendly B&Bs. **Pros:** complimentary breakfast; free Wi-Fi; comfy beds. **Cons:** small pool; not all rooms have balconies; needs updating. $ *Rooms from: $139* ⊠ *1997 S. Fletcher Ave.* ☎ *904/206–5600, 877/263–5428* ⊕ *www.ameliahotel.com* ⌔ *86 rooms* ⫶◯⫶ *Breakfast.*

$$
B&B/INN
🛏 **Elizabeth Pointe Lodge.** Guests at this oceanfront inn, built to resemble an 1890s sea-captain's house, can't say enough about the impeccable personal service, legendary breakfasts, and enjoyable evening social hour. **Pros:** beachfront location; hospitable staff; 24-hour desk attendant; convenient to recreation possibilities. **Cons:** pricey for a B&B; not all rooms are oceanfront; must reserve well in advance in high season. $ *Rooms from: $270* ⊠ *98 S. Fletcher Ave.* ☎ *904/277–4851, 800/772–3359* ⊕ *www.elizabethpointelodge.com* ⌔ *24 rooms, 1 2-bedroom cottage* ⫶◯⫶ *Breakfast.*

$
B&B/INN
🛏 **Florida House Inn.** Under new ownership, the recently restored inn has a rambling two-story clapboard main building, more than 150 years old, that is full of character. **Pros:** breakfast included; outstanding service; walk to restaurants and shops; free Wi-Fi; bridal suite. **Cons:** bar can be noisy; rooms are small. $ *Rooms from: $110* ⊠ *22 S. 3rd St.* ☎ *904/491–3322, 800/258–3301* ⊕ *www.floridahouseinn.com* ⌔ *16 rooms* ⫶◯⫶ *Breakfast.*

$$
RESORT
FAMILY
Fodor'sChoice
★
🛏 **Omni Amelia Island Plantation Resort and the Villas of Amelia Island Plantation.** Rebranded, and "reimagined" by the Omni hotel chain, this resort was transformed by an $85-million renovation and expansion in 2013, including 155 new oceanfront rooms and stunning oceanfront Beach Club pools. **Pros:** family-friendly; variety of outdoor activities;

shuttle service throughout property; kids' programs; "green" practices; largest poolscape in Northern Florida. **Cons:** some facilities require a golf cart or shuttle ride; quality of villas inconsistent; 11 am checkout. $ *Rooms from: $263* ⊠ *6800 1st Coast Hwy.* ☎ *904/261–6161, 800/843–6664* ⊕ *www.omnihotels.com* ⤺ *404 rooms, more than 300 1-, 2-, and 3-bedroom villas* ◉ *No meals.*

$ 🛏 **Residence Inn Amelia Island.** Discerning, value-driven travelers love this
HOTEL newer all-suites property for its great location, modern design features, and family-friendly amenities. **Pros:** proximity to beach and restaurants; complimentary breakfast; free Wi-Fi; bike rental on property; pet friendly (restrictions). **Cons:** no on-site restaurant or room service; historic district not within walking distance. $ *Rooms from: $145* ⊠ *2301 Sadler Rd.* ☎ *904/277–2440* ⊕ *www.residenceinnameliaisland. com* ⤺ *133 suites* ◉ *Breakfast.*

$$$ 🛏 **The Ritz-Carlton, Amelia Island.** Guests know what to expect from the
RESORT Ritz—elegance, superb comfort, excellent service—and the Amelia Island
FAMILY location is no exception. **Pros:** fine-dining restaurant; world-class spa;
Fodor'sChoice private beach access; accommodating staff; great programs, activities, and
★ amenities for kids, teens, and families. **Cons:** fee for Wi-Fi; no self-parking ($20 per day valet); a drive to sites and other restaurants. $ *Rooms from: $399* ⊠ *4750 Amelia Island Pkwy.* ☎ *904/277–1100* ⊕ *www.ritzcarlton. com/ameliaisland* ⤺ *446 rooms, 50 suites* ◉ *No meals.*

NIGHTLIFE

Falcon's Nest. The 7,000-square-foot, aviation-themed club in Amelia Island Plantation has a dance floor and outdoor deck. ⊠ *Omni Amelia Island Plantation, 39 Beach Lagoon* ☎ *904/261–6161* ⊕ *www. omnihotels.com/ameliaisland.*

Palace Saloon. Florida's oldest continuously operating bar entertained the Rockefellers and Carnegies at the turn of the 20th century but now caters to common folk. It also operates a package store, the only one in downtown Fernandina. ⊠ *117 Centre St.* ☎ *904/491–3332* ⊕ *www. thepalacesaloon.com.*

The Surf Restaurant & Bar. Locals like to congregate on the outdoor deck here for drinks and good old-fashioned bar food (burgers, wings, nachos). The restaurant has an extensive menu. ⊠ *3199 S. Fletcher Ave.* ☎ *904/261–5711* ⊕ *www.thesurfonline.com.*

SHOPPING

Amelia SanJon Gallery. One of a cluster of "Ash and Third" galleries, the Amelia SanJon offers watercolors, acrylic paintings, fused-glass art, custom jewelry, and large-scale, welded sculptures. ⊠ *218-A Ash St.* ☎ *904/491–8040* ⊕ *www.ameliasanjongallery.com.*

Book Loft. Popular for its readings and book signings, this old-fashioned bookstore fits perfectly in an old-fashioned town. In keeping with Fernandina's emphasis on its pirate heritage, the store includes kid-friendly pirate volumes like *The Pirate of Kindergarten* and *Do Pirates Change Diapers?* ⊠ *214 Centre St.* ☎ *904/261–8991* ⊕ *www.facebook.com/ thebookloftamelia.*

Celtic Charm. In addition to the obvious coffee cup with shamrocks and Irish-blessing plaque, this shop carries wonderful clothing—such as colorful and artistic Bill Baber Scottish sweaters—as well as Galway Irish crystal and Donegal Town Hana Hats. ⊠ *310 Centre St.* ☎ *904/277–8009* ⊕ *www.celticcharmamelia.com.*

Fantastic Fudge. Right there in the window, resting in splendor on several marble-topped tables, are huge blocks of fudge just calling your name—enough fudge to put every citizen of the town into a coma—not to mention hand-dipped chocolates, caramel corn, and so on. Indeed, if you hang out at one of the tables in front of this confectionery/ice cream shop, you'll see just about every kind of person imaginable pause by the door, sigh, and give in to temptation. The service is fast and friendly, and the ice cream is excellent, too. ⊠ *218 Centre St.* ☎ *904/277–4801* ⊕ *www.fantasticfudge.com.*

Gallery C. Up a wildly painted staircase, this gallery owned by artist Carol Winner (the "C" in the gallery's name) displays and sells one-of-a-kind semiprecious jewelry and mixed-media creations, as well as stunning paintings of local nature scenes. ⊠ *218-B Ash St.* ☎ *904/583–4676* ⊕ *www.carolwinnerart.com.*

Lindy's Jewelry. For tasteful jewelry that reflects beach life, Lindy's is a good place to shop. Those who collect charms will love the Fernandina Beach and Cumberland Island map charms to commemorate their vacation. ⊠ *202 Centre St.* ☎ *904/277–4880* ⊕ *www.lindysjewelry.com.*

Sea Jade. Inside, it's funny T-shirts and cheap souvenirs; outside, it's fishnet floats and stunning shells in all their natural beauty, heaped up in old-fashioned wooden baskets. Whether you want to buy sand dollars or saltwater taffy, if it's beach-related, there's a good chance you'll find it here. ⊠ *208 Centre St.* ☎ *904/277–2977.*

Slightly Off Centre Gallery & Gifts. Just a block off the main drag, this store sells artistic ceramics as well as vivid photographs, paintings, pottery, and metalwork. ⊠ *218-C Ash St.* ☎ *904/277–1147* ✪ *Closed Tues.*

SPORTS AND THE OUTDOORS
HORSEBACK RIDING
Kelly Seahorse Ranch. At this ranch within the Amelia Island State Park, you can arrange horseback rides on the beach. ⊠ *7500 1st Coast Hwy., Amelia Island* ☎ *904/491–5166* ⊕ *www.kellyranchinc.net* ✪ *Closed Mon.*

KAYAKING
Kayak Amelia. This outfitter takes adventurous types on guided tours of salt marshes and Fort George River and also rents equipment for those looking to create their own adventures. Reservations are required. ⊠ *4 N. 2nd. St.* ☎ *904/251–0016* ⊕ *www.kayakamelia.com.*

ST. AUGUSTINE

35 miles south of Jacksonville, on U.S. 1.

Along the banks of the shining Matanzas River lies St. Augustine, the nation's oldest city. It shows its age with charm, its history revealed in the narrow cobblestone streets, the horse-drawn carriages festooned with flowers, and the coquina bastions of the Spanish fort that guard the bay like sentinels. Founded in 1565 by Spanish explorers, St. Augustine is the site of the fabled Fountain of Youth, but travelers find additional treasures in the Historic District, which was built in the Spanish Renaissance Revival style. Terra-cotta roofs and narrow balconies overhang a wonderful hodgepodge of shops and eateries that can be happily explored for weeks.

St. Augustine also has miles of beaches on Anastasia Island to the east. From the idyllic, unspoiled beaches of Anastasia State Park to the more boisterous St. Augustine Beach, travelers have a full range of options when it comes to enjoying an ocean outing.

13

VISITOR INFORMATION

Centrally located between the south and north ends of St. Augustine's Historic District, the St. Augustine & St. Johns County Visitor Information Center is a smart place to start your day. You can park in the multistoried garage here ($1.25 per hour, $7.50 per day), as well as pick up maps, get information on and advice about attractions and restaurants, and hop aboard the sightseeing trolley.

Contacts St. Augustine, Ponte Vedra & the Beaches Visitors and Convention Bureau ☎ 904/829–1711, 800/653–2489 ⊕ www.floridashistoriccoast. com ⊘ Daily 8:30–5:30. **St. Augustine & St. Johns County Visitor Information Center** ✉ 10 W. Castillo Dr. ☎ 904/825–1000 ⊘ Daily 8:30–5:30.

TOURS

Old Town Trolley Tour. These fully narrated tours ($24) cover more than 100 points of interest and are, perhaps, the best way to take in the Historic District. Your pass is good for three days and, with parking at a premium and meters closely watched, it's nice to be able to park at one of the main stations (free) and get on and off at any of 22 stops throughout town. There are even shuttles to the beach. In the evening a macabre slant is added on the Ghosts and Graveyards Tour ($27), which includes visits to the Old Jail and Lighthouse. ✉ *167 San Marco Blvd.* ☎ *904/829–3800, 888/910–8687* ⊕ *www.trolleytours.com/staugustine.*

EXPLORING

St. Augustine's neighborhoods are fairly compact. Most include a stretch of waterfront—whether ocean, river, or creek—which, along with Mediterranean architectural details like curves, archways, and red-tile roofs gives the city its relaxed semitropical aura. Neighborhoods range from centuries old to mere decades, but all have sights worthy of attention.

It can be confusing to see references to the "Old City," "Old Town," and "Historic District." The Old City, like the Big Apple, refers not to a neighborhood but to the entire city of St. Augustine. Old Town is a small neighborhood, with the Plaza de la Constitución at its northern border, a row of shops and restaurants along King Street, many award-winning B&Bs, and the Oldest House museum toward the south. Old Town is actually within a larger neighborhood, the Historic District, a 144-block area filled with many of the city's most popular attractions,

Built to protect Spain's St. Augustine, the Castillo de San Marcos still stands along the shore.

including museums, parks, restaurants, nightspots, shops, and historic buildings.

St. Augustine's Uptown is filled with the shops, restaurants, and galleries along San Marco Boulevard, as well as museums, parks, and historic structures, all of which attract crowds. The narrow streets and hustle and bustle make for a vibrant atmosphere.

Heading east across the Bridge of Lions, you enter Anastasia Island, much of which is within city limits. In the 1920s, real estate developer D. P. Davis had big plans for a Mediterranean-style development here, but the Florida land boom went bust. Today Davis Shores has a mélange of styles and a casual beach vibe.

TOP ATTRACTIONS

FAMILY

Fodor's Choice

★

Castillo de San Marcos National Monument. The focal point of St. Augustine, this massive and commanding structure was completed by the Spaniards in 1695 (English pirates were handy with a torch back then), and it looks every day of its three centuries. The fort was constructed of coquina, a soft limestone made of broken shells and coral that, unexpectedly, could absorb the impact of British cannonballs. (Unlike solid stone, the softer coquina wouldn't shatter when hit by large munitions.) The fort was also used as a prison during the Revolutionary and Civil wars.

Park rangers provide an introductory narration, after which you're on your own to explore the moat, turrets, and 16-foot-thick walls. Garrison rooms depict the life of the era, and special cannon-firing demonstrations are held several times a day Friday through Sunday year-round. Children 15 and under are admitted free and must be accompanied by an adult. Save the receipt, since admission is valid for seven days. ⊠ *11 S. Castillo Dr.* ☎ *904/829–6506* ⊕ *www.nps.gov/casa* ✍ *$7* ⊙ *Daily 8:45–5:15, last ticket sold at 5.*

Cathedral Basilica of St. Augustine. This cathedral has the country's oldest written parish records, dating from 1594. The circa-1797 structure underwent changes after a fire in 1887 as well as restoration work in the mid 1960s. If you're around for the holidays, stop in for Christmas Eve's gorgeous midnight mass, conducted amid banks of flickering candles that reflect off gilded walls. Regular Sunday masses are held throughout the year at 7, 9, 11, and 5. ⊠ *38 Cathedral Pl.* ☎ *904/824–2806* ⊕ *www. thefirstparish.org* ✍ *Donations welcome* ⊙ *Daily 7–4:45.*

FAMILY **Colonial Quarter.** After being closed to the general public for yearlong renovations, the Colonial Quarter, formerly known as the Spanish Quarter, is now an even more appealing attraction. The 2-acre living history museum gives visitors a vivid sense of life in 16th-, 17th-, and 18th-century St. Augustine. The De Mesa–Sanchez House dates from the 1740s and the other buildings—including a soldier's home, print shop, blacksmith's shop, and gunsmith—are replicas, mostly built on the original foundations. Costumed re-enactors help make the history come alive. New additions to the complex include a 35-foot watchtower from which you have a panoramic view of the city. You can also dig for replica artifacts, create a leather medallion, take part in a musket drill, watch a 16th-century ship being built, and more. A family-style show, *The Colonial Crew Revue,* requires a separate admission. The complex also includes two restaurants: the Taberna del Caballo and the Bull and Crown British Publick House. ⊠ *37 St. George St.* ☎ *904/825–6830* ⊕ *www.colonialquarter.com* ✍ *$12.99, Colonial Crew Revue $29.99* ⊙ *Daily 9–8.*

Dow Museum of Historic Houses. An entire city block of historic homes is not a typical gift from a philanthropist, but that's what Kenneth Worcester Dow gave today's visitors to St. Augustine. Dow was not a St. Augustine native, but when he arrived in the 1930s, he bought the Prince Murat House, one of the city's oldest surviving colonial structures. (Murat was a nephew of Napoleon Bonaparte and also the crown prince of Naples, Italy.) Over the next two decades, Dow acquired the block's other nine historic homes and in 1989 donated them, along with his collections of art and antiques, but it took more than a decade to restore the buildings and open seven of them to the public. The houses were built between 1790 and 1910, demonstrating Florida history from the colonial era to the period when Henry Flagler established St. Augustine as a luxury resort location. The museum entrance is through the Star General Store, originally a dry-goods emporium built in 1899, which now houses the museum's gift shop. Both guided and self-guided tours are available. ⊠ *149 Cordova St.* ☎ *904/823–9722* ⊕ *www.moas. org/dowmuseum* ✍ *$8.95* ⊙ *Mon.–Sat. 10–4:30, Sun. 11–4:30.*

NEED A BREAK? **St. George Tavern.** Although they serve food (sandwiches, mostly), the appeal of this joint is that, in a city of historic recreations, this is the real deal: a noisy, packed, active bar where smokers smoke, drinkers drink, locals gather, and strangers blend right in. ⊠ *116-A St. George St.* ☎ *904/824–4204* ⊕ *www.stgeorgetavern.com.*

Lightner Museum. In his quest to turn Florida into an American Riviera, Henry Flagler built two fancy hotels in 1888: the Ponce de León, which became Flagler College, and the Alcazar. The latter, which closed during the Great Depression, was purchased by publisher Otto Lightner in 1946, and was donated to the city in 1948. It's now a museum with three floors of furnishings, costumes, Victorian art glass, not-to-be-missed ornate antique music boxes, and even an early 20th-century-era shrunken head from the Jivaro Indians of Ecuador. The Lightner Antiques Mall is on three levels of what was once the hotel's indoor pool. City staff occupy other floors since, apparently, the guest rooms of a former grand hotel also make nice municipal-government offices. ⊠ *75 King St.* ☎ *904/824–2874* ⊕ *www.lightnermuseum.org* ⌨ *$10* ☉ *Museum daily 9–5 (last admission at 4).*

Old Jail Museum. At this 19th-century prison, felons were detained and released or detained and hanged from the gallows in back. After learning the history of local crime and punishment and seeing displays of weapons and other artifacts, you can browse the surfeit of souvenirs in Cracker Bob's Trading Post and the adjacent Old Store Museum. Note that the museum is at the starting point for the Old Town Trolley Tour. ⊠ *167 San Marco Ave.* ☎ *904/829–3800* ⌨ *$9* ☉ *Daily 9–4:30.*

Ponce de León Hall, Flagler College. Originally one of two posh hotels Henry Flagler built in the 1880s, this building—which is now part of a small liberal-arts college—is a riveting Spanish Renaissance–revival structure with towers, turrets, and stained glass by Louis Comfort Tiffany. The former Hotel Ponce de León is a National Historic Landmark, having hosted U.S. presidents Grover Cleveland, Theodore Roosevelt, and Warren Harding. Visitors can view the building free or take a guided tour offered daily through Flagler's Legacy Tours. ⊠ *74 King St.* ☎ *904/829–6481, 904/823–3378 for tour info* ⊕ *legacy.flagler.edu* ⌨ *Tours $10* ☉ *Tours daily at 10 and 2 when school's in session, on the hr 10–3 when school's out.*

FAMILY **St. Augustine Alligator Farm Zoological Park.** Founded in 1893, the Alligator Farm is one of Florida's oldest (and, at times, smelliest) zoological attractions and is credited with popularizing the alligator in the national consciousness and helping to fashion an image for the state. In addition to oddities like Maximo, a 15-foot, 1,250-pound saltwater crocodile, and a collection of rare albino alligators, the park is also home to Land of Crocodiles, the only place in the world to see all 23 species of living crocodilians. Traversing the treetops in Crocodile Crossing is an inventive, ambitious, and expensive ($65) zipline/ropes course with more than 50 challenges and nine ziplines. In many places, a thin cable is all that keeps you from becoming croc cuisine. The shorter Sepik River course (three ziplines) is $35. Reptiles are the main attraction, but there's also a wading-bird rookery, an exotic-birds and mammals exhibit, and nature trails. Educational presentations are held throughout the day, and kids love the wild-animal shows. ⊠ *999 Anastasia Blvd.* ☎ *904/824–3337* ⊕ *www.alligatorfarm.com* ⌨ *$22.95* ☉ *Daily 9–5.*

St. Augustine

13

St. Augustine Lighthouse & Museum. It's unusual to find a lighthouse tucked into a residential neighborhood. This 1874 version replaced an earlier one built when the city was founded in 1565. Although its beacon no longer guides ships, it does draw thousands of visitors each year, in part because it has a reputation for being haunted. The visitor center has a museum with exhibits on the U.S. Coast Guard, historic boat building, maritime archaeology, and the life of a lighthouse keeper—whose work involved far more than light housekeeping. You have to climb 219 steps to reach the peak, 140 feet up, but the wonderful view and fresh ocean breeze are well worth it. Children must be at least 44 inches tall to make the ascent. The museum also conducts evening "Dark of the Moon Paranormal" tours ($25) and "Sunset-Moonrise" tours ($25) that include a champagne toast and light hors d'oeuvres. ⊠ *81 Lighthouse Ave.* 🕾 *904/829–0745* ⊕ *www.staugustinelighthouse. org* 🖼 *$9.75* ⊙ *Daily 9–6.*

FAMILY **St. Augustine Pirate and Treasure Museum.** Inside this small museum established by entrepreneur and motivational speaker Pat Croce is a collection of more than 800 pirate artifacts, including one of only two Jolly Rogers (skull-and-crossbones flags) known to have actually flown above a ship. Exhibits include a mock-up of a tavern, a captain's quarters, and a ship's deck. You'll learn about the lives of everyday and famous pirates, their navigation techniques, their weaponry, and the concoctions they drank (including something called Kill Devil, which is rum mixed with gunpowder). You'll get to touch an actual treasure chest; see piles of gold, jade, emeralds, and pearls; and leave knowing full well that there were pirates before Captain Jack Sparrow. ⊠ *12 S. Castillo Dr.* 🕾 *877/467–5863, 904/819–1444* ⊕ *www.thepiratemuseum.com* 🖼 *$12.99* ⊙ *Daily 10–8.*

WORTH NOTING

Anastasia State Park. This park draws families who like to hike, bike, swim, camp, and play on the beach to its 1,700 protected acres of bird sanctuary and 4 miles of secluded beachfront. ⊠ *1340-A Rte. A1A S* 🕾 *904/461–2033* ⊕ *www.floridastateparks.org/anastasia* 🖼 *$8 per vehicle; $2 pedestrians, bicyclists* ⊙ *Daily 8–sunset.*

City Gate. At the northernmost end of the colorful shops and sites of St. George Street, the gate is a relic from the days when the Castillo's moat ran westward to the river, and the Cubo Defense Line (defensive wall) protected against approaches from the north. The old coquina gates set the tone for St. George Street, a historic lane filled with old-world balconies and quaint little shops. ⊠ *St. George and Orange sts.*

Flagler Memorial Presbyterian Church. To look at a marvelous Venetian Renaissance–style structure, head to this church, built by Flagler in 1889 as a memorial to his daughter Jenny, who died during childbirth. In addition to Jenny, this is the final resting place for Flagler himself, his first wife Mary, and their granddaughter Marjorie. The dome of this stunning sanctuary towers more than 100 feet and is topped by a 20-foot Greek cross. ⊠ *32 Sevilla St.* 🕾 *904/829–6451* ⊕ *www.memorialpcusa.org* ⊙ *Sanctuary Mon.–Sat. 9–3:35; Sun. service hrs vary.*

The "Oldest Wooden Schoolhouse" is made of cedar and cypress wood and dates to the early 18th century.

Fountain of Youth National Archaeological Park. This once-dated attraction continues to undergo a major rejuvenation. There are still fun elements from the original "Old Florida" (admittedly somewhat kitschy), but there's much that's new and exciting, too. The timing is appropriate—in 2013, the park celebrated the 500th anniversary of Ponce de León's arrival. The 15-acre waterfront site is also the location where Spanish explorer Pedro Menéndez de Avilés, in 1565, established the first and oldest continuous European settlement in what's now the United States. Excavations have also shown it was the site of a Franciscan mission to the Timucuan Indians. The park includes a replica of the mission, a Timucuan village and burial grounds, a boatyard in which a 16th-century-style boat is being constructed, and a new observation platform over the marsh. Other highlights include cannon firings, Navigators Planetarium, a gift shop and snack bar, and the springhouse where you can still quench your thirst from "the fountain of youth." ⊠ *11 Magnolia Ave.* ☎ *904/829–3168, 800/356–8222* ⊕ *www.fountainofyouthflorida.com* 🖃 *$12* ⊗ *Daily 9–6.*

OFF THE BEATEN PATH

Ft. Matanzas National Monument. As you drive south on Anastasia Island, you head toward what was, in the 1700s, St. Augustine's farthest reaches. With Castillo de San Marcos guarding the town, in 1740 the Spanish created the relatively small Ft. Matanzas to defend their southern flank. A short ferry ride across the Matanzas River takes you to this national monument. Although it's only 15 miles from town, the fort feels eerily remote, and it takes little imagination to picture the demanding lives of the soldiers sent here to protect the young colony. Ferry shuttles are free and run on the half hour from 9:30 to 4:30, but you need to pick up a boarding pass from the visitor center. ✉ *8635 Rte. A1A S* ☎ *904/471–0116* ⊕ *www.nps.gov/foma* ☜ *Free* ◎ *Daily 9–5:30.*

Government House Museum. This historical building has been a hospital, a courthouse, a customs house, a post office, and, during the American Revolution, the home of the British governors. And it was from here, in 1821, that the Spanish governor ceded control of East Florida to the United States to conclude 256 years of colonial control. After a major renovation, the building reopened in Fall 2013 with a new exhibit, "First Colony: Our Spanish Origins." The exhibit presents the story of the founding of St. Augustine and focuses on the Hispanic aspect of American history. A shop on site sells history-related souvenirs and a wide selection of books. ✉ *48 King St.* ☎ *904/825–5034* ⊕ *www. staugustine.ufl.edu* ☜ *Free* ◎ *Thurs.–Mon. 10–4.*

OFF THE
BEATEN
PATH

Marineland Dolphin Adventure. The world's first oceanarium was constructed in 1938, 18 miles south of St. Augustine. This National Register of Historic Places designee, now part of the Georgia Aquarium, has come a long way from marine film studio to theme park to its current iteration as dolphin research, education, and entertainment center. The formal dolphin shows are history, but you can have a far more memorable experience with interactive programs that allow you to swim with and feed the animals, become a dolphin trainer for a day, or create dolphin art. Programs start at $29 a day (for the simple "touch-and-feed" option) and go as high as $450 (for "trainer for a day"). General admission allows you to observe the dolphins through 6-foot-by-10-foot acrylic windows. The 1.3-million-gallon facility is home to 13 dolphins, and until 2014 the park housed Nellie, the longest-lived dolphin in human care until her May 1, 2014 death at the age of 61. Reservations are required. ✉ *9600 Ocean Shore Blvd.* ☎ *904/471–1111, 877/933–3402* ⊕ *www.marineland.net* ☜ *$9.95* ◎ *Daily 9–4:30.*

Mission of Nombre de Dios. The site, north of the Historic District, commemorates where America's first mass was celebrated. A 208-foot-tall stainless-steel cross (purportedly the world's tallest) allegedly marks the spot where the mission's first cross was planted in 1565. Also on the property is the Shrine of Our Lady of La Leche, the first shrine devoted to Mary in the United States. The landscape is exquisitely maintained, and the mission is crisscrossed with paths. A museum and gift shop are also on the property. ✉ *27 Ocean Ave.* ☎ *904/824–2809, 800/342–6529* ⊕ *www.missionandshrine.org* ☜ *Donations welcome* ◎ *Site weekdays 9–5, weekends 10–5; museum Thurs.–Sat. 10–4, Sun. noon–4.*

Oldest House. Known as the Gonzalez-Alvarez House, Florida's oldest surviving Spanish-colonial dwelling is a National Historic Landmark. The current site dates from the early 1700s, but there's been a structure here since the early 1600s. Much of the city's history is seen in the building's modifications and additions, from the coquina blocks—which came into use to replace wood soon after the town burned in 1702—to the house's enlargement during the British occupation. The complex also includes the Manucy Museum, the Page L. Edwards Gallery and its rotating exhibits, a gift shop, and an ornamental garden. ✉ *14 St.*

Francis St. ☎ *904/824–2872* ⊕ *www.staugustinehistoricalsociety.org*
✉ *$8* ☉ *Daily 9–5, tours every ½ hr (last tour at 4:30).*

Oldest Wooden Schoolhouse. This tiny 18th-century building of cypress
and cedar served not only as a schoolhouse but also as a tearoom, a
farmhouse, and a guardhouse and sentry shelter during the Seminole
Wars. In 1939, members of the Class of '64 (1864, that is) dressed out
the school as they remembered it, and today automated mannequins
instruct you on the education of 150 years ago. Apparently teachers had
more leeway then because miscreants were given "time out" in a cubby
beneath the stairs. And the heavy chain wrapped around the building?
It was to hold the structure down during hurricanes. Kids will like the
school bell and wishing well in the charming courtyard garden. ⊠ *14
St. George St.* ☎ *888/653–7245* ⊕ *www.oldestwoodenschoolhouse.com*
✉ *$4.95* ☉ *Sun.–Thurs. 9–6, Fri.–Sat. 9–8.*

Plaza de la Constitución. At the foot of the Bridge of Lions, this central
area of the original settlement was laid out in 1598 by decree of Spain's
King Philip II. At its core is a monument to the Spanish constitution of
1812, and at its east end is a portico dating from early American days.
This is where products and, regrettably, people were sold, earning the
area the twin names of "public market" and "slave market." Today, it's
the gathering spot for holiday events, art shows, and evening concerts.
Toward the bridge, look for the life-size statue of Ponce de León. The
man who "discovered" Florida in 1513 was, apparently, all of 4'11".
⊠ *St. George St. and Cathedral Pl.*

FAMILY **Ripley's Believe It or Not! Museum.** The nation's first Ripley's museum is,
appropriately enough, in a historic structure—Castle Warden, an 1887
Moorish Revival–style mansion. Like its younger siblings, this "odditorium" is packed with plenty of unusual items, including Robert Ripley's
personal collections; a mummified cat; a death mask of Abraham Lincoln;
a scale model of the original Ferris Wheel created from an Erector set; and
life-size models of Robert Wadlow, the world's tallest man, and Robert
Hughes, the world's fattest man. ⊠ *19 San Marco Ave.* ☎ *904/824–1606*
⊕ *www.ripleys.com/staugustine* ✉ *$14.99* ☉ *Daily 9–8.*

World Golf Hall of Fame. This stunning tribute to the game of golf is
the centerpiece of World Golf Village, an extraordinary complex that
includes 36 holes of golf, a golf academy, several accommodations
options, a convention center, spa, and a variety of restaurants, including Murray Bros. Caddyshack. The Hall of Fame features an adjacent
IMAX theater and houses a variety of exhibits combining historical
artifacts and personal memorabilia with the latest in interactive technology. Stand up to the pressures of the TV camera and crowd noise
as you try to sink a final putt, take a swing on the museum's simulator,
or snap a photo as you walk across a replica of St. Andrews's Swilcan
Burn Bridge. Once you're sufficiently inspired, see how you fare on the
18-hole natural-grass putting course. Admission includes a chance to
score a hole-in-one on a 132-yard hole. If you do, you win a prize, such
as admission to THE PLAYERS Championship. ⊠ *1 World Golf Pl.*
☎ *904/940–4123* ⊕ *www.worldgolfhalloffame.org* ✉ *$19.50 (includes
museum, round on 18-hole putting course, and shot at hole-in-one*

challenge). IMAX $13 for features, $8.50 for documentaries ⊙ *Mon.–Sat. 10–6, Sun. noon–6.*

Ximenez-Fatio House Museum. Built as a merchant's house and store in 1798, the place became a boardinghouse in the 1800s and has been restored to look like it did during its inn days—romantic yet severe, with balconies that hearken back to Old Spain and sparely appointed rooms. Docents lead you around the property; be sure to look at the fascinating St. Augustine street scenes, painted in 1854 by an itinerant artist. Amazingly, much of what you see in the paintings is extant. ✉ *20 Aviles St.* ☎ *904/829–3575* ⊕ *www.ximenezfatiohouse.org* 🖃 *$7* ⊙ *Tues.–Sat. 11–4.*

BEACHES

Anastasia State Park Beach. If you don't mind paying a bit for beach access, this park offers some outstanding choices. At one end of the beach, there's a playground and snack bar, where you can order sandwiches and cold drinks or rent a beach chair, umbrella, surfboard, or other beach paraphernalia. If you walk north along the beach, however, all traces of civilization seem to vanish. An offshore break makes the park a good surfing spot, there's a boat launch, and canoes and kayaks can be rented. The campgrounds are very popular, too. **Amenities:** food and drink; lifeguards (seasonal); parking (no fee); showers; toilets; water sports. **Best for:** solitude; surfing; swimming; walking. ✉ *1340-A Rte. A1A S* ☎ *904/461–2033* ⊕ *www.floridastateparks/anastasia* 🖃 *$8 per vehicle, $2 pedestrians* ⊙ *Daily, 8–sundown.*

Butler Park Beach. In the days of racial segregation, Butler Beach, located south of St. Augustine and north of Crescent Beach, was an African-American beach. Today it is a small town that still provides access to the beachfront. **Amenities:** lifeguards (seasonal); parking (no fee); showers; toilets. **Best for:** swimming; walking. ✉ *5860 Rte. A1A S, south of St. Augustine Beach.*

Crescent Beach. A 15 minute-drive beyond the area's big tourist destinations, this quieter, less crowded spot offers wide, white-sand beaches with good shelling, making it particularly popular with beachcombers. Adding to the laid-back atmosphere are some good restaurants, where visitors can enjoy the beach from a distance, glass in one hand and plate of fresh seafood in the other. **Amenities:** lifeguards (seasonal); parking (no fee); showers; toilets. **Best for:** solitude; swimming; walking. ✉ *South of rtes. A1A and 206, Crescent Beach.*

North Beach. Just five minutes from St. Augustine, this site (aka Usina Beach) includes boat ramps, two campsites, and a picnic area with grills. If you'd rather opt for a restaurant than a picnic, you're in the right spot—a variety of eateries overlook the ocean or the Intracoastal Waterway. **Amenities:** lifeguards (seasonal); parking (no fee); showers; toilets. **Best for:** solitude; walking. ✉ *Rte. A1A, north of Vilano Beach.*

St. Augustine Beach. Just south of Anastasia State Park, this beach has a livelier setting, thanks to the restaurants, bars, and shops along Beachfront Avenue and the 4-acre St. Johns County Ocean Pier Park. The park includes a playground, small splash park, sand volleyball courts, and a covered pavilion, where from May to September a series of Music by the Sea concerts are offered free. Speaking of free, the beach doesn't charge a fee, but the popular fishing pier does ($3). In addition, there are some areas designated for driving on the beach. **Amenities:** lifeguards (seasonal); parking (no fee); showers; toilets. **Best for:** swimming. ⊠ *Old A1A/Beach Blvd., south of Rte. 312.*

Vilano Beach. This beach, just 2 miles north of St.Augustine, is sandwiched between the Tolomato River and the Atlantic. In the 1920s it was home to the Grand Vilano Casino, but that was destroyed by a hurricane in 1937. Until recently, Vilano Beach had deteriorated into a small, somewhat run-down area, though with a nice, laid-back '60s surf vibe. That's changed rapidly, however. Now it's home to new stores and restaurants, the Vilano Beach Fishing Pier, and other community improvements. A Hampton Inn & Suites is within a few minutes' walk. The beach has some nice breakers for surfing—skimboarding is also popular—but strong currents sometimes make it dangerous for swimming. It's also one of the few beaches on which you can still drive a car. **Amenities:** lifeguards (seasonal); showers; toilets. **Best for:** solitude, surfing, walking. ⊠ *3400 Coastal Hwy., Vilano Beach.*

13

WHERE TO EAT

$

ECLECTIC

✕ **Bull & Crown British Publick House.** A replica of an 18th-century "publick house," this pub's menu focuses primarily on sandwiches and salads. Since the restaurant was built on the homesite of Francisco Pellicer—a Minorcan carpenter who lived on St. George Street—it's only natural that you'd find a Minorcan-influenced dish, such as the Minorcan clam chowder infused with locally grown peppers. The pub also offers a full bar with beer, wine, and some creative martinis and bloody marys. Both indoor and courtyard seating are available. There's live music on weekends. ⑤ *Average main: $10* ⊠ *53 St. George St.* ☎ *904/342–2869* ⊕ *www.colonialquarter.com/dine/bull-and-crown-publick-house* ⌂ *Reservations not accepted* ⊗ *Sun.–Thurs. 11–10, Fri.–Sat. 11–11.*

$

CAFÉ

✕ **The Bunnery Bakery & Café.** Hidden among the art galleries and trinket shops of St. George Street is this cozy little restaurant, which is very popular at breakfast and nearly as popular during lunch. There's nothing fancy—just high-back booths and a menu of pancakes, bacon, eggs, cinnamon buns, salads, and sandwiches. It's the perfect spot when you want something familiar in a new place. ⑤ *Average main: $7* ⊠ *121 St. George St.* ☎ *904/829–6166* ⊕ *www.bunnerybakeryandcafe.com* ⌂ *Reservations not accepted* ⊗ *No dinner.*

$

CAFÉ

✕ **Café Alcazar.** Whether you browse the antiques shops and are drawn into having lunch or the other way around, there's plenty of temptation to go around here. Housed in the magnificent Lightner Museum—the luxurious Hotel Alcazar of the 1890s—this lovely little lunch spot sits where wealthy winter tourists once frolicked in the nation's largest indoor pool. The balconies that rise on all four sides are lined with intriguing stores, so it's easy for a relaxing lunch to expand into an entire afternoon of shopping pleasure. The food is good if slightly pricey, but it's beautifully presented in an atmosphere of elegance. Dinner is served on the first Friday of every month. ⑤ *Average main: $12* ⊠ *25 Granada St.* ☎ *904/825–9948* ⊕ *www.thecafealcazar.com* ⊘ *No dinner.*

$$$$
ECLECTIC
Fodor'sChoice
★

✕ **Collage.** Foodies seeking a new dining experience in the Oldest City head here for "artful global cuisine" in a warm and intimate setting. Tucked away on Hypolita Street in the Historic District, the 48-seat restaurant highlights local seafood, which, depending on the success of the fishermen, will include several fish entrées each day. The ever-changing menu also often has steak, lamb, or veal selections. For dessert, the bougainvillea, an original dessert inspired by the colorful flowering plants that frame the building, is made of strawberries, ice cream, and cabernet-vanilla sauce served in a leaf-shape phyllo cup. ⑤ *Average main: $36* ⊠ *60 Hypolita St.* ☎ *904/829–0055* ⊕ *www.collagestaug. com* ⊘ *No lunch.*

$$$
SPANISH

✕ **Columbia.** Arroz con pollo, fillet *salteado* (with a spicy sauce), and a fragrant seafood paella (allow 30 minutes for preparation) are the time-honored Cuban and Spanish dishes served at this branch of the original Columbia, which was founded in Tampa in 1905. Befitting its cuisine, the restaurant is more like an airy Spanish villa, with many archival family photos; a white-stucco exterior; and an atrium dining room full of palm trees, hand-painted tiles, and decorative arches. Table not ready? Linger in the courtyard, listen to the fountains, and enjoy a glass of homemade sangria or a refreshing mojito. ⑤ *Average main: $23* ⊠ *98 St. George St.* ☎ *904/824–3341* ⊕ *www.columbiarestaurant.com.*

$
MODERN
AMERICAN
FAMILY
Fodor'sChoice
★

✕ **The Floridian.** Although vegetarians flock to this artsy and inspired eatery for the veggie-centric menu, there's plenty to tantalize omnivores as well. Delicious Southern food with flair ranges from fried green tomato bruschetta to a choice of shrimp, fish, or tofu with polenta cakes (here called "grits"). Many dishes offer a choice of meat, tofu, or tempeh. Some gluten-free dishes are also available. The produce featured at this farm-to-table establishment is at the peak of freshness and plays a starring role in the Winter Salad and Florida Sunshine Salad. Attire is casual, and the oceanic hues and funky décor put you at ease. Kids' needs are handled with flexible good nature. It's a deservedly popular spot, especially on the weekends. Reservations aren't accepted, but if you call ahead with a time and the number of diners in your party you move to the front of the line, essentially, upon arrival. ⑤ *Average main: $15* ⊠ *39 Cordova St.* ☎ *904/829–0655* ⊕ *www.thefloridianstaug.com* ⊘ *No lunch Tues.*

$$$
ECLECTIC

✕ **95 Cordova.** On the first floor of the Casa Monica Hotel, this restaurant serves classic cuisine with an international flair. Sup in one of three dining rooms, including the main room with intricate Moroccan-style chandeliers, wrought-iron chairs, and heavy wood columns, or the Sultan's Room, a gold-dipped space accented with potted palms and a silk-draped ceiling. Innovative dishes with New World, Middle Eastern, and Asian flavors change seasonally and highlight local seafood and produce. Among the dinner items are several types of steak, duck two ways, braised pork osso buco, Bahamian lobster tail with crab risotto, and coriander-crusted sea scallops. The tasting menu offers five courses paired with outstanding wines. ⑤ *Average main: $28* ✉ *95 Cordova St.* ☎ *904/810–6810* ⊕ *www.casamonica.com* ⌖ *Reservations essential.*

$$$ ✗ **O.C. White's Seafood & Spirits.** Dining outside is a treat at this bustling
SEAFOOD little spot across from the marina. Set in the circa-1791 General Worth house, it has a homelike feel with a balanced clientele of locals, students, and visitors. Favorites include coconut shrimp, blue-crab cakes, and fresh local grouper. Beef lovers may want to try the filet mignon or the New York strip. From upstairs, you have a great marina view; in the courtyard, you might enjoy the perfume of blooming jasmine. Call ahead for "preferred seating." ⑤ *Average main: $23* ✉ *118 Av. Menendez* ☎ *904/824–0808* ⊕ *www.ocwhitesrestaurant.com* ⌖ *Reservations not accepted.*

13

$ ✗ **O'Steen's.** Across the Bridge of Lions from downtown, this hole-in-
SEAFOOD the-wall restaurant is recognizable for the line of customers who wait patiently for fried shrimp (their specialty), oysters, scallops, hush puppies, fried chicken, coleslaw, biscuits and cornbread with gravy, and banana cream pie. Needless to say it's been a popular local eatery for generations. Bring cash; credit cards are not accepted. ⑤ *Average main: $14* ✉ *205 Anastasia Blvd.* ☎ *904/829–6974* ⊕ *www.osteensrestaurant. com* ⌖ *Reservations not accepted* ▭ *No credit cards* ☾ *Closed Sun. and Mon.*

WHERE TO STAY

$ ⊡ **Bayfront Marin House Bed and Breakfast.** Children are rarely permitted
B&B/INN at B&Bs, but this is a charming exception, thanks to separate entrances,
FAMILY several units large enough to accommodate families, and the warm welcome of the inn's owners, Mike and Sandy Wieber. **Pros:** personal service; child- and pet-friendly; waterfront location; porches and balconies with river views; moderate prices outside high season. **Cons:** parking a block away; dining area small if weather forces breakfast indoors. ⑤ *Rooms from: $169* ✉ *142 Av. Menendez* ☎ *904/824–4301* ⊕ *www. bayfrontmarinhouse.com* ⇥ *15 units* ⦿*Breakfast.*

$ ⊡ **Bayfront Westcott House.** A bit more elegant and formal than the aver-
B&B/INN age B&B, this inn wows guests with a combination of English and American antiques and a wealth of complimentary food, from extravagant breakfasts to wine and canapés in the early evening. **Pros:** great views, most from private balconies; romantic rooms; free Wi-Fi. **Cons:** parking a short distance away; carriage house rooms not as elegant as main house. ⑤ *Rooms from: $189* ✉ *146 Av. Menendez* ☎ *904/825–4602, 800/513–9814* ⊕ *www.westcotthouse.com* ⇥ *16 rooms* ⦿*Breakfast.*

$ ⊡ **Carriage Way Bed and Breakfast.** When it comes to location, the Victo-
B&B/INN rian-era Carriage Way has the best of both worlds; it's far enough from the Historic District to avoid tourist noise but close enough to have easy access to excellent restaurants (try the nearby Floridian) and shops. **Pros:** great location; free on-site parking; personal attention; excellent breakfasts. **Cons:** some small rooms; street can get loud with traffic. ⑤ *Rooms from: $129* ✉ *70 Cuna St.* ☎ *904/829–2467, 800/908–9832* ⊕ *www.carriageway.com* ⇥ *13 rooms, 1 cottage* ⦿*Breakfast.*

$ ⊡ **Casa de Solana.** There's a reason you feel like you're stepping back in
B&B/INN time when you enter this 1820s-era inn made of coquina and handmade

bricks: it's on the oldest street in the oldest European-settled city in the country. **Pros:** excellent service; delicious breakfast; location. **Cons:** some small rooms; free parking is four blocks away; "forced" socialization. $ *Rooms from: $149* ⊠ *21 Aviles St.* ☎ *904/824–3555* ⊕ *www.casadesolana.com* ➥ *10 rooms* ⦿ *Breakfast.*

$
HOTEL
Fodor's Choice
★
 ⌂ **Casa Monica Hotel.** Hand-stenciled Moorish columns and arches, handcrafted chandeliers, and gilded iron tables decorate the lobby of this late-1800s Flagler-era masterpiece. **Pros:** location; affordable off-season rates; flat-screen TVs in all rooms. **Cons:** busy lobby; expensive parking ($24); small rooms. $ *Rooms from: $188* ⊠ *95 Cordova St.* ☎ *904/827–1888, 800/648–1888* ⊕ *www.casamonica.com* ➥ *127 rooms, 11 suites* ⦿ *No meals.*

$
B&B/INN
 ⌂ **Casablanca Inn Bed & Breakfast on the Bay.** Breakfast comes with scenic views of the Matanzas Bay at this restored 1914 Mediterranean-revival stucco-and-stone house, just north of the Bridge of Lions in the Historic District. **Pros:** comfy beds; friendly staff; free early evening snacks and beverages. **Cons:** some rooms have no view; street noise in some rooms. $ *Rooms from: $139* ⊠ *24 Av. Menendez* ☎ *904/829–0928, 800/826–2626* ⊕ *www.casablancainn.com* ➥ *21 rooms, 2 suites* ⦿ *Breakfast.*

$
HOTEL
FAMILY
 ⌂ **Hilton St. Augustine Historic Bayfront.** In the heart of historic St. Augustine, this Spanish-colonial-inspired hotel overlooking Matanzas Bay has 19 separate buildings in a village setting. **Pros:** location; comfortable beds; great for families. **Cons:** expensive valet parking only ($21); late-night noise at street level. $ *Rooms from: $189* ⊠ *32 Av. Menendez* ☎ *904/829–2277, 800/445–8667* ⊕ *www.hiltonhistoricstaugustine.com* ➥ *72 rooms* ⦿ *No meals.*

$
B&B/INN
 ⌂ **Inn on Charlotte Bed & Breakfast.** Innkeeper Rodney Holeman says guests comment that staying at his inn reminds them of visiting a friend or family member's home, assuming that person offers an elegant two-course breakfast and cozy rooms with whirlpool tubs. **Pros:** location; excellent service; free parking. **Cons:** strict cancellation policy; tight parking in compact lot; weekend street noise. $ *Rooms from: $149* ⊠ *52 Charlotte St.* ☎ *904/829–3819, 800/355–5508* ⊕ *www.innoncharlotte.com* ➥ *8 rooms* ⦿ *Breakfast.*

$
B&B/INN
 ⌂ **Old City House Inn & Restaurant.** Touches of Paris, Venice, and India are just a few of the surprises within this small two-story inn's coquina walls, where the rooms are decorated to reflect international cities or themes. **Pros:** location; romantic; free Wi-Fi; on-site restaurant. **Cons:** thin walls; may have to share room with a ghost! $ *Rooms from: $146* ⊠ *115 Cordova St.* ☎ *904/826–0113* ⊕ *www.oldcityhouse.com* ➥ *7 rooms, 2 suites* ⦿ *Breakfast.*

$
RESORT
Fodor's Choice
★
 ⌂ **Renaissance Resort at World Golf Village.** If you want to be within walking distance of all World Golf Village has to offer, this AAA Four Diamond resort is an excellent choice. **Pros:** breakfast buffet; large bathrooms; free shuttle to golf courses, spa, and downtown St. Augustine. **Cons:** small pool; daily fee for Internet/phone. $ *Rooms from: $169* ⊠ *500 S. Legacy Trail* ☎ *904/940–8000, 888/740–7020* ⊕ *www.worldgolfrenaissance.com* ➥ *271 rooms, 30 suites* ⦿ *Multiple meal plans.*

$
B&B/INN
 ⌂ **St. Francis Inn Bed & Breakfast.** If the walls of this late-18th-century house in the Historic District—and the oldest inn in the Oldest

City—could talk, they would tell of slave uprisings, buried doubloons, and Confederate spies. **Pros:** warm hospitality; family-friendly cottage; Southern breakfast buffet; short walk to Historic District attractions. **Cons:** small rooms; small pool. $ *Rooms from: $189* ⊠ *279 St. George St.* ☎ *904/824–6068, 800/824–6062* ⊕ *www.stfrancisinn.com* ↩ *12 rooms, 4 suites, 1 2-bedroom cottage* ⍾⊙⍾ *Breakfast.*

NIGHTLIFE

A1A Aleworks. The Aleworks always seems to be filled with students and visitors taste-driving the microbrews and other selections from the full bar. Seats on the 2nd-story balcony provide a great view of the marina and bay across the street. It's a little like being on Bourbon Street—but clean. ⊠ *1 King St.* ☎ *904/829–2977* ⊕ *www.A1Aaleworks.com.*

Mill Top Tavern. The rustic Mill Top is famous for its live, local music. ⊠ *19½ St. George St.* ☎ *904/829–2329* ⊕ *www.milltoptavern.com.*

The Original Cafe Eleven. This live music haven sets the stage for local groups, and tries to book national acts at least once a month. They also serve breakfast, lunch, and dinner seven days a week. ⊠ *501 Rte. A1A Beach Blvd.* ☎ *904/460–9311* ⊕ *www.originalcafe11.com.*

Scarlett O'Hara's. It's a popular and convenient spot to stop for lunch or dinner (preferably enjoyed on the front porch); later in the evening it turns up the volume with blues, jazz, disco, Top 40, or karaoke. Whatever's playing, it's always packed. ⊠ *70 Hypolita St.* ☎ *904/824–6535* ⊕ *www.scarlettoharas.net.*

Tini Martini Bar. The veranda overlooking Matanzas Bay at this Casablanca Inn bar is the perfect place to enjoy a cocktail, people-watch, and listen to live music. ⊠ *Casablanca Inn, 24 Av. Menendez* ☎ *904/829–0928* ⊕ *www.tini-martini-bar.com.*

Tradewinds. It's been showcasing bands—from country and western to rock and roll—since 1964. Thanks to the music, beer, and margaritas, you may feel as if you're in Key West. ⊠ *124 Charlotte St.* ☎ *904/826–1590* ⊕ *www.tradewindslounge.com.*

The World Famous Oasis Deck and Restaurant. If you're staying on Anastasia Island, this is your best nightlife bet. It has 24-ounce draft beers, beach access, and what many locals consider the best burgers in town. ⊠ *4000 Rte. A1A S, at Ocean Trace Rd.* ☎ *904/471–3424* ⊕ *www. worldfamousoasis.com.*

SHOPPING

One of the most pleasing pastimes in St. Augustine is a stroll along St. George Street, a pedestrian mall with shoulder-to-shoulder art galleries and one-of-a-kind shops selling candles, home accents, handmade jewelry, aromatherapy products, pottery, books, and clothing. There are also restaurants, clubs, and a veritable orchestra of street musicians.

Several blocks north of the Castillo and the popular St. George Street, a string of shops—galleries, antiques, a bookstore—line both sides of

San Marco Avenue. Although this strip isn't as eclectic as it used to be, you'll still find some interesting independent stores.

MALLS

Prime Outlets. Several miles outside of the city, Prime Outlets has more than 60 name-brand stores including Gucci, Saks 5th Avenue's OFF 5TH, and Michael Kors. ⊠ *500 Belz Outlet Blvd.* ☎ *904/826–1311* ⊕ *www.staugoutlets.com.*

St. Augustine Premium Outlets. Just north of St. Augustine, off Interstate 95, is this collection of 85 designer and brand-name outlet stores. ⊠ *2700 State Rd. 16* ☎ *904/825–1555* ⊕ *www.premiumoutlets.com.*

RECOMMENDED STORE

Whetstone Chocolate Factory. Chocolate fans won't want to miss a stop at Whetstone. Once upon a time the company operated a large factory in St. Augustine. They've scaled back to a small operation next door to their retail shop, but you can still take a quick-paced behind-the-scenes tour (reservations recommended). ⊠ *139 King St., Vilano Beach* ☎ *904/217–0275* ⊕ *www.whetstonechocolates.com* ⊠ *$8* ⊙ *Tours weekdays at 11, 1, 2:15, 3:30, Sat. at 10, 11:15, 1, 2:15, 3:30, Sun. at 1, 2:15, 3:30.*

SPORTS AND THE OUTDOORS

BIKING

Solano Cycle. Here you can rent bicycles, scooters, and "scoot coups," which look like the offspring of a scooter and a bumper car and are $49 for the first hour (one-hour minimum) and $69 for two. ⊠ *32 San Marco Ave.* ☎ *904/825–6766* ⊕ *www.solanocycle.com.*

BOAT TOURS

EcoTours. Amidst America's most enduring human history, EcoTours investigates St. Augustine's natural history. Scenic cruises, kayak tours, and catamaran excursions on Matanzas Bay offer a chance to see bottlenose dolphins, bird habitats, lakes, creeks, and saltwater marshes. Along the way are incredible photo ops of the city and the Castillo from the water. ⊠ *111 Av. Menendez* ☎ *904/377–7245* ⊕ *www. staugustineecotours.com.*

FAMILY **The Pirate Ship Black Raven.** Whether you prefer Captain Hook or Captain Jack Sparrow, it's a pirate's life for everyone aboard the Black Raven, even if you're only sailing on the Mantanzas River. This "floating performance theater" hosts live pirate shows that include sea shanties, black powder cannon firings, sword-fighting lessons for kids (with harmless foam blades), and treasure hunts on weekends. This is just entertainment, not historical education, so expect the jokes to be cheap and cheesy. However, the atmosphere's lively and the river's lovely. Kids can trade their "letters of marque" to get a share of the booty—if, that is, the crew and the kids can manage to get their treasure back from Blackbeard. There are also adults-only evening cruises—the ship includes a fully licensed bar, so grown-ups can live out the fantasy of "yo-ho-ho and a bottle of rum." Cruises can be cancelled for inclement weather, so call to check before making final travel plans. ⊠ *St.*

Augustine Municipal Marina, 111 Av. Menendez ☎ *904/826–0000, 877/578–5050* ⊕ *www.blackravenadventures.com* ⌛ *$29.95.*

Schooner Freedom. Cutting a sharp profile, this 72-foot replica of a 19th-century blockade-runner sails from the marina for excursions across Matanzas Bay. You can relax and savor the breeze, or you can help the crew prepare to set sail. There are two-hour day ($35 per person) and sunset ($45) sails as well as a 75-minute twilight–after dark sail ($35). Precise times vary by season. Reservations are advised. ☒ *St. Augustine Municipal Marina, 111 Av. Menendez, Slip 86* ☎ *904/810–1010* ⊕ *www.schoonerfreedom.com.*

FISHING

Sea Love Charters. Tackle and bait are included on this outfit's half- or full-day deep-sea fishing trips. ☒ *Cat's Paw Marina, 220 Nix Boat Yard Rd.* ☎ *904/824–3328* ⊕ *www.sealovefishing.com.*

GOLF

World Golf Village. The World Golf Hall of Fame complex has two 18-hole layouts named for and partially designed by golf legends Sam Snead, Gene Sarazen, Arnold Palmer, and Jack Nicklaus. The King & Bear course, a collaboration of Palmer and Nicklaus, features a design that symbolizes the styles of both golfing legends, including holes that especially reward outstanding power of the tees. Palmer chose the par-4 15th as one of his "Dream 18" in a *Sports Illustrated* report. It's the most picturesque hole on the course, with a dramatic rock wall surrounding the green. Snead and Sarazen consulted with designer Bobby Weed in creating the The Slammer & Squite course, which features generous fairways and lots of water hazards. Amenities for both courses include complimentary range balls and fresh chilled apples on the first and 10th tees. ☒ *1 World Golf Pl.* ☎ *904/940–6100 for Slammer & Squire, 904/940–6200 for King & Bear* ⊕ *www.worldgolfhalloffame. com* ⌛ *King & Bear $169 for 18 holes. Slammer & Squire $129 for 18 holes* ⚑ *King & Bear Course: 18 holes. 7279 yards. par 72. Slammer & Squite Course: 18 holes. 6939 yards. par 72.*

WATER SPORTS

Surf Station. Here you can rent surfboards, skimboards, and bodyboards. ☒ *1020 Anastasia Blvd.* ☎ *904/471–9463, 800/460–6394* ⊕ *www.surf-station.com.*

DAYTONA BEACH AND INLAND TOWNS

The section of the coast around Daytona Beach offers considerable variety, from the unassuming bedroom community of Ormond Beach to the spring-break and auto-racing capital of Daytona Beach. (Go 75 miles to the south, and you've got speeding rockets instead of speeding cars.)

Peaceful little inland towns are separated by miles of two-lane roads, running through dense forest and flat pastureland and skirting one lake after another. There's not much to see but cattle and the state's few hills. Gentle and rolling, they're hardly worth noting to people from true hill country, but they're significant enough in Florida for much of this area to be called the "hill and lake region."

DAYTONA BEACH

65 miles south of St. Augustine.

Best known for the Daytona 500, Daytona has been the center of automobile racing since cars were first raced along the beach here in 1902. February is the biggest month for race enthusiasts, and there are weekly events at the International Speedway. During race weeks, bike weeks, spring-break periods, and summer holidays, expect extremely heavy traffic. On the mainland, near the inland waterway, several blocks of Beach Street have been "streetscaped," and shops and restaurants open onto an inviting, broad, brick sidewalk.

GETTING HERE AND AROUND

Several airlines have regular service to Daytona Beach International Airport, which is next to Daytona International Speedway on International Speedway Boulevard, an east–west artery that stretches from Interstate 95 to the beaches. The average drive time from the airport to beachside hotels is 20 minutes; Yellow Cab–Daytona Beach makes the trip for $12–$40.

DOTS Transit Service has scheduled service ($35 one-way, $65 round-trip) connecting Daytona Beach, DeLand, Deltona, and the Orlando International Airport, which serves more airlines and has more direct flights but is about a 70-mile commute via Interstate 4 and State Road 417 (allow at least 90 minutes). Note that DOTS doesn't serve the Daytona airport. Indeed, outside of a few hotel shuttles, there's no shuttle service between the Daytona airport and town.

Daytona Beach has an excellent bus network, Votran, which serves the beach area, airport, shopping malls, and major arteries, including service to DeLand and New Smyrna Beach and the Express Link to Orlando ($3.50). Exact fare is required for Votran ($1.50) if using cash.

Contacts Daytona Beach International Airport (*DAB*). ✉ *700 Catalina Dr.* ☎ *386/248–8069* ⊕ *www.flydaytonafirst.com.* **DOTS Transit Service** ☎ *386/257–5411, 800/231–1965* ⊕ *www.dots-daytonabeach.com.* **Votran** ☎ *386/756–7496* ⊕ *www.votran.org.* **Yellow Cab–Daytona Beach** ☎ *386/255–5555, 888/333–3356* ⊕ *www.daytonataxi.com.*

VISITOR INFORMATION

Contact Daytona Beach Area Convention and Visitors Bureau ☎ *800/544–0415* ⊕ *www.daytonabeach.com.*

EXPLORING

The Casements. Built in 1912 for Reverend Harwood Huntington and named for its hand-crafted casement windows, the home was purchased by John D. Rockefeller Sr. in 1918 as a winter retreat. Once considered the richest man in the world, Rockefeller entertained famous friends such as Henry Ford, Will Rogers, and Henry Flagler at the home while remaining an active member of the Ormond Beach community. After Rockefeller's death in 1937, the property was bought and sold numerous times and is now a cultural center and museum. The waterfront estate and its formal gardens host daily tours and an annual lineup of events and exhibits; there's also a permanent exhibit of Hungarian folk art and Boy Scout memorabilia. ✉ *25 Riverside Dr., Ormond Beach* ☎ *386/676–3216* ⊕ *www.thecasements.net* ✉ *Donations accepted* ⊙ *Weekdays 10–3:30, Sat. 10–11:30.*

Halifax Historical Museum. Memorabilia from the early days of beach automobile racing are on display here, as are historic photographs, Native American and Civil War artifacts, a postcard exhibit, and a video that details city history. There's a shop for gifts and antiques, too. Admission is by donation on Thursday and on Saturday, kids 12-and-under are free. ✉ *252 S. Beach St.* ☎ *386/255–6976* ⊕ *www. halifaxhistorical.org* ✉ *$5* ⊙ *Tues.–Fri. 10:30–4:30, Sat. 10–4.*

13

FAMILY **Museum of Arts & Sciences.** This behemoth museum has displays of Chinese art and an eye-popping complete skeleton of a giant ground sloth that's 130,000 years old. The museum also boasts a new Visible Storage Building, one of the most significant collections of Cuban art outside of Cuba, a large Coca-Cola and Americana collection, a rare Napoleonic exhibit, and one of the more expansive collections of American art in the Southeast. Kids love the Charles and Linda Williams Children's Museum, which features interactive science, engineering, and physics exhibits; a nature preserve with half a mile of boardwalks and nature trails; and a planetarium with daily laser-light shows. ✉ *352 S. Nova Rd.* ☎ *386/255–0285* ⊕ *www.moas.org* ✉ *$12.95* ⊙ *Tues.–Sat. 9–5, Sun. 11–5.*

OFF THE
BEATEN
PATH

Ponce de León Inlet Light Station. At the southern tip of the barrier island that includes Daytona Beach is the sleepy town of Ponce Inlet, with a small marina, a few bars, and casual seafood restaurants. Boardwalks traverse delicate dunes and provide easy access to the beach, although storms have caused serious erosion. Marking this prime spot is the bright-red, century-old Ponce de León Inlet Light Station, a National Historic Monument and museum, the tallest lighthouse in the state and the third tallest in the country. Climb to the top of the 175-foot-tall lighthouse tower for a bird's-eye view of Ponce Inlet. ✉ *4931 S. Peninsula Dr., Ponce Inlet* ☎ *386/761–1821* ⊕ *www.ponceinlet.org* ✉ *$5* ⊙ *Sept.–May, daily 10–6; May–Sept., daily 10–9; last admission 1 hr before closing.*

BEACH

Daytona Beach. At the World's Most Famous Beach you can drive right onto the sand (at least from one hour after sunrise to one hour before sunset), spread out a blanket, and have all your belongings at hand (with the exception of alcohol, which is prohibited). All that said, heavy traffic during summer and holidays makes it dangerous for children, and families should be extra careful or stay in the designated car-free zones. The speed limit is 10 mph, and there's a $5 fee, collected at the beach ramps, for driving on the sands every month but December and January.

The wide, 23-mile-long beach can get crowded in the "strip" area (between International Speedway Boulevard and Seabreeze Boulevard) with its food vendors, beachfront bars, volleyball matches, and motorized water sports enthusiasts. Those seeking a quieter experience can head north or south in either direction toward car-free zones in more residential areas. The hard-packed sand that makes the beach suitable

If the action on Daytona Beach is too much for you, soar above it by parasailing.

for driving is also perfect for running and cycling. There's also excellent surf fishing directly from the beach. **Amenities:** food and drink; lifeguards; parking (some with fee); showers; toilets; water sports. **Best for:** sunrise; surfing; swimming; walking. ■ TIP→ **Signs on Route A1A indicate car access via beach ramps. Sand traps aren't limited to the golf course, though—cars can get stuck.** ⊠ *Rte. A1A* ⊕ *www.daytonabeach.com.*

WHERE TO EAT

$$$
SEAFOOD
✕ **Aunt Catfish's on the River.** Don't be surprised if your server introduces herself as your cousin, though you've never seen her before in your life. You see, everybody is "cousin" at Aunt Catfish's (as in, "Can I get you another mason jar of sweet tea, Cousin?"). The silly Southern hospitality is only one of the draws at this wildly popular seafood restaurant just south of Daytona. The main lure, of course, is the food: mouthwatering plates of fresh seafood and other Southern favorites. Hot cinnamon rolls, hush puppies, baked beans, cheese grits, and slaw come with every entrée and can be a meal in themselves. Bring your appetite and your patience—a wait is practically guaranteed. Sunday brunch lures empty stomachs with made-to-order eggs and French toast, and a chocolate fountain. ⑤ *Average main: $24* ⊠ *4009 Halifax Dr., Port Orange* ☎ *386/767–4768* ⊕ *www.auntcatfishontheriver.com* ⌳ *Reservations not accepted.*

$
AMERICAN
✕ **Daytona Brickyard.** It's not just the locals who swear that the Brickyard's charbroiled sirloin burgers are the best they've ever tasted—devotees have been known to drive from Georgia just for lunch. Given its name and location in the heart of NASCAR country, the popular bar and grill is covered in racing memorabilia. Dang, even the floor and the

tablecloths are black-and-white checkered. But don't mistake the racing theme to mean the place merely serves greasy bar food to Joe Sixpacks. It also feeds T-bone and New York strip steaks to doctors. ⑤ *Average main: $12* ✉ *747 International Speedway Blvd.* ☎ *386/253–2270* ⊕ *www.brickyardlounge.com* ⌨ *Reservations not accepted.*

$$$$ ✕ **Hyde Park Prime Steakhouse.** This chophouse provides an upscale alter-
STEAKHOUSE native to Daytona's more prevalent shorts-and-flip-flop joints. The lively dining room—done in dark wood with soft lighting and splashes of colorful artwork—is complemented by dramatic ocean views. Attentive servers carry chalkboards detailing specials such as lobster mac 'n' cheese. But steaks, especially the cuts named after race-car drivers, and mouthwatering sides (don't miss the potatoes Gruyère gratin) are the main attractions. The 22-ounce bone ribeye named after beefy Tony Stewart is, appropriately, the thickest, showing that these guys know their NASCAR. The popular Steak Earnhardt is a filet mignon over bordelaise crowned with lobster, béarnaise (yes, it has two sauces), asparagus, and mushroom caps. An expansive wine list includes over 40 options by the glass. And don't let this restaurant chain's Ohio roots fool you—the key lime pie is absolutely Florida-worthy. ⑤ *Average main: $38* ✉ *Hilton Resort, 100 N. Atlantic Ave.* ☎ *386/226–9844* ⊕ *www.hydeparkrestaurants.com* ⊘ *No lunch.*

$$$ ✕ **Martini's Chophouse.** Local beautiful people seem to flock to this trendy
CONTEMPORARY South Daytona eatery and lounge as much for the scene as for the food.
Fodor's Choice The bar area, done in gray with splashes of lime green, is a modern
★ meeting place for the after-work crowd, and the outdoor deck and bar attract a livelier bunch. Those who do deign to dine appreciate the chef's use of homegrown herbs and creative sauces in dishes such as Bahamian lobster sautée and natural grass-fed filet mignon with Amish blue cheese au jus, frizzled leeks, and mashed potatoes, which can be enjoyed in the sleek dining room or in the garden, complete with a 20-foot lighted waterfall and fire pit. ⑤ *Average main: $23* ✉ *1815 S. Ridgewood Ave., South Daytona Beach* ☎ *386/763–1090* ⊕ *www.martinischophouse. com* ⊘ *Closed Sun. and Mon. No lunch.*

$ ✕ **Tia Cori's Tacos.** Mexican street food is the specialty at this tiny, coun-
MEXICAN ter-service eatery in the downtown riverfront shopping district. The namesake tacos come Mexican style (with onion, cilantro, and lime), but for $0.50 more you can get an Americanized version with cheese. Fillings range from the familiar (chicken, steak, carnitas) to the less familiar (including beef tongue and spicy pork skin). Lines can get long during lunch hour, when surfers, college students, and the downtown business crowd converge for fresh, tasty, and cheap eats. The generously filled Mexican tacos are $1.50 apiece. Other favorites include fish tacos with pineapple and cabbage. The $9.99 steak dinner smothered with onions is another popular choice. Indoor and outdoor seating is available, and a mariachi band performs every Friday night. With a 3 am closing time on weekends, the restaurants is a late-night favorite for college students and the nightclub set. ⑤ *Average main: $6* ✉ *214 N. Beach St.* ☎ *386/947–4333* ⊕ *www.tiacoristacos.com* ⌨ *Reservations not accepted* ⊘ *Closed Sun.*

WHERE TO STAY

$ **Hilton Daytona Beach Oceanfront Resort.** Perched on the only traffic-
RESORT free strip of beach in Daytona, this high-rise is as popular with families as it is with couples. **Pros:** direct beach access; proximity to shops
and restaurants. **Cons:** inconvenient self-parking; extra charges; not all
rooms have balconies. $ *Rooms from: $139* ✉ *100 N. Atlantic Ave.*
☎ *386/254–8200, 866/536–8477* ⊕ *www.daytonahilton.com* ➦ *744
rooms, 52 suites* ⦿ *No meals.*

$ **Perry's Ocean Edge Resort.** Perhaps more than any other property in
RESORT Daytona, Perry's has a die-hard fan base, many of whom started coming
FAMILY to the oceanfront resort as children, then returned with their children
and their children's children. **Pros:** spacious rooms; helpful staff; nice
pools; family-friendly. **Cons:** small bathrooms; décor is dated. $ *Rooms
from: $119* ✉ *2209 S. Atlantic Ave.* ☎ *386/255–0581, 800/447–0002*
⊕ *www.perrysoceanedge.com* ➦ *170 rooms, 30 suites* ⦿ *Breakfast.*

$ **The Shores Resort & Spa.** Rustic furniture and beds swathed in mos-
RESORT quito netting are a nod to Old Florida at this 11-story beachfront resort,
Fodor's Choice but there's nothing rustic about the amenities, including a luxury four-
★ poster bed and a 42-inch plasma TV in every room. **Pros:** beachfront;
spa; friendly staff; 24-hour room service. **Cons:** expensive restaurant;
not all rooms have balconies. $ *Rooms from: $139* ✉ *2637 S. Atlantic
Ave., Daytona Beach Shores* ☎ *386/767–7350, 866/934–7467* ⊕ *www.
shoresresort.com* ➦ *212 rooms, 2 suites* ⦿ *No meals.*

$ **Wyndham Ocean Walk Resort.** Kids definitely won't be bored at this all-
RESORT suites high-rise beachfront resort with four swimming pools, a water-
FAMILY slide, lazy river, game room, indoor miniature-golf course, activities
Fodor's Choice center, and the only traffic-free beach in Daytona Beach. **Pros:** fam-
★ ily-friendly; beachfront; great facilities; in-room washers and dryers;
spacious accommodations. **Cons:** no room service; very slow elevators. $ *Rooms from: $155* ✉ *300 N. Atlantic Ave.* ☎ *386/323–4800,
888/743–2323* ⊕ *www.oceanwalk.com* ➦ *200 1-, 2-, and 3-bedroom
suites* ⦿ *No meals.*

NIGHTLIFE

BARS

Boot Hill Saloon. Despite its reputation as a biker bar, this place welcomes
nonbikers and even nonbiker tourists! ✉ *310 Main St.* ☎ *386/258–9506*
⊕ *www.boothillsaloon.com.*

Ocean Deck. It's the only oceanfront nightclub with live reggae music.
✉ *Ocean Village, 127 S. Ocean Ave.* ☎ *386/253–5224* ⊕ *www.
oceandeck.com.*

Ocean Walk Village. Lively and always hopping, Ocean Walk is a cluster of shops, restaurants, and bars (the Mai Tai Bar is a good bet)
stretching along Atlantic Avenue and the ocean. ✉ *250 N. Atlantic Ave.*
☎ *386/258–9544* ⊕ *www.oceanwalkshoppes.com.*

The Oyster Pub. Sports fans and oyster lovers congregate by the
thousands here. ✉ *555 Seabreeze Blvd.* ☎ *386/255–6348* ⊕ *www.
oysterpub.com.*

DANCE CLUBS

Razzle's Nightclub. DJs play high-energy dance music 8 pm–3 am. ✉ *611 Seabreeze Blvd.* ☎ *386/257–6236* ⊕ *www.razzlesnightclub.com.*

SHOPPING

Daytona Flea and Farmers' Market. One of the largest flea markets in the South draws residents from all over the state as well as visitors to the state. It's open weekends, including Friday, from 9 to 5. ✉ *2987 Bellevue Ave.* ☎ *386/253–3330* ⊕ *www.daytonafleamarket.com.*

Destination Daytona. This 100-acre biker enclave is complete with an expansive Harley-Davidson dealership; retail shops; a restaurant; bars; a tattoo parlor; a hotel; and a pavilion used for concerts, conventions—and even biker-inspired weddings. ✉ *1635 N. U.S. 1, Ormond Beach* ⊕ *www.brucerossmeyer.com.*

The Pavilion at Port Orange. Just off Interstate 95 (Port Orange exit), this outdoor shopping complex houses a 14-screen Hollywood Theaters; numerous restaurants; and retailers like the Southern department store, Belk, and ULTA beauty and cosmetics. ✉ *5501 S. Williamson Blvd., Port Orange* ⊕ *www.thepavilionatportorange.com.*

Volusia Mall. This mall has more than 125 stores, including anchors like JCPenney, Macy's, and Dillard's. ✉ *1700 W. International Speedway Blvd.* ☎ *386/253–6783* ⊕ *www.volusiamall.net.*

SPORTS AND THE OUTDOORS

BIRD-WATCHING

Tomoka State Park. With more than 160 species to see, this scenic park is perfect for bird-watching. It also has wooded campsites, bicycle and walking paths, and kayak and canoe rentals on the Tomoka and Halifax rivers. It's on the site of a Timucuan Indian settlement discovered in 1605 by Spanish explorer Alvaro Mexia. ✉ *2099 N. Beach St., 3 miles north of Ormond Beach* ☎ *386/676–4050* ⊕ *www.floridastateparks. org/tomoka* 🎟 *$5 per vehicle, up to 8 people; $2 pedestrians* ⊙ *Daily 8–sunset.*

BOATING

Cracker Creek. At this eco-adventure park you can rent kayaks, canoes, hydrobikes, and pontoon boats or take ecotours or a Pirate Cruise on scenic Spruce Creek. There are also on-site picnic facilities. ✉ *1795 Taylor Rd., Port Orange* ☎ *386/304–0778* ⊕ *www.crackercreek.com* ⊙ *Wed.–Sun. 8–5; canoeing and kayaking by reservation only.*

FISHING

Sea Spirit Fishing. Four- to 12-hour private and group charters are options with this operator. ✉ *Inlet Harbor Marina, 133 Inlet Harbor Rd., Ponce Inlet* ☎ *386/763–4388* ⊕ *www.seaspiritfishing.com.*

GOLF

Club at Pelican Bay South Course. Golfers rave about the great value of Pelican Bay South, but one word of caution: what you save in greens fees you might give back in lost balls. No, this isn't the most difficult track. But the abundance of water—and challenging ocean breezes—can result in a lot of splashes for novices or overaggressive advanced players. Designed by Lloyd Clifton in 1984, the course is open to the public and

Continued on page 696

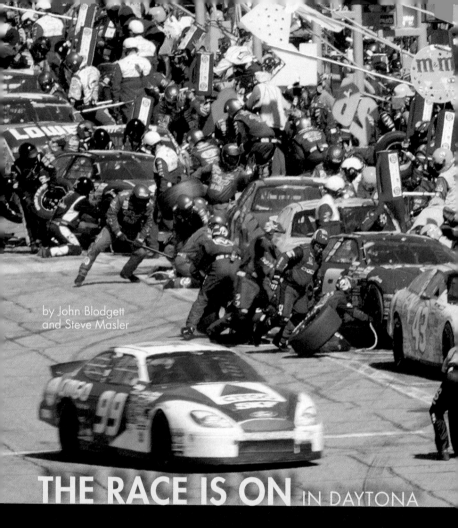

by John Blodgett
and Steve Masler

THE RACE IS ON IN DAYTONA

It's morning on race day. Check the weather—rain or shine? The race won't run if it's raining, but bring a poncho just in case, and pack some sunscreen, too. Oh, and don't forget your binoculars and ear plugs. Fill your cooler with snacks and drinks—yes, it's allowed. Got your waterproof padded seat? Good. If you have a radio scanner, bring it to listen in on the pit crews; if you don't, you can rent one at the track for $50 ($30 for Sprint customers). This handheld device, in addition to its scanning capabilities, provides live video feeds, driver statistics, and auto replay.

You're here! Welcome to Daytona International Speedway—the storied race track that is home to one of America's most famous races, the Daytona 500. Hope you like crowds, because you'll be jostling with upward of 150,000 fellow race fanatics. The gate generally opens at 8 AM, with the race starting at 1 PM. The hours in between are one of the best times to seek autographs from your favorite racers in their garages near the Sprint FANZONE (drivers also can be approached throughout race weekend as they hang out at their respective souvenir haulers).

Watching the race is a sensory experience: 43 cars powered by 500 or more horsepower make

DAYTONA ROARS ALL YEAR LONG

As the headquarter city for the National Association for Stock Car Auto Racing, better known as NASCAR, Daytona celebrates auto racing year-round. So while the Daytona 500 happens just one day out of 365, there's plenty for you to see and do every day at the speedway's 480-acre complex. You can go to other races, go on a tour, or, as part of the Richard Petty Driving Experience, maybe even jump into a stock car yourself. Major races are held during nine weekends, and an assortment of other races take place throughout the year. On non-race days the Speedway is host to R&D of racing vehicles, car shows, and other events. For motorcycles, there's the Daytona 200 and the Daytona Supercross by Honda.

for a constant roar; there's the smell of hot rubber, fuel, and exhaust; and, if you happen to be down low by the track itself, you might be pelted by flecks of tire as the pack blasts by at speeds approaching 190 mph. Every so often, let your binoculars wander—you might just see a past champion or other celebrity.

A few hours later the adrenaline-packed race is finished and your ears will be ringing (unless you remembered plugs). Now it's time to cheer the victor and wait in line to go find your car. This is when you grab another beverage from your cooler and relive the race with the fans next to you.

THE LAPS ALONG THE WAY

For more than 50 years, the world's top NASCAR drivers have competed in the Daytona 500, considered by many to be the sport's premier race.

The first official Daytona 500 was held on February 22, 1959, with 59 cars in front of 41,000 fans. It has been held each year in late February ever since. In the half century that followed, cash awards have grown from $68,000 to $18 million, with fewer drivers—43—but double the fans—150,000. Every year the 500-mile (200-lap) race marks the beginning of NASCAR's premier Sprint Cup series and generally offers the greatest monetary reward. Winning the Daytona 500 has been equated with a Super Bowl victory, and much as in that sport, the final moments can be the most memorable and most important.

GETTING TICKETS

For tickets to the Daytona 500 or any other races held at the speedway, contact the Daytona Speedway ticket office (✉ 1801 W. International Speedway Blvd., Daytona Beach ☎ 800/PIT-SHOP [748–7467] ⊕ www.daytonainternationalspeedway.com). Single ticket prices to the Daytona 500 range from $65 to $185, primo seats go quickly, so the sooner you order the better. Grandstand seats typically sell out days or weeks in advance.

NASCAR'S FINEST

David Pearson
"The Silver Fox"
105 NASCAR wins
retired in 1986.

Dale Earnhardt
"The Intimidator"
"Ironhead"
Killed during the
2001 Daytona 500.

Richard Petty
"King Richard,"
Most NASCAR wins
(200) and Daytona
victories (7).

Jimmie Johnson
Won his sixth
consecutive Sprint
Cup championship
in 2013.

Getting out and inspecting the track first hand is just one part of a Daytona Speedway tour.

You don't have to wait until race days to explore the World Center of Racing. Some of the best exploring can be done when the engines are silent. Narrated tours give you a look at the hallowed grounds where Fireball Roberts, Bobby Allison, Richard Petty, and Dale Earnhardt turned a regional sport into an international phenomenon.

The 90-minute All Access Tour ($23; hourly 10–3) brings you into the ritzy Daytona 500 Club and the Houston Lawing Press Box in the Sprint Tower, which features views not only of the 2.5-mile tri-oval, but also of the Atlantic Ocean nearby. You'll also visit the drivers' meeting room, the NASCAR Sprint Cup garages, Gatorade Victory Lane, and the Sprint FANZONE. There are three dramatic photo opportunities on the tour: Victory Lane, the start/finish line, and the daunting 31-degree banking in Turns 3 and 4.

Other options include the 30-minute Speedway Tour ($16; 11:30, 1:30, 3:30, and 4) and the three-hour VIP Tour ($50; by reservation on select days). ✉ 1801 W. International Speedway Blvd. ☎ 800/748–7467 ⊕ www.daytonainternationalspeedway.com.

If you're not satisfied with merely viewing the historic speedway, driving opportunities are also available through the Richard Petty

Driving Experience. You can ride shotgun—or, for more dough, drive yourself—in a stock car on Daytona International Speedway. You suit up, helmet and all, and slide into the car through the window, just like you're Jimmie Johnson. Be sure to get a photo afterward so your friends believe you when you tell them how you zoomed around at speeds in excess of 150 mph! Ride-alongs cost $135; call for driving prices and to reserve a ride. ☎ 800-BE PETTY (800/237–3389).

LADIES WELCOME

Stock-car racing has long been a male-dominated sport, but icons such as Dale Earnhardt Jr. and Jeff Gordon have been, on occasion, overshadowed by women. Danica Patrick, the pint-sized, telegenic driver of Indy Car fame made her NAS-CAR debut at Daytona in a 2010 Nationwide Series race. Patrick, who made her Sprint Cup debut in 2012, is among a growing number of women entering motorsports but one of only a few to break into NASCAR.

The Florida Trail goes through Ocala National Forest, taking hikers past hardwoods, pines, and prairies.

features an island green on the par-4 15th. It's worth sticking around for lunch or dinner at the 19th Hole Bar & Grill. ✉ *350 Pelican Bay Dr.* ☎ *386/756–0034* ⊕ *www.pelicanbaycc.com* 🖃 *$35 for 18 holes* 🏌 *18 holes. 6630 yards. par 72.*

LPGA International. This is where aspiring women professionals compete to earn a place on the LPGA Tour. The qualifying tournament—Q-school—is held every January, but the meticulously maintained courses are open to the public year-round. The Jones Course, designed by Rees Jones, is a links-style course with large, fast, undulating greens. Fairways are tighter on the Hills Course, designed by Arthur Hills, with long, difficult par 5s due to long carries and well-guarded greens. Wildlife is abundant, with bald eagles, owls, and deer as well as rattlesnakes and gators (some quite large). The course has driving, putting, and short-game practice areas, and an excellent restaurant, Malcolm's. ✉ *1000 Champions Dr.* ☎ *386/523–2001* ⊕ *www.lpgainternational. com* 🖃 *$74 for 18 holes* 🏌 *Jones Course: 18 holes. 7088 yards. par 72. Hills Course: 18 holes. 6984 yards. par 72.*

Spruce Creek Golf & Country Club. Golfers distracted by loud noise might want to avoid this course, which is part of a fly-in community whose residents have included John Travolta and NASCAR star Mark Martin. Most, however, find the air traffic a unique amenity to this semiprivate course, considered one of the best golf values in the Daytona Beach area. The front 9 are challenging off the tees, with some tight, tree-lined fairways. Wind is more of a challenge on the more open back 9, where water lines 8 of the holes. A virtual tour on the club website gives golfers shot-by-shot advice in managing the course, which boasts a driving range as well as putting and short-game practice areas. ✉ *1900 Country Club Dr., Port Orange* ☎ *386/756–6114* ⊕ *www.sprucecreekgolf.com* ✏ *$40 for 18 holes, $25 for 9 holes* ⚲ *18 holes. 6894 yards. par 72.*

MANATEE SPOTTING

Blue Spring State Park. January and February are the top months for sighting sea cows at this designated manatee refuge, but they begin to head here in November, as soon as the water gets cold enough (below 68°F). Your best bet for spotting a manatee is to walk along the boardwalk. The park, which is 30 miles southwest of Daytona Beach on Interstate 4, was once a river port where paddle wheelers stopped to take on cargoes of oranges. Home to the largest spring on the St. Johns River, the park offers hiking, camping, picnicking facilities, and two-bedroom cabins ($95 a night, 2-night minimum weekends and holidays). It also contains a historic homestead that's open to the public. ✉ *2100 W. French Ave., Orange City* ☎ *386/775–3663* ⊕ *www.floridastateparks. org/bluespring* ✏ *$6 per vehicle, up to 8 people; $2 pedestrians, bicyclists* ⊙ *Daily 8–sunset.*

FAMILY **Manatee Scenic Boat Tours.** This Ponce Inlet operator takes you on narrated cruises of the Intracoastal Waterway. Kids will love looking for the creatures also known as "sea cows," and your guide might tell you how (sun-delirious?) sailors may have mistaken them for mermaids. ✉ *133 Inlet Harbor Rd., Ponce Inlet* ☎ *386/761–2027, 800/881–2628* ⊕ *www.manateecruise.com* ✏ *$25.*

WATER SPORTS

Daytona Beach Parasail. Catch air with this Ponce Inlet outfitter. ✉ *4936 S. Peninsula Dr., Ponce Inlet* ☎ *386/547–6067* ⊕ *www. daytonaparasailing.com.*

Maui Nix. This is one of several outfitters that rent surf and body boards. ✉ *635 N. Atlantic Ave.* ☎ *386/253–1234* ⊕ *www.mauinix.com/store.*

Salty Dog Surf Shop. You can rent surfboards or paddleboards here. ✉ *700 E. International Speedway Blvd.* ☎ *386/258–0457* ⊕ *www. saltydogsurfshop.com.*

NEW SMYRNA BEACH

19 miles south of Daytona Beach, 56 miles northeast of Orlando.

The long, dune-lined beach of this small town abuts the Canaveral National Seashore. Behind the dunes sit beach houses, small motels, and an occasional high-rise (except at the extreme northern tip, where none is higher than seven stories). Canal Street, on the mainland, and Flagler Avenue, with many beachside shops and restaurants, have both been "streetscaped" with wide brick sidewalks and stately palm trees. The town is also known for its internationally recognized artists' workshop and some of the best surfing on the East Coast.

EXPLORING

Arts on Douglas. In a warehouse that has been converted into a stunning 5,000-square-foot, high-ceiling art gallery, Arts on Douglas has a new exhibit of works by a Florida artist every month. Representing more than 50 Florida artists, the gallery has hosted exhibits on the handmade jewelry of Mary Schimpff Webb and landscape and still-life oils by Barbara Tiffany. The gallery also holds an opening reception every first Saturday of the month from 4 to 7 pm. ⊠ *123 Douglas St.* ☎ *386/428–1133* ⊕ *www.artsondouglas.net* ☒ *Free* ⊙ *Tues.–Fri. 10–5, Sat. 11–3, and by appointment.*

Atlantic Center for the Arts. With exhibits that change every two months, the Atlantic Center for the Arts has works of internationally known artists. Mediums include sculpture, mixed materials, video, drawings, prints, and paintings. Intensive three-week residencies are periodically run by visual-, literary-, and performing-master artists such as Edward Albee, James Dickey, and Beverly Pepper. ⊠ *1414 Art Center Ave.* ☎ *386/427–6975* ⊕ *www.atlanticcenterforthearts.org* ☒ *Free* ⊙ *Tues.– Fri. 10–4, Sat. 10–2.*

Canaveral National Seashore. Miles of grassy windswept dunes and a virtually empty beach await you at this remarkable 57,000-acre park on a barrier island with 24 miles of undeveloped coastline spanning from New Smyrna to Titusville. The unspoiled area of hilly sand dunes, grassy marshes, and seashell-sprinkled beaches is a large part of NASA's buffer zone and is home to more than 1,000 species of plants and 300 species of birds and other animals. Surf and lagoon fishing are available, and a hiking trail leads to the top of an American Indian shell midden at Turtle Mound. For an additional charge, visitors can take a pontoon-boat tour ($20) or participate in the turtle-watch interpretive program ($14). Reservations are required. A visitor center is on Route A1A at Apollo Beach. Weekends are busy, and parts of the park are closed when mandated by NASA launch operations at the Kennedy Space Center, so call ahead. ⊠ *Visitor Information Center, 7611 S. Atlantic Ave.* ☎ *386/428–3384* ⊕ *www.nps.gov/cana* ☒ *$5 cars; $1 pedestrians, bicycles* ⊙ *Nov.–Mar., daily 6–6; Apr.–Oct., daily 6 am–8 pm.*

Smyrna Dunes Park. In this park, on a barrier island at the northernmost tip of New Smyrna Beach peninsula, 1½ miles of boardwalks criss-cross sand dunes and delicate dune vegetation to lead to beaches and a fishing jetty. Botanical signs identify the flora, and there are picnic tables and an information center. It's also one of the few county parks where pets are allowed (on leashes, that is). ⊠ *2995 N. Peninsula Ave.* ☎ *386/424–2935* ⊕ *www.volusia.org/parks/smyrnadunes.htm* ☒ *$5 per vehicle, up to 8 people* ⊙ *Daily sunrise–sunset.*

BEACHES

Apollo Beach. In addition to typical beach activities, visitors to this beach on the northern end of Canaveral National Seashore can also ride horses here (with a permit), hike self-guided trails, and tour the historic Eldora Statehouse. From I–95, take Exit 220 and head east. **Amenities:** lifeguards (seasonal); parking (fee); toilets. **Best for:** solitude; swimming; walking. ⊠ *Rte. A1A, at the southern end of New Smyrna Beach* ☎ *386/428–3384* ☒ *$5 per vehicle for national seashore.*

New Smyrna Beach. This public beach extends 7 miles from the north-ernmost part of New Smyrna's barrier island south to the Canaveral National Seashore. It's mostly hard-packed white sand, and at low tide can be stunningly wide in some areas. The beach is lined with heaps of sandy dunes, but because they're endangered, it's against the law to walk on or play in them or to pick the sea grass, which helps to stabilize the dunes. From sunrise to sunset cars are allowed on certain sections of the beach (speed limit: 10 mph). In season there's a $5 beach-access fee for cars. **Amenities:** food and drink; lifeguards; parking (some with fee); showers; toilets; water sports. **Best for:** sunrise; surfing; swimming; walking. ⊠ *Rte. A1A.*

WHERE TO EAT

$$
SEAFOOD
✕ **J. B.'s Fish Camp and Restaurant.** Better known simply as J. B.'s, this local landmark is on the eastern shore of the Indian River (i.e., the middle of nowhere). Crowds gather around the picnic-style tables inside and out, or belly up to the bar to dine on mounds of spicy seafood, Cajun alligator, J. B.'s famous crab cakes, and blue crabs by the dozen. It's a great place to catch the sunset, and there's live music weekend afternoons. Five bucks says at least one person at your table says their hush puppies are the best he's ever eaten. [$] *Average main: $17* ⊠ *859 Pompano Ave.* ☎ *386/427–5747* ⊕ *www.jbsfishcamp.com* ⟿ *Reservations not accepted.*

$
SEAFOOD
✕ **Norwood's Seafood Restaurant.** Fresh local fish and shrimp are the specialties at this bustling New Smyrna Beach landmark, open since 1946. Built as a gas station, the building later served as a general store and piggy-bank factory, but the remodeled interior belies this backstory; the place is replete with wood, from the chairs and booths to the walls and rafters. Order steak, pasta, or innovative seafood dishes such as seared grouper topped with wasabi cream and served over a Yukon gold potato cake (yeah, it's as good as it sounds). Prices are reasonable, and more than 3,000 bottles of wine are on hand. Don't be fooled by the fancy wine list and linen tablecloths; you can still wear shorts (business casual, however, is the norm). [$] *Average main: $12* ⊠ *400 2nd Ave.* ☎ *386/428–4621* ⊕ *www.norwoods.com.com* ⟿ *Reservations not accepted.*

$$$
CUBAN
✕ **Spanish River Grill.** Michele and Henry Salgado own this modern Cuban and Spanish eatery, which many locals think is the best restaurant in New Smyrna Beach. Though many consider the cuisine to represent fine dining, overall the restaurant is casual and unpretentious. Henry combines his Cuban grandmother's recipes with local ingredients for knockout results. Start with the fried green plantains or local clams steamed in white wine, garlic, and tomato. For your main course, try the yuca-crusted fresh fish or mojo-marinated grilled ribeye. Be sure to save room for one of Michele's desserts. Sunday sees a brunch from 11 to 3. [$] *Average main: $20* ⊠ *737 E. 3rd Ave.* ☎ *386/424–6991* ⊕ *www. thespanishrivergrill.com* ⟿ *Reservations not accepted* ☉ *Closed Mon.*

WHERE TO STAY

$
B&B/INN
Fodor'sChoice
★
▦ **Black Dolphin Inn.** On a quaint residential street, this Spanish-style, three-story inn combines the charm and hospitality of a B&B with modern sensibilities and a chic, coastal-casual vibe. **Pros:** hospitable staff; river views; comfy beds. **Cons:** no pool; must drive to the beach. [$] *Rooms from: $159* ⊠ *916 S. Riverside Dr.* ☎ *386/410–4868, 855/410–4868* ⊕ *www.blackdolphininn.com* ⟿ *14 rooms* ⏀ *Breakfast.*

$ ⬚ **Riverview Hotel and Spa.** A landmark since 1885, this former bridge
B&B/INN tender's home is set back from the Intracoastal Waterway at the edge of
the north causeway, which still has an operating drawbridge. **Pros:** on-
site spa and dining; hospitable staff; homey feel. **Cons:** small rooms in
main house; strict cancellation policy; blocks from the beach. ⑤ *Rooms
from: $142* ✉ *103 Flagler Ave.* ☎ *386/428–5858, 800/945–7416*
⊕ *www.riverviewhotel.com* ⤴ *17 rooms, 1 suite* ⦿ *Breakfast.*

OCALA NATIONAL FOREST

*Eastern entrance 40 miles west of Daytona Beach, northern entrance
52 miles south of Jacksonville.*

This breathtaking 383,000-acre national forest off Route 40 has lakes,
springs, rivers, hiking trails, campgrounds, and historic sites. It also has
the largest off-highway vehicle trail system in the Southeast and three
major recreational areas: Alexander Springs, Salt Springs, and Juniper
Springs. To get here, take Interstate 4 east to Exit 92, and head west
on Route 436 to U.S. 441, which you take north to Route 19 north.

Alexander Springs Recreation Area. In this recreation area you'll find a
stream for swimming and a campground. ✉ *49525 Rte. 445 S, off Rte
40, Altoona* ⊕ *www.recreation.gov* ✉ *$5.50.*

Juniper Springs Recreation Area. Here you'll find a stone waterwheel
house, a campground, a natural-spring swimming pool, and hiking
trails. The 7-mile Juniper Springs run is a narrow, twisting, and winding
canoe ride, which, although exhilarating, isn't for the novice. ✉ *14100
Rte. 40 N, Silver Springs* ⊕ *www.recreation.gov* ✉ *$5.*

Oklawaha Visitor Center. The busiest of the three visitor centers for Ocala
National Forest is just outside Silver Spring. Stop in to get information
on recreation and trails in the forest as well as maps. This is the center
that can give you information on recreation throughout the region.
✉ *Ocala National Forest, 3199 N.E. Rte. 315, and Gulf Dr., Silver
Springs* ☎ *352/236–0288* ⊕ *www.fs.usda.gov/Ocala.*

Salt Springs Recreation Area. The draw here is a natural saltwater spring
where Atlantic blue crabs come to spawn each summer. The forest has a
visitor center here as well. ✉ *Visitor Center, 14100 Rte. 19, Fort McCoy*
☎ *352/685–3070* ✉ *$5.50.*

SPORTS AND THE OUTDOORS
CANOEING
Juniper Springs Canoe Rentals. This operator inside the national forest
offers canoe rentals. ✉ *Juniper Springs Recreation Area, 26701 Rte.
40, Silver Springs* ☎ *877/444–6777.*

FISHING
Captain Tom's Custom Charters. Charter fishing trips offered by this company range from two hours to a full day. You can arrange sightseeing
cruises as well. Trips are by reservation only and are operated in a
variety of areas within the national forest. ☎ *352/236–0872* ⊕ *www.
captaintomscustomcharters.net.*

HORSEBACK RIDING

Adopt a Horse Club. Located within the Ocala National Forest, this outfitter offers trail riding and lessons (walk, gait, and canter) for all ages. ⊠ *22651 S.E. Rte. 42, Umatilla* ☎ *352/821–4756, 800/731–4756* ⊕ *www.adoptahorseclub.com.*

GAINESVILLE

98 miles northwest of Daytona Beach.

13

The University of Florida (UF) anchors this sprawling town. Visitors are mostly Gator football fans and parents of students, so the styles and costs of accommodations are aimed at budget-minded travelers rather than luxury-seeking vacationers. The surrounding area encompasses several state parks and interesting gardens and geological sites.

GETTING HERE AND AROUND

Gainesville Regional Airport is served by American, Delta, United, and US Airways. From the airport, taxi fare to the center of Gainesville is about $20; some hotels provide free airport pickup.

Contact Gainesville Regional Airport *(GNV).* ⊠ *3880 N.E. 39th Ave.* ☎ *352/373–0249* ⊕ *www.gra-gnv.com.*

VISITOR INFORMATION

Contact Gainesville/Alachua County Visitors and Convention Bureau ☎ *352/374–5260, 866/778–5002* ⊕ *www.visitgainesville.com.*

EXPLORING

Devil's Millhopper Geological State Park. Scientists surmise that thousands of years ago an underground cavern collapsed and created this geological wonder that is designated as a National Natural Landmark. You pass a dozen small waterfalls as you head down 236 steps to the bottom of this botanical wonderland: exotic subtropical ferns and trees growing in a 500-foot-wide, 120-foot-deep sinkhole. You can pack a lunch to enjoy in one of the park's picnic areas. And bring Spot, too; just keep him on a leash. Guided walks with a park ranger are offered Saturday mornings at 10. ⊠ *4732 Millhopper Rd., off U.S. 441* ☎ *352/955–2008* ⊕ *www.floridastateparks.org/devilsmillhopper* 🖾 *$4 per vehicle, up to 8 people; $2 pedestrians and bicyclists* ⊙ *Wed.–Sun. 9–5.*

FAMILY **Florida Museum of Natural History.** On the campus of the University of Florida, the state's official museum of natural history and the largest natural-history museum in the Southeast has holdings of more than 40 million objects and specimens. In addition to active collections in anthropology, archaeology, botany, mammalogy, and ornithology, the museum features several interesting replicas, including nearly complete fossil skeletons of a mastodon and mammoth from the last ice age as well as a full-size model of a Florida cave and mangrove forest. The Butterfly Rainforest houses 60 to 80 species in a 6,400-square-foot, screened, free-flight vivarium. Butterfly releases take place weekdays at 2, and weekends at 2, 3, and 4, weather permitting. ⊠ *University of Florida Cultural Plaza, S.W. 34th St. and Hull Rd.* ☎ *352/846–2000* ⊕ *www.flmnh.ufl.edu* 🖾 *Free; Butterfly Rainforest $10.50* ⊙ *Mon.–Sat. 10–5, Sun. 1–5.*

FAMILY **Marjorie Kinnan Rawlings Historic State Park.** One of America's most cherished authors found inspiration in this out-of-the-way hamlet about 20 miles outside of Gainesville. The 90-acre park, set amid aromatic citrus groves, has a playground for kids and short hiking trails, where you might see owls, deer, or Rawlings' beloved "red birds." But the main attraction is the restored Florida Cracker–style home, where Rawlings wrote classics such as *The Yearling* and *Cross Creek* and entertained the likes of poet Robert Frost, author Thornton Wilder, and actor Gregory Peck. Although the house is guarded closely by spirited roosters, guided tours ($3) are offered seasonally. ⊠ *18700 South County Rd. 325, Hawthorne* ☎ *352/466–3672* ⊕ *www.floridastateparks.org/marjoriekinnanrawlings* ⊠ *$3 per car, house tour $3* ⊙ *Daily 9–5; house tours Oct.–July, Thu.–Sun. at 10, 11, 1, 2, 3, and 4.*

> ## LATER, GATORS
>
> Depending on what time of year you visit, Gainesville's population could be plus or minus 50,000. Home to one of the largest colleges in the country, the University of Florida, Gainesville takes on a different personality during the summer, when most students return home. During the fall and spring terms, the downtown streets are teeming with students on bikes, scooters, and foot, but in summer it's much more laid-back.

Samuel P. Harn Museum of Art. This 112,800-square-foot museum has five main collections: Asian, with works dating back to the Neolithic era; African, encompassing costumes, domestic wares, and personal adornments; Modern, featuring the works of Georgia O'Keeffe, William Morris Hunt, Claude Monet, and George Bellows; Contemporary, with original pieces by Yayoi Kusama and El Anatsui; and Photography, including the work of Jerry N. Uelsmann, a retired University of Florida professor. ⊠ *3259 Hull Rd.* ☎ *352/392–9826* ⊕ *www.harn.ufl.edu* ⊠ *Free* ⊙ *Tues.–Fri. 11–5, Sat. 10–5, Sun. 1–5.*

WHERE TO EAT

$ ✕ **Bistro 1245.** You can get high-quality meals at bargain-basement prices
ECLECTIC at this trendy yet surprisingly down-to-earth restaurant, which shares a roof with Leonardo's by the Slice. Some call the small dining room cramped, while others find the close quarters romantic. However you look at it, the menu is full of comfort foods with a twist, such as maple-roasted chicken breast, spicy shrimp pasta, a seared-tuna club sandwich, and bison sirloin. In keeping with the bistro's lack of pretention, you're invited to pick your own wine from the restaurant's wine rack. For a lighter meal and a lighter price, order from the lunch menu in the evening. $ *Average main: $13* ⊠ *1245 W. University Ave.* ☎ *352/376–0000* ⊕ *www.leonardosgainesville.com.*

$ ✕ **Emiliano's Café.** Linen tablecloths and art deco–style artwork create
LATIN AMERICAN a casual, elegant feel at this Gainesville institution serving Pan-Latin cuisine for more than 20 years. Dine indoors or beneath the stars at the sidewalk café. Start with the Galician stew (a family recipe) or the black-bean soup, and then move on to one of the chef's signature dishes— Spanish saffron rice with shrimp, clams, mussels, fresh fish, chicken,

artichoke hearts, peas, asparagus, and pimientos. Emiliano's also offers an extensive tapas menu with nearly 40 items to mix and match, and tempting desserts like the original chipotle brownie cake. Live jazz fills the air Monday and Wednesday nights. ⑤ *Average main: $15* ✉ *7 S.E. 1st Ave.* ☎ *352/375–7381* ⊕ *www.emilianoscafe.com.*

$ ✕ **Leonardo's by the Slice.** It's ironic that the kitschy pizza joint with 1950s
ITALIAN   flair is surrounded by a white-picket fence, since most of its patrons and employees are far from conventional. College students, especially the pierced and tatted kind, flock to the Gainesville landmark not only because it's cheap but because it has the best pizza in town. Available in thick or thin varieties, by the pie and, of course, by the slice, Leonardo's pizza comes in a handful of varieties (like veggie, pepperoni, Greek, and spinach tomato). It also offers calzones, salads, and pasta such as baked ziti and fettuccine Alfredo, with no nonpizza entrée over $8.95. ⑤ *Average main: $12* ✉ *1245 W. University Ave.* ☎ *352/378–2001* ⊕ *www. leonardosgainesville.com* ⌔ *Reservations not accepted.*

$$$ ✕ **Paramount Grill.** This tiny, fine-dining restaurant may have single-
EUROPEAN   handedly changed the perception of Gainesville from a college town
Fodor's Choice   fueled by pizza, chicken wings, and pitchers of beer to an up-and-com-
★   ing culinary destination with imaginative menus driven by fresh Florida produce. What Paramount lacks in size and glitz it makes up for with its ever-changing menu. Try the organic beet salad and such entrées as sesame-roasted domestic red snapper with coconut milk and lemon-grass basmati rice, or grilled butcher-cut pork chops with white-cheddar polenta. If you miss lunch here, try the Sunday brunch. ⑤ *Average main: $26* ✉ *12 S.W. 1st Ave.* ☎ *352/378–3398* ⊕ *www.paramountgrill.com* ⊘ *No lunch Sat.*

WHERE TO STAY

$ ⚏ **Herlong Mansion.** Spanish moss clings to the stately oak trees sur-
B&B/INN   rounding this restored 1880s mansion, now a comfortable B&B in the town of Micanopy, 11 miles north of Gainesville. **Pros:** large private bathrooms; gourmet breakfast; evening wine-and-cookies reception. **Cons:** no phones in rooms; no TVs in some rooms; some small and windowless rooms; 14-day cancellation policy. ⑤ *Rooms from: $119* ✉ *402 N.E. Cholokka Blvd., Micanopy* ☎ *352/466–3322, 800/437–5664* ⊕ *www.herlong.com* ⋙ *10 rooms, 2 cottages* ⑪ *Breakfast.*

$ ⚏ **Hilton University of Florida Conference Center Gainesville.** With 25,000
HOTEL   square feet of meeting space, the University of Florida's flagship hotel caters most obviously to business travelers, but its location on the south-west corner of campus also makes it a good choice for UF visitors. **Pros:** proximity to college; spacious rooms; free use of business center. **Cons:** spotty service; overrated restaurant; charge for Wi-Fi. ⑤ *Rooms from: $109* ✉ *1714 S.W. 34th St.* ☎ *352/371–3600* ⊕ *www.hilton.com* ⋙ *245 rooms, 3 suites* ⑪ *No meals.*

$ ⚏ **Laurel Oak Inn.** Guests at this 1885 Queen Anne–style dwelling say
B&B/INN   they're so comfortable and at ease they feel like they're in a home, not an inn. **Pros:** three-course breakfast; location; hospitable staff. **Cons:** processing fee for cancellations; no pool. ⑤ *Rooms from: $140* ✉ *221 S.E. 7th St.* ☎ *352/373–4535* ⊕ *www.laureloakinn.com* ⋙ *5 rooms* ⑪ *Breakfast.*

13

$ ⬚ **Magnolia Plantation Inn.** Among only a handful of French Second
B&B/INN   Empire buildings in the southeastern United States, this inn consists of
Fodor's Choice   a main house, built in 1885, and nine adorable cottages. **Pros:** friendly
★   service; breakfast; nightly social hour. **Cons:** small rooms; seven-
day cancellation policy; some uncomfortable beds. ⑤ *Rooms from:
$145* ✉ *309 S.E. 7th St.* ☎ *352/375–6653, 800/201–2379* ⊕ *www.
magnoliabnb.com* ⇄ *5 rooms, 9 cottages* ⚬⧉ *Breakfast.*

$ ⬚ **Sweetwater Branch Inn Bed & Breakfast.** Modern conveniences such as
B&B/INN   hair dryers, complimentary Wi-Fi, a new pool, and business services mix
with Southern charm and hospitality, all wrapped up in two grand Victorian homes surrounded by lush tropical gardens. **Pros:** Southern-style
breakfast; Jacuzzi suites. **Cons:** occasional noise issues; frequent on-site
weddings. ⑤ *Rooms from: $139* ✉ *625 E. University Ave.* ☎ *352/373–
6760, 800/595–7760* ⊕ *www.sweetwaterinn.com* ⇄ *12 rooms, 7 cottages* ⚬⧉ *Breakfast.*

NIGHTLIFE

Lillian's Music Store. Gainesville's oldest bar has rock and Top 40 music,
bands, and karaoke. ✉ *112 S.E. 1st St.* ☎ *352/372–1010.*

1982 Bar. There's music five nights a week and a wide variety of video
games. ✉ *919 W. University Ave.* ☎ *352/371–9836* ⊕ *www.1982bar.
com.*

The Swamp Restaurant. This place attracts college students by the pitcher,
especially on game day. ✉ *1642 W. University Ave.* ☎ *352/377–9267*
⊕ *www.swamprestaurant.com.*

SPORTS AND THE OUTDOORS

AUTO RACING

Auto Plus Raceway. The site of professional and amateur auto and motorcycle races, including Gatornationals in March, is also home to Frank
Hawley's Drag Racing School (☎ *866/480–7223* ⊕ *www.frankhaw-
ley.com*). ✉ *11211 N. County Rd. 225* ☎ *352/377–0046* ⊕ *www.
autoplusraceway.com.*

FOOTBALL

Ben Hill Griffin Stadium. The University of Florida Gators play their
home games in the largest stadium in the state, also referred to as
"The Swamp." ✉ *Lemerand Dr. and Stadium Rd.* ☎ *352/375–4683.*

THE SPACE COAST

South of the Daytona Beach area and Canaveral National Seashore are
Merritt Island National Wildlife Refuge and the John F. Kennedy Space
Center. This area is also home to the laid-back town of Cocoa Beach,
which attracts visitors on weekends year-round because it's the closest
beach to Orlando, 50 miles to the east.

VISITOR INFORMATION

Contact Space Coast Office of Tourism ☎ *877/572-3224, 321/433-4470*
⊕ *www.visitspacecoast.com.*

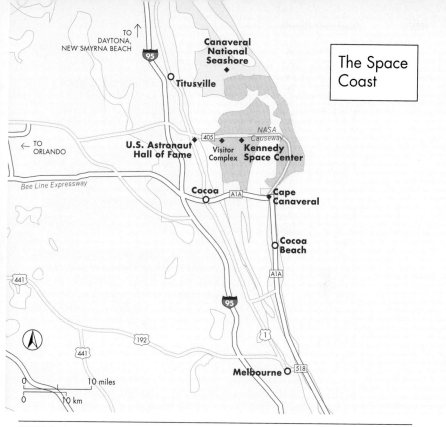

TITUSVILLE

34 miles south of New Smyrna Beach, 67 miles east of Orlando.

It's unusual that such a small, easily overlooked community could accommodate what it does, namely the magnificent Merritt Island National Wildlife Refuge and the entrance to the Kennedy Space Center, the nerve center of the U.S. space program *(➪ See In-Focus feature, "Soaring High at Kennedy Space Center").*

EXPLORING

American Police Hall of Fame & Museum. You know police officers deserve your respect, and you'll be reminded why at this intriguing attraction. In addition to memorabilia like the RoboCop costume and Blade Runner car from the films, informative displays offer insight into the dangers officers face every day: drugs, homicides, and criminals who can create knives from dental putty and guns from a bicycle spoke (really). Other exhibits spotlight the history of capital punishment (from hangings to the guillotine to the electric chair) and crime scene investigation, terrorism, and a rotunda where more than 9,000 names are etched in marble to honor police officers who have died in the line of duty. The 24-lane shooting range provides rental guns (Tuesday to Friday noon–8, weekends noon–6). ✉ *6350 Hori-zon Dr.* ☎ *321/264–0911* ⊕ *www.aphf.org* 🔁 *$13* 🕐 *Daily 10–6.*

Valiant Air Command Warbird Museum & Tico Airshow. Although its exterior looks sort of squirrelly, what's inside here is certainly impressive. Aviation buffs won't want to miss memorabilia from World Wars I and II, Korea, and Vietnam, as well as extensive displays of vintage military flying gear and uniforms. There are posters that were used to identify Japanese planes, plus there's a Huey helicopter and the

cockpit of an F-106 that you can sit in. In the north hangar it looks like activity day at the senior center as a volunteer team of retirees busily restores old planes. It's an inspiring sight, and a good place to hear some war stories. The lobby gift shop sells real flight suits, old flight magazines, bomber jackets, books, models, and T-shirts. ✉ *6600 Tico Rd.* ☎ *321/268–1941* ⊕ *www.vacwarbirds.org* 🔁 *$18* 🕐 *Daily 9–5.*

BEACH

Playalinda Beach. The southern access for the Canaveral National Seashore, remote Playalinda Beach has pristine sands and is the longest stretch of undeveloped coast on Florida's Atlantic seaboard. Hundreds of giant sea turtles come ashore here May through August to lay their eggs. Fourteen parking lots anchor the beach at 1-mile intervals. From Interstate 95, take Exit 249 and head east. Bring bug repellent in case of horseflies, and note that you may see some unauthorized clothing-optional activity. **Amenities:** lifeguards (seasonal); parking (fee); toilets. **Best for:** solitude; swimming; walking. ✉ *Rte. 402, at the northern end of Beach Rd.* ☎ *321/867–4077* ⊕ *www.nps.gov/cana* 🔁 *$5 per vehicle for national seashore.*

WHERE TO EAT

$$$
SEAFOOD
✕ **Dixie Crossroads.** This sprawling restaurant is always crowded and festive, but it's not just the rustic setting that draws the throngs—it's the seafood. The specialty is the difficult-to-cook rock shrimp, which are served fried, broiled, or steamed. Diners with a hearty appetite can opt for the all-you-can-eat rock shrimp, small shrimp, tilapia, or catfish. You might have to wait (up to 90 minutes) for a table, but if you don't have time to wait, you can order takeout or use the call-ahead seating option. And a word to the wise: as tempting as those corn fritters dusted with powdered sugar are, don't fill up on them. ⑤ *Average main: $23* ✉ *1475 Garden St., 2 miles east of I–95 Exit 220* ☎ *321/268–5000* ⊕ *www.dixiecrossroads.com* ⬢ *Reservations not accepted.*

WHERE TO STAY

$
HOTEL
🛏 **Hampton Inn Titusville.** Proximity to the Kennedy Space Center and reasonable rates make this four-story hotel a top pick for an overnight near the center. **Pros:** free Internet; extra-comfy beds; convenient to I–95.

Cons: thin walls; no restaurant on site; no room service. $ *Rooms from: $96* ⊠ *4760 Helen Hauser Blvd.* ☎ *321/383–9191* ⊕ *www.hamptoninn. com* ⇄ *86 rooms, 4 suites* ⦿| *Breakfast.*

SPORTS AND THE OUTDOORS

Fodor's Choice **Merritt Island National Wildlife Refuge.** Owned by the National Aero-
★ nautics and Space Administration (NASA), this 140,000-acre refuge,
which adjoins the Canaveral National Seashore, acts as a buffer around
Kennedy Space Center while protecting 1,000 species of plants and
500 species of wildlife, including 15 considered federally threatened
or endangered. It's an immense area dotted by brackish estuaries and
marshes and patches of land consisting of coastal dunes, scrub oaks,
pine forests and flatwoods, and palm and oak hammocks. You can
borrow field guides and binoculars at the visitor center (5 miles east of
U.S. 1 in Titusville on State Road 402) to track down falcons, ospreys,
eagles, turkeys, doves, cuckoos, owls, and woodpeckers, as well as
loggerhead turtles, alligators, wild boar and otters. A 20-minute video
about refuge wildlife and accessibility—only 10,000 acres are developed—can help orient you.

You might take a self-guided tour along the 7-mile Black Point Wildlife
Drive. On the Oak Hammock Foot Trail you can see wintering migratory waterfowl and learn about the plants of a hammock community.
If you exit the north end of the refuge, look for the Manatee Observation Area just north of the Haulover Canal (maps are at the visitor
center). They usually show up in spring and fall. There are also fishing
camps, fishing boat ramps, and six hiking trails scattered throughout
the area. Most of the refuge is closed 24 hours prior to a launch. ⊠ *Visitor Center, Rte. 402, 5 miles east of U.S. 1 across Titusville Causeway*
☎ *321/861–0667, 321/861–0669 for visitor center* ⊕ *www.fws.gov/
merrittisland* ⦿ *Free; $5 per vehicle on Black Point Wildlife Dr. only*
⊙ *Daily sunrise–sunset; visitor center weekdays 8–4:30, weekends 9–5.*

COCOA

17 miles south of Titusville.

Not to be confused with the seaside community of Cocoa Beach, the
small town of Cocoa sits smack-dab on mainland Florida and faces
the Intracoastal Waterway, known locally as Indian River. There's a
planetarium and a museum, as well as a rustic fish camp along the St.
Johns River, a few miles inland.

Folks in a rush to get to the beach tend to overlook Cocoa's Victorian-
style village, but it's worth a stop and is perhaps Cocoa's most interesting feature. Within the cluster of restored turn-of-the-20th-century
buildings and cobblestone walkways you can enjoy several restaurants,
indoor and outdoor cafés, snack and ice-cream shops, and more than
50 specialty shops and art galleries. The area hosts music performances
in the gazebo, arts-and-crafts shows, and other family-friendly events
throughout the year. To get to Cocoa Village, head east on Route 520—
named King Street in Cocoa—and when the streets get narrow and the

road curves, make a right onto Brevard Avenue; follow the signs for the free municipal parking lot.

EXPLORING

FAMILY **Brevard Museum of History & Natural Science.** This is the place to come to see what the lay of the local land looked like in other eras. Hands-on activities draw children, who especially migrate toward the Imagination Center, where they can act out history or reenact a space shuttle flight. Not to be missed are Ice Age–era creatures such as a fully articulated mastodon, giant ground sloth, and saber-tooth cat. The Windover Archaeological Exhibit features 7,000-year-old artifacts indigenous to the region. In 1984, a shallow pond revealed the burial ground of more than 200 American Indians who lived in the area about 7,000 years ago. Preserved in the muck were bones and, to the archeologists' surprise, the brains of these ancient people. Nature lovers appreciate the museum's butterfly garden and the nature center with 22 acres of trails encompassing three distinct ecosystems—sand pine hills, lake lands, and marshlands. ⊠ 2201 Michigan Ave. ☎ 321/632–1830 ⊕ www.brevardmuseum.org ⊇ $6 ⊙ Thurs.–Sat. 10–4.

WHERE TO EAT

$$$ ✕ **Café Margaux.** Eclectic, creative, and international is the best way to
ECLECTIC describe the cuisine and décor at this charming Cocoa Village spot. The
Fodor's Choice menu blends French, Italian, and Asian influences with dishes like lol-
★ lipop pork chop over English pea and orzo risotto, sweet onion–crusted fresh red snapper, and braised veal scaloppine, and also features more exotic fare such as duck and ostrich. Themed dining rooms are elaborately decorated with dramatic but not necessarily coordinating window treatments, wallpaper, and artwork. ⑤ Average main: $26 ⊠ 220 Brevard Ave. ☎ 321/639–8343 ⊕ www.margaux.com ⊙ Closed Sun.

$ ✕ **Lone Cabbage Fish Camp.** The word "rustic" doesn't even begin to
ECLECTIC describe this down-home, no-nonsense restaurant (translation: you eat off paper plates with plastic forks) housed in a weathered, old, clapboard shack along with a bait shop and airboat-tour company. Set your calorie counter for plates of catfish, frogs' legs, turtle, and alligator (as well as burgers and hot dogs). Dine inside or on the outdoor deck overlooking the St. Johns River with live music every Sunday. Who knows, you might even see your dinner swimming by. ⑤ Average main: $10 ⊠ 8199 Rte. 520, at St. Johns River ☎ 321/632–4199 ⌦ Reservations not accepted.

SHOPPING

Cocoa Flea Market. With more than 1,000 booths, this is, essentially, the largest outdoor shopping center in Brevard County. The market is open Friday, Saturday, and Sunday from 8 to 4. ⊠ 5605 N. U.S. 1 ☎ 321/631–0241.

Cocoa Village. You could spend hours browsing in the more than 50 boutiques here, along Brevard Avenue and Harrison Street (the latter has the densest concentration of shops). Although most stores are of the gift and clothing variety, the village is also home to antiques shops, art galleries, restaurants, a tattoo parlor, and a spa. ⊠ Rte. 520 and Brevard Ave. ☎ 321/631–9075.

Super Flea & Farmers' Market. You're sure to find a bargain at one of the 900 booths at this market, which is held every Friday, Saturday, and Sunday from 9 to 4. ✉ *4835 W. Eau Gallie Blvd., Melbourne* ☎ *321/242–9124* ⊕ *www.superfleamarket.com.*

SPORTS AND THE OUTDOORS
BOATING
Twister Airboat Rides. If you haven't seen the swampy, alligator-ridden waters of Florida, then you haven't really seen Florida. This thrilling wildlife tour goes where eagles and wading birds coexist with water moccasins and gators. The Coast Guard–certified deluxe airboats hit speeds of up to 45 mph and offer unparalleled opportunities to photograph native species. The basic tour lasts 30 minutes, but 60- and 90-minute ecotours are also available at an additional cost by reservation only. Twister Airboat Rides is inside the Lone Cabbage Fish Camp, about 9 miles west of Cocoa's city limits, 4 miles west of Interstate 95. ✉ *8199 Rte. 520, at St. Johns River* ☎ *321/632–4199* ⊕ *www. twisterairboatrides.com* 🖙 *$22* ⊙ *Daily 10–4:30.*

CAPE CANAVERAL

5 miles east of Cocoa via Rte. A1A.

The once-bustling commercial fishing area of Cape Canaveral is still home to a small shrimping fleet, charter boats, and party fishing boats, but its main business these days is as a cruise-ship port. This isn't the spiffiest place around, but what is becoming quite clean and neat is the north end of the port, where the Carnival, Disney, and Royal Caribbean cruise lines set sail. Port Canaveral is now Florida's second busiest cruise port for multiday cruises, which makes this a great place to catch a glimpse of these giant ships.

EXPLORING

FAMILY **Exploration Tower.** The best view at Port Canaveral is no longer from the top of your cruise ship. In fact, the view from atop this towering seven-story structure, which opened in late 2013, makes the cruise ships look—well, not so massive after all. The tower, a short walk from the cruise port, is equal parts museum and scenic overlook. The seventh-floor observation deck offers impressive views of the cruise port, the Atlantic Ocean, the Banana River, and even the Vehicle Assembly Building at Kennedy Space Center. Other floors house exhibits highlighting cultural history of the area, from space flight to surfing, bird and sea life to the rich maritime history. Kids will enjoy interactive exhibits, including a virtual ship bridge that allows you to pilot a boat through the Canaveral Channel and into the Atlantic. A theater shows a 20-minute film dedicated to the history of Brevard County, and a small café sells refreshments and baked goods. ✉ *670 Dave Nisbet Dr.* ☎ *321/394–3408* ⊕ *www.portcanaveral.com/welcomecenter/index.php* 🖙 *$6.50* ⊙ *Daily 9–6.*

Continued on page 718

The astronauts prepare for the launch
of Endeavour STS-118 on Pad 39-A.

SOARING HIGH

by John Blodgett
and Steve Master

AT THE KENNEDY SPACE CENTER

Ever since the National Aeronautics and Space Administration (NASA) was founded in 1958, the United States has been working on missions that launch us heavenward. When these dreams were about to become reality, and until 2011, when it was time for blastoff, Kennedy Space Center in Cape Canaveral, Florida, was where the action could be found.

NASA FROM COAST TO COAST

The Vehicle Assembly Building housed the space shuttle before a launch.

You've heard the words: "Houston, the *Eagle* has landed." And *Apollo 13*'s "Houston, we have a problem." But have you wondered, "Why are they talking to Houston if they left from Florida?"

NASA actually has operations at centers scattered across the United States. Its major centers are in Florida, Texas, and California. NASA's Launch Operations Center, known as the Kennedy Space Center, in Cape Canaveral, Florida, is where the famous countdowns are heard as a mission prepares for launch. You could say this is like NASA's big airport for outbound flights.

Once a mission (with a crew inside) is airborne, Houston takes over. In addition to operating all manned space flights, the Lyndon B. Johnson Space Center in Houston, Texas, is home base for American astronauts. They train here in laboratories that simulate weightlessness and other space-related concepts.

Not to be left out, the West Coast also gets a piece of the space-action pie. At Moffet Field, in California's Silicon Valley, the Ames Research Center is research and development central for NASA technology. If a mission can't happen because the technology isn't there yet, it's the job of the Ames Research Center to figure it out. Also in California is the Dryden Flight Research Center, at Edwards Air Force Base in Southern California. The center is where a lot of smart people who know a lot about aerodynamics get to test out their ideas; it's also where space shuttle orbiters land.

So, in a nutshell, you could say California is the brains of NASA's operations, Texas is its heart, and Florida is its wings.

NASA TIMELINE

OCT. 1958: NASA begins operating with 8,000 employees and $100 million. Ten days later, *Pioneer I* takes off.

MAY 1961: Alan B. Shepard, Jr., becomes the first American in space.

FEB. 1962: John Glenn is the first American to orbit the Earth.

JUNE 1965: Edward H. White II is the first American to walk in space.

DEC. 1968: Three astronauts orbit the moon aboard *Apollo 8.*

JULY 1969: *Apollo 11* brings man to the moon.

JULY 1976: *Viking 1* lands on Mars.

APRIL 1981: First space shuttle orbiter launches two astronauts into space.

JAN. 1986: Space shuttle *Challenger* explodes 73 seconds after launch; seven onboard astronauts die.

APRIL 1990: Hubble telescope launches.

JULY 1997: Mars Pathfinder lands on the red planet.

JULY 1999: Eileen Collins is the first woman to command a space shuttle mission.

FEB. 2002: Mars Odyssey begins mapping the red planet.

FEB. 1, 2003: Space shuttle *Columbia* explodes over Texas 15 minutes before scheduled landing; seven astronauts on board die.

JULY 2004: Cassini–Huygens spacecraft begins orbiting Saturn.

MAY 2010: Shuttle *Atlantis* delivers new Russian module and critical spare parts to International Space Station.

THE KENNEDY SPACE CENTER

The 140,000-acre Kennedy Space Center is one of central Florida's most popular sights. The must-see attraction gives you a hands-on opportunity to learn about the past, present, and future of America's space program. View old rockets and other artifacts from space flight operations, talk with astronauts during Q&As, experience a simulated launch, and become part of the awed crowd on launch days as you watch the blastoff from a viewing site on the grounds or nearby.

VISITOR COMPLEX

Space Walk of Honor

Space Education

Children's Pl Dome

Rocket Garden

Early Space Exploration

Early Space Exploration

PARKI

VISITOR COMPLEX

Kennedy Space Center Visitor Complex is the starting place for your visit. It's home to several attractions and is also where you can board the bus for tours of the center beyond the visitor complex.

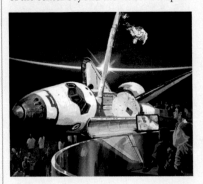

EXHIBITS

A **Space Shuttle Atlantis** exhibit puts visitors nose to nose with the historic spacecraft, which is tilted at a 43.21° angle with its payload door open and robot arm extended. The **Early Space Exploration** display highlights the Mercury and Gemini space programs; **Robot Scouts** is a walkthrough exhibit of unmanned planetary probes; and the **Exploration Space: Explorers Wanted** exhibit immerses visitors in exploration beyond Earth. Don't miss the outdoor **Rocket Garden**, winding around rockets, from early Atlas spacecraft to a Saturn IB. The most moving exhibit is the **Astronaut Memorial**, the imposing black-granite tribute to astronauts who lost their lives in the name of space exploration.

INTERACTIVE SHOWS AND RIDES

Astronaut Encounter Theater has two daily programs where NASA astronauts share their adventures in space travel and show a short film. More befitting Walt Disney World or Universal Studios (complete with the health warnings), the **Shuttle Launch Experience** is the center's spectacular attraction. Designed by a team of astronauts, NASA experts, and renowned attraction engineers, the 44,000-square-foot structure uses a sophisticated motion-based platform, special-effects seats, and high-fidelity visual and audio components to simulate the sensations experienced in an actual space-shuttle launch, including MaxQ, Solid Rocker Booster separation, main engine cutoff, and External Tank separation. The journey culminates with a breathtaking view of Earth from space. For those under 44 inches, **Children's Play Dome** enables kids to play among the next generation of spacecraft, climb a moon-rock wall, and crawl through rocket tunnels.

MOVIES

At the world's only back-to-back twin **IMAX Theater** the dream of space flight comes to life on a movie screen five stories tall with dramatic footage shot by NASA astronauts during missions. Realistic 3-D special effects will make you feel like you're in space with them. Films alternate throughout the year.

BEYOND THE VISITOR COMPLEX

SPACE CENTER TOURS

To explore the remainder of the space center, you will need to take a tour by bus. Buses depart every 15 minutes from the Visitor Complex; the tour duration is two hours, but you can get off and back on again at will at various sites. The bus tour takes guests past such iconic spots as the **Vehicle Assembly Building** and **Launch Pad 39-A.** At the **Apollo/Saturn V Center,** with a don't-miss presentation at the Firing Room Theater, the launch of America's first lunar mission, 1968's *Apollo VIII,* is re-created with a ground-shaking, window-rattling liftoff. The **Apollo/Saturn V Center** features one of the three remaining Saturn V moon rockets. This bus tour is included with admission; four others are available for additional fees (*see Add-Ons*).

U.S. ASTRONAUT HALL OF FAME

The original Mercury 7 team and the later Gemini, Apollo, Skylab, and shuttle astronauts contributed to make the United States Astronaut Hall of Fame the world's premium archive of astronauts' personal stories. Authentic memorabilia and equipment from their collections tell the story of human space exploration. This stand-alone attraction is across the river from the Kennedy Space Center; admission to it is included with your Visitor Complex ticket.

You can see one-of-a-kind items like Wally Schirra's relatively archaic Sigma 7 Mercury space capsule, Gus Grissom's spacesuit (colored silver only because NASA thought silver looked more "spacey"), and a flag that made it to the moon. The exhibit First of the Moon focuses on crew selection for Apollo 11 and the Soviet Union's role in the space race. One of the more challenging activities at the hall of fame is a space-shuttle simulator that lets you try your hand at landing the craft—and afterward replays a side view of your rolling and pitching descent. Don't miss Simulation Station, an area with interactive exhibits about space travel. There are also videos of historic moments.

The life of an astronaut can mean a tight squeeze! See for yourself at the U.S. Astronaut Hall of Fame.

ADD-ONS

The following tours and programs are available for extra cost beyond admission and should be reserved in advance.

■ A new **KSC Up-Close Tour** takes visitors past the launch pads, the Vehicle Assembly Building, and the Shuttle Landing Facility. This tour costs $25 and last 2 to 2½ hours.

■ See how far the space program has come on the **Cape Canaveral: Then and Now Tour** ($21). It puts you up close to the original launch pads, brings you to the Air Force Space and Missile Museum, and lets you watch the active unmanned rocket program.

■ During **Lunch With an Astronaut** ($24.99), astronauts talk about their experiences and engage in Q&A (kids often ask "How do you eat/sleep/relieve yourself in space?").

■ If you want to live the life of an astronaut, you can enroll in the **Astronaut Training Experience** (ATX) at the U.S. Astronaut Hall of Fame. The half-day program combines hands-on training and preparation for the rigors of space flight. NASA astronauts helped design the program, and you'll hear firsthand from them as you progress through an exciting day at the busiest launch facility on Earth. The $145 cost includes flight training simulators, a full-scale space shuttle mission simulation, a meet-and-greet with a NASA astronaut, and ATX Gear. Age restrictions apply. Reserve your spot well in advance.

PLANNING YOUR TRIP

GETTING HERE
Kennedy Space Center Visitor Complex and the U.S. Astronaut Hall of Fame are near Titusville, about a 45-minute drive from Orlando. From Orlando International Airport, take the north exit to 528 East (the Beachline Expressway) and drive east to the exit marked "407, Titusville, Kennedy Space Center." Take 407 until you reach Rte. 405 (Columbia Boulevard/NASA Parkway) and then turn right. After approximately 1 mile you will see the U.S. Astronaut Hall of Fame on your right. Continue another 5 mi until you reach the visitor complex, your starting point for all tours.

BUDGETING YOUR TIME
Plan to spend a full day at the Visitor Complex and hall of fame, or at the very least, several hours.

ADMISSION
Your $50 (plus tax) admission ticket grants you one day's admission to Kennedy Space Center Visitor Complex and related tours as well as a second day's free admission to the U.S. Astronaut Hall of Fame, which is just across the causeway.

CONTACT INFORMATION

✉ Off Rte. 405

☎ 877/313–2610

🌐 www.kennedyspacecenter.com

💲 $50

🕙 Daily 9 am; closing times vary. (Call ahead for restrictions if you're visiting on a launch day.)

Cape Canaveral Then and Now Tour.

13

IN FOCUS SOARING HIGH AT THE KENNEDY SPACE CENTER

BEACH

Jetty Park. A wonderful taste of the real Florida, this 4½-acre beach and oceanfront campground has picnic pavilions, bike paths, and a 1,200-foot-long fishing pier that doubles as a perfect vantage point from which to watch a liftoff from Cape Canaveral. Lifeguards are on duty all year, and beach wheelchairs are available for rent. A jetty constructed of giant boulders adds to the landscape, and a walkway that crosses it provides access to a less populated stretch of beach. Real and rustic, this is Florida without the theme-park varnish. **Amenities:** food and drink; lifeguards; parking (fee); showers; toilets; water sports. **Best for:** sunrise; surfing; swimming; walking. ⊠ *400 Jetty Rd.* ☎ *321/783–7111* ⊕ *www. jettyparkbeachandcampground.com* ⊑ *$5–$10 cars, $7–$15 RVs.*

WHERE TO EAT

$ ✕ **Seafood Atlantic.** Locals think of this casual waterfront seafood mar-

SEAFOOD   ket/eatery as a well-kept secret, but more and more cruise patrons are making their way here for a pre- or post-cruise treat. The market is connected to the restaurant, guaranteeing not only freshness but an array of choices. You don't just order a fish sandwich or plate of steamed shrimp; you choose from at least four varieties of fish (try the Golden Tile in season) and several varieties of shrimp (the Royal Reds may be the best you've ever tasted). Seating is alfresco, with views of the inland waterway and nearby cruise ships. Best for lunch or an early dinner, the restaurant closes at 8 on Friday and Saturday, earlier other nights. ⑤ *Average main: $12* ⊠ *520 Glen Cheek Dr.* ☎ *321/784–1963* ⊕ *www. seafoodatlantic.net* ⊲ *Reservations not accepted* ⊘ *Closed Tues.*

$$ ✕ **Thai Thai III.** The mouthwatering photos on the menu aren't just a

THAI   marketing ploy. The pictures don't do the real stuff justice. Locals and cruise-ship vacationers frequent this casual Thai-Japanese eatery within walking distance of cruise-port hotels. Seafood is an emphasis here, with specialties like lobster pad thai and snapper with ginger and scallion. The Thai curries, noodles, and soups can be prepared "Thai hot," but "medium" packs a subtle punch, too. On the sushi side, try the Beauty and the Beast roll: half tuna, half eel, with avocado, asparagus, scallions, and roe. Décor is eclectic and relaxing, with brightly painted walls and low-hanging sconces. Don't fret if you see a crowd out front. The place does a brisk take-out business. ⑤ *Average main: $16* ⊠ *8660 Astronaut Blvd.* ☎ *321/784–1561* ⊕ *www.thaithai3.com.*

WHERE TO STAY

$ 🏨 **Radisson Resort at the Port.** For cruise-ship passengers who can't wait

HOTEL   to get under way, this splashy resort, done up in pink and turquoise, already feels like the Caribbean. **Pros:** cruise-ship convenience; pool area; free shuttle. **Cons:** rooms around the pool can be noisy; loud air-conditioning in some rooms; no complimentary breakfast. ⑤ *Rooms from: $122* ⊠ *8701 Astronaut Blvd.* ☎ *321/784–0000, 888/201–1718* ⊕ *www. radisson.com/capecanaveralfl* ⇌ *284 rooms, 72 suites* ⑩ *No meals.*

$ 🏨 **Residence Inn Cape Canaveral/Cocoa Beach.** Billing itself as the closest

HOTEL   all-suites hotel to the Kennedy Space Center, this four-story Residence Inn, painted cheery yellow, is also convenient to other area attractions such as Port Canaveral, the Cocoa Beach Pier, the Brevard Zoo, and Cocoa Village, and is only an hour from the Magic Kingdom. **Pros:**

helpful staff; free breakfast buffet; pet-friendly. **Cons:** less-than-pictur-esque views; street noise in some rooms. ⑤ *Rooms from: $179* ✉ *8959 Astronaut Blvd.* ☎ *321/323–1100, 800/331–3131* ⊕ *www.marriott. com* ⤳ *150 suites* ⦿ *Breakfast.*

SHOPPING

Cove Marketplace. Whether you're at Port Canaveral for a cruise or are just passing through, this retail marketplace on the south side of the harbor has enough shops, restaurants, and entertainment venues to keep you occupied. Since most of the bars and eateries are located on the public waterfront area, you'll have a view of the cruise ships—and their colorful passengers. ✉ *Glen Cheek Dr., at Scallop Dr., Port Canaveral* ⊕ *www.portcanaveral.com/covemarketplace* ✆ *Free* ✆ *Hrs vary by business.*

COCOA BEACH

5 miles south of Cape Canaveral, 58 miles southeast of Orlando.

After crossing a long and high bridge just east of Cocoa Village, you drop down upon a barrier island. A few miles farther and you'll reach the Atlantic Ocean and picture-perfect Cocoa Beach at Route A1A.

In the early 1960s Cocoa Beach was a sleepy, little-known town. But in 1965 the sitcom *I Dream of Jeannie* premiered. The endearing show centered on an astronaut, played by Larry Hagman, and his "Jeannie" in a bottle, Barbara Eden, and was set in Cocoa Beach. Though the series was never shot in Florida, creator Sidney Sheldon paid homage to the town with local references to Cape Kennedy (now known as the Kennedy Space Center) and Bernard's Surf restaurant. Today the town and its lovely beach are mecca to Florida's surfing community.

ESSENTIALS

Visitor Information Cocoa Beach Convention and Visitors Bureau ☎ *321/454–2022, 877/321–8474* ⊕ *www.visitcocoabeach.com.*

EXPLORING

Cocoa Beach Pier. By day, it's a good place to stroll—if you don't mind weather-worn wood and sandy, watery paths. Although most of the pier is free to walk on, there's a $1 charge to enter the fishing area at the end of the 800-foot-long boardwalk, and a $5 fishing fee. You can rent rods and reels here for an additional $10. By night, visitors and locals—beach bums and surfers among them—head here to party. Come on Friday night for the Boardwalk Bash, with live acoustic and rock-and-roll music; Wednesday and Saturday also see live music. ▪ **TIP→ The pier is a great place to watch launches from Kennedy Space Center.** ✉ *401 Meade Ave.* ☎ *321/783–7549* ⊕ *www.cocoabeachpier.com.*

BEACH

Cocoa Beach. This is one of the Space Coast's nicest beaches—and the place where the great professional surfer Kelly Slater got his start. The beach boasts one of the steadiest surf breaks on the East Coast and has wide stretches that are excellent for biking, jogging, power walk-ing, and strolling. In some places there are dressing rooms, showers, playgrounds, picnic areas with grills, snack shops, and surfside parking lots. Beach vendors offer necessities, and lifeguards are on duty in the summer.

A popular entry road, Route 520 crosses the Banana River into Cocoa Beach. At its east end, 5-acre **Alan Shepard Park,** named for the famous astronaut, aptly provides excellent views of launches from Kennedy Space Center. Facilities here include 10 picnic pavilions, shower and restroom facilities, and more than 300 parking spaces. Beach vendors carry necessities for sunning and swimming. Parking is $7, $10 on weekends and holidays March through Labor Day. Shops and restaurants are within walking distance. Another enticing Cocoa Beach entry point is 10-acre **Sidney Fischer Park,** in the 2100 block of Route A1A in the central beach area. It has showers, playgrounds, changing areas, picnic areas with grills, snack shops, and plenty of well-maintained, inexpensive parking lots ($5 for cars). **Amenities:** food and drink; lifeguards (summer); parking (fee); showers; toilets; water sports. **Best for:** sunrise; surfing; swimming; walking. ⊠ *Rte. A1A from Cape Canaveral to Patrick Air Force Base, 401 Meade Ave.*

WHERE TO EAT

$$$
GERMAN

✕ **Heidelberg.** As the name suggests, the cuisine here is definitely German, from the sauerbraten served with potato dumplings and red cabbage to the beef Stroganoff and spaetzle to the classically prepared Wiener schnitzel. All the soups and desserts are homemade; try the Viennese-style apple strudel and the rum-zapped almond-cream tortes. Elegant interior touches include crisp linens and fresh flowers. There's live music Wednesday through Saturday evenings. You can also dine inside the jazz club, Heidi's, next door. ⑤ *Average main: $28* ⊠ *7 N. Orlando Ave., opposite City Hall* ☎ *321/783–6806* ⊕ *www.heidisjazzclub.com* ⊗ *Closed Mon. and Tues. No lunch Sun.*

$
SEAFOOD

✕ **Oh Shucks Seafood Bar.** At the only open-air seafood bar on the beach, at the entrance of the Cocoa Beach Pier, the main item is oysters, served on the half shell. You can also grab a burger here, crab legs by the pound, or Oh Shucks's most popular item, coconut beer shrimp. Some diners complain that the prices don't jibe with the ultracasual atmosphere (e.g., plastic chairs), but they're also paying for the "ex-Pierience." During high season, there's live entertainment on Wednesday, Friday, Saturday, and Sunday. ⑤ *Average main: $12* ⊠ *401 Meade Ave., Cocoa Beach Pier* ☎ *321/783–7549* ⊕ *www.cocoabeachpier.com.*

WHERE TO STAY

$
HOTEL

▦ **Best Western Oceanfront Hotel & Suites.** Families love this Best Western for its affordable suites; everyone loves it for its location—just a half block from the Cocoa Beach Pier—and great views of launches from Kennedy Space Center. **Pros:** free Internet; complimentary breakfast. **Cons:** not all rooms have an ocean view; small bathrooms; noise from the pier. ⑤ *Rooms from: $95* ⊠ *5600 N. Atlantic Ave.* ☎ *321/784–4343, 800/367–1223* ⊕ *www.bestwesterncocoabeach.com* ⇄ *230 rooms* ◎| *Breakfast.*

$
HOTEL

▦ **DoubleTree by Hilton Cocoa Beach Oceanfront.** Proximity to the beach and comforts like in-room microwaves and refrigerators—and DoubleTree's

The Cocoa Beach Pier is a magnet for nightlife in Cocoa Beach after dark.

famous chocolate chip–walnut cookies—make this six-story hotel a favorite of vacationing families, particularly Orlandoans on weekend getaways. **Pros:** private beach access; comfy beds; complimentary parking. **Cons:** extra charge for beach-chair rental; thin walls; slow elevators; no breakfast with standard room. ⑤ *Rooms from: $164* ✉ *2080 N. Atlantic Ave.* ☎ *321/783–9222* ⊕ *www.cocoabeachdoubletree.com* ⇆ *148 rooms, 12 suites* ⧖ *No meals.*

$ ⊞ **Hilton Cocoa Beach Oceanfront.** You can't get any closer to the beach
HOTEL than this seven-story oceanfront hotel. **Pros:** beachfront; friendly staff; clean. **Cons:** small pool and bathrooms; no balconies; room windows don't open; breakfast not included with standard rate. ⑤ *Rooms from: $124* ✉ *1550 N. Atlantic Ave.* ☎ *321/799–0003* ⊕ *www. hiltoncocoabeach.com* ⇆ *285 rooms, 11 suites* ⧖ *No meals.*

$ ⊞ **Inn at Cocoa Beach.** This charming oceanfront inn has spacious, indi-
B&B/INN vidually decorated rooms with four-poster beds, upholstered chairs, and balconies or patios; most have ocean views. **Pros:** quiet; romantic; honor bar. **Cons:** no on-site restaurant; "forced" socializing. ⑤ *Rooms from: $155* ✉ *4300 Ocean Beach Blvd.* ☎ *321/799–3460, 800/343–5307* ⊕ *www.theinnatcocoabeach.com* ⇆ *50 rooms* ⧖ *Breakfast.*

$ ⊞ **The Resort on Cocoa Beach.** Even if the beach weren't in its back-
RESORT yard, this family-friendly, oceanfront property offers enough activities
FAMILY and amenities—from tennis and basketball courts to a game room and
Fodor's Choice 50-seat movie theater—to keep everyone entertained. **Pros:** full kitch-
★ ens; in-room washers and dryers; large balconies. **Cons:** check-in not until 4 and checkout at 10; not all rooms are oceanfront; slow elevators. ⑤ *Rooms from: $180* ✉ *1600 N. Atlantic Ave.* ☎ *321/783–4000* ⊕ *www.theresortoncocoabeach.com* ⇆ *124 suites* ⧖ *No meals.*

NIGHTLIFE

The Cocoa Beach Pier has several nightspots as well as live-music sessions a couple of nights a week.

Heidi's Jazz Club. Local and nationally known jazz musicians (Boots Randolph and Mose Allison have taken the stage) play Tuesday through Sunday, with showcase acts appearing on weekends. ⊠ *7 Orlando Ave. N* ☎ *321/783–4559.*

SHOPPING

Merritt Square Mall. The area's only major shopping mall is about a 20-minute ride from the beach. Stores include Macy's, Dillard's, JCPenney, Sears, Foot Locker, Island Surf and Skate, and roughly 100 others. There's a 16-screen multiplex, along with a food court and several restaurant chains. ⊠ *777 E. Merritt Island Causeway, Merritt Island* ☎ *321/452–3270.*

SPORTS AND THE OUTDOORS

KAYAKING

Adventure Kayak of Cocoa Beach. Specializing in manatee encounters, this outfitter organizes one- and two-person kayak tours of mangroves, channels, and islands. Tours launch from various locations in the Cocoa Beach area. Rates run about $30 per person. ☎ *321/480–8632* ⊕ *www. kayakcocoabeach.com.*

SURFING

Cocoa Beach Surf Company. The world's largest surf complex has three floors of boards, apparel, sunglasses, and anything else a surfer, wannabe-surfer, or souvenir-seeker could need. Also on site are a 5,600-gallon fish and shark tank and the Shark Pit Bar & Grill. Here you can also rent surfboards, body boards, and wet suits, as well as umbrellas, chairs, and bikes. And staffers teach grommets (dudes) and gidgets (chicks)— from kids to seniors—how to surf. There are group, semi-private, and private lessons available in one-, two-, and three-hour sessions. Prices range from $40 (for a one-hour group lesson) to $120 (three-hour private). All gear is provided. ⊠ *4001 N. Atlantic Ave.* ☎ *321/799–9930.*

Fodor'sChoice
★
Ron Jon Surf Shop. It's impossible to miss Ron Jon: it takes up nearly two blocks along Route A1A and has a giant surfboard and an art-deco facade painted orange, blue, yellow, and turquoise. What started in 1963 as a small T-shirt and bathing-suit shop has evolved into a 52,000-square-foot superstore that's open every day 'round the clock. The shop rents water-sports gear as well as chairs and umbrellas, and it sells every kind of beachwear, surf wax, plus the requisite T-shirts and flip-flops. ⊠ *4151 N. Atlantic Ave., Rte. A1A* ☎ *321/799–8820* ⊕ *www.ronjonsurfshop.com*

Ron Jon Surf School. If you can't tell a tri-skeg stick from a hodaddy shredding the lip on a gnarly tube, then you may want to avail yourself of the Ron Jon Surf School. Private lessons and clinics are offered for surfers of all levels. The most popular sessions last two hours ($65 clinics, $95 private). Boards are provided, but you should bring your own towels and sunscreen. ⊠ *150 E. Columbia La.* ☎ *321/868–1980.*

MELBOURNE

20 miles south of Cocoa Beach.

Despite its dependence on the high-tech space industry, this town is decidedly laid-back. Most of the city is on the mainland, but a small portion trickles onto a barrier island, separated by the Indian River Lagoon and accessible by several inlets, including the Sebastian.

EXPLORING

FAMILY

Fodor'sChoice

★

Brevard Zoo. At the only Association of Zoo and Aquariums–accredited zoo built by a community, you can stroll along the shaded boardwalks and get a close-up look at rhinos, giraffes, cheetahs, alligators, crocodiles, giant anteaters, marmosets, jaguars, eagles, river otters, kangaroos, exotic birds, and kookaburras. Alligator, crocodile, and river-otter feedings are held on alternate afternoons—and no, the alligators don't dine on the otters. Stop by Paws-On, an interactive learning playground with a petting zoo, wildlife detective training academy, and the Indian River Play Lagoon. Hand-feed a giraffe in Expedition Africa or a lorikeet in the Australian Free Flight Aviary, and step up to the Wetlands Outpost, an elevated pavilion that's a gateway to 22 acres of wetlands through which you can paddle kayaks and keep an eye open for the 4,000 species of wildlife that live in these waters and woods. Adventurers seeking a chimp's-eye view can zipline through the zoo on Treetop Trek. ⊠ *8225 N. Wickham Rd.* ☎ *321/254–9453* ⊕ *www.brevardzoo.org* ⊜ *$16, $20.50 with train and giraffe and lorikeet food; Treetop Trek $22–$57* ⊙ *Daily 9:30–5 (last admission at 4:15).*

BEACHES

Paradise Beach. Small and scenic, this 1,600-foot stretch of sand is part of a 10-acre park north of Indialantic, about 20 miles south of Cocoa Beach on Route A1A. It has a refreshment stand, volleyball courts, outdoor showers, a beachfront park with pavilions, grills, picnic tables, and lifeguards in summer. **Amenities:** food and drink; lifeguards (seasonal); free parking; showers; toilets. **Best for:** sunrise; surfing; swimming; walking. ⊠ *2301 N. Rte. A1A.*

Satellite Beach. The sands of this sleepy little community just south of Patrick Air Force Base, about 15 miles south of Cocoa Beach on Route A1A, are cradled between the balmy Atlantic Ocean and biologically diverse Indian River Lagoon. It's a popular spot for family vacations because of its slow pace and lack of crowds as well as its beachfront park with playground, five pavilions, and picnic facilities. **Amenities:** food and drink; lifeguards; free parking; showers; toilets; water sports. **Best for:** sunrise; surfing; swimming; walking. ⊠ *Rte. A1A, Satellite Beach.*

SPORTS AND THE OUTDOORS

BASEBALL

Space Coast Stadium. Even though they play in our nation's capital during the regular season, the Washington Nationals use this stadium for their spring training site. For the rest of the season, the facility is home to the Brevard County Manatees (☎ *321/633–9200*), one of the

Milwaukee Brewers' minor-league teams. ⊠ *5800 Stadium Pkwy., Viera* ☎ *321/633–4487* ⊕ *www.viera.com.*

GOLF

Baytree National Golf Links. "Challenging but fair" is how golfers describe this links-style course, designed by PGA legend Gary Player (aka "The Black Knight."). This semi-private course, built in 1992, is known for its unique red shale–coquina waste areas. A round can be something of a rollercoaster ride, with an easy hole or two followed by a perplexingly challenging one. The 454-yard, par-4 18th, for instance, is rated among the toughest in Brevard County. It plays into the wind and requires an imposing carry over wetlands, followed by an approach into a green guarded by water on all sides. The club has a restaurant and full practice facility. ⊠ *8207 National Dr.* ☎ *321/259–9060* ⊕ *www. baytreenational.com* ✉ *$69 for 18 holes, $20 for 9 holes* ⅃ *18 holes. 7043 yards. par 72.*

Viera East Golf Club. Rated among the best public courses—and values— on the Space Coast, Viera East reflects course architect Joe Lee's credo that "golf should be enjoyable, not a chore." Novices appreciate the forgiving, open layout with generous landing areas; more advanced players embrace the challenge of Lee's strategically placed bunkers (there are 66), water hazards, and expansive, undulating greens. The coastal breezes can make club selection tricky at times. Opened in 1994, the course is framed by marshlands, lakes, ponds, pine and cypress trees. The par-5 14th is among the more picturesque and challenging holes, with a green surrounded by water. ⊠ *2300 Clubhouse Dr., Viera* ☎ *321/639–6500* ⊕ *www.vieragolf.com* ✉ *$60 for 18 holes* ⅃ *18 holes. 6720 yards. par 72.*

THE PANHANDLE

WELCOME TO THE PANHANDLE

TOP REASONS TO GO

★ **Snowy white beaches:** Most of the Panhandle's Gulf Coast shoreline is relatively unobstructed by high-rise condos and hotels, and the white-powder sand is alluring.

★ **Lots of history:** Spanish, Native American, and, later, French and English influences shaped the direction of this region and are well represented in its architecture, historic sites, and museums.

★ **Slower pace:** The Panhandle is sometimes referred to as "L.A.," or Lower Alabama. Southern through and through, the pace here is as slow as molasses—a fact Tallahassee plays up by claiming to be "Florida with a Southern accent."

★ **Capital sites:** As the state capital (chosen because it was midway between the two earlier Spanish head-quarters of St. Augustine and Pensacola), Tallahassee remains intriguing thanks to its history, historical museums, universities, and quiet country charm.

1 Around Pensacola Bay. By preserving architecture from early Spanish settlements, Pensacola earns points for retaining the influence of these early explorers. The downtown district is compact, plus there's the city's Naval Air Museum and beaches nearby. Inland are some small towns with Old Florida appeal.

GETTING ORIENTED

The Panhandle is a large area, and there are a number of airports to access the largest cities. Two major east–west routes offer alternatives to Interstate 10. Roughly parallel to its modern cousin, U.S. 90 is an early byway that goes from Tallahassee through small Old Florida towns like Marianna and DeFuniak Springs on its way to Pensacola. From Pensacola, U.S. 98 generally skirts along the Gulf of Mexico through seaside towns and communities like Fort Walton Beach, Destin, Panama City Beach, and Apalachicola, providing some breathtaking waterfront drives.

14

2 The Emerald Coast. A nature reserve spans thousands of square miles of Gulf Coast land, and miles of shoreline between Pensacola and Destin is nearly void of development. The area is known for its blue-green waters and sugarlike sand beaches made of Appalachian quartz crystals. Panama City offers unique attractions.

3 Tallahassee. In the state capital you can see the old and new capitols, visit the state's historical museum, attend an FSU football game, and go for a country ride down canopied roads.

By Ashley Wright

The sugar-white sands of the Panhandle's beaches stretch 227 miles from Pensacola east to Apalachicola. Sprinkle in clear emerald waters, towering dunes, and laid-back small towns where the fish are always biting and the folks are friendly, and you have a region with local color that's beloved by Floridians and visitors alike.

There are sights in the Panhandle, but sightseeing isn't the principal activity. The region is better known for its rich history, ample fishing and diving, and its opportunities for relaxation. Here it's about Southern drawls, a gentle pace, fresh seafood, and more grits and old-fashioned hospitality than anywhere else in the state. Sleepy beach towns offer world-class golf, deep-sea fishing, relaxing spa treatments, and unbeatable shopping.

There's glamour here, too. Look for it in winning resorts throughout the region and in the abundance of nightlife, arts, and culture—from local symphonies to boutique art galleries—particularly in the more metropolitan areas. And then there's the food: from fresh catches of the day to some of the nation's finest oysters to mom-and-pop favorites offering fried seafood goodness.

Jump in a car, rent a bike, or buy a spot on a charter boat—you're never too far from outdoor adventure, with more miles of preserved coastline than anywhere else in the state. Destin is, after all, dubbed "The World's Luckiest Fishing Village," and the sport of YOLO Boarding (this region's term for the popular paddleboarding craze) has invaded the area in full force, offering a unique waterborne view of all the region's unspoiled, natural beauty.

Don't forget to veer off the beach roads and venture into some of the area's picturesque historic districts. Pensacola is known as America's first settlement, and the rest of the region follows suit with rich history dating from the first settlers. The state's capital, Tallahassee, has its own unique history woven of politics, varying cultures, and innovation. Between the local charm, natural splendor, outdoor adventures, and miles of coastline, it's no wonder that the Panhandle is so beloved.

PLANNING

WHEN TO GO

Peak season is Memorial Day to Labor Day, with another spike during spring break. Inland, especially in Tallahassee, high season is during the fall (football) and March to April. Vendors, attractions, and other activities are in full swing in the summer. There's a "secret season" that falls around October and November: things quiet down as students go back to school, but restaurants and attractions keep normal hours and the weather is moderate.

GETTING HERE AND AROUND

AIR TRAVEL

The region is home to two primary airports—Northwest Florida Beaches International Airport (ECP) and Pensacola International Airport— which offer numerous flights from a number of major airlines. In addition, there are airports with regularly scheduled passenger service in Tallahassee, as well as a public airport—Northwest Florida Regional Airport—in Fort Walton Beach on the Eglin Air Force Base.

Contacts Northwest Florida Beaches International Airport (ECP). ✉ 6300 W. Bay Pkwy., Panama City ☎ 850/763–6751 ⊕ www.iflybeaches.com. **Northwest Florida Regional Airport** (VPS). ✉ Fort Walton Beach ☎ 850/651–7160 ⊕ www.flyvps.com. **Pensacola International Airport** (PNS). ✉ 2430 Airport Blvd., Pensacola ☎ 850/436–5000 ⊕ www.flypensacola.com. **Tallahassee Regional Airport** ✉ 3300 Capital Circle SW, Tallahassee ☎ 850/891–7800 ⊕ www.talgov.com/airport.

CAR TRAVEL

The main east–west arteries across the top of the state are Interstate 10 and U.S. 90. Interstate 10 can be monotonous, but U.S. 90 routes you along the main streets of several county seats. U.S. 98 snakes eastward along the coast, splitting into 98 and 98A at Inlet Beach before rejoining at Panama City and continuing on to Port St. Joe and Apalachicola. The view of the gulf from U.S. 98 can be breathtaking, especially at sunset.

If you need to get from one end of the Panhandle to the other in a timely manner, drive inland to Interstate 10, where the speed limit runs as high as 70 mph in places. Major north–south highways that weave through the Panhandle are (from east to west) U.S. 231, U.S. 331, Route 85, and U.S. 29. From U.S. 331, which runs over a causeway at the east end of Choctawhatchee Bay between Route 20 and U.S. 98, the panorama of barge traffic and cabin cruisers on the twinkling waters of the Intracoastal Waterway will get your attention.

HOTELS

Many of the lodging selections here revolve around extended-stay options: resorts, condos, and time-shares that allow for a week or more in simple efficiencies, as well as fully furnished homes. There are also cabins, such as the ones that rest between the dunes at Grayton Beach. In any case, these are great for families and get-togethers, allowing you to do your own housekeeping and cooking, and explore the area without tour guides.

14

Local visitors' bureaus often act as clearinghouses for these types of properties, and you can also search online for vacation rentals. On the coast, but especially inland, the choices seem geared more toward mom-and-pop motels in addition to the usual line of chain hotels. ■TIP→ During the summer and over holiday weekends, always reserve ahead for top properties.

Hotel reviews have been shortened. For full information, visit Fodors.com.

RESTAURANTS

An abundance of seafood is served at coastal restaurants: oysters, crab, shrimp, scallops, and a variety of fish. Of course, that's not all there is on the menu. This part of Florida still impresses diners with old-fashioned comfort foods such as meat loaf, fried chicken, beans and cornbread, okra, and fried green tomatoes. You'll also find small-town seafood shacks where you can dine on local favorites such as deep-fried mullet, cheese grits, coleslaw, and hush puppies. Restaurants, like resorts, vary their operating tactics off-season, so call first if visiting during winter months.

WHAT IT COSTS				
	$	$$	$$$	$$$$
RESTAURANTS	under $16	$16–$20	$21–$30	over $30
HOTELS	under $201	$201–$300	$301–$400	over $400

Restaurant prices are the average cost of a main course at dinner or, if dinner is not served, at lunch. Hotel prices are the lowest cost of a standard double room in high season.

PENSACOLA BAY

Nestled on the Gulf of Mexico at Florida's northwest tip, this region takes visitors back in time thanks to its rich cultural heritage. In 1559, Don Tristan de Luna first "discovered" the area, which today is divided into four distinct parts: North Pensacola, the walkable downtown historic district, Pensacola Beach, and Perdido Key. The historic district is the heart of the area. Just across the bay, Pensacola Beach is on Santa Rosa Island, while Perdido Key is farther west, hugging the Alabama state line.

PENSACOLA

59 miles east of Mobile, Alabama, via I–10.

Pensacola consists of four distinct districts—Seville, Palafox, East Hill, and North Hill—though they're easy to explore as a unit. Stroll down streets mapped out by the British and renamed by the Spanish, such as Cervantes, Palafox, Intendencia, and Tarragona.

An influx of restaurants and bars has brought new nightlife to the historic districts, especially Palafox Street, which is now home to a thriving entertainment scene. Taste buds water over fresh coastal cuisine from a number of award-winning, locally owned and operated restaurants, and the downtown entertainment district offers fun for any age throughout the year—festivals, events at bars and concert venues, and a growing Mardi Gras celebration.

At the southern terminus of Palafox Street is Plaza DeLuna, a 2-acre park with open grounds, interactive water fountains, and concessions. It's a quiet place to sit and watch the bay, fish, or enjoy an evening sunset.

GETTING HERE AND AROUND

Pensacola International Airport has dozens of daily flights and is served by American Airlines (American Eagle), Delta, Southwest, Silver Airways, United, and US Airways. From Pensacola International Airport via Yellow Cab, it costs about $14 to get downtown or about $32 to reach Pensacola Beach.

In Pensacola and Pensacola Beach, Escambia County Area Transit provides regular citywide bus service ($1.75), downtown trolley routes, tours through the historic districts, and free trolley service to the beach from mid-May to Labor Day on Friday, Saturday, and Sunday evenings as well as Saturday afternoon.

Contacts Escambia County Area Transit (*ECAT*). ☎ *850/595–3228* ⊕ *www. goecat.com.* **Yellow Cab** ☎ *850/433–3333.*

VISITOR INFORMATION

Contacts Pensacola Visitor Information Center ⊠ *1401 E. Gregory St.* ☎ *850/434–1234, 800/874–1234* ⊕ *www.visitpensacola.com.*

EXPLORING

TOP ATTRACTIONS

Historic Pensacola Village. Within the Seville Square Historic District is this complex of several museums and historic homes whose indoor and outdoor exhibits trace the area's history back 450 years. The Museum of Industry (⊠ *200 E. Zaragoza St.*), in a late-19th-century warehouse, is home to permanent exhibits dedicated to the lumber, maritime, and shipping industries—once mainstays of Pensacola's economy. A reproduction of a 19th-century streetscape is displayed in the Museum of Commerce (⊠ *201 E. Zaragoza St.*). Also in the village are the Julee Cottage (⊠ *210 E. Zaragoza St.*), the "first home owned by a free woman of color"; the 1871 Dorr House (⊠ *311 S. Adams St.*); and the 1805 French-Creole Lavalle House (⊠ *205 E. Church St.*).

Strolling through the area gives you a good (and free) look at many architectural styles, but to enter some of the buildings you must purchase an all-inclusive ticket at the Village gift shop in the Tivoli High House—which was once in the city's red-light district but now is merely a calm reflection of a restored home. A guided tour (at 11, 1, and 2:30 and lasting 60–90 minutes) lets you experience the history of Pensacola as you visit the Lavalle House, Dorr House, Old Christ Church, and 1890s Lear-Rocheblave House. ⊠ *Tivoli High House, 205 E. Zaragoza St.* ⊕ *www.historicpensacola.org* 🎟 *$6* ⊘ *Tues.–Sat. 10–4.*

14

National Museum of Naval Aviation. Within the Pensacola Naval Air Station, this 300,000-square-foot museum has more than 140 historic aircraft. Among them are the NC-4, which in 1919 became the first plane to cross the Atlantic; the famous World War II fighter the F-6 *Hellcat;* and the Skylab Command Module.

Other attractions include an atomic bomb (it's defused, we promise), and the restored Cubi Bar Café—a very cool former airmen's club transplanted here from the Philippines. Relive the morning's maneuvers in the 14-seat motion-based

> **TOP GUN**
>
> The National Museum of Naval Aviation is one of only two locations nationwide that feature "Top Gun," four real F-14 military flight-training simulators with all the actual controls. Experience mock air-to-air combat, practice carrier landings, or simply cruise over Las Vegas; Iraq; Miramar, California; and other simulated sites during a 20-minute joyride. The $25 experience includes "cockpit orientation training."

simulator as well as an IMAX theater playing *Fighter Pilot, The Magic of Flight,* and other educational films. Pensacola, also known as the "Cradle of Naval Aviation," celebrated the 100th Anniversary of Naval Aviation in 2011. ⊠ *Pensacola Naval Air Station, 1750 Radford Blvd.* ☎ *850/452–3604* ⊕ *www.navalaviationmuseum.org* ⊠ *Museum free, IMAX film $8.75* ⊘ *Daily 9–5.*

Pensacola Children's Museum. The Pensacola Children's Museum is the newest museum in the West Florida Historic Preservation, Inc. complex. The museum offers a variety of programs for children of all ages, including story time, art projects, as well as a plethora of interactive historical exhibits from maritime to multicultural themes. ⊠ *115 East Zaragoza St.* ☎ *850/595–1559* ⊕ *www.historicpensacola.org* ⊠ *$3* ⊘ *Tues.–Sat. 10–4.*

Fodor's Choice
★
Pensacola Naval Air Station. Locals almost unanimously suggest this as *the* must-see attraction of Pensacola. As you drive near it, don't be alarmed if you're suddenly struck with the shakes—they're probably caused by the U.S. Navy's Blue Angels' aerobatic squadron buzzing overhead. This is their home base, and they practice maneuvers here on Tuesday and Wednesday mornings at 11:30 from March to November.

Then stay late—the pilots stick around after the show to shake hands and sign autographs. During the show, cover your ears as the six F/A 18s blast off in unison for 45 minutes of thrills and skill. Watching the Blue Angels practice their aerobatics is one of the best "free" shows in all of Florida (your tax dollars are already paying for these jets). It's also home to the National Flight Academy, which teaches the principles of Science, Technology, Engineering, and Math (STEM) during an immersive experience for students aged 11–17. ⊠ *1750 Radford Blvd.* ☎ *850/452–3604, 850/452–3606.*

Seville Square Historic District. Established in 1559, this is the site of Pensacola's first permanent Spanish settlement (it beat St. Augustine's by six years). Its center is Seville Square, a live oak–shaded park bounded by Alcaniz, Adams, Zaragoza, and Government streets. Roam these brick streets past honeymoon cottages and homes set in a parklike setting. Many buildings have been converted into restaurants, bars, offices, and shops that overlook broad Pensacola Bay and coastal road U.S. 98, which provides access to the Gulf Coast and beaches. ☎ 850/595–5985.</R>

FAMILY **T. T. Wentworth, Jr. Florida State Museum.** Even if you don't like museums, this one is worth a look. Housed in the elaborate, Renaissance revival–style former city hall, it has an interesting mix of exhibits illustrating life in the Florida Panhandle over the centuries. One of these, the City of Five Flags, provides a good introduction to Pensacola's history. Mr. Wentworth was quite a collector (as well as a politician and salesman), and his eccentric collection includes a mummified cat (creepy) and the size-37 left shoe of Robert Wadlow, the world's tallest man (not creepy, but a really big shoe). A wide range of both permanent and traveling exhibits include a rare collection of dollhouses, Black Ink (a look at African-Americans' role in printing), Hoops to Hips (a review of fashion history), Civil War exhibits, and a kid-size interactive area with a ship and fort where kids can play and pretend to be colonial Pensacolans. ✉ 330 S. Jefferson St. ☎ 850/595–5990 ⊕ www.historicpensacola.org ▭ Free ⊗ Tues.–Sat. 10–4.

Vince J. Whibbs Sr. Community Maritime Park. The latest gem of the city sits on Pensacola's waterfront and offers a multiuse, public-private park development that is home to a 5,038-seat multipurpose stadium and Randall K. and Martha A. Hunter Amphitheater that overlooks beautiful Pensacola Bay. The stadium is also home to the Double-A Pensacola Blue Wahoos, part of Minor League Baseball's Southern League, and is considered one of the premier facilities in Minor League Baseball. Keep an eye out for tickets—they sell out fast—as well as a variety of other events that fill the stadium and surrounding park year-round. ✉ 301 W. Main St. ☎ 850/436–5670 ⊕ pensacolacommunitymaritimepark.com.

WORTH NOTING

Palafox Historic District. Palafox Street is the main stem of historic downtown Pensacola and the center of the Palafox Historic District. The commercial and government hub of Old Pensacola is now an active cultural and entertainment district, where locally owned and operated bars and restaurants attract flocks of locals and visitors. The opulent, renovated Spanish Renaissance–style Saenger Theater, Pensacola's 1925 movie palace, hosts performances by the local symphony and opera, as well as national acts.

On Palafox between Government and Zaragoza streets is a statue of Andrew Jackson, which commemorates the formal transfer of Florida from Spain to the United States in 1821. While in the area, stop by Veterans Memorial Park, just off Bayfront Parkway near 9th Avenue. The ¾-scale replica of the Vietnam Memorial in Washington D.C. honors the more than 58,000 Americans who lost their lives in the Vietnam War.

Pensacola Museum of Art. Pensacola's city jail once occupied the 1906 Spanish revival–style building that is now the secure home for the museum's permanent collection of paintings, sculptures, and works on paper by 20th- and 21st-century artists—and we do mean secure:

you can still see the actual cells with their huge iron doors. Traveling exhibits have focused on photography (Wegman, Leibovitz, Ansel Adams), Dutch masters, regional artists, and the occasional art-world icon, such as Andy Warhol or Salvador Dalí. ✉ *407 S. Jefferson St.* ☎ *850/432–6247* ⊕ *www.pensacolamuseumofart.org* ✉ *$5* ⊗ *Tues.– Fri. 10–5, Sat. noon–5.*

BEACHES

Perdido Key State Park. Part of Gulf Islands National Seashore, this state park is on Perdido Key, a 247-acre barrier island. Its beach, now referred to as Johnson Beach, was one of the few beaches open to African-Americans during segregation. Today the park offers primitive camping year-round. It is within walking distance of dining and nightlife on the key and is a short drive from Alabama. **Amenities:** showers; toilets. **Best for:** sunsets; swimming; walking. ✉ *5 miles southwest of Pensacola off Rte. 292, Perdido Key* ⊕ *www.floridastateparks.org/ perdidokey* ✉ *$3 per vehicle.*

WHERE TO EAT

$
ECLECTIC
✕ **Al Fresco.** Five different dining spots (including four airstream trailers serving as food trucks), complete with umbrella-shaded tables, sit within a sea of palm trees in downtown Pensacola. You will find a wide variety of flavors to suit any palate, with Jerry's Cajun Café as the anchor and four airstream trailers including Z Taco Fresh Mex, Gouda Stuff Gourmet Melts, Gunshot BBQ, and the Greenhouse. Have a taco before a baseball game, or enjoy a chilled glass of beer before walking through the shops downtown. Be warned: this is a fully alfresco dining experience. Hours vary by truck, but all are open for lunch and dinner daily. ⑤ *Average main: $8* ✉ *501 S. Palafox St.* ☎ *850/438–1999* ⊕ *www.eatalfresco.com.*

$$$
SEAFOOD
✕ **Fish House.** Come one, come all, come hungry, and come at 11 am to witness the calm before the lunch storm. By noon the Fish House is packed with professionals, power players, and poseurs. The wide-ranging menu of fish dishes is the bait, and each can be served in a variety of ways: ginger-crusted, grilled, blackened, pecan-crusted, or Pacific-grilled, which puts any dish over the top. The attentive service, bayfront setting, and signature Grits a Ya-Ya (fresh gulf shrimp on a bed of smoked-Gouda cheese grits smothered with a portobello mushroom sauce) keeps diners in the net. Steaks, delicious homemade desserts, a sushi bar, more than 300 varieties of wine, and a full-service bar don't hurt the popularity of this restaurant either. ⑤ *Average main: $28* ✉ *600 S. Barracks St.* ☎ *850/470–0003* ⊕ *www.fishhouse.goodgrits.com.*

$$$
ECLECTIC
✕ **Global Grill.** Come hungry to this trendy downtown Pensacola restaurant, and fill your eyes, plate, and belly from the selection of more than 40 different tapas, 11 entrées, and eight salads. Among the tapas are the high-demand lamb lollipops, Israeli couscous, sundried tomato au jus, spicy seared tuna with five-pepper jelly, and the andouille-Manchego empanadas with cucumber cream. To jazz things up, entrées like filet mignon, gulf shrimp, duck breast, fresh fish, and New York strip compete with the light appetizers. ⑤ *Average main: $26* ✉ *27 S. Palafox St.* ☎ *850/469–9966* ⊕ *globalgrillpensacola.com* ⚱ *Reservations essential* ⊗ *Closed Sun. and Mon. No lunch.*

Like an Old West town with a Victorian twist, historic Pensacola is eye candy for architecture buffs.

$$ ✕ **McGuire's Irish Pub.** Since 1977 this authentic Irish pub has promised
IRISH   its patrons "feasting, imbibery, and debauchery" seven nights a week.
Fodor's Choice   A sense of humor pervades the place, evidenced by the range of prices
★   on hamburgers—$10–$100 depending on whether you want it topped
with cheddar or served with caviar and champagne. Beer is brewed on
the premises, and the wine cellar has more than 8,500 bottles. Menu
items include corned beef and cabbage, great steaks, and a hickory-
smoked prime rib. In an old firehouse, the pub is replete with antiques,
moose heads, Tiffany-style lamps, and Erin-go-bragh memorabilia. As
for the "richness" of the décor—on the walls and ceiling are nearly
$1 million in bills signed and dated by "Irishmen of all nationalities."
$ *Average main: $20* ⊠ *600 E. Gregory St.* ☎ *850/433–6789* ⊕ *www.
mcguiresirishpub.com.*

WHERE TO STAY

$ ⊞ **Crowne Plaza–Pensacola Grand Hotel.** On the site of the restored historic
HOTEL   Louisville & Nashville (L&N) railroad passenger depot, the Crowne
Plaza has a 15-story glass tower, attached to the train depot by a glass
atrium, and incredible views of historic Pensacola. **Pros:** great location
near downtown; amenities perfect for business travelers. **Cons:** it's a
box; there are more intimate choices closer to downtown. $ *Rooms
from: $188* ⊠ *200 E. Gregory St.* ☎ *850/433–3336, 800/348–3336*
⊕ *www.pensacolagrandhotel.com* ⥱ *200 rooms, 10 suites* ⓘⓄⓘ *No meals.*

$ ⊞ **New World Inn.** If you like your inns small, warm, and cozy, with the
B&B/INN   bay on one side and a short two-block walk to the downtown historic
area on the other, then this is the inn for you. **Pros:** perfect location
downtown; unique boutique hotel. **Cons:** not well suited for kids or

large families. ⑤ *Rooms from: $109* ⊠ *600 S. Palafox St.* ☎ *850/432–4111* ⊕ *www.newworldlanding.com* ⤳ *14 rooms, 1 suite* �‖ *Breakfast.*

$ **⛫ Solé Inn and Suites.** If you want to stay in the middle of downtown
HOTEL action but within reasonable distance of Pensacola's beaches, Solé Inn
and Suites offers a bit of trendy style in a central location for a great
price. **Pros:** unique décor; complimentary happy hour; free Wi-Fi. **Cons:**
Small bathrooms; during peak season downtown location can be loud.
⑤ *Rooms from: $109* ⊠ *200 N. Palafox St.* ☎ *850/470–9298, 888/470–9298* ⊕ *www.soleinnandsuites.com* ⤳ *45 rooms* �‖ *Breakfast.*

NIGHTLIFE

Pensacola offers a wide variety of lively places to enjoy once the sun
goes down, from Irish pubs to local watering holes that were once the
haunts of old naval heroes. You can sample homegrown concoctions
at upscale martini bars and the tunes of local and national music acts
at numerous live-music venues.

Hopjacks Pizza Kitchen and Taproom. This restaurant and bar has one of
the Panhandle's most extensive selections of specialty beers—more than
150, including 36 on tap. A second location has opened at 204 Nine
Mile Road in North Pensacola. ⊠ *10 S. Palafox St.* ☎ *850/497–6073*
⊕ *www.hopjacks.com.*

McGuire's Irish Pub. Those of Irish descent and anyone else who enjoys
cold home-brewed ales, beers, or lagers will feel at home in this restaurant and microbrewery. Its 8,500-bottle wine cellar includes vintages
ranging from $14 to $20,000. If you want a quiet drink, steer clear
on Friday and Saturday nights—when crowds abound and live entertainment enlivens the masses. ⊠ *600 E. Gregory St.* ☎ *850/433–6789*
⊕ *www.mcguiresirishpub.com.*

Seville Quarter. In the heart of the Historic District is Pensacola's equivalent of New Orleans's French Quarter. In fact, you may think you've
traveled to Louisiana when you enter any of its seven bars and two
courtyards offering an eclectic mix of live music. College students pack
the place on Thursday, tourists come on the weekend, and military
men and women from six nearby bases are stationed here nearly all
the time. This is a classic Pensacola nightspot. ⊠ *130 E. Government
St.* ☎ *850/434–6211* ⊕ *www.sevillequarter.com.*

Vinyl Music Hall. Music now fills the space of this 112-year-old former
Masonic lodge. An impressive variety of bands and acts have floated
through the intimate music venue, which offers mostly standing room.
It's also home to 5½ Bar, where mixologists create unique, handcrafted
drinks from the classic to the contemporary in a swanky, downtown
loft atmosphere. The box office is open weekdays between noon and 5
as well as before all events (one hour before start time). ⊠ *2 S. Palafox
Place* ☎ *850/607–6758* ⊕ *www.vinylmusichall.com.*

SHOPPING

The Pensacola area is home to varied shopping. The Palafox and Seville
historic districts are enjoyable areas for browsing or buying; here boutiques sell trendy clothing and imported and eclectic home furnishings.

Meanwhile, the area's main shopping staple, Cordova Mall, contains national chain stores.

Cordova Mall. Ten miles north of the historic districts, this mall is anchored by large stores such as Dillard's, Dick's Sporting Goods, Best Buy, and World Market. There are also more than 125 specialty shops and a food court. ⊠ *5100 N. 9th Ave.* ☏ *850/477–5355.*

University Town Plaza. This renovated outdoor shopping center is anchored by Sports Academy + Outdoors, Toys "R" Us, Burlington Coat Factory, and Famous Footwear. Many dining options are nearby and in the complex. ⊠ *7171 N. Davis Hwy.* ☏ *850/477–7562* ⊕ *www.simon.com/mall/university-town-plaza.*

SPORTS AND THE OUTDOORS

14

CANOEING AND KAYAKING

The Pensacola Bay area is known as the "Canoe Capital of Florida," and the pure sand-bottom Blackwater River is a particularly nice place to paddle. You can rent canoes and kayaks from a number of local companies as well as from outfits on nearby Perdido Key, home to the picturesque Perdido Watershed.

Adventures Unlimited. This outfitter on Coldwater Creek rents light water-craft as well as campsites and cabins along the Coldwater and Blackwater rivers in the Blackwater State Forest. Though prime canoe season lasts roughly March through mid-November, Adventures Unlimited rents year-round. ⊠ *8974 Tomahawk Landing Rd., Milton* ☏ *850/623–6197, 800/239–6864* ⊕ *www.adventuresunlimited.com.*

Blackwater Canoe Rental. Canoe and kayak rentals for exploring the Blackwater River are available from this outfitter northeast of Pensacola off Interstate 10 Exit 31. ⊠ *6974 Deaton Bridge Rd., Milton* ☏ *850/623–0235, 800/967–6789* ⊕ *www.blackwatercanoe.com.*

FISHING

With 52 miles of coastline and a number of inland waterways, the Pensacola area is a great place to drop a line. Bottom fishing is best for amberjack and grouper; offshore trolling trips search for tuna, wahoo, and sailfish; and inshore charters are out to hook redfish, cobia, and pompano. For a complete list of local fishing charters, visit ⊕ *www.pensacolafishing.com.*

Beach Marina. For a full- or half-day deep-sea charter, try the Beach Marina, which represents several charter outfits. ⊠ *655 Pensacola Beach Blvd.* ☏ *877/650–3474.*

GOLF

The bay area has a number of award-winning and picturesque golf courses. Some offer beach views, and others are local haunts.

Club at Hidden Creek. Hidden Creek is known for its lush landscape, rolling terrain, and scenic layout. The public course, designed by Ron Garl, offers challenging play for all levels of golfers with water throughout and well-guarded greens. It's rated one of the "Top 201 Courses to Play in North America" by *Golf Digest.* A natural grass practice facility with driving, putting, and chipping areas offers another unique feature. ⊠ *3070 PGA Blvd., Navarre* ☏ *850/939–4604*

⊕ *theclubathiddencreek.com* ✍ *$30 nonmembers, $18.50 members;* ⚑ *18 holes. 6805 yards. par 72.*

Lost Key Golf Club. Framed by the natural beauty of Perdido Key, Lost Key is located a short drive from downtown Pensacola and features the new Sea Dwarf Paspalum grass from the tee through the green. The public Arnold Palmer Signature Design Course was the first golf course in the world to be certified as an Audubon International Silver Signature Sanctuary. The clubhouse has a full-service pro-shop, men's and ladies locker-room facilities with lounge areas, and a restaurant and bar with indoor and outdoor seating and panoramic views of the golf course. ✉ *625 Lost Key Dr.* ☎ *850/549–2160, 888/256–7853* ⊕ *www. lostkey.com* ✍ *$69 for 18 holes, $35 for 9 holes* ⚑ *18 holes. 6801 yards. par 71.*

SCUBA DIVING

Also called the "Mighty O," the USS *Oriskany,* a retired aircraft carrier, was sunk 24 miles off the Pensacola Pass in 2006 to serve as the superstructure of the world's largest artificial reef. The "island" is accessible just 67 feet down, and the flight deck can be reached at 137 feet. A number of dive shops offer charter trips to take divers to the site.

PENSACOLA BEACH

5 miles south of Pensacola via U.S. 98 to Rte. 399 (Bob Sikes) Bridge.

One of the longest barrier islands in the world, Pensacola Beach offers a low-key, family-friendly feel with many local hangouts, fishing galore, and historic Fort Pickens. Connected to Pensacola by two long bridges, the island offers both a gulf-front and "sound" side for those seeking a calmer seaside experience. Public beaches abound in the area, including Casino Beach at the tip of Pensacola Beach Road, which offers live entertainment at its pavilion in the summer, as well as showers and bathrooms. Quietwater Beach Boardwalk, across the street from Casino Beach, also offers boutique shopping, eateries, and nightlife.

Long home to chain hotels as well as locally owned motels, the beach has opened a number of condominiums and resorts in recent years. Don't miss renting a bike or taking a drive to explore both Fort Pickens Road and J. Earle Bowden Way (connecting Pensacola Beach to the Navarre Beach area), which have reopened after many years of being closed to vehicular traffic. They offer breathtaking, unobstructed views of the gulf.

GETTING HERE

Pensacola Beach is a short drive (just 5 miles) from Pensacola across the Bob Sikes Bridge (Rte. 399).

EXPLORING

Fort Pickens. Constructed of more than 21 million locally made bricks, this fort, dating back to 1834, once served as a prison for Apache chief Geronimo. A National Park Service plaque describes the complex as a "confusing jumble of fortifications," but the real attractions here are the beach, nature exhibits, a large campground, an excellent gift shop, and breathtaking views of Pensacola Bay and the lighthouse across the inlet. It's the perfect place for a picnic lunch and a bit of history, too. ✉ *Fort Pickens Rd. at western tip of island* ☎ *850/934–2635* 💲 *$8 per car* ⏱ *Daily 7 am–10 pm.*

BEACHES

Casino Beach. Named for the Casino Resort, the island's first tourist spot when it opened in 1931 (the same day as the first Pensacola Beach Bridge), this beach offers everything from seasonal live entertainment to public restrooms and showers. You can also lounge in the shade of the Pensacola Beach Gulf Pier. Casino Beach has the most parking for beach access on the island and is just a short stroll from dining, entertainment, and major hotels such as the Margaritaville Beach Hotel and Holiday Inn Resort Beachfront Hotel. **Amenities:** food and drink; lifeguards (seasonal); parking (no fee); showers; toilets. **Best for:** swimming; walking. ✉ *735 Pensacola Beach Blvd.*

Langdon Beach. The Panhandle is home to the Florida District of the Gulf Islands National Seashore, the longest tract of protected seashore in the United States. At the Ft. Pickens area of the park on the gulfside tip of Santa Rosa Island, this beach is one of the top spots to experience the unspoiled beauty and snow-white beaches this area is known for. Keep an eye out for wildlife of the flying variety; the Fort Pickens area is known for its nesting shorebirds. A large covered pavilion is great for picnicking and a few minutes of shade. **Amenities:** lifeguards; parking (no fee); showers; toilets; water sports. **Best for:** solitude; snorkeling; sunrise; sunset; walking. ✉ *Fort Pickens Rd., 3 miles west of Pensacola Beach on west end of Santa Rosa Island* ⊕ *www.nps.gov/guis/index.htm.*

WHERE TO EAT

$$ ✕ **Flounder's Chowder and Ale House.** The wide and peaceful gulf spreads
SEAFOOD out before you at this casual restaurant where, armed with a fruity libation, you're all set for a night of "floundering" at its best. Funkiness comes courtesy of an eclectic collection of objets d'art; tastiness is served in specialties such as seafood nachos and the shrimp-boat platter. Most signature dishes are charbroiled over a hardwood fire, and to cater to those who love the sea but not seafood, the extensive menu reveals more choices. Live entertainment is presented every night in season, with performances limited to weekends off-season. 💲 *Average main: $16* ✉ *800 Quietwater Beach Blvd.* ☎ *850/932–2003* ⊕ *www.flounderschowderhouse.com.*

$$$ ✕ **Grand Marlin Restaurant and Oyster Bar.** This restaurant offers unfor-
SEAFOOD gettable views of Santa Rosa Sound and Pensacola Bay along with mouthwatering fresh local cuisine. Top-notch seafood shares the menu—printed daily—with specials. A creative oyster bar carries the finest oysters from Apalachicola, East Bay, and beyond, shucked to order. 💲 *Average main: $21* ✉ *400 Pensacola Beach Blvd.* ☎ *850/677–9153* ⊕ *www.thegrandmarlin.com.*

WHERE TO STAY

$ 🏨 **Hilton Pensacola Beach Gulf Front.** The name is fitting; right on the gulf,
HOTEL this hotel offers incredible views at one of the beach's most affordable prices. **Pros:** impeccably well kept; great dining; affordable. **Cons:**

chain hotel. $ *Rooms from: $179* ✉ *12 Via De Luna* ☎ *850/916–2999, 866/916–2999* ⊕ *www.pensacolabeachgulffront.hilton.com* ⤳ *272 units* �‖ *No meals.*

$
RESORT
🏨 **Holiday Inn Resort Pensacola Beach.** Known for its 250-foot lazy river and cascading waterfall, this gulf-front hotel is one of the most family-friendly on the beach. **Pros:** indoor pool; beach-view fitness center. **Cons:** non-gulfside rooms have views of the parking lot. $ *Rooms from: $200* ✉ *14 Via de Luna* ☎ *850/932–5331* ⊕ *www.myholidayinnbeachresort. com* ⤳ *206 rooms* �‖ *No meals.*

$$
HOTEL
🏨 **Margaritaville Beach Hotel.** This tropical getaway, inspired by the lyrics of Jimmy Buffett, gives you the relaxed, fun Margaritaville experience with the amenities of a top-notch hotel that oozes barefoot elegance. **Pros:** clean, inviting atmosphere; lots of dining options; local spa services available. **Cons:** somewhat off the beaten path to other local dining and nightlife. $ *Rooms from: $299* ✉ *165 Fort Pickens Rd.* ☎ *850/916–9755* ⊕ *www.margaritavillehotel.com* ⤳ *162 rooms* �‖ *Multiple meal plans.*

SPORTS AND THE OUTDOORS

DOLPHIN-SPOTTING CRUISES

Chase-N-Fins. Climb aboard this 50-foot navy utility launch, which cruises Pensacola Bay along Ft. Pickens, Pensacola Pass, and the Lighthouse at Pensacola Naval Air Station in search of friendly dolphins. ✉ *655 Pensacola Beach Blvd.* ☎ *850/492–6337, 800/967–6789* ⊕ *www. chase-n-fins.com* ✉ *From $25.*

FISHING

Pensacola Beach Gulf Pier. The 1,471-foot-long pier touts itself as the "the most friendly pier around." It hosts serious anglers who find everything they'll need here—from pole rentals to bait—to land that big one, but those looking to catch only a beautiful sunset are welcome, too. Check the pier's website for the latest reports on what's biting. ✉ *41 Fort Pickens Rd.* ☎ *850/934–7200* ⊕ *www.fishpensacolabeachpier.com* ✉ *$7.50 fishers, $1.25 observers.*

DAYTRIPS FROM PENSACOLA

Inland, where the northern reaches of the Panhandle butt up against the back porches of Alabama and Georgia, you'll find a part of Florida that goes a long way toward explaining why the state song is "Swannee River" (and why its parenthetical title is "Old Folks at Home"). Stephen Foster's musical genius notwithstanding, the inland Panhandle area is definitely more Dixie than Sunshine State, with few lodging options other than the chain motels that flank the Interstate 10 exits and a decidedly slower pace of life than you'll find on the tourist-heavy Gulf Coast.

But the area's natural attractions—hills and farmland, untouched small towns, pristine state parks—make for great day trips from the coast should the sky turn gray or the skin red. Explore underground caverns where eons-old rock formations create bizarre scenes, visit one of Florida's up-and-coming wineries, or poke around small-town America in DeFuniak Springs. Altogether, the inland area of the Panhandle is one of the state's most satisfyingly soothing regions.

DEFUNIAK SPRINGS

77 miles northeast of Pensacola on U.S. 90 off I–10.

This scenic spot has a rather unusual claim to fame: at its center lies a nearly perfectly symmetrical spring-fed lake, one of only two such naturally circular bodies of water in the world (the other is in Switzerland). A sidewalk encircles Lake DeFuniak (also called Circle Lake), which is dotted by pine and shade trees, creating a very pleasing atmosphere for a long-distance mosey. In 1848 the Knox Hill Academy was founded here, and for more than half a century it was the only institution of higher learning in northwestern Florida.

In 1885 the town was chosen as the location for the New York Chautauqua educational society's winter assembly. The Chautauqua programs were discontinued in 1922, but DeFuniak Springs attempts to revive them, in spirit at least, by sponsoring a countywide Chautauqua Festival in April. Christmas is a particularly festive time, when the sprawling Victorian houses surrounding the lake are decorated to the nines.

There's not a tremendous amount to see here, but if you have the good sense to travel U.S. 90 to discover Old Florida, at least take the time to travel Circle Drive to see its beautiful Victorian homes. Also take a little time to walk around the small downtown area and drop in its bookstores, cafés, and small shops.

EXPLORING

Chautauqua Winery. Open since 1989, this winery and its vintages have slowly won respect from oenophiles wary of what was once considered to be an oxymoron at best: "Florida wine." The winery has won honors in national and international competitions, with wines that vary from dry, barrel-fermented wines to Southern favorites like sweet muscadine and blueberry wines. Fourteen vats ranging in size from 1,500 to 6,000 gallons generate a total of 70,000 gallons of wine. Take a free tour to see how ancient art blends with modern technology; then retreat to the tastefully decorated tasting room and gift shop. ✉ *364 Hugh Adams Rd.* ☎ *850/892–5887* ⊕ *www.chautauquawinery.com.*

TAKE A
TOUR

Circle Drive. Some of the finest examples of Victorian architecture in the state can be seen while you are walking or motoring around Circle Drive, the road that wraps around Circle Lake. The circumference is marked with beautiful Victorian specimens like the Walton-DeFuniak Public Library, the Dream Cottage, and the Pansy Cottage. Most of the other notable structures are private residences, but you can still admire them from the street.

WHERE TO STAY

$$
HOTEL

Hotel DeFuniak. This sweet, Depression-era two-story redbrick structure is on a quiet corner a few blocks from peaceful Lake DeFuniak—just look for the two-tone 1937 Buick permanently moored out front. **Pros:** applause for the owners who created a sweet little retreat in the heart of downtown. **Cons:** DeFuniak can be eerily empty and quiet at night. ⑤ *Rooms from: $105* ✉ *400 E. Nelson Ave.* ☎ *850/892–4383,*

877/333–8642 ⊕ *www.hoteldefuniak.com* ⊷ *8 rooms, 3 suites* ⫶○⫶ *Breakfast.*

FALLING WATERS STATE PARK
35 miles east of DeFuniak Springs via U.S. 90 and Rte. 77.

Falling Waters State Park. This site of a Civil War–era whiskey distillery and, later, an exotic-plant nursery (some species still thrive in the wild) is best known for also being the site of the Falling Waters Sink. The 100-foot-deep cylindrical pit provides the background for a waterfall, and there's an observation deck for viewing this natural phenomenon. The water freefalls 67 feet to the bottom of the sink, but where it goes after that is a mystery. ⊠ *1130 State Park Rd., Chipley* ☎ *850/638–6130* ⊕ *www.floridastateparks.org/fallingwaters* ⊠ *$5 per vehicle, up to 8 people* ⊙ *Daily 8–sunset.*

FLORIDA CAVERNS STATE PARK
13 miles northeast of Falling Waters off U.S. 90 on Rte. 166.

Florida Caverns State Park. A short drive from the center of Marianna, a cute and pristine community, you can see what's behind or—more accurately—what's beneath it all. Ranger-led cave tours reveal stalactites, stalagmites, soda straws, columns, rim stones, flowstones, and "waterfalls" of solid rock at these underground caverns, where the temperature hovers at an oh-so-pleasant 68°F year-round. Some of the caverns are off-limits to the public or open for scientific study by permit only, but you can still see enough to fill a half-day or more—and be amazed that caverns of this magnitude exist in the Sunshine State. Don't forsake the quiet, preserved, and peaceful woodlands, which encompass 10 distinct communities including upland glade, hardwood forests, floodplains, forests, and swamps. There are also hiking trails, campsites, and areas for swimming, horseback riding, and canoeing on the Chipola River. ⊠ *3345 Caverns Rd., off U.S. 90 on Rte. 166, Marianna* ☎ *850/482–9598, 800/326–3521 for camping reservations* ⊕ *www.floridastateparks.org/floridacaverns* ⊠ *Park $5 per vehicle, up to 8 people; caverns $8* ⊙ *Daily 8–sunset, cavern tours Thurs.–Mon. 9–4.*

THE EMERALD COAST

On U.S. 98, several towns, each with its own personality, are strung along the shoreline from Pensacola southeast to St. George Island. The side-by-side cities of Destin and Fort Walton Beach seemingly merge into one sprawling destination and continue to spread as more condominiums, resort developments, shopping centers, and restaurants crowd the skyline each year. The view changes drastically—and for the better—farther along the coast as you veer off 98 and enter Route 30A, the main coastal road that leads to a quiet stretch known as the Beaches of South Walton. Here building restrictions prohibit high-rise developments, and the majority of dwellings are privately owned homes, most of which are available to vacationers.

Continuing southeast on U.S. 98, you come to Panama City Beach, whose Miracle Strip, once crammed with carnival-like amusement parks, junk-food vendors, T-shirt shops, and go-kart tracks, has been nearly replaced by up-to-date shopping and entertainment complexes and new condos that have given the area a much-needed facelift. Farther east, past the up-and-coming sleeper cities of Port St. Joe and Mexico Beach, is the quiet blue-collar town of Apalachicola, Florida's main oyster fishery. Watch oystermen ply their trade, using long-handled tongs to bring in their catch. Cross the Apalachicola Bay via the Bryant Patton Bridge to St. George Island. This unspoiled 28-mile-long barrier island offers some of America's most scenic beaches, including St. George Island State Park, which has the longest beachfront of any state park in Florida.

14

GETTING HERE AND AROUND

Northwest Florida Regional Airport, on Highway 85 in North Eglin, is served by American Airlines (American Eagle), Delta (Delta Connection), United Airlines (Express Jet), and US Airways. From here you can take a number of car and cab services, including Checker Cab, to destinations such as Fort Walton Beach ($18) or Destin ($24).

Contacts Checker Cab ☎ *850/650–8294.*

VISITOR INFORMATION

Contacts Emerald Coast Convention and Visitors Bureau ☎ *850/651–7131, 800/322–3319* ⊕ *www.emeraldcoastfl.com.*

FORT WALTON BEACH

46 miles east of Pensacola via U.S. 98.

This coastal town dates from the Civil War but had to wait more than 75 years to come into its own. Patriots loyal to the Confederate cause organized Walton's Guard (named in honor of Colonel George Walton, onetime acting territorial governor of West Florida) and camped at a site on Santa Rosa Sound, later known as Camp Walton. In 1940 fewer than 90 people lived in Fort Walton Beach, but within a decade the city became a boomtown, thanks to New Deal money for roads and bridges and the development of Eglin Field during World War II.

Although off-limits to civilians, Eglin Air Force Base, which encompasses 724 square miles of land with 10 auxiliary fields and 21 runways, is Fort Walton Beach's main source of income. Tourism runs a close second. Despite inland sprawl, the town has a cute little shopping district with independent merchants along U.S. 98.

EXPLORING

Air Force Armament Museum. The collection at this museum just outside the Eglin Air Force Base's main gate contains more than 5,000 armaments (e.g., missiles, bombs, and aircraft) from World Wars I and II and the Korean and Vietnam wars. Included are uniforms, engines, weapons, aircraft, and flight simulators. You can't miss the museum—there's a squadron of aircraft including a B-17 Flying Fortress, an SR-71 Blackbird, a B-52, a B-25, and helicopters parked on the grounds in front. A continuously playing 32-minute movie, *Arming the Future*, features

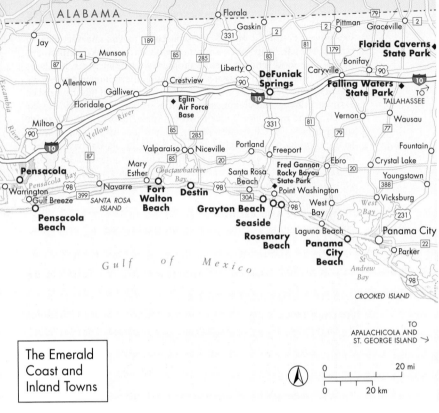

0   20 mi

0   20 km

current weapons and Eglin's history and its role in their development. ⊠ *100 Museum Dr. (Rte. 85), Eglin Air Force Base* ☏ *850/651–1808* ⊕ *www.afarmamentmuseum.com* ✉ *Free* ⊘ *Mon.–Sat. 9:30–4:30.*

Eglin Air Force Base Reservation. The 250,000 acres of the Eglin reservation conditionally open to the public include 21 ponds and plenty of challenging, twisting wooded trails that are all open to exploration. The area appeals to outdoors enthusiasts who want to hunt, fish, canoe, and swim. You can buy a day pass to hike or mountain bike on the Timberlake Trail. In order to gain access to the areas of the reservation that are open to the public (and many areas are closed all the time, others just some of the time), you must obtain a permit from the Natural Resource Division (also known locally as the Jackson Guard). ⊠ *Jackson Guard, 107 Rte. 85 N, Niceville* ☏ *850/882–4164* ⊕ *jacksonguard.com* ⊘ *Trail Mon.–Thurs. 7–4:30, Fri. 7–6, and Sat. 7:30–12:30.*

FAMILY **Gulfarium.** This marine adventure park has been a beloved attraction for locals and visitors alike for almost 60 years. In fact, it is the oldest continuously operating marine park in Florida. Species exhibited here include otters, penguins, alligators, harbor seals, and sharks. The summer of 2012 brought a number of fresh offerings, and now you can meander through renovated exhibits and get up close and personal with marine life thanks to several new interactive experiences, from swimming with our watery friends to feedings. For the not so faint of heart, the Stingray Bay Snorkel offers a chance to swim with the creatures as well as sharks, but for an even more intensive experience, there's a five-hour one-on-one with a marine-mammal trainer. ✉ *1010 Miracle Strip* ☎ *850/243–9046, 800/247–8575* ⊕ *www.gulfarium.com* 🎫 *$19.95, animal encounters extra* ⊘ *Daily 9–4:30.*

BEACHES

John Beasley Park. This tranquil seaside park rests among the rolling dunes on Okaloosa Island. Two dune walkovers lead to the beach, where there are a dozen covered picnic tables, pavilions, changing rooms, and freshwater showers—plus lifeguards in summer. The city's hottest nightlife is just down the road, but families can enjoy the scenic beauty. There is also an emphasis on wheelchair beach access. **Amenities:** lifeguards; parking; showers; toilets. **Best for:** sunset; walking. ✉ *Okaloosa Island.*

14

WHERE TO EAT

$$
AMERICAN

✕ **Angler's Beachside Grill and Sports Bar.** Unless you sit in the water, you can't dine any closer to the gulf than at this casual beachside bar and grill next to the Gulfarium. Located at the entrance to Okaloosa Island Pier (and within a complex of other nightclubs and restaurants), Angler's houses the requisite sports bar with televisions broadcasting sports events, including in the elevators and bathrooms. Outside, a volleyball net tempts diners onto the sands. Snack on nachos and quesadillas, sample fresh-catch dishes such as king crab and prawns, or try the smoked tuna dip, a lightly smoked yellowfin dip served with warm, crisp tortilla strips. The waterfront setting is the image of a picturesque Gulf Coast eatery. $ *Average main: $19* ✉ *1030 Miracle Strip Pkwy.* ☎ *850/796–0260* ⊕ *www.anglersbeachside.com.*

$$$
STEAKHOUSE

✕ **Pandora's Steakhouse and Lounge.** On the Emerald Coast, the name Pandora's is synonymous with prime rib. Steaks are cooked over a wood-burning grill, and you can order your prime rib regular or extra-thick cut; fish aficionados should try the char-grilled yellowfin tuna or one of the daily specials. Cozy up in an alcove to enjoy your meal in peace or head to the lounge, where the mood turns a bit more gregarious, with live entertainment Wednesday through Saturday. $ *Average main: $26* ✉ *1226 Santa Rosa Blvd.* ☎ *850/244–8669* ⊕ *www. pandorassteakhouse.com* ⊘ *Closed Mon. No lunch.*

WHERE TO STAY

$
B&B/INN

🏠 **Aunt Martha's Bed and Breakfast.** Although it has been pampering and charming its guests since 2001, Aunt Martha's can transport you back half a century to when Florida was still a sleepy little state. **Pros:** quiet sanctuary on the waterfront but with access to dining, shopping, and sites. **Cons:** not suited for kids and families; primarily for romance and privacy. $ *Rooms from: $105* ✉ *315 Shell Ave. SE* ☎ *850/243–6702* ⊕ *www.auntmarthasbedandbreakfast.com* 🛏 *5 rooms.* 🍴 *Breakfast.*

$
RESORT

🏠 **Ramada Plaza Beach Resort.** If your family loves the water, splash down at this beachside extravaganza, where activity revolves around a 194,000-gallon pool (allegedly the area's largest) with a spectacular swim-through waterfall that tumbles down from an island oasis;

there's also a separate kiddie Splash Garden, a beachwear and beach-toy shop, and an 800-foot private beach. **Pros:** extravagant offerings for a family-friendly vacation; the pool may please the kids more than the gulf. **Cons:** may be too busy for romance travelers or seniors seeking peace and quiet. $ *Rooms from: $199* ✉ *1500 Miracle Strip Pkwy. SE* ☎ *850/243–9161, 800/874–8962* ⊕ *www.ramadafwb.com* ↻ *335 rooms, 18 suites* ⫯⚪⫯ *No meals.*

NIGHTLIFE

The Boardwalk. This massive dining-and-entertainment complex at the entrance to the Okaloosa Island Pier includes several restaurants (Crab Trap, Oyster House, Floyd's Shrimp House, and Angler's) as well as an assortment of nightclubs. ✉ *1450 Miracle Strip Pkwy.* ⊕ *www. theboardwalkoi.com.*

Howl at the Moon. Dueling pianos and furious singalongs make this Boardwalk spot extremely popular. The show starts at 8 pm and rocks until 2. ✉ *1450 Miracle Strip Pkwy., Ste. 203* ☎ *850/301–0111* ⊕ *www. howlatthemoon.com.*

SPORTS AND THE OUTDOORS

FISHING

Okaloosa Island Pier. Don't miss a chance to go out to the end of this ¼-mile-long pier. There's an admission fee (and a fee to fish), and you can buy bait and tackle, and rent poles as well. ✉ *1030 Miracle Strip Pkwy. E* ☎ *850/244–1023* ⊕ *www.okaloosaislandpier.com.* ◈ *$2, $7.50 to fish.*

SCUBA DIVING

Discovery Dive World. Run by military veterans, this full-service snor-kleing and dive shop offers a variety of gear and lessons, though they specialize in spear fishing. ✉ *92 S. John Sims Pkwy., Valapariso* ☎ *850/678–5001* ⊕ *www.discoverydiveworld.com.*

DESTIN

8 miles east of Fort Walton Beach via U.S. 98.

Fort Walton Beach's "neighbor" lies on the other side of the strait that connects Choctawhatchee Bay with the Gulf of Mexico. Destin takes its name from its founder, Leonard A. Destin, a Connecticut sea captain who settled his family here sometime in the 1830s. For the next 100 years, Destin remained a sleepy little fishing village until the strait, or East Pass, was bridged in 1935. Then recreational anglers discovered its white sands, blue-green waters, and abundance of some of the most sought-after sport fish in the world. More billfish are hauled in around Destin each year than from all other gulf ports combined, giving credence to its nickname, the World's Luckiest Fishing Village.

But you don't have to be the rod-and-reel type to love Destin. There's plenty to entertain the sand-pail set as well as senior citizens, and there are many nice restaurants, which you'll have an easier time finding if you remember that the main drag through town is referred to as both U.S. 98 and Emerald Coast Parkway. The name makes sense, but part of what makes the gulf look so emerald in these parts is the contrasting

Live oaks draped with Spanish Moss are most common in the Panhandle.

whiteness of the sand on the beach. Actually, it's not sand—it's pure, powder-soft Appalachian quartz that was dropped off by a glacier a few thousand years back. Since quartz doesn't compress (and crews clean and rake the beach each evening), your tootsies get the sole-satisfying benefit of soft, sugary "sand." Sand so pure it squeaks.

ESSENTIALS

Visitor Information Destin Chamber of Commerce ☎ *850/837–6241* ⊕ *www.destinchamber.com.*

EXPLORING

FAMILY **Big Kahuna's Lost Paradise.** The water park is the big draw here, with the Honolulu Half Pipe (a perpetual surfing wave), flume rides, steep and slippery slides, and assorted other methods of expending hydro-energy appealing to travelers who prefer freshwater thrills over the gulf, which is just across the street. This complex also has dry family-friendly attractions: 54 holes of miniature golf, two go-kart tracks, an arcade, thrill rides, and an amphitheater. ✉ *1007 U.S. 98 E* ☎ *850/837–8319* ⊕ *www. bigkahunas.com* ✉ *Grounds free, water park $37.99, miniature golf $6.99, go-karts $6.99, Sky Coaster or Cyclone $16.99* ☉ *Water Park: early May–Labor Day, varying days 10–5 or 6. Adventure Park: early May–Labor Day, varying days 2–9 or 10; late Mar. and early Apr., varying days 2–9.*

BEACHES

Crab Island. All of the sugary, white-sand beaches of Destin and the surrounding Emerald Coast garner worldwide attention, but this is the locals' favorite. Actually a sandbar in East Pass rather than an island, Crab Island draws water-lovers and boaters, who wade the sandbar or drop anchor in droves on fair-weather days, especially weekends. People are friendly, so it's a great place to make new friends, and the shallow waters are good for families. A food barge comes around the "island" seasonally. **Amenities:** food and drink, water sports. **Best for:** partiers, snorkeling, swimming. ⊠ *North side of East Pass and Marler Bridge.*

WHERE TO EAT

$$$
SEAFOOD

✕ **Marina Café.** A harbor view, impeccable service, and sophisticated fare create one of the finest dining experiences on the Emerald Coast. An ocean motif is expressed in shades of aqua, green, and sand accented with marine tapestries and sea sculptures. The chef calls his creations contemporary Continental, offering diners a choice of thick USDA steaks, classic creole, Mediterranean, or Pan-Asian dishes. One regional specialty is the popular pan-seared yellow-edge grouper with a blue-crab-meat crust. A special sushi menu is available, the wine list is extensive, and happy hour runs from 5 to 7. ⑤ *Average main: $24* ⊠ *404 U.S. 98 E* ☎ *850/837–7960* ⊕ *www.marinacafe.com* ☉ *No lunch.*

WHERE TO STAY

$$$$
RESORT

▥ **Emerald Grande at HarborWalk Village.** Even locals seek out the views at this harborfront destination within a destination, with luxurious hotel accommodations and a full menu of amenities, including a full-service spa, marina, health club, and indoor-outdoor pools. **Pros:** great for larger families and groups; many top-rated amenities are part of the complex. **Cons:** very family-oriented, so it's not ideal for a romantic couple's getaway; must water-taxi to the beach. ⑤ *Rooms from: $487* ⊠ *10 Harbor Blvd.* ☎ *800/676–0091* ⊕ *www.emeraldgrande.com* ☞ *269 rooms* ⦿ *No meals.*

$$
RESORT
Fodor's Choice
★

▥ **Sandestin Golf and Beach Resort.** This place is its own little world—with shopping, charter fishing, spas, salons, tennis, water sports, golf, and special events—so it's no wonder newlyweds, conventioneers, and families all find something for them at this 2,400-acre resort. **Pros:** everything you'd ever need in a resort—and more. **Cons:** lacks the personal touches of a modest retreat. ⑤ *Rooms from: $211* ⊠ *9300 Emerald Coast Pkwy. W* ☎ *850/267–8000, 800/277–0800* ⊕ *www.sandestin. com* ☞ *1,400 rooms, condos, villas, and town homes* ⦿ *No meals.*

NIGHTLIFE

AJ's Seafood & Oyster Bar. Folks come by boat and car to this supercasual bar and restaurant overlooking the marina. Nightly live music means young lively crowds pack the dance floor. ⊠ *116 U.S. 98 E* ☎ *850/837–1913* ⊕ *www.ajs-destin.com.*

Harbor Docks. Affiliated with Pensacola's Dharma Blue, this favorite with the local seafaring set has been around since 1979. The incredibly casual feel is marked by picnic tables and hibachi grills. There's live music Thursday through Saturday. There's also a sushi bar. ⊠ *538 U.S. 98 E* ☎ *850/837–2506* ⊕ *www.harbordocks.com.*

Hog's Breath Saloon. The festive atmosphere is enhanced by good live music from a solo performer during the week and more musicians on the weekend. The food—steaks, burgers, salads—isn't bad, either. ⊠ *541 U.S. 98 E* ☎ *850/837–5991* ⊕ *www.hogsbreath.com.*

Nightown. This nightclub has an expansive dance floor, VIP access with bottle service, seven bars, live music, pool tables, and plenty of drink specials and theme evenings. It's open Wednesday through Saturday until 4 am. ⊠ *140 Palmetto St.* ☎ *850/837–7625* ⊕ *www.nightown. com.*

Sandestin Village of Baytowne Wharf. You can find funky blues, great sushi, and a set of dueling pianos here any night of the week. Music guests have included Graffiti & the Funky Blues Shack and John Wehner's Village Door Nightclub. ⊠ *9300 Emerald Coast Pkwy. W* ☎ *800/622–1038.*

SHOPPING

14

Destin Commons. Don't call it a mall. Call it an "open-air lifestyle center." More than 70 high-end specialty shops are here, as well as a 14-screen theater, Hard Rock Cafe, miniature train, and nautical theme park for kids. ⊠ *4300 Legendary Dr.* ☎ *850/337–8700* ⊕ *www. destincommons.com.*

Market at Sandestin. The two dozen or so upscale shops in this elegant Sandestin complex peddle everything from expensive chocolates to designer clothes. ⊠ *9300 Emerald Coast Pkwy. W* ☎ *850/267–8092.*

Shops at Grand Boulevard at Sandestin Town Center. This town center–style shopping and dining complex is on the area's main thoroughfare, just a hop, skip, and jump from the Sandestin Resort. For the high-end shopper, the center offers everything from Fusion Art Glass Gallery to Brooks Brothers Country Club. A number of boutiques, such as Hello, Sunshine and Magnolia House, carry fare you can't find anywhere else. Dining options include Mitchell's Fish Market, P. F. Chang's China Bistro, and Cantina Laredo Gourmet Mexican Food. ⊠ *600 Grand Blvd.* ☎ *850/654–5929* ⊕ *www.grandboulevard.com.*

Silver Sands Factory Stores. One of the Southeast's largest retail designer outlets has more than 100 shops selling top-name merchandise. ⊠ *10562 Emerald Coast Pkwy. W* ☎ *850/654–9771* ⊕ *www. silversandsoutlet.com.*

SPORTS AND THE OUTDOORS

FISHING

Destin has the largest charter-boat fishing fleet in the state. You can also pier-fish from the 3,000-foot-long Destin Catwalk and along East Pass Bridge.

Adventure Charters. This company represents more than 90 charter services that offer deep-sea, bay-bottom, and light-tackle fishing excursions. ⊠ *East Pass Marina, 288 U.S. 98 E* ☎ *850/837–1995* ⊕ *www. destinfishingservice.com* 🖃 *Private charters from $120 per hr.*

Destin Dockside. It's a great place to pick up bait, tackle, and most anything else you'd need for a day of fishing. ⊠ *East Pass Marina, 288 U.S. 98 E* ☎ *850/428–3313* ⊕ *www.boatrentalsindestin.com.*

HarborWalk Marina. At this rustic-looking waterfront complex you can get bait, gas, tackle, and food. Regularly scheduled party-fishing-boat excursions are offered and are a much cheaper alternative to chartering or renting your own boat. ⊠ *66 Harbor Blvd. (U.S. 98*

E) ☎ *850/337–8250* ⊕ *www.harborwalk-destin.com* ✉ *Excursions from $55.*

GOLF

For sheer number of holes, Sandestin tops the list with 72 (four courses): Baytowne Golf Club at Sandestin, the Burnt Pines Course, the Links Course, and the Raven Golf Club. For more information, see ⊕ *www.sandestin.com/golfers.*

Indian Bayou Golf Club. Indian Bayou offers three nine-hole courses with wide, forgiving fairways accented by well-manicured, lush greens, tall pines, and numerous lakes and water features. With challenging options for all skill levels, it is one of the more affordable options in the area. ✉ *1 Country Club Dr. E, off Airport Rd., off U.S. 98* ☎ *850/837–6191* ⊕ *www.indianbayougolf.com* ⛳. *Choctaw course: 9 holes. 3464 yards. par 36. Creek course: 9 holes. 3433 yards. par 36. Seminole course: 9 holes. 3614 yards. par 36.*

Kelly Plantation Golf Club. Designed by Fred Couples and Gene Bates, this semi-private course meanders along the Choctawhatchee Bay. The overall layout is encouraging for novice golfers from the forward tees, with hardly any forced carries; however, from the back tees, it's an entirely different game. Stretching 7,099 yards, the course offers a serious driving test for long hitters. Greens are unique on almost every hole. Keep an eye out for hole no. 4's spectacular, panoramic view of Choctawhatchee Bay, and take in the scents and sights of the surrounding magnolias and palmettos, native to the northwest Florida region. ✉ *307 Kelly Plantation Dr.* ☎ *850/650–7600* ⊕ *www.kellyplantationgolf.com* ✉ *$134* ⛳. *18 holes. 7099 yards. 72 par.*

Raven Golf Club. This picturesque course is a two-time home to the Boeing Championship—a stop on the PGA Champions Tour—and is carved through the marshes and pine trees of Sandestin Resort. Robert Trent Jones Jr. crafted the course as what he calls "a true modern traditional." The Raven Golf Club requires strategy on every tee as golfers are presented with a variety of shot options accompanied by changes in color and texture throughout the course. It will require almost every club and trick in your bag. ✉ *9300 Emerald Coast Pkwy. W* ☎ *850/267–8155* ⊕ *www.sandestin.com/Golfers* ✉ *$69* ⛳. *18 holes. 6931 yards. 71 par.*

Regatta Bay Golf and Country Club. Here you'll find a semi-private course nestled among nature preserves along Choctawhatchee Bay. You'll also enjoy the golf club's amenities, including a state-of-the-art Parview GPS system on golf carts, and small touches that make the course and club unique like chilled apples on the 1st and 10th tees and mango-scented iced towels. It's a favorite course for players in northwest Florida. ✉ *465 Regatta Bay Blvd.* ☎ *850/337–8080* ⊕ *www.regattabay.com* ✉ *$99* ⛳. *18 holes. 6894 yards. par 72.*

SCUBA DIVING

Although visibility here (about 50 feet) isn't on par with the reefs of the Atlantic Coast, divers can explore artificial reefs, wrecks, and a limestone shelf at depths of up to 90 feet.

Emerald Coast Scuba. You can take diving lessons, arrange excursions, and rent all the necessary equipment through this operation. ✉ *503*

Continued on page 757

GONE FISHIN'

by Gary McKechnie

My favorite uncle has a passion for fishing.

It was one I didn't really understand—I'm more of a motorcycle guy, not a fishing pole–toting one. But one day he piqued my curiosity by telling me that fishing has many of the same enticements as motorcycling. Come again? He beautifully described the peaceful process of it all—how the serenity and solitude of the sport wash away concerns about work and tune him into the wonder of nature, just like being on a bike (minus the helmet and curvy highways).

I took the bait, and early one morning a few weeks later, my Uncle Bud and I headed out in a boat to a secluded cove on the St. Johns River near DeLand. We'd brought our rods, line, bait, and tackle—plus hot chocolate and a few things to eat. We didn't need much else. We dropped in our lines and sat silently, watching the fog hover over the water.

There was a peaceful stillness as we waited (and waited) for the fish to bite. There were turtles sunning themselves on logs and herons perched in the trees. We waited for hours for just a little nibble. I can't even recall now if we caught anything, but it didn't matter. My uncle was right: it was a relaxing way to spend a Florida morning.

REEL TIME

Florida is recognized as the "Fishing Capital of the World" as well as the "Bass Capital of the World." It's also home to some of the nation's most popular crappie tournaments.

Florida and fishing have a bond that goes back to thousands of years before Christ, when Paleo-Indians living along Florida's rivers and coasts were harvesting the waters just as readily as they were harvesting the land. Jump ahead to the 20th century and along came amateur anglers like Babe Ruth, Clark Gable, and Gary Cooper vacationing at central Florida fishing camps in pursuit of bream, bluegill, and largemouth bass, while Ernest Hemingway was scouring the waters off Key West in hopes of snagging marlin, tarpon, and snapper. Florida was, and is, an angler's paradise.

A variety of fish and plentiful waterways—7,800 lakes and 1,700 rivers and creeks, not to mention the gulf and the ocean—are just two reasons why Florida is the nation's favorite fishing spot. And let's not forget the frost-free attributes: unlike their northern counterparts, Florida anglers have yet to

When he wasn't writing, Ernest Hemingway loved to fish in the Florida Keys. He's shown here in Key West in 1928.

drill through several feet of ice just to go fishing in the wintertime. Plus, a well-established infrastructure for fishing—numerous bait and tackle shops, boat rentals, sporting goods stores, public piers, and charters—makes it easy for experts and first-time fishermen to get started. For Floridians and the visitors hooked on the sport here, fishing in the Sunshine State is a sport of sheer ease and simplicity.

An afternoon on the waters of Charlotte County in southwest Florida.

CASTING WIDE

The same way Florida is home to rocket scientists and beach bums, it's home to a diverse variety of fishing methods. What kind will work for you depends on where you want to go and what you want to catch.

From the Panhandle south to the Everglades, fishing is as easy as finding a quiet spot on the bank or heading out on freshwater lakes, tranquil ponds, spring-fed rivers, and placid inlets and lagoons.

Perhaps the biggest catches are found offshore—in the Atlantic Ocean, Florida Straits, or the Gulf of Mexico. For saltwater fishing, you can join a charter, be it a private one for small groups or a large party one; head out along the long jetties or public piers that jut into the ocean; or toss your line from the shore into the surf (known as surf casting). Some attempt a tricky yet effective form of fishing called net casting: tossing a circular net weighted around its perimeter; the flattened net hits the surface and drives fish into the center of the circle.

Surf casting on Juno Beach, about 20 mi north of Palm Beach.

FRESHWATER FISHING VS. SALTWATER FISHING

FRESH WATER

With nearly 8,000 lakes to choose from, it's hard to pick the leading contenders, but a handful rise to the top: Lake George, Lake Tarpon, Lake Weohyakapka, Lake Istokpoga, Lake Okeechobee, Crescent Lake, Lake Kissimmee, Lake George, and Lake Talquin. Florida's most popular freshwater game fish is the largemouth bass. Freshwater fishermen are also checking rivers and streams for other popular catches, such as spotted bass, white bass, Suwannee bass, striped bass, black crappie, bluegill, redear sunfish, and channel catfish.

SALT WATER

The seas are filled with some of the most challenging (and tasty) gamefish in America. From piers, jetties, private boats, and charter excursions, fishermen search for bonefish, tarpon, snook, redfish, grouper, permit, spotted sea trout, sailfish, cobia, bluefish, snapper, sea bass, dolphinfish (the short, squat fish, not Flipper), and sheepshead.

Tarpon

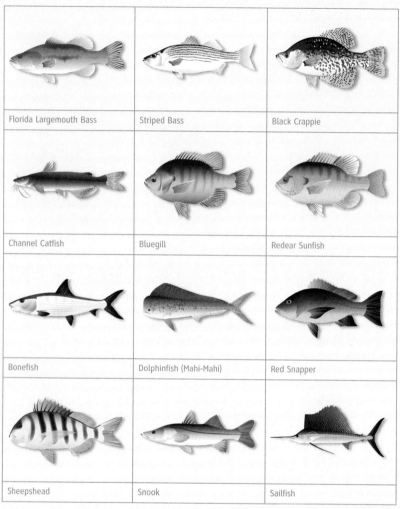

Florida Largemouth Bass

Striped Bass

Black Crappie

Channel Catfish

Bluegill

Redear Sunfish

Bonefish

Dolphinfish (Mahi-Mahi)

Red Snapper

Sheepshead

Snook

Sailfish

(top six) freshwater, (bottom six) saltwater

HERE'S THE CATCH

The type of fish you're after will depend on whether you fish in Florida's lake, streams, and rivers, or head out to sea. The Panhandle has an abundance of red snapper, while Lake Okeechobee is the place for bass fishing—although the largemouth bass is found throughout the state (they're easiest to catch in early spring, when they're in shallower waters). If you're looking for a good charter, Destin has a very large charter-boat fishing fleet. In the Florida Keys, you can fish by walking out in the very shallow water for hundreds of yards with the water only up to your knees; the fish you might reel in this way include bonefish, tarpon, and permit.

CHARTING THE WATERS

TYPE OF TRIP	COST	PROS	CONS
LARGE PARTY BOAT	Approx. $40/person for 4 hrs.	The captain's fishing license covers all passengers; you keep whatever you catch.	Not much privacy, assistance, or solitude: boats can hold as many as 35 passengers.
PRIVATE CHARTER	Roughly $1,200 for up to six people for 9 hrs.	More personal attention and more time on the water.	Higher cost ($200 per person instead of $40); tradition says you split the catch with the captain.
GUIDED TRIP FOR INLAND WATERS	Around $300–$400 for one or two people for 6 hrs.	Helpful if your time is limited and you want to make sure you go where the fish are biting.	Can be expensive and may not be as exciting as deep-sea fishing.
GOING SOLO	Cost for gear (rod, line, bait, and tackle) and license ($30–$100 depending on where you fish and if you need gear).	Privacy, flexibility, your time and destination are up to you; you can get fishing tips from your fellow anglers.	If you require a boat, you need to pay for and operate it yourself, plus pay for gear and a fishing license and find a fishing spot!

With a little hunting (by calling marinas, visiting bait and tackle stores, asking at town visitor centers), you can find a fishing guide who will lead you to some of the best spots on Florida's lakes and rivers. The guide provides the boat and gear, and his or her license should cover all passengers. A guide is not generally necessary for freshwater fishing, but if you're new to the sport, it might be a worthwhile investment.

On the other hand, if you're looking for fishing guides who can get you into the deep water for tarpon, redfish, snook, snapper, and dolphinfish, your best bet is to hang out at the marinas along the Florida coast and decide whether price or privacy is more important. If it's price, choose one of the larger party boats. If you'd prefer some privacy and the privilege of creating an exclusive passenger list, then sign up for a private charter. The average charter runs about nine hours, but some companies offer overnight and extended trips, too. Gear is provided in both charter-boat methods, and charters also offer the service of cleaning your catch. All guided trips encourage tipping the crew.

Most people new to the sport choose to do saltwater fishing via a charter party boat. The main reasons are expert guidance, convenience, and cost. Plus, fishing with others can be fun. Charter trips depart from marinas throughout Florida.

CREATING A FLOAT PLAN

If you're fishing in a boat on your own, let someone know where you're headed by providing a float plan, which should include where you're leaving from, a description of the boat you're on, how many are in the boat with you, what survival gear and radio equipment you have onboard, your cell phone number, and when you expect to return. If you don't return as expected, your friend can call the Coast Guard to search for you. Also be sure to have enough life jackets for everyone on board.

RULES AND REGULATIONS

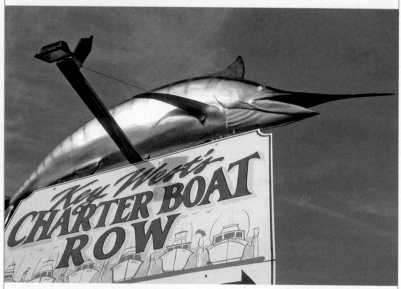

To fish anywhere in (or off the coast of) Florida, you need a license, and there are separate licenses for freshwater fishing and saltwater fishing.

For non-residents, either type of fishing license cost $47 for the annual license, $30 for the 7-day one, or $17 for a 3-day license. Permits/tags are needed for catching snook ($10), spiny lobster ($5), and tarpon ($51.50). License and permit costs help generate funds for the Florida Fish and Wildlife Conservation Commission, which reinvests the fees into ensuring healthy habitats to sustain fish and wildlife populations, to improve access to fishing spots, and to help ensure public safety.

You can purchase your license and permits at county tax collectors' offices as well as wherever you buy your bait and tackle, such as Florida marinas, specialty stores, and sporting goods shops. You can also buy it online at ⊕ license. myfwc.com and have it mailed to you; a surcharge is added to online orders.

If you're on a charter, you don't need to get a license. The captain's fishing license covers all passengers. Also, some piers have their own saltwater fishing licenses that cover you when you're fishing off them for recreational purposes—if you're pier fishing, ask the personnel at the tackle shop if the pier is covered.

RESOURCES

For the latest regulations on gear, daily limits, minimum sizes and seasons for certain fish, and other fishing requirements, consult the extraordinary **Florida Fish and Wildlife Conservation Commission** (☎ 850/488–4676 ⊕ www.myfwc.com).

WEB RESOURCES
Download the excellent, and free, Florida Fishing PDF at www.visitflorida.com/guides. Other good sites:
www.floridafishinglakes.net
www.visitflorida.com/fishing
www.floridasportsman.com

Harbor Blvd. ☎ *850/837–0955* ⊕ *www.divedestin.com* ✉ *Dive trips from $65, snorkel cruises from $30.*

BEACHES OF SOUTH WALTON

The 26-mile stretch of coastline between Destin and Panama City Beach is referred to as the Beaches of South Walton. From the middle of this mostly residential stretch of the Panhandle you can see the monolithic condos of Destin and Panama City Beach in either direction, like massive bookends in the distance, flanking the area's low-slung, less imposing structures. A decidedly laid-back, refined mood prevails in these parts, where vacation homes go for millions and selecting a dinner spot is usually the day's most challenging decision.

Accommodations consist primarily of private-home rentals, the majority of which are managed by local real-estate firms. Also scattered along Route 30A are a growing number of boutiques selling everything from fine art and unique hand-painted furniture to jewelry, gifts, and clothes.

ESSENTIALS

Visitor Information Beaches of South Walton Visitor Information Center ☎ *850/267–1216, 800/822–6877* ⊕ *www.beachesofsouthwalton.com.*

GRAYTON BEACH

18 miles east of Destin via U.S. 98 on Rte. 30A (Exit 85).

Inland, pine forests and hardwoods surround the area's 14 dune lakes, giving anglers ample spots to drop a line and kayakers a peaceful refuge. Grayton Beach, the oldest community in this area, was founded in 1890. You can still see some of the old weathered-cypress homes scattered along narrow, crushed-gravel streets. The secluded off-the-beaten-path town has been noticed with the addition of adjacent WaterColor, a high-end development of vacation homes with a stylish boutique hotel as its centerpiece. The architecture is tasteful, development is carefully regulated—no buildings taller than four stories are allowed—and bicycles and kayaks are the preferred methods of transportation. Stringent building restrictions, designed to protect the pristine beaches and dunes, ensure that Grayton maintains its small-town feel and look.

EXPLORING

Eden Gardens State Park. Scarlett O'Hara could be at home here on the lawn of an antebellum mansion amid an arcade of moss-draped live oaks in nearby Point Washington. Tours of the mansion are given every hour on the hour, and furnishings inside the spacious rooms date as far back as the 17th century. The surrounding grounds—the perfect setting for a picnic lunch—are beautiful year-round, but they're nothing short of spectacular in mid-March, when the azaleas and dogwoods are in full bloom. ✉ *Rte. 395, Point Washington* ☎ *850/267–8320* ✉ *Gardens $4, mansion tours $4* ☉ *Daily 8–sunset; mansion tours Thurs.–Mon. 10–3.*

BEACHES

Fodor's Choice ★ **Grayton Beach State Park.** This is the place to see what Florida looked like when only American Indians lived here. One of the most scenic spots along the Gulf Coast, this 2,220-acre park is composed primarily of untouched Florida woodlands within the Coastal Lowlands region. It also has salt marshes, rolling dunes covered with sea oats, crystal-white sand, and contrasting blue-green waters. The park has facilities for swimming, fishing, and snorkeling, and there's an elevated boardwalk that winds over the dunes to the beach, as well as walking trails around the marsh and into the piney woods. Notice that the "bushes" you see are actually the tops of full-size slash pines and Southern magnolias, an effect created by the frequent shifting of the dunes. Even if you're just passing by, the beach here is worth a stop. Thirty fully equipped cabins and a campground provide overnight options. **Amenities:** fishing; parking (fee); showers; toilets; water sports. **Best for:** snorkeling; sunrise; swimming; walking. ⌂ *357 Main Park Rd., off Rte. 30A* ☎ *850/267–8300* ⊕ *www.floridastateparks.org/graytonbeach* ⚏ *$5 per vehicle, up to 8 people; $2 pedestrians/cyclists* ☉ *Daily 8–sunset.*

WHERE TO EAT

$$$
ECLECTIC
Fodor's Choice
★

✕ **Fish Out of Water.** Time your appetite to arrive at sunset and you'll witness the best of both worlds: sea oats lumbering on gold-dusted dunes outside and a stylish interior that sets new standards of sophistication for the entire Panhandle. Colorful, handblown-glass accent lighting that "grows" out of the hardwood floors, plush taupe banquettes, oversize handmade lampshades, and a sleek bar area create an atmosphere worthy of the inventive cuisine. Menus are seasonal, but often range in influences from Southern (Low Country shrimp and scallops with creamy grits) to classic Continental, but all are convincingly wrought and carefully presented. The extensive wine list keeps pace with the menu offerings. $ *Average main: $26* ⌂ *WaterColor Inn, 34 Goldenrod Circle, 2nd fl., Santa Rosa Beach* ☎ *850/534–5050* ⊕ *www. watercolorresort.com* ☉ *No lunch.*

$$
SEAFOOD

✕ **Picolo Restaurant and Red Bar.** You could spend weeks here just taking in all the funky-junky, eclectic toy-chest memorabilia—from Marilyn Monroe posters to flags to dolls—dangling from the ceiling and tacked to every available square inch of wall. The contemporary menu is small, although it includes what you'd expect to find in the Panhandle: crab cakes, shrimp, and crawfish, to name a few. It also serves breakfast. In season, it can feed hundreds of people a day, so expect a wait. Blues and jazz musicians play nightly in the Red Bar. You can't make up a place like this. $ *Average main: $20* ⌂ *70 Hotz Ave., Santa Rosa Beach* ☎ *850/231–1008* ⊕ *www.theredbar.com* ⚌ *No credit cards.*

WHERE TO STAY

$
RENTAL

⌂ **Cabins at Grayton Beach State Park.** Back-to-nature enthusiasts and families love to visit these stylish accommodations set among the sand pines and scrub oaks of this pristine state park. **Pros:** rare and welcome preservation of Old Florida; pure peace and quiet; what a gulf vacation is meant to be. **Cons:** if you're accustomed to abundant amenities, you won't find them here. $ *Rooms from: $130* ⌂ *357 Main Park Rd., Santa Rosa Beach* ☎ *800/267–8300* ⌁ *30 cabins* ⦿ *No meals.*

$$$
HOTEL
Fodor's Choice
★

⌂ **WaterColor Inn and Resort.** Nature meets seaside chic at this boutique property, the crown jewel of the area's latest—and largest—planned communities. **Pros:** perhaps the ultimate vacation experience on the gulf; upscale and fancy. **Cons:** you may feel like it caters exclusively to Ivy Leaguers and CEOs, which might make it hard to relax. $ *Rooms*

If you saw *The Truman Show*, you may recognize several places in Seaside, where the movie was filmed.

from: $333 ⊠ 34 Goldenrod Circle, Santa Rosa Beach ☎ 850/534–5000 ⊕ www.watercolorresort.com ⇆ 60 rooms ⊚⏐ Breakfast.

NIGHTLIFE

Red Bar. The local watering hole presents red-hot blues or jazz acts every night. On Friday and Saturday nights it's elbow-to-elbow at the truly funky and colorful bar, which would be right at home on Miami's South Beach or in New York City's Greenwich Village. ⊠ *70 Hotz Ave., Santa Rosa Beach* ☎ *850/231–1008* ⊕ *www.theredbar.com.*

SHOPPING

Shops of Grayton. In the eight cottages of this colorful complex you can buy gifts, artwork, and antiques. ⊠ *Rte. 283, 2 miles south of U.S. 98.*

SPORTS AND THE OUTDOORS

GUSU Paddleboards. The biggest craze in the region is YOLO ("You Only Live Once") boarding, or stand-up paddling (SUP), on what looks like a surfboard. It can be found at many resorts in the region and also through businesses such as GUSU Paddleboards. The company's website offers a map of paddle trails throughout the region and state, as well as rates for lessons and tours. Try one out for $25 for a one-hour rental or a SUP-lates class. They're located inside TheXperience, a store that sells paddleboards and other wares in Destin. ⊠ *TheXperience, 111 Harbor Blvd., Destin* ☎ *850/460–7300* ⊕ *www.gusupaddlesports.com.*

SEASIDE

2 miles east of Grayton Beach on Rte. 30A.

This thriving planned community with old-fashioned Victorian architecture, brick streets, restaurants, retail stores, and a surfeit of art galleries was the brainchild of Robert Davis. Dubbed "new urbanism," the development style was designed to promote a neighborly, old-fashioned lifestyle. There's much to be said for an attractive, billboard-free village where you can park your car and walk everywhere you need to go. Pastel-color homes with white-picket fences, front-porch rockers, and captain's walks are set along redbrick streets, and all are within walking distance of the town center and its unusual cafés and shops. The community is so reminiscent of a storybook town that producers chose it for the set of the 1998 film *The Truman Show,* starring Jim Carrey.

The community has come into its own in the last few years, achieving a comfortable, lived-in look and feel that had escaped it since its founding in the late 1970s. Some of the once-shiny tin roofs are starting to rust around the edges and the foliage has matured, creating pockets of privacy and shade. There are also more signs of a real neighborhood with bars and bookstores added to the mix. Still, although Seaside's popularity continues to soar, it retains a suspicious sense of *Twilight Zone* perfection that can weird out some visitors.

Other planned neighborhoods, variations on the theme pioneered by Seaside's founders, have carved out niches along the dozen miles of Route 30A east to Rosemary Beach. The focus in the 107-acre planned community is on preserving the local environment (the landscape is completely made up of indigenous plants) and maintaining its small-town appeal. A nascent sense of community is sprouting at the Town Green, a perfect patch of manicured lawn fronting the beach, where locals gather with their wine glasses to toast the sunset. In total, the Beaches of South Walton tout 15 of these new urbanism–style beach communities and resorts.

WHERE TO EAT

$$$
EUROPEAN

✕ **Bud & Alley's.** This down-to-earth beachside bistro (named for a pet cat and dog) has been a local favorite since 1986. Tucked in the dunes by the gulf, the rooftop Tarpon Club bar makes a great perch for a sunset toast (guess the exact moment the sun will disappear and win a drink). Daily salad specials are tangy introductions to such entrées as grilled black grouper, seared diver scallops with creamy grits, a marinated pork chop with sweet-potato hash browns, and a taco and pizza bar. ⑤ *Average main: $30* ✉ *2236 E. Rte. 30A* ☎ *850/231–5900* ⊕ *www. budandalleys.com.*

$$$$
EUROPEAN

✕ **Café Thirty-A.** About a mile and a half east of Seaside in a beautiful Florida-style home with high ceilings and a wide veranda, this restaurant has an elegant look—bolstered by white linen tablecloths—and impeccable service. The menu changes nightly and includes such entrées as wood-oven-roasted wild king salmon, sesame-crusted rare yellowfin tuna, and grilled Hawaiian butterfish. Even if you're not a Southerner, you should try the appetizer of grilled Georgia quail with creamy grits and sage fritters. With nearly 20 creative varieties, the martini menu alone is worth the trip. ⑤ *Average main: $32* ✉ *3899 E. Rte. 30A, Seagrove Beach* ☎ *850/231–2166* ⊕ *www.cafethirtya.com* ⚑ *Reservations essential* ⊘ *No lunch.*

$$$
SEAFOOD

✕ **Great Southern Cafe.** Jim Shirley, founder of Pensacola's very popular Fish House, brought Grits a Ya-Ya to this restaurant on Seaside's town square. Breakfast is served from 8 to 11, when the menu segues to regional fare, including gulf shrimp, Apalachicola oysters, and fresh sides such as collards, okra, black-eyed peas, fried green tomatoes, and sweet potatoes. Oysters and po'boys stuffed with shrimp bring a little of N'awlins to the beach. Beer and wine and a full liquor bar are here to boot. $ *Average main: $24* ✉ *83 Central Sq.* ☎ *850/231–7327* ⊕ *www. thegreatsoutherncafe.com.*

WHERE TO STAY

$

RENTAL

🏠 **Seaside Cottage Rental Agency.** When residents aren't using their pricey one- to six-bedroom, porticoed, faux-Victorian cottages, they rent them out. $ *Rooms from: $198* ✉ *2311 E. Rte. 30A, Santa Rosa Beach* ☎ *850/231–2222, 866/966–2565 for reservations* ⊕ *www. cottagerentalagency.com* ⊅ *275 units* ○ *No meals.*

SHOPPING

Seaside's central square and open-air market, along Route 30A, offer a number of unusual and whimsical boutiques carrying clothing, jewelry, and arts and crafts. In the heart of Seaside in an area called Ruskin Place, there's a collection of small shops and artists' galleries that has everything from toys and pottery to fine works of art.

Perspicacity. This shop sells simply designed women's clothing and accessories perfect for easy, carefree, beach-town casualness. ✉ *178 Market St.* ☎ *850/231–5829.*

SPORTS AND THE OUTDOORS

Butterfly Bike & Kayak. A few miles from Seaside in Seagrove Beach, this outfitter rents bikes, kayaks, scooters, and golf carts and has free delivery and pickup. ✉ *3657 E. Rte. 30A* ☎ *850/231–2826* ⊕ *www. butterflybikerentals.com* ⊴ *From $20 per day, $45 per wk.*

SeaOats Beach Service. Whether it's a beach fire or surf lessons, this local couple's love for the beach shows through in a wide variety of luxury beach services. They don't have a brick-and-mortar store, but will meet you on the beach in Rosemary Beach instead. ☎ *850/951–3632* ⊕ *www. seaoatsbeachservice.com.*

PANAMA CITY BEACH

21 miles southeast of Seaside off U.S. 98.

In the early 2000s a dizzying number of high-rises built along the Miracle Strip—about two dozen in total—led to the formation of a new moniker for this stretch of the Panhandle: the "Construction Coast." This spate of invasive growth turned the main thoroughfare, Front Beach Road, into a dense mass of traffic that peaks in spring and between June and August, when college students descend en masse from neighboring states. The bright side of the changing landscape is that many of the attractions that gave parts of this area a seedy reputation (i.e., strip joints and dive bars) were driven out and replaced by new retailers and the occasional franchise "family" restaurant or chain store.

The one constant in this sea of change is the area's natural beauty, which, in some areas at least, manages to excuse its gross over-commercialization. The shoreline in town is 17 miles long, so even when a mile is packed with partying students, there are 16 more where you can toss a beach blanket and find the old motels that managed to survive. What's more, the beaches along the Miracle Strip, with their powder-soft sand and translucent emerald waters, are some of the finest in the state; in one sense, anyway, it's easy to understand why so many condos are being built here.

Cabanas, umbrellas, sailboats, WaveRunners, and floats are available from any of dozens of vendors along the beach. To get an aerial view, for about $30 you can strap yourself beneath a parachute and go parasailing as you're towed aloft behind a speedboat a few hundred yards offshore. And St. Andrews State Park, at the southeast end of the beaches, is treasured by locals and visitors alike. The incredible white sands, navigable waterways, and plentiful marine life that once attracted Spanish conquistadors today draw invaders of the vacationing kind—namely families, the vast majority of whom hail from nearby Georgia and Alabama. ■TIP→ When coming here, be sure to set your sights for Panama City Beach. Panama City is its beachless inland cousin.

GETTING HERE AND AROUND

The Northwest Florida Beaches International Airport opened in May 2010 on the east shore of Panama City's West Bay, with routes operated by Delta and Southwest. From the airport to the beach area, depending on the location of your hotel, it's about $15–$27 by taxi. Try Yellow Cab or Checker Cab.

When navigating Panama City Beach by car, don't limit yourself to Front Beach Road—the stop-and-go traffic will drive you nuts. You can avoid the congestion by following parallel roads like Back Beach Road and U.S. 98. Also, anywhere along this long stretch of beachfront, look for "sunrise" signs, which indicate an access point to the beach. They're a treasure to find, especially when you happen across one in the midst of a quiet residential neighborhood and know that a private, quiet beach experience is just a few feet away. The Baytown Trolley serves Bay County, including downtown Panama City and the beaches ($1.50, $4 for an all-day pass).

Contacts Baytown Trolley ☎ 850/769-0557 ⊕ www.baytowntrolley.org. **Checker Cab** ☎ 850/236-6666. **Yellow Cab** ☎ 850/763-4691.

VISITOR INFORMATION

Contacts Panama City Beach Convention and Visitors Bureau ☎ 850/233-5070, 800/722-3224 ⊕ www.visitpanamacitybeach.com.

EXPLORING

FAMILY **Gulf World Marine Park.** It's certainly no SeaWorld, but with a tropical garden, tropical-bird theater, plus alligator and otter exhibits, the park is still a winner with kids. The stingray-petting pool and the shark-feeding and scuba demonstrations are big crowd pleasers, and the old favorites—performing sea lions, otters, and bottlenose dolphins—still hold their own. If you're particularly interested, consider a specialty program, such as Trainer for a Day, which takes you behind the scenes to assist in food preparation and training sessions and lets you make an on-stage appearance in the Dolphin Show. The $250, six-hour program includes a souvenir photo, lunch, and trainer T-shirt. ✉ 15412

Get up close and personal with intriguing seashells on undeveloped Shell Island.

Front Beach Rd. ☎ *850/234–5271* ⊕ *www.gulfworldmarinepark.com* 🖅 *$28* ⊙ *Fall, Winter, Spring, daily 9:30–7; extended summer hrs vary.*

FAMILY
Fodor's Choice
★
St. Andrews State Park. At the southeastern tip of Panama City Beach, the hotels and condos and traffic stop, and there suddenly appears a pristine 1,260-acre park that offers a peek at what the entire beach area looked like before developers sank their claws into it. Here are beaches, pinewoods, and marshes with places to swim, pier-fish, and hike on clearly marked nature trails. A rock jetty creates a calm, shallow play area that is perfect for young children. There are also camping facilities and a snack bar. Board a ferry to Shell Island—a 700-acre barrier island in the Gulf of Mexico with some of the best shelling between here and southwest Florida's Sanibel Island. ✉ *4607 State Park La.* ☎ *850/233–5140* ⊕ *www.floridastateparks.org* 🖅 *$8 per vehicle, up to 8 people* ⊙ *Daily 8–sunset.*

FAMILY
Shipwreck Island Waterpark. Once part of the now-defunct Miracle Strip Amusement Park operation, this 6-acre water park has everything from speedy slides and tubes to the slow-moving Lazy River. Oddly enough, admission is based on height, with under 35 inches free. Wear flats. ✉ *12201 Middle Beach Dr.* ☎ *850/234–3333* ⊕ *www.shipwreckisland. com* 🖅 *$33* ⊙ *Mid-Apr.–May, weekends and some weekdays 10:30–4:30; June–early Aug., daily 10:30–5; mid-Aug.–early Sept., Sat. and some other days, 10:30–4:30.*

BEACHES

Mexico Beach. Just over 30 miles east of Panama City along scenic U.S. 98, this jewel of a beach is refreshingly free of the high-rises that populate many parts of Panama City Beach itself. Home to colorful, gracefully aging beach houses, the beach offers seclusion and a slower pace than its neighbor to the west. **Amenities:** food and drink; free parking. **Best for:** solitude. ⊠ *U.S. 98, 35 miles east of Panama City Beach* ☎ *888/723–2546.*

Panama City Beach. With 27 miles of shoreline, the beaches of Panama City offer the same pure white sand and emerald-green waters as its neighbors. Here, however, the coastline is dotted with high-rises rather than unspoiled nature. On the plus side, there are plenty of places to play, swim, splash, and feast, and there's no excuse for getting bored or hungry. Although it was once known as party central, Panama City Beach is becoming more family-friendly. **Amenities:** lifeguards; free parking; showers; toilets; water sports. **Best for:** partiers; swimming. ⊠ *Front Beach Rd., between U.S. 98 and St. Andrews State Park* ☎ *800/722–3224.*

WHERE TO EAT

$$ ✕ **Billy's Steamed Seafood Restaurant, Oyster Bar, and Crab House.** Join the
SEAFOOD throng of locals who really know their seafood. Then roll up your sleeves and dig into some of the gulf's finest blue crabs and shrimp seasoned to perfection with Billy's special recipe. Homemade gumbo, crawfish, shrimp, crab claws, fish tacos, whole lobsters, and the day's catch as well as sandwiches and burgers round out the menu. It's no-frills dining, but you may get a kick out of hanging out with some real Florida folks who consider table manners optional. ⑤ *Average main: $16* ⊠ *3000 Thomas Dr.* ☎ *850/235–2349* ⊕ *www.billysoysterbar.com.*

$$$ ✕ **Boar's Head.** An exterior that looks like an oversize thatch-roof
AMERICAN cottage sets the mood for dining in this ersatz-rustic restaurant and tavern. Inside you'll find the dark woods and dim lighting of steak restaurants of the 1970s, which is understandable considering that Boar's Head opened in 1978. From opening day, prime rib has been the number-one people pleaser—with blackened seafood and broiled shrimp with crabmeat stuffing always a close second. Its motto: "Good food, simply prepared." ⑤ *Average main: $25* ⊠ *17290 Front Beach Rd.* ☎ *850/234–6628* ⊕ *www.boarsheadrestaurant.com* ☽ *Closed Sun. and Mon. No lunch.*

$$$ ✕ **Capt. Anderson's.** Come early to watch the boats unload the catch of
SEAFOOD the day on the docks and to beat the long line that forms each afternoon at this noted restaurant with a real family feel. Here since 1953, it doesn't seem to have changed much and that's a good thing. A nautical theme is reinforced by tables made of hatch covers in the attached bar, which attracts longtime locals. The Greek specialties aren't limited to feta cheese and shriveled olives. Charcoal-broiled grouper, amberjack, and yellowfin tuna; crab-stuffed jumbo shrimp; stuffed fillet of grouper; and whole oven-broiled stuffed Florida lobster; and steaks are prominent on the menu as well. If you're visiting in the off-season, call to make sure it's adhering to the posted hours before venturing out. ⑤ *Average main: $30* ⊠ *5551 N. Lagoon Dr.* ☎ *850/234–2225* ⊕ *www. captainandersons.com* ⌂ *Reservations not accepted* ☽ *Closed Sun. and Nov.–Jan. No lunch.*

$$ ✕ **Schooners.** Thanks to a clientele that's mostly local, this beachfront
SEAFOOD spot—which is really tucked away down a small avenue—bills itself as

the "last local beach club," and more boldly, "the best place on Earth." It's actually a perfect spot for a casual family lunch or early dinner: kids can have burgers and play on the beach while Mom and Dad enjoy grown-up drinks and more substantial fare such as homemade gumbo, steak, or simply prepared seafood like crab-stuffed shrimp, gulf-fresh grouper, and grilled tuna steaks. One sign of Schooners' casual atmosphere is the ceremonial firing of the cannon when the sun disappears into the gulf, a crowd favorite that fires up an all-around good vibe. Late-night folks pile in for live music and dancing. ⑤ *Average main: $17* ✉ *5121 Gulf Dr.* ☎ *850/235–3555* ⊕ *www.schooners.com.*

WHERE TO STAY

$$ ⬚ **Edgewater Beach Resort.** You can sleep at least four and as many as
RESORT eight in the luxurious one-, two-, and three-bedroom apartments in beachside towers and golf course villas. **Pros:** variety of lodging options; 110 acres of beautiful beachfront property. **Cons:** overwhelming for those looking for a quiet getaway. ⑤ *Rooms from: $219* ✉ *11212 Front Beach Rd.* ☎ *855/874–8686 for info, 877/278–0544 for reservations* ⊕ *www.edgewaterbeachresort.com* ⤴ *520 apartments* ⭗ *No meals.*

$ ⬚ **Legacy by the Sea.** Nearly every room at this 14-story, pastel-peach
HOTEL hotel has a private balcony with commanding gulf views. **Pros:** shopping, dining, and attractions are within walking distance; all the amenities a family (or college kids) need. **Cons:** in the heart of a crowded and congested district; can be difficult to access in peak seasons. ⑤ *Rooms from: $179* ✉ *15325 Front Beach Rd.* ☎ *850/249–8601, 888/886–8917* ⊕ *www.legacybythesea.com* ⤴ *139 rooms and suites* ⭗ *Breakfast.*

$ ⬚ **Wyndham Bay Point Resort.** Across the Grand Lagoon from St. Andrews
RESORT State Park, this expansive property exudes elegance and offers quiet
Fodor's Choice away from the madness of Panama City Beach as well as proximity to
★ excellent golf. **Pros:** removed from the crush of tourists; complete range of services and activities. **Cons:** may be too expansive and generic for those seeking a small, intimate resort. ⑤ *Rooms from: $159* ✉ *4114 Jan Cooley Dr.* ☎ *850/236–6000, 877/999–3223 for reservations* ⊕ *www. wyndham.com/hotels/ECPWR/main.wnt* ⤴ *316 rooms, 60 1- and 2-bedroom golf villas* ⭗ *No meals.*

NIGHTLIFE

Club La Vela. Among the offerings that guarantee a full-tilt party here are a slate of concerts (acts have included Aerosmith, Creed, and Ludacris); international DJs; 48 bar stations; swimming pools; a tropical waterfall; and dance halls with names like Thunderdome, Underground, Night Gallery, Rock Arena, and the Pussykat Lounge. At spring-break time this club is transformed into a whirlpool of libido. ✉ *8813 Thomas Dr.* ☎ *850/234–1061, 850/234–3866* ⊕ *www.clublavela.com.*

Pineapple Willy's. This eatery and bar is geared to families and tourists— as well as sports fans. The signature rum drink, the Pineapple Willy, was the inspiration for its full slate of tropical drinks and the hangout's tiki attitude. ✉ *9875 S. Thomas Dr.* ☎ *850/235–0928* ⊕ *www.pwillys.com.*

14

SHOPPING

Pier Park. Occupying a huge swath of land that was once an amusement park, this diverse 900,000-square-foot entertainment/shopping/dining complex creates the downtown feel that Panama City Beach otherwise lacks. Anchor stores including Dillard's, JCPenney, and Target keep things active during the day, and clubs like Jimmy Buffett's Margaritaville and the 16-screen Grand Theatre keep things hopping after dark. Other stores, such as Ron Jon Surf Shop and Fresh Market, offer even more reason to see this vibrant and enjoyable complex. ⊠ *600 Pier Park Dr.* ☎ *850/236–9974* ⊕ *www.simon.com.*

SPORTS AND THE OUTDOORS

CANOEING

Econfina Creek Canoe Livery. Rentals for a trip down Econfina Creek—known as Florida's most beautiful canoe trail—are supplied by this outfitter, and they will pick you up from the end of the trail and bring you back to your vehicle (even if you bring your own canoe, albeit for a price). Single kayaks are $40; double kayaks and canoes rent for $50. No checks or credit cards. ⊠ *5641 Porter Pond Rd., north of Rte. 20, Youngstown* ☎ *850/722–9032* ⊕ *www.canoeeconfinacreek. net* ᄆ *From $40.*

GOLF

Bay Point Resort Golf Club. Two golf courses—the Nicklaus Course and the Meadows Course—are nestled on an 1,100 acre wildlife sanctuary and are open to the public. The Nicklaus Course is the only Nicklaus Design golf course in northwest Florida and features generous plateaus and uncharacteristic elevation changes unique to the Florida Panhandle region. A few holes offer panoramic views of the Grand Lagoon and St. Andrews Bay.

The Meadows Course is also picturesque, and its occasionally tight fairways, numerous lakes, and bunkers provide an ever-changing set of challenges. ⊠ *4701 Bay Point Rd.* ☎ *850/235–6950, 877/235–6950* ⊕ *www.baypointgolf.com* ᄆ *$26–$69 for Meadows Course; $34–$109 Nicklaus Course* 🏌 *Nicklaus Course: 18 holes. 7000 yards. par 72. Meadows Course: 18 holes. 6913 yards. par 72.*

Hombre Golf Club. The Hombre opened in 1989 with 18 holes and hosted its first PGA Tour event (The Panama City Beach Classic) in 1990. Hombre now gives golfers three different 18-hole options as well as four sets of tees for different levels of difficulty to best fit their game and handicap. The original 18 holes plays from 5,400 yards (senior tees) to 6,836 yards (championship tees) for the men, while the ladies layout is a 4,901 yards.

Each fall, Hombre hosts the PGA Tour Qualifying School, with the likes of Gary Nicklaus, Mike Weir, Michael Campbell having come in the past. ⊠ *120 Coyote Pass* ☎ *850/234–3673* ⊕ *www.hombregolfclub. com* ᄆ *$25 for "Good" course; $54 for "Bad" and "Ugly" courses* 🏌 *"Good" course: 9 holes. 3170 yards. par 35. "Bad" course: 9 holes. 3393 yards. par 36. "Ugly" course: 9 holes. 3427 yards. par 36.*

SCUBA DIVING

Snorkeling and scuba diving are extremely popular in the clear waters here. If you have the proper certification, you can dive among dozens of ships sunk by the city to create artificial reefs.

Panama City Dive Center. Here you can arrange for instruction, gear rental, and charters. Two-day "Wreck Daze," for those interested in wreck diving, include boat accommodations and guides. ⊠ *4823 Thomas Dr.* ☎ *850/235–3390* ⊕ *www.pcdivecenter.com* ☒ *From $34.*

APALACHICOLA

65 miles southeast of Panama City Beach off U.S. 98.

It feels like a long haul between Panama City Beach and here. Add an odd name and a town's below-the-radar reputation to that long drive and you may be tempted to skip Apalachicola. But you shouldn't. It's a weirdly fascinating town that, for some reason, has a growing cosmopolitan veneer. And that makes it worth a visit.

Meaning "land of the friendly people" in the language of its original Native American inhabitants, Apalachicola—known in these parts as simply Apalach—lies on the Panhandle's southernmost bulge. European settlers began arriving in 1821, and by 1847 the southern terminus of the Apalachicola River steamboat route was a bustling port town. Although the town is now known as the Oyster Capital of the World, oystering became king only after the local cotton industry flagged—the city's extra-wide streets, built to accommodate bales of cotton awaiting transport, are a remnant of that trade—and the sponge industry moved down the coast after depleting local sponge colonies.

But the newest industry here is tourism, and visitors have begun discovering the Forgotten Coast, as the area is known, flocking to its intimate hotels and bed-and-breakfasts, dining at excellent restaurants, and browsing in unique shops selling anything from handmade furniture to brass fixtures recovered from nearby shipwrecks. If you like oysters or want to go back in time to the Old South of Gothic churches and spooky graveyards, Apalachicola is a good place to start.

VISITOR INFORMATION

Contacts Apalachicola Bay Chamber of Commerce ☎ *850/653–9419* ⊕ *www.apalachicolabay.org.*

WHERE TO EAT

$ ✕ **Apalachicola Seafood Grill.** Where will you find the world's largest fish
SEAFOOD sandwich? Right here in downtown Apalachicola. Here since 1908, this is where the locals go for lunch and dinner, noshing on blue-crab cakes, seafood gumbo, fresh grouper, shrimp, and hamburgers. The décor is iconic diner, with a giant flamingo on the ceiling for that added Florida charm. ⑤ *Average main: $15* ⊠ *100 Market St.* ☎ *850/653–9510* ⊙ *No dinner Sun.*

$$ ✕ **Boss Oyster.** "Shut up and shuck." That's the advice from this rustic
SEAFOOD Old Florida restaurant—and it should know, since many consider this the top oyster restaurant in Florida's oyster capital. Located at the Apalachicola River Inn, this is where you can eat your oysters fried,

Twenty percent of the state's shrimp and 10% of the country's oysters come from Apalachicola Bay.

Rockefeller-style, on the half shell, or Greek, Mexican, English, with garlic, with shrimp, with crab, with hot peppers, with—oh, just eat 'em with gusto at this laid-back eatery overlooking the Apalachicola River. In addition to oysters, it lays down jumbo gulf shrimp, blue crabs, bay scallops, and fresh gulf grouper. Eat alfresco at picnic tables or inside in the busy, rustic dining room, but don't let the modest surroundings fool you—oysters aren't cheap here or anywhere in Apalach. The menu also includes such staples as steak and pizza. ⑤ *Average main: $20* ✉ *125 Water St.* ☎ *850/653–9364* ⊕ *www.bossoyster.com.*

$$$ ✗ **Owl Café.** Located in a behemoth clapboard building on a prime
AMERICAN corner in downtown Apalachicola, this old-fashioned, charming lunch-and-dinner spot pleases modern palates, both in the white-linen elegance of the dining room and in the colorful garden terrace. The food is an artful blend of old and new as well: the chicken wrap seems as much at home on the lunch menu as the crab quesadillas. Dinner seafood specials are carefully prepared and include lump-crab cakes, Atlantic salmon, and authentic jambalaya. Fine wines for adults and special menu selections for children along with a cluttered gift shop make this a family-friendly place. Later, the mood shifts to a casual lounge setting with a full bar—and if the liquor bar lacks enough choices, there's a 3,000-bottle wine cellar featuring 250 selections from around the world. ⑤ *Average main: $21* ✉ *15 Ave. D* ☎ *850/653–9888* ⊕ *www. owlcafeflorida.com.*

$$$ ✗ **Tamara's Café.** Mixing Florida flavors with South American flair,
LATIN AMERICAN Tamara, a native Venezuelan, opened this colorful bistro more than a decade ago. Now owned by her daughter and son-in-law, the restaurant resides in a 1920s-era building, complete with stamped-tin ceiling and

original brick walls. For starters, try the creamy black-bean soup or the pleasantly spicy oyster stew; for dinner choose from seafood paella, prosciutto-wrapped salmon with mango-cilantro sauce, or margarita chicken and scallops with a tequila-lime glaze. All entrées come with black beans and rice, fresh vegetables, and focaccia bread, but if you still have room for dessert, try the fried-banana split or the *tres leches* (cake soaked in three types of milk), a South American favorite. The chef, who keeps watch over the dining room from an open kitchen, is happy to accommodate most any whim. [$] *Average main: $23* ⊠ *71 Market St.* ☎ *850/653–4111* ⊕ *www.tamarascafe.com.*

WHERE TO STAY

$ 🛏 **The Consulate.** These four elegant suites, on the second story of the for-
RENTAL   mer offices of the French consul, range in size from 650 to 1,650 square feet and combine a 19th-century feel with 21st-century luxury. **Pros:** large rooms; more character than you'd find in a chain hotel. **Cons:** a bit pricey, especially for Apalachicola. [$] *Rooms from: $155* ⊠ *76 Water St.* ☎ *850/408–0556* ⊕ *www.consulatesuites.com* 🔀 *4 suites* ⭑◉⭑ *No meals.*

$ 🛏 **Coombs Inn.** A combination of neighboring homes and a carriage
B&B/INN   house, this entire complex was created with Victorian flair. **Pros:** clean and comfortable; on-site, friendly owner who's happy to assist with travel tips and suggestions. **Cons:** be prepared to meet and greet other guests at the inn; if you favor complete privacy, a hotel may suit you better. [$] *Rooms from: $119* ⊠ *80 6th St.* ☎ *850/653–9199* ⊕ *www. coombshouseinn.com* 🔀 *23 rooms* ⭑◉⭑ *Breakfast.*

$ 🛏 **Gibson Inn.** One of a few inns on the National Register of Historic
B&B/INN   Places still operating as a full-service facility, this turn-of-the-20th-century hostelry in the heart of downtown is easily identified by its wraparound porches, intricate fretwork, and widow's walk. **Pros:** smack-dab in the center of town; peaceful veranda. **Cons:** may get a little busy when weddings are taking place in the main lobby. [$] *Rooms from: $120* ⊠ *51 Ave. C* ☎ *850/653–2191* ⊕ *www.gibsoninn.com* 🔀 *28 rooms, 2 suites* ⭑◉⭑ *No meals.*

SHOPPING

The best way to shop in Apalachicola is just to stroll around the tiny downtown area. There are always new stores joining old favorites, and somewhere along the way you'll find something that'll pique your interest.

Grady Market. On the first floor of the Consulate Inn is a collection of more than a dozen boutiques, including several antiques dealers and the gallery of Richard Bickel, known for his stunning black-and-white photographs of local residents. ⊠ *76 Water St.* ☎ *850/653–4099* ⊕ *www. gradymarket.com.*

ST. GEORGE ISLAND

8 miles southeast of Apalachicola via Bryant Patton Bridge off U.S. 98.

Cross the long, long bridge leading east out of Apalachicola and then look to your right for another lengthy span that takes you south to pristine St. George Island. Sitting 5 miles out in the Gulf of Mexico, the island is bordered by both Apalachicola Bay and the gulf, offering the best of both to create a nostalgic seaside retreat.

The rich bay is an angler's dream, whereas the snowy-white beaches and clear gulf waters satisfy even the most finicky beachgoer. Indulge in bicycling, hiking, canoeing, and snorkeling, or find a secluded spot for reading, gathering shells, or bird-watching. Accommodations mostly take the form of privately owned, fully furnished condos and single-family homes.

EXPLORING

Fodor'sChoice **St. George Island State Park.** This is Old Florida at its undisturbed best.
★ On the east end of the island are 9 miles of undeveloped beaches and dunes—the longest beachfront of any state park in Florida. Sandy coves, salt marshes, oak forests, and pines provide shelter for many birds, including bald eagles and ospreys. Spotless restrooms and plentiful parking make a day at this park a joy. Campers and boaters also welcome. **Amenities:** free parking; showers; toilets. **Best for:** walking; swimming. ⊠ *1900 E. Gulf Beach Dr.* ☏ *850/927–2111* ⊕ *www. floridastateparks.org/stgeorgeisland* 🎫 *$6 per vehicle, up to 8 people* ⊙ *Daily 8–sunset.*

WHERE TO EAT

$ ✕ **BJs.** In any other locale you might think twice before dining at a res-
PIZZA taurant that advertises "kegs to-go" on the menu, but this is an island, so establishments tend to wear several hats (some even sell live bait). Fear not: This simple beach shack serves solid, if predictable, sandwiches (grilled chicken, turkey clubs, BLTs), salads (Caesar, tuna, fried chicken), and appetizers (buffalo wings, cheese sticks, onion rings), but the pizza is definitely worth stopping for. Pies range from white pizza with chicken and bacon to shrimp-and-mozzarella to build-your-own personal pie (choose from 15 toppings). Beer and wine are available, and there are pool tables to pass the time while you wait for your order. ⑤ *Average main: $7* ⊠ *105 W. Gulf Beach Dr.* ☏ *850/927–2805* ⊕ *www.sgipizza.com* 🍽 *Reservations not accepted.*

$$ ✕ **Blue Parrot.** You'll feel like you're sneaking in the back door as you
SEAFOOD climb the side stairs leading to an outdoor deck overlooking the gulf (this is Apalach's only restaurant on the beach). Or if you can, grab a table indoors. During special-event weekends, the place is packed, and service may be a little slow. The food is hard to beat if you're not looking for anything fancy. Baskets of shrimp, oysters, and crab cakes—fried or char-grilled and served with fries—are more than one person can handle. Daily specials are listed on the blackboard. ⑤ *Average main: $20* ⊠ *68 W. Gorrie Dr.* ☏ *850/927–2987* ⊕ *www.blueparrotsgi.com.*

TALLAHASSEE

103 miles east of Panama City, 78 miles northeast of Apalachicola.

Tallahassee is Florida with a Southern accent. It maintains a tranquility quite different from the sun-and-surf coastal towns. The only Southern capital spared in the Civil War, Tallahassee has preserved its history. Vestiges of the city's colorful past are found throughout. For example, in the capitol complex, the turn-of-the-20th-century Old Capitol building is strikingly paired with the New Capitol skyscraper.

The canopies of ancient oaks and spring bowers of azaleas line many streets; among the best "canopy roads" are St. Augustine, Miccosukee, Meridian, Old Bainbridge, and Centerville, all dotted with country stores and antebellum plantation houses. Between March and April, flowers bloom, the legislature is in session, and the Springtime Tallahassee festival is in full swing.

GETTING HERE AND AROUND

Just 14 miles south of the Georgia border and nearer to Atlanta than Miami, Tallahassee is midway between Jacksonville and Pensacola. Tallahassee Regional Airport is served by American, Delta, United Express, and US Airways. From the airport to downtown is around $20 via City Taxi or Yellow Cab.

Contacts City Taxi ☎ *850/562–4222.* **Yellow Cab** ☎ *850/575–1022.*

VISITOR INFORMATION

Contacts Tallahassee Area Convention and Visitors Bureau ☎ *850/606–2305, 800/628–2866* ⊕ *www.visittallahassee.com.*

EXPLORING

DOWNTOWN

FAMILY **Challenger Learning Center.** Visitors of all ages can't help but get excited about math and science exploration at this museum that features a space mission simulator, an IMAX 3D theater, and the Downtown Digital Dome Theatre and Planetarium. Every kid, and kid at heart, can re-enact a space mission with the Challenger Learning Center Space Mission Simulator. The next best thing to actual space flight, the simulator features a Mission Control room designed after NASA's Johnson Space Center and an orbiting space station modeled after the laboratory on the International Space Station. Hands-on or demonstrational science techniques and equipment can be found throughtout the museum. ⊠ *200 S. Duval St.* ☎ *850/645–7796, 850/644–4629 for IMAX theater* ⊕ *www.challengertlh.com* 🎟 *Planetarium $5, IMAX films $5.50–$7.75* ☉ *Showtimes vary.*

Downtown Tallahassee Historic Trail. A route originally mapped and documented by an eager Eagle Scout as part of a merit-badge project, this trail has become a Tallahassee sightseeing staple. The starting point is the New Capitol, where you can pick up maps and descriptive brochures at the visitor center. You'll walk through the Park Avenue and Calhoun Street historic districts, which will take you back to territorial days and the era of postwar reconstruction. The trail is dotted with landmark churches and cemeteries, along with outstanding examples of Greek revival, Italianate, and prairie-style architecture. Some houses are open to the public.

Meginnis-Monroe House. This house served as a field hospital during the Civil War and is now the home of the LeMoyne Center for the Visual Arts. ⊠ *125 N. Gadsden St.* ⊕ *www.lemoyne.org* 🎟 *Free* ☉ *Tues.–Sat. 10–5.*

Tallahassee Area

Museum of Florida History. If you thought Florida was founded by Walt Disney, stop in here. The displays explain the state's past by highlighting the unique geological and historical events that have shaped the state. Exhibits include a mammoth armadillo grazing in a savanna, the remains of a giant mastodon found in nearby Wakulla Springs, and a dugout canoe that once carried American Indians into Florida's backwaters. Florida's history also includes settlements by the Spanish, British, French, and Confederates who fought for possession of the state.

Gold bars, weapons, flags, maps, furniture, steamboats, and other artifacts underscore the fact that although most Americans date the nation to 1776, Florida's residents were building settlements hundreds of years earlier. If this intrigues you, one floor up is the Florida State Archives and Library, where there's a treasure trove of government records, manuscripts, photographs, genealogical records, and other materials. ■TIP➜ It was in these archives that researchers found footage of a young Jim Morrison appearing in a promotional film for Florida's universities. ⊠ 500 S. Bronough St. ☎ 850/245–6400, 850/245–6600 for library, 850/245–6700 for archives ⊕ www.museumoffloridahistory. com ☷ Free ⊙ Weekdays 9–4:30, Sat. 10–4:30, Sun. noon–4:30.

New Capitol. In the 1960s, when there was talk of relocating the capital to a more central location like Orlando, Panhandle legislators got to work and approved the construction of a 22-story skyscraper that would anchor the capital right where it was. It's perfectly placed at the crest of a hill, sitting prominently behind the low-rise Old Capitol. The governor's office is on the first floor, along with the Florida Artists Hall of Fame, a series of plaques that pay tribute to Floridians such as Ray Charles, Burt Reynolds, Tennessee Williams, Ernest Hemingway, and Marjorie Kinnan Rawlings.

The House and Senate chambers on the fifth floor provide viewer galleries for when the legislative sessions take place (March to May). Catch a panoramic view of Tallahassee and the surrounding countryside all the way into Georgia from the fabulous 22nd-floor observation deck. Although budget cuts have stopped scheduled guided tours, a free brochure can get you around; if you're traveling in a group, you can call ahead to have a guide usher you. To pick up information about the area, stop at the Florida Visitors Center on the plaza level, and check out the plaque on the north wall facing the elevators. It's dedicated to Senator Lee Wissenborn, "whose valiant effort to move the Capitol to Orlando was the prime motivation for the construction of this building." ⊠ *400 S. Monroe St.* 🕾 *850/488–6167* ⊕ *www.myfloridacapitol.com* ✉ *Free* ⊙ *Visitor center weekdays 8–5.*

Old Capitol. The centerpiece of the capitol complex, this 1842 structure has been added to and subtracted from several times. Having been restored, the jaunty red-and-white-striped awnings and combination gas-electric lights make it look much as it did in 1902. Inside, it houses a must-see museum of Florida's political history as well as the old Supreme Court chambers and Senate Gallery—a very interesting peek into the past. ⊠ *S. Monroe St. at Apalachee Pkwy.* 🕾 *850/487–1902* ✉ *Free* ⊙ *Self-guided tours weekdays 9–4:30, Sat. 10–4:30, Sun. noon– 4:30; call for guided tours.*

AWAY FROM DOWNTOWN

Alfred B. Maclay Gardens State Park. Starting in December, the grounds at this 1,200-acre estate are afire with azaleas, dogwood, Oriental magnolias, spring bulbs of tulips and irises, banana shrubs, honeysuckle, silverbell trees, pansies, and camellias. Allow half a day to wander past the reflecting pool into the tiny walled garden and around the lakes and woodlands. The Maclay residence (open January through April) is furnished as it was in the 1920s; picnic areas, gardens, and swimming and boating facilities are open to the public. ⊠ *3540 Thomasville Rd.* 🕾 *850/487–4556* ⊕ *www.floridastateparks.org/maclaygardens* ✉ *$6 per vehicle, up to 8 people; garden $6 per person Jan.–Apr. (blooming season), free rest of year* ⊙ *Daily 8–sunset.*

Fodor'sChoice ★ **Edward Ball Wakulla Springs State Park.** Known for having one of the deepest springs in the world, this very picturesque and highly recommended park remains relatively untouched, retaining the wild and exotic look it had in the 1930s, when the films *Tarzan* and *Creature from the Black Lagoon* were shot here. Even if they weren't, you'd want to come here and see what Florida really looks like. Beyond the lodge is the spring where glass-bottom boats set off deep into the lush, jungle-lined waterways to catch glimpses of alligators, snakes, nesting limpkins, and other

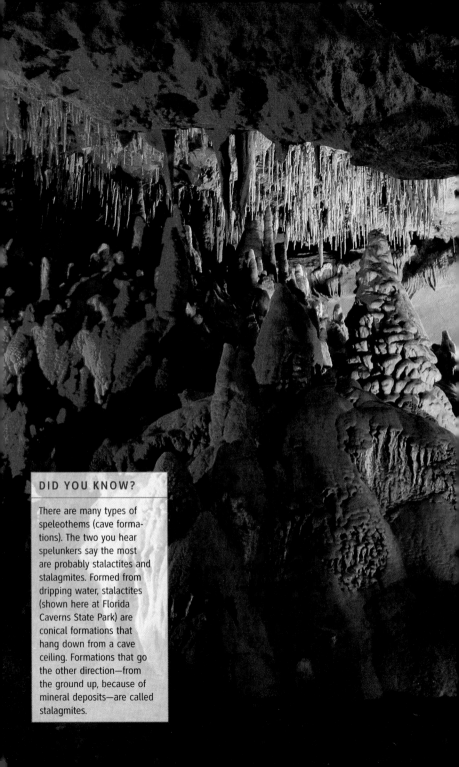

DID YOU KNOW?

There are many types of speleothems (cave formations). The two you hear spelunkers say the most are probably stalactites and stalagmites. Formed from dripping water, stalactites (shown here at Florida Caverns State Park) are conical formations that hang down from a cave ceiling. Formations that go the other direction—from the ground up, because of mineral deposits—are called stalagmites.

Guided tours are given daily at Florida's Old Capitol in Tallahassee. It sits in front of the 22-story New Capitol.

waterfowl. It costs $50 to rent a pontoon boat and go it alone—it may be worth it since an underground river flows into a pool so clear you can see the bottom more than 100 feet below. The park is 15 miles south of Tallahassee on Route 61. If you can't pull yourself away from this idyllic spot, spend the night in the 1930s Spanish Mediterranean–style lodge. ✉ *550 Wakulla Park Dr., Wakulla Springs* ☎ *850/926–0700* ⊕ *www. floridastateparks.org/wakullasprings* ✉ *$6 per vehicle, up to 8 people; boat tour $8* ⊙ *Daily 8–sunset, boat tours daily 9:30–4:30.*

Mission San Luis Archaeological and Historic Site. Long before New England's residents began gaining a foothold in North America, the native Apalachee Indians as well as Spanish missionaries settled here. On the site of a 17th-century Spanish mission and Apalachee Indian town, this museum focuses on the archaeology of the late 1600s, when the Apalachee village here had a population of at least 1,400. By 1704, however, threatened by Creek Indians and British forces, the locals burned the village and fled. About once a year, researchers conduct digs, and then they spend the rest of the year analyzing their findings. If you're here when they are, you can watch them dig. Otherwise, you'll have to be content with roaming around the re-creation of a 17th-century Spanish village and speaking with the living-history guides, who offer tours by advance arrangement. Even without seeing researchers digging for clues, this is still a cool experience and a great way to learn about Florida's impressive history. A 24,000-square-foot, state-of-the-art visitor center offers an expanded exhibit hall and gift shop. ✉ *2100 W. Tennessee St.* ☎ *850/245–6406* ⊕ *www.missionsanluis.org* ✉ *$5* ⊙ *Tues.–Sun. 10–4.*

St. Marks National Wildlife Refuge and Lighthouse. As its name suggests, this attraction is of both natural and historical interest. Natural salt marshes, tidal flats, and freshwater pools used by early natives set the stage for the once-powerful Fort San Marcos de Apalache, which was built nearby in 1639. Stones salvaged from the fort were used in the lighthouse, which is still in operation. In winter the 100,000-acre-plus refuge on the shores of Apalachee Bay is the resting place for thousands of migratory birds of more than 300 species, but the alligators seem to like it year-round (keep your camera ready). The visitor center has information on more than 75 miles of marked trails. Hardwood swamps and pine woodlands also provide habitat for wood ducks, black bears, otters, raccoons, deer, armadillos, coyotes, feral hogs, fox squirrels, gopher tortoises, and woodpeckers. Twenty-five miles south of Tallahassee, the refuge can be reached via Route 363. ⊠ *1255 Lighthouse Rd., St. Marks* ☎ *850/925–6121* ⊕ *saintmarks.fws.gov* ⊠ *$5 per vehicle* ⊙ *Refuge daily sunrise–sunset; visitor center weekdays 8–4, weekends 10–5.*

FAMILY **Tallahassee Museum.** Not exactly a museum, this is really an expansive, bucolic park that showcases a peaceful and intriguing look at Old Florida, located about 20 minutes from downtown. The theme and presentation here is of a working 1880s pioneer farm that offers daily hands-on activities for children, such as soap-making and blacksmithing. A boardwalk meanders through the 52 acres of natural habitat that make up the zoo, which has such varied animals as panthers, bobcats, white-tailed deer, bald eagles, red wolves, hawks, owls, otters, and black bears—many of which were brought here injured or orphaned. Also on site are nature trails, a one-room schoolhouse dating from 1897, and an 1840s Southern plantation manor, where you can usually find someone cooking on weekends. It's peaceful, pleasing, and educational. ⊠ *3945 Museum Dr.* ☎ *850/575–8684* ⊕ *www.tallahasseemuseum.org* ⊠ *$7.50* ⊙ *Mon.–Sat. 9–5, Sun. 11–5.*

WHERE TO EAT

$$$ ✕ **Andrew's 228.** Part of a smart complex in the heart of the political
ITALIAN district, this two-story "urban Tuscan villa" (contradiction noted) is the latest of owner Andy Reiss's restaurant incarnations to occupy the same space (the last was Andrew's Second Act). Leaning toward upscale, the menu includes a range of chicken, steak, pasta, and fish dishes such as grouper piccata, pesto salmon, wild-mushroom risotto, chicken marsala, and double-cut pork chops. If you're so inclined, try the specialty $6 martini. ⑤ *Average main: $26* ⊠ *228 S. Adams St.* ☎ *850/222–3444* ⊕ *www.andrewsdowntown.com* ⊙ *Closed Sun. No lunch.*

$$$ ✕ **Avenue Eat and Drink.** Elegant yet unpretentious, this cozy restaurant
SOUTHERN offers an eclectic mix of Southern fusion food that delights taste buds in small bites and larger plates. You can't go wrong with tuna two ways or the melt-in-your-mouth boneless shortribs served with mashed parsnip and potatoes with a rosemary-cabernet reduction. There is an extensive wine selection and a specialty martini menu. ⑤ *Average main: $28* ⊠ *115 E. Park Ave.* ☎ *850/224–0115* ⊕ *www.avenueeatanddrink.com.*

$$ **✗ Decent Pizza.** The name is terribly modest—the pizza here is much
PIZZA   more than decent, and the prices are more than reasonable. A couple
of Florida State University grads opened this simple pizzeria, which
became an instant hit with those on an undergraduate budget: slices
and salads start at $4 each, and at $1.25 each, the 9-ounce draft beers
are cheaper than sodas. Choose from more than 30 toppings for regu-
lar red-sauce, pesto, or white pies. ⑤ *Average main: $19* ⊠ *1026 N.
Monroe St.* ☎ *850/222–6400* ⊕ *www.decent-pizza.com* ⚑ *Reservations
not accepted.*

$ **✗ Hopkins' Eatery.** Locals in the know flock here for superb salads, home-
AMERICAN   made soups, and sandwiches—expect a short wait at lunchtime—via
simple counter service. Kids like the traditional peanut butter–and-jelly
sandwich (with bananas and sprouts, if they dare); adults might opt for
a chunky chicken melt, smothered beef, or garden vegetarian sub. The
spearmint iced tea is a must-have, as is a slice of freshly baked chocolate
cake. A second location on North Monroe Street offers the same menu;
a third location has also opened at 1208 Capital Circle SE. ⑤ *Average
main: $6* ⊠ *1415 Market St.* ☎ *850/668–0311* ⊕ *www.hopkinseatery.
com* ☾ *Closed Sun. No dinner Sat.*

$$ **✗ Kool Beanz Café.** The cuisine is as eclectic and cozy as the atmosphere
CARIBBEAN   at this Tallahassee staple, loved by locals and visitors alike. The décor
is part of the charm, with a vibrant setting of dark pastels and modern
art. The menu changes daily but typically includes seafood and vegetables served island-style. For a real treat, try brunch. ⑤ *Average main:
$20* ⊠ *921 Thomasville Rd.* ☎ *850/224–2466* ⊕ *www.kool-beanz.com.*

$$ **✗ The Mockingbird.** At this cozy café, contemporary gourmet dining
CONTEMPORARY   meets Southern staples set against a backdrop of eclectic artwork and
local musicians' tunes. The brunch is infamous, and locals flock here
to partake of such favorites as huevos rancheros and shrimp and grits.
The chef teases palates with creative specials on a regular basis, but the
sweet potato fries are a must and are a menu staple. Prices are reason-
able, and drink specials are always on tap. Try dining alfresco during the
warmer months. The lounge is open late. ⑤ *Average main: $18* ⊠ *1225
N. Monroe St.* ☎ *850/222–4956* ⊕ *www.mockingbirdtallahassee.com*
☾ *Closed Mon. No dinner Sun.*

WHERE TO STAY

$ **⌂ Aloft Tallahassee Downtown.** This urban-chic hotel provides the tree-
HOTEL   lined downtown district with a bit of trendy fun courtesy of loft-style
rooms with bright, minimalist décor. **Pros:** convenient to downtown,
universities, and nightlife/restaurants. **Cons:** small, utilitarian rooms;
lobby can get packed from the bar on weekend nights. ⑤ *Rooms from:
$139* ⊠ *200 N. Monroe St.* ☎ *850/513–0313, 866/513–0313* ⊄ *162
rooms* ❙○❙ *No meals.*

$ **⌂ Governors Inn.** Only a block from the capitol, this plushly restored
B&B/INN   historic warehouse is abuzz during the week with politicians, press,
and lobbyists. **Pros:** well run and well placed, a few steps from muse-
ums, restaurants, and the capitol; the rooms and lobby are warm and
inviting. **Cons:** during session and football season, the district can get
crowded and busy, and accessing the area may be a challenge. ⑤ *Rooms*

from: $169 ⊠ 209 S. Adams St. ☎ 850/681–6855 ⊕ www.thegovinn. com ⤳ 41 rooms, 8 suites ۱⊙۱ Breakfast.

$ 🛏 **Hotel Duval.** This boutique hotel, a renovated version of the landmark
HOTEL build in 1951, sets a high standard for small luxury hotels in the capital.
Fodor's Choice **Pros:** top-level amenities; good restaurants. **Cons:** not suited to families;
★ small rooms. *⑤ Rooms from: $109 ⊠ 415 N. Monroe St. ☎ 850/224–6000 ⊕ www.hotelduval.com ⤳ 108 rooms, 9 suites ۱⊙۱ No meals.*

NIGHTLIFE

There are endless options for after-dark entertainment for Tallahassee's government and university populations. When you're in town, be sure to check the college newspapers for the latest developments.

Level 8 Lounge. This rooftop lounge oozes a sleek, chic sophistication that matches the boutique hotel to which it's attached. Enjoy panoramic views of the capital city while you sip a drink from the custom drink menu (try the Cougarita), or nibble on small bites from the bar menu. *⊠ Hotel Duval, 415 N. Monroe St. ☎ 850/224–6000 ⊕ www. hotelduval.com.*

Midtown Filling Station. Comfort food and cold drinks abound at this gastropub in Midtown. Get a Dang Hippie burger or enjoy a Boiled Peanut of the Day while enjoying a good brew and live music. *⊠ 1122 Thomasville Rd. ☎ 850/224–8272 ⊕ www.midtownfillingstation.com.*

The Moon. For decades, this has been one of the capital city's most active nightclubs, capable of changing its music to suit the tastes of the new students attending FSU. Live bands and DJs have kept this club going since 1985 and will likely sustain its collegiate appeal for years to come. *⊠ 1105 E. Lafayette St. ☎ 850/878–6900, 850/222–6666 for events ⊕ tallahassee.moonevents.com.*

Tallahassee Symphony Orchestra. Concerts and events are held throughout the year; enjoy pre-concert lectures with composers as well as a variety of productions. Most concerts are held at Florida State University. *☎ 850/224–0461 ⊕ www.tallahasseesymphony.org.*

Theatre Tallahassee. This theater has a six-production season that runs September through June. *⊠ 1861 Thomasville Rd. ☎ 850/224–8474 ⊕ www.theatretallahassee.org.*

Waterworks. With its retro-chic tiki-bar fittings, Waterworks attracts the college art crowd, jazz fans, and hipsters of all ages for cocktails and DJ-spun dance music. On Friday night there's a banjo player, a retro-cool treat. *⊠ 1133 Thomasville Rd. ☎ 850/224–1887 ⊕ www. waterworkstallahassee.com.*

SHOPPING

Market District. Hop off I–10 at Exit 203 to head to this shopping and dining district filled with locally owned specialty shops, salons, cafés, and restaurants. My Favorite Things and Cotton Colors are popular, as are many other stores scattered around the area in smaller enclaves. Not to worry, though—most are within walking distance of one another.

The Market District is the place for a taste of true local culture. It's slightly west of Thomasville Road at the intersection of Timberline Road and Market Street. ✉ *Timberline Rd. at Market St.* ⊕ *www.themarketdistricttallahassee.com.*

Midtown District. This area mixes a little bit of Southern charm with city chic, offering everything from the stylish and cutting-edge fashions of Cole Couture and Divas and Devils to luxury beauty and spa services at Kanvas. Shops adorn the sides of North Monroe Street heading toward downtown, as well as some of the side streets. If you get hungry picking up purchases, try the delicious treats at Lucy & Leo's Cupcakery, featured on *Cupcake Wars.* ✉ *Between North Moore St. and Thomasville Rd., between W. 7th and W. 4th aves.*

TRAVEL SMART
FLORIDA

GETTING HERE AND AROUND

▮ AIR TRAVEL

Average flying times to Florida's international airports are 3 hours from New York, 4 hours from Chicago, 2¾ hours from Dallas, 4½–5½ hours from Los Angeles, and 8–8½ hours from London.

AIRPORTS

Florida has 21 commercial airports, the busiest being Orlando International Airport (MCO), Miami International Airport (MIA), Tampa (TPA), and Fort Lauderdale–Hollywood International Airport (FLL). Flying to alternative airports can save you both time and money. Fort Lauderdale is close to Miami, and Sarasota Bradenton International (SRQ) is close to Tampa. FLL is a 30-minute drive from MIA (and as close to certain neighborhoods of Miami). And what you might lose in driving time between Sarasota and downtown Tampa, you'll make up for in spades with shorter security lines and fewer in-terminal navigation woes at SRQ.

▮TIP➔ Flying to secondary airports can save you money—sometimes even when there are additional ground transportation costs—so price things out before booking. But sometimes one-way car rentals in Florida can be more cost-effective than shared van shuttles.

Airport Information Daytona Beach International Airport (*DAB*). ✉ *Daytona Beach* ☎ *386/248–8069* ⊕ *www.flydaytonafirst. com.* **Fort Lauderdale–Hollywood International Airport** (*FLL*). ✉ *Fort Lauderdale* ☎ *866/435–9355* ⊕ *www.broward.org/airport.* **Jacksonville International Airport** (*JAX*). ✉ *Jacksonville* ☎ *904/741–4902* ⊕ *www. flyjax.com.* **Key West International Airport** (*EYW*). ✉ *Key West* ☎ *305/809–5200* ⊕ *www. eywairport.com.* **Miami International Airport** (*MIA*). ✉ *Miami* ☎ *305/876–7000* ⊕ *www. miami-airport.com.* **Orlando International Airport** (*MCO*). ✉ *Orlando* ☎ *407/825–2001* ⊕ *www.orlandoairports.net.* **Palm Beach**

International Airport (*PBI*). ✉ *West Palm Beach* ☎ *561/471–7420* ⊕ *www.pbia. org.* **Northwest Florida Beaches International Airport** (*ECP*). ✉ *Panama City* ☎ *850/763–6751* ⊕ *www.iflybeaches. com.* **Sarasota Bradenton International Airport** (*SRQ*). ✉ *Bradenton* ☎ *941/359–5200* ⊕ *www.srq-airport.com.* **Southwest Florida International Airport** (*RSW*). ✉ *Fort Myers* ☎ *239/590–4800* ⊕ *www.flylcpa.com.* **St. Petersburg–Clearwater International Airport** (*PIE*). ✉ *Clearwater* ☎ *727/453–7800* ⊕ *www.fly2pie.com.* **Tampa International Airport** (*TPA*). ✉ *Tampa* ☎ *813/870–8700* ⊕ *www.tampaairport.com.*

GROUND TRANSPORTATION

There's SuperShuttle service from several Florida airports: Miami, Orlando, Sarasota-Bradenton, St. Petersburg/Clearwater, and Tampa. That said, most airports have some type of shuttle service or another.

If you book a shuttle from your hotel to the airport, allow at least 24 hours, and expect to be picked up 2½ hours before your scheduled departure.

Cab fares from Florida's larger airports into town can be high. Note that in some cities airport cab fares are a single flat rate; in others, flat-rate fares vary by zone; and in others still, the fare is determined by the meter. Private car service fares are usually more than taxi fares.

Shuttle Service SuperShuttle ☎ *800/258–3826* ⊕ *www.supershuttle.com.*

FLIGHTS

AirTran. AirTran flies to Miami, Fort Lauderdale, Fort Myers, Jacksonville, Key West, Orlando, Pensacola, Sarasota, Tampa, and West Palm Beach. ☎ *800/247–8726* ⊕ *www.airtran.com.*

American Airlines. Fort Lauderdale, Fort Myers, Fort Walton Beach, Gainesville, Jacksonville, Key West, Miami, Orlando, Pensacola, Tallahassee, Tampa, and West

Palm Beach. ☎ *800/433–7300* ⊕ *www. aa.com.*

Delta. Daytona Beach, Fort Lauderdale, Fort Myers, Fort Walton Beach, Gainesville, Jacksonville, Key West, Melbourne, Miami, Orlando, Panama City, Pensacola, Sarasota, Tallahassee, Tampa, and West Palm Beach. ☎ *800/221–1212 for U.S. reservations, 800/241–4141 for international reservations* ⊕ *www.delta.com.*

Frontier. Fort Lauderdale, Fort Myers, Jacksonville/St. Augustine, Orlando, and Tampa. Charges for a carry-on bag if you don't book on the airline's website. ☎ *800/432–1359* ⊕ *www.frontierairlines. com.*

JetBlue. Tampa, Fort Lauderdale, Sarasota, Fort Myers, Jacksonville, West Palm Beach, Orlando, and Key West. ☎ *800/538–2583* ⊕ *www.jetblue.com.*

Southwest. Fort Lauderdale, Fort Myers, Jacksonville, Key West, Orlando, Panama City, Pensacola, Tampa, and West Palm Beach. ☎ *800/435–9792* ⊕ *www. southwest.com.*

Spirit Airlines. Fort Lauderdale, Fort Myers, Orlando, Tampa, and West Palm Beach. This is one of a few airlines that charges for a carry-on bag. ☎ *801/401–2200* ⊕ *www.spirit.com.*

United. Daytona, Fort Lauderdale, Fort Myers, Fort Walton Beach, Gainesville, Jacksonville, Key West, Miami, Orlando, Pensacola, Sarasota/Bradenton, Tallahassee, Tampa, and West Palm Beach. ☎ *800/864–8331 for U.S. reservations, 800/538–2929 for international reservations* ⊕ *www.united.com.*

US Airways. Flies to Daytona Beach, Fort Lauderdale, Fort Myers, Fort Walton Beach, Gainesville, Jacksonville, Key West, Melbourne, Miami, Orlando, Pensacola, Sarasota, Tallahassee, Tampa, and West Palm Beach. ☎ *800/428–4322 for U.S. and Canadian reservations, 800/622–1015 for international reservations* ⊕ *www.usairways.com.*

▮ CAR TRAVEL

Three major interstates lead to Florida. I–95 begins in Maine, runs south through the Mid-Atlantic states, and enters Florida just north of Jacksonville. It continues south past Daytona Beach, the Space Coast, Vero Beach, Palm Beach, and Fort Lauderdale, ending in Miami.

I–75 begins in Michigan at the Canadian border and runs south through Ohio, Kentucky, Tennessee, and Georgia, then moves south through the center of the state before veering west into Tampa. It follows the west coast south to Naples, then crosses the state through the northern section of the Everglades, and ends in Miami.

California and most Southern and Southwestern states are connected to Florida by I–10, which moves east from Los Angeles through Arizona, New Mexico, Texas, Louisiana, Mississippi, and Alabama. It enters Florida at Pensacola and runs straight across the northern part of the state, ending in Jacksonville.

RENTAL CARS

Unless you plan to plant yourself at a beach or theme-park resort, you really need a car to get around in most parts of Florida. Rental rates usually start at $35 a day/$160 a week, plus tax ($2 per day), though rates have been going up lately and can more than double during busy periods. In Florida you must be 21 to rent a car, and rates are higher if you're under 25.

ROAD CONDITIONS

Downtown areas of such major cities can be extremely congested during rush hours, usually 7–9 am and 3:30–6:30 pm on weekdays. ▮TIP➔ Florida has a website (⊕ www.fl511.com) with real-time traffic information—including details on congestion owing to construction or accidents.

FROM–TO	MILES	HOURS +/-
Pensacola–Panama City	100	2
Tallahassee–Panama City	100	2
Tallahassee–Jacksonville	165	3
Jacksonville–St. Augustine	40	0:45
Cape/Port Canaveral–Orlando	60	1
Orlando–Tampa	85	1:30
Fort Lauderdale–Miami	30	0:30
Miami–Naples	125	2:15
Miami–Key Largo	65	1
Miami–Palm Beach	70	1:15
Key Largo–Key West	100	2

RULES OF THE ROAD

Speed limits are generally 60 mph on state highways, 30 mph within city limits and residential areas, and 70 mph on interstates and Florida's turnpike. Be alert for signs announcing exceptions. Children younger than four years old must be strapped into a separate carrier or child seat; children four through five can be secured in a separate carrier, an integrated child seat, or by a seat belt. The driver will be held responsible for passengers under the age of 18 who aren't wearing seat belts, and all front-seat passengers are required to wear seat belts.

Electronic tolls are becoming more common, and there's often no way of paying them in cash. Renting a toll pass may be a good idea in some areas (especially around Orlando), where it's almost impossible to get to Walt Disney World without paying a toll. You can also buy a mini-window transponder for your personal vehicle (and add value to the account) online for $4.99, and this will allow you to get the best rates on tolls. A regular transponder costs $25 and can also be purchased and recharged online.

Florida's Alcohol/Controlled Substance DUI Law is one of the toughest in the United States. A blood-alcohol level of 0.08 or higher can have serious repercussions even for a first-time offender.

CAR RENTAL RESOURCES

Local Agencies

Continental (Fort Lauderdale and Orlando)	800/221–4085 or 954/332–1125	www.continentalcar.com
Sunshine Rent A Car (Fort Lauderdale)	888/786–7446 or 954/467–8100	www.sunshinerentacar.com

Major Agencies

Alamo	877/222–9075	www.alamo.com
Avis	800/331–1212	www.avis.com
Budget	800/218–7992	www.budget.com
Hertz	800/654–3131	www.hertz.com
National Car Rental	800/227–7368	www.nationalcar.com

❚ FERRY TRAVEL

If you would like to avoid traffic to the Keys and make the trip less of a hassle, Key West Express ferries people from Fort Myers Beach on a daily basis (and Marco Island in season) to the historic seaport in Key West. The trip, just under four hours, is much cheaper than airfare, and doesn't require months-in-advance booking.

Contact Key West Express ☎ 888/539–2628 ⊕ www.keywestexpress.us.

ESSENTIALS

▌ ACCOMMODATIONS

In general, the peak seasons are during the Christmas holidays and late January through Easter in the southern half of the state, during the summer along the Panhandle and around Jacksonville and St. Augustine, and in both time frames in Orlando and Central Florida. Holiday weekends at any point during the year are packed; if you're considering home or condo rentals, minimum-stay requirements go up in these periods, too. Fall is the slowest season, with only a few exceptions (Key West is jam-packed for Fantasy Fest at Halloween). Rates are low and availability is high, but this is also the prime time for hurricanes.

Children are welcome generally everywhere in Florida, except for some Key West B&Bs and Inns; however, the buck stops at spring breakers. While most hotels allow them—and some even cater to them—almost all rental agencies won't lease units to anyone under 25 without a guardian present.

Pets, although allowed at hotels more and more often (one upscale chain, Kimpton, celebrates its pet-friendliness with treats in the lobby and doggie beds for rooms), often carry an extra flat-rate fee for cleaning and de-allergen treatments, and are not a sure thing. Inquire ahead if Fido is coming with you.

APARTMENT AND HOUSE RENTALS

The state's reputation for visiting snowbirds (Northerners who "flock" to Florida in the winter) has caused private home and condo rentals to be a booming business and at times a better option for vacationers, particularly families who want to have some extra space and cooking facilities. In some destinations, home and condo rentals are more readily available than hotels. Fort Myers, for example, doesn't have many luxury hotel properties downtown. Everything aside from beach towels is provided during a stay, but some things to consider are that sizable down payments must be made at booking (15% to 50%), and the full balance is often due before arrival. Check for any cleaning fees (usually not more than $150). If being on the beach is of utmost importance, carefully screen properties that tout "water views," because they might actually be of bays, canals, or lakes rather than of the Gulf of Mexico or the Atlantic.

Finding a great rental agency can help you weed through the junk. Target offices that specialize in the area you want to visit, and have a personal conversation with a representative as soon as possible. Be honest about your budget and expectations. For example, let the rental agent know if having the living room couch pull double-duty as a bed is not OK. Although websites listing rentals directly from homeowners are growing in popularity, there's a higher chance of coming across Pinocchios advertising "gourmet" kitchens that have one or two nice gadgets but fixtures from 1982. To protect yourself, talk extensively with the owners in advance, see if there's a system in place for accountability should something go wrong, and make sure there's a 24-hour phone number for emergencies.

Contacts American Realty of Captiva. Lower Gulf Coast (Captiva Island). ☎ 800/547–0127 ⊕ www.captiva-island.com. **Endless Vacation Rentals.** Unused time-share units from all major Florida cities and regions. ☎ 877/782–9387 ⊕ www.evrentals.com. **Florida Keys Rental Store.** Florida Keys ☎ 800/585–0584, 305/451–3879 ⊕ www. floridakeysrentalstore.com. **Freewheeler Vacations.** Florida Keys ☎ 866/664–2075, 305/664–2075 ⊕ www.freewheeler-realty.com. **Interhome.** Daytona Beach, Miami, Orlando, Sarasota, Florida Keys, Lower Gulf Coast, Tampa Bay Area ☎ 954/791–8282, 800/882–6864 ⊕ www.interhomeusa.com. **ResortQuest.**

Panhandle, Orlando ☎ *800/336–4853* ⊕ *www.resortquest.com.* **Sand Key Realty.** Tampa Bay Area (beaches) ☎ *800/257– 7332, 727/443–0032* ⊕ *www.sandkey.com.* **Suncoast Vacation Rentals.** Panhandle (St. George Island) ☎ *800/341–2021* ⊕ *www. uncommonflorida.com.* **Villas International.** Miami, Orlando, Broward County, Florida Keys, Lower Gulf Coast, Palm Beach County, Tampa Bay Area ☎ *415/499–9490, 800/221–2260* ⊕ *www.villasintl.com.*

BED-AND-BREAKFASTS

Small inns and guesthouses in Florida range from modest, cozy places with home-style breakfasts and owners who treat you like family, to elegantly furnished Victorian houses with four-course breakfasts and rates to match. Since most B&Bs are small, they rely on various agencies and organizations to get the word out and to help coordinate reservations.

Reservation Services BedandBreakfast.com ☎ *512/322–2710, 800/462–2632* ⊕ *www.bedandbreakfast.com.* **Bed & Breakfast Inns Online** ☎ *800/215–7365* ⊕ *www. bbonline.com.* **Florida Bed & Breakfast Inns** ☎ *561/223–9550* ⊕ *www.florida-inns.com.*

HOTELS AND RESORTS

Wherever you look in Florida, you'll find lots of plain, inexpensive motels and luxurious resorts, independents alongside national chains, and an ever-growing number of modern properties as well as quite a few classics. All hotels listed have a private bath unless otherwise noted.

Hotel reviews have been shortened. For full reviews, visit Fodors.com.

▌EATING OUT

Smoking is banned statewide in most enclosed indoor workplaces, including restaurants. Exemptions are permitted for stand-alone bars where food takes a backseat to the libations.

One caution: Raw oysters are a potential problem for people with chronic illness of the liver, stomach, or blood, or who have immune disorders. All Florida restaurants

---

FLORIDA'S SCENIC TRAILS

Florida has some 8,000 miles of land-based routes (plus another 4,000 miles for paddling!). About 1,400 miles of these connect to create the Florida Trail, one of only 11 National Scenic Trails in the United States. Info on top segments is available at ⊕ *www.floridatrail.org,* and you can find a searchable list of all trails at ⊕ *www. visitflorida.com/trails.*

---

that serve raw oysters must post a notice in plain view warning of the risks associated with consuming them.

MEALS AND MEALTIMES

Unless otherwise noted, you can assume that the restaurants we recommend are open daily for lunch and dinner.

RESERVATIONS AND DRESS

We discuss reservations only when they're essential (there's no other way you'll ever get a table) or when they're not accepted. It's always smart to make reservations when you can, particularly if your party is large or if it's high season. It's critical to do so at popular restaurants (book as far ahead as possible, often 30 days, and reconfirm on arrival).

We mention dress only when men are required to wear a jacket or a jacket and tie. Expect places with dress codes to truly adhere to them.

Contacts OpenTable ⊕ *www.opentable.com.*

▌HEALTH

Sunburn and heat prostration are concerns, even in winter. So hit the beach or play tennis, golf, or another outdoor sport before 10 am or after 3 pm. If you must be out at midday, limit exercise, drink plenty of nonalcoholic liquids, and wear a hat. If you feel faint, get out of the sun and sip water slowly.

Even on overcast days, ultraviolet rays shine through the haze, so use a sunscreen with an SPF of at least 15, and have children wear a waterproof SPF 30 or higher.

While you're frolicking on the beach, steer clear of what look like blue bubbles on the sand. These are Portuguese men-of-war, and their tentacles can cause an allergic reaction. Also be careful of other large jellyfish, some of which can sting.

If you walk across a grassy area on the way to the beach, you'll probably encounter the tiny, light-brown, incredibly prickly sand spurs. If you get stuck with one, just pull it out.

▍ HOURS OF OPERATION

Many museums are closed Monday but have late hours on another weekday and are usually open on weekends. Some museums have a day when admission is free. Popular attractions are usually open every day but Thanksgiving and Christmas Day. Watch out for seasonal closures at smaller venues; we list opening hours for all sights we recommend, but these can change on short notice. If you're visiting during a transitional month (for example, May in the southern part of the state), it's always best to call before showing up.

▍ MONEY

Prices here are given for adults. Substantially reduced fees are almost always available for children, students, and senior citizens.

CREDIT CARDS

We cite information about credit cards only if they aren't accepted at a restaurant or a hotel. Otherwise, assume that most major credit cards are acceptable.

Reporting Lost Cards American Express ☎ 800/528–4800 ⊕ www.americanexpress. com. **Discover** ☎ 800/347–2683 ⊕ www. discovercard.com. **MasterCard** ☎ 800/622–7747 ⊕ www.mastercard.com. **Visa** ☎ 800/847–2911 ⊕ www.visa.com.

▍ PACKING

Northern Florida is much cooler in winter than southern Florida, so pack a heavy sweater or more. Even in summer, ocean breezes can be cool, so it's good to have a lightweight sweater or jacket.

Aside from an occasional winter cold spell (when the mercury drops to, say, 50), Miami and the Naples–Fort Myers areas are usually warm year-round and extremely humid in summer. Be prepared for sudden storms all over in summer, and note that plastic raincoats are uncomfortable in the high humidity. Often storms are quick, usually in the afternoons, and the sun comes back in no time. (This also means that it's best to get in your beach time earlier in the day; if it's nice in the morning in August, go to the beach. Don't wait.)

Dress is casual throughout the state—sundresses, sandals, or walking shorts are appropriate. Palm Beach is more polos and pearls, Miami is designer jeans, and elsewhere the Tommy Bahama-esque look dominates. Even beach gear is OK at a lot of places, but just make sure you've got a proper outfit on (shirt, shorts, and shoes). A very small number of restaurants request that men wear jackets and ties, but most don't. Where there are dress codes, they tend to be fully adhered-to. Funnily enough, the strictest places are golf and tennis clubs. Many ask that you wear whites or at least special sport shoes and attire. Be prepared for air-conditioning working in overdrive anywhere you go.

You can generally swim year-round in peninsular Florida from about New Smyrna Beach south on the Atlantic coast and from Tarpon Springs south on the Gulf Coast. Bring a sun hat and sunscreen.

▌ SAFETY

Stepped-up policing of thieves who prey on tourists in rental cars has helped address what was a serious issue in the early 1990s. Still, visitors should be wary when driving in strange neighborhoods and leaving the airport, especially in the Miami area. Don't assume that valuables are safe in your hotel room; use in-room safes or the hotel's safety-deposit boxes. Try to use ATMs only during the day or in brightly lighted, well-traveled locales. Don't leave valuables unattended while you walk the beach or go for a dip. And never leave anything of value in a car; thefts from parked cars are on the rise in Florida, and visitors have reported the loss of their belongings while stopped for lunch or dinner as they travel to or from the airport.

If you're visiting Florida during the June through November hurricane season and a hurricane is imminent, be sure to follow directions from local authorities.

▌ TAXES

Florida's sales tax varies by locality but is between 6% and 7.5%. Hotel taxes vary between 11% and 13%. There are also hefty taxes on car rentals of up to 25% of rental rates.

▌ TIME

The western portion of the Panhandle is in the Central time zone, and the rest of Florida is in the Eastern time zone.

▌ TIPPING

Tip airport valets or hotel bellhops $1 to $3 per bag (there is also usually a charge to check bags outside the terminal, but this isn't a tip). Maids should get $1 to $2 per night per guest, more at expensive resorts, left each morning since your cleaner could change from day to day. Room service waiters still receive a 15% tip despite hefty room-service charges and service fees, which don't usually go to the waiters. A doorman or parking valet should get $1 to $3. Waiters should get 15% to 20% (on the before tax amount). Bartenders get $1 or $2 per round of drinks. Golf caddies get 15% of the greens fee.

▌ VISITOR INFORMATION

There are Florida welcome centers on I–10 (near Pensacola), I–75 (near Jennings), I–95 (near Yulee, north of Jacksonville), and U.S. 231 (near Campbellton), and in the lobby of the New Capitol in Tallahassee.

Contact Visit Florida ☎ 850/488–5607, 866/972–5280 ⊕ www.visitflorida.com.

INDEX

PHOTO CREDITS

Front cover: Martin Shields/Photo Researchers/Getty Images [Description: A variety of Atlantic calico scallop, Sanibel Island]. 1, Visit Florida. 2, timyyz, Fodors.com member. 5, jurvetson/flickr. Chapter 1: Experience Florida: 8-9, Sylvain Grandadam / age fotostock. 10, ACE STOCK LIMITED / Alamy. 11 (left), jeff gynane/Shutterstock. 11 (right), Jeff Greenberg/age fotostock. 12 (left), Cogoli Franco/SIME. 12 (right), Visit Florida. 13 (top left), Visit Florida. 13 (bottom left), Orlando CVB. 13 (top right), Universal Orlando Resort. 13 (bottom right), John Henshall / Alamy. 14 (top left), Jeremy Edwards/iStockphoto. 14 (bottom left), SeanPavonePhoto/Shutterstock. 14 (right), Visit Florida. 15 (left), Rob Keaton/ wikipedia.org. 15 (top right), RIEGER Bertrand/age fotostock. 15 (bottom right), Danita Delimont / Alamy. 16 (left), Jeff Greenberg / Alamy. 16 (top right), Ken Canning/Shutterstock. 16 (bottom right), Cogoli Franco/SIME/eStock Photo. 17 (left), Robert Harding Picture Library Ltd / Alamy. 17 (right), Dominika Sebjan/iStockphoto. 18, GlyndaK, Fodors.com member. 19, Jeff Greenberg/age fotostock. 20, The Breakers Palm Beach. 21 (left), culliganphoto / Alamy. 21 (right), Orlando CVB. 22, Cheryl Casey/Shutterstock. 23, St. Petersburg/Clearwater Area CVB. 24, j loveland/Shutterstock. Chapter 2: Miami and Miami Beach: 27, iStockphoto. 28, Stuart Westmorland/age fotostock. 29, Jeff Greenberg/ age fotostock. 30, Roxana Gonzalez/Shutterstock. 31 (top), JUPITERIMAGES/ Brand X / Alamy. 31 (bottom), iStockphoto. 32, Ivan Cholakov/Shutterstock. 52, Robert Harding Picture Library Ltd / Alamy. 93, John Tunney l Dreamstime.com. 105 (left), dk/Alamy. 105 (right), Nicholas Pitt/Alamy. 107 (top), M. Timothy O'Keefe/Alamy. 107 (bottom), Miami Design Preservation League. 108 (top), Nicholas Pitt/Alamy. 108 (2nd from top), Park Central Hotel. 108 (3rd from top), Ian Patrick Alamy. 108 (4th from top), Laura Paresky. 108 (bottom), ICIMAGE/Alamy. 109 (top), INTERFOTO Pressebildagentur/Alamy. 109 (bottom left), Ian Patrick/Alamy. 109 (bottom right), culliganphoto/Alamy. 110, PeskyMonkey/iStockphoto. Chapter 3: The Everglades: 115, David Lyons / Alamy. 116 (top), Visit Florida. 116 (bottom), Jeff Greenberg/age fotostock. 117 (top), FloridaStock/Shutterstock. 117 (bottom), Pamela McCreight/flickr. 118-19, tbkmedia.de/Alamy. 122 (left), inga spence/Alamy. 122 (top center), FloridaStock/Shutterstock. 122 (bottom center), Andrewtappert/wikipedia. org. 122 (top right), wikipedia.org. 122 (bottom right), David R. Frazier Photolibrary, Inc./Alamy. 123 (top left), Larsek/Shutterstock. 123 (bottom left), Caleb Foster/Shutterstock. 123 (bottom center), mlorenz/Shutterstock. 123 (top right), umar faruq/Shutterstock. 123 (bottom right), Peter Arnold, Inc./Alamy. 124 (left), John A. Anderson/Shutterstock. 124 (top right), FloridaStock/Shutterstock. 124 (bottom center), Norman Bateman/Shutterstock. 124 (bottom right), FloridaStock/Shutterstock. 125 (top left), David Drake & Deborah Jaffe. 125 (bottom left), Krzysztof Slusarczyk/Shutterstock. 125 (bottom center), Norman Bateman/Shutterstock. 125 (right), Jerry Zitterman/Shutterstock. 126, Patricia Schmidt/ iStockphoto. 127, (top left), Brett Charlton/iStockphoto. 127, (bottom left, bottom center, and right), David Drake & Deborah Jaffe. 128 (left), Walter Bibikow/age fotostock. 128 (right), Stephen Frink Collection/Alamy. 129, Leatha J. Robinson/Shutterstock. 131, Larsek/Shutterstock. 138, Steven Widoff / Alamy. 144, Marc Muench / Alamy. 148, Everglades National Park by http://www.flickr.com/photos/ jasonsewall/ 2277243977/ Attribution-NonCommercial-ShareAlike License. 156, Visit Florida. Chapter 4: The Florida Keys: 161, Patricia Schmidt/iStockphoto. 162 (top), Pawel Lipiec/iStockphoto. 162 (bottom), David L Amsler/iStockphoto. 163 (top), Sheri Armstrong/Shutterstock. 163 (bottom), Visit Florida. 164, Gregory Wrona / Alamy. 165 (top), Claudio Lovo/Shutterstock. 165 (bottom), Michael Ventura/Alamy. 166, iStockphoto. 173, Stephen Frink/ Florida Keys News Bureau. 181, flasporty/flickr. 188, (c) Korzeniewski l Dreamstime.com. 192, PBorowka/Shutterstock. 193 and 194 (top), Douglas Rudolph. 194 (bottom), ANDY NEWMAN/Visit Florida. 195, M. Timothy O'Keefe/Alamy. 196 (top), Bob Care/Florida Keys News Bureau. 196 (bottom), Julie de Leseleuc/iStockphoto. 197 (left), Visit Florida. 197 (right), Charles Stirling (Diving)/Alamy. 198 (top), Visit Florida. 198 (bottom), Gert Vrey/ iStockphoto. 199, Scott Wilson, FKCC Student. 200, Melissa Schalke/iStockphoto. 208, Henryk Sadura / Alamy. 220, CedarBendDrive/Flickr. 223, Visit Florida. 225, John P Franzis. 236, Starwood Hotels & Resorts. 238, Laure Neish/iStockphoto. 240, Laure Neish/iStockphoto. Chapter 5: Fort Lauderdale: 247, James Schwabel / age fotostock. 248, Rick Gomez. 249 (top), Dean Bergmann/iStockphoto. 249 (bottom), Jeff Greenberg /Alamy. 250, Jorg Hackemann/Shutterstock. 260, Nicholas Pitt /Alamy. 268, Eric Gevaert/Shutterstock. 277, Lago Mar Resort & Club. 288, Terrance Klassen / age fotostock. Chapter 6: Palm Beach and the Treasure Coast: 293, RIEGER Bertrand/age fotostock. 295 (top), Perry Correll/Shutterstock. 295 (bottom), Bill Bachmann / Alamy. 296, FloridaStock/Shutterstock. 301, The Breakers Palm Beach. 305, mrk_photo/flickr. 308, FloridaStock/Shutterstock. 325, Andre Jenny / Alamy. 328, wikipedia.org. 341 and 353, Visit Florida. Chapter 7: The Tampa Bay Area: 357, (c) Sayran l Dreamstime.com. 358 (top), gppilot, Fodors.com member. 358 (bottom), Visit Florida. 359 (top), Marje Cannon/iStockphoto. 359 (bottom), gracious_tiger/Shutterstock. 360, iStockphoto. 372, Martin Bennett / Alamy. 388, Seymour Levy, Fodors.com member. 397, Ed Wolfstein/Icon SMI. 398 (top),

Mtrommer I Dreamstime.com. 398 (bottom), Asklar I Dreamstime.com. 399 (top), Evan Meyer/Shutterstock. 399 (bottom) and 400 (bottom background photo), Mtrommer I Dreamstime.com. 400 (top), Gary I. Rothstein/Icon SMI. 401 (background photo), Bokdavid I Dreamstime.com. 403, watland, Fodors.com member. 406, Richard T. Nowitz / age fotostock. 415, TIPTON DONALD / age fotostock. 417, cogito ergo imago/Flickr (CC BY-SA 2.0). Chapter 8: The Lower Gulf Coast: 427, Dan Leffel/age fotostock. 429 (top), FloridaStock/Shutterstock. 429 (center), Visit Florida. 429 (bottom), FloridaStock/Shutterstock. 430, Philip Lange/Shutterstock. 436, Visit Florida. 444, World Pictures/age Fotostock. 446, Walter Bibikow / age fotostock. 449, blewisphotography/Shutterstock. 450, Mitch Aunger/Shutterstock. 474, Dennis Guyitt/ iStockphoto. Chapter 9: Orlando and Environs: 485, lightkey/iStockphoto. 486, SeaWorld Orlando. 487 (top), Nick Hotel. 487 (bottom), Universal Orlando Resort. 488, Universal Orlando Resort. 492, Orlando CVB. 496, Kissimmee - The Heart of Florida/Flickr. 498, spakattacks/Flickr. 533, Visit Florida. Chapter 10: Walt Disney World: 537, Disney. 538, d4rr3ll/Flickr. 539, vanguardist/Flickr. 540, Orlando CVB. 547, ckramer/Flickr. 553, JoshMcConnell/Flickr. 563, Disney. 565, yeowatzup/Flickr. 575, tom.arthur/Flickr. 584, PrincessAshley/Flickr. Chapter 11: Universal Orlando: 589-90, Universal Orlando Resort. 591, bea&txm/Flickr. 592, divemasterking2000/Flickr. 601, Universal Orlando Resort. 605, Jessica Walsh. 612, Universal Orlando Resort. 614, PCL / Alamy. 616, Wet 'n Wild. Chapter 12: SeaWorld Orlando: 619, SeaWorld Orlando. 620, Cybjorg/Wikimedia Commons. 621 (top), Fantaz/Flickr. 621 (bottom), Wendy Piersall (@eMom)/Flickr. 622, SeaWorld Orlando. 625, SeaWorld Orlando. 633, SeaWorld Parks & Entertainment. 634, Orlando CVB. Chapter 13: Northeast Florida: 637, FRILET Patrick/age fotostock. 638 (top), The Freewheeling Daredevil/Flickr. 638 (bottom), Henryk Sadura/Shutterstock. 639 (top), Diane Uhley/Shutterstock. 639 (bottom), Cogoli Franco/SIME/ eStockphoto. 640, Visit Florida. 644, Karel Gallas/Shutterstock. 650, Jeff Greenberg/age fotostock. 654, Therese McKeon/iStockphoto. 663, funinthetub, Fodors.com member. 670, (c) Arkorn I Dreamstime.com. 675, c) Paul65516 IDreamstime.com. 688, Visit Florida. 692-93, Visit Florida. 694 (top) Visit Florida. 694 (bottom left), David Allio/Icon SMI. 694 (bottom 2nd from left), JACK BRADEN/wikipedia.org. 694 (bottom 3rd from left), Arni Katz/Alamy. 694 (bottom right), Motorsports Images and Archives/Datona International Speedway. 695, Daytona Frontstretch Grandstand by Nancy Nally www.flicker.com/photos/scrapnancy/3289448500/Attribution-ShareAlike License. 696, greg pelt/iStockphoto. 710-11, jurvetson/Flickr. 712, thelastminute/Flickr. 713, yeowatzup/Flickr. 714 (all), Kennedy Space Center. 715 (left), thelastminute/Flickr. 715 (right), Kennedy Space Center Visitor Complex. 716, by jonworth/Flickr. 717, bnhsu/Flickr. 721, (c) Louishenault I Dreamstime.com. Chapter 14: The Panhandle: 725, Cheryl Casey/Shutterstock. 726 (top), Cheryl Casey/Shutterstock. 726 (bottom), Cheryl Casey/Shutterstock. 727 (top), Todd Taulman/Shutterstock. 727 (bottom), Visit Florida. 728, divemasterking2000/flickr. 735, Kathy Hicks/iStockphoto. 747, (c) Judykennamer I Dreamstime. com. 751, Visit Florida. 752 (top), Ernest Hemingway Photograph Collection, John F. Kennedy Presidential Library and Museum, Boston. 752 (bottom), Visit Florida. 753 (top), Linda Brinck, Fodors.com member. 753 (bottom), George Peters/iStockphoto. 756, Andrew Woodley/Alamy. 759, Central Square Records by THOR http://www.flickr.com/photos/geishaboy500/479513741/Attribution-NonCommercial License. 763, Gorilla/Shutterstock. 768, by nate steiner/flickr. 774-75, imagebroker / Alamy. 776, Dennis MacDonald/age fotostock. Back cover (from left to right): Cheryl Casey/Shutterstock; Brian Dunne/Shutterstock; Andreas Prott/iStockphoto. Spine: Garrett Nudd/iStockphoto.

About Our Writers: All photos are courtesy of the writers except for the following: Kate Bradshaw, courtesy of Tess Chibirka; Lynne Helm, courtesy of John Rude; Steve Master, courtesy of Daryl Labello; Avery Sumner, courtesy of André Bizard.

ABOUT OUR WRITERS

Tampa Bay and Naples updater and beach lover Kate Bradshaw lives in the small Gulf Coast town of St. Pete Beach and writes for various Tampa Bay news, environmental, and entertainment outlets. On weekends, you may spot her strumming her guitar at a local beach haunt. Born in the Chicago area, Kate has lived in Hawaii, New Zealand, and New Mexico, among other places. She is proud to now be a Florida resident, and, with her coverage for Fodor's, hopes to convey to visitors all the beauty and wonder of her adopted home.

After being hired sight unseen by a South Florida newspaper, Fort Lauderdale–based freelance travel writer and editor Lynne Helm arrived from the Midwest anticipating a few years of palm-fringed fun. More than a quarter century later (after covering the state for several newspapers, consumer magazines, and trade publications), she's still enamored of Florida's sun-drenched charms. Lynne updated the Everglades chapter.

Updating the Florida Keys and much of the Lower Gulf Coast is Miami native, Jill Martin. As a freelance writer, she has blogged more than 1,000 articles for the state's tourism website, Visit Florida, and also writes for various travel sites and print magazines. She has appeared on numerous TV and radio shows as a Florida travel expert and is the creator of Sunshine Brain Games, a trivia card game all about Florida. She resides full time in the Redland and part time on Sanibel.

Northeast Florida updater Steve Master can hear the engines roar, literally, from his home in Daytona Beach, 10 miles west of famed Daytona International Speedway. Steve spent 20 years as a sports writer for the *Daytona Beach News Journal*, where he won many awards, including a 2007 national honor from the Associated Press Sports Editors. He has written commentary for *NASCAR Illustrated* and covered travel for Orbitz Worldwide. Currently, he's an associate professor of communication at Embry-Riddle Aeronautical University in Daytona Beach.

Paul Rubio's quest to discover the world has taken him to 107 countries and counting. Paul graduated from Harvard in 2002 with master's degrees in both Public Administration and Economics, but in 2008 he gave into his passion and became a full-time travel writer. He's won over a dozen national awards for his articles and guidebooks. The prolific writer is the travel editor of *Palm Beach Illustrated, Naples Illustrated,* and *Weddings Illustrated* and regularly contributes to *Ultratravel US, Robb Report, Private Clubs,* and the full family of Modern Luxury publications.

Avery Sumner is a native Floridian from Tallahassee. She began her career in the Florida Keys as a newspaper staff writer and later set up camp on the edge of Everglades National Park as a restaurateur. Naples and Marco Island served as her beach and cultural centers during her time in the glades. For this edition, she updated Naples and Vicinity. Avery currently splits her time between Florida and southern France where she leads gourmet bicycle tours through wine country (⊕ *www. realtravelfrance.com*) and covers the Languedoc-Roussillon for *Fodor's France.* Like all the other snowbirds (human and feathered), Avery usually returns to her home state every winter.

Panhandle updater Ashley Wright is a northwest Florida native and a master-of-all-trades in the publishing world, including (but certainly not limited to) writing, editing, graphic design, and photography. She contributes to a number of local and regional publications, and loves sharing the hidden treasures of her native coast with travelers both near and far.

The Orlando and Walt Disney World chapters were updated by a talented team of writers, including Rona Gindin (Where to Eat), Jennifer Greenhill-Taylor (Where to Stay), Jennie Hess (all of Disney World), Gary McKechnie (Universal and SeaWorld), and Megan Peck (Orlando and environs sights and attractions).